Global Marketing

a decision-oriented approach

About the Supplements

Visit the *Global Marketing* Supplements at **www.booksites.net/hollensen** to access a rich, free resource of valuable teaching and learning material, including the following content:

General

- An **About the author** section, with a brief description of the author's academic credentials
- A full **table of contents**
- **Book features**, explaining what's new and what's changed in this new edition
- An **overview** of all the cases in the book, including weblinks so you are only one click away from exploring the subject

For the Lecturer

- A secure, **password-protected** site offering downloadable teaching support
- Customisable **PowerPoint slides**, including all the key figures and tables from the main text
- A fully updated **Instructor's Manual**, intended to be used by Lecturers as a guide to using the book as a supplement to their own resources
- **Teaching notes** for each of the extra case studies and the end-of-chapter discussion questions

For the Student

- Extra **case studies**, with questions and internet exercises, complete with weblinks
- A section on **global marketing information**, complete with an exhaustive array of specific, useful Internet resources to facilitate in-depth independent research

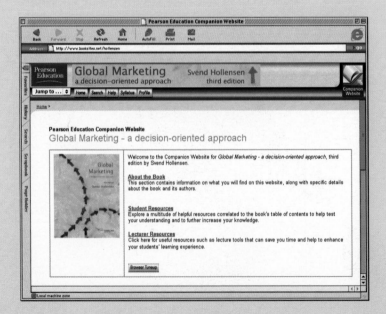

Global
Marketing

a decision–oriented approach

third edition

Svend Hollensen

FT Prentice Hall

FINANCIAL TIMES

An imprint of **Pearson Education**

Harlow, England • London • New York • Boston • San Francisco • Toronto
Sydney • Tokyo • Singapore • Hong Kong • Seoul • Taipei • New Delhi
Cape Town • Madrid • Mexico City • Amsterdam • Munich • Paris • Milan

Pearson Education Limited

Edinburgh Gate
Harlow
Essex CM20 2JE
England

and Associated Companies throughout the world

Visit us on the World Wide Web at:
www.pearsoned.co.uk

First published 1998 by Prentice Hall
Second edition published 2001 by Pearson Education Limited
Third edition published 2004

ISBN 0 273 67839 6

British Library Cataloguing-in-Publication Data
A catalogue record for this book is available from the British Library.

Library of Congress Cataloging-in-Publication Data
Hollensen, Svend.
 Global marketing : a decision-oriented approach / Svend Hollensen.—3rd ed.
  p. cm.
 Includes bibliographical references and index.
 ISBN 0-273-67839-6
  1. Export marketing. I. Title.

 HF1416.H65 2004
 658.8'4—dc22

                                        2003063526

10 9 8 7 6 5 4 3 2 1
08 07 06 05 04

Typeset in 9.5/12.5 pt Stone Serif by 25.
Printed and bound by Mateu-Cromo Artes Graficas, Madrid, Spain.

The publisher's policy is to use paper manufactured from sustainable forests.

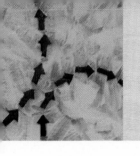

Short contents

Contents

Part I The decision whether to internationalize — 1

1 Global marketing in the firm — 3

2 Initiation of internationalization — 30

8 The international market selection process 218

Part II Case studies

16   Pricing decisions and terms of doing business   494

17   Distribution decisions   524

20 Organization and control of the global marketing programme   643

Part V Case studies

Preface to the third edition

Globalization is the growing interdependence of national economies – involving primarily customers, producers, suppliers and governments in different markets. Global marketing therefore reflects the trend of firms selling and distributing products and services in many countries around the world. It is associated with governments reducing trade and investment barriers, firms manufacturing in multiple countries and foreign firms increasingly competing in domestic markets.

For many years the globalization of markets, caused by the convergence of tastes across borders, was thought to result in very large multinational enterprises, which could use their advantages in scale economies to introduce world-standardised products successfully.

In his famous book from 1994, *The Global Paradox*, John Naisbitt has contradicted especially the last part of this myth:[1]

> The mindset that in a huge global economy the multinationals dominate world business couldn't have been more wrong. The bigger and more open the world economy becomes, the more small and middle sized companies will dominate. In one of the major turnarounds in my lifetime, we have moved from 'economies of scale' to 'diseconomies of scale'; from bigger is better to bigger is inefficient, costly and wastefully bureaucratic, inflexible and, now, disastrous. And the paradox that has occurred is, as we move to the global context: The smaller and speedier players will prevail on a much expanded field.

When the largest corporations (e.g. IBM, ABB) downsize, they are seeking to emulate the entrepreneurial behaviour of successful SMEs (small and medium-sized enterprises) where the implementation phase plays a more important role than in large companies. Since the behaviours of smaller and (divisions of) larger firms (according to the above quotation) are convergent, the differences in the global marketing behaviour between SMEs and LSEs (large-scale enterprises) are slowly disappearing. What is happening is that the LSEs are downsizing and decentralising their decision-making process. The result will be a more decision- and action-oriented approach to global marketing. This approach will also characterise this book.

In light of their smaller size, most SMEs lack the capabilities, market power and other resources of traditional multinational LSEs. Compared with the resource-rich LSEs, the complexities of operating under globalization are considerably more difficult for the SME. The success of SMEs under globalization depends in large part on the decision and implementation of the right international marketing strategy.

The primary role of marketing management, in any organization, is to design and execute effective marketing programmes that will pay off. Companies can do this in their home market or they can do it in one or more international markets. Going international is an enormously expensive exercise, in terms of both money and, especially, top management time and commitment. Due to the high cost, going international must generate added value for the company beyond extra sales. In other words, the company needs to gain a competitive advantage by going international. So, unless the company gains by going international, it should probably stay at home.

---

[1] Naisbitt, J. (1994) *The Global Paradox*, Nicholas Brealey Publishing, London p. 17.

The task of global marketing management is complex enough when the company operates in one foreign national market. It is much more complex when the company starts operations in several countries. Marketing programmes must, in these situations, adapt to the needs and preferences of customers that have different levels of purchasing power as well as different climates, languages and cultures. Moreover, patterns of competition and methods of doing business differ between nations and sometimes also within regions of the same nation. In spite of the many differences, however, it is important to hold on to similarities across borders. Some coordination of international activities will be required, but at the same time the company will gain some synergy across borders, in the way that experience and learning acquired in one country can be transferred to another.

Objectives

The book's value chain offers the reader an analytic decision-oriented framework for the development and implementation of global marketing programmes. Consequently, the reader should be able to analyse, select and evaluate the appropriate conceptual frameworks for approaching the five main management decisions connected with the global marketing process: (1) whether to internationalize, (2) deciding which markets to enter, (3) deciding how to enter the foreign market, (4) designing the global marketing programme and (5) implementing and coordinating the global marketing programme.

Having studied this book, the reader should be better equipped to understand how the firm can achieve global competitiveness through the design and implementation of market-responsive programmes.

Target audience

This book is written for people who want to develop effective and decision-oriented global marketing programmes. It can be used as a textbook for undergraduate or graduate courses in global/international marketing. A second audience is the large group of people joining 'global marketing' or 'export' courses on non-university programmes. The book is of special interest to the manager who wishes to keep abreast of the most recent developments in the global marketing field.

Prerequisites

An introductory course in marketing.

Special features

The book has been written from the perspective of the firm competing in international markets, irrespective of its country of origin. The book has the following key features:

- decision/'action'-oriented approach
- focus on SMEs as global marketing players

- buyer–seller relationships
- focus on SMEs as subsuppliers on the global market
- value chain approach
- market-responsive approach
- Internet marketing
- use of Internet in global marketing research.
- focus on global marketing in Far East countries (e.g. China)
- many up-to-date cases.

Outline

As the book has a clear **decision-oriented approach**, it is structured according to the five main decisions that marketing people in companies face in connection with the global marketing process. The 20 chapters are divided into five parts. The schematic outline of the book in Figure 1 shows how the different parts fit together. Compared to the second edition, 'global marketing research' is now considered to be an integral part of the decision-making process, therefore it has been moved to Chapter 5, so as to use it as an important input to the decision about which markets to enter (the beginning of Part II). Examples of the practice of global marketing by actual companies are used throughout the book, in the form of exhibits. Furthermore, each chapter and part end with cases, including questions for students.

Figure 1 Structure of the book

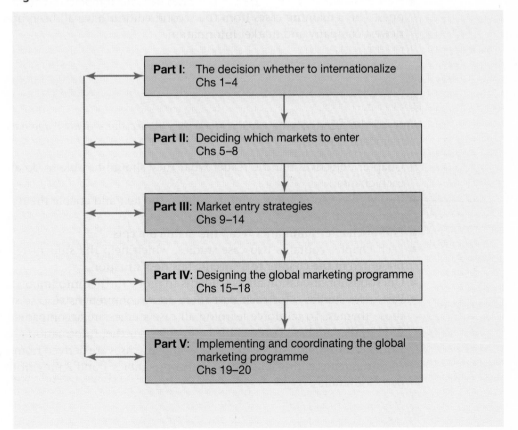

What's new in the third edition?

- Chapter 1 – Forces for 'global integration' and 'market responsiveness' (Section 1.4)
- Chapter 3 – The explanation of the transaction cost theory has been cut to a minimum, and only the key messages are further explained. The new sections are:
  - internationalization of SMEs (Section 3.5)
  - internationalization of services (Section 3.7)
- Chapter 5 – Now integrated into the text, this completely new chapter focuses on international marketing research. Compared to the second edition's Appendix, this chapter contains new sections on qualitative research, online surveys and scenario planning.
- Chapter 6 – A new section on The European Economic and Monetary Union (EMU) and the Euro (Section 6.4)
- Chapter 14 – As a consequence of developments in the communication technologies, this chapter now features a section about international mobile marketing (Section 14.9). There is also a new section about global strategy for Internet marketing (Section 14.8)
- Chapter 19 – Besides an expanded section on intercultural preparation, this chapter now includes comprehensive coverage of knowledge management and learning across borders and how to work in global project groups (Section 19.5)
- Chapter 20 – This chapter now includes more extensive coverage of the customer-oriented Global Account Management (GAM) organization (Section 20.3). Furthermore Section 20.5 on marketing control is supplemented by a better explanation of the underlying determinants in the global marketing budget.
- New and updated cases – Half of the cases have been replaced with new and updated ones. The remaining cases from the second edition have all been updated with the newest company and market information.

Pedagogical/learning aids

One of the strengths of *Global Marketing: A decision-oriented approach* is its strong pedagogical features.

- Chapter objectives tell the reader what they should be able to do after completing each chapter.
- Real world examples and exhibits enliven the text and enable the reader to relate to marketing models.
- End-of-chapter summaries recap the main concepts.
- Each chapter contains two case studies, which help the student relate the models presented in the chapter to a specific business situation.
- Questions for discussion allow students to probe further into important topics.
- Part cases studies – for each part there are 5 comprehensive case studies covering those themes. To reinforce learning all case studies are accompanied by questions. Case studies are based on real life companies. Further information about these companies can be found on the Internet. Company cases are derived from many different countries representing all parts of the world. Tables 1 and 2 present the chapter and part case studies.

Table 1 Chapter case studies: overview

Chapter	Case study title, subtitle and related websites	Country/area of company headquarters	Geographical target area	Target market	
				B-t-B	B-t-C
Chapter 1 Global marketing in the firm	*Case study 1.1* **Vermont Teddy Bear** Should Vermont Teddy Bear go abroad? www.vtbear.com	USA	USA/World	✓	✓
	Case study 1.2 **Arcor** A Latin American confectionary player is globalizing its business www.arcor.com.ar/eng/home.asp	Argentina	World		✓
Chapter 2 Initiation of internationalization	*Case study 2.1* **Blooming Clothing** A bumpy path to exports no website available	Ireland	Europe	✓	✓
	Case study 2.2 **Elvis Presley Enterprises Inc. (EPE)** Internationalization of a 'cult' icon www.elvis.com	USA	World		✓
Chapter 3 Internationalization theories	*Case study 3.1* **Cryos** They keep the stork busy around the world www.cryos.dk	Denmark	World	✓	✓
	Case study 3.2 **Fox Kids Europe** Rapid internationalization of a TV channel for kids www.foxkidseurope.com	Holland	Europe		✓
Chapter 4 Development of the firm's international competitiveness	*Case study 4.1* **Microsoft Xbox** The battle for gaming leadership against Nintendo's GameCube and Sony PlayStation 2 www.xbox.com www.microsoft.com/games	USA	World		✓
	Case study 4.2 **Sony Ericsson** Will pooling of competences in the mobile phone business create international competitiveness www.sonyericsson.com	Japan, Sweden	World	✓	✓
Chapter 5 Global marketing research	*Case study 5.1* **Teepack Spezialmaschinen GmbH** Organizing a global survey of customer satisfaction www.teepack.com	Germany	World	✓	
	Case study 5.2 **Tchibo** Expanding the coffee shops' business system in the United Kingdom and the rest of Europe www.tchibo.com	Germany	Germany	✓	

Table 1 continued

Chapter	Case study title, subtitle and related websites	Country/area of company headquarters	Geographical target area	Target market B-t-B	Target market B-t-C
Chapter 6 The political and economic environment	*Case study 6.1* **The World Bank and the IMF** What on earth is globalization about? Massive protests during a meeting in Washington www.worldbank.org www.imf.org	USA	World	✓	✓
	Case study 6.2 **Sauer-Danfoss** Which political/economic factor would affect a manufacturer of hydraulic components? www.sauer-danfoss.com	Germany, Denmark	World	✓	
Chapter 7 The sociocultural environment	*Case study 7.1* **Lifan** A Chinese subsupplier and brand manufacturer is aiming at the global market www.lifan.com/lifan	China	World	✓	✓
	Case study 7.2 **Playboy Enterprises** Internationalization of the Playboy Business compared with its major competitors (Hustler and Beate Uhse) www.playboyenterprises.com www.pornlegends.com/larryflynt.html www.hustler.com www.beate-uhse.ag	USA, Germany	World		✓
Chapter 8 The international market selection process	*Case study 8.1* **Jarlsberg** The king of Norwegian cheeses is seeking new markets www.tine.no/intmark/4735	Norway	World, USA	✓	✓
	Case study 8.2 **Durex** Using the 'Global Sex Survey' for seeking new condom markets www.durex.com	UK	World		✓
Chapter 9 Some approaches to the choice of entry mode	*Case study 9.1* **IO Interactive** A computer games developer is reconsidering its entry mode www.iointeractive-pr.com	Denmark	World	✓	✓
	Case study 9.2 **condomi AG** Evaluating its 'entry mode' strategy in Africa www.condomi.com	Germany	Africa	✓	✓

Table 1 **continued**

Chapters	Case study title, subtitle and related websites	Country/area of company headquarters	Geographical target area	Target market	
				B-t-B	B-t-C
Chapter 10 Export modes	*Case study 10.1* **Lysholm Linie Aquavit** Internationl marketing of the Norwegian Aquavit brand	Norway	Germany and the rest of World	✓	✓
	Case study 10.2 **Parle Products** An Indian biscuit brand is seeking agents and cooperation partners in new export markets **www.parleproducts.com**	India	World	✓	✓
Chapter 11 Intermediate entry modes	*Case study 11.1* **Ka-Boo-Ki** Licensing in the LEGO brand **www.lego.com/eng/wear**	Denmark	World	✓	✓
	Case study 11.2 **Bayer and GlaxoSmithKline** Can the X-coalition and the product Levitra challenge Viagra's market leader position? **www.bayergsk.com**	Germany, UK	World	✓	✓
Chapter 12 Hierarchical modes	*Case study 12.1* **Durex condoms** SSL will sell Durex condoms in the Japanese market through its own organization **www.durex.com**	UK	World	✓	✓
	Case study 12.2 **The Fred Hollows Foundation** A non-profit organization establishes lens production facilities in Nepal and Eritrea **www.hollows.org**	Australia	Less Developed Countries (LDCs)	✓	
Chapter 13 International sourcing decisions and the role of the subsupplier	*Case study 13.1* **LM Glasfiber A/S** Following its customers' international expansion in the wind turbine industry **www.lm.dk/uk**	Denmark	World	✓	
	Case study 13.2 **Lear Corporation** A leading supplier of automotive interior systems **www.lear.com**	USA	World	✓	
Chapter 14 Global e-marketing	*Case study 14.1* **Sonic innovations** A new US manufacturer of hearing aids is considering online sales in Europe **www.sonici.com**	USA	Europe	✓	✓
	Case study 14.2 **Auto-by-Tel** An example of reintermediation in the value chain **www.autobytel.com**	USA	Europe	✓	✓

Table 1 continued

Chapter	Case study title, subtitle and related websites	Country/area of company headquarters	Geographical target area	Target market B-t-B	B-t-C
Chapter 15 Product decisions	*Case study 15.1* **Danish Klassic** Launch of a cream cheese in Saudi Arabia **no website available**	Denmark	Saudi Arabia	✓	✓
	Case study 15.2 **Zippo Manufacturing Company** Has product diversification beyond the lighter gone too far? **www.zippo.com**	USA	World		✓
Chapter 16 Pricing decisions and the terms of doing business	*Case study 16.1* **Harley-Davidson** Does the image justify the price level? **www.harley-davidson.com**	USA	USA and Europe		✓
	Case study 16.2 **Gillette Co.** Is price standardisation possible for razor blades? **www.gillette.com**	USA	World	✓	✓
Chapter 17 Distribution decisions	*Case study 17.1* **De Beers** Forward integration into the diamond industry value chain **www.debeers.com**	South Africa, UK	Europe, World	✓	✓
	Case study 17.2 **Konka Group** Will an aggressive strategy help the Chinese television manufacturer to penetrate US retail distribution? **www.konka.com**	China	USA	✓	✓
Chapter 18 Communication decisions	*Case study 18.1* **Helly Hansen** Sponsoring fashion clothes in the US market **www.hellyhansen.com**	Norway	USA	✓	✓
	Case study 18.2 **Fisherman's Friend** Is sponsoring extreme motorsport events a good promotion tool? **www.fishermansfriend.com**	UK	Europe		✓
Chapter 19 Cross-cultural negotiations	*Case study 19.1* **Mecca Cola** Marketing of a Muslim cola to the European market **www.mecca-cola.com**	France	Europe	✓	✓
	Case study 19.2 **Toto** The Japanese toilet manufacturer seeks export opportunities for its high-tech brands in the United States **www.tot.co.jp**	Japan	USA	✓	✓

Table 1 continued

Chapter	Case study title, subtitle and related websites	Country/area of company headquarters	Geographical target area	Target market B-t-B	Target market B-t-C
Chapter 20 Organization and control of the global marketing programme	Case study 20.1 **Mars Inc.** Merger of the European food, petcare and confectionary divisions www.mars.com	USA	World	✓	✓
	Case study 20.2 **AGRAMKOW Fluid Systems** Reconsidering its global organization structure www.agramkow.com	Denmark	World	✓	

Table 2 Part case studies: overview

Part	Case study title, subtitle and related websites	Country/area of company headquarters	Geographical target area	Target market B-t-B	Target market B-t-C
Part I The decision whether to internationalize	Case study I.1 **Manchester United** Trying to establish a global brand www.manutd.com	UK	World (USA)	✓	✓
	Case study I.2 **Bridgestone Tyres** European Marketing Strategy www.bridgestone.com	Japan	Europe	✓	✓
	Case study I.3 **ResMed Inc.** Helping patients around the world suffering from obstructive sleep apnea (OSA) www.resmed.com	USA, Australia	World	✓	✓
	Case study I.4 **Steinway & Sons** Internationalizing the piano business www.steinway.com	USA	World		✓
	Case study I.5 **Titan Industries Ltd.** Is Titan Watches ready for globalization? www.titanworld.com	India	World		✓
Part II Deciding which markets to enter	Case study II.1 **CarLovers Carwash** Serendipity as a factor in foreign market selection: the case study of CarLovers of Australia no website available	Australia	World		✓
	Case study II.2 **Female Health Company** The female condom, Femidom, is seeking a foothold in the world market for contraceptive products www.femalehealth.com	USA	World (governmental organizations)	✓	✓

Table 2 continued

Part	Case study title, subtitle and related websites	Country/area of company headquarters	Geographical target area	Target market	
				B-t-B	B-t-C
	Case study II.3 **Tipperary Mineral Water Company** Market selection inside/outside Europe www.tipperary-water.ie	Ireland	Europe		✓
	Case study II.4 **Beverage Brands** Planning an international raid with the FABs (flavoured alcoholic beverages) www.shs-group.co.uk	UK	World		✓
	Case study II.5 **Village Roadshow/AOL Time Warner** Globalization of the theme park business www.villageroadshow.com.au	Australia, USA	World	✓	✓
Part III Market entry strategies	Case study III.1 **IKEA** Expanding through franchising to the South American market? www.ikea.com	Sweden, Holland	South America (Brazil)		✓
	Case study III.2 **NTT DoCoMo** Using a strong domestic position as a basis for international expansion. www.nttdocomo.com	Japan	World		✓
	Case study III.3 **Autoliv Air Bags** Transforming Autoliv into a global company www.autoliv.com	Sweden	World	✓	
	Case study III.4 **IMAX Corporation** Globalization of the film business www.imax.com	Canada	World	✓	✓
	Case study III.5 **Heineken/Al Ahram Beverages Co.** Marketing of alcoholic and non-alcoholic drinks to Egypt and other Muslim markets – does an acquisition help? www.heineken.com www.alahrambeverages.com	Holland, Egypt	Arabic world	✓	✓
Part IV Designing the global marketing programme	Case study IV.1 **Absolut Vodka** Defending and attacking for a better position in the global vodka market www.absolut.com	Sweden	World (Eastern Europe)		✓
	Case study IV.2 **3B Scientific** World market leader in the niche of anatomical models www.3bscientific.com	Germany	World	✓	✓

Table 2 continued

Part	Case study title, subtitle and related websites	Country/area of company headquarters	Geographical target area	Target market	
				B-t-B	B-t-C
	Case study IV.3 **BMG (A)** Global marketing strategy for the music business www.bmg.com	Germany/ USA	World	✓	✓
	Case study IV.4 **Dyson Vacuum Cleaner** Shifting from domestic to international marketing with the famous bagless vacuum cleaner www.dyson.co.uk	UK	USA and the rest of the World	✓	✓
	Case study IV.5 **Triumph Motorcycles Ltd** Rising from the ashes in the international motorcycle business www.triumph.co.uk	UK	World		✓
Part V Implementing and coordinating the global marketing programme	*Case study V.1* **Femilet** A SME is seeking foothold in the European lingerie market www.femilet.com	Denmark	Europe	✓	✓
	Case study V.2 **BMG (B)** New worldwide organizational structure and the marketing planning and budgeting of Dido's new album www.bmg.com	Germany/ USA	World, UK		✓
	Case study V.3 **Dandy/Cadbury Schweppes** Alliance building and corporate organizational considerations in the world chewing gum market www.cadburyschweppes.com	Denmark, UK	World	✓	✓
	Case study V.4 **SKF Rolling Bearings** The automotive division is facing a big challenge in Japan www.skf.com	Sweden	Japan	✓	
	Case study V.5 **Vipp AS** A SME uses global branding to break into the international waste bin business www.vipp.dk	Denmark	Europe		✓

Guided tour of the book

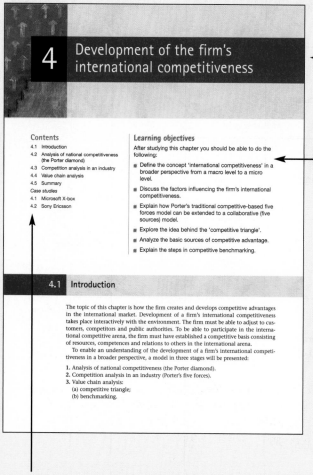

An attractive, user-friendly, full-colour text design colourfully highlights key aspects of the text for the reader

Learning objectives list the topics covered and what you should have learnt by the end of the chapter

Figures are used to illustrate key points, models, theories and processes

Brief contents allow you to get a clear picture of how the chapter is structured

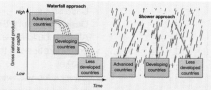

Exhibits appear throughout the text, applying theory to real-life examples of well-known brands

CASE STUDY 5.1   Teepack Spezialmaschinen GmbH

Organizing a global survey of customer satisfaction

Teepack (**www.teepack.com**) is a specialised manufacturer of tea bag machines for the world's best-known brands of tea and herbs and fruit teas, such as Lipton, Pickwick, Twinnings and Lyons/Tetley.

Teepack is a sister company of Teekanne,[1] the leading tea, herb, and fruit tea packing company in Germany, with the Teefix, Pompadour and Teekanne brands.

The invention of the automatic tea bag-packaging machine by Teepack in 1949 revolutionised the tea market with the double-chamber tea bag. It meant that production volumes could be increased dramatically. Today the latest generation of these machines is capable of production speeds of almost 400 tea bags per minute, i.e. some 4 billion per year.

The tea bag produced on Teepack machines is the most sold double-chamber tea bag in the world. Important benefits are that it has considerably larger space between the two bag chambers and offers maximum tea bag stability and durability without adding glue or heat sealing.

The popularity of this practical tea bag has continued to grow, for example in Germany 82 per cent of tea sales are in double-chamber tea bags; in the United States the figure is about 90 per cent and in Europe, if you omit the United Kingdom, the figure is close to 100 per cent. Even in the former UK colony, Australia, the double-chamber tea bag has almost convinced the consumers. 'Down under', sales of UK tea bags and the double-chamber tea bag more or less balance themselves out.

For over 50 years Teepack GmbH has been the number one producer of double-chamber tea packaging machines in the world and has sold more than 2,000 of its packaging machines 'Constanta'. Thanks to Teapack's packaging machines Lipton is the market leader of the international tea market. Up to 1957 Teepack had sold more than 100 tea bag packaging machines in the United States.

Technical innovation resulted in Teepack engineers developing a new, even more efficient machine – 'Perfecta'. Since 1990 more than 200 'Perfecta' machines have been sold worldwide.

Today Teepack has a market share of about 70 per cent of the global double chamber tea bag machine market.

Questions
(Please visit **www.teepack.com** before you answer the questions.)

1. How would you forecast worldwide demand for tea bag machines?

2. Argue the case for the market analysis method you would choose if you had to evaluate the competitiveness of Teepack Spezialmaschinen on the global tea bag packaging machine market.

3. In order to achieve better customer feedback, the top management of Teepack is interested in learning how to measure customer satisfaction. Propose a questionnaire design that contains some of the themes which it would be relevant to include in the questionnaire.

4. How would you organise the internal database with the customers' responses and the feedback of the questionnaire results to the customers?

[1] The Teekanne Group has production and sales subsidiaries in several countries. There are about 1,300 employees in the Group.

The colourfully illustrated, up-to-date **Case studies** help consolidate your learning of the major themes by encouraging you to apply what you have learnt to real-life marketing scenarios

Each chapter ends with **Questions for discussion**, which reinforce learning with problems and practical exercises

Questions for discussion

1. Why are joint ventures preferred by host countries as an entry strategy for foreign firms?

2. Why are strategic alliances used in new product development?

3. Under what circumstances should franchising be considered? How do these circumstances vary from those leading to licensing?

4. Do you believe that licensing in represents a feasible long-term product development strategy for a company? Discuss in relation to in-house product development.

5. Why would a firm consider forming partnerships with competitors?

6. Apart from the management fees involved, what benefits might a firm derive from entering into management contracts overseas?

References

Bleeke, J. and Ernst, D. (1994) *Collaborating to Compete: Using strategic alliances and acquisitions in the global marketplace*, John Wiley, New York.
Bradley, F. (1995) *International Marketing Strategy* (2nd edn), Prentice Hall, Hemel Hempstead.
Carstairs, R.T. and Welch, L.S. (1981) *A Study of Outward Foreign Licensing of Technology by Australian Companies*, Licensing Executives Society of Australia, Canberra.
Harrigan, K.R. (1985) *Strategies for Joint Ventures*, Lexington Books and D.C. Heath, Lexington, MA.
Lorange, P. and Roos, J. (1995) *Strategiske allianser i globale strategier*, Norges Eksportråd, Oslo.
Lowe, J. and Crawford, N. (1984) *Technology Licensing and the Small Firm*, Gower, Aldershot.
Luostarinen, R. and Welch, L. (1990) *International Business Operations*, Helsinki School of Economics, Helsinki.
Nanda, A. and Williamson, P.J. (1995) 'Use joint ventures to ease the pain of restructuring', *Harvard Business Review*, November–December, pp. 119–28.
Paliwoda, S. (1993) *International Marketing*, Heinemann, Oxford.
Perkins, J.S. (1987) 'How licensing and franchising differ', *Les Nouvelles*, vol. 22, no. 4, pp. 155–8.
Porter, M.E. and Fuller, M.B. (1986) 'Coalition and global strategy', in Porter, M.E. (ed.), *Competition in Global Strategies*, Harvard Business School Press, Boston, MA.
Walmsley, J. (1982) *Handbook of International Joint Ventures*, Graham & Trotman Ltd, London.
Young, S., Hamill, J. Wheeler, S. and Davies, J.R. (1989) *International Market Entry and Development*, Harvester Wheatsheaf/Prentice Hall, Hemel Hempstead.

Further reading

Andersen, P.H. (2000) 'A foot in the door: relationship marketing efforts towards transaction-oriented customers', *Journal of Market-Focused Management*, vol. 5, pp. 91–118.
BatNir, A. and Smith, A. (2002) 'Interfirm alliances in the small business: the role of social networks', *Journal of Small Business Management*, vol. 40, no. 3, pp. 219–32.
Berdrow, I. and Lane, H.W. (2003) 'International joint ventures: creating value through successful knowledge management', *Journal of World Business*, forthcoming.

Questions give you an opportunity to test your understanding of the material. Answers appear on the website, at www.booksites.net/hollensen

References provide sources for additional study on key topics and themes

Every chapter is supported by a **Further reading** section, giving many valuable printed and electronic sources for supplementary study

Acknowledgements

Writing any book is a long-term commitment and involves time-consuming effort. The successful completion of a book depends on the support and generosity of many people and the realisation of this book is certainly no exception.

I wish to thank the many scholars whose articles, books and other materials I have cited or quoted. However, it is not possible to acknowledge everyone by name. In particular I am deeply indebted to the following individuals and organizations. I thank you all for your help and contribution:

University of Southern Denmark

- Management at University of Southern Denmark provided the best possible environment for writing and completing this project.
- Colleagues provided encouragement and support during the writing process.
- Charlotte Hansen and Aase Simonsen took care of word processing of my drafts in a highly efficient manner. Furthermore they created many of the new figures in an imaginative way.
- The Library, Ole Krogh and the team behind him provided articles and books from different worldwide sources.

Reviewers

- Reviewers provided suggestions which were useful in improving many parts of the text.
- In the development of this text a number of reviewers have been involved, whom I would like to thank for their important and valuable contribution: Henrik Agndal, Jönköping International Business School; Grahame Fallon, University College Northampton; Poul Houman Andersen, Arhus School of Business.
- Professor Alkis Magdalinos, University of La Verne Athens Campus contributed with many necessary corrections and suggestions for improvement in different sections of the book.

Case contributors

- Dr. Mohan Lal Agrawal, Center for Services, Lucknow (India) for Case I.5: Titan Industries Ltd.
- Bill Merrilees and Dale Miller, Marketing Group, Department of Management, University of Newcastle, Australia for Case II.1: CarLovers Carwash.

I also wish to acknowledge the help from the following firms whose managers have provided valuable material that has enabled me to write the following cases. I have been in direct personal contact with most of the companies and I thank the managers involved for their very useful comments.

- Bridgestone/Firestone, Bruxelles, Belgium/Tokyo, Japan for Case I.2: Bridgestone Tyres.

- Bertelsmann Music Group (BMG), Gütersloh, Germany for Cases IV.3: BMG (A) and V.2: BMG (B).
- Autoliv AB, Stockholm, Sweden for Case III.3: Autoliv Air Bags.
- IMAX Corporation, Toronto, Canada for Case III.4: Imax Corporation.
- Dandy Group, Vejle, Denmark for Case V.3: Dandy/Cadbury Schweppes.
- The Absolut Company, a division of Vin & Sprit AB, Stockholm, Sweden for Case IV.1: Absolut Vodka.
- 3B Scientific, Poul Binhold, Lehrmittelfabrik, GmbH, Hamburg, Germany for Case IV.2: 3B Scientific.
- SKF, Göteborg, Sweden for Case V.4: SKF Rolling Bearings.

I am also grateful to the following international advertising agencies, which have provided me with examples of standardized and/or localized advertising campaigns:

- J. Walter Thompson (JWT Europe), London who contributed with a European ad for LUX soap.
- Hindustan Thompson (HTA), Bombay, India who contributed with an ad for Kellogg's Basmati Flakes in India and an ad for LUX soap in India.
- Ammirati Puris Lintas, Hamburg, Germany who contributed with an ad from the 'Me and my Magnum' campaign.

I would also like to thank LEGO and Langnese (special thanks to Silke for her efforts to get the Magnum ad) for their contributions to different examples in the book.

I am grateful to my publisher, Pearson Education. I would like to thank Development Editor Louise Lakey, and Editorial Assistant Ernestine Weller for their help with this edition. Joining the project were Senior Acquisitions Editor Thomas Sigel, Development Editor David Cox, Senior Editor Verina Pettigrew (and the team behind them) and Freelance Permissions Editor Lynette Miller; I thank them for their encouragement and professionalism in transforming the manuscript into the final book.

I also extend my greatest gratitude to my colleagues at the University of Southern Denmark for their constant help and inspiration.

Finally, I thank my family for their support through the revision process. I am pleased to dedicate this version to Jonna, Nanna and Julie.

Svend Hollensen
Sønderborg, Denmark
March 2004

svend@sam.sdu.dk

Publisher's acknowledgements

We are grateful to the following for permission to reproduce copyright material:

Figure 1.1 from A framework for analysis of strategy development in globalizing markets, *Journal of International Marketing*, Vol. 5 (1), reprinted by permission of American Marketing Association (Solberg, C.A. 1997); Figure 1.4 from The strategy concept I: five Ps for strategy, *California Management Review*, Vol. 30, No. 1, reprinted by permission of The Regents of the University of California (Mintzberg, H. 1987); Figure 1.5 from Rethinking incrementalism, *Strategic Management Journal*, Vol. 9, reprinted by permission of John Wiley & Sons Ltd. (Johnson, G. 1988); Figure 1.8 from *In Search of Excellence: Lessons from America's Best Run Companies*, reprinted by permission of HarperCollins Publishers Inc. (Peters, T.J. and Waterman, Jr., R.H. 1982); Figure 1.9 adapted from *Competitive Advantage: Creating and Sustaining Superior Performance*, reprinted by permission of The Free Press, a Division of Simon & Schuster Adult Publishing Group (Porter, M.E. 1985); Table 2.1 adapted from *International Marketing and Export Management, 2nd Edition*, pub Addison-Wesley, reprinted by permission of Pearson Education Ltd. (Albaum, G. *et al*. 1994); Figure 3.1 adapted from *International företagsekonomi*, pub Norstedts, reprinted by permission of Mats Forsgren (Forsgren, M. and Johanson, J. 1975); Figure 3.6 from Internationalization in industrial systems in *Strategies in Global Competition* edited by N. Hood and J.E. Vahlne, pub Croom Helm, reprinted by permission of Thomson Publishing Services (Johanson, J. and Mattson, L.G. 1988); Figure 4.4 adapted from Competitive advantage: merging marketing and competence-based perspective, *Journal of Business and Industrial Marketing*, Vol. 9, No. 4, reprinted by permission of Hans P. Wehrli (Jüttner, U. and Wehrli, H.P. 1994); Figure 4.5 from Exploiting the core competences of your organization, *Long Range Planning*, Vol. 27, No. 4, reprinted by permission of Elsevier (Tampoe, M. 1994); Case Study I.1, Table 1, from Big kick, Forbes Global 7 August, reprinted by permission of Forbes Global (Heller, R. 2002); Figure 5.6 from Gathering and interpreting strategic intelligence in Asia Pacific, *Long Range Planning*, Vol. 26, No. 3, reprinted by permission of Elsevier (Lasserre, P. 1993); Table 6.1 from *The Economist* 25 April 2003, reprinted by permission of The Economist Newspaper Ltd., London; Table 7.2 adapted from *International Marketing Strategy: Analysis, Development and Implementation*, pub Routledge, reprinted by permission of Thomson Publishing Services (Phillips, C. *et al*. 1994); Figure 7.3 from *International Marketing: A Cultural Approach*, reprinted by permission of Pearson Education Ltd. (Usunier, J.-C. 2000); Figure 7.4 from *Culture's Consequences: International Differences in Work-Related Values*, pub Sage, reprinted by permission of Geert Hofstede (Hofstede, G. 1980); Table 7.4 from *Going International*, pub Random House, reprinted by permission The Sagalyn Agency (Copeland, L. and Griggs, L. 1985); Figure 8.7 and Table 15.5 from *European Business: An Issue-Based Approach, 3rd Edition*, pub Pitman, reprinted by permission of Pearson Education Ltd. (Welford, R. and Prescott, K. 1996); Figure 8.10 from *Global Marketing Management*, pub Prentice Hall, reprinted by permission of Pearson Education, Inc. (Keegan, W.J. 1995); Figure 8.11 from *International Marketing Strategy*, pub Prentice Hall, reprinted by permission of Pearson Education Ltd. (Bradley, F. 1995); Figure 8.12 from Market expansion strategies in multinational marketing, *Journal of Marketing*, Vol. 43, Spring, reprinted by permission of American Marketing Association

(Ayal, I. And Zif, J. 1979); Table 10.1 from *Entry Strategies for International Markets: Revised and Expanded Edition*, pub Lexington Books, reprinted by permission of John Wiley & Sons, Inc. (Root, F.R. 1994); Table 11.3 adapted from *International Market Entry and Development*, pub Harvester Wheatsheaf/Prentice Hall, reprinted by permission of Pearson Education Ltd. (Young, S. *et al.* 1989); Figure 11.4 adapted from *Strategiske allianser i globale strategier*, pub Norges Eksportråd, reprinted by permission of Index Publishing/Norwegian Trade Council (Lorange, P. and Roos, J. 1995); Figures 11.5 and 11.6 from *Strategies for Joint Ventures*, reprinted by permission of K.R. Harrigan (Harrigan, K.R. 1985); Figure 12.3 from Organisational dimensions of global marketing, *European Journal of Marketing*, Vol. 23, No. 5, reprinted by permission of Emerald Publishing Ltd. (Raffée, H. and Kreutzer, R. 1989); Figure 12.4 from Regional headquarters: the spearhead for Asian Pacific markets, *Long Range Planning*, Vol. 29, No. 1, reprinted by permission of Elsevier (Lasserre, P. 1996); Figure 12.5 from Why are subsidiaries divested? A conceptual framework, *Working Paper No. 3–93*, reprinted by permission of Institute of International Economics and Management, Copenhagen Business School (Benito, G. 1996); Figure 13.1 adapted from Alihankintajarjestelma 1990-luvulla [subcontracting system in the 1990s], *Publications of SITRA*, No. 114, reprinted by permission of Sitra (Lehtinen, U. 1991); Table 13.1 and Figure 13.6 from Relationship marketing from a value system perspective, *International Journal of Service Industry Management*, No. 5, reprinted by permission of Emerald Publishing Ltd. (Jüttner, U. and Wehrli, H.P. 1994); Figure 13.3 from A total cost/value model for supply chain competitiveness, *Journal of Business Logistics*, Vol. 13, No. 2, reprinted by permission of Council of Logistics Management (Cavinato, J.L. 1992); Figure 13.4 adapted from Interactive strategies in supply chains: a double-edged portfolio approach to SME, *Subcontractors Positioning Paper* presented at the 8th Nordic Conference on Small Business Research, reprinted by permission of Per Blenker (Blenker, P. and Christensen, P.R. 1994); Figure 13.5 from *Strategies for International Industrial Marketing*, pub Croom Helm, reprinted by permission of Thomson Publishing Services (Turnbull, P.W. and Valla, J.P. 1986); Figure 13.7 from Developing buyer-seller relationships, *Journal of Marketing*, Vol. 51, April, reprinted by permission of American Marketing Association (Dwyer, R.F., *et al.* 1987); Figure 14.3 from Consumer purchasing on the Internet: process and prospects, *European Management Journal*, Vol. 16, No. 5, October, reprinted by permission of Elsevier Science (Butler, P. and Peppard, J. 1998); Part IV, Figure 3, p. 448, from Standardisation: an integrated approach to global marketing, *European Journal of Marketing*, Vol. 22, No. 10, reprinted by permission of Emerald Group Publishing Ltd. (Kreutzer, R. 1988); Table 15.2, Figure 15.9 and Figure 15.10 from New products: cutting the time to market, *Long Range Planning*, Vol. 28, No. 2, reprinted by permission of Elsevier (Töpfer, A. 1995); Table 15.3 adapted from The international dimension of branding: strategic considerations and decisions, *International Marketing Review*, Vol. 6, No. 3, reprinted by permission of Emerald Publishing Ltd. (Onkvisit, S. and Shaw, J.J. 1989); Table 15.4 from The future of consumer branding as seen from the picture today, *Journal of Consumer Marketing*, Vol. 12, No. 4, reprinted by permission of Emerald Group Publishing Ltd. (Boze, B.V. and Patton, C.R. 1995); Figure 15.5 partly reprinted from Competitive analysis using matrix displays, *Long Range Planning*, Vol. 17, No. 3, reprinted by permission of Elsevier (McNamee, P. 1984); Figure 15.6 from *International Marketing: Analysis and Strategy, 2nd Edition*, pub Macmillan, reprinted by permission of Sak Onkvisit (Onkvisit, S. and Shaw, J.J. 1993); Figure 15.13 adapted from *International Marketing: Analysis and Strategy, 2nd Edition*, pub Macmillan, reprinted by permission of Sak Onkvisit (Onkvisit, S. and Shaw, J.J. 1993); Figure 15.18 adapted from Environmentally responsible logistics systems, *International Journal of Physical Distribution and Logistics Management*, Vol. 25, No. 2, reprinted by permission of Emerald Group Publishing Ltd. (Wu, H.J. and Dunn, S.C. 1995); Figure 16.5 from

Pricing conditions in the European Common Market, *European Management Journal*, Vol. 12, No. 2, reprinted by permission of Elsevier (Diller, H. and Bukhari, I. 1994); Figure 16.6 from The European pricing bomb – and how to cope with it, *Marketing and Research Today*, February, reprinted by permission of ESOMAR (Simon, H. and Kucher, E. 1993); Figure 16.8 adapted from *International Marketing Strategy: Analysis, Development and Implementation*, pub Routledge, reprinted by permission of Thomson Publishing Services (Phillips *et al.* 1994); Table 17.1 from Are you tough enough to manage your channels?, *The McKinsey Quarterly*, No. 1, reprinted by permission of McKinsey and Company (Bucklin, C.B. *et al.* 1996); Table 17.2 from *Global Marketing Management: A Strategic Perspective, 2nd Edition*, pub Allyn & Bacon, reprinted by permission of Pearson Education, Inc. (Toyne, B. and Walters, P.G.P. 1993); Figure 17.3 from US-Japan distribution channel cost structures: is there a significant difference?, *International Journal of Physical Distribution and Logistics Management*, Vol. 27, No. 1, reprinted by permission of Emerald Group Publishing Ltd. (Pirog III, S.F. and Lancioni, R. 1997); Table 17.3 from *International Marketing Management, 5th Edition*, reprinted by permission of South-Western, a division of Thomson Learning (Jain, S.C. 1996); Figure 17.4 adapted from *Marketing Management: An Overview*, pub The Dryden Press, reprinted by permission of Dale M. Lewison (Lewison, D.M. 1996); Figure 17.5 from *Marketing Management: An Overview*, pub The Dryden Press, reprinted by permission of Dale M. Lewison (Lewison, D.M. 1996); Figure 17.8 from *International Marketing and Export Management, 2nd Edition*, pub Addison-Wesley, reprinted by permission of Pearson Education Ltd.; Figure 17.11 from *International Marketing*, pub Heinemann, reprinted by permission of Butterworth Heinemann Publishers, a division of Reed Educational & Professional Publishing Ltd. (Paliwoda, S. 1993); Table 18.3 from *International Marketing Strategy: Analysis, Development and Implementation*, pub Routledge, reprinted by permission of Thomson Publishing Services (Phillips *et al.* 1994); Figure 18.5 adapted from Trade fairs as international marketing venues: a case study, paper presented at the 12th IMP Conference, University of Karlsruhe, reprinted by permission of P.J. Rosson (Rosson, P.J. and Seringhaus, F.H.R. 1996); Table 18.5 from Guidelines for managing an international sales force, *Industrial Marketing Management*, Vol. 24, reprinted by permission of Elsevier (Honeycutt, E.D. and Ford, J.B. 1995); Table 20.1 adapted from *Principles and Practice of Marketing, 3rd Edition*, reprinted by permission of McGraw-Hill Publishing Company (Jobber, D. 1995); Table 20.3 adapted from *Marketing Management: Analysis, Planning, Implementation and Control, 9th Edition*, pub Prentice Hall, reprinted by permission of Pearson Education, Inc. (Kotler, P. 1997); Exhibit 20.1 Figure Sauer-Danfoss Production Locations reprinted by permission of Sauer-Danfoss Inc.

We are grateful to the following for permission to reproduce Case Study material:
Case Study 2.2 screen shot from www.elvis.com, Elvis image used by permission, Elvis Presley Enterprises, Inc.; Case Study 3.1 screen shot from www.cryos.dk reprinted by permission of Cryos International Sperm Bank Ltd.; Case Study 3.2 screen shot from www.foxkids.hu reprinted with kind permission of Fox Kids Europe; Case Study 4.1 screen shot from www.xbox.com reprinted by permission from Microsoft Corporation; Case Study 4.2 screen shot from www.sonyericsson.com included with the kind permission of Sony Ericsson. Sony is a trademark of Sony Corporation and Ericsson is a trademark of LM Ericsson; Case Study I.1 screen shot from www.manutd.com reprinted by permission of Manchester United plc; Case Study I.3 reprinted by permission of ResMed; Case Study I.4 screen shot from www.steinway.com reprinted by permission of Steinway & Sons; Case Study 5.1 screen shot from www.teepack.com reprinted by permission of Teepack Spezialmaschinen GmbH & Co. KG; Case Study 5.2 reprinted by

permission of Tchibo Frisch-Röst-Kaffee GmbH; Case Study 6.1 screen shot from www.worldbank.com republished with permission of The World Bank Group, from World Bank Online, 2003; permission conveyed through Copyright Clearance Center, Inc.; Case Study 6.2 screen shot from www.sauer-danfoss.com reprinted by permission of Sauer-Danfoss Inc.; Case Study 7.2 screen shot from www.playboyenterprises.com reprinted by permission of Playboy Enterprises, Inc.; Case Study 8.1 screen shot from www.norseland.com reprinted by permission of Norseland, Incorporated; Case Study 8.2 screen shot from www.durex.com reprinted by permission of SSL International plc; Case Study II.2 screen shot from www.femalehealth.com reprinted by permission of The Female Health Company; Case Study II.5 screen shot from www.movieworld. com.au reprinted by permission of Warner Village Theme Parks; Case Study 9.1 reprinted by permission of IO Interactive A/S; Case Study 9.2 reprinted by permission of Condomi AG; Case Study 10.1 reprinted by permission of Arcus; Case Study 12.2 screen shot from www.hollows.org courtesy of The Fred Hollows Foundation/www. hollows.org; Case Study III.1 screen shot from www.ikea.com reprinted by permission of IKEA Ltd; Case Study III.3 screen shot from www.autoliv.com reprinted by permission of Autoliv Inc.; Case Study III.4 reprinted by permission of IMAX Corporation; Case Study III.5 screen shot from www.alahrambeverages.com reprinted by permission of Al Ahram Beverages Company; Case Study 15.2 screen shot from www.zippo.com reprinted by permission of Zippo Manufacturing Company; Case Study IV.1 screen shot from www.absolut.com reprinted by permission of V&S Vin & Sprit AB; Case Study V3 reprinted by permission of Cadbury Schweppes plc and The Joyco Group; Case Study V5 reprinted by permission of SKF.

We are grateful to the following for permission to reproduce pictures:
Case Study 10.1 Linie Aquavit advertisement reprinted by permission of Arcus; Case Study 10.2 Parle-G advertisement reprinted by permission of Parle Products Pvt. Ltd.; Case Study 11.1 LEGO Kids Wear advertisement reprinted by permission of KA-BOO-KI A/S; Case Study 15.1, Plates 15.1, 15.2, 15.3 and 15.4 Danish Klassic advertising material and Plate 15.5 Puck Cream Cheese advertisement reprinted by permission of Arla Foods amba; Plate 18.9 Gammel Dansk advertisement reprinted by permission of Danisco Distillers Berlin GmbH; Case Study 18.1, Plate 18.14 Helly Hansen advertisement reprinted by permission of A/S Helly Hansen; Case Study IV.1, Plates IV-2, IV-3, IV-4 and IV-5 Absolut advertisements under permission by V&S Vin and Sprit AB; Case Study IV.2, Plates IV-8, IV-9, IV-10, IV-11 and IV-12 examples of 3B Scientific product programme reprinted by permission of 3B Scientific Hamburg; Case Study IV.5 Triumph motorcycle reprinted by permission of Triumph Motorcycles Ltd.; Case Study V.1 Femilet advertisement reprinted by permission of Femilet; Case Study V.5 Vipp waste bins, Vipp advertisements and 2003 Vipp Annonceplan reprinted by permission of Vipp AS.

We are grateful to the following for permission to reproduce texts:
Exhibit 13.1 from Network sourcing: A hybrid approach, *International Journal of Purchasing and Materials Management*, Vol. 31, No. 2, Spring, reprinted by permission of The National Association of Purchasing Management (Hines, P. 1995); Chapter 15, p. 455, extract from Developing global strategies for service businesses, *California Management Review*, Vol. 38, No. 2, reprinted by permission of The Regents of the University of California (Lovelock, C. and Yip, G.S. 1996).

In some instances we have been unable to trace the owners of copyright material, and we would appreciate any information that would enable us to do so.

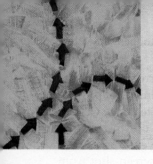

Abbreviations

ACs	advanced countries
APEC	Asia Pacific Economic Cooperation
ASEAN	Association of South East Asian Nations
B2B	business to business
B2C	business to consumer
C2B	consumer to business
C2C	consumer to consumer
CATI	computer-assisted telephone interviews
CEO	chief executive officer
CFR	cost and freight
CIF	cost, insurance and freight
CIP	carriage and insurance paid to
CPI	carriage paid to
DAF	delivered at frontier
DDP	delivered duty paid
DDU	delivered duty unpaid
DEQ	delivered ex-quay
DES	delivered ex-ship
DSS	decision support system
ECB	European Central Bank
ECO	ecology
EDI	electronic data interchange
EEG	European Economic Area
EFTA	European Free Trade Area
EMC	export management company
EMU	European Economic and Monetary Union
EU	European Union: title for the former EEC used since the ratification of the Maastricht Treaty in 1992
EXW	ex-works
FAS	free alongside ship
FCA	free carrier
FDI	foreign direct investment: a market entry strategy in which a company invests in a subsidiary or partnership in a foreign market (joint venture)
FMCG	fast-moving consumer goods
FOB	free on board: the seller quotes a price covering all expenses up to the point of shipment
FSC	foreign sales corporation
GAM	global account management
GDP	gross domestic product
GNP	gross national product: the total 'gross value' of all goods and services produced in the economy in one year
GRPs	gross rating points
HQ	headquarters

IDR	intermediation-disintermediation-reintermediation
IMF	International Monetary Fund
IMS	international market selection
IPLC	international product life cycle
ISO	International Standards Organization
IT	information technology
L/C	letter of credit
LDCs	less developed countries
LSEs	large-scale enterprises
MNCs	multinational corporations
NAFTA	North American Free Trade Agreement: a free trade agreement to establish an open market between the United States, Canada and Mexico
NICs	newly industrialised countries
OE	operational effectiveness
OECD	Organization for Economic Cooperation and Development: a multinational forum that allows the major industrialised nations to discuss economic policies and events
OEM	original equipment manufacturer (outsourcer)
OLI	ownership-location-internalization
OPEC	Organization for Petroleum Exporting Countries
PDAs	personal digital assistants
PLC	product life cycle: a theory that characterises the sales history of products as passing through four stages: introduction, growth, maturity, decline
PPP	purchasing-power parity
PR	public relations
QDF	quality deployment function
R&D	research and development
RMS	regional management centre
SBU	strategic business unit: a single business or a collection of related businesses that can be planned separately from the rest of the company
SMEs	small and medium-sized enterprises
SRC	self-reference criterion
TCA	transactional cost analysis
TFs	trade fairs
TQM	total quality management
USP	unique selling proposition
VER	voluntary export restraint
WTO	World Trade Organization

E-marketing terminology

Bandwidth Indicates the speed at which data are transferred using a particular network medium. It is measured in bits per second (bps).

Banner advertisement A graphic displayed on a Web page for purposes of brand building or driving traffic to a site.

Bricks-and-mortar Physical retail stores.

Browser Program such as Netscape Navigator or Microsoft Internet Explorer that enables users to view Web pages.

Channel conflicts A significant threat arising from the introduction of an Internet channel is that while disintermediation gives a company the opportunity to sell direct and increase the profitability of products it also threatens distribution arrangements with existing partners.

Cookies Bits of information about website visitors created by websites and stored on client computers.

Cost per mille (CPM) Cost per 1,000 ad impressions. An advertising pricing metric that equals the dollar amount paid to reach 1,000 persons in an estimated audience.

Cybermediaries Intermediaries who bring together buyers and sellers or those with particular information or service needs.

Cyberspace This term was preferred by science fiction writers to indicate the futuristic nature of using the Internet, the prefix 'cyber' indicating a blurring between humans, machines and communications.

Disintermediation The removal of intermediaries such as distributors or brokers that formerly linked a company to its customer. In particular, disintermediation enables a company to sell direct to the customer by cutting out the middle man.

Domain name The last part of a URL that includes the organization's unique name followed by a top-level domain name designating the type of organization, such as *.com* for 'commercial' or *.edu* for 'educational'.

E-business A term describing the use of digital and Internet technologies in the full range of business functions.

Electronic commerce (e-commerce) Business activities conducted using electronic data transmission via the Internet.

Electronic data interchange (EDI) The exchange, using digital media, of standardised business documents such as purchase orders and invoices between buyers and sellers.

Electronic mail (e-mail) A message transmitted electronically over the Internet or local area network to one or more receivers.

E-mail ads Personalised e-mail advertising messages sent to a particular customer, usually with a link to the advertiser's website.

Extranet A network system that extends a company's intranet and allows it to connect with the networks of business partners or other designated associates.

Infomediary An intermediary business whose main source of revenue derives from capturing consumer information and developing detailed profiles of individual customers for use by third parties.

Intermediaries Online sites that help bring different parties such as buyers and sellers together.

Internet The physical network that links computers across the globe. It consists of the infrastructure of network servers and communication links between them.

Intranet A private information network for company employees that is available only within the company's premises.

IPO Initial Public Offering. The first sales of stocks to the public.

Market space A virtual marketplace such as the Internet in which no direct contract occurs between buyers and sellers.

Mass customisation The ability to create tailored marketing messages or products for an individual customer or a group of similar customers yet retain the economies of scale and the capacity of mass marketing or production.

Mass marketing One-to-many communication between a company and potential customers with limited tailoring of the message.

Meta-site The prefix 'meta', from the Greek for 'between, with, or after' has come to mean 'going a level above or beyond'. So a meta-site would be a super site with many links, larger and more extensive than a customary website.

M-marketing Mobile marketing represents 'mobile' business and refers to the new communications and information delivery model created when telecommunications and the Internet converge. M-marketing combines the power and speed of the Internet with the geographic freedom of mobile telephony in terms of receiving and transmitting data and, importantly, the ability to conduct transactions.

MP3 A compression format that has revolutionised the way high-quality digital music can be delivered over the Internet.

One-to-many communication model A model of communications in which one entity communicates with a number of other entities.

One-to-one communication model A model of communications in which one entity communicates with one other entity.

Portal A website that acts as a gateway to the information on the Internet by providing search engines, directories and other services such as personalised news or free e-mail.

Reverse auction A type of auction in which sellers bid prices for which they are willing to sell items or services.

Spam Electronic junk mail.

Transaction costs The total of all costs incurred by a buyer and seller as they gather information and negotiate a transaction.

Virtual fairs Online sites that show new products, technologies and services to current or potential buyers.

Web addresses (universal resource locators–URLs) Web addresses refer to particular pages on a Web server, which is hosted by a company or organization. The technical name for Web addresses is uniform or universal resource locators.

Web application protocol (WAP) A standard that enables mobile phones to access text from websites.

Web server Computer that holds the pages and images that form a website and accepts requests from Web browsers to download them. The Web server is the host for the website.

World Wide Web (WWW) The subset of Internet computers that connects computers and the contents in a specific way, which allows for easy sharing of data using a standard interface.

About the author

Svend Hollensen is an Associate Professor of International Marketing at University of Southern Denmark. He holds an MSc (Business Administration) from Aarhus Business School. He has practical experience from a job as International Marketing Coordinator in a large Danish multinational enterprise as well as from being International Marketing Manager in a company producing agricultural machinery.

After working in industry he received his PhD in 1992 from Copenhagen Business School.

He has published articles in journals and is the author of two case books that focus on general marketing and international marketing (published by Copenhagen Business School Press).

In 2003 he published *Marketing Management – A Relationship Approach* with Pearson Education, as an alternative to the traditional mainstream marketing textbooks.

The author may be contacted via:

University of Southern Denmark
Grundtvigs Allé 150
DK-6400 Sønderborg
Denmark

fax: +45 65 5012 92
e-mail: svend@sam.sdu.dk

The decision whether to internationalize

PART I

Part I   Contents

Chapter 1   Global marketing in the firm
Chapter 2   Initiation of internationalization
Chapter 3   Internationalization theories
Chapter 4   Development of the firm's international competitiveness

Case studies

I.1   **Manchester United**
Trying to establish a global brand

I.2   **Bridgestone Tyres**
European marketing strategy

I.3   **ResMed Inc.**
Helping patients around the world suffering from obstructive sleep apnea
(OSA)

I.4   **Steinway & Sons**
Internationalizing the piano business

I.5   **Titan Industries Ltd**
Is Titan Watches ready for globalization?

Part I   Introduction

It is often the case that a firm going into an export adventure should have stayed in the home market because it did not have the necessary competences to start exporting. Chapter 1 discusses competences and global marketing strategies from the value chain perspective. Chapter 2 discusses the major motivations of the firm to internationalize. Chapter 3 concentrates on some central theories that explain firms' internationalization processes. Chapter 4 discusses the concept of 'international competitiveness' from a macro level to a micro level.

1 Global marketing in the firm

Contents

Learning objectives

After studying this chapter you should be able to do the following:

- Characterise and compare the management style in SMEs (small and medium-sized enterprises) and LSEs (large-scale enterprises).

- Identify drivers for 'global integration' and 'market responsiveness'.

- Explain the role of global marketing in the firm from a holistic perspective.

- Describe and understand the concept of the value chain.

- Identify and discuss different ways of internationalizing the value chain.

1.1 Introduction

In the face of globalization many firms attempt to expand their sales into foreign markets. International expansion provides new and potentially more profitable markets; helps increase the firm's competitiveness; and facilitates access to new product ideas, manufacturing innovations and the latest technology. However, internationalization is unlikely to be successful unless the firm prepares in advance. Advance planning has often been regarded as important to the success of new international ventures (Knight, 2000).

In the global/international marketing literature the 'staying at home' alternative is not discussed thoroughly. However, Solberg (1997) argues that with limited international experience and a weak position in the home market there is little reason for a firm to engage in international markets. Instead the firm should try to improve its performance in its home market. This alternative is window no. 1 in Figure 1.1.

Figure 1.1 The nine strategic windows

		Industry globalism		
		Local	Potentially global	Global
Preparedness for internationalization	*Mature*	3. Enter new business	6. Prepare for globalization	9. Strengthen your global position
	Adolescent	2. Consolidate your export markets	5. Consider expansion in international markets	8. Seek global alliances
	Immature	1. Stay at home	4. Seek niches in international markets	7. Prepare for a buyout

Source: Solberg, 1997, p. 11. Reprinted with kind permission.

If the firm finds itself in a global industry as a dwarf among large multinational firms, then Solberg (1997) argues that the firm may seek ways to increase its net worth so as to attract partners for a future buyout bid. This alternative (window no. 7 in Figure 1.1) may be relevant to SMEs selling advanced high-tech components (as subsuppliers) to large industrial companies with a global network. In situations with fluctuations in the global demand the SME (with limited financial resources) will often be financially vulnerable. If the firm has already acquired some competences in international business operations it can overcome some of its competitive disadvantages by going into alliances with firms representing complementary competences (window no. 8). The other windows in Figure 1.1 are further discussed by Solberg (1997).

1.2 Development of the 'global marketing' concept

Basically 'global marketing' consists of finding and satisfying global customer needs better than the competition, and of coordinating marketing activities within the constraints of the global environment. The form of the firm's response to global market opportunities depends greatly on the management's assumptions or beliefs, both conscious and unconscious, about the nature of doing business around the world. This worldview of a firm's business activities can be described as the **EPRG** framework, which four orientations are summarised in the following:

Ethnocentric: home country is superior and the needs of the home country are most relevant.

Polycentric (multidomestic): each country is unique and therefore each country should be targeted in a different way.

Regiocentric: the world consists of regions, e.g. Europe, Asia, the Middle East. The firm tries to standardise its marketing programme within regions, but not across them.

Geocentric (global): the world is getting smaller and smaller. The firm may offer global product concepts but with local adaptation ('think global, act local').

This leads us to a definition of global marketing:

Global marketing is defined as the firm's commitment to coordinate its marketing activities across national boundaries in order to find and satisfy global customer needs better than the competition. This implies that the firm is able to:

■ develop a global marketing strategy, based on similarities and differences between markets;
■ exploit the knowledge of the headquarters (home organization) through world-wide diffusion (learning) and adaptations;
■ transfer knowledge and 'best practices' from any of its markets and use them in other international markets.

There follows an explanation of some key terms:

Coordinate its marketing activities: coordinating and integrating marketing strategies and implementing them across global markets, which involves centralisation, delegation, standardisation, and local responsiveness.

Find global customer needs: this involves carrying out international marketing research and analysing market segments, as well as seeking to understand similarities and differences in customer groups across countries.

Satisfy global customers: adapting products, services and elements of the marketing mix to satisfy different customer needs across countries and regions.

Being better than the competition: assessing, monitoring and responding to global competition by offering better value, low prices, high quality, superior distribution, great advertising strategies or superior brand image.

The second part of the Global Marketing definition is also illustrated in Figure 1.2 and further commented on below.

Figure 1.2 The principle of transferring knowledge and learning across borders

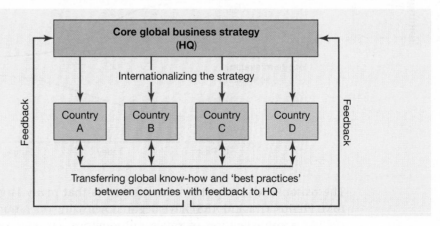

This global marketing strategy strives to achieve the slogan, 'think globally but act locally' (the so-called 'glocalisation' framework), through dynamic interdependence between headquarters and subsidiaries. Organizations following such a strategy coordinate their efforts, ensuring local flexibility while exploiting the benefits of global integration and efficiencies, as well as ensuring worldwide diffusion of innovation. A key element in knowledge management is the continuous learning from experiences. In practical terms, the aim of knowledge management as a learning-focused activity across borders is to keep track of valuable capabilities used in one market that could be used elsewhere (in other geographic markets), so that firms can continually update their knowledge. This is also illustrated in Figure 1.2 with the transfer of knowledge and 'best practices' from market to market. However, knowledge developed and used in one cultural context is not always easily transferred to another. The lack of personal relationships, the absence of trust and 'cultural distance' all conspire to create resistance, frictions and misunderstandings in cross-cultural knowledge management.

With globalization becoming a centrepiece in the business strategy of many firms – be they engaged in product development or providing services – the ability to manage the 'global knowledge engine' to achieve a competitive edge in today's knowledge-intensive economy is one of the keys to sustainable competitiveness. But in the context of global marketing the management of knowledge is de facto a cross-cultural activity, whose key task is to foster and continually upgrade collaborative cross-cultural learning (this will be further discussed in Chapter 19). Of course, the kind and/or type of knowledge that is strategic for an organization and which needs to be managed for competitiveness varies depending on the business context and the value of different types of knowledge associated with it.

1.3 Comparison of the global marketing and management style of SMEs and LSEs

In the Preface a change towards a 'convergence of orientation' in LSEs and SMEs was indicated. This 'convergence' is shown in Figure 1.3.

Figure 1.3 The 'convergence of orientation' in LSEs and SMEs

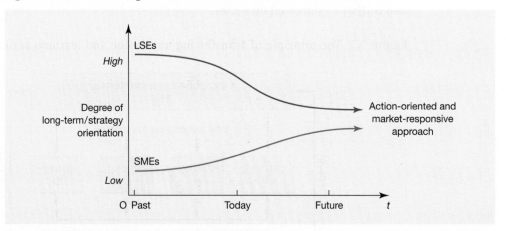

The reason underlying this 'convergence' is that many large multinationals (such as IBM, Philips, GM and ABB) have begun downsizing operations, so in reality many LSEs act like a confederation of small, autonomous, entrepreneurial and action-oriented companies. One can always question the change in orientation of SMEs. Some studies (e.g. Bonaccorsi, 1992) have rejected the widely accepted proposition that firm size is positively related to export intensity. Furthermore, many researchers (e.g. Julien *et al.*, 1997) have found that SMEs as exporters do not behave as a homogeneous group.

Table 1.1 gives an overview of the main qualitative differences between management and marketing styles in SMEs and LSEs. We will discuss each of the headings in turn.

Table 1.1 The characteristics of LSEs and SMEs

	LSEs	SMEs
Resources	Many resources Internalization of resources Coordination of – personnel – financing – market knowledge, etc.	Limited resources Externalization of resources (outsourcing of resources)
Formation of strategy/ decision-making processes	Deliberate strategy formation (Mintzberg, 1987; Mintzberg and Waters, 1985) (see Figure 1.4) Adaptive decision-making mode in small incremental steps (logical incrementalism) (e.g. each new product: small innovation for the LSE) (see Figure 1.5)	Emergent strategy formation (Mintzberg, 1987; Mintzberg and Waters, 1985) (see Figure 1.4) The entrepreneurial decision-making model (e.g. each new product: considerable innovation for the SME) The owner/manager is directly and personally involved and will dominate all decision making throughout the enterprise
Organization	Formal/hierarchical Independent of one person	Informal The owner/entrepreneur usually has the power/charisma to inspire/control a total organisation
Risk taking	Mainly risk averse Focus on long-term opportunities	Sometimes risk taking/sometimes risk averse Focus on short-term opportunities
Flexibility	Low	High
Take advantage of economies of scale and economies of scope	Yes	Only limited
Use of information sources	Use of 'advanced' techniques: – databases – external consultancy – Internet	Information gathering in an informal manner and an inexpensive way: – internal sources – face-to-face communication

Resources

■ *Financial*. A well-documented characteristic of SMEs is the lack of financial resources due to a limited equity base. The owners put only a limited amount of capital into the business, which quickly becomes exhausted.

■ *Business education/specialist expertise*. Contrary to LSEs, a characteristic of SME managers is their limited formal business education. Traditionally, the SME owner/manager is a technical or craft expert, and is unlikely to be trained in any of the major business disciplines. Therefore specialist expertise is often a constraint because managers in small businesses tend to be generalists rather than specialists. In addition, global marketing expertise is often the last of the business disciplines to be acquired by an expanding SME. Finance and production experts usually precede the acquisition of a marketing counterpart. Therefore it is not unusual to see owners of SMEs closely involved in sales, distribution, price setting and, especially, product development.

Formation of strategy/decision-making processes

As is seen in Figure 1.4, the realised strategy (the observable output of an organization's activity) is a result of the mix between the intended ('planned') strategy and the emergent ('not planned') strategy. No companies form a purely deliberate or intended strategy. In practice, all enterprises will have some elements of both intended and emergent strategy.

Figure 1.4 The intended and emergent strategy

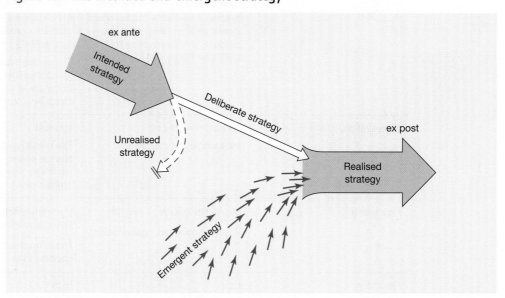

Source: Mintzberg, 1987, p. 14. Copyright © 1996 by the Regents of the University of California. Reprinted from the *California Management Review*, vol. 38, no. 2. By permission of the Regents.

In the case of the deliberate ('planned') strategy (mainly LSEs), managers try to formulate their intentions as precisely as possible and then strive to implement these with a minimum of distortion.

This planning approach 'assumes a progressive series of steps of goal setting, analysis, evaluation, selection and planning of implementation to achieve an optimal long-term direction for the organization' (Johnson, 1988). Another approach for the process of strategic management is so-called *logical incrementalism* (Quinn, 1980), where continual adjustments in strategy proceed flexibly and experimentally. If such small movements in strategy prove successful then further development of the strategy can take place. According to Johnson (1988) managers may well see themselves as managing incrementally, but this does not mean that they succeed in keeping pace with environmental change. Sometimes the incrementally adjusted strategic changes and the environmental market changes move apart and a *strategic drift* arises (Figure 1.5).

Figure 1.5 Incremental change and strategic drift

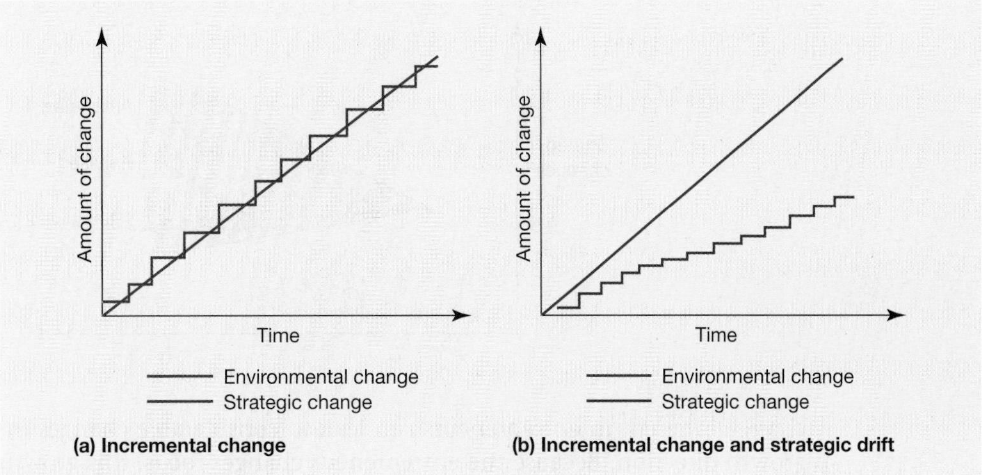

Source: Figure 1.5 – Johnson, G. (1988) 'Rethinking incrementalism', *Startegic Management Journal*, vol. 9, pp. 75–91. Copyright © of John Wiley & Sons Ltd. Reproduced with permission.

Exhibit 1.1 gives an example of strategic drift (LEGO).

Exhibit 1.1   LEGO'S strategic drift

The Danish family-owned LEGO group (**www.lego.com**) is today the world's fifth largest toy producer after Mattel (known for the Barbie doll), Hasbro (known for Trivial Pursuit and Disney figures, via a licensing agreement with Disney), Nintendo (computer games) and SEGA (computer games).

Until now LEGO has strongly believed that its unique concept was superior to other products, but today LEGO feels pressured into competing for children's time. The famous LEGO bricks receive increasing competition from TV, videos, CD-ROM games and the Internet. It seems that in LEGO's case a 'strategic drift' has arisen, where LEGO management's blind faith in its unique and pedagogical toys has not been harmonised with the way in which the world has developed. Many working parents have less and less time to 'control' children's play habits. Spectacular computer games win over 'healthy' and pedagogical toys that LEGO represents. This development has accelerated and has forced LEGO to re-evaluate its present strategy regarding product programmes and marketing.

The company suffered heavy losses in 1998 and 2000 and was forced to shed jobs, but in 2002 LEGO again showed some solid profits. However in 2003 LEGO again showed a net loss of approximately €190 million.

LEGO was trying to extend its traditional concepts and values into media products for children aged between 2 and 16. These new categories – including PC and console software, books, magazines, TV, film and music – aim to replicate the same feelings of confidence and trust already long established among children and their parents.

LEGO kits came as themed playsets under licensing deals with Harry Potter, Bob the Builder, Star Wars and Disney's Winnie the Pooh. It also went high-tech with products such as Mindstorms, and its popular Bionicles toys will appear in a full-length animated feature film. After the huge loss in 2003 (announced in the beginning of 2004) LEGO is now returning to LEGO's former concept. They will focus more on building bricks as their main product, concentrating on small kids' eagerness to assemble.

Source: adapted from different public media.

On the other hand, the SME is characterised by the entrepreneurial decision-making model (Figure 1.6). Here more drastic changes in strategy are possible because decision making is intuitive, loose and unstructured. In Figure 1.6 the range of possible realised strategies is determined by an interval of possible outcomes. SME entrepreneurs are noted for their propensity to seek new opportunities. This natural propensity for

Figure 1.6 The entrepreneurial decision–making model

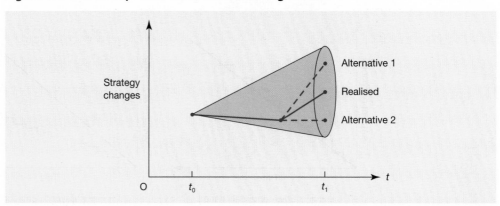

change inherent in entrepreneurs can lead to considerable changes in the enterprise's growth direction. Because the entrepreneur changes focus, this growth is not planned or coordinated and can therefore be characterised by sporadic decisions that have an impact on the overall direction in which the enterprise is going.

Organization

Compared to LSEs the employees in SMEs are usually closer to the entrepreneur, and because of the entrepreneur's influence these employees must conform to his or her personality and style characteristics if they are to remain employees.

Risk taking

There are, of course, different degrees of risk. Normally the LSEs will be risk averse because of their use of a decision-making model that emphasises small incremental steps with a focus on long-term opportunities.

In SMEs risk taking depends on the circumstances. Risk taking can occur in situations where the survival of the enterprise may be under threat, or where a major competitor is undermining the activities of the enterprise. The entrepreneur may also be taking risks when they have not gathered all the relevant information, and thus have ignored some important facts in the decision-making process.

On the other hand there are, of course, some circumstances in which an SME will be risk averse. This can often occur when an enterprise has been damaged by previous risk taking and the entrepreneur is therefore reluctant to take any kind of risk until confidence returns.

Flexibility

Because of the shorter communication lines between the enterprise and its customers, SMEs can react in a quicker and more flexible way to customer enquiries.

'Economies of scale' and 'economies of scope'

Economies of scale

Accumulated volume in production and sales will result in lower cost price per unit due to 'experience curve effects' and increased efficiency in production, marketing, etc. Building a global presence automatically expands a firm's scale of operations, giving it larger production capacity and a larger asset base. However larger scale will create competitive advantage only if the company systematically converts scale into economies of scale. In principle, the benefits of economies of scale can appear in different ways (Gupta and Govindarajan, 2001):

- Reducing operating costs per unit and spreading fixed costs over larger volume due to 'experience curve effects'.
- Pooling global purchasing gives the opportunity to concentrate global purchasing power over suppliers. This generally leads to volume discounts and lower transaction costs.
- A larger scale gives the global player the opportunity to build centres of excellence for development of specific technologies or products. In order to do this a company needs to focus a critical mass of talent in one location.

Because of size (bigger market share) and accumulated experience, the LSEs will normally take advantages of these factors. SMEs tend to concentrate on lucrative, small, market segments. Such market segments are often too insignificant for LSEs to target, but can be substantial and viable in respect of the SME. However, they will only result in a very limited market share of a given industry.

Economies of scope

Synergy effects and global scope can occur when the firm is serving several international markets. Global scope is not taking place if an international marketer is serving a customer that operates in just one country. The customer should purchase a bundle of identical products and services across a number of countries. This global customer could source these products and services either from a horde of local suppliers or from a single global supplier (international marketer) that is present in all of its markets. Compared with a horde of local suppliers, a single global supplier (marketer) can provide value for the global customer through greater consistency in the quality and features of products and services across countries, faster and smoother coordination across countries and lower transaction costs.

The challenge in capturing the economies of global scope lies in being responsive to the tension between two conflicting needs: the need for central coordination of most marketing mix elements, and the need for local autonomy in the actual delivery of products and services (Gupta and Govindarajan, 2001).

The LSEs often serve many different markets (countries) on more continents and are thereby able to transfer experience acquired in one country to another. Typically, SMEs serve only a very limited number of international markets outside their home market. Sometimes the SME can make use of economies of scope when it goes into an alliance or a joint venture with a partner that has what the particular SME is missing in the international market in question: a complementary product programme or local market knowledge.

Another example of economies of scale and scope can be found in the world car industry. Most car companies use similar engines and gearboxes across their entire product range so that the same engines or gearboxes may go into different models of cars. This generates enormous potential cost savings for such companies as Ford or Volkswagen. It provides both 'economies of scale' (decreased cost per unit of output) from producing a larger absolute volume of engines or gearboxes, and 'economies of scope' (reusing a resource from one business/country in additional businesses/countries). Therefore it is not surprising that the car industry has experienced a wave of mergers and acquisitions aimed at creating larger world car companies of sufficient size to benefit from these factors.

Use of information sources

Typically, LSEs rely on commissioned market reports produced by well-reputed (and well-paid!) international consultancy firms as their source of vital global marketing information.

SMEs usually gather information in an informal manner by use of face-to-face communication. The entrepreneur is able unconsciously to synthesise this information and use it to make decisions. The acquired information is mostly incomplete and fragmented, and evaluations are based on intuition and often guesswork. The whole process is dominated by the desire to find a circumstance that is ripe for exploitation.

Furthermore, the demand for complex information grows as the SME selects a more and more explicit orientation towards the international market and as the firm evolves from a production-oriented ('upstream') to a more marketing-oriented ('downstream') firm (Cafferata and Mensi, 1995).

As a reaction to pressures from international markets, both LSEs and SMEs evolve towards a globally integrated but market-responsive strategy. However, the starting points of the two firm types are different (see Figure 1.3). The huge global companies have traditionally based their strategy on taking advantage of 'economies of scale' by launching standardised products on a worldwide basis. These companies have realised that a higher degree of market responsiveness is necessary to maintain competitiveness in national markets. On the other side, SMEs have traditionally regarded national markets as independent of each other. But as international competences evolve they have begun to realise that there is interconnectedness between their different international markets. They recognise the benefits of coordinating the different national marketing strategies in order to utilise economies of scale in R&D, production and marketing.

Exhibit 1.2 is an example of an LSE (McDonald's) that has also moved from the left to the right in Figure 1.3, towards a higher degree of market responsiveness.

Exhibit 1.2	McDonald's is moving towards a higher degree of market responsiveness

McDonald's (**www.mcdonalds.com**) has now expanded to about 20,000 restaurants in over 100 countries. Executives at the headquarters of the McDonald's Corp. in Oak Brook, Illinois, have learned that despite the cost/savings inherent in standardisation, success is often about being able to adapt to the local environment. Here are some examples.

Japan

McDonald's first restaurant in Japan opened during 1971. At that time fast food here was either a bowl of noodles or miso soup.

With its first mover advantage, McDonald's kept its lead in Japan. By 1997 McDonald's had over 1,000 outlets across that nation, and these sold more food in Japan than any other restaurant company. This includes an annual 500 million burgers.

Among the offerings of McDonald's Co. (Japan) Ltd are chicken tatsuta, teriyaki chicken, and the Teriyaki McBurger. Burgers are garnished with a fried egg. Beverages include iced coffee and corn soup.

McDonald's in Japan imports about 70 per cent of its food needs, including pickles from the United States and beef patties from Australia. High volumes facilitate bargaining with suppliers, in order to guarantee sourcing at a low cost.

India

McDonald's, which now has seven restaurants in India, was launched there in 1996. It has had to deal with a market that is 40 per cent vegetarian; with the aversion to either beef or pork among meateaters; with a hostility to frozen meat and fish; with the general Indian fondness for spice with everything.

The Big Mac was replaced by the Maharaja Mac, made from mutton, and also on offer were vegetarian rice-patties flavoured with vegetables and spice.

Other countries

In tropical markets, guava juice was added to the McDonald's product line. In Germany, McDonald's did well selling beer as well as McCroissants. Bananafruit pies became popular in Latin America and McSpaghetti noodles became a favourite in the Philippines. In Thailand, McDonald's introduced the Samurai Pork Burger with sweet sauce. Meanwhile, McDonald's in New Zealand launched the Kiwiburger served with beetroot sauce and optional apricot pie.

In Singapore, where fries came to be served with chilli sauce, the Kiasuburger chicken breakfast became a bestseller. Singapore was among the first markets in which McDonald's introduced delivery service.

McDonald's also experimented with vegetarian needs. Its first meatless burger was the 'Hula Burger', consisting of grilled pineapple with cheese on a bun. This product was a failure, but in The Netherlands, during 1992, McDonald's tried to launch another vegetarian item, the Dutch veggie burger, made of spiced potatoes, peas, carrots and onions.

Despite success in many key markets, McDonald's also encountered difficulties marketing abroad. In October 1991 a poster illustrating the French celebrity Paul Bocuse was displayed in 66 outlets across The Netherlands; the problem was that it showed him with four other French chefs, examining a batch of dressed chickens, while the caption indicated that the chefs were dreaming of Big Macs. This was interpreted as an insult to French *haute cuisine*. McDonald's aggravated the situation with a letter of apology, in which it was claimed that the internationally famous chef was not well known in The Netherlands.

Source: adapted from a variety of public media.

Qualitative characteristics of SMEs and LSEs

Despite the convergence of behaviour in SMEs and LSEs, there are still some differences as indicated in Table 1.1 on page 7.

1.4 Forces for 'global integration' and 'market responsiveness'

In Figure 1.3 it is assumed that SMEs and LSEs are learning from each other.

The consequence of both movements may be an action-oriented approach, where firms use the strengths of both orientations. The following section will discuss the differences in the starting points of LSEs and SMEs in Figure 1.3. The rest of the book will concentrate on a common 'action/decision-oriented' approach. The result of the convergence movement of LSEs and SMEs into the upper right corner can be illustrated by Figure 1.7. The terms 'glocal strategy' and 'glocalization' have been introduced to reflect and combine the two dimensions in Figure 1.7: 'Globalization' (Y-axis) and 'Localization' (X-axis). The glocal strategy approach reflects the aspirations of a global integrated strategy, while recognising the importance of local adaptations/market responsiveness. In this way 'glocalization' tries to optimise the 'balance' between standardisation and adaptation of the firm's international marketing activities (Svensson, 2001; Svensson, 2002).

First let us try to explain the underlying forces for 'global coordination/integration' and 'market responsiveness' in Figure 1.7:

Figure 1.7 The global integration/market responsiveness grid: the future orientation of LSEs and SMEs

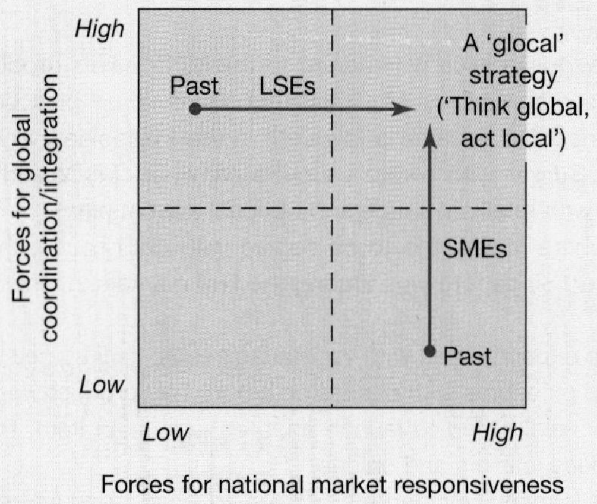

Forces for 'global coordination/integration'

In the shift towards integrated global marketing, greater importance will be attached to transnational similarities for target markets across national borders and less on cross-national differences. The major drivers for this shift are as follows (Sheth and Parvatiyar, 2001; Segal-Horn, 2002):

■ *Removal of trade barriers (deregulation)*. Removal of historic barriers, both tariff (such as import taxes) and non-tariff (such as safety regulations), which have constituted barriers to trade across national boundaries. Deregulation has occurred at all levels: national, regional (within national trading blocs) and international. Thus deregulation has an impact on globalization since it reduces the time, costs and complexity involved in trading across boundaries.

■ *Global accounts/customers*. As customers become global and rationalise their procurement activities they demand suppliers provide them with global services to meet their unique global needs. Often this may consist of global delivery of products, assured supply and service systems, uniform characteristics and global pricing. Several LSEs such as IBM, Boeing, IKEA, Siemens and ABB have such 'global' demands towards their smaller suppliers, typical SMEs. For these SMEs managing such global accounts requires cross-functional customer teams, in order to deploy quality consistency across all functional units. This issue is further discussed in Chapter 20 (section 20.3).

■ *Relationship management/network organization*. As we move towards global markets it is becoming increasingly necessary to rely on a network of relationships with external organizations, e.g. customer and supplier relationships to pre-empt competition. The firm may also have to work with internal units (e.g. sales subsidiaries) located in many and various parts of the world. Business alliances and network relationships help to reduce market uncertainties, particularly in the context of rapidly converging technologies and the need for higher amounts of resources to cover global markets. However, networked organizations need more coordination and communication.

■ *Standardised worldwide technology*. Earlier differences in world market demand were due to the fact that advanced technological products were primarily developed for the defence and government sectors before being scaled down for consumer applications. However, today the desire for gaining scale and scope in production is so high that worldwide availability of products and services should escalate. As a consequence we may witness more homogeneity in the demand and usage of consumer electronics across nations.

■ *Worldwide markets*. The concept of 'diffusions of innovations' from the home country to the rest of the world tend to be replaced by the concept of worldwide markets. Worldwide markets are likely to develop because they can rely on world demographics. For example, if a marketer targets its products or services to the teenagers of the world, it is relatively easy to develop a worldwide strategy for that segment and draw up operational plans to provide target market coverage on a global basis. This is becoming increasingly evident in soft drinks, clothing and sports shoes, especially in the Internet economy.

■ *'Global village'*. The term 'global village' refers to the phenomenon in which the world's population shares commonly recognised cultural symbols. The business consequence of this is that similar products and similar services can be sold to similar groups of customers in almost any country in the world. Cultural homogenisation therefore implies the potential for the worldwide convergence of markets and the emergence of a global marketplace, in which brands such as Coke, Nike and Levi's are universally aspired to.

■ *Worldwide communication*. New Internet-based 'low-cost' communication methods (e-mailing, e-commerce, etc.) ease communication and trade across different parts of the world. As a result customers within national markets are able to buy similar products and similar services across parts of the world.

■ *Global cost drivers*: Categorised as 'economies of scale' and 'economies of scope'. These were discussed in section 1.3.

Forces for 'market responsiveness'

■ *Cultural differences*. Despite the 'global village' cultural diversity clearly continues. Cultural differences often pose major difficulties in international negotiations and marketing management. These cultural differences reflect differences in personal values and in the assumptions people make about how business is organised. Every culture has its opposing values. Markets are people, not products. There may be global products, but there are not global people

■ *Regionalism/protectionism*. Regionalism is the grouping of countries into regional clusters based on geographic proximity. These regional clusters (such as the European Union or NAFTA) have formed regional trading blocs, which may represent a significant blockage to globalization, since regional trade is often seen as incompatible with global trade. In this case, trade barriers that are removed from individual countries are simply reproduced for a region and a set of countries. Thus all trading blocs create outsiders as well as insiders. Therefore one may argue that regionalism results in a situation where protectionism reappears around regions rather than individual countries.

■ *Deglobalisation trend*. More than 2,500 years ago the Greek historian Herodotus (based on observations) claimed that everyone believes their native customs and religion are the best. Current movements in Arab countries, or the big demonstrations accompanying conferences such as the World Economic Forum in Davos, or the World Trade Organization (WTO) meetings show that there could be a return to old values, promoting barriers to the further success of globalization. Rhetorical words such as 'McDonaldisation' and 'Coca-Colanisation' describe in a simple way fears of US cultural imperialism.

Whether or not 11 September 2001 means that globalization will continue is debatable. Quelch (2002) argues that it will, because 11 September is motivating greater cross-border cooperation among national governments on security matters, and this cooperation will reinforce interaction in other areas.

1.5   The role of global marketing in the firm: a holistic approach

Some firms are successful without having a complex marketing organization. Other firms have many subactivities belonging to the global marketing function, and yet fail to achieve success. However, marketing is not simply a structural matter that can be isolated from the firm's culture and its shared value system. A firm and a marketing infrastructure will have better chances of success if they operate in a corporate culture where the employees see their basic task as satisfying customers and their expectations. Every firm exists to satisfy the needs of its customers. The firm stands to win or lose by its ability to attain such a goal. This approach requires one to view the firm as a total system. Peters' and Waterman's book, *In Search of Excellence* (1982) views the firm from a holistic point of view by forcing managers to ask themselves many questions about the main elements of corporate excellence. The model, which is referred to as the 7-S framework for effective organizations, is based on the thesis that organizational effectiveness stems from the interaction of seven factors: structure, systems, style, staff, skills, strategy and shared values. Figure 1.8 shows the seven Ss and highlights their interconnectedness.

Figure 1.8 The 7–S framework

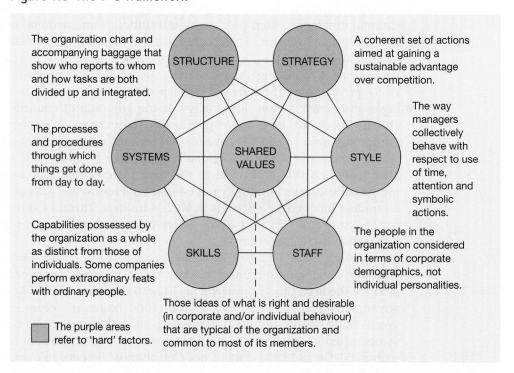

The organization chart and accompanying baggage that show who reports to whom and how tasks are both divided up and integrated.

A coherent set of actions aimed at gaining a sustainable advantage over competition.

The processes and procedures through which things get done from day to day.

The way managers collectively behave with respect to use of time, attention and symbolic actions.

Capabilities possessed by the organization as a whole as distinct from those of individuals. Some companies perform extraordinary feats with ordinary people.

The people in the organization considered in terms of corporate demographics, not individual personalities.

STRUCTURE   STRATEGY   SYSTEMS   SHARED VALUES   STYLE   SKILLS   STAFF

The purple areas refer to 'hard' factors.

Those ideas of what is right and desirable (in corporate and/or individual behaviour) that are typical of the organization and common to most of its members.

Source: 'McKinsey 7S Framework' from *In Search of Excellence: Lessons from America's Best Run Companies* by Thomas J. Peters and Robert H. Waterman, Jr. Copyright © 1982 by Thomas J. Peters and Robert H. Waterman, Jr. Reprinted by permission of HarperCollins Publishers, Inc.

According to the model, strategy is viewed as only one of seven elements typical of best-managed firms. Each of the seven Ss can be the driving force of change at a given point in time. Shared values are the centrepiece of the paradigm. A company has shared values when the employees share the same guiding values and missions. These are often unwritten and go beyond the conventional formal statement of corporate objectives. They are based on the firm's corporate philosophy and attitudes. The drive for their accomplishment pulls the firm's organization together; it provides the engine that pulls the firm in a desired direction.

One of the important features of the 7-S framework is the interconnectedness of the seven Ss. They must all work in harmony within the firm's changing international environment, with a view to creating and developing satisfied customers ('keeping the customers happy').

1.6 The value chain as a framework for identifying international competitive advantage

The 7-S framework studied in section 1.5 can be regarded as the roots from which the firm's different activities come. In particular, shared values should be a main determinant of the configuration of the value chain.

The concept of the value chain

The value chain shown in Figure 1.9 provides a systematic means of displaying and categorising activities. The activities performed by a firm in any industry can be grouped into the nine generic categories shown.

Figure 1.9 The value chain

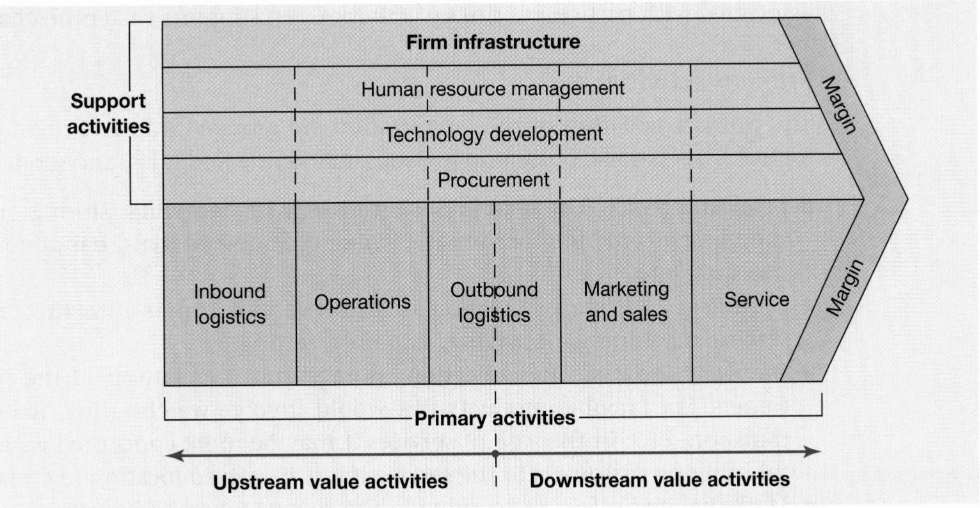

Source: Reprinted with the permission of The Free Press, a division of Simon & Schuster Adult Publishing Group, from *Competitive Advantage: Creating and Sustaining Superior Performance* by Michael E. Porter. Copyright © 1985, 1998 Michael E. Porter. All rights reserved.

At each stage of the value chain there exists an opportunity to contribute positively to the firm's competitive strategy by performing some activity or process in a way that is better than the competitors', and so provide some uniqueness or advantage. If a firm attains such a competitive advantage, which is sustainable, defensible, profitable and valued by the market, then it may earn high rates of return, even though the industry structure may be unfavourable and the average profitability of the industry modest.

In competitive terms, value is the amount that buyers are willing to pay for what a firm provides them with (perceived value). A firm is profitable if the value it commands exceeds the costs involved in creating the product. Creating value for buyers that exceeds the cost of doing so is the goal of any generic strategy. Value, instead of cost, must be used in analysing competitive position, since firms often deliberately raise their costs in order to command a premium price via differentiation. The concept of buyers' perceived value will be discussed further in Chapter 4.

The value chain displays total value and consists of value activities and margin. Value activities are the physically and technologically distinct activities that a firm performs. These are the building blocks by which a firm creates a product valuable to its buyers. Margin is the difference between total value (price) and the collective cost of performing the value activities.

Competitive advantage is a function of either providing comparable buyer value more efficiently than competitors (lower cost), or performing activities at comparable cost but in unique ways that create more customer value than the competitors are able to offer and, hence, command a premium price (differentiation). The firm might be able to identify elements of the value chain that are not worth the costs. These can then be unbundled and produced outside the firm (outsourced) at a lower price.

Value activities can be divided into two broad types, primary activities and support activities. *Primary activities*, listed along the bottom of Figure 1.9, are the activities involved in the physical creation of the product, its sale and transfer to the buyer, as well as after-sales assistance. In any firm, primary activities can be divided into the five generic categories shown in the figure. *Support activities* support the primary activities and each other by providing purchased inputs, technology, human resources and various firm-wide functions. The dotted lines reflect the fact that procurement, technology development and human resource management can be associated with specific primary activities as well as supporting the entire chain. Firm infrastructure is not associated with particular primary activities, but supports the entire chain.

Primary activities

The primary activities of the organization are grouped into five main areas: inbound logistics, operations, outbound logistics, marketing and sales, and service as, as follows:

- *Inbound logistics*. The activities concerned with receiving, storing and distributing the inputs to the product/service. These include materials, handling, stock control, transport, etc.
- *Operations*. The transformation of these various inputs into the final product or service: machining, packaging, assembly, testing, etc.
- *Outbound logistics*. The collection, storage and distribution of the product to customers. For tangible products this would involve warehousing, material handling, transport, etc.; in the case of services it may be more concerned with arrangements for bringing customers to the service if it is in a fixed location (e.g. sports events).
- *Marketing and sales*. These provide the means whereby consumers/users are made aware of the product/service and are able to purchase it. This would include sales administration, advertising, selling, etc. In public services, communication networks that help users access a particular service are often important.
- *Services*. All the activities that enhance or maintain the value of a product/service. Asugman *et al.* (1997) have defined after-sales service as 'those activities in which a firm engages after purchase of its product that minimize potential problems related

to product use, and maximise the value of the consumption experience'. After-sales service consists of the following: the installation and start-up of the purchased product, the provision of spare parts for products, the provision of repair services, technical advice regarding the product, and the provision and support of warranties.

Each of these groups of primary activities is linked to support activities.

Support activities

These can be divided into four areas:

- *Procurement.* This refers to the process of acquiring the various resource inputs to the primary activities (not to the resources themselves). As such, it occurs in many parts of the organization.
- *Technology development.* All value activities have a 'technology', even if it is simply 'know-how'. The key technologies may be concerned directly with the product (e.g. R&D, product design) or with processes (e.g. process development) or with a particular resource (e.g. raw material improvements).
- *Human resource management.* This is a particularly important area that transcends all primary activities. It is concerned with the activities involved in recruiting, training, developing and rewarding people within the organization.
- *Infrastructure.* The systems of planning, finance, quality control, etc., are crucially important to an organization's strategic capability in all primary activities. Infrastructure also consists of the structures and routines of the organization that sustain its culture.

As indicated in Figure 1.9, a distinction is also made between the production-oriented, 'upstream' activities and the more marketing-oriented, 'downstream' activities.

Having looked at Porter's original value chain model, a simplified version will be used in most parts of this book (Figure 1.10). This simplified version is characterised by the fact that it contains only the primary activities of the firm.

Although value activities are the building blocks of competitive advantage, the value chain is not a collection of independent activities, but a system of interdependent

Figure 1.10 A 'simplified' version of the value chain

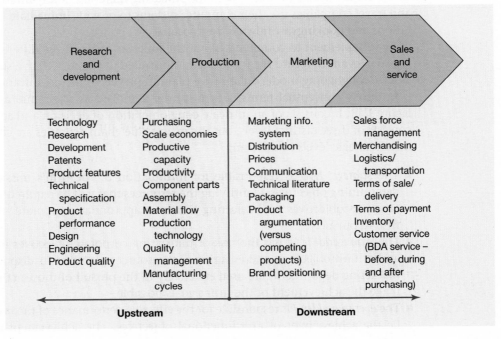

Research and development	Production	Marketing	Sales and service
Technology	Purchasing	Marketing info.	Sales force
Research	Scale economies	system	management
Development	Productive	Distribution	Merchandising
Patents	capacity	Prices	Logistics/
Product features	Productivity	Communication	transportation
Technical	Component parts	Technical literature	Terms of sale/
specification	Assembly	Packaging	delivery
Product	Material flow	Product	Terms of payment
performance	Production	argumentation	Inventory
Design	technology	(versus	Customer service
Engineering	Quality	competing	(BDA service –
Product quality	management	products)	before, during
	Manufacturing	Brand positioning	and after
	cycles		purchasing)

Upstream   **Downstream**

activities. Value activity is related by linkages within the value chain. Linkages are relationships between the way in which one value activity is dependent on the performance of another.

Furthermore, the chronological order of the activities in the value chain is not always as illustrated in Figure 1.10. In companies where orders are placed before production of the final product (build-to-order, e.g. seen at Dell) the sales and marketing function takes place before production.

In understanding the competitive advantage of an organization the strategic importance of the following types of linkage should be analysed in order to assess how they contribute to cost reduction or value added. There are two kinds of linkage:

- *internal linkages* between activities within the same value chain, but perhaps on different planning levels within the firm;
- *external linkages* between different value chains 'owned' by the different actors in the total value system.

Internal linkages

There may be important links between the primary activities. In particular, choices will have been made about these relationships and how they influence value creation and strategic capability. For example, a decision to hold high levels of finished stock might ease production scheduling problems and provide a faster response time to the customer. However, it will probably add to the overall cost of operations. An assessment needs to be made of whether the added value of 'stocking' is greater than the added cost. Suboptimisation of the single value chain activities should be avoided. It is easy to miss this point in an analysis if, for example, the marketing activities and operations are assessed separately. The operations may look good because they are geared to high-volume, low-variety, low-unit-cost production. However, at the same time the marketing team may be selling quickness, flexibility and variety to the customers. When put together these two potential strengths are weaknesses because they are not in harmony, which is what a value chain requires. The link between a primary activity and a support activity may be the basis of competitive advantage. For example, an organization may have a unique system for procuring materials. Many international hotels and travel companies use their computer systems to provide immediate 'real-time' quotations and bookings worldwide from local access points.

As a supplement to comments about the linkages between the different activities, it is also relevant to regard the value chain (illustrated in Figure 1.10 in a simplified form) as a thoroughgoing model on all three planning levels in the organization.

In purely conceptual terms, a firm can be described as a pyramid as illustrated in Figure 1.11. It consists of an intricate conglomeration of decision and activity levels. It consists of three distinct levels, but the main value chain activities are connected to all three strategic levels in the firm:

- The *strategic level* is responsible for formulation of the firm's mission statement, determining objectives, identifying the resources that will be required if the firm is to attain its objectives, and selecting the most appropriate corporate strategy for the firm to pursue.
- The *managerial level* has the task of translating corporate objectives into functional and/or unit objectives and ensuring that resources placed at its disposal (e.g. in the marketing department) are used effectively in the pursuit of those activities that will make the achievement of the firm's goals possible.
- The *operational level* is responsible for the effective performance of the tasks that underlie the achievement of unit/functional objectives. The achievement of operational

Figure 1.11 The value chain in relation to the strategic pyramid

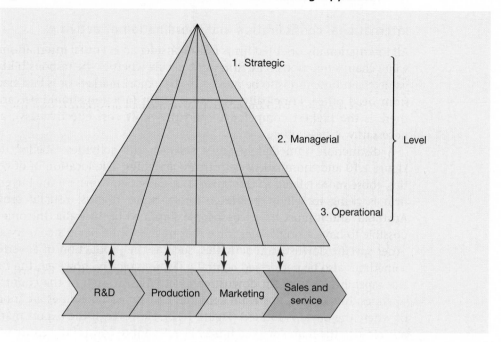

objectives is what enables the firm to achieve its managerial and strategic aims. All three levels are interdependent, and clarity of purpose from the top enables everybody in the firm to work in an integrated fashion towards a common aim.

External linkages

One of the key features of most industries is that a single organization rarely undertakes all value activities from product design to distribution to the final consumer. There is usually a specialisation of roles, and any single organization usually participates in the wider value system that creates a product or service. In understanding how value is created it is not enough to look at the firm's internal value chain alone. Much of the value creation will occur in the supply and distribution chains, and this whole process needs to be analysed and understood.

Suppliers have value chains (upstream value) that create and deliver the purchased inputs used in a firm's chain. Suppliers not only deliver a product, but can also influence a firm's performance in many other ways. For example Benetton, the Italian fashion company, managed to sustain an elaborate networks of suppliers, agents and independent retail outlets as the basis of its rapid and successful international development during the 1970s and 1980s.

In addition, products pass through the value chain channels (channel value) on their way to the buyer. Channels perform additional activities that affect the buyer and influence the firm's own activities. A firm's product eventually becomes part of its buyer's value chain. The ultimate basis for differentiation is a firm and its product's role in the buyer's value chain, which is determined by buyer needs. Gaining and sustaining competitive advantage depends on understanding not only a firm's value chain, but how the firm fits into the overall value system.

There are often circumstances where the overall cost can be reduced (or the value increased) by collaborative arrangements between different organizations in the value system. It will be seen in Chapter 11 that this is often the rationale behind joint ventures (e.g. sharing technology in the international motor manufacture and electronics industries).

Internationalizing the value chain

International configuration and coordination of activities

All internationally oriented firms must consider an eventual internationalization of the value chain's functions. The firm must decide whether the responsibility for the single value chain function is to be moved to the export markets or is best handled centrally from head office. Principally, the value chain function should be carried out where there is the highest competence (and the most cost effectiveness), and this is not necessarily at head office.

A distinction immediately arises between the activities labelled downstream on Figure 1.10 and those labelled upstream activities. The location of downstream activities, those more related to the buyer, is usually tied to where the buyer is located. If a firm is going to sell in Australia, for example, it must usually provide service in Australia, and it must have salespeople stationed in Australia. In some industries it is possible to have a single sales force that travels to the buyer's country and back again; other specific downstream activities, such as the production of advertising copy, can sometimes also be performed centrally. More typically, however, the firm must locate the capability to perform downstream activities in each of the countries in which it operates. In contrast, upstream activities and support activities are more independent of where the buyer is located (Figure 1.12). However, if the export markets are culturally close to the home market, it may be relevant to control the entire value chain from head office (home market).

Figure 1.12 Centralizing the upstream activities and decentralizing the downstream activities

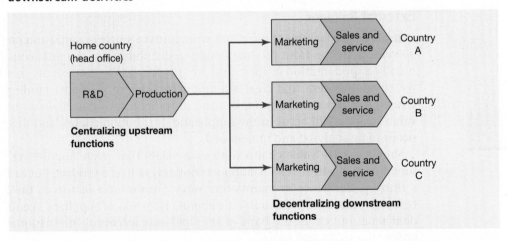

This distinction carries some interesting implications. First, downstream activities create competitive advantages that are largely country specific: a firm's reputation, brand name and service network in a country grow largely out of its activities and create entry/mobility barriers largely in that country alone. Competitive advantage in upstream and support activities often grows more out of the entire system of countries in which a firm competes than from its position in any single country.

Second, in industries where downstream activities or other buyer-tied activities are vital to competitive advantage, there tends to be a more multidomestic pattern of international competition. In many service industries, for example, not only downstream activities but frequently upstream activities are tied to buyer location, and global strategies are comparatively less common. In industries where upstream and support activities such as technology development and operations are crucial to competitive advantage, global competition is more common.

For example, there may be a large need in firms to centralise and coordinate the production function worldwide to be able to create rational production units that are able to exploit economies of scale.

Furthermore, as customers increasingly join regional cooperative buying organizations, it is becoming more and more difficult to sustain a price differentiation across markets. This will put pressure on the firm to coordinate a European price policy. This will be discussed further in Chapter 16.

The distinctive issues of international strategies, in contrast to domestic, can be summarised in two key dimensions of how a firm competes internationally. The first is called the *configuration* of a firm's worldwide activities, or the location in the world where each activity in the value chain is performed, including the number of places. The second dimension is called *coordination*, which refers to how identical or linked activities performed in different countries are coordinated with each other (Porter, 1986).

1.7 Information business and the virtual value chain

Most business managers would agree that we have recently entered a new era, 'the information age', which differs markedly from the industrial age. What have been the driving forces for these changes?

The consensus has shifted over time. To begin with it was thought to be the automation power of computers and computation. Then it was the ability to collapse time and space through telecommunications. More recently it has been seen as the value-creating power of information, a resource that can be reused, shared, distributed or exchanged without any inevitable loss of value; indeed value is sometimes multiplied. Today's fascination with competing on invisible assets means that people now see knowledge and its relationship with intellectual capital as the critical resource, because it underpins innovation and renewal.

One way of understanding the strategic opportunities and threats of information is to consider the 'virtual value chain' as a supplement to the 'physical value chain' (Figure 1.13).

Figure 1.13 The virtual value chain as a supplement to the physical value chain

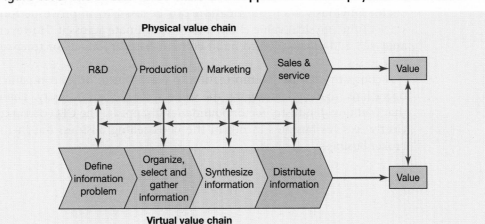

By introducing the *virtual value chain* Rayport and Sviokla (1996) have made an extension of the conventional value chain model, which treats information as a supporting element in the value-adding process. Rayport and Sviokla (1996) show how information in itself can be used to create value.

Fundamentally, there are four ways of using information to create business value (Marchand, 1999):

1. *Managing risks.* In the twentieth century the evolution of risk management stimulated the growth of functions and professions such as finance, accounting, auditing and controlling. These information-intensive functions tend to be major consumers of IT resources and people's time.
2. *Reducing costs.* Here the focus is on using information as efficiently as possible to achieve the outputs required from business processes and transactions. This process view of information management is closely linked with the re-engineering and continuous improvement movements of the 1990s. The common elements are focused on eliminating unnecessary and wasteful steps and activities, especially paperwork and information movements, and then simplifying and, if possible, automating the remaining processes.
3. *Offering products and services.* Here the focus is on knowing one's customers, and sharing information with partners and suppliers to enhance customer satisfaction. Many service and manufacturing companies focus on building relationships with customers and on demand management as ways of using information. Such strategies have led companies to invest in point-of-sale systems, account management, customer profiling and service management systems.
4. *Inventing new products.* Finally, companies can use information to innovate – to invent new products, provide different services and use emerging technologies. Companies such as Intel and Microsoft are learning to operate in 'continuous discovery mode', inventing new products more quickly and using market intelligence to retain a competitive edge. Here, information management is about mobilising people and collaborative work processes to share information and promote discovery throughout the company.

Every company pursues some combination of the above strategies.

In relation to Figure 1.13 each of the physical value-chain activities might make use of one or all four information processing stages of the virtual value chain, in order to create extra value for the customer. That is the reason for the horizontal double arrows (in Figure 1.13) between the different physical and virtual value-chain activities. In this way information can be captured at all stages of the physical value chain. Obviously such information can be used to improve performance at each stage of the physical value chain and to coordinate across it. However, it can also be analysed and repackaged to build content-based products or to create new lines of businesses.

A company can use its information to reach out to other companies' customers or operations, thereby rearranging the value system of an industry. The result might be that traditional industry sector boundaries disappear. The CEO of Amazon.com, Bezos, clearly sees his business as not in the book-selling business but in the information-broker business.

1.8 Summary

Global marketing is defined as the firm's commitment to coordinate its marketing activities across national boundaries in order to find and satisfy global customer needs better than the competition. This implies that the firm is able to do the following:

- develop a global marketing strategy, based on similarities and differences between markets;
- exploit the knowledge of the headquarters (home organization) through worldwide diffusion (learning) and adaptations;
- transfer knowledge and 'best practices' from any of its markets and use them in other international markets.

SMEs are often characterised by an entrepreneurial and action-oriented decision-making model, where drastic changes in strategy are possible because decision making is intuitive, sporadic and unstructured. On the other hand SMEs are more flexible than LSEs and are able to react more quickly to sudden changes in the international environment.

However, as a consequence of LSEs often acting as a confederation of SMEs, there seems to be a convergence of the marketing behaviour in SMEs and LSEs towards a market-responsiveness approach.

On the basis of the 7-S framework a simplified version of Porter's original value chain model was introduced, as a framework model for major parts of this book. In understanding how value is created it is not enough to look at the firm's internal value chain alone. In most cases the supply and distribution value chains are interconnected, and this whole process needs to be analysed and understood before considering an eventual internationalization of value chain activities. This also involves decisions about configuration and coordination of the worldwide value-chain activities.

At the end of this chapter the 'virtual value chain' was introduced as a supplement to the 'physical value chain', thus using information to create further business value.

CASE STUDY 1.1 Vermont Teddy Bear

Should Vermont Teddy Bear go abroad?

As Elisabeth B. Robert, CEO of The Vermont Teddy Bear Company (**www.vtbear.com**), leaves its annual meeting on 2 May 2003 she can look back on one of the best years in the history of the company:

2002

Net revenue:	$39.0 million
Net profit:	$2.5 million

The number of employees at the end of 2002 was 311.

But Elisabeth has further ambitions for the company:

> My longer-term vision for the company is to leverage our marketing and operational strengths with a sound brand strategy to grow our company with teddy bears and other products in the gift delivery service industry. Unlike other Internet companies, we have proven our ability to profitably market a gift delivery service using radio and the Internet. Unlike other Internet companies, we have an established, state-of-the-art, cost-effective fulfilment operation with integrated systems to customize, personalize, pick, pack, and ship and provide superior customer service. And, the people of The Vermont Teddy Bear Company are not only persistent and smart, they have become over the past several years extremely good at what they do. Why shouldn't we aspire to be one of the premier gift delivery services in the world?'

Source: Vermont Teddy Bear Annual Report.

The company

Vermont Teddy Bear's principal activity is direct marketing in the gift delivery industry. Founded in 1981 in Vermont (on the east coast of the United States) Vermont Teddy Bear expanded very quickly. In 1992 *Inc. Magazine* recognised The Vermont Teddy Bear Company as the 80th fastest growing private company in the United States. The same year, Vermont Teddy Bear went on the stock exchange in New York to finance further expansion. Building on its success with its bear delivery services, Vermont Teddy Bear began a new business segment in fiscal 2001, with its SendAMERICA subsidiary selling handcrafts and foodstuffs made by US artisans and growers. Vermont Teddy Bear launched PajamaGram in April 2002.

Vermont Teddy Bear has five operating segments:

- The *Bear-Gram service* segment involves sending personalised teddy bears directly to recipients for special occasions.
- The *SendAMERICA* segment extends the group's product offerings in the gift delivery service industry to include other US-made gift products in addition to teddy bears.
- The *Pajamagram* service segment involves sending pyjamas and related loungewear and spa products to recipients for special occasions and holidays.
- The *retail operation* segment involves two retail locations and family tours of the teddy bear factory and store.
- The *wholesale/corporate* segment proactively develops opportunities in the corporate affinity market and certain wholesale markets.

In 2002 the Bear-Gram service accounted for 88 per cent of revenue; retail operations, 8 per cent; corporate/wholesale (including licensing), 2 per cent; SendAMERICA, 1 per cent and the Pajamagram service, 1 per cent.

The company's Bear-Gram segment sales are heavily seasonal, with Valentine's Day and Mother's Day its largest sales seasons.

2002 Sales	%
Valentine's Day	30
Mother's Day	13
Birthdays	11
Get well	9
New births	9
Christmas	7
Other	21
Total	*100*

The company primarily uses the Internet to market its Bear-Gram gift delivery service.

The B-t-B - 'Bears-to-Business'

The B-t-B, or 'Bears-to-Business' programme is Vermont Teddy Bear's fastest growing segment, with year on year growth of more than 100 per cent. Its corporate sales programme offers promotional products and corporate gifts for mainly large companies.

One example of the 'Bears-to-Business' programme took place in late 1999 when the company had a co-promotion with Seagram's Ginger Ale. Across the country, 20 million litre bottles of Seagram's Ginger Ale were labelled with a chance to win a Vermont Teddy Bear and carried a coupon for a 20 per cent discount on any of the Vermont-made bears offered through the Bear-Gram gift delivery service.

Another example of a corporate customer is BMW of North America, which regularly uses the Bear-Gram gift delivery service to congratulate and thank both employees and clients for their dedication and service.

Among Vermont Teddy Bear's corporate customers are Johnson & Johnson, Kraft Foods, Marriott International and Pepsi Cola.

Online ordering

The company began taking orders on its website in March 1997, recognising that the website provided visual support of the company's radio advertising campaign across the country and was a convenient way for customers to place orders. In December 1997 online orders represented 7 per cent of total Bear-Gram orders. In April 2000 approximately 35 per cent of the Bear-Gram orders were received via the Company's website, triple the level of the prior year. In 2003 more than half of the orders are received via the Internet.

Competition

The company competes with a number of sellers of flowers, balloons, confectionery, cakes and other gift items, which can be ordered by telephone and over the Internet for special occasions and are delivered by express service in a manner similar to Bear-Gram gifts. The company also competes to a lesser degree with a number of companies that sell teddy bears in the United States, including, but not limited to, Steiff of Germany, Dakin, North American Bear and Gund. Many of these competitors have greater financial, sales and marketing resources than Vermont Teddy Bear.

The company sees its Bear-Gram gift delivery service as a 'creative alternative to flowers'. Approximately 62 per cent of Bear-Gram gifts are purchased by men, often at the last minute.

There are no material barriers to entry into this market, and accordingly there can be no assurance that additional companies will not seek to compete directly with Vermont Teddy Bear, including those with greater resources.

Approximately 350,000 bears are assembled per year. More than 50 per cent of this production is outsourced to overseas manufacturers, mainly in Asia. However, the management is exploring some opportunities in other parts of the world. As Elisabeth Robert says:

Gift giving is a deeply rooted tradition in many foreign cultures. Using common carriers such as FedEx and taking orders on the Internet, we avoid setting up an international distribution infrastructure. Handling an order from Tokyo is now no different than handling one from St Louis

Source: Vermont Teddy Bear Annual Report.

However, until now the company has only been selling to US customers, primarily in the big cities on the east coast: New York, Boston and Philadelphia.

Questions

1. What kind of difficulties would the Vermont Teddy Bear meet if it were to internationalize its business?

2. Could it be relevant for Vermont Teddy Bear to internationalize by following some of its US corporate customers abroad? How should this take place?

3. In what part of the world should the company start its internationalization?

4. How should the company penetrate the foreign markets:
   (a) by Internet?
   (b) by physical stores?
   (c) by a combination of the two?
   (d) by other means?

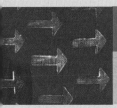

CASE STUDY 1.2   Arcor

A Latin American confectionary player is globalizing its business

Arcor (**www.arcor.com.ar/eng/home.asp**) was founded in 1951 to produce sweets. However, in order to tell the company's history fully we must go back to 1924, the year that Amos Pagani, a young Italian immigrant, decided to start up a bakery in the Province of Córdoba.

In the 1970s and 1980s Arcor transformed itself into a vast industrial complex, showing the way for other companies in the country. The company continued to grow both in Argentina and in different countries in the region. In 1976 Arcor started operations in Paraguay, in 1979 in Uruguay, in 1981 in Brazil and in 1989 in Chile.

In 1999 in Brazil Arcor opened the most advanced chocolate plant in the region, whose facilities also include the largest product distribution centre in that country. This was a start-up that put the company at the cutting edge of technology and production on the continent. It also permitted Arcor to consolidate its position in the very attractive Latin American market.

In order to continue with its expansion process Arcor established itself in Barcelona in 2002. Arcor's goal has always been to expand beyond the borders of its own country, and the opening of this new office allows the company to create closer bonds with customers from the European Economic Community, the Middle East and Africa.

Today the Arcor Group has a total of 31 plants. All are in Latin America: 25 in Argentina and the remaining 6 in Brazil (2), Chile (3) and Peru (1).

ARCOR prepares more than 1,500 products in the four areas that make up its business focus: foods, confectionery, chocolates and cookies and crackers. In all these segments the company has developed a very high degree of 'know-how' that has allowed it to become a true specialist in everything it produces.

At present Arcor is well established in Latin America, but outside this area they are relatively weak. Of the total sales of US$ 1,100 mill. less than 5 per cent derives from outside Latin America.

In the coming years, Arcor faces three big chal-lenges within its 'international expansion' framework: becoming the no. 1 Latin American confectionary and chocolate company; continuing to grow and establish itself in high development potential markets outside Latin America, such as the emerging Asian markets; and strengthening product penetration in the most demanding markets in the world: the United States, Japan and the European Union.

Recently the Arcor Group launched **www.arcorsales.com**, the first food industry website devoted to business-to-business (B-2-B) for the foreign market, a new trade channel for its products, to leverage those currently in use.

NUEVO ARCOR CEREAL MIX.

SPONSOR OFICIAL DE TODOS TUS ESFUERZOS.

ARCOR

Questions

1. What would be the major obstacles to Arcor's attempt to penetrate markets outside Latin America?

2. How could Arcor use the concept of the 'virtual value chain' to increase internationalization?

3. Where are Arcor's competitive advantages in the value chain?

For further exercises and cases, see this book's website at **www.booksites.net/hollensen**

Questions for discussion

1. What is the reason for the 'convergence of orientation' in LSEs and SMEs?

2. How can an SME compensate for its lack of resources and expertise in global marketing when trying to enter export markets?

3. What are the main differences between global marketing and marketing in the domestic context?

4. Explain the main advantages of centralising upstream activities and decentralising downstream activities.

5. How is the 'virtual value chain' different from the 'conventional value chain'?

References

Asugman, G., Johnson, J.L. and McCullough, J. (1997) 'The role of after-sales service in international marketing', *Journal of International Marketing*, vol. 5 (4), pp. 11–28.

Bonaccorsi, A. (1992) 'On the relationship between firm size and export intensity', *Journal of International Business Studies*, Fourth Quarter, pp. 605–35.

Cafferata, R. and Mensi, R. (1995) 'The role of information in the internationalization of SMEs: a typological approach', *International Small Business Journal*, vol. 13 (3), pp. 35–46.

Gupta, A.K. and Govindarajan, V. (2001) 'Converting global presence into global competitive advantage', *Academy of Management Executive*, vol. 15 (2), pp. 45–56.

Johnson, G. (1988) 'Rethinking incrementalism', *Strategic Management Journal*, vol. 9, pp. 75–91.

Julien, P.E., Joyal, A., Deshaies, L. and Ramangalahy, C. (1997) 'A typology of strategic behaviour among small and medium-sized exporting businesses: a case study', *International Small Business Journal*, vol. 15 (2), pp. 33–49.

Knight, G. (2000) 'Entrepreneurship and marketing strategy: the SME under globalization', *Journal of International Marketing*, vol. 8 (2), pp. 12–32.

Majaro, S. (1993) *The Essence of Marketing*, Prentice Hall, London.

Marchand, D.A. (1999) 'Hard IM choices for senior managers'. Part 10 of 'Your guide to mastering information management', *Financial Times*, 5 April.

Mintzberg, H. (1987) 'The strategy concept I: five Ps for strategy', *California Management Review*, vol. 30 (1), pp. 11–24.

Mintzberg, H. and Waters, A. (1985) 'Of strategies, deliberate and emergent', *Strategic Management Journal*, vol. 6, pp. 257–72.

Peters, T.J. and Waterman, R.H. (1982) *In Search of Excellence*, Harper & Row, New York.

Porter, M.E. (1985) *Competitive Advantage*, The Free Press, New York.

Porter, M.E. (1986) 'Competition in global industries: a conceptual framework', in Porter, M.E. (ed.), *Competition in Global Industries*, Harvard Business School Press, Boston, MA.

Quelch, J.A. (2002) 'Does globalization have staying power?', *Marketing Management*, March/April, pp. 18–23.

Quinn, J.B. (1980) 'Strategies for change: logical incrementalism', *Sloan Management Review*, vol. 20 (1), pp. 7–21.

Rayport, J.F. and Sviokla, J.J. (1996) 'Exploiting the virtual value chain', *McKinsey Quarterly*, no. 1, pp. 21–36.

Segal-Horn, S. (2002) 'Global firms: heroes or villains? How and why companies globalize', *European Business Journal*, vol. 14 (1), pp. 8–19.

Sheth, J.N. and Parvatiyar, A. (2001) 'The antecedents and consequences of integrated global marketing', *International Marketing Review*, vol. 18 (1), pp. 16–29.

Solberg, C.A. (1997) 'A framework for analysis of strategy development in globalizing markets', *Journal of International Marketing*, vol. 5 (1), pp. 9–30.

Svensson, G. (2001) ' "Glocalization" of business activities: a "glocal strategy" approach', *Management Decision*, vol. 39 (1), pp. 6–18.

Svensson, G. (2002) 'Beyond global marketing and the globalization of marketing activities', *Management Decision*, vol. 40 (6), pp. 574–83.

Further reading

Ali, A.J. (2001) 'Globalization: the great transformation' *ACR*, vol. 9 (1), pp. 1–9.

Fletcher, R. (2001) 'A holistic approach to internationalization', *International Business Review*, vol. 10, pp. 25–49.

Harvey, M., Nocicevic, M.M. and Kiessling, T. (2001) 'Hypercompetition and the future of global management in the twenty-first century', *Thunderbird International Business Review*, vol. 43 (5), pp. 599–616.

Mahajan, V., Moraes, M.V.P.D. and Wind, J. (2000) 'The invisible global market', *Marketing Management*, Winter, pp. 31–35.

Paul, H. (2000) 'Creating a global mindset', *Thunderbird International Business Review*, vol. 42, no. 2, pp. 187–200.

Rugman, A. and Hodgetts, R. (2001) 'The end of global strategy', *European Management Journal*, vol. 19 (4), pp. 333–343.

2 Initiation of internationalization

Contents

Learning objectives

After studying this chapter you should be able to do the following:

■ Discuss the reason (motives) why firms go international.

■ Explain the difference between proactive and reactive motives.

■ Analyse the triggers of export initiation.

■ Explain the difference between internal and external triggers of export initiation.

■ Describe different factors hindering export initiation.

■ Discuss the critical barriers in the process of exporting.

2.1 Introduction

Internationalization occurs when the firm expands its R&D, production, selling and other business activities into international markets. In many larger firms internationalization may occur in a relatively continuous fashion, with the firm undertaking various internationalization stages on various foreign expansion projects simultaneously, in incremental steps, over a period of time. However for SMEs internationalization is often a relatively discrete process; that is, one in which management regards each internationalization venture as distinct and individual.

In the pre-internationalization stages SME managers use information to achieve enough relevant knowledge to initiate internationalization (Freeman, 2002). Figure 2.1 illustrates the different stages in pre-internationalization, and the rest of this chapter refers to the stages in Figure 2.1.

Figure 2.1 Pre-internationalization: initiation of SME internationalization

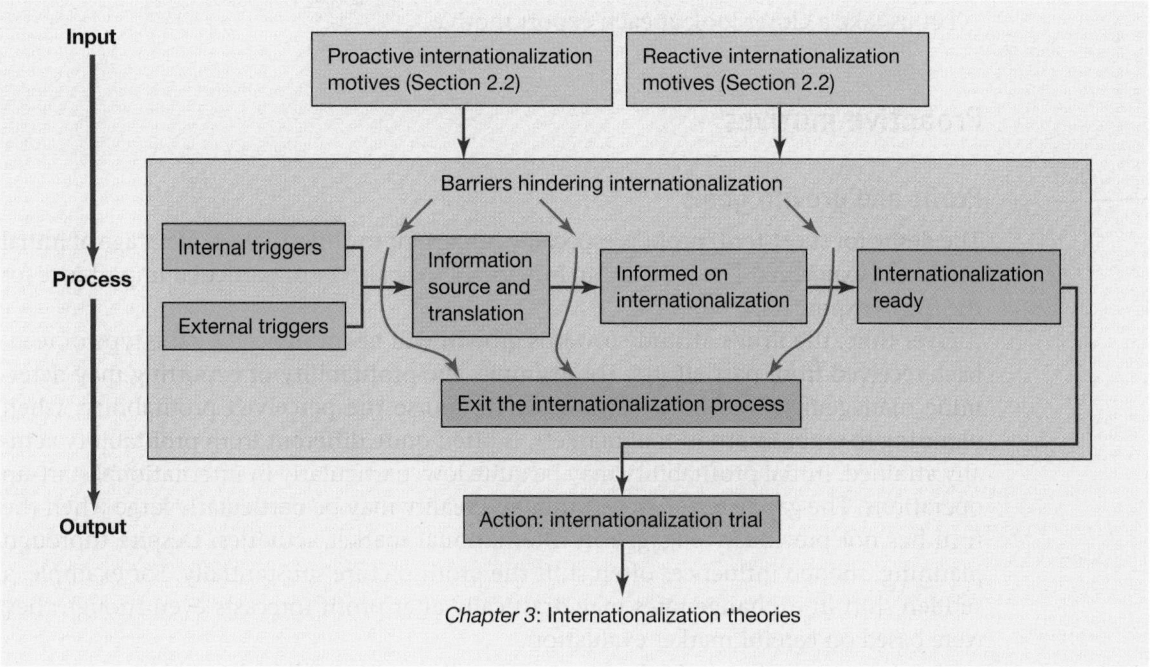

2.2   Internationalization motives

The fundamental reason for exporting, in most firms, is to make money. But, as in most business activities, one factor alone rarely accounts for any given action. Usually a mixture of factors results in firms taking steps in a given direction.

Table 2.1 provides an overview of the major motivations to internationalize. They are differentiated into proactive and reactive motives. *Proactive* motives represent stimuli to attempt strategy change, based on the firm's interest in exploiting unique competences (e.g. a special technological knowledge) or market possibilities. *Reactive*

Table 2.1 Major motives for starting export

Proactive motives	Reactive motives
● Profit and growth goals	● Competitive pressures
● Managerial urge	● Domestic market: small and saturated
● Technology competence/unique product	● Overproduction/excess capacity
● Foreign market opportunities/ market information	● Unsolicited foreign orders
● Economies of scale	● Extend sales of seasonal products
● Tax benefits	● Proximity to international customers/ psychological distance

Source: adapted from Albaum *et al.*, 1994, p. 31.

motives indicate that the firm reacts to pressures or threats in its home market or in foreign markets and adjusts passively to them by changing its activities over time.

Let us take a closer look at each export motive.

Proactive motives

Profit and growth goals

The desire for short-term profit is especially important to SMEs that are at a stage of initial interest in exporting. The motivation for growth may also be of particular importance for the firm's export start.

Over time, the firm's attitude towards growth will be influenced by the type of feedback received from past efforts. For example, the profitability of exporting may determine management's attitude towards it. Of course the perceived profitability, when planning to enter international markets, is often quite different from profitability actually attained. Initial profitability may be quite low, particularly in international start-up operations. The gap between perception and reality may be particularly large when the firm has not previously engaged in international market activities. Despite thorough planning, sudden influences often shift the profit picture substantially. For example, a sudden shift in exchange rates may drastically alter profit forecasts even though they were based on careful market evaluation.

The stronger the firm's motivation to grow, the greater will be the activities it generates, including search activity for new possibilities, in order to find means of fulfilling growth and profit ambitions.

Managerial urge

Managerial urge is a motivation that reflects the desire, drive and enthusiasm of management towards global marketing activities. This enthusiasm can exist simply because managers like to be part of a firm that operates internationally. Further, it can often provide a good reason for international travel. Often, however, the managerial urge to internationalize is simply a reflection of general entrepreneurial motivation – of a desire for continuous growth and market expansion.

Managerial attitudes play a critical role in determining the exporting activities of the firm. In SMEs export decisions may be the province of a single decision maker; in LSEs they can be made by a decision-making unit. Irrespective of the number of people involved in the export decision-making process, the choice of a foreign market entry strategy is still dependent on the decision maker's perceptions of foreign markets, expectations concerning these markets and the company's capability of entering them.

The internationalization process may also be encouraged by the cultural socialisation of the managers. Managers who either were born or have the experience of living or travelling abroad may be expected to be more internationally minded than other managers. Prior occupation in exporting companies, or membership in trade and professional associations, may also reinforce key decision makers' perceptions and evaluations of foreign environments.

Technology competence/unique product

A firm may produce goods or services that are not widely available from international competitors or may have made technological advances in a specialised field. Again, real and perceived advantages should be differentiated. Many firms believe that theirs are unique products or services, even though this may not be the case in the international market. If products or technology are unique, however, they can certainly provide a competitive edge and result in major business success abroad. One issue to consider is how long such a technological or product advantage will continue. Historically, a firm with a competitive edge could count on being the sole supplier to foreign markets for years to come. This type of advantage, however, has shrunk dramatically because of competing technologies and a frequent lack of international patent protection.

However, a firm producing superior products is more likely to receive enquiries from foreign markets because of the perceived competence of its offerings. Several dimensions in the product offering affect the probability that a potential buyer will be exposed to export stimuli. Furthermore, if a company has developed unique competences in its domestic market, the possibilities of spreading unique assets to overseas markets may be very high because the opportunity costs of exploiting these assets in other markets will be very low.

Foreign market opportunities/market information

It is evident that market opportunities act as stimuli only if the firm has or is capable of securing those resources necessary to respond to the opportunities. In general, decision makers are likely to consider a rather limited number of foreign market opportunities in planning their foreign entry. Moreover, such decision makers are likely to explore first those overseas market opportunities perceived as having some similarity with the opportunities in their home market.

From time to time certain overseas markets grow spectacularly, providing tempting opportunities for expansion-minded firms. The attraction of the south-east Asian markets is based on their economic successes, while the attraction of the eastern European markets is rooted in their new-found political freedoms and desire to develop trade and economic relationships with countries in western Europe, North America and Japan. Other countries that are likely to increase in market attractiveness as key internal changes occur include the People's Republic of China and South Africa.

Specialised marketing knowledge or access to information can distinguish an exporting firm from its competitors. This includes knowledge about foreign customers, marketplaces or market situations that is not widely shared by other firms. Such special knowledge may result from particular insights based on a firm's international research, special contacts a firm may have, or simply being in the right place at the right time (for example, recognising a good business situation during a vacation trip). Past marketing success can be a strong motivator for future marketing behaviour ('logical incrementalism' – see discussion in section 1.3). Competence in one or more of the major marketing activities will often be a sufficient catalyst for a company to begin or expand exports.

Economies of scale

Becoming a participant in global marketing activities may enable the firm to increase its output and therefore climb more rapidly on the learning curve. Ever since the Boston Consulting Group showed that a doubling of output can reduce production costs by up to 30 per cent this effect has been very much sought. Increased production for the international market can therefore also help in reducing the cost of production for domestic sales and make the firm more competitive domestically as well. This effect often results in seeking market share as a primary objective of firms. (See Exhibit 2.1 as an example of this.) At an initial level of internationalization it may mean an increased search for export markets; later on it can result in opening foreign subsidiaries and foreign production facilities.

Exhibit 2.1	Global marketing and economics of scale in Japanese firms

Japanese firms exploit foreign market opportunities by using a penetration pricing strategy – a low-entry price to build up market share and establish a long-term dominant market position. They do accept losses in the early years, as they view it as an investment in long-term market development. This can be achieved because much of Japanese industry is supported or owned by banks or other financial institutions with a much lower cost of capital.

Furthermore, because of the lifetime employment system, labour cost is regarded as a fixed expense, not a variable as it is in the west. Since all marginal labour cost will be at the entry salary level, raising volume is the only way to increase productivity rapidly. As a result market share, not profitability, is the primary concept in Japanese firms, where scale of operation and experience allow economies of scale, which also help to reduce distribution costs. The international trading companies typically take care of international sales and marketing, allowing the Japanese firm to concentrate on economies of scale and resulting in lower cost per unit.

Source: Genestre et al., 1995.

Through exporting, fixed costs arising from administration, facilities, equipment, staff work and R&D can be spread over more units. For some companies a condition for exploiting scale effects on foreign markets to the fullest extent is the possibility of standardising the marketing mix internationally. For others, however, standardised marketing is not necessary for scale economies.

Tax benefits

Tax benefits can also play a major motivating role. In the United States a tax mechanism called the Foreign Sales Corporation (FSC) has been instituted to assist exporters. It is in conformity with international agreements and provides firms with certain tax deferrals. Tax benefits allow the firm either to offer its products at a lower cost in foreign markets or to accumulate a higher profit. This may therefore tie in closely with the profit motivation.

Reactive motives

Competitive pressures

A prime form of reactive motivation is reaction to competitive pressures. A firm may fear losing domestic market share to competing firms that have benefited from economies of scale gained by global marketing activities. Further, it may fear losing foreign markets permanently to domestic competitors that decide to focus on these markets, knowing that market share is most easily retained by the firm that obtains it initially. Quick entry may result in similarly quick withdrawal once the firm recognises that its preparations have been insufficient. In addition to this, knowing that other firms, particularly competitors, are internationalizing provides a strong incentive to internationalize. Competitors are an important external factor stimulating internationalization. Coca-Cola became international much earlier than Pepsi did, but there is no doubt whatever that Coca-Cola's move into overseas markets influenced Pepsi to move in the same direction.

Domestic market: small and saturated

A company may be pushed into exporting because of a small home market potential. For some firms, domestic markets may be unable to sustain sufficient economies of scale and scope, and these companies automatically include export markets as part of their market entry strategy. This type of behaviour is likely for industrial products that have few, easily identified customers located throughout the world, or for producers of specialised consumer goods with small national segments in many countries.

A saturated domestic market, whether measured in sales volume or market share, has a similar motivating effect. Products marketed domestically by the firm may be at the declining stage of the product life cycle. Instead of attempting a push-back of the life cycle process, or in addition to such an effort, firms may opt to prolong the product life cycle by expanding the market. In the past such efforts were often met with success as customers in many developing countries only gradually reached a level of need and sophistication already attained by customers in industrialised nations. Some developing nations are still often in need of products for which the demand in the industrialised world is already on the decline. In this way firms can use the international market to prolong the life cycle of their product. (See also section 15.4, 'The product life cycle', for further discussion.)

Many US appliance and car manufacturers initially entered international markets because of what they viewed as near-saturated domestic markets. US producers of asbestos products found the domestic market legally closed to them, but because some overseas markets had more lenient consumer protection laws they continued to produce for overseas markets.

Another perspective on market saturation is also relevant for understanding why firms may expand overseas. Home market saturation suggests that unused productive resources (such as production and managerial slack) exist within the firm. Production slack is a stimulus for securing new market opportunities, and managerial slack can provide those knowledge resources required for collecting, interpreting and using market information.

Overproduction/excess capacity

If a firm's domestic sales of a product are below expectation the inventory can be above desired levels. This situation can be the trigger for starting export sales via short-term price cuts on inventory products. As soon as the domestic market demand returns to previous levels global marketing activities are curtailed or even terminated. Firms that have used such a strategy may encounter difficulties when trying to employ it again because many foreign customers are not interested in temporary or sporadic business relationships. This reaction from abroad may well lead to a decrease in the importance of this motivation over time.

In some situations, however, excess capacity can be a powerful motivation. If equipment for production is not fully utilised firms may see expansion into the international market as an ideal possibility for achieving broader distribution of fixed costs. Alternatively, if all fixed costs are assigned to domestic production, the firm can penetrate international markets with a pricing scheme that focuses mainly on variable costs. Although such a strategy may be useful in the short term it may result in the offering of products abroad at a lower cost than at home, which in turn may stimulate parallel importing. In the long run fixed costs have to be recovered to ensure replacement of production equipment. A market penetration strategy based on variable cost alone is therefore not feasible over the long term.

Sometimes excess production capacity arises because of changing demand in the domestic market. As domestic markets switch to new and substitute products companies making older product versions develop excess capacity and look for overseas market opportunities.

Unsolicited foreign orders

Many small companies have become aware of opportunities in export markets because their products generated enquiries from overseas. These enquiries can result from advertising in trade journals that have a worldwide circulation, through exhibitions and by other means. As a result a large percentage of exporting firms' initial orders were unsolicited.

Extend sales of seasonal products

Seasonality in demand conditions may be different in the domestic market from other international markets. This can act as a persistent stimulus for foreign market exploration that may result in a more stable demand over the year.

A producer of agricultural machinery in Europe had demand from its domestic market primarily in the spring months of the year. In an attempt to achieve a more stable demand over the year it directed its market orientation towards the southern hemisphere (e.g. Australia, South Africa), where it is summer when the northern hemisphere has winter and vice versa.

Proximity to international customers/psychological distance

Physical and psychological closeness to the international market can often play a major role in the export activities of a firm. For example, German firms established near the Austrian border may not even perceive their market activities in Austria as global marketing. Rather, they are simply an extension of domestic activities, without any particular attention being paid to the fact that some of the products go abroad.

Unlike US firms, most European firms automatically become international marketers simply because their neighbours are so close. As an example, a European firm operating in Belgium needs to go only 100 km to be in multiple foreign markets. Geographic closeness to foreign markets may not necessarily translate into real or perceived closeness to the foreign customer. Sometimes cultural variables, legal factors and other societal norms make a foreign market that is geographically close seem psychologically distant. For example, research has shown that US firms perceive Canada as psychologically much closer than Mexico. Even England, mainly because of similarity in language, is perceived by many US firms as much closer than Mexico or other Latin American countries, despite the geographic distances.

In a study of small UK firms' motives for going abroad, Westhead *et al.* (2002) found the following main reasons for starting exporting of their products/services:

- being contacted by foreign customers that place orders;
- one-off order (no continuous exporting);
- the availability of foreign market information;
- part of growth objective of the firm;
- export markets actively targeted by key founder/owner/manager.

The results in the study of Westhead *et al.* (2002) also showed that the bigger the firm the more likely that it would have cited *proactive* stimuli/motives.

| Exhibit 2.2 | Internationalization of Haier – proactive and reactive motives |

The Chinese manufacturer of home appliances (e.g. refrigerators), Haier Group, was near bankruptcy when Mr Zhang Ruimin was appointed plant director in 1984, the fourth one that year. It is Zhang Ruimin who has led the company to stand up and grow to the world's sixth largest home appliance manufacturer.

Proactive motives

Zhang Ruimin had an internationalization mindset for the initial stage of Haier's development. In 1984, soon after having joined the plant, he introduced technology and equipment from Liebherr, a German company, to produce several popular refrigerator brands in China. At the same time he actively expanded cooperation with Liebherr by manufacturing refrigerators based on its standards which were then sold to Liebherr, as a way of entering the German market. In 1986 the value of Haier's exports reached US$3 million for the first time. Zhang Ruimin later commented on this strategy: 'Exporting to earn foreign exchange was necessary at that time'.

When Haier invested in a plant in the United States Zhang Ruimin thought it gained location advantage by setting up plants overseas to avoid tariffs and reduce transportation costs. Internalization advantage had been attained through controlling services and marketing/distribution, and ownership advantage had been achieved by developing design and R&D capabilities through utilising high-quality local human resources.

Reactive motives

The entry of global home appliance manufacturers into the Chinese market forced Haier to seek international expansion. In particular, since China joined the WTO almost every international competitor has invested in China, establishing wholly owned companies. The best defensive strategy for Haier would be to have a presence in its competitors' home markets.

The saturation of the Chinese home appliance market, with intensifying competition, has been a major motive. After the mid-1990s price wars broke out one after another in various categories of the market. At the end of 2000 Haier's market shares in China of refrigerators, freezers, air conditioners and washing machines had reached 33, 42, 31 and 31 per cent, respectively. The potential for further development in the domestic market was therefore limited.

One of the important external triggers for the internationalization of Haier has been the Chinese government. Being an international player, Haier gained some special conditions that other Chinese companies could not obtain. For instance, Haier had already been approved to establish a financial company, to be the majority shareholder of a regional commercial bank, and to form a joint venture with a US insurance company. Without its active pursuit of internationalization as well as a dominant position in home appliance sectors it would normally be impossible for a manufacturer to get approval to enter the financial sector.

Source: adapted from Liu and Li, 2002.

2.3   Triggers of export initiation (change agents)

For internationalization to take place someone or something within or outside the firm (so-called change agents) must initiate it and carry it through to implementation (see Table 2.2).

Table 2.2 **Triggers of export initiation**

Internal triggers	External triggers
• Perceptive management	• Market demand
• Specific internal event	• Competing firms
• Importing as inward internationalization	• Trade associations
	• Outside experts

Internal triggers

Perceptive management

Perceptive managements gain early awareness of developing opportunities in overseas markets. They make it their business to become knowledgeable about these markets, and maintain a sense of open-mindedness about where and when their companies should expand overseas. Perceptive managements include many cosmopolites in their ranks.

A trigger factor is frequently foreign travel, during which new business opportunities are discovered or information received which makes management believe that such opportunities exist. Managers who have lived abroad, have learned foreign languages or are particularly interested in foreign cultures are likely, sooner rather than later, to investigate whether global marketing opportunities would be appropriate for their firm.

Often managers enter a firm having already had some global marketing experience in previous jobs and try to use this experience to further the business activities of their new firm. In developing their goals in the new job managers frequently consider an entirely new set of options, one of which may be global marketing activities.

Specific internal event

A significant event can be another major change agent. A new employee who firmly believes that the firm should undertake global marketing may find ways to motivate management. Overproduction or a reduction in domestic market size can serve as such an event, as can the receipt of new information about current product uses. For instance, a company's research activity may develop a by-product suitable for sale overseas, as happened with a food-processing firm that discovered a low-cost protein ideal for helping to relieve food shortages in some parts of Africa.

Research has shown that in SMEs the initial decision to export is usually made by the president, with substantial input provided by the marketing department. The carrying out of the decision – that is, the initiation of actual global marketing activities and the implementation of these activities – is then primarily the responsibility of marketing personnel. Only in the final decision stage of evaluating global marketing activities does the major emphasis rest again with the president of the firm. In order to influence a firm internally, it therefore appears that the major emphasis should be placed first on convincing the president to enter the international marketplace and then on convincing the marketing department that global marketing is an important activity. Conversely, the marketing department is a good place to be if one wants to become active in international business.

In a recent study of internationalization behaviour in Finnish SMEs, Forsman *et al.* (2002) found that the three most important triggers for starting up operations internationally were as follows:

■ management's interest in internationalization;

- foreign enquiries about the company's products/services;
- inadequate demand in the home market.

In this study it is interesting to notice that companies do not regard contacts from Chambers of Commerce or other support organizations as important for getting their international activities going.

Inward/outward internationalization

Internationalization has traditionally been regarded as an outward flow and most internationalization models have not dealt explicitly with how earlier inward activities, and thereby gained knowledge, can influence later outward activities. A natural way of internationalizing would be first to get involved in inward activities (imports) and thereafter in outward activities (exports). Relationships and knowledge gathered from import activities could thus be used when the firm engages in export activities (Welch *et al.*, 2001).

Welch and Loustarinen (1993) claim that inward internationalization (importing) may precede and influence outward internationalization (international market entry and marketing activities) – see Figure 2.2.

Figure 2.2 Inward/outward internationalization: a network example

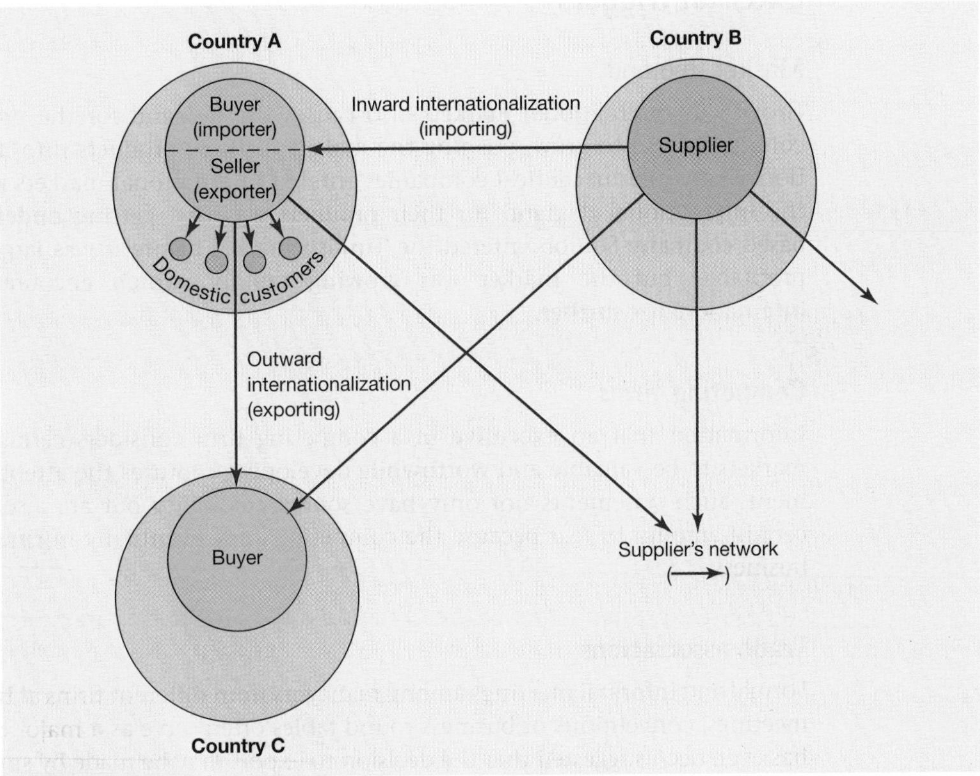

A direct relationship exists between inward and outward internationalization in the way that effective inward activities can determine the success of outward activities, especially in the early stages of internationalization. The inward internationalization may be initiated by one of the following:

- *the buyer*: active international search of different foreign sources (buyer initiative = reverse marketing)
- *the seller*: initiation by the foreign supplier (traditional seller perspective).

During the process from inward to outward internationalization the buyer's role (in country A) shifts to that of seller, both to domestic customers (in country A) and to foreign customers. Through interaction with the foreign supplier the buyer (importer) gets access to the network of the supplier, so that at some later time there may be an outward export to members of this network.

Inward international operations thus usually cover a variety of different forms used to strengthen a firm's resources. Of course inward flows imply importing products needed for the production process, such as raw materials and machinery. But inward operations can also include finances and technology through different operational forms, such as franchising, direct investments and alliances (Forsman *et al.*, 2002). In some cases inward foreign licensing may be followed by outward technology sales. According to Fletcher (2001) and Freeman (2002), inward and outward activities and the links between them can develop in different ways. The links are most tangible in counter-trade arrangements (where the focal firm initiates exporting to the same market from which importing takes place), but they can also be found in the networks of relationships between subunits within a multinational enterprise and in strategic alliances.

External triggers

Market demand

Growth in international markets also causes the demand for the products of some companies also to grow, pushing the makers of these products into internationalization. Many pharmaceutical companies entered international markets when growth in the international demand for their products was first getting under way. The US-based company Squibb entered the Turkish market before it was large enough to be profitable; but the market was growing rapidly, which encouraged Squibb to internationalize further.

Competing firms

Information that an executive in a competing firm considers certain international markets to be valuable and worthwhile developing captures the attention of management. Such statements not only have source credibility but are also viewed with a certain amount of fear because the competitor may eventually infringe on the firm's business.

Trade associations

Formal and informal meetings among managers from different firms at trade association meetings, conventions or business round tables often serve as a major change agent. It has even been suggested that the decision to export may be made by small firms on the basis of the collective experience of the group of firms to which they belong.

Outside experts

Several outside experts encourage internationalization. Among them are export agents, governments, Chambers of Commerce and banks.

- *Export agents* Export agents as well as export trading companies and export management firms generally qualify as experts in global marketing. They are already dealing internationally with other products, have overseas contacts and are set up to handle other exportable products. Many of these trade intermediaries approach prospective exporters directly if they think that their products have potential markets overseas.

- *Governments* In nearly all countries governments try to stimulate international business through providing global marketing expertise (export assistance programmes). For example, government stimulation measures can have a positive influence not only in terms of any direct financial effects that they may have, but also in relation to the provision of information.
- *Chambers of Commerce* Chambers of Commerce and similar export production organizations are interested in stimulating international business, both exports and imports. These organizations seek to motivate individual companies to get involved in global marketing and provide incentives for them to do so. These incentives include putting the prospective exporter or importer in touch with overseas business, providing overseas market information, and referring the prospective exporter or importer to financial institutions capable of financing global marketing activity.
- *Banks* Banks and other financial institutions are often instrumental in getting companies to internationalize. They alert their domestic clients to international opportunities and help them to capitalise on these opportunities. Of course, they look forward to their services being used more extensively as domestic clients expand internationally.

Information search and translation

Of all resources, information and knowledge are perhaps the most critical factor in the initiation of the internationalization process in the SME (see also Figure 2.1).

Because each international opportunity constitutes a potential innovation for the SME the management must acquire appropriate information. This is especially important to SMEs, which typically lack the resources to internationalize in the manner of LSEs. Consequently the management launches an *information search* and aquires relevant information from a number of sources, such as internal written reports, government agencies, trade associations, personal contacts or the Internet, relevant to the intended internationalization project. In the *information translation* stage the internationalization information is transformed by managers into knowledge within the firm. It is through the information search and translation into knowledge that management becomes informed on internationalization. At this stage the firm has entered a cycle of continuous search and translation into internationalization knowledge. This cycle continues until management is satisfied that it has sufficiently reduced the uncertainty associated with the internationalization project to ensure a relatively high probability of success. Once sufficient information has been acquired and translated into usable knowledge the firm leaves the cycle, becoming *internationalization ready*. It is here that the firm proceeds to action, that is, *internationalization trial*. 'Action' refers to behaviours and activities that management executes based on the knowledge that it has acquired. At this stage the firm could be said to have an embedded internationalization culture, where even the most challenging foreign markets can be overcome, leading to further internationalization and 'storage' of actual internationalization knowledge in the heads of the managers. The above description represents the firm more or less in isolation. However, the network theory recognises the importance of the firm's membership in a constellation of firms and organizations. By interacting within such a constellation the firm derives advantages well beyond what it could obtain in isolation.

At the most fine-grained level knowledge is created by individuals. Individuals acquire explicit knowledge via specific means and tacit knowledge through 'hands-on' experience.

The nature of the pre-internationalization process (illustrated in Figure 2.1) will be unique in each firm because of several factors at the organization and individual levels within the firm (Knight and Liesch, 2002).

Throughout the process depicted in Figure 2.1 the firm may exit from the pre-internationalization process at any time, as a result of the barriers hindering internationalization. The manager may decide to 'do nothing', an outcome that implies exiting from pre-internationalization.

2.4 Internationalization barriers/risks

A wide variety of barriers to successful export operations can be identified. Some problems mainly affect the export start; others are encountered in the process of exporting.

Barriers hindering export initiation

Critical factors hindering *internationalization initiation* include the following (mainly internal) barriers:

- insufficient finances;
- insufficient knowledge;
- lack of foreign market connections;
- lack of export commitment;
- lack of capital to finance expansion into foreign markets;
- lack of productive capacity to dedicate to foreign markets;
- lack of foreign channels of distribution;
- management emphasis on developing domestic markets;
- cost escalation due to high export manufacturing, distribution and financing expenditures.

Inadequate information on potential foreign customers, competition and foreign business practices are key barriers facing active and prospective exporters. Obtaining adequate representation for overseas distribution and service, ensuring payment, import tariffs and quotas, and difficulties in communicating with foreign distributors and customers are also major concerns. Serious problems can also arise from production disruptions resulting from a requirement for non-standard export products. This will increase the cost of manufacturing and distribution.

In a study of craft micro-enterprises (less than 10 employees) in the United Kingdom and Ireland, Fillis (2002) found that having sufficient business in the domestic market was the major factor in the decision not to export. Other reasons of above-average importance were: lack of export inquiries, relating to the reactive approach to business; complicated exporting procedures; poor levels of exporting assistance and limited government incentives. Similar results were supported by a study by Westhead *et al.* (2002), who found that for small firms 'focus on local market' was the main reason for not exporting any of their products.

Barriers hindering the process of internationalization

Critical barriers in the *process of internationalization* may be divided into three groups: general market risks, commercial risks and political risks.

General market risks

General market risks include the following:

- comparative market distance;
- competition from other firms in foreign markets;
- differences in product usage in foreign markets;
- language and cultural differences;
- difficulties in finding the right distributor in the foreign market;
- differences in product specifications in foreign markets;
- complexity of shipping services to overseas buyers.

Commercial risks

The following fall into the commercial risks group:

- exchange rate fluctuations when contracts are made in a foreign currency;
- failure of export customers to pay due to contract dispute, bankruptcy, refusal to accept the product or fraud;
- delays and/or damage in the export shipment and distribution process;
- difficulties in obtaining export financing.

Political risks

Among the political risks resulting from intervention by home and host country governments are the following:

- foreign government restrictions;
- national export policy;
- foreign exchange controls imposed by host governments that limit the opportunities for foreign customers to make payment;
- lack of governmental assistance in overcoming export barriers;
- lack of tax incentives for companies that export;
- high value of the domestic currency relative to those in export markets;
- high foreign tariffs on imported products;
- confusing foreign import regulations and procedures;
- complexity of trade documentation;
- enforcement of national legal codes regulating exports;
- civil strife, revolution and wars disrupting foreign markets.

The importance of these risks must not be overemphasised, and various risk-management strategies are open to exporters. These include the following:

- Avoid exporting to high-risk markets.
- Diversify overseas markets and ensure that the firm is not overdependent on any single country.
- Insure risks when possible. Government schemes are particularly attractive.
- Structure export business so that the buyer bears most of the risk. For example, price in a hard currency and demand cash in advance.

In Fillis (2002) over one-third of the exporting craft firms indicated that they encountered problems once they entered export markets. The most common problem was connected with the choice of a reliable distributor, followed by difficulties in promoting the product and matching competitors' prices.

2.5   Summary

This chapter has provided an overview of the pre-internationalization process. The chapter opened with the major motives for firms to internationalize. These were differentiated into proactive and reactive motives. Proactive motives represent internal stimuli to attempt strategy change, based on the firm's interest in exploiting unique competences or market possibilities. Reactive motives indicate that the firm reacts to pressures or threats in its home market or in foreign markets and adjusts passively to them.

For internationalization to take place someone or something ('triggers') inside or outside the firm must initiate it and carry it through. To succeed in global marketing the firm has to overcome export barriers. Some barriers mainly affect the export initiation and others are encountered in the process of exporting.

CASE STUDY 2.1   Blooming Clothing

A bumpy path to exports

It was 9 o'clock on a misty morning in February 1995. Martha O'Byrne cycled down the narrow avenue to the clothing factory of which she was managing director and the main shareholder. Wheeling her bicycle into her small office, she wondered if Janet Evans had called yet. Janet, the chief buyer with the Mothercare chain of stores in the United Kingdom, had promised to phone her that morning, to let her know if she would be placing a further order with Martha's company. Listening to the messages on her answering machine, Martha remembered the path she had taken to establish her own enterprise.

Blooming Clothing, the small company that Martha O'Byrne owns and manages, is situated in the Liberties, an old and historic part of Dublin, Ireland. Established in 1985, the firm employs 70 people manufacturing maternity wear for the Irish and export markets.

Martha O'Byrne had come to this business by an unusual route. Having established herself as a successful merchant banker, she had been considering setting up her own business for some time. 'Women, I think, can have a mid-life crisis at the menopause, but I got mine when I was 28,' she recalls. In 1984 a shopping trip with her pregnant sister-in-law revealed that the maternity wear available on the Irish market was dowdy and depressing. In that

A model in materinity wear from Blooming Clothing

moment the idea for Blooming Clothing was conceived. Martha resigned from her position at the investment bank in 1985 and set up in business with two partners as a retailer of maternity wear. Her shop, called 'Blooming', was located on South Leinster Street, on the fringes of Dublin's most prestigious shopping district. It quickly won recognition and sales for its more modern clothes, which proved particularly popular with working women. 'There was a need for a new, more vibrant look,' comments Martha, 'while still retaining the femininity and mystique of the pregnant woman.' The emphasis of the 'Blooming' label is on softly tailored separates – jackets, trousers, skirts and dresses – for office wear and special occasions. Having experienced problems with outsourcing garments Martha and her team started to manufacture their own lines in 1986.

By 1987 Blooming Clothing had a turnover of IR£250,000. The company built up further sales in Ireland through concession outlets in department stores and through a range of independent outlets. The break into exporting also came in 1987. Martha, herself six months pregnant at the time, made a presentation to a buyer from Harrods, the well-known department store in London. The store agreed to carry the Blooming label in its maternity wear section, and has been a good customer since. Arising out of this success Blooming appointed an agent, Favoro & Co., to build up further business in the United Kingdom.

By 1992 the firm had a turnover of IR£1.1 million and had moved manufacturing to the current premises at Carman's Hall, Francis Street. It had established a good sales base in Ireland and was selling in the United Kingdom to such prestigious retailers, in addition to Harrods, as John Lewis and Selfridges. The firm depended heavily on a personal approach to secure orders. It did not have a full-time salesperson as such or attend trade fairs. Would-be buyers would receive a presentation on the Blooming range from Martha O'Byrne herself or from Barbara Connolly, the firm's part owner and chief designer.

However, 1992 saw the UK economy go into deep recession, and clothing was one of the first industries to feel the pinch. As if this was not enough, 1992/3 also saw the development of a major currency crisis for the Irish pound vis-à-vis the pound sterling. The Irish pound, which had been trading at a rate of 96–98 pence to the pound sterling, rapidly appreciated in value, eventually trading at IR£1.10 to £1 sterling. Irish exporters, for whom the United Kingdom is the single most important market, found their prices increased and their customers falling away. Blooming

Clothing was not alone in experiencing these trends, and along with other companies received financial assistance from a state-funded scheme designed to help exporters through this crisis. In the meantime cash flow was squeezed and the aftermath was felt for two years. The management of Blooming spent 1993 trying to generate orders to make up for the business it had lost. Martha remained optimistic. 'There may be peaks and troughs in a business, but there are always opportunities in any market if you look,' she remarked.

In 1994 Blooming appointed an agent in Belgium. The agreement was signed just at the onset of a recession, and sales did not materialise. A foray into the Swedish market also proved disappointing. The agent selected by the firm did not generate worthwhile orders and the relationship gradually faded away.

The year 1995 marked a new departure. The firm began to build up increased sales through the appointment of new retail outlets. The British chain store Mothercare, part of the Storehouse group, agreed to stock a range of Blooming lines. Mothercare stores offer a range of nursery goods, children's clothes and associated items, through a network of over 330 outlets in the United Kingdom and international franchise operations in 25 countries with nearly 130 outlets. The order, worth £100,000 initially, would give both parties a chance to evaluate the success of the label and the fit with Mothercare's existing range of maternity wear. If the Blooming range was a success a partnership with Mothercare would allow Blooming the opportunity to penetrate the European market, with access to a broad range of outlets.

Martha gazed out of the window of her office and, as she waited in anticipation for a telephone call, she wondered what the future held for Blooming and more particularly for the company's export sales.

Questions

1. What could be the motives behind the start-up of exporting activities?

2. What do you think have been the main triggers for Blooming Clothing's export initiation?

3. The telephone rings. Janet Evans from Mothercare is on the line. What do you think is the outcome of the call?

International activities

From start-up, management at Blooming was aware of the need to seek new markets, and the relatively small size of the Irish market was also a strong impetus to move abroad. Like most other Irish companies, Blooming initially looked at the United Kingdom market, and in addition to England was actively seeking agents in Scotland and Northern Ireland to develop its business there. The United Kingdom's non-participation in the euro currency was however causing problems in price negotiations and profit forecasts for that market.

Blooming had searched for further international business. In 1995 orders were filled from a Japanese agent, but there were major differences in sizing that took some time to sort out. The slide in the value of the yen made the market unattractive, and Blooming did not pursue further business there.

In January 1999 the company took a stand at a specialist European clothing trade fair in Cologne. It had two objectives: to generate orders and to take a look at the European competition. En route to the trade fair, disaster struck, with half of the collection being stolen. Undeterred, the company exhibited at the show and came away with a strong positive feeling that its designs could match any of the European competitors regarding style and design.

Increasing international competition in the Irish market

During spring 2000 Martha saw that Blooming Clothing had increasing difficulties in keeping up sales of maternity wear in the Irish market. Chain stores from the United Kingdom and mainland Europe had made significant inroads in the Irish market. The Irish department stores and boutiques, which some years ago would have stocked only the Blooming brand as their range of maternity wear, were now stocking two or three European labels alongside it. These European chains usually locate their purchasing function in their home country offices. They rely on global sourcing and large volumes to keep prices down. For Irish suppliers such as Blooming Clothing access to these buying centres, and low-cost production capacity, is very difficult.

Also the day-to-day management of operations gave rise to several difficulties. The issues involved in keeping the Blooming factory going – sourcing supplies, filling orders and dealing with customers – took up a lot of Martha's time. The necessity to travel and be away from her desk for a couple of days at a stretch meant that, on her return, there was a list of problems pressing for the Martha's attention.

During the first months of 2000 she established contact with some low-cost production places in Eastern Europe. Blooming had earlier turned down offers to produce private label lines for other retailers and manufacturers, but maybe it was time to do something about it now.

Source: prepared by Edel Foley and Eibhlin Curley, College of Marketing and Design, Dublin Institute of Technology, Ireland. Information from company interviews and C. Flynn, 'A 40-something crisis', *Irish Independent*, 5 October 1995. The updating of the case to Spring 2000 is based on different sources.

Question

4. Evaluate the business situation regarding Blooming Clothing in spring 2000 and make recommendations for Martha O'Byrne to pursue.

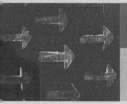

CASE STUDY 2.2   Elvis Presley Enterprises Inc. (EPE)

Internationalization of a 'cult icon'

Even more than 25 years after his death Elvis Presley has one of the most lucrative entertainment franchises in the world. Despite the sorry state of his affairs in 1977 the empire of Elvis has thrived due in large part to the efforts of the people who handled his estate after his grandmother died in 1980, including his ex-wife Priscilla Beaulieu Presley, his daughter Lisa Marie and Jack Soden, the CEO of Elvis Presley Enterprises Inc. (**www.elvis.com**), the company that handles all the official Elvis properties.

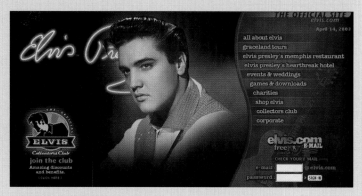

© Elvis Presley Enterprises, Inc. Used by permission.

Priscilla Presley was involved in the master-stroke decision to open Elvis's mansion, Graceland, to the public in 1982. Graceland gets more than 600,000 visitors per year, according to EPE's website. Over half of Graceland's visitors are under the age of 35. The visitors come from all parts of the world; however, the majority of the visitors still come from different parts of the United States. The Graceland tour costs US$25, which means that EPE makes US$15 million on those tickets alone, plus what it receives from photographs, hotel guests, meals and souvenirs.

EPE's other revenue streams include a theme restaurant called Elvis Presley's Memphis; a hotel, down at the end of Lonely Street, called Heartbreak Hotel; licensing of Elvis-related products, the development of Elvis-related music, film, video, TV and stage productions; and more.

Ironically, EPE gets very little money from Elvis's actual songs, thanks to a deal Elvis's infamous former manager, Colonel Tom Parker, made with RCA in 1973, whereby Elvis traded the rights for all future royalties from the songs he had recorded up to that point for a measly $5.4 million – half of which he had to give to Parker.

In 2000, the 25th anniversary was an international spectacle. A remix of the 1968 Elvis song 'A little less conversation' became a global hit single. Furthermore the CD 'Elvis: 30 #1 Hits' went tripple platinum. In August 2002, Priscilla Presely also unveiled plans to turn her romance with Elvis into a musical.

Source: **money.cnn.com/2002/08/15/news/elvis**

Questions

1. What are the main motives for the internationalization of EPE?

2. What can EPE do to maintain a steady income stream from abroad?

3. What are the most obvious assets for further internationalization of EPE?

For further exercises and cases, see this book's website at **www.booksites.net/hollensen**

Questions for discussion

1. Export motives can be classified as reactive or proactive. Give examples of each group of export motives. How would you prioritise these motives? Can you think of motives other than those mentioned in the chapter? What are they?

2. What is meant by 'change agents' in global marketing? Give examples of different types of change agent.

3. Discuss the most critical barriers to the process of exporting.

4. What were the most important change agents in the internationalization of Haier (Exhibit 2.2)?

5. What were the most important export motives in Japanese firms (Exhibit 2.1)?

References

Albaum, G., Strandskov, J., Duerr, E. and Dowd, L. (1994) *International Marketing and Export Management* (2nd edn), Addison-Wesley, Reading, MA.

Fillis, I. (2002) 'Barriers to internationalization: an investigation of the craft microenterprises', *European Journal of Marketing*, vol. 7–8, pp. 912–27.

Fletcher, R. (2001) 'A holistic approach to internationalization', *International Business Review*, vol. 10, pp. 25–49.

Forsman, M., Hinttu, S. and Kock, S. (2002) 'Internationalization from an SME perspective', Paper presented at the *18th Annual IMP Conference*, September, Lyon, pp. 1–12.

Freeman, S. (2002) 'A comprehensive model of the process of small firm internationalization: a network perspective', Paper presented at the *18th Annual IMP Conference*, September, Dijon, pp. 1–22.

Genestre, A., Herbig, D. and Shao, A.T. (1995) 'What does marketing really mean to the Japanese?', *Marketing Intelligence and Planning*, vol. 13 (9), pp. 16–27.

Knight, G.A. and Liesch, P.W. (2002) 'Information internalization in internationalizing the firm', *Journal of Business Research*, vol. 55, pp. 981–95.

Liu, H. and Li, K. (2002) 'Strategic implications of emerging Chinese multinationals: the Haier case study', *European Management Journal*, vol. 20 (6), pp. 699–706.

Welch, L.S., Benito, G.R.G., Silseth, P.R. and Karlsen, T. (2001) 'Exploring inward–outward linkages in firms' internationalization: a knowledge and network perspective', Paper presented at the *17th Annual IMP Conference*, September, Oslo, pp. 1–26.

Welch, L.S. and Loustarinen, R.K. (1993) 'Inward–outward connections in internationalization', *Journal of International Marketing*, vol. 1 (1), pp. 44–56.

Westhead P., Wright, M. and Ucbasaran, D. (2002) 'International market selection strategies selected by "micro" and "small" firms', *Omega – The International Journal of Management Science*, vol. 30, pp. 51–68.

Further reading

Craig, S.C. and Douglas, S.P. (2000) 'Configural advantage in global markets', *Journal of International Marketing*, vol. 8 (1), pp. 6–26.

Czinkota, M.R. (2002) 'Export promotion: a framework for finding opportunity in change', *Thunderbird International Business Review*, vol. 44 (3), pp. 315–24.

Halme, M., Park, J. and Chiu, A. (2002) 'Managing globalization for sustainability in the 21st century', *Business Strategy and the Environment*, vol. 11, pp. 81–9.

Schindehutte, M., Morris, M.H. and Kuratko, D.F. (2000) 'Triggering events, corporate entrepreneurship and the marketing function', *Journal of Marketing – Theory and Practice*, Spring, pp. 18–30

3 Internationalization theories

Contents

Learning objectives

After studying this chapter you should be able to do the following:

■ Analyse and compare the three theories explaining a firm's internationalization process:
  – the Uppsala internationalization model;
  – the transaction cost theory; and
  – the network model.

■ Explain the most important determinants for the internationalization process of SMEs.

■ Discuss the different factors which influence internationalization of services.

■ Explain and discuss the relevance of the network model for an SME serving as a subcontractor.

■ Explain the term 'Born Global' and its connection to Internet marketing.

3.1 Introduction

Having discussed the barriers to starting internationalization in Chapter 2, we will begin this chapter by presenting the different theoretical approaches to international marketing and then we will choose three models for further discussion in sections 3.2, 3.3 and 3.4.

Historical development of internationalization

Much of the early literature in internationalization was inspired by general marketing theories. Later on internationalization dealt with the choice between exporting and FDI (foreign direct investment). During the last 10–15 years there has been much focus on internationalization in networks, by which the firm has different relationships not only with customers but also with other actors in the environment.

The traditional marketing approach

The Penrosian tradition (Penrose, 1959; Prahalad and Hamel, 1990) reflects the traditional marketing focus on the firm's core competences combined with opportunities in the foreign environment.

The cost-based view of this tradition suggested that the firm must possess a 'compensating advantage' in order to overcome the 'cost of foreignness' (Kindleberger, 1969; Hymer, 1976). This led to the identification of technological and marketing skills as the key elements in successful foreign entry.

'Life cycle' concept for international trade

Sequential modes of internationalization were introduced by Vernon's 'Product Cycle Hypothesis' (1966), in which firms go through an exporting phase before switching first to market-seeking FDI, and then to cost-oriented FDI. Technology and marketing factors combine to explain standardisation, which drives location decisions.

Vernon's hypothesis is that producers in advanced countries (ACs) are 'closer' to the markets than producers elsewhere; consequently the first production facilities for these products will be in the ACs. As demand expands a certain degree of standardisation usually takes place. 'Economies of scale', through mass production, become more important. Concern about production cost replaces concern about product adaptations. With standardised products the less developed countries (LDCs) may offer competitive advantages as production locations. One example of this is the movement of production locations for personal computers from ACs to LDCs. The 'life cycle' concept is illustrated in Figure 15.3.

The Uppsala School approach

The Scandinavian 'stages' models of entry suggest a sequential pattern of entry into successive foreign markets, coupled with a progressive deepening of commitment to each market. Increasing commitment is particularly important in the thinking of the Uppsala School (Johanson and Wiedersheim-Paul, 1975; Johanson and Vahlne, 1977). The main consequence of this model is that firms tend to intensify their commitment towards foreign markets as their experience grows. Closely associated with the stages models is the notion of 'psychic distance', which attempts to conceptualise and, to some degree, measure the cultural distance between countries and markets (Hallen and Wiedersheim-Paul, 1979).

The internationalization/transaction cost approach

In the early 1970s intermediate forms of internationalization such as licensing were not considered interesting. Buckley and Casson (1976) expanded the choice to include licensing as a means of reaching customers abroad. But in their perspective the multinational firm would usually prefer to 'internalise' transactions via direct equity investment rather than license its capability. Joint ventures were not explicitly considered to be in the spectrum of governance choices until the mid-1980s (Contractor and Lorange, 1988; Kogut, 1988).

Buckley and Casson's focus on market-based (externalisation) versus firm-based (internalisation) solutions highlighted the strategic significance of licensing in market entry. internationalization involves two interdependent decisions – regarding location and mode of control.

The internalisation perspective is closely related to the transaction cost (TC) theory (Williamson, 1975). The paradigmatic question in internalisation theory is that, upon deciding to enter a foreign market, should a firm do so through internalisation within its own boundaries (a subsidiary) or through some form of collaboration with an external partner (externalisation)? The internalisation and TC perspectives are both concerned with the minimisation of TC and the conditions underlying market failure. The intention is to analyse the characteristics of a transaction in order to decide on the most efficient, i.e. TC minimising, governance mode. The internalisation theory can be considered the TC theory of the multinational corporation (Rugman, 1986; Madhok, 1997, 1998).

Dunning's eclectic approach

In his eclectic Ownership-Location-internalisation (OLI) framework Dunning (1988) discussed the importance of locational variables in foreign investment decisions. The word 'eclectic' represents the idea that a full explanation of the transnational activities of firms needs to draw on several strands of economic theory. According to Dunning the propensity of a firm to engage itself in international production increases if the following three conditions are being satisfied:

- *Ownership advantages*: A firm that owns foreign production facilities has bigger ownership advantages compared to firms of other nationalities. These 'advantages' may consist of intangible assets.
- *Locational advantages*: It must be profitable for the firm to continue these assets with factor endowments (labour, energy, materials, components, transport and communication channels) in the foreign markets. If not, the foreign markets would be served by exports.
- *Internalisation advantages*: It must be more profitable for the firm to use its advantages rather than selling them, or the right to use them, to a foreign firm.

The network approach

The basic assumption in the network approach is that the international firm cannot be analysed as an isolated actor but has to be viewed in relation to other actors in the international environment. Thus the individual firm is dependent on resources controlled by others. The relationships of a firm within a domestic network can be used as connections to other networks in other countries (Johanson and Mattson, 1988).

In the following three sections we will concentrate on three of the approaches presented above.

3.2 The Uppsala internationalization model

The stage model

During the 1970s a number of Swedish researchers at the University of Uppsala (Johanson and Wiedersheim-Paul, 1975; Johanson and Vahlne, 1977) focused their interest on the internationalization process. Studying the internationalization of Swedish manufacturing firms, they developed a model of the firm's choice of market and form of entry when going abroad. Their work was influenced by Aharoni's seminal (1966) study.

With these basic assumptions in mind, the Uppsala researchers interpreted the patterns in the internationalization process they had observed in Swedish manufacturing firms. They had noted, first of all, that companies appeared to begin their operations abroad in fairly nearby markets and only gradually penetrated more far-flung markets. Second, it appeared that companies entered new markets through exports. It was very rare for companies to enter new markets with sales organizations or manufacturing subsidiaries of their own. Wholly owned or majority-owned operations were established only after several years of exports to the same market.

Johanson and Wiedersheim-Paul (1975) distinguish between four different modes of entering an international market, where the successive stages represent higher degrees of international involvement/market commitment:

- Stage 1: No regular export activities (sporadic export).
- Stage 2: Export via independent representatives (export modes).
- Stage 3: Establishment of a foreign sales subsidiary.
- Stage 4: Foreign production/manufacturing units.

The assumption that the internationalization of a firm develops step by step was originally supported by evidence from a case study of four Swedish firms. The sequence of stages was restricted to a specific country market. This market commitment dimension is shown in Figure 3.1.

Figure 3.1 Internationalization of the firm: an incremental approach

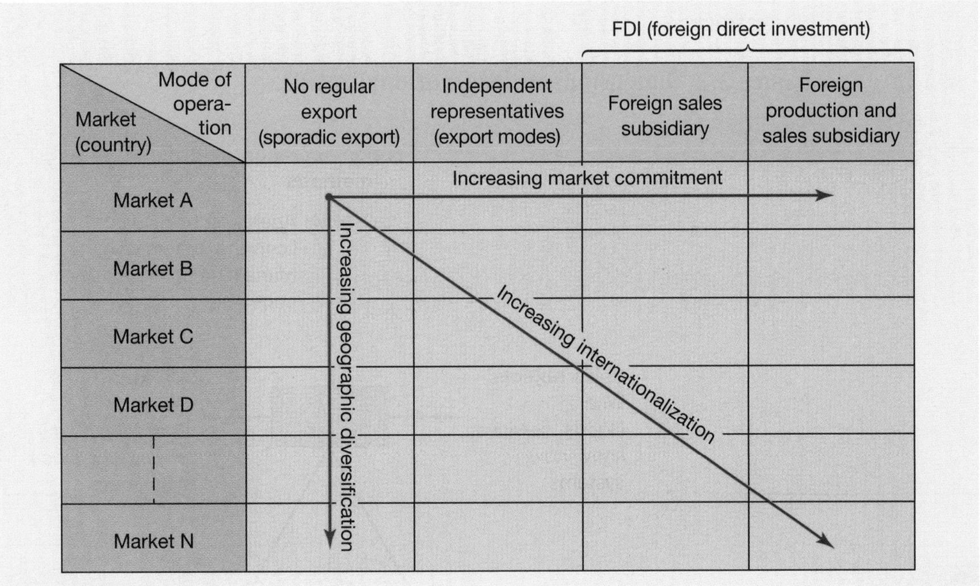

Source: adapted from Forsgren and Johanson, 1975, p. 16.

The concept of market commitment is assumed to contain two factors – the amount of resources committed and the degree of commitment. The amount of resources could be operationalised to the size of investment in the market (marketing, organization, personnel, etc.), while the degree of commitment refers to the difficulty of finding an alternative use for the resources and transferring them to the alternative use.

International activities require both general knowledge and market-specific knowledge. Market-specific knowledge is assumed to be gained mainly through experience in the market, whereas knowledge of the operations can be transferred from one country to another; the latter will thus facilitate the geographic diversification in Figure 3.1.

A direct relation between market knowledge and market commitment is postulated: knowledge can be considered as a dimension of human resources. Consequently, the better knowledge about a market, the more valuable are the resources and the stronger the commitment to the market.

Figure 3.1 implies that additional market commitment as a rule will be made in small incremental steps, both in the market commitment dimension and in the geographical dimension. There are, however, three exceptions. First, firms that have large resources experience small consequences of their commitments and can take larger internationalization steps. Second, when market conditions are stable and homogeneous, relevant market knowledge can be gained in ways other than experience. Third, when the firm has considerable experience from markets with similar conditions, it may be able to generalise this experience to any specific market (Johanson and Vahlne, 1990).

The geographical dimension in Figure 3.1 shows that firms enter new markets with successively greater psychic distance. Psychic distance is defined in terms of factors such as differences in language, culture and political systems, which disturb the flow of information between the firm and the market. Thus firms start internationalization by going to those markets they can most easily understand. There they will see opportunities, and there the perceived market uncertainty is low.

The original stage model has been extended by Welch and Loustarinen (1988), who operate with six dimensions of internationalization (see Figure 3.2):

- *sales objects* (what?): goods, services, know-how and systems:
- *operations methods* (how?): agents, subsidiaries, licensing, franchising management contracts;

Figure 3.2 Dimensions of internationalization

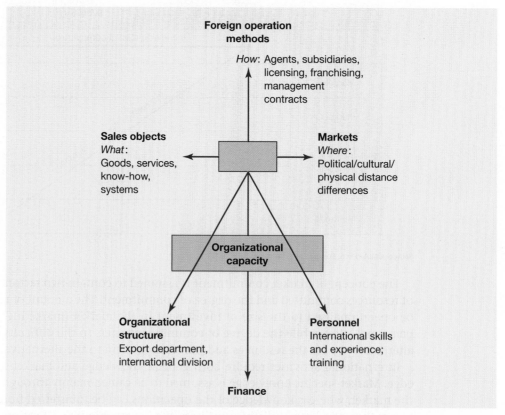

Source: Welch and Loustarinen, 1988. Reproduced with permission from The Braybrooke Press Ltd.

- *markets* (where?): political/cultural/psychic/physical distance differences between markets;
- *organizational structure*: export department, international division;
- *finance*: availability of international finance sources to support the international activities
- *personnel*: international skills, experience and training.

Critical views of the original Uppsala model

Various criticisms have been put forward. One criticism is that the model is too deterministic (Reid, 1983; Turnbull, 1987).

It has also been argued that the model does not take into account interdependencies between different country markets (Johanson and Mattson, 1986). It seems reasonable to consider a firm more internationalized if it views and handles different country markets as interdependent than if it views them as completely separate entities.

Studies have shown that the internationalization process model is not valid for service industries. In research into the internationalization of Swedish technical consultants – a typical service industry – it has been demonstrated that the cumulative reinforcement of foreign commitments implied by the process model is absent (Sharma and Johanson, 1987).

The criticism has been supported by the fact that the internationalization process of new entrants in certain industries has recently become more spectacular. Firms have lately seemed prone to *leapfrog* stages in the establishment chain, entering 'distant' markets in terms of psychic distance at an early stage, and the pace of the internationalization process generally seems to have speeded up.

Nordström's preliminary (1990) results seem to confirm this argument. The United Kingdom, Germany and the United States have become a more common target for the very first establishment of sales subsidiaries by Swedish firms than their Scandinavian neighbours.

The leapfrogging tendency not only involves entering distant markets. We can also expect a company to leapfrog some intermediate entry modes (foreign operation methods) in order to move away from the sequentialist pattern and more directly to some kind of foreign investment (Figure 3.3).

In market no. 1 the firm follows the mainstream evolutionary pattern, but in market no. 6 the firm has learned from the use of different operation methods in previous markets, and therefore chooses to leapfrog some stages and go directly to foreign investment.

Others have claimed that the Uppsala model is not valid in situations of highly internationalized firms and industries. In these cases, competitive forces and factors override psychic distance as the principal explanatory factor for the firm's process of internationalization. Furthermore, if knowledge of transactions can be transferred from one country to another, firms with extensive international experience are likely to perceive the psychic distance to a new country as shorter than firms with little international experience.

Nordström (1990) argues that the world has become much more homogeneous and that consequently psychic distance has decreased. He expects that recent starters are willing and able to enter directly into large markets as some of these are now as close to Sweden in a cultural sense as are other Scandinavian countries. Hence the explanatory value of psychic distance has decreased.

A similar way of reducing uncertainty is offered by international consulting firms. The consulting industry has experienced tremendous growth during the last 20 years.

Figure 3.3 Internationalization pattern of the firm as a sum of target country patterns

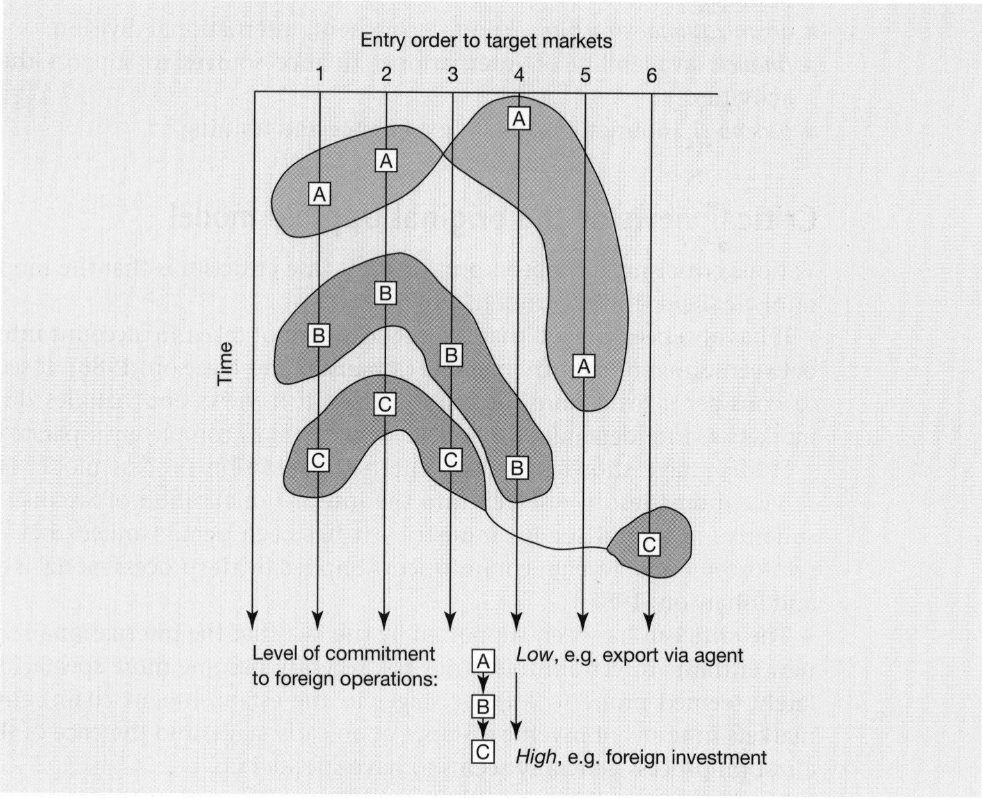

Entry order to target markets

Level of commitment to foreign operations:
A Low, e.g. export via agent
C High, e.g. foreign investment

Source: Welch and Loustarinen, 1988. Reproduced with permission from The Braybrooke Press Ltd.

It is possible to buy knowledge about legal and financial standards from international accounting firms and investment banks. Local and international consulting firms offer information about competitors, market potential, distribution systems, local buying standards, possible entry modes, etc. Thus there is a well-developed market for knowledge about foreign markets.

Firms today also have quicker and easier access to knowledge about doing business abroad. It is no longer necessary to build up knowledge in-house in a slow and gradual, trial-and-error process. Several factors contribute to this. For example, universities, business schools and management training centres all over the world are putting more and more emphasis on international business.

Probably even more important, the absolute number of people with experience of doing business abroad has increased. Hence it has become easier to hire people with the experience and knowledge needed, rather than develop it in-house. The number of people with experience of doing business abroad has increased over time as an effect of continuous growth in world trade and foreign direct investment.

The spectacular development of information technologies, in terms of both absolute performance and diminishing price/performance ratios, has made it easier for a firm to become acquainted with foreign markets, thus making a 'leapfrog' strategy more realistic (see also section 3.6 on Internet-based 'Born Globals').

In spite of the criticisms the Uppsala model has gained strong support in studies of a wide spectrum of countries and situations. The empirical research confirms that commitment and experience are important factors explaining international business behaviour. In particular, the model receives strong support regarding export behaviour, and the relevance of cultural distance has also been confirmed.

3.3   The transaction cost analysis (TCA) model

The foundation for this model was made by Coase (1937). He argued that 'a firm will tend to expand until the cost of organizing an extra transaction within the firm will become equal to the cost of carrying out the same transaction by means of an exchange on the open market' (p. 395). It is a theory which predicts that a firm will perform internally those activities it can undertake at lower cost through establishing an internal ('hierarchical') management control and implementation system while relying on the market for activities in which independent outsiders (such as export intermediaries, agents or distributors) have a cost advantage.

Transaction costs emerge when markets fail to operate under the requirements of perfect competition ('friction free'); the cost of operating in such markets (i.e. the transaction cost) would be zero, and there would be little or no incentive to impose any impediments to free market exchange. However, in the real world there is always some kind of 'friction' between buyer and seller, resulting in transaction costs (see Figure 3.4).

Figure 3.4 The principles of the TCA model

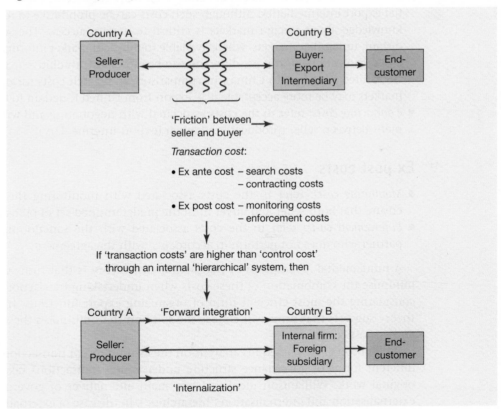

The friction between buyer and seller can often be explained by opportunistic behaviour. Williamson (1985) defines it as a 'self-interest seeking with guile'. It includes methods of misleading, distortion, disguise, and confusion. To protect against the hazards of opportunism, the parties may employ a variety of safeguards or governance structures. The term 'safeguard' (or alternatively 'governance structure') as used here can be defined as a control mechanism, which has the objective of bringing about the perception of fairness or equity among transactors. The purpose of safeguards is to provide, at minimum cost, the control and 'trust' that is necessary for transactors to believe that engaging in the exchange will make them better off. The most prominent safeguard is the legal contract. A legal contract specifies the obligations of each party and allows a transactor to go to a third party (i.e. a court) to sanction an opportunistic trading partner.

The transaction cost analysis (TCA) framework argues that cost minimisation explains structural decisions. Firms internalise, that is, integrate vertically, to reduce transaction costs.

Transaction costs can be divided into *different forms of costs* related to the transactional relationship between buyer and seller. The underlying condition for the following description of the cost elements is this equation:

$$\text{transaction cost} = \begin{array}{c} \text{ex ante costs} \\ + \\ \text{ex post costs} \end{array} = \begin{array}{c} (\text{search costs} + \text{contracting costs}) \\ + \\ (\text{monitoring costs} + \text{enforcement costs}) \end{array}$$

Ex ante costs

■ *Search costs*: include the cost of gathering information to identify and evaluate potential export intermediaries. Although such costs can be prohibitive to many exporters, knowledge about foreign markets is critical to export success. The search costs for distant, unfamiliar markets, where available (published) market information is lacking and organizational forms are different, can be especially prohibitive (e.g. exports from the United Kingdom to China). In comparison, the search costs for nearby, familiar markets may be more acceptable (e.g. export from United Kingdom to Germany).

■ *Contracting costs*: refer to the costs associated with negotiating and writing an agreement between seller (producer) and buyer (export intermediary).

Ex post costs

■ *Monitoring costs*: refer to the costs associated with monitoring the agreement to ensure that both seller and buyer fulfil the predetermined set of obligations.

■ *Enforcement costs:* refer to the costs associated with the sanctioning of a trading partner who does not perform in accordance with the agreement.

A fundamental assumption of transaction cost theory is that firms will attempt to minimise the combination of these costs when undertaking transactions. Thus, when considering the most efficient form of organizing export functions, transaction cost theory suggests that firms will choose the solution that minimises the sum of ex ante and ex post costs.

Williamson (1975) based his analysis on the assumption of transaction costs and the different forms of governance structure under which transactions take place. In his original work, Williamson identified two main alternatives of governance markets: externalisation and internalisation ('hierarchies'). In the case of externalisation, market transactions are by definition external to the firm and the price mechanism conveys all the necessary governance information. In the case of internalisation, the international firm creates a kind of internal market in which the hierarchical governance is defined by a set of 'internal' contracts.

Externalisation and internalisation of transactions are equated with intermediaries (agents, distributors) and sales subsidiaries (or other governance structures involving ownership control) respectively.

In this way, Williamson's framework provides the basis for a variety of research into the organization of international activity and the choice of international market entry mode. We will return to this issue in Part III of this book.

The conclusion of the transaction cost theory is:

> If the transaction costs (defined above) through externalisation (e.g. through an importer or agent) are higher than the control cost through an internal hierarchical system, then the firm should seek internalisation of activities, i.e. implementing the global marketing strategy in wholly owned subsidiaries. Or more popularly explained: if the 'friction' between buyer and seller is too high then the firm should rather internalise, in the form of its own subsidiaries.

Limitations of the TCA framework

Narrow assumptions of human nature

Ghoshal and Moran (1996) have criticised the original work of Williamson as having too narrow assumptions of human nature (opportunism and its equally narrow inter-pretation of economic objectives). They also wonder why the theory's mainstream development has remained immune to such important contributions as Ouchi's (1980) insight on social control. Ouchi (1980) points to the relevance of intermediate forms (between markets and hierarchies), such as the clan, where governance is based on a win–win situation (in contrast to a zero-sum game situation).

Sometimes firms would even build trust with their externalized agents and distributors by turning them into partners. In this way the firms would avoid large investments in subsidiaries around the world.

Excluding 'internal' transaction costs

The TCA framework also seems to ignore the 'internal' transaction cost, assuming zero friction within a multinational firm. One can imagine severe friction (resulting in transaction cost) between the head office of a firm and its sales subsidiaries when internal internal transfer prices have to be settled.

Relevance of 'intermediate' forms for SMEs

One can also question the relevance of the TCA framework to the internationalization process of SMEs (Christensen and Lindmark, 1993). The lack of resources and knowl-edge in SMEs is a major force for the externalisation of activities. But since the use of markets often raises contractual problems, markets in many instances are not real alternatives to hierarchies for SMEs. Instead, the SMEs have to rely on intermediate forms of governance, such as contractual relations and relations based on clan-like systems created by a mutual orientation of investments, skills and trust building. Therefore SMEs are often highly dependent on the cooperative environment available. Such an approach will be presented and discussed in the next section.

Importance of 'production cost' is understated

It can be argued that the importance of transaction cost is overstated and that the importance of production cost has not been taken into consideration. Production cost is the cost of performing a particular task/function in the value chain, such as R&D

costs, manufacturing costs and marketing costs. According to Williamson (1985), the most efficient choice of internationalization mode is one that will help *minimise the sum of production and transaction costs*.

3.4 The network model

Basic concept

Business networks are a mode of handling activity interdependences between several business actors. As we have seen, other modes of handling or governing interdependences in a business field are markets and hierarchies.

The network differs from the market with regard to relations between actors. In a market model, actors have no specific relations to each other. The interdependences are regulated through the market price mechanism. In contrast, in the business network the actors are linked to each other through exchange relationships, and their needs and capabilities are mediated through the interaction taking place in the relationships.

The industrial network differs from the hierarchy in the way that the actors are autonomous and handle their interdependences bilaterally rather than via a coordinating unit on a higher level. Whereas a hierarchy is organised and controlled as one unit from the top, the business network is organised by each actor's willingness to engage in exchange relationships with some of the other actors in the network. The networks are more loosely coupled than are hierarchies; they can change shape more easily. Any actor in the network can engage in new relationships or break off old ones, thereby modifying its structure. Thus business networks can be expected to be more flexible in response to changing conditions in turbulent business fields, such as those where technical change is very rapid.

It can be concluded that business networks will emerge in fields where coordination between specific actors can give strong gains and where conditions are changing rapidly. Thus the network approach implies a move away from the firm as the unit of analysis, towards exchange between firms and between a group of firms and other groups of firms as the main object of study. However, it also implies a move away from transactions towards more lasting exchange relationships constituting a structure within which international business takes place and evolves.

Evidently, business relationships and consequently industrial networks are subtle phenomena, which cannot easily be observed by an outsider: that is, a potential entrant. The actors are tied to each other through a number of different bonds: technical, social, cognitive, administrative, legal, economic, etc.

A basic assumption in the network model is that the individual firm is dependent on resources controlled by other firms. The companies get access to these external resources through their network positions. Since the development of positions takes time and depends on resource accumulations, a firm must establish and develop positions in relation to counterparts in foreign networks.

To enter a network from outside requires that other actors be motivated to engage in interaction, something which is resource demanding and may require several firms to make adaptions in their ways of performing business. Thus foreign market or network entry of the firm may very well be the result of interaction initiatives taken by other firms that are insiders in the network in the specific country. However, the chances of being the object of such initiatives are much greater for an insider.

The networks in a country may well extend far beyond country borders. In relation to the internationalization of the firm, the network view argues that the internationalizing firm is initially engaged in a network which is primarily domestic.

The relationships of a firm in a domestic network can be used as bridges to other networks in other countries. In some cases the customer demands that the supplier follows it abroad if the supplier wants to keep the business at home. An example of an international network is shown in Figure 3.5. It appears that one of the subsuppliers established a subsidiary in Country B. Here the production subsidiary is served by the local company of the subsupplier. Countries E and F, and partly Country C, are sourced from the production subsidiary in Country B. Generally it can be assumed that direct or indirect bridges exist between firms and different country networks. Such bridges can be important both in the initial steps abroad and in the subsequent entry of new markets.

The character of the ties in a network is partly a matter of the firms involved. This is primarily the case with technical, economic and legal ties. To an important extent, however, the ties are formed between the persons engaged in the business relationships. This is the case with social and cognitive ties. Industries as well as countries may differ with regard to the relative importance of firm and personal relationships. But it can be expected that the personal influence on relationships is strongest in the early establishment of relationships. Later in the process routines and systems will become more important.

When entering a network, the internationalization process of the firm will often proceed more quickly. In particular, SMEs in high-tech industries tend to go directly to more distant markets and to set up their own subsidiaries more rapidly. One reason

Figure 3.5 An example of an international network

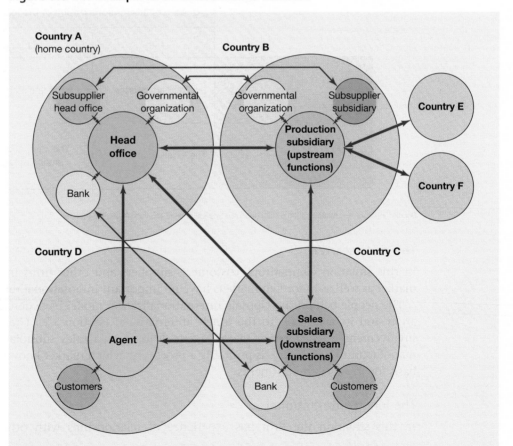

seems to be that the entrepreneurs behind those companies have networks of colleagues dealing with the new technology. Internationalization, in these cases, is an exploitation of the advantage that this network constitutes.

Four cases of internationalization

The Uppsala internationalization model treated internationalization independently of the situation and the competition in the market. In the following we will try to combine these two important aspects. A 'production net' contains relationships between those firms whose activities together produce functions linked to a specific area. The firm's degree of internationalization shows the extent to which the firm has positions in different national nets, how strong those positions are, and how integrated they are.

The network model also has consequences for the meaning of internationalization of the market. A production net can be more or less internationalized. A high degree of internationalization of a production net implies that there are many and strong relationships between the different national sections of the global production net. A low degree of internationalization means that the national nets have few relationships with each other.

We will distinguish between four different situations, characterised by, on the one hand, a low or a high degree of internationalization of the firm and, on the other, a low or high degree of internationalization of the market (the production network) (Figure 3.6).

Figure 3.6 Four cases of internationalization of a firm

		Degree of internationalization of the market	
		Low	High
Degree of internationalization of the firm	Low	The early starter	The late starter
	High	The lonely international	The international among others

Source: Johanson and Mattson, 1988 p. 298. Reprinted by permission of Thomson Publishing Services.

The early starter

In this situation competitors, customers, suppliers and other firms in the domestic market as well as in foreign markets have no important international relationships.

The people behind the Uppsala internationalization model have described this situation and its transition to the lonely international (section 3.2). Gradual and slow involvement in the market via an agent, leading to a sales subsidiary and then a manufacturing subsidiary, is primarily a process by which market knowledge gives the basis for stronger commitments.

The lonely international

In this situation the firm has experience of relationships with others in foreign countries. It has acquired knowledge and means to handle environments that differ with respect to culture, institutions and so on. The knowledge situation is also more favourable when establishing the firm in a new national net.

Initiatives to further internationalization do not come from other parties in the production nets, as the firm's suppliers, customers and competitors are less internationalized. On the contrary, the lonely international has the competences to promote internationalization of its production net and, consequently, the firms engaged in it. The firm's relationships with, and in, other national nets may function as a bridge to those nets for its suppliers and customers.

The late starter

In a situation with international customers and competitors, the less internationalized firm can be 'pulled out' of the domestic market by its customers or complementary suppliers to the customers. Sometimes the step abroad can be rather large in the beginning.

How will the firm go abroad in this situation? Here we will differentiate between SMEs and LSEs.

SMEs going abroad in an internationalized world probably have to be highly specialised and adjusted to solutions in specific sections of the production nets. Starting production abroad is probably a question of what bonds are important to the customers, and in this matter SMEs are very flexible.

LSEs that have become large in the domestic market are often less specialised than small firms, and their situation is often more complex than that of the small firm. One possibility is to get established in a foreign production net through acquisition or joint venture.

In general, it is probably more difficult for a firm that has become large at home to find a niche in highly internationalized nets. It cannot, as the small firm can, adjust in the flexible way which may be necessary in such a net.

Compared to the early starter, the late starter often finds it difficult to establish new positions in a tightly structured net. The best distributors are already linked to competitors. Competitors can, more or less legally, make the late newcomer unprofitable by predatory pricing. When we compare early and late starters we can see how important timing is in global marketing.

The international among others

In this situation the firm has the possibility of using positions in one net to bridge over to other nets, with regard to both extensions and penetration. There is a strong need for coordination of the international activities along the value chain (e.g. R&D, production and marketing/sales). Operations in one market may make it possible to utilise production capacity for sales in other markets. This may lead to production coordination by product specialisation and increased intra-firm trade across borders.

Establishment of sales subsidiaries is probably speeded up by high internationalization because the international knowledge level is higher and there is a stronger need to coordinate sales and marketing activities in different markets.

The relevance of the network model for the SME serving as a subcontractor

Until now a network has been connected with development of mutual trust and interests between firms in the network. In the following, domination and control characteristics will form the starting point for the formation of a more power-balanced network.

In the SME context it is clear that where, for example, a small firm derives a significant proportion of its turnover and profits from acting as a subcontractor to another, often larger firm, the small firm becomes dependent on the latter. In turn, the large firm may acquire power over its subcontractor. This power can be measured in terms of the larger company's influence on decision making within the smaller firm in areas such as pricing and investment.

Exchange networks are based on control, coordination and cooperation. By 'control' is understood quasi-hierarchical relationships allowing one company to dominate another: for example, the relationship that traditionally obtains in the car industry between the major manufacturers and their subcontractors. By 'coordination' is understood a situation in which a 'leading' or 'hub' firm in the network orchestrates the value-adding chain. This allows firms to specialise in those components of the value chain in which they have competitive advantage, abandoning and farming out those activities in which they are disadvantaged to network partners that do have strengths in these areas.

'Cooperation' is the result of increasing specialisation in small market niches, which has tended to encourage interdependency between firms in the value-added chain. Whereas in many subcontracting relationships in the past the subcontractor simply followed instructions of the dominating firm on design and manufacture, the need to adjust to ever-quicker changes in the marketplace can have the effect of making the subcontractor a more equal partner in the whole design to production process. The nature of the relationship between subcontractor and buyer thereby changes. Greater trust is required to make the partnership a success. Greater coordination is also required, creating a role for companies that simply 'manage' the value chain. In order to meet the pressures of these new circumstances the small firm will depend on the nature and number of its links to other firms. As a result the need for and value of networking have increased.

Where the network is dominated by a single firm and relationships are of the 'traditional' subcontracting kind, competition on price (or prices simply being imposed by the dominating firm) is the rule. Also, cooperating firms know that, while optimal networking is an effective strategy to reduce risk, less optimal networking will increase risk by increasing their dependence on, for example, a potentially unreliable supplier. To overcome the danger of dependence, 'traditional' risk reduction strategies can be implemented, such as the implementation of multiple sourcing by the purchasing company, or client diversification by the selling company.

3.5   Internationalization of SMEs

In the face of globalization threats many SMEs attempt to expand their sales into foreign markets. International expansion provides new and potentially more profitable markets; helps increase the firm's competitiveness; and facilitates access to new product ideas, manufacturing innovations and the latest technology.

At the macroenvironment and industry levels, globalization gives rise to market turbulence, increased competition from (especially) multinational firms, loss of protected markets due to trade liberalisation, and the emergence of international marketing opportunities, all of which can affect the operations and performance of the SME. In such an environment possession by management of an entrepreneurial orientation is expected to provide certain benefits.

It may be more appropriate to take a holistic view of the very small, entrepreneurial, or start-up firm's cross-border business activities, rather than to focus on discrete entry mode types. The challenge facing most entrepreneurial firms is to establish and develop a viable, competitive and sustainable business, usually with limited resources, and often by adopting flexible, imaginative and innovative business practices. International business activity for many firms, and particularly high-technology firms, may be an integral part of that process. In that respect too, internationalization is a firm-specific behaviour, in relation to and encompassing its international business activities.

The assumption made here therefore is that internationalization, for entrepreneurial firms, is a growth and development process. It may involve one or a number of value chain activities, some of which may be more internationalized, or more frequently subject to internationalization, than others. Internationalization may be part of the process, but for very small and very young firms internationalization is more likely to occur, in the first instance, through links and transactions with organizations and individuals in the external environment. The process may include both inward and outward links – see Table 3.1 and Figure 2.2 – and these are likely to reflect the firms' current areas of competence and expertise, and/or its current level of needs and perceived inadequacies.

Table 3.1 SMEs Inward–outward cross–border business activities

	Inward	Outward
R&D	Contract-in R&D License-in technology from overseas-based firms	License-out technology to overseas-based firm Contract-out R&D to overseas-based firm
Production	Technical service or consultancy performed in the home country for overseas-based clients Contract-in manufacture for overseas-based firms	Contract-out manufacture to overseas-based firm Technical service or consultancy performed overseas Minority investment in overseas production Majority investment in overseas production
Marketing and distribution	Import from overseas-based supplier Import with distribution in the home country Management or marketing service or consultancy performed in the home country for overseas-based clients	Exporting through home country-based intermediary Exporting through foreign-based agent/distributor Exporting through overseas-based sales representative or branch Management or marketing services or consultancy performed overseas

Source: adapted from Jones (2001), p. 197.

Initial international expansion may involve specific combinations of inward/outward value chain activities, which are not necessarily directly reciprocal. Efficiency and synergy in linkage combinations is an important concern for internationalizing firms.

The element of *time* is considered more important here than development stages, that, even if specifically determined, would vary considerably between firms.

Importance of personal factors

International entrepreneurship argues that the founders of international new ventures are more 'alert' to the possibilities of combing resources from different national markets because of the competences they have developed from their earlier activities.

Research results by Manolova and Brush (2002) indicate that owners/founders are likely to draw on their international experience, skills, or overall competences when internationalizing their own firms. Therefore, for managers with these sets of skills and positive environmental perceptions, the process of internationalization has 'less uncertainty', and hence is more likely to be pursued than it is for managers without comparable skills or perceptions.

Manolova and Bush (2002) clearly indicate that 'personal factors' matter with respect to SME internationalization but, more importantly, 'some personal factors matter more than others'. Owners/founders or managers who have more positive perceptions of the international environment would also be more likely to internationalize their own small businesses.

The most important finding from Manovala and Bush (2002) is that internationalization is not a function of 'demographics', but is instead a function of 'perceptions'. If the owner/founder or manager perceives that there is a lower level of environmental uncertainty in a particular international market, or perceives that there is the requisite skill set to internationalize, then chances are high that the small firm will be pursuing a strategy of internationalization. Additionally, the findings show that public policy directives, as well as education and training programmes, need to recognise that there are significant differences in small firm internationalization that are based upon the technology sector. Knowledge of these differences can be used to guide the development of small firm internationalization initiatives that match sector characteristics.

Entrepreneurial orientation is associated with opportunity seeking, risk taking, and decision action catalysed by a strong leader or an organization possessed of a particular value system. SMEs with an entrepreneurial orientation engage in product market innovations, undertake relatively risky ventures, and initiate proactive innovations.

Innovativeness refers to a corporate environment that promotes and supports novel ideas, experimentation and creative processes that may lead to new products, techniques or technologies. Risk taking reflects the propensity to devote resources to projects that entail a substantial possibility of failure, along with chances for high returns. Proactiveness is the opposite of reactiveness and implies taking initiative, aggressively pursuing ventures, and being at the forefront of efforts to shape the environment in ways that benefit the firm. Autonomy suggests the independent action of a person or a team in giving birth to an idea or a vision and then carrying it through to fruition. Finally, competitive aggressiveness refers to the firm's tendency to challenge its competitors intensely and directly in order to outperform them in the marketplace.

However, SMEs may lack the resources to compete head to head with larger rivals at home and invasions from abroad. Globalization may pose many challenges and can make the business milieu substantially more hostile for smaller firms. But all in all, given the turbulence posed by globalization, it is expected that SMEs with an entrepreneurial orientation will fare better than those that lack such an orientation.

Technology acquisition is one way of enabling the firm to compete more effectively or launch products that better satisfy customer needs. Innovation arising from acquired technology is a key source of competitive advantage, particularly in turbulent environments, that can enable firms to market new or improved goods faster than competitors. Technology acquisition can give rise to products that are better adapted to the specific needs of foreign markets. Firms can gain additional benefits by responding to the forces of globalization. SMEs that respond by appropriately adapting their marketing and other strategies to globalization demands are likely to perform better than firms which do not. Nature and pace of internationalization are conditioned by product, industry, and other external environmental variables, as well as by firm-specific factors. Therefore, at any given point in time, SMEs will be in a state of internationalization, which will be subject to both backward and forward momentum, instead of progressing through stages, as in the Uppsala model.

The SME's internationalization is unlikely to come off well unless the firm prepares in advance. Advance planning has often been regarded as important to the success of new ventures. Such planning is especially important in international ventures, in which the business environment can be considerably more complex than at home. Thus *internationalization preparation* describes a firm's efforts to prepare in advance as it seeks to expand into foreign markets. Such preparation involves conducting international market research; committing human, financial and other resources to supporting the international venture; and adapting products to suit the needs of target foreign markets.

In the next section we will look at a special case of SME internationalization – the so-called 'Born Globals'.

3.6   Born Globals

Introduction

In recent years research has identified an increasing number of firms that certainly do not follow the traditional stages pattern in their internationalization process. In contrast, they aim at international markets or maybe even the global market right from their birth.

A 'Born Global' can be defined as: 'a firm that from its inception derives competitive advantage from the use of resources and the sale of outputs in multiple countries' (Oviatt and McDougall, 1994, p. 49).

Born Globals represent an interesting case of firms operating under time and space compression conditions that have allowed then to assume a global geographic scope since their start up. This 'time–space compression' phenomenon (Harvey, 1996) means that geographical processes can be reduced and compressed into 'here and now' trade and information exchange over the globe – if available infrastructure, communication and IT devices are put in place together with skilled people. The global financial market is a good example of the phenomenon (Törnroos, 2002).

Oviatt and McDougall (1994) grouped Born Globals (or 'International New Ventures' as they call them) into four different categories, dependent on the number of value chain activities performed combined with the number of countries involved. For example, they distinguish the 'export/import start-up' from the 'global start-up', whereby the latter – contrary to the former – involves many activities coordinated across many countries.

Born Globals are typically characterised by being SMEs with less than 500 employees and annual sales under $100 million – and reliance on cutting-edge technology in the development of relatively unique product or process innovations. But the most distinguishing feature of Born Global firms is that they tend to be managed by entrepreneurial visionaries, who view the world as a single, borderless marketplace from the time of the firm's founding. Born Globals are small, technology-oriented companies that operate in international markets from the earliest days of their establishment. There is growing evidence of the emergence of Born Globals in numerous countries of the developed world.

More recently the concept of *born-again global firms* has been proposed, i.e. long-established firms that previously focused on their domestic markets but that suddenly embrace rapid and dedicated internationalization (Bell *et al.*, 2001).

The Born Global phenomenon suggests a new challenge to traditional theories of internationalization.

Born Globals are challenging traditional theories

Born Globals may be similar to the 'late starter' or the 'international among others' (Johanson and Mattson, 1988). In the latter situation both the environment and the firm are highly internationalized. Johanson and Mattson (1988) point out that internationalization processes of firms will be much faster in internationalized market conditions, among other reasons because the need for coordination and integration across borders is high. Since relevant partners/distributors will often be occupied in neighbouring markets, firms do not necessarily follow a 'rings in the water' approach to market selection. In the same vein their 'establishment chain' need not follow the traditional picture because strategic alliances, joint ventures, etc., are much more prevalent; firms seek partners with supplementary skills and resources. In other words internationalization processes of firms will be much more individual and situation specific in internationalized markets.

Many industries are characterised by *global sourcing activities* and also by networks across borders. The consequence is that innovative products can very quickly spread to new markets all over the world – because the needs and wants of buyers become more homogeneous. Hence the internationalization process of subcontractors may be quite diverse and different from the stages models. In other words, the new market conditions pull the firms into many markets very fast. Finally, financial markets have also become international, which means that an entrepreneur in any country may seek financial sources all over the world.

In the case of Born Globals we may assume that the background of the decision maker (founder) has a large influence on the internationalization path followed. Market knowledge, personal networking of the entrepreneur or international contacts and experience transmitted from former occupations, relations and education are examples of such international skills obtained prior to the birth of the firm. Factors such as education, experience from living abroad, experience of other internationally oriented jobs, etc., mould the mind of the founder and decrease the psychic distances to specific product markets significantly; the previous experience and knowledge of the founder extends the network across national borders, opening possibilities for new business ventures (Madsen and Servais, 1997).

Often Born Globals govern their sales and marketing activities through a specialised network in which they seek partners that complement their own competences; this is necessary because of their limited resources.

Most often Born Globals must choose a business area with homogeneous and minimal adaptation of the marketing mix. The argument is that these small firms cannot take a multi-domestic approach as can large firms, simply because they do not have sufficient scale in operations worldwide. They are vulnerable because they are dependent on a single product that they have to commercialise in lead markets first, no matter where such markets are situated geographically. The reason is that such markets are the key to broad and rapid market access, which is important because the fixed costs in these firms are relatively high. Since this is the key factor influencing the choice of the initial market the importance of psychic distance as market selection criteria is reduced.

Factors giving rise to the emergence of Born Globals

Several trends may explain the increasing importance of Born Globals and help explain why such companies can successfully enter international markets.

Increasing role of niche markets

There is a growing demand among customers in mature economies for specialised or customised products. With the globalization of markets and increasing worldwide competition from large multinationals, many smaller firms may have no choice but to specialise in the supplying of products that occupy a relatively narrow global niche.

Advances in process/technology production

Improvements in microprocessor-based technology imply that low-scale, batch-type production can be economical. New machine tools now permit the manufacture of complex, non-standard parts and components with relative ease. New technologies allow small companies to achieve comparable footing with large multinationals in the production of sophisticated products for sale around the world. Technology allows small importers to streamline production in ways that make their products highly competitive in the global marketplace. Furthermore, technology is facilitating the production of widely diverse products on an ever smaller scale. The consequence of this is increasing specialisation in many industries – more and more consumer goods will likely be tailor made to fit ever more diverse preferences.

Flexibility of SMEs/Born Globals

The advantages of small companies – quicker response time, *flexibility*, adaptability, and so on – facilitate the international endeavours of Born Globals. SMEs are more flexible and quicker to adapt to foreign tastes and international standards.

Global networks

Successful international commerce today is increasingly facilitated through partnerships with foreign businesses – distributors, trading companies, subcontractors, as well as more traditional buyers and sellers. Inexperienced managers can improve their chances for succeeding in international business if they take the time to build mutually beneficial, long-term alliances with foreign partners.

Advances and speed in information technology

A very important trend in favour of Born Globals is the recent advance in *communications technology*, which has accelerated the speed of information flows. Gone are the days of large, vertically integrated firms where information flows were expensive and took a considerable time to be shared. With the invention of the Internet and other telecommunication aids such as mobile phones, email and other computer-supported technologies such as electronic data interchange (EDI), managers even in small firms can efficiently manage operations across borders. Information is now readily and more quickly accessible to everyone. Everything gets smaller and faster and reaches more people and places around the globe.

Another important trend is the *globalization of technology*. Joint research and development platforms, international technology transfers, and the cross-border education and exchange of students in science, engineering and business have all exploded in recent years. As such, new and better approaches to manufacturing, product innovation and general operations have become much more readily available to smaller firms.

Internet–based Born Globals

The Internet revolution offers new opportunities for young SMEs to establish a global sales platform by developing e-commerce websites. Today many new and small firms are Born Globals in the way that they are 'start-ups' on the Internet and they sell to a global audience via a centralised e-commerce website. However, after some time many of these firms realise they cannot expand global sales to the next level without having some 'localised e-commerce websites'. If we compare the flow of financial results in physical ('bricks and mortar') companies with Internet-based companies we will often see a result such as that shown in Figure 3.7.

Figure 3.7 Models of economic efficiency

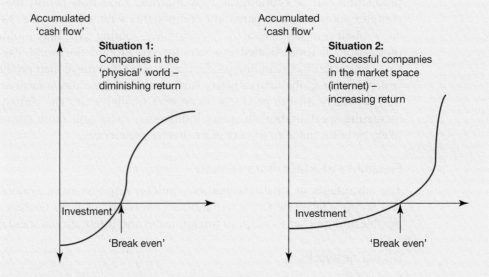

In the 'physical' companies we will often see the 'law of diminishing returns to scale' in function. This happens where the variable costs are relatively high compared to fixed costs of the company. We are learning that the law of diminishing returns does not always apply. In many cases the optimal production point is no longer determined by factory size, but by the point at which total market demand is satisfied. This occurs in markets in which fixed costs are much higher than variable costs. This is the case for products in digital form, where a single copy (of software, for instance) can satisfy total market needs, and for products with very high investment in intellectual content, such as pharmaceuticals.

In the successful Internet companies gains associated with increasing shares of markets do not diminish with time but actually increase. This increase creates 'increasing returns to scale'. In this environment companies must *win market shares rapidly*, which has driven many companies to create new strategies for market share capture. AOL Time Warner distributed CDs with software in everything from magazine inserts to fast-food giveaways, making its trial offer almost irresistible to millions of networks users.

Funding the large investments required to capture significant market share in the Internet economy does not come cheaply, especially if many companies are competing for the same market space. A substantial part of the investment must be made up front, sometimes years before revenues begin to outpace operating cost.

In a global economy companies must also be prepared, almost from the start, to serve larger market segments. Neither proposition is cheap. Amazon.com has achieved market dominance, but not without investing a half-billion dollars a year in sales and marketing.

Amazon.com is perhaps an example of Situation 2 in Figure 3.7 but, despite considerably increasing sales, it has just recently reached break-even. Many companies must also rethink their alliance strategies. No longer are alliances primarily about efficiency: 'How can I outsource certain functions to improve performance?' Now the emphasis is on gaining access to markets to exploit network effects, and on creating product and service synergies in aligning with larger, already dominant companies. For example, companies such as American Broadcasting Company (ABC) are partnering with Time Warner for access to its customer base and expected synergies with its offerings. Access has proved so valuable that companies are now paying a lot to such firms for the ability to reach its customers.

As economic fundamentals that have held true for decades begin to change, many traditional business strategies are becoming obsolete. The perfect profit formula for this new business environment is not yet clear. However, electronic commerce is changing the rules, and every business, even the most successful, needs a revised business plan.

3.7   Internationalization of services

As goods go through increasingly more complex value chains to increase firms' relative competitive advantage, services will play a more important role in their marketing. Services themselves are also getting more complex as information technology enables unlimited variations for both sales and after-sales support for target markets.

In the literature on international marketing of services an internationalization strategy is often considered more risky for service firms than for manufacturers. The main reason for this is that in many services the producer and the production facilities are part of the service, which requires that the firm has greater control of its resources than would otherwise be the case. In traditional international marketing models focusing on the needs of manufacturing firms the internationalization process can start in a minor scale using indirect export channels followed by a step-by-step move towards more direct channels. This enables the firm gradually to increase its understanding of quality expectations, personnel requirements, distribution and media structures, and buying behaviour peculiarities on the foreign market. For service firms the situation is different. They immediately face all this and other problems related to entering a foreign market. It has to find an entry mode and a strategy that helps it to cope with this situation as well as possible. The choice of course depends on the type of service and market.

First let us look at some characteristics of services.

Characteristics of services

A service is a complicated phenomenon. The word has many meanings, ranging from personal service to service as a product. Services are not things, they are processes or activities, and these activities are intangible in nature. The term can be even broader in scope. A machine, or almost any physical product, can be turned into a service to a customer if the seller makes efforts to tailor the solution to meet the most detailed demands of that customer. A machine is still a physical good, of course, but the way of treating the customer with an appropriately designed machine is a service.

Most often a service involves interactions of some sort with the service provider. However, there are situations where the customer as an individual does not interact with the service firm.

For most services, *three* basic characteristics can be identified.

1. **Services are at least to some extent produced and consumed simultaneously**. Services are produced and consumed simultaneously (this is also called the 'insepar-ability' characteristic) – it is difficult to manage quality control and to do marketing in the traditional sense, since there is no preproduced quality to control before the service is sold and consumed.

   One should realise that *it is the visible part of the service process that matters in the customer's mind*. As far as the rest is concerned, a customer can only experience the result; but the visible activities are experienced and evaluated in every detail. Quality control and marketing must therefore take place at the time and place of simultaneous service production and consumption.

   Most definitions of services imply that services do not result in *ownership* of any-thing. Normally this is true. When we use the services of an airline we are entitled, for example, to be transported from one place to another, but when we arrive at our destination there is nothing left but the remaining part of the ticket and the boarding card.

   Because of this it is not possible to keep services in stock in the same way as goods. If an aeroplane leaves the airport half-full the empty seats cannot be sold the next day; they are lost. Instead, capacity planning becomes a critical issue. Even though services cannot be kept in stock, one can try to *keep customers in stock*. For example, if a restaurant is full, it is always possible to try to keep the customer waiting in the bar until there is a free table.

2. **The customer participates in the service production process, at least to some extent**. The customer is not only a receiver of the service; the customer also partici-pates in the service process as a production resource in an interaction with the per-sonnel of the firm. Therefore service to one customer is not exactly the same as the 'same' service to the next customer.

   In many cases what the customer wants and expects is not known in detail at the beginning of the service process (service production process) or, consequently, what resources are needed, to what extent and in what configuration they should be used. A bank customer may only realise what their needs actually are during interactions with a teller or a loan officer. Thus the firm has to adjust its resources and its ways of using its resources accordingly. Customer-perceived value follows from a successful and customer-oriented management of resources relative to customer sacrifice, not from a preproduced bundle of features.

3. **Services are processes consisting of activities or a series of activities rather than things**. One important characteristic of services is their *process* nature. Services are

processes consisting of a series of activities where a number of different types of resources – people as well as other kinds of resources – are used, often in direct interactions with the customer, so that a solution is found to a customer's problem. Because the customer participates in the process, the process, especially the part in which the customer is participating, becomes part of the solution.

In order to understand service management and the marketing of services it is critical that one realises that the consumption of a service is *process consumption* rather than *outcome consumption*. The consumer or user perceives the service process (or service production process) as part of the service consumption, not simply the outcome of that process, as in traditional marketing of physical goods. When consuming a physical product customers make use of the product itself; that is they consume the outcome of the production process. In contrast, when consuming services customers perceive the process of producing the service to a greater or smaller degree, but always to a critical extent, as well as taking part in the process.

Factors to consider in the internationalization of services

Information technologies

Through information technologies service marketers can interact with customers to anticipate and serve their needs. Improving the service offering, providing alternative service delivery choices and communicating with the customer all foster better relationships with customers. The use of computerised communication allows the service marketer to establish an ongoing relationship with the customer at each stage of the consumption process. Online databases of customers can show consumption patterns and help track demand fluctuations. Automated service delivery mechanisms can provide a means for varying levels of self-service. In short, international services marketers need to examine information technologies to discover better ways to manage customer relationships.

The proliferation of information technology has made it possible for international service firms to serve customers 24 hours a day and seven days a week. Information technologies change the scale and the economics of service organizations. Home-based service organizations are now able to serve the needs of clients all over the world with a combination of computers, telephones, fax machines and electronic mail. In future it will be easy for groups of home-based service organizations to form flexible networks that quickly adapt to customer needs. However, even a firm that chooses to internationalize using electronic marketing cannot manage its service operations totally on its own. On foreign markets it has, for example, to rely on at least postal and delivery services. The possibility for the service firm to control such network partners may be very limited.

Cultural issues

Cultural issues will necessarily have a significant impact on the acceptability and adoption pattern of services. Since services inherently involve some level of human interaction the likelihood of cultural incompatibility is greater. For example, nations that culturally define the housewife's role as the family caretaker will probably not be very keen on using day-care centres.

However we design our service and whatever means of serving the market we choose there will be a need to adjust to *local cultural preferences*. Some means of internationalization – franchising, for example – provide an easier route to delivering culturally sensitive services by drawing on local management knowledge. Consumer services are likely to require greater cultural adaptation than do business-to-business services.

However, we cannot ignore culture and all firms providing services internationally should consider the provision of appropriate cultural training to staff, the use of local employees and, where needed, changes to the service offering itself. Without these provisions the company runs the risk of losing business to local companies or more culturally aware international service providers. Service businesses may be 'about people', but the technology and systems remain important. Even the best people struggle to deliver when systems are not in place to facilitate delivery.

Services do not necessarily require a physical presence. For established service businesses, confronting the competition from competitors trading via the Internet (or, in some industries, digital television) present a major challenge, especially for those firms that have extensive investments in property and staff around the globe.

Geographic locations

The strategic issue of location can be divided into two main aspects, that of where generally to locate a hospitality operation and then the specific issue of selecting suitable sites. In the hospitality industry the key factor in the location decision is demand. In simple terms, operations are located where demand is highest, and sited so that such demand can easily access the provision. Strategic success derives from matching the type and size of the business with the site available.

The factors that influence location in the accommodation and food service sectors are different. Hotels are primarily located near where people are travelling or at destinations that require them to stay away from home.

Standardisation versus customisation

An important strategic issue in marketing services internationally is the extent to which each service might be standardised. In addition to the necessity for customer contact for many service categories, many host government regulations in numerous services sectors make standardisation very difficult. Accounting and financial services markets are governed by very different rules around the world.

With globalization, the impact of cultural adaptation will need to be central to the study of operational topic areas such as joint venturing, materials management, purchasing, new product development, layout and process design, supervision and motivation, training, workforce scheduling, environmental management, and labour–management relations. These are all key areas of front room and back room management that are likely to require adaptation from country to country as services are globalized.

Local workers will need to be trained in their native language. The globalization of front room operations with its verbal customer contact still depends heavily on cultural adaptation of the service. The experience of The Walt Disney Company in its opening of Disneyland Paris is an example of the problems of controlling the customer contact experience in a foreign culture. Some concessions to French culture were made, such as adopting both the French and English languages for the park. However, a more troubling problem was training independently minded French nationals to act out the roles of Disney characters and perform their duties in a courteous manner. When the service is defined by the customer contact experience translating the required human behaviour of service personnel across national boundaries becomes a challenge.

Common customer needs for services vary more widely across nations than is the case for products, and addressing them requires localised solutions.

Retailing provides an excellent example of a service business that is difficult to standardise. Despite much talk about the internationalization of retail trade, local retailing regulations vary considerably, not only across countries (including within the European Union), but also within the provinces of each country.

Implications for international marketing of services

It is possible to distinguish between five main strategies for internationalizing services. These are not mutually exclusive, and in some cases some will also work well for manufactured goods (Grönroos, 1999):

1. direct export;
2. systems export/following the large customers abroad;
3. direct entry/own subsidiary;
4. indirect entry/intermediate mode;
5. electronic marketing/Internet.

1. **Direct export** of services may basically take place on industrial markets. Consultants and firms repairing and maintaining valuable equipment may have their base on the domestic market and whenever needed move the resources and system required to produce the service to the client abroad. Repair services on valuable equipment are often exported in this way. Some consultants work in a similar fashion. No step-by-step learning can take place as the service has to be produced immediately. Because of this, the risk of making mistakes can be substantial.

2. **Systems export/following the large customers abroad** is a joint export by two or more firms whose solutions complement each other. A service firm may support a goods-exporting firm or another firm. For example, when a manufacturer delivers equipment or turnkey factories to international buyers a need for engineering services, distribution, cleaning, security and other services is often present. This gives service firms an opportunity to expand their markets abroad. As the literature suggests, systems export is the traditional mode for service export. For example, advertising agencies and banks have extended their accessibility abroad because of their clients' activities on international markets. In systems export the services are mainly marketed in industrial markets abroad. For example, law firms expand into multiple cities in an attempt to align themselves with their corporate accounts, service companies are pushed by their customers to operate in the same countries as their clients. The truly global company wants and demands truly global service of its travel agents, it auditors, its consultants, and others. The weakness of this strategy for a company already committed to overseas operations is that it ignores the possible vast markets where clients are not represented.

3. **Direct entry/own subsidiary** means that the service firm establishes a service-producing organization of their own on the foreign market. For manufactured goods in the first stage of a learning process a sales office can be such an organization. For a service firm, a local organization normally has to be able to produce and deliver the service from the beginning. The time for learning becomes short. Almost from day one the firm has to be able to cope with problems with production, human resource management and consumer behaviour. In addition, the local government may consider the new, international service provider a threat to local firms and even to national pride.

4. **Indirect entry/intermediate mode** is used when the service firm wants to avoid establishing a local operation that is totally or partly owned by itself but wants to establish a permanent operation in the foreign market.

Table 3.2 Summary of the three models explaining the internationalization process of the firm

	Uppsala internationalization model	Transaction cost analysis model	Network mode
Unit of analysis	The firm	The transaction or set of transactions	Multiple interorganizational relationships between firms Relationships between one group of firms and other groups of firms
Basic assumptions about firms' behaviour	The model is based on behavioural theories and an incremental decision-making process with little influence from competitive market factors. A gradual learning-by-doing process	In the real world there is 'friction'/transactional difficulties between buyer and seller. This friction is mainly caused by opportunistic behaviour: the self-conscious attention of the single manager (i.e. seeking of self-interest with guile)	The 'glue' that keeps the network (relationships) together is based on technical, economic, legal and especially personal ties. Managers' personal influence on relationships is strongest in the early phases of the establishment of relationships. Later in the process routines and systems will become more important
Explanatory variables affecting the development process	The firm's knowledge/market commitment Psychic distance between home country and the firm's international markets	Transactional difficulties and transaction costs increase when transactions are characterised by asset specificity, uncertainty, frequency of transaction	The individual firms are autonomous. The individual firm is dependent on resources controlled by other firms. Business networks will emerge in fields where there is frequent coordination between specific actors and where conditions are changing rapidly
Normative implications for international marketers	Additional market commitments should be made in small incremental steps: – Choose new geographic markets with small psychic distances from existing markets – Choose an 'entry mode' with few marginal risks	Under the above-mentioned conditions (i.e. prohibitively high transaction costs), firms should seek internalisation of activities (i.e. implement the global marketing strategy in wholly owned subsidiaries)	The relationships of a firm in a domestic network can be used as bridges to other networks in other countries. Such direct or indirect bridges to different country networks can be important in the initial steps abroad and in the subsequent entry of new markets. Sometimes an SME can be forced to enter foreign networks: for example, if a customer requires that the subsupplier (an SME) follows it abroad. As an example see the case study in Chapter 13, LM Glasfiber.

- Licensing agreements give a local firm exclusive rights to use the professional concept of the firm. This of course requires that exclusive rights can be guaranteed.
- Franchising is a concept often used by restaurant and food service industries for indirect entry into a foreign market. Local service firms get the exclusive right to a marketing concept, which may also include rights to a certain operational mode, and in this way the concept can be replicated as much as existing demand allows throughout the foreign market. The internationalizing firm as the franchisor gets the local knowledge that the franchisees possess, whereas franchisees get an opportunity to grow with a new and perhaps well-established concept. With a reasonably standardised service offering, it would also be possible to franchise a consultancy overseas.
- Another form of indirect entry is *management contracts*, which are often used, for example, in the hotel business. As far as the need for market knowledge is concerned, indirect entry is probably the least risky of the internationalization strategies discussed so far. Conversely, the internationalizing firm's control over the foreign operations is normally more limited when using this entry strategy (own subsidiary).

5 Electronic marketing/Internet as an internationalizing strategy means that the service firm extends its accessibility through the use of advanced electronic technology. The Internet provides firms with a way of communicating their offerings and putting them up for sale, and a way of collecting data about the buying habits and patterns of its customers and using network partners to arrange delivery and payment. The electronic bookstore Amazon.com is a good example of a firm internationalizing its services using electronic marketing. When launching the concept it had to take into account the interest in its services that would automatically develop outside national borders. TV shops (satellite television) are examples of other ways of internationalizing services using advanced technology. When using electronic marketing the firm is not bound to any particular location. The service can be administered from anywhere on the globe and still reach customers throughout a vast international market, who are connected to the Internet or exposed to satellite television broadcasting.

3.8 Summary

The main conclusions of this chapter are summarised in Table 3.2.

Born Globals represent a relatively new research field in international marketing. Born Globals share some fundamental similarities: they possess unique assets, focus on narrow global market segments, are strongly customer oriented, the entrepreneur's vision and competences are of crucial importance. In the end, for these firms, being global does not seem to be an option but a necessity. They are pushed into globalization by global customers and too small national/regional market segments. They can sustain their immediate global reach thanks to entrepreneurial vision and competences, and a deep awareness and knowledge of their competitive advantage in foreign markets.

In this chapter, the importance of the personal factors in the internationalization process of SMEs is emphasized.

For internationalization of services the following five main strategies were identified: (1) direct export; (2) systems export/following the large customers abroad; (3) direct entry/own subsidiary; (4) indirect entry/intermediate mode; (5) electronic marketing/Internet.

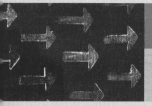

CASE STUDY 3.1   Cryos

They keep the stork busy around the world

Recent statistics indicate that 8 per cent of couples are infertile (**www.repromedltd.com**). Some decide they will live their lives together without children of their own. Others may pursue adoption – a procedure made more difficult because of the number of single women who choose to keep their children. A third option is for the couple to consult with their physician and to undergo artificial insemination using donor semen. It is many couples' deeply felt wish to have children that is the basis for the Danish-based Cryos International Sperm Bank.

Take artificial insemination. Sperm banking is now global; clients are no longer limited to the small donor pools at local sperm banks. For sperm banks technology plays a major role in the globalization drive. Concern about genetic defects and infectious diseases has led to sophisticated and expensive means of testing donations. Storage and transport methods have also grown more complicated. The improvements add to the investment required to operate a sperm bank. That, in turn, promotes consolidation in the industry.

Our main activity is worldwide delivery of high quality frozen tested semen from more than 200 donors on stock - mostly Scandinavians. Since 1991 more than 5,000 pregnancies have been reported from more than 30 countries all over the world.

History

Cryos International Sperm Bank was established in 1987 in Aarhus, Denmark, by Ole Schou. 'Cryos' is Greek and means 'ice' (from *crystallos*). The word is also known from 'cryobiology'. In English a sperm bank is often called a 'cryobank'.

The office and laboratory were initially established as a service both for men who were going to have a vasectomy and for cancer patients who wanted to have their sperm frozen before chemotherapy or radiation, which might make them infertile.

In 1990 the donor programme was established, and the first donor semen was released and delivered after six months' quarantine in May 1991. Demand increased very quickly. Clinics in Denmark started to receive semen from Cryos, quickly followed by clinics in Norway, Finland, Iceland, the United Kingdom, Greece, Germany, Italy, Switzerland, Belgium, and other countries. The clinics were

particularly satisfied with the good quality of semen, resulting in high pregnancy results (between 20 and 30 per cent per cyclus) and the professional service, with immediate supply from a relatively high selection of different donors.

In 1994 two new departments were opened, in the cities of Copenhagen and Odense, and Cryos had clients in 19 countries in Europe, Australia, Asia, Africa and north America.

In 1995 Cryos started distributing other sperm-related products such as preparation media. The same year Cryos started its own production of the culture media 'SpermWash'.

Today

Cryos markets three grades of sperm, including an 'Extra' grade, which contains twice as many sperm as the standard grade and exhibits the highest levels of motility, a measure of sperm's ability to reach its target.

In 2001 Cryos opened a branch in the United States in order to meet the specific market situation and the growing demand for Scandinavian donors. The sperm bank market in the United States is very different from that in other markets around the world, because it is not the clinics but the patients who choose a sperm bank and select the donor. The service includes patient access to donor lists, extended profiles, patient phone service, etc., which could not be organised within the 'clinic-only service' concept of Cryos. The US market for donor sperm is estimated at around €100 mill. per year.

Also in 2001, a new extensive homepage for the US market (**www.scandinaviancryobank.com**) was introduced with direct access to updated donor lists, online pregnancy reporting, a full product range with detailed information, prices and photos, online.

Today, Cryos can deliver sperm-related products to clinics or distributors in nearly 50 countries and donor semen to clinics in more than 35 countries. Cryos has become the largest sperm bank in the world, with more than 200 donors and almost 10,000 units of semen distributed each year, resulting in nearly 1,000 pregnancies.

Cryos employs a total of 26 people: 4 medical doctors, 1 biologist and 15 authorised laboratory technicians. An additional six people are employed in sales and administration.

The freezing of patients' own sperm has continued, involving several hundred patient deposits. Cryos's revenue in 2001 was around €1 million.

Of the income from donor semen 5 per cent is reserved for scientific and development purposes.

Cryos will continue to offer a high quality service related to its area of knowledge including donor semen, patient deposits and other semen-related clinical products. Furthermore, Cryos will continue to try to develop new and improved sperm-related knowledge and/or equipment for clinical use.

Using air freight and proprietary freezing techniques, Cryos can deliver to almost any customer in the world within 72 hours. The sperm travels in liquid-nitrogen tanks that, without refilling, can last a week. The quality of the sperm can be validated through laboratory tests.

Competition

Cryos's sperm generally costs less than US varieties, but still the company may find competing with US rivals difficult. The major reason is that US sperm banks are far more willing than Cryos and other overseas counterparts to reveal information about donors.

One of the main competitors, Xytex Corp., based in Augusta, Georgia, provides clients not only with photos of the donor and the offspring he's helped produce, but also with detailed biographical and physical information, including religion and educational background. The company even shows video footage of some donors. With seven sperm banks operating in the United States, from South Carolina to San Francisco, Xytex has another important advantage: steady access to donors of ethnic backgrounds, including Asians and African-Americans. This is important, because customers usually have a preference. In contrast, Cryos relies on three collection points in Denmark, ensuring that most of its donors will be white and of European descent.

Xytex provides physical, medical and social information about a donor to the patient. Donors are described by basic physical traits (hair and eye colour, height, weight, race, ethnic origin, skin tone and blood type), social traits (education, occupation, hobbies, special interests and skills), and medical histories on the donor and his family. In addition, donors provide a personal essay and physical and social information about their families.

In 1994 Xytex was the first sperm bank in the country to introduce photographs of its donors. Donors may choose to have their pictures taken to provide to the patient, or may voluntarily provide a childhood photograph. Though Cryos is not offering photographs of its donors, it is adapting to the environment in the US market. In order to avoid any recognition of the donors as they appear at Cryos, the donors listed with the Scandinavian Cryobank have been given names such as 'Oluf', 'Arne', 'Gorm', etc., instead of numbers.

The CEO of Cryos, Ole Schou, is considering the global launch of a franchising system focusing on quality so that the concept of Cryos can be copied in other clinics around the world. The franchising system involves a very comprehensive package of laboratory standards, control systems, training systems, franchising contracts, marketing plans, investment, financing, computer systems, etc.

Questions

1. Would you characterise Cyros as a 'Born Global'? Why/why not?

2. What do you think about Ole Schou's ideas of a 'global franchising system'?

3. What ethical and moral issues are involved for Cryos in this idea?

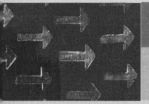

CASE STUDY 3.2   Fox Kids Europe

Rapid internationalization of a TV channel for kids

Early in 1997 a young Israeli television executive named Ynon Kreiz left the United States, headed for London. The task he had been given was to set up a pan-European children's television business from scratch. At the time he had less than two years' experience of full-time work in the entertainment business.

In 2000 Fox Kids Europe, **www.foxkidseurope. com**, had a presence in 30 countries in Europe and the Middle East, broadcast in 11 different languages, and reached 17 million households. In 2003 The Fox Kids Europe library includes major global programming franchises such as Power Rangers, Spiderman, X-Men, Inspector Gadget and Goosebumps. It includes diverse genres of programming (e.g. live action, animation, adventure, comedy, suspense, educational) and also has strong international appeal. The Fox Kids Europe library includes rights that, for most programming, cover all European markets and include most media (i.e. television, merchandising and the Internet).

Fox Kids Europe produces and broadcasts television programmes for children aged 2–14. It now broadcasts in 17 languages to 57 countries, reaching more than 32 million households across Europe and the Middle East. The content of each channel is tailored specifically to the local audience in each market, taking into account viewing habits, popularity of programmes, parental sensitivities and cultural trends. FOX KIDS Europe's main markets include the United Kingdom, the Netherlands, France, Germany, Poland, Spain, the Nordic Region, Romania, Turkey, Italy, Hungary, Russia and Israel. The company also operates 17 fully localised children's websites.

Source: © 2003 Fox Kids Europe. FOX KIDS and related names and logos are the exclusive property of the Twentieth Century Fox Film Corporation. IRON MAN™ & © 2003 Marvel. IRON MAN is the exclusive property of Marvel Characters, Inc. All rights Reserved. MAD JACK THE PIRATE™ & © 2003 BVS Entertainment, Inc., and BVS International N.V. All Rights Reserved. Reprinted with kind permission of Fox Kids Europe.

Questions

1. Which internationalization theory has the best match with the internationalization of Fox Kids Europe?

2. What are the drivers behind the internationalization of Fox Kids Europe?

Reprinted with kind permission of Fox Kids Europe.

For further exercises and cases, see this book's website at
www.booksites.net/hollensen

Questions for discussion

1. Explain why internationalization is an ongoing process in constant need of evaluation.

2. Explain the main differences between the three theories of internationalization: the Uppsala model, the transaction cost theory and the network model.

3. What is meant by the concept of 'psychological' or 'psychic distance'?

References

Aharoni, Y. (1966) *The Foreign Investment Decision Process*, Harvard Business School Press, Boston, MA.

Apte, U. and Mason, R.O. (1995) 'Global Disaggregation of Information Intensive Services', *Management Science*, vol. 41, No. 7, July, pp. 1250–1262.

Bell, J., McNaughton, R. and Young S. (2001) 'Born-Again global firms: an extension to the born global phenomenon', *Journal of International Management*, vol. 7 (3), pp. 173–90.

Buckley, P.J. and Casson, M. (1976) *The Future of the Multinational Enterprise*. Holmes & Meier, New York.

Christensen, P.R. and Lindmark, L.L. (1993) 'Location and internationalization of small firms', in Lindquist, L. and Persson, L.O. (eds) *Visions and Strategies in European Integration*, Springer Verlag, Berlin and Heidelberg.

Coase, R.H. (1937) 'The nature of the firm', *Economica*, pp. 386–405.

Contractor, F.J. and Lorange, P. (eds) (1998) *Cooperative Strategies in International Business*. Lexington Books, Lexington, MA.

Dunning, J.H. (1988) *Explaining International Production*, Unwin, London.

Forsgren, M. and Johanson, J. (1975) *International føretagsekonomi*, Norstedts, Stockholm.

Ghoshal, S. and Moran, P. (1996) 'Bad for practice: a critique of the transaction cost theory', *Academy of Management Review*, vol. 21 (1), pp. 13–47.

Grönroos, Christian (1999), 'Internationalization Strategies for Services.' *Journal of Services Marketing* 13 (4/5), 290–7.

Hallen, L. and Wiedersheim-Paul, F. (1979) 'Physical distance and buyer–seller interaction, *Organisasjon, Marknad och Samhalle*, vol. 16 (5), pp. 308–24.

Hymer, S.H. (1976) *The International Operations of National Firms: A study of direct foreign investment*, unpublished 1960 PhD thesis, MIT Press, Cambridge, MA.

Johanson, J. and Mattson, L.G. (1986) 'International marketing and internationalization processes: some perspectives on current and future research', in Paliwoda, S. and Turnbull, P. (eds), *Research in Developments in International Marketing*, Croom Helm, Beckenham (UK).

Johanson, J. and Mattson, L.G. (1988) 'Internationalization in industrial systems', in Hood, N. and Vahlne, J.E. (eds), *Strategies in Global Competition*, Croom Helm, Beckenham (UK).

Johanson, J. and Vahlne, J.E. (1977) 'The internationalization process of the firm: a model of knowledge development and increasing foreign market commitment', *Journal of International Business Studies*, vol. 8 (1), pp. 23–32.

Johanson, J. and Vahlne, J.E. (1990) 'The mechanism of internationalization', *International Marketing Review*, vol. 7 (4), pp. 11–24.

Johanson, J. and Wiedersheim-Paul, F. (1975) 'The internationalization of the firm: four Swedish cases', *Journal of Management Studies*, October, pp. 305–22.

Jones, M.V. (2001) 'First steps in internationalization: concepts and evidence from a sample of small high-technology firms', *Journal of International Management*, vol. 7, pp. 191–210.

Kindleberger, C.P. (1969) *American Business Abroad*, Yale University Press, New Haven, CT.

Kogut, B. (1988) 'Joint ventures: theoretical and empirical perspective', *Strategic Management Journal*, vol. 9, pp. 319–32.

Madhok, A. (1997) 'Cost, value and foreign market entry mode: the transaction and the firm', *Strategic Management Journal*, vol. 18, pp. 39–61.

Madhok, A. (1998) 'The nature of multinational firm boundaries: transaction cost, firm capabilities and foreign market entry mode', *International Business Review*, vol. 7, pp. 259–90.

Madsen, T.K. and Servais, P. (1997) 'The internationalization of Born Globals: an evolutionary process?', *International Business Review*, vol. 6 (6), pp. 561–83.

Manolova, T.S. and Brush, C.G. (2002) 'Internationalization of small firms – personal factors revisited', *International Small Business Journal*, vol. 20 (1), pp. 9–31.

Mclaughlin, Curtis P. and Fitzsimmons, James A. (1996): Strategies for Globalizing service operations. *International Journal of Service Industry Management*, vol. 7, No 4, pp. 43–57.

Nordström, K.A. (1990) *The internationalization Process of the Firm: Searching for new patterns and explanations*, Stockholm School of Economics.

Ouchi, W.G. (1980) 'Markets, bureaucracies and clans', *Administrative Science Quarterly*, vol. 25, pp. 129–42.

Oviatt, B. and McDougall, P. (1994) 'Towards a theory of international new ventures', *Journal of International Business Studies*, vol. 25 (1), pp. 45–64.

Penrose, E. (1959) *The Theory of the Growth of the Firm*. Blackwell, London.

Prahalad, C.K. and Hamel, G. (1990) 'The core competence and the corporation'. *Harvard Business Review*, May, pp. 71–97.

Reid, S.D. (1983) 'Firm internationalization, transaction costs and strategic choice', *International Marketing*, vol. 1 (2), p. 44.

Rugman, A.M. (1986) 'New theories of the multinational enterprise: an assessment of internationalization theory', *Bulletin of Economic Research*, vol. 38 (2), pp. 101–18.

Sharma, D.D. and Johanson, J. (1987) 'Technical consultancy in internationalization', *International Marketing Review*, Winter, pp. 20–9.

Turnbull, P.N. (1987) 'Interaction and international marketing: an investment process', *International Marketing Review*, Winter, pp. 7–19.

Törnroos, J.-Å. (2002) 'Internationalization of the firm: a theoretical review with implications for business network research', Paper presented at the *18th Annual IMP Conference*, September, Lyon, pp. 1–21.

Vernon, R. (1966) 'International investment and international trade in the product cycle', *Quarterly Journal of Economics*, vol. 80, pp. 190–207.

Welch, L.S. and Loustarinen, R. (1988) 'Internationalization: evolution of a concept', *Journal of General Management*, vol. 14 (2), pp. 36–64.

Williamson, O.E. (1975) *Markets and Hierarchies: Analysis and antitrust implications*, The Free Press, New York.

Williamson, O.E. (1985) *The Economic Institutions of Capitalization*, The Free Press, New York.

Further reading

Andersson, P. (2002) 'Connected internalizerings processes: the case of internationalization, *International Business Review*, vol. 11, pp. 365–83.

Chiara, A.D. and Minguzzi, A. (2002) 'Success factors in SMEs' internationalization processes: an Italian investigation', *Journal of Small Business Management*, vol. 40 (2), pp. 144–53.

Etemad, H., Wright, R.W. and Dana, L.P., (2002) 'Symbiotic international business networks: collaboration between small and large firms' *Thunderbird International Business Review*, vol. 43 (4), pp. 481–99.

Knight, G.A. and Liesch, P.W. (2002) 'Information internalization in internationalizing the firm', *Journal of Business Research*, vol. 55 (12), pp. 981–95.

Lindsay, V., Chadee, D., Mattsson, J., Johnston, R. and Millett, B. (2003) 'Relationship, the role of individuals and knowledge flows in the internationalization of service firms', *International Journal of Service Industry Management*, vol. 14, No. 1, pp. 7–35

Moen, Ø. and Servais, P. (2002) 'Born global or gradual global? Examining the export behavior of small and medium-sized enterprises', *Journal of International Marketing*, vol. 10 (3), pp. 49–72.

Rasmussen, E.S. and Madsen, T.K. (2002) 'The Born Global concept', Paper presented at the *28th EIBA Conference*, December.

Whitelock, J. (2002) 'Viewpoint (theories) theories of internationalization and their impact on marketing', *International Marketing Review*, vol. 19 (4), pp. 342–47.

Zucchella, A. (2002) 'Born Global versus gradually internationalizing firms: an analysis based on the Italian case', Paper presented at the *28th EIBA Conference*, December.

4 Development of the firm's international competitiveness

Contents

Learning objectives

After studying this chapter you should be able to do the following:

- Define the concept 'international competitiveness' in a broader perspective from a macro level to a micro level.

- Discuss the factors influencing the firm's international competitiveness.

- Explain how Porter's traditional competitive-based five forces model can be extended to a collaborative (five sources) model.

- Explore the idea behind the 'competitive triangle'.

- Analyse the basic sources of competitive advantage.

- Explain the steps in competitive benchmarking.

4.1 Introduction

The topic of this chapter is how the firm creates and develops competitive advantages in the international market. Development of a firm's international competitiveness takes place interactively with the environment. The firm must be able to adjust to customers, competitors and public authorities. To be able to participate in the international competitive arena the firm must have established a competitive basis consisting of resources, competences and relations to others in the international arena.

To enable an understanding of the development of a firm's international competitiveness in a broader perspective, a model in three stages (see Figure 4.1) will be presented:

1. analysis of national competitiveness (the Porter diamond);
2. competition analysis in an industry (Porter's five forces);
3. value chain analysis:
   (a) competitive triangle;
   (b) benchmarking.

Figure 4.1 Development of a firm's international competitiveness

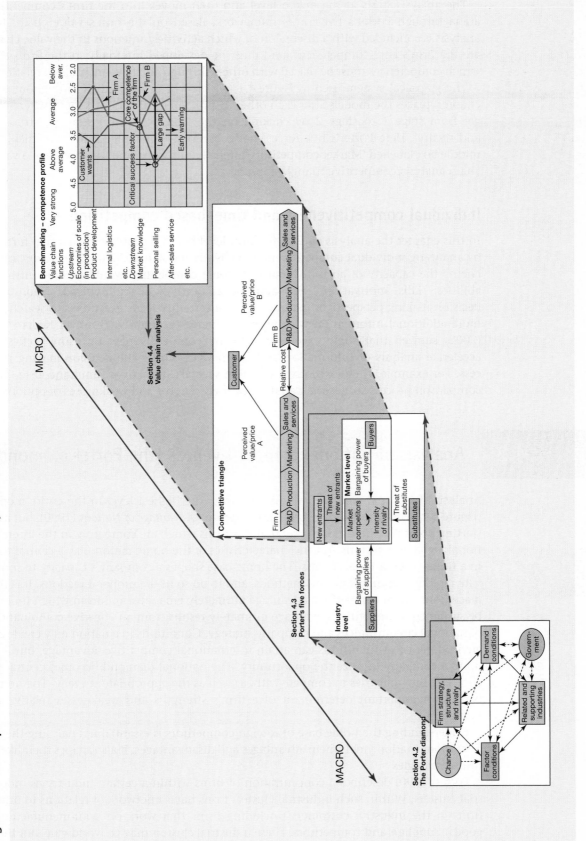

The analysis starts at the macro level and then moves into the firm's competitive arena through Porter's five forces framework. Based on the firm's value chain, the analysis is concluded with a discussion of which activities/functions in the value chain are the firm's core competences (and must be developed internally in the firm) and which competences must be placed with others through alliances and market relations.

The graphical system used in Figure 4.1 (which will be referred to throughout this chapter) places the models after each other in a hierarchical windows logic, where you get from stage 1 to stage 2 by clicking on the icon box: 'Firm strategy, structure and rivalry'. Here Porter's five forces model appears. From stage 2 to 3 we click the middle box labelled 'Market competitors/Intensity of rivalry' and the model for a value chain analysis/competitive triangle appears.

Individual competitiveness and time–based competition

In this chapter the analysis ends at the firm level but it is possible to go a step further by analysing individual competitiveness (Veliyath and Zahra, 2000). The factors influencing the capacity of an individual to become competitive would include intrinsic abilities, skills, motivation levels and the amount of effort involved. Traditional decision-making perspectives maintain that uncertainty leads executives to search for more additional information with which to increase certainty. However Kedia *et al.* (2002) showed that some executives increase competitiveness by using tactics to accelerate analysis of information and alternatives during the decision-making process. For example, these executives examine several alternatives simultaneously. The comparison process speeds their analysis of the strengths and weaknesses of options.

4.2 Analysis of national competitiveness (the Porter diamond)

Analysis of national competitiveness represents the highest level in the entire model (Figure 4.1). Porter called his work *The Competitive Advantage of Nations* (1990), but as a starting point it is important to say that it is firms which are competing in the international arena, not nations. Yet the characteristics of the home nation play a central role in a firm's international success. The home base shapes a company's capacity to innovate rapidly in technology and methods, and to do so in the proper directions. It is the place from which competitive advantage ultimately emanates and from which it must be sustained. Competitive advantage ultimately results from an effective combination of national circumstances and company strategy. Conditions in a nation may create an environment in which firms can attain international competitive advantage, but it is up to a company to seize the opportunity. The national diamond becomes central to choosing the industries to compete with, as well as the appropriate strategy. The home base is an important determinant of a firm's strengths and weaknesses relative to foreign rivals.

Understanding the home base of foreign competitors is essential in analysing them. Their home nation yields them advantages and disadvantages. It also shapes their likely future strategies.

Porter (1990) describes a concentration of firms within a certain industry as industrial clusters. Within such industrial clusters firms have a network of relations to other firms in the industry: customers (including firms that work on semi-manufactured goods), suppliers and competitors. These industrial clusters may go worldwide, but they will usually have their starting point and location in a certain country or region of a country.

A firm gains important competitive advantages from the presence in its home nation of world-class buyers, suppliers and related industries. They provide insight into future market needs and technological developments. They contribute to a climate for change and improvement, and become partners and allies in the innovation process. Having a strong cluster at home unblocks the flow of information and allows deeper and more open contact than is possible when dealing with foreign firms. Being part of a cluster localised in a small geographic area can be even more valuable, so the central question we can ask is: what accounts for the national location of a particular global industry? The answer begins, as does all classical trade theory, with the match between the factor endowments of the country and the needs of the industry.

Let us now take a closer look at the different elements in Porter's diamond, beginning with the factor conditions.

Factor conditions

In this connection it is important to mention that the most enduring competitive advantages for nations are created by those factors that have the least degree of mobility. Table 4.1 lists the various factors of production and indicates the mobility of each.

Table 4.1 **Factor conditions and their degree of mobility**

Factor	Degree of mobility
Climate	*Low*
Physical infrastructure (transport, etc.)	↑
Natural resources (minerals, oil)	
Educational system	
Human resources (movement of labour)	
Technological infrastructure (software, communication network)	↓
Capital	*High*

At one extreme, we have climate with no mobility. Finland will never be a major producer of citrus fruit, no matter what government and industry do to try to change the rest of the national diamond.

At the other end of the mobility scale we have capital, probably the most mobile of the factors of production. Over the years we have seen enormous increases in the inflow and outflow of foreign investment capital in the industrialised and developing countries of the world. This can be seen as part of the process of global economic integration. Technology and the loosening of currency restrictions throughout the world have improved the flow of capital across nations and suggest that differences in capital availability are no longer likely to constitute a very stable competitive advantage for an area.

Demand conditions

The nature and size of home demand is represented in the right-hand box of Porter's diamond (Figure 4.1). There exists an interaction between scale economies, transportation costs and the size of the home market. Given sufficiently strong economies of scale, each producer wants to serve a geographically extensive market from a single location. To minimise transportation costs the producer chooses a location with large local demand. When scale economies limit the number of production locations the size of a market will be an important determinant of its attractiveness. Large home markets will also ensure that firms located at that site develop a cost advantage based on scale and often on experience as well.

An interesting pattern is that an early large home market that has become saturated forces efficient firms to look abroad for new business. For example, the Japanese motorcycle industry with its large home market used its scale advantages in the global marketplace after an early start in Japan. The composition of demand also plays an important role.

A product's fundamental or core design nearly always reflects home market needs. In electrical transmission equipment, for example, Sweden dominates the world in the high-voltage distribution market. In Sweden there is a relatively large demand for transporting high voltage over long distances, as a consequence of the location of population and industry clusters. Here the needs of the home market shaped the industry that was later able to respond to global markets (with ABB as one of the leading producers in the world market).

The sophistication of the buyer is also important. The US government was the first buyer of chips and remained the only customer for many years. The price inelasticity of government encouraged firms to develop technically advanced products without worrying too much about costs. Under these conditions the technological frontier was clearly pushed much further and much faster than it would have been had the buyer been either less sophisticated or more price sensitive. Today the Japanese, who dominate the market for semiconductors, are influencing the shape of the industry and price issues have become more salient.

Related and supporting industries

In part, the advantages of clustering come from a reduction in the transportation costs for intermediate goods. In many other cases advantages come from being able to use labour that is attracted to an area to serve the core industry, but which is available and skilled for supporting industries. Coordination of technology is also eased by geographic proximity. Porter argues that Italian world leadership in gold and silver jewellery has been sustained in part by the local presence of manufacturers of jewellery-making machinery. Here the advantage of clustering is not so much transportation cost reductions but technical and marketing cooperation. In the semiconductor industry, the strength of the electronics industry in Japan (which buys the semiconductors) is a strong incentive to the location of semiconductors in the same area. It should be noted that clustering is not independent of scale economies. If there were no scale economies in the production of intermediate inputs, then the small-scale centres of production could rival the large-scale centres. It is the fact that there are scale economies in both semiconductors and electronics, coupled with the technological and marketing connections between the two, that give rise to clustering advantages.

Firm strategy, structure and rivalry

One of the most compelling results of Porter's study of successful industries in 10 different nations is the powerful and positive effect that domestic competition has on the ability to compete in the global marketplace. In Germany, the fierce domestic rivalry among BASF, Hoechst and Bayer in the pharmaceutical industry is well known. Furthermore, the process of competition weeds out inferior technologies, products and management practices, and leaves as survivors only the most efficient firms. When domestic competition is vigorous firms are forced to become more efficient, adopt new cost-saving technologies, reduce product development time, and learn to motivate and control workers more effectively. Domestic rivalry is especially important in stimulating technological developments among global firms.

The small country of Denmark has three producers of hearing-aids (William Demant, Widex and GN Resound/Danavox), which are all among the top 10 of the world's largest producers of hearing-aids. In 1996 Oticon (the earlier William Demant) and Widex fought a violent technological battle to be the first in the world to launch a 100 per cent digitalised hearing-aid. Widex (the smaller of the two producers) won, but forced Oticon at the same time to keep a leading edge in technological development.

Chance

When we look at the history of most industries we also see the role played by chance. Perhaps the most important instance of chance involves the question of who comes up with a major new idea first. For reasons having little to do with economics, entrepreneurs will typically start their new operations in their home countries. Once the industry begins in a given country scale and clustering effects can cement the industry's position in that country.

Government

Governments play a powerful role in encouraging the development of industries within their own borders that will assume global positions. One way governments do this is through their effect on other elements of the national diamond. Governments finance and construct infrastructure, providing roads, airports, education and health care, and can support use of alternative energy (e.g. windmills) or other environmental systems that affect factors of production.

From the firm's point of view the last two variables, chance and government, can be regarded as exogenous variables which the firm must adjust to. Alternatively, the government may be considered susceptible through lobbying, interest organizations and mass media.

In summary, we have identified six factors that influence the location of global industries: factors of production, home demand, the location of supporting industries, the internal structure of the domestic industry, chance and government. We have also suggested that these factors are interconnected. As industries evolve their dependence on particular locations may also change. For example, the shift in users of semiconductors from the military to the electronics industry has had a profound effect on the shape of the national diamond in that industry. To the extent that governments and firms recognise the source of any locational advantages that they have, they will be better able to both exploit those differences and anticipate their shifts.

4.3 Competition analysis in an industry

The next step in understanding the firm's competitiveness is to look at the competitive arena in an industry, which is the top box in the diamond model (see Figure 4.1).

One of the most useful frameworks for analysing the competitive structure has been developed by Michael E. Porter. Porter (1980) suggests that competition in an industry is rooted in its underlying economic structure and goes beyond the behaviour of current competitors. The state of competition depends upon five basic competitive forces, as shown in Figure 4.1. Together these factors determine the ultimate profit potential in an industry, where profit is measured in terms of long-run return on invested capital. The profit potential will differ from industry to industry.

To make things clearer we need to define a number of key terms. An *industry* is a group of firms that offer a product or class of products which are close substitutes for each other. Examples are the car industry and the pharmaceutical industry (Kotler, 1997, p. 230). A *market* is a set of actual and potential buyers of a product and sellers. A distinction will be made between industry and market level, as we assume that the industry may contain several different markets. This is why the outer box in Figure 4.1 is designated 'industry level' and the inner box 'market level'.

Thus the *industry level* consists of all types of actors (new entrants, suppliers, substitutes, buyers and market competitors) that have a potential or current interest in the industry.

The *market level* consists of actors with a current interest in the market: that is, buyers and sellers (market competitors). In section 4.4 (value chain analysis) this market level will be further elaborated on as the buyers' perceived value of different competitor offerings will be discussed.

Although division into the above-mentioned two levels is appropriate for this approach, Levitt (1960) pointed out the danger of 'marketing myopia', where the seller defines the competition field (i.e. the market) too narrowly. For example, European luxury car manufacturers showed this myopia with their focus on each other rather than on the Japanese mass manufacturers, who were new entrants into the luxury car market.

The goal of competition analysis is to find a position in industry where the company can best defend itself against the five forces, or can influence them in its favour. Knowledge of these underlying pressures highlights the critical strengths and weaknesses of the company, shows its position in the industry, and clarifies areas where strategy changes yield the greatest pay-off. Structure analysis is fundamental for formulating competitive strategy.

Each of the five forces in the Porter model in turn comprises a number of elements that combine to determine the strength of each force, and its effect on the degree of competition. Each force is now discussed.

Market competitors

The intensity of rivalry between existing competitors in the market depends on a number of factors:

- *The concentration of the industry.* Numerous competitors of equal size will lead to more intense rivalry. There will be less rivalry when a clear leader (at least 50 per cent larger than the second) exists with a large cost advantage.
- *Rate of market growth.* Slow growth will tend towards greater rivalry.
- *Structure of costs.* High fixed costs encourage price cutting to fill capacity.
- *Degree of differentiation.* Commodity products encourage rivalry, while highly differentiated products, which are hard to copy, are associated with less intense rivalry.
- *Switching costs.* When switching costs are high because the product is specialised, the customer has invested a lot of resources in learning how to use the product or has made tailor-made investments that are worthless with other products and suppliers (high asset specificity), rivalry is reduced.
- *Exit barriers.* When barriers to leaving a market are high due to such factors as lack of opportunities elsewhere, high vertical integration, emotional barriers or the high cost of closing down plant, rivalry will be more intense than when exit barriers are low.

Firms need to be careful not to spoil a situation of competitive stability. They need to balance their own position against the well-being of the industry as a whole. For example, an intense price or promotional war may gain a few percentage points in market share, but lead to an overall fall in long-run industry profitability as competitors respond to these moves. It is sometimes better to protect industry structure than to follow short-term self-interest.

Suppliers

The cost of raw materials and components can have a major bearing on a firm's profitability. The higher the bargaining power of suppliers, the higher the costs. The bargaining power of suppliers will be higher in the following circumstances:

- Supply is dominated by few companies and they are more concentrated than the industry they sell to.
- Their products are unique or differentiated, or they have built up switching costs.
- They are not obliged to contend with other products for sale to the industry.
- They pose a credible threat of integrating forwards into the industry's business.
- Buyers do not threaten to integrate backwards into supply.
- The market is not an important customer to the supplier group.

A firm can reduce the bargaining power of suppliers by seeking new sources of supply, threatening to integrate backwards into supply, and designing standardised components so that many suppliers are capable of producing them.

Buyers

The bargaining power of buyers is higher in the following circumstances:

- Buyers are concentrated and/or purchase in large volumes.
- Buyers pose a credible threat of integrating backwards to manufacture the industry's product.
- Products they purchase are standard or undifferentiated.
- There are many suppliers (sellers) of the product.
- Buyers earn low profits, which create a great incentive to lower purchasing costs.
- The industry's product is unimportant to the quality of the buyer's products, but price is very important.

Firms in the industry can attempt to lower buyer power by increasing the number of buyers they sell to, threatening to integrate forward into the buyer's industry, and producing highly valued, differentiated products. In supermarket retailing, the brand leader normally achieves the highest profitability, partially because being number one means that supermarkets need to stock the brand, thereby reducing buyer power in price negotiations.

Substitutes

The presence of substitute products can reduce industry attractiveness and profitability because they put a constraint on price levels.

If the industry is successful and earning high profits it is more likely that competitors will enter the market via substitute products in order to obtain a share of the potential profits available. If there are high prices for coffee, for example, tea will become more attractive.

The threat of substitute products depends on the following factors:

- the buyer's willingness to substitute;
- the relative price and performance of substitutes;
- the costs of switching to substitutes.

The threat of substitute products can be lowered by building up switching costs. These costs may be psychological. Examples are the creation of strong, distinctive brand personalities, and maintaining a price differential commensurate with perceived customer values.

New entrants

New entrants can serve to increase the degree of competition in an industry. In turn, the threat of new entrants is largely a function of the extent to which barriers to entry exist in the market. Some key factors affecting these entry barriers include the following:

- economies of scale;
- product differentiation and brand identity, which give existing firms customer loyalty;
- capital requirements in production;
- switching costs – the cost of switching from one supplier to another;
- access to distribution channels.

Because high barriers to entry can make even a potentially lucrative market unattractive (or even impossible) to enter for new competitors, the marketing planner should not take a passive approach but should actively pursue ways of raising barriers to new competitors.

High promotional and R&D expenditures and clearly communicated retaliatory actions to entry are some methods of raising barriers. Some managerial actions can unwittingly lower barriers. For example, new product designs that dramatically lower manufacturing costs can make entry by newcomers easier.

The collaborative 'five sources' model

Porter's original model is based on the hypothesis that the competitive advantage of the firm is best developed in a very competitive market with intense rivalry relations.

The five forces framework thus provides an analysis for considering how to squeeze the maximum competitive gain out of the context in which the business is located – or how to minimise the prospect of being squeezed by it – on the five competitive dimensions that it confronts.

Over the last decade, however, an alternative school (e.g. Reve, 1990; Kanter, 1994; Burton, 1995) has emerged which emphasises the positive role of cooperative (rather than competitive) arrangements between industry participants, and the consequent importance of what Kanter (1994) has termed 'collaborative advantage' as a foundation of superior business performance.

An all-or-nothing choice between a single-minded striving for either competitive or collaborative advantage would, however, be a false one. The real strategic choice problem that all businesses face is where (and how much) to collaborate, and where (and how intensely) to act competitively.

Put another way, the basic questions that firms must deal with in respect of these matters are as follows:

- choosing the combination of competitive and collaborative strategies that are appropriate in the various dimensions of the industry environment of the firm;

- blending the two elements together so that they interact in a mutually consistent and reinforcing, and not counterproductive, manner;
- in this way, optimising the firm's overall position, drawing upon the foundation and utilisation of both collaborative and competitive advantage.

This points to the imperative in the contemporary context of complementing the competitive strategy model with a sister framework that focuses on the assessment of collaborative advantage and strategy. Such a complementary analysis, which is called the *five sources framework* (Burton, 1995), is outlined below.

Corresponding to the array of five competitive forces that surround a company – as elaborated in Porter's treatment – there are also five potential sources for the building of collaborative advantage in the industrial environments of the firm. These sources are listed in Table 4.2.

In order to forge an effective and coherent business strategy, a firm must evaluate and formulate its collaborative and competitive policies side by side. It should do this for two purposes:

- to achieve the appropriate balance between collaboration and competition in each dimension of its industry environment (e.g. relations with suppliers, policies towards customers/channels);
- to integrate them in a way that avoids potential clashes and possibly destructive inconsistencies between them.

This is the terrain of composite strategy, which concerns the bringing together of competitive and collaborative endeavours.

Table 4.2 The five sources model and the corresponding five forces in the Porter model

Porter's five forces model	The five sources model
Market competitors	Horizontal collaborations with other enterprises operating at the same stage of the production process/producing the same group of closely related products (e.g. contemporary global partnering arrangements among car manufacturers).
Suppliers	Vertical collaborations with suppliers of components or services to the firm – sometimes termed vertical quasi-integration arrangements (e.g. the *keiretsu* formations between suppliers and assemblers that typify the car, electronics and other industries in Japan).
Buyers	Selective partnering arrangements with specific channels or customers (e.g. lead users) that involve collaboration extending beyond standard, purely transactional relationships.
Substitutes	Related diversification alliances with producers of both complements and substitutes. Producers of substitutes are not 'natural allies', but such alliances are not inconceivable (e.g. collaborations between fixed-wire and mobile telephone firms in order to grow their joint network size).
New entrants	Diversification alliances with firms based in previously unrelated sectors, but between which a 'blurring' of industry borders is potentially occurring, or a process (commonly due to new technological possibilities) that opens up the prospect of cross-industry fertilisation of technologies/business that did not exist before (e.g. the collaborations in the emerging multimedia field).

Source: from Burton, 1995. Reproduced with permission from The Braybrooke Press Ltd.

4.4   Value chain analysis

Until now we have discussed the firm's international competitiveness from a strategic point of view. To get closer to the firm's core competences we will now look at the market-level box in Porter's five forces model, which treats buyers and sellers (market competitors). Here we will look more closely at what creates a competitive advantage among market competitors towards customers at the same competitive level.

The competitive triangle

Success in the marketplace is dependent not only upon identifying and responding to customer needs, but also upon our ability to ensure that our response is judged by customers to be superior to that of competitors (i.e. high perceived value). Several writers (e.g. Porter, 1980; Day and Wensley, 1988) have argued that causes of difference in performance within a market can be analysed at various levels. The immediate causes of differences in the performance of different firms, these writers argue, can be reduced to two basic factors:

■ The *perceived value* of the product/services offered, compared to the perceived sacrifice. The *perceived sacrifice* includes all the 'costs' the buyer faces when making a purchase, primarily the *purchase price*, but also acquisition costs, transportation, installation, handling, repairs and maintenance (Ravald and Grönroos, 1996). In the models presented the (purchase) price will be used as a representative of the perceived sacrifice.
■ The firm-related *costs* incurred in creating this perceived value.

These two basic factors will be further discussed later in this section.

The more value customers perceive in a market offering relative to competing offerings, and the lower the costs in producing the value relative to competing producers, the higher the performance of the business. Hence firms producing offerings with a higher perceived value and/or lower relative costs than competing firms are said to have a competitive advantage in that market.

This can be illustrated by the 'competitive triangle' (see Figure 4.1). There is no one-dimensional measure of competitive advantage, and perceived value (compared to the price) and relative costs have to be assessed simultaneously. Given this two-dimensional nature of competitive advantage it will not always be clear which of the two businesses will have a competitive advantage over the other.

Looking at Figure 4.2, firm A will clearly have an advantage over firm B in case I, and clearly have a disadvantage in case IV, while cases II and III do not immediately allow such a conclusion. Firm B may have an advantage in case II, if customers in the market are highly quality conscious and have differentiated needs and low price elasticity, while firm A may have a similar advantage in case II when customers have homogeneous needs and high price elasticity. The opposite will take place in case III.

Even if firm A has a clear competitive advantage over firm B, this may not necessarily result in a higher return on investment for A, if A has a growth and B a hold policy. Thus performance would have to be measured by a combination of return on investment and capacity expansion, which can be regarded as postponed return on investment.

While the relationship between perceived value, relative costs and performance is rather intricate, we can retain the basic statement that these two variables are the cornerstone of competitive advantage. Let us take a closer look at these two fundamental sources of competitive advantage.

Figure 4.2 Perceived value, relative costs and competitive advantage

		Perceived value (compared to the purchase price)	
		Higher for A	*Higher for B*
Relative costs	*Lower for A*	I	II
	Lower for B	III	IV

Perceived value advantage

We have already observed that customers do not buy products, they buy benefits. Put another way, the product is purchased not for itself but for the promise of what it will 'deliver'. These benefits may be intangible: that is, they may relate not to specific product features but rather to such things as image or reputation. Alternatively, the delivered offering may be seen to outperform its rivals in some functional aspect.

Perceived value is the customer's overall evaluation of the product/service offered. So, establishing what value the customer is actually seeking from the firm's offering (value chain) is the starting point for being able to deliver the correct mix of value-providing activities. It may be some combination of physical attributes, service attributes and technical support available in relation to the particular use of the product. This also requires an understanding of the activities that constitute the customer's value chain.

Unless the product or service we offer can be distinguished in some way from its competitors there is a strong likelihood that the marketplace will view it as a 'commodity', and so the sale will tend to go to the cheapest supplier. Hence the importance of seeking to attach additional values to our offering to mark it out from the competition.

What are the means by which such value differentiation may be gained?

If we start in the value chain perspective (see section 1.6), we can say that each activity in the business system adds perceived value to the product or service. Value, for the customer, is the perceived stream of benefits that accrue from obtaining the product or service. Price is what the customer is willing to pay for that stream of benefits. If the price of a good or service is high it must provide high value, otherwise it is driven out of the market. If the value of a good or service is low its price must be low, otherwise it is also driven out of the market. Hence, in a competitive situation, and over a period of time, the price that customers are willing to pay for a good or service is a good proxy measure of its value.

If we look especially at the downstream functions of the value chain, a differential advantage can be created with any aspect of the traditional 4-P marketing mix: product, distribution, promotion and price are all capable of creating added customer perceived value. The key to whether improving an aspect of marketing is worthwhile is to know if the potential benefit provides value to the customer.

If we extend this model particular emphasis must be placed upon the following (see Booms and Bitner, 1981; Magrath, 1986; Rafiq and Ahmed, 1995):

■ *People*. These include both consumers, who must be educated to participate in the service, and employees (personnel), who must be motivated and well trained in order to ensure that high standards of service are maintained. Customers identify and associate the traits of service personnel with the firms they work for.

■ *Physical aspects.* These include the appearance of the delivery location and the elements provided to make the service more tangible. For example, visitors experience Disneyland by what they see, but the hidden, below-ground support machinery is essential for the park's fantasy fulfilment.

■ *Process.* The service is dependent on a well-designed method of delivery. Process management assures service availability and consistent quality in the face of simultaneous consumption and production of the service offered. Without sound process management balancing service demand with service supply is extremely difficult.

Of these three additional Ps, the firm's *personnel* occupy a key position in influencing customer perception of product quality. As a consequence the *image* of the firm is very much influenced by the personnel. It is therefore important to pay particular attention to the quality of employees and to monitor their performance. Marketing managers need to manage not only the service provider – customer interface, but also the actions of other customers; for example the number, type and behaviour of other people will influence a meal at a restaurant.

Relative cost advantage

Each activity in the value chain is performed at a cost. Getting the stream of benefits that accrue from the good or service to the customer is thus done at a certain 'delivered cost', which sets a lower limit to the price of the good or service if the business system is to remain profitable. Decreasing the price will thus imply that the delivered cost be first decreased by adjusting the business system. As mentioned earlier, the rules of the game may be described as *providing the highest possible perceived value to the final customer, at the lowest possible delivered cost.*

A firm's cost position depends on the configuration of the activities in its value chain versus that of competitors and its relative location on the cost drivers of each activity. A cost advantage is gained when the cumulative cost of performing all the activities is lower than competitors' costs. This evaluation of the relative cost position requires an identification of each important competitor's value chain. In practice, this step is extremely difficult because the firm does not have direct information on the costs of competitors' value activities. However, some costs can be estimated from public data or interviews with suppliers and distributors.

Creating a relative cost advantage requires an understanding of the factors that affect costs. It is often said that 'big is beautiful'. This is partly due to economies of scale, which enable fixed costs to be spread over a greater output, but more particularly it is due to the impact of the *experience curve*.

The experience curve is a phenomenon that has its roots in the earlier notion of the learning curve. The effects of learning on costs were seen in the manufacture of fighter planes for the Second World War. The time taken to produce each plane gradually fell as learning took place. The combined effect of economies of scale and learning on cumulative output has been termed the experience curve. The Boston Consulting Group estimated that costs reduced on average by approximately 15–20 per cent each time cumulative output doubled.

Subsequent work by Bruce Henderson, founder of the Boston Consulting Group, extended this concept by demonstrating that all costs, not just production costs, would decline at a given rate as volume increased. In fact, to be precise, the relationship that the experience curve describes is between real unit costs and cumulative volume.

This suggests that firms with greater market share will have a cost advantage through the experience curve effect, assuming that all companies are operating on the same curve. However, a move towards a new manufacturing technology can lower the experience curve for adopting companies, allowing them to leapfrog over more traditional firms and thereby gain a cost advantage even though cumulative output may be lower.

The general form of the experience curve and the above-mentioned leapfrogging to another curve are shown in Figure 4.3.

Figure 4.3 Leapfrogging the experience curve

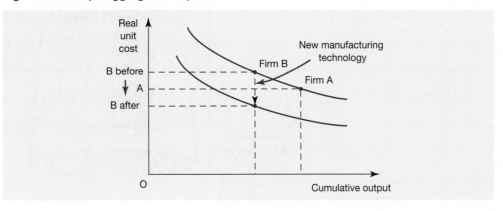

Leapfrogging the experience curve by investing in new technology is a special opportunity for SMEs and newcomers to a market, since they will (as a starting point) have only a small market share and thereby a small cumulative output.

The implications of the experience curve for the pricing strategy will be discussed further in Chapter 16. According to Porter (1980) there are other cost drivers that determine the costs in value chains:

- *Capacity utilisation*. Underutilisation incurs costs.
- *Linkages*. Costs of activities are affected by how other activities are performed. For example, improving quality assurance can reduce after-sales service costs.
- *Interrelationships*. For example, different SBUs' sharing of R&D, purchasing and marketing will lower costs.
- *Integration*. For example, deintegration (outsourcing) of activities to subsuppliers can lower costs and raise flexibility.
- *Timing*. For example, first movers in a market can gain cost advantage. It is cheaper to establish a brand name in the minds of the customers if there are no competitors.
- *Policy decisions*. Product width, level of service and channel decisions are examples of policy decisions that affect costs.
- *Location*. Locating near suppliers reduces in-bound distribution costs. Locating near customers can lower out-bound distribution costs. Some producers locate their production activities in eastern Europe or the Far East to take advantage of low wage costs.
- *Institutional factors*. Government regulations, tariffs, local content rules, etc., will affect costs.

The basic sources of competitive advantage

The perceived value created and the costs incurred will depend on the firm's *resources* and its *competences* (see Figure 4.4).

Resources

Resources are the basic units of analysis. They include all inputs into the business processes – that is, financial, technological, human and organizational resources.

Figure 4.4 The roots of performance and competitive advantage

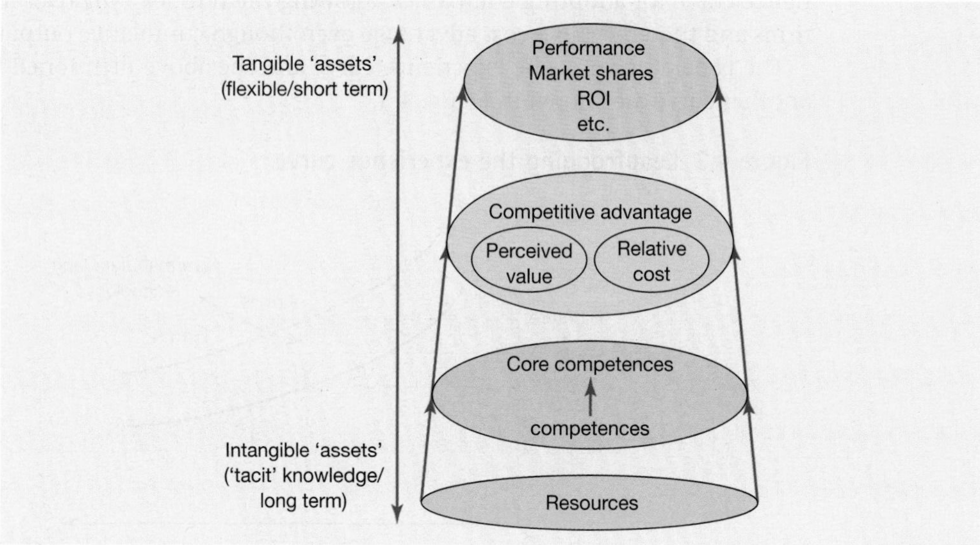

Source: adapted from Jüttner and Wehrli, 1994.

Although resources provide the basis for competence building, on their own they are barely productive.

Resources are necessary in order to participate in the market. The competitors in a market will thus not usually be very different with regard to these skills and resources, and the latter will not explain differences in created perceived value, relative costs and the resulting performance. They are failure preventers, but not success producers. They may, however, act as barriers to entry for potential new competitors, and hence raise the average level of performance in the market.

Competences

Competences – being components of a higher level – result from a combination of the various resources. Their formation and quality depend on two factors. The first factor is the specific capabilities of the firm in integrating resources. These capabilities are developed and improved in a collective learning process. On the other hand, the basis for the quality of a competence is the resource assortment. This forms a potential for competences, which should be exploited to the maximum extent.

A firm can have a lot of competences but only a few of them are core competences: that is, a value chain activity in which the firm is regarded as a better performer than any of its competitors (see Figure 4.5).

In Figure 4.5 a core competence is represented by a strategic resource (asset) that competitors cannot easily imitate and which has the potential to earn long-term profit. The objective of the firm will be to place products and services at the top-right corner. The top-left corner also represents profit possibilities, but the competitive advantage is easier to imitate, so the high profit will only be short term. The bottom-left corner represents the position of the price-sensitive commodity supplier. Here the profits are likely to be low because the product is primarily differentiated by place (distribution) and especially price.

Competitive benchmarking

The ultimate test of the efficiency of any marketing strategy has to be in terms of profit. Those companies that strive for market share, but measure market share in terms of

Figure 4.5 Illustration of the core competence

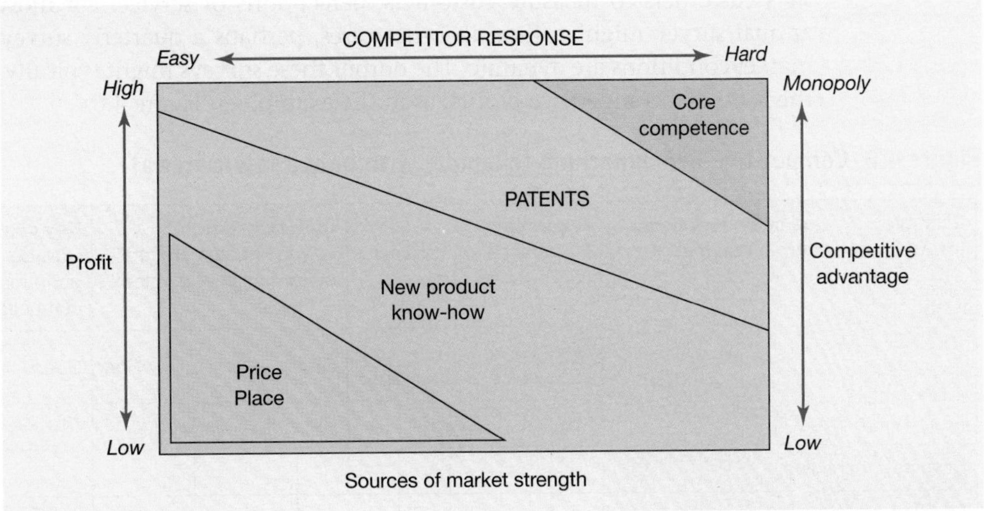

Source: Reprinted from *Long Range Planning*, Vol. 27, No. 4, Tampoe, M. (1994) 'Exploiting the core competences of your organization', p. 74, Copyright 1994, with permission from Elsevier.

volume sales, may be deluding themselves to the extent that volume is bought at the expense of profit.

Because market share is an 'after the event' measure, we need to utilise continuing indicators of competitive performance. This will highlight areas where improvements in the marketing mix can be made.

In recent years a number of companies have developed a technique for assessing relative marketplace performance, which has come to be known as *competitive benchmarking*. Originally the idea of competitive benchmarking was literally to take apart a competitor's product, component by component, and compare its performance in a value engineering sense with your own product. This approach has often been attributed to the Japanese, but many western companies have also found the value of such detailed comparisons.

The concept of competitive benchmarking is similar to what Porter (1996) calls operational effectiveness (OE), meaning performing similar activities better than competitors perform them. However, Porter (1996) also thinks that OE is a necessary but not a sufficient condition for outperforming rivals. Firms also have to consider strategic (or market) positioning, meaning the performance of *different* activities from rivals or performing similar activities in different ways. Only a few firms have competed successfully on the basis of OE over a long period. The main reason is the rapid diffusion of best practices. Competitors can rapidly imitate management techniques and new technologies with support from consultants.

However, the idea of benchmarking is capable of extension beyond this simple comparison of technology and cost effectiveness. Because the battle in the marketplace is for 'share of mind', it is customers' perceptions that we must measure.

The measures that can be used in this type of benchmarking programme include delivery reliability, ease of ordering, after-sales service, the quality of sales representation and the accuracy of invoices and other documentation. These measures are not chosen at random, but are selected because of their importance to the customer. Market research, often based on in-depth interviews, would typically be employed to identify what these 'key success factors' are. The elements that customers identify as being the most important (see Figure 4.6) then form the basis for the benchmark questionnaire. This questionnaire is administered to a sample of customers on a regular basis: for example, German

Telecom carries out a daily telephone survey of a random sample of its domestic and business customers to measure customers' perceptions of service. For most companies an annual survey might suffice; in other cases, perhaps a quarterly survey, particularly if market conditions are dynamic. The output these surveys might typically be presented in the form of a competitive profile, as in the example in Figure 4.6.

Figure 4.6 Competitive benchmarking (example with only a few criteria)

Examples of value chain functions (mainy donwstream functions)	Customer Importance to customer (key success factors)					Own firm (Firm A) How do customers rate performance of our firm?					Key competitor (Firm B) How do customers rate performance of key competitor?				
	High importance			Low importance		Good				Bad	Good				Bad
	5	4	3	2	1	5	4	3	2	1	5	4	3	2	1
Uses new technology															
High technical quality and competence															
Uses proved technology															
Easy to buy from															
Understands what customers want															
Low price															
Delivery on schedule															
Accessible for enquiries															
Takes full responsibility															
Flexible and quick															
Known contact person															
Provides customer training															
Take account of future requirements															
Courteous and helpful															
Specified invoices															
Gives guarantees															
ISO 9000 certified															
Right first time															
Can give references															
Environment counscious															

Most of the criteria mentioned above relate to downstream functions in the value chain. Concurrently with closer relations between buyers and suppliers, especially in the industrial market, there will be more focus on the supplier's competences in the upstream functions.

Development of a dynamic benchmarking model

On the basis of the value chain's functions, I will suggest a model for the development of a firm's competitiveness in a defined market. The model will be based on a specific market as the market demands are assumed to differ from market to market, and from country to country.

Before presenting the basic model for development of international competitiveness I will first define two key terms:

- *Critical success factors*. Those value chain functions where the customer demands/ expects the supplier (firm X) to have a strong competence.
- *Core competences*. Those value chain functions where firm X has a strong competitive position.

The strategy process

The model for the strategy process is shown in Figure 4.7.

Figure 4.7 Model for development of core competences

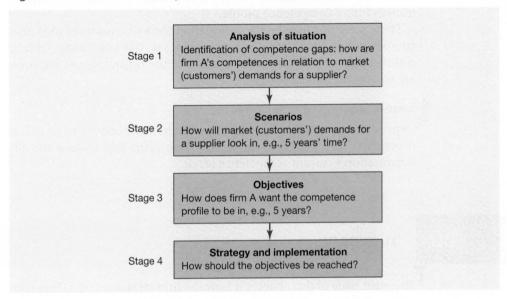

Stage 1	**Analysis of situation** Identification of competence gaps: how are firm A's competences in relation to market (customers') demands for a supplier?
Stage 2	**Scenarios** How will market (customers') demands for a supplier look in, e.g., 5 years' time?
Stage 3	**Objectives** How does firm A want the competence profile to be in, e.g., 5 years?
Stage 4	**Strategy and implementation** How should the objectives be reached?

Stage 1: Analysis of situation (identification of competence gaps)

We will not go into detail here about the problems there have been in measuring the value chain functions. The measurements cannot be objective in the traditional way of thinking, but must rely on internal assessments from firm representatives (interviews with relevant managers) supplemented by external experts ('key informants') who are able to judge the market's (customers') demand now and in the future.

The competence profile for firm A in Figure 4.1 (top-right diagram) is an example of how a firm is not in accordance with the market (= customer) demand. The company has its core competences in parts of the value chain's functions where customers place little importance (market knowledge in Figure 4.1).

If there is a generally good match between the critical success factors and firm A's initial position, it is important to concentrate resources and improve this core competence to create sustainable competitive advantages.

If, on the other hand, there is a large gap between customers' demands and the firm's initial position in critical success factors in Figure 4.1 (as with the personal selling functions), it may give rise to the following alternatives:

- Improve the position of the critical success factor(s).
- Find business areas where firm A's competence profile better suits the market demand and expectations.

As a new business area involves risk, it is often important to identify an eventual gap in a critical success factor as early as possible. In other words, an 'early warning' system must be established that continuously monitors the critical competitive factors so that it is possible to start initiatives that limit an eventual gap as early as possible.

In Figure 4.1 the competence profile of firm B is also shown.

Stages 2 and 3: Scenarios and objectives

To be able to estimate future market demand different scenarios are made of the possible future development. These trends are first described generally, then the effect of the market's future demand/expectations on a supplier's value chain function is concretised.

By this procedure the described 'gap' between market expectations and firm A's initial position becomes more clear. At the same time the biggest gap for firm A may have moved from personal sales to, for example, product development. From knowledge of the market leader's strategy it is possible to complete scenarios of the market leader's future competence profile.

These scenarios may be the foundation for a discussion of objectives and of which competence profile the company wants in, say, five years' time. Objectives must be set realistically and with due consideration of the organization's resources (the scenarios are not shown in Figure 4.1).

Stage 4: Strategy and implementation

Depending on which of firm A's value chain functions are to be developed, a strategy is prepared. This results in implementation plans that include the adjustment of the organization's current competence level.

4.5   Summary

The main issue of this chapter is how the firm creates and develops competitive advantages in the international marketplace. A three-stage model allows us to understand the development of a firm's international competitiveness in a broader perspective:

1. analysis of national competitiveness (the Porter diamond);
2. competition analysis (Porter's five forces);
3. value chain analysis:
   (a) competitive triangle;
   (b) benchmarking.

Analysis of national competitiveness

The analysis starts at the macro level, where the Porter diamond indicates that the characteristics of the home nation play a central role in the firm's international success.

Competition analysis

The next stage is to move to the competitive arena where the firm is the unit of analysis. Porter's five forces model suggests that competition in an industry is rooted in its underlying economic structure and goes beyond the behaviour of current competitors. The state of competition depends upon five basic competitive forces, which determine the profit potential in an industry.

Value chain analysis

Here we look at what creates a competitive advantage at the same competitive level (among industry competitors). According to the *competitive triangle*, it can be concluded that firms have a competitive advantage in a market if they offer products with the following:

- a higher perceived value to the customers;
- lower relative costs than competing firms.

A firm can find out its competitive advantages or core competences by using *competitive benchmarking*, which is a technique where customers measure marketplace performance of the firm compared to a 'first-class' competitor. The measures in the value chain that can be used include delivery reliability, ease of ordering, after-sales service and quality of sales representation. These value chain activities are chosen on the basis of their importance to the customer. As customers' perceptions change over time, it may be relevant to try and estimate customers' future demands on a supplier of particular products.

CASE STUDY 4.1   Microsoft Xbox

The battle for gaming leadership against Nintendo's GameCube and Sony PlayStation 2

In the video game market leadership has changed with each new generation of consoles, which come along every five years or so.

In a challenge that could have come from a 'beat-'em-up' computer game Microsoft – the world's biggest software company – has launched its own games console. But the Seattle company's attempts to muscle into a market that is worth £10 billion worldwide will meet stiff opposition from its rivals, which already have new, faster machines either released or planned. Microsoft's product, dubbed the 'Xbox', was launched in autumn 2000.

The Xbox is based on a 600 MHz microprocessor that is expected to be supplied by Advanced Micro Devices. The console has a DVD player, which can also be used to watch movies, and a high-capacity hard-disc drive that could be used to save game sessions as well as to bring full speech to video games. A sports game, for example, might include running commentary.

Like the PlayStation 2, the Xbox is linked to the Internet to enable multi- player games and downloadable games. However, Microsoft is gearing the Xbox to 'broadband' high-speed connections; unlike today's video game machines the Xbox will enable Internet chat among players, with voice communications rather than typed messages.

Source: Screenshot reprinted by permission from Microsoft Corporation.

Microsoft has subcontracted production of the Xbox to an unnamed third party, but it has chosen to market and sell the games console under its own name. As do other video games companies, Microsoft has 'certified' games software and takes a royalty on each game sold. Microsoft's initial price for the Xbox was around $300, a little more expensive than the price of the Sony PlayStation. Unlike Nitendo, which targets children aged 7–18, Microsoft is going after an older and more sophisticated user. Specifically, Xbox is geared towards men aged 16–35, the same market that Sony is targeting with its Sony PlayStation 2.

After sinking into the doldrums of the mid-1990s

the games console market has exploded in the past years, spurred on by Microsoft's biggest rival, Sony PlayStation, launched in 1995. PlayStation 2 was released in March 2000. An estimated 5 million PlayStations have been sold in the United Kingdom alone.

In February 2001 Sega announced its departure from the console market, intending to focus strictly on software development. This departure from the market left three global players: Sony, Nintendo and Microsoft.

Predictions for the future of gaming

In the United States and western Europe the online gaming market is set to be worth $4.9 billion, with 31 million gamers in Europe by 2004.

Datamonitor claims from its research that there is substantial consumer demand for online gaming and surf and play solutions. This will be met by two principal growth factors – games consoles and online gaming.

The introduction of better bandwidth – broadband – will increase popularity and consumer awareness, with the console gradually phasing out the PC as the main gaming device.

Recent market development

In May–June 2002 the prices of all three companies' consoles dropped from around $300 to $200. It is expected that as prices fall on consoles a new type of gamer will become important: children. Hardcore gamers and adults have so far been the only people able to afford the next generation of console systems. But with the price drops the audience base will expand dramatically.

In late June 2002 Microsoft said they had sold 3.9 million units of the Xbox worldwide. However, a source (BBC News, 26 June 2002) stated that Microsoft would lose $750 million (£490 million) on the Xbox console in the first half of 2002. A further loss of $1.1 billion (£720 million) was expected from 1 July 2002 until 30 June 2003.

Microsoft intends to have the world's largest online gaming community powered by its Xbox console. Microsoft stresses the 'plug and play' elements of the online service so that the non-technically minded may use it.

Sources: *Financial Times* (2000) 'Companies and Markets: Microsoft to take on video game leaders', 10 March; *New Media Age* (2000) 'Let the games begin', 8 March; BBC News, 26 June 2002: 'Works starts on new Xbox'; BBC News, 24 July 2002: 'Price cut boosts Xbox sales'; CNN news, May 22 2002: 'Console wars: Round two'.

Questions

1. What were Microsoft's motives in entering the games console market?

2. What are the chances that Microsoft will 'beat' the other games console suppliers, Nintendo and Sony?

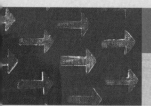

CASE STUDY 4.2   Sony Ericsson

Will pooling of competences in the mobile phone business create international competitiveness?

Sony Ericsson Mobile Communications (www.sonyericsson.com) was established on 28 August 2001 by telecommunications leader Ericsson and consumer electronics powerhouse Sony Corporation, partly as a consequence of sales problems (Ericsson had lost market shares to Nokia) and quality problems (Sony had to withdraw 1.1 million mobile telephones from the market) in the telecommunications industry. The company is equally owned as a joint venture by Ericsson and Sony, whose combined mobile phone businesses on a pro forma basis achieved annual sales of approximately 50 million units and sales of US$7.2 billion in 2000.

By combining the complementary strengths of Ericsson and Sony the joint venture aims to become an important player in mobile phones and multimedia handheld communication products within a few years, as the industry moves rapidly towards a mobile Internet.

Sony Ericsson is responsible for product research, design and development, as well as marketing and sales, distribution and customer service. The company's global corporate management is based in London and additionally it has approximately 3,500 employees in Germany, Japan, Sweden and the US.

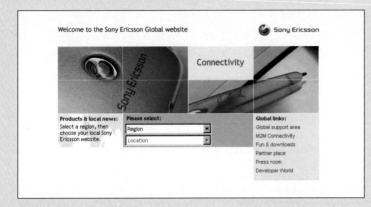

About Sony

Sony Corporation is a leading manufacturer of audio, video, game, communications and information technology products for the consumer and professional markets. With its music, pictures, computer entertainment and online businesses Sony is uniquely positioned to be the leading personal broadband entertainment company in the world. Sony recorded consolidated annual sales of nearly US$60 billion for the fiscal year ended 31 March 2001.

See Sony's home page at: **www.world.sony.com**

About Ericsson

Ericsson is shaping the future of mobile and broadband Internet communications through its technological competences. It is the leading communications supplier, combining innovation in mobility and the Internet in creating the new era of a mobile Internet. Ericsson provides total solutions covering everything from systems and applications to mobile phones and other communication tools. With a presence in 140 countries, Ericsson simplifies communications for customers all over the world

Read more at **www.ericsson.com/press**.

Questions

1. Describe how the competences of Sony and Eriscsson can complement each other.

2. What are the 'key success factors' in the mobile telephone business?

3. Will the Sony–Ericsson joint venture succeed in the global telecommunications market?

For further exercises and cases, see this book's website at
www.booksites.net/hollensen

Questions for discussion

1. How can analysis of national competitiveness explain the competitive advantage of the single firm?

2. Identify the major dimensions used to analyse a competitor's strengths and weaknesses profile. Do local, regional and global competitors need to be analysed separately?

3. How can a country with high labour costs improve its national competitiveness?

4. As the global marketing manager for Coca-Cola, how would you monitor reactions around the world to a major competitor such as Pepsi?

References

Booms, B.H. and Bitner, M.J. (1981) 'Marketing strategies and organization structures for service firms', in Donnelly, J.H. and George, W.R. (eds), *Marketing of Services*, American Marketing Association, Chicago, IL.

Burton, J. (1995) 'Composite strategy: the combination of collaboration and competition', *Journal of General Management*, vol. 21, no. 1, pp. 1–23.

Day, G.S. and Wensley, R. (1988) 'Assessing advantage: a framework for diagnosing competitive superiority', *Journal of Marketing*, vol. 52, no. 2, pp. 1–20.

Jüttner, U. and Wehrli, H.P. (1994) 'Competitive advantage: merging marketing and the competence-based perspective', *Journal of Business and Industrial Marketing*, vol. 9, no. 4, pp. 42–53.

Kanter, R.M. (1994) 'Collaborative advantage: the art of alliances', *Harvard Business Review*, July–August, pp. 96–108.

Kedia, B.L., Nordtvedt, R., Perez, L.M. (2002) 'International business strategies, decision-making theories, and leadership styles: an integrated framework', *CR*, vol. 12, no. 1, pp. 38–52.

Kotler, P. (1997) *Marketing Management: Analysis, planning, implementation, and control* (9th edn), Prentice-Hall, Englewood Cliffs, NJ.

Levitt, T. (1960) 'Marketing myopia', *Harvard Business Review*, July–August, pp. 45–56.

Magrath, A.J. (1986) 'When marketing service's 4 Ps are not enough', *Business Horizons*, May–June, pp. 44–50.

Porter, M.E. (1980) *Competitive Strategy*, The Free Press, New York.

Porter, M.E. (1990) *The Competitive Advantage of Nations*, The Free Press, New York.

Porter, M.E. (1996) 'What is strategy?', *Harvard Business Review*, November–December, pp. 61–78.

Rafiq, M. and Ahmed, P.K. (1995) 'Using the 7Ps as a generic marketing mix', *Marketing Intelligence and Planning*, vol. 13, no. 9, pp. 4–15.

Ravald, A. and Grönroos, C. (1996) 'The value concept and relationship marketing', *European Journal of Marketing*, vol. 30, no. 2, pp. 19–30.

Reve, T. (1990) 'The firm as a nexus of internal and external contracts', in Aoki, M., Gustafsson, M. and Williamson, O.E. (eds), *The Firm as a Nexus of Treaties*, Sage, London.

Tampoe, M. (1994) 'Exploiting the core competences of your organization', *Long Range Planning*, vol. 27, no. 4, pp. 66–77.

Veliyath. R. and Zahra, S.A. (2000) 'Competitiveness in the 21st century: reflections on the growing debate about globalization', *ACR*, vol. 8, no. 1, pp. 14–33

Further reading

Akhter, S.H. (2003) 'Strategic planning, hypercompetition, and knowledge management', *Business Horizons*, January-February, pp. 19–24.

Bergen, M. and Peteraf, M.A. (2002) 'Competitor identification and competitor analysis: a broad managerial approach', *Managerial and Decision Economics*, vol. 23, pp. 157–69.

Birkinshaw, J. (2001) 'Strategies for managing internal competition', *California Management Review*, vol. 44, no. 1, pp. 21–38.

Connor, T. (2002) 'The resource-based view of strategy and its value to practising managers', *Strategic Change*, vol. 11, pp. 307–16.

Connor, T. (2003) 'Managing for competitiveness: a proposed model for managerial focus', *Strategic Change*, June–July, pp. 195–207.

Czuchry, A.J. and Yasin, M.M. (2001) 'Enhancing global competitiveness of small and mid-sized firms: a rapid assessment methodology approach', *ACR*, vol. 9, no. 1, pp. 87–99.

Heelms, M.M. and Ettkin, L.P. (2000) 'Time-based competitiveness: a strategic perspective', *CR*, vol. 10, no. 2, pp. 1–14.

Hussey, D. (2002) 'Company analysis: determining strategic capability', *Strategic Change*, vol. 11, pp. 43–52.

Klein, J. (2002) 'Beyond competitive advantage', *Strategic Change*, vol. 11, pp. 307–16.

Ma, H. (2002) 'Competitive advantage: what's luck got to do with it?' *Management Decision*, vol. 40, no. 6, pp. 525–36.

Mills, J., Platts, K. and Bourne, M. (2003) 'Applying resource-based theory – Methods, outcomes and utility for managers', *International Journal of Operations & Production Management*, vol. 23, No. 2, pp. 148–66.

O'Donnell, A., Gilmore, A. Carson, D. and Cummins. D. (2003) 'Competitive advantage in small to medium-sized enterprises', *Journal of Strategic Marketing*, vol. 10, pp. 205–23.

Proff, H. (2002) 'Business unit strategies between regionalisation and globalization' *International Business Review*, vol. 11, pp. 231–50.

Zahra, S.A. (2000) 'Global competitiveness and corporate strategy in the 21st century', *CR*, vol. 10, no. 1, pp. 1–4.

Valentin, E.K. (2001) 'SWOT analysis from a resource-based view', *Journal of Marketing – Theory and Practice*, Spring, pp. 54–69.

CASE STUDY I.1 Manchester United

Trying to establish a global brand

Manchester United (abbreviated as ManUtd) has developed into one of the most famous and financially successful football clubs in the world, being recognised in virtually every country, even those with little interest in the sport.

Manchester United was listed on London's Stock Exchange in 1991 and has a market capitalisation of $466 million (see Table 1).

The most valuable US sports team, the National Football League's Washington Redskins, is worth $800 million. Baseball's New York Yankees are at $730 million. More than any US sports team, ManUtd has built a global brand, in part with 200 fan clubs: 151 in the United Kingdom, 25 in Ireland and 24 in the rest of the world, including one in the United States.

ManUtd's 1999 summer tour of Australia and China helped to raise the international profile of the brand even higher. The four-match tour attracted huge crowds, in the region of 70,000 per game. The tour was designed to take the club to places where it could build on existing support. The overseas supporters of Manchester United do not get many opportunities to see the team play live.

The club has launched a free Internet service (**www.manutd.com**). Although ManUtd was not the first UK club to offer free Internet access –

Arsenal launched its venture as early as the summer of 1997 – it was the first to offer its service with a worldwide audience in mind.

Prior to the Asian-Pacific tour an agreement was signed between the club, sportswear suppliers Umbro and the Australian Woolmark company to market a new fabric for the club's shirts for the 2000–01 season.

ManUtd had a fantastic year in 1999, when they won the treble: the Premier League (National) Championship, the FA Challenge Cup and the European Champions League. In 2000 they won their sixth Premiership title in eight years, and by a record 18 points margin. The club also won the International Cup for the first time (see Table 2).

Table 1 The market's top ten: highest valued of Europe's top-tier publicly traded soccer franchises

Company/country	Market cap ($mil)
Manchester United/England	466
Juventus/Italy	241
Rangers/Scotland	139
Arsenal/England	135
Lazio/Italy	111
Roma/Italy	96
Ajax/Netherlands	73
Borussia Dortmund/Germany	58
Newcastle United/England	50
Parken/Denmark	49

Source: Richard Heller: Big Kick, Forbes.com, 7 August 2002. Reprinted by permission of FORBES Global © 2003 Forbes Global Inc.

Table 2 ManUtd's recent successes

	2003	2002	2001	2000	1999	1998
FA Premier League	Champions	3rd	Champions	Champions	Champions	2nd
FA Challenge Cup	Winners	4th round	4th round	n/a	Winners	5th round
European Champions League	Quarter-final	Semi-final	Quarter-final	Quarter-final	Winners	Quarter-final

In what follows we present some key figures from the Manchester United financial report for 2002.

The ManUtd fanbase

More so than any US sports team, ManUtd has built a global brand, and it estimates it has a total of 50 million fans worldwide. The US fan club boasts 5 million members, accounting for 1 in 10 of fans worldwide. But 30 million fans are in Asia, where for the first time the soccer World Cup was held so successfully in 2002. The rest (15 million) live mainly in Europe.

Creating ManUtd's international brand power is expensive

ManUtd's brand power is derived from its football stars, who may choose to move on when their contracts expire. David Beckham, the England World Cup captain was a Manchester United midfielder, until July 2003, when Real Madrid acquired him for €35 million.

Beckham, one of the world's best-known athletes, is not the club's only valuable asset; there are other sporting icons in the club. Of the 23 men in the England World Cup team, 4 play for ManUtd. ManUtd's players also played for other national teams in the 2002 World Cup. They include Argentina's Juan Sebastian Veron, South Africa's Quinton Fortune and France's Fabien Barthez and Mikael Silvestre. Another ManUtd player, Roy Keane, the Ireland captain, quit in a disagreement with his national coach just before the World Cup in Korea.

These stars don't come cheap. ManUtd's compensation expenditure rose from 27 per cent of revenue five years ago to 39 per cent in 2001. Of the $74 million in compensation expenditure in 2001 an estimated $63 million (85 per cent of staff costs) was spent on players – that is 33 per cent of revenue. In 2002, estimated player costs increased to 36 per cent of revenue, still well below the 60 per cent average for the United States' National Football League.

Turnover, all of which arises from the Groups' principle activity, can be analysed into its main components as shown in Table 3.

Table 3 Key financial figures

Turnover	2002 £mil	2001 £mil
Gate receipts and programme sales	56.3	51.8
Media (mainly TV)	51.9	31.2
Commercial (mainly sponsorships)	26.5	27.4
Merchandising	11.4	19.2
Total turnover	146.1	129.6
Profit before tax	32.3	21.8

During 2000 ManUtd's flagship stores opened in Singapore, Dublin, Kuala Lumpur and Cape Town. In addition, the two financial services products launched in 1998, the 'Save and Support' savings account with Britannia and the club MasterCard, have been very successful and assisted in the increase in turnover.

Besides its own stores ManUtd has interests in two hotel projects. The quality hotel adjacent to the Old Trafford stadium in which Manchester United PLC has a 25 per cent stake continues to trade profitably. It has recently taken a 31.4 per cent stake in a 120-bedroom hotel (Sleep In) to be built adjacent to the Trafford Centre shopping complex, just a couple of miles from Old Trafford, which opened in late 2001.

Other promotional activities have included the following.

Sponsorship and new media

- £30 million four-year sponsorship deal with Vodafone.
- New £1.6 billion FA Premier League television contracts for season 2001/02.
- Expanded online access to the club through the official website: **www.manutd.com**.
- MUTV – the TV channel that lives and breathes Manchester United, seven days a week.

However MUTV, their joint venture television channel with BskyB (owning 10 per cent of Manchester United shares) and Canada, continued to incur losses in the year, although at a lower level than previously.

In 2002 the promotion activities were expanded with another activity, which has been outsourced to a subsupplier: fans of Manchester United are now able to play out their lifelong ambitions as they take control of the ManUtd team in the club's own football game, developed by UK-based games developer and publisher, Codemasters. Manchester United Club Football has been designed to be the ultimate game for fans of the Red Devils and launched on PlayStation 2 and XBOX.

The game opens at Old Trafford, which has been accurately modelled for the game. New technology will allow fans who have always wanted to play for Manchester United to create themselves as a digital player who can be slotted into the first team line up.

Global sponsorship alliances

ManUtd's objective was to seek new alliances that will encourage and reward investment in the club to the mutual advantage of both parties. This new model is based on aligning with companies that could contribute to the fan base with added-value products and services which were previously unavailable to them.

In the following some of the newest alliances will be further explained in chronological sequence, from the beginning of 2000 until the end of 2002.

Alliance with Vodafone

The arrangement with Vodafone (announced in February 2000) combines a traditional sponsorship element with a transactional aspect, with ManUtd benefiting from both. It will also link the mobile, multimedia operator in the development of a wireless Internet access portal.

ManUMobile has been launched as the first WAP-service of its kind to provide all the latest club news as it happens. Text messages provide live match day updates, kick-off times and other groundbreaking stories as they happen. The WAP site provides full news, match information, player biographies and a lot more, enabling supporters to keep up to date with their favourite team wherever they are. The deal with Vodafone also affords the opportunity to provide content through the much-anticipated 3G handsets. Ultimately ManUtd sees itself delivering self-produced content to a global audience through 3G wireless, the Internet and broadband TV.

Alliance with a retail partner in Japan

In November 2001 Manchester United PLC announced that it had appointed Japan Sports Vision (JSV) as its master merchandising licensee partner in Japan in a five-year deal. JSV is a leading sports retailer in Japan with over 25 stores across the country. The company is already an important customer for Nike.

The deal represents the first time that ManUtd has had a retail partner in Japan. The ManUtd merchandise was available for sale in JSV stores from the summer of 2002, at the same time as the start of the World Cup. This event created a huge interest in football in Japan and the whole Asian area.

Alliance with Budweiser

In December 2001 ManUtd signed a sponsorship alliance deal with Budweiser, the world's best-selling beer. Budweiser is brewed by St. Louis, Missouri-based Anheuser-Busch, Inc., and is available in more than 80 countries around the world.

Budweiser became a Platinum Sponsor of the club and the Official Beer of ManUtd, beginning with the 2002/03 season. As the club's official beer sponsor, Budweiser will have exclusive beer-pouring rights at the club's legendary Old Trafford stadium, receive on-field, in-stadium and concourse signage and have the right to use the official marks and logos of the club in advertising, promotions and packaging.

ManUtd is the latest addition to Budweiser's rich tradition in football. The brand is Official Beer of the 2002 and 2006 FIFA World Cups™, Official Beer of Chelsea Football Club (also a member of the English FA Premiership) and Official Beer of Major League Soccer and each of its 12 teams in the United States.

In addition to football, Budweiser was the Official Beer of the 2002 Salt Lake City Olympic Winter Games, the National Basketball Association (NBA), Major League Baseball and NASCAR racing in the United States, among others.

Alliance with Nike

In August 2002 the US-based sportswear firm, Nike, displaced the UK's Umbro as ManUtd's uniforms sponsor and merchandising partner in a deal worth £300 million over 13 years. Under the arrangement, the club will turn over to Nike the uniform-replica merchandising business. Nike will pay ManUtd a royalty for the use of the brand and develop merchandise to sell through its global network of outlets to ManUtd's estimated 50 million fans around the world. On the other hand ManUtd will market Nike products through different communication channels.

As part of their contractual arrangements, ManUtd and Nike will jointly launch a grass roots football programme that will focus on youth participation and skills development. The £1 million annual cost of the programme is fully funded by Nike out of its existing grass roots football commitment.

At the time the contract was announced (August 2002), Nike already supplied Teddy Sheringham, Ole Gunnar Solskjaer, Dwight Yorke and Andy Cole's boots.

Questions

1. Discuss and explain how the different alliances can increase the competitiveness of ManUtd.

2. Which environmental factors are most important for ManUtd to monitor in the international environment (political, economic or sociocultural factors)?

3. What are the main threats to retaining 'Manchester United' as a global brand?

CASE STUDY I.2   Bridgestone Tyres

European marketing strategy

It is a lovely spring morning in central Tokyo in 2003. Although the city is just awakening, with all its noise and stress, that does not bother the Chairman of Bridgestone Corporation, Shigeo Watanabe, as he is on his way to work. The Annual Report 2002 for Bridgestone has just been published, and shows an increase in net earnings to US$330 million based on a total turnover of US$18 billion.

The prospects look good. On his way into his office Shigeo Watanabe asks his assistant to give him a copy of the different manufacturers' 2002 market shares in the world market (Table 1), plus Bridgestone's 2002 market shares in the most important tyre markets in the world. Watanabe has a meeting with the board of directors the next day, when they will discuss Bridgestone's strategies in Europe, Asia and North America.

As can be seen from Table 1, together with Goodyear and Michelin, Bridgestone is among the world's largest manufacturers of tyres. Bridgestone

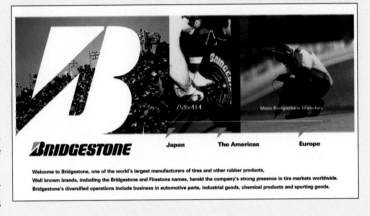

Welcome to Bridgestone, one of the world's largest manufacturers of tires and other rubber products. Well known brands, including the Bridgestone and Firestone names, herald the company's strong presence in tire markets worldwide. Bridgestone's diversified operations include business in automotive parts, industrial goods, chemical products and sporting goods.

has a 19 per cent worldwide market share (see Table 2), created by about 105,000 employees.

But still Bridgestone has a comparatively low market share (8%) and low brand awareness in Europe. The question for Shigeo Watanabe is: how can Bridgestone increase its market share in Europe? The following is a concentrated report on the market conditions for tyres in Europe.

The European tyre market

The European market for car tyres (including commercial vehicles) fell slightly from 2000 to 2002. Competition among tyre producers is fierce and tyre prices in real terms have fallen over the last few years.

In 2002 the total European market for tyres was 229.8 million. A breakdown of the total market is shown in Table 3. This table shows sales of new tyres

Table 1 Market share for tyres in the world market, 2002

Manufacturer	Market share (%)
Michelin	19.6
Bridgestone	18.9
Goodyear	18.2
Continental	7.2
Sumitomo	3.8
Pirelli	3.7
Yokohama	3.3
Cooper	2.5
Toyo	1.8
Kumho	1.8
Others	19.2
World total	100.0

Table 2 Bridgestone's market share for tyres in the most important markets, 2002

Market area	Bridgestone market share (%)
Asia	29
Europe	8
US	22
World total	19

Table 3 The European tyre market, 2002

Million units	Car tyres	Truck tyres	Total
New sales	65.4	9.3	74.7
Replacement sales	131.8	23.3	155.1
Total	197.2	32.6	229.8

for new cars (= new sales) and replacements of worn tyres (= replacement sales). Table 4 shows the total European tyre market broken down into countries, together with the market shares of the most important producers in the individual markets. On the basis of Table 4 the Boston Consulting Group (BCG) charts of the individual producers have been prepared (Figure 1). In this connection it should be noted that the areas of the circles show total sales in the respective countries and not the sales of the individual companies in the markets in question, which is normally the case in BCG charts.

Retreaded tyres

So far the markets have been described on the assumption that only the production and sale of new tyres was involved. For many years consumers have considered the retreaded tyre one of low price and low quality. In consequence European consumers have been somewhat reluctant to buy retreaded tyres. Tyres can be recycled. The main

problem is economic: recycling costs more than dumping, so many tyres end up in landfills or on illegal dumps, adding to those already polluting the landscape. Tyre dumps are potentially dangerous: they can catch fire and, when they do, toxic chemicals are released, leaving an oily residue that can contaminate groundwater.

Currently only about 12 per cent of the European Union's scrap tyres are retreaded and reused. The percentage has been decreasing over the last few years because new tyres are now so price competitive that many consumers prefer to buy new tyres. However retreaded tyres are still recommended by the European Commission, primarily for two reasons:

1. Waste problems connected to the accumulation of used tyres have made retreaded tyres an environmentally correct recycling solution.
2. The use of retreaded tyres reduces consumption of natural rubber, natural minerals, metal wire, oil and other chemicals that are normally used in the production of new tyres.

In 2002 sales of retreaded tyres were distributed as shown in Table 5. The European Commission encourages and recommends the increased use of retreaded tyres (rising to approximately 20 per cent of total sales).

One threat against such a development is, however, that the price of new imported tyres from the Far East is sometimes lower than that of retreaded tyres.

Table 4 The European market for tyres (cars and trucks)

	France	Germany	Italy	Spain	UK	Other markets	Total
Million units							
New sales	13.2	22.7	7.0	9.1	8.7	14.0	74.7
Replacement sales	24.2	36.7	15.8	8.9	22.0	47.5	155.1
Total	37.4	59.4	22.8	18.0	30.7	61.5	229.8
Producers' market shares (%)							
Michelin	55	24	31	44	30	—	35.0
Continental	4	26	8	7	13	—	14.4
Goodyear	7	16	11	4	16	—	11.3
Pirelli	5	6	23	13	11	—	10.4
SP (Dunlop)	10	10	4	4	14	—	8.9
Bridgestone/Firestone	7	5	8	18	7	—	8.0
Others	12	13	15	10	9	—	12.0
Total	100	100	100	100	100	—	100.0

Note: 'Other markets' include eastern Europe and Scandinavia, for which market shares are not available.

Figure 1 BCG charts for leading tyre producers

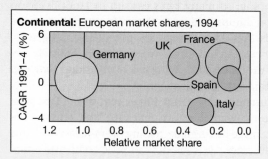

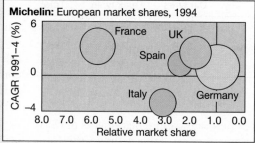

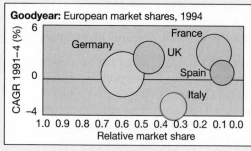

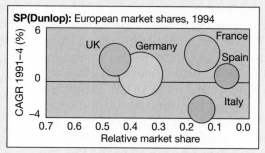

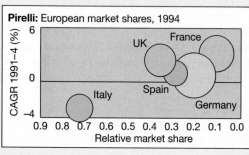

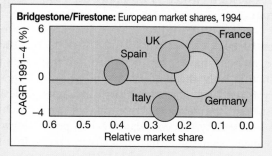

Notes:

CAGR = compound annual growth rate.

Relative market share = the market share of the individual producer in relation to the largest producer on the market.

Source: MarketLine.

Table 5 Sales of retreaded tyres in main European markets, 2002 (million units)

	France	Germany	Italy	Spain	UK
Cars	2.30	3.50	2.70	0.03	4.80
Trucks	0.85	1.40	0.95	0.44	0.95
Total	3.15	4.90	3.65	0.47	5.75

Table 6 Producers' nationality and different brand names

Producer	Nationality (ownership)	Brands
Michelin	France	Michelin, Kléber, Tyremaster
Continental	Germany	Continental, Uniroyal, Semperit, Barum, Viking, Gislaved, Mabor, Sava
Bridgestone/ Firestone	Japan	Bridgestone, Firestone, Dayton, Europa, First Stop
Pirelli	Italy	Pirelli, Curier
Goodyear	US	Goodyear, DunlOp, Kelly, Fulda
Others		Stomil, Tigar, Komho, Lassa, Marshal, Toyo

Characteristics of the leading producers (mentioned in Table 3)

In many countries the producers use several different brands to appeal to a larger clientele who have different preferences for different brands of tyres. A list of brand names is given in Table 6.

Europe's leading tyre suppliers may be briefly characterised as follows.

Michelin

Michelin is currently the largest tyre manufacturer in the world. The France-based company organises its operations into the following business units:

- passenger car and light truck tyres;
- truck tyres;
- earthmover tyres;
- agricultural tyres;
- aircraft tyres;
- two-wheel tyres;
- components (rubber and elastomers, reinforcement materials);
- suspension systems;
- tourism services (maps, guidebooks).

In contrast to its traditional single-brand strategy Michelin now has a long list of associate brands such as BF Goodrich, Kléber, Riken, Kormoran, Taurus, Laurent, Wolber, Tyremaster, Siamtyre, and Uniroyal (North America only). The company produces 3,500 different types of tyre, which are made in 67 factories in 13 countries. The Michelin Group employs over 100,000 people.

As part of the group's strategy to expand its share outside Europe, particularly in Asia and Latin America, Michelin has acquired MRF in the Philippines and the Colombian manufacturer, Icollantas. In Europe, meanwhile, Michelin has announced plans to improve productivity by 20 per cent within three years. It expects to achieve this through developing its products, services and multi-brand policy while restructuring all its European activities, possibly by closing plants or terminating technical activities and services.

In Europe Michelin is the clear market leader, with a market share of 32 per cent, well ahead of Continental and Goodyear.

Michelin's largest market is North America, which takes about 45 per cent of its tyre production, followed by Europe with 40 per cent and Asia with 5 per cent.

In 1993 Michelin registered a loss of nearly FFr4 billion. This led to widespread rationalisation: for example, the staff were reduced by 10,000. As early as 1994 the Michelin Group was back in the black. A turnover of some FFr67 billion resulted in a profit of FFr1.4 billion. Since then, there has been a lot of fluctuation in Michelin's results. However, in 2002 they had net profit of €614 million, based on a total sales of €16.5 billion.

Bridgestone/Firestone

Bridgestone was founded by Shojiro Ishibashi in 1931. The English translation of the surname Ishibashi is 'stone bridge'. Firestone was acquired by the Japanese-owned Bridgestone Corporation in 1988. Traditionally, Bridgestone has targeted the upper 'price-quality' segment, while Firestone appeals more to the 'mid-range' segment. Firestone has in particular contributed to strengthening the group's sales to car producers (new sales) in Europe (primarily Ford, Opel/Vauxhall, VW/Audi and Fiat).

There are 92,000 employees of the Bridgestone Corporation around the world. Of the total turnover around 25 per cent comes from non-tyre products, including conveyor belts, rubber crawlers, construction materials and vibration isolation parts (for vehicles). In Europe, Brussels-based Bridgestone/Firestone Europe SA oversees local production and R&D at the European facilities. There are five European tyre plants: one in France, one in Italy and three in Spain. Bridgestone's European sales subsidiaries are located in Austria, Benelux, Denmark, Finland, France, Germany, Italy, Portugal, Spain, Sweden, Switzerland and the United Kingdom.

However, brand awareness is still lower for Bridgestone than some of its its competitors, as shown in Table 7. As a consequence Bridgestone began supplying Bridgestone tyres to Formula One teams in 1996.

Table 7 Brand awareness in the major European markets: spontaneous (unaided) awareness (%)

Brand	UK	Germany	France	Italy	Spain	Total
Michelin	73	78	98	92	90	85
Pirelli	51	45	40	91	66	57
Goodyear	52	48	56	70	41	54
Dunlop	60	53	48	25	25	44
Firestone	32	25	40	37	69	38
Continental	12	65	15	26	20	31
Bridgestone	10	26	7	17	9	15
Population (million)	58	81	58	57	39	223

Source: Compiled by the author from different sources.

The company's status as tyre supplier to the Formula One World Championship is an important part of Bridgestone's promotional strategy and has helped increase awareness of the Bridgestone brand substantially in recent years, particularly in Europe.

Bridgestone is looking to increase its global market share to 20 per cent from 19 per cent and its European market share to around 15 per cent form 10 per cent. To achieve this the company admits that it needs to gain a much stronger presence in Europe and North America. However, its share in North America has been increasing by 1 per cent each year since 1993.

The company's main focus is on its Bridgestone and Firestone brands, although its multibrand approach to business extends to a range of budget and private brands such as Europa and First Stop in Europe or Dayton, Gillette and Peerless in North America.

Continental

Continental produces tyres for all forms of vehicles: cars, trucks, heavy vehicles, agricultural machinery, bicycles, motor cycles, etc. Continental bought (from Michelin) the rights to use the Uniroyal brand all over Europe.

Continental is the fourth largest tyre manufacturer in the world as well as being a world leader in the braking segment following the 1998 acquisition of ITT's Brake and Chassis Division. The Group's operations are split into five different sectors:

- the Passenger Tire Group (controlling the controlled distribution chains);
- the Commercial Vehicle Tire Group;
- the Automotive Systems Group (includes Continental Teves);
- Continental General Tire (the group's US subsidiary);
- ContiTech (industrial rubber products).

Continental was the first manufacturer to actively develop a multibrand strategy due to the uneven strength of its key brands across Europe. Today the company has eight main brands – Continental, Uniroyal (in Europe only), Semperit, General, Viking, Gislaved, Barum and Mabor. Part of its global strategy is to increase its strength in markets where it is underrepresented, considered by the company to be the United States, France, Italy, Spain and Asia. In 1998 Continental acquired Grupo Carso (Mexico), General Tyre and Rubber (Pakistan) and Gentyre South Africa as part of a move towards the developing markets, along with joint venture and technology agreements such as those made in Belarus, Slovakia and Argentina.

By reorganising its controlled distribution networks the company has been seeking to develop its share of the European market. The expansion of the Pneus Expert Europe-wide branded retail network has been central to this aim, combining Continental's wholly owned subsidiaries such as National Tyres (UK) and Vergoelst (Germany) with the activities of partner groups and nationally organised franchise networks. Since Continental began to actively develop Pneus Expert in mid-1997 it has grown to become the biggest branded retail network in Europe.

Continental's main strategy is to develop a position as a complete systems supplier to the automotive industry. It has been developing wheel assembly facilities in conjunction with vehicle manufacturers worldwide for some time and the company's Automotive Systems Group has also focused on high-tech automotive developments.

Continental is very dependent on the German market, which accounts for 33 per cent of its worldwide sales.

Goodyear

Goodyear has 86 factories in 26 different countries. The worldwide staff total more than 100,000, of whom 20,000 are employed in Europe. Some 55 per cent of the Group's sales relate to the US market, where Goodyear is the market leader. Besides tyres, the company makes several lines of belt, hose and other rubber products, rubber-related chemicals, and owns retail stores worldwide. It is split into six business units:

- Goodyear Asia;
- Goodyear European Union;
- Goodyear Latin America;
- North American Tire;
- Engineered and Chemical Products;
- Goodyear Eastern Europe, Africa, and Middle East.

Its tyres are sold under various brand names besides Goodyear, including Dunlop, Kelly, Fulda, Lee, Sava, Pneumant, India and Debica.

The Group's main aims are to maintain its current status by holding a number one or number two position in specific markets, keep up a fast and profitable growth in all core businesses and gain strategic acquisitions and expansions while being the lowest cost producer of the top three companies.

The alliance with Sumitomo Rubber Industries/ Dunlop was announced in January 1999 and covered the establishment of four joint venture sales companies, one in North America, two in Japan and one in Europe. The North American joint venture includes Dunlop's tyre activities in the region but not Goodyear's. In Europe, both Goodyear and Dunlop activities in western Europe are included but not Goodyear's activities in Poland, Turkey and Slovenia. The Japanese joint ventures will cover OE sales of both brands and replacement sales of Goodyear tyres with Sumitomo owning 75 per cent of both. Two further joint venture companies, majority owned by Goodyear, will be set up in the United States, one for purchasing and one for technology development. Activities by both companies in Asia and Latin America remain outside the deal. The alliance, unique in its scope and arrangement, means that Goodyear has gained control of the Dunlop brand in both Europe and North America, a move that is considered by some to be a precursor to a complete takeover of Dunlop's tyre activities.

Pirelli

The Italian Pirelli Group has two main activities: tyres and cables, and employs 3,800 employees worldwide.

Pirelli is the sixth largest tyre manufacturer in the world. The company has a presence in all areas of the tyre market but its particular strengths lie in the high-performance end of the passenger tyre market, where it can justifiably claim market leadership within Europe. The Pirelli brand is an out-and-out premium brand. However, the Group also owns a number of subsidiary brands including Courier, Ceat, Armstrong and the Metzeler brand of motorcycle tyres.

Within Europe Pirelli has key manufacturing plants in Italy, Germany, Spain and the United Kingdom.

Pirelli has the best market position in Italy, where it is second to Michelin. In 1992 Pirelli tried in vain to acquire its German competitor, Continental.

The distribution of tyres in Europe

The majority of replacement sales (replacement of tyres) take place through specialised tyre distributors:

- independent chains;
- producer-owned chains (e.g. in Germany Continental owns the Vergös chain and Michelin owns the Euromaster chain);
- franchise-based chains.

In addition, service stations have a certain share of replacement sales. This share is highest in newly developed eastern European markets, while it is decreasing in western Europe.

Questions

As a consultant for Chairman Shigeo Watanabe you are required to answer the following questions.

1. Make an assessment of the competitive strategies that Michelin, Continental and Goodyear, respectively may pursue to strengthen their European market positions.

2. Make an assessment of the alternative competitive strategies that Bridgestone can pursue to strengthen its European market position.

3. Give a well-reasoned proposal for criteria to be used by Bridgestone when choosing a market (country) that requires a larger marketing effort.

4. Give a well-reasoned proposal for Bridgestone's distribution and communication strategies in a market chosen by you.

CASE STUDY I.3   ResMed Inc.

Helping patients around the world suffering from obstructive sleep apnea (OSA)

Sleep apnea

Sleep apnea is a treatable disorder in which a person stops breathing during sleep, often hundreds of times during the night. Sleep apnea is a common disorder that affects millions of men, women, and children, but is often undiagnosed, despite its potentially serious consequences. It is estimated that at least 5 per cent of the world population have unrecognised sleep apnea.

Apnea is a Greek word meaning 'without breath'. An apnea is clinically defined in adults as a cessation of breath that lasts at least 10 seconds and in children as a cessation of breath that lasts the equivalent of two-and-a-half missed breaths. In addition to apneas, hypophneas are often present. *Hypopnea* also comes from the Greek: hypo meaning beneath or less than normal and phea meaning breath. A hypopnea is not a complete cessation of breath, but a reduction in airflow or a struggle to breathe. With each apnea and hypopnea the oxygen level in the bloodstream typically drops. The Apnea–Hypopnea Index (AHI) or Respiratory Disturbance Index refers to the total number of apneas and hypopneas divided by the total amount of sleep during the sleep study. The AHI is one measure of the severity of the sleep apnea. There are three different types of apnea: obstructive, central or mixed (a combination of obstructive and central). Obstructive Sleep Apnea (OSA) is the most common. Usually the soft tissue in the rear of the throat collapses and closes the airway so that sufferers of sleep apnea stop breathing repeatedly during sleep, as frequently as a hundred times an hour and often for a minute or longer.

With each apnea the brain receives a signal to arouse the person from sleep in order to resume breathing, but consequently sleep is extremely fragmented and of poor quality. People with untreated sleep apnea are generally not even aware of the awakenings, but only of being sleepy during the day. They may, however, realise that they snore or gasp for air during sleep. Loud snoring, punctuated with periods of silence (the apneas), is typical but is not always present, especially in children.

Consequences of untreated sleep apnea include high blood pressure and other cardiovascular diseases, and weight gain. People with untreated sleep apnea may also complain of falling asleep inappropriately, morning headaches, memory problems, feelings of depression, reflux, nocturia (a need to use the bathroom frequently at night), and impotence. Children with untreated apnea may be hyperactive. Untreated sleep apnea, as with sleep deprivation, may be responsible for job impairment and motor vehicle accidents. Apnea is a concern with certain medications and general anesthesia.

Risk factors for sleep apnea include a family history of sleep apnea, excess weight, a large neck, a recessed chin, male sex, abnormalities in the structure of the upper airway, ethnicity (African-Americans, Pacific Islanders and Mexicans), smoking, and alcohol use. Yet sleep apnea can affect both males and females of all ages, including children, and of any weight.

In its 'Wake Up America' report to Congress in 1993 the National Commission on Sleep Disorders Research estimated that approximately 10 per cent of the population in the United States suffer from chronic disorders of sleep and wakefulness, such as sleep apnea. According to this report sleep apnea is the most common sleep disorder. Health care professionals are often unable to diagnose OSA because they are unaware that such non-specific symptoms as fatigue, snoring and irritability are characteristic of OSA.

About ResMed (www.resmed.com)

ResMed is a leading respiratory medical device manufacturer, specialising in products for the diagnosis and treatment of Sleep Disordered Breathing (SDB). ResMed operates through direct offices in the United States, Australia, Germany, France, Sweden, the United Kingdom, Switzerland, Spain, the Netherlands, Finland, Austria, New Zealand,

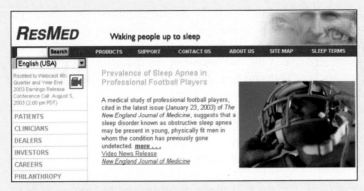
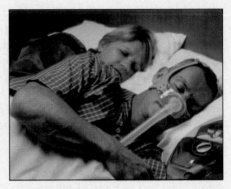

OSA (the problem) and CPAP (the solution)

Singapore, Malaysia, Japan, and through a network of distributors in more than 60 other countries. ResMed's principal manufacturing facilities are located in Sydney.

ResMed was born global – from day one the company operated in more than one country. When ResMed was formed in 1989 its primary purpose was to commercialise a device for treating Obstructive Sleep Apnea, a major subset of SDB. The company was founded by Peter Farrell, an Australian who had been an executive with Baxter (the US health care giant) and six colleagues. Their aim: to commercialise an invention first published in 1981 by a leading researcher in the field, Colin Sullivan of the University of Sydney Medical School.

Until Sullivan invented a treatment the only way to deal with the disease was to cut a hole in the sufferer's neck, circumventing the blockage in the throat. Sullivan's alternative is less drastic: to open the upper airway by blowing air in through the nose. He demonstrated the concept over 20 years ago by using a sophisticated vacuum cleaner in reverse mode as an airflow generator. The power was turned down by cutting a small hole in the rubber tube and releasing a stream of air, and a mask was taped to the patient's face. ResMed's machine works in a similar way: by applying what is known as continuous positive airway pressure (**CPAP**). CPAP therapy involves wearing a mask, which is connected to an electric device that delivers air at positive pressure. The air pressure acts as an air splint to keep the upper airway open and prevent apneas.

ResMed consults with physicians at major sleep centers throughout the world to identify technological trends in the treatment of SDB. These physicians serve as generators of new product ideas, but these new ideas can also come from ResMed's marketing staff, the direct sales force, the distribution network, manufacturers' representatives, customer, and patients. Typically, the internal development staff then perform the new product development.

In its commitment to technological innovation ResMed spends approximately 7–8 per cent of net revenue on research and product development. Together with a clear focus on growing market opportunities this dedication has enabled ResMed to create and maintain shareholder value. The company has a substantial number of patents issues both in- and outside the United States. Some of these patents and patent applications relate to significant aspects and features of ResMed's products.

Competition

The markets for ResMed's products are highly competitive. The company believes that the principal competitive factors in all of the markets are product features, reliability and price. Reputation and efficient distribution are also important. They compete on a market-by-market basis with various companies, some of which have greater financial, research, manufacturing and marketing resources than ResMed. In the United States, its principal market, Respironics Inc.; DeVilbiss, a division of Sunrise Medical Inc.; and Nellcor Puritan Bennett, a subsidiary of Tyco Inc., are the primary competitors for its CPAP products. Its principal European competitors are also Respironics, DeVilbiss, and Nellcor Puritan Bennett, as well as regional European manufacturers. The disparity between ResMed's resources and those of its competitors may increase as a result of the recent trend towards consolidation in the health care industry. In addition, the products compete with surgical procedures and dental appliances designed to treat OSA and other SDB-related respiratory conditions. The development of new or innovative procedures or devices by others could result in ResMed's products becoming obsolete or non-competitive, resulting in a material adverse effect on its business, financial condition and results of operations.

Any product developed by ResMed that gains regulatory clearance will have to compete for market acceptance and market share. An important factor in such competition may be the timing of market introduction of competitive products. Accordingly, the relative speed with which the company can develop and market products are expected to be important competitive factors. In addition, its ability to compete will continue to be dependent on the extent to which it is successful in protecting its patents and other intellectual property.

Respironics (www.respironics.com)

Respironics is a recognised resource in the medical device market. The company provides unique programmes, supported by knowledgeable people and innovative products, to assist health care providers to manage disease states for certain patient populations while helping them to grow and manage their businesses efficiently. A tradition of innovation and broad-based expertise uniquely positions Respironics in the $3.5 billion worldwide respiratory market of which the CPAPs equipment is only a part. The company is focused on homecare, hospital and international markets, providing programmes that manage sleep-disordered breathing, chronic obstructive pulmonary disease, asthma and infant care. Through the vision of its management team Respironics has entered a new phase of corporate development. For the fiscal year 2003 (ending 30 June) Respironics' revenue was $630 million with $47 million in net profits.

Employees

Respironics employs 2,600 individuals globally. As of 30 June 2003, ResMed had 1,464 employees or full-time consultants, of which 540 were employed in warehousing and manufacturing, 252 in research and development, 672 in sales, marketing and administration. Of the employees and consultants, 705 were located in Australia, 349 in the United States, 363 in Europe, and 47 in Asia. ResMed believes that the success of the business will depend, in part, on its ability to attract and retain qualified personnel.

Manufacturing

The principal manufacturing facilities are located in Sydney, Australia, and comprise a 120,000 sq ft manufacturing and research and development facility. The manufacturing operations consist primarily of assembly and testing of the flow generators, masks and accessories. Of the numerous raw materials, parts and components purchased for assembly of their therapeutic and diagnostic sleep

disorder products, most are off-the-shelf items available from multiple vendors. ResMed generally manufactures to its internal sales forecasts and fills orders as they are received. The quality control group performs tests at various steps in the manufacturing cycle to ensure quality.

Sales and marketing

ResMed products are typically purchased by a home health care worker dealer who then sells the products to the patient. The decision to purchase CPAP products is made or influenced by one or more of the following individuals or organizations: the prescribing physician and their staff, the home health care dealer, the insurer and the patient.

ResMed currently markets its products in over 60 countries using a network of distributors, independent manufacturers' representatives and its direct sales force through subsidiaries. ResMed attempts to tailor the marketing approach to each national market, based on regional awareness of SDB as a health problem, physician referral patterns, consumer preferences and local reimbursement policies.

ResMed employees created $155 million, $204 million and $274 million in revenue in fiscal years (ending 30 June) 2001, 2002 and 2003. The net profits in fiscal year 2003 were $46 million.

North America and Latin America

In the United States ResMed's sales and marketing activities are conducted through a field sales organization made up of regional territory representatives, programme development specialists and diagnostic system specialists, regional sales directors and independent manufacturers' representatives. The United States field sales organization markets and sells products to more than 4,000 home health care dealer branch locations throughout that country. The direct sales force receives a base salary, plus commissions, while the independent sales representatives receive higher commissions but no base salary.

ResMed also promotes and markets the products directly to sleep clinics. Patients who are diagnosed with OSA and prescribed CPAP treatment are typically referred by the diagnosing sleep clinic to a home health care dealer to fill the prescription. The home health care dealer, in consultation with the referring physician, will assist the patient in selecting the equipment, fit the patient with the appropriate mask and set the flow generator pressure to the prescribed level. In the United States the sales employees and manufacturers' representatives are managed by two regional sales managers, a director of sales and ultimately the senior vice-president, US sales and marketing.

The Canadian and Latin American sales are conducted through independent distributors. Sales in North America and Latin America accounted for 48 per cent, 49 per cent and 52 per cent of the net revenue for fiscal years 2003, 2002 and 2001 respectively.

Europe

ResMed markets its products in most major European countries. It has wholly owned subsidiaries in the United Kingdom, Germany, France, Spain, Austria, Finland and Sweden, and uses independent distributors to sell its products in other areas of Europe. Distributors are selected in each country based on their knowledge of respiratory medicine and a commitment to SDB therapy. In each country in which ResMed has a subsidiary a local senior manager is responsible for direct national sales.

The executive vice-president is responsible for the coordination of all European activities and, in conjunction with local management, the direct sales activity in Europe. Sales in Europe accounted for 42 per cent, 42 per cent and 39 per cent of the total net revenue for fiscal years 2003, 2002 and 2001 respectively. As a result of ResMed's acquisition of the German MAP, the company expects European sales to increase as a percentage of total net revenue in the near future.

Australia/rest of the world

Marketing in Australia and the rest of the world is the responsibility of the executive vice-president. Sales in Australia and the rest of the world accounted for 10 per cent, 9 per cent and 9 per cent of the total net revenue for the fiscal years ended 30 June 2003, 2002 and 2001 respectively.

Other marketing efforts

In addition to its sales efforts, ResMed works with the following organizations to promote public and clinical awareness of SDB and OSA:

- *National Stroke Association*: ResMed has developed a strategic alliance with the National Stroke Association to increase awareness about the high prevalence of SDB in the stroke survivor population.
- *American Heart Association:* It is working closely with the western affiliates of the American Heart Association on a number of local programmes to increase awareness and education about SDB. It is also in discussions with the national American Heart/American Stroke associations regarding national programmes, initially targeting clinicians on the impact of SDB on both heart disease and stroke patients, as well as its role in the development of hypertension, a major risk factor for both heart disease and stroke.
- *National Sleep Foundation:* The National Sleep Foundation is a non-profit organization dedicated to improving public health and safety by raising the level of awareness and education of sleep-related programmes and research. ResMed has been an active corporate partner and has supported the National Sleep Foundation for a number of years. The company believes that the affiliations and continued work with these organizations raises the awareness of SDB as a significant health concern.

Risks

The risks and uncertainties that may affect ResMed include the following.

ResMed's inability to compete successfully in its markets may harm its business. The markets for ResMed's SDB products are highly competitive. Competitors have greater financial R&D, manufacturing and marketing resources than ResMed. The past several years have seen a trend towards consolidation in the health care industry and in the markets for ResMed's products. Industry consolidation could result in greater competition if its competitors combine their resources or if competitors are acquired by other companies with greater resources than ResMed's. This competition could increase pressure on ResMed to reduce the selling prices of products or could cause it to increase its spending on R&D and sales and marketing. If it is unable to develop innovative new products, maintain competitive pricing, and offer products that consumers perceive to be as reliable as those of competitors, ResMed sales or gross margins could decrease, which would harm its business.

The business depends on its ability to market effectively to dealers of home health care products and sleep clinics. ResMed markets products primarily to home health care dealers and to sleep clinics that diagnose OSA and other sleep disorders. It believes that home health care dealers and sleep clinics play a significant role in determining which brand of CPAP product a patient will use. For example, in the United States, when a physician at a sleep clinic prescribes the use of a CPAP product, the patient typically purchases the product from a home health care dealer. The physician may or may not prescribe a specific brand of CPAP product. If a specific brand is prescribed, ResMed believes the brand prescribed depends upon the brand of CPAP product that is used in the sleep clinic. If a specific brand is not prescribed, the home health care dealer may recommend a specific brand. Occasionally, even if the physician prescribes a specific brand, a home health care dealer may substitute a competitive CPAP product. ResMed has limited resources to market to the more than 2,000 US sleep clinics and the more than 4,000 home health care dealer branch locations, most of which use, sell or recommend several brands of CPAP products. In addition, home health care dealers have experienced price pressures as government and third-party reimbursement have declined for home care products, and home health care dealers are requiring price discounts and longer periods of time to pay for products purchased from them.

On 16 February 2001, ResMed acquired all of the outstanding shares of MAP, located near Munich, Germany. It is currently in the process of integrating its operations with those of MAP. The integration requires significant efforts from both companies. ResMed may find it difficult to integrate the operations but, if it is unsuccessful, it may not realise the anticipated benefits of the MAP acquisition.

ResMed manufacturers substantially all of its products outside the United States and sells a signi-ficant portion of products in non-US markets, subjecting itself to various risks relating to international activities that could adversely affect overall profitability.

Sales outside North and Latin America accounted for approximately 52 per cent, 54 per cent and 57 per cent of their net revenues in fiscal years 2003, 2002 and 2001 respectively.

As a result of the MAP Medizin-Technologie acquisition it expects that sales within these areas will account for over 50 per cent of the company's net revenue in the foreseeable future. The sales outside North America and the operations in Europe, Australia and Asia are subject to several difficulties and risks that are separate and distinct from those ResMed faces in its domestic operations.

The global market for CPAP equipment is growing rapidly. Worldwide sales are rising by 20 per cent annually and should reach $900 million in 2003. ResMed has about 30% of the world market and is gaining share at the expense of its bigger but more diversified rival, Respironics, in Pittsburgh, Pennsylvania, which has a 40 per cent share.

Questions

1. How would you define ResMed's core competences?

2. Make a proposal for a ResMed competitive strategy that is able to capture further market share from Respironics.

Internationalizing the piano business

Steinway & Sons (www.steinway.com) remains one of the best-known producers of concert pianos in the world. Throughout the course of its 150-year history the company has shown a distinctive talent for innovation and quality workmanship, as evidenced by its 120 patents. In an age of mass production Steinway continues to build a limited number of handmade pianos.

Steinway & Sons was founded in 1853 by German immigrant Henry Engelhard Steinway in Manhattan. Henry was a master cabinet maker who built his first piano in the kitchen of his Seesen home in Germany. By the time Henry established Steinway & Sons he had built 482 pianos. The first piano produced by the company, number 483, was sold to a New York family for $500. It is now displayed in New York City's Metropolitan Museum of Art.

By 1860 Steinway & Sons had built a manufacturing facility at 52nd Street and Fourth Avenue. Here 350 men produced 30 square pianos and five grand pianos per week. In 1864 the firm opened a showroom on 14th Street. In 1865 sales topped $1,000,000.

From the beginning Steinway & Sons faced intense competition from rivals such as Chickering & Sons and Mason & Hamlin in the United States, and Erard and Broadway in Europe. Facing this competition, the firm sought to highlight not only the unique construction of the Steinway piano but its 'superior' sound.

Music historians consider the competition at the 1867 Paris Exhibition the turning point in the piano industry because it was there that the 'American' system of cast-iron frames, heavier strings, solid construction and more powerful tone took the competitive honours from European pianos. The jury awarded Steinway the prestigious 'Grand Gold Medal of Honour' for excellence in manufacturing and engineering. With this recognition, Steinway's domestic piano sales and exports grew rapidly,

requiring greater production capacity. In 1870 the firm purchased 400 acres of remote farmland in Queens with the idea of moving the factory from Manhattan. By 1873 the new factory was operating.

Virtually its own town, Steinway Village had its own foundries, factory, post office, parks and housing for employees. In 1875 the firm opened a showroom in London. In 1885, to build an early global presence, the firm built a factory in Hamburg, Germany. Pianos manufactured there were marketed in Europe and exported to the rest of the world. Today these two factories remain the firm's only manufacturing centres.

Steinway had a steady growth until the world economy entered a depression in the 1930s and the firm's survival was at stake. To market pianos to people of more modest means, with smaller homes, Steinway developed and introduced two new models – the 5ft 1in-'baby grand' and a 40-in upright piano. At the outbreak of the Second World War, production was stopped.

In the 1960s new competition emerged from Asia. Yamaha and Kawai began exporting thousands of pianos to the United States. A Yamaha piano sold for about one-half the price of the equivalent size Steinway model. By the early 1970s the Japanese threat raised questions about the future of Steinway & Sons and the entire US piano industry.

In 1972 the firm was acquired by CBS and merged into the CBS Musical Instruments Division. CBS sold

Steinway & Sons and the rest of its musical instruments division in December 1985 to John and Robert Birmingham, two brothers from Boston who had made their fortune through a family-owned heating-oil business.

In 1991 Steinway & Sons introduced a new line – the Boston pianos – designed to compete in the mid-range piano market. This line was designed by Steinway & Sons and manufactured at Kawai's factory in Japan. Steinway dealers had suggested that a logical step-up strategy to a Steinway piano was needed. The availability of many competent lower-prices pianos made making a Steinway sale to a novice pianist harder to justify.

Kawai is the second largest piano manufacturer in Japan after Yamaha. While the Boston piano is manufactured under contract by Kawai, Steinway controls the material handling process and owns the designs. Boston designs are not available under any other brand name and are distributed only by Steinway.

On 25 May 1995 Steinway & Sons merged with the Selmer Company, a manufacturer of brasswind, woodwind, percussion and stringed instruments, to form Steinway Musical Instruments Inc. The new company's strategy strives to capitalise on its strong brand names and leading market position.

Today

Although best known for handcrafting concert grand pianos that are played by the world's most esteemed musicians, 52 per cent of Steinway's sales come from band and orchestral instruments. Its Selmer subsidiary is the number one US maker of band instruments, including Selmer Paris saxophones, Bach trumpets and trombones, and Ludwig drums. Steinway sells three lines of pianos in three expense ranges (the elite Steinway, the mid-priced Boston, and the new lower-priced Essex) through ten company-owned showrooms and some 200 independent dealers worldwide. Chairman Kyle Kirland and CEO Dana Messina own 85 per cent of Steinway's voting shares.

Through a worldwide network of dealers, Steinway Musical Instrument's products are sold to professional, amateur and student musicians, as well as orchestras and educational institutions. The company employs a workforce of over 2,800. The company's net sales of $353 million for the year ended 31 December 2001 were comprised of $169 million in piano sales and £184 million in band and orchestral instruments sales. The total net income (profit) for Steinway Musical Instruments was $15.2 million in 2001.

Piano sales are influenced by general economic conditions, demographic trends and general interest in music and the arts. The operating results of this segment are primarily affected by Steinway & Sons grand piano sales. Given the total number of these pianos sold in any year (3,319 in 2001), a slight change in units sold can have a material impact on the company's business and operating results. The operating results of the piano segment are also influenced by sales of Boston and Essex pianos, which together represented approximately 50 per cent of total piano units sold and approximately 20 per cent of total piano revenue. The Boston and Essex piano lines are both manufactured in Asia, each by a single manufacturer. The ability of these manufacturers to produce and ship products to Steinway could also materially impact on the company's business and operating results.

The average ex-works unit price for a Steinway piano in 2001 was: $169 million/3,319 units = $51, 000. Prices for the Boston and Essex were lower, whereas prices for the high-end Steinway pianos were higher (up to $110,000).

The Steinway reputation

Though Steinway & Sons never offered to reduce the price of its pianos, it sought endorsements from the social elite. To this and other groups the firm presented itself as offering a high-quality product worthy of a high price. Today the Steinway pianos are the highest priced in the industry. Often the price is nearly double that of an equivalent Yamaha, the firm's most competitive rival in the United States.

Steinway & Sons has consistently emphasised its commitment to the cultural enrichment of the nation and the world. The firm's promotions argue, for example, that the act of buying a piano is not the same as the act of buying a Steinway. Buying a Steinway is depicted as an indication of appreciation for high cultural taste and, hence, a sign of high achievement.

Today more than 95 per cent of all classical music concerts worldwide featuring a soloist are performed on a Steinway concert grand piano. This endorsement has remained stable for many decades.

As we shall see, this high market share at classical music concerts has not resulted in a high overall market share in the piano market. The high reputation of the brand has resulted in many potential Steinway buyers not only being interested in music, but being greatly interested in class and status. Their interest in owning a Steinway would increase if the class and status associated with the Steinway name was emphasised.

Systematically, the firm has broadened the message in its promotions. The firm's advertising has emphasised, for example, that one does not 'buy', but 'invests' in a Steinway, and that a Steinway piano is always made just a little bit better than necessary. Steinway advertising has been targeted to emphasise family values, the contributions to art and music of Steinway & Sons, Steinway's technical excellence, or a combination of these. The 'timeless' excellence of a Steinway has also been emphasised.

International marketing of Steinway pianos

The piano market consists of two important segments – grands and uprights. Grand pianos are larger and give a louder, more resonant sound. The grands are more expensive and the market for such pianos is generally smaller than that for uprights, and fewer firms were involved in their manufacture.

Historically grand pianos have accounted for the bulk of Steinway's production. Grand pianos are at the premium end of the piano market in terms of quality and price, with the Steinway grands dominating the high end of the market. Retail prices in 1996 ranged from $30,000 to $111,000 in the United States.

Steinway pianos are primarily purchased by affluent individuals, highly knowledgeable about pianos with incomes over $120,000 per year. The typical customer is over 45 and has a serious interest in music. Steinway's core customer base consists of professional artists and amateur pianists as well as institutions such as concert halls, conservatories, colleges, universities and music schools. Customers purchase Steinway pianos either through one of the firm's five retail stores or through independently owned dealerships. The institutional segment of the world piano market, which includes music schools, conservatories and universities, represented less than 17 per cent of Steinway's sales. 80–85 per cent of the firm's piano sales are to individuals. In other countries, sales to individuals are a smaller percentage of the total sales.

Approximately 90 per cent of Steinway unit sales were made on a wholesale basis, with the remaining 10 per cent sold directly by Steinway at one of its eight company-owned retail locations (in big cities such as New York, London, Berlin and Hamburg).

Unlike many of its competitors in the piano industry, Steinway does not provide extended financing arrangements to its dealers. To facilitate the long-term financing required by some dealers Steinway has arranged financing through a third-party provider, which generally involves no guarantee by Steinway.

Education as a marketing parameter

Education continues to be an important focus for Steinway & Sons. William Steinway, managing director of Steinway & Sons in the late 1800s, is credited with the development of the Steinway Concert and Artist Program as well as many other successful marketing techniques. To foster this sense of creativity the William Steinway University was created. Through the Bachelors and Masters Programs offered the company provides product knowledge and sales skills to the Steinway & Sons family of dealers.

In order to train its highly skilled technicians to prepare pianos to Steinway & Sons' exacting standards, the company established the C.F. Theodore Steinway Technical Academy. The academy was a series of seminars for experienced piano technicians who wish to upgrade their skills.

New markets in Asia

Since Steinway opened a representative office in Beijing, China in 1999, it has signed agreements with five piano showrooms to represent Steinway & Sons in this market. It expanded this into a Chinese sales subsidiary in 2002. This is the same approach as in Japan – the Asian markets tend to be closed and Steinway's penetration of the Japanese market has been very slow. That was the trigger for setting up a sales subsidiary in Japan. In 1997 Steinway created a Japanese subsidiary to expand its distribution to consumer markets in Japan, one of the largest piano markets in the world. Since that time 23 dealers have been appointed to distribute Steinway & Sons pianos in this market. While the company expected it to take some time to fully develop the market, sales in Japan have more than doubled from 1997 to 2001, with revenue reaching $11 million in 2001.

Steinway also opened its own showroom, as property is at a premium in Japan, and the average piano dealer in Japan has a showroom probably no bigger than a living room. Steinway is still slowly developing its distribution network, and expects the same process to take place in China. In Japan, Steinway is up against high volume producers such as Yamaha, which can make grand pianos a lot more efficiently than Steinway, but cannot make them the same way that Steinway does. In Japan, Steinway charges four times more than Yamaha for a comparably sized piano, and still Steinway sells around 200 grand pianos there each year.

Competition

In the United States

In the 1960s US piano manufacturers were first confronted with Japanese piano imports. The Japanese firms offered consistent-quality pianos at a much lower price than US manufacturers. By the end of the 1960s two Japanese firms, Yamaha and Kawai, were selling 10,000 units annually. Together they captured 5 per cent of US upright piano sales and 28 per cent of US grand piano sales.

The 1980s saw further significant change in the US piano market. Yamaha introduced the first all-digital synthesiser, which could effectively produce a range of high-quality sounds. Yamaha's introduction of the synthesiser effectively undercut the low-end acoustic piano market.

Yamaha uses innovative engineering and automated manufacturing to produce its pianos and markets its pianos worldwide. By the end of the 1980s Yamaha was the world's leading musical instrument maker. It commanded 30 per cent of the world piano market.

As a consequence of the Asian competition several US firms have closed, and currently only two major US firms, Steinway & Sons and Baldwin, continue to make pianos.

Founded in 1862, Baldwin is best known for making grand and upright pianos under the Baldwin, Chickering and Wurlitzer names. It also makes ConcertMaster computerised player pianos and Baldwin Pianovelle digital keyboards. Baldwin has two manufacturing facilities in Arkansas. After selling off 11 of its retail stores and its retail finance business, the company filed for bankruptcy protection in May 2001. Today it is a member of the Gibson musical family.

In Europe

Although German piano manufacturers make high-quality, high-priced pianos they have been severely tested by the low-priced Asian competitors. As a consequence of this competition the number of piano makers has fallen from several hundred to around 10. All surviving firms faced financial difficulties in the 1990s.

Wilhelm Schimmel, Braunschweig, is not among the largest German piano manufacturers. It is a family-owned business run by the third and fourth generation. In 2001 Schimmel had about €25 million in total sales. Schimmel has a close relationship with Yamaha, which has marketed Schimmel pianos in Japan.

While English firms were world piano manufacturers during Steinway's earlier years, today there is little piano making in England. The manufacturing that does occur involves subcontracting from non-British makers. The most prominent is Kemble & Co., a firm that employs 100 people and makes pianos for Yamaha (Japan) and Schiedmeyer (Germany).

Steinway market shares

Though 95 per cent of worldwide concert solos are performed on a Steinway piano Steinway has 'only' a little less than 10 per cent world market share in the grand piano segment. This ranges from less than 1 per cent in China to 22–23 per cent in Switzerland. In the United States Steinway's market share is about 10 per cent. In the late 1980s Yamaha chose to enter the concert piano market in direct competition with Steinway. Developing new grand pianos provided Yamaha with the product offering to attack Steinway's 95 per cent market share in concert sales.

So there are reasons enough to conduct a review of the international marketing strategy of Steinway's grand piano business.

Sources: adapted from:
http://www.cantos.org/Piano/History/marketing.html 'Marketing history of the piano'
http://www.steinway.com
http://www.yamaha.com

Questions

1. Which of the four cases in Figure 3.6 could fit with Steinway's internationalization?

2. What are the core competences of Steinway & Sons?

3. How should Steinway cope with the increasing competition from Japanese manufacturers (such as Yamaha)?

CASE STUDY I.5   Titan Industries Ltd

Is Titan Watches ready for globalization?

Titan Industries Ltd

Titan Industries Ltd (Titan) came into being in 1986, as a venture of TATA, the leading business group of companies in India. The US$10 billion TATA Group is highly diversified, with business interests in automobiles, steel, power, engineering services and goods, chemicals, telecommunications, information technology, plantations, agro-industries, hotels and consumer goods. The TATA Group is internationally known and respected for its ethical business practices – a reputation that has helped the group to forge and cement international business partnerships in all sectors of industry.

Titan's head office is in Bangalore, a city known as the home of multiple computer software companies. The Titan plant is one of the most sophisticated watchmaking plants in India – costing over US$100 million in 1986. It now employs more than 2,500 employees. The plant has five extremely modern and well-equipped factories. The manufacturing of quartz watches and the standard of quality inspection are very stringent and world class. Titan claims that its watches are 'guaranteed to gain/lose no more than 30 seconds in a month'.

Producing around 6 million units of watches and clocks, Titan is presently among the largest integrated watch and jewellery manufacturers in the world. It also produces over 1,500,000 pieces of jewellery annually with the brand name Tanishq. Though Titan began with the objective of catering to the Indian market, it has now become international. It has offices in Australia, Singapore, London and Dubai. The Singapore office handles sales and marketing for countries in the Asia-Pacific region while the London office coordinates the pan-European management, marketing and distribution. The Middle East and Africa are centrally managed from Dubai. Titan continues the traditions of the TATA Group, its parent company. Like its parents,

Titan has transformed itself into a model corporate citizen. For six years, from 1992–1999, it kept its place as India's most admired company in consumer durables. The zenith of Titan was in 2000 when it was voted the most respected brand in India, ahead of such international names as Coca-Cola, Procter & Gamble and Pepsi, etc. The most liked attributes of Titan are its quality and brand image.

Generally, India is expanding its ties with the United States, Japan and western Europe. The Indian government promotes Indian exports aggressively and assists its exporters through a variety of incentives, finances and tax concessions.

Table 1 A financial snapshot of Titan

Financial year	Total sales (US$ million)	Net profits (US$ million)
2002	151	2.8
2001	148	5.0
2000	134	4.1
1999	103	3.6
1998	94	3.1

Note: based on the exchange rate: 1 US$ = Rs47 (Indian rupees) – April 2003.

Source: Titan Financial Reports

The Indian watch market

The Indian watch market has traditionally been a functional market for wristwatches. In a developing country where 40 per cent of the population live in poverty owning a wristwatch is itself a luxury and watches have in the past been bought of as time-keeping, functional devices. Until the arrival of Titan watches were not considered a fashion accessory at all. Naturally, the buying attributes for wristwatches were quality and functionality. For most Indians, wristwatches have also been regarded as durable items that, once bought, would be good for 10 years or until they were beyond repair. Price has been a major buying consideration in the Indian market. For instance, in 1999, watches costing less than Rs450 constituted half the market. Those between Rs450 and Rs1,000 constituted another 30 per cent, leaving only a fifth of the market for watches above Rs1,000.

In 1987 Titan changed the watch market for good. Offering premium quartz watches in a variety of styles, Titan succeeded in turning watch buyers into a style-conscious segment. Since then variety and design have become the attractions for Indians. Of course all this has had to come at a reasonable price. It has been the only way to make Indians buy more watches, and to make them replace old pieces more frequently and as and when fashion changed.

The watch market worldwide is comprised of 60 per cent quartz, 30 per cent digital and 10 per cent mechanical watches. By contrast in India the digital segment is very small (less than 5 per cent). Quartz watches probably account for 75 per cent of the Indian watch market, the rest being mechanical watches; however this is a declining segment.

A major segment of Indian watches is Indian made foreign quartz (IMFQ). Mostly operated by the unorganised sector, IMFQ watches are stylish, fashionable, cheap and disposable. The IMFQ category is driven solely by price, with most of the watches falling in the Rs200–400 price band. Mostly they are bought by children and youngsters and by low-income consumers. Estimated at 18 million pieces a year, this segment has often grown at the expense of the organised quartz watch market. In the last five years this market (in which Titan and Timex, the US watchmaker that was a partner of Titan until 1999) has shrunk by nearly 17 per cent. Timex entered the Indian market through a joint venture with Titan. Initially Titan operated in the high price segment with Timex at the low price end. But later the two companies entered each other's segments: Titan offering low-priced brands and Timex offering high-priced watches. This mixing of product segments was part of the reason for the break-up of the two companies.

The domestic marketing of Titan

Titan began with an undifferentiated marketing strategy in the domestic market. Its main aim was to sell to anyone who had an interest in buying quality and design together in wristwatches. Before Titan Indian consumers could not get quality and design simultaneously in a wristwatch at a reasonable price. Titan's main competitor was HMT (Hindustan Machine Tool), a public sector enterprise also located in Bangalore. HMT no doubt provided quality in wristwatches, but it did not have a marketing drive, or the designs, nor interest in its customers. The Japanese- and Swiss-made watches provided stylish and designs but their quality was suspect, as most of them entered India through 'grey' channels. Titan marketing changed all that. It provided huge competition to both HMT and global brands of watches in India. In fact Titan dwarfed both in a very short time and grew to be the first choice of Indian wristwatch customers.

The brands–segments matrix

Initially Titan sold watches without knowing who was buying them or who wanted more specific features. It graduated to a segmented marketing framework in the mid-1990s. It designed watches for specific segments and created a marketing pull for them through persuasive marketing efforts. It used a broad spectrum of segmentation variables and zeroed in on such demographic segments as male, female, children, businessmen and executives. It then identified segments based on functional as well as lifestyle reasons – marriage, seasonal gifts, multiunit ownership, occasion matching and suiting different seasons, etc.

The modular approach

By the end of 1998 the marketing strategy had the following goals for the Indian market:

- make Titan a mother brand and move it up the value chain;
- align it with international brands;
- enrich the choice range with low-end, independent brands;
- create specific segment subbrands to attract fast-rising children, businessmen, women, etc.
- relaunch existing brands (Royal, Exacta, Raga, etc.);
- create leverage on the Titan brand names for other products including jewellery.

Sensing a huge potential in the IMFQ segment, Titan decided to align itself with a global brand.

The IMFQ players offered flashy watches and more variety at a much lower price to Indian consumers. According to some estimates the segment accounted for as much as 75 per cent of the product category in India in 1999. Thus, assuming the total market size to be 40 million units, the IMFQ watch segment accounted for 20–30 million pieces. The IMFQ players imported watch movements and dials at very cheap prices. With a low-cost, low-overhead operation they were able to sell for as little Rs 350. Titan, due to its own movements manufacturing, was no match for the IMFQ segment. Therefore in 1995–6 Titan forged a joint venture with the US firm Timex, which continued for two years. The lack of success did not deter Titan from pursuing the same path again as better opportunities and options presented themselves. In 1999 the Indian government removed quantitative restrictions on imports, which encouraged Titan to take advantage of this opportunity by either aligning with global brands for distribution, supplying its own brands or even by marketing global brands via its own vast network of retailing.

Retailing power

From the beginning Titan made it a point of its marketing initiatives that its brands were available in as many locations and outlets as possible in India. The result was a vast retail network for Titan, which also included, so Titan claimed, the world's largest chain of exclusive showrooms for watches and jewellery. In 1999 the number of outlets where Titan could be bought exceeded 5,500 in more than 1,500 cities in 33 countries.

Titan's exclusive retail network consisted of two forms of outlets. The first was the World of Titan (WoT) that, up to the end of 1999, was in at 107 locations across 68 towns in India. Each shopper visiting and buying at the WoT was entitled to join the Signet Club, a customer loyalty plan offering additional privileges and benefits. Titan's other retailing outlet was Time Zone. All Titan showrooms were artistically designed and offered courteous service in a spacious and stylish retail ambience. By 1999 the Time Zone outlets were in 52 Indian cities. Since Titan also sold branded jewellery (Tanishq), it set up exclusive Tanishq outlets. These were more exclusive and up-market, premium showrooms and provided a rich ethnic Indian buying experience. The network of Tanishq showrooms covered almost every capital city and major town in India. The Titan retailing network was strongly supplemented by the bigger but very traditional independent watch retailers.

Titan was fairly successful in roping in the independent retailing network in India. In fact it was credited with having broken several traditions in Indian watch retailing. Before Titan's arrival wristwatches in India were never sold in high street shops – interested buyers had to search for specialised watch shops. These shops were poorly styled and lit and had virtually no retailing infrastructure or ambience to retain customers, who wanted to get out of the shop the moment they completed their purchase. Titan revolutionised this by bringing watch retailing in India to the high streets and introducing lifestyle buying. It also made its brands available in all those shops where customer traffic was expected to be higher and more frequent (such as general provision stores, clothes shops, electronics shops, etc.). These shops were fresh, younger looking and were also visited more by younger customers. Titan brands were also available in gift stores and departmental stores, to position them as gift items and encourage impulse purchases. To provide its customers with easy access to enhanced after-sales service Titan has over 350 watch care centres in India and around the world.

Going global

TATA Group, the promoter of Titan, always believed in global markets and in global alliances. This was necessary partly to be in tune with the changing global business environment and partly for business reasons in India. The demand pattern and growth in Indian markets began to mature. In keeping with TATA philosophy, Titan too initiated international forays in the mid-1990s. Titan has segmented its overseas world into four markets: the Middle East and Africa, Europe, the Far East and Australia. In each of these places Titan has an office that coordinates its international operations and promotes the brand image. These offices are also on the look-out to identify international partners and brand alliances. In May 1999 Titan was permitted to participate in the 1999 Basel Fair. It was the first time that Indian exhibitors had been allowed free and unfettered display of their products in the fair. Once in the Fair Titan tried to make the most of the opportunity and put on display its new range of jewellery and watches: Criterion, Concert, Chronata and Fastrack. Visitors, the media and, of course, watch connoisseurs visited the Titan stall and showed an appreciation of its designs and product range. Some retailers also showed their interest in retailing Titan watches in new markets and/or stocking them in more shops in the existing markets.

The global competition

After lording it over the Indian market with no meaningful competition for a decade, the year 1999 was altogether different. In that year the government of India removed quantitative restrictions on the import of watches, movements and parts, which meant that global majors such as Swatch, Citizen, Casio and Seiko could again enter Indian markets and pose a bigger challenge to Titan. Titan saw this as a positive development: in reality the new policy meant both opportunity and challenge. For instance, in the open era of global competition Titan will not be shackled by the need to first create an assembly before launching a product. If it spots an opportunity it can buy the products and put them on the market. On the other hand, the challenge is that the new global entrants might encourage brand switching; this would be at Titan's expense. A positive outcome of this new competition may be that the Indian market itself might grow. More players will create more interest in the product category by their physical presence and their communication. To date, Titan's had been the lone voice; the watch product category was overshadowed by colour televisions, garments and other consumer durables. The collective voice of Titan and global brands such as Swatch and Citizen may excite a new consumer interest in watches.

The dream

By 1999 Titan had begun to see itself as being in the business of personal adornment and as a global brand. It proclaimed in its media interactions that it was ready to move on beyond just wristwatches and jewellery. Its vision was to introduce Titan pens, sunglasses, leather products and more. Titan believed that, for instance, its watch brands for segments such as youth, children and women afforded it a unique opportunity to launch a whole new range of product categories for these segments. For instance, Dash!, the wristwatch for the youngsters, had entrenched itself as a fun children's brand. In other words, Titan could leverage in the children's market, extend itself and offer Dash! books, Dash! electronic toys, Dash! writing materials, etc. Titan officials are confident that they can use their marketing and distribution to sell other products in the personal adornment segment and a whole range of products related to the young – such as music. Four streams are on the agenda in this direction: brand extensions, leveraging Titan's expertise in marketing, retailing and skills in precision engineering areas.

Titan's other dream is to be a global brand. Having defeated domestic competition and having become the most respected brand in India, Titan believes that it is ready to take on the world.

The reality in Europe

Titan entered the European watch market (65 million watches per year) in 1995 in its quest to be a global brand. The rationale was that, as foreign brands were set to flood the Indian market, and given the preference of Indian consumers for things foreign, Titan had to be perceived as an international brand for its survival even in the Indian market. It was also assumed that there would be huge learning arising out of operating in the highly competitive European market.

Titan's European operations are handled by its associate company in London, Titan International Marketing. The Titan brand is reasonably well established in Spain, Portugal Greece, Austria and in the United Kingdom. However, the watchmaker's cumulative losses from this foray total close on to US$14 million. Titan admits that the cost of establishing and selling the Titan brand in Europe has been to a high, and considers the loss to be a 'matter of deep concern'. As a consequence, Titan has transferred the Indian manpower employed in managing the European operations from London to its HQ in Bangalore.

While Europe has proved to be a problem, Titan has fared better in other international markets such as the Middle East and Singapore.

Source: prepared by Dr Mohan Lal Agrawal, Professor of Marketing, XLRI Jamshedpur (India) and Associate Professor Svend Hollensen. Inputs for the case were sourced from a variety of public media.

Questions

1. Can Titan launch a true global brand?
2. What will be the criteria needed to examine its preparedness to become a global brand?
3. In what ways does a national brand differ from a global brand?
4. How should Titan solve its problems in Europe?

Deciding which markets to enter

PART II

Part II   Contents

Chapter 5   Global marketing research
Chapter 6   The political and economic environment
Chapter 7   The sociocultural environment
Chapter 8   The international market selection process

Case studies

II.1   CarLovers Carwash
Serendipity as a factor in foreign market selection: the case of CarLovers from Australia

II.2   Female Health Company (FHC)
The female condom is seeking a foothold in the world market for contraceptive products

II.3   Tipperary Mineral Water Company
Market selection inside/outside Europe

II.4   Beverage Brands
Planning an international raid with the FABs (flavoured alcoholic beverages)

II.5   Village Roadshow/AOL Time Warner
Globalization of the theme park business

Part II   Introduction

After considering the initial phase (Part I, The decision whether to internationalize) the structure of this part follows the process of selecting the 'right' international market. First of all, Chapter 5 presents the most important international marketing research tools for analysing the internal and external environment. Then the political and economic environment (Chapter 6) and the sociocultural environment (Chapter 7) are used as inputs to the process from which the output is the target market(s) that the firm should select as a basis for development of the international marketing mix (see Part IV). The structure of Part II is shown in Figure 1.

Figure 1 The structure and process of Part II

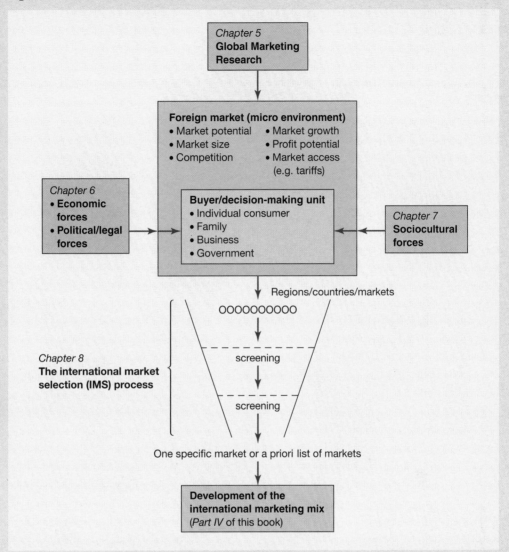

As Figure 1 shows, the research tools presented in Chapter 5, and the forces in Chapters 6 and 7, provide the environmental framework that is necessary for the following:

■ the selection of the right market(s) (Chapter 8);
■ the subsequent development of the global marketing mix.

The discussion following Chapters 6 and 7 will be limited to the major macro environmental dimensions affecting market and buyer behaviour and thus the global marketing mix of the firm.

5 Global marketing research

Contents

Learning objectives

After studying this chapter you should be able to do the following:

■ Explain the importance of having a carefully designed international information system.

■ Link global marketing research to the decision-making process.

■ Discuss the key problems in gathering and using international market data.

■ Distinguish between different research approaches, data sources and data types.

■ Discuss opportunities and problems with qualitative market research methods.

■ Understand how online surveys are carried out.

■ Understand the relevance of the World Wide Web as an important data source in global marketing research.

5.1   Introduction

Information is a key ingredient in the development of successful international marketing strategies. Lack of familiarity with customers, competitors and the market environment in other countries, coupled with the growing complexity and diversity of international markets makes it increasingly critical to collect information in relation to these markets.

In contrast to a researcher concerned with only one country, an international market researcher has to deal with a number of countries that may differ considerably in a number of important ways. Therefore many international marketing decisions are concerned with priorities and allocation of resources between countries.

The prime function of global marketing is to make and sell what international buyers want, rather than simply selling whatever can be most easily made. Therefore what customers require must be assessed through marketing research and/or through establishing a decision support system, so that the firm can direct its marketing activities more effectively by fulfilling the requirements of the customers.

The term 'marketing research' refers to gathering, analysing and presenting information related to a well-defined problem. Hence the focus of marketing research is a specific problem or project with a beginning and an end.

Marketing research differs from a decision support system (DSS), which is information gathered and analysed on a continual basis. In practice, marketing research and DSS are often hard to differentiate, so they will be used interchangeably in this context.

5.2   The changing role of the international researcher

The role of international market research is primarily to act as an aid to the decision maker. It is a tool that can help to reduce the risk in decision making caused by the environmental uncertainties and lack of knowledge in international markets. It ensures that the manager bases a decision on the solid foundation of knowledge and focuses strategic thinking on the needs of the marketplace rather than the product.

Earlier marketing research was regarded as a staff function and not a line function. Marketing researchers had little interaction with marketing managers and did not participate in marketing decision making. Likewise, external providers of marketing research had little interaction with marketing managers. However, as we have moved into the new millennium this line of demarcation between marketing research and marketing, and thus the distinction between marketing researchers and marketing managers, is becoming thinner and thinner.

As the line and staff boundary blurs marketing managers are becoming increasingly more involved in marketing research. This trend towards making marketing research more of a line function, rather than a staff function, is likely to continue and even accelerate in the near future where 'sense and respond' will increasingly characterise firms' approach to business. Thus the traditional marketing researcher in a commercial firm narrowly focused on the production of presentations and reports for management will become a rare breed. The transition of marketing researchers to researchers-cum-decision makers has already begun. Indeed some of the most effective researchers of customer satisfaction are not only participating in decision making but are also deployed as part of the team to implement organizational changes in response to customer satisfaction surveys.

The availability of better decision tools and decision support systems is facilitating the transition of research managers to decision makers. Senior managers can now directly access internal and external secondary data from computers and Internet sites around the world.

In this millennium good marketing researchers will be good marketing managers, and vice versa.

5.3   Linking global marketing research to the decision–making process

Global marketing research should be linked to the decision-making process within the firm. The recognition that a situation requires action is the initiating factor in the decision-making process.

Even though most firms recognise the need for domestic marketing research this need is not fully understood for global marketing activities. Most SMEs conduct no international market research before they enter a foreign market. Often decisions concerning entry into and expansion in overseas markets and the selection and appointment of distributors are made after a subjective assessment of the situation. The research done is usually less rigorous, less formal and less quantitative than in LSEs. Furthermore, once an SME has entered a foreign market, it is likely to discontinue any research of that market. Many business executives therefore appear to view foreign market research as relatively unimportant.

A major reason that firms are reluctant to engage in global marketing research is a lack of sensitivity to cross-cultural customer tastes and preferences. What information should the global marketing research/DSS provide?

Table 5.1 summarises the principal tasks of global marketing research, according to the major decision phases of the global marketing process. As can be seen, both internal (firm-specific) and external (market) data are needed. The role of a firm's internal information system in providing data for marketing decisions is often forgotten.

How the different types of information affect the major decisions are thoroughly discussed in the different parts and chapters of this book. Besides the split between

Table 5.1 Information for the major global marketing decisions

Global marketing decision phase	Information needed
1. Deciding whether to internationalize	Assessment of global market opportunities (global demand) for the firm's products
	Commitment of the management to internationalize
	Competitiveness of the firm compared to local and international competitors
	Domestic versus international market opportunities
2. Deciding which markets to enter	Ranking of world markets according to market potential of countries/regions
	Local competition
	Political risks
	Trade barriers
	Cultural/psychic 'distance' to potential market
3. Deciding how to enter foreign markets	Nature of the product (standard versus complex product)
	Size of markets/segments
	Behaviour of potential intermediaries
	Behaviour of local competition
	Transport costs
	Government requirements
4. Designing the global marketing programme	Buyer behaviour
	Competitive practice
	Available distribution channels
	Media and promotional channels
5. Implementing and controlling the global marketing programme	Negotiation styles in different cultures
	Sales by product line, sales force customer type and country/region
	Contribution margins
	Marketing expenses per market

internal and external data, the two major sources of information are primary data and secondary data:

- *Primary data*. These can be defined as information that is collected first-hand, generated by original research tailor-made to answer specific current research questions. The major advantage of primary data is that the information is specific ('fine grained'), relevant and up to date. The disadvantages of primary data are, however, the high costs and amount of time associated with its collection.
- *Secondary data*. These can be defined as information that has already been collected for other purposes and is thus readily available. The major disadvantage is that the data are often more general and 'coarse grained' in nature. The advantages of secondary data are the low costs and amount of time associated with its collection. For those who are unclear on the terminology, secondary research is frequently referred to as 'desk research'.

The two basic forms of research (primary and secondary) will be discussed in further detail later in this chapter.

If we combine the split of internal/external data with primary/secondary data, it is possible to place data in four categories. In Figure 5.1 this approach is used to categorise indicator variables for answering the following marketing questions. Is there a market for the firm's product A in country B? If yes, how large is it and what is the possible

Figure 5.1 Categorisation of data for assessment of market potential in a country

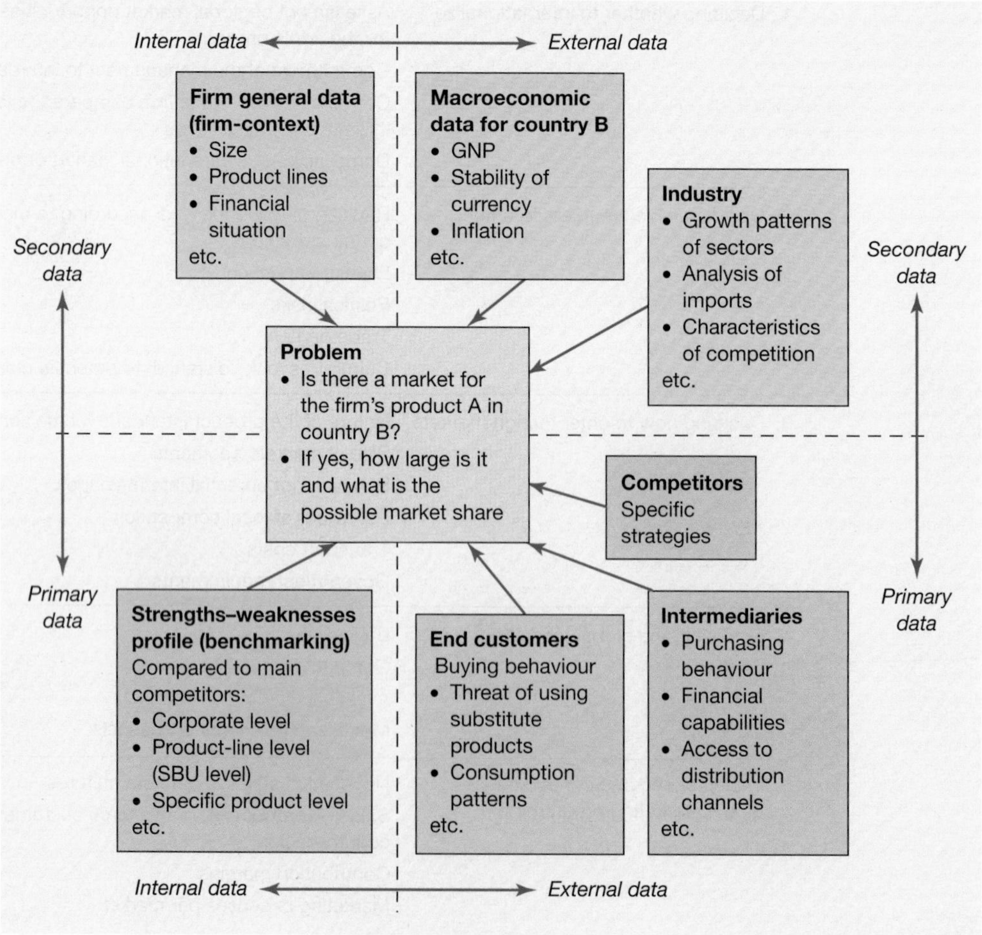

market share for the firm? Note that in Figure 5.1 only a limited number of indicator variables are shown. Of course the one-market perspective in Figure 5.1 could be expanded, to cover not only country B (as in Figure 5.1) but a range of countries, e.g. the EU.

As a rule, no primary research should be done without first searching for relevant secondary information, and secondary data should be used whenever available and appropriate. Besides, secondary data often help to define problems and research objectives. In most cases, however, secondary sources cannot provide all the information needed and the company must collect primary data.

In Figure 5.1 the most difficult and costly kind of data to obtain is probably the strengths–weaknesses profile of the firm (internal and primary data). However, because it compares the profile of the firm with those of its main competitors, this quadrant is a very important indicator of the firm's international competitiveness. The following two sections discuss different forms of secondary and primary research.

With many international markets to consider it is essential that firms begin their market research by seeking and utilising secondary data.

5.4   Secondary research

Advantages of secondary research in foreign markets

Secondary research conducted from the home base is less expensive and less time consuming than research conducted abroad. No contacts have to be made outside the home country, thus keeping commitment to possible future projects at a low level. Research undertaken in the home country about the foreign environment also has the benefit of objectivity. The researcher is not constrained by overseas customs. As a preliminary stage of a market-screening process secondary research can quickly generate background information to eliminate many countries from the scope of enquiries.

Disadvantages of secondary research in foreign markets

Problems with secondary research in foreign countries are as follows:

- *Non-availability of data*. In many developing countries secondary data are very scarce. These weak economies have poor statistical services – many do not even carry out a population census. Information on retail and wholesale trade is especially difficult to obtain. In such cases primary data collection becomes vital.
- *Reliability of data*. Sometimes political considerations may affect the reliability of data. In some developing countries governments may enhance the information to paint a rosy picture of the economic life in the country. In addition, due to the data collection procedures used, or the personnel who gathered the data, many data lack statistical accuracy. As a practical matter, the following questions should be asked to judge effectively the reliability of data sources (Cateora, 1993, p. 346):
  - Who collected the data? Would there be any reason for purposely misrepresenting the facts?
  - For what purpose was the data collected?
  - How was the data collected (methodology)?

- Are the data internally consistent and logical in the light of known data sources or market factors?

■ *Data classification.* In many countries the data reported are too broadly classified for use at the micro level.

■ *Comparability of data.* International marketers often like to compare data from different countries. Unfortunately the secondary data obtainable from different countries are not readily comparable because national definitions of statistical phenomena differ from one country to another. The term 'supermarket', for example, has a variety of meanings around the world. In Japan a supermarket is quite different from its UK counterpart. Japanese 'supermarkets' usually occupy two- or three-storey structures; they sell daily necessities such as foodstuff, but also clothing, furniture, electrical home appliances and sporting goods, and they have a restaurant.

In general the availability and accuracy of recorded secondary data increase as the level of economic development increases. However, there are many exceptions: India is at a lower level of economic development than other countries but has accurate and complete development of government-collected data.

Although the possibility of obtaining secondary data has increased dramatically the international community has grown increasingly sensitive to the issue of data privacy. Readily accessible, large-scale databases contain information valuable to marketers but considered privileged by the individuals who have provided the data. The international marketer must therefore also pay careful attention to the privacy laws in different nations and to the possible consumer response to using such data. Neglecting these concerns may result in research backfiring and the corporate position being weakened.

In doing secondary research or building a decision support system there are many information sources available. Generally these secondary data sources can be divided into internal and external sources (Figure 5.1). The latter can be classified as either international/global or regional/country-based sources.

Internal data sources

Internal company data can be a most fruitful source of information. However, it is often not utilised as fully as it should be.

The global marketing and sales departments are the main points of commercial interaction between an organization and its foreign customers. Consequently a great deal of information should be available, including the following:

■ *Total sales.* Every company keeps a record of its total sales over a defined time period: for example, weekly records, monthly records and so on.

■ *Sales by country.* Sales statistics should be split up by countries. This is partly to measure the progress and competence of the export manager or the salesperson (sometimes to influence earnings because commission may be paid on sales) and partly to measure the degree of market penetration in a particular country.

■ *Sales by products.* Very few companies sell only one product. Most companies sell a range of products and keep records for each kind of product or, if the range is large, each product group.

■ *Sales volume by market segment.* Such segmentation may be geographical or by type of industry. This will give an indication of segment trends in terms of whether they are static, declining or expanding.

■ *Sales volume by type of channel distribution.* Where a company uses several different distribution channels it is possible to calculate the effectiveness and profitability of each type of channel. Such information allows marketing management to identify and develop promising channel opportunities, and results in more effective channel marketing.

■ *Pricing information.* Historical information relating to price adjustments by product allows the organization to establish the effect of price changes on demand.

■ *Communication mix information.* This includes historical data on the effects of advertising campaigns, sponsorship and direct mail on sales. Such information can act as a guide to the likely effectiveness of future communication expenditure plans.

■ *Sales representatives' records and reports.* Sales representatives should keep a visit card or file on every 'live' customer. In addition, sales representatives often send reports to the sales office on such matters as orders lost to competitors and possible reasons why, as well as on firms that are planning future purchasing decisions. Such information could help to bring improvements in marketing strategy.

External data sources

A very basic method of finding international business information is to begin with a public library or a university library. The Internet can also help in the search for data sources. The Internet has made available thousands of databases for intelligence research (i.e. research on competitors). In addition, electronic databases carry marketing information ranging from the latest news on product development to new thoughts in the academic and trade press and updates in international trade statistics. However, the Internet will not totally replace other sources of secondary data. Cost compared to data quality will still be a factor influencing a company's choice of secondary data sources.

International/global sources (web addresses)

The links to the international data sources may be reached at **www.booksites.net/ hollensen**

Secondary data used for estimation of foreign market potential

Secondary data are often used to estimate the size of potential foreign markets. In assessing current product demand and forecasting future demand reliable historical data are required. As previously mentioned, the quality and availability of secondary data are frequently inadequate. Nevertheless estimates of market size must be attempted in order to plan effectively. Despite limitations there are approaches to forecasting future demand in a market with a minimum of information. A number of techniques are available (see Craig and Douglas, 2000), but here only two are further explained: lead–lag analysis and estimation by analogy.

Lead–lag analysis

This technique is based on the use of time-series data from one country to project sales in other countries. It assumes that the determinants of demand in the two countries are the same, and that only time separates them. This requires that the diffusion process and specifically the rate of diffusion is the same in all countries. Of course this is not always the case, and it seems that products introduced more recently diffuse more quickly (Craig and Douglas, 2000).

Figure 5.2 shows the principle behind the lead–lag analysis with an illustrative example in the DVD market. By the end of 2003 it is assumed that 55 per cent of the

Figure 5.2 Lead–lag analysis of penetration of DVDs (Digital Versatile Discs) in the USA and Italy (illustrative examples)

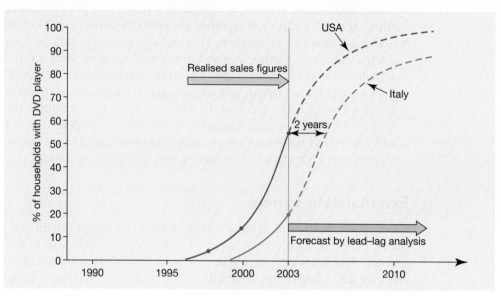

US households will have at least one DVD in their home, whereas it is assumed that 'only' 20 per cent of the Italian households will have a DVD. We define the time-lag between the American and the Italian DVD market as two years. So if we were to estimate the future penetration of DVDs in Italian households (and as a consequence also demand) we could make a parallel displacement of the S-formed US penetration curve by two years, as illustrated in Figure 5.2. This also shows how rapidly new products today are diffused from market to market. The difficulty in using the lead–lag analysis includes the problem of identifying the relevant time lag and the range of factors that impact future demand. However, the technique has considerable intuitive appeal to managers and is likely to guide some of their thinking.

When data are not available for a regular lead–lag analysis, estimation by analogy can be used.

Estimation by analogy

This is essentially a single-factor index with a correlation value (between a factor and demand for a product) obtained in one country applied to a target international market. First a relationship (correlation) must be established between the demand to be estimated and the factor, which is to serve as the basis for the analogy. Once the known relationship is established the correlation value then attempts to draw an analogy between the known situation and the market demand in question.

Example

We want to estimate the market demand for refrigerators in Germany. We know the market size in the United Kingdom but we do not know it in Germany.

As nearly all households in the two countries already have a refrigerator, a good correlation could be number of households or population size in the two countries. In this situation we choose to use population size as the basis for the analogy:

Population size in the United Kingdom: 60 million
Population size in Germany: 82 million
Furthermore we know that the number of refrigerators sold in the United Kingdom in 2002 was 1.1 million units.

Then by analogy we estimate the sales to be the following in Germany:

$$(82/60) \times 1.1 \text{ million units} = 1.5 \text{ million units}$$

Generally caution must be used with 'estimation by analogy' because the method assumes that factors other than the correlation factor used (in this example population size) are similar in both countries, such as the same culture, buying power of consumers, tastes, taxes, prices, selling methods, availability of products, consumption patterns and so forth. Despite the apparent drawbacks to analogy it is useful where international data are limited.

5.5   Primary research

Qualitative and quantitative research

If a marketer's research questions are not adequately answered by secondary research it may be necessary to search for additional information in primary data. These data can be collected by qualitative and quantitative research. Quantitative and qualitative techniques can be distinguished by the fact that quantitative techniques involve getting data from a large, representative group of respondents.

The objective of qualitative research techniques is to give a holistic view of the research problem, and therefore these techniques must have a large number of variables and few respondents (illustrated in Figure 5.3). Choosing between quantitative and qualitative techniques is a question of trading off breadth and depth in the results of the analysis.

Figure 5.3 The 'trade-off' in the choice between quantitative and qualitative research

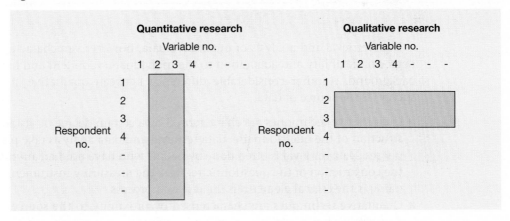

Other differences between the two research methodologies are summarised in Table 5.2. Data retrieval and analysis of quantitative respondent data are based on a comparison of data between all respondents. This places heavy demands on the measuring instrument (the questionnaire), which must be well structured (with different answering categories) and tested before the survey takes place. All respondents are given identical stimuli: that is, the same questions. This approach will not usually give any problems, as long as the respondent group is homogeneous. However, if it is a heterogeneous group of respondents it is possible that the same question will be understood in different ways. This problem becomes especially intensified in cross-cultural surveys.

Table 5.2 **Quantitative versus qualitative research**

Comparison dimension	Quantitative research (e.g. a postal questionnaire)	Qualitative research (e.g. a focus group interview or the case method)
Objective	To quantify the data and generalise the results from the sample to the population of interest	To gain an initial and qualitative understanding of the underlying reasons and motives
Type of research	Descriptive and/or casual	Exploratory
Flexibility in research design	Low (as a result of a standardised and structured questionnaire: one-way communication)	High (as a result of the personal interview, where the interviewer can change questions during the interview: two-way communication)
Sample size	Large	Small
Choice of respondents	Representative sample of the population	Persons with considerable knowledge of the problem (key informants)
Information per respondent	Low	High
Data analysis	Statistical summary	Subjective, interpretative
Ability to replicate with same result	High	Low
Interviewer requirements	No special skills required	Special skills required (an understanding of the interaction between interviewer and respondent)
Time consumption during the research	Design phase: high (formulation of questions must be correct) Analysis phase: low (the answers to the questions can be coded)	Design phase: low (no 'exact' questions are required before the interview) Analysis phase: high (as a result of many 'soft' data)

Data retrieval and analysis of qualitative data, however, are characterised by a high degree of flexibility and adaptation to the individual respondent and his or her special background. Another considerable difference between qualitative and quantitative surveys is the source of data:

- Quantitative techniques are characterised by a certain degree of distance as the construction of the questionnaire, data retrieval and data analysis take place in separate phases. Data retrieval is often done by people who have not had anything to do with the construction of the questionnaire. Here the measuring instrument (the questionnaire) is the critical element in the research process.
- Qualitative techniques are characterised by proximity to the source of data, where data retrieval and analysis are done by the same person, namely, the interviewer. Data retrieval is characterised by interaction between the interviewer and the respondent, where each new question is to a certain degree dependent on the previous question. Here it is the interviewer and his or her competence (or lack of the same) which is the critical element in the research process.

Qualitative techniques imply a less sharp separation between data retrieval and analysis/interpretation, since data retrieval (for example the next question in a personal interview) will be dependent on the interviewer's interpretation of the previous answer. The researcher's personal experience from fieldwork (data retrieval) is generally a considerable input into the analysis phase. In the following section the two most important qualitative research methods are presented.

Triangulation: mixing qualitative and quantitative research methods

Quantitative and qualitative research methods often complement each other. Combined use of quantitative and qualitative research methods in the study of the same phenomenon is termed triangulation (Denzin, 1978; Jick, 1979). The triangulation metaphor is from navigation and military strategy, which use multiple reference points to locate an object's exact position. Similarly, market researchers can improve the accuracy and validity of their judgements by collecting both quantitative and qualitative data. Sometimes qualitative research methods explain or reinforce quantitative findings and even reveal new information.

Sometimes it is relevant to use qualitative data collected by, for example, in-depth interview of a few key informants as exploratory input to the construction of the best possible questionnaire for the collection of quantitative data. In this way triangulation can enrich our understanding of a research question before a structured and formalised questionnaire is designed.

Research design

Figure 5.4 shows that designing research for primary data collection calls for a number of decisions on research approaches, contact methods, sampling plan and research

Figure 5.4 Primary data collection: research design

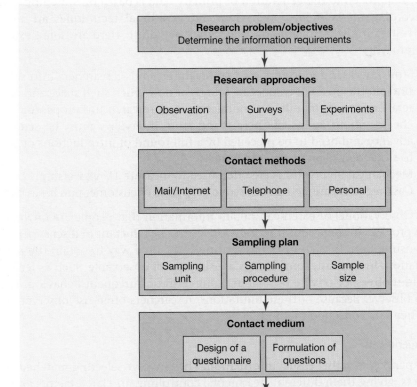

instruments. The following pages will look at the various elements of Figure 5.4 in further detail.

Research problem/objectives

Companies are increasingly recognising the need for primary international research. As the extent of a firm's international involvement increases, so does the importance and complexity of its international research. The primary research process should begin with a definition of the research problem and the establishment of specific objectives. The major difficulty here is translating the business problem into a research problem with a set of specific researchable objectives. In this initial stage researchers often embark on the research process with only a vague grasp of the total problem. Symptoms are often mistaken for causes, and action determined by symptoms may be oriented in the wrong direction.

Research objectives may include obtaining detailed information for better penetrating the market, for designing and fine-tuning the marketing mix, or for monitoring the political climate of a country so that the firm can expand its operations successfully. The better defined the research objective is, the better the researcher will be able to determine the information requirement.

Research approaches

In Figure 5.4 three possible research approaches are indicated: observation, surveys and experiments.

Observation

This approach to the generation of primary data is based on watching and sometimes recording market-related behaviour. Observational techniques are more suited to investigating what people do than why they do it. Here are some examples of this approach:

- Store checks: a food products manufacturer sends researchers into supermarkets to find out the prices of competing brands or how much shelf space and display support retailers give its brands. To conduct in-store research in Europe, for example, store checks, photo audits of shelves and store interviews must be scheduled well in advance and need to be preceded by a full round of introductions of the researchers to store management and personnel.
- Mechanical observations are often used to measure TV viewership.
- Cash register scanners can be used to keep track of customer purchases and inventories.

Observational research can obtain information that people are unwilling or unable to provide. In some countries individuals may be reluctant to discuss personal habits or consumption. In such cases observation is the only way to obtain the necessary information. In contrast, some things are simply not observable, such as feelings, attitudes and motives, or private behaviour. Long-term or infrequent behaviour is also difficult to observe. Because of these limitations, researchers often use observation along with other data collection methods.

Experiments

Experiments gather casual information. They involve selecting matched groups of subjects, giving them different treatments, controlling unrelated factors and checking for differences in group responses. Thus experimental research tries to explain cause-and-effect relationships.

The most used marketing research application of experiments is in test marketing. This is a research technique in which a product under study is placed on sale in one or more selected localities or areas, and its reception by consumers and the trade is observed, recorded and analysed. In order to isolate, for example, the sales effects of advertising campaigns, it is necessary to use relatively self-contained marketing areas as test markets.

Performance in these test markets gives some indication of the performance to be expected when the product goes into general distribution. However, experiments are difficult to implement in global marketing research. The researcher faces the task of designing an experiment in which most variables are held constant or are comparable across cultures. To do so represents a major challenge. For example, an experiment that intends to determine a casual effect within the distribution system of one country may be difficult to transfer to another country where the distribution system is different. As a result experiments are used only rarely, even though their potential value to the international market researcher is recognised.

Surveys

The survey research method is based on the questioning of respondents and represents, both in volume and in value terms, perhaps the most important method of collecting data. Typically the questioning is structured: a formal questionnaire is prepared and the questions are asked in a prearranged order. The questions may be asked verbally, in writing or via a computer.

Survey research is used for a variety of marketing issues, including the following:

- customer attitudes;
- customer buying habits;
- potential market size;
- market trends.

Unlike experimental research, survey research is usually aimed at generating descriptive rather than casual data. Unlike observational research, survey research usually involves the respondent.

Because of the importance and diversity of survey research in global marketing, it is on this particular aspect that we now concentrate.

Contact methods

The method of contact chosen is usually a balance between speed, degree of accuracy and costs. In principle there are three possibilities when choosing a contact method: personal (face-to-face) interviews, telephone interviews and mail surveys. Each method has its own strengths and weaknesses. Table 5.3 gives an overview of these.

Mail/Internet surveys

These can collect a large amount of data that can be quantified and coded into a computer. A low research budget combined with a widely dispersed population may mean that there is no alternative to the mail/Internet survey. However, the major problem is its potentially low response rate.

Telephone interviews

In some ways these are somewhere between personal and mail surveys. They generally have a response rate higher than mail questionnaires but lower than face-to-face interviews, their cost is usually less than with personal interviews, and they allow a degree

Table 5.3 **Strengths and weaknesses of the three contact methods**

Questions/questionnaire	Mail/Internet	Telephone	Personal
Flexibility (ability to clarify problems)	Poor	Good	Excellent
Possibility of in-depth information (use of open-ended questions)	Fair	Fair	Excellent
Use of visual aids	Good	Poor	Good
Possibility of a widely dispersed sample	Excellent	Excellent	Fair
Response rates	Poor	Good	Good
Asking sensitive questions (anonymity of respondent is assumed)	Good	Poor	Fair
Control of interviewer effects (no interviewer bias)	Excellent	Fair	Poor
Speed of data collection	Poor	Excellent	Good
Costs	Good	Excellent	Poor

of flexibility when interviewing. However, the use of visual aids is not possible and there are limits to the number of questions that can be asked before respondents either terminate the interview or give quick (invalid) answers to speed up the process. With computer-aided telephone interviewing (CATI), centrally located interviewers read questions from a computer monitor and input answers via the keyboard. Routeing through the questionnaire is computer controlled, helping the process of interviewing. Some research firms set up terminals in shopping centres, where respondents sit down at a terminal, read questions from a screen and type their answers into the computer.

Personal interviews

Personal interviews take two forms – individual and group interviewing. *Individual interviewing* involves talking with people in their homes or offices, in the street or in shopping arcades. The interviewer must gain the cooperation of the respondents. *Group interviewing* (*focus-group interviewing*) consists of inviting 6 to 10 people to gather for a few hours with a trained moderator to talk about a product, service or organization. The moderator needs objectivity, knowledge of the subject and industry, and some understanding of group and consumer behaviour. The participants are normally paid a small sum for attending.

Personal interviewing is quite flexible and can collect large amounts of information. Trained interviewers can hold a respondent's attention for a long time and can explain difficult questions. They can guide interviews, explore issues and probe as the situation requires. Interviewers can show subjects actual products, advertisements or packages, and observe reactions and behaviour.

The main drawbacks of personal interviewing are the high costs and sampling problems. Group interview studies usually employ small sample sizes to keep time and costs down, but it may be hard to generalise from the results. Because interviewers have more freedom in personal interviews the problem of interviewer bias is greater.

Thus there is no 'best' contact method – it all depends on the situation. Sometimes it may even be appropriate to combine the three methods.

Sampling plan

Except in very restricted markets it is both impractical and too expensive for a researcher to contact all the people who could have some relevance to the research problem. This total number is known statistically as the 'universe' or 'population'. In marketing terms, it comprises the total number of actual and potential users/customers of a particular product or service.

The population can also be defined in terms of elements and sampling units. Suppose that a lipstick manufacturer wants to assess consumer response to a new line of lipsticks and wants to sample females over 15 years of age. It may be possible to sample females of this age directly, in which case a sampling unit would be the same as an element. Alternatively, households might be sampled and all females over 15 in each selected household interviewed. Here the sampling unit is the household, and the element is a female over 15 years old.

What is usually done in practice is to contact a selected group of consumers/customers to be representative of the entire population. The total number of consumers who could be interviewed is known as the 'sample frame', while the number of people who are actually interviewed is known as the 'sample'.

Sampling procedure

There are several kinds of sampling procedure, with probability and non-probability sampling being the two major categories:

- *Probability sampling.* Here it is possible to specify in advance the chance that each element in the population will have of being included in a sample, although there is not necessarily an equal probability for each element. Examples are simple random sampling, systematic sampling, stratified sampling and cluster sampling (see Malhotra (1993) for more information).
- *Non-probability sampling.* Here it is not possible to determine the above-mentioned probability or to estimate the sampling error. These procedures rely on the personal judgement of the researcher. Examples are convenience sampling, quota sampling and snowball sampling (see Malhotra (1993) for more information).

Given the disadvantages of non-probability samples (results are not projectable to the total population, and sampling error cannot be computed) one may wonder why they are used so frequently by marketing researchers. The reasons relate to the inherent advantages of non-probability sampling:

- Non-probability samples cost less than probability samples.
- If accuracy is not critical non-probability sampling may have considerable appeal.
- Non-probability sampling can be conducted more quickly than probability sampling.
- Non-probability sampling, if executed properly, can produce samples of the population that are reasonably representative (e.g. by use of quota sampling) (Malhotra, 1993, p. 359).

Sample size

Once we have chosen the sampling procedure the next step is to determine the appropriate sample size. Determining the sample size is a complex decision and involves financial, statistical and managerial considerations. Other things being equal the larger the sample, the less the sampling error. However, larger samples cost more money, and the resources (money and time) available for a particular research project are always limited.

In addition the cost of larger samples tends to increase on a linear basis, whereas the level of sampling error decreases at a rate only equal to the square root of the relative increase in sample size. For example, if sample size is quadrupled data collection costs will be quadrupled too, but the level of sampling error will be reduced by only one-half. Among the methods for determining the sample size are the following:

- *Traditional statistical techniques* (assuming the standard normal distribution).
- *Budget available.* Although seemingly unscientific this is a fact of life in a business environment, based on the budgeting of financial resources. This approach forces the researcher to consider carefully the value of information in relation to its cost.
- *Rules of thumb.* The justification for a specified sample size may boil down to a 'gut feeling' that this is an appropriate sample size, or it may be a result of common practice in the particular industry.
- *Number of subgroups to be analysed.* Generally speaking the more subgroups that need to be analysed, the larger the required total sample size.

In transnational market research, sampling procedures become a rather complicated matter. Ideally a researcher wants to use the same sampling method for all countries in order to maintain consistency. Sampling desirability, however, often gives way to practicality and flexibility. Sampling procedures may have to vary across countries in order to ensure reasonable comparability of national groups. Thus the relevance of a sampling method depends on whether it will yield a sample that is representative of a target group in a certain country, and on whether comparable samples can be obtained from similar groups in different countries.

Contact medium/measurement instrument

Designing the questionnaire

A good questionnaire cannot be designed until the precise information requirements are known. It is the vehicle whereby the research objectives are translated into specific questions. The type of information sought, and the type of respondents to be researched, will have a bearing upon the contact method to be used, and this in turn will influence whether the questionnaire is relatively unstructured (with open-ended questions), aimed at depth interviewing, or relatively structured (with closed-ended questions) for 'on the street' interviews.

In cross-cultural studies open-ended questions appear useful because they may help to identify the frame of reference of the respondents. Another issue is the choice between direct and indirect questions. Societies have different degrees of sensitivity to certain questions. Questions related to the income or age of the respondent may be accepted differently in different countries. Thus the researcher must be sure that the questions are culturally acceptable. This may mean that questions which can be asked directly in some societies will have to be asked indirectly in others.

Formulation (wording) of questions

Once the researcher has decided on specific types of questions the next task is the actual writing of the questions. Four general guidelines are useful to bear in mind during the wording and sequencing of each question:

- *The wording must be clear.* For example, try to avoid two questions in one.
- *Select words so as to avoid biasing the respondent.* For example, try to avoid leading questions.
- *Consider the ability of the respondent to answer the question.* For example, asking respondents about a brand or store that they have never encountered creates a problem. Since respondents may be forgetful, time periods should be relatively short. For example: 'Did you purchase one or more cola(s) within the last week?'

■ *Consider the willingness of the respondent to answer the question.* 'Embarrasing' topics that deal with things such as borrowing money, sexual activities and criminal records must be dealt with carefully. One technique is to ask the question in the third person or to state that the behaviour or attitude is not unusual prior to asking the question. For example: 'Millions of people suffer from haemorrhoids. Do you or does any member of your family suffer from this problem?'

The impact of language and culture is of particular importance when wording questions. The goal for the global marketing researcher should be to ensure that the potential for misunderstandings and misinterpretations of spoken or written words is minimised. Both language and cultural differences make this issue an extremely sensitive one in the global marketing research process.

In many countries different languages are spoken in different areas. In Switzerland German is used in some areas and French and Italian in others. And the meaning of words often differs from country to country. For example, in the United States the concept of 'family' generally refers only to the parents and children. In the southern part of Europe, the Middle East and many Latin countries it may also include grandparents, uncles, aunts, cousins and so forth.

When finally evaluating the questionnaire, the following items should be considered:

■ Is a certain question necessary? The phrase 'It would be nice to know' is often heard, but each question should either serve a purpose or be omitted.
■ Is the questionnaire too long?
■ Will the questions achieve the survey objectives?

Pretesting

No matter how comfortable and experienced the researcher is in international research activities, an instrument should always be pretested. Ideally such a pretest is carried out with a subset of the population under study, but a pretest should at least be conducted with knowledgeable experts and/or individuals. The pretest should also be conducted in the same mode as the final interview. If the study is to be 'on the street' or in the shopping arcade, then the pretest should be the same. Even though a pretest may mean time delays and additional cost the risks of poor research are simply too great for this process to be omitted.

Data collection

The global marketing researcher must check that the data are gathered correctly, efficiently and at a reasonable cost. The market researcher has to establish the parameters under which the research is conducted. Without clear instructions the interviews may be conducted in different ways by different interviewers. Therefore the interviewers have to be instructed about the nature of the study, start and completion time, and sampling methodology. Sometimes a sample interview is included with detailed information on probing and quotas. Spot checks on these administration procedures are vital to ensure reasonable data quality.

Data analysis and interpretation

Once data have been collected the final steps are the analysis and interpretation of findings in the light of the stated problem. Analysing data from cross-country studies calls for substantial creativity as well as scepticism. Not only are data often limited, but frequently results are significantly influenced by cultural differences. This suggests that there is a need for properly trained local personnel to function as supervisors and interviewers; alternatively international market researchers require substantial advice from knowledgeable local research firms that can also take care of the actual collection of data. Although data in cross-country analyses are often of a qualitative nature the researcher should, of course, use the best and most appropriate tools available for analysis. On the other hand, international researchers should be cautioned against using overly sophisticated tools for unsophisticated data. Even the best of tools will not improve data quality. The quality of data must be matched with the quality of the research tools.

Problems with using primary research

Most problems in collecting primary data in international marketing research stem from cultural differences among countries, and range from the inability of respondents to communicate their opinions to inadequacies in questionnaire translation (Cateora *et al.*, 2000).

Sampling in field surveys

The greatest problem of sampling stems from the lack of adequate demographic data and available lists from which to draw meaningful samples. For example, in many South American and Asian cities street maps are unavailable, and streets are neither identified nor houses numbered. In Saudi Arabia, the difficulties with probability sampling is so acute that non-probabilistic sampling becomes a necessary evil. Some of the problems in drawing a random sample include:

- no officially recognised census of population;
- incomplete and out-of-date telephone directories;
- no accurate maps of population centres, therefore no area samples can be made.

Furthermore, door-to-door interviewing in Saudi Arabia is illegal.

Non–response

Non-response is the inability to reach selected elements in the sample frame. As a result opinions of some sample elements are not obtained or properly represented. A good sampling method can only identify elements who should be selected; there is no guarantee that such elements will ever be included.

The two main reasons for non-response errors are as follows:

- *Not being at home.* In countries where males are still dominant in the labour force it may be difficult to contact a head of household at home during working hours. Frequently only housewives or servants are at home during the day.
- *Refusal to respond.* Cultural habits in many countries virtually prohibit communication with a stranger, particularly for women. This is the case in the Middle East, much of the Mediterranean area and throughout most of south-east Asia – in fact wherever strong traditional societies persist. Moreover, in many societies such matters as preferences for hygienic products and food products are too personal to be shared with an outsider. For example, in many Latin American countries a woman may feel ashamed to talk with a researcher about her choice of brand of sanitary towel, or even hair shampoo or perfume. Respondents may also suspect that the interviewers are agents of the government, seeking information for the imposition of additional taxes. Finally, privacy is becoming a big issue in many countries: for example, in Japan the middle class is showing increasing concern about the protection of personal information.

Language barriers

This problem area includes the difficulty of exact translation that creates problems in eliciting the specific information desired and in interpreting the respondents' answers.

In some developing countries with low literacy rates written questionnaires are completely useless. Within some countries the problem of dialects and different languages can make a national questionnaire survey impractical – this is the case in India, which has 25 official languages.

The obvious solution of having questionnaires prepared or reviewed by someone fluent in the language of the country is frequently overlooked. In order to find possible translation errors marketers can use the technique of *back translation*, where the questionnaire is translated from one language to another, and then back again into the original language. For example, if a questionnaire survey is going to be made in France, the English version is translated into French and then translated back to English by a different translator. The two English versions are then compared and, where there are differences, the translation is checked thoroughly.

Measurement

The best research design is useless without proper measurements. A measurement method that works satisfactorily in one culture may fail to achieve the intended purpose in another country. Special care must therefore be taken to ensure the *reliability* and *validity* of the measurement method.

If we measure the same phenomenon over and over again with the same measurement device and we get similar results then the method is reliable. There are three types of validity: construct, internal and external.

Construct validity

Construct validity establishes correct operational measures for the concepts being studied. If a measurement method lacks construct validity it is not measuring what it is supposed to.

Internal validity

Internal validity establishes a causal relationship, whereby certain conditions are shown to lead to other conditions.

External validity

External validity is concerned with the possible generalisation of research results to other populations. For example, high external validity exists if research results obtained for a marketing problem in one country will be applicable to a similar marketing problem in another country. If such a relationship exists it may be relevant to use the analogy method for estimating market demand in diffrent countries. Estimating by analogy assumes, for example, that the demand for a product develops in much the same way in countries that are similar.

The concepts of reliability and validity are illustrated in Figure 5.5. In the figure, the bull's eye is what the measurement device is supposed to 'hit'.

Situation 1 shows holes all over the target, which could be due to the use of a bad measurement device. If a measurement instrument is not reliable there are no circumstances under which it can be valid. However, just because an instrument is reliable, the instrument is not automatically valid. We see this in *situation 2*, where the instrument

Figure 5.5 Illustrations of possible reliability and validity situations in measurement

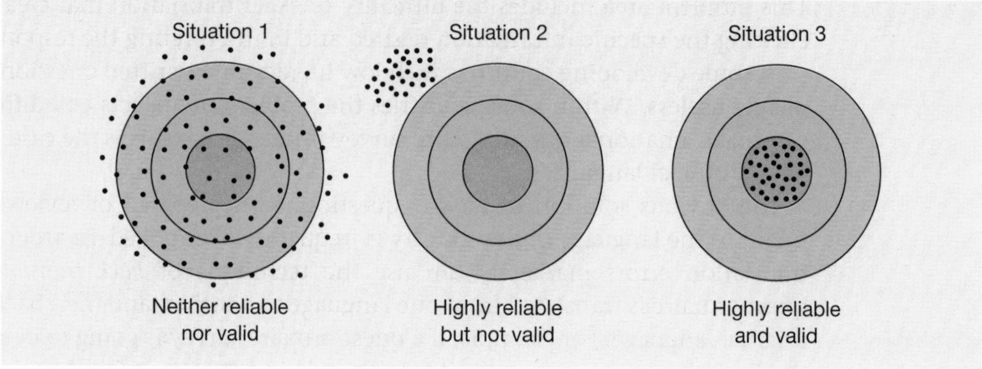

Source: McDaniel and Gates, 1993, p. 372.

is reliable but is not measuring what it is supposed to measure. The shooter has a steady eye, but the sights are not adjusted properly. *Situation 3* is the ideal situation for the researcher to be in. The measurement method is both reliable and valid.

An instrument proven to be reliable and valid in one country may not be so in another culture. The same measurement scales may have different reliabilities in different cultures because of various levels of consumers' product knowledge. Therefore it may be dangerous simply to compare results in cross-country research. One way to minimise the problem is to adapt measurement scales to local cultures by pretesting measures in each market of interest until they show similar and satisfactory levels of reliability.

However, as different methods may have varying reliabilities in different countries, it is essential that these differences can be taken into account in the design of a multicultural survey. Thus, a mail survey could be most appropriate to use in country A and personal interviews in country B. In collecting data from different countries it is more important to use techniques with equivalent levels of reliability than to use the same techniques across countries.

Exhibit 5.1   Gathering and interpreting information in Asia-Pacific

The Asia-Pacific market has been highlighted as a key market area for this decade, so obtaining reliable information in the region is of crucial importance to companies wishing to develop these markets. However, a recent survey by Lasserre (1993), with results from 167 European marketing and planning executives operating in the Asia-Pacific region, found that only in Japan, Singapore and Hong Kong were companies able easily to access data that were viewed as being of good quality (see Figure 5.6)

Vietnamese data, in particular, are not trusted by researchers. The fact that Vietnam is characterised by an almost total lack of reliable data on virtually every aspect of doing business is confirmed by Dang and Speece (1996). The infrastructure to support marketing research is very bad in Vietnam. For example, telephones are rare and government development plans hope to reach a telephone density of 5 per cent by the year 2002. As mail is also a very difficult and slow contact method face-to-face interviews seem to be the only way to learn something about what potential Vietnamese customers think and want.

The most important data sources in Asia-Pacific are the personal sources of companies (primary research, whether from customers, from other business relations or from their own in-house surveys). The importance of primary research confirms the widely held opinion that business in Asia-Pacific depends more heavily on the network of personal relationships than on analysis of hard data (secondary research).

Figure 5.6 Information base in Asia–Pacific

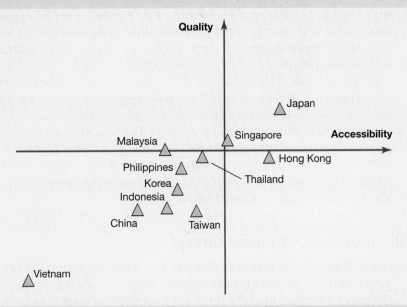

Source: Lasserre, 1993, p. 57.

This pattern is valid from country to country, with the exception of Japan, where secondary data are both accessible and of good quality. The only problem for western firms here seems to be the cost of acquiring it. Government data sources are also important in Singapore. Generally, however, personal contacts and in-house surveys are very important data sources in Asia-Pacific.

Source: Reprinted from *Long Range Planning*, Vol. 26, No. 3, Lasserre, P. (1993) 'Gathering and interpreting strategic intelligence in Asia Pacific', p. 57, Copyright 1993, with permission from Elsevier.

5.6   Online (Internet) primary research methods

Although the Internet is still confined to the boundaries of the personal computer screen this will soon be a thing of the past; it is now clear that the Internet is definitely going to be a medium for the masses. Many researchers are amazed at how efficiently surveys can be conducted, tabulated and analysed on the Web. Additionally, online data collection lets marketers use complex study designs once considered either too expensive or too cumbersome to execute via traditional means. While initial forays were fraught with technical difficulties and methodological hurdles recent developments have begun to expose the medium's immense potential.

The earliest online tools offered little more than the ability to deploy paper-based questionnaires to Internet users. Today, however, online tools and services are available with a wide range of features at a wide range of prices.

For the international market researcher the major advantages and disadvantages of online surveys are the following (Grossnickle and Raskin, 2001).

Advantages of online surveys

- *Low financial resource implications*: The scale of the online survey is not associated with finance, i.e., large-scale surveys do not require greater financial resources than small surveys. Expenses related to self-administered postal surveys are usually in the form of outward and return postage, photocopying, etc., none of which is associated with online surveys.
- *Short response time*: Online surveys allow questionnaires to be delivered instantly to their recipients, irrespective of their geographical location. Fast survey execution allows for most interviews to be completed within a week or so.
- *Saving time with data collection and analysis*: The respective questionnaire can be programmed so that responses can feed automatically into the data analysis software (SPSS, SAS, Exel, etc.), thus saving time and resources associated with data entry process. Furthermore, this avoids associated data transcription errors.
- Visual stimuli can be evaluated, unlike CATI.

Disadvantages of online surveys

- *Respondents have no physical addresses*: The major advantage of postal over online surveys is that respondents have physical addresses, whereas yet not everyone has an electronic address. Especially is this an international marketing research problem in geographical areas where the penetration of the Internet is not as high as in Europe and North America. For cross-country surveys the multimode approach (i.e. a combination of online and postal survey) compensates for the misrepresentation of the general population.
- *Guarding respondents' anonymity*: Traditional mail surveys have advantages in guarding respondents' anonymity. Sensitive issues, which may prevent respondents from giving sincere answers, should be addressed via the post rather than online.
- *Time necessary to download pages*: Problems may arise with older browsers, which failed to properly display HTML questionnaires, with the appearance of the questionnaires in different browsers (Internet Explorer, Netscape)

Online quantitative market research (e-mail and Web-based surveys)

Online surveys can be conducted through e-mail or they can be posted on the Web and the URL provided (a password is optional depending on the nature of the research) to the respondents who have already been approached. When a wide audience is targeted the survey can be designed as a pop-up survey, which would appear as a Web-based questionnaire in a browser window while users are browsing the respective websites. Such a Web-based survey is appropriate for a wide audience, where all the visitors to certain websites have an equal chance to enter the survey.

However, the researcher's control over respondents entering the Web-based surveys is lower than for e-mail surveys. One advantage of Web-based surveys is the better display of the questionnaire, whereas e-mail software still suffers from certain limitations in terms of design tools and offering interactive and clear presentation. However, these two modes of survey may be mixed, combining the advantages of each (Ilieva *et al.*, 2002).

Online qualitative market research

There are many interesting opportunities to conduct international qualitative market research quickly and at relatively low cost, without too much travelling involved (Scholl *et al.*, 2002).

- *Saving money on travelling costs, etc*: Many qualitative researchers often have to travel to countries in which research is conducted, briefing local moderators and viewing some groups or holding interviews to get a grasp of the local habits and attitudes. This leads to high travelling costs and increases the time needed to execute the field-work. It usually takes one or two weeks to recruit the respondents, and one or two weeks before the analysis can start. In online research the respondents can be recruited and interviewed from any computer anywhere in the world. Nearly everyone who is connected to the Internet knows how to use chat rooms and they speak English. Fieldwork may start two days after briefing, and the analysis may start right after the last interview on the basis of complete and accurate transcripts, with each comment linked to the respective respondent.
- *Cross-country qualitative research*: International online research is particularly inter-esting for multinational companies that sell their products on a global scale and are afraid to build the global marketing strategy on research which has been conducted in only a few of these countries. Online qualitative research could serve as an addi-tional multicountry check. This is not intended to give insight into the psychology of customers but rather to check whether other countries or cultures may add to the general picture, which has been made on the basis of qualitative face-to-face research.

One of the limitations with, e.g., online focus groups is that they seem to generate less interaction between members than the face-to-face groups. Discussions between respondents occur, but they are less clear and coherent.

5.7   Other types of marketing research

A distinction is made between ad hoc and continuous research.

Ad hoc research

An ad hoc study focuses on a specific marketing problem and collects data at one point in time from one sample of respondents. Examples of ad hoc studies are usage and atti-tude surveys, and product and concept tests via custom-designed or multiclient studies. More general marketing problems (e.g. total market estimates for product groups) may be examined by using Delphi studies.

Custom-designed studies

These are based on the specific needs of the client. The research design is based on the research brief given to the marketing research agency or internal marketing researcher. Because they are tailor-made such surveys can be expensive.

Multiclient studies

These are a relatively low-cost way for a company to answer specific questions without embarking on its own primary research. There are two types of multiclient study:

- *Independent research studies*. These are carried out totally independently by research companies (e.g. Frost and Sullivan) and then offered for sale.
- *Omnibus studies*. Here a research agency will target specified segments in a particular foreign market and companies will buy questions in the survey. Consequently

interviews (usually face to face or by telephone) may cover many topics. Clients will then receive an analysis of the questions purchased. For omnibus studies to be of use the researcher must have clearly defined research needs and a corresponding target segment in order to obtain meaningful information.

Delphi studies

This type of research approach clearly aims at qualitative rather than quantitative measures by aggregating the information of a group of experts. It seeks to obtain answers from those who possess particular in-depth expertise instead of seeking the average responses of many with only limited knowledge.

The area of concern may be future developments in the international trading environment or long-term forecasts for market penetration of new products. Typically 10–30 key informants are selected and asked to identify the major issues in the area of concern. They are also requested to rank their statements according to importance and explain the rationale behind the ranking. Next the aggregated information is returned to all participants, who are encouraged to state clearly their agreements or disagreements with the various rank orders and comments. Statements can be challenged and then, in another round, participants can respond to the challenges. After several rounds of challenge and response a reasonably coherent consensus is developed.

One drawback of the technique is that it requires several steps, and therefore months may elapse before the information is obtained. However the emergence of e-mail may accelerate the process. If done properly the Delphi method can provide insightful forecast data for the international information system of the firm.

Continuous research (longitudinal designs)

A longitudinal design differs from ad hoc research in that the sample or panel remains the same over time. In this way a longitudinal study provides a series of pictures that give an in-depth view of developments taking place. The panel consists of a sample of respondents who have agreed to provide information at specified intervals over an extended period.

There are two major types of panel:

■ *Consumer panels*. These provide information on their purchases over time. For example, a grocery panel would record the brands, pack sizes, prices and stores used for a wide range of supermarket brands. By using the same households over a period of time measures of brand loyalty and switching can be achieved, together with a demographic profile of the type of person or household who buys particular brands.
■ *Retailer panels*. By gaining the cooperation of retail outlets (e.g. supermarkets) sales of brands can be measured by laser scanning the bar codes on goods as they pass through the checkout. Although brand loyalty and switching cannot be measured in this way retail audits can provide accurate assessments of sales achieved by store. A major provider of retail data is the A.C. Nielsen company.

Sales forecasting

A company can forecast its sales either by forecasting the market sales (called *market forecasting*) and then determining what share of this will accrue to the company or by forecasting the company's sales directly. Techniques for doing this are dealt with later in the chapter. The point is that planners are only interested in forecasts when the forecast comes down to individual products in the company.

We shall now examine the applicability and usefulness of the short-, medium- and long-term forecasts in so far as company planners are concerned and shall then look at each from individual company departmental viewpoints.

■ *Short-term forecasts*. These are usually for periods up to three months ahead, and as such are really of use for tactical matters such as production planning. The general trend of sales is less important here than short-term fluctuations.

■ *Medium-term forecasts*. These have direct implications for planners. They are of most importance in the area of business budgeting, the starting point for which is the sales forecast. Thus if the sales forecast is incorrect the entire budget is incorrect. If the forecast is over-optimistic then the company will have unsold stocks which must be financed out of working capital. If the forecast is pessimistic then the firm may miss out on marketing opportunities because it is not geared up to produce the extra goods required by the market. More to the point is that when forecasting is left to accountants they will tend to err on the conservative side and will produce a forecast that is less than actual sales, the implications of which have just been described. This serves to re-emphasise the point that sales forecasting is the responsibility of the sales manager. Such medium-term forecasts are normally for one year ahead.

■ *Long-term forecasts*. These are usually for periods of three years or more depending on the type of industry being considered. In industries such as computers 3 years is considered long term, whereas for steel manufacture 10 years is a long-term horizon. They are worked out from macroenvironmental factors such as government policy, economic trends, etc. Such forecasts are needed mainly by financial accountants for long-term resource implications, but such matters of course are boards of directors' concerns. The board must decide what its policy is to be in establishing the levels of production needed to meet the forecast demand; such decisions might mean the construction of a new factory and the training of a workforce. Forecasts can be produced for different horizons, starting at an international level and then ranging down to national levels, by industry and then by company levels until we reach individual product-by-product forecasts. This is then broken down seasonally over the time span of the forecasting period, and geographically right down to individual salesperson areas. It is these latter levels that are of specific interest to sales management, or it is from this level of forecasting that the sales budgeting and remuneration system stems.

Figure 5.7 shows an example of trend forecasting.

Figure 5.7 An example of trend forecasting

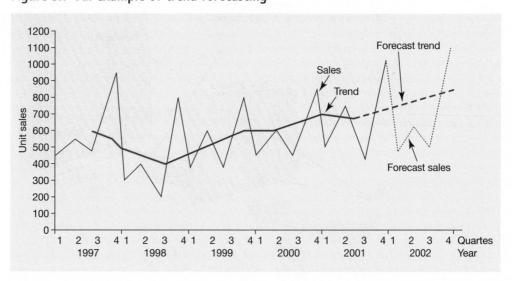

The unit sales and trend are drawn in as in Figure 5.7. The trend line is extended by sight (and it is here that the forecaster's skill and intuition must come in). The deviations from trend are then applied to the trend line, and this provides the sales forecast.

In this particular example it can be seen that the trend line has been extended slowly upwards, similar to previous years. The technique, as with many similar techniques, suffers from the fact that downturns and upturns cannot be predicted, and such data must be subjectively entered by the forecaster through manipulation of the extension to the trend line.

Scenario planning

Scenarios are diverging – but plausible – views of the future. They differ from forecasts in that they explore possible futures rather than predict a single point future. Figure 5.8 shows two different scenarios – A and B – where the outcome – measured on two dimensions – is influenced by both convergent and diverging forces.

Figure 5.8 shows that the diverging and converging factors have to be balanced. Time flows from the left to the right. The courses of the scenarios pass through a number of time windows, each made up of the key dimensions the scenario writers want to highlight. In Figure 5.8 two 'time windows' are shown: One in two years from now and another one in five years from now. The two dimensions could be e.g. 'worldwide market share' and 'worldwide market growth' for one of the company's main product. The 'convergent forces' would mean that Scenario A and B would come nearer to each other over time. The 'divergent forces' would have the opposite effect.

Examples of convergent forces would be:

- High degree of macroeconomic stability in key international markets.
- Increasing standardization of product across borders.

Scenario planning allows us to consider a range of 'alternative futures', each of which is dramatically different from the other and from the current operating environment. Rather than rely on a single 'most likely' forecast it is possible to compare and contrast alternative opinions on how your industry may evolve.

Figure 5.8 Development of scenarios A and B over time

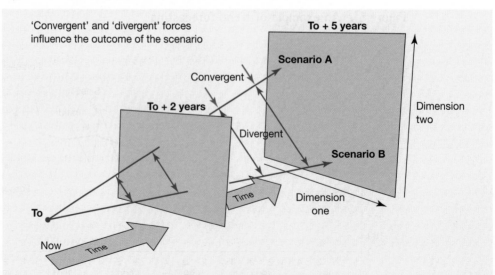

Since it is externally oriented scenario planning is very effective at identifying growth strategies for the company as well as potential threats to its market position. Scenarios can also help to identify the specific external industry changes that are causing falling market share or margins.

Guidelines for scenario planning

- *Establish a core planning team.* Analysing the strategic implications of scenarios is best done in teams. The creative dynamics of an effective group are likely to provide the types of breakthrough that will make the scenario process worthwhile. What seems obvious to one person will be surprising to another. A good rule of thumb is to have five to eight people in the planning group.
- *Get a cross-section of expertise.* Include the heads of all functional areas – sales, marketing, operations, purchasing, information technology, personnel, etc. We also recommend including individuals beyond the top executives. This injects new perspectives on your company or your line of trade. This is a great time to involve the rising stars and innovative thinkers in the organization.
- *Include outside information and outside people.* Focus on injecting interesting and challenging perspectives into the discussion. In a group composed solely of insiders it will be hard to achieve breakthrough insights. Outsiders may be customers, suppliers or consultants. If possible, involve an executive from another line of trade or even from outside wholesale distribution. However, many executives feel uncomfortable letting outsiders participate in the planning process of their companies.

5.8 Summary

The basic objective of the global marketing research function is to provide management with relevant information for more accurate decision making. The objective is the same for both domestic and global marketing. However, global marketing is more complex because of the difficulty of gathering information about multiple and different foreign environments.

In this chapter, special attention has been given to the information collection process and the use of marketing information. This coverage is far from being exhaustive, and the reader should consult marketing research textbooks for specific details related to particular research topics.

An international marketer should initiate research by searching first for any relevant secondary data. Typically a great deal of information is already available, and the researcher needs to know how to identify and locate the international sources of secondary data.

If it is necessary to gather primary data the international marketer should be aware that it is simply not possible to replicate elsewhere the methodology used in one country. Some adaptation of the research method to different countries is usually necessary.

The firm should set up a decision support system to handle the gathered information efficiently. This system should integrate all information inputs, both internal and external. However, in the final analysis, every international marketer should keep in mind that an information system is no substitute for sound judgement.

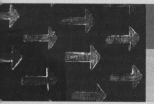

CASE STUDY 5.1   Teepack Spezialmaschinen GmbH

Organizing a global survey of customer satisfaction

Teepack (**www.teepack.com**) is a specialised manufacturer of tea bag machines for the world's best-known brands of tea and herbs and fruit teas, such as Lipton, Pickwick, Twinnings and Lyons/Tetley.

Teepack is a sister company of Teekanne,[1] the leading tea, herb, and fruit tea packing company in Germany, with the Teefix, Pompadour and Teekanne brands.

The invention of the automatic tea bag-packaging machine by Teepack in 1949 revolutionised the tea market with the double-chamber tea bag. It meant that production volumes could be increased dramatically. Today the latest generation of these machines is capable of production speeds of almost 400 tea bags per minute, i.e. some 4 billion per year.

The tea bag produced on Teepack machines is the most sold double-chamber tea bag in the world. Important benefits are that it has considerably larger space between the two bag chambers and offers maximum tea bag stability and durability without adding glue or heat sealing.

The popularity of this practical tea bag has continued to grow, for example in Germany 82 per cent of tea sales are in double-chamber tea bags; in the United States the figure is about 90 per cent and in Europe, if you omit the United Kingdom, the figure is close to 100 per cent. Even in the former UK colony, Australia, the double-chamber tea bag has almost convinced the consumers. 'Down under', sales of UK tea bags and the double-chamber tea bag more or less balance themselves out.

For over 50 years Teepack GmbH has been the number one producer of double-chamber tea bag packaging machines in the world and has sold more than 2,000 of its packaging machine 'Constanta'. Thanks to Teepack's packaging machines Lipton is the market leader of the international tea market. Up to 1957 Teepack had sold more than 100 tea bag packaging machines in the United States.

Technical innovation resulted in Teepack engineers developing a new, even more efficient machine – 'Perfecta'. Since 1990 more than 200 'Perfecta' machines have been sold worldwide.

Today Teepack has a market share of about 70 per cent of the global double chamber tea bag machine market.

Questions

(Please visit **www.teepack.com** before you answer the questions.)

1. How would you forecast worldwide demand for tea bag machines?

2. Argue the case for the market analysis method you would choose if you had to evaluate the competitiveness of Teepack Spezialmaschinen on the global tea bag packaging machine market.

3. In order to achieve better customer feedback, the top management of Teepack is interested in learning how to measure customer satisfaction. Propose a questionnaire design that contains some of the themes which it would be relevant to include in the questionnaire.

4. How would you organise the internal database with the customers' responses and the feedback of the questionnaire results to the customers?

---

[1] The Teekanne Group has production and sales subsidiaries in several countries. There are about 1,300 employees in the Group.

CASE STUDY 5.2 Tchibo

Expanding the coffee shops' business system in the United Kingdom and the rest of Europe

Tchibo Frisch-Röst-Kaffee GmbH (Hamburg, Germany) was founded in 1949 by Max Herz. Tchibo was originally set up as a mail order company. At that time Tchibo sent coffee by post. The original mail-order coffee company has grown into a multinational enterprise, active in many more sectors than just traditional coffee retailing. For example, at the end of 2003 Tchibo was one of the top two online shops in Germany.

The first Tchibo specialist coffee shop with coffee counter service opened in Hamburg in 1955. The idea was that customers would have the chance to try the coffee before they bought a whole packet. This idea has been consistently developed ever since.

The retailing concept typical of Tchibo combines sales of roasted coffee with counter sales of coffee specialities, surrounded by an attractive merchandise world that changes every week.

Table 1 shows the Tchibo coffee shops in Europe Tchibo is market leader in the German, Austrian, Czech, Hungarian and Polish household roasted coffee market with its coffee brands Tchibo, Gala von Eduscho and local brands. This success is partly based on the systematic development of a business 'system', which combines Tchibo roasted coffee and coffee bar sales with a rich variety of innovative consumer merchandise and services. The product range in this business system is being developed on a continual basis and expanded by offering innovative weekly changing new products. Tchibo's uniqueness is emphasized by the fact that not all products are offered at the same time but that the assortment changes 52 times a year. The motto 'A new experience every week' enables Tchibo to surprise its customers every Wednesday with introduction of a new theme, made of around 25 products.

In the United Kingdom, Tchibo has successfully opened about 30 coffee shops mainly in the Greater London area.

Tchibo is planning to expand its business system in the United Kingdom. However, in order to develop the right promotion to the right customer group, Tchibo asks you as an international marketing consultant to answer the following questions.

Questions

1. Which market analysis should be made in the United Kingdom in order to target the right promotion campaign to the right customer group?

2. How would you estimate the potential market for coffee shops (in general) in Europe?

3. How will you use market analysis methods for estimating the possible European market share of Tchibo coffee shops?

Table 1 Tchibo Coffee shops in Europe in 2003

Country	Number of coffee shops
Germany	around 250
United Kingdom	around 30
Switzerland	around 20
Austria	around 160
Poland	around 10

Source: Tchibo.

Questions for discussion

1. Explore the reasons for using a marketing information system in the international market. What are the main types of information you would expect to use?

2. What are some of the problems that a global marketing manager can expect to encounter when creating a centralised marketing information system? How can these problems be solved?

3. What are the dangers of translating questionnaires (which have been designed for one country) for use in a multicountry study? How would you avoid these dangers?

4. Identify and classify the major groups of factors that must be taken into account when conducting a foreign market assessment.

5. A US manufacturer of shoes is interested in estimating the potential attractiveness of China for its products. Identify and discuss the sources and the types of data that the company will need in order to obtain a preliminary estimate.

6. Identify and discuss the major considerations in deciding whether research should be centralised or decentralised.

7. Distinguish between internal and external validity. What are the implications of external validity for international marketers?

8. Would Tokyo be a good test market for a new brand planned to be marketed worldwide? Why or why not?

9. If you had a contract to conduct marketing research in Saudi Arabia what problems would you expect in obtaining primary data?

10. Do demographic variables have universal meanings? Is there a chance that they may be interpreted differently in different cultures?

11. In forecasting sales in international markets, to what extent can the past be used to predict the future?

12. How should the firm decide whether to gather its own intelligence or to buy it from outside?

References

Cateora, P.R. (1993) *International Marketing* (8th edn), Irwin, Homewood, IL.

Cateora, P.R., Graham, J.L. and Ghauri, P.N. (2000), *International Marketing*, European Edition, McGraw-Hill Publishing Company, England.

Craig, S.C. and Douglas, S.P. (2000), *International Marketing Research*, (2nd edn) John Wiley & Sons, England.

Dang, T. and Speece, M. (1996) 'Marketing research in Vietnam', *Journal of International Marketing and Marketing Research*, vol. 21, no. 3, pp. 145–61.

Denzin, N.K. (1978) *The Research Act* (2nd edn), McGraw-Hill, New York.

Grossnickle, J. and Raskin, O. (2001) 'What's ahead on the Internet: new tools, sampling methods, and applications help simplify Web research', *Market Research*, Summer, pp. 9–13.

Jick, T.D. (1979) 'Mixing qualitative and quantitive methods: triangulation in action', *Administrative Science Quarterly*, vol. 24, December, pp. 602–11.

Ilieva, J., Baron, S. and Healey, N.M. (2002) 'Online surveys in marketing research: pros and cons', *International Journal of Market Research*, vol. 44, quarter 3, pp. 361–76.

Lasserre, P. (1993) 'Gathering and interpreting strategic intelligence in Asia Pacific', *Long Range Planning*, vol. 26, no. 3, pp. 55–66.

Malhotra, N.K. (1993) *Marketing Research: An applied orientation*, Prentice-Hall, Englewood Cliffs, NJ.

McDaniel, C. Jr. and Gates, R. (1993) *Contemporary Marketing Research* (2nd edn), West Publishing Co., Minneapolis, MN.

Scholl, N., Mulders, S. and Drent, R. (2002) 'On-line qualitative market research: interviewing the world at a fingertip', *Qualitative Market Research: An International Journal*, vol. 5, no. 3, pp. 210–23.

Further reading

Brown, J., Culkin, N. and Fletcher, J. (2001) 'Human factors in business-to-business research over the Internet', *International Journal of Market Research*, vol. 43, quarter 4, pp. 425–40.

Chowdhury, S. (2003) 'Databases, Data Mining and beyond', *Journal of American Academy of Business*. March, pp. 576–580.

Craig, C.S. and Douglas, S.P. (2000), *International Marketing Research*, Wiley, Chichester.

Demirdjian, Z.S. (2003) 'Marketing Research and Information systems: the Unholy Seperation of the Siamese Twins', *The Journal of American Academy of Business*, Cambridge, pp. 218–23.

Kumar, K. (2000), *International Marketing Research*, Prentice-Hall, Englewood Cliffs, NJ.

McPhee, N. (2002) 'Gaining insight on business and organizational behaviour: the qualitative dimension', *International Journal of Market Research*, vol. 44, quarter 1, pp. 53–70.

Severson, J. (2002) 'What every manager needs to know about consumer research', *Management Quarterly*, Summer, pp. 17–35.

Vyas, R. and Souchon, A.L. (2003) 'Symbolic use of export information', *International Marketing Review*, vol. 20, No. 1, pp. 67–94.

6 The political and economic environment

Contents

Learning objectives

After studying this chapter you should be able to do the following:

- Discuss how the political/legal environment will affect the attractiveness of a potential foreign market.

- Distinguish between political factors in the home country environment and the host country environment.

- Explain the steps in a political risk analysis procedure.

- Distinguish between tariff barriers and non-tariff barriers.

- Describe the major trading blocs.

- Explore why the structure of consumption is different from country to country.

- Explain how managers can influence local politics.

- Define regional economic integration and identify different levels of integration.

- Discuss the benefits and drawbacks associated with regional economic integration.

- Evaluate consequences of the EMU and the euro on European business.

6.1 Introduction

This chapter is devoted to macroenvironmental factors that explain the many forces to which a firm is exposed. The marketer has to adapt to a more or less uncontrollable environment within which they plan to operate. In this chapter the environmental factors in the foreign environment are limited to the political/legal forces and the economic forces.

6.2   The political/legal environment

This section will concentrate mainly on political issues. The political/legal environment comprises primarily two dimensions:

■ the home country environment;
■ the host country environment.

Besides these two dimensions there is also a third:

■ The general international environment (see Figure 6.1).

Figure 6.1 Barriers in the political/legal environment

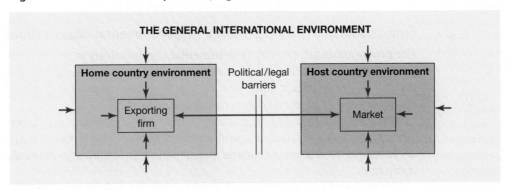

Home country environment

A firm's home country political environment can constrain its international operations as well as its domestic operations. It can limit the countries that the international firm may enter.

The best-known example of the home country political environment affecting international operations was South Africa. Home country political pressure induced some firms to leave the country altogether. After US companies left South Africa the Germans and the Japanese remained as the major foreign presence. German firms did not face the same political pressure at home that US firms had. However, the Japanese government was embarrassed when Japan became South Africa's leading trading partner. As a result some Japanese companies reduced their South African activity.

One challenge facing multinationals is the triple-threat political environment. Even if the home country and the host country do not present problems, they may face threats in third markets. Firms that did not have problems with their home government or the South African government, for example, could be troubled or boycotted about their South African operations in third countries, such as the United States. Today European firms face problems in the United States if they do business in Cuba. Nestlé's problems with its infant formula controversy were most serious, not at home in Switzerland, or in African host countries, but in a third market – the United States.

A third area in which some governments regulate global marketing concerns bribery and corruption. In many countries payments or favours are a way of life, and an 'oiling of the wheels' is expected in return for government services. In the past many companies doing business internationally routinely paid bribes or did favours for foreign officials in order to gain contracts.

Many business managers argue that their home country should not apply its moral principles to other societies and cultures in which bribery and corruption are endemic. If they are to compete globally, these managers argue, they must be free to use the most common methods of competition in the host country. Particularly in industries that face limited or even shrinking markets, such stiff competition forces firms to find any edge possible to obtain a contract.

On the other hand, applying different standards to management and firms, depending on whether they do business abroad or domestically, is difficult to envisage. Also, bribes may open the way for shoddy performance and loose moral standards among managers and employees, and may result in a concentration on how best to bribe rather than on how best to produce and market products.

The global marketer must carefully distinguish between reasonable ways of doing business internationally – including compliance with foreign expectations – and outright bribery and corruption.

Promotional activities (sponsored by governmental organizations)

The programmes adopted by governmental organizations to promote exporting are an increasingly important force in the international environment. Many of the activities involve implementation and sponsorship by government alone, while others are the results of the joint efforts of government and business.

Furthermore, so-called regulatory supportive activities are direct government attempts to make its country's products more competitive in world markets. Also, there are attempts to encourage greater participation in exporting, particularly by smaller companies.

The granting of subsidies is of special interest: export subsidies are to the export industries what tariffs are to domestic industries. In both cases the aim is to ensure the profitability of industries and individual firms that might well succumb if exposed to the full force of competition. For export industries, revenue is supplemented by subsidies, or costs are reduced by subsidies to certain input factors. Subsidies can be given through lower taxes on profits attributable to export sales, refunding of various indirect taxes, etc. Furthermore, a subsidy may take the form of a direct grant, which enables the recipient to compete against companies from other countries that enjoy cost advantages, or may be used for special promotion by recipient companies.

In a broader sense, government export promotion programmes, and programmes for global marketing activities in general, are designed to deal with the following internal barriers (Albaum *et al.*, 2002):

- lack of motivation, as global marketing is viewed as more time consuming, costly and risky, and less profitable, than domestic business;
- lack of adequate information;
- operational/resource-based limitations.

Some of these programmes are quite popular in developing countries, especially if they enjoy the support of the business community.

Financial activities

Through the membership of international financial organizations such as the International Monetary Fund and the World Bank the national government can assume its role as an international banker. The granting of subsidies is another financially based promotional activity of national governments.

One of the most vital determinants of the results of a company's export marketing programme is its credit policy. The supplier that can offer better payment terms and financing conditions may make a sale, even though its price may be higher or the quality of its product inferior to that of its competitors.

If the credit terms are extended, the risks of non-payment increase, and many exporters are reluctant to assume the risks. Consequently, it may be necessary to offer exporters the opportunity of transferring some of the risk to governmental organizations through credit insurance. *Export credit insurance* and guarantees cover certain commercial and political risks that might be associated with any given export transaction.

Information services

Many large companies can collect the information they need themselves. Other firms, even if they do not possess the expertise to do their own research, can afford to hire outside research agencies to do the necessary research. However, a large number of companies are not in a position to take either of these approaches. For these firms, generally smaller companies or newcomers to global marketing, their national government is the major source of basic marketing information.

Although the information relevant for international/export marketers varies from country to country, the following kinds are typically available (Albaum *et al.*, 2002, p. 119–20):

- economic, social and political data on individual countries, including their infrastructure;
- summary and detailed information on aggregate global marketing transactions;
- individual reports on foreign firms;
- specific export opportunities;
- lists of potential overseas buyers, distributors and agents for various products in different countries;
- information on relevant government regulations both at home and abroad;
- sources of various kinds of information not always available from the government: for example, foreign credit information;
- information that will help the company manage its operation: for example, information on export procedures and techniques.

Most types of information are made available to firms through published reports or through the Internet. In addition, government officials often participate in seminars and workshops aimed at helping the international marketer.

Export-facilitating activities

A number of national government activities can stimulate export. These include the following (Albaum *et al.*, 2002, p. 119–20):

- Trade development offices abroad, either as a separate entity or as part of the normal operations of an embassy or consulate.
- Government-sponsored trade fairs and exhibitions. A trade fair is a convenient marketplace in which buyers and sellers can meet, and in which an exporter can display products.
- Sponsoring trade missions of businesspeople who go abroad for the purpose of making sales and/or establishing agencies and other foreign representation.
- Operating permanent trade centres in foreign market areas, which run trade shows often concentrating on a single industry.

From the national government's point of view, each of these activities represents a different approach to stimulating the growth of exports. From the point of view of an individual company, these activities provide relatively low-cost ways of making direct contact with potential buyers in overseas markets.

Promotion by private organizations

Various non-governmental organizations play a role in the promotion of global marketing. These include the following (Albaum *et al.*, 2002, p. 120):

- industry and trade associations, national, regional and sectoral industry associations, associations of trading houses, mixed associations of manufacturers and traders, and other bodies;
- chambers of commerce: local chambers of commerce, national chambers, national and international associations of chambers, national chambers abroad and binational chambers;
- other organizations concerned with trade promotion: organizations carrying out export research, regional export promotion organizations, world trade centres, geographically oriented trade promotion organizations, export associations and clubs, international business associations, world trade clubs and organizations concerned with commercial arbitration
- export service organizations, banks, transport companies, freight forwarders, export merchants and trading companies.

The type of assistance available to firms includes information and publications, education and assistance in 'technical' details, and promotion in foreign countries.

State trading

Many of the former communist countries are now allowing some private trading activities, either through joint ventures or as a result of privatisation of state-owned enterprises. However, there are still countries with active state trading, such as Cuba and to some extent China.

Private businesses are concerned about state trading for two reasons. First, the establishment of import monopolies means that exporters have to make substantial adjustments in their export marketing programmes. Second, if state traders wish to utilise the monopolistic power they possess, private international marketers will have a difficult time.

Host country environment

Managers must continually monitor the government, its policies and its stability to determine the potential for political change that could adversely affect operations of the firm.

Political risks

There is political risk in every nation, but the range of risks varies widely from country to country. In general, political risk is lowest in countries that have a history of stability and consistency. Three major types of political risk can be encountered:

- *ownership risk*, which exposes property and life;
- *operating risk*, which refers to interference with the ongoing operations of a firm;
- *transfer risk*, which is mainly encountered when companies want to transfer capital between countries.

Political risk can be the result of government action, but it can also be outside the control of government. The types of action and their effects can be classified as follows:

- *Import restrictions*. Selective restrictions on the import of raw materials, machines and spare parts are fairly common strategies to force foreign industry to purchase more supplies within the host country and thereby create markets for local industry. Although this is done in an attempt to support the development of domestic industry, the result is often to hamstring and sometimes interrupt the operations of established industries. The problem then becomes critical when there are no adequately developed sources of supply within the country.

- *Local-content laws*. In addition to restricting imports of essential supplies to force local purchase, countries often require a portion of any product sold within the country to have local content: that is, to contain locally made parts. This requirement is often imposed on foreign companies that assemble products from foreign-made components. Local-content requirements are not restricted to Third World countries. The European Union has a 45 per cent local-content requirement for foreign-owned assemblers. This requirement has been important for Far East car producers.

- *Exchange controls*. Exchange controls stem from shortages of foreign exchange held by a country. When a nation faces shortages of foreign exchange, controls may be levied over all movements of capital or, selectively, against the most politically vulnerable companies to conserve the supply of foreign exchange for the most essential uses. A problem for the foreign investor is getting profits and investments into the currency of the home country (transfer risks).

- *Market control*. The government of a country sometimes imposes control to prevent foreign companies from competing in certain markets. Some years ago the US government threatened to boycott foreign firms trading with Cuba. The EU countries have protested against this threat.

- *Price controls*. Essential products that command considerable public interest, such as pharmaceuticals, food, petrol and cars, are often subjected to price controls. Such controls can be used by a government during inflationary periods to control the environmental behaviour of consumers or the cost of living.

- *Tax controls*. Taxes must be classified as a political risk when used as a means of controlling foreign investments. In many cases they are raised without warning and in violation of formal agreements. In underdeveloped countries, where the economy is constantly threatened with a shortage of funds, unreasonable taxation of successful foreign investments appeals to some governments as the most convenient and quickest way of finding operating funds.

- *Labour restrictions*. In many nations labour unions are very strong and have great political influence. Using their strength, unions may be able to persuade the government to pass very restrictive laws that support labour at heavy cost to business. Traditionally labour unions in Latin America have been able to prevent lay-offs and plant shutdowns. Labour unions are gradually becoming strong in western Europe as well. For example, Germany and a number of other European nations require labour representation on boards of directors.

- *Expropriation*. Defined as official seizure of foreign property, this is the ultimate government tool for controlling foreign firms. This most drastic action against foreign firms is fortunately occurring less often as developing countries begin to see foreign direct investment as desirable.

- *Domestication*. This can be thought of as creeping expropriation and is a process by which controls and restrictions placed on the foreign firm gradually reduce the control of the owners. The firm continues to operate in the country while the host government is able to maintain leverage on the foreign firm through imposing different controls. These controls include: greater decision-making powers accorded to nationals; more products produced locally rather than imported for assembly; gradual transfer of ownership to nationals (demand for local participation in joint ventures); and promotion of a large number of nationals to higher levels of management. Domestication provides the host country with enough control to regulate the activities of the foreign firm carefully. In this way, any truly negative effects of the firm's operations in the country are discovered and prompt corrective action may be taken.

Trade barriers from home country to host country

Free trade between nations permits international specialisation. It also enables efficient firms to increase output to levels far greater than would be possible if sales were limited to their own domestic markets, thus permitting significant economies of scale. Competition increases, prices of goods in importing countries fall, while profits increase in the exporting country.

While countries have many reasons for wishing to trade with each other, it is also true to say that all too frequently an importing nation will take steps to inhibit the inward flow of goods and services.

One of the reasons why international trade is different from domestic trade is that it is carried on between different political units, each one a sovereign nation exercising control over its own trade. Although all nations control their foreign trade, they vary in the degree of control. Each nation or trading bloc invariably establishes trade laws that favour its indigenous companies and discriminate against foreign ones.

There are two main reasons why countries levy tariffs:

- *To protect domestic producers*. First, tariffs are a way of protecting domestic producers of a product. Because import tariffs raise the effective cost of an imported good, domestically produced goods can appear more attractive to buyers. In this way domestic producers gain a protective barrier against imports. Although producers receiving tariff protection can gain a price advantage, protection can keep them from increasing efficiency in the long run. A protected industry can be destroyed if protection encourages complacency and inefficiency when it is later thrown into the lion's den of international competition.
- *To generate revenue*. Second, tariffs are a source of government revenue. Using tariffs to generate government revenue is most common among relatively less developed nations. The main reason is that less developed nations tend to have less formal domestic economies that presently lack the capability to record domestic transactions accurately. The lack of accurate record keeping makes the collection of sales taxes within the country extremely difficult. Nations solve the problem by simply raising their needed revenue through import and export tariffs. Those nations obtaining a greater portion of their total revenue from taxes on international trade are mainly the poorer nations.

Trade distortion practices can be grouped into two basic categories: tariff and non-tariff barriers.

Tariff barriers

Tariffs are direct taxes and charges imposed on imports. They are generally simple, straightforward and easy for the country to administer. While they are a barrier to trade they are a visible and known quantity and so can be accounted for by companies when developing their marketing strategies.

Tariffs are used by poorer nations as the easiest means of collecting revenue and protecting certain home industries. They are a useful tool for politicians to show indigenous manufacturers that they are actively trying to protect their home markets.

The most common forms of tariffs are as follows:

- *Specific*. Charges are imposed on particular products, by either weight or volume, and usually stated in the local currency.
- *Ad valorem*. The charge is a straight percentage of the value of the goods (the import price).
- *Discriminatory*. In this case the tariff is charged against goods coming from a particular country, either where there is a trade imbalance or for political purposes.

Non–tariff barriers

In the last 40 years the world has seen a gradual reduction in tariff barriers in most developed nations. However, in parallel to this, non-tariff barriers have substantially increased. Non-tariff barriers are much more elusive and can be more easily disguised. However, in some ways the effect can be more devastating because they are an unknown quantity and are much less predictable.

Among non-tariff barriers the most important (not mentioned earlier) are as follows.

Quotas

A restriction on the amount (measured in units or weight) of a good that can enter or leave a country during a certain period of time is called a *quota*. After tariffs, a quota is the second most common type of trade barrier. Governments typically administer their quota systems by granting quota licences to the companies or governments of other nations (in the case of import quotas), and domestic producers (in the case of export quotas). Governments normally grant such licences on a year-by-year basis.

- *Reasons for import quotas*. There are two reasons why a government imposes *import quotas*. First, it may wish to protect its domestic producers by placing a limit on the amount of goods allowed to enter the country. This helps domestic producers maintain their market shares and prices because competitive forces are restrained. In this case, domestic producers win because of the protection of their markets. Consumers lose because of higher prices and less selection due to lower competition. Other losers include domestic producers whose own production requires the import to be slapped with a quota. Companies relying on the importation of so-called 'intermediate' goods will find the final cost of their own products increases.

  Second, a government may impose import quotas to force the companies of other nations to compete against one another for the limited amount of imports allowed. Thus those wishing to get a piece of the action will likely lower the price that they are asking for their goods. In this case, consumers win from the resulting lower prices. Domestic producers of competing goods win if external producers do not undercut their prices, but lose if they do.
- *Reasons for export quotas*. There are at least two reasons why a country imposes *export quotas* on its domestic producers. First, it may wish to maintain adequate supplies of a product in the home market. This motive is most common among countries exporting natural resources that are essential to domestic business or the long-term survival of a nation.

  Second, a country may restrict exports to restrict supply on world markets, thereby increasing the international price of the good. This is the motive behind the formation and activities of the Organization of Petroleum Exporting Countries

(OPEC). This group of nations from the Middle East and Latin America attempts to restrict the world's supply of crude oil to earn greater profits.

■ *Voluntary export restraints.* A unique version of the export quota is called a voluntary export restraint (VER) – a quota that a nation imposes on its exports usually at the request of another nation. Countries normally self-impose a voluntary export restraint in response to the threat of an import quota or total ban on the product by an importing nation. The classic example of the use of a voluntary export restraint is the automobile industry in the 1980s. Japanese carmakers were making significant market share gains in the US market. The closing of US carmakers' production facilities in the United States was creating a volatile anti-Japan sentiment among the population and the US Congress. Fearing punitive legislation in Congress if Japan did not limit its auto exports to the United States, the Japanese government and its carmakers self-imposed a voluntary export restraint on cars headed for the United States.

Consumers in the country that imposes an export quota benefit from greater supply and the resulting lower prices if domestic producers do not curtail production. Producers in an importing country benefit because the goods of producers from the exporting country are restrained, which may allow them to increase prices. Export quotas hurt consumers in the importing nation because of reduced selection and perhaps higher prices. However, export quotas might allow these same consumers to retain their jobs if imports were threatening to put domestic producers out of business. Again, detailed economic studies are needed to determine the winners and losers in any particular export quota case.

Embargoes

A complete ban on trade (imports and exports) in one or more products with a particular country is called an *embargo*. An embargo may be placed on one or a few goods or completely ban trade in all goods. It is the most restrictive non-tariff trade barrier available and is typically applied to accomplish political goals. Embargoes can be decreed by individual nations or by supranational organizations such as the United Nations. Because they can be very difficult to enforce, embargoes are used less today than in the past. One example of a total ban on trade with another country has been the United States' embargo on trade with Cuba.

Administrative delays

Regulatory controls or bureaucratic rules designed to impair the rapid flow of imports into a country are called *administrative delays*. This non-tariff barrier includes a wide range of government actions such as requiring international air carriers to land at inconvenient airports; requiring product inspections that damage the product itself; purposely understaffing customs offices to cause unusual time delays; and requiring special licences that take a long time to obtain. The objective of such administrative delays for a country is to discriminate against imported products – in a word, it is protectionism.

Although Japan has removed some of its trade barriers many subtle obstacles to imports remain. Products ranging from cold pills and vitamins to farm products and building materials find it hard to penetrate the Japanese market.

Local-content requirements

Laws stipulating that a specified amount of a good or service be supplied by producers in the domestic market are called local-content requirements. These requirements can state that a certain portion of the end product consist of domestically produced goods, or that a certain portion of the final cost of a product have domestic sources.

The purpose of local-content requirements is to force companies from other nations to employ local resources in their production processes – particularly labour. Similar to other restraints on imports, such requirements help protect domestic producers from the price advantage of companies based in other, low-wage countries. Today companies can circumvent local-content requirements by locating production facilities inside the nation stipulating such restrictions.

Historical development of barriers

Non-tariff barriers become much more prevalent in times of recession. The United States and Europe have witnessed the mobilisation of quite strong political lobby groups as indigenous industries, which have come under threat, lobby their governments to take measures to protect them from international competition. The last major era of protectionism was in the 1930s. During that decade, under the impact of the most disastrous trade depression in history, most countries of the world adopted high tariffs.

After the Second World War there was a reaction against the high tariff policy of the 1930s and significant efforts were made to move the world back to free trade. World organizations (such as GATT and its successor, WTO) have been developed to foster international trade and provide a trade climate in which such barriers can be reduced.

The general international environment

In addition to the politics and laws of both the home and the host countries, the marketer must consider the overall international political and legal environment. Relations between countries can have a profound impact on firms trying to do business internationally.

The international political environment involves political relationships between two or more countries. This is in contrast to our previous concern for what happens only within a given foreign country. The international firm almost inevitably becomes somewhat involved with the host country's international relations, no matter how neutral it may try to be. It does so because its operations in a country are frequently related to operations in other countries, either on the supply or the demand side or both. East–West relations are a good example of a situation in the international political environment that is continually evolving.

The effect of politics on global marketing is determined by both the bilateral political relations between home and host countries and the multilateral agreements governing the relations among groups of countries. One aspect of a country's international relations is its relationship with the firm's home country.

A second critical element affecting the political environment is the host country's relations with other nations. If a country is a member of a regional group, such as the European Union or ASEAN, this influences the firm's evaluation of the country. If a nation has particular friends or enemies among other nations, the firm must modify its international logistics to comply with how that market is supplied and to whom it can sell.

Another clue to a nation's international behaviour is its membership of international organizations. Membership of the IMF or the World Bank may aid a country's financial situation, but it also puts constraints on the country's behaviour. Many other international agreements impose rules on their members. These agreements may affect, for example, patents, communication, transportation and other items of interest to the international marketer. As a rule, the more international organizations a country belongs to, the more regulations it accepts, and the more dependable is its behaviour.

Figure 6.2 Three-step process of political risk analysis

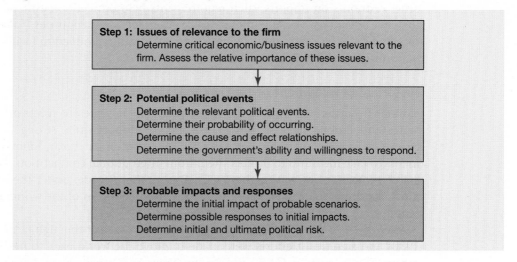

Step 1: Issues of relevance to the firm
Determine critical economic/business issues relevant to the firm. Assess the relative importance of these issues.

Step 2: Potential political events
Determine the relevant political events.
Determine their probability of occurring.
Determine the cause and effect relationships.
Determine the government's ability and willingness to respond.

Step 3: Probable impacts and responses
Determine the initial impact of probable scenarios.
Determine possible responses to initial impacts.
Determine initial and ultimate political risk.

The political risk analysis procedure

We now outline in general terms a procedure for analysing political risk and avoiding the common error of over- or underestimating such risk at the firm level. The goal of this procedure is to help firms make informed decisions based on the ratio of the return to risk, so that firms can enter or stay in a country when the ratio is favourable and avoid or leave a country when the ratio for them is poor. This procedure involves three major steps (Figure 6.2).

Step 1: Assessing issues of relevance to the firm

Clearly, the relevant issues and the magnitude of their importance will vary by firm even within a given country. For one firm the repatriation of profits (and therefore policies and changes that affect that issue) could be the most important. For another firm in the same country repatriation of profits may be less of a concern, but product quality (and therefore policies and changes that affect labour, material or technology) may be of the highest concern.

Step 2: Assessing potential political events

In general, political instability is more likely during greater periods of economic depression. However, the more the event is controllable and the more government is able and willing to exercise control, the lower the probability that the event will have a direct impact on foreign firms.

It is important to estimate not only the probability of a single political event occurring or the confidence with which that prediction is made, but also the sequence of related events. For example, suppose it was highly likely that Russian president Vladimir Putin was going to be replaced by a new president. Would this have any effect on policies on the repatriation of profits, the regulations of exports and other related issues?

Step 3: Assessing probable impacts and responses

Step 3 is really where 'political risk' for the particular firm is assessed. Because political instability in a country does not equal political risk for a firm, the same scenario of politically destabilising events could have very different associated risks for different firms in the same industry or for those in different industries. The fact that firms can be differentially affected by political events because of their unique mix of inputs, outputs and goals reinforces the usefulness of constructing political scenarios rather than single-item forecasts.

Influencing local politics

Managers must be able to deal with the political risks, rules and regulations that apply in each national business environment. Moreover, laws in many nations are susceptible to frequent change, with new laws continually being enacted and existing ones modified. To influence local politics in their favour, managers can propose changes that positively affect their local activities:

- *Lobbying*. Influencing local politics always involves dealing with local lawmakers and politicians, either directly or through lobbyists. Lobbying is the policy of hiring people to represent a company's views on political matters. Lobbyists meet with local public officials and try to influence their position on issues relevant to the company. They describe the benefits that a company brings to the local economy, natural environment, infrastructure and workforce. Their ultimate goal is getting favourable legislation passed and unfavourable legislation rejected.
- *Corruption*. Bribes are one method of gaining political influence. They are routinely used in some countries to get distributors and retailers to push a firm's products through distribution channels. Sometimes they mean the difference between obtaining important contracts and being completely shut out of certain markets.

In summary, the political risk perspective of a nation can be studied using factors such as those in the following list:

- change in government policy;
- stability of government;
- quality of host government's economic management;
- host country's attitude towards foreign investment;
- host country's relationship with the rest of the world;
- host country's relationship with the parent company's home government;
- attitude towards the assignment of foreign personnel;
- closeness between government and people;
- fairness and honesty of administrative procedures.

The importance of these factors varies from country to country and from firm to firm. Nevertheless, it is desirable to consider them all to ensure a complete knowledge of the political outlook for doing business in a particular country.

6.3   The economic environment

Market size and growth are influenced by many forces, but the total buying power in the country and the availability or non-availability of electricity, telephone systems, modern roads and other types of infrastructure will influence the direction of that spending.

Economic development results from one of three types of economic activity:

- *Primary*. These activities are concerned with agriculture and extractive processes (e.g. coal, iron ore, gold, fishing).
- *Secondary*. These are manufacturing activities. There are several evolutions. Typically countries will start manufacturing through processing the output of primary products.
- *Tertiary*. These activities are based upon *services* – for example tourism, insurance and health care. As the average family income in a country rises the percentage of income spent on food declines, the percentage spent on housing and household activities remains constant, and the percentage spent on service activities (e.g. education, transport and leisure) will increase.

How exchange rates influence business activities

Times of crisis are not the only occasions during which companies are affected by exchange rates. In fact movement in a currency's exchange rate affects the activities of both domestic and international companies. Let us now examine how exchange rate changes affect the business decisions of companies, and why stable and predictable rates are desirable.

Exchange rates affect demand for a company's products in the global marketplace. When a country's currency is *weak* (valued low relative to other currencies), the price of its exports on world markets declines and the price of imports increases. Lower prices make the country's exports more appealing on world markets. They also give companies the opportunity to take market share away from companies whose products are highly priced in comparison.

Furthermore, a company selling in a country with a *strong* currency (one that is valued high relative to other currencies) while paying workers in a country with a weak currency improves its profits.

The international lowering of the value of a currency by the nation's government is called devaluation. The reverse, the intentional raising of its value by the nation's government, is called revaluation. These concepts are not to be confused with the terms *weak* and *strong* currencies, although their effects are similar.

Devaluation lowers the price of a country's exports on world markets and increases the price of imports because the country's currency is now worth less on world markets. Thus a government might devalue its currency to give its domestic companies an edge over competition from other countries. It might also devalue to boost exports so that a trade deficit can be eliminated. However, such a policy is not wise because devaluation reduces consumers' buying power. It also allows inefficiencies to persist in domestic companies because there is now less pressure to be concerned with production costs. In such a case, increasing inflation may be the result. Revaluation has the opposite effect: it increases the price of exports and reduces the price of imports.

As we have seen, unfavourable movements in exchange rates can be costly for both domestic and international companies. Therefore, managers prefer that exchange rates be *stable*. Stable exchange rates improve the accuracy of financial planning, including cash flow forecasts. Although methods do exist for insuring against potentially adverse exchange rate movements, most of these are too expensive for small and medium-sized businesses. Moreover, as the unpredictability of exchange rates increases, so too does the cost of insuring against the accompanying risk.

Law of one price

An exchange rate tells us how much of one currency we must pay to receive a certain amount of another. But it does not tell us whether a specific product will actually cost us more or less in a particular country (as measured in our own currency). When we travel to another country we discover that our own currency buys more or less than it does at home. In other words, we quickly learn that exchange rates do not guarantee or stabilise the buying power of our currency. Thus we can lose purchasing power in some countries while gaining it in others.

The law of one price stipulates that an identical product must have an identical price in all countries when price is expressed in a common-denominator currency. For this principle to apply products must be identical in quality and content in all countries, and must be entirely produced within each particular country.

Big Mac Index/Big MacCurrencies

The usefulness of the law of one price is that it helps us determine whether a currency is overvalued or undervalued. Each year *The Economist* magazine publishes what it calls its 'Big MacCurrencies' exchange-rate index (see Table 6.1).

The index is based on the theory of purchasing-power parity (PPP), the notion that a dollar should buy the same amount in all countries. The theory naturally relies on certain assumptions, such as negligible transportation costs, that goods and services must be 'tradable', and that a good in one country does not differ substantially from the same good in another country. Thus, in the long run, the exchange rate between two currencies should move towards the rate that equalises the prices of an identical basket of goods and services in each country. In this case the 'basket' is a McDonald's Big Mac, which is produced in about 120 countries. The Big Mac PPP is the exchange rate that would mean hamburgers cost the same in the United States as abroad. Comparing actual exchange rates with PPP indicates whether a currency is under- or overvalued.

This index uses the law of one price to determine the exchange rate that should exist between the US dollar and other major currencies. It employs the McDonald's Big Mac

Table 6.1 The hamburger standard

	Big Mac prices		Implied PPP[a] of the dollar	Actual dollar exchange rate 22 April 2003	Under (−)/over (+) valuation against the dollar, %
	In local currency	In dollars			
United States	$2.71	2.71			
Argentina	Peso 4.10	1.40	1.51	2.88	−47
Australia	A$3.00	1.80	1.11	1.61	−31
Brazil	Real 4.55	1.44	1.68	3.07	−45
Britain	£1.99	3.08	1.36[b]	1.58[b]	+16
Canada	C$3.20	2.17	1.18	1.45	−18
Chile	Peso 1,400	1.95	517	716	−28
China	Yuan 9.90	1.20	3.65	8.28	−56
Czech Rep	Koruna 56.57	1.91	20.9	28.9	−28
Denmark	DKr27.75	3.99	10.2	6.78	+51
Egypt	Pound 8.00	1.38	2.95	5.92	−50
Euro area	€2.71	2.89	1.00[c]	1.10[c]	+10
Hong Kong	HK$11.50	1.47	4.24	7.80	−46
Hungary	Forint 490	2.14	181	224	−19
Indonesia	Rupiah 16,100	1.81	5,941	8,740	−32
Japan	¥262	2.18	96.7	120	−19
Malaysia	M$5.04	1.33	1.86	3.80	−51
Mexico	Peso 23.00	2.14	8.49	10.53	−19
New Zealand	NZ$3.95	2.15	1.46	1.78	−18
Norway	Kroner 39.5	5.51	14.6	7.16	+64
Peru	New Sol 7.90	2.28	2.92	3.46	−16
Philippines	Peso 65.00	1.23	24.0	52.5	−54
Poland	Zloty 6.30	1.56	2.32	3.89	−40
Russia	Rouble 41.00	1.31	15.1	31.1	−51
Singapore	S$3.30	1.85	1.22	1.78	−31
South Africa	Rand 13.95	1.74	5.15	7.56	−32
South Korea	Won 3,300	2.63	1,218	1,220	nil
Sweden	SKr30.00	3.50	11.1	8.34	+33
Switzerland	SFr6.30	4.52	2.32	1.37	+69
Taiwan	NT$70.00	2.01	25.8	34.8	−26
Thailand	Baht 59.00	1.37	21.8	42.7	−49
Turkey	Lira 3,750,000	2.28	1,383,764	1,600,500	−14
Venezuela	Bolivar 3,700	2.32	1,365	1,598	−15

a. Purchasing-Power Parity: Local price divided by price in United States
b. Dollars per pound
c. Dollars per euro

Source: **Economist.com**: Economic Focus McCurrencies, 25 April 2003 © *The Economist* Newspaper Limited, London (25.4.03)

as its single product to test the law of one price. Why the Big Mac? Because each Big Mac is fairly identical in quality and content across national markets and almost entirely produced within the nation in which it is sold. The underlying assumption is that the price of a Big Mac in any world currency should, after being converted to dollars, equal the price of a Big Mac in the United States. A country's currency would be overvalued if the Big Mac price (converted to dollars) is higher than the US price. Conversely, a country's currency would be undervalued if the converted Big Mac price was lower than the US price.

Such large discrepancies between a currency's exchange rate on currency markets and the rate predicted by the Big Mac Index are not surprising, for several reasons. For one thing, the selling price of food is affected by subsidies for agricultural products in most countries. Also, the Big Mac is not a 'traded' product in the sense that one can buy Big Macs in low-priced countries and sell them in high-priced countries. Prices can also be affected because Big Macs are subject to different marketing strategies in different countries. Finally, countries impose different levels of sales tax on restaurant meals.

The drawbacks of the Big Mac Index reflect the fact that applying the law of one price to a single product is too simplistic a method for estimation of exchange rates. Nonetheless, a recent study finds that currency values in 8 out of 12 industrial countries do tend to change in the direction suggested by the Big Mac Index. And for 6 out of 7 currencies that change more than 10 per cent the Big Mac Index was as good a predictor as more sophisticated methods.

Table 6.1 also uses the concept of purchasing-power parity (PPP), which economists use when adjusting national income data (GNP, etc.) to improve comparability. PPPs are the rates of currency conversion that equalise the purchasing power of different currencies by eliminating the differences in price levels between countries. In their simplest form PPPs are simply price relatives that show the ratio of the prices in national currencies of the same good or service in different countries.

The easiest way to see how a PPP is calculated is to consider Table 6.1 for a product that is identical in several countries. For example, a Big Mac costs C$3.20 in Canada. If we divide 3.20 with the price in the United States, $2.71, the result will be the PPP of the dollar = 1.18 (the 'theoretical' exchange rate of the Canadian dollar). Then if we divide 1.18 with the actual exchange rate, 1.45, we find that the Canadian dollar is undervalued by $1 - (1.18/1.45) \times 100 = 18$ per cent.

PPPs are not only calculated for individual products; they are calculated for a 'basket' of products, and PPP is meaningful only when applied to such a 'basket'.

Classification by income

Countries can be classified in a variety of ways. Most classifications are based on national income (GDP or GNP per capita) and the degree of industrialisation. The broadcast measure of economic development is *gross national product* (GNP) – the value of all goods and services produced by a country during a one-year period. This figure includes income generated both by domestic production and by the country's international activities. *Gross domestic product* (GDP) is the value of all goods and services produced by the domestic economy over a one-year period. In other words, when we add to GDP the income generated from exports, imports, and the international operations of a nation's companies, we get GNP. A country's GNP per capita is simply its GNP divided by its population. GDP per capita is calculated similarly.

Both GNP per capita and GDP per capita measure a nation's income per person.

Less developed countries (LDCs)

This group includes underdeveloped countries and developing countries. The main features are a low GDP per capita (less than $3,000), limited amount of manufacturing activity and a very poor and fragmented infrastructure. Typical infrastructure weaknesses are in transport, communications, education and health care. In addition, the public sector is often slow moving and bureaucratic.

It is common to find that LDCs are heavily reliant on one product and often on one trading partner. The typical pattern for single-product dependence is the reliance on one agricultural crop, or on mining. Colombia (coffee) and Cuba (sugar) are examples of extreme dependence upon agriculture. The risks posed to the LDC by changing patterns of supply and demand are great. Falling commodity prices can result in large decreases in earnings for the whole country. The resultant economic and political adjustments may affect exporters to that country through possible changes in tariff and non-tariff barriers.

A wide range of economic circumstances influences the development of the less developed countries in the world. Without real prospects for rapid economic development private sources of capital are reluctant to invest in such countries. This is particularly the case for long-term infrastructure projects. As a result, important capital spending projects rely heavily on world aid programmes.

The quality of distribution channels varies considerably between countries. There are often great differences between the small-scale, undercapitalised distribution intermediaries in LDCs and the distributors in more advanced countries. Retailers, for example, are more likely to be market traders. The incidence of large-scale self-service outlets will be comparatively low.

Newly industrialised countries (NICs)

NICs are countries with an emerging industrial base: one that is capable of exporting. Examples of NICs are the 'tigers' of south-east Asia: Hong Kong, Singapore, South Korea and Taiwan. Brazil and Mexico are examples of NICs in South America. In NICs, although the infrastructure shows considerable development, high growth in the economy results in difficulties with producing what is demanded by domestic and foreign customers.

Advanced industrialised countries

These countries have considerable GDP per capita, a wide industrial base, considerable development in the services sector and substantial investment in the infrastructure of the country.

This attempt to classify the economies of the world into neat divisions is not completely successful. For example, some of the advanced industrialised countries (e.g. the United States and France) have important agricultural sectors.

Regional economic integration

Economic integration has been one of the main economic developments affecting world markets since the Second World War. Countries have wanted to engage in economic cooperation to use their respective resources more effectively and to provide large markets for member-country producers.

Some integration efforts have had quite ambitious goals, such as political integration; some have failed as a result of perceptions of unequal benefits from the arrangement or a parting of the ways politically. Figure 6.3, a summary of the major forms of economic cooperation in regional markets, shows the varying degrees of formality with which integration can take place. These economic integration efforts are dividing the world into trading blocs.

The levels of economic integration will now be described.

Figure 6.3 Forms of economic integration in regional markets

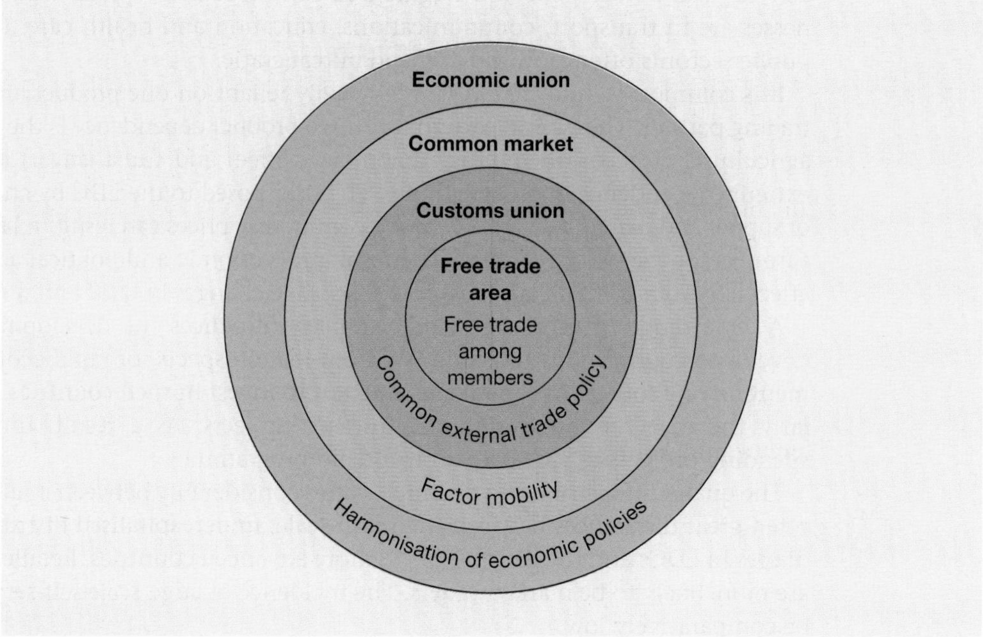

Source: Czinkota and Ronkainen, 1996, p. 112.

Free trade area

The free trade area is the least restrictive and loosest form of economic integration among nations. In a free trade area all barriers to trade among member countries are removed. Each member country maintains its own trade barriers vis-à-vis non-members.

The European Free Trade Area (EFTA) was formed in 1960 with an agreement by eight European countries. Since that time EFTA has lost much of its original significance due to its members joining the European Union. All EFTA countries have cooperated with the European Union through bilateral free trade agreements, and since 1994 through the European Economic Area (EEA) arrangement that allows for free movement of people, products, services and capital within the combined area of the European Union and EFTA. Of the EFTA countries, Iceland and Liechtenstein have decided not to apply for membership of the European Union and Norway turned down membership after a referendum in 1994. Switzerland has also decided to stay out of the European Union.

After three failed tries during the last century the United States and Canada signed a free trade agreement that went into effect in 1989. North American free trade expanded in 1994 with the inclusion of Mexico in the North American Free Trade Agreement (NAFTA).

Customs union

The customs union is one step further along the spectrum of economic integration. As in the free trade area, goods and services are freely traded among members. In addition, however, the customs union establishes a common trade policy with respect to non-members. Typically this takes the form of a common external tariff, whereby imports from non-members are subject to the same tariff when sold to any member country. The Benelux countries formed a customs union in 1921 that later became part of wider European economic integration.

Common market

The common market has the same features as a customs union. In addition, factors of production (labour, capital and technology) are mobile among members. Restrictions on immigration and cross-border investment are abolished. When factors of production are mobile capital, labour and technology may be employed in their most productive uses.

The removal of barriers to the free movement of goods, services, capital and people in Europe was ratified by the passing of the Single European Act in 1987 with the target date of 31 December 1992 to complete the internal market. In December 1991 the EEC agreed in Maastricht that the so-called 1992 process would be a step towards cooperation beyond the economic dimension. While many of the directives aimed at opening borders and markets were completed on schedule some sectors, such as cars, will take longer to open up.

Economic union

The creation of true economic union requires integration of economic policies in addition to the free movement of goods, services and factors of production across borders. Under an economic union members harmonise monetary policies, taxation and government spending. In addition, a common currency is used by members and this could involve a system of fixed exchange rates. The ratification of the Maastricht Treaty in late 1993 resulted in the European Union being effective from 1 January 1994. Clearly the formation of a full economic union requires the surrender of a large measure of national sovereignty to a supranational body. Such a union is only a short step away from political unification, but many countries in the European Union (especially in the northern part of Europe) are sceptical about this development because they fear a loss of national identity.

Enlargement of EU

The EU can already look back on a history of successful enlargements. The Treaties of Paris (1951), establishing the European Coal and Steel Community (ECSC), and Rome (1957), establishing the European Economic Community (EEC) and EURATOM, were signed by six founding members: Belgium, France, Germany, Italy, Luxembourg and the Netherlands. The EU then underwent four successive enlargements: 1973: Denmark, Ireland and the United Kingdom; 1981: Greece; 1986: Portugal and Spain; 1995: Austria, Finland and Sweden.

After growing from 6 to 15 members, the European Union is now preparing for its biggest enlargement ever in terms of scope and diversity. 13 countries have applied to become new members: 10 of these countries – Cyprus, the Czech Republic, Estonia, Hungary, Latvia, Lithuania, Malta, Poland, the Slovack Republic, and Slovenia are set to join on 1st May 2004. They are currently known by the term 'acceding countries'. Bulgaria and Romania hope to do so by 2007, while Turkey is not currently negotiating its membership. However, Turkey wants to be a member of the EU and the issue is taken up again in the future.

New countries wanting to join the Union, need to fulfil the economic and political conditions known as the 'Copenhagen criteria', according to which a prospective member must (http://europa.eu.int/comm/enlargement): be a stable democracy, respecting human rights, the rule of law, and the protection of minorties; have a functioning market economy; and adopt the common rules, standards and policies that make up the body of EU law.

6.4   The European Economic and Monetary Union and the euro

The Maastricht Treaty resulted in the European Economic and Monetary Union (EMU), which also included the new common European currency, the euro. Although the EMU is currently limited to 12 of the 15 member states, it nevertheless involves the extension of the 'law of one price' across a market comprising 300 million consumers, representing one-fifth of the world economy, which should promote increased trade and stimulate greater competition. Consequently the development of this 'new' Europe has an importance beyond the relatively small group of nations currently involved in its creation. The former eastern European nations, eager to gain full EU membership, for political and economic reasons, will be required to accept full participation in EMU. Unaided, this could conceivably preoccupy their economies for decades (Whyman, 2002).

The consequences of European economic integration will not be restricted to so-called 'European' business. Most obviously the developments associated with the EMU will have a direct impact upon all foreign subsidiaries located within the new euro market. These companies will be forced to adapt their accounting, personnel and financial processes to accommodate the new currency.

The EMU will also affect the international competitiveness of European companies. Reductions in transaction costs, exchange rate risk, intensified domestic competition and the possibilities of gleaning additional economies of scale should all facilitate reductions in the cost structures of European firms, with inevitable consequences upon their external competitors. However, this may be negated by the impact of demands for wage equalisation and restrictions imposed by regulations.

With so many important issues in the EMU there is no single economic consensus concerning the likely development of the European economy.

Supporters of EMU claim that the greater nominal exchange rate stability, lower transaction costs (by the introduction of the euro) and price transparency (across European borders) resulting in reduction of information costs will increase the international competitiveness of European business, raising consumer welfare together with their demand for cheaper products. The establishment of an independent European Central Bank (ECB) is anticipated to ensure a low level of inflation, reduce real interest rates and thereby stimulate investment, output and employment.

Opponents of the EMU claim the following:

■ The loss of national economic policy tools will have a destabilising impact.
■ The lack of 'real' convergence of participating economies is likely to increase the problem of asymmetric shocks.
■ The ECB's attempts at stabilisation by the use of a single instrument, a common interest rate, are likely to prove insufficient because the common monetary policy affects EU members differently due to differences in factors, including the concentration of owner-occupation and variable interest borrowing.

Benefits of regional integration

Nations engage in specialisation and trade because of the gains in output and consumption, and higher standards of living for all should result from higher levels of trade between nations.

Trade creation

As we have seen, economic integration removes barriers to trade and/or investment for nations belonging to a trading bloc. The increase in the level of trade between nations that results from regional economic integration is called trade creation. One result of trade creation is that consumers and industrial buyers in member nations are faced with a wider selection of goods and services.

Another result of trade creation is that buyers can acquire goods and services at less cost following the lowering of trade barriers such as tariffs. Furthermore, lower costs tend to lead to higher demand for goods because people have more money left over after a purchase to buy other products.

Greater consensus

The World Trade Organization works to lower barriers on a global scale. Efforts at regional economic integration differ in that they comprise smaller groups of nations – ranging anywhere from several countries to as many as 30 or more nations. The benefit of trying to eliminate trade barriers in smaller groups of countries is that it can be easier to gain consensus from fewer members as opposed to, say, the 133 countries that comprise the WTO.

Political cooperation

There can also be political benefits from efforts at regional integration. A group of nations can have significantly greater political weight in the world than the nations have individually. Thus nations can have more say when negotiating with other countries. Moreover, integration involving political cooperation can reduce the potential for military conflict between member nations.

Drawbacks of regional integration

Although trade tends to benefit countries, it can also have substantial negative effects. Let us now examine the more important of these.

Trade diversion

The flip side of trade creation is trade diversion – the diversion of trade away from nations not belonging to a trading bloc towards member nations. Trade diversion can occur after formation of a trading bloc because of the lower tariffs charged between member nations. It can actually result in reduced trade with a more efficient non-member producer and increased trade with a less efficient producer within the trading bloc. In this sense economic integration can unintentionally reward a less efficient producer within the trading bloc. Unless there is other internal competition for the producer's good or service buyers will be paying more after trade diversion due to the inefficient production methods of the producer.

Shifts in employment

Perhaps the most controversial aspect of regional economic integration is how people's jobs are affected. Industries requiring mostly unskilled labour, for example, will tend to shift production to low-wage nations within a trading bloc.

Thus trade agreements do cause dislocations in labour markets – some jobs are lost while others are gained.

It is highly likely that countries protecting low-wage domestic industries from competition will see these jobs move to the country where wages are lower once trade and investment barriers are removed. But this is also an opportunity for workers to upgrade their skills and gain more advanced job training. This can help nations increase their competitiveness because a better educated and more skilled workforce attracts higher paying jobs than does a less skilled workforce. However, an opportunity for a nation to improve some abstract 'factors of production' is little consolation to people finding themselves suddenly without work.

Loss of national sovereignty

Successive levels of integration require that nations surrender more of their national sovereignty. A certain amount of sovereignty has to be surrendered to the trading bloc.

Major trading blocs

Table 6.2 shows the major trading blocs together with their population, GNP and GNP per capita. The size and economic importance of the USA and Japan stand out. The affluence of Luxembourg and Switzerland – both small countries – is marked by high values of GNP per head.

Besides the major trading blocs mentioned in Table 6.2 the most important global market will be the 'triad'.

The triad of Europe, North America and Japan

The global economic size of these three, Europe, the United States and Japan, is disproportionate to their actual number or physical size. Ohmae (1985) cites Japan and the United States alone as accounting for 30 per cent of the free world total, and that with the addition of the United Kingdom, Germany, France and Italy this increases to 45 per cent. Aside from economic wealth these countries share other similarities: mature, stagnant economies; ageing populations; dynamic technological developments and constantly escalating costs of research and development and production facilities. This is all part of the new reality as Ohmae sees it.

This triad creates a market of 600 million with marked demographic similarities and levels of purchasing power as a result of the following:

- growth of capital intensive manufacturing;
- accelerated tempo of new technology;
- concentrated pattern of consumption.

A reaction to any of those forces above is protectionism. Ohmae shows that industries critical to wealth generation in the 1980s were all concentrated in Japan, the United States and Europe, constituting more than 80 per cent of global production and consumption. The implication of the triad is that these 600 million consumers share the same desire for the same goods: Gucci bags, Sony Walkmans, McDonald's hamburgers, etc. While there is an international youth market for denims, CDs and tapes, tastes are not the same, nor is purchasing power equal. Psychographic segmentation based on values and attitudes that may also be shared across national boundaries is what is important.

The answer to market entry in each of the triad regions comes through consortia and joint ventures that pose a new challenge for the corporation, as Ohmae points out, of learning how to communicate institutionally with the very different corporate cultures and languages of other companies.

Table 6.2 Major trading blocs

Organization	Type	Members	Population (million)	GNP ($bn)	GNP per capita ($)
European Union	Political and economic union	Belgium	10.2	259.0	25,380
		Luxembourg	0.4	19.2	45,100
		Denmark	5.3	176.2	33,040
		France	58.8	1,466.4	24,210
		Germany	82.0	2,179.8	26,570
		Ireland	3.7	69.3	18,710
		Italy	57.6	1,157.0	20,090
		UK	59.1	1,264.3	21,410
		Netherlands	15.7	389.1	24,780
		Greece	10.5	123.4	11,740
		Portugal	10.0	106.4	10,670
		Spain	39.4	556.2	14,100
		Sweden	8.9	226.5	25,580
		Austria	8.1	216.7	26,830
		Finland	5.2	125.1	24,280
		Total	374.9	8,331.6	22,224
Association of South East Asian Nations (ASEAN)	Limited trade and cooperation agreement	Indonesia	203.7	130.6	640
		Brunei	n.a.	n.a.	n.a.
		Vietnam	76.5	26.5	350
		Malaysia	22.2	81.3	3,670
		Singapore	3.2	96.5	30,170
		Philippines	76.2	78.9	1,050
		Thailand	61.2	131.9	2,160
		Total	442.0	414.1	937
Asia Pacific Economic Cooperation (APEC, excl. ASEAN, USA and Canada)	Formal institution	China	1,238.6	923.6	750
		Japan	126.4	4,089.1	32,350
		South Korea	46.4	398.8	8,600
		Taiwan*	21.8	261.6	12,000
		Australia	18.8	387.0	20,640
		New Zealand	3.8	55.4	14,600
		Total	1,456.8	6,115.5	4,201
North American Free Trade Area (NAFTA)	Free trade area	US	270.3	7,903.0	29,240
		Canada	30.3	580.9	19,170
		Mexico	96.8	368.1	3,840
		Total	396.4	8,852.0	22,331

* Estimated from different sources as Taiwan is not in the World Bank Statistics.

Source: Adapted from *World Bank* (2000), Section 1.1.

Per capita income

The statistic most frequently used to describe a country economically is its per capita income. This figure is used as a shorthand expression for a country's level of economic development as well as its degree of modernisation and progress in health, education and welfare. Partial justification for using this figure in evaluating a foreign economy lies in the fact that it is commonly available and widely accepted. A more pertinent justification is that it is, in fact, a good indicator of the size or quality of a market.

The per capita income figures vary widely among the countries of the world. The World Bank finds over half the world's population living in countries with an average per capita income of only $330.

However, a number of criticisms can be made of per capita income figures:

- *Purchasing power is not reflected.* Per capita income comparisons are expressed in a common currency – usually US dollars – through an exchange rate conversion. The dollar figure for a country is derived by dividing its per capita income figure in national currency by its rate of exchange against the dollar. The resulting dollar statistic for a country's per capita income is accurate only if the exchange rate reflects the relative domestic purchasing power of the two currencies. There is often reason for doubting that it does. For example, the impact of speculation can pull a currency away from its 'true' value.

- *Lack of comparability.* Another limitation to the use of per capita income figures is that there is a twofold lack of comparability in the figures themselves. Goods entering the national income totals of the developed economies are only partially in the money economy in less developed countries. A large part of a European's budget, for example, goes on food, clothing and shelter. In many less developed nations these items may be largely self-provided and are therefore not reflected in national income totals.

- *Sales are not related to per capita income.* Another limitation to using per capita income figures to indicate market potential is that the sales of many goods show little correlation with per capita income. Many consumer goods sales correlate more closely with population or household figures than with per capita income. Some examples might be Coca-Cola, ballpoint pens, bicycles, sewing machines and radios. Industrial goods and capital equipment sales generally correlate better with industrial structure or total national income than with per capita income.

- *Uneven income distribution.* Finally, per capita figures are less meaningful if there is great unevenness of income distribution in the country. This has already been discussed. Per capita income figures are averages and are meaningful if most people in the country are near the average. Frequently, however, this is not the case. Among world nations the Scandinavian countries have a relatively equal distribution of income among people. Even here, however, marketers are very attentive to differences in income levels when studying potential for their product if the product is at all income sensitive. Many countries have a relatively uneven distribution of income. An extreme example is Brazil, where the lowest 20 per cent of the population receive less than 3 per cent of the national income, whereas the highest 20 per cent receive 63 per cent of that income.

Structure of consumption

While it is important to measure the volume of consumption among various cultures, nations and societies, the characteristics of that consumption reveal its structure. Depending on economic factors, a country may have to emphasise producer goods over consumer goods. Moreover, what are considered necessities in one economy may be luxuries in another. In addition, consumption in most advanced countries is characterised by a higher proportion of expenditure devoted to capital goods than in poor countries, where substantially more is spent on consumer goods.

The structural differences with regard to expenditure among nations can be explained by a theory propounded by the German statistician Engel. The law of consumption (Engel's law) states that poorer families and societies spend a greater proportion of their income on food than well-to-do people. Housing, in particular, receives a much smaller share of income in underdeveloped countries than in the advanced nations.

The structure of consumption varies among developed countries. While the average person in England eats 13 pounds of cereal a year, per capita consumption in France is just 1 pound, and in Japan less than one-quarter of a pound. Americans eat about 10 pounds of cereal each per year (Jain, 1996, p. 193).

6.5   Summary

In this chapter we have concentrated on analysing the political/legal and the economic environment as it affects the firm in international markets. Most companies are unable to influence the environment of their markets directly, but their opportunities for successful business conduct largely depend on the structure and content of that environment. A marketer serving international markets or planning to do so, therefore, has to assess carefully the political and legal environments of the markets served or under consideration to draw the appropriate managerial consequences.

Political environment

The international marketer's political environment is complex because of the interaction among domestic, foreign and international politics. When investing in a foreign country firms have to be sensitive to that country's political concerns. The firm should prepare a monitoring system that allows it systematically to evaluate the political risks – such as expropriation, nationalisation and restrictions against exports and/or imports. Through skilful adaptation and control political risks can be reduced or neutralised.

Tariffs have traditionally been used as barriers to international trade. International trade liberalisation during the last decade of the twentieth century led to a significant reduction of tariff barriers. Therefore governments have been increasingly using non-tariff barriers to protect those of their countries' industries that they think are unable to sustain free international competition. A government may also support or deter international business through its investment policy, that is, the general rules governing legislation concerning domestic as well as foreign participation in the equity or ownership of businesses and other organizations of the country.

There are various trade barriers that can inhibit global marketing. Although nations have used the WTO to lessen many of the restrictions many of these barriers will undoubtedly remain.

Economic environment

The economic environment is a major determinant of market potential and opportunity. Significant variations in national markets originate in economic differences. Population characteristics, of course, represent one major dimension. The income and wealth of the nation's people are also extremely important because these key figures determine people's purchasing power. Countries and markets may be at different stages of economic development, each stage having different characteristics.

The Maastricht Treaty resulted in the European Economic and Monetary Union, which also included the new common European currency, the euro. Although the EMU is currently limited to 12 of the 15 member states it nevertheless involves the extension of the 'law of one price' across a market comprising 300 million consumers, representing one-fifth of the world economy, which should promote increased trade and stimulate greater competition. Consequently the development of this 'new' Europe has an importance beyond the relatively small group of nations currently involved in its creation.

Formal methods for gauging economic development in other nations include: (a) national production, such measures as gross national product and gross domestic product; (b) purchasing-power parity, or the relative ability of two countries' currencies to buy the same 'basket' of goods in those two countries. This index is used to correct comparisons that are made.

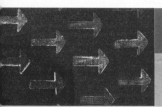

CASE STUDY 6.1   The World Bank and the IMF

What on earth is globalization about? Massive protests during a meeting in Prague

The Internet may be spearheading a global communications revolution; fashion designers may embrace 'ethnic' hues and styles; McDonald's may spread its restaurants across the globe. Globalization is a reality that, for better or worse, touches our lives in ways most of us never stop to think about. Many would certainly say it was a good thing. Increased international trade has made us wealthier and allowed us to lead more diverse lifestyles.

However, the annual meeting of the IMF and the World Bank, held in the Czech capital Prague in September 2002, was marred by large demonstrations outside the conference centre. The protesters said both organizations are actually worsening the life of many poor people in developing countries.

Some would say the world was as globalized 100 years ago as it is today, with international trade and migration. But the 1930s depression put paid to that. Nation states drew back into their shell on realising that international markets could deliver untold misery in the form of poverty and unemployment. The resolve of western states to build and strengthen international ties in the aftermath of the Second World War laid the groundwork for today's globalization. It has brought diminishing national borders and the fusing of individual national markets. The fall of protectionist barriers has stimulated free movement of capital and paved the way for companies to set up several bases around the world. The rise of the Internet and recent advances in telecommunications have spurred on the already surging train.

For consumers and avowed capitalists this is largely a good thing. Vigorous trade has made for more choice in the high street, greater spending, rising living standards and a growth in international travel. Supporters of globalization say it has promoted information exchange, led to a greater understanding of other cultures and allowed democracy to triumph in most countries.

But as the street protests indicate there is a growing opposition to the forces of globalization. Critics say the West's gain has been at the expense of developing countries. Demonstrators say rich countries should forgive debts of the poorest nations. Rock star Bono of U2, who attended the meeting to press for debt relief, condemned any violence but said that people's concerns needed to be heard and addressed. He urged ministers to go further to provide debt relief to alleviate what he called a 'holocaust' in poor developing countries.

The already meagre share of the global income of the poorest people in the world has dropped from 2.3 per cent to 1.4 per cent in the last decade. But even in the developed world not everyone has been a winner. The freedoms granted by globalization are

leading to increased insecurity in the workplace. Manual workers in particular are under threat as companies shift their production lines overseas to low-wage economies.

At the heart of the demonstrators' concerns is the fact that huge transnational companies are becoming more powerful and influential than democratically elected governments, putting shareholder interests above those of communities and even customers. Ecological campaigners say corporations are disregarding the environment in the stampede for worldwide mega-profits. Human rights groups say corporate power is restricting individual freedom. Even business people behind small firms have sympathy for the movement, afraid as they are that global economies of scale will put them out of work.

The mere fact that the debate can take place simultaneously across countries and continents, however, may well show that the celebrated global village is already here.

Source: adapted from BBC News, 26 September 2003, **news.bbc.co. uk/1/hi/business/2283666.stm**

Questions

1. What were the the key arguments of the demonstrators at the annual meeting of the IMF and World Bank?

2. How could these protests affect the operations of multinational companies?

3. How could the IMF and World Bank do a better marketing job in communicating their views to the global audience?

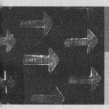

CASE STUDY 6.2   Sauer–Danfoss

Which political/economic factor would affect a manufacturer of hydraulic components?

Sauer-Danfoss (**www.sauer-danfoss.com**) is a comprehensive subsupplier of mobile hydraulic solutions as either components or integrated systems to manufacturers of mobile equipment in agriculture, construction, material handling and road building, as well as specialty vehicles in forestry and on-highway. With more than 7,000 employees and 24 factories in North America, Europe and East Asia, Sauer-Danfoss is among the largest manufacturers and suppliers of mobile hydraulics in the world today. Sauer-Danfoss has principal business center in Ames, Iowa (US), Neumünster (Germany) and Nordborg (Denmark).

Questions

1. Which political and economic factors in the global environment would have the biggest effect on the future global sales of Sauer-Danfoss hydraulic components/systems to:

(a) manufacturers of construction and mining equipment (e.g. Caterpillar)?
(b) manufacturers of agricultural machinery (e.g. John Deere)?

2. What are the biggest problems in forecasting future demand for a subsupplier such as Sauer-Danfoss?

Questions for discussion

1. Identify different types of barrier to the free movement of goods and services.
2. Explain the importance of a common European currency to firms selling goods to the European market.
3. How useful is GNP when undertaking a comparative analysis of world markets? What other approaches would you recommend?
4. Discuss the limitations of per capita income in evaluating market potential.
5. Distinguish between: (a) free trade area, (b) customs union, (c) common market, (d) economic and monetary union and (e) political union.
6. Why is the international marketer interested in the age distribution of the population in a market?
7. Describe the ways in which foreign exchange fluctuations affect: (1) trade, (2) investments, (3) tourism.
8. Why is political stability so important for international marketers? Find some recent examples from the press to underline your points.
9. How can the change of major political goals in a country have an impact on the potential for success of an international marketer?
10. A country's natural environment influences its attractiveness to an international marketer of industrial products. Discuss.
11. Explain why a country's balance of trade may be of interest to an international marketer.

References

Albaum, G., Strandskov, J. and Duerr, E. (2002) *International Marketing and Export Management* (4th edn), Financial Times/Pearson Education, Harlow.

Czinkota, M.R. and Ronkainen, I.A. (1996) *Global Marketing*, The Dryden Press, Fort Worth, TX.

Jain, S.C. (1996) *International Marketing Managment*, South-Western College Publishing, Cincinnati, OH.

Ohmae, K. (1985) *Triad Power: The coming shape of global competition*, The Free Press, New York.

Whyman, P. (2002) 'Living with the euro: the consequences for world business', *Journal of World Business*, vol. 37, issue 3, Autumn, pp. 208–15.

World Bank (2000) *World Bank Atlas*, Washington, DC.

Further reading

Forlani, D. and Parthasarathy, M. (2003) 'Dynamic market definition: an international marketing perspective', *International Marketing Review*, volume 20, No. 2, pp. 142–60.

Keillor, B.D., Pettijohn, C.E. and Bashaw, R.E. (2000) 'Political activities in the global marketplace', *Industrial Marketing Management*, vol. 29, pp. 613–22.

LeClair, D.T. (2000) 'Marketing planning and the policy environment in the European Union', *International Marketing Review*, vol. 17, No. 3, pp. 193–215.

Tinsley, S. (2002) 'EMS models for business strategy development', *Business Strategy and the Environment*, Vol. 11, pp. 376–90.

7 The sociocultural environment

Contents

Learning objectives

After studying this chapter you should be able to do the following

■ Discuss how the sociocultural environment will affect the attractiveness of a potential market.

■ Define culture and name some of its elements.

■ Explain the '4 + 1' dimensions in Hofstede's model.

■ Discuss the strengths and weaknesses of Hofstede's model.

■ Discuss whether the world's cultures are converging or diverging.

7.1   Introduction

Culture as a concept is very difficult to define. Every author who has dealt with culture has given a different definition. Hofstede's (1980) definition is perhaps the best known to management scholars and is used here: 'Culture is the collective programming of the mind which distinguishes the members of one human group from another ... Culture, in this sense, includes systems of values; and values are among the building blocks of culture' (p. 21).

The importance of culture to the international marketer is profound. It is an obvious source of difference. Some cultural differences are easier to manage than others. In tackling markets in which buyers speak different languages or follow other religions, for instance, the international marketer can plan in advance to manage specific points of difference. Often a greater problem is to understand the underlying attitudes and values of buyers in different countries.

The concept of culture is broad and extremely complex. It encompasses virtually every part of a person's life. The way in which people live together in a society is influenced by religion, education, family and reference groups. It is also influenced by legal, economic, political and technological forces. There are various interactions between these influences. We can look for cultural differences in the ways different societies communicate: different spoken languages are used, and the importance of spoken and other methods of communication (e.g. the use of space between people) will vary. The importance of work, the use of leisure, and the types of reward and recognition that people value vary from culture to culture. In some countries people are highly motivated by monetary rewards, while in other countries and cultures social position and recognition are more important.

Culture develops through recurrent social relationships which form patterns that are eventually internalised by members of the entire group. In other words, a culture does not stand still, but changes slowly over time. Finally, cultural differences are not necessarily visible but can be quite subtle, and can surface in situations where one would never notice them.

It is commonly agreed that a culture must have these three characteristics:

- *It is learned*: that is, acquired by people over time through their membership of a group that transmits culture from generation to generation. In the case of a national culture, you learn most intensively in the early years of life. By the age of five you are already an expert in using your language. You have internalised values associated with such functions as:
  - interacting with other members of your family;
  - eliciting rewards and avoiding punishments;
  - negotiating for what you wanted;
  - causing and avoiding conflict.
- *It is interrelated*: that is, one part of the culture is deeply connected with another part such as religion and marriage, business and social status.
- *It is shared*: that is, tenets of a culture extend to other members of the group. The cultural values are passed on to an individual by other members of the culture group. These include parents, other adults, family, institutions such as schools, and friends.

Culture can be thought of as having three other levels (Figure 7.1). The tangible aspects of a culture – things you can see, hear, smell, taste or touch – are artefacts or manifestations of underlying values and assumptions that a group of people share. The structure of these elements is like that of an iceberg.

The part of the iceberg that you see above the water is only a small fraction of what is there. What you cannot see are the values and assumptions that can sink your ship if you mistakenly run into them. Daily behaviour is influenced by values and social morals that work closer to the surface than the basic cultural assumptions. The values and social norms help people to make adjustments to their short-term daily behaviour; these standards change over shorter periods of time (10 or 20 years), whereas the basic cultural assumptions are probably formed over centuries.

For the purposes of this book we will define culture as the learned ways in which a society understands, decides and communicates.

One way to approach the analysis of cultural influences is to examine cultures by means of a high context/low context analysis. Because languages are an important component of culture and an important means of communication we will look at both spoken languages and silent languages.

The differences between some cultures may be large. Language and value differences between the Swiss and Chinese cultures, for instance, are considerable. There are also

Figure 7.1 The visible and invisible parts of culture

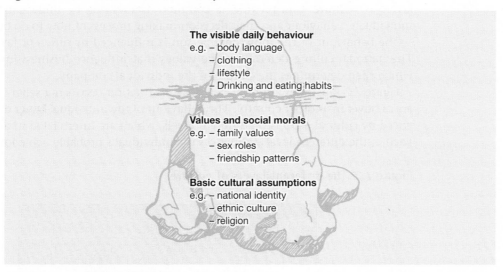

differences between the Spanish and Italian cultures, but they are much fewer. Both have languages based on Latin – they use the same written form of communication and they have similar, although not identical, values and norms.

Exhibit 7.1	Scotch whisky crossing international borders

Scotch whisky is consumed globally but bought for many different reasons. The right image has to be communicated for each culture, without of course losing any of the product's core brand values. The key value for Scotch generally is status.

In the United Kingdom this tends to be underplayed, never brash or 'in-your-face'. In Italy the image is more tied to machismo and any Scotch ad would have to show a man with a woman on his arm, flaunting the status the drink confers. In Japan, however, the status value is all about going with the majority. It is not aspirational to be individualistic in Japan.

Thus the understated drinker image that might work in the United Kingdom is inappropriate in other countries.

Source: adapted from Boundary Commission, *Marketing Week*, London, 29 January 1998; Sophie MacKenzie.

The use of communication techniques varies in different cultures. In some languages communication is based strictly on the words that are said or written; in others the more ambiguous elements such as surroundings or the social status of the message giver are important variables in the transmission of understanding. Hall (1960) used this finding to make a generalised division between what he referred to as 'low-context cultures' and 'high-context cultures'.

7.2   Layers of culture

The norms of behaviour accepted by the members of the company organization become increasingly important with the company's internationalization. When people with increasingly diverse national cultural backgrounds are hired by international firms the layers of culture can provide a common framework to understand the various individuals' behaviour and their decision-making process of how to do business.

The behaviour of the individual person is influenced by different layers of culture. The national culture determines the values that influence business/industry culture, which then determines the culture of the individual company.

Figure 7.2 illustrates a typical negotiation situation between a seller in one country and a buyer in another country. The behaviour of the individual buyer or seller is influenced by cultural aspects on different levels, which are interrelated in a complex way. Each of the different levels influences the individual's probable behaviour.

Figure 7.2 The different layers of culture

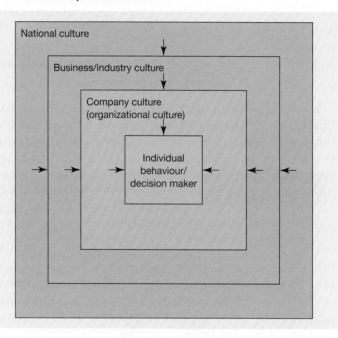

In Figure 7.2 the different levels are looked at from a 'nesting' perspective, where the different culture levels are nested into each other in order to grasp the cultural interplay between the levels. The total nest consists of the following levels:

- *National culture*. This gives the overall framework of cultural concepts and legislation for business activities.
- *Business/industry culture*. Every business is conducted within a certain competitive framework and within a specific industry (or service sector). Sometimes these may overlap but, in general, a firm should be able to articulate quite clearly what business it is in. This level has its own cultural roots and history, and the players within this level know the rules of the game. Industry culture is very much related to a branch of industry, and this culture of business behaviour and ethics is similar across borders. For example, shipping, the oil business, international trading and electronics have similar characteristics across national borders.
- *Company culture (organizational culture)*. The total organization often contains subcultures of various functions. Functional culture is expressed through the shared values, beliefs, meanings and behaviours of the members of a function within an organization (e.g. marketing, finance, shipping, purchasing, top management and blue-collar workers).

■ *Individual behaviour.* The individual is affected by the other cultural levels. In the interaction environment the individual becomes the core person who 'interacts' with the other actors in industrial marketing settings. The individual is seen as important because there are individual differences in perceiving the world. Culture is learned; it is not innate. The learning process creates individuals due to different environments in learning and different individual characteristics.

7.3   High- and low-context cultures

Edward T. Hall (1960) introduced the concept of high and low contexts as a way of understanding different cultural orientation. Table 7.1 summarises some of the ways in which high- and low-context cultures differ.

■ *Low-context cultures* rely on spoken and written language for meaning. Senders of messages encode their messages, expecting that the receivers will accurately decode the words used to gain a good understanding of the intended message.
■ *High-context cultures* use and interpret more of the elements surrounding the message to develop their understanding of the message. In high-context cultures the social importance and knowledge of the person and the social setting add extra information, and will be perceived by the message receiver.

Table 7.1 General comparative characteristics of cultures

Characteristic	Low-context/individualistic (e.g. western Europe, US)	High-context/collectivistic (e.g. Japan, China, Saudi Arabia)
Communication and language	Explicit, direct	Implicit, indirect
Sense of self and space	Informal handshakes	Formal hugs, bows and handshakes
Dress and appearance	Dress for individual success, wide variety	Indication of position in society, religious rule
Food and eating habits	Eating is a necessity, fast food	Eating is social event
Time consciousness	Linear, exact, promptness is valued, time = money	Elastic, relative, time spent on enjoyment, time = relationships
Family and friends	Nuclear family, self-oriented, value youth	Extended family, other oriented, loyalty and responsibility, respect for old age
Values and norms	Independence, confrontation of conflict	Group conformity, harmony
Beliefs and attitudes	Egalitarian, challenge authority, individuals control destiny, gender equity	Hierarchical, respect for authority, individuals accept destiny, gender roles
Mental process and learning	Linear, logical, sequential, problem solving	Lateral, holistic, simultaneous, accepting life's difficulties
Business/work habits	Deal oriented ('Quickly getting down to business'), rewards based on achievement, work has value	Relationship oriented ('First you make a friend, then you make a deal'), rewards based on seniority, work is a necessity

Figure 7.3 shows the contextual differences in the cultures around the world. At one extreme are the low-context cultures of northern Europe. At the other extreme are the high-context cultures. The Japanese and Arabs have a complex way of communicating with people according to their sociodemographic background.

Figure 7.3 The contextual continuum of differing cultures

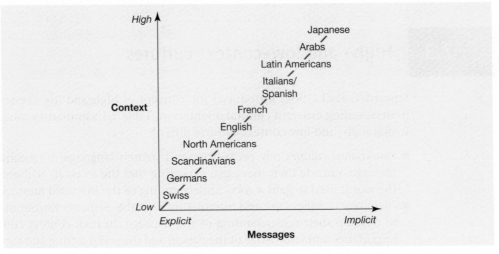

Source: Usunier, J.-C., 2000, Reprinted by *International Marketing*, Pearson Education Limited.

In an analysis of industrial buyer behaviour in Arab countries Solberg (2002) found that building trust with partners willing to endorse one's products takes more time in Arab countries than is customary in the West. Networking – using the power of other partners – seems to play a far greater role for Arab buyers. In Arab countries the position of the agent and his network with prominent families may be critical for success. 'Falling in love' with the wrong agent may therefore spoil the exporter's chances of spending a long period of time in the market.

The greater the context difference between those trying to communicate, the greater the difficulty in achieving accurate communication.

7.4 Elements of culture

There are varying definitions of the elements of culture, including one (Murdoch, 1945) that counts 73 'cultural universals'.

The following elements are usually included in the concept of culture.

Language

A country's language is the key to its culture and can be described as the mirror of the culture. Thus, if one is to work extensively with any one culture, it is imperative to learn the language. Learning a language well means learning the culture because the words of the language are merely concepts reflecting the culture from which it derives.

Language can be divided into two major elements. The verbal language of vocal sounds in patterns that have meaning is the obvious element. Non-verbal language is less obvious, but it is a powerful communicator through body language, silences and social distance.

Verbal language

Verbal language is an important means of communication. In various forms, such as plays and poetry, the written word is regarded as part of the culture of a group of people. In the spoken form, the actual words spoken and the ways in which the words are pronounced provide clues to the receiver about the type of person who is speaking.

Language capability plays four distinct roles in global marketing:

- Language is important in information gathering and evaluation efforts. Rather than rely completely on the opinions of others, the manager is able to see and hear personally what is going on. People are far more comfortable speaking their own language, and this should be treated as an advantage. The best intelligence is gathered on a market by becoming part of the market rather than observing it from the outside. For example, local managers of a global corporation should be the firm's primary source of political information to assess potential risk.
- Language provides access to local society. Although English may be widely spoken, and may even be the official company language, speaking the local language may make a dramatic difference. For example, firms that translate promotional materials and information are seen as being serious about doing business in the country.
- Language capability is increasingly important in company communications, whether within the corporate family or with channel members. Imagine the difficulties encountered by a country manager who must communicate with employees through an interpreter.
- Language provides more than the ability to communicate; it extends beyond mechanics to the interpretation of contexts.

A very important dimension of the language that can vary by culture is the extent to which communication is explicit or implicit. In explicit-language cultures managers are taught that to communicate effectively you should 'say what you mean, and mean what you say'. Vague directives and instructions are seen as a sign of poor communication abilities. The assumption in explicit-language cultures is that the burden of effective communication is on the speaker. In contrast, in implicit-language cultures (mostly high context) the assumption is that the speaker and listener both share the burden of effective communication. Implicit communication also helps avoid unpleasant and direct confrontations and disagreements.

Estimates of the main spoken languages around the world are given in Table 7.2.

Table 7.2 Official languages and spoken languages in the world

Mother tongue (first language)	No. of speakers (million)
Chinese	1,000
English	350
Spanish	250
Hindi	200
Arabic	150
Bengali	150
Russian	150
Portuguese	135
Japanese	120
German	100
French	70
Punjabi	70

Note: Chinese is composed of a number of dialects of which Mandarin is the largest.

Source: adapted from Phillips et al., 1994, p. 97.

Chinese is spoken as the mother tongue (or first language) by three times more people than the next largest language, English. However, Chinese is overtaken by English when spoken business-language population numbers are taken into account.

It should be noted that official languages are not always spoken by the whole population of a country. For example, French is an official language in Canada, but many Canadians have little or no fluency in French.

Hence English is often, but by no means always, the common language between businesspeople of different nationalities.

Non–verbal language

Non-verbal language is a powerful means of communication. The importance of non-verbal communication is greater in high-context countries. In these cultures people are more sensitive to a variety of different message systems, while in the low-context Anglo-Germanic cultures many of these non-verbal language messages would not be noticed.

Non-verbal language messages, according to Hall (1960), communicate up to 90 per cent of the meaning in high-context cultures. Table 7.3 describes some of the main non-verbal languages.

Table 7.3 **The main non–verbal languages in international business**

Non-verbal language	Implications for global marketing and business
Time	The importance of being 'on time'. In the high-context cultures (Middle East, Latin America), time is flexible and not seen as a limited commodity.
Space	Conversational distance between people. *Example*: Individuals vary in the amount of space they want separating them from others. Arabs and Latin Americans like to stand close to people they are talking with. If an American, who may not be comfortable with such close range, backs away from an Arab, this might be taken incorrectly as a negative reaction.
Material possessions	The relevance of material possessions and interest in the latest technology. This can have a certain importance in both low-context and high-context countries.
Friendship patterns	The significance of trusted friends as a social insurance in times of stress and emergency. *Example*: In high-context countries extended social acquaintance and the establishment of appropriate personal relations are essential to conducting business. The feeling is that one should often know one's business partner on a personal level before transactions occur.
Business agreements	Rules of negotiations based on laws, moral practices or informal customs. *Example*: Rushing straight to business will not be rewarded in high-context cultures because deals are made not only on the basis of the best product or price, but also on the entity or person deemed most trustworthy. Contracts may be bound by handshakes, not complex agreements – a fact that makes some, especially western, businesspeople uneasy.

Manners and customs

Changes occurring in manners and customs must be carefully monitored, especially in cases that seem to indicate a narrowing of cultural differences between peoples. Phenomena such as McDonald's and Coca-Cola have met with success around the world.

Exhibit 7.2	Sensuality and touch culture in Saudi Arabian versus European advertising

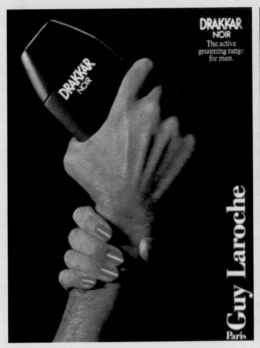 

Drakkar Noir: Sensuality and touch culture in Europe and Saudi Arabia   Source: Field, 1986.

Although Saudi Arabia has a population of only about 9 million people (including 2 million immigrants) the country is the sixth biggest fragrance market in the world behind the United States, Japan, Germany, France and Italy. Saudi Arabia also has the world's highest per capita consumption of fragrance, leaving all other countries far behind.

In promoting perfumes the big importers generally use the same advertising materials used by marketers in Europe. What is specifically Arabian in the campaigns is often dictated by Arabian morals.

Normally Saudi Arabia is a high-touch culture, but inappropriate use of touch in advertising messages may cause problems. The Drakkar Noir pictures show two advertisements for the men's perfume, in which Guy Laroche (via the advertising agency Mirabelle) tones down the sensuality for the Arab version. The European ad (left) shows a man's hand clutching the perfume bottle and a woman's hand seizing his bare forearm. In the Saudi version (right), the man's arm is clothed in a dark jacket sleeve, and the woman is touching the man's hand only with her fingertip.

Understanding manners and customs is especially important in negotiations because interpretations based on one's own frame of reference may lead to a totally incorrect conclusion. To negotiate effectively abroad one needs to read correctly all types of communication.

In many cultures certain basic customs must be observed by the foreign business-person. One of them concerns the use of the right and left hands. In so-called right-hand societies the left hand is the 'toilet hand' and using it to eat, for example, is considered impolite.

Technology and material culture

Material culture results from technology and is directly related to how a society organises its economic activity. It is manifested in the availability and adequacy of the basic economic, social, financial and marketing infrastructures.

With technological advancement comes cultural convergence. Black-and-white television sets extensively penetrated the US market more than a decade before they reached similar levels in Europe and Japan. With colour television, the lag was reduced to five years. With videocassette recorders, the difference was only three years, but this time the Europeans and the Japanese led the way, while Americans concentrated on cable systems. With the compact disc, penetration rates were even after only one year. Today, with Internet or MTV available by satellite across Europe, no lag exists at all.

Social institutions

Social institutions – business, political, family or class related – influence the behaviour of people and the ways in which people relate to each other. In some countries, for example, the family is the most important social group, and family relationships sometimes influence the work environment and employment practices.

In Latin America and the Arab world a manager who gives special treatment to a relative is considered to be fulfilling an obligation. From the Latin point of view, it makes sense only to hire someone you can trust. In the United States and Europe, however, it is considered favouritism and nepotism. In India there is a fair amount of nepotism. But there too it is consistent with the norms of the culture. By knowing the importance of family relationships in the workplace and in business transactions embarrassing questions about nepotism can be avoided.

An important part of the socialisation process of consumers worldwide is *reference groups*. These groups provide the values and attitudes that become influential in shaping behaviour. Primary reference groups include the family, co-workers and other intimate groupings, whereas secondary groups are social organizations in which less continuous interaction takes place, such as professional associations and trade organizations.

Social organizations also determine the roles of managers and subordinates and how they relate to one another. In some cultures managers and subordinates are separated. In other cultures managers and subordinates are on a more common level, and work together in teams.

Education

Education includes the process of transmitting skills, ideas and attitudes, as well as training in particular disciplines. Even primitive peoples have been educated in this broader sense. For example, the Bushmen of South Africa are well educated for the culture in which they live.

One function of education is the transmission of the existing culture and traditions to the new generation. However, education can also be used for cultural change. The promotion of a communist culture in the People's Republic of China is a notable example, but this, too, is an aspect of education in most nations. Educational levels will have an impact on various business functions. Training programmes for a production facility will have to take the educational backgrounds of trainees into account.

The global marketing manager may also have to be prepared to overcome obstacles in recruiting a suitable sales force or support personnel. For example, Japanese culture places a premium on loyalty, and employees consider themselves to be members of the corporate family. If a foreign firm decides to leave Japan employees may find themselves stranded in mid-career, unable to find a place in the Japanese business system. University graduates are therefore reluctant to join all but the largest and most well known of foreign firms.

If technology is marketed the level of sophistication of the product will depend on the educational level of future users. Product adaptation decisions are often influenced by the extent to which targeted customers are able to use the product or service properly.

Values and attitudes

Our attitudes and values help determine what we think is right or appropriate, what is important, and what is desirable. Some relate to marketing, and these are the ones we will look at here.

The more rooted values and attitudes are in central beliefs (such as religion), the more cautiously the global marketing manager has to move. Attitude towards change is basically positive in industrialised countries, whereas in more tradition-bound societies change is viewed with great suspicion, especially when it comes from a foreign entity.

In a conservative society there is generally a greater reluctance to take such risks. Therefore the marketer must also seek to reduce the risk involved in trying a new product as perceived by customers or distributors. In part this can be accomplished through education; guarantees, consignment selling or other marketing techniques can also be used.

Aesthetics

Aesthetics refers to attitudes towards beauty and good taste in the art, music, folklore and drama of a culture. The aesthetics of a particular culture can be important in the interpretation of symbolic meanings of various artistic expressions. What is and what is not acceptable may vary dramatically even in otherwise highly similar markets. Sex in advertising is an example.

It is important for companies to evaluate in depth such aesthetic factors as product and package design, colour, brand name and symbols. For instance, some conventional brand names that communicate positive messages in the United States have a totally different meaning in another country, which may substantially damage corporate image and marketing effectiveness (see Table 7.4).

Religion

The major religions are shared by a number of national cultures:

Table 7.4 US brand names and slogans with offensive foreign translations

Company	Product	Brand name or slogan	Country	Meaning
ENCO	Petroleum	Former name of EXXON	Japan	'Stalled car'
American Motors	Automobile	Matador	Spain	'Killer'
Ford	Truck	Fiera	Spain	'Ugly old woman'
Pepsi	Soft drink	'Come alive with Pepsi'	Germany	'Come out of the grave'

Source: Copeland and Griggs, 1985, p. 62.

- Christianity is the most widely practised. The majority of Christians live in Europe and the Americas, and numbers are growing rapidly in Africa.
- Islam is practised mainly in Africa, the Arab counties and around the Mediterranean, and in Indonesia. There has been a recent rise in Islamic fundamentalism in Iran, Pakistan, Algeria and elsewhere.
- Hinduism is most common in India. Beliefs emphasise the spiritual progress of each person's soul rather than hard work and wealth creation.
- Buddhism has adherents in central and south-east Asia, China, Korea and Japan. Like Hinduism it stresses spiritual achievement rather than wealth, although the continuing development of these regions shows that it does not necessarily impede economic activity.
- Confucianism has adherents mainly in China, Korea and Japan. The emphasis on loyalty and obligation between superiors and subordinates has influenced the development of family companies in these regions.

Religion can provide the basis for transcultural similarities under shared beliefs in Islam, Buddhism or Christianity, for example. Religion is of utmost importance in many countries. In the United States and Europe substantial efforts are made to keep government and church matters separate. Nevertheless there remains a healthy respect for individual religious differences. In some countries, such as Lebanon and Iran, religion may be the very foundation of the government and a dominant factor in business, political and educational decisions.

Religion may affect the global marketing strategy directly in the following ways:

- Religious holidays vary greatly among countries, not only from Christian to Muslim, but even from one Christian country to another. In general, Sundays are a religious holiday in all nations where Christianity is an important religion. In the Muslim world, however, the entire month of Ramadan is a religious holiday for all practical purposes.

   In Saudi Arabia, for example, during the month of Ramadan, Muslims fast from sunrise to sunset. As a consequence worker production drops. Many Muslims rise earlier in the morning to eat before sunrise and may eat what they perceive to be enough to last until sunset. This affects their strength and stamina during the working day. An effort by management to maintain normal productivity levels will probably be rejected, so managers must learn to be sensitive to this custom and to similar ones.
- Consumption patterns may be affected by religious requirements or taboos. Fish on Friday for Catholics used to be the classic example. Taboos against beef for Hindus and pork for Muslims and Jews are other examples. The pork restriction exists in Israel as well as in Islamic countries in the Middle East such as Saudi Arabia, Iraq and Iran, and south-east Asian countries such as Indonesia and Malaysia.

■ Islamic worshippers pray facing the holy city of Mecca five times each day. Visiting westerners must be aware of this religious ritual. In Saudi Arabia and Iran it is not unusual for managers and workers to place carpets on the floor and kneel to pray several times during the day.

■ The economic role of women varies from culture to culture, and religious beliefs are an important cause. In the Middle East women may be restricted in their capacity as consumers, as workers or as respondents in a marketing study. These differences can require major adjustments in the approach of a management conditioned to western markets. Women are, among other things, required to dress in such a way that their arms, legs, torso and faces are concealed. An American female would be expected to honour this dress code while in the host country.

Exhibit 7.3	Polaroid's success in Muslim markets

During the past 30 years Polaroid's instant photography has been largely responsible for breaking down taboos against picture taking in the Arab world, especially those concerning women revealing their faces.

When Polaroid entered the market in the mid-1960s it discovered that instant photography had a special appeal. Because of religious constraints there were only a few photo-processing laboratories. But with Polaroid's instant cameras Arab men were able to photo-graph their wives and daughters without fear of a stranger in a film laboratory seeing the women unveiled and without the risk of someone making duplicates.

Source: Harper, 1986.

7.5 Hofstede's original work on national cultures (the '4 + 1' dimensions model)

While an international manager may have neither the time nor the resources to obtain a comprehensive knowledge of a particular culture, a familiarity with the most perva-sive cultural 'differentiators' can provide useful guidance for corporate strategy devel-opment. One approach to identifying these pervasive fundamental differences of national cultures is provided by Hofstede (1983). Hofstede tried to find an explanation for the fact that some concepts of motivation did not work in the same way in all coun-tries. Hofstede based his research on an extensive IBM database from which – between 1967 and 1973 – 116,000 questionnaires (from IBM employees) were used in 72 coun-tries and in 20 languages.

According to Hofstede, the way people in different countries perceive and interpret their world varies along four dimensions: power distance, uncertainty avoidance, indi-vidualism and masculinity.

1. *Power distance* refers to the degree of inequality between people in physical and edu-cational terms (i.e. from relatively equal to extremely unequal). In high power dis-tance societies power is concentrated among a few people at the top who make all the decisions. People at the other end simply carry these decisions out. They accept differences in power and wealth more readily. In low power distance societies, on the other hand, power is widely dispersed and relations among people are more

egalitarian. The lower the power distance the more individuals will expect to participate in the organizational decision-making process. A high power distance score was observed in Japan. The United States and Canada record a middle-level rating on power distance, but countries such as Denmark, Austria and Israel exhibit much lower ratings.

2. *Uncertainty avoidance* concerns the degree to which people in a country prefer formal rules and fixed patterns of life, such as career structures and laws, as means of enhancing security. Another important dimension of uncertainty avoidance is risk taking. High uncertainty avoidance is probably associated with risk aversion. Organization personnel in low uncertainty avoidance societies face the future as it takes shape without experiencing undue stress. In high uncertainty avoidance cultures managers engage in activities such as long-range planning to establish protective barriers to minimise the anxiety associated with future events. On uncertainty avoidance the United States and Canada score quite low, indicating an ability to be more responsive in coping with future changes. But Japan, Greece, Portugal and Belgium score high, indicating their desire to meet the future in a more structured and planned fashion (see Figure 7.4).

3. *Individualism* denotes the degree to which people in a country learn to act as individuals rather than as members of groups. In individualistic societies people are self-centred and feel little need for dependency on others. They seek fulfilment of their

Figure 7.4 Uncertainty avoidance versus power distance

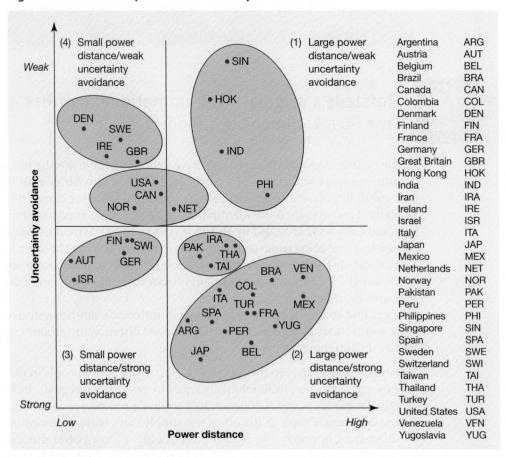

Source: Hofstede, 1980, p. 317. Reprinted by permission of Geert Hofstede.

own goals over the group's. In collectivistic societies members have a group mentality. They are interdependent on each other and seek mutual accommodation to maintain group harmony. Collectivistic managers have high loyalty to their organizations, and subscribe to joint decision making. The United Kingdom, Australia, Canada and the United States show very similar high ratings on individualism, while Japan, Brazil, Colombia, Chile and Venezuela exhibit very low ratings.

4. *Masculinity* relates to the degree to which 'masculine' values, such as achievement, performance, success, money and competition, prevail over 'feminine' values, such as quality of life, maintaining warm personal relationships, service, care for the weak, preserving the environment and solidarity. Masculine cultures exhibit different roles for men and women, and perceive anything big as important. The feminine cultures value 'small as beautiful', and stress quality of life and environment over materialistic ends. A relatively high masculinity index was observed for the United States, Italy and Japan. In low-masculinity societies such as Denmark and Sweden people are basically motivated by a more qualitative goal set as a means to job enrichment. Differences on masculinity scores are also reflected in the types of career opportunity available in organizations and associated job mobility.

5. *Time perspective* In a 23-country study, some years after Hofstede's original work, Hofstede and Bond (1988) identified a fifth dimension that they first termed Confucian Dynamism and then renamed 'time orientation'. This time orientation is defined as the way members in an organization exhibit a pragmatic future-oriented perspective rather than a conventional history or short-term point of view. The consequences of a high score on the long-term orientation (LTO) index are: persistence, ordering relationships by status and observing this order. The opposite is short-term orientation, which includes personal steadiness and stability.

Most south-east Asian markets, such as China, Hong Kong, Taiwan and South Korea, score high on the LTO index. This tendency has something to do with the Confucian traditions prevalent there. On the other hand many European countries are short-term oriented. They believe in preserving history and continuing past traditions.

7.6 The strengths and weaknesses of Hofstede's model

The strengths are as follows:

- Though the data are 30 years old no study since then has been based on such a large sample (116,000 respondents).
- The *information population* (IBM employees) is *controlled* across countries, which means comparisons can be made. This is a strength despite the difficulties of generalising to other occupational groups within the same national culture.
- The *four dimensions* tap into deep cultural values and make significant comparisons between national cultures.
- The connotations of each dimension are highly *relevant*. The questions asked of the respondents relate to issues of importance to international managers.
- No other study compares so many other national cultures in so much detail. Simply, this is *the best there is*.

The weaknesses are as set out below:

- As with all national cultural studies, this one assumes that *national territory* and the limits of the culture correspond. But cultural homogeneity cannot be taken for granted in countries that include a range of culture groups or with socially dominant and inferior culture groups, such as the United States, Italy (North/South debate), Belgium (French and Flemish cultures) and Spain (Basque, Catalan and Castillian). The break-up of Yugoslavia during the 1990s demonstrates the futility of trying to create tight political units from disparate national cultures.

■ Hofstede's respondents worked within a *single industry* (the computer industry) and a single multinational. This is misleading for two reasons. In any one country the values of IBM employees are typical only to a small group (educated, generally middle class, city dwelling); other social groups (for instance unskilled manual workers, public sector employees, family entrepreneurs, etc.) are more or less unrepresented. This problem of representation would occur whichever single company provided respondents.

■ There may be technical difficulties in Hofstede's research due to an overlap between the four dimensions, e.g. small power distance/feminine and large power distance/ masculine.

■ Likewise the definition of the dimensions may be different from culture to culture, e.g. collectivist behaviour in one context might have different connotations elsewhere. For instance, Japanese collectivism is organization based but Chinese collectivism is family based. In Japanese terms, a Taiwanese employee who places his family interests above the interests of the Japanese-owned multinational is disloyal and cannot be fully trusted.

7.7   Managing cultural differences

Having identified the most important factors of influence from the cultural environment on the firm's business and having analysed those factors, the international marketer is able to take decisions about how to react to the results of the analysis.

In accordance with Chapter 8 (The international market selection process) less attractive markets will not be considered further. On the other hand, in the more attractive markets, marketing management must decide to what extent adaptions to the given cultural specifics are needed.

For example, consider *punctuality*. In the most low-context cultures – the Germans, Swiss and Austrians, for example – punctuality is considered extremely important. If you have a meeting scheduled for 9.00 a.m. and you arrive at 9:07 a.m. you are considered 'late'. Punctuality is highly valued within these cultures, and to arrive late for a meeting (thus 'wasting' the time of those forced to wait for you) is not appreciated.

By contrast, in some southern European nations, and within Latin America, a somewhat 'looser' approach to time may pertain. This does not imply that one group is 'wrong' and the other 'right'. It simply illustrates that different approaches to the concept of time have evolved for a variety of reasons, over many centuries, within different cultural groups. Culture can and does influence the business sector in different parts of the world to function in distinct ways.

Another example of how cultural differences influence the business sector concerns the presentation of business cards. Within the United States – which has a very 'informal' culture – business cards are typically presented in a very casual manner. Cards are often handed out quickly and are just as quickly placed into the recipient's pocket or wallet for future reference.

In Japan, however – which has a comparatively 'formal' culture – the presentation of a business card is a more carefully orchestrated event. There, business cards are presented by holding the card up with two hands while the recipient carefully scrutinises the information it contains. This procedure ensures that one's title is clearly understood: an important factor for the Japanese, where one's official position within one's organizational 'hierarchy' is of great significance.

To simply take the card of a Japanese and immediately place it in one's card holder could well be viewed (from a Japanese perspective) in a negative light. However, within the United States, to take several moments to carefully and deliberately scrutinise an American's business card might also be taken in a negative way, perhaps suggesting that one's credibility is in doubt.

These examples – the sense of time/punctuality and the presentation of the business card – illustrate just two of the many ways in which cultural factors can influence business relationships.

In attempting to understand another culture we inevitably interpret our new cultural surroundings on the basis of our existing knowledge of our own culture.

In global marketing it is particularly important to understand new markets in the same terms as buyers or potential buyers in that marketplace. For the marketing concept to be truly operational the international marketer needs to understand buyers in each marketplace and be able to use marketing research in an effective way.

Lee (1966) used the term *self-reference criterion* (SRC) to characterise our unconscious reference to our own cultural values. He suggested a four-step approach to eliminate SRC:

1. Define the problem or goal in terms of home country culture, traits, habits and norms.
2. Define the problems or goals in terms of the foreign culture, traits, habits and norms.
3. Isolate the SRC influence in the problem and examine it carefully to see how it complicates the problem.
4. Redefine the problem without the SRC influence and solve for the foreign market situation.

It is therefore of crucial importance that the culture of the country is seen in the context of that country. It is better to regard the culture as different from, rather than better or worse than, the home culture. In this way differences and similarities can be explored and the reasons for differences can be sought and explained.

7.8 Convergence or divergence of the world's cultures

As we have seen earlier in this book the right mix between local knowledge of different cultures and globalization/integration of national marketing strategies is the key to success in global marketing.

There seems to be a great difference in attitude towards the globalization of cultures among different age groups, the youth culture being more international/global than other age groups (Smith, 2000).

Youth culture

Countries may be at different stages in the evolution of particular product and service categories, but in most cases youth is becoming more homogeneous across national markets. Youth cultures are more international than national. There are still some strong national characteristics and beliefs, but they are being eroded. The McDonald's culture is spreading into southern Europe, and at the same time we can see satellite TV taking the values of MTV, *The Simpsons*, and Ricky Lake all over the world, with English language culture in their wake.

Differences between youth and adult markets are changing in several key respects, the professionals agree. Younger consumers differ from adults in emphasising quality and being both discerning and technically literate. Younger consumers are now much more self-reliant and take responsibility far earlier. They are sensible, sophisticated and grown-up at an early age.

Generational barriers are now very blurred. The style leaders for many young people–musicians, sports stars and so on – are often in their 30s and 40s. Cultural and family influences remain very strong throughout Europe and the rest of the world. Few young people have 'role models', but they respect achievers particularly in music and sport – and their parents, particularly if their parents have succeeded from humble beginnings.

The lack of clarity in age-group targeting has to be weighed against a growth in cross-border consistencies. But marketers should beware of strategies aimed too blatantly at younger consumers. Young people tend to reject marketing and promotions that are obviously targeted at 'youth'. They perceive it to be false and hypocritical (Smith, 1998).

Today's youth have greater freedom than previous generations had. They are more culturally aware and are reluctant to take anything – or anyone – at face value. Pasco (2000) argues that getting youngsters to relate to celebrities is increasingly difficult. Celebrities often fail or disappoint young people, and again they 'sell out', giving up the integrity for which they were admired in the first place.

Disillusion with celebrities has led youth to look elsewhere for inspiration. They select values from a range of individuals rather than buy wholesale into one. Despite their mistrust of corporations youth increasingly aspire to, and engage with, brands. It appears safer to invest emotionally in brands than in celebrities.

7.9   The effects of cultural dimensions on ethical decision making

As more and more firms operate globally an understanding of the effects of cultural differences on ethical decision making becomes increasingly important for avoiding potential business pitfalls and for designing effective *international marketing* management programmes.

Culture is a fundamental determinant of ethical decision making. It directly affects how an individual perceives ethical problems, alternatives and consequences. In order to succeed in today's international markets managers must recognise and understand how ideas, values and moral standards differ across cultures, and how these in turn influence marketing decision making.

Some countries, such as India, are well known for 'requiring' small payments if customs officials are to allow goods to enter the country. While this may indeed be a bribe and illegal, the ethics of that country seem to allow it (at least to a certain extent). The company is then left with a problem: does it bribe the official, or does it wait for normal clearance and let its products sit in the customs warehouse for a considerably longer time?

Fees and commissions paid to a firm's foreign intermediate or to consultant firms for their services are a particular problem – when does the legal fee become a bribe? One reason for employing a foreign representative or consultants is to benefit from their contacts with decision makers, especially in a foreign administration. If the export intermediary uses part of the fee to bribe administrators there is little that the firm can do.

Thus every culture – national, industry, organizational or professional – establishes a set of moral standards for business behaviour, that is, a code of business ethics. This set of standards influences all decisions and actions in a company, including, for example, what and how to manufacture (or not), what wages are appropriate to pay, how many hours personnel should work under what conditions, how to compete, and what communication guidelines to follow. Which actions are considered right or wrong, fair or unfair, in the conduct of business and which are particularly susceptible to ethical norms is heavily influenced by the culture in which they take place (the bribery theme is further discussed in Chapter 19).

The ethical commitment of an international company is illustrated in Figure 7.5 as a continuum from unacceptable ethical behaviour to most ethical decision making.

Figure 7.5 Ethical decision making

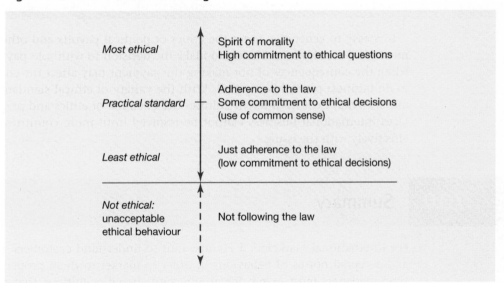

The adherence only to the letter of the law reflects minimally acceptable ethical behaviour. A classification of a company as 'most ethical' requires that the firm's code of ethics should address the following six major issues:

- *Organizational relations*, including competition, strategic alliances and local sourcing.
- *Economic relations*, including financing, taxation, transfer prices, local reinvestment, equity participation.
- *Employee relations*, including compensation, safety, human rights, non-discrimination, collective bargaining, training, and sexual harassment.
- *Customer relations*, including pricing, quality and advertising.
- *Industrial relations*, including technology transfer, research and development, infrastructure development and organizational stability/longevity.
- *Political relations*, including legal compliance, bribery and other corrupt activities, subsidies, tax incentives, environmental protection and political involvement.

| Exhibit 7.4 | Levi Strauss: An example of a multinational company's ethics code |

Levi Strauss's policy of being a responsible employer in developing countries, where poverty and social problems are endemic, is not something it shouts about. But it is at least partly designed to maintain that good image. Levi's is better able to pursue such a policy because it remains a private, family-run business. That means it does not have to answer to big shareholders on Wall Street, who might want a greater emphasis on short-term profitability. But finding the balance between efficiency and social responsibility is a challenge to Levi's.

In May 1993 Levi's announced that it planned to end most of its business in the People's Republic of China. This meant phasing out the use of Chinese subcontractors, which at that time accounted for about 2 per cent of total production (approximately $50 million a year). The reason given was China's record of 'pervasive human rights abuses'.

The decision to leave China reflected principles embodied in the company's organizational culture. This culture was expressed in sets of standards for doing business abroad, which emphasised a commitment to fair working conditions. If the company could not operate in a country without compromising its principles it should withdraw – as it had done in Myanmar and had threatened in Bangladesh.

Source: Various public media.

It is easy to generalise about the ethics of political payoffs and other types of payments; it is much more difficult to make the decision to withhold payment of money when the consequences of not making the payment may affect the company's ability to do business profitably or at all. With the variety of ethical standards and levels of morality that exist in different cultures the dilemma of ethics and pragmatism which faces international business cannot be resolved until more countries decide to deal effectively with the issue.

7.10 Summary

For international marketers it is important to understand customers' personal values and accepted norms of behaviour in order to market to them properly. At the same time marketers must search for groups with shared cognitions that result in shared views of the marketer's offerings and in similar product-related behaviour to simplify their task. Such groups may even exist across country borders.

How we perceive other cultures stems from our own cultural mind-set, and it is very difficult not to take the ethnocentric point of view when classifying other cultures. Classification of cultures is necessary to develop marketing and advertising strategies in the global marketplace. Classifying cultures on dimensions has proved to be the most constructive method. It helps in vocalising and labelling cultural differences and similarities. Many of the cultural differences are reflected in the type of communication culture used. In this chapter different models for classification have been discussed.

High/low context cultures

The difference between high- and low-context communication cultures helps us understand why, for example, Asian (high-context) and western (low-context) styles are so different, why the Asians prefer indirect verbal communication and symbolism over the direct assertive communication approaches used by western people. Other dimensions, such as different concepts of time, can also explain major differences between East and West.

Hofstede's model

In order to construct a more refined classification system, Hofstede developed a model of '4 + 1' dimensions for comparing work-related values, based on data collected in an extensive study. This model also proves useful for comparing cultures with respect to consumption-related values. As a result it can explain the variety of values and motivations used in marketing and advertising across cultures.

It can also explain differences in actual consumption behaviour and product use and can thus assist in predicting consumer behaviour or effectiveness of marketing strategies for cultures other than one's own. This will be particularly useful for companies that want to develop global marketing and advertising strategies.

The problem of business ethics is infinitely more complex in the international marketplace because value judgements differ widely among culturally diverse groups. What is commonly accepted as right in one country may be completely unacceptable in another. Giving business gifts of high value, for example, is generally condemned in western countries, but in many countries of the world gifts are not only accepted but expected.

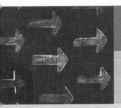

CASE STUDY 7.1   Lifan

A Chinese subsupplier and brand manufacturer of motorcycles is aiming at the global market

In 1992 Yin Mingshan established the Lifan Group (**www.lifan.com.cn**) in Chongqing together with nine employees. Yin Mingshan was then 54 years old. He came from a job as an editor in the Chongqing Publishing Agency. Lifan started out being a supplier of motorcycle parts to original equipment manufacturers (OEMs) of complete motorcycles and, later became a supplier of complete motorcycle engines. Today it is a producer of its own branded Lifan motorcycle.

In 10 years Lifan has developed into a state-level, large private enterprise – Chongqing Lifan Industrial (Group) Co., Ltd. There are more than 3,800 employees in the Group, which includes eight companies, three marketing companies and one city-level technical centre. Lifan was the first private company to establish a Party Committee within the company to help in the development of the company.

In September 2001 Lifan motorcycles were first sold to Japan, and overwrote the history of no motorcycles being exported to Japan from China. In Vietnam Lifan motorcycles have absolute predominance; the commercial counsellor of the Vietnam Embassy in China said: 'In Vietnam, the Lifan brand is more famous than Honda.'

In order to make the best use of its brand Lifan is

manufacturing as an outsourcer household electrical goods, wine, anti-theft doors, mineral water, garniture, sports shoes, etc. and building a 'Lifan Pyramid' with motorcycles, engines, automobile electrics, agricultural machines and media.

In 2002 the Lifan Group achieved the following sales:

- 714,000 branded motorcycles, placing it fourth in the Chinese motorcycle industry;
- 1,840,000 motorcycle engines, which made it number one in the Chinese motorcycle industry.

More than 1 million motorcycle engines were exported to foreign markets. In 2002 Lifan had total sales of $478 million, of which $117 million came from export. Its motorcycles were exported to over 70 countries.

World market for motorcycles

The Japanese company Yamaha has published a market survey result, which shows the demand for motorcycles in the world will reach 27.5 million units, 60 per cent higher than in 2001. This survey indicated that, due to the continuous expansion of the Vietnamese and Indian motorcycle markets, the demand in 2002 in the Asian market (excluding China) is expected to reach 10.2 million units, 10 per cent higher than in 2001. The demand in China will reach 11.7 million units, 5 per cent higher than in 2001. The demand in Japan is expected to be 810,000 units in 2002, 3.8 per cent higher than in 2001 and in North America demand will be around 800,000 units, about 3 per cent higher than in 2001.

Since 1995 Chinese motorcycle production has ranked first in the world. In 2001 28.8 million units were exported from China and made China the number one motorcycle export country. However, there is still a gap between the motorcycle great powers such as Japan in areas such as sales income, brand, R&D and quality.

The management philosophy of Yin Mingshan, CEO of Lifan

Here are some statements, taken directly from the Lifan website:

Fellows, our burden is heavy, but we have confidence. Honda and Yamaha are all over, what shall we Lifan people do? I believe, with our plan of 'Big Lifan', 'New Lifan', with enterprise culture integration, the Lifan people will work together. When the civil industry is in the most dangerous situation, Lifan people are forced to shout out: 'innovation, innovation, innovation'. Then the ideal of 'Long live Lifan' will come true.

Finally, I wish all staff a Happy New Year and a Happy Family

(Yin Mingshan at the Spring Festival (Chinese New Year), March 2003)

The penetration of Lifan motorcycles in the world market has caused panic in the Japanese motorcycle manufacturing industry. This is the main reason why the Japanese press showed an interest in the Lifan Group. Another reason mentioned by Japanese journalists is that most Japanese think 90 per cent of Chinese motorcycles are copying Japanese motorcycles. They will give Japanese citizens an objective report on the existing situation in the Chinese motorcycle industry, and try to change the thinking of Japanese citizens.

To earn money in China is a success, to earn profit overseas is glory.

Hundreds of people will lose their jobs without strict management.

Three treasures of Lifan: innovation, export, high credit.

If you do not work hard today – you will look very hard for a job tomorrow.

If one contaminates Lifan's brand – Lifan will get rid of one's job.

Lifan invests 600 million yuan in automobiles

Lifan has long held the ambition to enter the automobile industry. Last year the Group and the Chongqing Bus Plant had a short-time contract and in April the Lifan Group started to reorganise the Chongqing Bus Plant, but within six months they separated due to a conflict between the state-owned system and the private system. Lifan called back all its staff who had been dispatched to the Chongqing Bus Plant and the plan for reorganising it was announced a failure. (We reported this on 28 January 2003).

Though thwarted in the bus field Lifan did not give up hope of entering the automobile industry, on the contrary, its will became stronger. Lifan management made slight adjustments to its automobile industry strategy and changed from buses to touring cars.

Lifan will input 600 million yuan in the touring car project. The project started at the beginning of this year, and it is estimated to be complete within two years. On completion and the putting into service of this project it will output 100,000 units of automobiles and 100,000 units of automobile engines each year, mainly for the middle class in cities and higher income class in agricultural areas.

Sales income is estimated at 4 billion yuan and the profit after tax 400 million yuan.

Yang Zhou, the president of the Lifan Group, said:

'It is definitely not just a dream for Lifan to enter automobile manufacturing. Lifan is trying to reach its target of 10 billion yuan. It is hard to achieve this target by motorcycles alone – Lifan has an order worth $150 million for automobiles. It is negotiating with a Shenzhen company and companies from the United Kingdom and Germany regarding high grade chassis and electric cars, to increase the technical content of its products.'

Chongqing motorcycle manufacturers turn to automobiles

As Lifan aggressively enters automobile manufacturing another two motorcycle manufacturers in Chongqing, Loncin and Zongshen, are also targeting the automobile industry. Loncin and Chendu Shanlu Automobile Co., Ltd established Loncin Chendu Automobile Co., Ltd and plan to reach an annual output of 30 million automobiles in three years.

Data shows that the domestic motorcycle market capacity has reached 12 million units, and will reach 15 million units within five years. This is the saturated capacity of the market. Meanwhile, owing to tough market competition, the profit of each motorcycle manufacturer is reducing rapidly.

The worst is that Honda has pushed forward a cheap style to the south-east Asia market, only $700+ against the price advantage of Chongqing motorcycles. This is a great threat to Chongqing motorcycle manufacturers and their overseas markets. Though

they have been exploring new bases and seeking new markets in the Middle East, south Asia, South America and Africa, they know the motorcycle industry is at the top of the growth curve.

Compared to the sad state of affairs in the motorcycle industry, the automobile manufacturing industry has a wonderful future. In recent years the bus market has been increasing at better than 20 per cent. Especially under the push of expanding financial policies, the highway is being laid out all over the country, which has brought senior grade buses a broad market space. Besides, the existing urban buses are old, but with the development of cities they will be updated. A survey by Lifan shows that in the coming 10 years, market capacity for buses will be still over 20 per cent. The huge market demands ensures profit. The profit on automobiles is about 10 per cent, the net profit is 8 per cent, twice that of motorcycles. In the coming five years this figure won't be changing much. (Lifan News, 6 March 2003.)

Source: adapted from the Lifan website.

Questions

1. Based on the information in the case, how is the international marketing management philosophy in Lifan different from a typical company in western Europe?

2. How can the difference in marketing management philosophy be explained by the differences in culture between western Europe and China?

3. How should Lifan overcome the cultural differences if they decide to enter the western European market?

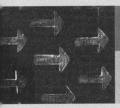

CASE STUDY 7.2 Playboy Enterprises

Internationalization of the Playboy business compared with its major competitors (Hustler and Beate Uhse)

Playboy Enterprises Inc. (PEI; **www.playboy enterprises.com**) is an international multimedia entertainment company that sells and markets branded products and services in almost 200 countries worldwide. The company's six business groups (SBUs) are Publishing, Entertainment, Product Marketing, Catalog, Casino Gaming and Playboy.com, Inc.

'We're going from a domestic print-oriented magazine to a global entertainment company.

This has been the vision that I had since becoming CEO,' Christie Hefner, chairman and CEO of PBE and PEI ('New Hefner at helm is trying fresh focus – The famous bunny is going global', *USA Today*, 6 October 1999).

Christie Hefner adds: 'To have long-term surviv-ability, brands shouldn't be identified in the con-sumer's mind with a single product. They should reflect a point of view that you can own and adapt what products will best express it, given trends, lifestyle, and technology. What we've done is extract from the magazine the essence of what the brand stands for as a lifestyle, and a sense of fun, sexy entertainment and then marry that with the right content of the right product to represent the brand in a different format, whether that be Playboy Television or Playboy Online' ('Pulling rabbits out of hats', *Chief Executive*, New York, September 1999).

Although most analysts have been impressed by Ms Hefner's approach to the business there are also some who remain critical about the future value of PBE: 'Playboy is no longer unique. Each one of these magazines has taken on a part of Playboy's niche. It is hard to find a way to grow' (magazine industry analyst Samir Husni, 'New Hefner at helm is trying fresh focus – The famous bunny is going global', *USA Today*, 6 October 1999).

Questions

1. Make an evaluation of the internationalization potential of the Playboy brand compared to its competitors such as Hustler (**www.hustler.com**) or the European market leader Beate Uhse (**www.beate-uhse.ag**)

2. Playboy would like to have a larger market share in Europe: which of the six SBUs in the product port-folio should it focus on in order to gain market shares from Beate Uhse in the erotic business?

3. Should PBE try to transfer its brand image to other product areas? Which ones and how?

For further exercises and cases, see this book's website at **www.booksites.net/hollensen**

Questions for discussion

1. Because English is the world language of business, is it necessary for UK managers to learn a foreign language?

2. According to Hofstede and Hall, Asians are (1) more group oriented, (2) more family oriented and (3) more concerned with social status. How might such orientations affect the way you market your product to Asian consumers?

3. Do you think that cultural differences between nations are more or less important than cultural variations within nations? Under what circumstances is each important?

4. Identify some constraints in marketing to a traditional Muslim society. Use some of the examples in the chapter.

5. What layers of culture have the strongest influence on business people's behaviour?

6. The focus of this chapter has mainly been the influence of culture on international marketing strategies. Try also to discuss the potential influences of marketing on cultures.

7. What role does the self-reference criterion play in international business ethics?

8. Compare the role of women in your country to their role in other cultures. How do the different roles affect women's behaviour as consumers and as business people?

References

Copeland, L. and Griggs, L. (1985) *Going International*, Random House, New York.

Field, M. (1986) 'Fragrance marketers sniff out rich aroma', *Advertising Age* (special report on 'Marketing to the Arab world'), 30 January, p. 10.

Hall, E.T. (1960) 'The silent language in overseas business', *Harvard Business Review*, May–June, pp. 87–97.

Harper, T. (1986) 'Polaroid clicks instantly in Moslem market', *Advertising Age* (special report on 'Marketing to the Arab world'), 30 January, p. 12.

Hofstede, G. (1980) *Culture's Consequences: International differences in work-related values*, Sage, Beverly Hills, CA, and London.

Hofstede, G. (1983) 'The cultural relativity of organizational practices and theories', *Journal of International Business Studies*, Fall, pp. 75–89.

Hofstede, G. and Bond, M.R. (1988) 'The Confucius connection: from cultural roots to economic growth', *Organizational Dynamics*, vol. 16, no. 4, pp. 4–21.

Lee, J. (1966) 'Cultural analysis in overseas operations', *Harvard Business Review*, March–April, pp. 106–14.

MacKenzie, S. (1998) 'Boundary commission', *Marketing Week*, London, 29 January.

Murdoch, G.P. (1945) 'The common denominator of cultures', in Linton, R. (ed.), *The Science of Man in the World Crises*, Columbia University Press, New York.

Pasco, M. (2000) 'Brands are replacing celebrities as role models for today's youth', *Kids Marketing Report*, 27 January.

Phillips, C., Doole, I. and Lowe, R. (1994) *International Marketing Strategy: Analysis, development and implementation*, Routledge, London.

Smith, D.S. (1998) 'Europe's youth is our future', *Marketing*, London, 22 January.

Smith, K.V. (2000) 'Why SFA is a tough sell in Latin America', *Marketing News*, Chicago, 3 January.

Solberg, C.A. (2002) 'Culture and industrial buyer behavior: the Arab experience, Paper presented at the 18th *IMP Conference*, pp. 1–34.

Usunier, J.C. (2000) *International Marketing*, Pearson Education, Harlow.

Further reading

Chaker, M.N. (2003) 'The Impact on Cultural Industries in United Arab Emirates', *Journal of American Academy of Business*, vol. 3, No. 1–2, pp. 323–25.

Eckhardt, G.M. and Houston, M.J. (2002) 'Cultural paradoxes reflected in brand meaning: McDonald's in Shanghai, China', *Journal of International Marketing*, vol. 10, no. 2, pp. 68–82.

Friedman, H.H. (2001) 'The impact of Jewish values on marketing and business practices', *Journal of Macromarketing*, vol. 21, no. 1 (June), pp. 74–80.

Gehrt, K.C. and Shim, S. (2002) 'Situational influence in the international marketplace: an examination of Japanese gift-giving', *Journal of Marketing Theory and Practice*, vol. 10, no. 1, pp. 11–22.

Gesteland, R. (2002) *Cross-cultural Business Behavior* (3rd edn), Copenhagen Business School Press.

Haley, G.T. and Tan, C.-T. 'East vs. West: strategic marketing management meets the Asian networks', *Journal of Business & Industrial Marketing*, vol. 14, no. 2, pp. 91–101.

Hamilton, J.B. and Knouse, S.B. (2001) 'Multinational enterprise decision principles for dealing with cross-cultural ethical conflicts', *Journal of Business Ethics*, vol. 31, pp. 77–94.

Jallat, F. and Kimmel, A.J. (2002) 'Marketing in culturally diverse environments: the case of Western Europe, *Business Horizons*, July–August, pp. 30–6.

Souiden, N. (2002) 'Segmenting the Arab markets on the basis of marketing stimuli', *International Marketing Review*, vol. 19, no. 6, pp. 611–36.

Sullivan, D.P. and Weaver, G.R. (2000) 'Cultural cognition in international business research', *Management International Review*, vol. 40, no. 3, pp. 269–97.

Warner, M. and Joynt, P. (2002) *Managing Across Cultures* (2nd edn), Thomson Learning, London.

8 The international market selection process

Contents

Learning objectives

After studying this chapter you should be able to do the following:

- Define international market selection and identify the problems in achieving it.
- Explore how international marketers screen potential markets/countries using secondary and primary data (criteria).
- Distinguish between preliminary and 'fine-grained' screening.
- Realise the importance of segmentation in the formulation of the global marketing strategy.
- Choose among alternative market expansion strategies.
- Distinguish between concentration and diversification in market expansion.

8.1 Introduction

Identifying the 'right' market(s) to enter is important for a number of reasons:

- It can be a major determinant of success or failure, especially in the early stages of internationalization.
- This decision influences the nature of foreign marketing programmes in the selected countries.
- The nature of geographic location of selected markets affects the firm's ability to coordinate foreign operations.

In this chapter a systematic approach to International Market Selection (IMS) is presented. A study of recently internationalized US firms showed that on average firms do not follow a highly systematic approach. However, those firms using a systematic sequence of steps in IMS also showed a better performance (Yip *et al.*, 2000).

8.2   International market selection: SMEs versus LSEs

The international market selection process seems different in small and medium-sized enterprises and large-scale enterprises.

In the SME the IMS is often simply a reaction to a stimulus provided by a change agent. This agent can appear in the form of an unsolicited order. Government agencies, chambers of commerce and other change agents may also bring foreign opportunities to the firm's attention. Such cases constitute an externally driven decision in which the exporter simply responds to an opportunity in a given market.

In other cases the IMS of SMEs is based on the following criteria (Johanson and Vahlne, 1977):

- Low 'psychic' distance: low uncertainty about foreign markets and low perceived difficulty of acquiring information about them. 'Psychic' distance has been defined as differences in language, culture, political system, level of education or level of industrial development.
- Low 'cultural' distance: low perceived differences between the home and destination cultures ('cultural' distance is normally regarded as part of 'psychic' distance).
- Low geographic distance.

Using any one of these criteria often results in firms entering new markets with successively greater psychic distance. The choice is often limited to the SMEs' immediate neighbours, since geographic proximity is likely to reflect cultural similarity, more knowledge about foreign markets and greater ease in obtaining information. When using this model the decision maker will focus on decision-making based on incrementalism where the firm is predicted to start the internationalization by moving into those markets they can most easily understand. It is generally believed that SMEs and firms which are early in their internationalization process are more likely to use a 'psychic' distance or other 'rules of thumb' procedures than LSEs with international experience (Andersen and Buvik, 2002).

By limiting their consideration to a nearby country SMEs effectively narrow the IMS into one decision: to go or not to go to a nearby country. The reason for this behaviour can be that SME executives, usually being short of human and financial resources, find it hard to resist the temptation of selecting target markets intuitively.

In a study of internationalization in Danish SMEs Sylvest and Lindholm (1997) found that the IMS process was very different in 'old' SMEs (established before 1960) from that in 'young' SMEs (established in 1989 or later). The young SMEs entered more distant markets much earlier than the older SMEs, which followed the more traditional 'step-by-step' IMS process. The reason for the more rapid internationalization of young SMEs may be their status as subsuppliers to larger firms, where they are 'pulled out' to international markets by their large customers and their international networks.

While SMEs must make first entry decisions by selecting targets among largely unknown markets, LSEs with existing operations in many countries have to decide in which of them to introduce new products. By drawing on existing operations LSEs have easier access to product-specific data in the form of primary information that is more accurate than any secondary database. As a result of this the LSEs can be more proactive. Although selecting markets based on intuition and pragmatism can be a satisfying way for SMEs, the following will be based on a more proactive IMS process, organised in a systematic and step-by-step analysis.

However, in 'real life' the IMS process will not always be a logical and gradual sequence of activities, but an iterative process involving multiple feedback loops (Andersen and Strandskov, 1998). Furthermore, in many small subcontracting firms exporting firms do not actively select their foreign markets. The decision about IMS is made by the partner obtaining the main contract (main contractor), thus pulling the SME into international markets (Brewer, 2001; Westhead *et al.*, 2002).

8.3   Building a model for international market selection

Research from the Uppsala school on the internationalization process of the firm has suggested several potential determinants of the firm's choice of foreign markets. These can be classified into two groups: (1) environmental and (2) firm characteristics (see Figure 8.1).

Figure 8.1 Potential determinants of the firm's choice of foreign markets

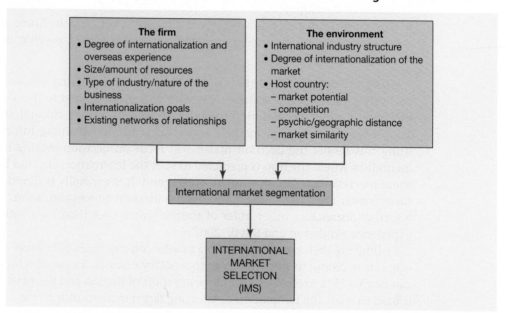

Let us look first at the environment. How do we define 'international markets'? The following approach suggests two dimensions:

- The international market as a country or a group of countries.
- The international market as a group of customers with nearly the same characteristics. According to this latter definition a market can consist of customers from several countries.

Most books and studies in global marketing have attempted to segment the world market into the different countries or groups of countries. This has been done for two principal reasons:

- International data are more easily (and sometimes exclusively) available on a nation-by-nation basis. It is very difficult to acquire accurate cross-national statistical data.
- Distribution management and media have also been organised on a nation-by-nation basis. Most agents/distributors still represent their manufacturers only in one single country. Few agents sell their products on a cross-national basis.

However, country markets or multicountry markets are not quite adequate. In many cases boundary lines are the result of political agreement or war and do not reflect a similar separation in buyer characteristics among people on either side of the border.

Presentation of a market–screening model

In Figure 8.1 an outline model for IMS was presented. In the following we will look in more detail at the box labelled 'international market segmentation'. The elements of IMS are shown in Figure 8.2.

Figure 8.2 International market segmentation

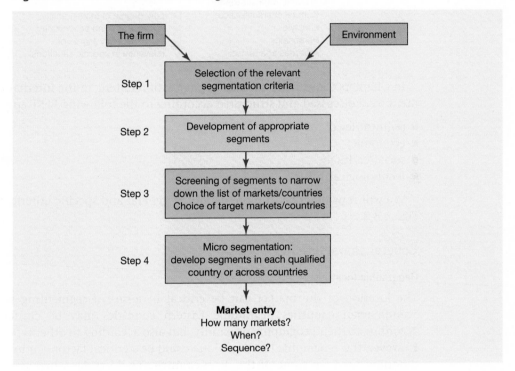

Steps 1 and 2: Defining criteria

In general, the criteria for effective segmentation are as follows:

- *measurability*: the degree to which the size and purchasing power of resulting segments can be measured;
- *accessibility*: the degree to which the resulting segments can be effectively reached and served;
- *substantiality/profitability*: the degree to which segments are sufficiently large and/or profitable;
- *actionability*: the degree to which the organization has sufficient resources to formulate effective marketing programmes and 'make things happen'.

A high degree of measurability and accessibility indicates more general characteristics as criteria (at the top of Figure 8.3) and vice versa.

It is important to realise that more than one measure can be used simultaneously in the segmentation process.

Figure 8.3 The basis of international market segmentation

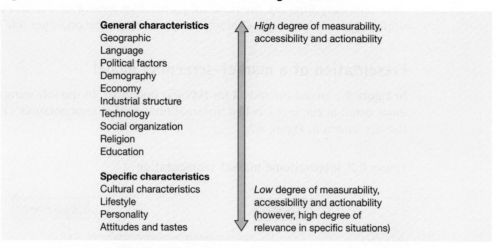

In Chapters 6 and 7 the different segmentation criteria in the international environment were discussed and structured according to the following PEST approach:

- political/legal;
- economic;
- social/cultural;
- technological.

We will now describe in more detail the general and specific criteria mentioned in Figure 8.3.

General characteristics

Geographic location

The location of the market can be critical in terms of segmenting world markets. Scandinavian countries or Middle Eastern countries may be clustered not only according to their geographic proximity, but also according to other types of similarity. However, the geographic location alone could be a critical factor. For instance, air conditioning needs in some of the Arab countries could make a manufacturer consider these countries as specific clusters.

Language

Language has been described as the mirror of the culture. On one level its implications for the international marketer are self-evident: advertising must be translated; brand names must be vetted for international acceptability; business negotiations must often be conducted through expensive interpreters or through the yet more expensive acquisition of a foreign translator. In the latter case genuine fluency is essential; persuasion and contract negotiation present enough difficulties even in a mother tongue.

Less obvious is the fact that foreign language may imply different patterns of thought and different customer motivations. In such cases a knowledge – again, a good knowledge – of the language will do more than facilitate communication; it provides automatic insight into the relevant culture.

Political factors

Countries may be grouped and world markets segmented according to broad political characteristics. Until recently the Iron Curtain was the basis of one such division. In general terms, the degree of power that the central government has may be the general criterion for segmentation. It is possible, for instance, that a company is producing certain chemicals but that, due to government regulations, many of the world markets may be considered too difficult to enter.

Demography

Demographics is a critical basis for segmentation. For instance, it is often necessary to analyse population characteristics in terms of the proportion of elderly people or children in the total population.

If the country's population is getting older and the number of infants per thousand is declining, which is the case in some European countries, a baby food company would not consider entering that country. In Europe birth rates are tumbling and life spans lengthening. Baby-based industries from toys to foods and nappies face sharp competition. Consumer electronics and housing may also be affected.

Economy

As the earlier studies have indicated, economic development level could be a critical variable for international market segmentation. Electric dishwashers or washer–dryers require a certain level of economic development. There is not a good market for these products in India. However, in western European countries these products are becoming almost a basic necessity. On the basis of the level of economic development certain specific consumption patterns emerge. Societies with high personal income spend more time and money on services, education and recreation. Thus it may be possible to arrange certain income groups from different countries into certain clusters.

Industrial structure

A country's industrial structure is depicted by the characteristics of its business population. One country may have many small retailers; another country may rely on a large number of department stores for retail distribution. One country may be thriving on small manufacturers; another may have very concentrated and large-scale manufacturing activity. The type of competition that exists at the wholesale level may be the critical specific factor for clustering international markets. The international marketer may wish to work with a series of strong wholesalers.

Technology

The degree of technological advancement or the degree of agricultural technology may easily be the basis for segmentation. A software company planning to enter international markets may wish to segment them on the basis of the number of PCs per thousand of the population. It may not be worthwhile for this company to enter markets below a certain number of PCs per thousand of the population. For example, it may find Pakistan, Iran and most Arab countries, all of Africa and all of eastern Europe less than satisfactory for entry.

Social organization

The family is an important purchasing group in any society. In Europe marketers are accustomed to either the so-called nuclear family, with father, mother and children all living together under one roof, or, increasingly as society changes, the single-parent family. In other countries the key unit is the extended family, with three or four generations all in the same house.

In the United States, for instance, socioeconomic groupings have been used extensively as segmentation tools. A six-category classification is used: upper upper class, lower upper, upper middle, lower middle, upper lower and lower lower. The US high-income professionals are relegated to the lower upper class, described as those 'who have earned their position rather than inherited it', the *nouveaux riches*.

In contrast, it would have been hard to find useful socioeconomic groupings in Russia beyond white-collar worker, blue-collar worker and farm worker.

Religion

Religious customs are a major factor in marketing. The most obvious example, perhaps, is the Christian tradition of present giving at Christmas, yet even in this simple matter pitfalls lie in wait for the international marketer: in some Christian countries the traditional exchange of presents takes place not on Christmas Day but on other days in December or early January.

The impact of religion on marketing becomes most evident in the case of Islam. Islamic laws, based on the Koran, provide guidance for a whole range of human activities, including economic activity.

Education

Educational levels are of importance to the international marketer from two main standpoints: the economic potential of the youth market and, in developing countries, the level of literacy.

Educational systems vary a lot from country to country. The compensation for on-the-job training also varies a great deal. As a result the economic potential of the youth market is very different from country to country.

In most industrialised countries literacy levels are close to 100 per cent and the whole range of communications media is open to the marketer. In developing countries literacy rates can be as low as 25 per cent, and in one or two 15 per cent or less, although at such low levels the figures can be no more than estimates. In those same countries television sets and even radios are economically beyond the reach of most of the population, although communal television sets are sometimes available. The consumer marketer faces a real challenge in deciding on promotional policies in these countries, and the use of visual material is more relevant.

Specific characteristics

Cultural characteristics

Cultural characteristics may play a significant role in segmenting world markets. To take advantage of global markets or global segments firms require a thorough understanding of what drives customer behaviour in different markets. They must learn to detect the extent to which similarities exist or can be achieved through marketing activities. The cultural behaviour of the members of a given society is constantly shaped by a set of dynamic variables that can also be used as segmentation criteria: language, religion, values and attitudes, material elements and technology, aesthetics, education and social institutions. These different elements were dealt with more extensively in Chapters 6 and 7.

Lifestyles

Typically activity, interest and opinion research is used as the tool for analysing lifestyles. However, such a research tool has not quite been developed for international purposes. Perhaps certain consumption habits or practices may be used as an indication of the lifestyle that is being studied. Food consumption habits can be used as one such general indicator. Types of food eaten can easily indicate lifestyles that an international food company should be ready to consider. For example, Indian-style hot curries are not likely to be very popular in Germany given its rather bland cooking. Very hot Arab dishes are not likely to be very popular in western Europe.

Personality

Personality is reflected in certain types of behaviour. A general characteristic may be temper, so that segmentation may be based on the general temper of people. Latin Americans or Mediterranean people are known to have certain personality traits. Perhaps those traits are a suitable basis for the segmentation of world markets. One example is the tendency to haggle. In pricing, for instance, the international firm will have to use a substantial degree of flexibility where haggling is widespread. Haggling in a country such as Turkey is almost a national pastime. In the underground bazaars of Istanbul the vendor would be almost offended if the customer accepted the first asking price.

Attitudes, tastes or predispositions

These are all complex concepts, but it is reasonable to say that they can be utilised for segmentation. Status symbols can be used as indicators of what some people in a culture consider would enhance their own self-concept as well as their perception among other people.

Step 3: Screening of markets/countries

This screening process can be divided in two:

- *Preliminary screening.* This is where markets/countries are screened primarily according to external screening criteria (the state of the market). In the case of SMEs the limited internal resources (e.g. financial resources) must also be taken into account. There will be a number of countries that can be excluded in advance as potential markets.
- *Fine-grained screening.* This is where the firm's competitive power (and special competences) in the different markets can be taken into account.

Preliminary screening

The number of markets is reduced by 'coarse-grained', macro-oriented screening methods based on criteria such as the following:

- restrictions in the export of goods from one country to another;
- gross national product per capita;
- cars owned per 1,000 of the population;
- government spending as a percentage of GNP;
- population per hospital bed.

When screening countries it is particularly important to assess the political risk of entering a country. Over recent years marketers have developed various indices to help assess the risk factors in the evaluation of potential market opportunities. One of these indices is the Business Environment Risk Index (BERI).

BERI measures the general quality of a country's business climate. Launched in 1972, it was developed by Frederich Haner of the University of Delaware in the United States. It has since expanded into country-specific forecasts and country risk forecasts for international lenders, but its basic service is the Global Subscription Service. This assesses countries several times a year on different economic, political and financial factors on a scale from 0 to 4. The overall index ranges from 0 to 100 (see Table 8.1).

Table 8.1 **Criteria included in the overall BERI index**

Criteria	Weights	Multiplied with the score (rating) on a scale of 0–4[a]	Overall BERI index[b]
Political stability	3		
Economic growth	2.5		
Currency convertibility	2.5		
Labour cost/productivity	2		
Short-term credit	2		
Long-term loans/venture capital	2		
Attitude towards the foreign investor and profits	1.5		
Nationalization	1.5		
Monetary inflation	1.5		
Balance of payments	1.5		
Enforceability of contracts	1.5		
Bureaucratic delays	1		
Communications: phone, fax, internet-access	1		
Local management and partner	1		
Professional services and contractors	0.5		
Total	25	× 4 (max.)	= Max. 100

[a] 0 = unacceptable; 1 = poor; 2 = average conditions; 3 = above average conditions; 4 = superior conditions.
[b] Total points: >80 favourable environment for investors, advanced economy. 70–79 not so favourable, but still an advanced economy. 55–69 an immature economy with investment potential, probably an NIC. 40–54 a high-risk country, probably an LDC. Quality of management has to be superior to realise potential. <40 very high risk. Would only commit capital if some extraordinary justification.

The BERI index has been questioned as a general management decision tool and should therefore be supplemented by in-depth country reports before final market entry decisions are made.

Among other macro-oriented screening methods is the *shift-share approach* (Green and Allaway, 1985; Papadopoulos and Denis, 1988; Papadopoulos *et al.*, 2002). This approach is based upon the identification of relative changes in international import shares among various countries. The average growth rate of imports for a particular product for a 'basket' of countries is calculated and then each country's actual growth rate is compared with the average growth rate. The difference, called the 'net shift', identifies growing or declining markets. This procedure has the advantage that it takes into account both the absolute level of a country's imports and their relative growth rate. On the other hand, it examines only those criteria and does not take into account other macro-oriented criteria.

'Fine-grained' screening

As the BERI index focuses only on the political risk of entering new markets a broader approach that includes the competences of the firm is often needed.

For this purpose a powerful aid to the identification of the 'best opportunity' target countries is the application of the market attractiveness/competitive strength matrix (Figure 8.4). This market portfolio model replaces the two single dimensions in the BCG growth–share matrix with two composite dimensions applied to global marketing issues. Measures on these two dimensions are built up from a large number of possible variables, as listed in Table 8.2. In the following, one of the important dimensions will be described and commented upon.

Figure 8.4 **The market attractiveness/competitive strength matrix**

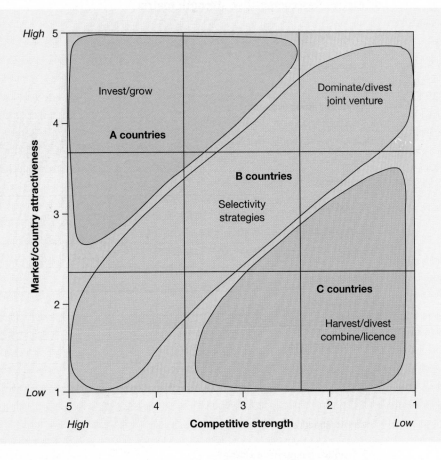

Table 8.2 **Dimensions of market/country attractiveness and competitive strength**

Market/country attractiveness	Competitive strength
Market size (total and segments)	Market share
Market growth (total and segments)	Marketing ability and capacity (country-specific know-how)
Buying power of customers	Products fit to market demands
Market seasons and fluctuations	Price
Average industry margin	Contribution margin
Competitive conditions (concentration, intensity, entry barriers, etc.)	Image
Market prohibitive conditions (tariff/non-tariff barriers, import restrictions, etc.)	Technology position
Government regulations (price controls, local content, compensatory exports, etc.)	Product quality
Infrastructure	Market support
Economic and political stability	Quality of distributors and service
Psychic distance (from home base to foreign market)	Financial resources
	Access to distribution channels

Figure 8.5 Underlying questionnaire for locating countries on a market attractiveness/competitive strength matrix

Time of analysis:
Analysis of product area:
In country:

A. Market attractiveness

	1 Very poor	2 Poor	3 Medium	4 Good	5 Very good	% Weight factor	Result (grading × weight)
Market size							
Market growth							
Buying structure							
Prices							
Buying power							
Market access							
Competitive intensity							
Political/economic risks							
etc.							
Total						100	

Market attractiveness = Result : 100 = ...

B. Relative competitive strength
with regard to the strongest competitor = ...

	1 Very poor	2 Poor	3 Medium	4 Good	5 Very good	% Weight factor	Result (grading × weight)
Products fit to market demands							
Prices and conditions							
Market presence							
Marketing							
Communication							
Obtainable market share							
Financial results							
etc.							
Total						100	

Relative competitive strength = Result : 100 = ...

Market size

The total market volume per year for a certain country/market can be calculated as:

> Production (of a product in a country)
> + import
> − export
> = theoretical market size
> +/− changes in stock size
> = effective market size

Production, import and export figures can usually be found in the specific country's statistics, if it is a standardised product with an identifiable customs position.

A more precise location of a particular country (in Figure 8.4) may be determined by using the questionnaire in Figure 8.5.

As seen from Figure 8.4 one of the results of this process is a prioritised classification of countries/markets into distinct categories:

- *A countries*. These are the primary markets (i.e. the key markets), which offer the best opportunities for long-term strategic development. Here companies may want to establish a permanent presence and should therefore embark on a thorough research programme.
- *B countries*. These are the secondary markets, where opportunities are identified but political or economic risk is perceived as being too high to make long-term irrevocable commitments. These markets would be handled in a more pragmatic way due to the potential risks identified. A comprehensive marketing information system would be needed.

Exhibit 8.1	Market assessment for Ford Tractors

The large multinational company Ford Tractors used many market analysis responses to produce the matrix shown in Figure 8.6. The information inputs required may sometimes be beyond the reach of an SME. In such cases there is still value in using this approach as a framework for identifying key markets; however, the analysis will then have to be based on more subjectively assessed criteria.

Source: Harrell and Kiefer, 1995, p. 98.

Figure 8.6 Country attractiveness: the example of Ford Tractors

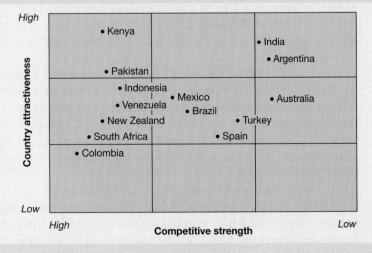

■ *C countries*. These are the tertiary or 'catch what you can' markets. They will be perceived as high risk, and so the allocation of resources will be minimal. Objectives in such countries would be short term and opportunistic; companies would give no real commitment. No significant research would be carried out.

Step 4: Develop subsegments in each qualified country and across countries

Once the prime markets have been identified firms then use standard techniques to segment markets within countries, using variables such as the following:

■ demographic/economic factors;
■ lifestyles;
■ consumer motivations;
■ geography;
■ buyer behaviour;
■ psychographics, etc.

Thus the prime segmentation basis is geographic (by country) and the secondary is within countries. The problem here is that, depending on the information basis, it may be difficult fully to formulate secondary segmentation bases. Furthermore, such an approach can run the risk of leading to a differentiated marketing approach, which may leave the company with a very fragmented international strategy.

The drawback of traditional approaches lies in the difficulty of applying them consistently across markets. If a company is to try to achieve a consistent and controlled marketing strategy across all its markets it needs a transnational approach to its segmentation strategy.

It can be argued that companies competing internationally should segment markets on the basis of consumers, not countries. Segmentation by purely geographical factors leads to national stereotyping. It ignores the differences between customers within a nation and ignores similarities across boundaries.

Cluster analysis can be used to identify meaningful cross-national segments, each of which is expected to evoke a similar response to any marketing mix strategy. Figure 8.7 shows an attempt to segment the western European market into six clusters.

Once the firm has chosen a certain country as a target market the next stage in the micro segmentation process is to decide with which products or services the company wishes to become active in the individual countries. Here it is necessary to make a careful market segmentation, especially in the larger and more important foreign markets, in order to be in a position to exhaust the market potential in a differentiated manner (Figure 8.8).

In this context it is necessary to draw attention to a specific strategic procedure, which is oriented worldwide towards similar market segments. Here it is not the country-specific market attractiveness that influences the decision on specific markets, but the recognition of the existence of similar structures of demand and similar consumer habits in segments (and perhaps only in small segments) of different markets.

An illustration of the whole international market segmentation/screening process (steps 1–4 in Figure 8.2) is seen in Figure 8.9.

The model in Figure 8.9 begins by regarding the world market as the potential market for a firm's product. However, if the firm only regards western Europe as a possible market, then the firm may start the screening process at this lower level. The six western European clusters are based on the transnational clustering in Figure 8.7. The further down in the model, the greater the use of primary data (personal interviews, field

Figure 8.7 Transnational clustering of the western European market

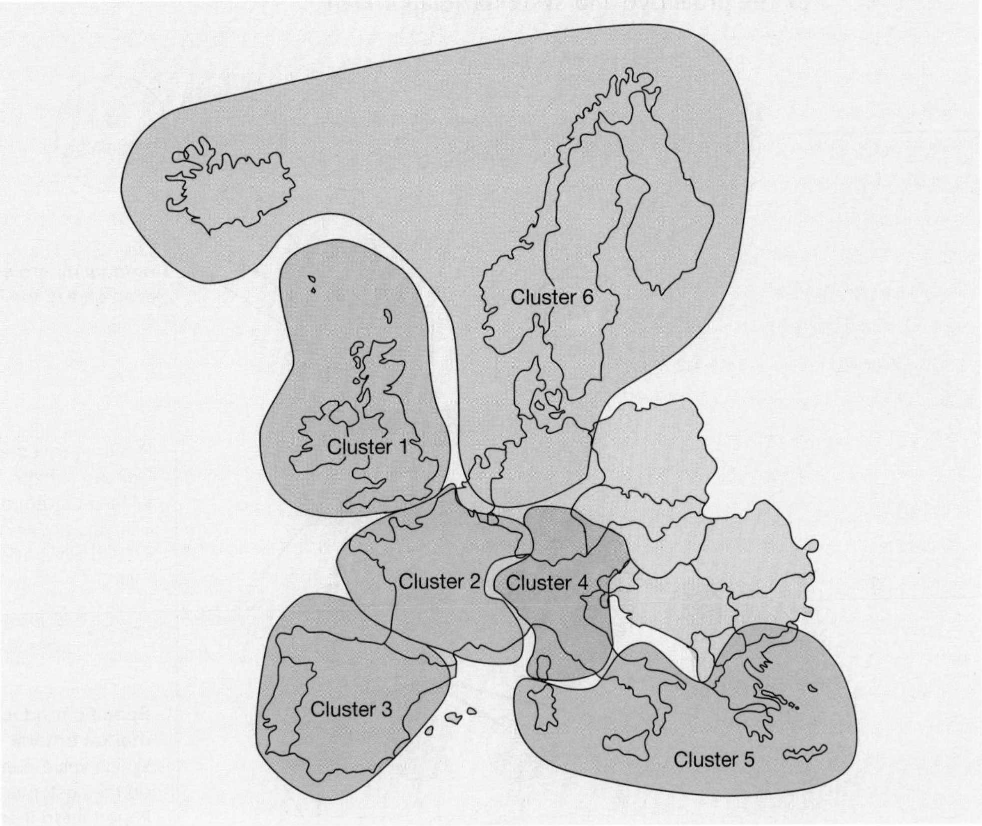

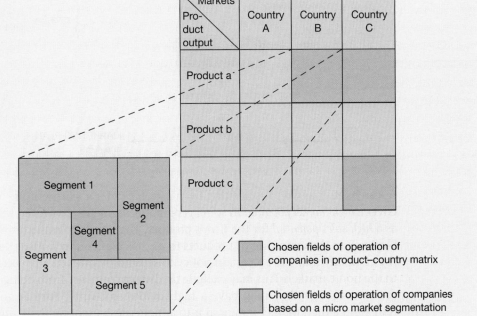

Source: Welford and Prescott, 1996. *European Business: An issue-based approach*, 3rd Edition. Reprinted by permission of Pearson Education Ltd.

Figure 8.8 Micro market segmentation

Figure 8.9 The international market segmentation/screening process: an example of the proactive and systematic approach

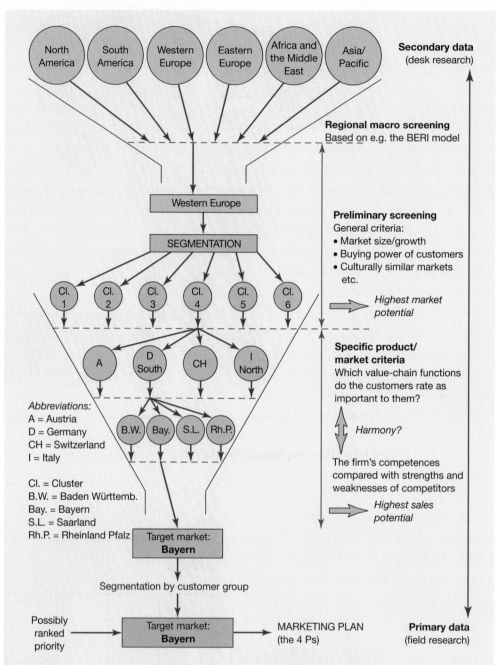

research, etc.), as well as screening from internal criteria. Furthermore, the firm may discover a *high market potential* in some geographic segments. However, this is not the same as a *high sales potential* for the firm's product. There may be some restrictions (e.g. trade barriers) on the exporting of products to a particular country. Also the management of the company may have a certain policy to select only markets that are culturally similar to the home market. This may exclude far distant countries from being selected as target markets, though they may have a high market potential. Furthermore, to be able to transform a high market potential into a high sales potential, there must be a harmony between the firm's competences (internal criteria) and the value-chain functions that customers rate as important to them. Only in this situation will a customer regard the firm as a possible supplier, equal to other possible suppliers. With other words, in making the International Market Selection, the firm must seek the synergy between the possible new target market and its own strengths, objectives, and strategy. The firm's choice of new international markets is very much influenced by the existence of complementary markets and marketing skills gained in these markets.

In general, Figure 8.9 is based on proactive and systematic decision-making behaviour by the firm. This is not always a realistic condition, especially not in SMEs, where a *pragmatic approach* is required. Often firms are not able to segment from their own criteria but must expect to be evaluated and chosen (as subsuppliers) by much larger firms. The pragmatic approach to IMS can also give rise to the firm choosing customers and markets with a background similar to the managers' own personal network and cultural background. Contingencies, serendipity and 'management feel' play an important role in both early and late phases of IMS. In a qualitative study of Australian firms Rahman (2003) found, that an important factor that firms take into consideration at the final stage of evaluating the attractiveness of foreign markets is 'management feel'. One of the companies said:

> At the end of the day much of the decision depends on the management's feel about the market. There will always be some uncertainties in the market, particularly when you are deciding about the future, and international markets are no exception in this regard. So, we managers will have to make the decision within the limited information available to us, and 'gut feel' plays a big role in that (Rahman, 2003, p. 124)

8.4 Market expansion strategies

The choice of a market expansion strategy is a key decision in export marketing. First, different patterns are likely to cause development of different competitive conditions in different markets over time. For example, a fast rate of growth into new markets characterised by short product life cycles can create entry barriers towards competitors and give rise to higher profitability. On the other hand, a purposeful selection of relatively few markets for more intensive development can create higher market shares, implying stronger competitive positions.

In designing their strategy firms have to answer two underlying questions:

- Will they enter markets incrementally (the waterfall approach) or simultaneously (the shower approach) (see Figure 8.10 on p. 234)?
- Will entry be concentrated or diversified across international markets?

Incremental versus simultaneous entry

A firm may decide to enter international markets on an incremental or experimental basis, entering first a single key market in order to build up experience in international operations, and then subsequently entering other markets one after the other. Alternatively, a firm may decide to enter a number of markets simultaneously in order to leverage its core competence and resources rapidly across a broader market base. (Read about Sanex's shower approach in Exhibit 8.2 on p. 234.)

For the big global company the two strategies can be translated into the concept of the *international product life cycle* (Vernon, 1966), as illustrated in Figure 8.10. See also Figure 15.6, p. 458.

Figure 8.10 The incremental strategy (waterfall approach) and simultaneous strategy (the shower approach)

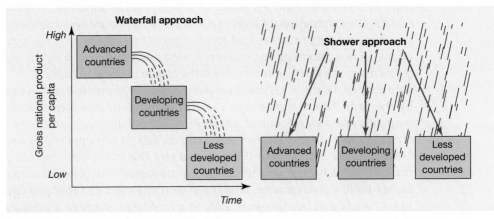

Source: Keegan, 1995. *Global Marketing Management*, © Reprinted by permission of Pearson Education, Inc., Upper Saddle River, NJ.

Exhibit 8.2	Sanex's aggressive search for cross-border niches: an example of the diversification approach

Sanex was developed as a liquid personal soap in 1984. Its success was established quickly – within a year it had gained market leadership in Spain. Soon afterwards it was bought by the US consumer giant Sara Lee, which has four main product sectors:

- packaged meats and bakery products.
- personal products;
- coffee and groceries;
- household and personal care products.

The market basis for Sanex was the growing shower gel market in Europe. Consumers were moving from the ritual of bathing to the more hygienic routine of showering. The Sanex concept of healthy skin fitted perfectly with this trend. The word 'Sanex' is derived from sano, which is Spanish for 'healthy'. The idea behind the positioning was to build up a cross-border (European) concept of health in consumers' minds. This positioning strategy was in contrast to the positioning of the established players such as Procter & Gamble, Unilever, Colgate-Palmolive and Henkel. They were marketing their products under the cosmetic umbrella with strong perfume and colours, and high levels of detergents, supported by the sort of advertising familiar in the cosmetic industry, using beautiful women and exotic surroundings.

The market expansion strategy of Sanex was to launch the product simultaneously on a number of European markets (the 'shower approach' in Figure 8.10). The idea behind this strategy was that Sanex should obtain a 'first-mover advantage', which meant that the big competitors did not have time to copy the product concept before Sanex had product extensions ready for international market launching. The concept of Sanex's shower gel was well understood in most countries, but the potential for the brand would be different. If the habit of showering was well established, the opportunity for Sanex would be better. But in the United Kingdom, for example, baths are still very important, although the frequency of showering has increased. In another big potential market, the United States, people use bars of soap, although they have recently begun to switch to liquid soap.

In a relatively short time Sanex succeeded in developing and launching a broad range of products, including deodorants, colognes and body milk. With 1995 revenues of almost $100 million a year, Sanex is now marketed throughout Europe and the Far East.

Sources: Mazur and Lannon, 1993, p. 23.

Entry on an incremental basis, especially into small markets, may be preferred where a firm lacks experience in foreign markets and wishes to edge gradually into international operations. Information about, and familiarity with, operating in foreign markets are thus acquired step by step. This strategy may be preferable if a company is entering international markets late and faces entrenched local competition. Equally, if a firm is small and has limited resources, or is highly risk averse, it may prefer to enter a single or a limited number of markets and gradually expand in a series of incremental moves rather than making a major commitment to international expansion immediately.

Some companies prefer a rapid entry into world markets in order to seize an emerging opportunity or forestall competition. Rapid entry facilitates early market penetration across a number of markets and enables the firm to build up experience rapidly. It also enables a firm to achieve economies of scale in production and marketing by integrating and consolidating operations across these markets. This may be especially desirable if the product or service involved is innovative or represents a significant technological advance, in order to forestall pre-emption or limitation by other competitors. While increasingly feasible due to developments in global information technology, simultaneous entry into multiple markets typically requires substantial financial and management resources and entails higher operating risk.

The appropriate expansion strategy for the SME

The SME often exploits domestic market opportunities to build up company resources, which later may be used in international markets (Figure 8.11).

The company strategy for market expansion should be concentrated on the product-market segment where the core competences of the company give it a competitive advantage (here product A, B, C and market 1, 2).

The process might evolve step by step, taking one market at a time, market 1, niche 1, learning from it, and then using it as a bridgehead to transfer that competence to the same niche in the next market (market 2, niche 1). The company may develop its international operations by continuing to develop new markets in a step-by-step process, ensuring consolidation and profitability before moving on.

Figure 8.11 Appropriate global marketing strategies for SMEs

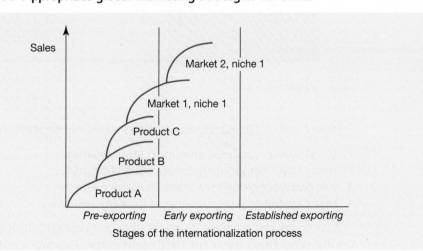

Source: Bradley, 1995. *International Marketing Strategy*. Reproduced by permission of Pearson Education Ltd.

Concentration versus diversification

The firm must also decide whether to concentrate resources on a limited number of similar markets, or alternatively to diversify across a number of different markets. A company may concentrate its efforts by entering countries that are highly similar in terms of market characteristics and infrastructure to the domestic market. Management could also focus on a group of proximate countries. Alternatively, a company may prefer to diversify risk by entering countries that differ in terms of environmental or market characteristics. An economic recession in one country could be counterbalanced by growth in another market. The strength of competition also often varies from one market to another, and profits in a relatively protected or less competitive market may be funnelled into more fiercely competitive markets. Spreading out operations over a broader geographic base, and investing in different regions throughout the world, may also diversify risk, since in some industries markets in different regions are not interdependent (i.e. trends in one region will not spill over into another).

The question of concentrating or diversifying on the country level can be combined with concentration or diversification on the customer (segment) level. The resulting matrix (Figure 8.12) illustrates the four possible strategies.

Figure 8.12 The market expansion matrix

		Market/customer target group	
		Concentration	*Diversification*
Country	*Concentration*	1	2
	Diversification	3	4

Source: Ayal and Zif, 1979, p. 84.

From Figure 8.12 four expansion alternatives can be identified:

1. few customer groups/segments in few countries;
2. many customer groups/segments in few countries;
3. few customer groups/segments in many countries;
4. many customer groups/segments in many countries.

A company can calculate its degree of export concentration and compare it over time or with other firms, using the Herfindahl index. This index is defined as the sum of the squares of the percentage of sales in each foreign country.

$$C = \sum S_i^2 \qquad i = 1, 2, 3, 4 \ldots n \text{ countries}$$

where C = the export concentration index of the firm

S_i = exports to country i as a percentage (measured in decimal numbers from 0 to 1) of the firm's total exports

$$\sum S_i = 1$$

Maximum concentration ($C = 1$) occurs when all the export is made to one country only, and minimum concentration ($C = 1/n$) exists when exports are equally distributed over a large number of countries.

The factors favouring country diversification versus concentration are shown in Table 8.3.

Table 8.3 **International market diversification versus market concentration**

Factors favouring country diversification	Factors favouring country concentration
Company factors	
High management risk consciousness	Low management risk consciousness
Objective of growth through market	Objective of growth through market penetration
Development	Ability to pick 'best' markets
Little market knowledge	
Product factors	
Limited specialist uses	General uses
Low volume	High volume
Non-repeat	Repeat-purchase product
Early or late in product life cycle	Middle of product life cycle
Standard product saleable in many markets	Product requires adaptation to different markets
Market factors	
Small markets – specialised segments	Large markets – high-volume segments
Unstable markets	Stable markets
Many similar markets	Limited number of markets
New or declining markets	Mature markets
Low growth rate in each market	High growth rate in each market
Large markets are very competitive	Large markets are not excessively competitive
Established competitors have large share of key markets	Key markets are divided among many competitors
Low customer loyalty	High customer loyalty
High synergy effects between countries	Low synergy effect between countries
Short competitive lead time	Long competitive lead time
Marketing factors	
Low communication costs for additional markets	High communication costs for additional markets
Low order-handling costs for additional markets	High order-handling costs for additional markets
Low physical distribution costs for additional markets	High physical distribution costs for additional markets
Standardized communication in many markets	Communication requires adaptation to different markets

Source: Adapted from Ayal and Zif, 1979 and Piercy, 1981.

Figure 8.13 Unilever's global portfolio

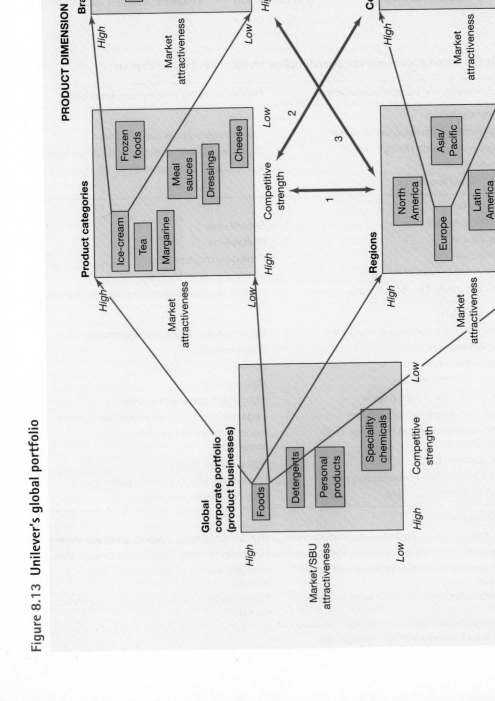

8.5   The global product/market portfolio

The corporate portfolio analysis provides an important tool to assess how to allocate resources, not only across geographic areas but also across the different product business (Douglas and Craig, 1995). The global corporate portfolio represents the most aggregate level of analysis and it might consist of operations by product businesses or by geographic areas.

As illustrated in Figure 8.13 (based on the market attractiveness/competitive strength matrix of Figure 8.4), Unilever's most aggregate level of analysis is its different product businesses. With this global corporate portfolio as a starting point, the further analysis of single corporate product business can go in a product dimension, a geographic dimension or a combination of the two.

It appears from the global corporate portfolio in Figure 8.13 that Unilever's 'foods' business is characterised by high market attractiveness and high competitive strengths. However, a more distinct picture of the situation is obtained by analysing underlying levels. This more detailed analysis is often required to give an operational input to specific market-planning decisions.

By combining the product and geographic dimensions it is possible to analyse the global corporate portfolio at the following levels (indicated by the arrows in the example of Figure 8.13):

1. product categories by regions (or vice versa);
2. product categories by countries (or vice versa);
3. regions by brands (or vice versa);
4. countries by brands (or vice versa).

Of course, it is possible to make further detailed analysis of, for example, the country level by analysing different customer groups (e.g. food retailers) in certain countries.

Thus it may be important to assess the interconnectedness of various portfolio units across countries or regions. A customer (e.g. a large food retail chain) may have outlets in other countries, or the large retailers may have formed cross-border alliances in retailing with central purchasing from suppliers (e.g. Unilever) – see also section 17.7 on international retailing.

8.6   Summary

Especially in SMEs international market selection is simply a reaction to a stimulus provided by a change agent, in the form of an unsolicited order.

A more proactive and systematic approach to IMS entails the following steps:

1. selection of relevant segmentation criteria;
2. development of appropriate segments;
3. screening of segments to narrow down the list of appropriate countries (choice of target);
4. micro segmentation: development of subsegments in each qualified country or across countries.

However, the *pragmatic approach* to IMS is often used successfully by firms. Often coincidences and the personal network of top managers play an important role in the 'selection' of the firm's first export market. In making the International Market Selection, the firm must seek the synergy between the possible new target market and its own strengths, objectives, and strategy. The firm's choice of new international markets is very much influenced by the existence of complementary markets and marketing skills gained in these markets.

After the four steps described above the market expansion strategy of the chosen market is a key decision. In designing this strategy the firm has to answer two underlying questions:

- Will it enter markets incrementally (the waterfall approach) or simultaneously (the shower approach)?
- Will entry be concentrated or diversified across international markets?

Corporate portfolio analysis represents an excellent way of combining the international market selection (the geographic dimension) with the product dimension. It is important to assess how to allocate resources across geographic areas/product businesses. However, it is also important to evaluate the interconnectedness of various portfolio units across geographic borders. For example, a particular customer (located in a certain country) may have businesses in several countries

CASE STUDY 8.1   Jarlsberg

The king of Norwegian cheeses is seeking new markets

Jarlsberg cheese (**www.norseland.com**) has been well received in the US market. Nearly 40 years after going to the United States it is now the imported cheese with the biggest market share of its category in the competitive US supermarkets. The total export of Norwegian cheese to the United States in 2001 was approximately 7,000 tons, of which the majority was Jarlsberg. This means that the quota, which the WTO has set up between Norway and United States, was full. Therefore Jarlsberg has to find other ways of selling cheese in the United States.

The story
Professor Ole M. Ystgaard and his employees at the Norwegian Agricultural School developed Jarlsberg in the 1950s. The cheese is based on traditions from Swiss cheese makers, who developed cheese with holes in the 1830s.

Jarlsberg cheese arrived in the United States in 1963. In the beginning the Jarlsberg management team travelled around the country to demonstrate how the cheese could be used for 'everyday' and at parties. After just two years Jarlsberg had a sales volume of 450.000 kg in the market, and the managers understood they had a 'hot' product.

product, served by celebrities at 'high society' parties.

Norseland Inc.
Norseland Inc. was founded in 1978. The purpose of the company was to market and distribute Jarlsberg and other Norwegian cheese in the United States. The company is a 100 per cent

owned subsidiary of TINE Norwegian Dairies, which has the main responsibility for the production and marketing of Jarlsberg cheese. In 2002 Norseland had net sales of $130 million, about half of this derived from imported Norwegian Jarlsberg, about 25 per cent from Jarlsberg produced in Ohio and the remainder from sales of products from other companies, among them Danish Tholstrup Cheese and French Unilever Boursin. Norseland's strategy is to sell exclusive cheeses only, and the company commands respect in the US retail trade where a 90 per cent distribution coverage has been achieved. Norseland has a regional office in Montreal, Canada, where an additional 800 tonnes of Jarlsberg were sold in 2001.

The US cheese market

The total market for 'hard cheese' is approximately 400.000 tons, but the market also consumes a lot of 'soft cheese'. Though Jarlsberg only has a small market share in the total cheese market this represents the largest market share in the Swiss-like cheese category.

The largest producer of cheese for the US market is Philip Morris, including the company Nabisco, which Philip Morris bought in December 2000. The most well-known brands from Philip Morris come from Kraft, which markets the popular 'soft cheese', Philadelphia. The second largest cheese producer for the US market is Con Agra, which had total sales of $26 billion in 2001.

In general, the tendency to consume cheese is higher in the eastern part of the United States, whereas 'healthy' food products are focused on more in the western part of the country. There is a tendency to eat more imported cheese as personal income increases.

Jarlsberg's customers and marketing

Jarlsberg cheese has some snob appeal. Customers want to show they have 'good taste'. Without complaining they accept the higher price of Jarlsberg compared to other competitive products. The mild and creamy taste appeals to Americans, and many think that the taste of the traditional Swiss cheese, Emmenthale, is too sharp.

Characteristics of the typical Jarlsberg buyer:

- female;
- earning more than US$80,000 per year;
- over 40 years old.

It is important to buyers that it is an imported cheese. That it is a Norwegian cheese plays a minor role and Norseland does not use this fact in their marketing.

Norseland has the objective of attracting new and younger consumers for its Jarlsberg cheese. To achieve this objective Norseland wants to make contracts and deals with retail chains like 7-Eleven, which also sells sandwiches, etc.

Besides its own sales force Norseland uses nearly 500 'brokers' (distributors), who sell all over the United States. These are 'external' sales representatives who visit shops, retail chains and restaurants in order to sell and market products, among their Jarlsberg.

Five years from now Jarlsberg aims to be present in at least five new countries, either through local production, supplied from Norway, or from other locations of production.

Questions

1. Which screening criteria should Norseland use in its selection process for new markets/countries for its Jarlsberg cheese?

2. Which five new countries should Norseland choose to penetrate over the next five years? What should be the timing of these new country penetrations?

CASE STUDY 8.2   Durex

Durex Global Sex Survey

The Durex Global Sex Survey 2002 focuses exclusively on the sexual attitudes and behaviour of today's youth in 20 countries around the world. The survey is sponsored by SSL International, manufacturer of Durex, which is the world's leading condom brand (**www.durex.com**).

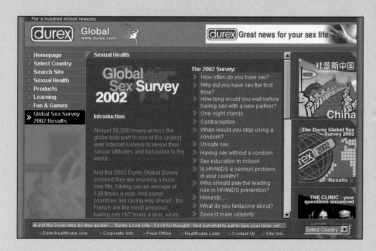

Questions

1. Which sociocultural factors are important to consider in the global marketing of condoms?

2. How could Durex use the survey in their international market selection?

3. Which of the 22 markets in the survey would you recommend Durex concentrates on?

Questions for discussion

1. Why is screening of foreign markets important? Outline the reasons why many firms do not systematically screen countries/markets.

2. Explore the factors which influence the international market selection process.

3. Discuss the advantages and disadvantages of using only secondary data as screening criteria in the IMS process.

4. What are the advantages and disadvantages of an opportunistic selection of international markets?

5. What are the differences between a global market segment and a national market segment? What are the marketing implications of these differences for a firm serving segments on a worldwide basis?

6. Discuss the possible implications that the firm's choice of geographic expansion strategy may have on the ability of a local marketing manager of a foreign subsidiary to develop and implement marketing programmes.

References

Andersen, O. and Buvik, A. (2002) 'Firms' internationalization and alternative approaches to the international customer/market selection', *International Business Review*, vol. 11, pp. 347–63.

Andersen, P.H. and Strandskov, J. (1998) 'International market selection', *Journal of Global Marketing*, vol. 11, no. 3, pp. 65–84.

Ayal, I. and Zif, J. (1979) 'Market expansion strategies in multinational marketing', *Journal of Marketing*, vol. 43, Spring, pp. 84–94.

Bradley, F. (1995) *International Marketing Strategy*, Prentice Hall, London.

Brewer, P. (2001) 'International market selection: developing a model from Australian case studies', *International Business Review*, vol. 10, pp. 155–74.

Crick, D. and Chaudhry, S. (1995) 'Export practices of Asian SMEs: some preliminary findings', *Marketing Intelligence and Planning*, vol. 13, no. 11, pp. 13–21.

Douglas, S. and Craig, C.A. (1995) *Global Marketing Strategy*, McGraw-Hill, New York.

Green, R.T. and Allaway, A.W. (1985) 'Identification of export opportunities: a shift-share approach', *Journal of Marketing*, vol. 49, Winter, pp. 83–8.

Harrell, G.D. and Kiefer, R.O. (1995) 'Multinational market portfolios' in Paliwoda, S.J. and Ryans Jr, J.K., *International Marketing Reader*, Routledge, London/New York.

Johanson, J. and Vahlne, J.E. (1977) 'The internationalization process of the firm: a model of knowledge development and increasing foreign market commitment', *Journal of International Business Studies*, vol. 8, no. 1, pp. 23–32.

Keegan, W. (1995) *Global Marketing Management*, Prentice-Hall, Englewood Cliffs, NJ.

Mazur, L. and Lannon, J. (1993) 'Crossborder marketing lessons from 25 European success stories', *EIU Research Report*, the Economist Intelligence Unit Limited, London, pp. 17–19.

Papadopoulos, N. and Denis, J.E. (1988) 'Inventory, taxonomy and assessment of methods for international market selection', *International Marketing Review*, Autumn, pp. 38–51.

Papadopoulos, N., Chen, H. and Thomas, D.R. (2002) 'Toward a tradeoff model for international market selection', *International Business Review*, vol. 11, pp. 165–92.

Piercy, N. (1981) 'Company internationalization: active and reactive exporting', *European Journal of Marketing*, vol. 15, no. 3, pp. 26–40.

Rahman, S.H. (2003), Modelling of international market selection process: a qualitative study of successful Australian international businesses', *Qualitative Market Research: An International Journal*, vol 6, no. 2, pp. 119–32.

Sylvest, J. and Lindholm, C. (1997) 'Små globale virksomheder', *Ledelse & Erhvervsøkonomi*, vol. 61, April, pp. 131–43.

Vernon, R. (1966) 'International investment and international trade in product cycle', *Quarterly Journal of Economics*, vol. 80, pp. 190–208.

Welford, R. and Prescott, K. (1996) *European Business: An issue-based approach*, Pitman, London.

Westhead, P., Wright, M., Ucbasaran, D. (2002) 'International market selection strategies selected by "micro" and small firms', *Omega*, vol. 30, pp. 51–68.

Yip, G.S., Biscarri, J.G. and Monti, J.A. (2000), 'The role of the internationalization process in the performance of newly internationalizing firms', *Journal of International Marketing*, vol. 8, no. 3, pp. 10–35.

Further reading

Aurifeille, J.-M. (2002) 'Global vs international involved-based segmentation: a cross-national exploratory study', *International Marketing Review*, vol. 19, no. 4, pp. 369–86.

Brewer, P. (2001) 'International market selection: developing a model from Australian case studies', *International Business Review*, vol. 10, pp. 155–74.

Dow, D. (2000), 'A note on psychological distance and export market selection', *Journal of International Marketing*, vol. 8, no. 1, pp. 51–64.

Koch, A.J. (2001a) 'Selecting overseas markets and entry modes: two decision processes or one?', *Marketing Intelligence & Planning*, vol. 19, no. 1, pp. 65–75.

Koch, A.J. (2001b) 'Factors influencing market and entry mode selection: developing the MEMS model', *Marketing Intelligence & Planning*, vol. 19, no. 5, pp. 351–61.

Kumar, V. and Nagpal, A. (2001) 'Segmenting global markets: look before you leap', *Marketing Research*, Spring, pp. 8–13.

Petersen, B., Lawrence, S. and Liesch, P.W. (2002) 'The Internet and foreign market expansion by firms', *Management International Review*, vol. 42, no. 2, pp. 207–21.

Rahman, S.H. 'Modelling of international market selection process: a qualitative study of successful Australian international businesses', *Qualitative Market Research: An international Journal*, vol. 6, No. 2, pp. 119–32.

Robertson, K. and Wood, V.R. (2001) 'The relative importance of types of information in the foreign market selection process', *International Business Review*, vol. 10, pp. 363–79.

Steenkamp, J.-B. and Hofstede, F.-T. (2002) 'International market segmentation: issues and perspectives', *International Journal of Research in Marketing*, vol. 19, pp. 185–213.

CASE STUDY II.1   CarLovers Carwash

Serendipity as a factor in foreign market selection: the case of CarLovers from Australia

The CarLovers brand was introduced into the Australian market in March 1989 by three Australian and two American businessmen, and was incorporated and fully Australianised in December 1990. The concept was to revolutionise the car-washing industry, which is dominated in most countries by the major petrol companies.

Approximately 20 million people live on the Australian continent, a mass of land roughly the size of the United States. According to Pro Wash, an Australian carwash company, there are presently only 500 automatic carwashes in operation in the country. This leaves a lot of room for growth, and operators are seizing the opportunities that lie in this relatively new market. In comparison, the United States has more than 10,000 automatic car washes in operation.

The Australian carwash industry got its start, as did many, with carwashes at petrol stations about 25 years ago. It was not until 1993 that CarLovers began to build stand-alone washes. While most existing commercial carwashes are owned by individual owners/operators, CarLovers has 100 loca-

tions in Australia; half are company owned and half are franchised. Approximately 50 per cent of the CarLovers locations have in-bay automatics, which are the most popular wash option in Australia along with self-serves. In these cases vehicles are washed by attendants at these bays and owners can choose from the menu of washes and other ancillary services that include polish, cleaning of engine, wheels and tyres, interior vacuuming, upholstery shampooing and a complete range of associated products. Some operators are hesitant about letting customers load themselves onto the automatic carwash without an attendant close by. Customer safety is the main reason. However, after one or two carwashes many customers can handle themselves.

So, CarLovers Carwash's principal activities are the development and operation of franchised and company-operated video stores (Video Ezy Australasia) and self-serve and automatic carwashes.

The brand is strong on environmental considerations, with less polluting grease and chemicals being released into public drains, and 80 per cent reclaiming and recycling of all water used in the car-washing process. These public benefits are supplemented by private benefits to consumers, since the laser technology also results in less damage to cars when they are washed. Additionally the facility is easy to use in a bright, clean retailing atmosphere, as opposed to the often greasy facilities and low service priority offered at petrol stations.

Business activities initially laid emphasis on the Australian operations, resulting in 48 car washes by 1995, 14 company owned and 34 franchised. Franchising was seen as an important way to grow the business in the first five years. Since 1995 the number of car washes has increased to about 80, with all additions being company owned.

Facilities at a CarLovers Carwash

The original strategy was to develop the concept, prove that it could be multiplied in the mode of McDonald's, and then take it to other countries. *The decision to internationalize* was therefore present at the beginning of the company's life. However, it was more of 'a dream, rather than a grand plan', according to Steve Spencer, managing director of CarLovers International, in an interview for this case study. The McDonald's experience was always an inspirational factor, providing a lesson in developing a good concept, proving it domestically and then going international.

The success of the concept relative to the offer of competitors is clearly evident in the rapid and sustained growth of carwashes. Within a few years it would have been clear that the concept was ready for internationalization. The focus of this case study is the selection of country markets: that is, *which countries to enter in what order*. The managing director of CarLovers made it quite clear that the standard textbook model of market selection (see Figure 8.2) was *not* used. Business does not work that way, he said. Instead he gives emphasis to opportunities, chance meetings, rejecting the less viable options, and seizing the best opportunities as they present themselves. This is the way business works in practice. The textbook model may be appropriate for larger firms, but for small and medium-sized firms in general, and certainly in the case of CarLovers, the pragmatic model better describes the internationalization process.

To illustrate this process in more detail, here are five steps taken by CarLovers to enter foreign markets:

1. In mid-1993 executives of CarLovers were in the United States holding discussions with their equipment suppliers. This led to a chance meeting with some Mexican businessmen visiting the same supplier. Following discussions with the Mexicans, agreement was reached for them to start a Mexican franchise of the business. One could say that the choice of country (Mexico) and partners was based on chance.

2. A year later, further discussions with business contacts in the United States led to a US franchise being established in Grand Rapids. To avoid council red tape an existing carwash site was used and refitted to the CarLovers design. The success of this operation can be seen in the tripling of turnover at the site. A second US site has since been refitted.

3. In late 1994 an executive from CarLovers held discussions with the Malaysian manager of Caltex and this led to CarLovers introducing two outlets *within* Caltex service stations. The CarLovers brand was not prominent in this arrangement. In this case a particular friendship and business contact in Malaysia determined both the third foreign market to be entered and the partner involved.

4. Later in 1994 further business contacts led to meetings in Kuala Lumpur with representatives from a Malaysian conglomerate called the Berjaya Group. These discussions were so fruitful that the Berjaya Group purchased 24 per cent of the equity of CarLovers. Further equity and more planning led to the January 1997 go-ahead to build four new CarLover carwashes in Malaysia in 1997 and more later.

5. The January 1997 decision also flagged Kuala Lumpur as the training centre for all of the Asian operations. Three countries, Indonesia, the Philippines and Korea, are the priority target markets, followed by China.

Formal planning has been greater for this wave of foreign entry, perhaps a reflection that CarLovers is now a bigger operation (though still a medium-sized company) and needs to satisfy a large conglomerate partner. The factors leading to the selection of the top three target markets included size of market, degree of development, cost of land, opportunity and the emerging mass of middle-class consumers. These factors are closer to the textbook model of market selection.

These phases of foreign market selection provide great insight into the actual process used by a service-based exporter (though CarLovers also sells some manufactured products as well). *The pragmatic model*, reflecting the cut and thrust of seeking business opportunities, plays an important role in the selection of country, partner, distributor and distribution system (company owned, franchised or concession arrangement). Business contacts and networking are at the heart of this cut and thrust. In many cases, the business relationships were determined first and the choice of target markets came second. However, as a small business gets larger, although serendipity may continue to play a part, it is a smaller part of the target market selection process.

The CarLovers case study is also a good example of the need to be flexible in terms of both entry modes and international marketing programmes. The entry mode for Mexico was less restricted than for the United States, which was strongly influenced by local government regulations. Two different entry modes were used in Malaysia, initially a concession approach and then a fully branded franchised system, to reflect the different nature of the distributors. Slightly different marketing programmes are needed across countries. Although the basic concept of less damage to cars, a clean and pleasant retailing environment and environmental care holds true in most countries, there can be subtle differences that need to be taken into account at the specific country level. For example, the benefit of water conservation is more important in a low-rainfall country such as Australia than in tropical Malaysia.

Postscript/Latest developments

At the beginning of 2003 the biggest shareholder of CarLovers, Malaysian investment company Berjaya Group, launched a share buy-back offer to take the company off the Australian Stock Exchange after several cash injections over the past three years. Berjaya owns 88.44 per cent of CarLovers stock.

CarLovers has performed below expectations since it was listed in January 1994: it lost $6.1 million in the 12 months to 30 April 2002 compared with a AUS.$3.5 million loss in 2000–1. In May CarLovers sold its 60 per cent share in Video Ezy Australasia to three investment companies for $12.3 million. It used the proceeds to pay off several creditors, including the Australian Taxation Office.

Questions

1. How would you characterise the IMS process in this case compared to the textbook model?

2. What are the general differences in the IMS process between LSEs and SMEs?

3. In this case the management implicitly have some screening criteria in the IMS process. Could there be other relevant screening criteria?

Source: prepared by Bill Merrilees and Dale Miller, Marketing Group, Department of Management, University of Newcastle, Australia. Updated 2003 by Svend Hollensen.

CASE STUDY II.2   The Female Health Company (FHC)

The female condom is seeking a foothold in the world market for contraceptive products

It's time to take control. Give your vagina a choice.

Toronto Public Health Department Female Condom Campaign Slogan
Source: FHC 2001 Annual Report

On one of her few days off before Christmas 2002 President of FHC, Mary Ann Leeper, is thinking about the great opportunities for the female condom. The potential market for the product of her company, the female condom, is huge, but still FCH has been making net losses during the last few years. Mary Ann is thinking about how to turn the 'minus' figures into 'plus' figures. She accepts that the product is still relatively young in the world market for contraceptives, but she thinks it must be possible to produce positive financial results with such a high quality product. The big question is how ...

Background to the contraceptive market

The market for contraceptives has long been heavily influenced by social and political considerations. From the early days of the pill, the growing numbers of abortions and the decision to make the pill freely available in the early 1970s to the emergence of the AIDS threat in the 1980s, this sector has always been more than a mere product category.

Of the 44 million people infected with HIV world-wide an estimated 29 million (or about 70 per cent) are African. In some countries (such as Botswana) more than 20 per cent of the population are infected by HIV. The number of African AIDS orphans is expected to reach 15 million in 2003. Over 30 million people have already died from AIDS – more than the number of deaths from all African wars – and 11,000 new cases are diagnosed every day. The deadly disease is decimating Africa's labour force and seriously impeding the continent's economic recovery and development.

The increase in the pandemic has been linked to such cultural practices as polygamy, female genital mutilation, widow inheritance and sexual practices and behaviour that are culturally imposed in some societies. In Swaziland, for example, the local culture celebrates virility or the *Ingwanwa* – a man who engages in multiple sexual encounters, while the female equivalent, *Igwandla* is shunned. The AIDS disease is also fuelled by a popular myth that sex with a virgin cures AIDS.

The total market consists of a very broad range of products, with oral contraceptives (the pill) and male condoms the most popular. Other, 'natural' forms of contraception are also practised, such as withdrawal and the safe period. Men and women may also be surgically sterilised.

Contraceptive products are available in pharmacies or general retail outlets, over the counter (OTC), or via prescription. Contraceptive products are also widely distributed in public clinics. In terms of the two leading forms of contraception, the contraceptive pill is available only on prescription, while condoms are widely available in chemists, supermarkets and vending machines, etc. Growth in distribution channels has been a feature of the condom market since the second half of the 1980s in response to the AIDS crisis.

Condom usage has risen substantially over the past six years, while use of the pill has remained broadly stable. The pill remains a popular contraceptive (based upon surveys of women – surveys of men and women show use of condom and pill as about equal).

The product

The female condom is made of polyurethane – a thin but strong material that is resistant to tearing. The female condom consists of a soft, loose-fitting sheath and two flexible O rings. One of the rings is used to insert the device and helps to hold it in place. The other ring remains outside the vagina after insertion. The female condom lines the vagina, preventing skin from touching skin during intercourse. The female condom is prelubricated and disposable and is intended for use only once. The product offers an additional benefit to the 10–15 per cent of the population that are allergic to latex and who, as a result, may be irritated by latex male condoms.

FHC and the female condom

The female condom was invented by a Danish physician who obtained a US patent for the product in 1988, and subsequently sold certain rights to the female condom to a US company. The first female condom became available in 1992, since which time more than 50 million have been sold around the world. The female condom is marketed under the name FC female condom in the United States, Femidom in the United Kingdom, and Myfemy in other markets, such as Japan.

The Female Health Company manufactures, markets and sells the female condom, the only approved product under a woman's control. FHC is based in Chicago, but has production in London. FHC's UK manufacturing subsidiary received a Queen's Award for enterprise in April, 2002, in recognition of international trade achievements. FHC owns worldwide rights to the female condom, including patents that have been issued in a number of countries. The problem in many less developed countries (such as many in Africa) is that most men do not want to use condoms and, when it comes to sexual relationships, women do not have power to negotiate. In many cultures it is accepted that men can do what they like, so the female condom is a way of empowering and protecting women in those countries.

The female condom can prevent unintended pregnancy and sexually transmitted diseases (STDs), including HIV/AIDS. It is the only HIV/AIDS product specifically developed and approved by regulatory agencies in the United States, the European Union, Japan and the People's Republic of China, among others, since the epidemic began about 20 years ago, for the prevention of the transmission of HIV/AIDS through sexual contact.

The product is currently sold or available in various venues including commercial (private sector) outlets, public sector clinics and research programmes in over 75 countries. It is commercially marketed in 21 countries, including the United States, the United Kingdom, Canada, France and Japan. However, the female condom is mainly sold to the global public sector. In the United States it is marketed to city and state public health clinics as well as not-for-profit organizations. Following several years of testing the efficacy and acceptability of the female condom, in 1996 FHC entered into a three-year agreement with the Joint United Nations Programme on AIDS (UNAIDS), which has subsequently been extended. Under the agreement UNAIDS facilitates the availability and distribution of the female condom in the developing world and the FHC will sell the product to developing countries at a reduced price based on the total number of units purchased. The current price per unit is approximately £0.38, or €0.55. Pursuant to this agreement, the product is currently available in over 80 countries with major UN health programmes in about 10 countries including Zimbabwe, Tanzania, Brazil, Uganda, South Africa, Namibia, Ghana and Haiti.

Global market potential and FHC sales

It is estimated the global annual market for male condoms is 12.4 billion units. The major segments are in the global public sector, the United States, Japan, India and the People's Republic of China. However, the majority of all acts of sexual intercourse, excluding those intended to result in pregnancy, are completed without protection. As a result it is estimated that the potential market for barrier contraceptives is much larger than the identified male condom market.

Currently it is estimated that more than 5 billion male condoms are distributed worldwide by the public sector each year. The female condom is seen as an important addition to prevention strategies by the public sector because studies show that its availability decreases the amount of unprotected sex by as much as one-third over offering only a male condom.

FHC expects to derive the vast majority, if not all, of its future revenue from the female condom, its sole current product. While management believe the global potential for the female condom is significant, the product is in the early stages of commercialisation. To date sales of the female condom have not been sufficient to cover the company's operating costs.

FHC's total net revenue in 2001 was approximately $8.4 million, but with operating losses (of $1.2 million). The total revenue in 2001 per geographic area were as shown in Table 1.

The Brazilian case

After the United States and South Africa, Brazil comes as a major market for the female condom. The way Brazil handles the AIDS problem fits well with the visions of FHC. On 4 November 2002 FHC announced that it had signed a contract with the Ministry of Health in Brazil to provide 4 million female condoms for the Ministry's groundbreaking National AIDS Programme. Under the terms of the contract 2 million units were shipped immediately, with two subsequent shipments of 1 million units each to follow. The Brazil Ministry of Health has created a model programme where the female condom is part of a comprehensive AIDS prevention strategy that includes training, counselling, outreach, education and support for women and men to change their behaviour.

Since 1998 the Ministry of Health has ordered more than 8 million female condoms. The programme began with a very successful acceptability trial, which included 100,000 units for distribution. The order expanded in 1999 to allow 13,000 Brazilians access to the female condom. During 2000 and 2001 the Ministry bought 2 million units each year. This new 4 million unit order will allow the Ministry an even broader reach in its comprehensive prevention programme.

In one Brazilian study to evaluate the acceptance and use of the female condom among HIV infected women high rates of use (87 per cent), acceptability (68 per cent) and continuation (78 per cent) were observed, with a reduction in the proportion of unprotected sexual acts from 14 per cent to 6 per cent. The study concluded that adding the female condom to contraceptive options with appropriate counselling was able to reduce unprotected sex among HIV infected women, a key target group of the programme.

In addition to the continued expansion of the Ministry's public sector female condom programme, the product is also available commercially through *DKT do Brasil*, FHC's Brazilian marketing partner, which markets the product under the brand name Reality.

The Female Health Foundation

In order to educate women worldwide about reproductive health, actress Drew Barrymore and representatives of FHC announced the launch of the not-for-profit Female Health Foundation on 9 December 1996. This organization is dedicated to improving women's health by raising awareness of women's health issues and developing programmes to inform women how they can protect themselves and their partners against sexually transmitted diseases such as AIDS.

Questions

1. How would you explain FHC's internationalization process up to now?

2. What are the main cultural barriers for expanding global sales of the female condom?

3. Refer back to Case Study 8.2 p. 242. Go to the contraception part of the Global Sex Survey 2002 at **www.durex.com**. Which of the countries mentioned in the 'world survey 2002', (PDF file) offers the best chances for selling the female condom?

4. How can FHC increase its profitability?

The Irish firm Tipperary Mineral Water Company (TMWC) was founded in 1986 by Patrick and Nicholas Cooney. It has since developed into a major national brand in the £40 million Irish mineral water market, with about 15 per cent market share there. The market share outside Ireland is very small.

In 1998 the 60 employees in the company generated a total turnover of about £7 million Irish (IEP). The net profit was IEP 0.3 million (IEP 1 = $1.2).

TMWC is a part of the Gleeson Group, which has a solid base in the Irish drinks market and ranks among the top 200 companies in Ireland. As a consequence TMWC has a solid and sound financial background.

Tipperary mineral water (sparkling and still) is available in a range of packaging options including 200 ml, 500 ml, 1 litre, 1.5 litre and 2 litre bottles. All bottles are recyclable and all labels bear the recyclable symbol. The product range has been extended into the office and leisure market, with 19 litre Tipperary Cooler Dispensers for offices (you can see the product range at **www.tipperary-water.ie/products.html**).

Mineral water in Ireland

General acceptance of bottled water as an alternative to alcohol when socialising is a relatively recent phenomenon in Ireland and Britain. However, it has long been a way of life in continental Europe and the United States. This has as much to do with historical traditions as the quality of tap water. France has a tradition of drinking bottled water going back to Roman times. French consumers today use different brands on different occasions and have a highly developed palate for water, which could be said for most continental countries.

Ireland is therefore at an early stage of development as regards the consumption of bottled water. Few consumers can distinguish between alternative brands and sales of sparkling water are greater than still water. In Europe and the United States bottled

water is part of the way of life and sales of still water greatly outweigh sales of sparkling water, with much substitution of bottled for tap water.

Consumption per capita of bottled water in Ireland is perhaps 5 litres per capita per annum, with the United Kingdom consuming 8 litres. However, consumption per capita in France is in excess of 80 litres per capita per annum, with Germany averaging 80, and the United States over 60.

Tipperary as a brand name abroad gains instant recognition from the song 'It's a long way from Tipperary', which is one of the most international of songs. It was particularly popular during the First and Second World Wars as a marching song and was

Table 1 **Value sales of mineral waters in US dollars by country, 1997**

Country	US$ (millions)
Germany	3,491
Italy	2,421
France	2,087
UK	657
Spain	415
Benelux	354

Source: Based on date from *Euromonitor*

Table 2 Characteristics of four major mineral water markets (sales in hotels, restaurants and catering are not included), 1999

	UK	France	Germany	US
Market sectors (millions litres)	*Type* Flavoured 33 Still 518 Carbonated 290 Total 841	*Type* Flavoured 125 Still 5750 Carbonated 1120 Total 6995	*Type* Flavoured 63 Still 2308 Carbonated 3758 Total 6129	*Type* Flavoured 139 Still 4709 Carbonated 315 Total 5163
Market shares (%)	*Companies (brands)* Premier Waters Ltd 17 Perrier Vittel (UK) Ltd 9 Eden Valley Mineral Water Co. Ltd 5 Highland Ltd 5 Strathmore Ltd 2 Spadel (UK) Ltd 1 Coca-Cola Schweppes Beverages Ltd 1 Ballygowan Ltd 1 Private label 45 Other 14 Total 100	*Companies (brands)* Group Danone (Evian) 40 Perrier Vittel SA 26 Groupe Neptune SA 12 St Amand 2 Private label 8 Other 12 Total 100	*Companies (brands)* Gerolsteiner Brunnen GmbH & Co 11 Die Blauen Quellen Mineral- und Heilbrune AG 6 Mineralbrunnen berkingen-Teinach AG 4 Visla Brunnen 3 Apollinaris Schweppes GmbH & Co. 3 Coca-Cola Schweppes Beverages Ltd 2 Frankenbrunnen 2 Rheinfelsquell 2 Richard Haringer Getränke 3 Private label 3 Other 61 Total 100	*Companies (brands)* Nestlé SA (Perrier, Poland Spring) 19 Group Danone SA (Evian) 10 PepsiCo 5 McKesson BHOC 4 Suntory Ltd 2 Private label 26 Other 34 Total 100
Distribution of mineral water and comments (%)	*Channels* Supermarkets/hypermarkets 69 Other stores 13 Small food outlets 9 General merchandisers 4 Outdoor 3 Vending machine 1 Other 1 Total 100 In the supermarkets/hypermarkets J. Sainsbury and Tesco are the two leading mineral water retailers. As demand grows, mineral water is starting to be delivered to British homes by milkmen.	*Channels* Supermarkets/hypermarkets 75 General merchandiser 15 Small food outlets 5 Other stores 2 Outdoor 2 Vending machine 1 Total 100 The three giants of the hypermarket operators are Carrefour, Leclerc and Intermarché, the latter being mainly large supermarkets. Wholesalers are under threat as large supermarkets and hypermarkets are increasingly dealing directly with manufacturers. Very hot summer weather will drive impulse sales through local outlets.	*Channels* Supermarkets/hypermarkets 39 Specialist bulk stores 32 Traditional food retailers 17 Discount stores 8 Other 4 Total 100 Unlike other food markets, traditional retailers hold a comparatively high share of the distribution breakdown (17%) because mineral water is seen as an everyday essential item. Discount stores are of particular importance for the distribution of carbonated mineral water, predominantly selling private label products.	*Channels* Supermarkets/hypermarkets 43 Small food outlets/superettes 21 Vending machine 15 General merchandisers 11 Other stores 8 Outdoor 2 Total 100 Private label sales accounted for over 26% of volume sales distribution in 1999, reflecting the strength of major supermarket/hypermarket retailers. Vending is a convenient, clean way for consumers to obtain water.
Comments on consumer profiles	Private label products have benefited from the fact that mineral water is a fairly homogenous product, making pricing the most important consideration for many consumers. Mineral water is consumed more by women than by men in the UK. This is particularly noticeable with sparkling water where consumption by females is almost twice the level of male consumption. Consumers in higher income socioeconomic groups drink much more mineral water than lower earners.	According to a study carried out by Credoc (a consumer research body) in 1998, 35.6% of French households refused to drink tap water. The low share of the carbonated type is due to the fact that most French people continue to drink still water with meals. Flavoured waters, particularly the sparkling variety, can compete more directly with soft drinks and therefore appeal to a younger market. The emergence and popularity of the five litre bottles demonstrates that more and more people are using mineral water not only for drinking, but also for preparation of tea, coffee and in cooling.	The Germans are the fourth largest group of mineral water consumers in Europe behind the Italians, French and Belgians with a per capita consumption of 97 litres in 1999. The trend towards a healthy lifestyle is responsible for the recent surge in the number of teenagers who drink mineral water. Climate also plays an important role in the consumption of mineral water with 85% of Bavarians drinking it regularly, compared to 72% of their northern counterparts.	Mineral water consumption is higher among women than it is among men, as the former tend to be more conscious about their eating habits and the latest health trends. Consumers between the ages of 35 and 44 consume mineral water more frequently than consumers in other age groups. Consumption is related to household income, as usage is higher in wealthier households. Consumption is lowest among consumers aged 65 and over, a group that has not accepted the concept of paying for water, when tap water is free.

Source: adapted from different sources.

broadcast to a worldwide cinema audience through Movietone news reports.

The location of Ireland to source bottled water is a good idea in that Ireland is generally perceived as green, unspoiled and lacking in industrialisation or pollution.

The European market for mineral water

The following examines the retail market for mineral water in six major markets: France, Italy, the United Kingdom, Germany, Spain and Benelux (Belgium, the Netherlands and Luxembourg). Sales through 'horeca' (hotels, restaurants and catering establishments) are for the main part excluded.

Mineral water originates from a pure earth source and contains healthy constituents such as minerals and trace elements. It must be bottled at source and must not undergo any form of treatment except that of separating the iron from sulphur to avoid any discoloration or smell. Nothing may be added or taken away from the water, except carbon dioxide to make sparkling water. Mineral water has benefited from the shift away from alcohol consumption due to stricter drink-drive laws and health awareness generally. Greater concern over the quality of municipal tap water supplies has also underpinned rising demand for mineral water.

Table 1 shows the total market values of mineral water in the major European markets. The mineral water market is broken down into the following sectors:

- still;
- sparkling;
- flavoured.

Still water is the dominant sector in the mineral water market, offering a direct, healthy alternative to tap water. Sparkling water demand is more meal/occasion specific, and the digestive properties on offer mean that sparkling water tends to attract a higher margin. Flavoured water remains a negligible influence on most markets, but is the most dynamic sector where sales exist.

An increased spread of distribution outlets and wider availability have exposed mineral water to a greater audience. So mineral water has established a commodity status in several countries and this is increasingly affecting trends apparent in the market. As a consequence the mineral water market is characterised by high levels of private label penetration.

Competitive situation in the European mineral water market

The global bottled water market underwent dramatic changes in terms of brand ownership in 1992, when the Swiss food giant Nestlé bought all Perrier's mineral water brands except Volvic, which was sold to BSN (now known as Groupe Danone). Today Nestlé (with brands such as Perrier and Vittel) and Danone (with brands including Evian and Volvic) are the leading mineral water producers, both in Europe and throughout the world. The market shares of the manufacturers in the major markets are shown in Table 2.

Domestic producers continue to have a significant presence, despite increasing consolidation, in France (Groupe Neptune with Castel), Italy (San

Table 3 Volume and value of all mineral waters by country

	Per capita volume 1997 (litres)	Total value 1997 (US$ million)	% change 1993/ 1997 (US$ value)	Per capita value 1997 (US$)
Argentina	13.1	300	46.6	8.40
Australia	8.4	133	48.6	7.20
Brazil	8.9	1,244	219.9	7.78
Canada	18.6	436	44.6	14.39
Chile	5.2	46	33.3	3.13
China	0.4	447	48.9	0.36
Columbia	14.2	755	92.5	20.87
Hong Kong, China	7.1	47	40.5	7.21
India	0.0	12	923.6	0.01
Indonesia	4.1	270	52.9	1.34
Israel	22.8	117	71.0	20.13
Japan	5.4	757	60.3	6.01
Malaysia	1.2	28	28.0	1.30
Mexico	4.6	365	39.3	3.79
New Zealand	2.3	9	53.7	2.46
Philippines	3.3	136	170.8	1.85
Singapore	7.0	47	97.1	15.16
South Africa	0.3	17	165.6	0.38
South Korea	11.5	408	48.5	8.87
Taiwan	7.6	149	83.7	6.95
Thailand	0.0	1	54.1	0.01
Turkey	2.6	165	56.0	2.59
USA	44.7	8,567	48.8	31.98
Venezuela	5.7	86	88.2	3.72
Vietnam	0.5	26	991.9	0.33

Source: Based on data from *Consumer International*, 1999.

Benedetto), Spain (Vichy Catlan) and Benelux (Spadel from Belgium is the market leader with 29 per cent of total value sales in 1997).

As an international marketing consultant you are contacted by the management group of TMWC. They want you to prepare a report in which you give well-founded solutions to the following tasks.

Questions

1. Which country or countries in Europe (outside Ireland) would you recommend TMWC to concentrate on?

2. Which country or countries outside Europe would you recommend TMWC to concentrate on (use Table 3)?

CASE STUDY II.4   Beverage Brands

Planning an international raid with the FABs (flavoured alcoholic beverages)

The term **FAB** (flavoured alcoholic beverage) describes a whole category of 'new flavoured drinks', including spirits, sodas, ciders, 'alcopops' and 'designer drinks'.

FABs offer great potential for innovation in the premium sector through new flavours, new alcohol mixes and packaging designs. Image and marketing in the premium sector are closely interlinked, and one will impact on the other. For example, Kahlua, a coffee-flavoured liqueur from Allied Domecq, had an image as staid, after-dinner drinking for women in the 30+ age group. This was changed by a spell of integrated marketing featuring television, radio and print advertising. The drink was positioned as a highly mixable and credible product and following this a range of Kahlua-based premixed drinks named after actual cocktails, such as B52 and White Russian, were released.

Although accounting for only 2 per cent of the global alcoholic drinks market, sales of FABs have risen 60 per cent in the years from 1997 to 2001 – see Figure 1.

One of the players in the FAB industry is the UK-based firm, **Beverage Brands**.

Beverage Brands

Beverage Brands was founded by Joe Woods,

Managing Director, in 1992 and has offices in Torquay and Bristol. Beverage Brands had an annual turnover of £110 million in 2001 and employed 40 full-time staff, mainly concerned with sales. Beverage Brands is part of the SHS Group Ltd (**www.shs-group.co.uk**). The annual turnover for Group in the year ending 31 December 2001 was £180 million, indicating a strong, financially sound company.

Beverage Brands produces innovative premium soft and alcoholic (FAB) drinks. Boosted by its own New Product Development, Finance, Production Control and Marketing Departments, Beverage Brands has become the number three player in the premium packaged spirit market in the United Kingdom (Source: A.C. Nielsen, November 2001). You can find a short video about Beverage Brands at **http://www.shs-group.co.uk/case_studies/index.shtml**.

WKD brand

WKD was launched by Beverage Brands in March 1996 and is available in two flavours – Original Alcoholic Iron Brew and Original Vodka Blue. The brand sells in excess of 2.25 million bottles per week in the United Kingdom, assuring its position as an innovative brand for vibrant young people (primarily males). Currently it is No. 3 in the UK Premium Packaged spirit brand (Source: AC Nielsen, Nov. 2001).

- ABV (Alcohol by volume) of 5.5 per cent per 330 ml bottle.
- The new 700 ml pack was launched in July 2001, aimed at in-home and party consumption.
- Consumer site at **www.wkd.co.uk**

Woody's Cocktails

Launched in May 1998, Woody's Cocktails are a quality range of well-known, premixed cocktail blends. The product is largely aimed at women, and its features are as follows:

- ABV of 5.3 per cent per bottle;
- the perfect endorsement of any festive occasion;
- aimed at working females, 20–30 years old;

Figure 1 The world market for alcoholic drinks by sector: % volume growth 1997–2001

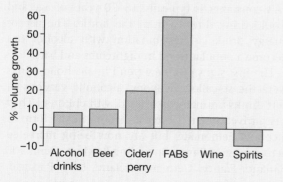

Source: Based on data from Euromonitor.

- particular strong brand in the off-licence sector and stocked by most major multiple retailers;
- 700 ml multiserve pack launched January 2001, for in-home consumption;
- new long-neck pack for on-trade customers.

Managing Director Joe Woods admits that up until now his company has mainly been represented in the UK market. Maybe it is time to take a look at a new potential market? Joe is also unsure of which brand to use for the internationalization process.

Total drinks market in the United Kingdom

The total spirits market is now worth £27 billion. With a third of the UK spirits sales, gin and vodka together are now the largest sector by volume (33 per cent) in the United Kingdom. In the off trade supermarkets, multiples, grocers and off licences dominate sales in volume terms, where 70 per cent of gin and vodka are sold. The rest of the gin and vodka market is in the on trade – pubs, clubs and licensed premises

Figure 2 Composition of the UK spirits market by volume

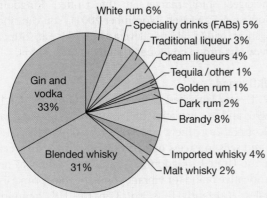

White rum 6%
Speciality drinks (FABs) 5%
Traditional liqueur 3%
Cream liqueurs 4%
Tequila / other 1%
Golden rum 1%
Dark rum 2%
Brandy 8%
Gin and vodka 33%
Blended whisky 31%
Imported whisky 4%
Malt whisky 2%

Source: Adapted from different Euromonitor statistics.

On trade

The on trade is moving towards being more of an interactive experience, as the clientele influence the image of the place, and vice versa. The newer city-centre 'style bars' are sophisticated venues that attract affluent, image-conscious consumers – exactly the type of on-trade establishment designer alcoholic drinks thrive on. Manufacturers are attempting to capitalise on the exclusivity of location, which translates into exclusivity for the product, making it a 'must-have'.

The club scene is also important – allying a product with the nightclubbing market increases brand exposure and means that the product acquires acceptance from the socially influential nightclub audience. Both of these are integral to the development of designer alcoholic drinks.

'Opinion leaders' form the segment of the consumer base that is socially influential in terms of fashions. Taking the product to places where opinion leaders congregate is an attempt to secure acceptance of the product by these trend-setters. This consequently expands the appeal of the product to consumers who are driven by more peer-led drinking. In the designer alcoholic drinks market opinion leaders tend to be young professional adults who frequent city-centre bars.

The trend for going to stylish bars and drinking expensive cocktails mixed at the bar is an affirmation of wealth and style and it has experienced a resurgence due to rising disposable incomes. 'Cocktail culture' has influenced flavour trends, especially in the premixed spirits market. Premixed spirits can be seen as being bottled cocktails, using as they do a spirit base and flavoured mixer, and this is the most notable influence of cocktail culture on flavour trends.

New flavourings have tended to be drawn from trends in cocktail mixtures, for instance the current trend for cranberry flavourings began as an on-trade development whereby vodka was mixed with cranberry juice. Strong and vibrant colouring in drinks is another aspect of the influence of cocktail culture on the FAB market.

The UK market for FABs

Although FABs' fast growth has brought them much attention, they constitute only 5 per cent of the total UK market by volume (in litres of pure alcohol). Following considerable capital investment to bring these products to market, their success has led to increased employment and a significant export business is now being built up.

The majority is consumed in the on trade with modern town bars and nightclubs being the most popular venues for consuming these products. The FAB consumer is typically 18–30 years of age and would drink directly from the bottle. The use of energy drinks in combination with alcohol has become a popular trend in nightclubs and bars.

The first signs of a new trend in alcoholic drinks were the so-called alcopops, alcoholic versions of soft drinks normally associated with children. They first arrived in the United Kingdom in the form of alcoholic lemonade, but are now being marketed across most of Europe including Belgium, Denmark, Finland, France, Germany, Ireland, Italy, Portugal, Spain and Sweden.

The broader category FABs are perceived as trendy, desirable products and are particularly popular among image-conscious consumers within the 18–30 age group. To a large extent, it is through strong branding that the industry has managed the transition from alcopops, with its connotation of under-age drinking, to the positive, premium image FABs currently enjoy.

The UK market for flavoured alcoholic beverages has grown significantly year on year since its conception, disproving any evidence suggesting that it is simply a fad. As the market expands, so do the number of variants available. New flavours/styles, including the increasingly popular cranberry, appear on a regular basis in a bid to retain and stimulate consumer interest. Although the majority of spirit bases comprise white rum and vodka, tequila is not uncommon and dark spirit entries are anticipated shortly, mainly from the United States. Key for brand owners is consumer loyalty: in the hope that today's 18–34-year-old drinkers will continue drinking these branded beverages in later life brand owners must keep the consumers' attention and interest.

Despite the astounding growth of this market, retailers in both the on and off trades are still allocating insufficient space to the category, which remains highly display sensitive. Merchandising is, therefore, particularly important, as is the ambience and music in the on trade. There are likely to be more chillers, probably branded, introduced in both the on and off trade. Packaging is also moving to accommodate changing lifestyles. As with beer, multipacks and multiserve bottles are now on the supermarket shelves, resulting in unit retail prices falling. Cans, PET bottles and pouches have all made their debut in the on trade, where sometimes glass is forbidden.

Consumption of FABs is seen generally to decline steadily with age (particularly after the age of 34) although the category is beginning to attract a wider audience. Consumer research, however, shows that brands such as Bacardi Breezer are popular with consumers right up to the age of 65! It is clear that there is scope to push the category further among consumers of all ages and backgrounds. Although women continue to consume more than men, the difference in consumption levels by gender is narrowing.

Designer drinks are mainly wine or spirit based but also include some ciders. They are normally considerably stronger than alcopops but like them are sold in trendy bottles and packaging and given names thought likely to appeal particularly to children and teenagers.

Both types of drinks have caused much controversy and have come under sustained attack not only from alcohol control groups but also from politicians, educationalists, police, the media and even some alcohol retailers for encouraging under-age drinking and alcohol abuse. For example, in Scotland 4,000 members of the Licensed Traders' Association (alcohol retailers) refused to stock alcopops. In the United Kingdom the new drinks and those who produce them have clearly tried the patience of even politicians not normally associated with 'anti-alcohol' views.

Flavoured alcoholic beverages continue their drive, however mainstream, boosted by more billboards and commercials.

Demand for FABs has grown sharply in the United Kingdom with spirit-based beverage brands Bacardi Breezer and Smirnoff Ice being the key brands driving the market. A host of smaller brands are jostling for position, with Red Square one of the more successful of the new entrants.

Vodka forms the main base for FABs, especially in the United Kingdom. However, other spirits are slowly entering the market to liven up competition: whisky and absinthe. On test in Spain, and expected to be launched in the United Kingdom is J&B Twist, a Jim Beam whiskey-based premium packaged spirit with 5.6 per cent ABV.

Packaging is also playing a role in premiumisation. Long-necked 275 ml glass bottles have become the norm in packaging for premium drinks, particularly for premixed drinks and bottled beer. Glass bottles in general are particularly synonymous with premium status. In this case it is not the actual quality of the product that impacts on the consumer's purchase decision, as this is a largely an unknown entity; it is the perception that the product is premium by because of the packaging.

The development of a 'food culture' has played a major part in changing consumer attitudes. There is increased sophistication in eating habits, and people are more willing to experiment with new food trends. This has impacted on the drinks market in the sense that consumers are now more willing to try out newer drinks, or perhaps new ways of drinking more established drinks. Exotic flavour combinations are more readily tested and accepted, as are unconventional drink combinations. All of this is driving sales for flavoured premixed drinks and cocktail-style drinks.

The 'cult of the individual' is a major aspect of

culture and is a growing trend across all markets. This term refers to the trend for individuality in consumption. For instance, rather than drinking the same brand as one's peers, consumers drink something that is particular to their own consumption habits in order to assert their own character and individuality.

This trend is manifesting itself in both an assertion of individuality and a rejection of blanket marketing. This is a strong driver for sales of designer alcoholic drinks, even though brands have targeted opinion leaders in an attempt to capture more peer-led consumption. Ultimately, the brands' contribution to the consumers' perception of their own individuality is key to the success of designer alcoholic drinks, despite the inherent contradictions in this.

Consumers are becoming more adept at discerning which products are qualitatively better than others. They are also becoming quicker to abandon those that do not appeal to them. This is increasing the impetus on producers to create products that are obviously better than others in a tangible way. Despite the importance of image, poor quality in the premium market is less tolerated among consumers now.

Some FAB competitors

Recent 2003 growth figures in the flavoured alcoholic beverage (FAB) market in the UK seems to indicate that the majority phase has been reached for the product category, according to The FAB Report from Bacardi-Martini, which claims to be the leading producer of premium-packaged spirits, the driving force in the FAB market. Bacardi Breezer is the number one FAB brand according to the report, with sales of more than 10,000 cases in the on trade every hour.

French Connection, the clothing chain famous for its controversial ad campaigns, is to encourage dedicated followers of fashion to not only wear its brand, but to drink it as well. The company launched the FCUK-branded, vodka-based alcoholic drinks which are sold in bars, clubs and off-licences in November 2002. FCUK is a new flavoured alcoholic beverage being launched by Matthew Clark Brands under licence from French Connection. The venture brings together a drinks company with a broad portfolio and a deep understanding of the marketplace with a brand that has an exceptional approval rating among core FAB consumers.

FCUK Spirit aims to cash in on 18–24-year-olds' enthusiasm for the fashion brand. The 1 million people who buy FCUK T-shirts each year are the same people who drink premixed drinks such as Vodka Source, Smirnoff Ice and Bacardi Breezer. Two flavours of FCUK Spirit – lemon, and cranberry and grapefruit – will be launched first. Other flavours, as well as a non-alcoholic variant, are in development.

French Connection has already extended its brand into condoms, make-up, toiletries and accessories. But the launch into the highly competitive alcohol market is its most challenging departure yet.

A recent report by Datamonitor said the unstoppable rise of alcoholic designer drinks is set to continue as consumers become more interested in the label on the bottle than the taste of the contents.

Questions

1. Does Beverage Brands have the right competences for the internationalization process?

2. Which product (WKD or Woody's Cocktails) would you recommend for the international marketing activities of Beverage Brands?

3. Which new countries would you recommend Beverage Brands to select (use Tables 1 and 2) for the internationalization?

Table 1 Total volume and revenue of FAB sales

	Volume: litres (000s)			Revenue: euro (millions – fixed exchange rate)		
	1999	2000	2001	1999	2000	2001
Western Europe	270,246.03	320,774.00	375,056.62	n/a	n/a	n/a
Austria	8,188.50	10,644.43	11,309.93	16.98	21.08	22.77
Belgium	1,432.00	2,575.00	3,924.00	10.34	18.98	29.13
Denmark	216.20	228.80	233.00	3.11	3.33	3.50
Finland	15,376.00	13,863.00	12,296.00	73.53	68.87	62.84
France	63,786.36	61,037.05	60,793.24	106.75	100.86	105.43
Germany	112,254.00	136,803.00	161,956.10	116.17	135.70	161.66
Greece	670.00	1,500.00	2,900.00	3.82	8.80	17.57
Ireland	1,073.70	1,167.00	1,289.00	8.18	9.15	10.41
Italy	17,100.00	17,405.00	17,503.25	85.57	86.46	85.95
The Netherlands	2,720.00	2,897.00	3,143.00	28.36	30.43	32.81
Norway	681.00	520.00	474.00	6.91	5.38	4.99
Portugal	230.05	635.82	627.57	1.10	3.18	3.20
Spain	12,119.00	12,397.40	12,707.00	14.12	14.38	14.69
Sweden	896.00	478.80	386.40	4.14	2.61	2.25
Switzerland	757.80	1,480.90	1,574.60	4.98	9.64	10.27
United Kingdom	32,500.00	56,800.00	83,480.00	227.62	390.99	594.71
Eastern Europe	129,296.62	154,211.17	190,783.27	n/a	n/a	n/a
Bulgaria	39.99	119.90	260.00	0.10	0.26	0.60
Hungary	—	—	112.00	—	—	0.62
Romania	—	—	7.00	—	—	0.02
Russia	122,000.00	146,290.20	182,005.00	232.64	262.55	316.44
Ukraine	6,200.00	6,603.00	6,990.00	5.52	5.74	6.46
North America	365,123.60	407,612.12	596,183.26	n/a	n/a	n/a
Canada	38,523.10	41,681.82	45,503.36	168.53	181.71	202.95
USA	326,600.50	365,930.30	550,679.90	1,288.16	1,461.02	2,083.75
Latin America	29,659.44	28,569.71	28,626.52	n/a	n/a	n/a
Argentina	205.00	207.80	208.00	0.45	0.46	0.47
Brazil	14,720.00	13,220.00	12,932.84	35.50	31.64	37.08
Chile	188.00	197.00	202.91	0.84	0.88	0.88
Colombia	592.76	589.59	595.88	1.66	1.78	1.95
Mexico	11,727.56	11,971.60	12,267.39	32.76	34.55	37.90
Venezuela	462.00	533.00	503.00	2.60	3.44	4.38
Asia Pacific	275,030.38	308,394.52	377,039.82	n/a	n/a	n/a
Hong Kong, China	170.02	178.59	187.37	1.11	1.15	1.19
Indonesia	32.00	34.00	35.70	0.04	0.05	0.05
Japan	265,844.00	297,946.00	364,062.00	1,209.48	1,323.54	1,581.79
Malaysia	151.76	161.48	162.31	1.38	1.43	1.34
Philippines	709.50	906.95	1,204.90	2.57	3.88	5.67
Singapore	123.10	127.50	127.54	1.05	1.10	1.11
Taiwan	—	—	—	—	—	—
Thailand	8,000.00	9,040.00	11,260.00	14.96	17.52	21.63

(continued)

Table 1 continued

	Volume: litres (000s)			Revenue: euro (millions – fixed exchange rate)		
	1999	2000	2001	1999	2000	2001
Australasia	67,172.00	87,239.97	119,684.92	n/a	n/a	n/a
Australia	57,039.00	75,676.97	106,035.75	328.68	422.35	591.17
New Zealand	10,133.00	11,563.00	13,649.17	30.66	35.23	41.84
Israel	355.78	365.12	373.72	2.37	2.46	2.53
Sum selected rows	1,136,883.90	1,307,166.60	1,687,748.10	4,487.60	5,097.10	6,224.90

Definition: FABs (flavoured alcoholic beverages) (off trade): This is the aggregation of wine, spirit and other types of flavoured alcoholic beverages. These drinks have an alcohol content of around 5% and a maximum content 8% abv.

Note: Historical value data is shown at current prices. Cross-country differences may also be a result of differences in making up the statistical figures regarding sales of FABs. Furthermore some important countries (e.g. China) are also missing.

Source: adapted from Euromonitor data

Table 2 Per capita volume and revenue of FAB sales

	Volume: millilitres			Revenue: euro (fixed exchange rate)		
	1999	2000	2001	1999	2000	2001
Western Europe	n/a	n/a	n/a	n/a	n/a	n/a
Austria	1,013.07	1,316.52	1,398.11	2.10	2.61	2.82
Belgium	140.20	251.61	382.63	1.01	1.85	2.84
Denmark	40.69	42.91	43.55	0.58	0.63	0.65
Finland	2,980.05	2,680.53	2,372.08	14.25	13.32	12.12
France	1,081.62	1,032.99	1,027.06	1.81	1.71	1.78
Germany	1,368.33	1,668.95	1,977.26	1.42	1.66	1.97
Greece	63.68	142.45	275.12	0.36	0.84	1.67
Ireland	287.48	309.08	337.63	2.19	2.42	2.73
Italy	296.81	301.75	302.95	1.49	1.50	1.49
The Netherlands	172.59	182.58	196.74	1.80	1.92	2.05
Norway	153.19	116.25	105.32	1.55	1.20	1.11
Portugal	23.05	63.58	60.60	0.11	0.32	0.31
Spain	307.63	314.34	321.83	0.36	0.36	0.37
Sweden	101.19	54.03	43.57	0.47	0.29	0.25
Switzerland	106.38	207.15	219.44	0.70	1.35	1.43
United Kingdom	548.25	955.66	1,403.00	3.84	6.58	9.99
Eastern Europe	n/a	n/a	n/a	n/a	n/a	n/a
Bulgaria	4.86	14.66	31.95	0.01	0.03	0.07
Hungary	—	—	11.14	—	—	0.06
Romania	—	—	0.31	—	—	0.00
Russia	833.74	1,005.03	1,255.66	1.59	1.80	2.18
Ukraine	124.37	133.73	142.57	0.11	0.12	0.13

(continued)

Table 2 continued

	Volume: millilitres			Revenue: euro (fixed exchange rate)		
	1999	2000	2001	1999	2000	2001
North America	n/a	n/a	n/a	n/a	n/a	n/a
Canada	1,263.63	1,361.59	1,477.05	5.53	5.94	6.59
USA	1,202.80	1,335.20	1,991.22	4.74	5.33	7.53
Latin America	n/a	n/a	n/a	n/a	n/a	n/a
Argentina	5.64	5.65	5.58	0.01	0.01	0.01
Brazil	90.38	80.11	76.56	0.22	0.19	0.22
Chile	12.60	13.03	13.26	0.06	0.06	0.06
Colombia	15.48	15.15	15.08	0.04	0.05	0.05
Mexico	120.45	121.07	122.22	0.34	0.35	0.38
Venezuela	19.49	22.05	20.42	0.11	0.14	0.18
Asia Pacific	n/a	n/a	n/a	n/a	n/a	n/a
Hong Kong, China	25.13	25.77	26.51	0.16	0.17	0.17
Indonesia	0.15	0.16	0.17	—	—	—
Japan	2,098.46	2,346.89	2,867.00	9.55	10.43	12.46
Malaysia	6.95	7.24	7.18	0.06	0.06	0.06
Philippines	9.50	11.88	15.58	0.03	0.05	0.07
Singapore	38.58	39.28	38.75	0.33	0.34	0.34
Thailand	131.46	147.06	182.40	0.25	0.29	0.35
Australasia	n/a	n/a	n/a	n/a	n/a	n/a
Australia	3,026.19	3,967.41	5,509.04	17.44	22.14	30.71
New Zealand	2,648.66	3,004.46	3,530.12	8.01	9.15	10.82
Israel	59.01	59.21	59.49	0.39	0.40	0.40
Sum selected rows	225.90	257.00	328.90	0.90	1.00	1.20

Note: Historical value data is shown at current prices. Cross-country differences may also be a result of differences in making up the statistical figures regarding sales of FABs. Furthermore some important countries (e.g. China) are also missing.

Source: adapted from Euromonitor data

Globalization of the theme park business

Based in Melbourne, Australia, Village Roadshow is a leading international media and entertainment company with its core businesses in cinema, movie production, film distribution, radio and theme parks. Village Roadshow has now exported its cinema development and management expertise to 11 countries. Export of management expertise in Radio and the group's movie production business means it now has operations in 13 countries.

Village Roadshow's assets include:

- An international cinema circuit of around 1,139 screens in 134 separate sites.
- A majority shareholding in Austereo Group Limited, managing Australia's leading radio networks – Triple M and Today.
- A 50 per cent stakeholding in Warner Bros. Movie World, Sea World and Wet 'n' Wild Water World, Australia's most popular theme parks.
- A major movie production business based in Los Angeles. In movie production, the company is one of the most successful independent producers in Hollywood with recent successes, e.g. 'The Matrix Relaoded'.
- A film distribution business with operations in Australia, New Zealand, Singapore and Greece.

History

Village Roadshow commenced operating in 1954, owning and managing one of the first drive-in cinemas in Australia (Melbourne). From these modest beginnings the company gradually expanded its drive-in cinema circuit with the addition of more traditional or 'hardtop' cinemas in major population centres. To strengthen its position through business diversification Village Roadshow entered the vertically related businesses of film distribution in the 1960s and film production in the 1970s.

In the 1980s Village Roadshow was a pioneer in the development of state of the art multiplex cinema complexes. The group's developments raised cinema exhibition standards to new levels by utilising stadium seating, the latest sound systems and advanced projection technologies. These cinemas were the forerunners of the high quality multiplexes that operate around the world today.

In the 1990s Village Roadshow sought to further strengthen its position by diversifying into entertainment businesses. This included the purchase and development of theme parks, which are at focus here.

Theme parks

With its three parks on Australia's Gold Coast, Village Roadshow is the country's largest theme park operator. Around 3 million people per annum visit the three parks, Warner Bros. Movie World, Sea World and Wet 'n' Wild Water World. The group is also a part owner of Sea World Nara Resort, a 405-room hotel adjacent to Sea World. A brief comment on each of the parks follows:

Village Roadshow's 50 per cent partner in the group's theme parks is AOL Time Warner. The combined business, Village Roadshow and AOL Time Warner is here abbreviated to VR/AOL.

Warner Bros. Movie World

Based on Warner Bros. successful movies and movie characters, Warner Bros. Movie World is Australia's number

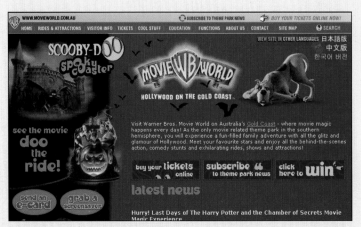

one tourist attraction. Conveniently situated just north of Australia's Gold Coast, the park covers over 100 hectares (252 acres), offering a full day of entertainment for all. Warner Bros. Movie World has consolidated its position as a worldwide leader in tourism and theme park marketing by winning numerous state, national and international awards in the last 10 years, including its membership in the coveted Australian Tourism Hall of Fame.

Employing approximately 800 staff, the park contains a number of rides and attractions including behind the scenes movie action, comedy stunts and animatronics from Warner Bros. movies and cartoons and an array of rides. Access to the attractions and rides is available for a single entry fee. In addition, visitors can take some of the magic home with them through Warner Bros. souvenirs, vintage portraits, screen test photos, video recordings, as well as photos of their favourite movie stars and characters.

The Warner Roadshow Movie World Studios are located next to the Warner Bros. Movie World theme park. The Studios are purpose built – a one-stop shop of studio and production facilities incorporating sound stages, casting production offices, water tanks, editing suites, wardrobe, make-up, construction workshops, preview theatrette, visual effects studio, film processing, post production, travel and freight services, and much more.

Over the last 10 years the studios have been home to countless feature films, telemovies, TV series and mini series.

For more information on the attractions of Warner Bros. Movie World visit its website at **www.movieworld.com.au**

Sea World

Sea World originally opened in 1971 to showcase the Water Ski Spectacular and has since grown to become Australia's premier marine park. For a single entry fee visitors can experience all of the park's attractions covering 25 hectares (55 acres), a few minutes north of Queensland's Gold Coast.

Visitors to the park are able to participate in a range of interactive activities including marine mammal interactive programmes involving dolphins and seals, a behind the scenes tour of Polar Bear Shores as well as a range of watersports. Through Sea World Helicopters the park also offers scenic helicopter flights around the Gold Coast and hinterland.

Sea World Research and Rescue Foundation is an independent, non-profit organization supported by Sea World. The foundation has been responsible for countless rescues of marine mammals, turtles and sea birds throughout Australia and its expertise in the care of these animals is sought worldwide. In addition to conducting its own marine research, the Foundation also funds a number of independent marine research projects.

Sea World employs over 600 staff and is a pioneer in Gold Coast tourism. The first theme park in Australia to be inducted into the Australian Tourism Hall of Fame in 1992 and winner of Major Tourist Attraction in the 2001 Queensland Tourism Awards, Sea World has set the standards other Australian theme parks have followed.

For more information about the attractions visit the Sea World Website at **www.seaworld.com.au**

Wet 'n' Wild Water World

Located alongside Warner Bros. Movie World, Wet 'n' Wild Water World is Australia's premier water theme park. The park comprises a wide range of water-based fun, including Australia's largest water slides, a giant wave pool and a variety of leisure pools.

Wet 'n' Wild Water World has been one of the group's most successful theme parks, with consistent growth in attendances. The park relies to a large extent on local visitors although the introduction of the 3 Park Super Pass in conjunction with Warner Bros. Movie World and Sea World has increased both the awareness of the park and interstate attendances.

The park employs over 70 people with employee numbers swelling to over 250 in peak periods. Wet 'n' Wild Water World was judged Best Major Attraction in the 2001 Brisbane Tourism Awards.

For more information visit the Wet 'n' Wild Water World Website at **www.wetnwild.com.au**

Theme parks in international tourism

The theme park has several historical antecedents, including the ride-based amusement parks of the early twentieth-century United States and the garden parks of Europe, e.g. Tivoli in Copenhagen. The birth of the modern theme park, however, is commonly recognised as occurring with the opening of Disneyland about 30 years ago.

Economics Research Associates (**ERA**) has completed many assignments for the Walt Disney Company over the years, and since Disneyland, theme parks have multiplied throughout the world. And they all bear the following primary characteristics:

1. They have family appeal.
2. They contain one or more themed environments.

3. They have some form of 'ambient entertainment', that is, strolling musicians, performers, costumed characters and so on, who perform for 'free'.
4. They have a high investment level per unit of ride or show capacity.
5. They have high standards of service, maintenance and cleanliness.
6. They contain enough activities (entertainment content) to create an average visitor length of stay of typically five to seven hours.
7. They will usually, but not always, have a pay-one-price admission policy.

Recently there have been variations from the formula. These include theme parks oriented around one theme or towards one market, for example aquatic parks and children's parks. A second departure from the traditional theme park is indoor theme parks combined with retail shopping centres. The largest examples of these are West Edmonton Mall in Canada, Lotte World in Seoul and Mall of America in Minneapolis.

State of the industry

The theme park industry has witnessed fairly rapid international expansion in recent years, with growth focused mostly in Europe and Japan. It is instructive to compare industry development in the United States with where other world markets stand.

The US industry has had about a 30-year growth to maturity. This is characterised by an inception period pioneered by Disney in the late 1950s and early 1960s, rapid growth through the 1970s, and maturity in the 1980s. Europe and North Asia are currently in the rapid growth phase of their theme park industries with the developing countries in the inception period. While the US experience cannot be directly translated to foreign markets, we can be reasonably assured that Europe and North Asia will continue to have fairly strong growth over the next 10 years or so, and it will be 5 years or more before we see any significant growth in the developing countries.

In the following the main theme park regions in North America, Europe, North Asia and the developing world will be discussed.

North America

The US theme park industry is by far the largest in the world. There are approximately 40 large-scale parks with annual attendance of over 1 million, and approximately 55 moderate-scale parks with attendance between 500,000 and 1 million. Annual attendance at these attractions totals 159 million, with revenue of $4.5 billion. The US industry dominates the world, in scale, product innovation, marketing savvy, and operating knowledge.

The United States has a mature industry. Growth has been at a compounded annual rate of about 3 per cent over the last 10 years. About half of this growth has come from the addition of new parks and not from increased attendance in existing parks. Per capita expenditure has slightly exceeded the rate of inflation, reflecting admission price increases and strong growth in merchandise sales and games revenue. When we combine attendance growth with per capita expenditure increases we see an annual revenue growth of about 9 per cent over the last 10 years.

The watchwords for the US industry are: (1) maturation, (2) consolidation, (3) diversification and (4) destination tourism.

1. Maturation

The majority of US markets capable of supporting large-scale, outdoor theme parks already have them. It is unlikely that a significant number of major regional theme parks will be developed in the future. Growth in this industry has stabilised, and there should not be any huge fluctuations in attendance or development activity. However, there are opportunities for adjusting product to suit changing markets and to effectively compete with other entertainment for consumers' leisure time and expenditure.

2. Consolidation

Typical of a maturing industry, there have been numerous changes in theme park ownership over the last several years. This indicates a strong consolidation trend. Much of the control of the industry is now focused into a few multipark operating companies: Disney, Time Warner/Six Flags, Paramount/KECO, Anheuser Busch and MCA-Universal.

Three major corporations have left the industry (Taft Broadcasting, Marriott Corporation and Harcourt Brace Javonavich (HBJ)). The Marriott Corporation sold its two parks to divest itself of the industry. One was in Santa Clara and is now owned by KECO, and the other was in the Chicago area and is now owned by Six Flags. HBJ, previous owners of the Sea World parks, sold all its parks to Busch, which already owned two parks. Busch's theme park holdings now total seven, with a planned attraction in Spain.

The seven Six Flags parks have been sold as a group several times and are now owned by

Time/Warner. Four of the Six Flags parks were started by independent operators.

Disney continues to increase its leadership in the industry by building more attractions. Within the last several years they have opened three: the Disney/MGM Studio Tour, Typhoon Lagoon and Pleasure Island. Disney has also announced plans for additional attractions in Anaheim on property adjacent to Disneyland.

3. Diversification

The US theme park industry is diversifying into new, smaller-scale targeted products for 'niche' markets that may not be covered by the large-scale theme parks.

ERA feels that this trend is being driven by market opportunities such as those that drove expansion of the theme park industry several decades ago. The theme park development boom in the 1970s represented a massive, heavily capitalised response to the need to provide baby boomers with family entertainment. Theme parks fit into the urban fabric of the United States by being located next to large, built-up metropolitan markets, and on relatively inexpensive land.

The 1980s witnessed a narrowing of market and product focus with the smaller investment waterparks. This was the first major diversification of the industry. Waterparks appealed to a narrower market, usually teens and young families, and were suitable for smaller, secondary markets.

The new entertainment attractions of the 1990s represent a further diversification. These attractions narrow the niche appeal even more, with smaller capital investment, and an appeal usually to very specific market groups such as children, teens, young singles, etc. Many of these attractions tap the 'baby boomlet' sector, and respond to the need to regenerate under-performing suburban real estate properties by locating in shopping centres.

Examples of the new entertainment attractions include the family entertainment centres being developed in malls, the expansion of outdoor family recreation and mini-golf attractions, entertainment centres combined with urban mixed-use projects, sports bars, themed restaurants, children's attractions, mini-aquariums, and a host of others.

Diversification should continue as entrepreneurs attempt to seek out untapped entertainment markets.

4. Destination Tourism

Within the last 10 years the only major parks developed in the United States have been destination market parks focusing on the tourist markets of the sunbelt states of Florida and Texas. These attractions have included Disney's EPCOT Center, Disney's MGM Studio Theme Park, Universal Studios – Florida, and Sea World Texas in San Antonio. One exception was Marine World Africa U.S.A., which was relocated from one area of the San Francisco Bay region to another.

Additionally, the major planned attractions, Disney's new California attraction, Fiesta Texas in San Antonio, and the possible Columbia Pictures attraction in California, will all be destination in nature.

Theme park development in the United States has changed from selling a seven-hour experience to a seven-day experience. Disney, of course, is the pioneer in this way of thinking. Developers have realised the huge economic value created by the impact of a tourism-oriented theme park on surrounding complementary properties such as hotels, resorts and shopping centres.

Europe

Europe has a number of parks spread throughout western Europe, with a large concentration of attractions in Germany, France, the Benelux countries and the United Kingdom. Expansion of the industry into southern Europe is now taking place, with several planned or implemented projects in Spain, Italy, Turkey and Greece. There are also a number of proposed projects in North Africa and the Middle East.

Currently the European theme park industry consists of 19 major attractions, with annual attendance of over 1 million, and some 45 moderate-scale attractions with attendance between 500,000 and 1 million. Europe's parks generate annual attendance of about 70 million, and revenue of around $1.5 billion. The European industry is about one-third the size of the US industry in terms of revenue.

The European market changed with the opening of EuroDisney:

1. EuroDisney (ED) will expand the overall European theme park industry and focus the industry in Paris by creating a multi park destination attraction complex.
2. Disney will educate the market as to the theme park product, the quality of the theme park experience, and the value of the pay-one-price admission for a day of quality entertainment.
3. Disney will provide price leadership in the market. This will allow others to price up to Disney levels.

4. EuroDisney will create marketing awareness through its well-established and creative marketing programmes and will also enlighten competitors as to the use of effective marketing techniques.

5. EuroDisney will improve management expertise in the European theme park business. ED will train and create a labour pool of experienced theme park managers that will in the future help to enhance the performance of the European theme park business as a whole.

The key words for Europe are: (1) anticipation, (2) repositioning, (3) expansion and (4) consolidation.

1. Anticipation
Wherever Disney theme parks enter new markets there are significant structural changes to the indigenous theme park industries. In the United States, Disney's first attraction, Disneyland, founded the industry. In Florida Disney's attraction converted an unknown swamp into the United States' premier tourist destination and attraction market, and in Japan Tokyo Disneyland spurred growth of the Japanese theme park industry. It is believed Disney will have a significant impact on the attractions' industry in France and Europe.

2. Repositioning
Many of the European parks have been expanding and repositioning with a renewed emphasis on reinvestment and marketing. Many have undertaken major expansion programmes, increasing ride and show capacity and expanding visitor services such as restaurants and merchandise areas (areas where European parks have traditionally lagged behind those in the United States). Major expansion programmes have occurred at, among others, Alton Towers in England, De Efteling in Holland, Gardaland in Italy, Parc Asterix in France, Walibi in Belgium.

Several European parks have repositioned themselves in the marketplace. In the past the parks relied on steady repeat business from the immediate resident market. This market responded to the attraction's low admission prices, picnic areas and relatively passive environments, which offered a quasi-public park experience. Through recent reinvestment programmes parks have repositioned themselves as more active and commercial attractions with higher admission prices, thus drawing from somewhat larger markets. EDL will create the need for proper product positioning to complement Disney in the market area.

3. Expansion
The European theme park industry has also been marked by new development activity in recent years. In the last four years new attraction development has been focused primarily on France. EuroDisney opened in 1992 but was preceded (perhaps unwisely) by four other new attractions:

- Parc Asterix;
- The Smurf Park;
- Mirapolis; and
- Zygofolis.

Disney has yet to be well accepted by the French market although it does quite well with tourists. The other new French parks have struggled financially, due to flaws in design, development and management. Two (Mirapolis and Zygofolis) have gone bankrupt and significantly damaged the enthusiasm of investors and lenders. Busch is proceeding with its park in Tarragona, Spain and several other new projects are proposed in southern Europe.

Legoland is also expanding to several new key markets, including United States, UK, Germany and Japan.

4. Consolidation
A final trend in the European theme park business is the consolidation of the industry into key ownership groups. This occurs in industries as they mature and has also been a trend in the United States. In Europe, several attraction acquisitions have begun this process. In 1990 Madame Tussauds purchased Alton Towers (Madame Tussauds also owns several smaller attractions on the continent and the Rock Circus attraction in London). The Walibi organization purchased The Smurf Park (now called Walibi Smurf), increasing its theme park industry holdings to four parks. Finally, Accor, France's largest hotel operator, acquired a controlling interest in Parc Asterix. With European unification and the continuing maturation of the European theme park industry this trend will continue.

It is too early to determine trends for eastern Europe but a number of schemes have surfaced, including theme parks oriented towards increasing tourism-based foreign exchange. Because of the rapid changes in these markets we may have to wait some time before we see any significant development in the amusement and theme park industry. However, we should keep our eye on them.

North Asia
Asia is the world's next leading international theme

park market. It includes a mature industry in Japan, strong growth in Korea, strong performance in Hong Kong, underserved markets in Taiwan, and a rapidly changing China.

A substantial amusement park industry has been established in Japan since the recovery from the post-war period. A variety of themed attractions and numerous amusement parks are located throughout the country. The growth of this business has been assisted by the presence of major amusement ride manufacturers in Japan.

There are strong concentrations of amusement and theme parks in the Kanto region around Tokyo and the Kansai region near Osaka and Kobe. These are the two main urban areas in Japan and they both have huge population bases that support a variety of attractions. A third concentration, now in the formative stages, is on the southern island of Kyushu, which is developing as a resort destination area and has several parks and attractions, including Harmonyland.

Tokyo Disneyland, which opened in 1983, brought the large-scale theme park product to Japan, and since that time several large projects have been built, including the $630 million Puroland in Tama, and Nippon Space World in Kyushu. Several other large projects are currently being planned or are under way.

The Japanese industry at present has about 29 large parks with annual attendance over 1 million, and 30 moderate-scale parks with attendance between 500,000 persons and 1 million. As a whole, the Japanese industry generates about 75 million attendees and about $1.5 billion in annual revenue. This places the Japanese industry at about 30 per cent of the US industry in terms of revenue. On a revenue per capita basis, however, they are reasonably close.

The watchwords for Asia are: (1) selective growth and (2) short-term retrenchment.

1. Growth

For the last five to seven years there has been strong interest in theme park development in Japan and Korea. Much of this was catalysed by the success of Tokyo Disneyland. Other factors driving Japanese interest in theme parks have been the high level of discretionary income available for entertainment and a heightened national interest in leisure. Also, the Japanese government, until very recently, has provided strong incentives for leisure development.

There are several large-scale theme park projects under consideration at this time. These include a second-gate attraction at Tokyo Disneyland, which may be a movie studio park or the Disney Sea attraction originally planned for Long Beach, California; a major sea life park in the Awaji area near Osaka; a large-scale theme park proposed for a landfill area in Kobe; MCA's Universal Studios Japan project; expansion of Yongin Farmland in Korea; expansion of Ocean Park, Hong Kong; several proposed projects in Taiwan; and a push by China to encourage theme park investment. There are also numerous other projects being discussed.

2. Retrenchment

In the last year or so there has been something of a retrenchment of the theme park industry in Japan. In the late 1980s major Japanese corporations entered the industry with gusto. Unfortunately their efforts were met in many cases with design, operating and financial difficulties at some of the major projects. Several poorly performing projects that have been financial drains on the major corporations which developed them have created an air of caution in Japan about the theme park business. This, combined with economic ills being faced in different segments of the country's economy, have slowed down the growth of the theme park industry as the Japanese reassess what makes the industry work, and what the model for Japan should be.

The developing world

Developing countries are concerned with many economic and social development issues. Some see tourism as a major force for economic improvement and look to themed attractions as part of the tourism product. There is also a growing resident market with the income necessary to afford attractions.

It is instructive to look at the world's population distribution. Right now, 78 per cent of the world's 5.4 billion people, or 4.2 billion people, live in developing countries. By the year 2010 82 per cent of the world's population will live in these countries. Even if 20 per cent of these people are income qualified for a theme park product, that is a market approaching 1 billion people! And many of these economies, particularly in Asia, are expanding and have rising income levels.

It will be some time before the developing countries have major theme or amusement park industries, but some countries should be seeing development activity in the near future. Countries to keep an eye on are Brazil, Mexico, India, Thailand, the Middle East, and the south-east Asian growth triangle of Singapore, Malaysia and Indonesia.

Theme parks and tourism

Let us turn now to the relationship of theme parks to tourism. The relationship is complex and highly dependent on the park's scale, quality and uniqueness.

Typically residents (from within 1.5 to 2 hours travelling distance) will account for 80 per cent of traditional theme park visitation. Even the tourist visitors are often in the area for other reasons (such as visiting friends and relatives). Thus just having a theme park does not automatically insure an influx of tourism. Rather, to impact on destination tourism, a theme park must meet the following criteria.

Be unique, a 'must see' destination

This can be accomplished through character development (Mickey and his friends), architectural form, natural features, special events and programming (Opryland) or a combination thereof.

Have large-scale and a critical mass of attractions

Investment levels to impact on international tourism generally must exceed $150 million. There should be a combination of high technology with human scale and quality service. Investments in the 'thrill hardware' must be combined with a high level of service from the 'hosts and hostesses' so that a unique local culture and friendly human contact is balanced with the high technology.

Encourage overnight stays

The principal economic benefits of tourism comes when overnight stays are generated. Day visitors or tourists who stay with friends and relatives generate only 20 per cent of the economic impact of tourists staying in hotels and motels ($50 versus $250 per day). Thus in designing a theme park for tourism a multiple attraction destination (with experiences that can occupy two or three days) is more likely to have the desired impact.

Have complementary destination activities

Tourist-oriented theme parks should be part of a mix of recreation and leisure activities. A true tourist destination would also have supporting recreation uses such as high quality hotels, convention and conference facilities, resorts, recreational shopping and dining experiences, and sports activities including golf, tennis, and water-related activities, and excursions into nearby local tourism areas.

Support media (TV) coverage and exposure

As with many other things in life, future theme parks must be designed for television. The use of theme parks and resorts as backdrops for variety programmes, celebrity games, sports competitions, and convention/conference broadcasting is increasing rapidly and the resultant TV exposure is very important in creating awareness in tourism markets.

Given that these criteria are part of the theme park/tourist destination programme, the results can be dramatic and provide a sustaining economic base. For example, at Walt Disney World tourism increased from 2.8 million visitors in 1970 to over 35 million by 1992. The increase in the number of air visitors alone was 20 million. This increase in visitation (particularly overnight visitation) spurred the development of over 50,000 hotel rooms and resulted in the direct employment of over 250,000 people – quite a success story for what was once only a mosquito-infested swamp bought for an average price of $200 per acre. Smaller-scale attractions, such as the Polynesian Cultural Center in Hawaii, have also built a steady business of nearly 1 million visitors a year through strong penetration of the tourism market.

Developing trends

As we move further into the twenty-first century, how will theme parks evolve as a component of international tourism? They will not blindly follow the US model, but evolve new forms of attractions where tourism is a more important source of market support. From our perspective in analysing development trends and proposed new parks we see the following changes.

Themed to country/region

New parks will have stronger theming tied to the country or local region. Theme parks are increasingly becoming a symbol and showcase for regional pride, culture and technological achievement. The danger here, of course, is that by being too serious about 'cultural' tourism the parks can cease to be fun. We have to constantly counsel our clients that a theme park's prime objective is entertainment. This is the 'sugar' that makes the learning and culture pill work.

Part of larger, mixed-use destination projects

In the urban/suburban context, we now see theme parks and large-scale attractions being designed into regional and speciality shopping complexes, mixed-use waterfront developments, and even some multiuse office buildings. In more rural settings, additional components often include destination resorts, bungalow parks, shopping/restaurant villages, and special events centres/trade expositions.

Greater visitor participation and interaction
New attractions are being designed to provide greater participant control and encourage interplay between the visitor and their environment. This is a natural outgrowth of both available technology and the demonstrated appeal of such involvement at places such as the San Francisco Exploratorium. New thrill rides are being offered where the rider can individually control the experience and intensity of the ride. Future thematic concepts will be based more on participative activities (sports, music) that relate to the audience rather than comic book characterisations.

Use of simulation experiences and virtual reality
Perhaps one of the most exciting areas of development is in the area of simulation. Advances in technology have allowed attractions designers to realistically duplicate virtually any natural or special effects experience. By combining extremely high quality visual imagery with seats that are programmed to move with the action, visitors can realistically enjoy experiences that were previously unavailable in a theme park environment. The first highly popular example of this technology is the Star Tours attraction at Disneyland. However, new simulation presentations include river rafting in New Zealand, runaway sports cars in the Italian Alps, and intergalactic space races. These simulations are produced for a fraction of the cost of traditional attractions. The technology is also more flexible (you can change the experience by simply changing the software (film) rather them creating a new attraction), and more land efficient (a 45-seat simulator needs only about 300 square meters). A major challenge, however, will be to have the technology breakthrough and still maintain the thrill and spontaneity of perceived personal risk and group interaction.

Greater water orientation
A greater use of water-related activities, attractions and landscaping is occurring in theme park design as well as in nearly all forms of real estate development. Several parks (Ocean Park, Hong Kong; Dreamland, Australia; Walibi, Belgium) combine an active water park with more traditional themed rides and amusements. Performance parks such as Sea World are still popular but future expansion will be limited by restrictions on capturing and displaying aquatic mammals. We see a continuing acceptance of new, high technology aquariums using acrylic tunnel concepts that combine a scuba diver's view of the undersea world with a ride experience. Some of these will be developed in the open ocean.

Design for all-weather operation/artificial environments
New theme parks are designed to have more covered attractions as well as climate-controlled walkways and rest areas. This allows for shorter amortisation of high capital investment and fixed cost components. New theme parks are being designed with a greater degree of weather protection in order to enable a longer operating season and longer operating hours per day.

When one looks ahead at the larger number of tourists who are expected to travel to new destinations (particularly within the Asia-Pacific region), there will be increasing pressure on sensitive environmental and social resources at the destination. A new role for theme parks is emerging. By their nature, they are designed to handle large numbers of people within a controlled space and with manageable impacts. In future they will embody a greater educational function to introduce, interpret and sensitise the overseas tourist to the environment and to the host community and its values. They can become a new gateway for host country tourism. Rather than being viewed as a stand-alone attraction theme parks will become part of a balanced leisure product and tourism system that contributes to the economic development, employment and resource preservation of an entire region.

Source: adapted from **www.villageroadshow.com.au** and **www.econres.com** (Economics Research Associates)

Questions

1. Which are the key success factors in VR/AOL's operations of a theme park?

2. Which criteria should VR/AOL use in order to select the best locations for the opening of new theme parks?

Market entry strategies

Part III   Contents

Case studies

Part II   Introduction

Once the firm has chosen target markets abroad (see Part II) the question arises as to the best way to enter those markets. In Part III we will consider the major market entry modes and criteria for selecting them. An international market entry mode is an institutional arrangement necessary for the entry of a company's products, technology and human capital into a foreign country/market.

To separate Part III from later chapters, let us take a look at Figure 1. The figure shows the classical distribution systems in a national consumer market.

In this context the chosen market entry mode (here, own sales subsidiary) can be regarded as the first decision level in the vertical chain that will provide marketing and distribution to the next actors in the vertical chain. In Chapter 17 we will take a closer look at the choice between alternative distribution systems at the single national level.

Figure 1 Examples of different market entry modes and the distribution decision

```
Part III
Deciding between
alternative market                    HQ
entry modes                                              Border
- - - - - - - - - - - - - - - - - - - - - - - - - -    --- etc.

  ┌──────────┐   ┌──────────────┐   ┌───────────┐   ┌──────────┐
  │Distributor│  │ Own sales    │   │ Licensing │   │  Joint   │
  └──────────┘   │ subsidiary   │   └───────────┘   │ venture  │
                 └──────────────┘                    └──────────┘

                 ┌──────────────┐
                 │  Wholesaler  │
                 └──────────────┘

                 ┌──────────────┐
                 │   Retailer   │
                 └──────────────┘

                 ┌──────────────┐
                 │ End customer │
                 └──────────────┘

                    Chapter 17
                Distribution decisions
```

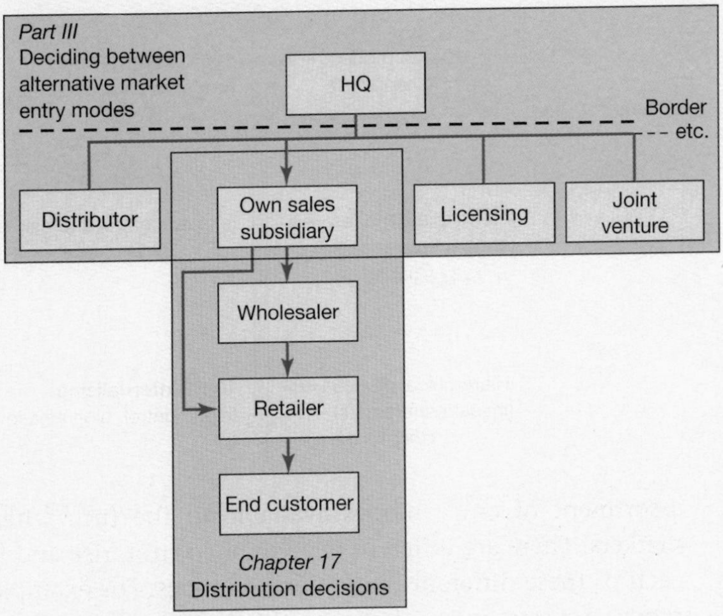

Some firms have discovered that an ill-judged market entry selection in the initial stages of its internationalization can threaten its future market entry and expansion activities. Since it is common for firms to have their initial mode choice institutionalized over time, as new products are sold through the same established channels and new markets are entered using the same entry method, a problematic initial entry mode choice can survive through the institutionalisation of this mode. The inertia in the shift process of entry modes delays the transition to a new entry mode. The reluctance of firms to change entry modes once they are in place, and the difficulty involved in so doing, makes the mode of entry decision a key strategic issue for firms operating in today's rapidly internationalizing marketplace (Hollensen, 1991).

For most SMEs the market entry represents a critical first step, but for established companies the problem is not how to enter new emerging markets, rather how to exploit opportunities more effectively within the context of their existing network of international operations.

There is, however, no ideal market entry strategy, and different market entry methods might be adopted by different firms entering the same market and/or by the same firm in different markets. Petersen and Welch (2002) found that a firm often combines modes to enter or develop a specific foreign market. Such 'mode packages' may take the form of concerted use of several operation modes in an integrated, complementary way. In some cases a firm uses a combination of modes that compete with each other. Sometimes this occurs when a firm attempts a hostile takeover of an export market. The existing local distributor might be able to resist giving up the market, depending on the nature of existing obligations, but the exporter nevertheless may establish a wholly owned sales subsidiary.

As shown in Figure 2, three broad groupings emerge when one looks at the

Figure 2 Classification of market entry modes

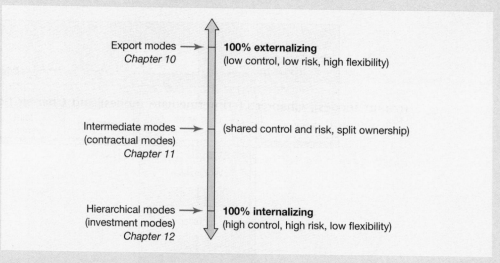

assortment of entry modes available to the firm when entering international markets. There are different degrees of control, risk and flexibility associated with each of these different market entry modes. For example, the use of hierarchical modes (investment modes) gives the firm ownership and thereby high control, but committing heavy resources to foreign markets also represents a higher potential risk. At the same time heavy resource commitment creates exit barriers, which diminish the firm's ability to change the chosen entry mode in a quick and easy way. So the entry mode decision involves trade-offs, as the firm cannot have both high control and high flexibility.

Figure 3 shows three examples representing the main types of market entry mode. By using hierarchical modes, transactions between independent actors are

Figure 3 Examples of the different market entry modes in the consumer market

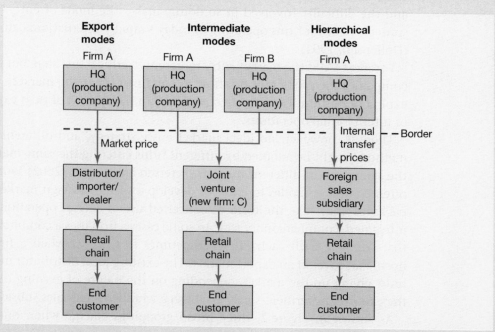

substituted by intra-firm transactions, and market prices are substituted by internal transfer prices.

Many factors should be considered in deciding on the appropriate market entry mode. These factors (criteria) vary with the market situation and the firm in question.

Chapter 9 will examine the different decision criteria and how they influence the choice among the three main groupings of market entry modes. Chapter 10 (Export modes), Chapter 11 (Intermediate modes) and Chapter 12 (Hierarchical modes) will discuss in more detail the three main types of entry mode. A special issue for SMEs is how their internationalization process is related to their much bigger customers and their sourcing and entry mode decisions. This will be discussed further in Chapter 13. Finally in Chapter 14 (Global e-commerce) the special online entry modes will be discussed.

The simple version of the value chain (see Figure 1.10) will be used to structure the different entry modes in Chapters 10, 11 and 12.

References

Hollensen, S. (1991) 'Shift of market servicing organization in international markets: a Danish case study', in Vestergaard, H. (ed.), *An Enlarged Europe in the Global Economy*, EIBA's 17th Annual Conference, Copenhagen.

Petersen, B. and Welch, L.S. (2002), 'Foreign operation mode combinations and internationalization', *Journal of Business Research*, vol. 55, pp. 157–162.

9 Some approaches to the choice of entry mode

Contents

Learning objectives

After studying this chapter you should be able to do the following:

- Identify and classify different market entry modes.
- Explore different approaches to the choice of entry mode.
- Explain how opportunistic behaviour affects the manufacturer/intermediary relationship.
- Identify the factors to consider when choosing a market entry strategy.

9.1 Introduction

We have seen the main groupings of entry modes which are available to companies that wish to take advantage of foreign market opportunities. At this point we are concerned with the question: what kind of strategy should be used for the entry mode selection?

According to Root (1994) there are three different rules:

- *Naive rule*. The decision maker uses the same entry mode for all foreign markets. This rule ignores the heterogeneity of the individual foreign markets.
- *Pragmatic rule*. The decision maker uses a workable entry mode for each foreign market. In the early stages of exporting the firm typically starts doing business with a low-risk entry mode. Only if the particular initial mode is not feasible or profitable will the firm look for another workable entry mode. In this case not all potential alternatives are investigated, and the workable entry may not be the 'best' entry mode.
- *Strategy rules*. This approach requires that all alternative entry modes are systematically compared and evaluated before any choice is made. An application of this decision rule would be to choose the entry mode that maximises the profit contribution over the strategic planning period subject to (1) the availability of company resources, (2) risk and (3) non-profit objectives.

Although many SMEs probably use the pragmatic or even the naive rule, this chapter is mainly inspired by an analytical approach, which is the main principle behind the strategy rule.

9.2   The transaction cost approach

The principles of transaction cost analysis have already been presented in Chapter 3 (section 3.3). This chapter will go into further details about 'friction' and opportunism.

The unit of analysis is the transaction rather than the firm. The basic idea behind this approach is that in the real world there is always some friction between the buyer and seller in connection with market transactions. This friction is mainly caused by opportunistic behaviour in the relation between a producer and an export intermediary.

In the case of an agent, the producer specifies sales-promoting tasks that the export intermediary is to solve in order to receive a reward in the shape of commission.

In the case of an importer, the export intermediary has a higher degree of freedom as the intermediary itself, to a certain extent, can fix sales prices and thus base its earnings on the profit between the producer's sales price (the importer's buying price) and the importer's sales price.

No matter who the export intermediary may be, there will be some recurrent questions that may result in conflicts and opportunistic actions:

- stock size of the export intermediary;
- extent of technical and commercial service that the export intermediary is to carry out for its customers;
- division of marketing costs (advertising, exhibition activities, etc.) between producer and export intermediary;
- fixing of prices: from producer to export intermediary, and from the export intermediary to its customers;
- fixing of commission to agents.

Opportunistic behaviour from the export intermediary

In this connection the export intermediary's opportunistic behaviour may be reflected in two activities:

- In most producer–export intermediary relations a split of the sales promoting costs has been fixed. Thus statements by the export intermediary of too high sales promotion activities (e.g. by manipulating invoices) may form the basis of a higher payment from producer to export intermediary.
- The export intermediary may manipulate information on market size and competitor prices in order to obtain lower ex-works prices from the producer. Of course, this kind of opportunism can be avoided if the export intermediary is paid a commission of realised turnover (the agency case).

Opportunistic behaviour from the producer

In this chapter we have so far presumed that the export intermediary is the one who has behaved opportunistically. The producer may, however, also behave in an opportunistic way, as the export intermediary must also use resources (time and money) on building up the market for the producer's product programme. This is especially the case if the producer wants to sell expensive and technically complicated products.

Thus the export intermediary carries a great part of the economic risk, and will always have the threat of the producer's change of entry mode hanging over its head. If the export intermediary does not live up to the producer's expectations it risks being replaced by another export intermediary, or the producer may change to its own export organization (sales subsidiary), as the increased transaction frequency (market size) can obviously bear the increased costs.

The last case may also be part of a deliberate strategy from the producer: namely, to tap the export intermediary for market knowledge and customer contacts in order to establish a sales organization itself.

What can the export intermediary do to meet this situation?

Heide and John (1988) suggest that the agent should make a number of further 'offsetting' investments in order to counterbalance the relationship between the two parties. These investments create bonds that make it costly for the producer to leave the relationship: that is, the agent creates 'exit barriers' for the producer (the principal). Examples of such investments are as follows:

- Establish personal relations with the producer's key employees.
- Create an independent identity (image) in connection with selling the producer's products.
- Add further value to the product, such as BDA service (before–during–after service), which creates bonds in the agent's customer relations.

If it is impossible to make such offsetting investments Heide and John (1988) suggest that the agent reduces its risk by representing more producers.

These are the conditions that the producer is up against, and when several of these factors appear at the same time the theory recommends that the company (the producer) internalises rather than externalises.

9.3 Factors influencing the choice of entry mode

A firm's choice of its entry mode for a given product/target country is the net result of several, often conflicting forces. The need to anticipate the strength and direction of these forces makes the entry mode decision a complex process with numerous trade-offs among alternative entry modes.

Generally speaking the choice of entry mode should be based on the expected contribution to profit. This may be easier said than done, particularly for those foreign markets where relevant data are lacking. Most of the selection criteria are qualitative in nature, and a quantification is very difficult.

As shown in Figure 9.1, four groups of factors are believed to influence the entry mode decision:

- internal factors;
- external factors;
- desired mode characteristics;
- transaction-specific behaviour.

Figure 9.1 Factors affecting the foreign market entry mode decision

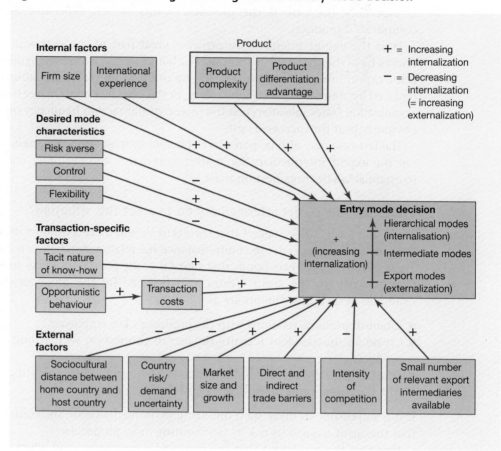

In what follows a proposition is formulated for each factor: how is each factor supposed to affect the choice of foreign entry mode? The direction of influence is also indicated both in the text and in Figure 9.1. Because of the complexity of the entry mode decision the propositions are made under the condition of other factors being equal.

Internal factors

Firm size

Size is an indicator of the firm's resource availability; increasing resource availability provides the basis for increased international involvement over time. Although SMEs may desire a high level of control over international operations and wish to make heavy resource commitments to foreign markets, they are more likely to enter foreign markets using export modes because they do not have the resources necessary to achieve a high degree of control or to make these resource commitments. Export entry modes (market modes), with their lower resource commitment, may therefore be more suitable for SMEs. As the firm grows it will increasingly use the hierarchical model.

International experience

Another firm-specific factor influencing mode choice is the international experience of managers and thus of the firm. Experience, which refers to the extent to which a firm has been involved in operating internationally, can be gained from operating either in a particular country or in the general international environment. International experience reduces the cost and uncertainty of serving a market, and in turn increases the probability of firms committing resources to foreign markets.

In developing their theory of internationalization Johanson and Vahlne (1977) assert that uncertainty in international markets is reduced through actual operations in foreign markets (experiential knowledge) rather than through the acquisition of objective knowledge. They suggest that it is direct experience with international markets that increases the likelihood of committing extra resources to foreign markets.

Product

The physical characteristics of the product or service, such as its value/weight ratio, perishability and composition, are important in determining where production is located. Products with high value/weight ratios, such as expensive watches, are typically used for direct exporting, especially where there are significant production economies of scale, or if management wishes to retain control over production. Conversely, in the soft drinks and beer industry, companies typically establish licensing agreements, or invest in local bottling or production facilities, because shipment costs, particularly to distant markets, are prohibitive.

The nature of the product affects channel selection because products vary so widely in their characteristics and use, and because the selling job may also vary markedly. For instance, the technical nature of a product (high complexity) may require service both before and after sale. In many foreign market areas marketing intermediaries may not be able to handle such work. Instead firms will use one of the hierarchical modes.

Products distinguished by physical variations, brand name, advertising and after-sales service (e.g. warranties, repair and replacement policies) that promote preference for one product over another may allow a firm to absorb the higher costs of being in a foreign market. Product differentiation advantages give firms a certain amount of impulse in raising prices to exceed costs by more than normal profits (quasi rent). They also allow firms to limit competition through the development of entry barriers, which are fundamental in the competitive strategy of the firm, as well as serving customer needs better and thereby strengthening the competitive position of the firm compared to other firms. Because these product differentiation advantages represent a 'natural monopoly' firms seek to protect their competitive advantages from dissemination through the use of hierarchical modes of entry.

External factors

Sociocultural distance between home country and host country

Socioculturally similar countries are those that have similar business and industrial practices, a common or similar language, and comparable educational levels and cultural characteristics.

Sociocultural differences between a firm's home country and its host country can create internal uncertainty for the firm, which influences the mode of entry desired by that firm.

The greater the perceived distance between the home and host country in terms of culture, economic systems and business practices, the more likely it is that the firm will shy away from direct investment in favour of joint venture agreements. This is because the latter institutional modes enhance firms' flexibility to withdraw from the host market, if they should be unable to acclimatise themselves comfortably to the unfamiliar setting. To summarise, other things being equal, when the perceived distance between the home and host country is great, firms will favour entry modes that involve relatively low resource commitments and high flexibility.

Country risk/demand uncertainty

Foreign markets are usually perceived as riskier than the domestic market. The amount of risk the firm faces is a function not only of the market itself but also of its method of involvement there. In addition to its investment the firm risks inventories and receivables. When planning its method of entry the firm must do a risk analysis of both the market and its method of entry. Exchange rate risk is another variable. Moreover, risks are not only economic; there are also political risks.

When country risk is high a firm would do well to limit its exposure to such risk by restricting its resource commitments in that particular national domain. That is, other things being equal, when country risk is high, firms will favour entry modes that involve relatively low resource commitments (export modes).

Unpredictability in the political and economic environment of the host market increases the perceived risk and demand uncertainty experienced by the firm. In turn this disinclines firms to enter the market with entry modes requiring heavy resource commitments; on the other hand, flexibility is highly desired.

Market size and growth

Country size and rate of market growth are key parameters in determining the mode of entry. The larger the country and the size of its market, and the higher the growth rate, the more likely management will be to commit resources to its development, and to consider establishing a wholly owned sales subsidiary or to participate in a majority-owned joint venture. Retaining control over operations provides management with direct contact and allows it to plan and direct market development more effectively.

Small markets, on the other hand, especially if they are geographically isolated and cannot be serviced efficiently from a neighbouring country, may not warrant significant attention or resources. Consequently they may be best supplied via exporting or a licensing agreement. While unlikely to stimulate market development or maximise market penetration this approach enables the firm to enter the market with minimal resource commitment, and frees resources for potentially more lucrative markets.

Direct and indirect trade barriers

Tariffs or quotas on the import of foreign goods and components favour the establishment of local production or assembly operations (hierarchical modes).

Product or trade regulations and standards, as well as preferences for local suppliers, also have an impact on mode of entry and operation decisions. Preferences for local suppliers, or tendencies to 'buy national', often encourage a company to consider a joint venture or other contractual arrangements with a local company (intermediate modes). The local partner helps in developing local contacts, negotiating sales and establishing distribution channels, as well as in diffusing the foreign image.

Product and trade regulations and customs formalities similarly encourage modes involving local companies, which can provide information about and contacts in local markets, and can ease access. In some instances, where product regulations and standards necessitate significant adaptation and modification, the firm may establish local production, assembly or finishing facilities (hierarchical modes).

The net impact of both direct and indirect trade barriers is thus likely to be a shift towards performing various functions such as sourcing, production and developing marketing tactics in the local market.

Intensity of competition

When the intensity of competition is high in a host market firms will do well to avoid internalisation, as such markets tend to be less profitable and therefore do not justify heavy resource commitments. Hence, other things being equal, the greater the intensity of competition in the host market the more the firm will favour entry modes that involve low resource commitments (export modes).

Small number of relevant intermediaries available

In such a case the market field is subject to the opportunistic behaviour of the few export intermediaries, and this will favour the use of hierarchical modes in order to reduce the scope for opportunistic behaviour.

Desired mode characteristics

Risk averse

If the decision maker is risk averse they will prefer export modes (e.g. indirect and direct exporting) or licensing (an intermediate mode) because they typically entail low levels of financial and management resource commitment. A joint venture provides a way of sharing risk, financial exposure and the cost of establishing local distribution networks and hiring local personnel, although negotiating and managing joint ventures often absorb considerable management time and effort. However, modes of entry that entail minimal levels of resource commitment and hence minimal risks are unlikely to foster the development of international operations and may result in significant loss of opportunity.

Control

Mode-of-entry decisions also need to consider the degree of control that management requires over operations in international markets. Control is often closely linked to the level of resource commitment. Modes of entry with minimal resource commitment, such as indirect exporting, provide little or no control over the conditions under which the product or service is marketed abroad. In the case of licensing and contract manufacturing management needs to ensure that production meets its quality standards. Joint ventures also limit the degree of management control over international operations and can be a source of considerable conflict where the goals and objectives of partners diverge. Wholly owned subsidiaries (hierarchical mode) provide the most control, but also require a substantial commitment of resources.

Flexibility

Management must also weigh up the flexibility associated with a given mode of entry. The hierarchical modes (involving substantial equity investment) are typically the most costly but the least flexible and most difficult to change in the short run. Intermediate modes (contractual agreements and joint ventures) limit the firm's ability to adapt or change strategy when market conditions are changing rapidly.

Transaction-specific factors

The transaction cost analysis approach was discussed in Chapter 3 (section 3.3) and earlier in this chapter. We will therefore refer to only one of the factors here.

Tacit nature of know-how

When the nature of the firm-specific know-how transferred is tacit it is by definition difficult to articulate. This makes the drafting of a contract (to transfer such complex know-how) very problematic. The difficulties and costs involved in transferring tacit know-how provide an incentive for firms to use hierarchical modes. Investment modes are better able to facilitate the intra-organizational transfer of tacit know-how. By using a hierarchical mode the firm can utilize human capital, drawing upon its organizational routines to structure the transfer problem. Hence, the greater the tacit component of firm-specific know-how, the more a firm will favour hierarchical modes.

9.4 Summary

Seen from the perspective of the manufacturer (international marketer), market entry modes can be classified into three groups:

- *export modes:* low control, low risk, high flexibility;
- *intermediate modes* (contractual modes): shared control and risk, split ownership;
- *hierarchical modes* (investment modes): high control, high risk, low flexibility.

It cannot be stated categorically which alternative is the best. There are many internal and external conditions which affect this choice and it should be emphasised that a manufacturer wanting to engage in global marketing may use more than one of these methods at the same time. There may be different product lines, each requiring a different entry mode.

CASE STUDY 9.1   IO Interactive

A computer games developer is reconsidering its entry mode

If you visit IO Interactive's homepage (**www.ioi.dk**) you can download a demo version of 'Hitman' and there is a link to the international publisher, Eidos.

The global computer games industry

In 2000 computer games had an annual turnover of €13 billion in the United States and Europe. This market increases yearly by approximately 20 per cent, and competition with the film industry is keener still.

Revenues in the games industry have overtaken the film industry, and it is the most widespread entertainment. Via the Internet computer games have become enormously popular. The online game 'Everquest' alone has 300,000 active players from all over the world.

Approximately 60 per cent of all Americans, 145 million people, play computer games. 35 per cent of

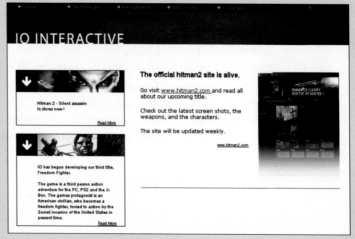

all Americans regard computer games as the most entertaining pastime – twice as many as films, TV, and books. In five years the average American is expected to spend more time on computer games than books and magazines. The active gamers spend on average 10 hours per week, with either PC games or console games.

In addition to computer games the console market is increasing. It is expected to be dominated by the following three products: Nintendo Gamecube, Sony Playstation 2, and Microsoft X BOX. A pessimistic estimate is that there will be approximately 150–200 million private games consoles worldwide in 2005.

The big landslide from films to games has many consequences. By 1992 Nintendo showed a greater profit than all US film companies and the three biggest TV networks together. The James Bond film, *Golden Eye*, was a solid success, but when Nintendo launched the Golden Eye game turnover doubled. Recently there has been an attempt to transfer computer games to films. *Tomb Raider: Lara Croft* had its first performance in the United States in June 2001. The film turned out to be a commercial success in spite of production costs being more than $100 million.

Two of the biggest publishers in the games software market are: in the United States, Electronic Arts (EA); and the United Kingdom, Eidos plc.

Electronic Arts

Electronic Arts is the world's largest publisher and distributor of games software. In 2002 it realised total turnover of €1.7 billion. The company systematically works at buying rights to develop games based on books, films, and sport, and recently bought the rights to the Harry Potter books.

Today EA has the sole right to game icons such as James Bond, Tiger Woods and FIFA. It recently hived off online games to an independent business. Its goal is to establish a strong position in the rapidly growing online market. In March 2000 EA entered into an agreement with AOL Time Warner on the sole right to AOL's games channel. The agreement gives EA access to AOL's 60 million online customers.

In 2002 EA's top title was 'Harry Potter and the Sorcerer's Stone', which sold 9 million units.

Eidos

Eidos is the UK's largest publisher and developer of entertainment software.

Eidos has 499 employees worldwide. The company only came into existence in 1995 and today is home to some of the interactive industry's best-known brands, including Commandos, Championship Manager and Tomb Raider – featuring the world's most famous cyber-babe, Lara Croft. Eidos develops and publishes a diverse mix of titles for the PC, PlayStation® game console, PlayStation®2 computer entertainment system, Nintendo GameCube and the XBOX video game system from Microsoft.

Table 1 Comparison of EA and Eidos as distributors of entertainment software

Region	EA	Eidos
Total turnover	€1,700 millions	€280 millions
	% of total turnover	% of total turnover
Europe	30	54
US	63	39
Rest of the World	7	7
Total	100	100

Table 1 compares EA and Eidos plc as distributors.

Besides size and geographical focus the main difference between EA and Eidos is, that EA is both a publisher and a distributor, whereas Eidos is only a publisher, but has made business alliances with distributors around the world. The different coverage of the industry value chain is also illustrated in Figure 1.

IO Interactive

IO Interactive was founded in 1998, as a joint venture between Reto-Moto and Nordisk Film/Egmont. (Nordisk Film Egmont owns 40 per cent of the shares in IO Interactive. The rest is owned by the seven original founder of IO Interactive and some employees). The Managing Director of IO Interactive, Janos Flösser, was headhunted from Nordisk Film and straight away began providing capital for developing the first game (Hitman). Eidos and 2–3 other publishers were contacted, and Eidos was immediately interested in the Hitman concept. IO Interactive received an advance on their royalties of €2.27 million from Eidos in order to develop Hitman. Thus IO Interactive acted as a subsupplier to Eidos, which took care of financing and distribution. IO Interactive did, however, gain experience in the global market, because most of the time Eidos distributed the game and left the player contact to IO Interactive.

Hitman 1 and 2 are 3D games, in which you play a ruthless, bald, hired assassin with the code name 47. The game is inspired by movies such as *The Godfather*.

International launch of Hitman

About a month after the launch Hitman 1 had sold 250,000 copies – 100,000 copies alone were sold in the United States 24,000 in England and 33,000 in Germany. The rest were distributed in a number of markets, including Denmark, where the game topped the hit list.

Every time a copy of Hitman is sold IO Interactive receives so-called royalties. The company will not make any money until the break-even point is reached, for which for Hitman 1 was 420,000. Until then all the money would go into Eidos's cash box. Once Hitman had passed sales of 420,000, every copy sold will place approximately €6.5 (a 10 per cent royalty) in IO Interactive's account. Hitman 2: Silent Assassin passed the breakeven point on the release day and generated royalties to the company in excess of DKK 69.1 million in 2002. In August

Figure 1 The value chain in the computer game industry, seen from IO Interactive's perspective

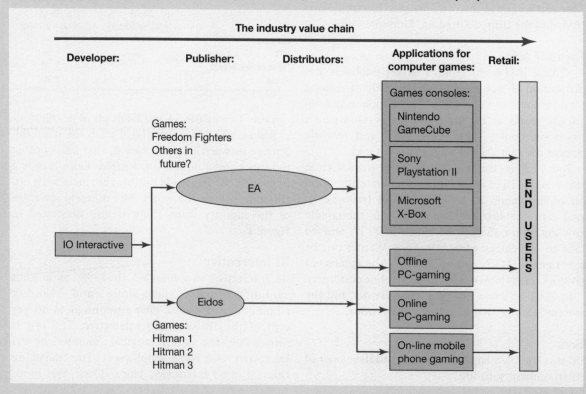

2003, Hitman 2 had reached sales fo more than 2 million units.

IO Interactive might have made a bigger profit by distributing the game itself, but this would have meant investment in distribution and marketing in the range of $20–40 million. The relationship with Eidos is a risk-minimising business model for Interactive, and at the same time it has made the company a well-known games developer in international circles.

The total industry value chain is illustrated in Figure 1.

Until now most computer games have been sold to offline PCs without access to the Internet. In future a larger part of the games is expected to be distributed to game consoles or through Internet suppliers or mobile phone companies offering these services to their subscribers. The tendency towards online games is accelerated by the broadband development, with the effect that in future advanced games can be distributed over the Internet or the mobile net. This part of the market will be characterised as Business-to-Business. Direct B-t-B customers become owners of Internet portals (e.g. AOL, Jubii) or mobile phone companies. When Internet and TV merge, TV companies (or suppliers of channels for cable TV) will also be possible B-t-B customers for online games.

IO Interactive can be considered as a games developer for Eidos, but with its own brand IO Interactive is one of the large players in the market, and the relationship with Eidos offers IO Interactive the opportunity of getting into its international network, and may be in touch with other producers or distributors who can benefit from IO Interactive's competences in the technology area and in developing games. At any rate, the access to Eidos's distribution network has meant that right from its birth IO Interactive is characterised as a genuine 'Born Global' (see Chapter 3).

The most important end user application for IO Interactive is the games console market. The number of installed of consoles reached 50 million units in 2002, with Playstation 2 being by far the most important platform. The size of the market has been seen by many as an opportunity to publish a lot of games of very inconsistent quality, but the experience of 2002 showed that the market is increasingly discerning and demands games of the highest quality – both in terms of game play and technological quality. High quality games now stay in the market considerably longer than the first three months following release, which was the norm for most games released in earlier years.

Table 2 shows the sales of the existing games, Hitman 1 and 2.

IO Interactive's latest production, Freedom Fighters was presented at the 2003 (May) games exhibition in Los Angeles. The game was released in the autumn of 2003 on Playstation 2, XBOX, GameCube and PC. It will be published by the world's biggest games publisher, Electronic Arts.

The future

Recently the number of new titles in development has been decreasing. As a result the prospects for smaller publishers and game developers look uncertain, especially if they are unable to deliver the high quality products now demanded by the market. Consequently IO Interactive expects the sector to witness further mergers and acquisitions, as well as the closure of many smaller publishers and developers, during 2003, as the consolidation that started in 2002 accelerates in 2003.

IO Interactive expects that the next generation of consoles (Playstation 3/XBOX2) will be launched towards the end of 2005 or the beginning of 2006 but publishers are already tending to reduce the number of contracts for the development of new games on existing consoles. There is no doubt that the more advanced technologies that will be used in the next generation of consoles will translate into a reduction in the number of games released (due to longer and more costly development processes) and that the developers capable of developing games for the next generation of consoles will be fewer and significantly larger, on average, than at present.

Table 2   Sales of IO Interactive games (includes all formats)

Games	Release date	Sales year 2002 units	Lifetime sales units
Hitman 1: Code name 47	November 2000	116,679	523,614
Hitman 2: Silent Assassin	October 2002	1,721,838	1,721,838
Total		1,840,519	2,245,452

The management of IO Interactive realise that they did very well financially in 2002, but maybe they could have received a larger share of the value-added 'cake' (than the 10 per cent royalty they get now) if they changed the entry mode?

Questions

1. What entry mode should IO Interactive change to, in order to get a larger slice of the total profits in the industry value chain? Would you recommend it to change to another entry mode?

2. Let us assume that IO Interactive keeps the existing entry mode. Is Eidos the right distributor for Hitman 3 (to be developed during 2003 and 2004) or should it change to EA, which is the distributor for IO Interactive's latest production, Freedom Fighters?

3. One day in October 2003, the top management of IO Interactive receive information from Eidos that Paramount (which made the Lara Croft film) is interested in developing Hitman into a Hollywood movie. Eidos asks IO Interactive if it has any reservations in relation to the project. From IO Interactive's point of view, what do you think should be the key issues in its forthcoming negotiations with Paramount?

CASE STUDY 9.2   condomi AG

Evaluating its 'entry mode' strategy in Africa

condomi AG is one of the world's leading condom manufacturers.

Founded in 1988, condomi opened the first condom only shop in Cologne/Germany. With a very young and fun oriented marketing approach, condomi embarked on its success story. In only a few years, condomi was operating a chain of franchise shops and had developed its own brand – 'CONDOMIS'.

In 1997, condomi incorporated a well-established condom manufacturing plant (in operation since 1929) located in Erfurt/Germany. Since 1999 condomi holds a majority interest in unimil S.A. the leading Polish condom manufacturer.

In 1999 condomi was listed on the Frankfurt Stock Exchange as the first and only domestic condom manufacturer to float. Since then, condomi's production has increased in capacity and further improved in quality, operating one of the world's most modern and fully automated condom manufacturing plants. Today the condomi Group is Europe's largest condom manufacturer.

The marketing strategy for Africa

An estimated five million people have HIV/AIDS in South Africa – one in nine of the population – and condoms form a major part of the prevention programme.

condomi is actively developing its condom social marketing in Africa. condomi has developed its own innovative approach to condom social marketing in developing countries.

condomi defines social marketing in this way:

> The aim of social marketing is to change people's attitude and behaviour towards safe sex, we believe that educating the population is extremely important. In this way, both the target group and the whole population can benefit.

Source: (**http://www.condomi-plus.org/**)

condomi's social marketing drive is based on increasing condom accessibility and acceptability within the target markets/regions.

condomi is working to reduce the number of new HIV infections, by promoting the use of condoms and offering partnerships in social marketing related projects, focusing on primary prevention. condomi has produced culturally adapted information brochures on HIV/AIDS in local African languages. condomi constantly tries to destigmatize the use of condoms in African countries and influence behavior towards convincing people to use condoms naturally to protect themselves from HIV/AIDS. condomi's marketing campaign in Africa (especially South Africa) is about targeting companies which purchase condoms for distribution to their employees and as novelties for business partners. In connection with this condomi will offer consulting on HIV/AIDS issues.

condomi works closely with domestic and international AIDS relief organisations, as well as with family planning organisations and countless health organisations and advisory services. condomi is one of the pre-qualified suppliers of UNFPA. Their activities currently focus on Africa and provide an example of the economic and ethical values that condomi stands for.

Currently most African countries have to import almost all their complete demand for condoms, e.g. for South Africa the total demand is estimated at about 500 million condoms for the year 2002.

condomi will help to create a network between NGO's (Non Government organisations), government organisations, private institutions and businesses involved in the fight against HIV/AIDS. condomi is a member of the Global Business Coalition on HIV/AIDS.

Socio-cultural adaption is an integral part of condomi's social marketing approach. condomi has therefore developed a series of training tools for certain cultural target groups, e.g. within South Africa, i.e. Xhosa, Zulu, Sesotho and Afrikaans.

The slogan **'be safe and have fun'** is of key importance in the way condomi promotes its products. Destigmatisation, done in a culturally sensitive manner, is important to them. All of their activities focus on these basic doctrines.

The latest development

After having considered a joint venture solution (involving local production of condoms) in the Republic of South Africa, condomi has now decided that all the African countries will be sourced with condoms from the production plants in Germany and Poland (condomi press release 1st September, 2003)

Sources:

Material from **www.condomi.com**, and related websites

Different press releases from Condomi, especially

Condomi Press release, 01.09.2003 (**http://www.condomi.com/ag-en/press/news/daten/249071/index.html**

Global Business Coalition on HIV/AIDS (**http://www.businessfightsaids.org/members_companies.asp?alpha**=all&CompanyID=60)

For further exercises and cases, see this book's website at **www.booksites.net/hollensen**

Questions for discussion

1. Why is choosing the most appropriate market entry and development strategy one of the most difficult decisions for the international marketer?

2. Do you agree with the view that LSEs use a 'rational analytic' approach ('strategy rule') to the entry mode decision, while SMEs use a more pragmatic/opportunistic approach?

3. Use Figure 9.1 to identify the most important factors affecting the choice of foreign entry mode. Prioritise the factors.

References

Heide, J.B. and John, G. (1988) 'The role of dependence balancing in safeguarding transaction-specific assets in conventional channels', *Journal of Marketing*, vol. 52, January, pp. 20–35.

Johanson, J. and Vahlne, J.E. (1977) 'The internationalization process of the firm – a model of knowledge', *Journal of International Business Studies*, vol. 8, no. 1, pp. 23–32.

Maio, P. (2001) 'Video-Game Industry is seen expanding at a rapid clip during next five years', *Wall Street Journal*, May 25, New York.

Root, F.R. (1994) *Entry Strategies for International Markets: Revised and expanded edition*, The New Lexington Press, Lexington, MA.

Further reading

Burgel, O. and Murray, G.C. (2000) 'The international market entry choices of start-up companies in high-technology industries', *Journal of International Marketing*, vol. 8, no. 2, pp. 33–62.

Lotayif, M. (2003) 'A theoretical Model for Matching Entry Modes with Defensive Marketing Strategies', *Journal of American Academy of Business*, vol. 2, No. 2 (March), pp. 460–66.

McNaughton, R.B. and Bell, J. (2000) 'Channel switching between domestic and foreign markets', *Journal of International Marketing*, vol. 9, no. 1, pp. 24–39.

Pehrsson, A. (2002) 'The PSE model: entry into emerging markets', *Strategic Change*, vol. 11, pp. 143–54.

Rundh, B. (2001) 'International market development: new patterns in SMEs' international market behaviour', *Marketing Intelligence & Planning*, vol. 19, No. 5, pp. 319–29.

10 Export modes

Contents

Learning objectives

After studying this chapter you should be able to do the following:

- Distinguish between indirect, direct and cooperative export modes.

- Describe and understand the five main entry modes of indirect exporting:
  - export buying agent;
  - broker;
  - export management company/export house;
  - trading company; and
  - piggyback.

- Describe the two main entry modes of direct exporting: distributor;
  - agent.

- Discuss the advantages and disadvantages of the main export modes.

- Discuss how manufacturers can influence intermediaries to be effective marketing partners.

10.1 Introduction

With export entry modes a firm's products are manufactured in the domestic market or a third country and then transferred either directly or indirectly to the host market.

Export is the most common mode for initial entry into international markets. Sometimes an unsolicited order is received from a buyer in a foreign country, or a domestic customer expands internationally and places an order for its international operations. This prompts the firm to consider international markets and to investigate their growth potential.

Exporting is thus typically used in initial entry and gradually evolves towards foreign-based operations. In some cases where there are substantial scale economies or

Figure 10.1 Export modes

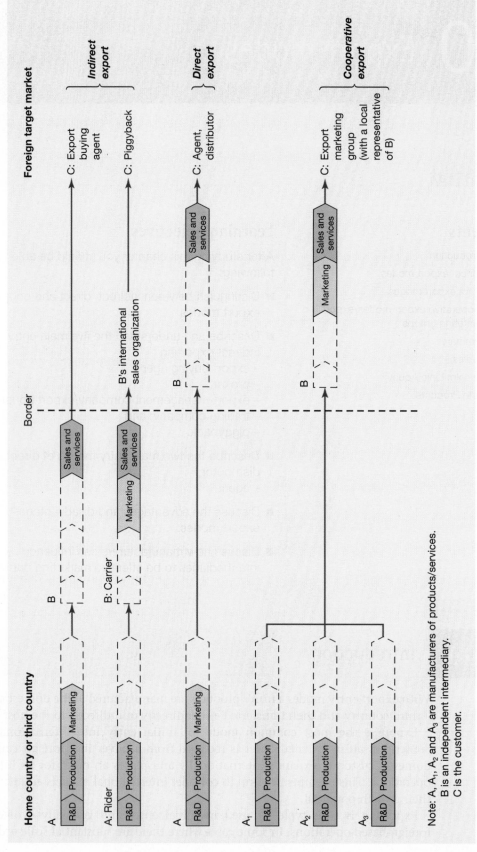

Note: A, A₁, A₂ and A₃ are manufacturers of products/services.
B is an independent intermediary.
C is the customer.

a limited number of buyers in the market worldwide (for example, aerospace), production may be concentrated in a single or a limited number of locations, and the goods then exported to other markets.

Exporting can be organised in a variety of ways, depending on the number and type of intermediaries. As in the case of wholesaling, export and import agents vary considerably in the range of functions performed. Some, such as export management companies, are the equivalent of full-service wholesalers and perform all functions relating to export. Others are highly specialised and handle only freight forwarding, billing or clearing goods through customs.

In establishing export channels a firm has to decide which functions will be the responsibility of external agents and which will be handled by the firm itself. While export channels may take many different forms, for the purposes of simplicity three major types may be identified: indirect, direct and cooperative export marketing groups.

- *Indirect export.* This is when the manufacturing firm does not take direct care of exporting activities. Instead another domestic company, such as an export house or trading company, performs these activities, often without the manufacturing firm's involvement in the foreign sales of its products.
- *Direct export.* This usually occurs when the producing firm takes care of exporting activities and is in direct contact with the first intermediary in the foreign target market. The firm is typically involved in handling documentation, physical delivery and pricing policies, with the product being sold to agents and distributors.
- *Cooperative export.* This involves collaborative agreements with other firms (export marketing groups) concerning the performance of exporting functions.

In Figure 10.1 the different export modes are illustrated in a value chain.

10.2   Indirect export modes

Indirect export occurs when the exporting manufacturer uses independent organizations *located in the producer's country*. In indirect exporting the sale is like a domestic sale. In fact the firm is not really engaging in global marketing, because its products are carried abroad by others. Such an approach to exporting is most likely to be appropriate for a firm with limited international expansion objectives. If international sales are viewed primarily as a means of disposing of surplus production, or as a marginal, use of indirect export modes may be appropriate. This method may also be adopted by a firm with minimal resources to devote to international expansion, which wants to enter international markets gradually, testing out markets before committing major resources and effort to developing an export organization.

It is important for a firm to recognise, however, that the use of agents or export management companies carries a number of risks. In the first place the firm has little or no control over the way the product or service is marketed in other countries. Products may be sold through inappropriate channels, with poor servicing or sales support and inadequate promotion, or be under- or overpriced. This can damage the reputation or image of the product or service in foreign markets. Limited effort may be devoted to developing the market, resulting in lost potential opportunities.

Particularly significant for the firm interested in gradually edging into international markets is that, with indirect exporting, the firm establishes little or no contact with markets abroad. Consequently the firm has limited information about foreign market potential, and obtains little input to develop a plan for international expansion. The firm will have no means to identify potential sales agents or distributors for its products.

While exporting has the advantage of the least cost and risk of any entry method, it allows the firm little control over how, when, where and by whom the products are sold. In some cases the domestic company may even be unaware that its products are being exported.

Moreover, an SME that is already experienced in traditional exporting may have resources that are too limited to open up a great number of export markets by itself. Thus, through indirect export modes the SME is able to utilise the resources of other experienced exporters and to expand its business to many countries.

There are five main entry modes of indirect exporting:

- export buying agent;
- broker;
- export management company/export house;
- trading company;
- piggyback (shown as a special case of indirect exporting in Figure 10.1).

Export buying agent (export commission house)

Some firms or individuals do not realise that their products or services have potential export value until they are approached by a buyer from a foreign organization, which might make the initial approach, purchase the product at the factory gate and take on the task of exporting, marketing and distributing the product in one or more overseas markets.

The export buying agent is a representative of foreign buyers who resides in the exporter's home country. As such, this type of agent is essentially the overseas customer's hired purchasing agent in the exporter's domestic market, operating on the basis of orders received from these buyers. Since the export buying agent acts in the interests of the buyer, it is the buyer that pays a commission. The exporting manufacturer is not directly involved in determining the terms of purchase; these are worked out between the export buying agent and the overseas buyer.

The export commission house essentially becomes a domestic buyer. It scans the market for the particular merchandise it has been requested to buy. It sends out specifications to manufacturers inviting bids. Other conditions being equal, the lowest bidder gets the order and there is no sentimentality, friendship or sales talk involved.

From the exporter's point of view, selling to export commission houses represents an easy way to export. Prompt payment is usually guaranteed in the exporter's home country, and the problems of physical movement of the goods are generally taken completely out of its hands. There is very little credit risk and the exporter has only to fulfil the order, according to specifications. A major problem is that the exporter has little direct control over the global marketing of products.

Small firms find that this is the easiest method of obtaining foreign sales but, being totally dependent on the purchaser, they are unlikely to be aware of a change in consumer behaviour and competitor activity, or of the purchasing firm's intention to terminate the arrangement. If a company is intent upon seeking longer-term liability for its export business it must adopt a more proactive approach, which will inevitably involve obtaining a greater understanding of the markets in which its products are sold.

Broker

Another type of agent based in the home country is the export/import broker. The chief function of a broker is to bring a buyer and a seller together. Thus the broker is a specialist in performing the contractual function, and does not actually handle the products sold or bought. For its services the broker is paid a commission (about 5 per cent) by the principal. The broker commonly specialises in particular products or classes of product. Being a commodity specialist there is a tendency for the broker to concentrate on just one or two products. Because the broker deals primarily in basic commodities, for many potential export marketers this type of agent does not represent a practical alternative channel of distribution. The distinguishing characteristic of export brokers is that they may act as the agent for either the seller or the buyer.

Export management company/export house

Export houses or export management companies (EMCs) are specialist companies set up to act as the 'export department' for a range of companies. As such the EMC conducts business in the name of each manufacturer it represents. All correspondence with buyers and contracts are negotiated in the name of the manufacturer, and all quotations and orders are subject to confirmation by the manufacturer.

By carrying a large range EMCs can spread their selling and administration costs over more products and companies, as well as reducing transport costs because of the economies involved in making large shipments of goods from a number of companies.

EMCs deal with the necessary documentation, and their knowledge of local purchasing practices and government regulations is particularly useful in markets that might prove difficult to penetrate. The use of EMCs, therefore, allows individual companies to gain far wider exposure of their products in foreign markets at much lower overall costs than they could achieve on their own, but there are a number of disadvantages, too:

- The export house may specialise by geographical area, product or customer type (retail, industrial or institutional), and this may not coincide with the supplier's objectives. So the selection of markets may be made on the basis of what is best for the EMC rather than for the manufacturer.
- As EMCs are paid by commission they might be tempted to concentrate upon products with immediate sales potential, rather than those that might require greater customer education and sustained marketing effort to achieve success in the longer term.
- EMCs may be tempted to carry too many product ranges and as a result the manufacturer's products may not be given the necessary attention from sales people.
- EMCs may carry competitive products that they may promote to the disadvantage of a particular firm.

Manufacturers should therefore take care in selecting a suitable EMC and be prepared to devote resources to managing the relationship and monitoring its performance.

As sales increase the manufacturer may feel that it could benefit from increased involvement in international markets, by exporting itself. However, the transition may not be very easy. First, the firm is likely to have become very dependent on the export house and, unless steps have been taken to build contacts with foreign customers and to build up the firm's knowledge of its markets, moving away from using an EMC could prove difficult. Second, the firm could find it difficult to withdraw from its contractual commitments to the export house. Third, the EMC may be able to substitute products from an alternative manufacturer and so use its existing customer contacts as a basis for competing against the original manufacturer.

Trading company

Trading companies are part of the historical legacy from colonial days and, although different in nature now, they are still important trading forces in Africa and the Far East. Although international trading companies have been active throughout the world, it is in Japan that the trading company concept has been applied most effectively. There are thousands of trading companies in Japan involved in exporting and importing, and the largest firms (varying in number from 9 to 17 depending upon source of estimate) are referred to as general trading companies or *Soge Shosha*. This group of companies, which includes C. Itoh, Mitsui & Company and Mitsubishi Shoji Kaisha, handle 50 per cent of Japan's exports and 67 per cent of its imports. While the smaller trading companies usually limit their activities to foreign trade, the larger general trading companies are also heavily involved in domestic distribution and other activities.

They play a central role in such diverse areas as shipping, warehousing, finance, technology transfer, planning resource development, construction and regional development (for example, turnkey projects), insurance, consulting, real estate and deal making in general (including facilitating investment and joint ventures). In fact it is the range of financial services offered that is a major factor distinguishing general trading companies from others. These services include the guaranteeing of loans, the financing of both accounts receivable and payable, the issuing of promissory notes, major foreign exchange transactions, equity investment and even direct loans.

Another aspect of their operations is to manage counter-trade activities, in which sales into one market are paid for by taking other products from that market in exchange. The essential role of the trading company is to find a buyer quickly for the products that have been taken in exchange. Sometimes this can be a very resource-demanding process.

Counter trade is still a very widespread trading form in eastern Europe and developing countries because of their lack of 'hard' currency. One of the motivations for western firms to go into counter trade is the low-cost sources of production and raw materials for use in the firm's own production (Okoroafo, 1994).

Piggyback

In piggybacking the export-inexperienced SME, the 'rider', deals with a larger company (the 'carrier') which already operates in certain foreign markets and is willing to act on behalf of the rider that wishes to export to those markets. This enables the carrier to utilise fully its established export facilities (sales subsidiaries) and foreign distribution. The carrier is either paid by commission and so acts as an agent or, alternatively, buys the product outright and so acts as an independent distributor. Piggyback marketing is typically used for products from unrelated companies that are non-competitive (but related) and complementary (allied).

Sometimes the carrier will insist that the rider's products are somewhat similar to its own, in view of the need to deal with technical queries and after-sales service 'in the field'. Branding and promotional policies are variable in piggybacking. In some instances the carrier may buy the products, put its own brand on them, and market them as its own products (private labels). More commonly the carrier retains the brand name of the producer and the two work out promotional arrangements between them. The choice of branding and promotional strategy is a function of the importance of brand to the product and of the degree to which the brand is well established.

Piggybacking has the following advantages/disadvantages for the carrier and the rider.

Carrier

Advantages

A firm that has a gap in its product line or excess capacity in its export operation has two options. One is to develop internally the products necessary to round out its line and fill up its exporting capacity. The other option is to acquire the necessary products outside by piggybacking (or acquisition). Piggybacking may be attractive because the firm can get the product quickly (someone already has it). It is also a low-cost way to get the product because the carrier firm does not have to invest in R&D, production facilities or market testing for the new product. It can just pick up the product from another firm. In this way the firm can broaden its product range without having to develop and manufacture extra products.

Disadvantages

Piggybacking can be extremely attractive for the carrier, but some concerns exist about quality control and warranty. Will the rider maintain the quality of the products sold by another firm? This depends in part on whose brand name is on the product. If the rider's name is on the product the quality incentive might be stronger. A second concern is continuity of supply. If the carrier develops a substantial market abroad, will the rider firm develop its production capacity, if necessary? Each of these items should be a subject in the agreement between the two parties. If the piggybacking arrangement works out well there is another potential advantage for the carrier. It might find that the rider is a good acquisition candidate or joint-venture partner for a stronger relationship.

Rider

Advantages

Riders can export conveniently without having to establish their own distribution systems. They can observe carefully how the carrier handles the goods and hence learn from the carrier's experience – perhaps to the point of eventually being able to take over its own export transactions.

Disadvantages

For the smaller company this type of agreement means giving up control over the marketing of its products – something that many firms dislike doing, at least in the long run. Lack of commitment on the part of the carrier and the loss of lucrative sales opportunities in regions not covered by the carrier are further disadvantages.

In summary, piggyback marketing provides an easy, low-risk way for a company to begin export marketing operations. It is especially well suited to manufacturers that either are too small to go directly into exports or do not want to invest heavily in foreign marketing.

10.3   Direct export modes

Direct exporting occurs when a manufacturer or exporter sells directly to an importer or buyer located in a foreign market area. In our discussion of indirect exporting we examined ways of reaching foreign markets without working very hard. Indeed, in the indirect approaches, foreign sales are handled in the same way as domestic sales: the producer does the global marketing only by proxy (that is, through the firm that carries its products overseas). However, both the global marketing know-how and the sales achieved by these indirect approaches are limited.

As exporters grow more confident they may decide to undertake their own exporting task. This will involve building up overseas contacts, undertaking marketing research, handling documentation and transportation, and designing marketing mix strategies. Direct exporting modes include export through foreign-based agents and distributors (independent intermediaries).

The terms 'distributor' and 'agent' are often used synonymously. This is unfortunate because there are distinct differences: distributors, unlike agents, take title to the goods, and are paid according to the difference between the buying and selling prices rather than by commission. Distributors are often appointed when after-sales service is required, as they are more likely than agents to possess the necessary resources.

Distributors

Exporting firms may work through distributors, which are the exclusive representatives of the company and are generally the sole importers of the company's product in their markets. As independent merchants, distributors buy on their own accounts and have substantial freedom to choose their own customers and to set the conditions of sale. For each country exporters deal with one distributor, take one credit risk, and ship to one destination. In many cases distributors own and operate wholesale and retail establishments, warehouses and repair and service facilities. Once distributors have negotiated with their exporters on price, service, distribution and so on their efforts focus on working their own suboperations and dealers.

The distributor category is broad and includes more variations, but distributors usually seek exclusive rights for a specific sales territory and generally represent the manufacturer in all aspects of sales and servicing in that area. The exclusivity is in return for the substantial capital investment that may be required on the part of the distributor in handling and selling products.

Agents

Agents may be exclusive, where the agent has exclusive rights to specified sales territories; semi-exclusive, where the agent handles the exporter's goods along with other non-competing goods from other companies; or non-exclusive, where the agent handles a variety of goods, including some that may compete with the exporter's products.

An agent represents an exporting company and sells to wholesalers and retailers in the importing country. The exporter ships the merchandise directly to the customers, and all arrangements on financing, credit, promotion, etc., are made between the exporter and the buyers. Exclusive agents are widely used for entering international markets. They cover rare geographic areas and have subagents assisting them. Agents and subagents share commissions (paid by the exporter) on a pre-agreed basis. Some agents furnish financial and market information, and a few also guarantee the payment of customers' accounts. The commissions that agents receive vary substantially, depending upon services performed, the market's size and importance, and competition among exporters and agents.

The advantages of both agents and distributors are that they are familiar with the local market, customs and conventions, have existing business contacts and employ foreign nationals. They have a direct incentive to sell through either commission or profit margin, but since their remuneration is tied to sales they may be reluctant to devote much time and effort towards developing a market for a new product. Also, the amount of market feedback may be limited as the agent or distributor may see itself as a purchasing agent for its customers rather than as a selling agent for the exporter.

Choice of an intermediary

The selection of a suitable intermediary can be a problematic process. But the following sources may help a firm to find such an intermediary:

- asking potential customers to suggest a suitable agent;
- obtaining recommendations from institutions such as trade associations, chambers of commerce and government trade departments;
- using commercial agencies;
- poaching a competitor's agent;
- advertising in suitable trade papers.

In selecting a particular intermediary the exporter needs to examine each candidate firm's knowledge of the product and local markets, experience and expertise, required margins, credit ratings, customer care facilities and ability to promote the exporter's products in an effective and attractive manner.

Figure 10.2 shows the matchmaking of a manufacturer and his 'wish'-profile and two potential intermediaries and their performance profile on a particular market.

If Partner 1 and 2 were the only potential candidates for the manufacturer, Partner 2 would probably be chosen because of the better match of profiles between what the manufacturer wants on the market ('wish'-profile) and the performance profile of Partner 2.

The criteria listed in Figure 10.2 would probably not be the only criteria in a selection process. Some other specific desirable characteristics of an intermediary (to be included in the decision-making process) are listed below (Root, 1994, pp. 86–7):

- size of firm;
- physical facilities;
- willingness to carry inventories;
- knowledge/use of promotion;
- reputation with suppliers, customers and banks;
- record of sales performance;
- cost of operations;
- overall experience;
- knowledge of English or other relevant languages;
- knowledge of business methods in manufacturer's country.

When an intermediary is selected by the exporting manufacturer it is important that a contract is negotiated and developed between the parties. The foreign representative agreement is the fundamental basis of the relationship between the exporter and the intermediary. Therefore the contract should clearly cover all relevant aspects and define the conditions upon which the relationship rests. Rights and obligations should be mutually defined and the spirit of the agreement must be one of mutual interest. The agreement should cover the provisions listed in Table 10.1.

Figure 10.2 An example of matchmaking between a manufacturer and two potential distribution partners

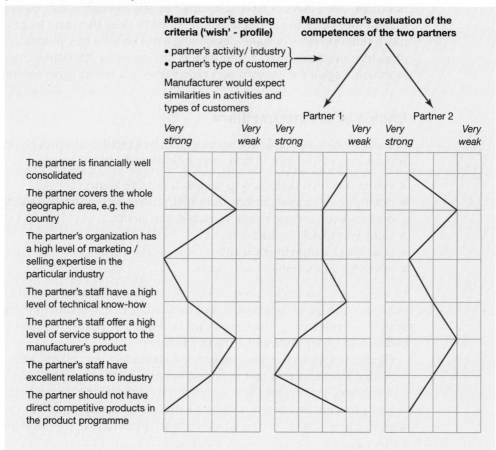

Table 10.1 Contracts with intermediaries

1. **General provisions**

Identification of parties to the contract	Definition of territory or territories
Duration of the contract	Sole and exclusive rights*
Definition of covered goods	Arbitration of disputes

2. **Rights and obligations of manufacturer**

Conditions of termination	Inspection of distributor's books
Protection of sole and exclusive rights	Trademarks/patents
Sales and technical support	Information to be supplied to the distributor
Tax liabilities	Advertising/promotion
Conditions of sale	Responsibility for claims/warranties
Delivery of goods	Inventory requirements
Prices	Termination and cancellation*
Order refusal	

3. **Rights and obligations of distributor**

Safeguarding manufacturer's interests	Customs clearance
Payment arrangements	Observance of conditions of sale
Contract assignment	After-sales service
Competitive lines*	Information to be supplied to the manufacturer

*Most important and contentious issues.

Source: Root, F.R. (1998) *Entry Strategies for International Markets: Revised and Expanded Edition*, pp. 90–1. Copyright © Jossey-Bass 1998. This material is used by permission of John Wiley & Sons, Inc.

For most exporters the three most important aspects of their agreement with foreign representatives are sole or exclusive rights, competitive lines and termination of the agreement. The issue of agreeing territories is becoming increasingly important, as in many markets distributors are becoming fewer in number, larger in size and sometimes more specialised in their activity. The trend to regionalization is leading distributors increasingly to extend their territories through organic growth, mergers and acquisitions, making it more difficult for firms to appoint different distributors in individual neighbouring markets.

In general there are some principles that apply to the law of agency in all nations:

- An agent cannot take delivery of the principal's goods at an agreed price and resell them for a higher amount without the principal's knowledge and permission.
- Agents must maintain strict confidentiality regarding their principal's affairs and must pass on all relevant information.
- The principal is liable for damages to third parties for wrongs committed by an agent 'in the course of his or her authority' (e.g. if the agent fraudulently misrepresents the principal's firm).

During the contract period the support and motivation of intermediaries is important. Usually this means financial rewards for volume sold, but there can also be other means:

- significant local advertising and brand awareness development by the supplying firm;
- participation in local exhibitions and trade fairs, perhaps in cooperation with the local intermediary;
- regular field visits and telephone calls to the agent or distributor;
- regular meetings of agents and distributors arranged and paid for by the supplying company in the latter's country;
- competitions with cash prizes, free holidays, etc., for intermediaries with the highest sales;
- provision of technical training to intermediaries;
- suggestion schemes to gather feedback from agents and distributors;
- circulation of briefings about the supplying firm's current activities, changes in personnel, new product developments, marketing plans, etc.

Even if the firm has been very careful in selecting intermediaries a need can arise to extricate oneself quickly from a relationship that appears to be going nowhere. Cancellation clauses usually involve rights under local legislation, and it is best that a contract is scrutinised by a local lawyer before signature, rather than after a relationship has ended and a compensation case is being fought in the courts.

Termination laws differ from country to country, but the European Union situation has been largely reconciled by a Directive on agency that has been effective in all EU nations since 1994. Under the Directive, an agent whose agreement is terminated is entitled to the following:

- full payment for any deal resulting from its work (even if concluded after the end of the agency);
- a lump sum of up to one year's past average commission;
- compensation (where appropriate) for damages to the agent's commercial reputation caused by an unwarranted termination.

Outside western Europe some countries regard agents as basically employees of client organizations, while others see agents as self-contained and independent businesses. It is essential to ascertain the legal position of agency agreements in each country in which a firm is considering doing business.

10.4   Cooperative export modes/export marketing groups

Export marketing groups are frequently found among SMEs attempting to enter export markets for the first time. Many such firms do not achieve sufficient scale economies in manufacturing and marketing because of the size of the local market or the inadequacy of the management and marketing resources available. These characteristics are typical of traditional, mature, highly fragmented industries such as furniture and clothing. Frequently the same characteristics are to be found among small, recently established high-technology firms.

Figure 10.1 shows an export marketing group with manufacturers A_1, A_2 and A_3, each having separate upstream functions but cooperating on the downstream functions through a common, foreign-based agent.

One of the most important motives for SMEs to join with others is the opportunity of effectively marketing a complementary product programme to larger buyers. The following example is from the furniture industry.

Manufacturers A_1, A_2 and A_3 have their core competences in the upstream functions of the following complementary product lines:

A_1 Living room furniture.

A_2 Dining room furniture.

A_3 Bedroom furniture.

Together they form a broader product concept that could be more attractive to a buyer in a furniture retail chain, especially if the total product concept targets a certain lifestyle of the end customers.

The cooperation between the manufacturers can be tight or loose. In a loose cooperation the separate firms in a group sell their own brands through the same agent, whereas a tight cooperation often results in the creation of a new export association. Such an association can act as the exporting arm of all member companies, presenting a united front to world markets and gaining significant economies of scale. Its major functions are the following:

- exporting in the name of the association;
- consolidating freight, negotiating rates and chartering ships;
- performing market research;
- appointing selling agents abroad;
- obtaining credit information and collecting debts;
- setting prices for export;
- allowing uniform contracts and terms of sale;
- allowing cooperative bids and sales negotiation.

Firms in an association can research foreign markets more effectively together, and obtain better representation in them. By establishing one organization to replace several sellers they may realise more stable prices, and selling costs can be reduced. Through consolidating shipments and avoiding duplicated effort firms realise transportation savings, and a group can achieve standardisation of product grading and create a stronger brand name, just as the California fruit growers did with Sunkist products.

Considering all the advantages for an SME in joining an export marketing group, it is surprising that so few groups are actually running. One of the reasons for this could be that the firms have conflicting views as to what the group should do. In many SMEs there are strong feelings of independence inspired by their founders and entrepreneurs, which may be contrary, for example, to the common goal setting of export marketing groups. One of the major tasks of the export group is to balance the interests of the different stakeholders in the group.

10.5 Summary

The advantages and disadvantages of the three main types of export mode are summarised in Table 10.2.

Table 10.2 Advantages and disadvantages of the different export modes for the manufacturer

Export mode	Advantages	Disadvantages
Indirect exporting (e.g. export buying agent, broker or export management company)	Limited commitment and investment required. High degree of market diversification is possible as the firm utilises the internationalization of an experienced exporter. Minimal risk (market and political). No export experience required.	No control over marketing mix elements other than the product. An additional domestic member in the distribution chain may add costs, leaving smaller profit to the producer. Lack of contact with the market (no market knowledge acquired). Limited product experience (based on commercial selling).
Direct exporting (e.g. distributor or agent)	Access to local market experience and contacts with potential customers. Shorter distribution chain (compared to indirect exporting). Market knowledge acquired. More control over marketing mix (especially with agents). Local selling support and services available.	Little control over market price because of tariffs and lack of distribution control (especially with distributors). Some investment in sales organization required (contact from home base with distributors or agents). Cultural differences, providing communication problems and information filtering (transaction costs occur). Possible trade restrictions.
Export marketing groups	Shared costs and risks of internationalization. Provide a complete product line or system sales to the customer.	Risk of unbalanced relationships (different objectives). Participating firms are reluctant to give up their complete independence.

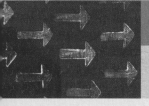

CASE STUDY 10.1 Lysholm Linie Aquavit

International marketing of the Norwegian Aquavit brand

Aquavit, which translates as 'water of life', a slightly yellow or colorless alcoholic liquor, is produced in the Scandinavian countries by redistilling neutral spirits such as grain or potatoes and flavoring it with caraway seeds. It is often consumed as an aperitif.

The alcohol content in the various aquavits varies somewhat, starting at 37.5 per cent. Most brands contain about 40 per cent alcohol. Lysholm Linie Aquavit has an alcohol content of 41.5 per cent. ('Lysholm' is the name of the distillery in Trondheim, where the aquavit is made, and from this point the name 'Linie Aquavit' is used).

The history of Aquavit

Originally, aquavit was used for medicinal purposes, but from the 1700s stills became commonplace in Scandinavian homes.

The definition of aquavit gets slightly complicated when you try to draw the line between it and other spirits popular in the northern climate. The term 'schnapps' for instance, is widely used in Germany, Switzerland and Scandinavia (the Danish say 'snaps') to mean any sort of neutral spirits, flavoured or otherwise. Then there's 'brannvin' a term used similarly in Sweden. (Like the Dutch word 'brandewijn' from which we derive the word 'brandy' it means 'burnt wine'.) The famous Swedish vodka Absolut began life in 1879 as a product called 'Absolut Renat Brannvin' which might be translated as 'absolutely pure schnapps', said to have been distilled ten times. However, when the Swedish government's alcohol monopoly launched Absolut's descendant as an international brand in 1979, they labelled it vodka.

Making of the 'Linie Aquavit'

Caraway is the most important herb in aquavit, but the mixture of herbs varies from brand to brand. Linie Aquavit is derived from Norwegian potato alcohol blended with spices and herbal infusions, and caraway and aniseed predominate. After the alcohol and the herbs have been mixed the aquavit is poured into 500-litre oak barrels, the choice of which has not been left to chance. Norwegian specialists travel to Spain for the express purpose of selecting the best barrels, from those used in the production of Olorso sherry for several years.

Sherry casks are used because they remove the rawer, more volatile aspects of the liquor; the aquavit takes on a golden hue, and the residual sherry imparts a gentle sweetness.

Many theories have been put forward to explain how the man behind Linie Aquavit, Jørgen B. Lysholm, came up with the idea of sending aquavit around the world on sailboats in order to produce a special flavour. History tells us that, in the early 1800s, his family tried to export aquavit to the West Indies, but the ship 'Trondheim's Prøve' returned with its unsold cargo. That is when they discovered the beneficial effects that the long ocean voyage and the special storage had had on the aquavit: the length of the journey, the constant gentle rocking of the boat, and the variation in temperature on deck, all helped give Linie Aquavit its characteristic taste.

Jørgen B. Lysholm subsequently commercialized his maturation method, and this is still how things are done today. Linie Aquavit has one of Norway's long-established shipping companies as its steady travel partner, the first Wilhelmsen liner vessel carrying Lysholm Linie Aquavit set sail in 1927. Since that time, Wilhelmsen has been the sole carrier of this distinguished product. The barrels are tightly secured in specially designed cribs before being loaded onto containers, which remain on deck during the entire journey. The journey from Norway to Australia and

THE CONTENT OF THIS BOTTLE HAS BEEN TO S[ ] FOR 146 DAYS.
YOU'LL NOTICE AFTER A COUPLE OF GLASSE[ ]

The content of this bottle has travelled around the world crossing the equator twice. This might sound as an exotic gimmick, but it's not. Sending the sherry casks containing Linie Aquavit to Australia and back on Norwegian ships is an old tradition. Furthermore it's the most important part of Linies famous recipe. The length of the voyage, the constant rolling of the ship and the variation in temperatures combine in a unique maturation process making Linie the most exclusive aquavit in the world.

Arcus
ARCUS PRODUKTER AS

LINIE AQUAVIT. AROUND THE WORLD IN SHERRY CASKS.
ARCUS PRODUKTER AS. OSLO, NORWAY.
TEL. +47 2297 5500. FAX +47 2263 7338

back again, takes four and a half months and crosses the equator (or the line, as sailors prefer to call it) twice. In fact, this is where Linie Aquavit gets its name. On the back of each label is the name of the ship and the date that it first crossed the equator.

International sales of Linie Aquavit

Arcus AS is Norway's sole manufacturer of hard liquor and it is this company which produces Linie Aquavit. The company also taps wine from wine producers all over the world, and imports a select range of bottled wines. With a market share of approx. 30 per cent, Arcus AS is the leading player in the Norwegian wine and spirits market.

The international aquavit markets (primarily Sweden, Norway, Denmark, Germany and United States) are dominated (except United States) by local Aquavit brands. At the moment Linie Aquavit is the market leader in Norway, with 20 per cent market share. In Denmark and Sweden the market share is 3–5 per cent. Germany is the most important export market, where Linie Aqavit holds 12 per cent of the Aquavit market in competition with brands like Malteserkreutz and Bommerlunde.

Arcus is using export modes (foreign-based intermediaries) in all export markets. In 2000 the main distributors in Germany (Berentzen-Gruppe) and Denmark (Hans Just) became part-owners of Arcus AS, because they wanted to be sole distributors of Linie Aquavit in their countries. In the German market Berentzen offers a whole range of different types of alcoholic drinks. The company ranked number three in spirits in 2001, with a volume share of 7 per cent. Berentzen aims to expand its international spirits business during the next few years, in order to achieve long-term growth.

Questions

1. What are the main advantages and disadvantages for Arcus of using export modes, compared to other entry modes, to their Linie Aquavit?

2. What are the advantages for Arcus of having distributors as part-owners?

3. What should be Arcus' main criteria for selecting new distributors, or cooperation partners, for Linie Aquavit in new markets?

4. Would it be possible to pursue an international branding strategy for Linie Aquavit?

Sources: **www.arcus.no/english/**, Christian Brink, Head of Marketing, Sales and R&D at Arcus AS

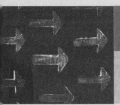

CASE STUDY 10.2   Parle Products

An Indian biscuit is seeking agents and cooperation partners in new export markets

A long time ago, when the British ruled India, a small factory was set up in the suburbs of Mumbai city to manufacture sweets and toffees. The year was 1929 and the market was dominated by famous international brands that were freely imported. Despite the odds and unequal competition the company, called Parle Products (**www.parleproducts.com**), survived and succeeded, by adhering to high quality and improvising from time to time

Today, Parle enjoys a 40 per cent share of the total Indian biscuit market and a 15 per cent share of the total confectionary market in India. The Parle Biscuit brands, such as Parle-G, Monaco and Krackjack, and confectionery brands, such as Melody, Poppins, Mangobite and Kismi, enjoy a strong image and appeal among consumers.

If you thought that a typical family-run Indian company could not top the worldwide charts, think again. The homegrown biscuit brand, Parle G, has proved the belief wrong by becoming the largest

selling biscuit brand in the world. However in most European markets Parle Products has to fight against a particular competitor, United Biscuits (producer of McVitie's). In all European markets the market share of Parle Prosucts is very small.

United Biscuits (UB)

United Biscuits was founded in 1948 following the merger of two Scottish family businesses – McVitie & Price and McFarlane Lang. In 1960 UB added to its portfolio with the acquisition of Crawford's Biscuits and MacDonald's Biscuits.

In 2000 UB was bought by Finalrealm, a consortium of investors, and reverted to private limited company status.

Brand muscle

UB's brands rank number one or two in seven countries, they have 5 of the top 10 biscuit brands in the United Kingdom, France and Spain, and 4 out of the top 10 leading snack brands in the United Kingdom. More than 89 per cent of UK households bought McVitie's products in 2001. Anyone would agree that they have 'brand muscle'.

Consumer insight

UB's unique position as the largest UK snack food player, with a balanced portfolio of both sweet and savoury brands, gives us a unique understanding of how to respond effectively to changing consumer needs and wants.

Parle Products

Parle Products is the leader in the glucose and salty biscuit category but do not have a strong presence in the premium segment, with Hide-n-Seek being its only brand.

The extensive distribution network, built over the years, is a major strength for Parle Products. Its biscuits and sweets are available to consumers even in the most remote places and in the smallest of villages in India, some with a population of just 500.

Parle has nearly 1,500 wholesalers, catering to 425,000 retail outlets directly or indirectly. A 200-strong dedicated field force services these wholesalers and retailers. Additionally, there are 31 depots and C&F agents supplying goods to the wide distribution network.

The Parle marketing philosophy emphasises catering to the masses. They constantly endeavour to design products that provide nutrition and fun for everyone. Most Parle offerings are in the low and mid-range price segments. This is based on the understanding of the Indian consumer psyche. The value-for-money positioning helps generate large sales volumes for the products.

The other global biscuit brands include Oreo from Nabisco and McVitie's from UK-based United Biscuits. According to market reports Parle Products commands (with Parle G as the market leader) a 40 per cent market share in the R3,500 core biscuit market in India. In the confectionery segment the company enjoys a mere 15 per cent market share. The Parle G brand faces competition from Britannia's Tiger brand of biscuits, among others.

The company's flagship brand, Parle G, contributes more than 50 per cent to the company's total turnover. The other biscuits in the Parle Products' basket include Marie, Cheeslings, Jeffs, Sixer and Fun Centre.

Source: adapted from: Jain and Zachariah, 2002.
http://www.bsstrategist.com/archives/2002/mar/

Questions

1. Which region of the world would you recommend Parle Products to penetrate as its first choice?

2. What kind of export mode would be most relevant for Parle Products?

3. How could Parle Products conduct a systematic screening of potential distributors or agents in foreign markets?

4. What would be the most important issues for Parle Products to discuss with a potential distributor/agent before final preparation of a contract?

For further exercises and cases, see this book's website at
www.booksites.net/hollensen

Questions for discussion

1. Why is exporting frequently considered the simplest way of entering foreign markets and thus favoured by SMEs?

2. What procedures should a firm follow in selecting a distributor?

3. Why is it difficult – financially and legally – to terminate a relationship with overseas intermediaries? What should be done to prevent or minimise such difficulties?

4. Identify the ways to reach foreign markets by making a domestic sale.

5. What is the difference between direct and indirect exporting?

6. Discuss the financial and pricing techniques for motivating foreign distributors.

7. Which marketing tasks should be handled by the exporter and which ones by its intermediaries in foreign markets?

8. How can the carrier and the rider both benefit from a piggyback arrangement?

9. When a firm begins direct exporting, what tasks must it perform?

10. Discuss the various ways of communicating with foreign distributors.

11. 'When exporting to a market, you're only as good as your intermediary there.' Discuss.

12. The international marketer and the intermediary will have different expectations concerning the relationship. Why should these expectations be spelled out and clarified in the contract?

References

Jain, S. and Zachariah, R. (2002), in *Business Standard* (Mumbai) 14 March.

Okoroafo, S.C. (1994) 'Implementing international countertrade: a dyadic approach', *Industrial Marketing Management*, vol. 23, pp. 229–34.

Root, F.R. (1994) *Entry Strategies for International Markets: Revised and expanded edition*, The New Lexington Press, Lexington, MA.

Wilkinson, A. (1999) 'Pepsi plans global hit with chart show', *Marketing Week*, 4 March.

Further reading

Albaum, G., Strandskov, J. and Duerr. E. (2002) *International Marketing and Export Management* (4th edn), Financial Times Pearson Education, Harlow.

McNaughton, R.B. (2001) 'The export mode decision-making process in small knowledge-intensive firms', *Marketing Intelligence & Planning*, vol. 19, no. 1, pp. 12–20.

O'Cass, A. and Julian, C. (2003) 'Examining firm and environmental influences on export marketing mix strategy and export performance of Australian exporters', *European Journal of Marketing*, vol. 37, Number 3/4, pp. 366–84.

Solberg, C.A. and Nes, E.B. (2002) 'Exporter trust, commitment and marketing control in integrated and independent export channels', *International Business Review*, vol. 11, pp. 385–405.

Wells, L.F. and Dulat, K.B. (1996) *Exporting from Start to Finance* (3rd edn), McGraw-Hill, New York.

11 Intermediate entry modes

Contents

Learning objectives

After studying this chapter you should be able to do the following:

- Describe and understand the main intermediate entry modes:
    contract manufacturing;
    licensing;
    franchising; and
    joint venture/strategic alliances.

- Discuss the advantages and disadvantages of the main intermediate entry modes.

- Explain the different stages in joint-venture formation.

- Explore the reasons for the 'divorce' of the two parents in a joint-venture constellation.

- Explore different ways of managing a joint venture/strategic alliance.

11.1 Introduction

So far we have assumed that the firm entering foreign markets is supplying them from domestic plants. This is implicit in any form of exporting. However, sometimes the firm may find it either impossible or undesirable to supply all foreign markets from domestic production. Intermediate entry modes are distinguished from export modes because they are primarily vehicles for the transfer of knowledge and skills, although they may also create export opportunities. They are distinguished from the hierarchical entry modes in the way that there is no full ownership (by the parent firm) involved, but ownership and control can be shared between the parent firm and a local partner. This is the case with the (equity) joint venture.

Intermediate entry modes include a variety of arrangements, such as licensing, franchising, management contracts, turnkey contracts, joint ventures and technical

Figure 11.1 Intermediate modes

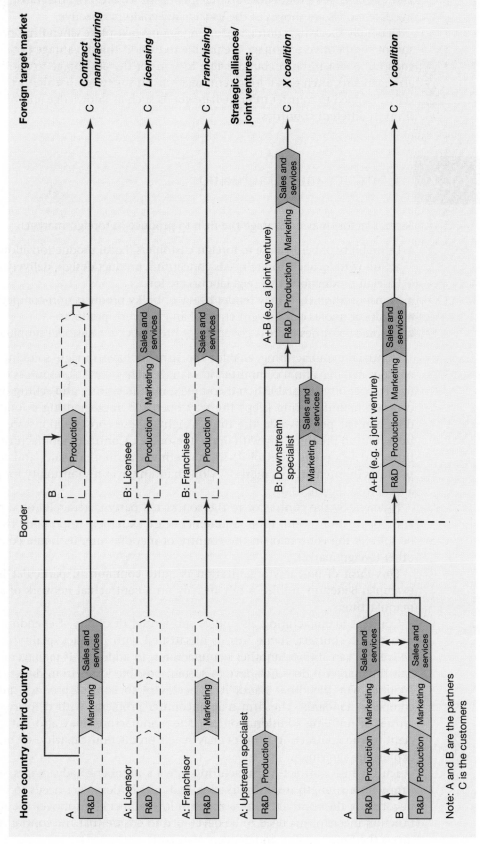

know-how or co-production arrangements. In Figure 11.1 the most relevant intermediate modes are shown in the usual value chain perspective.

Generally speaking, contractual arrangements take place when firms possessing some sort of competitive advantage are unable to exploit this advantage because of resource constraints, for instance, but are able to transfer the advantage to another party. The arrangements often entail long-term relationships between partner firms and are typically designed to transfer intermediate goods such as knowledge and/or skills between firms in different countries.

11.2 Contract manufacturing

Several factors may encourage the firm to produce in foreign markets:

- Desirability of being close to foreign customers. Local production allows better interaction with local customer needs concerning product design, delivery and service.
- Foreign production costs (e.g. labour) are low.
- Transportation costs may render heavy or bulky products non-competitive.
- Tariffs or quotas can prevent entry of an exporter's products.
- In some countries there is government preference for national suppliers.

Contract manufacturing enables the firm to have foreign sourcing (production) without making a final commitment. Management may lack resources or be unwilling to invest equity to establish and complete manufacturing and selling operations. Yet contract manufacturing keeps the way open for implementing a long-term foreign development policy when the time is right. These considerations are perhaps most important to the company with limited resources. Contract manufacturing enables the firm to develop and control R&D, marketing, distribution, sales and servicing of its products in international markets, while handing over responsibility for production to a local firm (Figure 11.1).

Payment by the contractor to the contracted party is generally on a per unit basis, and quality and specification requirements are extremely important. The product can be sold by the contractor in the country of manufacture, its home country, or some other foreign market.

This form of business organization is quite common in particular industries. For example, Benetton and IKEA rely heavily on a contractual network of small overseas manufacturers.

Contract manufacturing also offers substantial flexibility. Depending on the duration of the contract, if the firm is dissatisfied with product quality or reliability of delivery it can shift to another manufacturer. In addition, if management decides to exit the market it does not have to sustain possible losses from divesting production facilities. On the other hand, it is necessary to control product quality to meet company standards. The firm may encounter problems with delivery, product warranties or fulfilling additional orders. The manufacturer may also not be as cost efficient as the contracting firm, or may reach production capacity, or may attempt to exploit the agreement.

Thus, while contract manufacturing offers a number of advantages, especially to a firm whose strength lies in marketing and distribution, care needs to be exercised in negotiating the contract. Where the firm loses direct control over the manufacturing function mechanisms need to be developed to ensure that the contract manufacturer meets the firm's quality and delivery standards.

11.3   Licensing

Licensing is another way in which the firm can establish local production in foreign markets without capital investment. It differs from contract manufacturing in that it is usually for a longer term and involves much greater responsibilities for the national firm, because more value chain functions have been transferred to the licensee by the licensor (see Figure 11.1).

A licensing agreement

A licensing agreement is an arrangement wherein the licensor gives something of value to the licensee in exchange for certain performance and payments from the licensee. The licensor may give the licensee the right to use one or more of the following things:

- a patent covering a product or process;
- manufacturing know-how not subject to a patent;
- technical advice and assistance, occasionally including the supply of components, materials or plant essential to the manufacturing process;
- marketing advice and assistance;
- the use of a trade mark/trade name.

In the case of trade mark licensing the licensor should try not to undermine a product by overlicensing it. For example, Pierre Cardin diluted the value of his name by allowing some 800 products to use the name under licence. Overlicensing can increase income in the short run, but in the long run it may mean killing the goose that laid the golden egg.

In some situations the licensor may continue to sell essential components or services to the licensee as part of the agreement. This may be extended so that the total agreement may also be one of cross-licensing, wherein there is a mutual exchange of knowledge and/or patents. In cross-licensing there might not be a cash payment involved.

Licensing can be considered a two-way street because a licence also allows the original licensor to gain access to the licensee's technology and product. This is important because the licensee may be able to build on the information supplied by the licensor. Some licensors are very interested in grantbacks and will even lower the royalty rate in return for product improvements and potentially profitable new products. Where a product or service is involved the licensee is responsible for production and marketing in a defined market area. This responsibility is followed by all the profits and risks associated with the venture. In exchange the licensee pays the licensor royalties or fees, which are the licensor's main source of income from its licensing operations and that usually involve some combination of the following elements:

- A lump sum not related to output. This can include a sum paid at the beginning of an agreement for the initial transfer of special machinery, parts, blueprints, knowledge and so on.
- A minimum royalty – a guarantee that at least some annual income will be received by the licensor.
- A running royalty – normally expressed as a percentage of normal selling price or as a fixed sum of money for units of output.

Other methods of payment include conversions of royalties into equity, management and technical fees, and complex systems of counter purchase, typically found in licensing arrangements with eastern European countries.

If the foreign market carries high political risk then it would be wise for the licensor to seek high initial payments and perhaps compress the timescale of the agreement. Alternatively, if the market is relatively free of risk and the licensee is well placed to develop a strong market share, then payment terms will be somewhat relaxed and probably influenced by other licensors competing for the agreement.

The licensing agreement or contract should always be formalised in a written document. The details of the contract will probably be the subject of detailed negotiation and hard bargaining between the parties, and there can be no such thing as a standard contract.

In the following we see licensing from the viewpoint of a *licensor* (licensing out) and a *licensee* (licensing in). This section is written primarily from the licensor's viewpoint, but licensing in may be an important element in smaller firms' growth strategies, and therefore some consideration is given to this issue too.

Licensing out

Generally there is a wide range of strategic reasons for using licensing. The most important motives for licensing out are as follows:

- The licensor firm will remain technologically superior in its product development. It wants to concentrate on its core competences (product development activities) and then outsource production and downstream activities to other firms.
- The licensor is too small to have financial, managerial or marketing expertise for overseas investment (own subsidiaries).
- The product is at the end of its product life cycle in the advanced countries because of obsolescent technology or model change. A stretching of the total product life cycle is possible through licensing agreements in less developed countries.
- Even if direct royalty income is not high margins on key components to the licensee (produced by the licensor) can be quite handsome.
- If government regulations restrict foreign direct investment or if political risks are high licensing may be the only realistic entry mode.
- There may be constraints on imports into the licensee country (tariff or non-tariff barriers).

When setting the price for the agreement the costs of licensing should not be underestimated. Table 11.1 presents a breakdown of costs of licensing out by Australian firms.

Licensing in

Empirical evidence shows (Young *et al.*, 1989, p. 143) that many licensing agreements actually stem from approaches by licensees. This would suggest that the licensee is at an immediate disadvantage in negotiations and general relations with the licensor. In other cases licensing in is used as the easy option, with the licence being renewed regularly and the licensee becoming heavily dependent on the technology supplier (the licensor).

As Figure 11.2 shows, licensing in can improve the net cash flow position of the licensee, but mean lower profits in the longer term. Because technology licensing allows the firms to have products on the market sooner than otherwise, the firm benefits from an earlier positive cash flow. In addition, licensing means lower development costs. The immediate benefits of quick access to new technology, lower development costs and a relatively early cash flow are attractive benefits of licensing.

Table 11.1 Relative costs of licensing overseas (%)

Breakdown of total costs of licensing overseas	
Protection of industrial property	24.4
Establishment of licensing agreement	46.6
Maintenance of licensing agreement	29.0
	100.0
Breakdown of establishment costs	
Search for suitable licensee	22.8
Communication between involved parties	44.7
Adoption and testing of equipment for licensee	9.9
Training personnel for licensee	19.9
Other (additional marketing activity and legal expenses)	2.7
	100.0
Breakdown of maintenance costs	
Audit of licensee	9.7
Ongoing market research in market of licensee	7.2
Back-up services for licensee	65.0
Defence of industrial property rights in licensee's territory	11.0
Other	7.1
	100.0

Sources:Based on Carstairs and Welch (1981) and Young *et al*. (1989), p. 132.

Figure 11.2 Life cycle benefits of licensing

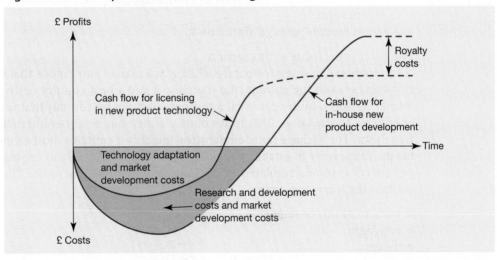

Sources: Lowe and Crawford, 1984; Bradley, 1995, p. 388.

Table 11.5 (see section 11.6) summarises the advantages and disadvantages of licensing for the licensor.

11.4   Franchising

The term 'franchising' is derived from the French, meaning 'to be free from servitude'. Franchise activity was almost unknown in Europe until the beginning of the 1970s. The concept was popularised in the United States, where over one-third of retail sales are derived from franchising, in comparison with about 11 per cent in Europe (Young *et al*., 1989, p. 111).

A number of factors have contributed to the rapid growth rate of franchising. First, the general worldwide decline of traditional manufacturing industry and its replacement by service-sector activities has encouraged franchising. It is especially well suited to service and people-intensive economic activities, particularly where these require a large number of geographically dispersed outlets serving local markets. Second, the growth in popularity of self-employment is a contributory factor to the growth of franchising. Government policies in many countries have improved the whole climate for small businesses as a means of stimulating employment.

A good example of the value of franchising is the Swedish furniture manufacturer IKEA, which franchises its ideas throughout the western world, especially in Europe and North America. In terms of retail surface area and the number of visitors to retail stores, this company has experienced very significant growth through franchising in recent years.

Franchising is a marketing-oriented method of selling a business service, often to small independent investors who have working capital but little or no prior business experience. However, it is something of an umbrella term that is used to mean anything from the right to use a name to the total business concept. Thus there are two major types of franchising:

- Product and trade name franchising. This is very similar to trade mark licensing. Typically it is a distribution system in which suppliers make contracts with dealers to buy or sell products or product lines. Dealers use the trade name, trade mark and product line. Examples of this type of franchising are soft drink bottlers such as Coca-Cola and Pepsi.
- Business format 'package' franchising.

The latter is the focus of this section.

International business format franchising is a market entry mode that involves a relationship between the entrant (the franchisor) and a host country entity, in which the former transfers, under contract, a business package (or format) that it has developed and owns, to the latter. This host country entity can be either a franchisee or a subfranchisor. The package transferred by the franchisor contains most elements necessary for the local entity to establish a business and run it profitably in the host country in a prescribed manner, regulated and controlled by the franchisor. The package can contain the following items:

- trade marks/trade names;
- copyright;
- designs;
- patents;
- trade secrets;
- business know-how;
- geographic exclusivity.

The package may also include the right for the local entity, a subfranchisor, to establish and service its own subsystem of subfranchisees within its appointed territory.

In addition to this package the franchisor also typically provides local entities with managerial assistance in setting up and running local operations. All locally owned franchisees, subfranchisees and subfranchisors can also receive subsupplies from the franchisor and benefit from centrally coordinated advertising. In return for this business package the franchisor receives from the franchisee or subfranchisor an initial fee up front and/or continuing franchise fees, based typically on a percentage of annual turnover as a mark-up on goods supplied directly by the franchisor.

There is still a lively debate about the differences between licensing and franchising, but if we define franchising in the broader 'business format' (as here), we see the differences presented in Table 11.2.

Table 11.2 How licensing and franchising differ

Licensing	Franchising
The term 'royalties' is normally used.	'Management fees' is regarded as the appropriate term.
Products, or even a single product, are the common element.	Covers the total business, including know-how, intellectual rights, goodwill, trade marks and business contacts. (Franchising is all-encompassing, whereas licensing concerns just one part of the business.)
Licences are usually taken by well-established businesses.	Tends to be a start-up situation, certainly as regards the franchisee.
Terms of 16–20 years are common, particularly where they relate to technical know-how, copyright and trademarks. The terms are similar for patents.	The franchise agreement is normally for 5 years, sometimes extending to 11 years. Franchises are frequently renewable.
Licensees tend to be self-selecting. They are often established businesses and can demonstrate that they are in a strong position to operate the licence in question. A licensee can often pass its licence on to an associate or sometimes unconnected company with little or no reference back to the original licensor.	The franchisee is very definitely selected by the franchisor, and its eventual replacement is controlled by the franchisor.
Usually concerns specific existing products with very little benefit from ongoing research being passed on by the licensor to its licensee.	The franchisor is expected to pass on to its franchisees the benefits of its ongoing research programme as part of the agreement.
There is no goodwill attached to the licence as it is totally retained by the licensor.	Although the franchisor does retain the main goodwill, the franchisee picks up an element of localised goodwill.
Licensees enjoy a substantial measure of free negotiation. As bargaining tools they can use their trade muscle and their established position in the marketplace.	There is a standard fee structure and any variation within an individual franchise system would cause confusion and mayhem.

Sources: Based on Perkins (1987), pp. 22, 157 and Young *et al*. (1989), p. 148.

Types of business format franchise include business and personal services, convenience stores, car repairs and fast food. US fast-food franchises are some of the best-known global franchise businesses, and include McDonald's, Burger King and Pizza Hut.

The fast-food business is taken as an example of franchising in the value chain approach of Figure 11.1. The production (e.g. assembly of burgers) and sales and service functions are transferred to the local outlets (e.g. McDonald's restaurants), whereas the central R&D and marketing functions are still controlled by the franchisor (e.g. McDonald's head office in the United States). The franchisor will develop the general marketing plan (with the general advertising messages), which will be adapted to local conditions and cultures.

As indicated earlier, business format franchising is an ongoing relationship that includes not only a product or a service but also a business concept. The business concept usually includes a strategic plan for growth and marketing, instruction on the operation of the business, elaboration of standards and quality control, continuing guidance for the franchisee, and some means of control of the franchisee by the franchisor. Franchisors provide a wide variety of assistance for franchisees, but not all franchisors provide the same level of support. Some examples of assistance and support provided by franchisors are in the areas of finance, site selection, lease negotiation, cooperative advertising, training and assistance with store opening. The extent of ongoing support to franchisees also varies among franchisors. Support areas include central data processing, central purchasing, field training, field operation evaluation, newsletters, regional and national meetings, a hotline for advice and franchisor–franchisee advisory councils. The availability of these services is often a critical factor in the decision to purchase a franchise, and may be crucial to the long-term success of marginal locations or marginally prepared owners.

International expansion of franchising

Franchisors, as other businesses, must consider the relevant success factors in making the decision to expand their franchising system globally. The objective is to search for an environment that promotes cooperation and reduces conflict. Given the long-term nature of a franchise agreement country stability is an important factor.

Where should the international expansion start? The franchising development often begins as a response to a perceived local opportunity, perhaps as an adaptation of a franchising concept already operating in another foreign market. In this case the market focus is clearly local to begin with. In addition, the local market provides a better environment for testing and developing the franchising format. Feedback from the marketplace and franchisees can be obtained more readily because of the ease of communication. Adjustments can be made more quickly because of the close local contact. A whole variety of minor changes in the format may be necessary as a result of early experience in areas such as training, franchisee choice, site selection, organization of suppliers, promotion and outlet decoration. The early stages of franchise development represent a critical learning process for the franchisor, not just about how to adapt the total package to the market requirements but also regarding the nature of the franchising method itself. Ultimately, with a proven package and a better understanding of its operation, the franchisor is in a better position to attack foreign markets, and is more confident about doing so with a background of domestic success.

Developing and managing franchisor–franchisee relationships

Franchising provides a unique organizational relationship in which the franchisor and franchisee each bring important qualities to the business. The franchise system combines the advantages of economy of scale offered by the franchisor with the local knowledge and entrepreneurial talents of the franchisee. Their joint contribution may result in success. The franchisor depends on franchisees for fast growth, an infusion of capital from the franchise purchase fee, and an income stream from the royalty fee paid by franchisees each year. Franchisors also benefit from franchisee goodwill in the community and, increasingly, from franchisee suggestions for innovation. The most important factor, however, is the franchisee's motivation to operate a successful independent business. The franchisee depends on the franchisor for the strength of the trade mark, technical advice, support services, marketing resources and national advertising that provides instant customer recognition.

There are two additional key success factors, which rest on the interdependence of the franchisee and the franchisor:

- integrity of the whole business system;
- capacity for renewal of the business system.

Integrity of the business system

The business will be a success in a viable market to the extent that the franchisor provides a well-developed, proven business concept to the franchisee and the franchisee is motivated to follow the system as it is designed, thereby preserving the integrity of the system. Standardisation is the cornerstone of franchising: customers expect the same product or service at every location. Deviations from the franchising business concept by individual franchisees adversely affect the franchisor's reputation. The need for the integrity of the system requires that the franchisor exerts control over key operations at the franchise sites.

Capacity for renewal of the business system

Although most franchisors conduct research and development within the parent company, the highest proportion of innovation originates from franchisees in the field. Franchisees are most familiar with customers' preferences. They sense new trends and the opportunity to introduce a new product and service. The issue is getting the franchisee to share new ideas with the parent company. Not all franchisees are willing to share ideas with the franchisor, for a number of reasons. The most common is failure of the franchisor to keep in close contact with the franchisees; the most troubling is a lack of trust in the franchisor. The franchisor needs to promote a climate of trust and cooperation for mutual benefit.

Handling possible conflicts

Conflict is inherent in the franchisor–franchisee relationship, since all aspects that are good for the franchisor may not be good for the franchisee. One of the most basic conflicts is failure of either the franchisor or the franchisee to live up to the terms of the legal agreement.

Disagreement over objectives may be the result of poor communication on the part of the franchisor, or failure on the part of the franchisee to understand the franchisor's objectives. Both franchisor and franchisee agree on the need for profits in the business, not only to provide a living but to stay competitive. However, the two parties may disagree on the means of achieving profits. The number of conflicts between franchisors and franchisees may be reduced by establishing extensive monitoring of the franchisee (e.g. computer-based accounting, purchasing and inventory systems). Another way of reducing the number of conflicts is to view franchisors and franchisees as partners in running a business; both objectives and operating procedures have to be in harmony. This view requires a strong common culture with shared values established by the use of intensive communication between franchisor and franchisees in different countries (e.g. cross-national/regional meetings, cross-national/regional advisory councils).

11.5   Joint ventures/strategic alliances

A joint venture or a strategic alliance is a partnership between two or more parties. In international joint ventures these parties will be based in different countries, and this obviously complicates the management of such an arrangement.

A number of reasons are given for setting up joint ventures, including the following:

- Complementary technology or management skills provided by the partners can lead to new opportunities in existing sectors (e.g. multimedia, in which information processing, communications and the media are merging).
- Many firms find that partners in the host country can increase the speed of market entry.
- Many less developed countries, such as China and South Korea, try to restrict foreign ownership.
- Global operations in R&D and production are prohibitively expensive, but are necessary to achieve competitive advantage.

The formal difference between a joint venture and a strategic alliance is that a strategic alliance is typically a non-equity cooperation, meaning that the partners do not commit equity into or invest in the alliance. The joint venture can be either a contractual non-equity joint venture or an equity joint venture.

In a contractual joint venture no joint enterprise with a separate personality is formed. Two or more companies form a partnership to share the cost of investment, the risks and the long-term profits. An equity joint venture involves the creation of a new company in which foreign and local investors share ownership and control. Thus, according to these definitions, strategic alliances and non-equity joint ventures are more or less the same (Figure 11.3).

Figure 11.3 Joint ventures and strategic alliances

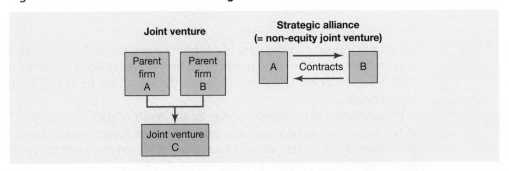

The question of whether to use an equity or a non-equity joint venture is a matter of how to formalise the cooperation. Much more interesting is to consider the roles that partners are supposed to play in the collaboration.

In Figure 11.4 two different types of coalition are shown in the value chain perspective. These are based on the possible collaboration pattern along the value chain. In Figure 11.4 we see two partners, A and B, each having its own value chain. Three different types of value chain partnership, appear:

1. *Upstream-based collaboration.* A and B collaborate on R&D and/or production.
2. *Downstream-based collaboration.* A and B collaborate on marketing, distribution, sales and/or service.

Figure 11.4 Collaboration possibilities for partners A and B in the value chain

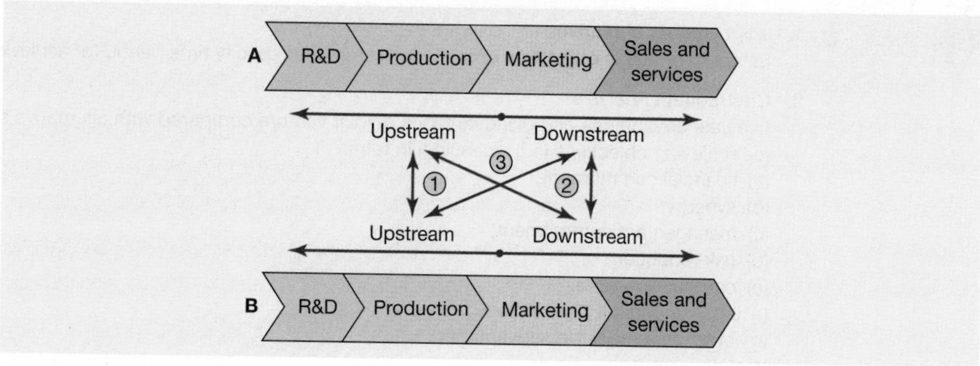

Source: Adapted from Lorange and Roos, 1995, p. 16.

3. *Upstream/downstream-based collaboration*. A and B have different but complementary competences at each end of the value chain.

Types 1 and 2 represent the so-called Y coalition and type 3 represents the so-called X coalition (Porter and Fuller, 1986, pp. 336–7):

- *Y coalitions*. Partners share the actual performance of one or more value chain activities: for example, joint production of models or components enables the attainment of scale economies that can provide lower production costs per unit. Another example is a joint marketing agreement where complementary product lines of two firms are sold together through existing or new distribution channels, and thus broaden the market coverage of both firms.
- *X coalitions*. Partners divide the value chain activities between themselves: for example, one partner develops and manufactures a product while letting the other partner market it. Forming X coalitions involves identifying the value chain activities where the firm is well positioned and has its core competences. Take the case where A has its core competences in upstream functions but is weak in downstream functions. A wants to enter a foreign market but lacks local market knowledge and does not know how to get access to foreign distribution channels for its products. Therefore A seeks and finds a partner, B, which has its core competences in the downstream functions but is weak in the upstream functions. In this way A and B can form a coalition where B can help A with distribution and selling in a foreign market, and A can help B with R&D or production.

In summary, X coalitions imply that the partners have asymmetric competences in the value chain activities: where one is strong the other is weak and vice versa. In Y coalitions, on the other hand, partners tend to be more similar in the strengths and weaknesses of their value chain activities.

Stages in joint–venture formation

The various stages in the formation of a joint venture are shown in Table 11.3.

Step 1: Joint-venture objectives

Joint ventures are formed for a variety of reasons: entering new markets, reducing manufacturing costs, and developing and diffusing new technologies rapidly. Joint ventures are also used to accelerate product introduction and overcome legal and trade barriers expeditiously. In this period of advanced technology and global markets implementing strategies quickly is essential. Forming alliances is often the fastest, most

Table 11.3 Stages in joint–venture formation

1. **Joint venture objectives**
   Establish strategic objectives of the joint venture and specify time period for achieving objectives.

2. **Cost/benefit analysis**
   Evaluate advantages and disadvantages of joint venture compared with alternative strategies for achieving objectives (e.g. licensing) in terms of:
   (a) financial commitment;
   (b) synergy;
   (c) management commitment;
   (d) risk reduction;
   (e) control;
   (f) long-run market penetration; and
   (g) other advantages/disadvantages.

3. **Selecting partner(s)**
   (a) profile of desired features of candidates;
   (b) identifying joint-venture candidates and drawing up short list;
   (c) screening and evaluating possible joint-venture partners;
   (d) initial contact/discussions; and
   (e) choice of partner.

4. **Develop business plan**
   Achieve broad agreement on different issues.

5. **Negotiation of joint-venture agreement**
   Final agreement on business plan.

6. **Contract writing**
   Incorporation of agreement in legally binding contract, allowing for subsequent modifications to the agreement.

7. **Performance evaluation**
   Establish control systems for measuring venture performance.

Source: Adapted from Young *et al.*, 1989, p. 233. Reproduced by permission of Pearson Education Ltd.

effective method of achieving objectives. Companies must be sure that the goal of the alliance is compatible with their existing businesses, so their expertise is transferable to the alliance. Firms often enter into alliances based on opportunity rather than linkage with their overall goals. This risk is greatest when a company has a surplus of cash.

There are three principal objectives in forming a joint venture:

1. *Entering new markets.* Many companies recognise that they lack the necessary marketing expertise when they enter new markets. Rather than trying to develop this expertise internally the company may identify another organization that possesses those desired marketing skills. Then, by capitalising on the product development skills of one company and the marketing skills of the other, the resulting alliance can serve the market quickly and effectively. Alliances may be particularly helpful when entering a foreign market for the first time because of the extensive cultural differences that may abound. They may also be effective domestically when entering regional or ethnic markets.

2. *Reducing manufacturing costs.* Joint ventures may allow companies to pool capital or existing facilities to gain economies of scale or increase the use of facilities, thereby reducing manufacturing costs.

3. *Developing and diffusing technology.* Joint ventures may also be used to build jointly on the technical expertise of two or more companies in developing products that are technologically beyond the capability of the companies acting independently.

Step 2: Cost/benefit analysis

A joint venture/strategic alliance may not be the best way of achieving objectives. Therefore this entry mode should be evaluated against other entry modes. Such an analysis could be based on the factors influencing the choice of entry mode (see section 9.3).

Step 3: Selecting partner(s)

If it is accepted that a joint venture is the best entry mode for achieving the firm's objectives, the next stage is the selection of the joint-venture partner. This normally involves five stages.

Establishing a desired partner profile

Companies frequently search for one or more of the following resources in a partner:

- development know-how;
- sales and service expertise;
- low-cost production facilities;
- strategically critical manufacturing capabilities;
- reputation and brand equity;
- market access and knowledge;
- cash.

Identifying joint-venture candidates

Often this part of partner selection is not performed thoroughly. The first candidate, generally discovered through contacts established by mail, arranged by a banker or a business colleague already established in the country, is often the one with whom the company undertakes discussions. Little or no screening is done, nor is there an in-depth investigation of the motives and capabilities of the candidate. At other times the personal network that executives maintain with senior managers from other firms shapes the set of prospective joint-venture partners that companies will generally consider. All too often, however, alliances are agreed upon informally by these top managers without careful attention to how appropriate the partner match may be. Instead of taking this reactive approach the firm should proactively search for joint-venture candidates. Possible candidates can be found among competitors, suppliers, customers, related industries and trade association members.

Screening and evaluating possible joint-venture partners

Relationships get off to a good start if partners know each other. Table 11.4 gives some criteria that may be used to judge a prospective partner's effectiveness.

These suggestions form only an outline sketch of the type of information that can be used to grade partners. They cover areas where there is a reasonable chance of forming a view by the appraisal of published information and by sensible observation and questioning.

Initial contacts/discussions

Since relationships between companies are relationships between people it is important that the top managers of the firm meet personally with top managers from the remaining two or three possible partners. It is important to highlight the personal side of a business relationship. This includes discussion of personal and social interests to see if there is a good 'chemistry' between the prospective partners.

Table 11.4 Analysis of prospective partners: examples of criteria that may be used to judge a prospective partner's effectiveness by assessing existing business ventures and commercial attitudes

1. **Finance**
   Financial history and overall financial standing (all the usual ratios).
   Possible reasons for successful business areas.
   Possible reasons for unsuccessful business areas.

2. **Organization**
   Structure of organization.
   Quality and turnover of senior managers.
   Workforce conditions/labour relations.
   Information and reporting systems; evidence of planning.
   Effective owner's working relationship with business.

3. **Market**
   Reputation in marketplace and with competitors.
   Evidence of research/interest in service and quality.
   Sales methods; quality of sales force.
   Evidence of handling weakening market conditions.
   Results of new business started.

4. **Production**
   Condition of existing premises/works.
   Production efficiencies/layouts.
   Capital investments and improvements.
   Quality control procedures.
   Evidence of research (internal/external); introduction of new technology.
   Relationship with main suppliers.

5. **Institutional**
   Government and business contacts (influence).
   Successful negotiations with banks, licensing authorities, etc.
   Main contacts with non-national organizations and companies.
   Geographical influence.

6. **Possible negotiating attitudes**
   Flexible or hardline.
   Reasonably open or closed and secretive.
   Short-term or long-term orientation.
   Wheeler-dealer or objective negotiator.
   Positive, quick decision making or tentative.
   Negotiating experience and strength of team support.

Sources: Walmsley, 1982; Paliwoda 1993.

Choice of partner

The chosen partner should bring the desired complementary strength to the partnership. Ideally the strengths contributed by the partners will be unique, for only these strengths can be sustained and defended over the long term. The goal is to develop synergies between the contributions of the partners, resulting in a win–win situation for both. Moreover, the partners must be compatible and willing to trust one another.

It is important that neither partner has the desire to acquire the other partner's strength, or the necessary mutual trust will be destroyed. Dow Chemical Company, a frequent and successful alliance practitioner, uses the negotiation process to judge other corporate cultures and, consequently, their compatibility and trustworthiness.

Commitment to the joint venture is essential. This commitment must be both financial and psychological. Unless there is senior management endorsement and enthusiasm at the operating level an alliance will struggle, particularly when tough issues arise.

Step 4: Develop business plan

Issues that have to be negotiated and determined prior to the establishment of the joint venture include the following:

- ownership split (majority, minority, 50–50);
- management (composition of board of directors, organization, etc.);
- production (installation of machinery, training, etc.);
- marketing (the four Ps, organization).

Figure 11.5 Partner–to–partner relationships creating a joint venture

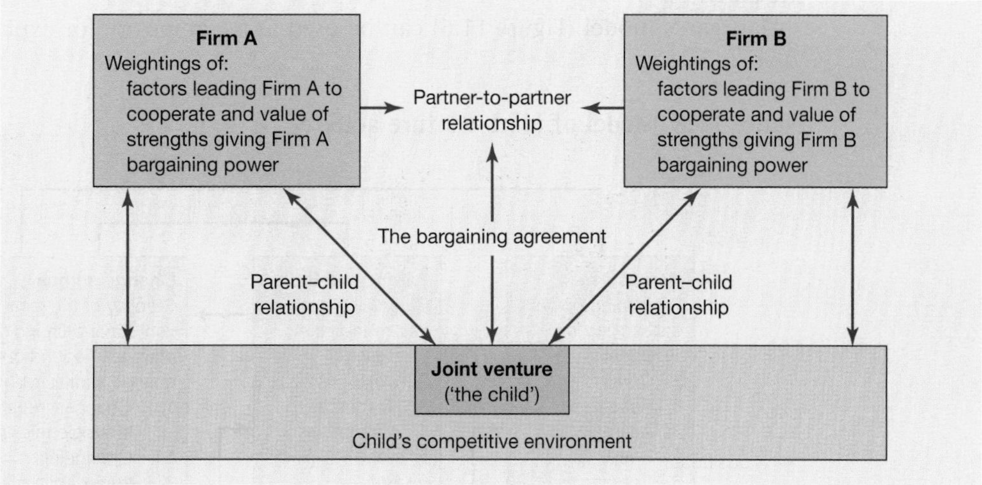

Source: Harrigan, 1985, p. 50.

Step 5: Negotiation of joint–venture agreement

As Figure 11.5 shows, the final agreement is determined by the relative bargaining power of both prospective partners.

Step 6: Contract writing

Once the joint-venture agreement has been negotiated it needs to be written into a legally binding contract. Of course, the contract should cover the 'marriage' conditions of the partners, but it should also cover the 'divorce' situation, such as what happens with 'the child' (the joint venture).

Step 7: Performance evaluation

Evaluating joint-venture performance is a difficult issue. Managers often fall into the trap of assessing partnerships as if they were internal corporate divisions with unambiguous goals operating in low-risk, stable environments. Bottom-line profits, cash flow, market share and other traditional financially oriented output measures become standard indicators of performance. These measures may be inappropriate for two reasons. First, they reflect a short-term orientation, and maximisation of initial output too soon can jeopardise the prospects for alliances positioned for the long term. Second, the goals of many alliances may not be readily quantifiable. For instance, a partnership's objectives may involve obtaining access to a market or blocking a competitor.

Many alliances need considerable time before they are ready to be judged on conventional output measures. Only after partnerships mature (i.e. when the operations of the alliance are well established and well understood) can managers gradually shift to measure output, such as profits and cash flows.

Thus expecting too much too soon in terms of profit and cash flows from an alliance working under risky conditions can endanger its future success.

Managing the joint venture

In recent years we have seen an increasing number of cross-border joint ventures. But it is dangerous to ignore the fact that the average lifespan for alliances is only about seven years, and nearly 80 per cent of joint ventures ultimately end in a sale by one of the partners.

Harrigan's model (Figure 11.6) can be used as a framework for explaining this high 'divorce rate'.

Figure 11.6 Model of joint-venture activity

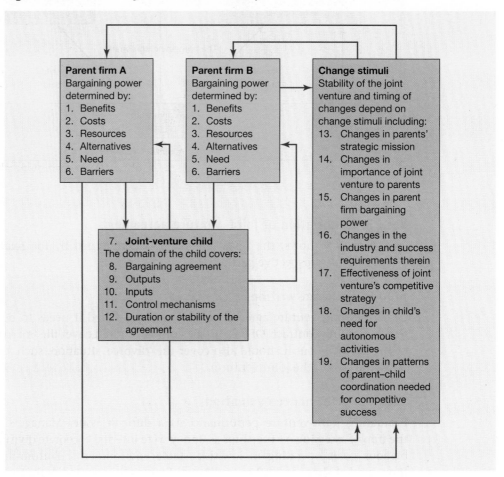

Source: Harrigan, 1985, p. 52.

Changes in bargaining power

According to Bleeke and Ernst (1994), the key to understanding the 'divorce' of the two parents is changes in their respective bargaining power. Let us assume that we have established a joint venture with the task of penetrating markets with a new product. In the initial stages of the relationship the product and technology provider generally has the most power. But unless those products and technologies are proprietary and unique power usually shifts to the party that controls distribution channels and thus customers.

The bargaining power is also strongly affected by the balance of learning and teaching. A company that is good at learning can access and internalise its partner's capabilities more easily, and is likely to become less dependent on its partner as the alliance evolves. Before entering a joint venture some companies see it as an inter-mediate stage before acquiring the other partner. By entering a joint venture the prospective buyer of the partner is in a better position to assess the true value of such intangible assets as brands, distribution networks, people and systems. This experience reduces the risk that the buyer will make an uninformed decision and buy an expensive 'lemon' (Nanda and Williamson, 1995).

Other change stimuli and potential conflicts

Diverging goals

As the joint venture progresses the goals of the two partners may diverge. For example, unacceptable positions can develop in the local market when the self-interest of one partner conflicts with the interest of the joint venture as a whole, as in the pricing of a single-source input or raw material.

Double management

A potential problem is the matter of control. By definition, a joint venture must deal with double management. If a partner has less than 50 per cent ownership that partner must in effect let the majority partner make decisions. If the board of directors has a 50–50 split it is difficult for the board to make a decision quickly if at all.

Repatriation of profits

Conflicts can also arise with regard to issues such as repatriation of profits, where the local partner desires to reinvest them in the joint venture while the other partner wishes to repatriate them or invest them in other operations.

Mixing different cultures

An organization's culture is the set of values, beliefs and conventions that influence the behaviour and goals of its employees. This is often quite different from the culture of the host country and the partner organization. Thus, developing a shared culture is central to the success of the alliance.

Partnering is inherently very people oriented. To the extent that the cultures of the partners are different, making the alliance work may prove difficult. Cultural differences often result in an 'us versus them' situation. Cultural norms should be consistent with management's vision of the alliance's ideal culture. This may entail creating norms as well as nurturing those that already exist. The key to developing a culture is to acknowledge its existence and to manage it carefully. Bringing two organizations together and letting nature take its course is a recipe for failure. Language differences are also an obvious hurdle for an international alliance.

Ignoring the local culture will almost certainly destroy the chances of it accepting the alliance's product or service. Careful study of the culture prior to embarking on the venture is vital. Again, extensive use of local managers is usually preferred.

Shared equity

Shared equity may also involve an unequal sharing of the burden. Occasionally, international companies with 50–50 joint ventures believe that they are giving more than 50 per cent of the technology, management skill and other factors that contribute to the success of the operation, but are receiving only half the profits. Of course, the national partner contributes local knowledge and other intangibles that may be underestimated. Nevertheless, some international companies believe that the local partner gets too much of a 'free ride'.

Developing trust in joint ventures

Developing trust takes time. The first times that companies work together their chances of succeeding are very slight. But once they find ways to work together all sorts of opportunities appear. Working together on relatively small projects initially helps develop trust and determine compatibility while minimising economic risk. Each partner has a chance to gauge the skills and contributions of the other, and further investment can then be considered. Of course, winning together in the marketplace on a project of any scale is a great way to build trust and overcome differences. It usually serves as a precursor to more ambitious joint efforts.

Providing an exit strategy

As indicated earlier, there is a significant probability that a newly formed joint venture will fail, even if the previously mentioned key principles are followed. The anticipated market may not develop, one of the partner's capabilities may have been overestimated, the corporate strategy of one of the partners may have changed, or the partners may simply be incompatible. Whatever the reason for the failure, the parties should prepare for such an outcome by addressing the issue in the partnership contract. The contract should provide for the liquidation or distribution of partnership assets, including any technology developed by the alliance.

11.6   Other intermediate entry modes

Management contracting emphasises the growing importance of services and management know-how. The typical case of management contracting is where one firm (contractor) supplies management know-how to another company that provides the capital and takes care of the operating value chain functions in the foreign country. Normally the contracts undertaken are concerned with management operating/control systems and training local staff to take over when the contracts are completed. It is usually not the intention of the contractor to continue operating after the contract expires. Normally it is the philosophy to operate, transfer know-how to the local staff and then depart. This will usually give a strong competitive position to pick up other management contracts in the area.

Management contracts typically arise in situations where one company seeks the management know-how of another company with established experience in the field. The lack of management capability is most evident for developing countries. Normally the financial compensation to the contractor for the management services provided is a management fee, which may be fixed irrespective of the financial performance or may be a percentage of the profit (Luostarinen and Welch, 1990). The advantages and disadvantages of management contracting are listed in Table 11.5.

Other management contracts may be part of a deal to sell a processing plant as a project or a turnkey operation. This issue will be dealt with more intensively in Chapter 13 (section 13.8).

Table 11.5 Advantages and disadvantages of the different intermediate modes

Intermediate entry mode	Advantages	Disadvantages
Contract manufacturing (seen from the contractor's viewpoint)	Permits low-risk market entry. No local investment (cash, time and executive talent) with no risk of nationalisation or expropriation. Retention of control over R&D, marketing and sales/after-sales service. Avoids currency risks and financing problems. A locally made image, which may assist in sales, especially to government or official bodies. Entry into markets otherwise protected by tariffs or other barriers. Possible cost advantage if local costs (primarily labour costs) are lower. Avoids intra-corporate transfer-pricing problems that can arise with a subsidiary.	Transfer of production know-how is difficult. Contract manufacture is only possible when a satisfactory and reliable manufacturer can be found – not always an easy task. Extensive technical training will often have to be given to the local manufacturer's staff. As a result, at the end of the contract, the subcontractor could become a formidable competitor. Control over manufacturing quality is difficult to achieve despite the ultimate sanction of refusal to accept substandard goods. Possible supply limitation if the production is taking place in developing countries.
Licensing (seen from the licensor's viewpoint)	Increases the income on products already developed as a result of expensive research. Permits entry into markets that are otherwise closed on account of high rates of duty, import quotas and so on. A viable option where manufacture is near the customer's base. Requires little capital investment and should provide a higher rate of return on capital employed. There may be valuable spin-off if the licensor can sell other products or components to the licensee. If these parts are for products being manufactured locally or machinery, there may also be some tariff concessions on their import. The licensor is not exposed to the danger of nationalisation or expropriation of assets. Because of the limited capital requirements, new products can be rapidly exploited, on a worldwide basis, before competition develops. The licensor can take immediate advantage of the licensee's local marketing and distribution organization and of existing customer contacts. Protects patents, especially in countries that give weak protection for products not produced locally. Local manufacture may also be an advantage in securing government contracts.	The licensor is ceding certain sales territories to the licensee for the duration of the contract; should it fail to live up to expectations, renegotiation may be expensive. When the licensing agreement finally expires, the licensor may find he or she has established a competitor in the former licensee. The licensee may prove less competent than expected at marketing or other management activities. Costs may even grow faster than income. The licensee, even if it reaches an agreed minimum turnover, may not fully exploit the market, leaving it open to the entry of competitors, so that the licensor loses control of the marketing operation. Danger of the licensee running short of funds, especially if considerable plant expansion is involved or an injection of capital is required to sustain the project. This danger can be turned to advantage if the licensor has funds available by a general expansion of the business through a partnership. Licence fees are normally a small percentage of turnover, about 5%, and will often compare unfavourably with what might be obtained from a company's own manufacturing operation. Lack of control over licensee operations. Quality control of the product is difficult – and the product will often be sold under the licensor's brand name. Negotiations with the licensee, and sometimes with local government, are costly. Governments often impose conditions on transferral of royalties or on component supply.

(continued)

Table 11.5 continued

Intermediate entry mode	Advantages	Disadvantages
Franchising (seen from franchisor's viewpoint)	Greater degree of control compared to licensing. Low-risk, low-cost entry mode (the franchisees are the ones investing in the necessary equipment and know-how). Using highly motivated business contacts with money, local market knowledge and experience. Ability to develop new and distant international markets, relatively quickly and on a larger scale than otherwise possible. Generating economies of scale in marketing to international customers. Precursor to possible future direct investment in foreign market.	The search for competent franchisees can be expensive and time consuming. Lack of full control over franchisee's operations, resulting in problems with cooperation, communications, quality control, etc. Costs of creating and marketing a unique package of products and services recognised internationally. Costs of protecting goodwill and brand name. Problems with local legislation, including transfers of money, payments of franchise fees and government-imposed restrictions on franchise agreements. Opening up internal business knowledge may create potential future competitor. Risk to the company's international profile and reputation if some franchisees underperform ('free riding' on valuable brand names).
Joint venture (seen from parent's viewpoint)	Access to expertise and contacts in local markets. Each partner agrees to a joint venture to gain access to the other partner's skills and resources. Typically, the international partner contributes financial resources, technology or products. The local partner provides the skills and knowledge required for managing a business in its country. Each partner can concentrate on that part of the value chain where the firm has its core competence. Reduced market and political risk. Shared knowledge and resources: compared to wholly owned subsidiary, less capital and fewer management resources are required. Economies of scale by pooling skills and resources (resulting in e.g. lower marketing costs). Overcomes host government restrictions. May avoid local tariffs and non-tariff barriers. Shared risk of failure. Less costly than acquisitions. Possibly better relations with national governments through having a local partner (meets host country pressure for local participation).	Objectives of the respective partners may be incompatible, resulting in conflicts. Contributions to joint venture can become disproportionate. Loss of control over foreign operations. Large investments of financial, technical or managerial resources favour greater control than is possible in a joint venture. Completion might overburden a company's staff. Partners may become locked into long-term investments from which it is difficult to withdraw. Transfer pricing problems as goods pass between partners. The importance of the venture to each partner might change over time. Cultural differences may result in possible differences in management culture among participating firms. Loss of flexibility and confidentiality. Problems of management structures and dual parent staffing of joint ventures. Nepotism perhaps the established norm.
Management contracting (seen from contractor's viewpoint)	If direct investment or export is considered too risky – for commercial or political reasons – this alternative might be relevant. As with other intermediate entry modes, management contracts may be linked together with other forms of operation in foreign markets. Allows a company to maintain market involvement, so puts it in a better position to exploit any opportunity that may arise. Organizational learning: if a company is in its early development stages of internationalization, a management contract may offer an efficient way of learning about foreign markets and international business.	Training future competitors: the management transfer package may in the end create a competitor for the contractor. Creates a great demand for key personnel. Such staff are not always available, especially in SMEs. Considerable effort needs to be put into building lines of communication at local level as well as back to contractor. Potential conflict between the contractor and the local government as regards the policy of the contract venture. Little control, which also limits the ability of a contractor to develop the capacity of the venture.

| Exhibit 11.1 | McDonald's + Coca-Cola + Disney = a powerful alliance |

Today business is being driven by two fashionable ideas: globalization and core competences. The first compels companies to look for ways to sell their product in as many different places as possible, which often requires other people to help them. The second, the fashion for a firm sticking to what it does best, means that they must often let outsiders help them with everything else.

The ties binding Coca-Cola, McDonald's and Disney vary enormously.

McDonald's ⟷ Disney

In 1997 McDonald's and Disney began a formal 10-year alliance. The first specific outcome was a Disney film, *Flubber*, whose box-office returns were helped by tie-ins at McDonald's. In July 1998 a promotion started of *Armageddon*, a $111 million film starring Bruce Willis, with McDonald's selling tickets and special 'Astromeals' at each of its 23,500 restaurants worldwide. This time the target was not children but young adults – a market in which McDonald's is weaker.

McDonald's ⟷ Coca-Cola

This alliance has no formal agreement – no piece of paper to fall back on. Although Coca-Cola sells drinks to other restaurants, its relationship with McDonald's goes far beyond that of a mere supplier. It has helped its partner to set up new operations around the world. Coca-Cola is sold in almost twice as many countries as McDonald's.

Coca-Cola ⟷ Disney

Coca-Cola's ties to Disney are probably the weakest of the three – but they are still considerable. Coca-Cola has been the sole provider of soft drinks at Disney parks since 1955, and it has had a marketing alliance in place since 1985. Coca-Cola has also helped Disney overseas.

Figure 11.7 McDonald's + Coca-Cola + Disney = a powerful alliance

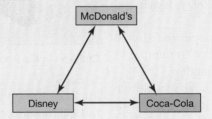

Questions

1. What is it that makes the Coca-Cola–Disney–McDonald's triumvirate so powerful in the globalization process?
2. Which factors could make the alliance of Coca-Cola–Disney–McDonald's break up?

| 11.7 | Summary |

The advantages and disadvantages of the different intermediate entry modes are summarised in Table 11.5.

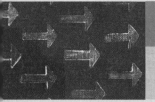

CASE STUDY 11.1   Ka-Boo-Ki

Licensing in the LEGO brand

The Danish toy manufacturer LEGO is known worldwide for its LEGO bricks. LEGO is a strong and well-known brand. At the end of 1991 LEGO management received the result of three consumer surveys:

■ Landour Associates completed a survey at the end of 1991 of the best brands' 'image power' among 11,000 representatively chosen adults aged between 18 and 65 in the United States, Japan and Europe (Belgium, France, the Netherlands, Italy, Spain, the United Kingdom and Sweden). 'Image power' is a measure of brands' impact, where consumers' awareness of the world's leading brands is combined with their judgement of the brands' quality. In the United States and Japan LEGO was not placed among the top 10, but the results from Europe were impressive. Here LEGO was placed at number 5 after four car brands: Mercedes-Benz, Rolls-Royce, Porsche and BMW. LEGO was in front of brands such as Nestlé, Rolex, Jaguar and Ferrari.

■ A US survey, conducted in Europe, the United States and Japan, showed that LEGO is number 13 in the list of most appreciated brands.

■ A survey by a German market analysis institute showed that LEGO is one of the most well-known brands in toys in the new German Federal Republic, with an awareness share of 67 per cent. Matchbox is number 2 with 41 per cent.

The LEGO management has decided to exploit this strong brand image. A managing director for the new business area LEGO Licensing A/S has been appointed. The company's objective is to generate income from licensing suitable partners, which will use the LEGO brand in marketing their own products.

The LEGO management has noticed that Coca-Cola has an income of DKK3 billion from licensing alone. Coca-Cola's strategy can be characterised as 'brand milking', where a brand is sold to the highest bidder in each product area.

Children in Ka-Boo-Ki clothes (Lego licence)

Ideas become viable

In 1993 the idea of licensing the LEGO brand became viable for the Danish textile firm Ka-Boo-Ki, as it was given the rights to use the LEGO brand in connection with the production and sale of children's clothes. For Ka-Boo-Ki's Managing Director, Torben Klausen, the idea of producing children's clothes is not new. He was earlier employed in LEGO's international marketing department, where he was in charge of coordinating the European marketing of LEGO bricks. From this position he was able to follow the development of the licensing concept. Since 1993 things have been developing very fast. In mid-1997 Ka-Boo-Ki, which has invested a considerable amount of money in the R&D of LEGO children's clothes, was selling to approximately 900 shops, primarily in Scandinavia and England.

Torben Klausen says:

> We received a strong international brand from the first day. But in selling LEGO children's comes an obligation to live up to the LEGO company's unique quality demands. LEGO must approve all new models that are put on the market, and that is between 350 and 400 a year.

LEGO children's clothes distinguish themselves from other brands by being functional and having strong colours and an uncompromising quality. This means a relatively high price for the clothes, and that the products are not sold in discount shops. The clothes are sold on the basis of a shop-in-shop concept, where merchandising and display facilities are very important.

You have just been employed by LEGO Licensing A/S in connection with the development of the licensing data. You are given the following assignments.

Questions

1. What are the most important factors determining future market demand for LEGO children's clothes from Ka-Boo-Ki?

2. Which other products could be considered for licensing out the LEGO brand?

3. List some criteria for choosing suitable licensees and future products for the LEGO brand (licensing out).

4. What values/benefits can LEGO transfer to the licensee (e.g. Ka-Boo-Ki) apart from the use of the LEGO brand?

5. What values/benefits can the licensee transfer to the licensor?

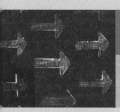

CASE STUDY 11.2   Bayer and GlaxoSmithKline

Can the X–coalition and the product Levitra challenge Viagra's market leader position

In November 2001 Bayer and GlaxoSmithKline (GSK) signed a worldwide co-promotion and co-development agreement (**www.bayergsk.com**) to launch a new treatment for men seeking to improve their erectile function, Levitra. Since then both companies have been working together on the development and future marketing of the product. Under the terms of a joint promotion agreement Bayer will mainly take care of up-stream activities (manufacturing the product and being responsible for all regulatory work required to obtain product approval), whereas GSK will promote Levitra worldwide. Selling and future development expenses, along with all the profits, will be shared by the two companies. Bayer and GSK will form a committee to oversee the marketing and future development of the product. If Bayer is seeking sales force strength in the alliance GSK's sales performance indicates that the choice has been a wise one. GSK's US sales force is the largest of all the pharmaceutical companies, with 8,000 representatives.

In March 2003 German drug maker Bayer won approval to sell the new impotence drug, Levitra, across the European Union In August, 2003, the same thing happened in the US market. The US Food and Drug Administration (FDA) approved Levitra, an orange pill compared to Viagra's blue, based on studies showing that men were on average five times more likely to achieve an erection suitable for intercourse when taking the pill compared with those given a dummy medicine. It hopes it will win market share from Pfizer's breakthrough blockbuster Viagra. It took more than a year

to whittle about 700 possible names down to Levitra, derived from *le*, the French masculine pronoun, and *vita*, Latin for life.

Like Pfizer Inc.'s market-leading Viagra, Levitra is an oral drug. But Levitra has been shown in clinical trials to work much faster – in around 20 minutes compared with around 40 minutes for Viagra. In one large-scale trial submitted to European regulators, 80 per cent of men taking Levitra reported an improvement in erectile function, compared with 28 per cent on a placebo.

Viagra is forecast to reap sales of over $1.5 billion in 2002, while Bayer expects Levitra, which is marketed by the UK's GlaxoSmithKline, to reach its sales peak when some $1 billion worth will have been realised by 2006, once it secures approval in the United States. Bayer was introducing the round, orange pills in the beginning of April 2003. The product is already approved in several Latin American countries.

The battle for dominance in a condition that affects about one in five men is expected to be fierce. Cialis, a drug from Indianapolis-based Eli Lilly/Ico, a joint venture between Eli Lilly & Co. (**www.lilly.com**) and Icos Corp. (**www.icos.com**) won European approval in 2002 and hit pharmacies in the United States the following year, so Cialis is a little ahead of Levitra.

All the drugs work in the same manner so some doctors believe it may be difficult for Levitra and Cialis to establish themselves when Viagra has been around for five years. Others say the drugs are an option for those whose conditions are not helped by Viagra.

The price of Levitra in Britain is £19.34 ($30.86)

for a pack of four 10 mg tablets, or £23.50 for a pack of four 20 mg tablets – identical to the price of Viagra 50 mg and 100 mg. Cialis is priced at £19.34 for four pills, irrespective of whether patients use the 10 mg or 20 mg dose.

Sales of Pfizer's blue, diamond-shaped Viagra pills totalled $1.7 billion in 2001. At that time it was the only significant prescription product for erectile dysfunction. Estimates suggest sales of erectile dysfunction drugs will reach £4 billion globally within six to seven years. In the United States 30 million men suffer from some form of erectile dysfunction and only 10 per cent receive treatment. Worldwide the number of sufferers is 152 million.

Leverkusen-based Bayer is still suffering from the 2001 withdrawal of the cholesterol lowering drug Lipobay. The company that invented aspirin said in 2002 it was prepared to merge its drugs business with a larger rival. But taking on Pfizer, the biggest drug company in the world, will not be easy. It spent about $100 million on marketing Viagra last year and has an army of sales people.

Source: 'Germany's Bayer gets green light for new impotence drug in Europe', Associated Press, 7 March (**www.miami.com/mld/miamiherald/business/5342464.htm**)

Questions

1. Explain the term 'X-coalitition' (Figure 11.1), by describing the role of the two partners in the alliance.

2. What are the benefits of the alliance for each partner?

3. Are there any disadvantages in this alliance for either partner?

4. Describe a possible course of internationalization.

For further exercises and cases, see this book's website at
www.booksites.net/hollensen

Questions for discussion

1. Why are joint ventures preferred by host countries as an entry strategy for foreign firms?

2. Why are strategic alliances used in new product development?

3. Under what circumstances should franchising be considered? How do these circumstances vary from those leading to licensing?

4. Do you believe that licensing in represents a feasible long-term product development strategy for a company? Discuss in relation to in-house product development.

5. Why would a firm consider forming partnerships with competitors?

6. Apart from the management fees involved, what benefits might a firm derive from entering into management contracts overseas?

References

Bleeke, J. and Ernst, D. (1994) *Collaborating to Compete: Using strategic alliances and acquisitions in the global marketplace*, John Wiley, New York.

Bradley, F. (1995) *International Marketing Strategy* (2nd edn), Prentice Hall, Hemel Hempstead.

Carstairs, R.T. and Welch, L.S. (1981) *A Study of Outward Foreign Licensing of Technology by Australian Companies*, Licensing Executives Society of Australia, Canberra.

Harrigan, K.R. (1985) *Strategies for Joint Ventures*, Lexington Books and D.C. Heath, Lexington, MA.

Lorange, P. and Roos, J. (1995) *Strategiske allianser i globale strategier*, Norges Eksportråd, Oslo.

Lowe, J. and Crawford, N. (1984) *Technology Licensing and the Small Firm*, Gower, Aldershot.

Luostarinen, R. and Welch, L. (1990) *International Business Operations*, Helsinki School of Economics, Helsinki.

Nanda, A. and Williamson, P.J. (1995) 'Use joint ventures to ease the pain of restructuring', *Harvard Business Review*, November–December, pp. 119–28.

Paliwoda, S. (1993) *International Marketing*, Heinemann, Oxford.

Perkins, J.S. (1987) 'How licensing and franchising differ', *Les Nouvelles*, vol. 22, no. 4, pp. 155–8.

Porter, M.E. and Fuller, M.B. (1986) 'Coalition and global strategy', in Porter, M.E. (ed.), *Competition in Global Strategies*, Harvard Business School Press, Boston, MA.

Walmsley, J. (1982) *Handbook of International Joint Ventures*, Graham & Trotman Ltd, London.

Young, S., Hamill, J. Wheeler, S. and Davies, J.R. (1989) *International Market Entry and Development*, Harvester Wheatsheaf/Prentice Hall, Hemel Hempstead.

Further reading

Andersen, P.H. (2000) 'A foot in the door: relationship marketing efforts towards transaction-oriented customers', *Journal of Market-Focused Management*, vol. 5, pp. 91–118.

BatNir, A. and Smith, A. (2002) 'Interfirm alliances in the small business: the role of social networks', *Journal of Small Business Management*, vol. 40, no. 3, pp. 219–32.

Berdrow, I. and Lane, H.W. (2003) 'International joint ventures: creating value through successful knowledge management', *Journal of World Business*, forthcoming.

Chetty, S. and Wilson, H.I.M. (2003) 'Collaborating with competitors to acquire resources', *International Business Review*, vol. 12, pp. 61–81.

Clarke-Hill, C., Li, H. and Davies, B. (2003) 'The Paradox of Co-Operation and Competition in Strategic Alliances: Towards a Multi-Paradigm Approach', *Management Research News*, vol. 26, No.1, pp. 1–20.

Buckley, P.J., Glaister, K.W and Husan, R. (2002) 'International joint ventures: partnering skills and cross-cultural issues', *Long Range Planning*, vol. 35, pp. 113–34.

Glaister, K.W., Husan, R. and Buckley, P.J. (2003) 'Learning to manage international joint ventures', *International Business Review*, vol. 12, no. 1, pp. 83–108.

Hougaard, S. and Bjerre, M. (2000), *Strategic Relationship Management*, Samfundsliteratur, Copenhagen.

Sashi, C.M and Karuppur, D.P. (2002) 'Franchising in global markets: towards a conceptual framework', *International Marketing Review*, vol. 19, no. 5, pp. 499–52.

Wilkinson, I. and Young, L. (2002) 'On cooperating: firms, relations and networks', *Journal of Business Research*, vol. 55, pp. 123–132.

12 Hierarchical modes

Contents

Learning objectives

After studying this chapter you should be able to do the following:

- Describe the main hierarchical modes:
  - domestic-based representatives;
  - resident sales representatives;
  - foreign sales subsidiary;
  - sales and production subsidiary; and
  - region centres.

- Compare and contrast the two investment alternatives: acquisition versus greenfield.

- Explain the different determinants that influence the decision to withdraw investments from a foreign market.

12.1 Introduction

The final group of entry modes is the hierarchical modes, where the firm completely owns and controls the foreign entry mode. Here it is a question of where the control in the firm lies. The degree of control that head office can exert on the subsidiary will depend on how many and which value chain functions can be transferred to the market. This again depends on the allocation of responsibility and competence between head office and the subsidiary, and how the firm wants to develop this on an international level. An organization that is not 100 per cent owned will here be viewed as an export mode or an intermediate mode. The following example, though, may suggest some of the problems involved in this sharp division: a majority-owned (e.g. 75 per cent) joint venture is according to definition an intermediate mode, but in practice a firm with 75 per cent will generally have nearly full control, similar to a hierarchical mode.

If a producer wants greater influence and control over local marketing than export modes can give it is natural to consider creating own companies in the foreign markets. However, this shift involves an investment, except in the case of the firm having its own sales force, which is considered an operating cost (Figure 12.1).

As a firm goes through Figure 12.1 it chooses to decentralise more and more of its activities to the main foreign markets. In other words, it transfers the responsibility of performing the value chain functions to the local management in the different countries. While moving through Figure 12.1 the firm also goes from one internationalization stage to another (Perlmutter, 1969):

- *Ethnocentric orientation*, represented by the domestic-based sales representatives. This orientation represents an extension of the marketing methods used in the home country to foreign markets.
- *Polycentric orientation*, represented by country subsidiaries. This orientation is based on the assumption that markets/countries around the world are so different that the only way to succeed internationally is to manage each country as a separate market with its own subsidiary and adapted marketing mix.
- *Regiocentric orientation*, represented by a region of the world (section 12.5).

Figure 12.1 Hierarchical modes in a value chain perspective

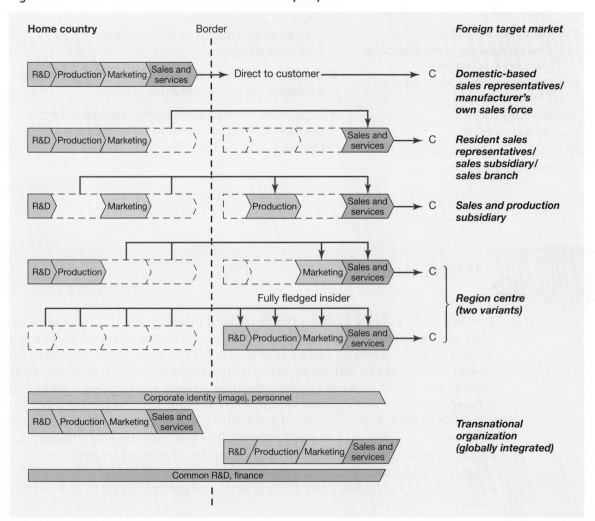

- *Geocentric orientation*, represented by the transnational organization. This orientation is based on the assumption that the markets around the world consist of similarities and differences and that it is possible to create a transnational strategy which takes advantage of the similarities between the markets by using synergy effects to leverage learning on a worldwide basis.

The following description and discussion concerning hierarchical modes takes Figure 12.1 as its starting point.

12.2   Domestic-based sales representatives

A domestic-based sales representative is one who resides in one country, often the home country of the employer, and travels abroad to perform the sales function. As the sales representative is a company employee better control of sales activities can be achieved than with independent intermediaries. Whereas a company has no control over the attention that an agent or distributor gives to its products or the amount of market feedback provided, it can insist that various activities be performed by its sales representatives.

The use of company employees also shows a commitment to the customer that the use of agents or distributors may lack. Consequently they are often used in industrial markets, where there are only a few large customers that require close contact with suppliers, and where the size of orders justifies the expense of foreign travel. This method of market entry is also found when selling to government buyers and retail chains, for similar reasons.

12.3   Resident sales representatives/foreign sales branch/foreign sales subsidiary

In all these cases the actual performance of the sales function is transferred to the foreign market. These three options all display a greater customer commitment than using domestic-based sales representatives. In making the decision whether to use travelling domestic-based representatives or resident sales representatives in any particular foreign market a firm should consider the following:

- *Order making or order taking*. If the firm finds that the type of sales job it needs done in a foreign market tends towards order taking it will probably choose a travelling domestic-based sales representative; and vice versa.
- *The nature of the product*. If the product is technical and complex in nature and a lot of servicing/supply of parts is required the travelling salesperson is not an efficient entry method. A more permanent foreign base is needed.

Sometimes firms find it relevant to establish a formal branch office, to which a resident salesperson is assigned. A foreign branch is an extension and a legal part of the firm. A foreign branch also often employs nationals of the country in which it is located as salespeople. If foreign market sales develop in a positive direction the firm (at a certain point) may consider establishing a wholly owned sales subsidiary. A foreign subsidiary is a local company owned and operated by a foreign company under the laws of the host country.

The sales subsidiary provides complete control of the sales function. The firm will often keep a central marketing function at its home base, but sometimes a local marketing function can be included in the sales subsidiary. When the sales function is organised as a sales subsidiary (or when sales activities are performed) all foreign orders are channelled through the subsidiary, which then sells to foreign buyers at normal wholesale or retail prices. The foreign sales subsidiary purchases the products to be sold from the parent company at a price. This, of course, creates the problem of intra-company transfer pricing. In Chapter 16 this problem will be discussed in further detail.

One of the major reasons for choosing sales subsidiaries is the possibility of transferring greater autonomy and responsibility to these subunits, being close to the customer. However, another reason for establishing sales subsidiaries may be the tax advantage. This is particularly important for companies headquartered in high-tax countries. With proper planning companies can establish subsidiaries in countries having low business income taxes and gain an advantage by not paying taxes in their home country on the foreign-generated income until such income is actually repatriated to them. Of course the precise tax advantages that are possible with such subsidiaries depend upon the tax laws in the home country compared to the host country.

12.4   Sales and production subsidiary

Especially in developing countries sales subsidiaries may be perceived as taking money out of the country and contributing nothing of value to the host country in which they are based. In those countries a sales subsidiary will generally not be in existence long before there are local demands for a manufacturing or production base.

Generally, if the company believes that its products have long-term market potential in a politically relatively stable country, then only full ownership of sales and production will provide the level of control necessary to meet fully the firm's strategic objectives. However, this entry mode requires great investment in terms of management time, commitment and money. There are considerable risks, too, as subsequent withdrawal from the market can be extremely costly – not simply in terms of financial outlay but also in terms of reputation in the international and domestic market, particularly with customers and staff.

Japanese companies have used this strategy to build a powerful presence in international markets over a long period of time. Their patience has been rewarded with high market shares and substantial profits, but this has not been achieved overnight. They have sometimes spent more than five years gaining an understanding of markets, customers and competition, as well as selecting locations for manufacturing, before making a significant move.

The main reasons for establishing some kind of local production are as follows:

- *To defend existing business.* Japanese car imports to Europe were subject to restrictions, and as their sales increased so they became more vulnerable. With the development of the single European market Nissan and Toyota set up operations in the United Kingdom.
- *To gain new business.* Local production demonstrates strong commitment and is the best way to persuade customers to change suppliers, particularly in the industrial markets where service and reliability are often the main factors when making purchasing decisions.

- *To save costs.* By locating production facilities overseas costs can be saved in a variety of areas such as labour, raw materials and transport.
- *To avoid government restrictions* that might be in force to restrict imports of certain goods.

Assembly operations

An assembly operation is a variation of the production subsidiary. Here a foreign production plant might be set up simply to assemble components manufactured in the domestic market or elsewhere. The firm may try to retain key component manufacture in the domestic plant, allowing development, production skills and investment to be concentrated, and maintaining the benefit from economies of scale. Some parts or components may be produced in various countries (multisourcing) in order to gain each country's comparative advantage. Capital-intensive parts may be produced in advanced nations, and labour-intensive assemblies may be produced in a less developed country, where labour is abundant and labour costs are low. This strategy is common among manufacturers of consumer electronics. When a product becomes mature and faces intense price competition it may be necessary to shift all of the labour-intensive operations to LDCs. This is the principle behind the international product life cycle (IPLC): see also Chapter 15 (section 15.4).

12.5   Region centres (regional headquarters)

Until now choice of foreign entry mode has mainly been discussed in relation to one particular country. If we suspend this condition, we consider option 3 in Figure 12.2, where 'geographically focused start-up' is an attempt to serve the specialised needs of a particular region of the world. It is very difficult for competitors to imitate a successful coordination of value chain activities in a particular region, as it involves tacit knowledge and is socially complex.

The world is increasingly being regionalised through the formation of such groupings as the European Union, the North American Free Trade Area and the Association of South-East Asian Nations.

Figure 12.2 Types of international new venture

		Number of countries involved	
		Few	*Many*
Coordination of value chain activities	*Few activities coordinated across countries (primarily logistics)*	New international market makers	
		Export/import start-up ①	Multinational trader ②
	Many activities coordinated across countries	③ Geographically focused start-up	④ Global start-up

Source: Oviatt and McDougall, 1994, p. 59. Reprinted with permission by *Journal of International Business Studies (JIBS)*: Georgetown University, Washington DC.

In Figure 12.2 two examples of region centres are shown. The first variant shows that the downstream functions have been transferred to the region. In the second variant even greater commitment is shown to the region because here all the value chain activities are moved to the region, whereby the firm has become a fully fledged insider in the region. At this stage the firm has all the necessary functions in the region to compete effectively against local and regional competitors. At the same time, the firm can respond to local customer needs.

Formation of region centres implies creation of a regional headquarters or appointment of a 'lead country', which will usually play the role of coordinator and stimulator with reference to a single homogeneous product group (see Figure 12.3).

Figure 12.3 The lead country concept

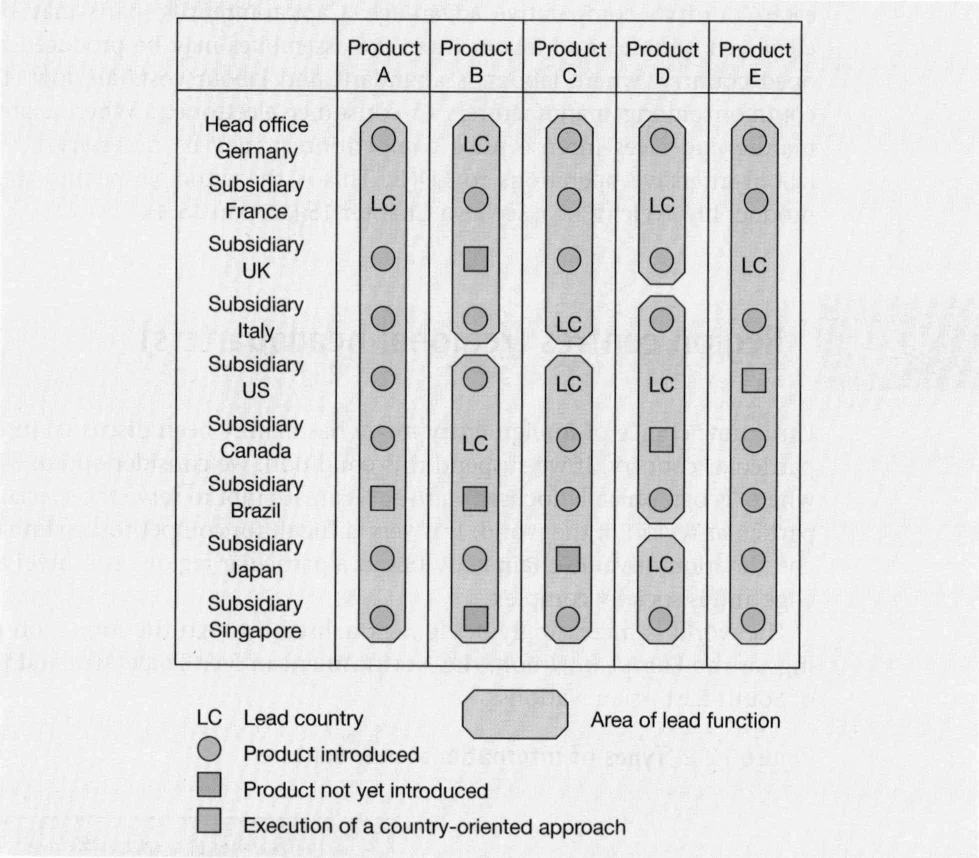

	Product A	Product B	Product C	Product D	Product E
Head office Germany	○	LC	○	○	○
Subsidiary France	LC	○	○	LC	○
Subsidiary UK	○	◻	○	○	LC
Subsidiary Italy	○	○	LC	○	○
Subsidiary US	○	○	LC	LC	◻
Subsidiary Canada	○	LC	○	◻	○
Subsidiary Brazil	◻	◻	○	○	○
Subsidiary Japan	○	○	◻	LC	○
Subsidiary Singapore	○	◻	○	○	○

LC   Lead country   Area of lead function
○   Product introduced
◻   Product not yet introduced
◻   Execution of a country-oriented approach

Source: Raffée and Kreutzer, 1989. Published with permission of Emerald Publishing Ltd.; **www.emeraldinsight.com**

The coordination role consists of ensuring three things:

- Country and business strategies are mutually coherent.
- One subsidiary does not harm another.
- Adequate synergies are fully identified and exploited across business and countries.

The stimulator role consists of two functions:

- facilitating the translation of 'global' products into local country strategies;
- supporting local subsidiaries in their development (Lasserre, 1996).

Figure 12.3 (an example of a multinational company having its head office in Germany) shows that different countries/subsidiaries can have a leading function for different product groups. In the diagram there is a world market such that for products A and E only one country/subsidiary has the coordination function on a global basis (France and the United Kingdom, respectively). For product D there are three regions with a lead country in each region.

The choice of a lead country is influenced by several factors:

- the marketing competences of the foreign subsidiaries;
- the quality of human resources in the countries represented;
- the strategic importance of the countries represented;
- location of production;
- legal restrictions of host countries.

The country with the best 'leading' competences should be chosen for the job as lead country.

Figure 12.4 shows how a firm can develop the region centre concept in the Asia-Pacific area. The countries in the Asia-Pacific area are so different that you have to proceed in a sequential way. The example is based on a country-by-country approach together with developing a regional view (Lasserre, 1995).

Figure 12.4 Developing the region centre concept in Asia–Pacific

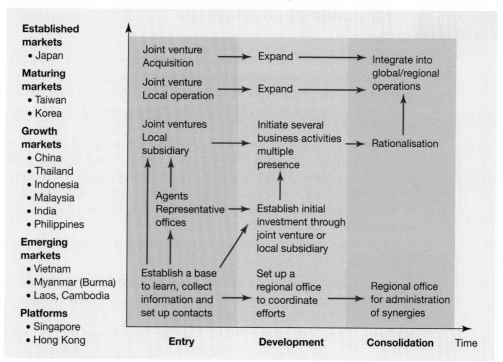

Source: Reprinted from *Long Range Planning*, Vol. 29, No. 1, Lasserre, P. (1996) 'Regional headquarters: the spearhead for Asian Pacific markets', p. 21, Copyright 1996, with permission from Elsevier.

One can distinguish five types of country in Asia, which are represented in Figure 12.4.

- The *platform countries*, such as Singapore or Hong Kong, which can be used in the starting phase as bases for gathering intelligence and initiating first contacts that can later become the centre of regional coordination. For instance, medium-sized companies with no prior experience in the region could establish their presence by setting up a 'listening post' in these countries.
- The *emerging countries*, such as Vietnam today and Myanmar (Burma) and Cambodia in the near future. The task in these countries is to establish an initial presence

through a local distributor and build the necessary relationships in order to prepare for the establishment of a local operation, either directly or through a joint venture.

- The *growth countries*, such as China and the ASEAN countries, where it is becoming urgent to establish a significant presence in order to capitalise on the opportunities generated by rapid economic development.
- The *maturing* and *established countries*, such as Korea and Taiwan, which already have significant economic infrastructures and well-established local and international competitors. In the entry phase the task here is to find a way to acquire, through massive investment, the necessary operational capability to catch competitors up.

The particular entry and pathway to development will depend upon the company's prior experience and capabilities, and on the particular strategic attractiveness of an industrial sector in a country.

Gradually the firm will start to look at all the countries in one region, because some activities, notably strategic, intelligence, financial, engineering, R&D, training and specialised services, can reap the benefits of economies of scale only by servicing the whole region.

12.6   Transnational organization

In this final stage of internationalization companies attempt to coordinate and integrate operations across national boundaries so as to achieve potential synergies on a global scale. Management views the world as a series of interrelated markets. At this stage the employees tend to identify more strongly with their company than with the country in which they operate.

Common R&D and frequent geographical exchange of human resources across borders are among the characteristics of a transnational company. The overall goal for the transnational company will be to achieve global competitiveness through recognising cross-border market similarities and differences, and linking the capabilities of the company across national boundaries. One of the relatively few international companies that have reached this stage is Unilever – see also section 8.5.

In summary, managing a transnational company requires the sensitivity to know the following:

- when a global brand makes sense or when local requirements should take precedence;
- when to transfer innovation and expertise from one market to another;
- when a local idea has global potential;
- when to bring international teams together fast to focus on key opportunities.

12.7   Establishing wholly owned subsidiaries – acquisition or greenfield

All the hierarchical modes presented in this chapter (except domestic-based sales representatives) involve investment in foreign-based facilities. In deciding to establish wholly owned operations in a country a firm can either acquire an existing company or build its own operations from scratch (greenfield investment).

Acquisition

Acquisition enables rapid entry and often provides access to distribution channels, an existing customer base and, in some cases, established brand names or corporate reputations. In some cases, too, existing management remains, providing a bridge to entry into the market and allowing the firm to acquire experience in dealing with the local market environment. This may be particularly advantageous for a firm with limited international management expertise, or little familiarity with the local market.

In saturated markets the industry is highly competitive or there are substantial entry barriers, and therefore there is little room for a new entrant. In these circumstances acquisitions may be the only feasible way of establishing a base in the host country.

Acquisitions take many forms. According to Root (1987) acquisition may be horizontal (the product lines and markets of the acquired and acquiring firms are similar), vertical (the acquired firm becomes supplier or customer of the acquiring firm), concentric (the acquired firm has the same market but different technology, or the same technology but different markets) or conglomerate (the acquired firm is in a different industry from that of the acquiring firm). No matter what form the acquisition takes, coordination and styles of management between the foreign investor and the local management team may cause problems.

Greenfield investment

The difficulties encountered with acquisitions may lead firms to prefer to establish operations from the ground up, especially where production logistics is a key industry success factor, and where no appropriate acquisition targets are available or they are too costly.

The ability to integrate operations across countries, and to determine the direction of future international expansion, is often a key motivation to establish wholly owned operations, even though it takes longer to build plants than to acquire them.

Furthermore, if the firm builds a new plant, it can not only incorporate the latest technology and equipment, but also avoid the problems of trying to change the traditional practices of an established concern. A new facility means a fresh start and an opportunity for the international company to shape the local firm into its own image and requirements.

12.8   Foreign divestment: withdrawing from a foreign market

While a vast theoretical and empirical literature has examined the determinants of entering into foreign direct investments, considerably less attention has been given to the decision to exit from a foreign market.

Most of the studies undertaken show a considerable 'loss' of foreign subsidiaries over time:

- Between 1967 and 1975 the 180 largest US-based multinationals added some 4,700 subsidiaries to their networks, but more than 2,400 affiliates were divested during the same period (Boddewyn, 1979).
- Out of 225 FDIs undertaken by large Dutch multinationals in the period 1966–88, only just over half were still in existence in 1988 (Barkema et al., 1996).

Closing down a foreign subsidiary or selling it off to another firm is a strategic decision, and the consequence may be a change of foreign entry mode (e.g. from a local sales and production subsidiary to an export mode or a joint venture), or a complete withdrawal from a host country.

The most obvious incentive to exit is profits that are too low, which in turn may be due to high costs, permanent decreases in local market demand or the entry into the industry of more efficient competitors. Besides being voluntary, the divestment may also be a result of expropriation or nationalisation in the foreign country.

In order to investigate further the question of why foreign divestments take place it is necessary to look at the specific factors that may influence incentives and barriers to exit, and thereby the probability of exiting from a foreign subsidiary. Benito (1996) classifies the specific factors into four main groups (Figure 12.5).

Figure 12.5 Divestment of foreign operation: a framework

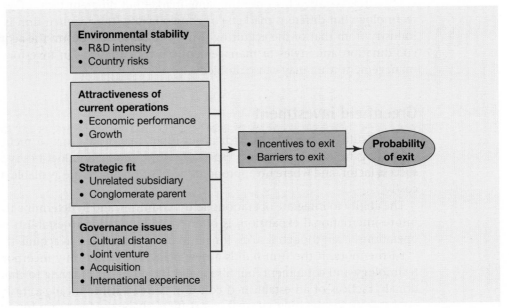

Source: Benito, 1996, Figure 2.

Environmental stability

This is a question of the predictability of the environment – competitively and politically – in which the foreign subsidiary operates:

■ *R&D intensity*. Perceived barriers to exit are likely to increase due to large market-specific investments made in R&D and the marketing of the products.
■ *Country risks*. These risks are typically outside the firm's scope of control. Political risks may often lead to forced divestment, with the result that expropriation takes place.

Attractiveness of current operations

■ *Economic performance*. Unsatisfactory economic performance (i.e. inability to produce a net contribution to overall profits) is the most obvious reason why particular subsidiaries are sold off or shut down. On the other hand, if the subsidiary is a good economic performer, the owners may see an opportunity to obtain a good price for the unit while it is performing well.

- *Growth.* Economic growth in the host country would normally make FDI even more attractive, thereby increasing the barriers to exit from such a country. However, the attractiveness of the location would make such operations more likely targets for takeovers by other investors.

Strategic fit

Unrelated expansion (i.e. diversification) increases the governance cost of the business, and economies of scale and scope are also rarely achieved by unrelated subsidiaries. Hence these factors increase the incentives to exit.

The same arguments apply to a conglomerate parent.

Governance issues

- *Cultural distance.* Closeness between home country and host countries results in easier monitoring and coordination of production and marketing activities in the various locations. Thus culturally close countries increase the barriers to exit and vice versa.
- *Joint venture and acquisition.* A joint venture with a local partner can certainly reduce barriers to the penetration of a foreign market by giving rapid access to knowledge about the local market. On the other hand, whenever a joint venture is set up with a foreign partner, both different national and corporate cultures may have an impact on its success. Joint ventures and acquisitions are put in a difficult situation in the often critical initial phases of the integration process. Thus a lack of commitment in the parent company or companies may increase the incentive to exit.
- *Experience.* Firms learn from experience how to operate in the foreign environment, and how to search for solutions to problems that emerge. As experience is accumulated it becomes easier to avoid many of the problems involved in running foreign subsidiaries and to find workable solutions if problems should arise. This also includes the unpleasant decision to close down a subsidiary.

12.9 Summary

The advantages and disadvantages of the different hierarchical entry modes are summarised in Table 12.1.

Furthermore, this chapter discussed under what circumstances foreign divestment is likely to take place. The most obvious reason to exit from a market seems to be low profits earned in the market.

Table 12.1 Advantages and disadvantages of different hierarchical entry modes

Hierarchical entry mode	Advantages	Disadvantages
Domestic-based sales representatives	Better control of sales activities compared to independent intermediaries. Close contact with large customers in foreign markets close to home country.	High travel expenses. Too expensive in foreign markets, far away from home country.
Foreign sales, branch/sales and production subsidiary	Full control of operation. Eliminates the possibility that a national partner gets a 'free ride'. Market access (sales subsidiary). Acquire market knowledge directly (sales subsidiary). Reduce transport costs (production subsidiary). Elimination of duties (production subsidiary). Access to raw materials and labour (production subsidiary).	High initial capital investment required (subsidiary). Loss of flexibility. High risk (market, political and economic). Taxation problems.
Region centres/transnational organization	Achieves potential synergies on a regional/global scale. Regional/global scale efficiency. Leverage learning on a cross-national basis. Resources and people are flexible and can be put into operating units around the world.	Possible threats: – increasing bureaucracy. Limited national-level responsiveness and flexibility. A national manager can feel he or she has no influence. Missing communication between head office and region centres.
Acquisition	Rapid entry to new markets. Gaining quick access to: – distribution channels; – a qualified labour force; – existing management experience; – local knowledge; – contacts with local market and government; – established brand names/ reputation.	Usually an expensive option. High risk (taking over companies that are regarded as part of a country's heritage can raise considerable national resentment if it seems that they are being taken over by foreign interests). Possible threats: – lack of integration with existing operation. Communication and coordination problems between acquired firm and acquirer.
Greenfield investment	Possible to build in an 'optimum' format, i.e. in a way that fits the interests of the firm (e.g. integrating production with home base production). Possible to integrate state-of-the-art technology (resulting in increased operational efficiency).	High investment cost. Slow entry of new markets (time-consuming process).

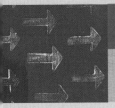

CASE STUDY 12.1   Durex condoms in Japan

SSL will sell Durex condoms in the Japanese market through its own organization

Durex condoms will go on sale in Japan for the first time after SSL International, the manufacturer and distributor of healthcare products, announced it is to expand its operation in the country. SSL International was formed in June 1999 by the merger of Seton Scholl Health Care with LIG (London International Group). Durex is the most sold condom brand in the world, available in more than 140 countries, and with approximately 22 per cent of the global branded condom market. The Durex brand name was registered in 1929, with the name Durex derived from Durability, Reliability and Excellence.

Generally the SSL managers run a brand-oriented strategy: 'We want Durex to be the Coca-Cola of the condom world'. The move into Japan was made possible by the 1999 merger. Seton Scholl has its own presence in Japan, with marketing and distribution networks set up, whereas LIG did not. Through Seton Scholl Japan it already distributes Scholl products such as shoes and other footwear products throughout the country as well as surgical gloves, which are manufactured by the old LIG company.

SSL has terminated a long-term contract with Okamoto, the largest supplier of condoms in Japan, freeing it to vie for a share of the country's 200 million condom market. The Chief Executive, said, 'It now makes sense for us to take control of our own destiny in Japan.' SSL aims to have won 5 per cent of the market within five years, generating £10 million worth of new revenue. SSL has bought out its partner in Seton Scholl Japan, giving it full control. Iain Carter again: 'We saw more prospect of generating value for shareholders by going it alone in Japan.' He added that Durex was already well known as an international brand in the country.

The Japanese market for condoms is said to be the world's largest, with annual turnover worth about £200 million. It is dominated by Okamoto (42 per cent market share) and other locally produced products. The Japanese market is as large because until June 1999 the contraceptive pill was banned and most people had to rely on condoms for birth control. Experts say that it will still take one or two generations before the pill is widely used in Japan.

One reason why it took 40 years for the contraceptive pill to be legalised in Japan was because of lobbying by condom-makers against its introduction. Japanese health officials said they were concerned that use of the pill, instead of condoms, would spread sexually transmitted diseases. It was even claimed, by other opponents, that the urine of women on the pill would pollute rivers and deform fish.

Source: adapted from: *Financial Times* (2000) 'SSL goes it alone in Japan with Durex', 3 February; *New Media Age* (1997) 'Condom brand goes global on web', 1 May.

Questions

1. What were the main motives for SSL establishing their own distribution channels for condoms in Japan?

2. What are the major barriers to SSL reaching a higher market share for condoms in Japan?

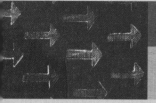

CASE STUDY 12.2   The Fred Hollows Foundation

A non-profit organization establishes lens production factories in Nepal and Eritrea

The Fred Hollows Foundation (**www.hollows.org**) is a non-profit and non-government organization that was established in Sydney, Australia in 1992. Its main aim is to raise funds to continue the work of Professor Fred Hollows in reducing the problems of cataract blindness in developing countries by offering a relatively cheap and quick solution. Cataract blindness is a huge problem in developing countries but it can be treated or reversed with a relatively simple operation using an intraocular lens (**IOL**). Normally such an operation costs too much for people in developing countries, so, in 1994 The Fred Hollows Foundation built IOL manufacturing facilities in Eritrea and Nepal. The IOLs produced by commercial manufacturers are more expensive than those produced by organizations like The Fred Hollows IOL Laboratories in these two countries. At the two factories IOLs are now produced for approximately $5–6 and are sold for about $10. IOLs produced in western Europe or North America are at least ten times as expensive and cost from $150 upwards.

The Fred Hollows Foundation has equiped and trained over 750 doctors in more than 29 developing countries in Africa, Asia and the Pacific since it was established in 1992. Europe is now being considered as the next export market for the lens. However, in Europe there is most demand for soft lenses, as opposed to the hard lenses that The Fred Hollows Foundation produces.

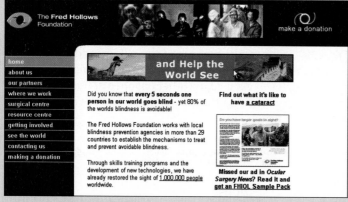

Courtesy of The Fred Hollows Foundation

Questions

1. What could have been the motives for choosing Eritrea and Nepal as the countries for investment?

2. Is it a good idea to start exporting IOLs to Europe?

3. Which marketing initiatives would you recommend be implemented in order to raise funding for The Fred Hollows Foundation?

For further exercises and cases, see this book's website at **www.booksites.net/hollensen**

Questions for discussion

1. By what criteria would you judge a particular foreign direct investment activity to have succeeded or failed?

2. What are a firm's major motives in deciding to establish manufacturing facilities in a foreign country?

3. Is the establishment of wholly owned subsidiaries abroad an appropriate international market development mode for SMEs?

4. What is the idea behind appointing a 'lead country' in a region?

5. Why is acquisition often the preferred way to establish wholly owned operations abroad? What are the limitations of acquisition as an entry method?

6. What are the key problems associated with profit repatriation from subsidiaries?

References

Barkema, H.G., Bell, J. and Pennings, J.M. (1996) 'Foreign entry, cultural barriers and learning', *Strategic Management Journal*, vol. 17, pp. 151–66.

Benito, G. (1996) 'Why are subsidiaries divested? A conceptual framework', Working Paper No. 3–93, Institute of International Economics and Management, Copenhagen Business School.

Boddewyn, J.J. (1979) 'Foreign divestment: magnitude and factors', *Journal of International Business Studies*, vol. 10, pp. 21–7.

Lasserre, P. (1995) 'Corporate strategies for the Asia Pacific region', *Long Range Planning*, vol. 28, no. 1, pp. 13–30.

Lasserre, P. (1996) 'Regional headquarters: the spearhead for Asian Pacific markets', *Long Range Planning*, vol. 29, no. 1, pp. 30–7.

Oviatt, B.M. and McDougall, P.P. (1994) 'Toward a theory of international new ventures', *Journal of International Business Studies*, vol. 25, no. 1, pp. 45–64.

Perlmutter, H. (1969) 'The torturous evolution of multinational corporations', *Columbia Journal of World Business*, January–February, pp. 9–18.

Raffée, H. and Kreutzer, R. (1989) 'Organizational dimensions of global marketing', *European Journal of Marketing*, vol. 23, no. 5, pp. 43–57.

Root, F.R. (1987) *Entry Strategies for International Markets*, Lexington Books, Lexington, MA.

Further reading

Anders, G.C. and Usachev, D.A. (2003) 'Strategic Elements of Eastman Kodak's Successful Market Entry in Russia', *Thunderbird International Business Review*, vol. 45, No. 2 (March–April), pp. 171–83.

Buckley, P.J. and Ghauri, P.N. (2002) *International Mergers and Acquisitions: A reader*, Thomson, London.

Hoffmann, W.H. and Schaper-Rinkel, W. (2001), 'Acquire or ally?: a strategy framework for deciding between acquisition and cooperation', *Management International Review*, vol. 41, no. 2, pp. 131–59.

Moore, K.J. (2001) 'A strategy for subsidiaries: Centres of Excellence to build subsidiary specific advantages', *Management International Review*, vol. 41, no. 3, pp. 275–290.

Rodgers, I., Gancel, C. and Raynauld, M. (2002) *Successful Mergers, Acquisitions and Strategic Alliances: How to bridge corporate cultures*, McGraw-Hill, London.

13 International sourcing decisions and the role of the subsupplier

Contents

Learning objectives

After studying this chapter you should be able to do the following:

- Describe the role of subcontractors in the vertical chain.

- Explore the reasons for international outsourcing.

- Explain the development of a buyer–seller relationship.

- Discuss alternative routes of subcontractor internationalization.

- Explain how turnkey contracts differ from conventional subcontracting.

13.1 Introduction

Recent studies of subcontracting and competitiveness have emphasised the importance of outsourcing: moving functions or activities out of an organization. Outsourcing is often more efficient, except in the case of the firm's core competences, which are considered central to its success. Thus the issue is whether an organization should perform certain functions itself ('make') or source ('buy') these activities from outside. If LSEs outsource an increasing number of value chain functions it provides business opportunities for SMEs as subcontractors to LSEs (main contractors).

A subcontractor can be defined as a person or a firm that agrees to provide semi-finished products or services needed by another party (main contractor) to perform another contract to which the subcontractor is not a party. According to this definition, the characteristics of subcontractors that distinguish them from other SMEs are as follows:

- Subcontractors' products are usually part of the end product, not the complete end product itself.

- Subcontractors do not have direct contact with the end customers, because the main contractor is usually responsible to the customer.

The position of subcontractors in the vertical production chain is shown in Figure 13.1.

Figure 13.1 Subcontractor's position in the vertical chain

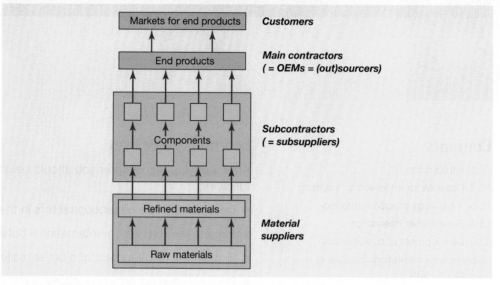

Source: adapted from Lehtinen, 1991, p. 22.

In the OEM contract (where OEM stands for original equipment manufacturer), the contractor is called the OEM or 'sourcer', whereas the parts suppliers are regarded as 'manufacturers' of OEM products (= subcontractors = subsuppliers). Typically the OEM contracts are different from other buyer–seller relationships because the OEMs (contractors) often have much stronger bargaining power than the subcontractors. However, in a partner-based buyer–seller relationship the power balance will be more equal. There are cases where a subcontractor improved its bargaining position and went on to become a major force in the market (Cho and Chu, 1994).

The structure of the remainder of this chapter is shown in Figure 13.2.

Figure 13.2 Structure of Chapter 13

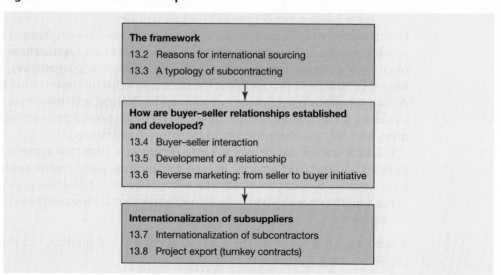

13.2   Reasons for international sourcing

More and more international firms are buying their parts, semi-finished components and other supplies from international subcontractors. Creating competitiveness through the subcontractor is based on the understanding that the supplier can be essential to the buyer (contractor) for a number of reasons.

Concentration on in-house core competences

A contractor wishes to concentrate management time and effort on those core business activities that make the best use of in-house skills and resources. There may also be special difficulties in obtaining suitably skilled labour in-house.

Lower product/production costs

In this respect there are two underlying reasons for outsourcing:

- *Economies of scale.* In many cases the subcontractor produces similar components for other customers, and by use of the experience curve the subcontractor can obtain lower production costs per unit.
- *Lower wage costs.* The labour costs involved in the domestic country can make the in-house operation uneconomic and motivate international sourcing. For example, 80 per cent of the labour cost of clothing manufacture is in the sewing stage. Short production runs of different sizes of clothes permit only a low degree of mechanisation. Moreover, adjusting the tooling for each run is relatively labour intensive (Hibbert, 1993). Therefore a large part of labour-intensive clothing production is moved to low-wage countries in eastern Europe and the Far East.

General cost efficiency

If a firm plans to be more cost efficient than its competitors it has to minimise the total costs towards the end (ultimate) customer. Figure 13.3 shows a model of the different cost elements, from the basic price of materials to the ultimate customer cost.

Each element of the supply chain is a potential candidate for outsourcing. Quality costs, inventory costs (not explicitly mentioned in Figure 13.3) and buyer/supplier transaction costs are examples of costs that should be included in every calculation. However, some of these costs are difficult to estimate and are consequently easily overlooked when evaluating a subcontractor.

For example, the quality of a subcontractor's product or service is essential to the buyer's quality. However, it is not only a question of the quality of the product or service. The quality of the delivery processes also has a major impact on the buyer's performance. Uncertainties, as far as lead times are concerned, have an impact on the buyer's inventory investments and cost efficiency, and they may cause delays in the buyer's own delivery processes. Thus the buyer's own delivery times towards the end customers are determined by the subcontractors and their delivery. Another important fact is that the cost of components and parts is to a large extent already determined at the design stage. Thus, close cooperation between buyer and seller at this stage can give rise to considerable cost advantages in production and distribution.

Figure 13.3 The total cost/value hierarchy model

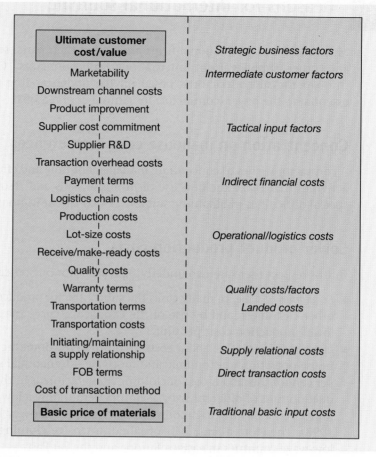

Source: Cavinato, 1992.

Increased potential for innovation

Ideas for innovation can be generated by the subcontractor due to its more in-depth understanding of the component. New ideas can also be transferred from other customers of the subcontractor.

Fluctuating demand

If the main contractor is confronted with fluctuating demand levels, external uncertainty and short product life cycles, it may transfer some risk and stock management to the subcontractor, leading to better cost and budget control.

Finally, it should be mentioned that, when buying from international sources, fluctuations in exchange rates become particularly important, especially when there is a lag from the time the contract is signed to when payment is made. When the currency in the country of the main contractor is very strong against a particular country this can be an incentive for the main contractor to buy from this country.

In summary, price is a very important reason for (international) outsourcing, but the main contractors increasingly regard cooperation with critical subcontractors as advantageous to the buying firm's competitiveness and profitability.

13.3   A typology of subcontracting

Traditionally, a subcontractor has been defined as a firm carrying out day-to-day production based on the specifications of another firm (the main contractor). The variety of subcontracting relationships that are appearing indicates a need for a more differentiated typology.

Figure 13.4 displays a typology of subcontractors based on differences in the contractor–subcontractor relationship. The typology displays the interplay between the degree of coordination needed and the complexity of the tasks to be solved.

Figure 13.4 Typology of subcontracting

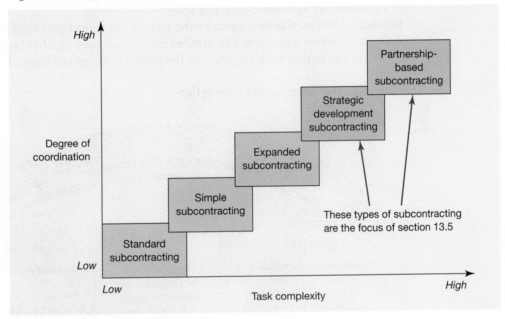

Source: adapted from Blenker and Christensen, 1994

- *Standard subcontracting.* Economies of scale often operate in the global market with standardised products, in which case no adaptation to specific customers is needed.
- *Simple subcontracting.* Information exchange is simple since the contractor specifies criteria for contribution. The contractor's in-house capacity is often a major competitor.
- *Expanded subcontracting.* There is some mutual specialisation between the two parties and exit costs are higher for both parties. Therefore single sourcing (one supplier for a product/component) may replace multisourcing (more suppliers for a product/component).
- *Strategic development subcontracting.* This is very important to the contractor. Subcontractors possess a critical competence of value to the contractor. They are involved in the contractor's long-term planning, and activities are coordinated by dialogue.
- *Partnership-based subcontracting.* This is a relationship based on a strong mutual strategic value and dependency. The subcontractor is highly involved in the R&D activities of the contractor.

There is a certain overlap between the different types of subcontractor and in a specific relationship it can be very difficult to place a subcontractor in a certain typology.

Depending primarily on the task complexity, a main contractor may have both standard subcontractors and partnership-based subcontractors. Also a subcontractor may play more than one role in Figure 13.4, but only one at a time.

13.4   Buyer–seller interaction

Traditionally, subcontracting has been defined as the production activities that one firm carries out on the day-to-day specification of another firm. Outsourced activities increasingly include R&D, design and other functions in the value chain. Thus what starts with simple transactions (so-called episodes) may, if repeated over time, evolve into a relationship between buyer and seller.

Interaction theory was developed by the Swedes but spread into France, Britain, Italy and Germany when a group of like-minded researchers formed what became known as the IMP Group, basing their research on the interaction model (Figure 13.5).

Figure 13.5 The buyer–seller interaction

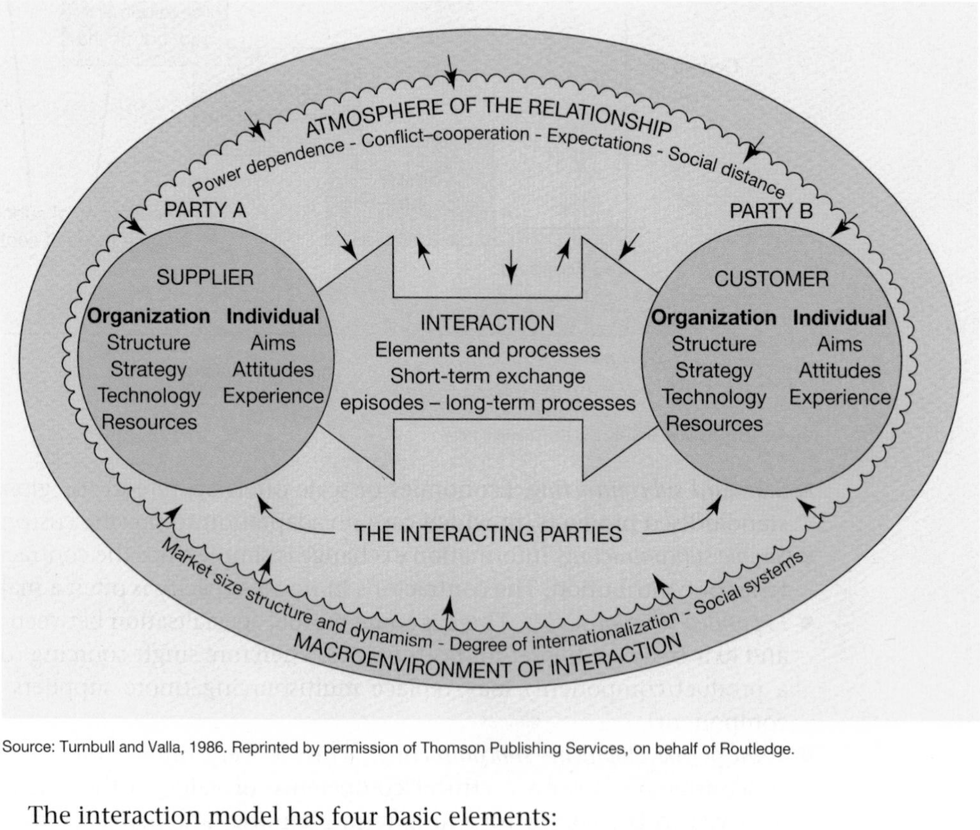

Source: Turnbull and Valla, 1986. Reprinted by permission of Thomson Publishing Services, on behalf of Routledge.

The interaction model has four basic elements:

1. The interaction process, which expresses the exchanges between the two organizations along with their progress and evolution throughout time.
2. The participants in the interaction process, meaning the characteristics of the supplier and the customer involved in the interaction process.
3. The atmosphere affecting and being affected by the interaction.
4. The environment within which interaction takes place.

Interaction process

The interaction process can be analysed in both a short-term and a long-term perspective. Over time the relationship is developed by a sequence of episodes and events that tends to institutionalize or destabilize it, depending on the evaluations made by the two firms in the interaction. These episodes may vary in terms of types of exchange: commercial transactions, periods of crisis caused by delivery, price disputes, new product development stages, etc.

Through social exchange with the supplier the customer attempts to reduce decision-making uncertainty. Over time and with mutual adaptation a relationship-specific mode of operation emerges and may act as a 'shock absorber' in case of crisis. This mode of operation can take the form of special procedures, mutual developments, communication style between individuals, and more or less implicit rules. These rules are modified through past exchanges and form the framework for future exchanges.

Interacting parties

The participants' characteristics strongly influence the way they interact. Three analytical perspectives of buyer and seller, at different levels, may be taken into account.

The social system perspective

Dimensions such as culture – languages, values and practices – and the operating modes of the firm influence the distance between actors that will limit or encourage collaboration.

The organizational perspective

The relationship between buyer and seller is influenced by three organizational dimensions:

- The characteristics of each firm's technology (i.e. products and production technology) strongly influence the nature of the interaction between the two organizations.
- The complexity of products sold, for example, conditions the very nature and the density of the interaction between supplier and customer.
- Relationship characteristics: a supplier can choose to develop a stable relationship with a customer, or the supplier can regard the relationship as a pure transaction-based exchange where the supplier typically makes 'one-shot' business with a customer purely to increase sales volume and with no further involvement.

The individual perspective

The individuals' characteristics, their objectives and their experience will influence the way social exchanges and social contacts take place, and subsequently the development of supplier–customer interaction.

Atmosphere of the relationship

The atmosphere is the 'climate' that has developed between the two firms. This atmosphere can be described in terms of power–dependence, cooperation–conflict and trust–opportunism, and in terms of understanding and social distance. The atmosphere concept is central to the understanding of the supplier–customer relationship. In the case of key account management, atmosphere plays a particularly important role. As buyer and seller approach each other the marketing exchanges are changing from single transactions to a relationship. The further characteristics of these two situations are described in Table 13.1 and Figure 13.6.

Table 13.1 Marketing exchange understanding

	Transaction	Relationship
Objective	To make a sale (sale is end result and measure of success). Customer needs satisfaction (customer buys values).	To create a customer (sale is beginning of relationship). Customer integration (interactive value generation)
Customer understanding	Anonymous customer. Independent buyer and seller.	Well-known customer. Interdependent buyer and seller.
Marketers' task and performance criteria	Assessment on the basis of products and prices. Focus on gaining new customers.	Assessment on the basis of problem-solving competence. Focus on value enhancing of existing customers.
Core aspects of exchange	Focus on products. Sale as a conquest. Discrete event. Monologue to aggregated broad customer segments.	Focus on service. Sale as an agreement. Continuing process. Individualized dialogue.

Source: Jüttner and Wehrli 1994. Published with permission of Emerald Publishing Ltd. **www.emeraldinsight.com**

Figure 13.6 Market exchange understanding

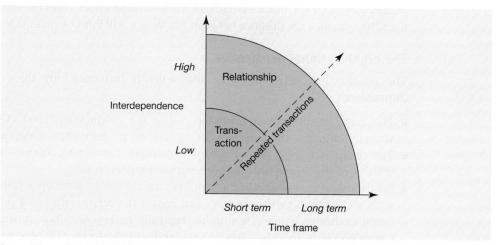

Source: Jüttner and Wehrli 1994. Published with permission of Emerald Publishing Ltd. **www.emeraldinsight.com**

Interaction environment

Supplier–customer relationships evolve in a general macroenvironment that can influence their very nature. The following analytical dimensions are traditionally considered: political and economic context, cultural and social context, market structure, market internationalization and market dynamism (growth, innovation rate).

13.5   Development of a relationship

A relationship between two firms begins, grows and develops – or fails – in ways similar to relationships between people. The development of a relationship has been mapped out in a five-phase model: awareness, exploration, expansion, commitment and dissolution. The first four phases are shown in Figure 13.7. Within such a

Figure 13.7 The relationship development process

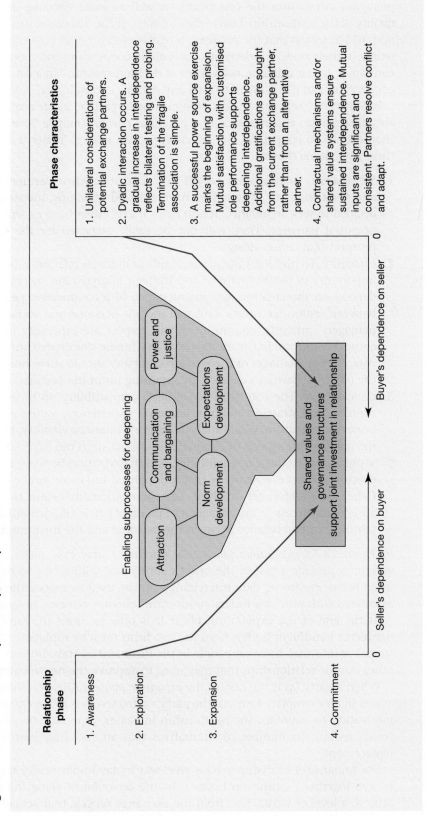

Relationship phase

1. Awareness
2. Exploration
3. Expansion
4. Commitment

Enabling subprocesses for deepening

Attraction — Communication and bargaining — Power and justice

Norm development — Expectations development

Shared values and governance structures support joint investment in relationship

0 Seller's dependence on buyer

0 Buyer's dependence on seller

Phase characteristics

1. Unilateral considerations of potential exchange partners.

2. Dyadic interaction occurs. A gradual increase in interdependence reflects bilateral testing and probing. Termination of the fragile association is simple.

3. A successful power source exercise marks the beginning of expansion. Mutual satisfaction with customised role performance supports deepening interdependence. Additional gratifications are sought from the current exchange partner, rather than from an alternative partner.

4. Contractual mechanisms and/or shared value systems ensure sustained interdependence. Mutual inputs are significant and consistent. Partners resolve conflict and adapt.

Source: Dwyer et al., 1987, p. 15.

framework one might easily characterise a marketing relationship as a marriage between a seller and a buyer (the dissolution phase being a 'divorce'). The use of the marriage metaphor emphasises the complexity as well as some affective determinants of the quality of the relationship. Dwyer *et al.* (1987) call the first phase in a relationship *awareness*, which means that the partners recognise each other as potential partners. In other words, in their model the decisions made about cooperating and choosing the partner are combined. In our opinion, both types of decision making can exist at the beginning of cooperation, but it is difficult to state any definite chronological order between them.

In SMEs it is likely that the decision making is reactive, in the way that the SME probably first realises the existence of a potential partner (maybe 'love at first sight') and then decides to cooperate. The selection process may go better if companies look for three key criteria (Kanter, 1994):

1. *Self-analysis*. Relationships get off to a good start when partners know themselves and their industry, when they have assessed changing industry conditions and decided to seek an alliance. It also helps if executives have experience in evaluating potential partners. They will not be easily attracted by the first good-looking prospect that comes along.

2. *Chemistry*. To highlight the personal side of business relationships is not to deny the importance of sound financial and strategic analysis. But successful relations often depend on the creation and maintenance of a comfortable personal relationship between senior executives. This will include personal and social interests. Signs of managers' interests, commitment and respect are especially important in high-context countries. In China, as well as in Chinese-dominated businesses throughout Asia, the top manager of the western company should show honour and respect to the potential partner's decision by investing his or her personal time.

3. *Compatibility*. The courtship period tests compatibility on broad historical, philosophical and strategic grounds: common experiences, values and principles, and hopes for the future. While analysts examine financial viability, managers can assess the less tangible aspects of compatibility. What starts out as personal rapport, philosophical and strategic compatibility, and shared vision between two companies' top executives must eventually be institutionalized and made public ('getting engaged'). Other stakeholders get involved, and the relationship begins to become depersonalised. But success in the engagement phase of a new alliance still depends on maintaining a careful balance between the personal and the institutional.

In Figure 13.7's *exploration phase* trial purchases may take place and the exchange outcomes provide a test of the other's ability and willingness to deliver satisfaction. In addition, electronic data interchange can be used to reduce the costly paperwork associated with purchase orders, production schedule releases, invoices and so on.

At the end of the exploration phase it is time to 'meet the family'. The relations between a handful of leaders from the two firms must be supplemented with approval, formal or informal, by other people in the firms and by stake holders. Each partner has other outside relationships that may need to approve the new relationship.

When a party (as is the case in the *expansion phase*) fulfils perceived exchange obligations in an exemplary fashion, the party's attractiveness to the other increases. Hence motivation to maintain the relationship increases, especially because high-level outcomes reduce the number of alternatives that an exchange partner might use as a replacement.

The romance of courtship quickly gives way to day-to-day reality as the partners begin to live together ('setting up house'). In the *commitment phase* the two partners can achieve a level of satisfaction from the exchange process that actually precludes other primary exchange partners (suppliers) that could provide similar benefits. The buyer has not ceased attending other alternative suppliers, but maintains awareness of alternatives without constant and frequent testing.

During the description of the relationship development, the possibility of a withdrawal has been implicit. The *dissolution phase* may be caused by the following problems:

- Operational and cultural differences emerge after collaboration is under way. They often come as a surprise to those who created the alliance. Differences in authority, reporting and decision-making styles become noticeable at this stage.
- People in other positions may not experience the same attraction as the chief executives. The executives spend a lot of time together both informally and formally. Other employees have not been in touch with one another, however, and in some cases have to be pushed to work with their overseas counterparts.
- Employees at other levels in the organization may be less visionary and cosmopolitan than top managers and less experienced in working with people from different cultures. They may lack knowledge of the strategic context in which the relationship makes sense and see only the operational ways in which it does not.
- People just one or two tiers from the top might oppose the relationship and fight to undermine it. This is especially true in organizations that have strong independent business units.
- Termination of personal relationships, because managers leave their positions in the companies, is a potential danger to the partnership.

Firms have to be aware of these potential problems before they go into a relationship, because only in that way can they take action to prevent the dissolution phase.

13.6   Reverse marketing: from seller to buyer initiative

Reverse marketing describes how purchasing actively identifies potential subcontractors and offers suitable partners a proposal for long-term cooperation. Similar terms are proactive procurement and buyer initiative (Ottesen, 1995). In recent years the buyer–seller relationship has changed considerably. The traditional relationship, in which a seller takes the initiative by offering a product, is increasingly being replaced by one in which the buyer actively searches for a supplier that is able to fulfil its needs.

Today, many changes are taking place in the utilisation of the purchasing function:

- Reduction in the number of subcontractors.
- Shorter product life cycles, which increase the pressure to reduce the time to market (just in time).
- Upgraded demands on subcontractors (zero defects). In addition, firms are demanding that their suppliers become certified. Those that do not comply may be removed from the approved supplier list.
- Purchasing that no longer just serves the purpose of getting lower prices. The traditional arm's-length relationships are increasingly being replaced by long-term partnerships with mutual trust, interdependence and mutual benefits.

Implementing a reverse marketing strategy starts with fundamental market research and with an evaluation of reverse marketing options (i.e. possible suppliers). Before choosing suppliers the firm may include both present and potential suppliers in the analysis as well as current and desired activities (Figure 13.8).

Figure 13.8 **Supplier development strategies**

	Current activities	New activities
Existing suppliers	Intensify current activities	Develop and add new activities
New potential suppliers	Replace existing suppliers Add suppliers: secure deliveries	Develop new activities not covered by existing suppliers

Based on this analysis the firm may select a number of suitable partners as suppliers and rank them in order of preference.

13.7 Internationalization of subcontractors

In Chapter 3 the internationalization process was described as a learning process (the Uppsala school). Generally speaking it is something that can be described as a gradual internationalization. According to this view the international development of the firm is accompanied by an accumulation of knowledge in the hands of management and by growing capabilities and propensities to manage international affairs. The main consequence of this way of thinking is that firms tend to increase their commitment towards foreign markets as their experience grows. The number of adherents to this theory has grown, but there has also been much criticism of it.

The main problem with the model is that it seems to suggest the presence of a deterministic and mechanistic path that firms implementing their internationalization strategy must follow. Sometimes it happens that firms leapfrog one or more stages in the establishment chain; at other times firms stop their internationalization altogether (Welch and Luostarinen, 1988).

Concerning internationalization among contractors and subcontractors, there is a central difference. The internationalization of subcontractors is closely related to their customers. The concept of subcontractor indicates that the strategies of such a firm, including its internationalization strategy, cannot be seen in isolation from the strategies of its partner, the contractor. Therefore the internationalization of subcontractors may show irregular paths, such as leapfrogging.

Andersen *et al.* (1995) introduce four basic routes of internationalization (note that sometimes there is an overlap between the different routes, e.g. between routes 2 and 3).

Route 1: Following domestic customers

If a contractor is internationalizing and establishing a production unit in a foreign market some subcontractors (standard or simple in Figure 13.4) may be replaced with local suppliers, because they might be able to offer the standard components at cheaper prices. However, subcontractors in the upper part of Figure 13.4 and with a strategic value to the contractor will be maintained if they commit themselves to foreign direct investment: claims for direct delivery to the foreign production unit or claims for after-sales service on delivered components may result in the establishment of a local sales and/or production subsidiary by the subcontractor. In most cases such a direct foreign investment related directly to a specific contractor is based on a guarantee of procurement over some years (until the payback period has passed).

When the furniture chain IKEA established itself in the North American market it took along some strategically important Scandinavian subcontractors, some of which also established subsidiaries in North America. Other examples are the Japanese car manufacturers that established production units in the United States and pulled along a lot of Japanese subcontractors to establish subsidiaries there. This route is similar to the 'late starters' in the model of Johanson and Mattson (1988) in Figure 3.6.

Route 2: internationalization through the supply chain of an multinational corporation

Deliveries to one division of a multinational corporation may lead to deliveries to other divisions, or to parts of its network. One case is when mergers and acquisitions take place between firms, and create new business opportunities for dynamic subcontractors.

The strategic alliance between the French car manufacturer Renault and the Swedish Volvo is one example, where Swedish subcontractors have become involved in the subcontracting system of Renault, and French subcontractors have opportunities to get into the subcontracting system of Volvo (Christensen and Lindmark, 1993).

Route 3: Internationalization in cooperation with domestic or foreign system suppliers

In collaboration with other specialised subcontractors, system suppliers may be involved in international system supplies by taking over the management of whole supplies of subsystems (Figure 13.9).

Systems supplies result in the development of a new layer of subcontractors (second-tier subcontractors). Through the interaction between a system supplier and a domestic main contractor the system supplier can get access to the network of a global contractor (the dotted line in Figure 13.9) because of the network/contract between the contractor and the global contractor. For example, a Japanese car seat supplier supplies the Japanese Toyota factory (domestic main contractor). This can eventually give the

Figure 13.9 Possible internationalization of system suppliers

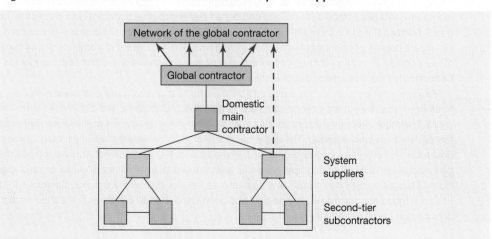

supplier access to other Toyota factories around the world (global contractors) and their global networks.

In many cases the collaboration between the subcontractors will be characterised by exchange of tacit, not easily transferable, knowledge. The reason for this is that the complete subsystem is frequently based on several fields of competence, which have to be coordinated by use of tacit knowledge and communication. In the case of the Japanese car seat supplier, the system supplier should have a tight relationship with the subcontractors (suppliers of leather head rests, etc.) in order to adapt the car seat to the individual car models. (See also Exhibit 13.1.)

Route 4: Independent internationalization

The need to gain economies of scale in production forces the standard contractor, in particular, to use the route of independent internationalization. In other cases it cannot be recommended that small subcontractors follow the independent route. The barriers of independent internationalization are too high for small firms with limited resources. For these firms, route 3 (collaboration with other subcontractors) seems to be a more realistic way to internationalize.

Exhibit 13.1	An example of Japanese network sourcing: the Mazda seat-sourcing case

Mazda adopts a policy of splitting its seat purchases between two suppliers, Delta Kogyo and the Toyo Seat Company. The present division is approximately 60 per cent to Delta and 40 per cent to Toyo. Each of these companies is responsible for different models of seats. Note that each individual item, such as a seat for the Mazda 626, is single sourced for the product life cycle of typically three to five years, but seat production in general is, in effect, dual sourced.

Both Delta Kogyo and the Toyo Seat Company are informally assured of a certain percentage of the Mazda seat business at any one time. This percentage is approximately one-third of the total Mazda seat purchases. Thus each firm has an assured long-term share of Mazda's seat business. Indeed, when asked about the length of relationship that Mazda has with its suppliers, Mr Nakamichi of Mazda's marketing division noted that relationships with all suppliers, whether they are affiliates, subcontractors or common part suppliers, were established for an 'indefinite' period of time. In addition, the last third of the seat business was available to whichever of the suppliers had performed the best over the life cycle of previous car models.

The two seat makers rely on Mazda for a very high percentage of their business. In the case of Delta Kogyo, Mazda business represents around two-thirds of its total sales. In addition, both suppliers are members of Mazda's *Keiretsu* (network) and hence come into direct contact with each other on a regular basis. Additionally, since they are direct competitors for only a third of Mazda's seat business, there is a significant degree of openness between the two firms. This openness in some instances takes the form of cooperation in solving mutual or individual problems, because the other seat supplier is often in a better position to give advice than Mazda itself.

However, competition for the remaining third of the Mazda seat business is very intense, since both firms know that they have only one chance to gain the orders for a new car model every three to five years. The most interesting aspect of this competition is that it is based primarily on performance since the last contract was awarded. The areas of competition include design abilities, management strength, cost reduction progress, quality record and, perhaps surprisingly, the amount of assistance that the supplier has given to its direct competitor either within the auspices of the *Keiretsu* or on separate occasions. Thus either firm can obtain new business as long as the other does not fall below 33 per cent of Mazda's total seat purchases. A situation has been created in which there is creative tension between cooperation and competition.

Indeed, when one of the suppliers approaches the lower limit of its 33 per cent supply Mazda typically uses its own engineers, and possibly those of the supply competitor, to help the weaker supplier in terms of a joint value analysis/value engineering programme. Because neither supplier wants to be forced into this situation both will work diligently to avoid this fate – and at the same time to enhance their own competitiveness.

Mazda is careful to ensure that neither supplier is forced into a situation of unprofitability, since this would obviously mean that Mazda would suffer in the long term. This is not to say that either supplier is allowed to make excessive profits. Indeed profit as a percentage of sales is roughly equalised throughout the supply network, including the Mazda organization itself. During recessionary periods Mazda and its network of suppliers would make no more than about 2 per cent profit on sales. Thus members of the supply network stand or fall together, increasing the shared bonds and the willingness to help any member of the network.

Source: Reproduced with permission from the publisher, the National Association of Purchasing Management, 'Network Sourcing: A Hybrid Approach', *The International Journal of Purchasing and Materials Management*, by Peter Hines, Spring 1995, Volume 31, #2, pp. 18–24.

13.8   Project export (turnkey contracts)

This chapter has dealt mainly with sourcing (subcontracting) in the industrial market. Although marketing of subsupplies to international projects has a number of similarities with subsupplies in the industrial market in general, it also has the characteristics of the special marketing situation in the project market: for example, the long and often very bureaucratic selection of subsuppliers for ad hoc supplies.

The subsupplier market in project export, however, is also very internationalized, and the main part of marketing should be conducted in those centres or countries where the main contractor is domiciled. For example, London is the domicile of a number of building contracting businesses, which work in those countries that used to be in the British Empire.

Project export is a very complex international activity, involving many market players. The preconditions for project export are a technology gap between the exporting and importing countries and that the exporter possesses the specific product and technology know-how that is being demanded in the importing country.

Project export involves supplies or deliveries that contain a combination of hardware and software. When the delivery is concluded it will constitute an integrated system that is able to produce the products and/or the services which the buyer requires. An example of this type of project is the construction of a dairy in a developing country.

Hardware is the blanket term for the tangible, material or physical contribution of the project supply. Hardware is buildings, machines, inventory, transport equipment, etc., and is specified in the quotation and contract between buyer and seller in the form of drawings, unit lists, descriptions and so on.

Software is the blanket term for the intangible contributions in a project supply. Software includes know-how and service. There are three types of know-how:

- *technology know-how*, comprising product, process and hardware know-how;
- *project know-how*, comprising project management, assembly and environmental know-how;
- *management know-how*, which in general terms involves tactical and operational management, and specifically includes marketing and administrative systems.

Service includes advisory services and assistance in connection with various applications and approvals (environmental approval, financing of the project, planning permission, etc.).

The marketing of projects is different from the marketing of products in the following respects:

- Decision of purchase, apart from local business interests, often involves decision processes in national and international development organizations. This implies the participation of a large number of people and a heavily bureaucratic system.
- The product is designed and created during the negotiation process, where the requirements are put forward.
- It often takes years from the disclosure of needs to the purchase decision being taken. Therefore total marketing costs are very large.
- When the project is taken over by the project buyer, the buyer–seller relations cease. However, by cultivating these relations before, during and after the project, a 'sleeping' relationship can be woken again in connection with a new project (Hadjikhani, 1996).

Financing a project is a key problem for the seller as well as the buyer. The project's size and the time used for planning and implementation result in financial demands that make it necessary to use external sources of finance. In this connection the following main segments can be distinguished. The segments arise from differences in the source of financing for the projects:

- Projects where *multilateral organizations*, such as the World Bank or regional development banks, are a primary source of finance.
- Projects where *bilateral organizations* are a primary or essential source of finance.
- Projects where a *government institution* acts as buyer. This was normal in the command economies, where government companies acted as buyers. However, it can also be found in liberal economies: for example in connection with the development of social infrastructure or the building of a bridge.
- Projects where a *private person or firm* acts as buyer, as when Unilever builds a factory in Vietnam for the production of ice cream.

Organizing export projects involves establishing an interaction between different firms from the West on the one side, and firms and authorities typically from developing countries on the other. Creating or adapting an organization that is able to function under these conditions is a precondition of project marketing.

13.9 Summary

This chapter has analysed the buyer–seller relationship from different angles in the internationalized environment. The advantages and disadvantages for the contractor and subcontractor of going into a relationship are summarised in Table 13.2.

The project export situation differs from the 'normal' buyer–seller relationship in the following ways:

- The buying decision process often involves national and international development organizations. This often results in very bureaucratic selection of subcontractors.
- Financing of the project is a key problem.

Table 13.2 Advantages and disadvantages of buyer–seller relationships for contractor and subcontractor

	Advantages	Disadvantages
Contractor (buyer)	The contractor is flexible by not investing in manufacturing facilities. The subcontractor can source the products more cheaply (because of e.g. cheaper labour costs) than by own production. The contractor can concentrate on in-house core competences. Complement of the contractor's product range. New ideas for product innovation can be carried over from the subcontractor.	The availability of suitable manufacturers (subcontractors) cannot be assumed. Outsourcing tends to be relatively less stable than in-house operations. The contractor has less control over the activities of the subcontractor. Subcontractors can develop into competitors. Quality problems of outsourced products can harm the business of the contractor. Assistance to the subcontractor may increase the costs of the whole operation.
Subcontractor (seller)	Access to new export markets because of the internationalization of the contractor (especially relevant for the so-called late starters). Exploits scale economies (lower cost per unit) through better capacity utilization. Learns product technology of the contractor. Learns marketing practices of the contractor.	Risk of becoming dependent on the contractor because of expanding production capacity and concurrent overseas expansion of sales and marketing activities in order to meet the demands of the contractor.

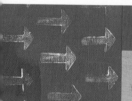

CASE STUDY 13.1   LM Glasfiber A/S

Following its customers' international expansion in the wind turbine industry

LM Glasfiber A/S is the world's leading supplier of rotor blades for wind turbines. Its headquarters is located in Lunderskov, Denmark. It has 14 manufacturing bases in 10 Danish towns, with more than 1,700 employees in modern production areas covering some 100,000 sq m.

The company is internationally represented, with manufacturing facilities and sales offices in Germany, the Netherlands, Spain, the United States, India and China. Its customers are thus guaranteed prompt and punctual delivery with a high level of service worldwide.

LM Glasfiber's establishment in India is explained and illustrated in Figure 1. Typically, rotor blades represent approximately 20 per cent of a wind turbine's value (excluding mounting, installation etc.).

Figure 1 shows the phases that LM Glasfiber (as subsupplier) went through in order to globalize via the buyers'/wind turbine manufacturers' network, especially Micon's network.

The ① in the figure indicates that LM Glasfiber has very large deliveries of rotor blades to the Danish

Source: www. lmglasfiber.com. Copyright LM Glasfiber A/S

Figure 1 LM Glasfiber's globalization through the network of the customer

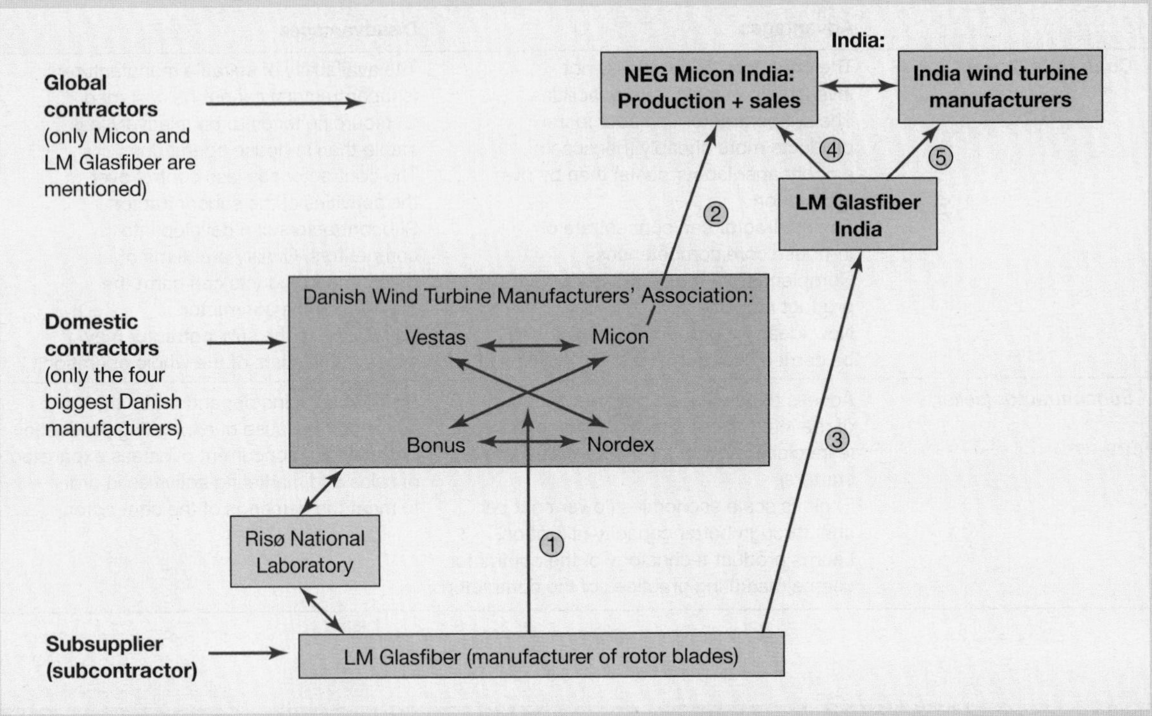

network of wind turbine manufacturers ('domestic contracts'), the largest being NEG Micon (in 1999), Vestas (wind systems), Bonus (energy), and Nordex. Even though the total Danish network covers more than 50 per cent of the world market for wind turbines it should be remembered that competition between the companies in the international market is very keen. Having exceeding close relations with and deliveries to the Danish Wind Turbine Manufacturers' Association, LM Glasfiber also cooperates very closely with the research environment within wind turbine technology by way of relations with the Ris National Laboratory.

This example is based on LM Glasfiber's relations with Micon – the second-biggest wind turbine manufacturer in the world (Micon is fighting with Vestas for first place). As regards subsuppliers Micon's strategy has been to outsource the biggest part of its rotor blade production. However, Micon has always aimed at having an adequate share of internal subsuppliers of rotor blades, in order for the company to have the necessary technological preparedness compared to competitors and external subsuppliers. This flexible sourcing concept is an essential precondition for Micon's continued globalization process.

② shows Micon's establishment of a sales and manufacturing company in India at the beginning of the 1990s. India is an attractive market for wind turbines, as India's power supply is poor, especially in the countryside. The Indian government has therefore supported the mounting of wind turbines that can contribute to stabilising the power supply (often in cooperation with foreign development aid organizations).

LM Glasfiber realised that it had to start manufacturing rotor blades in India to continue being one of India's subsupplies. ③ shows the 1994 establishment of LM Glasfiber India Ltd. – a joint venture between LM Glasfiber A/S, the Industrialization Fund for Developing Countries, and the Indian wind turbine manufacturer NEPC. ④ therefore shows the local deliveries of rotor blades and the back-up service that LM Glasfiber India can provide by being a local company. As a consequence of the partnership with NEPC, LM Glasfiber has now (via the local joint venture) gained access to NEPC's network, which includes several markets in Asia. ⑤ thus shows that LM Glasfiber has been able to use its relationship with NEPC as a 'springboard' to other markets in Asia.

Questions

1. Are there any threats to LM Glasfiber's strategy in following the key customer abroad?

2. How does this case relate to the network model in Chapter 3?

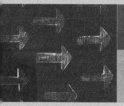

CASE STUDY 13.2   Lear Corporation

A leading supplier of automotive interior systems

Lear Corporation (**www.lear.com**) is one of the 10 largest independent automotive suppliers in the world. The company is also the leading supplier of automotive interior systems in the global automotive interior market and the third largest supplier in the global automotive electrical distribution systems market. The company has established in-house capabilities in all five principal segments of the automotive interior market: seat systems; flooring and acoustic systems; door panels; headliners; and instrument panels. The company is the largest supplier in the global seat systems market. In North America it is one of the two largest suppliers in each of the other principal automotive interior markets, with the exception of the instrument panels market, in which it is the fourth largest. The company is also one of the leading global suppliers of automotive electrical distribution systems.

Questions

1. How can Lear Corp. be characterised as a subsupplier?

2. Describe the relationships that Lear Corp. has with its customers.

3. How would you consider the international competitiveness of Lear Corp. compared with its Japanese customers?

Questions for discussion

1. What are the reasons for the increasing level of outsourcing to international subcontractors?

2. Describe the typology of subcontractors based on the differences in the contractor/subcontractor relationship.

3. Explain the shift from seller to buyer initiative in subcontracting.

4. Explain the main differences between the US and the Japanese subsupplier systems.

5. How are project exports/turnkey projects different from general subcontracting in the industrial market?

6. Project export is often characterised by a complex and time-consuming decision-making process. What are the marketing implications of this for the potential subcontractor?

References

Andersen, P.H., Blenker, P. and Christensen, P.R. (1995) *Internationalization of Subcontractors: In search of a theoretical framework*, The Southern Denmark Business School, Kolding.

Blenker, P. and Christensen, P.R. (1994) 'Interactive strategies in supply chains: a double-edged portfolio approach to SME', *Subcontractors Positioning Paper* presented at the 8th Nordic Conference on Small Business Research.

Cavinato, J.L. (1992) 'A total cost/value model for supply chain competitiveness', *Journal of Business Logistics*, vol. 13, no. 2, pp. 285–301.

Cho, Dong-Sung and Chu, Wujin (1994) 'Determinants of bargaining power in OEM negotiations', *Industrial Marketing Management*, vol. 23, pp. 342–55.

Christensen, P.R. and Lindmark, L. (1993) 'Location and internationalization of small firms', in Lindquist, L. and Persson, L.O. (eds), *Visions and Strategies in European Integration*, Springer Verlag, Berlin/Heidelberg.

Dwyer, R.F., Schurr, P.H. and Oh, S. (1987) 'Developing buyer–seller relationships', *Journal of Marketing*, vol. 51, April, pp. 11–27.

Hadjikhani, A. (1996) 'Project marketing and the management of discontinuity', *International Business Review*, vol. 5, no. 3, pp. 319–36.

Hibbert, E.P. (1993) 'Global make or buy decisions', *Industrial Marketing Management*, vol. 22, pp. 67–77.

Hines, P. (1995) 'Network sourcing: a hybrid approach', *International Journal of Purchasing and Materials Management*, Spring, pp. 18–24.

Johanson, J. and Mattson, L.G. (1988) 'Internationalization in industrial systems', in Hood, N. and Vahlne, J.E. (eds), *Strategies in Global Competition*, Croom Helm, Beckenham.

Jüttner, U. and Wehrli, H.P. (1994) 'Relationship marketing from a value system perspective', *International Journal of Service Industry Management*, no. 5, pp. 54–73.

Kanter, R.M. (1994) 'Collaborative advantage', *Harvard Business Review*, July–August, pp. 96–107.

Lehtinen, U. (1991) 'Alihankintajarjestelma 1990-luvulla [Subcontracting system in the 1990s]', *Publications of SITRA*, no. 114, Helsinki.

Ottesen, O. (1995) 'Buyer initiative: ignored, but imperative for marketing theory', Working Paper, Department of Business Administration, Stavanger College, Norway.

Turnbull, P.W. and Valla, J.P. (1986) *Strategies for International Industrial Marketing*, Croom Helm, London.

Welch, L.S. and Luostarinen, R. (1988) 'Internationalization: evolution of a concept', *Journal of General Management*, vol. 14, no. 2, pp. 36–64.

Further reading

Alvarez, S.A. and Barney, J.B. (2001) 'How entrepreneurial firms can benefit from alliances with large partners', *Academy of Management Executive*, vol. 15, No. 1, pp. 139–48.

Andersen, P.H. and Christensen, P.R (2000) 'Inter-partner learning in global supply chains: lessons from NOVO Nordisk', *European Journal of Purchasing & Supply Management*, vol. 6, pp. 105–16.

Gelderman, C.J. and Weele, A.J. van (2002) 'Strategic direction through purchasing portfolio management: a case study', *The Journal of Supply Chain Management*, Spring, pp. 30–37.

Holmström, J., Hoover, W.E., Louhiluoto, P. and Vasara, A. (2000) 'The other end of the supply chain', *The McKinsey Quarterly*, no. 1, pp. 63–71.

Hvolby, H.-H. and Trienekens, J. (2002) 'Supply chain planning opportunities for small and medium sized companies', *Computers in Industry*, vol. 49, pp. 3–8.

Lambert, D.M. and Pohlen, T.L. (2001) 'Supply chain metrics', *The International Journal of Logistics Management*, vol. 12, no. 1, pp. 1–19.

Leminen, S. (2001) 'Seven glasses for buyer–seller relationships: a framework for analysing gaps', *Management Decisions*, vol. 39, no. 5, pp. 379–87.

Murray, J.Y. (2001) 'Strategic Alliance-based global sourcing strategy for competitive advantage: a conceptual framework and research proposition', *Journal of International Marketing*, vol. 9, no. 4, pp. 30–58.

Ritter, T., Wilkinson, I.F. and Johnston, W.J. (2002) 'Measuring network competence: some international evidence', *Journal of Business & Industrial Marketing*, vol. 17, no. 2/3, pp. 119–38.

Sarkis, J. and Talluri, S. (2002) 'A model for strategic supplier selection', *The Journal of Supply Chain Management*, Winter, pp. 18–28.

Trent, R.J. and Monczka, R.M. (2003) 'Understanding integrated global sourcing', *International Journal of Physical Distribution & Logistics Management*, vol. 33, No. 7, pp. 607–29.

Weele, A.J. van (2002) *Purchasing and supply chain management* (3rd edition), Thomson Learning.

14 Global e-marketing

Contents

Learning objectives

After studying this chapter you should be able to do the following:

■ Describe the development of Internet and e-marketing in the main regions of the world.

■ Explain the reasons for the rapid development of e-marketing.

■ Explore how e-marketing functions in the two main market types: B-t-B, B-t-C, C-t-B, C-t-C.

■ Discuss the reality behind 'disintermediation' (bypassing resellers).

■ Discuss alternative routes of global e-marketing strategies.

■ Discuss the global marketing opportunities with 'mobile' marketing (m-marketing)

14.1   Introduction

In the past few years there has been an explosion of online commercial activity enabled by the Internet or World Wide Web. This is generally referred to as electronic marketing (e-marketing), with a major component of e-marketing being electronic transactions taking place on Internet-based markets (electronic markets or e-markets).

The development of the Internet as a 'new' distribution channel will result in a shift of power from the manufacturers and the traditional retail channels to the consumers. This increasing consumer power can be explained in the following ways:

1. *The search for convenience.* The Internet gives people a new tool to gather information and purchase more easily than do traditional channels.
2. *The incorporation of the net into the purchase process.* Pre-purchase and post-sale use of the net is exploding, regardless of where the product is bought.

3. *A shift in loyalties*. Consumers reward online merchants with higher repeat-purchase behaviour.
4. *Future buying plans*. Survey results indicate an increasing consumer disposition to buy online (Boston Consulting Group, 2000; IDC, 2000a).

Today's technology only scratches the surface of efficient comparison shopping and product search. The development of automated buying profiles, networked buying clubs and online auctions will bring greater price competition to the Internet. Merchants must be prepared to live up to 'We will match any price' marketing guarantees (see also Chapter 16, Pricing decisions).

Competing on the Internet is different from the traditional industrial world. Competition no longer takes place in the physical *marketplace*, but in the *market space* (Rayport and Sviokla, 1996). This computer-mediated environment has profound implications for how business is transacted between buyer and seller. The nature of transaction is different in that it is based on information about the product or services rather than on its physical appearance or attributes. The context of the transaction is different; instead of taking place in a physical world it occurs in a computer-mediated environment with the buyer conducting the transaction from a personal computer screen. Consequently, to be a player in many industries does not require a physical infrastructure such as buildings and machinery; a computer and communications platform are sufficient.

Like so many 'buzz words' in use today, e-marketing tends to mean different things to different people. For the purpose of introducing the subject, e-marketing is defined in this way: *The enablement of a business vision supported by advanced information technology to increase the effectiveness of the business relationships between trading partners.*

Examples of e-marketing transactions are:

- An individual purchases a book on the Internet.
- A government employee reserves a hotel room over the Internet.
- A business calls a toll-free number and orders a computer using the seller's interactive telephone system.
- A retailer orders merchandise using an EDI network or a supplier's extranet.
- A manufacturing plant orders electronic components from another plant within the company using the company's intranet.
- An individual withdraws funds from an automatic teller machine.

14.2   Types of products

The products sold in e-marketing markets can roughly be grouped into two categories: physical products and purely digital goods and services.

Physical products

Marketing physical products over the Web has led to some of the biggest success stories in e-marketing. The key to success is marketing that takes advantage of the interface and the networked environment. Transferring a conventional mail-order business to the Web adds little value.

The potential advantages of the Internet include the scope for real-time interaction within a vast networked community, the possibility of using sophisticated market mechanisms, and the illusion of almost infinite inventory (when an intermediary acts for many suppliers). Businesses that exploit these opportunities, such as Amazon.com and eBay, have been very successful.

Digital goods and services

This category includes information goods and services, such as financial information, news services, reference and learning material, entertainment and multimedia products, software distribution services, distributed database services and remote computation services. In addition, the Internet has spawned innovative digital products such as online gaming, chat rooms, search engines, online advertising, yellow pages and certification services. These products are characterised by being difficult to value and easy to copy.

Companies use different strategies to price and market these goods. They include customisation and bundling, bundling valuable content with advertising to provide 'free' goods, introducing different versions of the same product to suit different users, charging subscriptions and, most important, using market mechanisms to help set prices.

The individualisation of goods

The digital world, in which information can be acquired and processed with ease, lets sellers tailor their products to individual customers. Further, the electronic environment allows companies to respond quickly to consumer feedback.

The ease of customisation, and the ability to adapt to variations in consumer preferences, lead to the possibility of individualising goods in the electronic markets. As each consumer will prefer (and be offered) a different version of the basic product, the total perceived value of the same (basic) product may be higher than with only one version of the product.

Comparison between the industrial economy (the physical marketplace) and the digital economy (the market space)

Electronic commerce is more than home shopping. It encompasses a range of electronic interactions between organizations and their up- and downstream trading partners. Many of their transactions have been occurring for quite some time, long before the Internet opened to commercial traffic. Platforms for electronic commerce that precede the Internet include the use of the Teletel in France for inter-organizational commercial transactions, as well as the use of EDI over private networks.

The Internet has become a powerful business tool. This new approach to the communication and distribution of information and services has transformed the fundamental dynamics behind many social and business interactions. The barriers and obstacles that often accompanied traditional commerce are giving way to new business approaches. Consumers, producers and distributors now all have flexible, fast and inexpensive ways of participating in the market for products and services around the world. Individual and corporate customers can approach the marketplace differently as the variety and depth of information on products and services speed up decision-making processes. Moreover, this new virtual marketplace is providing a significant boost to economic activity.

The Internet's unprecedented impact on the way the world does business stems from the way it has altered basic business dynamics. The dynamics that have shaped markets and market leaders since the nineteenth century – dynamics rooted in an industrial economy – have been replaced with a new set of fundamental principles based on a digital economy (Figure 14.1).

Figure 14.1 **The new business dynamics**

Industrial economy (Marketplace = physical products)	**Digital economy** (Marketplace = e-marketing)
• Manufacturing dominates	• Knowledge and relationships dominate
• Barrier: physical distribution	• E-distribution is the new barrier
• Barrier: lack of capital	• Capital is a commodity
• First-mover advantage was years	• First-mover advantage is months
• Innovative ideas contained internally	• Innovation is the public domain
• Relationships constrained by human capital	• Relationships can be established electronically

In the industrial economy, manufacturing dominates. The physical production of goods is the principal driver of economic activity. In the digital economy, knowledge and relationships dominate. It is a world where information and ideas are becoming more important than physical objects.

In the industrial economy, the most serious market barriers were lack of a physical distribution infrastructure and lack of capital. These significant barriers to entry in the physical world meant first-mover advantage could typically be measured in years. The Internet, however, has turned traditional distribution models upside down. With distribution models changing and capital roadblocks removed, markets are wide open and first-mover advantage is now measured in months. The new distribution roadblock is 'e-distribution', or the first-mover advantage earned by companies that are able to lock up exclusive business relationships with the new e-business drivers, such as the leading Web portals. Becoming an exclusive retail partner of a portal such as AOL, for example, would enable a retailer to leapfrog ahead of its competition.

14.3 Types of e-marketing – defining new business models

The impact of e-marketing on the economy extends far beyond the dollar value of e-marketing activity. Businesses use e-marketing to develop competitive advantages by providing more useful information, expanding choice, developing new services, streamlining purchasing processes and lowering costs. The Internet also imposes price discipline as customers have access to price and product information from many sources.

The different e-marketing markets may be divided into four categories. In the following the four markets shown in Table 14.1 will be further discussed.

Today *the market volume in the B-t-B is much bigger than in the B-t-C market* – five times more, according to Forrester (**www.forrester.com/**).

Table 14.1 Four different e-marketing markets

	Business	Consumer
Business	**B-t-B** • EDI relation • GM, Ford and DaimlerChrysler join forces in sourcing of autoparts in e-markets	**B-t-C** • Dell • amazon.com • eToys • Cdnow
Consumer	**C-t-B (reverse auctions)** • Priceline • MobShop (formerly Accompany) • LetsBuyIt	**C-t-C (traditional auctions)** • eBay • QXL

Business–to–business (B–to–B) e–marketing

Electronic-based commerce is not a new phenomenon in the B-to-B market. Instead of Internet-based solutions many industries have been using electronic data interchange for years to streamline business processes and reduce the cost of doing business. Suppliers, manufacturers, wholesalers, distributors and retailers share inventory information and send orders, invoices and shipping data electronically. EDI enhances the flow of information and goods through the supply chain and eliminates a manual re-entry of data, thereby eliminating errors and costly delays.

EDI is used for the exchange of structured data between the computer systems of trading partners. It is frequently used as an electronic replacement for traditional 'paper' documents such as the order form or invoice but EDI is developed also in the world of finance, administration, etc. In essence EDI is used for the exchange of structured data between originators and recipients of such information. EDI can be defined as *the transfer of structured data, by agreed message standards, from one computer system to another by electric means.*

A brief definition of the terms used in this definition will help readers understand the concept, which is also known as 'paperless trading':

■ The use of *structured data* refers to a precise, recognised method of assembling data. Such data items as item code, customer reference, delivery point and limit price all come together to form a purchase order invoice, packing list, acknowledgement of order, etc.

■ The phrase *by agreed message standards* implies that such discrepancies between documents (an invoice is one such message) will be minimised by providing a fixed and agreed method of specifying and presenting the data. Much effort has been expended by respected national and international bodies (ISO bodies) in producing standards for presenting the data, via syntax rules and message guidelines.

■ The definition also uses the phrase *from one computer system to another*, and implies that the two systems belong to distinct organizations. However, EDI can be used for both intra-company and inter-company communications.

■ The phrase *by electronic means* implies no human intervention. In Table 14.2 a comparison between the traditional EDI and the Internet is made.

Table 14.2 A comparison between EDI and the Internet

Traditional EDI	Internet
Proprietary, dedicated network	Open network
Highly structured, machine-readable data	E-mail, video, voice, image
High cost	Low cost
More secure	Less secure

Traditional EDI, however, is expensive and time consuming to implement. Many smaller companies simply cannot justify the price of entry. According to *Business Week*, adding a single trading partner to an EDI network can cost up to $50,000. In contrast, some Internet-based EDI links cost less than $1,000, making them affordable for a much broader audience.

EDI on the Web supports much richer information exchange. Traditional EDI supports only highly structured documents such as purchase orders and invoices. The Internet supports the exchange of multimedia information, including engineering drawings, full-colour photographs, audio and even video clips. As a result, Internet-based EDI fosters much tighter relationships among participants, providing a sense of teamwork and shared goals, and enabling all components and systems of a value chain to communicate with each other. Today, EDI has further developed and hybrid solutions are now available, most of them based on Web technology.

Many of the same advantages that arise from retail e-marketing hold for business-to-business e-marketing. For example, e-marketing can permit businesses to increase services they can offer their business customers. By opening an immediate and convenient channel for communicating, exchanging and selecting information, e-marketing is allowing firms to reconsider which functions they should perform 'in-house' and which are best provided by others. The new technology has helped to create new relationships and to streamline and augment supply chain processes. As these changes are occurring the roles of logistic and financial intermediaries (e.g. FedEx, UPS, American Express) are expanding.

These changes will result in aggressive growth rates during the next few years: in January 2000 Gartner Group forecast the worldwide B-t-B market would grow from $145 billion in 1999 to $7.29 trillion in 2004. (Gartner Group, 2000.)

The catalyst for B-t-B e-marketing is e-market maker activity. E-market makers are projected to facilitate $2.71 trillion e-marketing sales transactions in 2004, representing 37 per cent of the overall B-t-B market. (See also Figure 14.2 for the illustration of the principle behind e-markets.)

Boston Consulting Group's (BCG's) research shows that the size of the business-to-business e-marketing is far greater than is commonly reported, in part because it recognises the establishment of EDI over private networks and its extensions to the Internet. While EDI over private networks represented the biggest share of 1998 volume (86 per cent), nearly all of the additional volume until 2003 (90 per cent, or $2.0 trillion) will be Internet-based transactions. BCG predicts that business-to-business e-marketing will account for *24 per cent* of total business-to-business commerce by 2003.

Figure 14.2 illustrates the shift from EDI to Internet-based B-t-B e-marketing.

While business-to-business e-marketing is a global phenomenon, the North American market currently dominates. The $700 billion North American market is twice the size of business-to-business e-marketing in the rest of the world combined

Figure 14.2 The development of B-t-B e-marketing

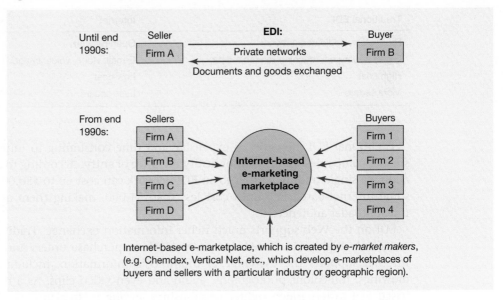

Internet-based e-marketplace, which is created by *e-market makers*, (e.g. Chemdex, Vertical Net, etc., which develop e-marketplaces of buyers and sellers with a particular industry or geographic region).

($330 billion). North America will likely retain its significant lead over the next few years, but the global dynamics of business-to-business e-marketing will shift. In western Europe, which lags 18 months behind North America in e-marketing adoption, several countries have accelerated their e-marketing investments and will significantly close this gap. Asia and Latin America remain further behind, but this may change rapidly as global supply chains go online. For local suppliers in local markets, business-to-business e-marketing presents significant growth opportunities, as they expand their networks and customer bases by accessing new export markets.

Business–to–consumer (B-t-C) e-marketing

Many of the advantages of e-marketing were first exploited (in the mid-1990s) by retail 'e-businesses' such as Amazon.com, eTrade, and Auto-by-tel that were created as Internet versions of traditional bookstores, brokerage firms and auto dealerships. Freed from the geographic confines and costs of running actual stores, such firms could deliver almost unlimited content on request and could react and make changes in close to real time. Compared to traditional retail or catalogue operations, this new way of conducting business is changing cost structures. The emergence of these e-businesses has made their competitors consider their own e-marketing strategies, and many now operate their own online stores (e.g. Barnes and Noble, Merrill Lynch).

E-marketing does more than simply provide alternative shipping sites to real-world stores; it can also expand existing markets and even create new ones. Not included in the cost savings listed above are the additional value that Internet-based businesses can provide in terms of increased information and choice and time savings. These advantages make it possible for buyers and sellers to come together in significantly more efficient ways than would otherwise be possible. For example, musicfile.com serves as a clearing house where music collectors and retailers can post their out-of-print vinyl records and CDs, and buyers can post their 'wants'.

The move towards providing goods and services through a digital medium does not need to be 'all or nothing'. In the retail business the Web store and the physical store can support each other in many different ways, capitalising on natural complementarities. These include cross-promotions, joint-service provisions and value-added services. Cross-promotions are perhaps the most straightforward example of a natural complementarity. Web stores may provide the bargains that people may expect when shopping on the Internet, but also offer coupons for in-store purchases. Marketers are accustomed to the use of 'loss-leaders' as an approach to increasing store traffic, and realise that once in the store other purchases for non-discounted merchandise are more likely. A physical store can use its website to highlight local events, such as a reading or performance at the store, helping to bring in traffic. The Web store may also provide information about additional services, available at the store, that add value to products purchased online. A company might use electronic mail for direct marketing not only to advertise the website, but also to provide information about in-store products and services. Some services might be provided jointly, leveraging the investment in physical and Web presence. A good example would be when a computer store offers a product online, but provides installation and repair services at its premises for customers purchasing from their website. Finally, the Web store may function as a source of value-added service for customers who have purchased or plan to purchase goods at the physical store.

With the emergence of Web-based grocery sites customers gain convenience by shopping online. A local grocery store then delivers the chosen items. Finally, a number of stores have initiated in-store Web kiosks as a means of lowering costs and improving service. In-store shoppers gain the ability to search for products not on display, gather in-depth information without taking up the salesperson's time, and even purchase or pay for products for immediate or subsequent delivery. These various complementary approaches represent a sampling of strategies a retailer might use to leverage its investment in physical and Web distribution channels.

Exhibit 14.1   **Priceline.com – consumer-to-business e-marketing**

Priceline.com has a type of e-marketing known as a 'demand collection system' that enables consumers to use the Internet to save money on a wide range of products and services while enabling sellers to generate incremental revenue. Using a simple and compelling consumer proposition – 'name your price' – Priceline.com collects consumer demand (in the form of individual customer offers guaranteed by a credit card) for a particular product or service at a price set by the customer and communicates that demand directly to participating sellers or to their private databases. Consumers agree to hold their offers open for a specified period of time to enable Priceline.com to fulfil their offers from inventory provided by participating sellers. Once fulfilled, offers generally cannot be cancelled. By requiring consumers to be flexible with respect to brands, sellers and/or product features, they enable sellers to generate incremental revenue without disrupting their existing distribution channels or retail pricing structures

Let us say that a customer wants a hotel room in San Francisco on a certain date, but only wants to pay $100 per night. Priceline will take this offer to its participating, name-brand hotels in San Francisco to see if any will agree to the price. If they are successful, the customer has the room they want at the price they want to pay! Since airlines fly with many empty seats every day, and thousands of hotel rooms go unsold every night, it is easy to understand why companies would be willing to consider the offer from a potential customer.

Consumer-to-business (C-t-B) e-marketing

This type of e-marketing is a kind of 'reverse auction' where the buyer (consumer) rather than the seller initiates the transaction.

Exhibit 14.1 illustrates an example where Priceline.com collects demand for a product at a price set by the customer. The 'reverse auction' also covers cases where a buyer sends out a tender and invites suppliers to put in bids. An example is Sainsbury, which has tendered a contract for a three-month supply of mild Chedder cheese, in a retail e-marketplace.

Consumer-to-consumer (C-t-C) e-marketing

This e-marketing type covers the new fashion for consumer-to-consumer auctions. They are not so much a new marketplace as a new form of entertainment. Auctions did not develop by chance; for many products they suit both buyers and sellers. Fixed prices did not develop by chance; for many (standardised) products they suit both buyers and sellers. However, despite these reservations, the new auction-pricing portals will not disappear, because they are great fun for many people. The bidding and close interaction between buyers and sellers promotes a sense of community – a near addiction that keeps them coming back.

The US-based eBay Inc. is the world's largest and most popular person-to-person trading community on the Internet. eBay pioneered online, person-to-person trading by developing a Web-based community in which buyers and sellers are brought together in an efficient and entertaining auction format to buy and sell personal items such as antiques, coins, collectibles, computers, memorabilia and toys. The eBay service permits sellers to list items for sale, buyers to bid on items of interest and all eBay users to browse through listed items in a fully automated, topically arranged, intuitive and easy-to-use online service that is available 24 hours a day, seven days a week.

The eBay user spends 130 minutes a month at the site – 10 times more than the typical Amazon user. Of all consumer e-marketing spending in 1998 some 15 per cent came through auctions (*Business Week*, 1999b).

Amazon's response to this development came on 12 April 1999 when it announced its plans to acquire the Internet-based auction company, LiveBid.com Inc., after eBay also approached the company about a possible buyout. In *Business Week* (1999b) Amazon's founder Jeff Bezos was asked if he thought that the dynamic pricing of auctions would come to other products of Amazon.com. Bezos answered (*Business Week*, 1999b):

> No, no, no. Auction pricing is most useful when it's hard to assess a fair value. So that means either that the thing you are selling is unique, or maybe it's not unique, but its value fluctuates rapidly. Stock prices are sort of like that. For most things, fixed prices are more efficient. The reason is that you don't have to negotiate. You don't want to negotiate the price of simple things you buy every day.

This answer is in line with the principles of the transactions cost analysis model, which implies that transaction costs increase when the transactions are characterised by a high degree of complexibility (see the TCA approach in Chapter 3).

QXL.com is eBay's direct European competitor. It is a pan-European auction community, conducting consumer-to-consumer and business-to-consumer auctions across seven countries in western Europe.

14.4　Exploring buying behaviour in e-marketing

This section deals with buying behaviour on the two main markets: the business-to-consumer (B-t-C) market and the business-to-business (B-t-B) market.

Segmenting and exploring consumer behaviour in the B-t-C market

Hofacker (1999) divides Internet users into two main segments:

1. *Hedonic surfers*. Hedonic surfers use a website by experiencing it in the same way they do movies and sports events. Often there is a strong non-verbal aspect to the hedonic experience – the images are quite important. Surfers are relatively unfocused and their browsing is spontaneous. The goal is escapist, to achieve immersion in the site, or at least a high degree of personal enjoyment either through arousal or pleasure or both. The idea is to gather interesting and exciting experiences from the Web.

   A unique site works best for these surfers, one which is novel and interesting. They can be drawn into a website via links everywhere and ad banners on other sites.

2. *Utilitarian searchers*. In contrast to hedonic surfers, utilitarian searchers are on a mission and they have a work mentality. The utilitarian searcher uses the Web in a way that is instrumental and rational. Such a visitor is looking for some kind of specific information. A well-organised and searchable site works best for these seekers.

   Utilitarian searchers often use search engines and they can often find a Web address that is easy to guess.

In the following we will further discuss consumer buying behaviour in the B-to-C market. Despite the fundamental difference between the 'physical marketplace' and the 'virtual market space', one principle still holds true in both worlds: the marketer must understand how the consumer makes decisions as to purchase choice before they can effectively respond to these demands.

Figure 14.3 provides an overview of the main differences between 'marketplace' and 'market space' in the consumer decision process. Of course, iteration exists between the different stages.

Each of these stages is now examined in turn and compared in the context of the marketplace and the market space.

Problem recognition

The first stage, consumer decision, triggers all subsequent activity. The consumer is compelled to fill the gap between the actual and the desired state. When problem awareness is reached problem recognition may be triggered by a number of external and internal factors.

In traditional markets, conventional marketing communications stimulate demand via conventional media, e.g. an advertisement on television. However, on the Internet the medium is new, and so new kinds of communications are required. In the traditional mass marketing approaches much of the audience will not be interested, and there is considerable wastage. But new information technologies fundamentally change that. Computer-mediated environments enable identification of individual

Figure 14.3 Consumer purchasing decision process: the marketplace vs market space

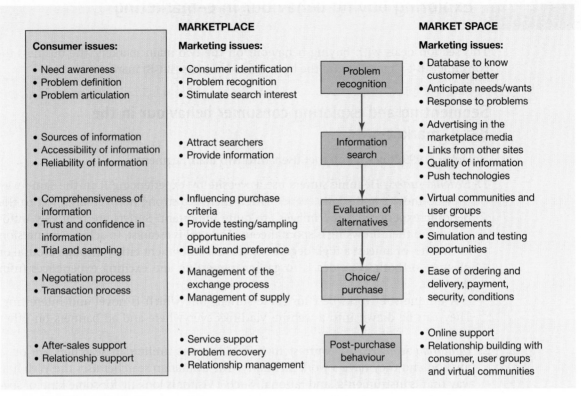

Source: Butler and Peppard, 1998, p. 603.

consumer needs and wants, and subsequent design and delivery of individual and customised communications.

Information search

The information gathered, be it from internal sources (e.g. memory) or external sources (e.g. discussions, brochures, sales promotions) provides the basis for this stage. The physical marketplace imposes limitations on information. Economic and access barriers constrain what can efficiently be known, and consequently what can realistically be evaluated. On the Internet, however, intelligent shopping agents can scan the entire Web to find the data necessary for comparison. The relevant criteria can be presented and explained and can be ordered to suit individual needs.

The management of information is the primary role of the agent or broker in the marketplace. The intermediary function is here largely based on information provision and exchange. This is the effective function of travel agents, for instance. But, in the market space, when an airline sets up its own website with interactive flight information and booking facilities, for example, then the traditional intermediary is bypassed in a classic case of disintermediation. As channel disintermediation and re-intermediation become important, a match between information content and consumer requirements also becomes important. As individuals come to utilise the Internet for consumer purchases a situation of perfect information is almost attainable. However, it must be noted that consumers' sense of uncertainty can actually increase as they gain more information. Information 'overload' occurs when we learn more about the alternatives available to us, and the search becomes 'psychologically costly'.

Evaluation of alternatives

In the marketplace word-of-mouth communication, the references of family, colleagues and friends, are a central influence at this stage. In the market space, new reference groups appear. The virtual community, consisting of discussion groups of interested parties, can have the power of the traditional reference groups, but with even greater quality and quantity of evaluative information. A simple version of a virtual community is Amazon.com's open book reviews, whereby a potential buyer can read book reviews by other website visitors.

Purchase decision

This stage involves decisions on *where* and *how* to buy. *Where* to buy is a decision regarding the choice of seller. Competition on the Web is driven by sellers attempting to build more exciting and interesting sites than their competitors, attracting the right customers to those sites, and providing superior shopping experiences to induce purchase. *How* to buy concerns the nature of the transaction and contract. Many of the products and services currently available to individual consumers on the Internet are digital, e.g. software and upgrades, or easily physically transported, e.g. music CDs and books. The future broadening of the base will require particular analysis of physical delivery issues. The actual delivery routines for such a service are probably more complex than the ordering, packing and payment routines. Whereas the order can be met within the one organization and under one roof, the logistics of physical delivery of relatively bulky but relatively low-value grocery orders is an entirely different proposition.

Post-purchase behaviour

In this stage the actual sale should be perceived as a starting point rather than an end. How the customer takes delivery of the product, how the product is used, the degree and satisfaction, quality of the service dimensions, customer complaints and suggestions are all critical to understanding consumer behaviour. This, of course, applies both in the *marketplace* and in the *market space*.

The main difference between relationship development in the two types of markets is that the *market space* emphasises 'high-tech', and is more characterised by the power of information and communication technologies to satisfy customer needs and thereby continue business relationships. For the seller in the market space the big issue is to update the website continuously. Post-purchase activity involves consumers returning to the seller's site with queries, for *new* information, and to repurchase.

Finally, how do features from marketplace retail stores relate to market space retail stores? Table 14.3 illustrates analogies between physical stores (also called 'bricks-and-mortar') and online retail stores. Obviously some features such as atmosphere are difficult to measure and characterise in online retail stores. Other features such as store promotions are less difficult to measure in online retail stores.

Exploring business behaviour in the B–t–B market

Web information systems hold great potential to streamline and improve business-to-business transactions. Instead of regarding the Internet as a mere sales channel, companies also utilise emerging technologies to cut costs out of the supply chain by streamlining procurement processes and improving collaboration. In times of intense competition and increasingly open markets the ability to achieve efficiency improvements can become key to commercial success.

Table 14.6 Differences between physical and online stores

Physical store: marketplace	Online retail store: market space
Salesclerk service	Product descriptions, information pages, gift services, search function, clerk on the phone/e-mail
Store promotion	Special offers, online games and lotteries, links to other sites of interest, appetiser information
Store window displays	Home page
Store atmosphere	Interface consistency, store organization, interface and graphics
Aisle products	Featured product on hierarchical levels of the store
Store layout	Screen depth, browse and search functions, indices, image maps
Number of floors in the store	Hierarchical levels of the store
Number of store entrances and store outlets/branches	Number of links to a particular online retail store
Checkout cashier	Online shopping basket and/or order form
Look and touch of the merchandise	Limited to image quality and description, potential for sound and visual applications
Number of people entering the store	Number of unique visits to the online retail store
Sales per period	Sales per period

Source: Lohse and Spiller, 1999, p. 4.

In the following we will look at how businesses make buying decisions and how they can be supported by an e-marketing information system. A conceptual framework is introduced in Figure 14.4. The interorganisational transactions are analysed from a process-oriented perspective. We distinguish between four phases: information, negotiation, settlement, and after-sales and transaction analysis.

Participants

Transactions usually involve three categories of participants: buyers, sellers and intermediaries. Buyers and sellers are the active groups in terms of exchanging goods and services (sellers) for some form of compensation (buyer). Regarding the third group,

Figure 14.4 The buyer/seller transaction process model

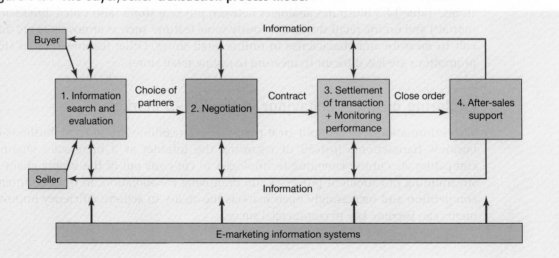

intermediaries, we will expand the role from a traditional distributor of goods as described in Chapters 10 and 11. The intermediaries are supposed to offer a variety of services to support and facilitate transactions. This includes financial institutions such as banks, credit card companies and insurance brokers; providers of shipping, logistics and warehousing services; and consultants, industry associations and market researchers offering advice, product data or market information. Providers of information technology to automate transactions or to help set up electronic marketplaces can be characterised as intermediaries as well.

In the case of business-to-business transactions, both buyers and sellers are business organizations, whereas business-to-consumer and consumer-to-consumer transactions involve end consumers or private households as buyers or sellers, respectively.

In the following we refer to the four phases of the buyer/seller transaction process model (Figure 14.4). In particular the role of the e-marketing information system will be described.

Phase 1: Information search and evaluation

In the information phase of a transaction both buyers and sellers reach out to the world in search of information. In the physical world (marketplace), buyers locate information sources such as product catalogues, use them to scan product listings, obtain offerings from prospective suppliers and gather additional information about products, vendor or transaction-specific requirements. Before a purchasing transaction can be performed internal approval frequently has to be obtained from upper-level management.

The information phase comprises both searching for a particular electronic catalogue or source of information and locating required information and commodities within the information repository. In this phase buyers and sellers are not yet focused on specific transaction partners. Information gathering and knowledge creation are the centre of attention, and information is the primary object of exchange between prospective transaction partners.

A variety of Web-based information systems and other applications are available to provide support for the information phase of a transaction. Electronic catalogues, for example, feature comprehensive product descriptions and search tools, configuration support for complex purchases, workflow routing for approval processes, and access to additional information such as market research data and product review. Catalogues can be provided by suppliers, set up by the buyer, or developed by a third party. They can be hosted on the supplier's Web server, or be integrated into internal systems. Links to back-end systems provide access to human resources data, as they are required to manage purchasing authorisation.

Phase 2: Negotiation

Of all transaction phases, the negotiation phase shows the broadest range of variations, from simple processes where price is the most important factor ('always-a-share'), to very complex arrangements where the buyer–seller relationship is regarded as a long-term strategic partnership ('lost-for-good'), according to Jackson (1985). Negotiations are often perceived as processes where a small number of prospective customers and sellers (often only one participant on each side) bargain on product prices and other terms of a deal. The parties jointly identify possible solutions with the goal of reaching a consensus, usually in the form of a contract. Bargaining processes alter with decisions whether to accept or reject the offering, and with the outlining of counter-suggestions until a mutually satisfactory agreement is reached. As prospective buyers and sellers start communicating directly with each other interaction is the centre of attention. In this phase influence is the primary object of exchange between the transaction partners. Not every transaction process features such complex negotiations. In fact the negotiation phase is very often quite simple or even non-existent, such as in the case of retail buys and pre-negotiated contracts.

Negotiations can range from a single transaction to multiple-year contracts. The longer the time span that is covered, the more complex the structure of the bargaining process tends to be. In the following, we focus on complex forms of negotiations (be it for one transaction or a large number), but acknowledge the simpler forms as well.

Information systems support negotiations in a number of ways. They can provide transaction information and decision support by assessing the value of specific offerings, by identifying new bargaining options, and by increasing the negotiation's productivity. Participants may improve their bargaining positions through additional online information, such as the volume of previous business, supplier performance or spending patterns.

Phase 3: Settlement of transaction + monitoring performance

Upon execution of the contract the objects of the transaction are exchanged according to the conditions previously stipulated. In addition, the settlement phase regularly includes some form of mutual performance monitoring. After the rather unstructured negotiation phase the process of executing a transaction can be relatively straightforward. It is formally initiated as soon as a purchase order is confirmed by the supplier. The supplier ships the goods (often in collaboration with a third party, for example a local provider of logistic services), announces the shipment, and sends out a corresponding invoice. On the buyer side, orders are tracked, items are received, and payment is initiated after matching the invoice with the delivery. Naturally there are many variations of this standard scenario. Consider, for example, the differences between the shipment of physical goods and the online delivery of information goods.

In the settlement phase of a transaction activities and procedures are comparatively well defined, as they are part of the contract. Thus attention centres on execution and efficiency. At this point the main objects of exchange are goods and services. Information technologies to support transaction settlement may include EDI systems on the Web and various tools to process orders internally and between transaction partners, facilitate order tracking and support payment processes.

Phase 4: After-sales analysis

After a transaction has taken place both sellers and buyers store the transaction data to provide after-sales support (seller), or to assess supplier performance and analyse internal buying patterns (buyer). On the buyer side the information flow is often split. While the purchase data is stored with central procurement, the end user keeps the product-related documentation. In case of unexpected irregularities it is often the end user who contacts the supplier (e.g. to request a repair). Without proper access to the transaction file communication problems and delays can occur. Capturing, storing and managing data are vital at this point. Similar to the first phase (information), it is mainly information that is being exchanged between buyer and seller.

The electronic support of after-sales activities ranges from simple electronic mail services to automated help desks and sophisticated electronic maintenance manuals. Ideally systems to support after-sales and transaction analysis provide central access to the transaction information. Data warehousing applications support the storing, accessing and processing of large amounts of data. They allow the firm to assess supplier performance, analyse internal buying patterns, provide the basis for consolidation corporate buys, and improve future bargaining positions with suppliers. On the supplier side, data about past transactions – including information of system configurations, preferred payment options and so forth – support the maintenance process and subsequently improve the quality of the information phase of future transactions.

14.5   Disintermediation in e-marketing – myth or reality?

According to transaction cost analysis firms will choose the entry and distribution mode that economises on transaction cost, e.g. in particular the coordination cost between producer and intermediaries.

Today, as information technology continues its rapid cost performance, information infrastructures are extending to reach individual consumers. The potential for transformations in the value chain of many firms is thus far greater now than it has been in the past, as technology begins to enable producers to interact directly with consumers. It has been noted that intermediaries add significant costs to the value chain, which are reflected in a higher prices of products or services to the end customers. One fundamental question, therefore, is to what extent producers would take advantage of direct electronic links with consumers, and whether, in the process, intermediaries will be eliminated from the value system.

The essential argument is that the use of IT allows manufacturers to internalise activities that have been traditionally performed by intermediaries. Producers will 'capture value' and in the resultant redistribution of profits along the value system traditional intermediaries will disappear. Benjamin and Wigand (1995) argue that if transactions take place directly between manufacturers and consumers both manufacturers and consumers will benefit: the manufacturers will try to retain a higher portion of surplus value or profits that are generated along the value system, while the consumers will benefit from both a larger choice and lower prices. In other words the network's ability to support direct exchanges efficiently will increase both producer and consumer welfare. Thus it is predicted that manufacturers will sell directly to consumers, and consumers will prefer to buy directly from manufacturers.

Thus the myth has been that the Internet will eliminate the need for intermediaries. Early predictions called for *disintermediation* (e.g. Wunderman, 1998), that is, the disappearance of physical distribution chains as people moved from buying through distributors and resellers to buying directly from manufacturers. The reality is that the Internet may eliminate the traditional 'physical' distributors, but in the transformation process of the value chain new types of intermediaries may appear. So the disintermediation process has come to be balanced by a re-intermediation force – the evolution of new intermediaries tailor-made for the online world (Figure 14.5).

The transformation of any industry structure in the Internet economy is likely to go through the intermediation–disintermediation–reintermediation (IDR) cycle – as shown in Figure 14.5. The IDR cycle will occur because new technologies are forcing change in the relationships among buyers, suppliers and middlemen. Intermediation occurs when a firm begins as a middleman between two industry players (e.g. buyer–supplier, buyer–established intermediary or established intermediary–supplier). Disintermediation occurs when an established middleman is pushed out of the value chain. Reintermediation occurs when a once disintermediated player is able to re-establish itself as an intermediary. Exhibit 14.2 and Case Study 14.2 give two examples of dis- and reintermediation.

Reintermediation occurs when new intermediaries use electronic networks to add

Figure 14.5 Disintermediation and reintermediation

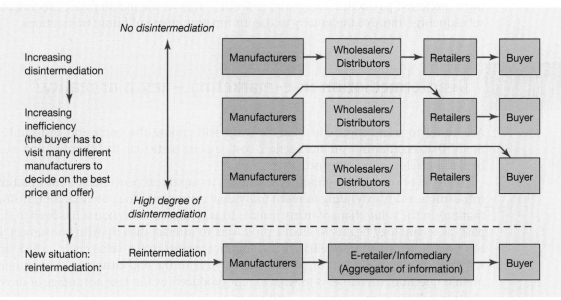

value to the intermediation electronic networks to add value to the intermediation process. In the IDR cycle some elimination of traditional intermediaries may occur in the short run, but the disintermediated players could also fight back and reintermediate themselves. The IDR cycle can react differently based on the structure of the marketplace.

The traditional distribution model is linear. The manufacturer builds products. Wholesalers and distributors aggregate products from multiple manufacturers and

---

Exhibit 14.2   **Dell – an example of disintermediation**

Disintermediation is not a new phenomenon. As far as Dell is concerned it began in 1983 when Michael Dell used the direct sales model, first by telephone and catalogue via Dell Direct, then, in July 1996, via its electronic site, Dell online. Founder Michael Dell's original idea was simple: sell computers directly, bypassing IT distributors. This disintermediation meant the company could avoid retail margins, make computers on demand, and lower the costs of stocking the finished product. Cutting the time lapse between production and delivery to the end customer is an undeniable advantage in an area where prices for components change rapidly and innovation seems ever present and exponential. If this new configuration gives Dell a key cost advantage and greater flexibility in terms of its formula, other factors reinforce its capacity to compete. Dell's virtual integration combines the wise use of IT with the systematic subcontracting of low added-value elements of the business. This combination has enabled it to gain from the dual advantages of coordination among the links of the value chain and a level of flexibility that comes with a virtual company.

Dell Computers as a manufacturing company gains efficiency by working closely with key suppliers to eliminate having to carry any inventory. Dell requires its suppliers of PC components to locate their inventory within 15 minutes of its factory. Dell also outsources with third-party warehouses that specialise in running technology-driven supply chains. On the logistics side, Dell links with UPS to store and deliver a specified monitor with the computer. Dell computer targets large corporate customers that order large quantities of PCs frequently, and the second and third time buyers of household PCs who do not need extensive sales information.

Source: adapted from **www.dell.com**; Jallat and Capek, 2001; Morris and Morris, 2002.

bring them through several levels of distribution in small lots to resellers who deal directly with consumers. The value added of the distribution chain lies in shipping, warehousing and delivering products.

With the Internet, value chains are being deconstructed and reconstructed in different ways – into value webs. *This process has given rise to a new class of intermediary.* Companies such as Yahoo! aggregate information and make it easier to access information and see new possibilities of doing business. *The value added is no longer in logistic aggregation but rather in information aggregation* – or eyeball aggregation. Consumers come to these sites looking for information and opportunities to purchase.

Companies such as Amazon.com and E*Trade are dramatically changing traditional models of selling goods and services by acting as a new type of intermediary. These new types of intermediary offer new opportunities for existing companies as well as start-ups. Companies need to examine their current value chain and determine how the Internet might change it. Then they can adapt their business processes to take advantage of the new model – protecting their major sources of revenue and also developing new ones.

As an example, consider the airline industry. In the physical economy, who are the distributors of travel tickets? Thousands of travel agents, spread around the world. In the online economy, who are the distributors? Travel-related websites such as Microsoft's Expendia, among others. Consider another data point: in some big cities of the United States various reports indicate that almost 30 per cent of automobile sales take place on Internet sites. The distribution channels have not gone away; they have simply shifted to new intermediaries (see Case Study 14.2).

14.6   Developing dynamic global e-marketing

Many commercial websites have moved from providing basic company and product information to becoming an integral part of product and service launch strategies. Yet many firms are realising that even this more coordinated approach is not taking full advantage of the Internet environment.

Figure 14.6 explores the development of a firm's Web strategy from a low-level strategy with the same one-way communication to a fully integrated e-marketing strategy, where the customer feels that they are treated on a one-to-one interactive basis. The following discusses the three commitment levels in detail.

Level 1: One-to-many broadcast ('use Internet representation as a company and product brochure')

Companies use the Internet for something that could be considered little else than a formal presence. These companies feel that they have to be present on the Web, but do not follow any concrete marketing objectives with the establishment of their website.

The motivation of the management in establishing such a page is most probably mainly reactive: as competitors move on to the Web it is felt that a presence has become necessary. Often, however, management will doubt that few if any customers or prospects will ever care to go near the page. The only tangible benefit from the Web is seen in the ability to use the website in traditional marketing channels in order to project a 'high-tech' image, an image of a company that keeps abreast of the latest developments. Although such an Internet 'strategy' will certainly not double

Figure 14.6 **Increasing commitment to e-marketing**

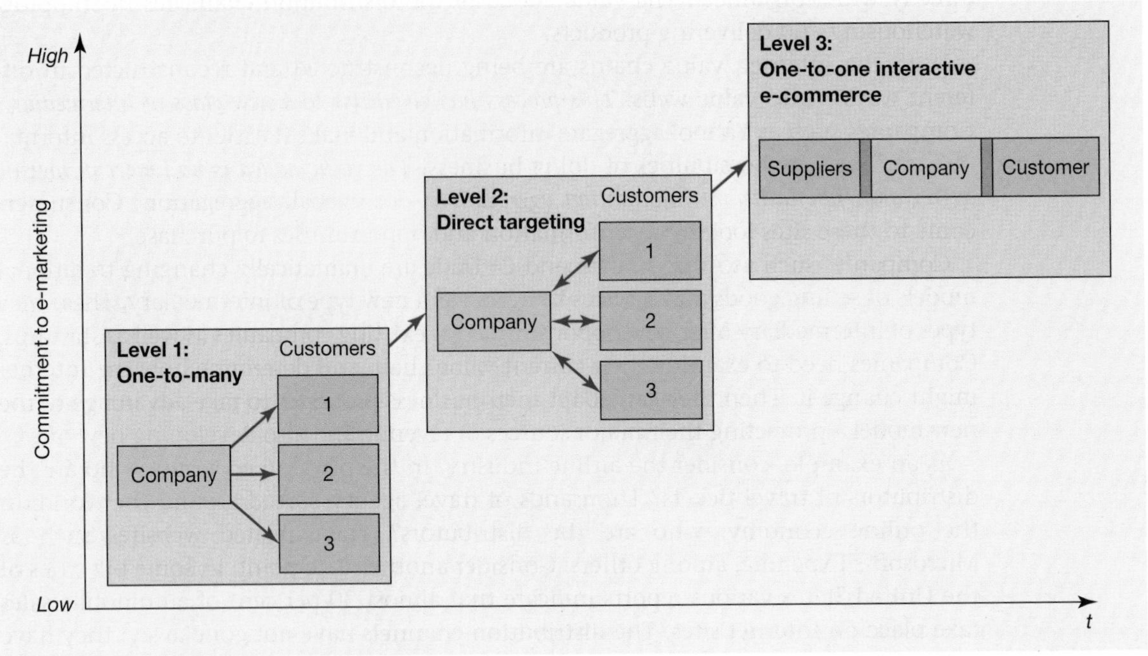

the company's turnover it can nonetheless be an economically plausible move because investments are low.

The Web representation is regarded as an additional tool to channel information on a firm's products or services to potential and existing customers. Companies following this strategy do consider the World Wide Web a useful tool, but perceive it more or less as no different from the traditional one-to-many marketing channels. The focus of such a Web presence will therefore lie in the firm providing as much information as possible through the Web rather than establishing a dialogue with the customer. Consequently these companies will spend considerable time designing their website and ensuring the information is complete, accurate and kept up to date. The site will be easy to access, quick to load, and easily found using search engines. Products or services may be displayed in great detail in this virtual showroom to enhance their visibility and exposure in the marketplace and thus increase purchase probability.

However, these sites will not be designed as a communication device. The site will not explicitly encourage customer feedback such as service requests or complaints beyond product enquiries. Moreover, if a customer wants to purchase a product they will often have to use the traditional channels to do so. In summary, these informational sites represent company and product brochures. Economically speaking this is a valid strategy for companies that rely heavily on mass communication. The Web presence will allow these firms to keep their customers and prospects constantly up to date. It will also decrease the amount of printed information and the likelihood of having boxes full of outdated brochures awaiting disposal.

Level 2: Direct targeting

For the firms on this level the key difference between traditional marketing media and the new cyber marketing is the degree of interactivity. Communication is no longer based on businesses feeding information to customers. Rather, the customers play an active role not only in looking for information relevant to the specific product and service needs in their buying process, but also in communicating these needs to the company. Hence some degree of segmentation is possible. In some cases the customers can also buy standard products on the website. The interaction (feedback) is still not on the highest level, as the basic exchange of information takes place through e-mails.

The most fundamental capability of a website is the presentation of information about products, services, people, events or ideas. Websites with a strategic orientation emphasise both the gathering (feedback) and diffusion of information. It is possible to evaluate the extent to which an organization fulfils the informing function by examining the efforts to exchange information with key stakeholders. These stakeholders are customers, investors, suppliers, affiliates, employees, managers and community members. In addition to providing information on the company's vision, history, products and services, many websites include information on organizational structure, financials, recruiting, executive teams and customer surveys.

After establishing a presence on the Internet one of the primary objectives of a new website is to attract a variety of interested parties to visit the company's online presence. This is done in a variety of ways. It may simply be a matter of mentioning the address of the firm's home page in all possible connections. On the other hand, the company may have found differences among the customers and have differentiated the home page to its different customer groups around the world.

Many companies try to duplicate their US e-marketing strategy in European countries, but it is not as easy as it might seem. Companies cannot create a single website and expect to reach customers and distributors around the world.

Global e-marketing with one worldwide standardised website will probably not be successful in the long run, but for the small company ('Born Global') it may be the only way to get started in global e-marketing, without using too many resources. The moment a company has to deliver physical goods it is up against every piece of legislation that exists in the real world (e.g. tariff barriers, VAT). Not to mention every cultural, legal, ethical and language barrier.

Let us further explore the language barrier. Today there are only seven countries where English is the primary language spoken and where the combined economies represent 30 per cent of the world's economy. The combined population of these countries (some half a billion people) represent 8 per cent of the world's population. Companies that continue to target this small fraction of the world market will miss out on capturing a large potential market.

An example of the use of multilingual websites is Eastman Kodak, which has region-specific versions of its Kodak.com websites in 16 countries. Also, search engines such as Yahoo! and Alta Vista have country-specific websites, at least in their major markets.

Level 3: One-to-one interactive e-marketing strategy

This is the final level, where we see a high degree of interaction between buyer and seller. Here the company is moving from providing company and product information to becoming an integral part of the whole vertical value chain from supplier to end consumer. This virtual integration works faster than Level 2 (direct targeting) by blurring traditional boundaries between suppliers, manufacturers and customers in the value chain. Dell Computers gained the position as a market leader in the personal computer industry by using this model (Magretta, 1998).

A website that supports e-marketing can provide an important strategic asset for a business. A successful site has many benefits:

- It tightens relationships with existing customers and business partners.
- It offers new revenue-generating opportunities – through new channels as well as new business models.
- It offers opportunities to reduce costs by streamlining processes.
- It provides a competitive advantage.

Building a site can represent a significant investment in time and resources. A haphazard approach often results in wasted money and lost opportunity. To be successful companies must integrate e-marketing into their overall business strategies and processes. They must understand the role of e-marketing in the context of other revenue-generating channels as well as re-engineering and cost-reduction initiatives.

Companies must also recognise that e-marketing may have a dramatic impact on existing business models and distribution channels. It may be necessary to redefine the current business model and perhaps modify relationships with the current channel or supply chain – or develop entirely new relationships or supply chains. Some industries will be more affected than others by the supply chain transformation that the Internet is causing. In some industries a complete redefinition of the business model may be the only way to maintain a competitive edge. As a result, a careful examination of the existing business model and how e-marketing may affect it is essential for success in the online arena.

The following phases are involved in developing and implementing a successful e-marketing strategy:

1. *Identification of the process, product or business area that is most applicable for an e-marketing initiative.*
2. *The company's e-marketing goods.* Questions that need to be answered include:
   (a) What portion of the business will e-marketing represent in 12 months, two years and five years?
   (b) What volume of business does the company expect over the next five years?
   (c) What level of return on investment does the company expect?
   (d) How will return on investment be measured?
   (e) What cost savings can the company realise through e-marketing?
   (f) Will online sales reduce the sales volumes in existing channels? If so, what will be the impact on each channel?
3. *Definition of 'internal' and 'external' actors.* Defining the audience or customer is one of the primary tasks because it determines how and when internal and external actors should be involved. This includes identifying internal audiences such as marketing, sales, channel sales, finance, IT and other internal groups, as well as external customers, suppliers, vendors, resellers and other business partners. This element of the overall plan affects many other aspects of the e-marketing system, from site design to online marketing techniques.
4. *Evaluation of competitor strategies.* The company's traditional competitors may already have an e-marketing initiative. It is essential to identify what these competitors are doing. Are they aggressively pursuing an e-marketing strategy or are they taking a wait-and-see approach? Are they extending their existing offerings to the new channel or are they creating an entirely new business? Although current competitors are a threat, non-traditional competitors often represent the biggest competitive risk. These are the companies that find new ways to reconstruct traditional value chains into value webs – gaining a significant head-start over companies that simply move existing business processes to the Internet.
5. *Integration of e-marketing with existing distribution channels and partners.* E-marketing is one component of an overall business value chain. It integrates with existing busi-

ness processes and systems, and should complement existing channels rather than compete with them.

6. *Putting the right internal competences/skills in place*. Moving into the electronic commerce area requires new skills, knowledge and expertise in the three areas of strategy, technology and creativity:

   (a) *Strategy*: Strategic planning must be approached in a totally different way because of the dynamic nature of the Internet. Therefore the time perspective of strategic plans in the 'physical' firms (e.g. five years) should normally be shortened to maybe one year in 'virtual' firms.

   (b) *Technology*: Internet technologies are rapidly evolving, and keeping pace with the new breakthroughs is difficult. Technological expertise involves in-depth understanding of current hardware and software solutions, new technologies, site development, systems integration and security issues.

   (c) *Creativity*: Creative skills involve more than just basic website design. This discipline encompasses the entire user experience – what users see, how they navigate, how they obtain information and how they conduct transactions. It also encompasses the audience development activities that drive traffic to the site. Marketing and promotional techniques that are effective in traditional media do not always translate well into the online marketplace.

After considering these phases the company may go on to the phase with design and implementation of the desired e-marketing system.

Companies that conduct e-marketing are subject to the same laws, regulations and taxes that govern operations of all businesses. Companies operating on the Web face at least one complicating factor as they try to follow the laws. A company that uses the Web immediately becomes an international business, and as such the company can become subject to many more laws, more quickly, than it would if it had been a traditional bricks-and-mortar company tied to one specific physical location. Furthermore, any country's legal issues are difficult to interpret and follow because of the newness of electronic commerce and the unsettled nature of the laws. Some of the legal issues

14.7   The legal environment of e-marketing

(in different countries) on which companies might need to seek specific legal advice are: ownership of company's domains (URLs), advertising/marketing standards and taxation on e-marketing.

If the Internet is used to promote and sell product overseas the company has to be aware of various marketing legislation in the different countries; for example, Germany has specific laws that prohibit explicit comparisons between products.

One interesting issue is the *data protection and privacy laws*. The European Union's comprehensive privacy legislation, the Directive on Data Protection (the Directive), became effective on 25 October 1998. It requires that transfers of personal data take place only to non-EU countries that provide an 'adequate' level of privacy protection.

The United States and the European Union have been trying to set common rules on data privacy. The former is concerned that strict EU laws would stop companies from sending some data to the United States from the European Union. The United States also says the EU rules are likely to give US consumers a false sense of security because such rules are impossible to enforce. In November 1999 the Commerce Department released a plan to issue 'safe harbor' regulations that would protect US companies operating in Europe from sanctions under a new EU law as long as they meet certain guidelines. The European Union, meanwhile, is concerned that the United States may not enforce privacy guidelines strictly enough. It also wants the United States to set clear rules that allow consumers access to their own personal information that has been collected by businesses.

14.8 A global strategy for Internet marketing

The Internet was often seen as an embodiment of globalization and terms such as 'borderless cyberspace' were previously used to refer to it. It was hailed as a space where individuals and firms could escape the control of nation-states. Governments would not be able to effectively regulate the Internet and such regulation could even be considered illegitimate, so there would be unlimited freedom of speech, no taxes and no government regulation.

But maybe the World Wide Web is not so global after all. When Theodore Levitt wrote his influential article 'The globalization of markets' (1983) he proposed that companies standardise their approach to foreign markets, emphasising the similarities rather than the differences. Although current technological, economic and demographic changes give some credence to Levitt's view it is not clear that a global strategy always delivers the highest profits. In fact, depending on the nature of the product and the industry, local adaptation may be a better way of making money. Contrary to conventional wisdom, local responsiveness may contribute to sustainable profitability for certain types of goods or services, and in certain Internet markets. Globalization and the net are not simply and not always about standardisation and homogenisation.

Businesses are finding it hard to service the global e-market as if it were of one piece. Different national regulations, local consumer preferences and habits, currencies, languages, user demographics and attitudes toward pricing and quality militate against global Internet strategies that approach all national markets as if they were the same. At long last (measured in Internet time) companies such as Yahoo!, Amazon and eBay are recognising that some measure of local adaptation to each specific national market is a hallmark of a successful, and profitable, Internet strategy. Yahoo!, for instance, operates in 22 country-specific portals in 13 different languages (Guillen, 2002).

Vast differences in online behaviour, connectivity, platforms, regulatory conditions and cultural aspects have emerged as Internet use increases worldwide. The different dominant delivery platforms in many countries suggest that online experiences are very diverse. Europe and Japan are already experiencing a wireless-based online experience. A dial-up experience is prevalent in Mexico and Brazil. European and Japanese users prefer wireless or Internet services to PC-based access, given the high cost of computers and small home environments. German online top sites are those that offer financial reports, whereas UK top sites are sports and entertainment. Brazilian Internet use is dominated by chat room activity (Robles, 2002).

Although there are substantial differences in online use and experience worldwide, there are a few similarities that are worth mentioning. Online user concerns for privacy and security seem to be important across countries and cultures. Another universal trait is the emergence of particular clusters of users with common interests and online use. The culture of intense online socialisation using multiple platforms seems common to youth in Japan or England. Others include the emergence of female and senior users.

In the following we discuss some of the factors influencing the creation of a global e-marketing strategy.

Diversity of regulations

Online regulations such as privacy laws, taxes or commerce have a direct impact on online providers, and thus shape usage behaviour in a given country. The type of competition emerging in a given country or region depends on the type of regulatory framework. Strict European privacy guidelines prohibit the transfer of data across borders. In fact the transfer of any data requires the customer's permission. In Italy bank regulations require customers to open accounts in person, forcing online banking providers to establish an offline presence.

Furthermore, as the consumers may come from many different jurisdictions with different consumption tax regimes, the administration of tax is particularly complex in e-marketing. It is also more difficult to locate the place of consumption and the place of origin of the delivered good/service for tax purposes, particularly with regard to 'all-digital' transactions such as the purchase of music files on the Internet using electronic cash (Frynas, 2002).

Infrastructure

Telecommunication and Internet infrastructures differ markedly from country to country. Perhaps two aspects are especially relevant to strategy formulation. First, installed international bandwidth sets limits on the speed at which information flows back and forth between a foreign website and a local buyer. One way a firm can react to these slow speeds is by redesigning its website to make downloading pages less time-consuming. The number of 'click-throughs' necessary to complete a purchase may also have to be reduced. Second, there are stunning differences between countries in terms of the proportions of users accessing the Web through a PC, their TV set or a mobile phone.

Geographical distance

The world may have shrunk as a result of globalization and the net, but distance is still an issue. It is hard to underestimate the need for smooth and cost-effective distribution logistics when it comes to fulfilling international orders for tangible goods. The ability to deliver physical products on a timely basis is not the only challenge to online marketers, however. Processing and restocking product returns can be a nightmare, especially given widely different cross-national regulations and customer preferences on returns policies.

Language

The world would be very simple (though perhaps boring) if English were the only language. Too many an e-company has ignored the golden rule of marketing: that marketing activities should always take place in the language of the customer. Buyers like to purchase products and services in their own language, especially if the purchasing process requires understanding contractual clauses.

User demographics

Although online populations are growing rapidly throughout the world no one should assume that they are homogeneous. For instance, only 10 per cent of Internet users in most Latin American countries are women, whereas women represent close to 50 per cent in the United States and Europe. Companies looking to sell, say, health care goods and services online will find it hard to grow sales in countries with few women Web surfers, since it is women who make most of the family decisions on health care. Similarly, in some countries most Internet users are located in the major metropolitan areas, which considerably simplifies distribution logistics.

Buyer behaviour

As if language were not enough of a complication, there are countless differences in tastes and preferences. These are especially pronounced in the case of 'cultural' goods, such as food, wine and entertainment. Even consumer durables are subject to tremendous cross-national variations in taste. Companies need to consider customer tastes and preferences when it comes to merchandise selection and stocking. Portals with online stores are now offering different selections and special discounts in each country.

Payment systems

Payment methods and customs vary widely from country to country. Much e-marketing growth has been based on the assumption that people have credit cards, but rare is the country in which most adults have one. In most countries more than 75 per cent of the adult population does not. In many countries even people with a credit card are reluctant to use it online for security reasons.

The challenges to credit-card-based e-marketing are enormous even in affluent western Europe. Many buyers and sellers alike prefer bank transfers and cash on demand. But let us not forget that legal and cultural norms of credit vary significantly throughout the world.

Currency

Many Internet companies are also stymied by how difficult it is to decide the currency in which to quote prices when buyers from different countries can visit the website; for example, eBay alienated many foreign customers by quoting prices only in dollars.

Some sites therefore offer currency conversion engines, but that may just add to the customer's frustration when the exchange rate applicable to a particular purchase depends on the payment method used. It seems that e-companies may have to accept the reality of multiple currencies and try to leverage it as a price discrimination tool. They should also keep an eye on currency fluctuations, since the time lag between order and payment exposes them to exchange rate risk.

Firms that perceive a high level of pressure to respond to local needs use a nationally responsive strategy. Localisation strategy of global portals is challenging because of lack of local content, the diversity of platforms, regulations, and lack of flexibility of off-the-shelf operational programs. The areas of the portal architecture that require substantial localisation are content, commerce and connectivity platforms. Content needs to be adapted to local user culture in terms of language, formats and iconography. For instance, content adaptation of interfaces and applications features should support local data formats such as dates, currencies, numbers and addresses. This localisation effort requires the redesign of forms and dynamic content generation and even back-office support systems such as help and customer support. The commerce architecture also needs to be localised to support different payment mechanisms, tax systems, currencies, fulfilment options and compliance with privacy and decency regulations. A third important area of localisation is the connectivity platforms in the local market. The local telecommunication options and capacity will determine the mix and richness of text, graphics, voice and video that can be delivered online.

To reduce the local responsiveness pressure some global e-marketers have concentrated on particular niches. These niches are either language based (Chinese or Spanish language portals) or business-segment based (sports, entertainment, financial information). For instance, an online financial portal has developed a successful business model, focused on the needs of Latin American investors.

Development of a global portal strategy

An international expansion strategy triggers a number of questions that the Internet portal needs to address. The decisions at the early stage include which markets or regions to enter first, whether or not to use local partners, what functions of the portal architecture to offer on international sites, what to host in the home base and abroad, and how to develop local content, commerce and connectivity. Robles (2002) found that the Internet firms' global portal strategy develops through different stages.

Stage 1: Translation of content (from home base)

The first stage of internationalization implies the translation of content and other relevant information to the language of the visitor. At this early stage of internationalization traffic to the portal and information thereon is given to international visitors from home-based operations.

Stage 2: Presence in international markets

At the second stage the portal establishes a presence in international markets in a variety of ways. Portals moved first to countries with large online populations through joint ventures and partnerships with local media companies or telecommunications firms. The local site at this stage was a copy of the home-based portal. The portal transferred the basic functionality (technology) of the site while keeping some of the most advanced back-end systems at home and also providing host services for the new venture while it took off. The local partner contributed with marketing, promotion and customer service, local network and connectivity, billing, securing local content, and recruiting local commerce partners.

Stage 3: Extensive localisation

At the third stage extensive localisation and local development of services and tools took place. Alliances with local firms to provide local language search engines, local directories and more local content were central at this stage. An important effort at this stage was to increase the depth of local commerce. As part of the localisation, portals leveraged the information captured from visitors to fine-tune the local interface. This decentralised approach resulted in a variety of interfaces, sites and connectivity platforms in national markets, but kept a uniform template for all. At this stage innovation and upgrading of services took place on the home site. Some, but not all, of these innovations were transferred to international sites.

Stage 4: A common global platform

As international expansion gains momentum Internet firms may reconsider the diversity of local strategies, by attempting to consolidate and introduce efficiencies. The pressure for consistency and universal architecture stems from the challenge of rivals, whether global or local portals. Most firms realise that only one or two viable global portals will remain so in the long run. Several strategies emerge at this stage. The most common approach is to develop a common global platform and a distributed architecture that make sense on grounds of efficiency. Under this strategy the portal firm seeks global partnerships with content, commerce and infrastructure providers. Another strategy is to focus on a region, seeking to dominate a particular geography. The regional strategy allows firms to become highly focused on a given community by aggregating commerce and media to a target segment, based on culture and language.

Robles (2002) uses the international expansion of AOL to illustrate this global portal evolution framework.

The global evolution of portals seems to fit the theory of stages of internationalization described in Chapter 3 of this book. The main differences seem to be explained by the nature of the technology. In the early stages portal firms export the service and enter international markets without committing large resources or taking large risks. As they learn, they replicate the portal infrastructure for local markets and provide shared services to national operations. Later stages require a greater degree of control and integration. At this stage global portals may either try to integrate by acquiring full control, such as AOL's evolving European strategy, or develop a web of national partnership such as MSN is using.

In global portals, in addition to cost efficiency reasons, the need for integration stems from the view of corporate offices, desire to achieve consistent branding. Another reason for integration is to provide users with the same online experiences through uniform look-and-feel interfaces. Global portal integration is achieved through the use of common technology platforms and standards that allow remote sites to share central corporate resources (information) and assets (servers), use the same style guides and templates, and pre-approved reference applications. For instance, hosting services in one central location would reduce costs to all network operations. With a distributed architecture the host and control server could customise and deliver the service to clients worldwide. One example could be serving banner advertising for a global partner, where a uniform copy and message can be translated and customised on demand for a variety of languages and geographies.

The characteristics of integrated global networks provide the architecture to attempt to not only be able to centralise certain processes but be responsive and able to coordinate the variety of localised sites and complex collaboration agreements at the global, regional and local level.

Another area where global portals have been able to develop strong competences is in the integration of the value chain. The value chain for a portal can be defined as the design, production and delivery of content and commerce through a rule-based system that permits the creation of value to the user. Broad-based portals have benefited largely from transactional completeness in the value chain because their operating costs to aggregate and manage large pools of providers of content, engage in commerce and develop communities are very low. As integrators, portals create online user value at a minimal cost. Their operating costs are mostly related to network communications and operations. This architecture allows portal firms to separate common content from content that is specific to local sites through centralised hubs. The key to building such architecture is to build in the flexibility to support multiple localised versions in the e-network.

Given the recent nature of globalization of the Internet an effective global portal strategy has not yet emerged. The potential to develop one depends on firms' abilities to formulate an adequate balance of global integration and local responsiveness. Finding the right mix of efficiency, local responsiveness and transaction completeness and a global configuration of assets, competences, partners, content, commerce and community is a challenge.

The success of any global portal strategy also depends on their ability to conquer the massive online populations in the developing world. Current strategies have been based on the online experiences of first-time users in China, Brazil or Mexico, which tend to be highly educated, affluent and cosmopolitan. The needs, concerns and experiences of the larger masses of middle class and poor income segments could be radically different.

In summary, the bottom line is that in the new economy a company still needs to maximise the chances that customers will be aware of its existence, take a liking to its products or services, decide to buy them, and be happy about the overall experience – preferably in their own language.

14.9 International mobile marketing

In this chapter mobile marketing (**m-marketing**) is defined as the application of marketing to the mobile environment of smart phones, mobile phones, personal digital assistants (PDA) and telematics. M-marketing is characterised by both the interaction with the World Wide Web and the location-specific context that enhances communication and delivery of information. Marketing communication and information can be delivered to mobile devices via voice activated portals or 'vortals', text applications such as SMS, using e-mail (the current I-Mode application) and via Web-mediated delivery using the 3G spectrum. These applications provide ideal opportunities for making m-marketing a pervasive electronic presence that senses and responds not only to who the customer is, but where they are and what they are doing. It is clear that adding value to the consumer experience will require that organizations anticipate and meet the needs of customers not only based on psychographics, demographics and behaviours, but also on their real-time personal physical location, and to travel alongside the customer to provide them with tailored messages and information at the point of need.

M-marketing should be considered within the context of m-commerce. Emerging from recent developments in communications technology, m-business represents 'mobile' business and refers to the new communications and information delivery model created when telecommunications and the Internet converge. M-marketing combines the power and speed of the Internet with the geographic freedom of mobile telephony in terms of receiving and transmitting data and, importantly, the ability to conduct transactions. The emerging capacity to communicate with any individual, from any place, over any network, and to any device, regardless of time or geographical location, provides enormous potential for marketers. For this reason the impact on marketing strategies for direct marketers needs to be addressed.

Thus m-marketing is the use of wireless technology to provide convenient, personalised and location-based information for a commercial purpose to consumers and businesses. Consequently a transaction in m-marketing involves a unique combination of time, location and personalisation of the service. At the same time m-marketing has two important limitations:

1. *Form factor*. The physical form of mobile devices invokes very different user experiences from those of a desktop. Manufacturers will have to develop larger screens for PDAs, convenient keyboards for two-way pagers, or voice recognition for mobile phones.

2. *Bandwidth*. There are still several constraints for transmitting audio and video over mobile devices. However applications, not bandwidth, will drive m-commerce

Exhibit 14.3	Adidas – m-marketing

The Adidas short message service (SMS) campaign provides an illustration of this potential. By utilising the 24/7 Media Europe opt-in SMS database and using a text message to alert a specific demographic group, Adidas was able to increase brand awareness and drive users to watch the Adidas advertisements in the first break of the televised Brit Awards (an annual music award in the United Kingdom). The media agency Mindseye Communication was looking for a new and original method to market the Adidas brand consistent with its image and to co-promote the Brit Awards. This method allowed a direct response by precisely timing the messages and alerting the target audience, people in the United Kingdom aged under 30, to a specific event in a specified time frame.

growth. Many applications requiring large bandwidth are not necessary for mobile commerce.

Figure 14.7 shows how the three characteristics of m-marketing are interlinked and dependent on each other.

Figure 14.7 The three unique characteristics of m-marketing

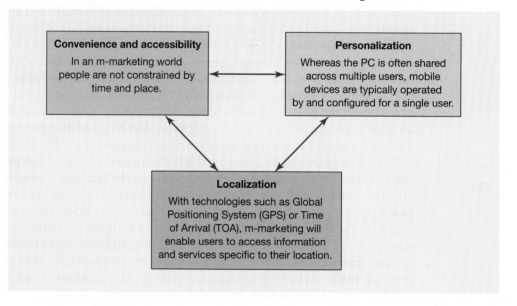

Each country/market has its own marketing mix

Distinction between e-marketing and m-marketing

A key distinction between e-marketing and m-marketing lies in the different enabling technologies. Most notably, the facilitative mode for traditional e-marketing, the PC, is a relatively large and cumbersome device that is probably deskbound and equipped with a Web browser through standard connectivity. Even when configured as a laptop it is not easy to move.

M-marketing is faced with the challenge of developing capabilities in a much more diverse technical context, albeit within the single framework of mobility. Mobile devices currently vary in terms of the network to which they are connected – the 'European' standard or the North American standard.

Rapidly emerging innovations will deliver the possibility of smart phones able to use product bar codes to access product-related information and phones able to act as e-wallets, as either a prepaid card for small purchases or a fully functioning credit/debit card unit.

Benefits of m-marketing

The introduction of m-marketing should bring a series of benefits to consumers, merchants and telecommunication companies. As with all technologies, many benefits will arise in the future that are not yet even imagined. Some benefits that are apparent now, however, include the following

For consumers

- *Comparison shopping*: Consumers can access on demand, at the point of purchase, the best prices in the marketplace. This can be done now without mobility, with services such as pricescan.com.
- *Bridge the gap between bricks and clicks*: Services permitting users to examine merchandise in a store and still shop electronically for the best price.
- *Opt-in searches*: Customers may receive alerts from merchants when products they are looking for become available.
- *Travel*: Ability to change and monitor scheduled travel any time, any place.

For merchants

- *Impulse buying*: Consumers may buy discounted products from a Web page promotion or a mobile alert, increasing their willingness to buy as they are right near or even inside the store, and thus increasing merchants' sales.
- *Drive traffic*: Companies will guide their customers to where it is easier to carry out the transaction, to either online or offline stores, due to the time-sensitive, location-based and personalised characteristics of the mobile device
- *Education of consumers*: Companies will send information to customers about product benefits or new products.
- *Perishable products*: This is especially important for products that do not retain their value when unused, such as service-based products. For example, the use of an aeroplane seat, that, when unused, generates no revenue and is lost value. This will enable companies to better manage inventory.
- *Drive efficiency*: Companies will save time with their clients. Because information is readily available on the mobile device they will not have to talk about the benefits of the different products or about prices.
- *Target market*: Companies will be better able to target their products and promotions to those in a given geographic area at a specific time.

For telecommunication companies the advantages are primarily more airtime used by the consumers and higher fees charged to content providers for each m-commerce transaction.

M-marketing requires direct marketers to rethink their strategies to tap into already existing communities such as sports fans, surfers, music fans, and time-context communities such as spectators at sports events and festivals, and location-sensitive communities such as gallery visitors and small shoppers, and develop ways to get them to opt in to m-marketing.

Applications must be responsive to location, customer needs and device capabilities. For example, time and location-sensitive applications, such as travel reservations, cinema tickets and banking will be excellent vehicles for young, busy and urban people.

Finally, as highlighted, mobile marketing enables distribution of information to the consumer at the most effective time, place and in the right context. This suggests that m-marketing, via mobile devices, will cement further the interactive marketing relationship.

The players in the mobile value chain

Wireless Internet access promises great potential for all the players in the value chain, but the key to a rapid take-up, and faster revenues, is finding a way to provide services to as wide a customer base as possible.

Figure 14.8 highlights the players in the value chain in the mobile commerce market.

Figure 14.8 The interaction of the main actors in the mobile value chain

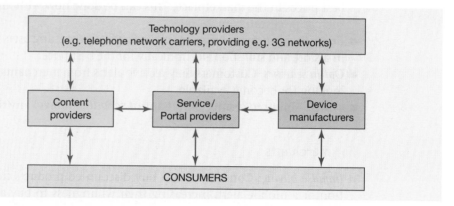

Technology providers

The way the world views mobile communications is expected to change in the coming years. All the power of the World Wide Web is expected to be available, at high speeds, for those who are on the move. High-speed Web connections, always-on systems and a concentration on data rather than voice are the major changes that are anticipated.

These developments will be achieved via telephone network carriers (with 3G protocols). The first generation (1G) protocols included analogue cell phones. Second generation (2G) protocols included digital systems used by several mobile devices. The third generation (3G) will allow users to enjoy the broadband experience with mobility.

Content providers

Content is a strong determinant of the benefit users get out of applications. Content providers are, for example, weather channels, news companies, banks and travel bureaus. Content providers such as Amazon.com, Barnes and Noble, eBay and many others are deploying wireless front-end access in their e-marketing engines. Though their offerings are still rudimentary, features include single-click buying, auction alerts, and some interesting bonuses such as the ability to listen to music clips over the phone.

Brand names that are associated with trustworthy and reliable fulfilment will translate effectively in the wireless domain.

Economic models for content providers ideally include creation of incentives for consumers, assessments of technical and form factor limitations, marketing investment versus incremental airtime, and building of customer relationships. Advertising is also possible, but form factor limitations and airtime costs for downloaded ads are hurdles. Advertisers are interested in this market, but have not yet figured out how to leverage it.

CNN fits into the value chain as a content provider by making its branded services available wherever and whenever people want news. Users are looking for brands they know, and many people turn to CNN for news.

CNN has signed 20 wireless operators worldwide to its mobile service. CNN is also working with Oracle to create personalised content and custom news delivery using hundreds of sources. News services will leverage extensive online audio and video. Audio is very important because people spend so much time in their cars and cannot safely read phone screens while driving.

CNN, a part of AOL, Time Warner, is part of a huge content conglomerate. The entry of companies such as AOL/Time Warner into the wireless space will help increase user awareness because they have such strong brands. CNN mobile is moving from simple licensing to a cable TV model of shared risk and growth for content distribution.

Service providers/portals

Service providers are players that bundle together access, content and the device, presenting the consumer with a simplified purchase and subscription decision, and a packaged mobile data experience.

Portals are companies that aggregate different types of content and distribute them to the user in a single site, making for simplified search, navigation and information resource management. The benefit of the portal for the user is that all one needs is in one place; the benefit of the portal for the content owner is that it provides another channel to the end user.

Traditional portals are well positioned to play a key role in m-commerce. They already have some key ingredients, such as Web-based communications (e-mail, unified messaging) and content. However, they do need to adjust to new requirements to perform in a mobile device, meaning that they have to strip out graphics and other graphic-intensive features compared with conventional portals. Major initiatives have been announced at MSN, AOL and Yahoo!, giving them a good chance at market leadership from the start. In addition, new portals will try to break into these markets, some of them backed by deals with companies at the carrier side of the value chain (e.g. mobile portals owned by carriers such as Vodophone).

As shown in Figure 14.9, mobile services have progressed from being simple informational services and transactional tools to being an integral part of strengthening customer relationships through value-added problem solving.

An example of the bandwidth-driven services is video conferencing/multimedia. As the devices get faster with 3G technology users will be able to utilise video conferencing in the air, as well as download different video applications.

Device manufacturers

Two important groups of device manufacturers are starting to play an active role in the wireless Internet market. The first group includes mobile manufacturers such as Nokia, Motorola and Ericsson and the second includes PDA manufacturers such as Palm, Handspring and Microsoft.

Cellular phone and PDA manufacturers are both fighting for leadership in m-commerce. It is unclear which kind of device will eventually win, or whether a hybrid between the PDA and cell phone will emerge. As hardware costs decrease devices will

Figure 14.9 Evolution of mobile services

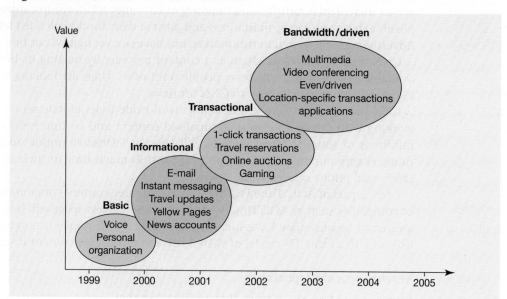

most likely continue to specialise, with each device optimised for its required task. There is of course a limit to the number of devices consumers will carry with them.

Despite growth estimations many players in the mobile manufacturing industry (e.g. Ericsson) have recently decided to outsource the business. Increasing competition in the mobile market, together with a slowdown in the growth of the industry (the actual current figure is smaller than previous estimates), has triggered many mobile makers to redefine their core business.

Recently PDA manufacturers also had sales problems – the total number of PDAs sold was less in 2002 than in 2001.

Taking into account the potential of 3G, the competition and the fact that PDAs and mobile phones have increasingly overlapping features, we will probably see mergers and joint ventures among the players in the next couple of years.

Crossing the chasm and competition in the mobile value chain

Geoffrey Moore, in his book called *Inside the Tornado*, explains that in an early market period margins are typically high and solutions tend to be customised. Product leadership is key during this phase, since innovators and early adopters are attracted to leading products and applications. The foundation for growing a customer base is built in this early cycle, and as Sun-Tzu (the author of *The Art of War*) states, 'Opportunities multiply as they are seized'. The market for mobile data has seen adoption by many innovators and early adopters, and many of the early winners in the value chain have been either enabling-software and services companies or solution providers that have been able to cobble together leading-edge solutions for specific industries or a narrow set of horizontal applications such as messaging. Moore also writes in *Inside the Tornado* that as the early majority adopts a product margins start decreasing. Solutions are still somewhat customised, but operational excellence becomes key, along with product leadership. As the product moves to the late majority low margins can be expected, and products tend to be more standardised. At that point operational excellence and customer intimacy play a bigger role. Dell Computers is an excellent example in the now mature PC industry.

Figure 14.10 illustrates Moore's chasm applied to the m-marketing industry. When the WAP technology was introduced in the late 1990s it did not succeed in creating the sufficient customer base that was necessary for crossing the chasm. An example of a successful crossing of the chasm is NTT DoCoMo, which has succeeded with their broad and standardised functionality.

Figure 14.10 Crossing the chasm at the diffusion curve can be very hard – the WAP did not make it – NTT DoCoMo did (also see Case Study III.2)

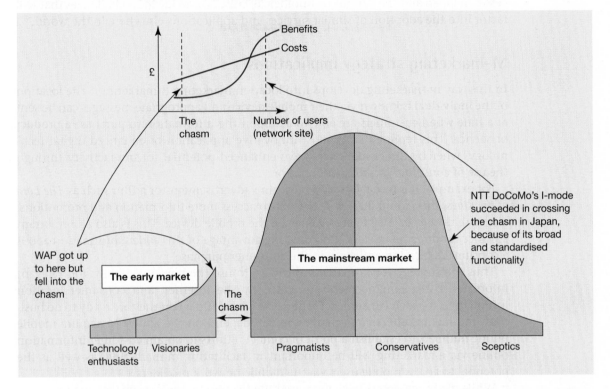

At the 'early market' stage the total costs are greater than the benefits. Apart from fixed costs, costs increase linearly with network size. Benefits grow slowly at first, then exponentially with network size. Since the number of users (or network size) is the critical success factor, what will influence this network size? Generally, there are two important factors:

1. *Standardisation* of the infrastructure behind the application drives down the costs to the user. At a lower cost the application addresses a much larger market, and what was once useful in one industry is now worth paying for in another. The cost of the application drops as the infrastructure standardises, because economies of scope accompany standards. For example, once a company owns a PC, the marginal cost of adding an additional application is small. The cost of the PC, or underlying infrastructure, is amortised over the benefits received from the numerous applications it can run.

2. The second factor that will influence widespread adoption of applications across industries is *broad functionality*. An application created for a specific vertical probably has some functionality that is specific to that vertical and some functionality that is useful to many industries. Before a vertical application starts its migration a modified version must be created that removes the industry-specific functionality. Obviously not every vertical application has enough common functionality to drive demand in the broad market. The process is more akin to natural

selection. Certainly it is possible to discover a horizontal application for businesses, however it is more likely that a vertical application will be modified to target a larger market.

The 2G mobile WAP application did not succeed in achieving the necessary network size and fell into the 'chasm'. However, a tantalising example of strong branding and widespread consumer adoption of mobile data has occurred in Japan through the phenomenal success of I-Mode. Part III concludes with a case study (III.2) of I-Mode's successes in Japan and the various technological, cultural and business challenges that will factor into the adoption of similar services and applications elsewhere in the world.

M-marketing strategy implications

In this way m-marketing develops into location marketing (l-marketing). The location of the individual is known via their mobile device and appropriate messages can be sent at a time when customers are able to act upon the information to purchase a product or service. This represents the most innovative application of enhanced digital technology, whereby direct marketers have enhanced potential for interactivity through the use of consumer location information.

For example, if a teenager sees a magazine advertisement for a film such as *The Lord of the Rings*, they could dial *R_I_N_G_S* to access more information and promotions, purchase tickets, or play related games on the mobile device. This is also an important advance for direct marketers, who can take advantage of this added information about a consumer's location and stage in the consumer purchase.

Thus the strategy for m-marketing will be to use the power of timely and relevant information, the enhancements provided by the Internet, and consumer location information to reach consumers at the point where and when they are ready to do business. In practice, effective m-marketing will depend on the ability to acquire mobile phone numbers to establish a point of contact. Efforts to obtain customer information online via e-marketing will be important in facilitating m-marketing, as well as the potential to access mobile users via the mobile network providers.

While direct marketers have long used the telephone, they are challenged to understand more clearly the relationship between the consumer and their mobile device. For example, mobile phone users are generally reluctant to make their phone number widely known and may restrict the listing of their number in formal and informal directories. Users have adopted the mobile phone and in effect taken it into their personal space for the simple reason that they find a personal, mobile communication device valuable and useful. The challenge to direct marketers is to develop the potential of m-marketing around providing relevant information, 'being with' the user, and being responsive to needs while being determined not to impose unsolicited or unwelcome information. Strategists need technical and managerial solutions that enable them to identify when they are needed, to become a partner to the access, use and management of information to enhance consumers' real-world embedded experience with direct m-marketing.

Gathering data from mobile phone users can be done by utilising other media such as television or radio. For example, some television programmes encourage their audiences to send SMS messages to answer a quick quiz with the opportunity to win prizes.

Transactions via the mobile phone should appeal to direct marketers for a number of reasons. Mobile technology offers personalised consumer interaction, often resulting from consumers opting in to the enhanced information environment, customer-location information and the possibility of continuous connection to the Internet.

With the proliferation of mobile devices, user liberation and technological divergence, direct marketers can link to customers to develop new, stronger relationships and interactions that will provide them with enhanced prospects for investment return.

The employment of these strategies by direct marketers will play an increasingly important role in adding value for consumers.

14.10   Summary

During the last few years there has been an explosion of online commercial activity enabled by the Internet or World Wide Web. This is generally referred to as electronic commerce (e-marketing), with a major component of e-marketing being electronic transactions taking place on Internet-based markets (electronic markets, or e-markets).

The development of the Internet as a 'new' direct distribution channel has resulted in a shift of power from the manufacturers and the traditional retail channels to the consumer.

Generally, the development of e-marketing in Europe has been behind that in the United States. A major factor inhibiting growth of consumer e-marketing in Europe is lack of confidence in online security. However, for those selling via the Internet, the new European currency, the euro, will make it easier to do business, and give encouragement to companies selling to European customers. Since Europeans will now be able to shop and compare prices at the click of a mouse, they will be more favourably inclined towards e-marketing.

The market volume of e-marketing in the B-t-B is much bigger than in the B-t-C market – five times more, according to some research results. The reason for this difference is that e-marketing is not a new phenomenon in the B-to-B market. Instead of Internet-based solutions many industries have been using electronic data interchange for years to streamline business processes and reduce the cost of doing business.

The main difference between buying behaviour in the 'physical marketplace' and the 'virtual market space' is that the market space emphasises 'high-tech', and is more characterised by the power of information and communication technologies to satisfy customer needs and thereby continue business relationships.

The myth has been that the Internet will eliminate the need for intermediaries. Early predictions called for *disintermediation*, that is, the disappearance of physical intermediaries, as people moved from buying through distributors and resellers to buying directly from manufacturers. The reality is that the Internet may eliminate the traditional 'physical' distributors, but the transformation process of the value chain *has given rise to a new class of intermediaries*. Companies such as Yahoo aggregate information and make it easier to access new information and see new business possibilities. *The value-added is no longer in logistic aggregation but rather in information aggregation.*

Three alternative strategy levels of e-marketing commitment have been presented:

- *Level 1*. One-to-many strategy: use Internet presence as a company- and product-brochure.
- *Level 2*. Direct targeting: here the company starts selling on the Internet.
- *Level 3*. One-to-one interactive e-marketing.

On Level 3 the company is moving from providing company and product information to becoming an integral part of the whole vertical value chain from supplier to end consumer. This virtual integration works faster than Level 2 (direct targeting) by blurring traditional boundaries between suppliers, manufacturers and customers in the value chain.

Companies that conduct e-marketing must be subject to the same laws, regulations and taxes that govern operations of all businesses. But a company that uses the Web immediately becomes an international business, and as such the company can become subject to many more laws, more quickly, than if it were a traditional bricks-and-mortar company tied to one specific physical location. Furthermore many countries' legal issues are difficult to interpret and follow because of the newness of electronic commerce.

What are the drivers and barriers of e-marketing?

Drivers
- For the supplier:
  - reduced working capital (less inventory, reduced administration);
  - global reach;
  - more efficient distribution (disintermediation means fewer distribution channels);
  - ability to develop relationships with customers.
- For the customer:
  - more choices (greater product depth and global reach);
  - ease of purchase and monitoring delivery;
  - more individual products (via 'mass customisation' of products);
  - cost savings;
  - faster product cycle time (ordering, shipping, billing);
  - in the B-t-B market the customer has better possibilities of swapping between suppliers than with EDI.

Barriers (for both supplier and customer)
- When entering the global market there may be different barriers to different countries: language barriers, cultural barriers, limited Internet access, different legislation, logistical barriers, etc.
- Web-technology is not user friendly.
- Security fears.
- E-marketing is not suitable for certain types of product, for example 'high-touch' products (fashion clothes) or very complex products or projects, where face-to-face communication is necessary.
- Conflicting interests (distributor and manufacturer may have different interests).
- WWW = World Wide Wait (poor performance leading to slow download).

M-marketing (marketing by mobile telephone) is defined as the application of marketing to the mobile environment of smart phones, mobile phones and personal digital assistants. M-marketing is characterised by both the interaction with the World Wide Web and the location-specific context that enhances communication and delivery of information. The emerging capacity to communicate with any individual, from any place, over any network, and to any device, regardless of time or geographical location, provides enormous potential for marketers. The location of the individual is known via their mobile device and appropriate messages can be sent at a time when they are able to act upon the information to purchase a product or service. This represents the most innovative application of enhanced digital technology, whereby direct marketers have enhanced potential for interactivity through the use of consumer location information.

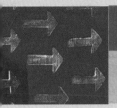

CASE STUDY 14.1   Sonic Innovations

A new US manufacturer of hearing aids is considering online sales in Europe

Sonic Innovations, Inc. (**www.sonici.com**), a producer of advanced digital hearing aids, has been named number 117 on the 2003 Deloitte Technology Fast 500, a ranking of the 500 fastest growing technology companies in North America. The ranking is based on Sonic's average percentage revenue growth from 1998 (when it was founded) to 2002. However, the profits have been very limited until now, in fact Sonic had an accumulated deficit of $52 million by the end of 2002.

In 2002 total sales of Sonic's hearing aids were $68 million; and by geography: North America: $40 million; Europe: $15 million; and Rest-of-World: $13 million.

Sonic Innovations designs, develops, manufactures and markets advanced digital hearing aids which provide a high level of satisfaction for hearing impaired consumers. The company has developed patented digital signal processing (DSP) technologies and embedded them in the smallest single-chip DSP platform ever installed in a hearing aid. By the end of 2002, Sonic had 288 employees (in the U.S.), including 27 in administration, 72 in sales and marketing, 46 in research and 143 in operations.

Market potential for hearing aids

It is estimated that 10 per cent of the world's population suffer from hearing problems. With a world population of about 6 billion people, this gives a potential 600 million clients who may use hearing aids.

Of course this figure is not realistic because the great majority of the world's population is living in areas where hearing aids are not easily accessible. Nevertheless, potential figures are estimated at about 70 million hearing-impaired people in Europe and 30 million people in North America. At the same time, figures show that more young people are beginning to suffer from hearing problems at an earlier age, which may be due to exposure to excessive noise. This shows the enormous potential of this market.

Today, around two thirds of users of hearing aids are 60 years and older. The gap between the potential users and the real users of hearing aids is due to several facts: First, in some cases, there is the stigma of hearing loss. This means that people with hearing problems are reluctant to accept their hearing loss, so they wait an estimated five to fifteen years before they seek professional help. Some people do not

want to admit that they need a hearing aid because this will make them seem older or even partly handicapped. The development of Completely-In-the-Channel Instruments, that are practically invisible to other people, may help to reduce the fear of exposing one's handicap towards other people, but will not remove the problem that using a hearing aid often means to admitting that 'I am getting old'. In order to improve sales to the full market potential it will be necessary, in some instances, to change public opinion to the problems.

A second crucial factor for sales is the way different countries' social security systems subsidize costs. Figures show that every technological development, which has achieved success in the recent years, is not able to improve the sales volume at all if social security departments reduce subsidies for hearing aids, due to budget cuts. This may even lead to counter-cyclical market developments such as in Germany, where the market share of BTE-Instruments (Behind-the-Ear) has been increasing in the last years, simply because they are cheaper than ITE (In-the-Ear) products. Whilst in the rest of Europe and in North America the ITE technology is steadily gaining importance. As a result, lobbying in order to avoid public subsidy cuts seems the most important key to successful sales for the hearing aids industry. Sonic believes that the poor economic climate has caused consumers to chose lower-priced digital aids.

The hearing aids market can be divided into two segments, analog and digital. Digital hearing aids were first introduced in 1996 and currently represent an estimated 46 per cent of the U.S. hearing aid sales and 33 per cent of global hearing aid sales. Digital-based hearing aids continue to gain market share at the expense of the older (analog-based) technology.

Competition

Sonic meets competition from a number of worldwide competitors, six of which have far greater sales (see Table 1).

In 2001 some six million hearing aids were sold globally. This market is made up of industrialized countries, two thirds of which are the United States, Germany and Japan. The United States alone accounts for 40 per cent of the market volume, and Europe for around 30 per cent.

Table 1 World market shares of main hearing aids manufacturers

Company	Country	Number of years on the hearing aids market	Market share (%)
Siemens	Germany	93	20%
William Demant (the earlier Oticon)	Denmark	99	19%
GN ReSound	Denmark	60	15%
Starkey	USA	32	13%
Phonak	Switzerland	56	10%
Widex	Denmark	47	8%
Sonic	USA	4	4%
Others (around 30 manufacturers)	–	–	11%
Total			100%

Generally, the market share of Sonic in United States is higher than in Europe.

Most hearing aids in the US and Europe are custom-made to each individual ear. Until now, hearing aids have traditionally been dispensed (sold to consumer) by hearing-care professionals in clinics. Due to the hearing-care professional's influence over the consumer's choice of hearing aid brand, Sonic has believed that developing and maintaining strong relationships with hearing-care professionals in hearing clinics has been the most critical aspect of their international marketing strategy. In the United States there are more than 13,000 hearing-care professionals who sell hearing aids. In this market Sonic position their products as premium-priced, premium-performance hearing aids and their direct sales force select hearing-care professionals who are capable of, and interested in, dispensing premium digital hearing aids.

Outside the U.S., Sonic sells its products to hearing aids retailers or through a network of established distributors, who in turn sell to hearing aid care clinics.

However, there seems to be a growing market (both in Europe and the United States) for cheaper and standardized digital hearing aids, sold over the Internet. Sonic is considering forming an independent online company, with the sole purpose of selling low-priced hearing aids on the Internet.

Questions

1. What are the advantages and disadvantages for a hearing aid manufacturer like Sonic to sell hearing aids online?

2. Would it be possible for Sonic to sell other products or services online? If yes, how should it be done?

Sources:
http://www.sonici.com/; http://www.hearing-siemens.com/; http://www.demant.com/; http://www.resound.com/; http://www.starkey.com/; http://www.phonak.com/; http://www.widex.com/

CASE STUDY 14.2 Auto–by–Tel

An example of reintermediation in the value chain

Auto-by-Tel was founded in 1995 by Peter Ellis, who based his business around the simple concept that he could take advantage of the Net's interactivity to sell cars on the Web (**www.autobytel.com**). In just four years Ellis became a heavyweight in the vehicle distribution business. Since its inception the company has helped more than 2 million online buyers find a car. With a staff of fewer than 200, the company currently grosses 1 per cent of new car sales in the United States.

The goal of a cybermediary is to step in at several points along the economic chain and integrate buyer/seller relationships. Some cybermediaries specialise and become Internet brokers, allowing clients access to a broader information base and enhancing

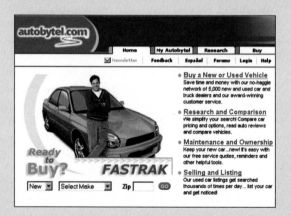

both selection processes and negotiating power. This is what Auto-by-Tel has achieved.

Based on a network of 2,700 dealers, Auto-by-Tel matches buyers with the nearest car dealer that meets their criteria. When clients put in an order for a specific model the request is sent to a server that contacts all qualified dealers geographically close to the client. Within 48 hours a product proposal is sent to the client. The network is composed of certified car dealers ready to sell cars at the price listed on the website. Auto-by-Tel updates its database continually and has a staff of 35 working on site maintenance alone. The service it provides is free for clients and has the advantage of being cheaper than traditional advertising. Car dealers who want to be an Auto-by-Tel franchisee pay an entrance fee as well as a monthly fee.

Auto-by-Tel is an e-alliance with a solution strategy. The Auto-by-Tel website offers a complete solution for car owners, integrating a number of services that are relevant for car owners and buyers. More specifically, four different services are offered via its website. The first service is new car purchases: customers select cars on the Auto-by-Tel website; Auto-by-Tel then e-mails the nearest dealer to ask for a price and checks that it is fair; dealer and customer are then left to themselves to conclude their deal. A second service is

buying and selling used cars: both dealers and private persons may offer used cars for sale; private sellers pay a fee to do so. Third, a number of insurance companies offer their products via the Auto-by-Tel website, and finally, clients can also obtain finance from Auto-by-Tel. Customers can compare both insurance and finance on the Auto-by-Tel website.

Auto-by-Tel has also entered into relationships with contractual partners. There are two categories: the dealer network and the insurance and finance partners. The car dealers with which it has concluded partnerships do the actual car selling. The objective is to have a number of dealers, who profit because Auto-by-Tel expands their marketing and sales channel.

Source: adapted from: De Man *et al.* (2002), Jallat and Capek (2001); **www.autobytel.com**

Questions

1. Is it possible to sell cars on the Internet?

2. Explain how reintermediation is working in the case of Auto-by-Tel

3. Which elements of Auto-by-Tel's concept is it possible to internationalize and standardize across borders, and which elements should be localised?

For further exercises and cases, see this book's website at
www.booksites.net/hollensen

Questions for discussion

1. Explain the term virtual value chain.

2. Explain what is meant by electronic marketing.

3. What are transaction costs and why are they important in e-marketing?

4. 'The WWW represents a pull medium for marketing rather than a push medium.' Discuss.

5. What types of channel conflict are caused by the Internet?

6. How does the demographic profile of Internet users differ from the general population of a country?

7. Explain the main benefits that a company selling fast-moving consumer products could derive by creating a website.

8. Describe sticky features that websites use to attract and keep visitors. Why is stickiness important to companies operating websites?

9. How do companies that create global Web strategies need to accommodate cultural differences and can they turn them to their advantage?

10. For the following stages in the buying process, explain how the Internet can be used to help achieve the communication objectives: supplier search, evaluation and selection, purchase, post-purchase.

11. Why is the Internet a suitable medium for one-to-one marketing?

12. 'Companies should spend a higher proportion of their website budgets on promotion than on designing and developing the site.' Discuss.

14. 'It is inevitable that the transparency of information on products and price on the World Wide Web will drive down product prices.' Discuss.

References

Benjamin, R. and Wigand, R. (1995) 'Electronic markets and virtual chains on the information highway', *Sloan Management Review*, Winter, pp. 62–72.

Boston Consulting Group (2000) *The Race for Online Riches: E-Retailing in Europe* (**http://www.bcg.com/new_ideas/new_ideas_subpage3.asp**).

Business Week (1999b) 'In the ring: eBay vs. Amazon.com', *Business Week*, 31 May, pp. 49–55.

Butler, P. and Peppard, J. (1998) 'Consumer purchasing on the Internet: process and prospects', *European Management Journal*, vol. 16, no 5, pp. 600–10.

De Man, A.-P., Stienstra, M. and Volberda, H.W. (2002) 'E-partnering: moving bricks and mortar online', *European Management Journal*, vol. 20, no. 4, pp. 329–39.

Frynas, J.G. (2002) 'The limits of globalization: legal and political issues in e-commerce', *Management Decisions*, vol. 40, no. 9, pp. 871–80.

Gartner Group (2000), 'GartnerGroup forecasts worldwide business-to-business e-commerce to reach $7.29 trillion in 2004', GartnerGroup Corporate Headquarters, Connecticut, January.

Grant, L. (1998) 'On-line shopping soars: Net sales nag retailers', *USA Today*, 15 December.

Guillen, M. (2002) 'What is the best global strategy for the Internet?', *Business Horizons*, May–June, pp. 39–46.

Hofacker, C.F. (1999) *Internet Marketing* (2nd edn), Digital Springs, Inc, Dripping Springs, TX.

IDC (2000) 'Europe sees big gains in Internet usage, 2000' (**cyberatlas.internet.com/big_picture/demographics/article/0,1323,5911_281021,00.html**)

Jackson, B. (1985) 'Build customer relationships that last', *Harvard Business Review*, November–December, pp. 120–28.

Jallat, F. and Capek, M.J. (2001) 'Disintermediation in question: new economy, new networks, new middlemen', *Business Horizons*, March–April, pp. 55–60.

Jastrow, D. (1999) 'Saying no to Web sales', *Computer Reseller News*, 29 November.

Levitt, T. (1983) 'The Globalization of Markets', *Harvard Business Review*, May/June, pp 92–102.

Lohse, G.L. and Spiller, P. (1999) 'Internet retail store design: how the user interface influences traffic and sales', *Journal of Computer Mediated Communication*, vol. J, no. 2, December, pp. 1–20.

Magretta, J. (1998) 'The power of virtual integration: an interview with Dell Computer's Michael Dell', *Harvard Business Review*, March–April, pp. 73–84.

Moore, G. (1995) Inside the Tornado – Marketing Strategies form Silicon Valley's Cuting Edge, HarperCollins, CA.

Morris, L.J. and Morris, J.S. (2002) 'The changing role of middlemen in the distribution of personal computers', *Journal of Retailing and Consumer Services*, vol. 9, pp. 97–105.

Rayport, J.F. and Sviokla, J.J. (1996) 'Exploiting the virtual value chain', *McKinsey Quarterly*, no. 1, pp. 21–36.

Robles, F. (2002) 'The evolution of global portal strategy', *Thunderbird International Business Review*, vol. 44, no. 1, pp. 25–46.

Rosenbush, S. (1998) 'Personalizing service on Web', *USA Today*, 16 November.

Wunderman, W. (1998) 'The future of selling via the Internet: the online progress of disintermediation', *Web Commerce Today*, issue 10, 15 May.

Further reading

Chakrabarti, R. and Scholnick, B. (2002) 'International expansion of e-retailers: where the Amazon flows', *Thunderbird International Business Review*, vol. 44, no. 1, pp. 85–104.

Clarke, I. and Flaherty, T.B. (2003) 'Web-based B2B portals' *Industrial Marketing Management*, vol. 32, no. 1, pp. 15–23.

Emiliani, M.L. and Stec, D.J. (2002) 'Realizing savings from online reverse auctions', *Supply Chain Management: An International Journal*, vol. 7, no. 1, pp. 12–23.

Gulledge, T. (2002) 'B2B emarketplaces and small- and medium-sized enterprises', *Computers in Industry*, vol 49, no. 1, pp. 47–58.

Jalassi, T. and Leenen, S. (2003) 'An e-commerce sales model for manufacturing companies: a conceptual framework and a European example', *European Management Journal*, vol. 21, no. 1, pp. 38–47.

Joergensen, J.L. and Blythe, J. (2003) 'A guide to a more effective World Wide Web presence', *Journal of Marketing Communications*, vol. 9, pp. 45–58.

Sashi, C.M and O'Leary, B. (2002) 'The role of Internet auctions in the expansion of B2B markets', *Industrial Marketing Management*, vol. 31, pp. 103–10.

Standifer, R.L. (2003) 'Managing conflict in B2B e-commerce', *Business Horizons*, March–April, pp. 65–70.

Thiessen, J.H., Wright, R.W. and Turner I. (2001), 'A model of e-commerce use by international SMEs', *Journal of International Management*, vol. 7, no. 3, pp. 211–33.

Turban, E. (2002) *Electronic Commerce: A Managerial Perspective*, Prentice Hall, International Edition Upper Saddle River, N.J.

Wilson, S.G. and Abel, I. (2002) 'So you want to get involved in e-commerce', *Industrial Marketing Management*, vol. 31, pp. 85–94.

Expanding through franchising to the South American market?

At the beginning of 2003 Ingvar Kamprad, founder of the Swedish furniture retailing giant IKEA, is concerned 'his' firm may be growing too quickly. He used to be in favour of rapid expansion, but he has now become worried that the firm may be forced to close stores in the event of a sustained economic downturn.

In 2002 *Forbes Magazine* ranked Ingvar Kamprad as the world's sixteenth richest man, estimating his personal fortune at $13.4 billion. However in January 2003 Kamprad said to a local newspaper in Smaaland: 'I was something of an engine before. But in the last 10 years I have in that way become an unhappy man, I see the responsibility and what the consequences can be. It's not fun to sit and feel this responsibility.' (BBC News, 2003)

Now Ingvar Kamprad has heard that the top management of the IKEA Group plans to make a further international expansion, into South America, because of the growth opportunities there. Kamprad is very sceptical about these plans and his personal assistant has asked you, as an international marketing specialist, to get an expert opinion about the plans ...

IKEA – an international retailer

IKEA Svenska AB, founded in 1943, is the world's largest furniture retailer and specialises in stylish but inexpensive Scandinavian designed furniture.

Brief timeline

1943 The founder of IKEA, Ingvar Kamprad from Agunnaryd, Sweden, registers the name IKEA. The name was formed from the founder's initials (I.K.) plus the first letters of

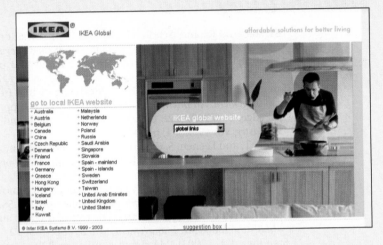

Elmtaryd and Agunnaryd, the farm and village where he grew up.

1950 Furniture enters the IKEA product range for the first time.

1951 The first IKEA catalogue is published.

1953 The first IKEA furniture showroom is opened in Älmhult, Sweden, to better display the products' quality.

1955 IKEA begins to design its own furniture.

1956 IKEA introduces self-assembly furniture in flat packs.

1958 The first IKEA store opens in Älmhult, Sweden.

1963 The second IKEA store is opened in Oslo, Norway.

1965 The IKEA Stockholm store opens. The self-service, open warehouse is introduced.

1969 The first IKEA store in Denmark opens.

1973 The first store outside Scandinavia is opened in Spreitenbach, Switzerland.

1974 The first IKEA store opens in Germany, in Munich.

1975 The first IKEA store in Australia.

1976   The first IKEA store in Canada.

1977   The first IKEA store in Austria.

1978   The first IKEA store in Singapore.

1979   The first IKEA store in the Netherlands.

1980   The first IKEA store in the Canary Islands.

1981   The first IKEA stores in France and Iceland.

1983   The first IKEA store in Saudi Arabia.

1984   The first IKEA stores in Belgium and Kuwait.

1985   The first IKEA store in the United States.

1987   The first IKEA stores in the United Kingdom and Hong Kong.

1989   The first IKEA store in Italy.

1990   The first IKEA stores in Hungary and Poland.

1991   The first IKEA stores in the Czech Republic and the United Arab Emirates.

1992   The first IKEA stores in Mallorca and Slovakia.

1994   The first IKEA store in Taiwan.

1996   The first IKEA stores in Finland, Malaysia and mainland Spain.

1997   IKEA appears on the Internet with the World Wide Living Room website.

1998   The first IKEA store in mainland China.

IKEA has grown into the world's largest furniture retailer, with 148 stores in 22 countries and a workforce of some 70,000 people since its first outlet opened in Aelmhult in 1958. The firm is noted for its rapid international expansion and has recently set up stores in eastern Europe and Russia.

IKEA's success in the retail industry can be attributed to its vast experience in the retail market, product differentiation, and cost leadership. The company is one of the world's most successful multinational retailing firms, operating as a global organization, with its unique concept that its furniture is sold in kits that are assembled by the customer at home.

The firm, which remains in private ownership, racked up sales of nearly €12 billion in 2002.

About corporate IKEA

The IKEA business idea is to offer a wide range of home furnishing items of good design and function, excellent quality and durability, at prices so low that the majority of people can afford them. The company targets the customer who is looking for value and is willing to do a little bit of work serving themselves, transporting the items home and assembling the furniture. The typical IKEA customer is a young low- to middle-income family.

IKEA's retailing, with its Swedish roots, is based on a franchise system. Inter IKEA Systems B.V., located in Delft (the Netherlands), is the owner and franchisor of the IKEA concept. The IKEA Group is a private group of companies owned by a charitable foundation in the Netherlands. It is active in developing, purchasing, distributing and selling IKEA products. The IKEA experience is more than just products, however, it is a retail concept. For the concept to work all aspects must be in place. IKEA products are therefore sold only in IKEA stores franchised by Inter IKEA Systems B.V. However, most of the global product policy (including product development) and the global marketing is centralised to the Swedish part of the company, IKEA of Sweden.

Product development

The team behind each product consists of designers, product developers and purchasers who get together to discuss design, materials and suitable suppliers. Everyone contributes with their specialist knowledge. Purchasers, for example, use their contacts with suppliers all over the world via IKEA Trading Service Offices. Who can make this product of the best quality for the right price at the right time? Products are often developed in close cooperation with suppliers and often only one supplier is appointed to supply all the stores around the world.

IKEA does not have its own manufacturing facilities but uses subcontracted manufacturers all over the world. In order to keep costs low, IKEA shoppers are pro-sumers – half producers and half consumers. In other words, they have to assemble the products themselves. To facilitate shopping, IKEA provides catalogues, tape measures, shopping lists and an Internet website to help the consumer with fitting the furniture into the room. Car roof racks are available for purchase at cost and IKEA pick-up vans/mini-trucks are available to rent. IKEA's success is based on the relatively simple idea of keeping the cost between manufacturers and customers down. Costs are kept under control starting at the design level of the value-added chain. IKEA also keeps costs down by packing items compactly in flat standardized packaging and stacking them as high as possible to reduce storage space during and after distribution.

Effective marketing through catalogues is what usually attracts the customer first; what keeps customers coming back is good service. IKEA believes that a strong in-stock position, in which the most popular style and design trends are correctly anticipated, is crucial to keep customers satisfied. For that IKEA depends on leading-edge technology and the company has developed its own global distribution network. By utilising control points in the distribution cycle the firm is able to insure timely delivery of products to retail stores all over the world.

IKEA thinks that consumer tastes are merging globally. To take one example, IKEA, which has been exporting the 'streamlined and contemporary Scandinavian style' to the United States since 1985, found several opportunities to export US style to Europe, as Europeans picked up on some US furnishing concepts. To respond to this new demand IKEA now markets 'American-style' furnishings in Europe.

Bureaucracy is fought at all levels in the organization. Kamprad believes that simplicity and common sense should characterise planning and strategic direction. In addition, the culture emphasises efficiency and low cost, which is not to be achieved at the expense of quality or service. Symbolic policies, such as only flying economy class and stay at economical hotels, employing young executives and sponsoring university programmes, have been integrated into the corporate culture and have further inspired the spirit of entrepreneurship in the organization. For instance, all design teams enjoy complete autonomy in their work, but are expected to design new and appealing products regularly.

IKEA has improved its value chain by a cooperative focus on suppliers and customers. The firm emphasizes centralised control and standardisation of the product mix.

In order to maintain cost leadership in the market, internal production efficiencies must be greater than those of competitors. Under IKEA's global strategy suppliers are usually located in low-cost nations, with close proximity to raw materials and reliable access to distribution channels. These suppliers produce highly standardised products intended for the global market, which size provides the firm with the opportunity to take advantage of economies of scale. IKEA's role is not only to globally integrate operations and centrally design products, but also to find an effective combination of low cost, standardisation, technology and quality.

In the case of IKEA, a standardised product strategy does not mean complete cultural insensitivity. The company is, rather, responding to globally emerging consumer tastes and preferences. Retail outlets all over the world carry the basic product range, which is universally accepted, but also place great emphasis on the product lines that appeal to local customer preferences.

IKEA has modified the value chain approach by integrating the customer into the process and introducing a two-way value system between customers, suppliers and IKEA's headquarters. In this global sourcing strategy the customer is a supplier of time, labour, information, knowledge and transport. On the other hand, the suppliers are customers, receiving technical assistance from IKEA's corporate technical headquarters through various business services. The company wants customers to understand that their role is not to consume value, but rather to create it.

IKEA's role in the value chain is to mobilise suppliers and customers to help them further add value to the system. Customers are clearly informed in the catalogues of what the firm's business systems provide, and what they are expected to add to the final process.

In order to furnish the customer with good quality products at a low cost, the firm must be able to find suppliers that can deliver high quality items at low cost per unit. The company's headquarters provides carefully selected suppliers with technical assistance, leased equipment and the necessary skills needed to produce high quality items. This long-term supplier relationship not only produces superior products, but also adds internal value to the suppliers. In addition, this value chain modification differentiates IKEA from its competitors.

Directly linked to its mission statement, IKEA has built its cost leadership position on these processes. It furnishes the customer with a quality product with components derived from all over the world utilising multi-level competitive advantages, low cost logistics, and large simple retail outlets in suburban areas. Furthermore, cost leadership has been effectively incorporated into the organization's culture through symbols and efficient processes. In return for high sales volumes IKEA accepts low profit margins. In addition, IKEA's marketing emphasis on budget prices and good value clearly communicates cost leadership to customers. IKEA's strategy demonstrates that the perception that cost leadership equals poor quality in products and services is incorrect. High quality is associated with input and process variables. Cost reduction, on the other hand, does not mean reducing the quality of these variables, but rather doing things better, and more efficiently. Cost leadership is a part of the management process and culture.

From this discussion it is possible to conclude that IKEA effectively aligns its cost leadership platform, focusing on the needs of its target market segment. Differentiation, as indicated in the modification of the value chain, also focuses on this particular segment.

The internationalization of IKEA

IKEA has applied a conservative policy to internationalization. As a general rule, the firm does not enter a new potential market by opening a retail outlet. Instead, a supplier link with the host nation is established. This is a strategic, risk-reducing approach in which local suppliers can provide valuable input on political and legal, cultural, financial and other issues that provide opportunities and/or threats to the IKEA concept. In the 1970s and 1980s IKEA concentrated its international expansion in Europe and in North America mainly through company-owned subsidiaries. On the other hand, over the last 20 years franchising has been extensively utilised in expanding to other areas of the world.

Expansion by franchising

IKEA approaches unknown, relatively small and high risk markets by franchising. Franchises are granted by Inter IKEA Systems B.V. as part of a detailed international expansion plan. Serious applicants are carefully researched and evaluated and franchises are granted only to companies and/or individuals with strong financial backing and a proven record in retail. Franchisees have to carry basic items, but have the freedom to design the rest of the product mix to fit local market needs. The basic core items number approximately 12,000 simple and functional products. The centralised head office is actively involved in the selection processes and provides advice. In addition, all products have to be purchased from IKEA's product lines. In order to maintain service, quality and logistic standards, individual franchisees are periodically audited and compared to overall corporate performance. Extensive training and operational support is provided from headquarters. All franchisees pay franchise fees to IKEA Holdings. All catalogues and promotional advertising is the responsibility of headquarters. Franchising has been used as a vehicle for the company's generic focus strategy.

Balance of autonomy and strategic direction

As IKEA continues to expand overseas the significance of centralised strategic direction will increase. Naturally rapid internationalization will trigger a range of challenges imposed on the headquarters, such as the following:

- The complexity of the logistics system will increase.
- It will be more difficult to respond to national needs and cultural sensitivity issues.
- Franchisees may demand more control over operations.

- Emerging demographic trends will force the organization to broaden its focus strategy to respond to varying nation-level consumer groups.

With all these challenges emerging it might be very difficult to maintain a central organizational structure. The best way to meet these challenges is to find the proper balance between country level autonomy and centralised intervention. With reference to IKEA's long-term relationship and control over its suppliers in exchange for quality assurance, technology transfers and economies of scale factors may trigger potential suppliers to integrate forward and produce competitive products for IKEA's local competitors. With logistics complications and long lead times IKEA is forced to maintain high control levels over its suppliers. For instance, if the supplier responsible for the screws component to a table cannot deliver on time, the supplier of the table-top has to adapt its production to the new scenario. Without IKEA's centralised logistics system this example could lead to severe store shortages, leading to losses in sales.

The Brazilian market for furniture

According to the Brazilian Association of Furniture Manufacturers (ABIMOVEL), the Brazilian furniture market was estimated at approximately $3.6 billion in 2000, of which about $111 million were imports. The market can be broken down into three main categories: residential (60 per cent), office (25 per cent), and institutional organizations, such as schools, hospitals and hotels (15 per cent).

Brazil has 4.6 million hectares of planted forests, almost all of which is located in the south of the country. Wood from such forests is mainly used in the production of furniture, pulp and paper. The main furniture production centres, as well as the most important markets, are also located in southern Brazil.

The production of particleboard, which was 494,000 m^3 in 1990, jumped to 1.3 million m^3 in 1998, an annual growth rate of 13 per cent. This pattern is expected to continue in the near future. Approximately 80 per cent of Brazil's particleboard production is consumed by the furniture sector. A smaller volume is marketed by resellers and destined for small furniture manufacturers.

As the Brazilian furniture market continues to reap more and more of its profits from exports, production is increasingly tailored to satisfy market niches that demand differentiated products. To meet this need the Brazilian industry is investing more in design and development, although investments are smaller in comparison to investments made in the United States, Italy and Germany. Brazil is also importing state-of-the-art equipment to address quality issues mandated by foreign markets, e.g. the U.S., Italian and German. Today the segment requires import of equipment such as wood-drying machinery, finishing machinery and tools.

According to the Brazilian Furniture Association there are approximately 13,500 Brazilian furniture manufacturers, most of which are small. These firms are typically family-owned companies whose capital is exclusively Brazilian. Historically, the greater proportion of Brazilian manufacturers have been concentrated in areas of large population density in southern Brazil.

The process of trade liberalisation initiated in 1990 introduced significant changes in Brazil's trade regime, resulting in a more open and competitive economy.

The Brazilian economy was deeply affected by the crises in the Asian and Russian markets. As a consequence the currency suffered deeply from the devaluation in January 1999. Brazilian imports of furniture were also seriously affected by this devaluation, and the industry is currently suffering from the unfavourable (for Brazilians) *real*–dollar exchange rate.

US exports of furniture to Brazil reached US$43 million in 2000 (39 per cent of total Brazilian furniture imports) and are expected to decrease to $36 million in 2001. US exports to Brazil were particularly strong in the area of seats, new-design office furniture, and high-end, high-value-added residential furniture. Market analysts estimate that in the next 3–4 years imports of institutional furniture, such as that used in hospitals and hotels, will increase considerably, mainly imports from the United States.

Imports

Brazilian furniture imports totalled US$111 million in 2000, and decreaseed to US$96 million in 2001. This represents 3 per cent of the total furniture market in Brazil. The USA holds 39 per cent of the imported furniture market, followed by Germany with 36 per cent, Italy with 10 per cent, and other countries with 15 per cent. US exports to Brazil were particularly strong in the area of seats, new-design office furniture, and high-end, high-value-added residential furniture. Market analysts estimate that in the next 3–4 years imports of institutional furniture, such as that used in hospitals and hotels, will increase considerably, mainly imports from the United States.

End–user analysis

Different industry segments, such as automotive, aviation and furniture (residential, commercial and institutional) make up the Brazilian market. Each of those areas has its own purchasing approach. For example, the automotive industry may import directly from its headquarters and, in the case of the furniture industry, the end user might be an importer or a store chain.

It is important to mention that there are no major distributor chains in Brazil. Most furniture imports are made through direct importers and, in a smaller proportion, local manufacturers wishing to complement their product line.

High-end furniture and mattresses are commonly imported into Brazil by direct importers or furniture stores. Interior decorators and architects are also considered decision makers, since they are the ones who recommend brands and styles to their final clients.

Import climate

Brazil has a tariff-based import system and has simplified the process for obtaining import licences. Import tariffs are levied *ad valorem* on the CIF value of the imports. Import tax (IPI) for furniture varies from 5–15 per cent.

The Industrial Products Tax (IPI) is a federal tax levied on most domestic and imported manufactured products. It is assessed at the point of sale by the manufacturer or processor in the case of domestically produced goods, and at the point of customs clearance in the case of imports. The tax rate varies by product and is based on the product's CIF value plus duties.

Interest rates in Brazil are high (estimated at 18.3 per cent per year in June 2001) and discourage demand for bank loans. The few sources of funds available for long-term financing are provided by the National Bank for Economic and Social Development (BNDES), through leasing operations and by foreign government export agencies.

Distribution and business practices

Major end users of furniture will only purchase from well-known and reliable suppliers. Although large end users may import directly from foreign suppliers, they are always concerned with after-sales service. Technical assistance and availability of replacement parts are considered important factors in the purchasing decision. In some segments, such as commercial and institutional, this factor may determine from whom the end user will purchase. A physical presence in the market, either through an agent or a manufacturing plant, increases the end user's trust in the supplier's commitment to this market and facilitates the sale.

The retail scene in Brazil

For many years the popular wisdom in Brazil was that shopping malls were only for rich people. The 1984 opening of Center Norte mall in São Paulo changed all that. It is strategically placed next to a subway and a bus terminal. Proximity to mass transit is essential, since many low-income consumers do not own cars. Center Norte was followed by other shopping malls in other cities, such as Rio de Janeiro and Belo Horizonte.

Economic instability, difficulties in obtaining financing at reasonable interest rates and customs barriers for certain imports have slowed down the the entry of foreign retailers to Brazil. Among the international chains that have been attracted by Brazil's 80 million consumers are JC Penney, Zara and the Dutch chain C&A, that leads the fashion sector in Brazil. International franchisors such as Benetton, Lacoste, Hugo Boss, Polo Ralph Lauren and McDonald's operate in Brazilian shopping centres, some on a large scale.

Those who have set up shops in Brazil have varied results directly related to their ability to adapt to local conditions. Sears, for example, had extremely negative results, due to the centralisation of decision making in Chicago. Similarly, Zara tried to bring to Brazil its European management policy and market approach and is now facing poor financial results. The contrast is the excellent performance of C&A, whose policies and procedures were defined in Brazil for the local market. JC Penney acquired a local chain (Renner) and accelerated its expansion with good results (ICSC Worldwide Commission, 2000).

Sources: IKEA Annual Report 2002 (preliminary results); www.ikea.com; BBC News (2003), news.bbc.co.uk, 'IKEA founder worried over growth', 3 January; ICSC Worldwide Commission (2000), 'Shopping centres: a world of opportunities', www.icsc.org

Questions

1. Until now IKEA international marketing strategy has been tightly and centrally controlled by corporate headquarters. However, high local pressures emerging due to demographic and cultural differences might force the local IKEA shops to take strategic initiatives to respond to local market needs. In this connection discuss the regional headquarters and transnational organization (presented in Chapter 12) as hierarchical 'entry mode' alternatives to the very centralised strategy emanating from IKEA's headquarters.

2. IKEA has not yet explored joint venture and strategic alliances strategies. Evaluate the pros and cons regarding these two entry strategies versus the traditional IKEA entry mode of franchising.

3. Should IKEA penetrate the South American market by establishing a shop in Brazil?

4. In the light of the political and economic situation in South America, outline the sourcing concept that should be implemented in the South American market.

CASE STUDY III.2   NTT DoCoMo

Using a strong domestic position as a basis for international expansion

NTT DoCoMo is a Tokyo-based company whose main services include: cellular phones (including i-mode), personal handyphone system, pagers, maritime telephones, in-flight telephones and an international service.

After the deregulation of Japanese telecommunications in 1992 the telecommunications giant NTT spun off DoCoMo, maintaining two-thirds ownership. To date DoCoMo's greatest success has been **i-mode (information mode)** mobile phone data service.

How NTT DoCoMo created Japan's mobile Internet (i-mode)

In 1996 Koji Oboshi, President of NTT DoCoMo, foresaw that the demand for new mobile phones would soon peak unless mobiles were developed with new capabilities and services so that consumers would trade in their old mobile for a new, improved one. However, Oboshi believed that the future lay in non-voice, or data, communications. In January 1997 he charged Keiichi Enoki with building a new organization that would concentrate on non-voice communications for retail consumers.

The organization was called Gateway Business and began with a staff of 10, recruited from both within and outside the parent organization. By August 1997 it had a total of 70 staff. It was working on a new service, called i-mode, which would offer a mobile Internet service to customers over their mobile phones. In order to achieve the i-mode goal, Gateway had to accomplish the following:

- develop a network that could deliver the content;
- develop the mobile phone that could receive the content; and
- bring on board the Internet service providers to design the content that would attract the end-user customers.

Keiichi Enoki realised that Gateway would be unable to deliver all this on its own. He saw that the way forward lay in collaboration with others:

- other divisions within DoCoMo;
- Internet service providers (**ISPs**); and
- terminal manufacturers and platform vendors.

Initially Enoki faced objections to the idea of the new mobile Internet service from within DoCoMo itself. He opted to lead the Gateway team that was working with the other departments to convince them of i-mode's potential. Instead of running away from conflicts he tried to make them a source of dialogue and discussion.

The i-mode service was launched in February 1999, with the aim of making it as attractive as possible to end users and thus triggering an explosive growth in the take-up of the service. NTT DoCoMo knew that this growth would only happen if all the elements of the service were right. This included the following:

- developing attractive new content, known within DoCoMo as the portal strategy;
  - developing new mobile phones with add-on features, known as the terminal strategy; and
  - developing platforms other than phones, known as the platform strategy.

A portal community, comprising DoCoMo outside ISPs, developed the portal strategy. As well as developing content, an advertisement delivery service and a financial service linked to the net-based banking service were set up.

The technical community covered alliances with companies such as Sony Computer Entertainment and Sun Microsystems. DoCoMo hoped that, by keeping on top of technical advances and making improvements to the phones, customers would be keen to pay to add new features to their phones, and that in turn these new features would create a new source of revenue for DoCoMo.

Looking to the future, the platform community worked on new platforms, such as games consoles and car navigation systems, as a source of new revenues.

By January 2001 the i-mode service had 25 million subscribers, well within the 30-month target originally set. In July 2001 Gateway became the i-mode business division and began work on IMT-2000, the third generation mobile service (see also Figure 1).

At the start of 2003 the Japanese population was a little under 130 million. Around 40 million (see Figure 2) of these are NTT DoCoMo subscribers, and 90 per cent (36 million people) have i-mode on their mobile phones. Together with other m-Internet users this also means that 80 per cent of the world's mobile Internet users are Japanese.

In summary, the i-mode concept consists of the following elements:

- focus on fresh, entertaining and informative services rather than technology;
- strong i-mode branding, not technology specific, open to future technologies;
- content provided by alliance partners and other 'voluntary' sites;
- information, transactions and fun sold in small, convenient, inexpensive packets;
- uses successful micropayment system through NTT DoCoMo phone bill;

Figure 1 i-mode step-by-step introduction

C-mode = Paying for drinks–Coca Cola–on the vending machine, through the mobile phone.

L-mode = Fixed-line services similar to the earlier French 'Minitel' services. The user can use the Internet and e-mail from an L-mode compatible telelphone or fax using the buttons on the fixed-line telephone.

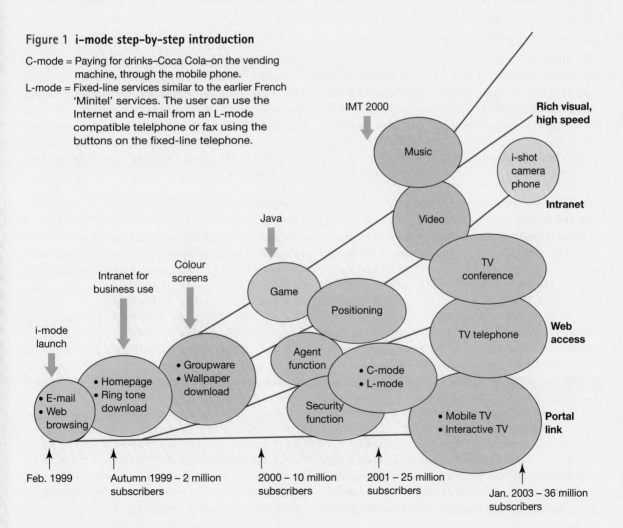

Figure 2 The development of NTT DoCoMo subscribers in Japan

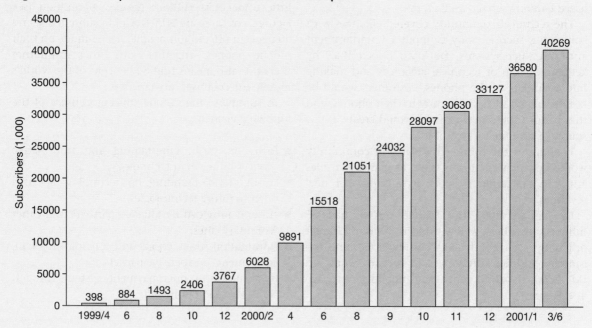

- i-mode websites are easy to create and build on existing Internet;
- i-mode's success accelerated introduction of 3G (IMT 2000) to Japan, bringing 200 times the then current bandwidth;
- technology: packet switched (Internet protocol, always on, no dial-in) overlaid over circuit-switched digital voice mobile;
- i-mode uses cHTML (subset of HTML), not WAP.

DoCoMo's core competences

The key factors that enabled DoCoMo to secure its dominant position in the Japanese market are its excellent management and marketing skills, investment in R&D and relationships with manufacturers.

DoCoMo has built a very strong brand name, projecting the image of a new, young and dynamic company. It has challenged traditional Japanese management practice by bringing in people from outside the company to join the management team. It has also relied on various types of external consulting to make internal management changes. These competences in management and marketing have created a strong image for DoCoMo within the 'new generation' of consumers in Japan, and as a result a high penetration in that demographic.

DoCoMo has also invested heavily in technology development. It has constantly improved acquired technologies so it can sell them in other markets, thus establishing a platform for itself and developing

competences in technology. This has been a key strength in DoCoMo's gaining market share at home.

Finally, DoCoMo's relationship with suppliers has been very effective and it has developed a strong network with handset manufacturers such as Motorola, Nokia and Ericsson. These companies sell handsets marketed under the DoCoMo brand name so they benefit from DoCoMo's growing pool of subscribers.

Competition in mobile Internet

DoCoMo's significant market power has helped it maintain its dominant position as it has been able to influence the development of both phones and content. DoCoMo works with phone manufacturers to design i-mode phones that are user friendly, light, and boast the latest in technological advances. In January 2000 DoCoMo introduced phones with colour screens capable of 256-bit colour graphics that can display animated GIF files just like Web browsers. In addition, the extensive market penetration of i-mode makes its application a must for content developers.

i-mode now commands approximately 60 per cent market share in Japan. Two other players complete the wireless data market in Japan. KDDI markets a service called EZWeb, based on WAP protocols. Japan Telecom's J-Phone offers its J-SkyWalker service, based on its own protocol, called Mobile Markup Language.

One of the competitive advantages of i-mode is the amount of service and content available at the user's fingertips with relative ease. Types of transactions fall into four categories:

1. *M-commerce*. Banking, books and CDs, trading, airline and concert tickets. Sony's online store now also takes orders via i-mode. The stockbroker DLJ Direct receives 30 per cent of its transactions in Japan over i-mode. Japan Airlines and Nippon Travel get many reservations the same way.
2. *Database access*. Telephone and restaurant directories.
3. *Weather, news, and stock information*.
4. *Entertainment*. Games, karaoke and club events.

i-mode designates 10–20 official i-mode sites from the thousands of applications it receives each month. In January 2003 there were around 3,000 official sites in the portal. For example, one popular site helps the user 'trick' the system to send and receive longer text messages than allowed by DoCoMo. Some other popular sites on i-mode include the following:

- *Yamaha Corp*. Maintains a site enabling users to download hit songs to use as dial tones.
- *Olympus*. Has launched a camera designed to transmit digital photos when connected to an i-mode phone.
- *DoCoMo*. Launched a global positioning system that tells users where they are and gives directions to a destination.

See also Tables 1 and 2 regarding users' purchases of I-Mode services. Although 95 per cent of i-mode users purchase content or use premium sites primarily for entertainment (cartoon sites are especially popular), 42 per cent of i-mode traffic is e-mail and messages. A recent survey by InforCom Research found that i-mode phone users spend 34.2 per cent of their total use time making and receiving calls (an average of 3.67 calls pers day), 41.8 per cent send e-mail (an average of 9.08 e-mail messages sent and received per day), and 24 per cent surf i-modes sites. Only 26.2 per cent use i-mode at work or school (July 2000, **www.japaninc.net**. The elements contributing to i-mode's success are detailed below.

Market power
The company leveraged its channel dominance to get handset developers such as Sony, Sharp, Kyocerea, and even Nokia to do its bidding. i-mode

Table 1 i-mode users vs the Internet (Japan)

	i-mode	Internet
Sex of users	Men 43% Women 57%	Men 55% Women 45%
Price	Monthly basic charge of ¥300 + ¥0.3 per 1 packet	Monthly basic charge of ¥1.480 yen + ¥8 yen per 3 minutes
Number of users	21.70 million	17.25 million

Source: **www.japaninc.net** 2002

Table 2 Survey of purchasers' use (in %) of DoCoMo i-mode services, by age in Japan (multiple responses possible)

Service	13–19	20–29	30–39	40–49
Ringtones	83	81	67	65
Information	38	36	39	48
Online games	38	27	28	20
Photos/video clips	31	27	21	22
News (audio and video)	21	14	19	28
Story/fortune telling	21	18	15	13
CD/Video/DVD (e.g. watching video clips from latest film movie)	17	19	14	0
Books	10	12	11	15

was thus able to provide phones that were technologically advanced, appealing to consumers wanting cutting-edge technology. At a recent industry show in Japan nearly 40 new i-mode devices were shown, resembling everything from a traditional cell phone to a cosmic egg to a TV-like palm device.

Consumer focus
DoCoMo recognised the tremendous opportunity of connecting consumers to the Internet when landline access was limited. After seeing the potential, DoCoMo's concentration on connecting with young consumers, early adopters of mobile technologies, tapped a lucrative market. In addition it realised that, with the large amount of time the Japanese spend commuting, an application capitalising on that idle time could be very successful.

In metropolitan areas of Japan such as Tokyo daily commutes can take two hours or more. Though automobile ownership is not unheard of, commutes are typically via public transport – train and bus. Anyone who has ridden a packed-to-the-gills train in

Tokyo during the rush hour knows that at times it can be difficult even to open a newspaper. Long commutes on public transport provide an obvious opportunity for i-mode usage, which at times can be logistically more tenable for commuters than other forms of entertainment.

Lifestyle

- *Leisure time*: Outside of work hours it appears that many Japanese prefer to be 'out' rather than at home. Restaurants, bars and public places are crowded every day of the week until late at night, particularly in the cities. In other parts of the world personal Internet usage is largely from home. Japanese social habits thus encourage the use of alternative means to access the Internet – such as I-Mode.
- *Disposable income among young people*: In Japan, the age at which people marry is rising. Due to the astonishing property prices in metropolitan Japan these young, single, gainfully employed individuals – many of them women – often continue to live at home with their parents. Since these people's living expenses are almost zero their salary is virtually completely disposable. Many choose to spend their income on food and fashion, but this generation has contributed to the financial success of i-mode.
- *Cultural and demographic idiosyncrasy*: i-mode's success has undoubtedly been catalysed by idiosyncrasies that simply are not found in other countries and cultures. Less than pervasive English language ability falls into this category, but there are many others.
- *Fascination with gadgets*: The Japanese – by their own admission – are fascinated by gadgets. The smaller and the more clever, the better. Japanese cellular handsets offer features such as colour displays, digital cameras, on-board voicemail/voice note recorders, polyphonic ringers, external keyboards for e-mail and short messaging and many others. Foreign cellular handsets seem almost dull in comparison. The gap between Japanese and foreign handsets was most apparent when i-mode was taking off in 1998 and 1999. i-mode and its cousins from J-Phone and KDDI thus represent a new genre in gadgets and thus were bound to attract a following in Japan.
- *Fashion*: Informal surveys of i-mode demographics indicate that a large portion of the user base and the overwhelming volume of usage is by young women and teenage girls. One need only spend a few minutes at the Shibuya train station in Tokyo to witness literally hundreds of teenage girls being entranced by their i-mode handset's display. Young Japanese women seem to have a passion for 'cuteness'. *Kawaii* ('Oh, how cute') is often heard in the streets of Tokyo, and is invariably used as a means of product promotion. This undoubtedly contributes to the volume of 'screen saver', 'wallpaper' and ringing tone downloads that comprise a significant portion of i-mode traffic. A famous example is a service that sends an image of the Hello Kitty character to the subscriber's handset every day. The service costs ¥100 per month and has millions of subscribers. More generally, young Japanese women have a well-known predilection for fashion and trends. This applies to clothing, physical appearance and cuisine, as well as to cellular handsets. Some of i-mode's popularity might well be the result of fashion sense.
- *Politeness*: The Japanese use their handsets for voice calls in inconspicuous ways. It is considered unacceptably rude in Japan to have loud conversations on mobile phones and people seem – for the most part – to respect the 'no mobile phones' signs that dot public places, including trains and buses. The extreme politeness of Japanese culture itself might tend to increase the use of i-mode-based e-mail in lieu of voice calls.

Brand development

In its marketing DoCoMo did not refer to established interactive mediums such as the Web. Instead it focused on services that are available uniquely on i-mode, such as the ability to send messages to friends, which created strong brand awareness among consumers.

User interface

To create a better consumer experience, DoCoMo developed a friendly and intuitive user interface – for example, train schedules are retrievable in two clicks. Packet-switching technology made mobile surfing and access easy, since the customer is connected whenever the phone is on and it takes only one button to enter the i-mode services. Compact HTML is flexible enough to accommodate multibyte *kanji* characters and other graphical elements, further improving the user interface. Since only 13 per cent of the Japanese have access to the Internet through a home computer they were more amenable to accessing the Internet on a small phone screen.

Content quality

The development team focused on including content that would be valuable to individuals on the move. The i-mode system was also attractive to content developers since, unlike WAP, it allows site designers to write programs in a stripped-down version of HTML. That further encouraged the development of content and the creation of valuable unofficial i-mode sites. DoCoMo recently allied with Sony to jointly develop PlayStation and i-mode technologies, further strengthening its strong content position.

Economical positioning

DoCoMo took advantage of the high cost of installing and maintaining a land-line connection by developing an economical cost structure. A new telephone line connection costs $600 (¥72,000) in Japan before usage charges; by contrast, i-mode costs $28 for the connection, and monthly bills average $17. For the wireless version the cost is linked to usage in terms of data downloaded and not on a time basis, which allows users to explore i-mode without incurring high costs.

Existing customer base

As a pre-existing provider of mobile voice services to the Japanese market, NTT DoCoMo had an established customer base. At the launch of i-mode all but the very basic phones came equipped with i-mode, thereby removing the impact of switching costs. That is particularly important in the Japanese market, where mobile phones are often perceived as a fashion accessory and regularly updated.

Conclusion

While i-mode is undoubtedly a well-designed and marketed service, its rise is intimately tied to the Japanese marketplace, Japanese culture and uniquely Japanese personal traits. Thus its viability – let alone runaway popularity and attendant profits – outside of Japan is highly questionable.

The i-mode business model

The business model is quite simple, as shown in Figure 3.

Using the i-mode service, content providers pay a commission fee of 9 per cent of sales and DoCoMo collects fees on their behalf for using the content. The monthly basic fee is ¥300 ($2.50) + a data transmission fee of ¥0.3 per 1 packet (128 bytes transferred). If the user downloads 1 MB it is equal to $20. This is approximately 10 times the price in the

Figure 3 DoCoMo's business modes

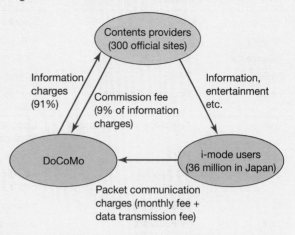

European and US markets or other highly competitive Asian markets, e.g. Hong Kong.

In 2002 the average i-mode mobile telephone user spent the following amount per month:

Mobile telephone usage	¥6360
i-mode	¥1670
Total	**¥8030**
	(approximately $70)

The percentage used for i-mode services is 20.8 per cent.

Internationalization of DoCoMo – i-mode

With its huge success at home, DoCoMo has been looking at ways to expand abroad. It wants to market i-mode worldwide, but unlike its US and European counterparts, who have been merging feverishly to enter new markets, DoCoMo believes friendly alliances will be more effective, especially in the Asian market. DoCoMo has taken equity stakes in several Asian companies and plans to woo Asian operators with funds and state-of-the-art technology. With its newly developed 3G wireless networks, DoCoMo has negotiated additional joint experimental projects with China, Malaysia, Singapore and South Korea.

Rivalry with competitors in the domestic markets does not deter DoCoMo from cooperating with them in foreign markets. Because DoCoMo is relatively new in the wireless market it has relatively limited experience in human resources, management, marketing and the technological expertise necessary to deal in countries outside of Asia. Therefore forming strategic alliances with more experienced competitors helps DoCoMo market its technology abroad and become a player in the global industry.

Table 3 i-mode's markets

UK	H3GUK	Under study for i-mode deployment
Germany	E-Plus	i-mode: launched on 16 March 2002
Netherlands	KPN-M NL	i-mode: launched on 18 April 2002
Belgium	BASE	i-mode: launched on 15 October 2002
France	Bouygues Telecom	i-mode licence agreement concluded in April 2002: launched in Nov. 2002
Spain	Telefonica Moviles Espana	Licence agreement concluded in July 2002. Planned for launch as 'e-mocion' in 1H/03
Hong Kong	HTCL	Orange World: launched in May 2000
Taiwan	KG Telecom	i-mode: licence agreement concluded in June 2001. Service launched on 20 June 2002
US	AT&T Wireless	mMode: launched in April 2002
Brazil	TeleSudeste	e-mocion: launched in July 2002

After establishing itself as the key player in the wireless industry, NTT DoCoMo has sought aggressive global diversification by acquiring selected wireless and Internet-type companies in Asia, Europe, and the United States. As of August 2001 NTT DoCoMo's selected overseas acquisitions and shareholdings include: KPN, The Netherlands (15 per cent); Hutchison Whampoa, Hong Kong (13 per cent); KG Telecom, Taiwan (20 per cent); AT&T Wireless Group (16 per cent); Verio, United States (100 per cent); and SK Telecom, South Korea. In the last three years the company has created a multitude of alliances and partnerships with companies such as: America Online, Coca-Cola Japan, Denstu, Itochu, Microsoft, SEGA Corp., Sony, Sun Microsystems, 3Com, Walt Disney, and others. Regarding the nature of its long-term shareholdings in foreign markets, NTT DoCoMo has avoided acquiring companies and instead preferred to take minority ownership in Asia, Europe and North America.

The company has taken a low-profile approach in its acquisitions but still exercises some control over the management. In the area of alliances and collaborations the company's strategy is to tie up with other high-tech and mobile operators that have significant national and global visibility, i.e. AOL, Coca-Cola, Denstu, Microsoft, and others.

At the global level, more opportunities are available to the wireless and mobile phone companies because of deregulations, privatisations and a surge in consumer demand. Mobile phone companies are able to bypass obstacles that were faced by traditional multinationals in the process of internationalization. Vodafone is an interesting example, where the company has sought internationalization in over 30 countries in a very short time because of the above-mentioned opportunities. Unlike traditional multinationals from Japan, NTT DoCoMo is more risk prone and innovative in the areas of its global acquisitions, alliances and expansion.

DoCoMo has also internationalised its R&D strategies by establishing R&D centres at the following locations:

- YRP R&D Center, Yokosuka, Japan, founded March 1998
- DoCoMo USA LAB, San Jose, California, founded November 1999
- DoCoMo EURO LAB, Munich, Bavaria, Germany, founded April 2001

At the global level, the Internet and e-commerce industry is a complex market because of the regulatory environment and country-specific standards. Besides this, e-commerce and its business models have been scrutinised because of valuation problems and long-term viability issues.

To expand and compete effectively in the global markets NTT DoCoMo may seek additional expansion into and acquisitions in Europe, North America and Asia. Long-term synergies are difficult to emulate in high-tech acquisitions.

Questions

1. Will DoCoMo be able to repeat its success with i-mode outside of Japan?

2. If yes, how should it do it? What entry modes should it consider and choose?

CASE STUDY III.3   Autoliv Air Bags

Transforming Autoliv into a global company

Chief executive officer of Autoliv Inc., Lars Westerberg, is in the middle of a board of directors' meeting in Stockholm in September 2003, discussing how it is possible to further globalize Autoliv. He takes out a situation report for the business area of air bags. As there are a couple of new members on the board Lars takes the opportunity to give a broader introduction to the business area than he usually does. The following is Lars Westerberg's status report.

Situation report for the business area of air bags

Business concept

Autoliv Inc., which is a Fortune 500 company, is the world's largest automotive safety supplier with sales to all the leading car manufacturers in the world. Autoliv's shares are listed on the New York Stock Exchange and on the Stockholm Stock Exchange. The company develops, markets and manufactures airbags, seat belts, safety electronics, steering wheels, anti-whiplash systems, seat components and child seats. Autoliv has 80 subsidiaries and joint ventures in 30 vehicle-producing countries, with about 30,000 employees. In addition, Autoliv has technical centres in 9 countries with 20 crash test tracks – more than any other automotive safety supplier.

Autoliv aims to develop, manufacture and market systems and components worldwide for *personal safety* in automobiles. This includes the mitigation of injuries to autombile occupants and pedestrians and the avoidance of accidents. In this aspect, Autoliv wants to be the systems supplier and the development partner to car producers that satisfy all the needs in the area of personal safety. To fulfil its business concept Autoliv has strong product lines:

- frontal and side-impact airbags (including all key components such as inflators with initiators, textile cush-

ions, electronics with sensors and software, steel and plastic parts);
- seat belts (including all key components such as webbing, retractors and buckles);
- seat belt features (including pretensioners, load limiters, height adjusters and belt grabbers);
- seat SubSystems (including anti-whiplash systems);
- steering wheels (including integrated driver airbags);
- roll-over protection (including sensors, pretensioners and airbag curtains).

The following will concentrate on the business area of air bags.

Production strategy

Autoliv has final assembly of restraint systems, located close to major customers' plants for just-in-time supply. The company also has six specialised component groups where the production is concentrated in relatively few locations for achieving economies of scale. The component companies are generally located in the same countries as the assembly plants. Autoliv is one of the most vertically integrated automotive safety system suppliers, with in-house divisions for all key components.

Since major automobile manufacturers are continually expanding production into more countries, it is also Autoliv's strategy to have manufacturing capacity where the major vehicle manufacturers have or are likely to set up production facilities. As a consequence Autoliv has more plants for automo-

tive safety products in more countries than any other supplier.

The product: the air bag

Even the best belt designs cannot prevent all head and chest injuries in serious head-on crashes. This is where air bags help, by creating an energy-absorbing cushion between an occupant's upper body and the steering wheel, instrument panel or windshield. Independent research has shown that driver deaths in head-on crashes are about 20 per cent lower in cars with frontal air bags than in similar cars with belts only. In all kinds of crash deaths are down by about 15 per cent over and above lives already being saved by belts.

Although air bags may seem complicated they are in fact relatively simple. In moderate and severe head-on crashes sensors signal inflators to fill the bags with harmless gas. The bags fill in a fraction of a second and begin deflating the instant they cushion people. Peak inflation is in less than $\frac{1}{20}$th of a second, faster than the blink of an eye. The speed and force of air bag inflation may occasionally cause injuries, mostly minor abrasions or bruises, but in the United States some occupants have died of broken necks caused by air bags that inflated with great force. Those at the greatest risk of injury caused by an air bag are those who drive or ride unbelted, small children, short or obese adults, and certain disabled people.

Injury risk from the bag itself can be reduced by choosing a driving or passenger position that does not put your face or chest close to the steering wheel or instrument panel. The combination of seat belt and air bag provides maximum protection in all kinds of crash.

Together with Volvo Autoliv has also developed the first side air bags to protect drivers and front-seat passengers in side-impact crashes. These bags are typically smaller than frontal air bags and they inflate more quickly. Volvo was the first manufacturer to offer side air bags in its 850 model in 1994. Volvo's bag is mounted on the outside of driver and front-seat passenger seat backs. Since 1996 side bags have been standard in all Volvo models.

The history of air bags goes back to the early 1950s. The product idea was patented in 1951 by Walter Linderer from Munich. It was in the United States, however, that the concept came into existence, driven by the North Americans' reluctance to use seat belts and hindered by the car manufacturers, which initially ridiculed the idea. In 1981 only 2,636 air bag systems were produced.

However, in late 1989 automatic restraint systems became compulsory in all passenger cars in the United States on the driver's side and, while this included automatically fastening seat belts, it seemed that the air bag had at last arrived. By 1992 10 million air-bag-equipped cars had been delivered to the United States. In 1993 came the requirement that all new light vehicles of model year 1999 produced in the United States had to be fitted with frontal air bags for the driver and the front-seat occupant. The next stage will be the compulsory fitting of air bags to both the driver and front passenger sides.

Autoliv introduced its first air bag system in 1990. It was designed to meet US requirements, where not all states have laws on wearing seat belts. The air bag therefore had to be relatively large. Autoliv has developed a special system (the Eurobag system) for markets where wearing a seat belt is compulsory. In this system the air bags have less volume (but they are still effective) and therefore the price can be kept at a lower level than some of the competitors. In the Eurobag system the air bags are 30–45 litres on the driver's side and 60–100 litres on the passenger's side. Furthermore, the Eurobag system is lighter and less bulky.

An air bag system consists of an electronic control unit and an air bag module. The electronic control unit contains (among other things) a sensor, while the module essentially consists of a gas generator, a nylon bag and a cover for the steering wheel centre or the instrument panel, depending on where the air bag module is placed. Autoliv typically supplies entire systems adapted to individual car models.

Organization

In France, Germany, Spain, Sweden, the United Kingdom and the United States, local management is regionally responsible for Autoliv's operations in countries other than their own. As a result the main customers have the advantage of dealing with Autoliv both in their home market and when they have or are going to establish production in other markets. Together with two regional coordination offices this organization contributes to low corporate overheads and short response times for the customers. (Autoliv's global headquarters has only 35 employees.) Autoliv's business directors and their organizations coordinate all activities with major customers on a global basis.

The world market for air bags

With its successful growth strategy, Autoliv has become the global leader in the $16 billion automobile occupant restraint market. Airbags account

Figure 1 **Autoliv's corporate structure**

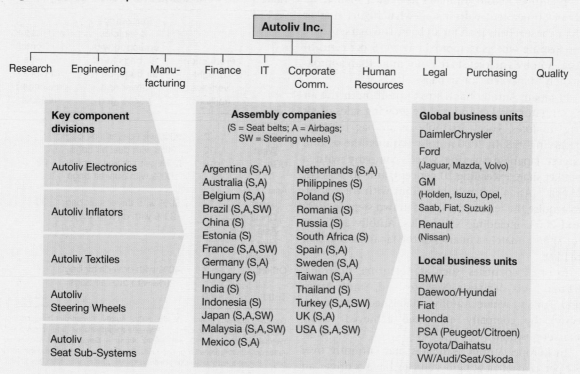

for just over 50 per cent of that market, seat belts for almost 30 per cent and electronics for nearly 20 per cent.

The global steering wheel market, which Autoliv entered in 1995 to promote the integration of driver air bags into steering wheels, amounts to over $1 billion.

The world market for air bags was an area of spectacular growth during the 1990s. In 2001 the number of frontal air bag units was almost 90 million and the number of side-impact air bags nearly 40 million.

In the United States frontal air bags – both on the driver and the passenger side – are compulsory under federal law in all new light vehicles sold after 1 September, 1998. The US market for frontal air bags therefore fluctuates with the car production cycle, but sales of side air bags are now about to take off. Their penetration rate was less than 20 per cent among new US light vehicles in 2001. Both Ford and General Motors have announced aggressive plans for curtain side air bags such as Autoliv's Inflatable Curtain. In addition, new regulations in the United States will require vehicle manufacturers to phase in more valuable 'advanced air bags' during a three-year period starting on 1 September, 2003.

Autoliv estimates that it currently has approximately one-third of the global market for car occu-

pant restraint products and that it has a somewhat larger global market share for air bags than for seat belts. For side air bags, which were invented by Autoliv and introduced in 1994, Autoliv's global market share is still approximately 50 per cent. For other recent safety improvements, such as seat belt pretensioners and load limiters, Autoliv's global market position is strong.

In North America, Autoliv estimates that in 2001 it accounted for approximately one-third the air bag products market and for one-quarter of the seat belt market compared with just over 10 per cent in 1999. (Autoliv did not sell seat belts in the United States until 1993.) Autoliv made its big entry into the North American market in 1996 when it acquired Morton Automotive Safety Products, which at that time was North America's largest air bag producer. The air bag business has given Autoliv an opportunity to expand its seat belt business now as complete systems sourcing takes place. In 2000 Autoliv acquired the North American seat belt business of NSK. Autoliv's market share for seat belts also increased as a result of new contracts, and the increasing number of new United States vehicles with seat belt pretensioners. Steering wheel sales in the United States commenced in 1998. Based on orders received so far, Autoliv expects its steering wheel market share to approach 10 per cent in just a couple of years.

In Europe, Autoliv estimates its market share to be about 50 per cent with a somewhat higher market share for seat belts than for air bags. The market share for steering wheels is approximately 15 per cent. In Asia, Autoliv's market share is not more than approximately 10 per cent for air bags.

In Japan, Autoliv has a strong position in the air bag inflator market and rapidly growing sales of air bag modules. Local assembly of air bag modules began in 1998. In 2000 Autoliv acquired the second largest Japanese steering wheel company with a market share exceeding 20 per cent, and 40 per cent of NSK's Asian seat belt operations with the option to acquire the remaining shares in two steps in 2002 and 2003. Including NSK's sales, Autoliv accounts for approximately a quarter of the Japanese seat belt market.

In other countries, such as Argentina, Australia, China, India, Malaysia, New Zealand, South Africa and Turkey, where Autoliv established production early, the company has often achieved strong market positions.

In Europe, Autoliv estimates that currently over 90 per cent of new light vehicles have a driver air bag, and 80 per cent also have an air bag for the front seat occupant. Installations of side impact air bags began in 1994, but in 2001 two-thirds of all new vehicles in Europe had such systems for chest protection. In addition, 25 per cent had a separate side impact air bag for head protection (such as the Inflatable Curtain or the ITS).

In Japan, where development started later than in Europe, penetration rates for frontal air bags are already as high as in Europe, while the penetration rate for side air bags is just over 10 per cent.

In the rest of the world, penetration rates vary greatly from country to country, but the average is still less than 50 per cent for both driver and passenger air bags (see Table 1). Installations of side air bags has just started.

The potential market for side air bags is difficult to assess. This is because side impact air bags will be optional accessories in many cars – at least initially – until the car producers have had time to evaluate the reaction of the market.

Competitors

In the late 1990s the number of major suppliers of occupant restraint systems was reduced from nine to four. As a result of the consolidation among producers of light vehicles the new entities that have been formed require suppliers to be cost efficient and have the capability to deliver the same products

Table 1 The world market for frontal air bags, 2001

	Production of light vehicles (millions)	Percentage of vehicles equipped with air bags (dual air bags, both driver and passenger)	Total market for frontal air bags (driver + passenger) (millions)
Europe			24
East	2	90% with driver's air bag	
West	12	80% with dual air bags	
USA	16	100% with driver's air bag	32
		100% with dual air bags	
Asia			
Japan	13	50% with driver's air bag	30
China	5	30% with dual air bags	
Asia (exc. Japan)	5		
Others	7	40% with driver's air bag	4
		20% with dual air bags	
Total	60		90

Sources: Autoliv Financial Report 2002, Autoliv PowerPoint presentations, W.J. Trein, Wirtschaftsordnung, *Unternehmensorganisation und internationale Wettbewerbsfähigkeit – Ein intergrativer Ansatz – Dargestellt am Beispiel der Automobilindustrie* (Peter Lang, 1994); EIU, 'The European market passenger car air bags', *Europe's Automotive Components Business*, 3rd quarter, 1995, pp. 52–63.

to all the companies' plants worldwide.

The four leading car occupant restraint suppliers now account for approximately 80 per cent of the world market (worth $16 billion) as opposed to 50 per cent five years ago. During this period Autoliv has increased its share to slightly more than 30 per cent and has replaced TRW (a US publically traded company) as the market leader. Another important auto safety supplier is Takata (a privately owned Japanese company). Both TRW and Takata have about 25 per cent market share. Delphi (the world's largest automotive components supplier) and Breed (a US company that in 2000 emerged from bankruptcy) have less than 5 per cent each.

Customers

Several of the world's largest car producers are among Autoliv's customers (see Table 2). Autoliv typically accounts for between 25 and 75 per cent of customers' purchases of seat belts and air bags. Autoliv supplies all major car makers in the world and most car brands. In the development of a new car model, a process that takes several years, Autoliv in many cases functions as a development partner for the car manufacturer. This typically means that Autoliv gives advice on new safety-enhancing products and assists in adaptation and conduct testing

Table 2 Autoliv's customer mix, 2001

Car manufacturer	Share of global vehicle production (60 million vehicles) %	Share of Autoliv's total sales ($4,443 million) %
General Motors	15	15
Renault/Nissan	9	13
Ford	11	17
Daimler/Chrysler	8	9
PSA (Citroën and Peugeot)	5	8
VW	10	9
Volvo	1	6
Toyota	11	5
BMW	2	4
Hyundai	4	4
Honda	5	2
Mitsubishi	3	1
Fiat	4	1
Others	12	6
Total	100	100

(including full-scale crash tests with the vehicle) of the safety systems.

No customer group accounts for more than 23 per cent of Autoliv's sales. The contracts are generally divided among a car maker's different car models, with each contract usually running for the life of the car model. No contract accounts for more than 5 per cent of consolidated sales. Of the total sales in Table 3, Europe accounts for 53 per cent, North America 33 per cent, Japan 9 per cent and the rest of the world 5 per cent.

Table 3 Three years of economic development at Autoliv Inc.

Key figures	2002	2001	2000
Sales ($million)	4,443	3,991	4,116
Pre-tax profit ($million)	287	117	291

The total number of employees (whole Autoliv Group, including subsidiaries) in December 2002 was about 30,0000.

With this positive news Lars Westerberg finishes his presentation of Autoliv's position in the air bags market. He would like a discussion of the following, to which you are asked to contribute.

Questions

1. Describe Autoliv's role as a subsupplier for large auto manufacturers in a market that is characterised by consolidation.

2. Which car manufacturer should Autoliv target to strengthen its global competitive position?

3. What strategic alternative does Autoliv have to strengthen its competitive position outside Europe?

Globalization of the film business

Back in 1997 the CEO of IMAX, Richard L. Gelfond, was a bit sceptical about building a story with Hollywood movie stars into the big screen format. At that time his answer to the criticism of IMAX® films' missing story was: 'It is too expensive and risky for us to put all our eggs in one basket and hire a major movie star.'

However, in 2003 new technological achievements have made it possible to show, e.g. *Matrix Reloaded* on the huge screen format. This is not just the projection of the standard theatrical print on an IMAX screen – the film will undergo the patented IMAX DMR (digital re-mastering) process, which enhances the quality of the image and soundtrack to the huge IMAX 15/70 format. The same has happened to *Apollo 13*, featuring Oscar®-winning actor Tom Hanks.

So though IMAX have been through financial tough times the company now seems to be looking towards a brighter future.

The IMAX Corporation

The IMAX Corporation is involved in a wide variety of out-of-home entertainment business activities. It designs and manufactures projection and sound systems for giant-screen theatres based on a patented technology. The IMAX Corporation is the world's largest producer and distributor of films for giant-screen theatres.

The IMAX Corporation, together with its wholly owned subsidiaries, is one of the world's leading entertainment technology companies whose principal activities are the following:

- the design, manufacture, marketing and leasing of proprietary projection and sound systems for Imax theaters principally owned and operated by institutional and commercial customers in more than 36 countries (September 1, 2003);
- the development, production, digital re-mastering, post-production and distribution of certain films shown in the IMAX theatre network;
- the operation of certain IMAX theatres located primarily in the United States and Canada; and
- the provision of other services to the IMAX theatre network including designing and manufacturing IMAX camera equipment for rental to film-makers and providing ongoing maintenance services for the IMAX projection and sound systems.

The IMAX theatre network is the most extensive large-format network in the world, with 239 theatres operating in more than 36 countries. Of these, 115 are in institutional locations and 102 in commercial locations. While IMAX's roots are in the institutional market, it believes that the commercial market is potentially larger. To increase the demand for IMAX theatre systems, it is currently working to position the network as a new window for Hollywood event films. To this end IMAX has both developed a technology that allows standard 35 mm movies to be converted to its format and is also working to build strong relationships with Hollywood studios and commercial exhibition companies.

In 2000 Buena Vista Pictures Distribution, a unit of The Walt Disney Company, released Disney's animated feature *Fantasia 2000: The Imax Experience®* to 75 IMAX theatres around the world. *Fantasia 2000* was the first full-length feature film to be reformatted into 15/70-format film and became the fastest grossing large-format film in history ($80.5 million to date). In January 2002 Disney released *Beauty and the Beast* to 77 IMAX theatres around the world and has stated that it will release an additional three films in the next 12 months. IMAX believes that the commercial success of *Fantasia 2000* and *Beauty and the Beast*, coupled with its new digital remastering technology, has the potential to lead to the release of additional Hollywood films into IMAX theaters, which could create further demand worldwide for commercial IMAX theatres.

IMAX theatre systems combine advanced, high-resolution projection systems, sound systems and screens as much as eight storeys high (approximately 80 feet) that extend to the edge of a viewer's peripheral vision to create the audio-visual experience. As a result audiences feel as if they are a part of the on-screen action in a way that is more intense and exciting than in traditional theatres. In addition, IMAX's 3D theatre systems combine the same projection and sound systems and up to eight storey screens with 3D images that further increase the audience's feeling of immersion in the film. IMAX believes that its network of 3D theatres is the largest out-of-home, 3D distribution network in the world.

History

The IMAX system has its roots in EXPO '67 in Montreal, Canada, where multiscreen films were the hit at the fair. A small group of Canadian film-makers/entrepreneurs (Graeme Ferguson, Roman Kroitor and Robert Kerr), who had made some of those popular films, decided to design a new system using a single powerful projector rather than the cumbersome multiple projectors used at that time. The result was the IMAX motion picture projection system, which would revolutionise giant-screen theatre. As the IMAX screen is about 10 times the size of a conventional movie screen picture quality has to be very good. The camera required is also much bigger than a conventional movie camera, but for anyone with film experience it is not hard to learn to use.

The much acclaimed *Fires of Kuwait* was nominated for an Academy Award in the Feature Documentary category in 1993. Since the premiere in 1970 more than 700 million people have enjoyed the IMAX® Experience™.

In 1977, IMAX was awarded the sole Oscar® for Scientific and Technical Achievement by the Academy of Motion Picture Arts and Sciences. The award recognized IMAX's innovation in creating the world's best film capture and projection system as well as IMAX's acceptance as part of the entertainment mainstream.

IMAX Ridefilm: entry and departure

Historically, another part of the corporation was the IMAX® Simulation Ride System, which combined giant-screen technology with aspects of an amusement park ride.

So until March 2001 IMAX subsidiaries also included Ridefilm Corporation, manufacturers and producers of motion simulation theaters or movie rides. IMAX Ridefilm (Ridefilm Corporation) was originally founded in 1989 by visionary film-maker and entrepreneur Douglas Trumbull as a privately owned company specialising in the development and production of simulation rides. As early as 1974 Trumbull combined 35 mm film with a flight simulator, creating the world's first movie ride. To simulate the experience of physical movement within a theater environment, Trumbull synchronised the audio and visual elements of the film with a hydraulic motion system, which persuaded the audience that they were actually flying, diving and accelerating. One of Ridefilm Corporation's new state-of-the-art projects became reality in 1993. *Back to the Future – The Ride*, directed by Douglas Trumbull, premiered in June at Universal Studios, Hollywood. This high-tech attraction was considered by entertainment industry experts to be the paradigm for the film experience of the future. The Ridefilm concept consisted of 18-person projection rooms in which the seats are equipped with seat belts and move with the action on the screen. The film is projected on a 180-degree screen, with digital surround sound.

In March 1994 Ridefilm Corporation and the former Trumbull Company, Inc. were purchased by an investment group as part of a transaction involving the acquisition of IMAX Corporation. Ridefilm was now a US-based, wholly owned subsidiary of IMAX. In June 1994 IMAX Corporation became a publicly traded company listed on the Nasdaq Exchange. Douglas Trumbull served as Vice-Chairman of IMAX Corporation and President/CEO of Ridefilm Corporation until 1 March 1997, when he left IMAX.

From 1995 IMAX deliveries of the system grew, climbing from 2 in 1995 to 15 in 1997. In 1999

IMAX listed 21 Ridefilm system locations. They are in shopping malls, hotels and interactive play centres, including the Luxor Hotel in Las Vegas, Fantasy Island in England, and two Sega Enterprises Ltd high-tech theme parks in Japan. IMAX Ridefilm simulator systems and films were marketed worldwide to such venues as theme parks, shopping malls, multiplex theatres, festival retail centres, urban entertainment centres, speciality retail chains and other high-traffic locations.

However, SimEx Inc., a competitor and a Toronto-based simulator ride company, emerged as the consolidator in the tough ridefilm business, announcing deals to merge with a US-based competitor and buy the ridefilm library of Canada's IMAX.

SimEx went on a buying spree in March 2001, coming up with agreements to buy Iwerks Entertainment Inc., a maker of giant-screen theaters and theme park rides, as well as acquiring the rights to seven simulation films held by the now defunct Ridefilm Corp. As a result of the transactions SimEx would have almost 150 simulation ride theatres under its wing, up from 45 and about half of the total market worldwide.

IMAX never succeeded in becoming profitable in the ridefilm business. One of the reasons for that might be that it never reached the critical mass of about 100 cinemas needed in order to support the three or four ridefilms that must be made each year to make the business profitable. The simulation ride business has been tough for Iwerks and IMAX's Ridefilm division, which have both lost money. SimEx has actually been profitable in eight of the nine years it has been operating. In 2000 it had revenue of about $25 million, and $36 million in 2001. In 2002 SimEx's annual revenue jumped to about $80 million. The deal with SimEx to buy the Ridefilm library puts to an end IMAX's venture in the simulation business, which had turned into a fiasco for the company. While sales of the ride systems were initially successful they declined steadily, and exhibitors complained about the software and maintenance problems. IMAX was forced to write off Ridefilm's assets in fiscal 1999, resulting in a charge of $13.6 million. Iwerks had been IMAX's main competitor when it came to giant-screen projection systems, a fact that caused bitter disputes and lawsuits between the two companies.

IMAX's business today

Generally speaking IMAX does not own its theatres, but leases its projection and sound systems and licenses the use of its trade marks. IMAX derives revenue principally from theatre system lease agreements, maintenance agreements, film production agreements and distribution of films.

In film production and distribution, IMAX has an agreement with Warner Bros. Pictures to continue digitally re-mastered event films into IMAX's 15/70 format using IMAX DMR technology. After successfully releasing the second and third Matrix films in IMAX's format in 2003. Warner Bros. announced plans to release the third Harry Potter film in 2004 and is in discussions to potentially release Charlie and the Chocolate Factory (directed by Tim Burton and starring Johnny Depp), as well as Polar Express in IMAX 3D. Such films add value to the IMAX film library by giving IMAX theatre more choice for their programming.

Theatre system leases

IMAX's system leases generally have 10–20-year initial terms and are typically renewable by the customer for one or more additional 10-year terms. As part of the lease agreement IMAX advises the customer on theater design and custom assemblies and supervises the installation of the system; provides training in using the equipment to theatre personnel; and for a separate fee provides ongoing maintenance of the system. Prospective theatre owners are responsible for providing the location, the design and construction of the building, the installation of the system and any other necessary improvements. Under the terms of the typical lease agreement the title to all theatre system equipment (including the projection screen, the projector and the sound system) remains IMAX's. IMAX has the right to remove the equipment for non-payment or other defaults by the customer. The contracts are generally not cancellable by the customer unless IMAX fails to perform its obligations. The contracts are generally denominated in US dollars, except in Canada and Japan, where contracts are generally denominated in Canadian dollars and Japanese yen, respectively.

The typical lease agreement provides for three major sources of revenue: (i) initial rental fees, (ii) ongoing additional rental payments and (iii) ongoing maintenance fees. Rental payments and maintenance fees are generally received over the life of the contract and are usually adjusted annually based on changes in the local consumer price index. The terms of each lease agreement vary according to the system technology provided and the geographic location of the customer.

IMAX films

IMAX produces films that are financed internally and through third parties. With respect to the latter, IMAX generally receives a film production fee in exchange for producing the films and is appointed the exclusive distributor of the film. When IMAX produces films it typically hires production talent and specialists on a project-by-project basis, allowing the company to retain creative and quality control without the burden of significant ongoing overhead expenses. Typically the ownership rights to films produced for third parties are held by the film sponsors, the film investors and IMAX.

IMAX is a significant distributor of 15/70 format films, with distribution rights to more of these films than any competing distributor. IMAX generally distributes films that it produces and it has acquired distribution rights to films produced by independent producers. As a distributor, IMAX generally receives a percentage of box office receipts.

The library of 15/70 format films includes general entertainment and educational films on subjects such as space, wildlife, music, history and natural wonders, and consisted of 200 films at the end of 2002, of which IMAX had distribution rights to 59. In recent years several 15/70 format commercial films have been successfully released, including *Space Station*, which was released in April 2002 and had grossed over $66 million as of 31 December 2003; *T-Rex: Back to the Cretaceous*, released by IMAX in 1998 and has grossed over $75 million to date; *Everest*, released by MacGillivray Freeman Films in 1998 and has grossed over $120.6 million.

15/70 format films have significantly longer exhibition periods than conventional 35 mm films and many of the films in the library have remained popular over the years, including *To Fly!* (1976), *Grand Canyon – The Hidden Secrets* (1984) and *The Dream Is Alive* (1985). In 2002 there were 21 new films released in the 15/70 format by all distributors.

In 2002 IMAX commenced production of 15/70 format films that are re-mastered from 35 mm studio films using IMAX's IMAX DMR technology. IMAX generally receives a processing fee for the re-mastering, the cost of which is borne by the rights holder of the 35 mm film. IMAX may also receive distribution rights to the 15/70 format films produced using the its technology.

International marketing

IMAX markets its theatre systems through a direct sales force and marketing staff located in offices in Canada, the United States, Europe, China and Japan. In addition, IMAX has agreements with consultants,

Table 1 Breakdown of installations by geographic segment as at 31 December 2002

	2002 Installed base	2001 Installed base
Canada	23	23
United States	113	110
Europe	43	41
Japan	18	20
Rest of World	35	33
Total	232	227

Table 2 Revenue by geographic area

	Years ended 31 December		
	2002 US$	2001 US$	2000 US$
Canada	7,236	5,524	8,454
United States	75,620	71,357	82,987
Europe	23,846	21,880	43,141
Japan	6,395	3,971	4,512
Rest of World	17,553	15,927	34,022
Total	$130,650	$118,659	$173,116

business brokers and real estate professionals to find potential customers and theater sites for IMAX on a commission basis.

IMAX has experienced an increase in the number of commercial theatre and international signings since 1995. The commercial theatre segment of IMAX's network is now its largest, with a total of 120 theatres opened. As at 31 December 2002, 38.0 per cent of all theatres are outside North America. IMAX's institutional customers include science and natural history museums, zoos, aquaria and other educational and cultural centres. IMAX also leases its systems to theme parks, tourist destination sites, fairs and expositions. See Table 1 for an outline of IMAX's operations by area.

For information on revenue breakdown by geographic area see Table 2.

No one customer represents more than 3.0 per cent of IMAX's installed base of theaters. IMAX has no dependence upon a single customer, or a few customers, the loss of any one or more of which would have a material adverse effect on the company.

As of 31 December 2002 IMAX had 288 employees, excluding hourly employees at company-owned and operated theatres.

Competition in the industry

Imax competes with a number of manufacturers of large-format film projection systems, most of which utilise smaller film formats, including 8-perforation film frame, 70 mm and 10-perforation film frame,

Audience watching 'Apollo 13' in a IMAX theatre.

70 mm formats, which IMAX believes deliver an image that is inferior to the IMAX experience. As already mentioned, the IMAX theatre network and the number of 15/70 format films to which IMAX has distribution rights are substantially larger than those of its competitors, and IMAX DMR films are available exclusively to the IMAX network. IMAX's customers generally consider a number of criteria when selecting a large-format theatre, including quality, reputation, brand name recognition, type of system, features, price and service. IMAX believes that its competitive strengths include the value of the IMAX® brand name, the quality and historic up-time of IMAX cinema systems, the number and quality of 15/70 format films that it distributes, the quality of the sound system in the IMAX theater, the potential availability of Hollywood event films to IMAX cinimas through IMAX DMR technology and the level of IMAX's service and maintenance efforts. Nearly all of the best performing large-format theaters in the world are IMAX's.

The commercial success of IMAX's products is ultimately dependent on consumer preferences. The out-of-home entertainment industry in general continues to go through significant changes, primarily due to technological developments and changing consumer tastes. Numerous companies are developing new entertainment products for the out-of-

home entertainment industry and there are no guarantees that some of these new products will not be competitive with, superior to or more cost effective than IMAX's products.

IMAX introduces the IMAX MPX theatre system

IMAX recently (2003) developed a new large-format theatre system designed specifically for use in multiplex theatres. Known as IMAX® MPX(TM), this new lower cost system allows commercial exhibitors to add an IMAX® theatre to an existing multiplex building or to retrofit two existing multiplex auditoriums into an IMAX theatre. By reducing system, construction, installation, facility and operation costs, the IMAX MPX theatre system significantly improves the economics of enterng into the IMAX theatre business for commercial theatre exhibitors. The IMAX MPX system was created to show Hollywood event films that have been digitally re-mastered into IMAX's 15/70 format using IMAX(R) DMR(TM) technology. The system also gives cinema operators access to the library of popular traditional IMAX 2D and IMAX(R) 3D film product. The development advances the Company's commercial strategy and is expected to have a significant impact on the growth of the commercial IMAX theatre network.

For example, in January 2004 IMAX signed a deal

with the leading film exhibitor in Spain for three IMAX theatre systems based on IMAX MPX theatre system. Each theatre will be located in shopping mall-based multiplexes in Spain.

Sources: Imax press release, 9 April 2001, 'Imax Corporation forms strategic partnership with DHJ Media to produce networked digital billboards'
Imax financial reports, 2002
other public media.
www.imax.com
IMAX press release, December 18, 2003, 'Third instalment of Harry Potter film series to be released as IMAX Film in Summer 2004'
IMAX press release, January 7, 2004, 'IMAX launches retrofit strategy by signing multiple theatre deal with Spain's leading exhibitor, Yelmo Cineplex SL'

Questions

1. Discuss the statement back in 1997: 'Technology is the star of the show. People don't go for a story.'

2. What are the main reasons for the failure of the Imax SBU Ridefilm?

3. Can IMAX's core competences be transferred to the marketing of high volume commercial products? Which types of product could these be?

4. What are possibilities of growing the IMAX business with the new IMAX MPX system combined with their new IMAX DMR technology, which enables Hollywood studios to digitally re-master their films into IMAX's 15/70?

CASE STUDY III.5 Heineken/Al Ahram Beverages Co.

Marketing of alcoholic and non-alcoholic drinks to Egypt and to other Muslim markets – does an acquisition help?

Heineken/Al Ahram Beverages Co. is eyeing the growing Islamic market with an ambitious plan to use its vast distribution network for a line of non-alcoholic, fruit-flavoured beers. As a first step Heineken, one of the world's largest brewers, paid $287 million in October 2002 to buy Al Ahram Beverages Co. (**ABC**) of Cairo, the biggest financial deal in Egypt's history. Al Ahram uses a special brewing process that yields no alcohol, thus allowing its malt beverages to be certified fit for consumption by Muslims, whose religion prohibits drinking alcohol.

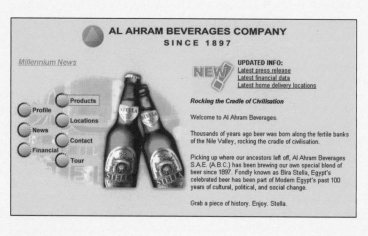

Background

Modern Egyptian beer-brewing officially began 100 years ago. On 15 May 1897 the Crown Brewery Company (ABC's oldest forerunner) registered itself in the Kingdom of Belgium – home of the well-known Stella Artois beer – to start operations in Alexandria. Two years later a different group of entrepreneurs from Brussels and Antwerp opened a brewery in Cairo, which came to be known as Pyramids Brewery. In July 1953 the Cairo brewery became known as Al Ahram (the pyramids) Beer Company.

Ten years later all companies traded on the Cairo and Alexandria stock exchanges were either nationalised or sequestered. Al Ahram Beer Company was first sequestered in 1961, then nationalised in 1963 when it was forcibly merged with the Crown Brewery Company of Alexandria.

This was the beginning of a state-run economy. Although contracts with the West slowed to a trickle and revenues were drying up under new public sector financial systems, Al Ahram Beer Company kept brewing beer and introducing new products including the Stella Export brand in 1967, created for foreign tastes.

Beginning in the 1970s the population of Egypt began to explode, and tourism became increasingly important. Demand for Stella beer grew with the crowds, foreigners and Egyptians alike, despite a rise in anti-secular sentiment throughout the Nile Valley.

In an attempt to counter these social trends and appease general sentiment Al Ahram Beverages (the company's new name as of May 1985) diversified its production line and launched several non-alcoholic drinks including the non-alcoholic beer Birell, and Fayrouz, a malt-based apple/lemon-flavoured beverage. These new drinks complemented Stella beer in an increasingly diverse and competitive market. The introduction of two more soft drinks, Yusfino (mandarin) in 1993 and Citrino (lemon–lime) in 1994 further varied the company's innovative product line.

Alcoholic drinks in Egypt

The alcoholic beverages market in Egypt, despite the large growth in values and volumes across all sectors and improvements in the quality of products available, is still characterised by unsatisfied demand. Unlike most other consumer markets, there are severe restrictions that thwart the development of this market in Egypt. Egypt is a Muslim country, with 85 per cent of the population practising Muslims. Islam condemns alcohol consumption and considers it a very serious sin. Even the Christian population, influenced by the general Islamic atmosphere, considers drinking alcohol a very bad habit, although they are not bound by religious law regarding consumption.

Shariaa Law prohibits the manufacture and sale of alcoholic beverages or even being in the same physical space as those drinking alcohol. A regular drinker in Egypt is seen as untrustworthy and particularly weak in terms of their desires. Hence, despite the significant number of drinkers, consumption usually takes place outside the family except in rare cases. Parents who drink tend not to drink in front of their children and children would consider it disrespectful to drink in front of their parents. So there is a great deal of discretion, sometimes amounting to secrecy, surrounding the buying and drinking of alcohol in Egypt.

Discretion is paramount when retailing alcohol. Most off-trade outlets operate in large open shopping malls or areas where the police are present. In fact some stores have police outside the front doors. This caution is due to the tension that flares up between Islamic groups and the government, the former tending to target such outlets as expressions of western influence on Egyptian society. Discretion is also used in order to avoid offending the large number of Egyptian Muslims who do not want to see alcohol being sold.

Retailers in more remote areas do not have access to the same level of security as their urban counterparts and tend to be very discrete about selling alcoholic beverages. These outlets usually sell such products only to known customers. If the owner does not know the person asking for alcohol, for example, they will deny that alcohol is sold in the store. This is because Islamic groups are known to attack shops selling alcohol.

The Egyptian government places its legitimacy on being a Muslim state, which derives its legislation from the Shariaa. However, it has never tried to prohibit the drinking of alcohol as it is a very lucrative business and has been a cash cow for the government. Duties on imports of alcoholic beverages are very high, at 300 per cent for beer and 3,000 per cent for wine and other spirits, making it almost impossible for someone to pay this duty. The tourism sector, however, which accounts for more than 30 per cent of national foreign currency earnings, is the main reason behind the government's attitude and the overall social compromise regarding alcoholic beverages.

It is believed that Egypt's competitiveness in terms of tourism would be harmed if alcohol was banned. Thus the state imposes these very high duties to prevent locals from buying alcoholic drinks, reserving them almost exclusively for tourists, who have access to duty free quotas of alcoholic beverages. The local population is denied access to such privileges, and this encourages black market trading, as high demand from those who do drink far outstrips supply. Current supply is hampered by limited local production and the limited supply of alcohol from duty free shops, and as such this market has huge gaps that have yet to be filled. As a result it certainly represents an opportunity for new players.

Dominant position in beer and wine

Local production has always dominated beer and wine sales in Egypt. The presence of prohibitive tariffs mean that off-trade purchases of such items are rather small compared to on-trade sales in tourist compounds and high-class restaurants. The general trend has been towards the monopoly of these particular products. In February 2001 ABC bought its only rival in beer and wine sales, El-Gouna Beverages Co., which accounted for 15 per cent and 40 per cent of beer and wine sales respectively. Thus ABC became the main producer of beer and wine in Egypt, accounting for around 98 per cent and 60 per cent of local production respectively.

ABC has an absolute monopoly of wine and beer sales in the absence of local rivals. The state also helps prevent foreign competitors from gaining a foothold as it imposes extremely high import duties on alcoholic drinks. Hence beer and wine account for the largest proportion of the total alcoholic beverages market in both volume and value terms. In addition, Egyptian consumers prefer low-alcohol percentage beverages to very high percentage products. This makes them preferable due to Egypt's very hot climate. In volume terms, beer accounted for 96 per cent of the total market while wine accounted for 3.3 per cent. The rest was mainly accounted for by spirits, as neither flavoured alcoholic drinks or cider/perry demonstrated significant sales. Sales of these products were limited to the extent that they remained negligible.

Market expansion potential

Led by ABC's monopoly, the market is expanding rapidly. Fuelled by the boom in tourism, which is growing by 11 per cent per annum on average, the market has a renewable source of consumers with high purchasing power. Most tourists drink alcohol in Egypt and they tend to drink rather heavily while on holiday. The year 2001 saw rapid development in this market. New products are being launched, and expansion of production facilities has also been rapid in response to the high unsatisfied demand. Expansion of outlets has also been increasing.

Over the past three years more than 150 outlets were opened or reopened by ABC. The company also operates a telesales system, which provides consumers with the discretion and convenience necessary in image-conscious Egypt, where many people do not want others to know that they are buying alcoholic beverages. The introduction of telesales has greatly boosted sales.

Beer sales are expected to grow by an average approaching 24 per cent per annum over the forecast period, while wine is expected to see average annual growth of more than 33 per cent. This will mainly occur as a result of growth in production, as demand is still higher than the production capacity of the single company in this business. Foreign imports have no chance of penetrating the market due to the duties imposed on them, which place their products beyond the reach of Egyptian consumers.

ABC also dominates distribution

Retail outlets are undeveloped in Egypt. The majority are very old, owned by either Coptic or Greek families who have lived in Egypt for a long time. ABC is the only company to have really developed a sophisticated distribution network of specialised off-licence shops in Egypt. In fact ABC distribution network has been so successful that it accounted for the majority of off-trade sales over 2000–1. ABC expanded its outlets after privatisation in late 1997 to reach a total of 150 outlets by 2001. Outlets are present throughout the country but are still restricted to the big cities. Their locations are well planned and the shops themselves are remarkably clean, unlike the old specialist shops, which tend to be very dusty and unpleasant.

Legal restriction on sales

Egyptian law is rather tough on drinking in general. It is a violation of the law to drink in public, and it is also illegal to be drunk in public. However, the police in Egypt are rather lax in the application of these laws with regard to the wealthy, and certainly do not apply them to tourists. Lower classes are usually the target of these laws.

Al Ahram Beverages Co.

ABC's Pilsener beer brand Stella is almost synonymous with beer in Egypt. With a volume of 620,000 hectolitres of non-alcoholic malt beverages, particularly the promising malt-based drink Fayrouz, ABC is also the market leader in this segment. In addition ABC has wineries producing the brands Gianaclis and Obélisque that account for 85 per cent of domestic consumption. The market share of the spirits division is around 35 per cent while its soft drinks operations have a market share of 3 per cent. In 2001 ABC derived 52 per cent of its sales from beer, 29 per cent from non-alcoholic malt beverages, 11 per cent from spirits and wine and 8 per cent from soft drinks. Total net turnover in 2001 amounted to $105 million, operating profit to $30.8 million and net profit to $22.8 million. ABC employs 3,860 people.

Heineken aquires Al Ahram Beverages Co.

It is no secret that the local Egyptian economy is thirsty for foreign investment. Now, the biggest private sector acquisition in national history could be the thrust that stokes western investors' interest in Egypt, which has been badly on the wane of late.

On 25 September 2002 Netherlands-based brewer Heineken bought up Al Ahram Beverages Co., whose shareholders agreed to sell 98 per cent of the local company at the $14 share price offered by the Dutch giant. This brings the total acquisition price to $280 million.

Heineken

Heineken has the widest global presence of all the international brewing groups, operating in over 170 countries and employing 40,000 people. In 2001 Heineken brewed a total of 105 million hectolitres of beer at over 110 breweries in more than 60 countries. In 2002 Heineken reached a turnover of approximately €10.3 billion. The net profits were €800 million.

The company's main international brands are Heineken and Amstel. Amstel holds strong positions in a number of European and African markets and is as a rule positioned as a mainstream beer. In the United States Amstel Light profits from its good taste and the success of the light beer segment, which makes up more than 44 per cent of the US beer market.

In order to remain one of the top global brewers, Heineken focuses on a combined portfolio of local brands and international brands, first their flagship Heineken, but also Amstel and speciality beers such as Desperados and Murphy's. This combination has enabled Heineken to achieve strong market positions and an efficient cost structure in many countries.

Heineken's overall beer market share in the European Union is 14 per cent, in Europe 12 per

cent, and globally it is 6 per cent.

Heineken's growth strategy in the Middle East

ABC had long been considered the darling of the Egyptian privatisation drive – a shining example of an uncompetitive, state-owned dinosaur turned into a star in the private sector.

Ahmed Zayat's Luxor Group bought 75 per cent of ABC in February 1997. While maintaining the well-known Stella as its flagship label, the new management also introduced new brand names, delving deeply into the non-alcoholic beverage market with heavy promotion of Fayrouz.

Four years after privatisation ABC bought out its only local competitor, Gouna Beverages, previously owned by Samih Sawiris' Orascom Projects & Touristic Development. From that point Ahmed Zayat's beverage empire held a 95 percent market share in Egypt, while pushing rapidly into the Gulf countries on the basis of its growing non-alcoholic range.

Heineken was obviously impressed by ABC's near domination of the Egyptian market within five years: 'We believe this is a very good brewery with excellent management, and well equipped,' Heineken spokesman Albert Holtzappel was quoted as saying in an Oxford Business Group bulletin, adding, 'We think that the Egyptian beer market in the long term will be attractive.'

Heineken is hardly new to Egypt. The Dutch brewer owned part of ABC before it was nationalised in 1963. For Heineken the deal is part of a larger strategy – to secure a dominant market share in the

A different kind of investor

Regional political frictions have led many foreign investors to avoid pumping money into the Middle East market altogether. This is not the case for Heineken.

Since the outbreak of the second Palestinian intifada in October 2000 and the attacks of 11 September 2001, the Middle East has been hit hard, with foreign investors pulling out of the region 'in droves'. ABC was – as were most Egyptian companies – badly bruised by these events, with its stock price falling below its 1997 Initial Public Offering (IPO) price.

Major multinational brewers, for their part, began to recognise the potential of a well-run beverage monopoly in a market of 65 million – within striking range of Africa and the Middle East. Heineken, along with Belgian Interbrew and South African Breweries, expressed interest in ABC.

ABC officials do not anticipate drastic changes to the company's local operations as a result of the takeover. ABC products, they assured, would continue to be marketed under their existing, regionally recognised brand names. ABC's 3,860 employees, meanwhile, will keep their jobs, according to ABC's corporate communications director Hala Al-Khatib.

Still, Egypt's opposition press, notoriously distrustful of the privatisation process and of foreign investment, were satisfied with the deal. The newspaper *Al-Neba Al-Watany* went so far as to suggest that Ahmed Zayat should buy other loss-making Egyptian companies and reform them, too.

Questions

1. In what circumstances would acquisitions be an advantage to Heineken, compared to 'greenfield' investments (use Chapter 12 as an starting point)?

2. Will Heineken's acquisition of ABC help with selling more alcoholic and non-alcoholic beverages in Egypt and in other international markets?

3. Is Heineken's acquisition a good strategic move from Heineken's viewpoint?

4. If you were a consultant for Budweiser would you also recommend Budweiser to select acquisition as a main 'entry mode' in the Middle East? If not, which entry mode would you recommend?

Designing the global marketing programme

PART IV

Part IV   Contents

Part IV   Introduction

Once the firm has decided how it will enter the international market(s) (Part III), the next issue is how to design the global marketing mix.

Since the beginning of the 1980s the term 'globalization' has increasingly become a matter of debate. Levitt's contribution on 'The globalization of markets' (Levitt, 1983) provoked much controversy concerning the most appropriate way for companies to become international. Levitt's support of the globalization strategy received both support and criticism. Essentially the two sides of this debate represented local marketing versus global marketing and focused on the central question of whether a standardized, global marketing approach or a country-specific differentiated marketing approach has the most merits. In Part IV we learn that there are different forces in the international environment that may favour either 'increasing globalization' or 'increasing adaptation' of a firm. The starting point is illustrated by the existing balance point on the scale illustrated in Figure 1. Which force will win not only depends on the environmental forces but also on the specific international marketing strategy that the firm might favour. Figure 2 shows the extremes of these two strategies.

Hence, a fundamental decision that managers have to make regarding their global marketing strategy is the degree to which they should standardise or adapt

Figure 1 Environmental factors influencing the balance between standardisation and adaptation

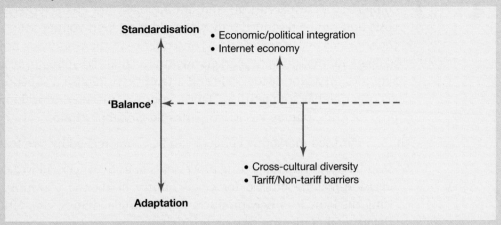

Figure 2 Standardisation and adaptation of the international marketing mix

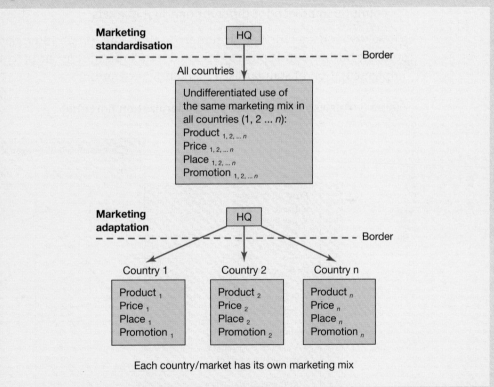

their global marketing mix. The following three factors provide vast opportunities for marketing standardization (Meffert and Bolz, 1993):

■ *Globalization of markets.* Customers are increasingly operating on a worldwide basis and are characterised by an intensively coordinated and centralised purchasing process. As a countermeasure, manufacturers establish a global key account management in order to avoid individual country subsidiaries being played off against each other in separate negotiations with, for example, global retailers.

■ *Globalization of industries*. Many firms can no longer depend on home markets for sufficient scale economies and experience curve effects. Many industries, such as computers, pharmaceuticals and automobiles, are characterised by high R&D costs that can be recouped only via worldwide, high-volume sales.

■ *Globalization of competition*. As a consequence of the worldwide homogenization of demand, the different markets are interrelated. Therefore firms can plan their activities on a worldwide scale and attempt to establish a superior profile vis-à-vis other global competitors. Hence, country subsidiaries no longer operate as profit centres, but are viewed as parts of a global portfolio.

The standardised marketing concept can be characterized by two features:

1. Standardisation of marketing processes is mainly concerned with a standardised decision-making process for cross-country marketing planning. By standardising the launch of new products, controlling activities, etc., rationalisation of the general marketing process is sought.

2. Standardisation of marketing programmes and the marketing mix is concerned with the extent to which individual elements of the 4 Ps can be unified into a common approach for different national markets.

These two characteristics of standardisation are often interrelated: for many strategic business units process-oriented standardisation is the precondition for the implementation of standardised marketing programmes.

Figure 3 Analysis of a company's standardization potential

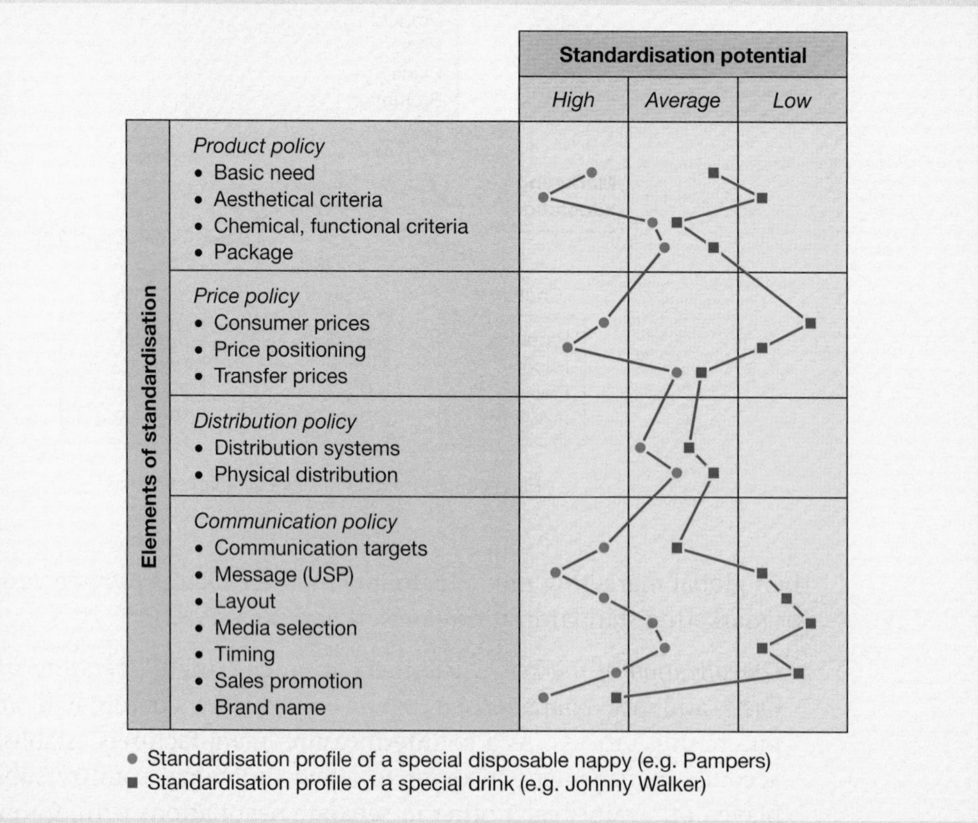

● Standardisation profile of a special disposable nappy (e.g. Pampers)
■ Standardisation profile of a special drink (e.g. Johnny Walker)

Source: adapted from Kreutzer, 1988. Reproduced with kind permission from MCB University Press; **www.mcb.co.uk**.

Many writers discuss standardisation and adaptation as two distinct options. The commercial reality, however, is that few marketing mixes are totally standardised or adapted. Instead it is more relevant to discuss *degrees* of standardisation. Therefore Figure 3 shows a standardisation-potential profile for two different products by the same company (Procter & Gamble).

The results indicate that there are different ways of realising a standardised concept within the marketing mix. In the case of both products it is possible to standardise the package at least on an average level. Difficulties arise as far as the price policy is concerned. Here it is possible to reach a standardised price positioning only for disposable nappies. So Procter & Gamble selects only those markets that possess the necessary purchasing power to pay a price within the target price range. In the case of alcoholic drinks it is nearly impossible to gain a standardised price positioning due to legal constraints. In Denmark, for example, consumers have to pay twice as much for the same Johnny Walker whisky as they do in Germany because of tax regulations. In many cases it is possible to use one brand name on a worldwide basis. There are negative effects connected with particular names in only a few cases; you have to change brand names to avoid these unintentional images.

We end this introduction to Part IV by listing in Table 1 the main factors favouring standardisation versus adaptation of the global marketing programme.

Table 1 **Main factors favouring standardisation versus adaptation**

Factors favouring standardisation	Factors favouring adaptation
• Economies of scale in R&D, production and marketing (experience curve effects)	• Local environment-induced adaptation: government and regulatory influences (no experience curve effects)
• Global competition	• Local competition
• Convergence of tastes and consumer needs (consumer preferences are homogeneous)	• Variation in consumer needs (consumer needs are heterogeneous)
• Centralised management of international operations	• Fragmented and decentralised management with independent country subsidiaries
• A standardised concept is used by competitors	• An adapted concept is used by competitors

References

Kreutzer, R. (1988) 'Standardisation: an integrated approach in global marketing', *European Journal of Marketing*, vol. 22, no. 10, pp. 19–30.

Levitt, T. (1983) 'The globalization of markets', *Harvard Business Review*, May–June, pp. 92–102.

Meffert, H. and Bolz, J. (1993) 'Standardization of marketing in Europe', in Halliburton, C. and Hünerberg, R. (eds) *European Marketing: Readings and cases*, Addison–Wesley, Wokingham, England.

Further reading

Berman, B. (2002) 'Should your firm adopt a mass customisation strategy?', *Business Horizons*, July–August, pp. 51–60.

Biemans, W. (2001) 'Designing a dual marketing program', *European Management Journal*, vol. 19, no. 6, December, pp. 670–677.

Solberg, C.A. (2000) 'Educator insights: standardization or adaptation of the international marketing mix: the role of the local subsidiary/representative', *Journal of International Marketing*, vol. 8, no. 1, pp. 78–98.

15 Product decisions

Contents

Learning objectives

After studying this chapter you should be able to do the following:

■ Discuss the influences that lead a firm to standardise or adapt its products.

■ Explore how international service strategies are developed.

■ Distinguish between the product life cycle and the international product life cycle.

■ Discuss the challenge of developing new products for foreign markets.

■ Explain and illustrate the alternatives in the product communication mix.

■ Define and explain the different branding alternatives.

■ Explain what is meant by a 'green' product.

■ Discuss alternative environmental management strategies.

■ Define and explain the different standards of ISO 9000.

15.1 Introduction

The product decision is among the first decisions that a marketing manager makes in order to develop a global marketing mix. This chapter examines product-related issues and suggests conceptual approaches for handling them. Also discussed are international brand (labelling) strategies and service policies.

15.2   The dimensions of the international product offer

In creating an acceptable product offer for international markets it is necessary to examine first what contributes to the 'total' product offer. Kotler (1997) suggests five levels of the product offer that should be considered by marketers in order to make the product attractive to international markets. In the product dimensions of Figure 15.1 we include not just the core physical properties, but also additional elements such as packaging, branding and after-sales service that make up the total package for the purchaser.

We can also see from Figure 15.1 that it is much easier to standardise the core product benefits (functional features, performance, etc.) than it is to standardise the support services, which often have to be tailored to the business culture and sometimes to individual customers.

Figure 15.1 The three levels of a product

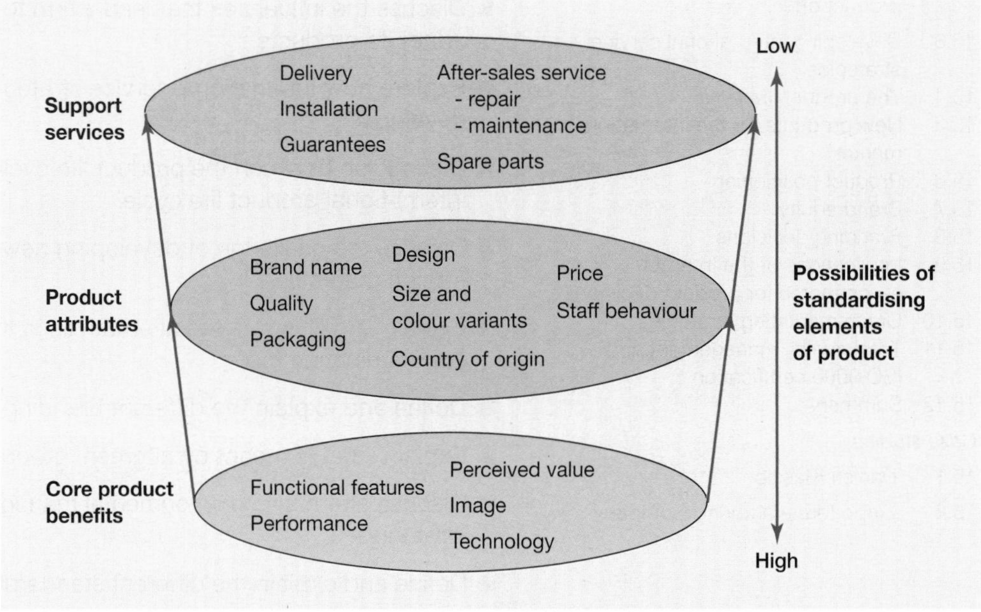

15.3   Developing international service strategies

We have seen from the definition of a product that services often accompany products, but products are also an increasingly important part of our international economy in their own right. As Figure 15.2 shows, the mix of product and service elements may vary substantially.

Characteristics of services

Before considering possible international service strategies it is important to consider

Figure 15.2 Scale of elemental dominance

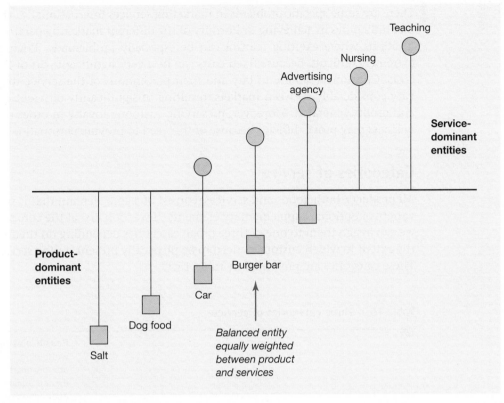

Source: Czinkota and Ronkainen, 1995, p. 526.

the special nature of global service marketing. Services are characterised by the following features:

- *Intangibility.* As services such as air transport or education cannot be touched or tested, the buyers of services cannot claim ownership or anything tangible in the traditional sense. Payment is for use or performance. Tangible elements of the service, such as food or drink on airlines, are used as part of the service in order to confirm the benefit provided and to enhance its perceived value.
- *Perishability.* Services cannot be stored for future use – for example, unfilled airline seats are lost once the aircraft takes off. This characteristic causes considerable problems in planning and promotion in order to match supply and demand. To maintain service capacity constantly at levels necessary to satisfy peak demand will be very expensive. The marketer must therefore attempt to estimate demand levels in order to optimise the use of capacity.
- *Heterogeneity.* Services are rarely the same because they involve interactions between people. Furthermore, there is high customer involvement in the production of services. This can cause problems of maintaining quality, particularly in international markets where there are quite different attitudes towards customer service.
- *Inseparability.* The time of production is very close to or even simultaneous with the time of consumption. The service is provided at the point of sale. This means that economies of scale and experience curve benefits are difficult to achieve, and supplying the service to scattered markets can be expensive, particularly in the initial setting-up phase.

Global marketing of services

There are some specific problems in marketing services internationally. There are particular difficulties in achieving uniformity of the different marketing parameters in remote locations where exerting control can be especially problematic. Pricing, too, can be extremely difficult, because fixed costs can be a very significant part of the total service costs. Consumers' ability to buy and their perceptions of the service they receive may vary considerably between markets, resulting in significantly different prices being set and profits generated. Moreover, preserving customer loyalty in order to obtain repeat business may prove difficult because of the need to provide personalised services.

Categories of service

All products, both goods and services, consist of a core element that is surrounded by a variety of optional supplementary elements. If we look first at the core service products we can assign them to one of three broad categories depending on their tangibility and the extent to which customers need to be physically present during service production. These categories are presented in Table 15.1.

Table 15.1 Three categories of service

Categories of service	Characteristics	Examples (service provider)	Possibilities of worldwide standardisation (hence utilising economies of scale, experience effects, lower costs)
People processing	Customers become part of the production process. The service firm needs to maintain local geographic presence.	Education (schools, universities). Passenger transport (airlines, car rental). Health care (hospitals). Food service (fast food, restaurants). Lodging service (hotel).	No good possibilities: because of 'customer involvement in production' many local sites will be needed, making this type of service very difficult to operate globally.
Possesion processing	Involves tangible actions to physical objects to improve their value to customers. The object needs to be involved in the production process, but the owner of the object (the customer) does not. A local geographic presence is required.	Car repair (garages). Freight transport (forwarding agent). Equipment installation (e.g. electrician). Laundry service (launderette).	Better possibilities: compared to people-processing services, this involves a lower degree of contact between the customer and the service personnel. This type of service is not so culture sensitive.
Information-based services	Collecting, manipulating, interpreting and transmitting data to create value. Minimal tangibility. Minimal customer involvement in the production process.	Telecommunication services (telephone companies). Banking. News. Market analysis. Internet services (producers of homepages on the WWW, database providers).	Very good possibilities: of worldwide standardisation from one central location (single sourcing) because of the 'virtual' nature of these services.

Categories of supplementary service

The core service provider, whether a bed for the night or a bank account, is typically accompanied by a variety of supplementary elements, which can be grouped into eight categories (Lovelock and Yip, 1996):

- *Information.* To obtain full value from any good or service, customers need relevant information about it, ranging from schedules to operating instructions, and from user warnings to prices. Globalization affects the nature of that information (including the languages and format in which it is provided). New customers and prospects are especially information hungry and may need training in how to use an unfamiliar service.

- *Consultation and advice.* Consultation and advice involve a dialogue to probe customer requirements and then develop a tailored solution. Customers' need for advice may vary widely around the world, reflecting such factors as level of economic development, nature of the local infrastructure, topography and climate, technical standards and educational levels.

- *Order taking.* Once customers are ready to buy suppliers need to make it easy for them to place orders or reservations in the language of their choice, through telecommunications and other channels, at times and in locations that are convenient to them.

- *Hospitality: taking care of the customer.* Well-managed businesses try, at least in small ways, to treat customers as guests when they have to visit the supplier's facilities (especially when, as is true for many people-processing operations, the period extends over several hours or more). Cultural definitions of appropriate hospitality may differ widely from one country to another, such as the tolerable length of waiting time (much longer in Brazil than in Germany) and the degree of personal service expected (not much in Scandinavia, but lavish in Indonesia).

- *Safekeeping: looking after the customer's possessions.* When visiting a service site customers often want assistance with their personal possessions, ranging from car parking to packaging and delivery of new purchases. Expectations may vary by country, reflecting culture and levels of affluence.

- *Exceptions.* Exceptions fall outside the routine of normal service delivery. They include special requests, problem solving, handling of complaints/suggestions/compliments, and restitution (compensating customers for performance failures). Special requests are particularly common in people-processing services, such as in the travel and lodging industries, and may be complicated by differing cultural norms. International airlines, for example, find it necessary to respond to an array of medical and dietary needs, sometimes reflecting religious and cultural values. Problem solving is often more difficult for people who are travelling overseas than it would be in the familiar environment of their native country.

- *Billing.* Customers need clear, timely bills that explain how charges are computed. With abolition of currency exchange restrictions in many countries bills can be converted to the customer's home currency. Hence currencies and conversion rates need to be clarified on billing statements. In some instances prices may be displayed in several currencies, even though this policy may require frequent adjustments in the light of currency fluctuations.

- *Payment.* Ease and convenience of payment (including credit) are increasingly expected by customers when purchasing a broad array of services. Major credit cards and travellers cheques solve the problem of paying in foreign funds for many retail purchases, but corporate purchasers may prefer to use electronic fund transfers in the currency of their choice.

Not every core service is surrounded by all eight supplementary elements. In practice the nature of the product, customer requirements and competitive pressures help to determine which supplementary service must be offered. In many cases the provider of the supplementary services can be located in one part of the world and the services delivered electronically to another. For example, order taking/reservations and payment can be handled through telecommunication channels, ranging from voice telephone to the World Wide Web. As long as appropriate languages are available many such service elements could be delivered from almost anywhere.

In summary, the information-based services offer the best opportunities of global standardisation. The two other types of service (people processing and possession processing) both suffer from their inability to transfer competitive advantages across borders. For example, when Euro Disneyland in Paris opened Disney suffered from not being able to transfer the highly motivated staff of its US parks to Europe.

The accelerating development within information technology (the Internet/WWW) has resulted in the appearance of new types of information service (e.g. information on international flight schedules), which offer great opportunities for standardisation.

Service in the business–to–business market

Business-to-business markets differ from customer markets in many ways:

- fewer and larger buyers, often geographically concentrated;
- a derived, fluctuating and relatively inelastic demand;
- many participants in the buying process;
- professional buyers;
- a closer relationship;
- absence of intermediaries;
- technological links.

For services in consumer markets an alternative for dissatisfied consumers is always to exit from the supplier–consumer relationship, as the number of firms offering the same kind of products is usually high. Therefore it is easy to switch between products and firms.

In the business-to-business market, however, bonds between the buyer and seller make the firms more unwilling to break the relationship. Of course the exit opportunity also exists to some extent in the business-to-business market, but the loss of investment in bonds and commitment tends to create exit barriers, because the costs of changing supplier are high. Furthermore, it can be difficult to find a new supplier.

Professional service firms, such as consulting engineering firms, have similarities with typical business-to-business service firms, but they involve a high degree of customisation and have a strong component of face-to-face interaction. The service frequently takes the form of a hundred-million-dollar project and is characterised by the development of long-term relationships between firms, but also the management of day-to-day relationships during the project. When a professional service firm (whether it be an accountant, architect, engineer or management consultant) sells to its clients it is less the services of the firm than the services of specific individuals that it is selling. As a consequence professional service firms require highly skilled individuals.

Filiatrault and Lapierre (1997) made a study of the cultural differences in consulting engineering projects between Europe (France) and North America (Canada). In North America the consulting engineering firms are generally smaller and they work in an economic environment closer (than in Europe) to pure competition. The contracts in Europe are very large and often awarded by governments. The French consultants recognise that there is more flexibility in managing in North America than in Europe. Subcontracting also appears to be more popular in North America.

15.4   The product life cycle

The concept of the product life cycle (PLC) provides useful inputs into making product decisions and formulating product strategies.

Products, like individuals, pass through a series of stages. Each stage is identified by its sales performance and characterised by different levels of profitability, various degrees of competition and distinctive marketing programmes. The four stages of the product life cycle are introduction, growth, maturity and decline. The basic model of the PLC is shown in Figure 15.3.

Figure 15.3 The product life cycle

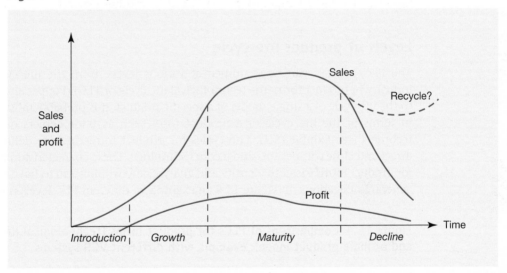

The PLC emphasises the need to review marketing objectives and strategies as products pass through various stages. It is helpful to think of marketing decisions during the lifetime of a product, but managers need to be aware of the limitations of the PLC so they are not misled by its prescriptions.

Limitations of the product life cycle

Misleading strategy prescriptions

The PLC is a dependent variable that is determined by the marketing mix; it is not an independent variable to which firms should adapt their marketing programmes (Dhalla and Yuspeh, 1976). If a product's sale is declining management should not conclude that the brand is in the decline stage. If management withdraws marketing resources from the brand it will create a self-fulfilling prophecy and the brand's sales will continue to decline. Instead management might increase marketing support in order to create a recycle (see Figure 15.3). This could be realised by the use of one or more of the following measures:

- product improvements (e.g. new product packaging).
- reposition perception of the product;
- reach new users of the product (via new distribution outlets);
- promote more frequent use of the product (fulfilling same need);
- promote new uses of the product (fulfilling new needs).

Fads

Not all products follow the classic PLC curve. Fads are fashions that are adopted very quickly by the public, peak early and decline very fast. It is difficult to predict whether something will be only a fad, or how long it will last. The amount of mass-media attention together with other factors will influence the fad's duration.

Unpredictability

The duration of the PLC stages is unpredictable. Critics charge that markets can seldom tell what stage the product is in. A product may appear to be mature when actually it has only reached a temporary plateau prior to another upsurge.

Levels of product life cycle

The PLC concept can be examined at various levels, from the life cycle of a whole industry or product form (the technological life cycle or TLC) (Popper and Buskirk, 1992) to the life cycle of a single model of a specific product. It is probably most useful to think in terms of the life cycle of a product form such as photocopiers or video cassette recorders (see Exhibit 15.1). Life cycles for product forms include definable groups of direct and close competitors and a core technology. These characteristics make life cycles for product forms easier to identify and analyse, and would seem to have more stable and general implications. In Figure 15.4 an example of different PLC levels is shown.

Figure 15.4 Comparisons of PLCs for product forms (technological life cycles, TLCs) and a single product model: example with different VCR systems

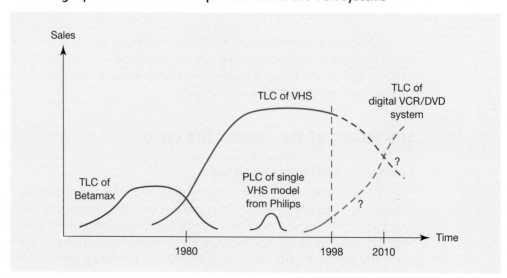

| Exhibit 15.1 | The global VHS/Betamax contest in the VCR business |

Figure 15.4 shows that the Betamax format introduced by Sony lost ground when the VHS standard (introduced by JVC) was adopted worldwide as the VCR diffused into global markets. The VHS/Betamax contest was a fight to the death by two virtually equal but incompatible formats. Market forces decided that there was room for only one successful format. Product performance was apparently not the crucial factor in the outcome, as an independent test found little difference between Betamax and VHS in, for example, picture and sound quality. However JVC was quicker than Sony to add features that consumers could immediately see the value of, such as longer recording and extended delay times. In promoting Betamax Sony evidently created an awareness of VCRs from which VHS subsequently benefited. The fierce competition between the formats (resulting in lower prices) accelerated total VCR sales. Today the VHS system is in the late maturity stage and a new digital DVD system has been introduced.

Another example of a TLC shift happened when the compact disc (CD) format was introduced as a result of a joint development between Philips and Sony. A key factor in the success of the CD format displacing the old LP record format was the ownership by Sony of CBS in the United States, and by Philips of Polygram in Europe, two of the biggest music software companies in the world. This contributed to the new CD format establishing itself as the industry standard. However, there were also a number of barriers to the adoption of the new format. The potential users had already invested in LP record collections and the prices of discs and players were relatively high at the beginning of the TLC.

Product life cycles for different products of the firm

So far in this chapter we have treated products as separate, distinct entities. However, many firms are multiproduct, serving multimarkets. Some of these products are 'young' and some are 'older'. Young products will require investment to finance their growth, others will generate more cash than they need. Somehow firms have to decide how to spread their limited resources among the competing needs of products so as to achieve the best performance of the firm as a whole. Figure 15.5 shows an example of a company (British Leyland) that did not succeed in achieving a balanced product portfolio (note that the PLC curves are represented by profit and not sales).

Product life cycles for different countries

When expanding the concept of the PLC to international markets two different approaches appear:

- international product life cycle (IPLC): a macroeconomic approach
- PLCs across countries: a microeconomic approach.

The international product life cycle

The IPLC theory (originally Vernon, 1966) describes the diffusion process of an innovation across national boundaries (Figure 15.6). For each curve net export results when the curve is above the horizontal line; if the curve is below the horizontal line net import results for a particular country.

Figure 15.5 Situation of British Leyland in the late 1970s

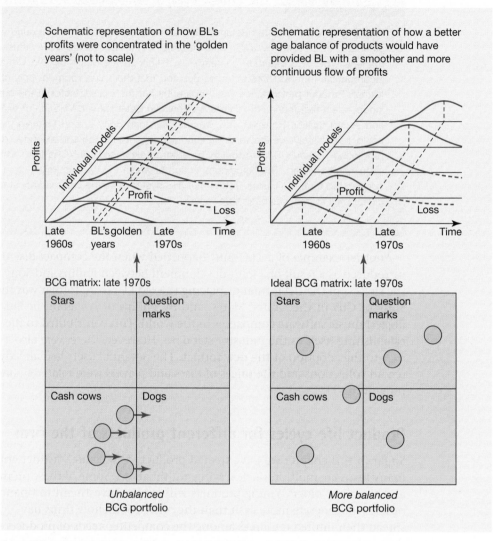

Source: Partly reprinted from *Long Range Planning*, Vol. 17, No. 3, McNamee, P. (1984) 'Competitive analysis using matrix displays', pp. 98–114, Copyright 1984, with permission from Elsevier.

Figure 15.6 IPLC curves

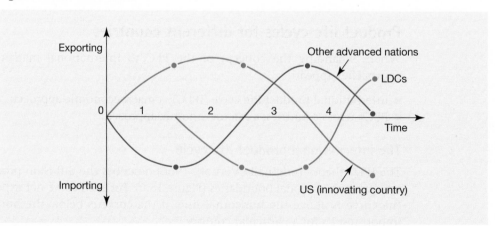

Source: Onkvisit and Shaw, 1993, p. 483.

Typically, demand first grows in the innovating country (here the United States). In the beginning excess production in the innovating country (greater than domestic demand) will be exported to other advanced countries where demand also grows. Only later does demand begin in less developed countries. Production, consequently, takes place first in the innovating country. As the product matures and technology is diffused production occurs in other industrialised countries and then in less developed countries. Efficiency/comparative advantages shift from developed countries to developing countries. Finally, advanced countries, no longer cost effective, import products from their former customers.

Examples of typical IPLCs can be found in the textile industry and the computer/software industry. For example, many software programs today are made in Bangalore, India.

Product life cycles across countries: a microeconomic approach

In foreign markets the time span for a product to pass through a stage may vary from market to market. In addition, due to different economic levels in different countries, a specific product can be in different PLC stages in different countries. Figure 15.7 shows that the product (at a certain time, t_1) is in the decline stage in the home market, while it is in the maturity stage for country A and in the introduction stage for country B (Majaro, 1982).

Figure 15.7 **PLCs of different countries for a specific product**

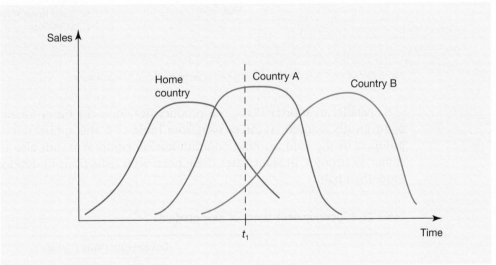

15.5   New products for the international market

Customer needs are the starting point for product development, whether for domestic or global markets. In addition to customer needs conditions of use and ability to buy the product form a framework for decisions on new product development for international markets.

Developing new products/cutting the time to market

As a consequence of increasing international competition, time is becoming a key success factor for an increasing number of companies that manufacture technologically sophisticated products. This time competition and the level of technological development mean that product life cycles are getting shorter and shorter (see Figure 15.8).

Figure 15.8 Gillette's product life cycles are getting shorter

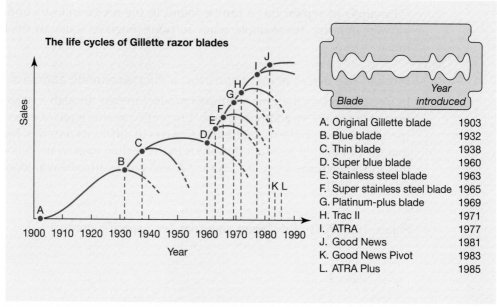

The life cycles of Gillette razor blades

Blade	Year introduced
A. Original Gillette blade	1903
B. Blue blade	1932
C. Thin blade	1938
D. Super blue blade	1960
E. Stainless steel blade	1963
F. Super stainless steel blade	1965
G. Platinum-plus blade	1969
H. Trac II	1971
I. ATRA	1977
J. Good News	1981
K. Good News Pivot	1983
L. ATRA Plus	1985

Source: Zikmund and D'Amico, 1989, p. 247. Reprinted by permission of John Wiley & Sons, Inc.

In parallel to shorter PLCs, the product development times for new products are being greatly reduced. As can be seen from Table 15.2, this applies not only to technical products in the field of office communication equipment, but also to cars and consumer electronics. In some cases there have been reductions in development times of more than half.

Table 15.2 Development times of new products

Company	Product	Development time in years 1980	1990
Rank Xerox	Copiers	5	3
Brother	Printers	4	2
Hewlett-Packard	Printers	4.5	2
Apple	Computers	3.5	1
Volvo	Trucks	7	5.5
Honda	Cars	8	3
AT&T	Telephone systems	2	1
Sony	Television Sets	2	0.75

Source: Reprinted from *Long Range Planning*, Vol. 28, No. 2, Töpfer, A. (1995) 'New products: cutting the time to market', p. 68, Copyright 1995, with permission from Elsevier.

Similarly, the time for marketing/selling, and hence also for R&D cost to pay off, has gone down from about four years to only two years. This new situation is illustrated in Figure 15.9.

For all types of technological product it holds true that the manufactured product must have as good a quality as required by the customer (i.e. as good as necessary), but not as good as technically feasible. Too frequently technological products are over-optimised and therefore too expensive from the customer's point of view (a good analysis of 'quality' is to be found in Guiltinan *et al.*, 1997).

Figure 15.9 Compression of R&D cycles and product life cycles

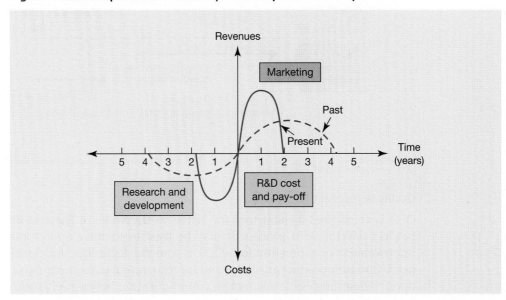

Source: Reprinted from *Long Range Planning*, Vol. 28, No. 2, Töpfer, A. (1995) 'New products: cutting the time to market', p. 64, Copyright 1995, with permission from Elsevier.

As we have indicated in earlier chapters, Japanese and European suppliers to the car industry have different approaches to the product development process. Figure 15.10 shows an example with suppliers of dashboard instruments for cars. The two Japanese manufacturers start the engineering design phase two years later than the European manufacturer. This enables the Japanese fully to develop a product in a shorter time using the newest technology and to launch it almost simultaneously with their competitors.

The reason for the better time competition of the Japanese manufacturers is the intensive use of the following measures:

- early integration of customers and suppliers;
- multiskilled project teams;
- interlinking of R&D, production and marketing activities;
- total quality management;
- parallel planning of new products and the required production facilities (simultaneous engineering);
- high degree of outsourcing (reduction of internal manufacturing content).

Today product quality is not enough to reach and to satisfy the customer. Quality of design and appearance play an increasingly important role. A highly qualified product support and customer service is also required.

Figure 15.10 Development and test periods for suppliers to the car industry

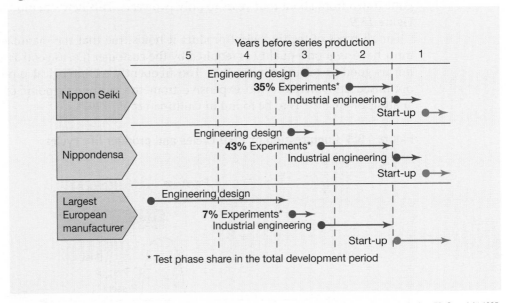

Source: Reprinted from *Long Range Planning*, Vol. 28, No. 2, Töpfer, A. (1995) 'New products: cutting the time to market', p. 72, Copyright 1995, with permission from Elsevier.

Quality Deployment Function

QFD is considered a main tool for 'listen to the voice of the customer' in the new product development process. It may be used to identify opportunities for product improvement or differentiation. QFD is a useful technique for translating customer needs into new product attributes and for responding to requirements of the successful development process. It encourages communication between engineering, production and marketing. Besides the involvement of customer requirements in the new product development process QFD permits the reduction of design time and design cost while maintaining or enhancing the quality of the design. QFD originated in 1972 at Mitsubishi's Kobe shipyard and is used widely both in Japan and the United States. It has reduced design time and cost at Toyota by 40 per cent. The time and cost reducing effect arises because more effort is allocated in the early stages of the product innovation process.

Degrees of product newness

A new product can have several degrees of newness. A product may be an entirely new invention (new to the world) or it may be a slight modification of an existing product. In Figure 15.11 newness has two dimensions: newness to the market (consumers, channels and public policy) and newness to the company. The risk of market failure also increases with the newness of the product. Hence the greater the newness of the product, the greater the need for a thorough internal company and external environment analysis, in order to reduce the risk involved.

The product communication mix

Having decided upon the optimum standardisation/adaptation route and the newness of the product, the next most important (and culturally sensitive) factor to be considered is that of international promotion.

Figure 15.11 Different degrees of product newness

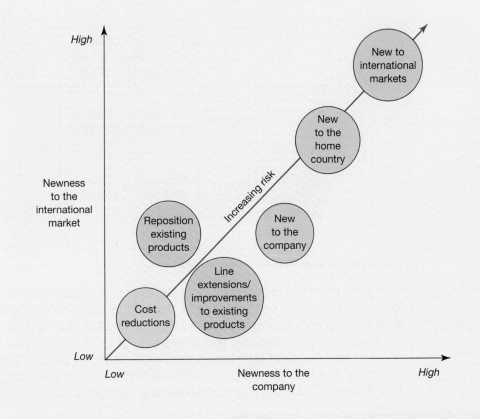

Product and promotion go hand in hand in foreign markets and together are able to create or destroy markets in very short order. We have considered above the factors that may drive an organization to standardise or adapt its product range for foreign markets. Equally important are the promotion or the performance promises that the organization makes for its product or service in the target market. As with product decisions, promotion can be either standardised or adapted for foreign markets.

Keegan (1995) has highlighted the key aspects of marketing strategy as a combination of standardisation or adaptation of the product and promotion of elements of the mix, and offers five alternative and more specific approaches to product policy. These approaches are shown in Figure 15.12 overleaf.

Straight extension

This involves introducing a standardised product with the same promotion strategy throughout the world market (one product, one message worldwide). By applying this strategy successfully major savings can be made on market research and product development. Since the 1920s Coca-Cola has adopted a global approach, which has allowed the company to make enormous cost savings and benefits from continual reinforcement of the same message. While a number of writers have argued that this will be the strategy adopted for many products in the future, in practice only a handful of products might claim to have achieved this already. A number of firms have tried and failed. Campbell's soups, for example, found that consumers' taste in soup was by no means international.

Figure 15.12 Product/communication mode

Promotion		Product		
		Standard	*Adapt*	*New*
	Standard	Straight extension	Product adaptation	Product invention
	Adapt	Promotion adaptation	Dual adaptation	

Source: adapted from Keegan, 1995. With permission of Prentice-Hall, Inc.

An example of successful extension is Unilever's worldwide introduction of Organics Shampoo, which was first launched in Thailand in late 1993 after joint development work by Unilever's Hair Innovation Centres in Bangkok and Paris. By 1995 the brand was sold in over 40 countries, generating sales of £170 million. You can see below a two-page advertisement from a magazine, used during the product's introduction into Argentina. The basic advertising concept all over the world (including Argentina) has been 'Organics – the first ever root-nourishing shampoo'.

'Straight extension' of Organics Shampoo to Argentina

도전하는 자만이
새로운 세계를 열 수 있습니다.

Star TAC™ 폴더

Ⓜ **MOTOROLA**

Motorola's 'promotion adaption' for the Korean market

Promotion adaptation

Use of this strategy involves leaving a product unchanged but fine-tuning promotional activity to take into account cultural differences between markets. It is a relatively cost-effective strategy as changing promotion messages is not as expensive as adapting products. An example of this strategy is illustrated on the left, which shows Motorola's cellular phone advertisement for the Korean market. An advertising campaign for the south-east Asian market was developed in Singapore. However, the advertising proposal from Singapore was redeveloped in Korea. A juggler was switched to a well-known Korean drummer as it was thought to be more familiar and appealing to Korean consumers. The English translation of the Korean script is as follows:

Only those who challenge the limits can open the new world of possibilities
Percussionist Kim Dae Hwan challenges the boundaries of performance technique and creates a new world of sound that no one previously has imagined. We sometimes meet situations in our lives that seem too difficult to overcome, but with our constant challenging spirit we can certainly overcome them. Motorola Cellular constantly challenges the boundaries of technology. We create a new world of cellular technology that no one could have thought possible by creating smaller and lighter cellular phones. The new world of cellular phones, a result of our challenging spirit, helps many of us in the world to accomplish more in our lives. Rest assured, only those who challenge the limits can open the new world of possibilities.

Motorola. A world you never thought possible.

Product adaptation

By modifying only the product a manufacturer intends to maintain the core product function in the different markets. For example, electrical appliances have to be modified to cope with different electrical voltages in different countries. A product can also be adapted to function under different physical environmental conditions. Exxon changed the chemical composition of petrol to cope with the extremes of climate, but still used the 'Put a tiger in your tank' campaign unchanged around the world.

Dual adaptation

By adapting both product and promotion for each market the firm is adopting a totally differentiated approach. This strategy is often adopted by firms when one of the previous three strategies has failed, but particularly if the firm is not in a leadership position and is therefore reacting to the market or following competitors. It applies to the majority of products in the world market. The modification of both product and promotion is an expensive but often necessary strategy.

An example of dual adaptation is shown overleaf, with the launch of Kellogg's Basmati Flakes in the nascent breakfast cereal market in India. This product was specially created to suit Indian tastes, India being a large rice-eating country. The advertising campaign was a locally adapted concept based on international positioning. Note that the product is available only in the Bombay area.

Kellogg's dual adaption for the Indian market

Product invention

Product invention is adopted by firms usually from advanced nations that are supplying products to less developed countries. Products are specifically developed to meet the needs of the individual markets. Existing products may be too technologically sophisticated to operate in less developed countries, where power supplies may be intermittent and local skills limited. Keegan (1995) uses a hand-powered washing machine as a product example.

15.6 Product positioning

Product positioning is a key element in the successful marketing of any organization in any market. The product or company that does not have a clear position in the customer's mind consequently stands for nothing and is rarely able to command more than a simple commodity or utility price. Premium pricing and competitive advantage are largely dependent upon the customer's perception that the product or service on offer is markedly different in some way from competitive offers. How can we achieve a credible market position in international markets?

Since it is the buyer/user perception of benefit-generating attributes that is important, product positioning is the activity by which a desirable 'position' in the mind of the customer is created for the product. Positioning a product for international markets begins with describing specific products as comprising different attributes that are capable of generating a flow of benefits to buyers and users.

The global marketing planner puts these attributes into bundles so that the benefits generated match the special requirements of specific market segments. This product design problem involves not only the basic product components (physical, package, service and country of origin) but also brand name, styling and similar features.

Viewed in a multidimensional space (commonly denoted as 'perceptual mapping'), a product can be graphically represented at a point specified by its attributes. The location of a product's point in perceptual space is its 'position'. Competitors' products are similarly located (see also Johansson and Thorelli, 1985). If points representing other products are close to the point of the prototype then these other products are close competitors of the prototype. If the prototype is positioned away from its closest competitors in some international markets and its positioning implies important features for customers, then it is likely to have a significant competitive advantage.

Country-of-origin effects

The country of origin of a product, typically communicated by the phrase 'made in [country]', has a considerable influence on the quality perception of that product. Some countries have a good reputation and others have a poor reputation for certain products. For example, Japan and Germany have good reputations for producing cars. The country-of-origin effects are especially critical among eastern European consumers. A study (Ettensén, 1993) examined the brand decision for televisions among Russian, Polish and Hungarian consumers. These consumers evaluated domestically produced television products much lower than western-made products, regardless of brand name. There was a general preference for televisions manufactured in Japan, Germany and the United States.

The country of origin is more important than the brand name and can be viewed as good news for western firms that are attempting to penetrate the eastern European region with imports whose brand name is not yet familiar. Another study (Johansson *et al.*, 1994) showed that some products from eastern Europe have done well in the West, despite negative country-of-origin perceptions. For example, Belarus tractors have sold well in Europe and the United States not only because of their reasonable price but also because of their ruggedness. Only the lack of an effective distribution network has hindered the firm's ability to penetrate western markets to a greater degree.

When considering the implications of product positioning it is important to realise that positioning can vary from market to market, because the target customers for the product differ from country to country. In confirming the positioning of a product or service in a specific market or region it is therefore necessary to establish in the consumer's perception exactly what the product stands for and how it differs from existing and potential competition. In developing a market-specific product positioning the firm can focus upon one or more elements of the total product offer, so the differentiation might be based upon price and quality, one or more attributes, a specific application, a target consumer or direct comparison with one competitor.

15.7   Brand equity

A study by Citibank and Interbrand in 1997 found that companies basing their business on brands had outperformed the stock market for 15 years. The same study does, however, note the risky tendency of some brand owners to have reduced investments in brands in the mid-1990s with negative impacts on their performance (Hooley *et al.*, 1998, p. 120).

The following two examples show that brands add value for customers:

- The classic example is that in blind test 51 per cent of consumers prefer Pepsi to Coca-Cola, but in open tests 65 per cent prefer Coca-Cola to Pepsi: soft drink preferences are based on brand image, not taste (Hooley *et al.*, 1998, p. 119).
- Skoda cars have been best known in the United Kingdom as the butt of bad jokes, reflecting a widespread belief that the cars are of very low quality. In 1995 Skoda was preparing to launch a new model in the United Kingdom, and did 'blind and seen' tests of the consumers' judgement of the vehicle. The vehicle was rated as better designed and worth more by those who did not know the make. With the Skoda name revealed perceptions of the design were less favourable and estimated value was substantially lower. This leads us from the reputation of the company to branding (Hooley *et al.*, 1998, p. 117).

Definitions of 'brand equity'

Although the definition of brand equity is often debated, the term deals with the brand value, beyond the physical assets associated with it manufacture.

David Aaker of the University of California at Berkeley, one of the leading authorities on brand equity, has defined the term as 'a set of *brand assets and liabilities* linked to the brand, its name and symbol, that add to or subtract from the value provided by a product or service to a firm or to the firm's customers (Aaker, 1991, p. 15).

Aaker has clustered those assets and liabilities into five categories:

1. *Brand loyalty.* Encourages customers to buy a particular brand time after time and remain insensitive as competitors' offerings.
2. *Brand awareness.* Brand names attract attention and convey images of familarity. May be translated to: how big a percentage of the customers know the brand name.
3. *Perceived quality.* 'Perceived' means that the customers decide upon the level of quality, not the company.
4. *Brand associations.* The values and the personality linked to the brand.
5. *Other proprietary brand assets.* Include trademarks, patents and marketing channel relationships.

Brand equity can be thought of as the additional cash flow achieved by associating a brand with the underlying values of the product or service. In this connection it is useful (although incomplete) to think of a brand's equity as *the premium a customer/ consumer would pay for the branded product or service compared to an identical unbranded version of the same product/service.*

Hence brand equity refers to the strength, depth and character of the consumer–brand relationship. A strong equity implies a positive force that keeps the consumer and the brand together, in the face of resistance and tension. The strength, depth and character of the customer–brand relationship is referred to as the *brand relationship quality* (Marketing Science Institute, 1995).

15.8 Branding decisions

Closely linked to product positioning is the question of branding. The basic purposes of branding are the same everywhere in the world. In general, the functions of branding are as follows:

- to distinguish a company's offering and differentiate one particular product from its competitors;

Table 15.3 Advantages and disadvantages of branding alternatives

	Advantages	Disadvantages
No brand	Lower production cost. Lower marketing cost. Lower legal cost. Flexible quality control.	Severe price competition. Lack of market identity.
Branding	Better identification and awareness. Better chance for production differentiation. Possible brand loyalty. Possible premium pricing.	Higher production cost. Higher marketing cost. Higher legal cost.
Private label	Possibility of larger market share. No promotional problems.	Severe price competition. Lack of market identity.
Co-branding/ ingredient branding	Adds more value to the brand. Sharing of production and promotion costs Increases manufacturer's power in gaining access to retailers' shelves. Can develop into long-lasting relationships based on mutual commitment.	Consumers may become confused. Ingredient supplier is very dependent on the success of the final product. Promotion cost for ingredient supplier.
Manufacturer's own brand	Better price due to higher price inelasticity. Retention of brand loyalty. Better bargaining power. Better control of distribution.	Difficult for small manufacturer with unknown brand. Requires brand promotion.
Single market, single brand	Marketing efficiency. Permits more focused marketing. Eliminates brand confusion. Good for product with good reputation (halo effect).	Assumes market homogeneity. Existing brand's image harmed when trading up/down. Limited shelf space.
Single market, multiple brands	Market segmented for varying needs. Creates competitive spirit. Avoids negative connotation of existing brand. Gains more retail shelf space. Does not harm existing brand's image.	Higher marketing cost. Higher inventory cost. Loss of economies of scale.
Multiple markets, local brand	Meaningful names. Local identification. Avoidance of taxation on international brand. Allows variations of quantity and quality across markets.	Higher marketing cost. Higher inventory cost. Loss of economies of scale. Diffused image.
Multiple markets, global brand	Maximum marketing efficiency. Reduction of advertising costs. Elimination of brand confusion. Good for culture-free product. Good for prestigious product. Easy identification/recognition for international travellers. Uniform worldwide image.	Assumes market homogeneity. Problems with black and grey markets. Possibility of negative connotation. Requires quality and quantity consistency. LDCs' opposition and resentment. Legal complications.

Source: Adapted from Onkvisit and Shaw 1989. Published with permission from Emerald Publishing Ltd. www.emeraldinsight.com

- to create identification and brand awareness;
- to guarantee a certain level of quality and satisfaction;
- to help with promotion of the product.

All of these purposes have the same ultimate goals: to create new sales (market shares taken from competitors) or induce repeat sales (keep customers loyal).

As seen from Figure 15.13 there are four levels of branding decisions. Each alternative at the four levels has a number of advantages and disadvantages, which are presented in Table 15.3. We will discuss these options in more detail below.

Figure 15.13 Branding decisions

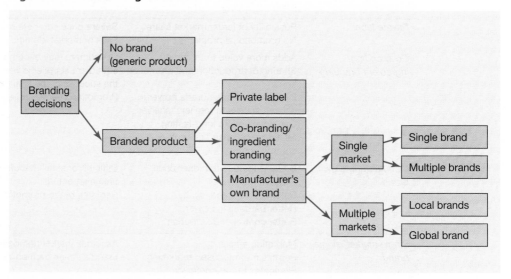

Source: adapted from Onkvisit and Shaw, 1993, p. 534.

Brand versus no brand

Branding is associated with added costs in the form of marking, labelling, packaging and promotion. Commodities are 'unbranded' or undifferentiated products. Examples of products with no brand are cement, metals, salt, beef and other agricultural products.

Private label versus co-branding versus manufacturer's own brand

These three options can be graded as shown in Figure 15.14.

The question of consumers having brand loyalty or shop loyalty is a crucial one. The competitive struggle between the manufacturer and the retailer actualises the need for a better understanding of shopping behaviour. Both actors need to be aware of determinants of shop choice, shopping frequency and in-store behaviour. Where manufacturers pay little attention to the shopping behaviour of their consumers, this helps to anticipate the increasing power of certain retail chains.

Private label

Private labelling is most developed in the United Kingdom, where Marks & Spencer, for instance, only sell own-label products. At Sainsbury's own labels account for 60 per cent of the sales. Compared with the high share of private labelling in northern Europe, the share in southern Europe (e.g. Spain and Portugal) is no higher than 10 per cent.

Figure 15.14 **The three brand options**

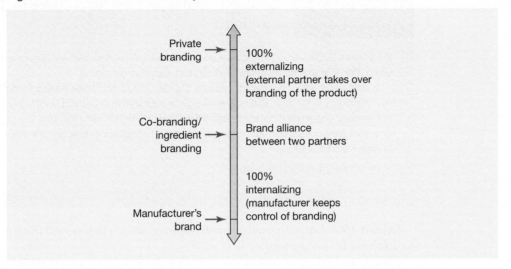

The retailer's perspective

For the retailer there are two main advantages connected with own-label business:

- *Own labels provide better profit margins*. The cost of goods typically makes up 70–85 per cent of a retailer's total cost (*The Economist*, 4 March 1995, p. 10). So if the retailer can buy a quality product from the manufacturer at a lower price this will provide a better profit margin for the retailer. In fact private labels have helped UK food retailers to achieve profit margins averaging 8 per cent of sales, which is high by international standards. The typical figure in France and the United States is 1–2 per cent.
- *Own labels strengthen the retailer's image with its customers*. Many retail chains try to establish loyalty to their particular chain of shops by offering their own quality products. In fact premium private-label products (e.g. Marks & Spencer's St Michael) that compete in quality with manufacturers' top brands have seen a growth in market share, whereas the share of cheap generics is tiny and declining.

The manufacturer's perspective

Although private brands are normally regarded as threats for manufacturers there may be situations where private branding is a preferable option:

- Since there are no promotional expenses associated with private branding for the producer, the strategy is especially suitable for SMEs with limited financial resources and limited competences in the downstream functions.
- The private brand manufacturer gains access to the shelves of the retail chains. With increasing internationalization of the big retail chains this may also result in export business for the SME that has never been in international markets.

There are also a number of reasons why private branding is bad for the manufacturer:

- By not having its own identity, the manufacturer must compete mainly on price, because the retail chain can always switch supplier.
- The manufacturer loses control over how its products should be promoted. This may become critical if the retailer does not do a good job in pushing the product to the consumer.
- If the manufacturer is producing both its own brands and private brands there is a danger that the private brands will cannibalise the manufacturer's brand-name products.

Exhibit 15.2	Kellogg is under pressure to produce under Aldi's own label

In February 2000 Kellogg (the cereal giant) made an own-label deal with German supermarket chain Aldi. It is the first time that Kellogg has supplied own label.

A slogan on Kellogg's cereal packets claims: 'If you don't see Kellogg's on the box ... it isn't Kellogg's in the box. But now Kellogg has negotiated a deal with Aldi to supply products in Germany bearing a different brand name. Reports in Germany say that the deal was made after Aldi announced it would no longer pay brand suppliers' prices and threatened to cut top brands from its shelves.

Source: adapted from various public media.

Exhibit 15.2 shows an example with Kellogg, which has moved from a brand strategy to a private brand strategy.

Quelch and Harding (1996) argue that many manufacturers have over reacted to the threat of private brands. Increasing numbers of manufacturers are beginning to make private-label products to take up excess production capacity. According to Quelch and Harding (1996), more than 50 per cent of US manufacturers of branded consumer packaged goods already make private-label goods as well.

Managers typically examine private-label production opportunities on an incremental marginal cost basis. The fixed overhead costs associated with the excess capacity used to make the private-label products would be incurred anyway. But if private-label manufacturing were evaluated on a full-cost basis rather than on an incremental basis it would, in many cases, appear much less profitable. The more private-label production grows as a percentage of total production, the more an analysis based on full costs becomes relevant (Quelch and Harding, 1996).

Manufacturer's own brand

From the Second World War until the 1960s brand manufacturers managed to build a bridge over the heads of the retailers to the consumers. They created consumer loyalty for their particular brand by using sophisticated advertising (culminating in TV advertising) and other promotional techniques.

Since the 1960s various sociological changes (notably the car) have encouraged the rise of large, efficient retailers. Nowadays the distribution system is being turned upside down. The traditional supply chain, powered by manufacturer 'push', is becoming a demand chain, driven by consumer 'pull'. Retailers have won control over distribution not just because they decide the price at which goods are sold, but also because both individual shops and retail companies have become much bigger and more efficient. They are able to buy in bulk and to reap economies of scale, mainly due to advances in transport and, more recently, in information technology. Most retail chains have not only set up computer links between each store and distribution warehouses, they are also hooked up with the computers of the firm's main suppliers, through an (electronic data interchange) system.

After some decades of absence private labels reappeared in the 1970s as generic products pioneered by Carrefour in France but were soon adopted by UK and US retailers. Ten years ago there was a distinct gap in the level of quality between private-label and brand-name products. Today the gap has narrowed: private-label quality levels are much higher than ever before, and they are more consistent, especially in categories historically characterised by little product innovation.

Co-branding/ingredient branding

Despite the similarities between co-branding and ingredient branding there is also an important difference, as we shall see below.

Co-branding

Co-branding is a form of cooperation between two or more brands with significant customer recognition, in which all the participants' brand names are retained. It is of medium to long-term duration and its net value creation potential is too small to justify setting up a new brand and/or legal joint venture. The motive for co-branding is the expectation of synergies that create value for both participants, above the value they would expect to generate on their own.

In the case of co-branding, the products are often complementary, in the way that one product can be used or consumed independently of the other (e.g. Bacardi Rum and Coca-Cola). Hence co-branding may be an efficient alternative to traditional brand extension strategies (Figure 15.15).

Figure 15.15 Illustration of co-branding and ingredient branding

---

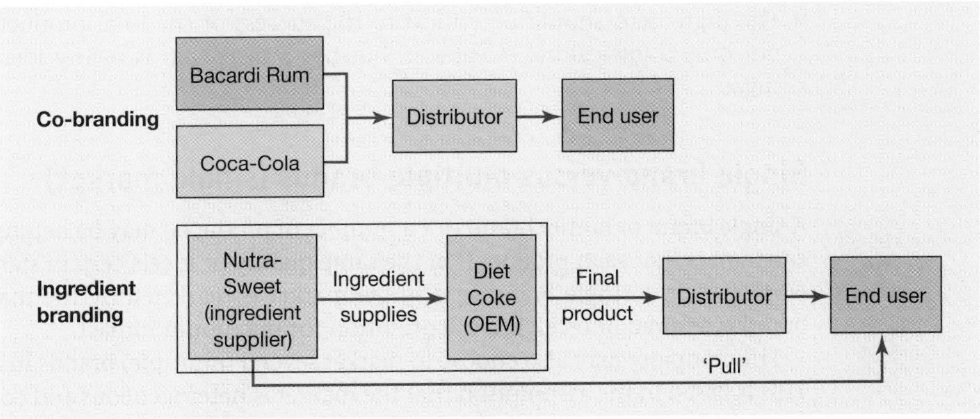

Exhibit 15.3   Shell's co-branding with Ferrari and LEGO

In 1999–2000 Shell ran a £50 million co-branding campaign with Ferrari and LEGO. Some people might have thought that this was an attempt to persuade people, mainly in the West, that Shell's controversial attempt to dump the Brent Spar oil platform in the North Sea was not a true reflection of the company.

However, it may be more accurate to say that Shell was seeking a 'brand image transfer'. In the petrol retailer market traditionally driven by price and more price promotions, Shell wanted both Ferrari's sexy, sporty image and the family values of LEGO. Furthermore Shell was and is no longer only in the petroleum and oils business, where price promotions are the main focus of marketing activity. They are also involved in food retailing, where loyalty programmes are also important.

What were the benefits for Ferrari and LEGO?

Ferrari gained sponsorship and royalty income from model car sales, while LEGO got improved global distribution. The co-branding strategy involved the use of 10 exclusive small boxed toys and a big Ferrari LEGO car carrying a Shell logo. Shell wanted to sell between 20 and 40 million units of LEGO globally. It made Shell one of the world's largest toy distributors.

Source: adapted from various public media.

Ingredient branding

Normally the marketer of the final product (OEM) creates all of the value in the consumer's eyes. But in the case of Intel (see ad to the left) and NutraSweet the ingredient supplier is seeking to build value in its products by branding and promoting the key component of an end product. When promotion ('pull' strategy: see Figure 15.15) of the key component brand is initiated by the ingredient supplier the goal is to build awareness and preference among consumers for that ingredient brand. Simultaneously, it may be the manufacturer (OEM) that seeks to benefit from a recognised ingredient brand. Some computer manufacturers are benefiting from the quality image of using an Intel chip.

However, ingredient branding is not suitable for every supplier of components. An ingredient supplier should fulfil the following requirements:

- The ingredient supplier should be offering a product that has a substantial advantage over existing products. DuPont's Teflon, NutraSweet, Intel chips and the Dolby noise reduction system are all examples of major technological innovations, the result of large investments in R&D.
- The ingredient should be critical to the success of the final product. NutraSweet is not only a low-calorie sweetener, but has a taste that is nearly identical to that of sugar.

Single brand versus multiple brands (single market)

A single brand or family brand (for a number of products) may be helpful in convincing consumers that each product is of the same quality or meets certain standards. In other words, when a single brand in a single market is marketed by the manufacturer, the brand is assured of receiving full attention for maximum impact.

The company may also choose to market several (multiple) brands in a single market. This is based in the assumption that the market is heterogeneous and consists of several segments.

Local brands versus a global brand (multiple markets)

A company has the option of using the same brand in most or all of its foreign markets or of using individual, local brands. A single, global brand is also known as an international or universal brand. A Eurobrand is a slight modification of this approach, as it is a single product for a single market of 15 or more European countries, with an emphasis on the search for intermarket similarities rather than differences.

A global brand is an appropriate approach when a product has a good reputation or is known for quality. In such a case a company would be wise to extend the brand name to other products in the product line. Examples of global brands are Coca-Cola, Shell and the Visa credit card. Although it is possible to find examples of global brands, local brands are probably more common among big multinational companies than people realise. Boze and Patton (1995) have studied the branding practices in 67 countries all over the world of six multinational companies:

- Colgate-Palmolive – headquartered in the US.
- Kraft General Foods (now part of Philip Morris) – headquartered in the US.
- Nestlé – headquartered in Switzerland.

- Procter & Gamble – headquartered in the US.
- Quaker Oats – headquartered in the US.
- Unilever – headquartered in the UK and the Netherlands.

The findings of the research are summarised in Table 15.4. Of the 1,792 brands found in the 67 countries, 44 per cent were only marketed in one country. Only 68 brands (4 per cent) could be found in more than half of the countries. Of these 68 brands, only the following 6 were found in all 67 countries: Colgate, Lipton, Lux, Maggi, Nescafé and Palmolive. Hence these were the only true world brands.

Table 15.4 Brands of six multinational companies in 67 countries

Company	Total no. of brands	Brands found in 50% or more countries		Brands in only one country	
		Number	% of total	Number	% of total
Colgate	163	6	4	59	36
Kraft GF	238	6	3	104	44
Nestlé	560	19	4	250	45
P & G	217	18	8	80	37
Quaker	143	2	1	55	38
Unilever	471	17	4	236	50
Total	1792	68	4	784	44

Source: Boze and Patton, 1995, p. 22. Reproduced with kind permission from the *Journal of Consumer Marketing*, MCB University Press.

Surprisingly, each of the six multinationl corporations (MNCs) seems to follow the practice of multiple brands in a single market. No official explanation was offered for this strategy, but a Nestlé manager explained 'that he believed it is a very important marketing advantage to provide a brand name not found in any other country, especially those adjacent to the nation or bigger than it' (Boze and Patton, 1995, p. 24).

The use of umbrella brands varies a lot among the MNCs examined. Of the six MNCs Colgate is the most intensive user of its two company names:

- *Colgate*. Mostly dental products: toothpaste, tooth powder, toothbrushes, dental floss, mouthwash, and shaving cream.
- *Palmolive*. Hair products, shaving products, hand lotion, talc, deodorant, sun screen, toilet soap, bath products, liquid detergent (dishes and fine fabrics) and automatic dishwasher detergent.

It should be emphasised that the big MNCs prefer to acquire some local brands instead of using a global brand.

15.9   Implications of the Internet/e-commerce for product decisions

Types of product

The products sold via electronic markets were roughly grouped in Chapter 14 into two categories: *physical products* and purely *digital goods and services*.

Customization and closer relationships

The new business platform recognises the increased importance of customization of products and services. Increased commoditisation of standard features can only be countered through customization, which is most powerful when backed up by sophisticated analysis of customer data.

Mass-marketing experts such as Nike are experimenting with ways of using digital technology to enable customization. Websites that can display three-dimensional images, for example, will certainly boost the attractiveness of custom tailoring.

The challenge is clear: to use IT to get closer to customers. There are already many examples of this. Dell is building a closer relationship with its end customer by letting them design their own PC on the Internet. Customers who have ordered their computers from Dell can then follow their computers along the various stages of the production process in real time on their personalized website. Such experimentation is advisable because the success of 'build-to-order' models such as Dell's represents a challenge to current 'build-to-stock' business platforms, which Compaq generally uses. In Exhibit 15.4 there is a comparison of the business models of Dell and Compaq. Dell's

---

Exhibit 15.4   Business models of Dell and Compaq

In the personal computer industry Dell and Compaq are worldwide market leaders. However, the business models of the two companies differ a lot, as the following table demonstrates.

Compaq has business systems of the type traditionally associated with branded products. It has high R&D expenditure, low-cost, low-variety, large-run manufacturing systems, one month finished products inventory.

	Dell	Compaq
Target customer	Knowledgeable customer buying multiple units	Multiple customer segments with varied needs
Value proposition	Customised PC at competitive price	'Brand' with quality image
Value capture	Through pushing latest components upgrades and low-cost distribution system	Through premium for the 'brand' and reseller push
Buiness system *R&D*	Limited	Considerable
Manufacturing	Flexible assembly, cost advantage	High speed, low-variety, low-cost manufacturing system
Supply chain	Made to order; inventory: one week, mainly component	Made to stock; delivery; inventory: one month, finished product
Marketing	Moderate advertising	Expensive brand advertising
Sales and distribution	Primarily through sales force, telemarketing and the Internet	Primarily through third-party resellers

Dell primarily targets corporate accounts but with built-to-order, customized PCs at reasonable prices. Dell has minimal R&D expenditure, a made-to-order, flexible manufacturing system (which puts Dell at a slight disadvantage compared to Compaq), one-week parts inventory and an efficient distribution system. Dell has been a pioneer in PC sales through the Internet.

Source: adapted from Kumar, 1999.

basic business principle is the close relationship between the PC manufacturer and the end customer, without further intermediaries in the distribution channel. This allows Dell to individualise the computers to the specific needs of the customers.

Computers can also be remotely diagnosed and fixed over the network today; this may soon be true of many other appliances. Airlines now communicate special fares to preferred customers through e-mails and special websites. Cars will soon have Internet protocol addresses, which will make possible a range of personal, in-vehicle information services.

Customers can also be involved in the early stages of product development so that their inputs can shape product features and functionality. Pharmaceutical companies are experimenting with the possibility of analysing patients' genes to determine precisely what drugs should be administered in what dosages.

The transformation in the business platform can be seen in university textbook publishing. This industry – which has seen little innovation since the advent of the printing press – is now in the midst of major changes. Publishers are creating supplementary website links to provide additional ways for students and professors to be connected during courses (e.g. **www.pearsoneduc.com** and **www.wiley.com**). The publisher's role, which traditionally was selling textbooks at the beginning of term, is becoming that of an educational consultant or value-adding partner throughout the term.

Dynamic customisation of product and services

The second stage of the customer interaction vector focuses on the opportunities and challenges in dynamically customising products and services. Competitive markets are rapidly eroding margins due to price-based competition, and companies are seeking to enhance margins through customised offerings. Dynamic customization is based on three principles: modularity, intelligence, and organization.

- *Modularity:* An approach for organizing complex products and processes efficiently. Product or service modularity requires the partitioning of a task into independent modules that function as a whole within overall architecture.
- *Intelligence:* Continuous information exchange with consumers allows companies to create products and processes using the best possible modules. Website operators can match buyer and seller profiles and make recommendations based on their shared interests. The result is intelligent sites that learn their visitors' (potential buyers') tastes and deliver dynamic, personalised information about products and services.
- *Organization:* Dynamic customisation of products and services requires a customer-oriented and flexible approach that is fundamentally committed to operating in this new way.

How can the Internet be integrated in the future product innovation?

Figure 15.16 shows some of the implications of the Internet on future product innovation. The Internet is seen as the medium through which each 'box' communicates with the R&D function in the company.

- *Design.* Data is gathered directly from the product and is part of designing and developing the product. New product features (such as new versions of software programs) may be built into the product directly from the Internet.

Figure 15.16 Product innovation through the Internet

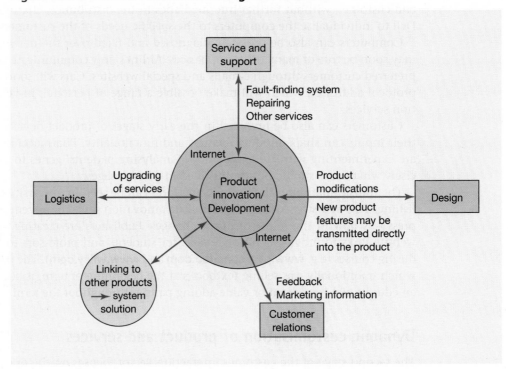

- *Service and support.* The service department can perform troubleshooting and correction directly through the Internet set-up. For example a Mercedes car driving on the highway may be directly connected to the Mercedes service department. It will monitor the main functions of the car and if necessary make online repairs of e.g. the software of the car.
- *Customer relations.* Data gathered from the product may form part of statistics, comparisons between customers, etc. In this way the customer can compare the performance of their product (e.g. a car) with other customers' product (a kind of benchmarking). This may also strengthen an existing customer relationship.
- *Logistics.* Concurrently with increasing demands for just-in-time deliveries, the Internet will automatically find the distribution and transport that will take the goods from the subsupplier to the producer and then to the customers in the cheapest and most efficient way (and on time).

A fundamental shift in thinking is to replace the term 'supply chain' with 'demand chain'. The critical difference is that demand-chain thinking starts with the customers and works backwards. This breaks away from parochial approaches that focus solely on reducing transport costs. It supports a 'mass customisation' viewpoint, in which bundles of goods and services are offered in ways that support customers' individual objectives.

This does not necessarily imply product differentiation. In fact the service aspects often require differentiation. For example, a company such as Unilever will provide the same margarine to both Tesco and Sainsbury's. However, the ways in which the product is delivered, transactions are processed and other parts of the relationship are managed, can and should be different, since these two competing supermarket chains each have their own ways of evaluating performance. The information systems required to coordinate companies along the demand chain require a new and different approach to that required within individual companies. Some managers believe that if they and their suppliers choose the same standard software package, such as SAP, they will be able to integrate their information systems.

■ *Link to other products*. Sometimes a product is used as a subcomponent in other products. Through links in the Internet such subcomponents may be essential inputs for more complex product solutions. The car industry is an example of an industry that already makes a targeted effort in this direction. New 'stylish' cars are linked together by the Internet. In the wake of this development a new industry is created, the purpose of which is to provide integrated transport. In this new industry developing and producing cars is only one of several important services. Instead systems are to be developed that can diagnose cars (and correct the error) while the car is running, systems for regulation of traffic, interactive systems that enable drivers to have the desired transport at their disposal when and where they want it without tiresome rental agreements, etc.

The music industry is also undergoing a change. Today you can buy portable 'players' that can download music from the Internet using the MP3 format, and subsequently play the music that is stored in the 'player'. The CD is skipped – and so is the whole distribution facility. The music industry will become completely altered through the different economic conditions. The struggle will be about creating the best portal to the Internet, where the consumer can find the best information on music and the largest selection of music. The problems regarding rights are, however, still being discussed, and the lawyers and politicians have to find a final solution before the market can increase significantly.

Thus innovative product development of the future demands that a company possesses the following characteristics:

■ *Innovative product development and strategic thinking*. Product development will contain much technology and demand an interdisciplinary, strategic overview and knowledge in order to find out what new services are worth aiming at.
■ *Management of alliances*. Few companies have all the necessary qualifications themselves – innovative product development and the resulting services demand that companies enter into alliances very dynamically and yet in a structured way.
■ *New customer relations*. The above-mentioned car industry example clearly shows that the customers are not car buyers any longer but *buyers of transport services*, and that is quite another matter. This means that companies have to focus on understanding the customers' needs in a quite different way.

Developing brands on the Internet

Clearly consumer product companies such as Procter & Gamble, Colgate, Kraft Foods, and consumer durables and business-to-business companies such as General Motors, General Electric, Allied Signal and Caterpillar have crafted their business strategies by leveraging physical assets and developing powerful global brands supported by mass advertising and mass distribution. But remote links with customers apply equally well to these companies. Remote and continuous links with customers become critical as the concepts of brand identity and brand equity are redefined by the Internet.

Kraft Interactive Kitchen (**www.kraftfoods.com**) is an example of a consumer products company keeping in touch with its consumers by providing information-based services such as meal planners, recipes, tips and cooking techniques. Kraft's intention is to have remote connections and interactions with consumers in new ways.

However, some companies find it difficult to translate a strong offline brand (such as Nike and Levi's) to the Internet, because many of the well-known brands are based on an extensive 'physical' retail distribution system, and many of the retailers are reluctant to support online brands because of the fear of disintermediation (see section 14.6 for more discussion of this issue).

In fact many sites that are run by top brands register minimal online traffic, according to a report by Forrester Research. Forrester studied brand awareness and Web surfing behaviour among 16–22-year-olds, whom advertisers consider to be strongly brand conscious.

Companies are taking a broad approach to branding, integrating it with an overall advertising and marketing strategy. On the net branding is more than logos and colour schemes; it is about creating experiences and understanding customers. Consequently Web brand building is not cheap. Building a brand requires a persistent online presence. For some brands that entails a mass-appeal site; for others brand building requires a combination of initiatives, from banner ads to sponsorships.

15.10 Green marketing strategies

Environmentalists were once considered the only people concerned about the depletion of natural resources, waste accumulation and pollution. Environmentalists around the world are now becoming global in their scope and scale of operations. Their aim is to increase people's awareness of the importance of environmental preservation on a global scale and how the lack of it will have a harmful effect on our planet. Global awareness about the environment is also being aroused by media reports on ecological disasters such as Chernobyl, the *Exxon Valdez* oil spill, acid rain and global warming.

The scientific community asserts that atmospheric pollution is having a damaging effect on the ozone layer. Two major factors influencing the depletion of the ozone layer are the use of aerosol sprays and the manufacture of certain types of plastic and foam insulation.

Because ecological grassroot campaigns gain widespread recognition and support, and global media networks such as CNN continue to report on environmental issues and disasters, today's consumer is becoming more environmentally conscious. Various polls and surveys reveal that many consumers are taking environmental issues into consideration as they buy, consume and dispose of products. Consequently there is a direct connection between a company's ability to attract and keep consumers and its ability to develop and execute environmentally sound strategies.

As consumer preferences and government policies increasingly favour a balanced business approach to the environment, managers are paying more attention to the strategic importance of their environmental decisions. Irresponsible behaviour by some firms has led to consumer boycotts, lengthy lawsuits and large fines. Such actions may have harmed firms in less direct ways, such as negative public relations, diversion of management attention and difficulty in hiring top employees.

In Europe particularly the green consumer movement is large and growing, and certain countries can be considered leaders and standard setters in green awareness. Of

German consumers, for instance, 80 per cent are willing to pay premiums for household goods that are recycled, recyclable and non-damaging to the environment; in France 50 per cent of consumers will pay more at the supermarket for products they perceive as being environmentally friendly. This trend is growing elsewhere too: according to a European study, consumers throughout the OECD area are willing to pay more for green goods (Vandermerwe and Oliff, 1991).

Several retailers have also committed themselves to marketing green products. Clearly, failing to consider the environmental impact of strategic decisions may affect the financial stability of the firm and the ability of that firm to compete with others in the industry.

Strategic options

Figure 15.17 presents four strategic options that are available for the firm with environmental concerns. The choice of strategic environmental posture will depend on how an organization wants to create value for its green customers and how change oriented its approach is.

Figure 15.17 Types of environmental strategic posture

		Value creation approach	
		Benefit enhancement for customers	Cost reduction
Change orientation	Proactive	Green product Innovation (major modification) ①	Pollution prevention Beyond compliance ③
	Accommodative	Green product ② Differentiation (minor modification)	④ Pollution prevention Compliance

Source: adapted from Starik *et al.*, 1996, p. 17.

As can be seen from Figure 15.17, if a firm is more oriented to cost reduction than to benefit enhancement for customers, pollution prevention strategies (options 3 and 4) would probably be chosen in preference to the development of green products: for example by using natural or recycled materials. If a firm is more proactive than accommodative, it tends to be more innovative than otherwise (options 1 and 3).

Although going beyond compliance (i.e. doing more than required according to environmental legislation) is generally perceived as highly desirable, SMEs may not have the resources to act proactively, and hence need to focus on compliance and minor product modification (options 2 and 4).

Environmental management in the value chain perspective

Management cannot afford to be myopic in looking at the finished product without considering the manufacturing and R&D phases as they relate to consumers' perceptions of what constitutes a green product. Nor can a company use traditional marketing principles to gain product acceptance. Put differently, both the input and output activities associated with the design, manufacture and delivery of products must be considered, and each step within the value-creating process must be assessed in the light of its overall environmental impact and consequences.

Figure 15.18 illustrates the resource conversion and pollutant generation relationships. As resources are used to create desired utilities, pollutants are implicitly produced as byproducts during each step of the integrated supply chain process. For example, packaging is used to protect the products from damage and is an undesired item once they are consumed. Proper management and awareness of the environmental implications of logistical activities can significantly reduce their negative impact.

Figure 15.18 Value-adding logistics and the environmental interface

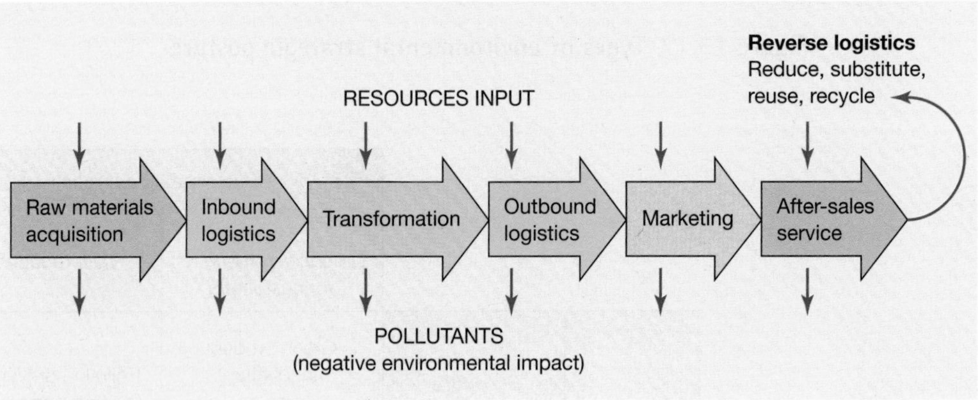

Source: adapted from Wu and Dunn, 1995, p. 23 with permission from *International Journal of Physical Distribution and Logistics Management*, MCB University Press; **www.mcb.co.uk**

Integrative environmental management means that every element in the corporate value chain is involved in the minimization of the firm's total environmental impact from start to finish of the supply chain, and also from beginning to end of the product life cycle.

Reverse logistics in Figure 15.18 results in the shipment of packaging waste, recyclable packages and consumer returns in the logistics system.

Germany and other European countries state that consumers have the right to leave packaging materials at retail stores and that stores must dispose of them properly. Denmark has for many years also required beer bottles to be reusable. The shipment of these packaging materials back to original sites creates demand for logistical capacity and adds no direct value to the goods.

Management has to consider how to reduce the reverse flows. In relation to Figure 15.18, reverse logistics emphasises source reduction and substitution over reuse and recycling. Source reduction refers to doing the same things with less resources. The practice reduces total waste in the system. Substitution means using more environmentally friendly materials instead of regular ones that end up as pollutants. Reuse is employing the same item many times in its original form so that little is discarded. Recycling gives discarded materials a new life after some chemical or physical processes.

Eco-labelling schemes

Over the years eco-labelling schemes have been implemented in a number of EU countries in an attempt to promote the use of products and production methods that are less harmful to the environment. The first scheme was introduced in West Germany in 1978. Today the organisers of the scheme claim that 80 per cent of German households are aware of the scheme and it receives widespread support from manufacturers.

The label should affect all businesses along the supply chain because the suppliers have to provide detailed information about their own components and their manufacturing process. The criteria for the award of an eco-label for a product are based on a cradle-to-grave analysis or life cycle assessment (Table 15.5). National bodies that award the eco-labels for products act as a kind of jury, assessing the environmental performance of a product by reference to agreed specific environmental criteria for each product group.

Table 15.5 **Eco-labelling scheme indicative assessment**

Environmental fields	Product life cycle				
	Pre-production	Production	Distribution	Utilization	Disposal
Waste relevance	× ×	× ×	× ×	× ×	× ×
Soil pollution and degradation	× ×	× ×	× ×	× ×	× ×
Water contamination	× ×	× ×	× ×	× ×	× ×
Air contamination	× ×	× ×	× ×	× ×	× ×
Noise	× ×	× ×	× ×	× ×	× ×
Consumption of energy	× ×	× ×	× ×	× ×	× ×
Consumption of natural resources	× ×	× ×	× ×	× ×	× ×
Total effects on eco-systems	× ×	× ×	× ×	× ×	× ×

Source: Welford and Prescott, 1996, *European Business: An issue-based approach, 3rd Edition*. Reprinted by permission of Pearson Education Ltd.

Green alliances between business and environmental organizations

Strategic alliances with environmental groups (e.g. Greenpeace) can provide five benefits to marketers of consumer goods (Mendleson and Polonsky, 1995):

- *They increase consumer confidence in green products and their claims.* It can be assumed that, if an environmental group supports a firm, product or service, consumers are more likely to believe the product's environmental claims.
- *They provide firms with access to environmental information.* It is in their role as an information clearing house that environmental groups may be of immense benefit to organizations with which they form strategic alliances. Manufacturers facing environmental problems may turn to their strategic partners for advice and information. In some cases environmental partners may actually have technical staff who can be used to assist in solving organizational problems or implementing existing solutions.
- *They give the marketer access to new markets.* Most environmental groups have an extensive support base, which in many cases receives newsletters or other group mailings. Their members receive catalogues marketing a variety of licensed products, all of which are less environmentally harmful than other commercial alternatives.

Environmental group members represent a potential market that can be utilised by producers, even if these groups do not produce specialised catalogues. An environmental group's newsletter may discuss how a firm has formed a strategic alliance with the group, as well as the firm's less environmentally harmful products. Inclusion of this information in a newsletter is a useful form of publicity.

- *They provide positive publicity and reduce public criticism.* Forming strategic alliances with environmental groups may also stimulate increased publicity. When the Sydney Olympic Bid Committee announced that Greenpeace was the successful designer for the year 2000 Olympic Village the story appeared in all major newspapers and on the national news. It is highly unlikely that this publicity would have been generated if a more conventional architect had been named as the designer of the village. Once again the publicity associated with the alliance was positive and credible.
- *They educate consumers about key environmental issues for the firm and its product(s).* Environmental groups are valuable sources of educational information and materials. They educate consumers and the general public about environmental problems and also inform them about potential solutions. In many cases the public views these groups as credible sources of information, without a vested interest. Marketers can also play an important role as providers of environmental information through their marketing activities. In doing so they create environmental awareness of specific issues, their products and their organizations. For example, Kelloggs in Norway educated consumers and promoted its environmental concern by placing environmental information on the packaging of its cereals relating to various regional environmental problems (World Wide Fund for Nature, 1993).

Choosing the correct alliance partner is not a simple task, as environmental groups have different objectives and images. Some groups may be willing to form exclusive alliances, where they partner only one product in a given product category. Other groups may be willing to form alliances with all products that comply with their specific criteria.

The marketer must determine what capabilities and characteristics an alliance partner can bring to the alliance. As with any symbiotic relationship, each partner must contribute to the success of the activity. Poor definition of these characteristics may result in the firm searching out the wrong partner.

15.11   Total quality management and ISO 9000 certification

With product quality becoming the cornerstone of global competition companies are increasingly requiring assurances of standard performance from suppliers. In this sense total quality management (TQM) is a broad organizational approach. TQM may be defined as follows:

- *Total.* All persons in the firm are involved (and where possible also the customers and suppliers of the firm).
- *Quality.* Customer requirements are met precisely.
- *Management.* Senior executives are fully committed.

As part of TQM, ISO 9000 does not relate to specific products but is the registration and certification of a manufacturer's quality system. The ISO 9000 standards ensure that products are produced using certified methods of manufacture, thereby eliminating product quality variation. However, the ISO 9000 certification does not guarantee that a manufacturer produces a 'quality' product. The end product is only as good as the design and process specifications require.

Headquartered in Geneva, Switzerland, the International Standards Organization (ISO) promotes the development of standardization and standards with a view to facilitating the international exchange of goods and services. Currently made up of the national standard bodies of 91 countries, ISO initiated the ISO 9000 standards in 1987. The standards are revised periodically to ensure that they do not become outdated.

The five standards of ISO 9000

The five standards that collectively make up the ISO 9000 are as follows:

- *ISO 9000*. This is the road map for the series. It is the overall term covering the other four standards in the series: 9001, 9002, 9003 and 9004.
- *ISO 9001*. This is the most comprehensive of the standards. It is a quality assurance that requires the demonstration of a supplier's capability to fulfil the requirements during all phases of operation: design, development, production, installation and servicing.
- *ISO 9002*. This standard is a subset of ISO 9001 with the areas of design and development of the product removed. The standard is sometimes used as an interim standard before expanding to the more comprehensive ISO 9001. It is also the most commonly used standard for service companies. The quality guidelines are used to ensure that the service is provided using a consistent process that is described in the quality documents.
- *ISO 9003*. This model provides a standard of quality assurance for firms only involved in final inspection and testing of products. Firms using this standard are basically performing the inspection function of the product that would normally be done by the customer when the product is received.
- *ISO 9004*. This standard provides a set of guidelines by which the management of a company can implement and develop an effective quality management system. There is heavy emphasis on meeting company and customer needs.

Implementing ISO 9000

Considerable work is needed before obtaining a certification to a chosen ISO 9000 standard. The costs can also be large, especially for small companies when external consultants are needed to perform much of the work.

When the firm is ready it requests a certifying body (a third party authorised to provide an ISO 9000 audit) to conduct a registration assessment: that is, an audit of the key business processes in the company. In some countries there is more than one registration body. For example, in the United Kingdom companies can register under BSI, Lloyd's, Yardsley and others approved by the National Council for Certification Award Bodies (Ho, 1995). When accreditation is granted the company receives certification. A complete assessment for recertification will be done every four years, with intermediate evaluations during the four-year period.

The strong level of interest in ISO is being driven by market requirements, and ISO 9000 is becoming an important competitive marketing tool in international markets, especially in the European Union. Industrial buyers often use the list of ISO-registered suppliers as a screening device to identify potential suppliers (Ferguson, 1996).

15.12 Summary

In deciding the product policy abroad, it is important to decide what parts (product levels) should be standardised and what parts should be adapted to the local environment. This chapter has discussed the variety of factors that are relevant to this decision.

A very important issue is the question of branding. Different branding alternatives have been discussed. For example, because large (often transnational) retail chains have won control over distribution, they try to develop their own labels. For the retailer, private labels provide better profit margins and strengthen the retailer's image with its customers. Because of the power shift to the retailers the percentage of retail grocery sales derived from private brands has increased in recent years.

This chapter has also discussed two issues that are experiencing increasing interest: total quality management/ISO 9000 and green marketing strategies, including the need for product adaptation in a 'green' direction.

CASE STUDY 15.1 Danish Klassic

Launch of a cream cheese in Saudi Arabia

In the spring of 1987 the product manager of Danish Cheese Overseas, KA, was pleased to note that after some decline, e.g. in Iran, feta sales were improving in the Middle East. However, the company was a little concerned that the feta, according to several expert opinions, could lose ground to the cream cheese that was apparently becoming more and more popular among Arabs in both the cities and provincial areas.

Saudi Arabia in general

Because of its immense income from oil, Saudi Arabia has developed fantastically over the past 30 years. With the Islamic tradition as its basis, the country has become more modern.

In 1987 the population was 11.5 million, more than 50 per cent of whom were under 15 years of age, which makes Saudi Arabia a 'young' nation. According to the Saudi Arabian Ministry of Agriculture, the population was forecast to rise to 19 million in 2000. The expected development in population in the three biggest cities is shown in Table 1.

The cheese market in Saudi Arabia

Traditionally Danish Cheese Overseas has had a strong position in Saudi Arabia, having been the market leader for several years, especially as regards feta and some other types of cheese. However, Danish Cheese Overseas has had some difficulties in the cream cheese market. The market has risen, but

Table 1 Development in population in the three biggest cities in Saudi Arabia

	Population (million) 1974	Population (million) 2000
Riyadh	0.7	2.4
Jeddah	0.6	2.1
Dammam	0.2	0.8

Source: *Demographic Yearbook 1985*, p. 270, and prognosis from the Saudi Arabian Ministry of Agriculture.

to date two globally large exporters of cheese have dominated the market – that is France and Australia.

The total import of cheese into Saudi Arabia (there is very little local production) is shown in Table 2. So far the share of cheese from Denmark has been about 25 per cent (£10 million). On the basis of this Danish Cheese decided to develop a new cream cheese in order to compete with the big exporters of cheese within the cream/processed segment. The product was to be targeted at the Middle East, where Saudi

Table 2 Total import of cheese in 1986 (tons)

	Total import
Processed cheese (including cream cheese)	29,500
Feta	18,400
Other types of cheese	2,400
Total	50,300

Source: Saudi Arabian import statistic.

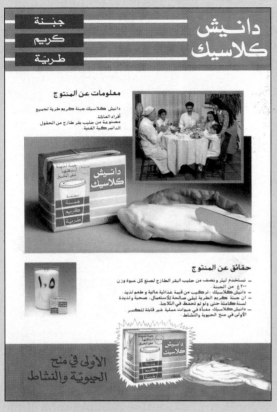

(a) product information

Arabia is the main market, but was also to form the basis for an international brand: *Danish Klassic*.

In order to plan the specific details of the product parameter Danish Cheese contacted an international market research bureau that specialised in the Middle East. The objective was to analyse the cream cheese consumption among typical Middle East families living in cities. The final result showed that between 85 and 100 per cent of all family members eat cream cheese on a regular basis (mostly in the middle of the day), and that consumption is especially high among children. Thus the company could set forth on product development of the new cheese. Different product concepts were tested among typical families, with the final result being a 200-gram cream cheese in brick cartons. This is a new type of packaging – until then cream cheese had mostly been sold in glass packaging.

Marketing plan for Danish Klassic

The following describes the launch actually made by Danish Cheese Overseas in 1987.

An introduction was held in October 1987, in the form of three trade seminars in the three big cities – Riyadh, Jeddah and Dammam. Here the product concept and the advertising campaign were presented to a large number of distributors and wholesalers (see Plates (a)–(e)).

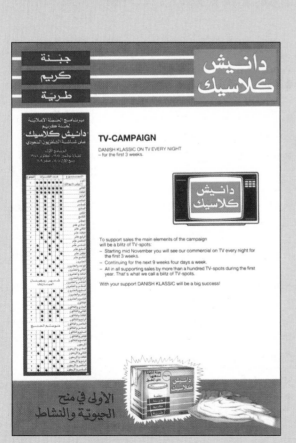

(b) TV advertising information

(c) print advertising information

(d) point-of-sale equipment

(e) packaging system

TV commercials

In Saudi Arabia television is considered the most effective medium for mass communication. It therefore became the foundation of the company's marketing. In total, 128 commercial spots were planned for the first year (plate (b)).

Print advertisements

- *Consumer oriented*: the most popular newspapers and family magazines in the big cities, especially directed at women as the decisive buyer unit; (plate (c));
- *Distributor oriented*: trade magazines.
- *In-store promotion*: displays, taste sample demonstrations etc. (plate (d)).

The campaign material was introduced in both Arabic and English.

The campaign was influenced by a high degree of pull strategy (consumer influence). In this way distributors were induced to build up stocks in order to meet the expected end-user demand. The risk the distributors would face when buying large quantities was limited because the cheese could be kept for a year without being refrigerated.

Plate (a) can be translated as follows:

Product information:

- *Danish Klassic* – cream cheese spread for the whole family.
- Created from fresh cow's milk from the vigorous fields of Denmark.

Product facts:

- It takes 1.5 litres of fresh cow's milk to produce a single box of 200 g.
- *Danish Klassic* is packed in a practical, unbreakable box.
- This cream cheese spread will remain healthy and delicious for a whole year after production – even if not kept under refrigeration.
- *Danish Klassic*, a combination of high nutrition value and a delicious taste.

This enclosure was also used as an advertisement for many consumer-oriented newspapers and magazines.

Plate (d) can be translated as follows:

Shop demonstrations:

- To let your customers know *Danish Klassic* is in town we plan shop demonstrations in a number of supermarkets all over the country.

- The selected shops will be decorated with giant *Danish Klassic* boxes.
  - Your customers are bound to notice this cream cheese.
  - Samples will be distributed.
  - Taste it. It's delicious. It's healthy, and full of energy.

What happened to Danish Klassic?

About six months after the introduction in Saudi Arabia, the following was part of an article in *Jyllandsposten*, a Danish newspaper (24 October 1988):

So far MD Foods has shipped 700–800 tons of the new, long-life cheese from the harbour of Esbjerg, but sales are expected to rise to 5,000 tons per year during the next few years ... According to the plan, 'Danish Klassic' is to be marketed in Denmark and in other parts of the world such as South America, where it has scored top marks in recent taste tests.

The new long-life cheese that comes in completely sealed 200 g packages is marketed massively through TV spots, the company's own sales representatives, shop promotions and print advertisements. About half of the total investment of DKK30–35 million is allocated to marketing. In this way MD Foods is challenging the multinational food concern, Kraft Food, which, through its various types of cheese in glass packaging, controls the majority of the markets in the Middle East.

However, at the beginning of 1993 MD Foods realised that Danish Klassic could not meet the international sales budgets and therefore, later in 1993, MD Foods withdrew the product from the market.

Today MD Foods sells cheese to the Middle East through its sales company, Chesco Cheese Ltd. The cream cheese and other types of cheese are now sold under the brand 'Puck' (plate (e)) in glass packaging (the 140 g and 240 g round containers). Its market share of cream cheese is increasing again and today the total sales are very close to those of the market leader Kraft Food.

Questions

1. What could be the reasons for Danish Klassic not being able to meet expectations? Comment on the following:
   - the change of packaging – from glass to plastic brick carton;
   - the consumer-oriented advertisement (Plate 15.5a) – is it targeted at the Saudi Arabian market?
2. What do you think of the brand name Danish Klassic?

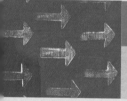

CASE STUDY 15.2   Zippo Manufacturing Company

Has product diversification beyond the lighter gone too far?

History

Zippo (**www.zippo.com**) was founded in Bradford, Pennsylvania in 1932 when George G. Blaisdell decided to create a lighter that would look good and be easy to use. Blaisdell obtained the rights for an Austrian windproof lighter with a removable top, and redesigned it to his own requirements. He made the case rectangular and attached the lid to the bottom with a welded hinge, and surrounded the wick with a windhood. Fascinated by the sound of the name another recent invention, the zipper, Blaisdell called his new lighter 'Zippo', and backed it with a Lifetime Guarantee. The 70-year old brand's fame took off during the Second World War, when Zippo's entire production was distributed through commercial outlets run by the US military.

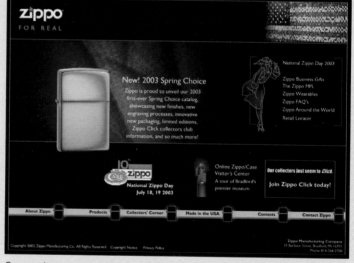

Source: zippo.com

Today

Zippo has produced over 375 million windproof lighters since its founding in 1932. Except for improvements in the flint wheel and modifications in case finishes, Blaisdell's original design remains virtually unchanged. The Lifetime Guarantee that accompanies every Zippo lighter still guarantees that 'It works or we fix it free™'.

Although the windproof lighter is the most popular Zippo product, Zippo has been hurt by the anti-smoking campaigns. Its business is fundamentally tied to smokers, and it has suffered from US tobacco regulations. Cigarette makers order thousands of Zippos to promote their brands, distributing them to smokers in exchange for coupons. One of the company's recent advertising campaigns suggested 101 ways to use your Zippo. Warming your hands and de-icing car locks were on the list; lighting a cigarette was not.

The success of this product led Zippo to expand the line to its current product family of tape measures, pocket knives, money clips, writing instruments, key holders and its newest product, the Multi-Purpose Lighter. All of these items can be imprinted with company logos or trademarks.

In 1993 Zippo licensed its name to Itochu Fashion System Co., a large clothing manufacturer in Japan. Zippo leather jackets, Zippo jeans and Zippo gloves are now available in Tokyo, and Zippo may license clothes in the United States too. Today Japan is still the biggest export market for Zippo.

Zippo has expanded its sales operations nationally and internationally through a wide network of sales representatives. In more than 120 countries throughout the world Zippo is synonymous with US-made quality and craftsmanship.

Zippo windproof lighters enjoy a widespread and enviable reputation as valuable collectibles. The company produces the Zippo Lighter Collectors' Guide, containing illustrations of the lighters and descriptions of the series, as well as an explanation of the date code found on the bottom of every Zippo lighter. Clubs for lighter collectors have been organized in the United Kingdom, Italy, Switzerland, Germany, Japan and the United States. Zippo also sponsors it own collectors club, Zippo Click.

Questions

1. What are the pros and cons of the product diversification strategy that Zippo has been following recently?

2. On **www.sramarketing.com/OutDoors/experience /outdoor** (click on Case studies) you will find a case story, where Zippo in the late 1990s was repositioned as an essential tool for avid outdoorsmen. However the outdoor market was entirely new to the Zippo salesforce, who were accustomed to calling on tobacconists and convenience stores. How would you use the PLC concept for this case story?

3. What obstacles would Zippo Manufacturing Company face if they repeated the outdoor campaign in other countries?

For further exercises and cases, see this book's website at **www.booksites.net/hollensen**

Questions for discussion

1. How would you distinguish between services and products? What are the main implications of this difference for the global marketing of services?

2. What implications does the product life cycle theory have for international product development strategy?

3. To what degree should international markets be offered standardised service and warranty policies that do not differ significantly from market to market?

4. Why is the international product policy likely to be given higher priority in most firms than other elements of the global marketing mix?

5. Describe briefly the IPLC theory and its marketing implications.

6. What are the requirements that must be met so that a commodity can effectively be transformed into a branded product?

7. Discuss the factors that need to be taken into account when making packaging decisions for international product lines.

8. When is it appropriate to use multiple brands in (a) a single market and (b) several markets/countries?

9. What is the importance of 'country of origin' in international product marketing?

10. What are the distinguishing characteristics of services? Explain why these characteristics make it difficult to sell services in foreign markets.

11. Identify the major barriers to developing international brands.

12. Discuss the decision to add or drop products to or from the product line in international markets.

13. Why should customer-service levels differ internationally? Is it, for example, ethical to offer a lower customer-service level in developing countries than in industrialized countries?

14. What are the characteristics of a good international brand name?

References

Aaker, D. (1991) *Managing the Brand Equity: Capitalizing on the Value of the Brand Name*, The Free Press, New York.

Boze, B.V. and Patton, C.R (1995) 'The future of consumer branding as seen from the picture today', *Journal of Consumer Marketing*, vol. 12, no. 4, pp. 20–41.

Czinkota, M.R. and Ronkainen, I.A. (1995) *International Marketing* (4th edn), Dryden Press, Fort Worth, TX.

Dhalla, N.K. and Yuspeh, S. (1976) 'Forget the product life concept', *Harvard Business Review*, January–February, pp. 102–12.

Ettensén, R. (1993) 'Brand name and country of origin: effects in the emerging market economies of Russia, Poland and Hungary', *International Marketing Review*, no. 5, pp. 14–36.

Ferguson, W. (1996) 'Impact of ISO 9000 series standards on industrial marketing', *Industrial Marketing Management*, vol. 25, pp. 305–10.

Filiatrault, P. and Lapierre, J. (1997) 'Managing business-to-business marketing relationships in consulting engineering firms', *Industrial Marketing Management*, vol. 26, pp. 213–22.

Guiltinan, J.P., Paul, G.W., Madden, T.J. (1997), *Marketing Management: Strategies and Programs* (6th edn), McGraw-Hill Companies, Inc., New York.

Ho, S.K.M. (1995) 'Is the ISO 9000 series for total quality management?', *International Journal of Physical Distribution and Logistics Management*, vol. 25, no. 1, pp. 51–66.

Hooley, G.J., Saunders, J.A. and Piercy, N. (1998) *Marketing Strategy and Competitive Positioning* (2nd edn), Prentice Hall, Hemel Hempstead.

Johansson, J.K. and Thorelli, H.B. (1985) 'International product positioning', *Journal of International Business Studies*, vol. 16, Fall, pp. 57–75.

Johansson, J.K., Ronkainen, I.A. and Czinkota, M.R. (1994) 'Negative country-of-origin effects: the case of the new Russia', *Journal of International Business Studies*, vol. 25, 1st quarter, pp. 1–21.

Keegan, W.J. (1995) *Global Marketing Management* (5th edn), Prentice-Hall, Englewood Cliffs, NJ.

Kotler, P. (1997) *Marketing Management: Analysis, planning, implementation and control* (9th edn), Prentice-Hall, Englewood Cliffs, NJ.

Kumar, N. (1999) 'Internet distribution strategies: dilemmas for the incumbent', Mastering Information Management Part 7, Electronic Commerce, *Financial Times*, 15 March.

Lovelock, C.H. and Yip, G.S. (1996) 'Developing global strategies for service business', *California Management Review*, vol. 38, no. 2, pp. 64–86.

Majaro, S. (1982) *International Marketing: A Strategic Approach to World Markets* rev. edn, George Allen & Unwin, London.

Marketing Science Institute (1995) *Brand Equity and Marketing Mix: Creating customer value*, Conference Summary, Report no. 95–111, September, p. 14.

McNamee, P. (1984) 'Competitive analysis using matrix displays', *Long Range Planning*, vol. 17, no. 3, pp. 98–114.

Mendleson, N. and Polonsky, M.J. (1995) 'Using strategic alliances to develop credible green marketing', *Journal of Consumer Marketing*, vol. 12, no. 2, pp. 4–18.

Onkvisit, S. and Shaw, J.J. (1989) 'The international dimension of branding: strategic considerations and decisions', *International Marketing Review*, vol. 6, no. 3, pp. 22–34.

Onkvisit, S. and Shaw, J.J. (1993) *International Marketing: Analysis and strategy* (2nd edn), Macmillan, London.

Popper, E.T. and Buskirk, B.D. (1992) 'Technology life cycles in industrial markets', *Industrial Marketing Management*, vol. 21, pp. 23–31.

Quelch, J.A. and Harding, D. (1996) 'Brands versus private labels: fighting to win', *Harvard Business Review*, January–February, pp. 99–109.

Starik, M., Throop, G.M., Doody, J.M. and Joyce, M.E. (1996) 'Growing on environmental strategy', *Business Strategy and the Environment*, vol. 5, pp. 12–21.

Töpfer, A. (1995) 'New products: cutting the time to market', *Long Range Planning*, vol. 28, no. 2, pp. 61–78.

Vandermerwe, J. and Oliff, M.D. (1991) 'Corporate challenges for an age of reconsumption', *Columbia Journal of World Business*, vol. 26, no. 3, pp. 6–25.

Vernon, R. (1966) 'International investment and international trade in the product life cycle', *Quarterly Journal of Economics*, May, pp. 190–207.

Welford, R. and Prescott, K. (1996) *European Business: An issue-based approach* (3rd edn), Pitman, London.

World Wide Fund for Nature (1993) *Corporate Relationships*, Sydney.

Wu, H.J. and Dunn, S.C. (1995) 'Environmentally responsible logistics systems', *International Journal of Physical Distribution and Logistics Management*, vol. 25, no. 2, pp. 20–38.

Zikmund, W. and D'Amico, M. (1989) *Marketing* (3rd edn), John Wiley, New York.

Further reading

Abratt, R. and Motlana, P. (2002) 'Managing co-branding strategies: global brands into local markets', *Business Horizons*, September–October, pp. 43–50.

Alashban, A.A., Hayes, L.A., Zinkham, G.M. and Balazs, A.L. 'International brand-name standardisation/adaptation: antecedents and consequences', *Journal of International Marketing*, vol. 10, no. 3, pp. 22–48.

Campbell, M.C. 'Building brand equity', *International Journal of Medical Marketing*, vol. 2, no. 3, May, pp. 208–18.

Javalgi, R.G. and White, D.S. (2002) 'Viewpoint: strategic challenges for the marketing of services internationally', *International Marketing Review*, vol. 19, no. 6, pp. 563–81.

Keller, K.L. (2003), *Strategic Brand Management – Building, Measuring, and Managing Brand Equity*, Second Edition (International Edition), Prentice Hall/Pearson Education International, New Jersey.

Keller, K.L. and Moorthi, Y.L.R. (2003) 'Branding in developing markets', *Business Horizons*, May–June, pp. 49–59.

Meinders, H. and Meuffels. M. (2001) 'Product chain responsibility: an industry perspective', *Corporate Environmental Strategy*, vol. 8, no. 4, pp. 348–54.

Oliva, R. and Kallenberg, R. (2003) 'Managing the transition from products to services', *International Journal of Service Industry Management*, vol. 14, no. 2, pp. 160–72.

Prakash, A. (2002) 'Green marketing, public policy and managerial strategies', *Business Strategy and the Environment*, vol. 11, pp. 285–297.

Roellig, L. (2001) 'Designing global brands: critical lessons', *Design Management Journal*, Fall, pp. 40–5.

16 Pricing decisions and terms of doing business

Contents

Learning objectives

After studying this chapter you should be able to do the following:

- Explain how internal and external variables influence international pricing decisions.

- Explain why and how prices escalate in export selling.

- Discuss the strategic options in determining the price level for a new product.

- Explain the necessary sales volume increase as a consequence of a price decrease.

- Explain what is meant by experience curve pricing.

- Explore the special roles and problems of transfer pricing in global marketing.

- Discuss how varying currency conditions challenge the international marketer.

- Identify and explain the different terms of sale (price quotations).

- Discuss the conditions that affect terms of payment.

- Discuss the role of export credit and financing for successful export marketing.

16.1 Introduction

Pricing is part of the marketing mix. Pricing decisions must therefore be integrated with the other three Ps of the marketing mix. Price is the only area of the global marketing mix where policy can be changed rapidly without large direct cost implications. This characteristic, plus the fact that overseas consumers are often sensitive to price changes, results in the danger that pricing action may be resorted to as a quick fix instead of changes being made in other areas of the firm's marketing programme. It is thus important that management realises that constant fine-tuning of prices in overseas markets should be avoided and that many problems are not best addressed by pricing action.

Generally, pricing policy is one of the most important yet often least recognised of all the elements of the marketing mix. The other elements of the marketing mix all lead to costs. The only source of profit to the firm comes from revenue, which in turn is dictated by pricing policy. In this chapter we focus on a number of pricing issues of special interest to international marketers.

16.2 International pricing strategies compared with domestic pricing strategies

For many SMEs operating in domestic markets pricing decisions are based on the relatively straightforward process of allocating the total estimated cost of producing, managing and marketing a product or service and adding an appropriate profit margin. Problems for these firms arise when costs increase and sales do not materialise or when competitors undercut them. In international markets, however, pricing decisions are much more complex, because they are affected by a number of additional external factors, such as fluctuations in exchange rates, accelerating inflation in certain countries and the use of alternative payment methods such as leasing, barter and counter-trade.

Of special concern to the global marketing manager are pricing decisions on products made or marketed locally, but with some centralised influence from outside the country in which the products are made or marketed. Broadly speaking, pricing decisions include setting the initial price as well as changing the established price of products from time to time.

16.3 Factors influencing international pricing decisions

An SME exporting for the first time, with little knowledge of the market environment that it is entering, is likely to set a price that will ensure that the sales revenue generated at least covers the costs incurred. It is important that firms recognise that the cost structures of products are very significant, but they should not be regarded as sole determinants when setting prices.

Pricing policy is an important strategic and tactical competitive weapon that, in contrast to the other elements of the global marketing mix, is highly controllable and inexpensive to change and implement. Therefore pricing strategies and action should be integrated with the other elements of the global marketing mix.

Figure 16.1 presents a general framework for international pricing decisions. According to this model, factors affecting international pricing can be broken down into two main groups (internal and external factors) and four subgroups, which we will now consider in more detail.

Firm-level factors

International pricing is influenced by past and current corporate philosophy, organization and managerial policies. The short-term tactical use of pricing in the form of discounts, product offers and reductions is often emphasised by managers at the expense of its strategic role, and yet pricing over recent years has played a very significant part in the restructuring of many industries, resulting in the growth of some

Figure 16.1 International pricing framework

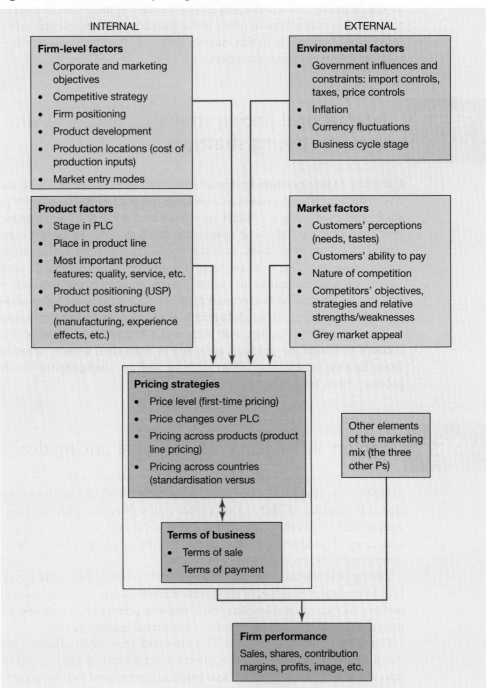

businesses and the decline of others. In particular, Japanese firms have approached new markets with the intention of building market share over a period of years by reducing price levels, establishing the brand name, and setting up effective distribution and servicing networks. The market share objectives of the Japanese firms have usually been accomplished at the expense of short-term profits, as international Japanese firms have consistently taken a long-term perspective on profit. They are usually prepared to wait much longer for returns on investments than some of their western counterparts.

The choice of foreign market entry mode also affects the pricing policy. A manufacturer with a subsidiary in a foreign country has a high level of control over the pricing policy in that country.

Product factors

Key product factors include the unique and innovative features of the product and the availability of substitutes. These factors will have a major impact on the stage of the product life cycle, which will also depend on the market environment in target markets. Whether the product is a service or a manufactured or commodity good sold into consumer or industrial markets is also significant.

The extent to which the organization has had to adapt or modify the product or service, and the level to which the market requires service around the core product, will also affect cost and thereby have some influence on pricing.

Costs are also helpful in estimating how rivals will react to the setting of a specific price, assuming that knowledge of one's own costs helps in the assessment of competitors' reactions. Added to the above is the intermediary cost, which depends on channel length, intermediary factors and logistical costs. All these factors add up and lead to price escalation.

The example in Table 16.1 shows that, due to additional shipping, insurance and distribution charges, the exported product costs some 21 per cent more in the export

Table 16.1 Price escalation (examples)

| | Domestic channel | Foreign marketing channel | |
	(a)	(b)	(c)
	Firm	Firm	Firm
	↓	--------↓--------Border	--------↓--------Border
	Wholesaler	Wholesaler	Importer
	↓	↓	↓
	Retailer	Retailer	Wholesaler
	↓	↓	↓
	Consumer	Consumer	Retailer
			↓
			Consumer
	£	£	£
Firm's net price	100	100	100
Insurance and shipping costs	—	10	10
Landed cost	—	110	110
Tariff (10% of landed cost)	—	11	11
Importer pays (cost)	—	—	121
Importer's margin/mark-up (15% of cost)	—	—	18
Wholesaler pays (cost)	100	121	139
Wholesaler'/mark-up (20% of cost)	20	24	28
Retailer pays (cost)	120	145	167
Retail margin/mark-up (40% of cost)	48	58	67
Consumer pays (price) (exclusive of VAT)	168	203	234
% price escalation over domestic channel	—	21	39

market than at home. Through the use of an additional distribution link (an importer), the product costs 39 per cent more abroad than at home.

Many exporters are not aware of rapid price escalation; they are preoccupied with the price they charge to the importer. However, the final consumer price should be of vital concern because it is on this level that the consumer can compare prices of different competitive products and it is this price that plays a major role in determining the foreign demand.

Price escalation is not a problem for exporters alone. It affects all firms involved in cross-border transactions. Companies that undertake substantial intracompany shipment of goods and materials across national borders are exposed to many of the additional charges that cause price escalation.

The following management options are available to counter price escalation:

- *Rationalising the distribution process.* One option is to reduce the number of links in the distribution process, either by doing more in-house or by circumventing some channel members.
- *Lowering the export price from the factory* (firm's net price), thus reducing the multiplier effect of all the mark-ups.
- *Establishing local production of the product* within the export market to eliminate some of the cost.
- *Pressurising channel members to accept lower profit margins.* This may be appropriate if these intermediaries are dependent on the manufacturer for much of their turnover.

It may be dangerous to overlook traditional channel members. In Japan, for example, the complex nature of the distribution system, which often involves many different channel members, makes it tempting to consider radical change. However, existing intermediaries do not like to be overlooked, and their possible network with other channel members and the government may make it dangerous for a foreign firm to attempt to cut them out.

Environmental factors

The environmental factors are external to the firm and thus uncontrollable variables in the foreign market. The national government control of exports and imports is usually based on political and strategic considerations.

Generally speaking, import controls are designed to limit imports in order to protect domestic producers or reduce the outflow of foreign exchange. Direct restrictions commonly take the form of tariffs, quotas and various non-tariff barriers. Tariffs directly increase the price of imports unless the exporter or importer is willing to absorb the tax and accept lower profit margins. Quotas have an indirect impact on prices. They restrict supply, thus causing the price of the import to increase.

Since tariff levels vary from country to country there is an incentive for exporters to vary the price somewhat from country to country. In some countries with high customs duties and high price elasticity the base price may have to be lower than in other countries if the product is to achieve satisfactory volume in these markets. If demand is quite inelastic the price may be set at a high level, with little loss of volume, unless competitors are selling at lower prices.

Government regulations on pricing can also affect the firm's pricing strategy. Many governments tend to have price controls on specific products related to health, education, food and other essential items. Another major environmental factor is fluctuation in the exchange rate. An increase (revaluation) or decrease (devaluation) in the relative value of a currency can affect the firm's pricing structure and profitability.

Market factors

One of the critical factors in the foreign market is the purchasing power of the customers (customers' ability to pay). The pressure of competitors may also affect international pricing. The firm has to offer a more competitive price if there are other sellers in the market. Thus the nature of competition (e.g. oligopoly or monopoly) can influence the firm's pricing strategy.

Under conditions approximating pure competition price is set in the marketplace. Price tends to be just enough above costs to keep marginal producers in business. Thus, from the point of view of the price setter, the most important factor is cost. The closer the substitutability of products, the more nearly identical the prices must be, and the greater the influence of costs in determining prices (assuming a large enough number of buyers and sellers).

Under conditions of monopolistic or imperfect competition the seller has some discretion to vary the product quality, promotional efforts and channel policies in order to adapt the price of the total product to serve preselected market segments. Nevertheless the freedom to set prices is still limited by what competitors charge, and any price differentials from competitors must be justified in the minds of customers on the basis of differential utility: that is, perceived value.

When considering how customers will respond to a given price strategy, Nagle (1987) has suggested nine factors that influence the sensitivity of customers to prices. Price sensitivity is reduced in the following cases:

- More distinctive product.
- Greater perceived quality of products.
- Consumers less aware of substitutes in the market.
- Difficulty in making comparisons (e.g. in the quality of services such as consultancy or accountancy).
- The price of a product represents a small proportion of total expenditure of the customer.
- The perceived benefit for the customer increases.
- The product is used in association with a product bought previously, so that, for example, components and replacements are usually extremely highly priced.
- Costs are shared with other parties.
- The product or service cannot be stored.

In the following sections we discuss the different available pricing strategies.

16.4   International pricing strategies

In determining the price level for a new product the general alternatives are as shown in Figure 16.2.

Skimming

In this strategy a high price is charged to 'skim the cream' from the top end of the market, with the objective of achieving the highest possible contribution in a short time. For a marketer to use this approach the product has to be unique, and some segments of the market must be willing to pay the high price. As more segments are

Figure 16.2 Strategies for pricing a new product

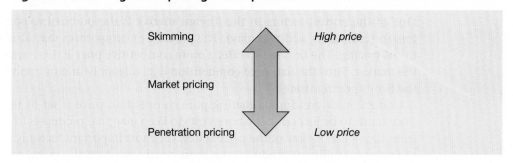

targeted and more of the product is made available the price is gradually lowered. The success of skimming depends on the ability and speed of competitive reaction.

Products should be designed to appeal to affluent and demanding consumers, offering extra features, greater comfort, variability or ease of operation. With skimming the firm trades off a low market share against a high margin.

Problems with skimming are as follows:

- Having a small market share makes the firm vulnerable to aggressive local competition.
- Maintenance of a high-quality product requires a lot of resources (promotion, after-sales service) and a visible local presence, which may be difficult in distant markets.
- If the product is sold more cheaply at home or in another country grey marketing (parallel importing) is likely.

Market pricing

If similar products already exist in the target market, market pricing may be used. The final customer price is based on competitive prices. This approach requires the exporter to have a thorough knowledge of product costs, as well as confidence that the product life cycle is long enough to warrant entry into the market. It is a reactive approach and may lead to problems if sales volumes never rise to sufficient levels to produce a satisfactory return. Although firms typically use pricing as a differentiation tool the global marketing manager may have no choice but to accept the prevailing world market price.

From the price that customers are willing to pay it is possible to make a so-called retrograde calculation where the firm uses a 'reversed' price escalation to calculate backwards (from market price) to the necessary (ex factory) net price. If this net price can create a satisfactory contribution margin then the firm can go ahead.

Penetration pricing

A penetration pricing policy is used to stimulate market growth and capture market shares by deliberately offering products at low prices. This approach requires mass markets, price-sensitive customers and reduction in unit costs through economies of scale and experience curve effects. The basic assumption that lower prices will increase sales will fail if the main competitors reduce their prices to a correspondingly low level. Another danger is that prices might be set so low that they are not credible to consumers. There exist 'confidence levels' for prices below which consumers lose faith in the product's quality.

Motives for pricing at low levels in certain foreign markets might include the following:

■ Intensive local competition from rival companies.
■ Lower income levels of local consumers.
■ Some firms argue that, since their R&D and other overhead costs are covered by home sales, exporting represents a marginal activity intended merely to bring in as much additional revenue as possible by offering a low selling price.

Japanese companies have used penetration pricing intensively to gain market share leadership in a number of markets, such as cars, home entertainment products and electronic components.

Price changes

Price changes on existing products are called for when a new product has been launched or when changes occur in overall market conditions (such as fluctuating foreign exchange rates).

Table 16.2 shows the percentage sales volume increase or decrease required to maintain the level of profit. An example (the figure in bold type in Table 16.2) shows how the table functions. A firm has a product with a contribution margin of 20 per cent. The firm would like to know how much the sales volume should be increased as a consequence of a price reduction of 5 per cent, if it wishes to keep the same total profit contribution.

Table 16.2 Sales volume increase or decrease (%) required to maintain total profit contribution

	Profit contribution margin (price – variable cost per unit as % of the price)								
Price reduction (%)	5	10	15	20	25	30	35	40	50
	Sales volume increase (%) required to maintain total profit contribution								
2.0	67	25	15	11	9	7	7	5	4
3.0	150	43	25	18	14	11	9	8	6
4.0	400	67	36	25	19	15	13	11	9
5.0		100	50	33	25	20	17	14	11
7.5		300	100	60	43	33	27	23	18
10.0			200	100	67	50	40	33	25
15.0				300	150	100	75	60	43

	Profit contribution margin (price – variable cost per unit as % of the price)								
Price increase (%)	5	10	15	20	25	30	35	40	50
	Sales volume increase (%) required to maintain total profit contribution								
2.0	29	17	12	9	7	6	5	5	4
3.0	37	23	17	13	11	9	8	7	6
4.0	44	29	21	17	14	12	10	9	7
5.0	50	33	25	20	17	14	12	11	9
7.5	60	43	33	27	23	20	18	16	13
10.0	67	50	40	33	29	25	22	20	17
15.0	75	60	50	43	37	33	30	27	23

The calculation is as follows:

Before price reduction

Per product | sales price | £100
| variable cost per unit | £80
| contribution margin | £20

Total contribution margin: 100 units @ £20 = £2,000

After price reduction (5%)

Per product | sales price | £95
| variable cost per unit | £80
| contribution margin | £15

Total contribution margin: 133 units @ £15 = £1,995

As a consequence of a price reduction of 5 per cent, a 33 per cent increase in sales is required.

If a decision is made to change prices, related changes must also be considered. For example, if an increase in price is required it may be accompanied, at least initially, by increased promotional efforts.

When reducing prices the degree of flexibility enjoyed by decision makers will tend to be less for existing products than for new products. This follows from the high probability that the existing product is now less unique, faces stronger competition and is aimed at a broader segment of the market. In this situation the decision maker will be forced to pay more attention to competitive and cost factors in the pricing process.

The timing of price changes can be nearly as important as the changes themselves. For example, a simple tactic of time lagging competitors in announcing price increases can produce the perception among customers that you are the most customer-responsive supplier. The extent of the time lag can also be important.

In one company an independent survey of customers (Garda, 1995) showed that the perception of being the most customer-responsive supplier was generated just as effectively by a six-week lag in following a competitor's price increase as by a six-month lag. A considerable amount of money would have been lost during the unnecessary four-and-a-half-month delay in announcing a price increase.

Experience curve pricing

Price changes usually follow changes in the product's stage in the life cycle. As the product matures more pressure will be put on the price to keep the product competitive because of increased competition and less possibility of differentiation.

Let us also integrate the cost aspect into the discussion. The experience curve has its roots in a commonly observed phenomenon called the learning curve, which states that as people repeat a task they learn to do it better and faster. The learning curve applies to the labour portion of manufacturing cost. The Boston Consulting Group extended the learning effect to cover all the value-added costs related to a product – manufacturing plus marketing, sales, administration and so on.

The resulting experience curves, covering all value chain activities (see Figure 16.3), indicate that the total unit costs of a product in real terms can be reduced by a certain percentage with each doubling of cumulative production. The typical decline in cost is 30 per cent (termed a 70 per cent curve), although greater and lesser declines are observed (Czepiel, 1992, p. 149).

Figure 16.3 Experience curves of value chain activities

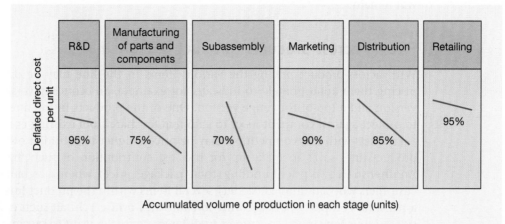

Source: Czepiel, 1992, p. 154.

If we combine the experience curve (average unit cost) with the typical market price development within an industry we will have a relationship similar to that shown in Figure 16.4.

Figure 16.4 shows that after the introduction stage (during part of which the price is below the total unit cost), profits begin to flow. Because supply is less than demand prices do not fall as quickly as costs. Consequently the gap between costs and prices widens, in effect creating a price umbrella, attracting new competitors. However, the competitive situation is not a stable one. At some point the umbrella will be folded by one or more competitors reducing the prices in an attempt to gain market share. The result is that a shake-out phase will begin: inefficient producers will be shaken out by

Figure 16.4 Product life cycle stages and the industry price experience curve

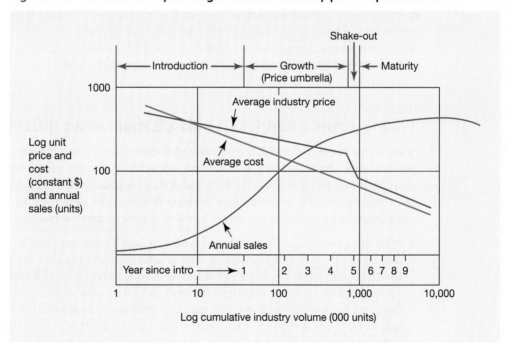

Source: Czepiel, 1992, p. 167.

rapidly falling market prices, and only those with a competitive price/cost relationship will remain.

Pricing across products (product line pricing)

With across-product pricing the various items in the line may be differentiated by pricing them appropriately to indicate, for example, an economy version, a standard version and a top-of-the-range version. One of the products in the line may be priced to protect against competitors or to gain market share from existing competitors.

Products with less competition may be priced higher to subsidise other parts of the product line, so as to make up for the lost contribution of such 'fighting brands'. Another strategy is price bundling (total 'package' price), where a certain price is set for customers who simultaneously buy several items within the product line (one price for a personal computer package with software and printer). In all such cases a key consideration is how much consumers in different countries want to save money, to spend time searching for the 'best buy' and so forth. Furthermore, some items in the product line may be priced very low to serve as loss leaders and induce customers to try the product. A special variant of this is the so-called buy in–follow on strategy (Weigand, 1991). A classic example of this strategy is the razor blade link where Gillette, for example, uses a penetration price on its razor (buy in) but a skimming pricing (relatively high price) on its razor blades (follow on). Thus the linked product or service – the follow on – is sold at a significant contribution margin. This inevitably attracts hitchhikers who try to sell follow-on products without incurring the cost of the buy in.

The buy in–follow on strategy is different from a low introductory price, which is based on the hope that the customer (of habit) will return again and again at higher prices. With the buy in–follow on strategy sales of two products or services are powerfully linked by factors such as legal contracts, patents, trade secrets, experience curve advantages and technological links.

Other examples of the strategy are as follows:

- The price of a Polaroid instant camera is very low, but Polaroid hopes that this will generate sales of far more profitable films for many years.
- The telephone companies sell mobile (cellular) telephones at a near giveaway price, hoping that the customer will be a 'heavy' user of the profitable mobile telephone network.

Pricing across countries (standardization versus differentiation)

A major problem for companies is how to coordinate prices between countries. There are two essential opposing forces: first, to achieve similar positioning in different markets by adopting largely standardized pricing; and second, to maximise profitability by adapting pricing to different market conditions. In determining to what extent prices should be standardized across borders two basic approaches appear:

- *Price standardization*. This is based on setting a price for the product as it leaves the factory. At its simplest it involves setting a fixed world price at the headquarters of the firm. This fixed world price is then applied in all markets after taking account of factors such as foreign exchange rates and variance in the regulatory context. For the firm this is a low-risk strategy, but no attempt is made to respond to local conditions and so no effort is made to maximise profits. However, this pricing strategy might be appropriate if the firm sells to very large customers, who have companies in several countries. In such a situation the firm might be under pressure from the customer only to deliver at the same price to every country subsidiary, throughout the customer's multinational organization. In Figure 16.5 this is exemplified, e.g. by the 'International activities of large retail organizations'. Another advantage of price standardization includes the potential for rapid introduction of new products in international markets and the presentation of a consistent (price) image across markets.

■ *Price differentiation.* This allows each local subsidiary or partner (agent, distributor, etc.) to set a price that is considered to be the most appropriate for local conditions, and no attempt is made to coordinate prices from country to country. Cross-cultural empirical research has found significant differences in customer characteristics, preference and purchasing behaviour among different countries (Theodosiou and Katsikeas, 2001). The weakness with 'price differentiation' is the lack of control that the headquarters has over the prices set by the subsidiary operations or external partner. Significantly different prices may be set in adjacent markets, and this can reflect badly on the image of multinational firms. It also encourages the creation of parallel importing/grey markets (which are dealt with in greater detail in Chapter 17), whereby products can be purchased in one market and sold in another, undercutting the established market prices in the process.

The underlying forces favouring standardization or differentiation are shown in Figure 16.5.

Figure 16.5 Structural factors of standardized versus differentiated pricing in European consumer goods markets

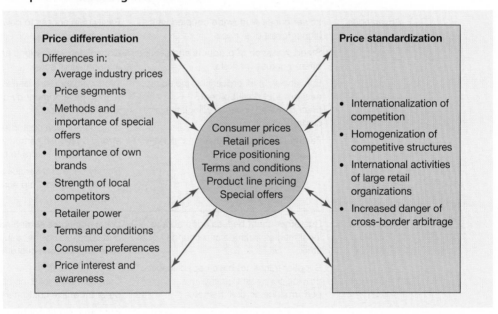

Price differentiation

Differences in:
- Average industry prices
- Price segments
- Methods and importance of special offers
- Importance of own brands
- Strength of local competitors
- Retailer power
- Terms and conditions
- Consumer preferences
- Price interest and awareness

Consumer prices
Retail prices
Price positioning
Terms and conditions
Product line pricing
Special offers

Price standardization

- Internationalization of competition
- Homogenization of competitive structures
- International activities of large retail organizations
- Increased danger of cross-border arbitrage

Source: Reprinted from *European Management Journal*, Vol. 12, No. 2, Diller. H. and Bukhari, I. (1994) 'Pricing conditions in the European Common Market', p. 168, Copyright 1994, with permission from Elsevier.

Establishing global-pricing contracts (GPCs)

As globalization increases the following sentence is heard frequently among global suppliers and global customers: 'Give me a global-pricing contract (GPC) and I'll consolidate my worldwide purchase with you.' Increasingly global customers are demanding such contracts from suppliers. For example, in 1998 General Motor's Powertrain Group told suppliers of components used in GM's engines, transmissions and subassemblies to charge GM the same for parts from one region as they did for parts from another region.

Suppliers do not need to lose out when customers globalize. The most attractive global-pricing opportunities are those that involve suppliers and customers working together to identify and eliminate inefficiencies that harm both. Sometime suppliers do not have a choice. They do not want to shut themselves out of business with their largest and fastest-growing customers.

Suppliers and customers have different advantages and disadvantages with global-pricing contracts. Table 16.3 illustrates some of them.

One chemicals manufacturer concentrated on relationships with a few select customers. It had decided that its strength lay in value-added services but that potential customers in emerging markets were fixated on price. The select customers, however, were interested in money-saving supply and inventory management initiatives developed jointly with the supplier.

Global customers' demands for detailed cost information can also put suppliers at risk. Toyota, Honda, Xerox and others force suppliers to open their books for inspection. Their stated objectives: to help suppliers identify ways to improve processes and quality while reducing costs – and to build trust. But in an economic downturn the global customer might seek price reductions and supplementary services.

Table 16.3 Global pricing contracts (GPCs): advantages and disadvantages

	Customers	Suppliers
Advantages	Lower prices worldwide coupled with higher levels of service.	Easily gain access to new markets and grow the business.
	Standardisation of products and services offered across markets.	Consolidate operations and achieve economies of scale.
	Efficiencies in all processes, including new product development, manufacturing, inventory, logistics and customer service	Work with industry leaders and influence market development by using them as showcase accounts.
	Faster diffusion of innovations globally.	Collaborate with customers and develop strong relationships that are difficult for potential competitors to break into.
		Rectify price and service anomalies in a customer relationship across country markets.
Disadvantages	Customer might be less adaptable to local market variance and changes over time.	Local managers sometimes resist change, and supplier may get caught in the crossfire between customer's HQ and country managers.
	Supplier might not have capabilities to provide consistent quality and performance across markets.	Supplier might lose the ability to serve other attractive customers.
	Supplier might use customer's over-dependence to extract higher prices.	Customer might not be able to deliver on promises.
	Local managers might resist global contracts and prefer dealing with local suppliers.	Customer might take advantage of cost information shared in the relationship.
	Costs of monitoring global contracts might outstrip the benefits.	Supplier might become over-dependent on one customer, even when there are other more attractive customers to serve.
		Supplier might have a conflict with existing channels of distribution in the new markets.

Source: adapted from Narayandas, Quelch and Swartz, 2000, p. 61–70.

European pricing strategy

In 1991 price differentials for identical consumer goods across Europe were around 20 per cent on average, but much greater differences were apparent in certain products (Simon and Kucher, 1993). In another study (Diller and Bukhari, 1994) there were also considerable price differences for identical take-home ice-cream products.

The causes of price differentials are differences in regulations, competition, distribution structures and consumer behaviour, such as willingness to pay. Currency fluctuations can also influence short-term price differences. The pressures of regionalisation are accelerating the move to uniform pricing, but Simon and Kucher (1993) warn that this is a potential time bomb, as the pressure is for uniform pricing to be at the lowest pricing levels.

Europe was a price differentiation paradise as long as markets were separated. But it is becoming increasingly difficult to retain the old price differentials. There are primarily two developments that may force companies to standardise prices across European countries:

- International buying power of cross-European retail groups.
- Parallel imports/grey markets. Because of differentiated prices across countries, buyers in one country are able to purchase at a lower price than in another country. As a result there will be an incentive for customers in lower-price markets to sell goods to higher-price markets in order to make a profit. Grey marketing will be examined further in section 17.8.

Simon and Kucher (1993) suggest a price 'corridor' (Figure 16.6). The prices in the individual countries may only vary within that range. Figure 16.6 is also interesting in the light of the euro, which had been fully implemented by January 2002. However, price differences that can be justified by transportation costs and short-term competitive conditions, etc., may still be maintained.

They recommend that business in smaller countries should be sacrificed, if necessary, in order to retain acceptable pricing levels in the big markets such as France, Germany, the United Kingdom and Italy. For example, for a pharmaceutical manufacturer it is

Figure 16.6 Development of prices in Europe

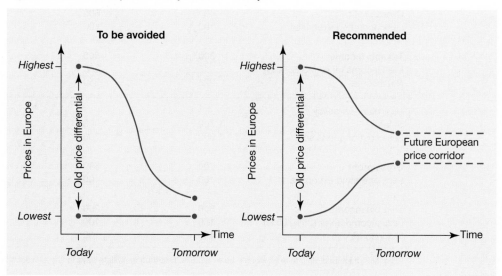

more profitable not to sell in the Portuguese pharmaceutical market than to accept a price reduction of 10 per cent in the German market due to parallel imports from Portugal.

Transfer pricing

Transfer prices are those charged for intracompany movement of goods and services. Many purely domestic firms need to make transfer-pricing decisions when goods are *transferred* from one domestic unit to another. While these transfer prices are internal to the company they are important externally because goods being transferred from country to country must have a value for cross-border taxation purposes.

The objective of the corporation in this situation is to ensure that the transfer price paid optimises corporate rather than divisional objectives. This can prove difficult when a company internationally is organised into profit centres. For profit centres to work effectively a price must be set for everything that is transferred, be it working materials, components, finished goods or services. A high transfer price – for example, from the manufacturing division to a foreign subsidiary – is reflected in an apparently poor performance by the foreign subsidiary (see the high mark-up policy in Table 16.4), whereas a low price would not be acceptable to the domestic division providing the goods (see the low mark-up policy in Table 16.4). This issue alone can be the cause of much mistrust between subsidiaries.

The 'best' of Table 16.4's two mark-up policies seen from the consolidated point of view is to use a high mark-up policy, since it generates a net income of $550, as against

Table 16.4 Tax effect of low versus high transfer price on net income ($)

	Manufacturing affiliate (division)	Distribution/selling affiliate (subsidiary)	Consolidated company total
Low mark-up policy			
Sales	1,400	2,000	2,000
Less cost of goods sold	1,000	1,400	1,000
Gross profit	400	600	1,000
Less operating expenses	100	100	200
Taxable income	300	500	800
Less income taxes (25%/50%)	75	250	325
Net income	225	250	475
High mark-up policy			
Sales	1,700	2,000	2,000
Less cost of goods sold	1,000	1,700	1,000
Gross profit	700	300	1,000
Less operating expenses	100	100	200
Taxable income	600	200	800
Less income taxes (25%/50%)	150	100	250
Net income	450	100	550

Note: Manufacturing affiliate pays income taxes at 25%. Distribution affiliate pays income taxes at 50%.

Source: adapted from Eiteman and Stonehill, 1986.

$475 from using a low mark-up policy. The 'best' solution depends on the tax rates in the countries of the manufacturing and distribution affiliates (subsidiaries).

There are three basic approaches to transfer pricing:

- *Transfer at cost.* The transfer price is set at the level of the production cost, and the international division is credited with the entire profit that the firm makes. This means that the production centre is evaluated on efficiency parameters rather than profitability. The production division normally dislikes selling at production cost because it believes it is subsidising the selling subsidiary. When the production division is unhappy the selling subsidiary may get sluggish service, because the production division is serving more attractive opportunities first.
- *Transfer at arm's length.* Here the international division is charged the same as any buyer outside the firm. Problems occur if the overseas division is allowed to buy elsewhere when the price is uncompetitive or the product quality is inferior, and further problems arise if there are no external buyers, making it difficult to establish a relevant price. Nevertheless the arm's-length principle has now been accepted worldwide as the preferred (not required) standard by which transfer prices should be set (Fraedrich and Bateman, 1996).
- *Transfer at cost plus.* This is the usual compromise, where profits are split between the production and international divisions. The actual formula used for assessing the transfer price can vary, but usually it is this method that has the greatest chance of minimising executive time spent on transfer-price disagreements, optimising corporate profits and motivating the home and international divisions. A senior executive is often appointed to rule on disputes.

A good transfer-pricing method should consider total corporate profile and encourage divisional cooperation. It should also minimise executive time spent on transfer-price disagreements and keep the accounting burden at a minimum.

Currency issues

A difficult aspect of export pricing is the decision about what currency the price should be quoted in. The exporter has the following options:

- the foreign currency of the buyer's country (local currency);
- the currency of the exporter's country (domestic currency);
- the currency of a third country (usually US dollars);
- a currency unit such as the euro.

If the exporter quotes in the domestic currency then not only is it administratively much easier, but also the risks associated with changes in the exchange rate are borne by the customer, whereas by quoting prices in the foreign currency the exporter bears the exchange rate risk. However, there are benefits to the exporter in quoting in foreign currency:

- Quoting in foreign currency could be a condition of the contract.
- It could provide access to finance abroad at lower interest rates.
- Good currency management may be a means of gaining additional profits.
- Customers normally prefer to be quoted in their own currency in order to be able to make competitive comparisons and know exactly what the eventual price will be.

Another difficult problem that exporters face is caused by fluctuating exchange rates. A company in a country with a devalued currency can (all other things being equal) strengthen its international competitive position. It can choose to reduce prices in foreign currencies or it can leave prices unchanged and instead increase profit margins.

When the Italian lira dropped by 15–20 per cent in value against the German mark it gave the Italian car producer Fiat a competitive advantage in pricing. The German car exporters, such as Volkswagen, were adversely affected and had to lower the list prices. In this respect the geographic pattern of a firm's manufacturing and sales subsidiaries compared with those of its main competitors becomes very important, since a local subsidiary can absorb most of the negative effects of a devaluation.

16.5 Implications of the Internet/e-commerce for pricing across borders

Europe's single currency, the euro (**http://europa.eu.int/euro/**) has finally become a reality after more than a decade of planning and preparation. In one stroke the single currency has created the largest single economy in the world, with a larger share of global trade and a greater number of consumers than in the United States.

The implication is that Europe suddenly became a single market by the end of 2000, and people can purchase from another country as easily as they can from a shop across the road. The same currency will be used; only the language issue remains. Opinion in Europe is that, as more of the population goes online, and as Europe starts using its new single currency, online shopping will experience a tremendous growth.

Most of this growth has been fuelled by aggressive price cutting from Internet service providers. A number of UK companies, for example, are now offering free Internet access or pay-as-you-go models, which have encouraged new sections of the population to try the Internet for the first time.

A European single currency was a long-held ambition for members of the European Union. The idea was first considered in the 1970s, but knocked off-course by oil price rises. It re-emerged in the early 1980s, and was finally agreed to in the 1992 Maastricht Treaty. There were many accounting criteria to be met by each country, such as the control of the rate of inflation and the debt/GDP ratio. Most countries have met these criteria and were permitted to join the European Monetary Union.

This goal has now been achieved by 11 countries. EU currencies such as the German mark, the French franc and the Italian lira are now replaced by the euro. The Eurozone includes all EU countries except the United Kingdom, Sweden and Denmark. The United Kingdom being outside the euro region will be quite inconvenient for many US companies who trade heavily with UK companies or have subsidiaries there.

The exact timetable was as follows:

- *1 January 1999*: the euro became an official currency.
- *1999–2002*: existing national currencies and the euro operated side by side at fixed rates. The euro was not imposed as currency, but interbank transfer could be made in euros.
- *By January 2002*: new euro notes and coins were circulated.
- *By July 2002*: local currencies were completely phased out and no longer allowed. Only euro transactions (cash or transfer) possible.

The current value of the euro is now (May 2003) equal to the value of one US dollar.

The main detailed implications of the euro will be that it will:

- lower prices for consumers by making prices transparent across Europe;
- create a real single market by reducing 'friction' to trade caused by high transaction costs and fluctuation currencies;
- enhance competition by forcing companies to concentrate on price, quality and production instead of hiding behind weak currencies;
- benefit SMEs and consumers by making it easier for the former to enter 'foreign' markets, and allowing the latter, increasingly via the Internet, to shop in the lowest priced markets;
- establish inflation and interest rate stability via the new European Central Bank; and
- lower the costs of doing business through lower prices, lower interest rates, no transaction costs or loss through exchanging currencies, and the absence of exchange rate fluctuations.

In short, the single currency will significantly increase competition, lower transaction costs, and bring about greater certainty. These new forces will bring about structural reforms in Europe. Almost every aspect of Europe's business and political environment will be affected.

Perhaps most importantly, marketing and pricing strategies need rethinking. Because the euro will allow easy price comparison across Europe (especially via the Internet), it will reveal the differences between higher and lower priced markets.

For those selling via the Internet the euro will make it easier to do business, and give encouragement to companies selling to European customers. Since Europeans will now be able to shop and compare prices at the click of a mouse they will also be more favourably inclined towards e-commerce.

In any single European country there is not usually much competition for a given product, since purchasing habits have always been local (in one's own country). Now that Europeans will be able to shop internationally via the Internet they will become aware of other choices and prices for the same product that were not previously known. Competition will heat up for the buyer's euro, and this should put a downward pressure on prices.

However, recent research has also stated that the Internet is not creating a state of perfect competition with decreasing prices as a result. In fact in some cases online prices are higher than those of conventional retail outlets. Research has also shown that online consumers are not as price sensitive as had previously been thought. Consumers become less price sensitive and more loyal as the level of quality information on a site increases (Kung and Monroe, 2002).

16.6 Terms of sale/delivery terms

The price quotation describes a specific product, states the price for the product as well as a specified delivery location, sets the time of shipment and specifies payment terms. The responsibilities of the buyer and the seller should be spelled out as they relate to what is and what is not included in the price quotation and when ownership of goods passes from seller to buyer. Incoterms are the internationally accepted standard definitions for terms of sale set by the International Chamber of Commerce. They have been fully revised for the new millennium in line with developments in commercial practice. Published in September 1999, *Incoterms 2000* may be used to define the responsibilities of buyer and seller in contracts effective from 1 January 2000.

The 13 terms contained in *Incoterms 2000* are the following:

EXW: *Ex-works* (... named place)
FCA: *Free carrier* (... named place)
FAS: *Free alongside ship* (... named port of shipment)
FOB: *Free on board* (... named port of shipment)
CFR: *Cost and freight* (... named port of destination)
CIF: *Cost, insurance and freight* (... named port of destination)
CPT: *Carriage paid to* (... named place of destination)
CIP: *Carriage and insurance paid to* (... named place of destination)
DAF: *Delivered at frontier* (... named place)
DES: *Delivered ex-ship* (... named port of destination)
DEQ: *Delivered ex-quay* (... named port of destination)
DDU: *Delivered duty unpaid* (... named place of destination)
DDP: *Delivered duty paid* (... named place of destination)

Table 16.5 describes the point of delivery and risk shift for some terms of sale.

Table 16.5 Point of delivery and where risk shifts from seller to buyer

	EXW	FAS	FOB	CFR	CIF	DEQ	DDP
Supplier's factory/warehouse	×						
Dock at port of shipment (export dock)		×					
Port of shipment (on board vessel)			×	×	×		
Port of destination (import dock)					×*	×	
Buyer's warehouse (destination)							×
Main transit risk on	buyer	buyer	buyer	buyer	seller	seller	seller

* The seller transfers the risk to its insurance company.

Source: adapted from Onkvisit and Shaw, 1993, p. 799. Reprinted by permission of Macmillan.

The following is a description of some of the most popular terms of sale:

- *Ex-works (EXW).* The term 'Ex' means that the price quoted by the seller applies at a specified point of origin, usually the factory, warehouse, mine or plantation, and the buyer is responsible for all charges from this point. This term represents the minimum obligation for the exporter.
- *Free alongside ship (FAS).* Under this term the seller must provide for delivery of the goods free alongside, but not on board, the transportation carrier (usually an ocean vessel) at the point of shipment and export. This term differs from that of FOB, since the time and cost of loading are not included in the FAS term. The buyer has to pay for loading the goods on to the ship.
- *Free on board (FOB).* The exporter's price quote includes coverage of all charges up to the point when goods have been loaded on to the designated transport vehicle. The designated loading point may be a named inland shipping point, but is usually the port of export. The buyer assumes responsibility for the goods the moment they pass over the ship's rail.
- *Cost and freight (CFR).* The seller's liability ends when the goods are loaded on board a carrier or are in the custody of the carrier at the export dock. The seller pays all the

transport charges (excluding insurance, which is the customer's obligation) required to deliver goods by sea to a named destination.

- *Cost, insurance and freight (CIF)*. This trade term is identical with CFR except that the seller must also provide the necessary insurance. The seller's obligations still end at the same stage (i.e. when goods are loaded or aboard), but the seller's insurance company assumes responsibility once the goods are loaded.
- *Delivered ex-quay (DEQ)*. Ex-quay means from the import dock. The term goes one step beyond CIF and requires the seller to be responsible for the cost of the goods and all other costs necessary to place the goods on the dock at the named overseas port, with the appropriate import duty paid.
- *Delivered duty paid (DDP)*. The export price quote includes the costs of delivery to the importer's premises. The exporter is thus responsible for paying any import duties and costs of unloading and inland transport in the importing country, as well as all costs involved in insuring and shipping the goods to that country. These terms imply maximum exporter obligations. The seller also assumes all the risks involved in delivering to the buyer. DDP used to be known as 'Franco domicile' pricing.

Export price quotations are important because they spell out the legal and cost responsibilities of the buyer and seller. Sellers favour a quote that gives them the least liability and responsibility, such as ex-works, which means the exporter's liability finishes when the goods are loaded on to the buyer's carrier at the seller's factory. Buyers, on the other hand, would prefer either DDP, where responsibility is borne by the supplier all the way to the customer's warehouse, or CIF port of discharge, which means that the buyer's responsibility begins only when the goods are in its own country.

Generally, the more market-oriented pricing policies are based on CIF, which indicates a strong commitment to the market. By pricing ex-works an exporter is not taking any steps to build a relationship with the market and so may be indicating only short-term commitment.

16.7 Terms of payment

The exporter will consider the following factors in negotiating terms of payment for goods to be shipped:

- practices in the industry;
- terms offered by competitors;
- relative strength of the buyer and the seller.

If the exporter is well established in the market with a unique product and accompanying service, price and terms of trade can be set to fit the exporter's desires. If, on the other hand, the exporter is breaking into a new market or if competitive pressures call for action, pricing and selling terms should be used as major competitive tools.

The basic methods of payment for exports vary in terms of their attractiveness to the buyer and the seller, from cash in advance to open account or consignment selling. Neither of the extremes will be feasible for longer-term relationships, but they do have their uses in certain situations. The most common payment methods are presented in Figure 16.7.

The most favourable term to the exporter is cash in advance because it relieves the exporter of all risk and allows for immediate use of the money. On the other hand, the

Figure 16.7 Different terms of payment

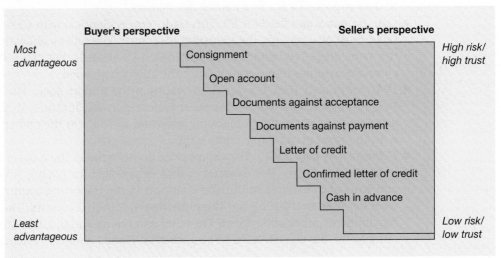

Source: Chase Manhattan Bank, 1984, p. 5.

most advantageous option seen from the buyer's perspective would be consignment or open account.

The most common arrangements, in decreasing order of attractiveness to the exporter, will now be described.

Cash in advance

The exporter receives payment before shipment of the goods. This minimises the exporter's risk and financial costs, since there is no collection risk and no interest cost on receivables. However, importers will rarely agree to these terms, since it ties up their capital and the goods may not be received. Consequently such terms are not widely used. They are most likely either when the exporter lacks confidence in the importer's ability to pay (often the case in initial export transactions) or where economic and political instability in the importing country may result in foreign exchange not being made available for importers.

Letter of credit

Worldwide letters of credit are very important and very common. A letter of credit is an instrument whereby a bank agrees to pay a specified amount of money on presentation of documents stipulated in the letter of credit, usually the bill of lading, an invoice and a description of the goods. In general, letters of credit have the following characteristics:

- They are an arrangement by banks for settling international commercial transactions.
- They provide a form of security for the parties involved.
- They ensure payment, provided that the terms and conditions of the credit have been fulfilled.
- Payment by such means is based on documents only and not on the merchandise or services involved.

The process for handling letters of credit is illustrated in Figure 16.8.

Figure 16.8 The process for handling letters of credit

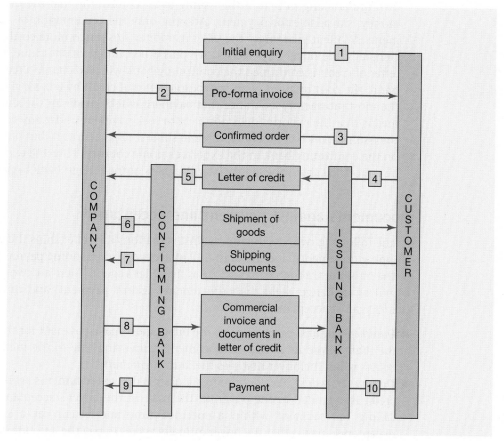

Source: Phillips *et al.*, 1994, p. 454, with permission from ITBP Ltd.

In the process the customer agrees to payment by a confirmed letter of credit. The customer begins the process by sending an enquiry for the goods (1). The price and terms are confirmed by a pro-forma invoice (2) by the supplier, so that the customer knows for what amount (3) to instruct its bank (the issuing bank) to open a letter of credit (L/C)(4). The L/C is confirmed by a bank (5) in the supplier's country.

When the goods are shipped (6) the shipping documents are submitted by the supplier to his bank (7), so that shipment is confirmed by their presentation (8) together with the L/C and all other stipulated documents and certificates for payment (9). The money is automatically transmitted from the customer's account via the issuing bank. The customer may collect the goods (10) only when all the documents have been delivered to it by its bank – the issuing bank (adapted from Phillips *et al.*, 1994, p. 453).

The letter of credit has three forms:

- *Revocable L/C*. Now a rare form, this gives the buyer maximum flexibility as it can be cancelled without notice to the seller up to the moment of payment by the bank.
- *Irrevocable but unconfirmed L/C*. This is as good as the credit status of the establishing bank and the willingness of the buyer's country to allow the required use of foreign exchange. An unconfirmed L/C should not necessarily be viewed with suspicion. The reason for the lack of confirmation may be that the customer has been unwilling to pay the additional fee for confirmation.

- *Confirmed irrevocable L/C.* This means that a bank in the seller's country has added its own undertaking to that of the issuing bank, confirming that the necessary sum of money is available for payment, awaiting only the presentation of shipping documents. While it guarantees the seller its money it is much more costly to the buyer. Generally the buyer pays a fixed fee plus a percentage of the value, but where the letter of credit is confirmed the confirming bank will also charge a fee. On the other hand, the confirmation of an irrevocable letter of credit by a bank gives the shipper the most satisfactory assurance that payment will be made for the shipment. It also means that the exporter does not have to seek payment under any conditions from the issuing bank – invariably located in some foreign country – but has a direct claim on the confirming bank in the exporter's home country. Thus the exporter need not be concerned about the ability or willingness of the foreign bank to pay.

Documents against payment and acceptance

In the following two 'documents against' situations the seller ships the goods and the shipping documents, and the draft (bill of exchange) demanding payment is presented to the importer through banks acting as the seller's agent. There are two principal types of bill of exchange: sight draft (documents against payment) and time draft (documents against acceptance).

- *Documents against payment.* Here the buyer must make payment for the face value of the draft before receiving the documents conveying title to the merchandise. This occurs when the buyer first sees the draft (*sight draft*).
- *Documents against acceptance.* When a draft is drawn 'documents against acceptance' credit is extended to the buyer on the basis of the buyer's acceptance of the draft calling for payment within a specified time and usually at a specified place. Acceptance means that the buyer formally agrees to pay the amount specified by the draft on the due date. The specified time may be expressed as certain number of days after sight (*time draft*). A time draft offers less security for the seller than a sight draft, since the sight draft demands payment prior to the release of shipping documents. The time draft, on the other hand, allows the buyer a delay of 30, 60 or 90 days in payment.

Open account

The exporter ships the goods without documents calling for payment, other than the invoice. The buyer can pick up the goods without having to make payment first. The advantage of the open account is its simplicity and the assistance it gives to the buyer, which does not have to pay credit charges to banks. The seller in return expects that the invoice will be paid at the agreed time. A major weakness of the method is that there are no safeguards for payment. Exporters should sell on open account only to importers they know very well or that have excellent credit ratings, and to markets with no foreign exchange problems. Open account sales are less complex and expensive than drafts, since there are no documentation requirements or bank charges.

Consignment

Here the exporter retains title of the goods until the importer sells them. Exporters own the goods longer in this method than any other, and so the financial burden and risks are at their greatest. The method should be offered only to very trustworthy importers with an excellent credit rating in countries where political and economic risk is very low. Consignments tend to be mainly used by companies trading with their own subsidiaries.

The credit terms given are also important in determining the final price to the buyer. When the products of international competitors are perceived to be similar the purchaser may choose the supplier that offers the best credit terms, in order to achieve a greater discount. In effect the supplier is offering a source of finance to the buyer.

16.8 Export financing

Exporters need financing support in order to obtain working capital and because importers will often demand terms that allow them to defer payment. Principal sources of export finance include commercial banks, government export financing programmes, export credit insurance, factoring houses and counter-trade.

Commercial banks

The simplest way of financing export sales is through an overdraft facility with the exporter's own bank. This is a convenient way to finance all the elements of the contract, such as purchasing, manufacturing, shipping and credit. The bank is generally more favourably disposed towards granting an overdraft if the exporter has obtained an export credit insurance policy.

Export credit insurance

Export credit insurance is available to most exporters through governmental export credit agencies or through private insurers. Such insurances usually cover the following:

- *political risks* and non-convertibility of currency;
- *commercial risks* associated with non-payment by buyers.

Exporters may be able to use credit insurance to enable them to grant more liberal credit terms or to encourage their banks to grant them financing against their export receivables. The costs of such insurance are often quite low in many markets, ranging from 1–2 per cent of the value of the transaction. Specialised insurance brokers handle such insurance.

Factoring

Factoring means selling export debts for immediate cash. In this way the exporter shifts the problems of collecting payment for completed orders over to organizations or factors that specialise in export credit management and finance.

Ideally the exporter should go to the factor before any contract is signed or shipment made, and secure its willingness to buy the receivable. The factor will check out the credit rating and so forth of the prospective buyer(s) typically by having a correspondent in the importer's country do the necessary checking. Thus the factor acts as a credit approval agency as well as a facilitator and guarantor of payment.

The factor does not usually purchase export debts on terms exceeding 120 days. The factor normally charges a service fee of between 0.75 and 2.5 per cent of the sales value, depending on the workload and the risk carried by the factor.

Forfeiting

This is a finance method developed in Switzerland in the 1950s. It is an arrangement whereby exporters of capital goods can obtain medium-term finance (between one and seven years). The system can briefly be explained as follows.

An exporter of capital goods has a buyer that wishes to have medium-term credit to finance the purchase. The buyer pays some of the cost at once and pays the balance in regular instalments for, say, the next five years. The principal benefit is that there is immediate cash for the exporter and, along with the first cash payment by the buyer, forfeiting can finance up to 100 per cent of the contract value.

Bonding

In some countries (e.g. in the Middle East) contracts are cash or short term. Whereas this is an ideal situation for suppliers, it means that the buyer loses some of its leverage over the supplier as it cannot withhold payment. In this situation a bond or guarantee is a written instrument issued to an overseas buyer by an acceptable third party, either a bank or an insurance company. It guarantees compliance of its obligations by an exporter or contractor, or the overseas buyer will be indemnified for a stated amount against the failure of the exporter/contractor to fulfil its obligations under the contract.

Leasing

Exporters of capital equipment may use leasing in one of two ways:

- to arrange cross-border leases directly from a bank or leasing company to the foreign buyer;
- to obtain local leasing facilities either through overseas branches or subdivisions of international banks or through international leasing associations.

With leasing the exporter receives prompt payment for goods directly from the leasing company. A leasing facility is best set up at the earliest opportunity, preferably when the exporter receives the order.

Counter-trade

Counter-trade is a generic term used to describe a variety of trade agreements in which a seller provides a buyer with products (commodities, goods, services, technology) and agrees to a reciprocal purchasing obligation with the buyer in terms of an agreed percentage (full or partial) of the original sales value.

Barter

This is a straightforward exchange of goods for goods without any money transfer. Bilateral barter, where only two parties are involved, is relatively uncommon. The bartering process can, however, be facilitated when a third (trilateral barter) or even more countries (multilateral barter) become involved in a trading chain.

Compensation deal

This involves the export of goods in one direction. The 'payment' of the goods is split into two parts:

- Part payment in cash by the importer.

■ For the rest of the 'payment' the original exporter makes an obligation to purchase some of the buyer's goods. These products can be used in the exporter's internal production or they may be sold on in the wider market.

Buy-back agreement

The sale of machinery, equipment or a turnkey plant to the buyer's production is financed at least in part by the exporter's purchase of some of the resultant output. Whereas barter and compensation deals are short-term arrangements, buy-back agreements are long-term agreements. The contract may last for a considerable period of time, such as 5–10 years. The two-way transactions are clearly linked, but are kept financially separate.

Counter-trade has arisen because of shortages of both foreign exchange and international lines of credit. Some have estimated that the size of counter-trade is as high as 10–15 per cent of world trade.

16.9 Summary

The major issues covered in this chapter include the determinants of price, pricing strategy, how foreign prices are related to domestic prices, price escalation, the elements of price quotation, and transfer pricing.

Several factors must be taken into consideration in setting price, including cost, competitors' prices, product image, market share/volume, stage in product life cycle and number of products involved. The optimum mix of these ingredients varies by product, market and corporate objectives. Price setting in the international context is further complicated by such factors as foreign exchange rates, different competitive situations in each export market, different labour costs and different inflation rates in various countries. Also local and regional regulations and laws in setting prices have to be considered.

The international marketer must quote a meaningful price by using proper international trade terms. When there is doubt about how to prepare a quotation freight forwarders may be consulted (see section 17.5). These specialists can provide valuable information with regard to documentation (e.g. invoice, bill of lading) and the costs relevant to the movement of goods. Financial documents, such as letters of credit, require a bank's assistance. International banks have international departments that can facilitate payment and advise clients regarding pitfalls in preparing and accepting documents.

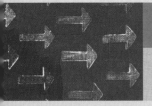

CASE STUDY 16.1   Harley-Davidson

Does the image justify the price level?

The Harley-Davidson (**HD**) Corporation has been dominating the motorcycle industry for many decades. Today, it continues to have a strong presence in the world market for the heavyweight cruisers. The mission statement of the company is to fulfil dreams through the experience of motorcycling, by providing to the motorcyclists and the general public an expanding line of motorcycles, and branded products and services, in selected market segments. HD offers a complete range of motorcycles, parts, accessories, apparel, and general merchandise. Strategic licensing of the HD brand helps create future generations of Harley-Davidson enthusiasts. The U.S. market launch of the Fisher-Price Power Wheels Harley-Davidson Lil' motorcycle, a four-wheeled, battery-operated a ride-on-toy, has become the most successful Power Wheels product introduced in the last ten years.

In 2003 HD celebrated its 100-year anniversary. Over the previous century the company managed to create a strong brand image and a loyal customer base within the market place. Much of the value of a Harley resides in its tradition – the look, sound, and heritage that has made it an all-American symbol. The bikes represent something very basic – a desire for freedom, adventure, and individualism.

HD maintains a close relationship with its customers through a variety of programs (Harley Owners Group), product offerings, and events such as the Daytona bike week, motor shows, and rallies, etc. However, the company is facing rigorous competition from Japanese manufacturers, specifically Honda and Yamaha. Harley-Davidson's strength is their brand image within the market place, but their weakness is related to production capacity and unfulfilled demand for their products. HD tries to continue to strengthen its positioning strategy by building on the 'Own an American Icon' slogan.

As its average customer's age raises, and sales go down, Harley-Davidson faces the task of attracting younger customers. Part of retooling their image includes releasing a new motorcycle, the Buell, designed for young professionals and women.

According to the Motorcycle Industry Council (**www.mic.org**), an industry trade group based in Irvine, California no one doubts that the women's market is real, although it still accounts for only 9 per cent of the total motorcycling population. In 2001, according to the Council, 10 per cent of new motorcycle buyers were women.

Pricing

The international price competition is getting tougher. Compared to similar models from Honda, Harley-Davidson has still has a 30 per cent price premium; even though Harley bikers still wear t-shirts saying 'I'd rather push a Harley than drive a Honda'.

Today, Harley's overseas business outside the USA is around 25 per cent of its annual total. Europeans like cruiser bikes, but not Harley prices. In fact some Harley bikes are believed to have been shipped back from Europe due to lack of demand. At the moment (2004), the European market share of HD in the heavyweight segment (over 650 cc) is around 7 per cent. The market leaders in Europe are Honda (20 per cent market share), Yamaha (18 per cent market share), Suzuki and BMW (each with around 15 per cent market share).

Questions

1. Describe the HD's general pricing strategy. What does the company's positioning have to do with its pricing strategy?

2. Should Harley alter its price, given strong price pressures from rivals?

3. What should HD do to improve its market share in Europe?

Sources:
www.harley-davidson.com/
www.mic.org/
www.motorcyclenewswire.com/
www.neobike.net/industry

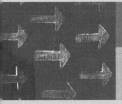

CASE STUDY 16.2   Gillette Co.

Is price standardization possible for razor blades?

The latest Gillette (**www.gillette.com**) shaving innovation, the MACH3 triple-blade shaving system, is now available in North America, western Europe, the former Soviet Union and selected markets in Asia-Pacific, eastern Europe and Latin America. Gillette extended their distribution of the MACH3 system to nearly all major world-wide markets in 1999.

This new product has further strengthened the worldwide leadership position Gillette holds in blades and razors, its principal line of business.

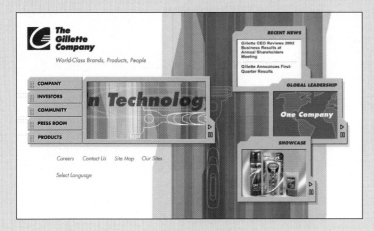

Question

1. Discuss whether it is possible for Gillette to standardize pricing across borders for their MACH3 triple-blade. Which factors would favour price standardization and which factors would favour price differentiation?

For further exercises and cases, see this book's website at
www.booksites.net/hollensen

Questions for discussion

1. What are the major causes of international price escalation? Suggest possible courses of action to deal with this problem.

2. Explain how exchange rate and inflation affect the way you price your product.

3. In order to protect themselves, how should marketers price their product in a country with high inflation?

4. International buyers and sellers of technology frequently disagree on the appropriate price for knowledge. Why?

5. What methods can be used to compute a transfer price (for transactions between affiliated companies)?

6. What relevance has the international product life cycle theory for pricing strategy in international firms?

7. Why is it often difficult to compute fair arm's-length transfer prices?

8. Explain these terms of sale: EXW, FAS, FOB, CFR, CIF, DEQ and DDP. Which factors will determine the terms of sale?

9. Explain these types of letter of credit: revocable/irrevocable, confirmed/unconfirmed. Under what sets of circumstances would exporters use the following methods of payment:
    (a) revocable letter of credit;
    (b) confirmed letter of credit;
    (c) confirmed irrevocable letter of credit;
    (d) time draft (i.e. bill of exchange)?

10. Name some of the financing sources for exporters.

11. How does inflation affect a country's currency value? Is it a good idea to borrow or obtain finance in a country with high inflation?

12. How and why are export credit financing terms and conditions relevant to international pricing?

13. What is counter-trade? Why should firms be willing to consider counter-trade arrangements in their global marketing efforts?

References

Chase Manhattan Bank (1984) *Dynamics of Trade Finance*, New York.

Czepiel, J.A. (1992) *Competitive Marketing Strategy*, Prentice-Hall, Englewood Cliffs, NJ.

Diller, H. and Bukhari, I. (1994) 'Pricing conditions in the European Common Market', *European Management Journal*, vol. 12, no. 2, pp. 163–70.

Eitman, D.K. and Stonehill, A.I. (1986) *Multinational Business Finance* (4th edn), Addison-Wesley, Reading, MA.

Fraedrich, J.P. and Bateman, C.R. (1996) 'Transfer pricing by multinational marketers: risky business', *Business Horizons*, vol. 39, no. 1, pp. 17–22.

Garda, R.A. (1995) 'Tactical pricing', in Paliwoda, S.J. and Ryans, J.K. (eds), *International Marketing Reader*, Routledge, London.

Kung, M. and Monroe, K.B. (2002) 'Pricing on the Internet', *Journal of Product & Brand Management*, vol. 11, no. 5, pp. 274–87.

Nagle, T.T. (1987) *The Strategies and Tactics of Pricing*, Prentice-Hall, Englewood Cliffs, NJ.

Narayandas, D., Quelch, J. and Swartz, G. (2000), Prepare your company for global pricing, *Sloan Management Review*, Fall, pp. 61–70.

Onkvisit, S. and Shaw, J.J. (1993) *International Marketing Analysis and Strategy* (2nd edn), Macmillan, London.

Phillips, C., Doole, I. and Lowe, R. (1994) *International Marketing Strategy: Analysis, development and implementation*, Routledge, London.

Simon, H. and Kucher, E. (1993) 'The European pricing bomb – and how to cope with it', *Marketing and Research Today*, February, pp. 25–36.

Theodosiou, M. and Katsikeas, C.S. (2001) 'Factors influencing the degree of international pricing strategy standardization of multinational corporations', *Journal of International Marketing*, vol. 9, no. 3, pp. 1–18.

Valenti, C. (1999) 'Coke denies pricing plan', ABCNEWS.com from TheStreet.com, 28 October.

Weigand, R.E. (1991) 'Buy in–follow on strategies for profit', *Sloan Management Review*, Spring, pp. 29–38.

Further reading

Abdallah, W.M. (2002) 'Global transfer pricing of multinationals and e-commerce in the twenty-first century', *Multinational Business Review*, Fall, pp. 62–71.

Bergstein, H. and Estelami, H. (2002) 'A survey of emerging technologies for pricing new-to-the-world products', *Journal of Product & Brand Management*, vol. 11, no. 5, pp. 303–18.

Dozoretz, J. and Malanovich, T. (2002) 'The deadly dynamics of price competition', *Marketing Research*, Winter, pp. 26–30.

Elliott, J. and Emmanuel, C. (2000) 'International Transfer Pricing: Searching for Patterns', *European Management Journal*, vol. 18, No. 2, pp. 216–22.

Hanlon, D. and Luery, D. (2002) 'The role of pricing research in assessing the commercial potential of new drugs in development', *International Journal of Market Research*, vol. 44, No. 4, pp. 423–47.

Iyer, G.R., Miyaazaki, A.D., Grewal, D. and Giordano, M. (2002) 'Linking Web-based segmentation to pricing tactics', *Journal of Product & Brand Management*, vol. 11, no. 5, pp. 288–302.

Monroe, K.B. and Cox. J.L. (2001) 'Pricing practices that endanger profits', *Marketing Management*, September/October, pp. 42–46.

Stöttinger, B. (2001) 'Strategic export pricing: a long and winding road', *Journal of International Marketing*, vol. 9, no. 1, pp. 40–63.

17 Distribution decisions

Contents

Learning objectives

After studying this chapter you should be able to do the following:

- Explore the determinants of channel decisions.

- Discuss the key points in putting together and managing global marketing channels.

- Discuss the factors influencing channel width (intensive, selective or exclusive coverage).

- Explain what is meant by integration of the marketing channel.

- Describe the most common export documents.

- Define and explain the main modes of transportation.

- Explain how the internationalisation of retailing affects the manufacturer.

- Define grey markets and explain how to deal with them.

17.1 Introduction

Access to international markets is a key decision area facing firms into the 2000s. In Part III we considered the firm's choice of an appropriate market entry mode that could assure the entry of a firm's products and services into a foreign market.

After the firm has chosen a strategy to get its products into foreign markets the next challenge (and the topic of this chapter: see Figure 17.1) is the distribution of the products within those foreign markets. The first part of this chapter concerns the structure and management of foreign distribution. The second part is concerned with the management of international logistics.

According to Table 17.1, distribution channels typically account for 15–40 per cent of the retail price of goods and services in an industry.

Figure 17.1 Channel decisions

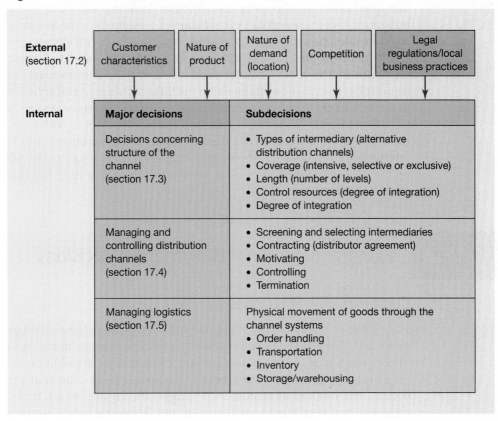

| External (section 17.2) | Customer characteristics | Nature of product | Nature of demand (location) | Competition | Legal regulations/local business practices |

Internal	**Major decisions**	**Subdecisions**
	Decisions concerning structure of the channel (section 17.3)	• Types of intermediary (alternative distribution channels) • Coverage (intensive, selective or exclusive) • Length (number of levels) • Control resources (degree of integration) • Degree of integration
	Managing and controlling distribution channels (section 17.4)	• Screening and selecting intermediaries • Contracting (distributor agreement) • Motivating • Controlling • Termination
	Managing logistics (section 17.5)	Physical movement of goods through the channel systems • Order handling • Transportation • Inventory • Storage/warehousing

Table 17.1 Value added in the vertical chain (% of retail price, estimated)

Actor in the vertical chain	Cars	Software	Petrol	Laser printers	Packaged goods
Supplier of raw materials/components	45	10	53	40	26
Manufacturer of finished goods	40	65	19	30	33
Distribution channel	15	25	28	30	41
Total	100	100	100	100	100

Source: Bucklin *et al.*, 1996, p. 106. The figures in the table are based on research conducted by, among others, the Economist Intelligence Unity and McKinsey.

Over the next few years the challenges and opportunities for channel management will multiply, as technological developments accelerate channel evolution. Data networks are increasingly enabling end users to bypass traditional channels and deal directly with manufacturers and service providers.

Electronic data interchange is now used for the exchange of orders and invoices between suppliers and their customers. By online monitoring of stocks customers are also able to order directly from suppliers on a just-in-time basis, and thereby to avoid holding stock altogether or to minimise the time it is held.

At the same time new channels are continuing to emerge in one industry after another, opening up opportunities for companies to cut costs or improve their effectiveness in reaching specific market segments. Catalogue retailing, telephone ordering, cable TV shopping and Internet ordering are all becoming increasingly important to consumer goods manufacturers. Despite the scale and importance of these opportunities, however, few companies manage to take full advantage of them.

The following presents a systematic approach to the major decisions in international distribution. The main channel decisions and their determinants are illustrated in Figure 17.1. Distribution channels are the links between producers and final customers. In general terms, an international marketer distributes either directly or indirectly. As we saw in Chapter 10, direct distribution amounts to dealing with a foreign firm, while the indirect method means dealing with another home country firm that serves as an intermediary. Figure 17.1 shows that the choice of a particular channel link will be strongly influenced by various characteristics of the host markets. We will now consider these in more detail.

17.2 External determinants of channel decisions

Customer characteristics

The customer, or final consumer, is the keystone in any channel design. Thus the size, geographic distribution, shopping habits, outlet preferences and usage patterns of customer groups must be taken into account when making distribution decisions.

Consumer product channels tend to be longer than industrial product channels because the number of customers is greater, the customers are more geographically dispersed, and they buy in smaller quantities. Shopping habits, outlet preferences and usage patterns vary considerably from country to country and are strongly influenced by sociocultural factors.

Nature of product

Product characteristics play a key role in determining distribution strategy. For low-priced, high-turnover convenience products, the requirement is an intensive distribution network. On the other hand it is not necessary or even desirable for a prestigious product to have wide distribution. In this situation a manufacturer can shorten and narrow its distribution channel. Consumers are likely to do some comparison shopping and will actively seek information about all brands under consideration. In such cases limited product exposure is not an impediment to market success.

Transportation and warehousing costs of the product are also critical issues in the distribution and sale of industrial goods such as bulk chemicals, metals and cement. Direct selling, servicing and repair, and spare parts warehousing dominate the distribution of such industrial products as computers, machinery and aircraft. The product's durability, ease of adulteration, amount and type of customer service required, unit costs and special handling requirements (such as cold storage) are also significant factors.

Nature of demand/location

The perceptions that the target customers hold about particular products can force modification of distribution channels. Product perceptions are influenced by the customer's income and product experience, the product's end use, its life cycle position and the country's stage of economic development.

The geography of a country and the development of its transportation infrastructure can also affect the channel decision.

Competition

The channels used by competing products and close substitutes are important because channel arrangements that seek to serve the same market often compete with one another. Consumers generally expect to find particular products in particular outlets (e.g. speciality stores), or they have become accustomed to buying particular products from particular sources. In addition, local and global competitors may have agreements with the major wholesalers in a foreign country that effectively create barriers and exclude the company from key channels.

Sometimes the alternative is to use a distribution approach totally different from that of the competition and hope to develop a competitive advantage.

Legal regulations/local business practices

A country may have specific laws that rule out the use of particular channels or intermediaries. For example, until recently all alcoholic beverages in Sweden and Finland had to be distributed through state-owned outlets. Other countries prohibit the use of door-to-door selling. Channel coverage can also be affected by law. In general, exclusive representation may be viewed as a restraint of trade, especially if the product has a dominant market position. EU antitrust authorities have increased their scrutiny of exclusive sales agreements. The Treaty of Rome prohibits distribution agreements (e.g. grants of exclusivity) that affect trade or restrict competition.

Furthermore, local business practices can interfere with efficiency and productivity and may force a manufacturer to employ a channel of distribution that is longer and wider than desired. Because of Japan's multitiered distribution system, which relies on numerous layers of intermediaries, foreign companies have long considered the complex Japanese distribution system as the most effective non-tariff barrier to the Japanese market.

Exhibit 17.1 shows how the Japanese distribution system differs from its counterparts in the United States and Europe.

Exhibit 17.1	The distribution system in Japan

The distribution network in Japan has more wholesalers and retailers per capita than any other industrial nation (Onkvisit and Shaw, 1993, p. 598). Figure 17.2 illustrates the difference between shorter US channels and the long and complex Japanese channels.

A consequence of the more complex Japanese distribution system is the considerable price escalation from producer to consumer, as shown in Figure 17.3. (The principle behind price escalation is shown in Table 16.1.)

The first transaction in Figure 17.3, from producer to wholesaler, is a *vertical* exchange, whereas the next transaction (from one wholesaler to another) is a *horizontal* exchange. Small Japanese distributors often lack adequate inventory to serve another distributor at the same vertical level (i.e. horizontal exchange). According to economic criteria, the Japanese distribution system would seem to be inefficient, resulting in higher consumer prices.

However, the complex Japanese distribution system exists to serve social as well as economic purposes. Channel members are like family members and their relationships to each other are tightly interlocked by tradition and emotion. Because of these social considerations inefficient channel members are sometimes retained and tolerated in order to maintain employment and income flows. For example, one of the primary concerns of Japanese channel managers is to help other channel members preserve their dignity. Going out of business is viewed as disgraceful, so stronger channel members (typically producers) must often support weak distributors. The Japanese system is often seen as a trade barrier by western firms, but it is likely that these foreign firms have merely failed to understand the system.

Sources: Cateora (1993); Onkvisit and Shaw (1993); Pirog and Lancioni (1997).

Figure 17.2 Comparison of distribution channels in car parts between Japan and the USA

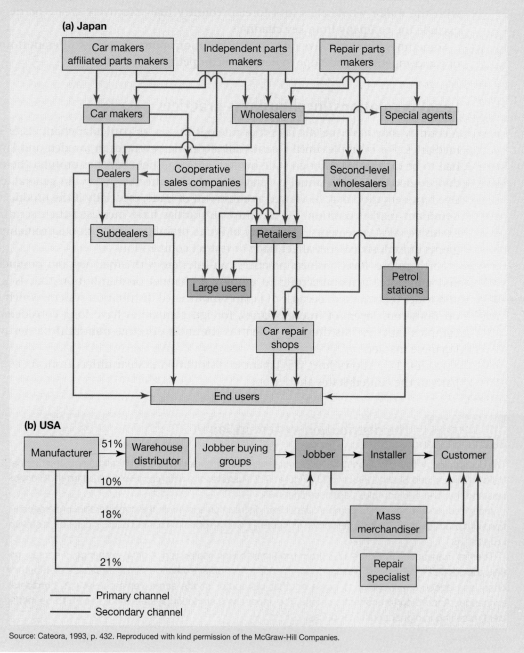

Source: Cateora, 1993, p. 432. Reproduced with kind permission of the McGraw-Hill Companies.

Figure 17.3 A hypothetical channel sequence in the Japanese consumer market

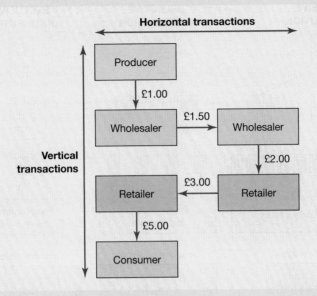

Source: Pirog and Lancioni, 1997, p. 57. Adapted with kind permission from *International Journal of Physical Distribution and Logistics Management*, MCB University Press; http://www.mcb.co.uk

Let us now return to the major decisions concerning the structure of the distribution channel (Figure 17.1).

17.3   The structure of the channel

Market coverage

The amount of market coverage that a channel member provides is important. Coverage is a flexible term. It can refer to geographical areas of a country (such as cities and major towns) or the number of retail outlets (as a percentage of all retail outlets). Regardless of the market coverage measure(s) used the company has to create a distribution network (dealers, distributors and retailers) to meet its coverage goals.

As shown in Figure 17.4, three different approaches are available:

- *Intensive coverage*. This calls for distributing the product through the largest number of different types of intermediary and the largest number of individual intermediaries of each type.
- *Selective coverage*. This entails choosing a number of intermediaries for each area to be penetrated.
- *Exclusive coverage*. This involves choosing only one intermediary in a market.

Channel coverage (width) can be identified along a continuum ranging from wide channels (intensive distribution) to narrow channels (exclusive distribution). Figure 17.5 illustrates some factors favouring intensive, selective and exclusive distribution.

Figure 17.4 Three strategies for market coverage

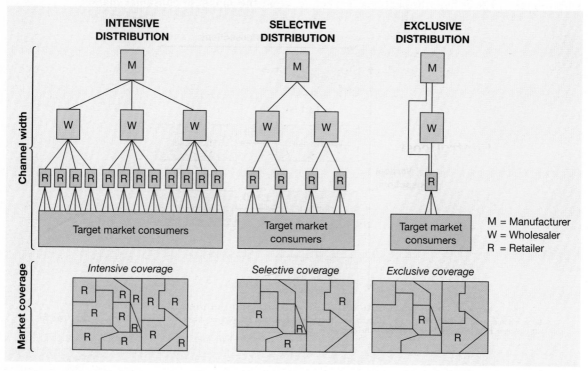

Source: Lewison, 1996, p. 271.

Figure 17.5 Factors influencing channel width

		Channel width		
		Intensive distribution ⟷	Selective distribution ⟷	Exclusive distribution
Factor	Product type	Convenience products	⟷	Speciality products
	Product life cycle stage	Mature products	⟷	New products
	Product price	Low-price products	⟷	High-price products
	Brand loyalty	Brand-preferred products	⟷	Brand-insisted products
	Purchase frequency	Frequently purchased products	⟷	Infrequently purchased products
	Product uniqueness	Common products	⟷	Distinctive products
	Selling requirement	Self-service products	⟷	Personal-selling products
	Technical complexity	Non-technical products	⟷	Technical products
	Service requirements	Limited-service products	⟷	Extensive-service products

Source: adapted from Lewison, 1996, p. 279

Channel length

This is determined by the number of levels or different types of intermediaries. Longer channels, those with several intermediaries, tend to be associated with convenience goods and mass distribution. As seen in Exhibit 17.1, Japan has longer channels for convenience goods because of the historical development of its system. One implication is that prices increase considerably for the final consumer (price escalation: see section 16.3).

Control/cost

The 'control' of one member in the vertical distribution channel means its ability to influence the decisions and actions of other channel members. Channel control is of critical concern to international marketers wanting to establish international brands and a consistent image of quality and service worldwide.

The company must decide how much control it wants to have over how each of its products is marketed. The answer is partly determined by the strategic role assigned to each market. It is also a function of the types of channel member available, the regulations and rules governing distribution activity in each foreign market, and to some extent the roles traditionally assigned to channel members.

Normally a high degree of control is provided by the use of the firm's own sales force in international markets. The use of intermediaries will automatically lead to loss of some control over the marketing of the firm's products.

An intermediary typically performs certain functions:

- carrying of inventory;
- demand generation, or selling;
- physical distribution;
- after-sales service;
- extending credit to customers.

In getting its products to end-user markets a manufacturer must either assume all of these functions or shift some or all of them to intermediaries. As the old saying goes, 'You can eliminate the intermediary, but not the functions of the intermediary.'

In most marketing situations there is a trade-off between a producer's ability to control important channel functions and the financial resources required to exercise that control. The more intermediaries involved in getting a supplier's product to user customers, the less control the supplier can generally exercise over the flow of its product through the channel and the way it is presented to customers. On the other hand, reducing the length and breadth of the distribution channel usually requires that the supplier perform more functions itself. In turn this requires the supplier to allocate more financial resources to activities such as warehousing, shipping, credit, field selling or field service.

In summary, the decision to use an intermediary or to distribute via a company-owned sales force requires a major trade-off between the desire to control global marketing efforts and the desire to minimise resource commitment costs.

Degree of integration

Control can also be exercised through integration. Channel integration is the process of incorporating all channel members into one channel system and uniting them under one leadership and one set of goals. There are two different types of integration:

- *vertical integration*: seeking control of channel members at different levels of the channel;
- *horizontal integration*: seeking control of channel members at the same level of the channel (i.e. competitors).

Integration is achieved either through acquisitions (ownership) or through tight cooperative relationships. Getting channel members to work together for their own mutual benefit can be a difficult task. However, today cooperative relationships are essential for efficient and effective channel operation.

Figure 17.6 shows an example of vertical integration.

Figure 17.6 Vertical integration

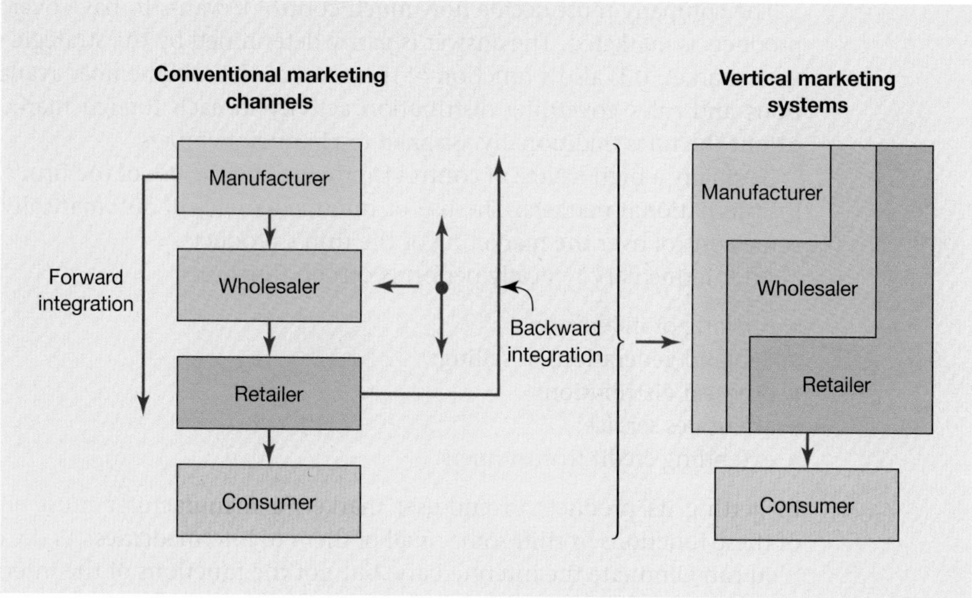

The starting point in Figure 17.6 is the conventional marketing channels, where the channel composition consists of isolated and autonomous participating channel members. Channel coordination is here achieved through arm's-length bargaining. At this point, the vertical integration can take two forms – forward and backward.

- The manufacturer can make forward integration when it seeks control of businesses of the wholesale and retail levels of the channel.
- The retailer can make backward integration, seeking control of businesses at wholesale and manufacturer levels of the channel.
- The wholesaler has two possibilities: both forward and backward integration.

The result of these manoeuvres is the vertical marketing system (Figure 17.6). Here the channel composition consists of integrated participating members, where channel stability is high due to assured member loyalty and long-term commitments.

17.4 | Managing and controlling distribution channels

Once the basic design of the channel has been determined the international marketer must begin to fill it with the best available candidates, and must secure their cooperation.

Screening and selecting intermediaries

At this stage the international marketer knows the type of distributor that is needed. The potential candidates must now be compared and contrasted against determining criteria.

The example in Table 17.2 uses 13 criteria for screening potential channel members. The criteria to be used depend on the nature of a firm's business and its distribution objectives in given markets. The list of criteria should correspond closely to the

Table 17.2 **Examples of distributor (dealer) selection criteria**

Criteria (no ranking implied)	Weight	Distributor 1 Rating	Distributor 1 Score	Distributor 2 Rating	Distributor 2 Score	Distributor 3 Rating	Distributor 3 Score
Financial soundness and depth of channel member	4	5	20	4	16	3	12
Marketing management expertise and sophistication	5	4	20	3	15	2	10
Satisfactory trade, customer relations and contacts	3	4	12	3	9	3	9
Capability to provide adequate sales coverage	4	3	12	3	12	3	12
Overall positive reputation and image as a company	3	5	15	4	12	4	12
Product compatibility (synergy or conflict?)	3	3	9	4	12	4	12
Pertinent technical know-how at staff level	—	—	—	—	—	—	—
Adequate technical facilities and service support	—	—	—	—	—	—	—
Adequate infrastructure in staff and facilities	1	5	5	3	3	3	3
Proven performance record with client companies	2	4	8	3	6	3	6
Positive attitude towards the company's products	1	3	3	3	3	3	3
Mature outlook regarding the company's inevitable progression in market management	1	3	3	3	3	3	3
Excellent government relations	1	4	4	3	3	3	3
Score			**111**		**94**		**85**

Scales:

Rating	Weighting	Rating	Weighting
5 Outstanding	5 Critical success factor	2 Below average	2 Of some importance
4 Above average	4 Prerequisite success factor	1 Unsatisfactory	1 Standard
3 Average	3 Important success factor		

Source: Global Marketing Management: A Strategic Perspective 2/E by Toyne/Walters, Copyright 1993. Reprinted by permission of Pearson Education, Inc., Upper Saddle River, NJ.

marketer's own determinants of success – all the things that are important to beating the competition.

The hypothetical consumer packaged goods company used in Table 17.2 considered the distributor's marketing management expertise and financial soundness to be of greatest importance. These indicators will show whether the distributor is making money and is able to perform some of the necessary marketing functions such as extension of credit to customers and risk absorption. Financial reports are not always complete or reliable, or may lend themselves to differences of interpretation, pointing to the need for a third-party opinion. In the example, Distributor 1 would be selected by the company.

Alternatively, an industrial goods company may consider the distributor's product compatibility, technical know-how and technical facilities and service support of high importance, and the distributor's infrastructure, client performance and attitude towards its products of low importance. Quite often global marketers find that the most desirable distributors in a given market are already handling competitive products and are therefore unavailable.

A high-tech consumer goods company, on the other hand, may favour financial soundness, marketing management expertise, reputation, technical know-how, technical facilities, service support and government relations. In some countries religious or ethnic differences might make an agent suitable for one part of the market coverage but unsuitable for another. This can result in more channel members being required in order to give adequate market coverage.

Contracting (distributor agreements)

When the international marketer has found a suitable intermediary a foreign sales agreement is drawn up. Before final contractual arrangements are made it is wise to make personal visits to the prospective channel member. The agreement itself can be relatively simple but, given the numerous differences in the market environments, certain elements are essential. These are listed in Table 17.3.

The long-term commitments involved in distribution channels can become particularly difficult if the contract between the company and the channel member is not carefully drafted. It is normal to prescribe a time limit and a minimum sales level to be achieved, in addition to the particular responsibilities of each party. If this is not carried

---

Table 17.3 Items to include in an agreement with a foreign intermediary (distributor)

- Names and addresses of both parties.
- Date when the agreement goes into effect.
- Duration of the agreement.
- Provisions for extending or terminating the agreement.
- Description of sales territory.
- Establishment of discount and/or commission schedules and determination of when and how paid.
- Provisions for revising the commission or discount schedules.
- Establishment of a policy governing resale prices.
- Maintenance of appropriate service facilities.
- Restrictions to prohibit the manufacture and sale of similar and competitive products.
- Designation of responsibility for patent and trade mark negotiations and/or pricing.
- The assignability or non-assignability of the agreement and any limiting factors.
- Designation of the country and state (if applicable) of contract jurisdiction in the case of dispute.

---

out satisfactorily the company may be stuck with a weak performer that either cannot be removed or is very costly to buy out from the contract.

Contract duration is important, especially when an agreement is signed with a new distributor. In general, distribution agreements should be for a specified, relatively short period (one or two years). The initial contract with a new distributor should stipulate a trial period of either three or six months, possibly with minimum purchase requirements. Duration is also dependent on the local laws and their stipulations on distributor agreements.

Geographic boundaries for the distributor should be determined with care, especially by smaller firms. Future expansion of the product market might be complicated if a distributor claims rights to certain territories. The marketer should retain the right to distribute products independently, reserving the right to certain customers.

The *payment section* of the contract should stipulate the methods of payment as well as how the distributor or agent is to draw compensation. Distributors derive compensation from various discounts, such as the functional discount, whereas agents earn a specific commission percentage of net sales (typically 10–20 per cent). Given the volatility of currency markets the agreement should also state the currency to be used.

Product and conditions of sale need to be agreed on. The products or product lines included should be stipulated, as well as the functions and responsibilities of the intermediary in terms of carrying the goods in inventory, providing service in conjunction with them, and promoting them. Conditions of sale determine which party is to be responsible for some of the expenses (e.g. marketing expenses) involved, which will in turn have an effect on the price to the distributor. These conditions include credit and shipment terms.

Means of communication between the parties must be stipulated in the agreement if a marketer–distributor relationship is to succeed. The marketer should have access to all information concerning the marketing of its products in the distributor's territory, including past records, present situation assessments and marketing research.

Motivating

Geographic and cultural distance make the process of motivating channel members difficult. Motivating is also difficult because intermediaries are not owned by the company. Since intermediaries are independent firms they will seek to achieve their own objectives, which will not always match the objective of the manufacturer. The international marketer may offer both monetary and psychological rewards. Intermediaries will be strongly influenced by the earnings potential of the product. If the trade margin is poor and sales are difficult to achieve intermediaries will lose interest in the product. They will concentrate upon products with a more rewarding response to selling efforts, since they make their sales and profits from their own assortment of products and services from different companies.

It is important to keep in regular contact with agents and distributors. A consistent flow of all relevant types of communication will stimulate interest and sales performance. The international marketer may place one person in charge of distributor-related communications and put into effect an exchange of personnel so that both organizations gain further insight into the workings of the other.

Controlling

Control problems are reduced substantially if intermediaries are selected carefully. However, control should be sought through the common development of written performance objectives. These performance objectives might include some of the following: sales turnover per year, market share growth rate, introduction of new products, price charged and marketing communications support. Control should be exercised through periodic personal meetings.

Evaluation of performance has to be done against the changing environment. In some situations economic recession or fierce competition activity prevents the possibility of objectives being met. However, if poor performance is established, the contract between the company and the channel member will have to be reconsidered and perhaps terminated.

Termination

Typical reasons for the termination of a channel relationship are as follows:

- The international marketer has established a sales subsidiary in the country.
- The international marketer is unsatisfied with the performance of the intermediary.

Open communication is always needed to make the transition smooth. For example, the intermediary can be compensated for investments made, and major customers can be visited jointly to assure them that service will be uninterrupted.

Termination conditions are among the most important considerations in the distribution agreement. The causes of termination vary and the penalties for the international marketer may be substantial. It is especially important to find out what local laws say about termination and to check what type of experience other firms have had in the particular country.

In some countries terminating an ineffective intermediary can be time consuming and expensive. In the European Union one year's average commissions are typical for termination without justification. A notice of termination has to be given three to six months in advance. If the cause for termination is the manufacturer's establishment of a local sales subsidiary, then the international marketer may consider engaging good employees from the intermediary as, for example, managers in the new sales subsidiary. This can prevent a loss of product know-how that has been created at the intermediary's firm. The international marketer could also consider an acquisition of this firm if the intermediary is willing to sell.

17.5 Managing logistics

Logistics is used as a term to describe the movement of goods and services between supplier(s) and end users.

Two major phases in the movement of materials are of logistical importance. The first phase is *materials management*, or the timely movement of raw materials, parts and supplies into and through the firm. The second phase is *physical distribution*, or the movement of the firm's finished product to its customers. The basic goal of logistics management is the effective coordination of both phases and their various components to result in maximum cost effectiveness while maintaining service goals and requirements.

The primary area of concern in this section is the second phase: that is, order handling, transportation, inventory and storage/warehousing.

Order handling

The general procedure for order handling, shipment and payment is shown in Figure 17.7:

1. The sale

   Importer makes enquiry of potential supplier.
   Exporter sends catalogues and price list.
   Importer requests pro-forma invoice (price quote).
   Exporter sends pro-forma invoice.
   Importer sends purchase order.
   Exporter receives purchase order.

2. Importer arranges financing through its bank.
3. Importer's bank sends letter of credit (most frequently used form of payment).
4. Exporter's bank notifies exporter that letter of credit is received.
5. Exporter produces or acquires goods.
6. Exporter arranges transportation and documentation (obtained by exporter or through freight forwarding company).

   Space reserved on ship or aircraft.
   Documents acquired or produced, as required:
   (a) exporter's licence;
   (b) shipper's export declaration;
   (c) commercial invoice;
   (d) bills of lading;
   (e) marine insurance certificate;
   (f) consular invoice;
   (g) certificate of origin;
   (h) inspection certificates;
   (i) dock receipts.

Figure 17.7 The export procedure

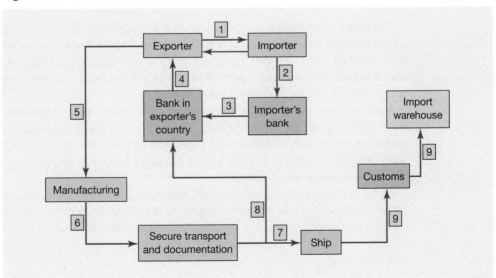

Source: Albaum *et al.*, 1994, p. 419.

7. Exporter ships goods to importer.
8. Exporter presents documents to bank for payment.
9. Importer has goods cleared through customs and delivered to its warehouse.
   Source: Albaum *et al.*, 1994, p. 419.

Most common export documents

This section is drawn from Albaum *et al.* (1994), p. 440.

Transportation documents

- *Bill of lading.* This is a receipt for the cargo and a contract for transportation between a shipper and a transport carrier. It may also be used as an instrument of ownership.
- *Dock receipt.* This is the document acknowledging receipt of the cargo by an ocean carrier.
- *Insurance certificate.* This is evidence that insurance is provided to cover loss or damage to the cargo while in transit.

Banking documents

- *Letter of credit.* This is a financial document issued by a bank at the request of the importer, guaranteeing payment to the exporter if certain terms and conditions surrounding a transaction are met.

Commercial documents

- *Commercial invoice.* This is a bill for the products from the exporter to the buyer.

Government documents

- *Export declaration.* This includes complete information about the shipment.
- *Consular invoice.* This is a document signed by a consul of the importing country that is used to control and identify goods shipped there.
- *Certificate of origin.* This is a document certifying the origin of products being exported, so that the buying country knows in which country the products were produced.

The enquiry or order for products and/or services may be unsolicited or the result of a firm's efforts (the manufacturer or the agent). When the actual order is received the international marketer will normally send a confirmation of receipt, followed by a commitment to fulfil the order if all of the terms and payment arrangements are acceptable for the international marketer.

A pro-forma invoice may be prepared by the exporter to indicate the terms that have been agreed upon (or are proposed). The pro-forma invoice normally shows the type and amount of merchandise, unit costs and extensions, expected weights and measures, and often other terms (including payment terms). If accepted by the prospective buyer it may serve as a contract.

Order cycles are shortened by rapid processing of orders, and the role of communications technology (such as electronic data interchange) is critical in reducing the time factor. Few countries have efficient and reliable communication systems; however, possessing an efficient international order-processing system would give a firm a competitive advantage.

Transportation

This deals primarily with the mode of transport, which usually constitutes 10–15 per cent of the retail costs of imported goods. There are four main modes of transport: road, water, air and rail.

Road

Roads are very efficient for short hauls of high-value goods, being very flexible in route and time. Goods can be delivered direct to customers' premises. However, restrictions at border controls can be time consuming, and long distances and the need for sea crossings reduce the attractiveness of freight transport by road. In some parts of the world, particularly in LDCs, road surfaces are poor.

Water

Water transportation is a key mode for international freight movements because it provides a very low-cost way to transport bulky products such as coal and oil. However, water transport is slow and is subject to difficulties caused by the weather – for example, some ports are iced over for part of the winter. Water transport usually needs to be combined with other modes of transport to achieve door-to-door delivery.

Increasingly nations have begun to recognise the importance of appropriate port structures and are developing such facilities in spite of the heavy investment necessary. If such investments are accompanied by concurrent changes in the overall infrastructure transportation efficiency should, in the long run, more than recoup the original investment.

Air

Air freight is available to and from most countries. There has been a tremendous growth in international air freight over recent decades. Air freight is considerably more expensive per tonne/kilometre than the other modes of transport. It accounts for less than 1 per cent of the total volume of international transport, but represents more than 20 per cent of the value shipped by industrialized countries (Sletmo and Picard, 1984). High-value items are more likely to be shipped by air, particularly if they have a high weight-to-volume ratio.

Rail

Rail services provide a very good method of transporting bulky goods over long distances. The increasing use of containers provides a flexible means to use rail and road modes, with minimal load transfer times and costs. High-speed trains are also emerging in Europe and the United States as attractive alternatives. For example, in Europe trains travelling at 190 miles per hour have cut the travel time between major European cities.

The decision about which transportation mode to use is affected by a number of factors, including the following:

- cost of different transport alternatives;
- distance to the location;
- nature of the product;
- frequency of the shipment;
- value of the shipment;
- availability of transport.

The level of economic development is a major determinant of the availability of transportation – in some markets air freight is highly developed compared to rail transportation.

Freight forwarders

Freight forwarders provide an important service to exporters. The full-service foreign freight forwarder can relieve the producer of most of the burdens of distribution across national borders. This is particularly so for small and medium-sized companies and those that are inexperienced in exporting. Freight forwarders provide a wide range of services, but the general activities and services are as follows:

- coordination of transport services;
- preparation and processing of international transport documents;
- provision of warehousing;
- expert advice.

The traditional view of the freight forwarder is that of a provider of services, a company that does not own transport facilities but which buys from the most appropriate transport provider, and a company that acts as the agent of the exporter. Various changes have taken place that have impacted upon freight forwarders. There has been a tendency for transport companies to extend their activities to include an in-house forwarding function. In addition, larger and more experienced exporters have developed their own in-house transport and documentation expertise. Both these trends have threatened the freight forwarder.

Inventory (at the factory base)

The purpose of establishing inventory – to maintain product movement in the delivery pipeline, in order to satisfy demand – is the same for domestic and international inventory systems.

There are many different cost elements involved in managing an inventory: storage, interest on capital tied up, taxes, lost sales, etc. Since these costs may sometimes be sizeable management must be concerned about inventory control. This involves determining the proper level of inventory to hold so that a balance is maintained between customer service and inventory cost.

In deciding the level of inventory to be maintained the international marketer must consider two factors:

1. *Order cycle time*: the total time that passes between the placement of an order by a customer and the receipt of the goods. Depending on the choice of transportation mode, delivery times may vary considerably. As a result the marketer has to keep larger safety stock in order to be able to satisfy demand in any circumstance. However, the marketer could attempt to reduce order cycle time, thereby reducing costs, by altering transportation method, changing inventory locations or shifting order placement to direct computer-order entry (EDI).
2. *Customer service levels*: the ability to fulfil customer orders within a certain time. For example, if within three days 80 per cent of the orders can be fulfilled, the customer service level is 80 per cent. The choice of customer service level for the firm has a major impact on the inventories needed. Because high customer service levels are costly (inventory constitutes tied-up capital) the goal should not be the highest level possible but rather an acceptable level, based on customer expectations. For some

products customers may not demand or expect quick delivery. In addition, if higher customer service levels result in higher prices, this may reduce the competitiveness of a firm's product.

Besides these two factors, international inventories can also be used as a strategic tool in dealing with currency valuation changes or hedging against inflation.

Storage/warehousing (in foreign markets)

Sometimes goods and materials need to be stored in the export markets. However, this activity involves more than just storage. In addition to storing products in anticipation of consumer demand warehousing encompasses a broad range of other activities, such as assembling, breaking bulk shipments into smaller sizes to meet customer needs, and preparing products for reshipment.

Warehousing decisions focus on three main issues:

1. where the firm's customers are geographically located;
2. the pattern of existing and future demands;
3. the customer service level required (i.e. how quickly a customer's order should be fulfilled).

The following general observations can be made about warehousing facilities:

- If products need to be delivered quickly storage facilities will be required near the customer.
- For high-value products (e.g. computer software) the location of the warehouse will be of minimal importance as these lightweight products can be air freighted.

Exhibit 17.2	How Bosch–Siemens improved customer service and reduced costs by closing warehouses

Bosch-Siemens (BS) is a leading European manufacturer of consumer white goods, with handsome market shares in Germany, Scandinavia, Spain and Greece. Recently the company decided to reduce the number of its European warehouses from 36 to 10. BS aimed to cut costs and reduce the amount of stock it held. The company also wanted to improve its distribution, enhance customer service and reform its logistics structure to boost its share in other markets, particularly the United Kingdom and France.

The process of continent-wide rationalisation took three years to plan. BS fixed on 10 sites as its current optimum, based on effective delivery criteria. It wanted to be able to reach customers within 24–48 hours. On the other hand, the optimum size of a warehouse in terms of cost is 20,000–30,000 sq m. Hence BS arrived at 10 as its optimum number of warehouses in Europe. These are shown in Figure 17.8.

BS seeks to serve several territories from each warehouse. Thus, for example, it has a warehouse in Sweden that also covers Norway and Finland; and its south German warehouse supplies Luxembourg, Austria and parts of France.

By cutting warehouses it has reduced total distribution and warehousing costs, brought down staff numbers, holds fewer items of stock, provides greater access to regional markets, makes better use of transport networks and has improved service to customers.

The financial benefit is a saving of DM30 million a year, or a reduction of 21 per cent in total logistics costs. BS has also achieved greater flexibility in the use of transport systems such as rail and waterways. It has brought stock numbers down from 1 million items to 700,000.

Source: EIU (1995).

Figure 17.8 Bosch-Siemens' European distribution centres

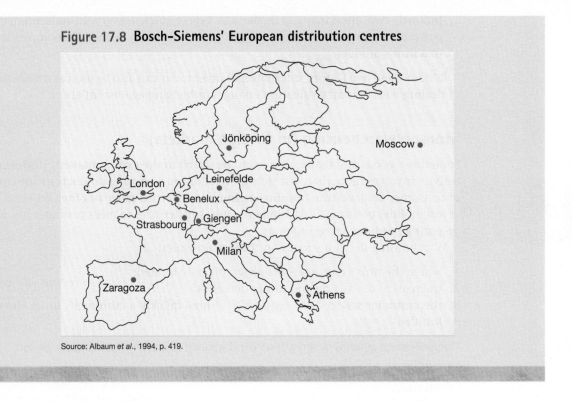

Source: Albaum et al., 1994, p. 419.

Packaging

A good balance needs to be achieved between the high costs of the substantial export packing required to eliminate all damage and the price and profit implications that this has for the customer and the exporter.

Export packing has been modified over the years from wooden crates. Different countries have different regulations about what materials are acceptable. One example of this is the recycling of containers for reuse, which requires a system for deposits and returns into the distribution channels. In addition, export packing influences customer satisfaction through its appearance and its appropriateness to minimise handling costs for the customer.

During recent years packaging has been simplified by palletisation. Computer software is now available from packaging suppliers that can design individual product packaging to maximise the number of units per pallet, and thus per container load. Palletisation with shrink-wrap protection, together with containerisation, has served both to protect goods against damage and to diminish losses through theft.

Third-party logistics (contract logistics)

A growing preference among international firms is to employ outside logistical expertise. The main thrust behind the idea is that individual firms are experts in their industry and should therefore concentrate only on their operations. Third-party logistics providers, on the other hand, are experts solely at logistics, with the knowledge and means to perform efficient and innovative services for those companies in need. The goal is improved service at equal or lower cost.

One of the greatest benefits of contracting out the logistics function in a foreign market is the ability to take advantage of an in-place network complete with resources and experience. The local expertise and image are crucial when a business is just starting up.

One of the main arguments levelled against contract logistics is the loss of the firm's control in the supply chain. Yet contract logistics does not and should not require the handing over of control. Rather, it offers concentration on one's core competence, a division of labour. The control and responsibility towards the customer remain with the firm, even though operations may move to a highly trained outside organization.

17.6	Implications of the Internet/e-commerce for distribution decisions

The Internet has the power to change drastically the balance of power among consumers, retailers, distributors, manufacturers and service providers. Some participants in the distribution chain may experience an increase in their power and profitability. Others will experience the reverse; some may even find that they have been bypassed and have lost their market share.

Physical distributors and dealers of goods and services that are more conveniently ordered and/or delivered online are indeed subject to increasing pressure from e-commerce. This *disintermediation* process, with increasing direct sales through the Internet, leads manufacturers to compete with their resellers, which results in *channel conflict*. The extent to which these effects are salient depends upon which of the following *four Internet distribution strategies* are adopted by the manufacturer.

1. Present only product information on the Internet

As less than 5 per cent of retail sales (in both Europe and the United States) presently occur over the Internet, only a few manufacturers would be willing to endanger their relationships with their distributors for that volume. The risk of conflicts with the existing distributors would be too great. So manufacturers may decide not to sell their products through the Internet and also prohibit their resellers from using the Internet for sales. Only product information is provided on the Internet, with any customer queries being passed on to the appropriate channel member. In industries such as aircraft manufacturing, where sales are large, complex and customised, this may be an appropriate strategy.

2. Leave Internet business to resellers

Some companies prefer distributors to leave the Internet business for resales and not to sell directly through the Internet. How effective this strategy is depends on the existing distribution structure. It can be effective when manufacturers assign exclusive territories to resellers, since resellers can be restricted to either delivering only to customers within their assigned territory or they can be compensated through profit pass-over agreements if they are adversely affected. Any leads generated by the manufacturer's website are passed on to the appropriate regional reseller.

By contrast, for intensively distributed products where resellers have no assigned territories, resellers simply compete with each other as they would do in the normal, physical marketplace. The global nature of the Internet creates price transparency, which may conflict with differential prices charged by the manufacturer in various markets. Another limitation of this approach is that most consumers search for manufacturers' websites rather than resellers' websites. Inability to purchase from the manufacturer's website can be frustrating for the consumer and can result in lost sales for the manufacturer.

3. Leave Internet business to the manufacturer only

A third strategy for the manufacturer is to restrict Internet sales exclusively to itself. This strategy is only profitable if the manufacturer has a business model that is aligned with sales through the Internet. The business system of most manufacturers (such as consumer packaged goods companies) is not set up for sales to end users who place numerous small orders. Alternatively, by selling through the Internet a manufacturer may aim not to generate profits, but rather to learn about this new channel of distribution, collect information on consumers or build its brand. But regardless of a manufacturer's objectives resellers dislike having to yield the market space to manufacturers.

If the manufacturer uses this strategy it also risks channel conflicts, i.e. creating competition with its own customers (distributors). The PC manufacturer Compaq realised this when it struggled to exploit the Internet, because to do so properly would mean bypassing its distributors. For Compaq it was difficult to remit sales through the Internet without upsetting their distributors and jeopardising their historically strong relationships with them. In order to limit the direct competition with its customers Compaq introduced a differentiated product line of PCs, Prosignia, for sales through the Internet (Kumar, 1999).

4. Open Internet business to everybody

The fourth strategy is to let the market decide the winners and open the Internet to everybody – for direct sales and resellers. Manufacturers who have ventured online, either through the third or the fourth strategy, usually sell at retail prices and/or provide only a limited line because of their desire not to compete with their resales. However, this limits the attractiveness of the Internet's value proposition.

Conclusion

The fear of cannibalising existing distribution channels and potential channel conflict requires manufacturers to trade off existing sales through the traditional distribution network and potential future sales through the Internet. Unfortunately, history suggests that most companies tend to stay with declining distribution networks for too long.

17.7   Special issue 1: International retailing

In the continuing integration of the world economy, internationalization not only concerns advertising, banking and manufacturing industries, it also affects the retailing business. The trend in all industrialised countries is towards larger units and more self-service. The number of retail outlets is dwindling, but the average size is increasing.

However, retailing still shows great differences between countries, reflecting their different histories, geography, culture and economic development. The cultural importance attached to food in Italy provides an opportunity for small specialist food retailers to survive and prosper. In other developed countries, such as the United States, the trend is towards very large superstores that incorporate a wide range of speciality foods. The Italian approach relies on small-scale production by the retail proprietor. The US approach encourages mass production, branding and sophisticated distribution systems to handle inventory and freshness issues.

A consequence of the greater economies of scale and efficiency in US retailing is that the United States tends to have larger retail outlets and a smaller number per capita than other developed countries. Some industrialised countries do not have an extensive modern retail sector. Among them are Japan, France and Italy. Japan has more retail outlets than the United States with only half the population (Jain, 1996, p. 536).

Legislation

A major reason for the lack of growth of large-scale retailing in these countries is legislation. Compared to the United States, retailing in Europe and to some extent Japan is subject to rather stringent legislation. In order to protect the independent retailer in town centres legislation primarily targets competition, new shops, and days and hours of opening.

Legislative conditions differ across Europe. In the United Kingdom legislation is liberal, which explains the rapid development of large supermarkets in the 1980s and large specialised stores in the 1990s. In Italy, where legislation is much stricter, the opening of department stores and hypermarkets has been limited.

Legislation can hamper the development of some forms of retailing. Though France was one of the creators of the hypermarket (a giant market), the country passed a law regulating the establishment or expansion of retail stores in 1973. The effect of this law and similar laws in Italy is to allow existing retailers to protest against the establishment of any new, large-scale retailers in their area.

Internationalization of retailing

Both US and European retailers are internationalizing their business. Among large international US retailers are: 7-eleven, McDonald's, Pizza Hut, Blockbuster Video and Toys Я Us. Among the large international European retailers are IKEA, Benetton, The Body Shop and Carrefour.

The Japanese are relative newcomers to this internationalization of retailing, but they are getting deeply involved. One of the Japanese food retailers, Jusco, has supermarkets in Hong Kong, Thailand and Malaysia. South-east Asia seems to be the natural zone of influence for Japanese retailers, and they have spread throughout the region.

Despite the trend towards internationalization in retailing a prospective international retailer also faces some serious challenges and problems. The problems begin with the consumers. Retailers' performance in local markets is highly sensitive to variations in consumer behaviour. These are differences in consumer tastes, buying habits and spending patterns from country to country. Such differences have implications for a more differentiated merchandise offering along dimensions such as colour, fabric and site for clothing, and flavour for confectionery and snack foods.

Other problems that retailers will encounter when operating internationally include shortages of key resources such as land and labour, unfavourable tax and tariff structures, restrictions on trading hours and foreign ownership, and impenetrable established supplier relationships.

A case study of one US speciality retailer (Barth *et al.*, 1996) has pinpointed the problems of establishing a retail business in Europe. The reasons for the relatively bad financial performance in European retailing can be sought in the following factors:

■ higher costs of acquiring real estate in Europe;
■ more expensive labour in Europe;
■ the complex legislation for establishing large retail stores in Europe.

Stages of internationalization

The 'stages' concept (the Uppsala school: see section 3.2) has been applied to depict the typical movement by retailers towards internationalization. Given the considerable risks and costs involved in expansion outside home markets, most have viewed the prospect with a degree of reluctance. Retail companies will typically move from reluctance to cautious expansion abroad, starting with the closest markets.

The internationalization of retailing has produced different styles of international operation, ranging from multinational to global (Figure 17.9). Global retailers such as Toys Я Us vary their format very little across national boundaries, achieving the greatest economies of scale but showing the least local responsiveness. Multinational retailers, on the other hand, operate as autonomous entities within each country. A middle course is termed 'transnational' retailing, whereby the company seeks to achieve global efficiency while responding to national opportunities and constraints.

Figure 17.9 International development positions

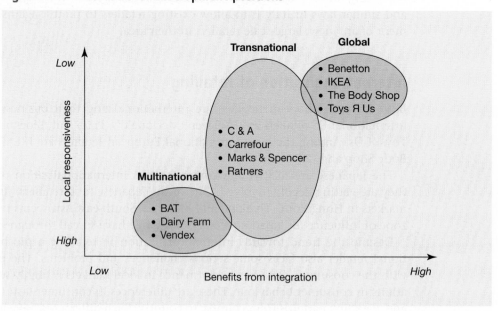

Source: McGoldrick and Davies, 1995, p. 7.

Trade marketing

For too long manufacturers have viewed vertical marketing channels as closed systems, operating as separate, static entities. The most important factors creating long-term, integrated strategic plans and fostering productive channel relationships were largely ignored. Fortunately a new philosophy about channel management has emerged, but to understand its potential we must first understand how power has developed at the retailer level.

Power in channel relationships can be defined as the ability of a channel member to control marketing decision variables of any other member in a channel at a different level of distribution. A classic example of this is the amount of power wielded by retailers against the food and grocery manufacturers. As the balance of power has shifted, more merchandise is controlled by fewer and fewer retailers (Table 17.4).

Table 17.4 **Concentration in food retailing: food market share of the top five retailers**

	Belgium	Germany	France	Italy	Netherlands	UK
Top five retailers	GIB	Aldi	Leclerc	Crai	Ahold	Sainsbury's
	Delhaize	Rewe	Intermarche	Conad	Super-Unie	Tesco
	Aldi	Edeka	Carrefour	Coop	Vendex	Argyll
	Colruyt	Markant	Promodes	Vege	Aldi	Asda
	Edeku	Asko	Auchan	Rinascente	Hermans	Co-op
Food market share of top five retailers	43%	41%	40%	20%	44%	48%

Source: adapted from McGoldrick and Davies, 1995, p. 20.

There is a worldwide tendency towards concentration in retailing. As Table 17.4 shows, the concentration in the European food sector is most evident in the northern part of Europe. Since the mid 90s (when Table 17.4 was created) new players have arrived on the European grocery market, e.g. the German discount-chain, Lidl, which is now second in the German discount-sector after Aldi. Lidl is also expanding to the remaining European area, e.g. to Scandinavia, UK and France. In UK Tesco is now no. 1 and Sainsbury no. 2.

A consequence of this development is that there has been a worldwide shift from manufacturer to retailer dominance. Power has become concentrated in the hands of fewer and fewer retailers, and the manufacturers have been left with little choice but to accede to their demands. This often results in manufacturing of the retailers' own brands (private labels). This phenomenon was discussed in section 15.8.

Therefore we can see that traditional channel management, with its characteristics of power struggles, conflict and loose relationships, is no longer beneficial. New ideas are emerging to help channel relationships become more cooperative. This is what is known as 'trade marketing'. Trade marketing is when the manufacturer (supplier) markets directly to the trade (retailers) to create a better fit between product and outlet. The objective is to create joint marketing and strategic plans for mutual profitability.

For the manufacturer (supplier), it means creating twin marketing strategies: one to the consumer and another to the trade (retailers). However, as Figure 17.10 shows, potential channel conflicts exist because of differences in the objectives of the channel members.

Despite potential channel conflicts what both parties share, but often forget, is their common goal of consumer satisfaction. If the desired end result is to create joint

Figure 17.10 Channel relationships and the concept of trade marketing

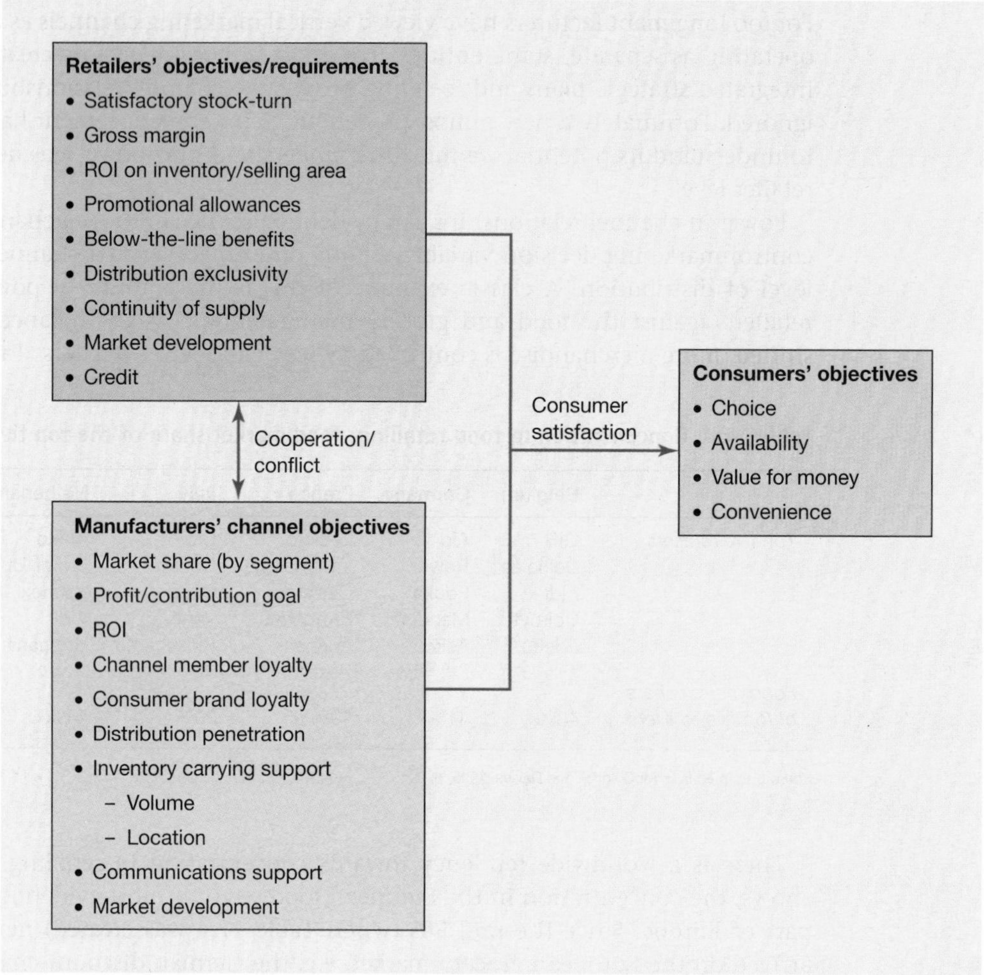

Retailers' objectives/requirements
- Satisfactory stock-turn
- Gross margin
- ROI on inventory/selling area
- Promotional allowances
- Below-the-line benefits
- Distribution exclusivity
- Continuity of supply
- Market development
- Credit

Cooperation/
conflict

Manufacturers' channel objectives
- Market share (by segment)
- Profit/contribution goal
- ROI
- Channel member loyalty
- Consumer brand loyalty
- Distribution penetration
- Inventory carrying support
    - Volume
    - Location
- Communications support
- Market development

Consumer
satisfaction

Consumers' objectives
- Choice
- Availability
- Value for money
- Convenience

marketing plans a prerequisite must be an improved understanding of the other's perspective and objectives.

Retailers are looking for potential sales, profitability, exclusivity in promotions and volume. They are currently in the enviable position of being able to choose brands that fulfil those aims.

A private label manufacturer has to create different packages for different retailers. By carefully designing individual packages the manufacturer gains a better chance of striking up a relationship with the best-matched retailer.

Manufacturers can offer retailers a total 'support package' by stressing their own strengths. These include marketing knowledge and experience, market position, proven new product success, media support and exposure, and a high return on investment in shelf space.

If a joint strategy is going to be successful manufacturers and retailers must work together at every level, perhaps by matching counterparts in each organization. As a consequence of the increasing importance of the individual customer the concept of the key account (key customer) was introduced. Key accounts are often large retail chains with a large turnover (in total as well as of the supplier's products), which are able to decide quantity and price on behalf of different outlets.

Segmentation of customers is therefore no longer based only on size and geographic position but also on customers' (retailers') structure of decision making. This results in a gradual restructuring of sales from a geographic division to a customer division. This reorganization is made visible by creating key account managers (managers responsible for customers).

Cross–border alliances in retailing

The focus of this section is alliances between retailers that are both horizontal (i.e. retailer to retailer) and also international, in that they cross the boundaries of nation states. Cross-border retailer alliances are emerging predominantly between western European retailers and can, in many cases, be interpreted as explicit responses to the perceived threats and opportunities of the EU internal market.

None of the cross-border alliances in Europe can be described as 'equity participating alliances', which include a cross-shareholding between members. None of the alliances involves the sharing of equity, but they all have a central secretariat with the function of coordinating operational activities – buying, branding, expertise exchange and product marketing.

Until now the range of activities performed by the secretariats of the alliances has been limited and excludes actual processing and central payments. The present advantage for an individual retail member in a cross-border alliance lies primarily in central purchasing from suppliers, where price advantages flow to all members, suggesting that the alliance is attempting to countervail the power of the manufacturer (supplier). Cross-border central buying can be a relevant starting point for both manufacturers and retailers attempting to move towards a pan-European supply network.

17.8 | Special issue 2: Grey marketing (parallel importing)

Grey marketing or parallel importing can be defined as the importing and selling of products through market distribution channels that are not authorised by the manufacturer. It occurs when manufacturers use significantly different market prices for the same product in different countries. This allows an unauthorised dealer (in Figure 17.11, a wholesaler) to buy branded goods intended for one market at a low price and then sell them in another, higher-priced market, at a higher profit than could have been achieved in the 'low-price' market.

Grey marketing often occurs because of the fluctuating value of currencies between different countries, which makes it attractive for the 'grey' marketer to buy products in markets with weak currencies and sell them in markets with strong currencies.

Grey markets can also be the result of a distributor in one country having an unexpected oversupply of a product. This distributor may be willing to sell its excess supply for less than the normal margin to recover its investment. Other reasons for lower prices in some countries (which can result in grey marketing) might be lower transport costs, fiercer competition and higher product taxes (high product taxes put pressure on the ex-works price to keep the end-consumer price at an acceptable level).

The particular problem with grey marketing for the manufacturer is that it results in authorised intermediaries losing motivation. The grey marketer usually competes only

Figure 17.11 Grey marketing (parallel importing)

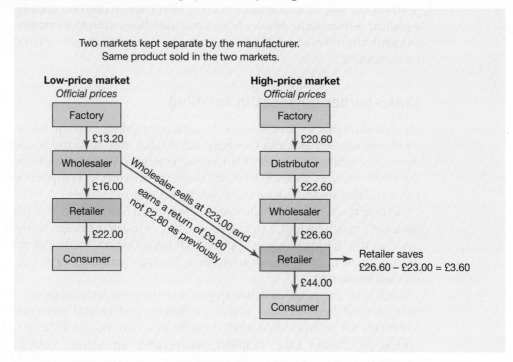

Source: Paliwoda, 1993, p. 300. Reprinted with permission from Butterworth-Heinemann Publishers; **http://www.heinemann.co.uk**

on price and pays little attention to providing marketing support and after-sales service.

Possible strategies to reduce grey marketing

Sometimes companies hope that it is a short-term problem and that it will disappear. Indeed it might be if the price difference is the result of the fluctuating value of currencies. At other times a more proactive approach to the problem is needed:

- *Seek legal redress*. Although the legal option can be time consuming and expensive, some companies (e.g. Seiko) have chosen to prosecute grey marketers.
- *Change the marketing mix*.

The latter involves three elements:

- *Product strategy*. This strategy is about moving away from the standardisation concept (same product for all markets), and introducing a differentiated concept with a different product for each main market.
- *Pricing strategy*. The manufacturer can change the ex-works prices to the channel members to minimise price differentials between markets. The manufacturer can also narrow the discount schedules it offers for large orders. This will reduce the incentive for intermediaries to over-order to get lower prices and later sell unsold stock on the grey market, still at a profit.
- *Warranty strategy*. The manufacturer may reduce or cancel the warranty period for grey market products. This will require that the products can be identified through the channel system.

17.9 Summary

In this chapter we have examined the management of international distribution channels and logistics. The main structure of this chapter was given in Figure 17.1, and from the discussion it is evident that the international marketer has a broad range of alternatives for selecting and developing an economical, efficient and high-volume international distribution channel.

In many instances the channel structure is affected by external factors and it may vary from nation to nation. Physical distribution (external logistics) concerns the flow of goods from the manufacturer to the customer. This is one area where cost savings through efficiency are feasible, provided the decision is systematically made. The changing nature of international retailing influences distribution planning. During the last decade the balance of power (between manufacturers and retailers) has shifted in favour of the retailers. The manufacturer often has no other choice than to cooperate with large and increasingly concentrated retailers in terms of the 'trade marketing' concept.

A phenomenon of growing importance in international markets is the grey market, which consists of unauthorised traders buying and selling a company's product in different countries. Companies confronted with a grey market situation can react in many ways. They may decide to ignore the problem, take legal action or modify elements of their marketing mix. The option chosen is strongly influenced by the nature of the situation and its expected duration.

CASE STUDY 17.1 De Beers

Forward integration into the diamond industry value chain

Since the late 1800s the South African multinational De Beers (**www.debeers.com**) has regulated both the industrial and gemstone diamond markets and effectively maintained an illusion of diamond scarcity. It has developed and nurtured the belief that diamonds are precious, invaluable symbols of romance. Every attitude consumers hold today about diamonds exists – at least in part – because of the persistent efforts of De Beers.

Moreover, by monitoring the supply and distribution of diamonds throughout the world, De Beers has introduced and maintained an unprecedented degree of price stability for a surprisingly common mineral: compressed carbon. Such unique price stability lies within the cartel's tight control over the distribution of diamonds. De Beers' operating strategy has been pure and simple:

to restrict the number of diamonds released into the market in any given year and to perpetuate the myth that they are scarce and should therefore command high prices.

De Beers spends about $200 million a year to promote diamonds and diamond jewellery. 'A diamond is forever' and the firm controls nearly 70 per cent of the rough diamond market.

De Beers controls a producer's cartel that operates as a quantity-fixing entity by setting production quotas for each member (as does OPEC). De Beers has successfully convinced the producers that the diamond supply must be regulated in order to maintain favourably high prices and profits.

During the early part of the last century much of the diamond cartel's strength rested with De Beers' control of the South African mines. Today the source of power no longer comes from rough diamond production alone, but from a sophisticated network of production, marketing sales and promotion arrangements, all administered by De Beers.

It is interesting to note that diamond prices have little or no relation to the cost of extraction (production).

Table 1 shows average or 'normal' price mark-ups on gemstones along the channel of distribution.

Table 1   Mark-ups on diamonds

Stage of distribution	Mark-up (%)	Average value of 0.5 carat gem ($/carat)
Cost of mining	—	100
Mine sales	67	167
Dealers of rough gems	20	200
Cutting units	100	400
Wholesaler dealers	15	460
Retail	100	920

Source: adapted from Ariovich, 1985 and Bergenstock and Maskula, 2001.

A diamond that may cost $100 to mine can end up costing a consumer $920 at a local jewellery store. Business cycles and individual commercial practices may positively or negatively influence these figures, together with the gemstone quality. Diamond sales, known in the trade as 'sights', are held 10 times a year in London, in Lucerne, Switzerland, and in Kimberley, South Africa. The sales are limited to approximately 160 privileged 'sightholders', primarily owners of diamond-cutting factories in New York, Tel Aviv, Bombay and Antwerp, who then sell to the rest of the diamond trade.

Diamond output from De Beers' self-owned and self-operated mines constitutes only 43 per cent of the total world value of rough diamonds. Because it is not the sole producer of rough stones in the world De Beers has had to join forces with other major diamond-producing organizations, forming the international diamond cartel that controls nearly three-quarters of the world market.

De Beers has constructed a controlled supply and distribution chain whereby all cartel producers are contracted to sell the majority of their entire output to a single marketing entity: the De Beers-controlled Central Selling Organization (CSO) (see Figure 1).

The total rough diamond supply controlled by the CSO comes from three sources: De Beers/Centenary-owned mines, outside suppliers contracted to the CSO (cartel members) and open market purchases via buying offices in Africa, Antwerp and Tel Aviv (rough output purchased from countries that have not signed an agreement with De Beers). De Beers functions as the sole diamond distributor. In any given year approximately 75 per cent of the world's diamonds pass through the CSO to cutters and brokers.

The economic success of the cartel depends highly on strict adherence to their rules, written or unwritten. Clients who follow the rules are rewarded with consistent upgrades in the quality and quantity of rough stones in their boxes, while those who circumvent them find progressively worse allocations and risk not being invited back to future sights.

De Beers' 'forward integration' decision

Until 2001 De Beers concentrated on supplying its diamonds to brand manufacturers, such as Cartier. The core business of the De Beers Group remains the mining and marketing of rough diamonds. However, in January 2001 the De Beers Group, the world's premier diamond group, and LVMH Moet Hennessy Louis Vuitton, the world's leading luxury products group, agreed to establish an independently managed joint venture, De Beers LV, to develop the global consumer brand potential of the De Beers name.

LVMH Moet Hennessy Louis Vuitton is the home of premier brands in the categories of fashion and leather goods, watches and jewellery, wine and spirits, cosmetics and perfumes. LVMH will contribute with its extensive experience in both developing luxury brands and rolling out premium retail concepts.

The 'mother' company, De Beers SA, contributes to the joint venture with its over 100 years of experience in the form of technology and individual experts to allow for the selection of the most beautiful diamonds.

Figure 1 De Beers' diamond distribution

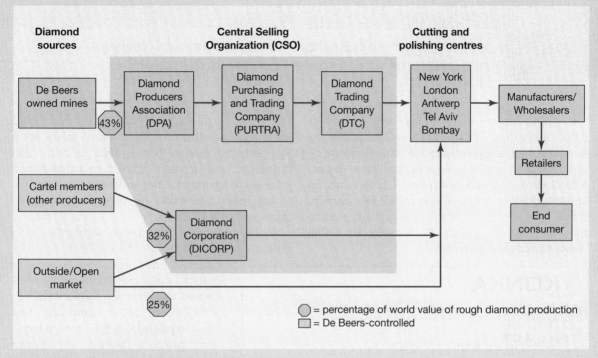

Sources: adapted from De Beers Annual Report and Bergenstock and Maskula, 2001.

As part of the joint venture agreement De Beers SA has transferred to De Beers LV the worldwide rights to use the De Beers brand name for luxury goods in consumer markets. From now on, De Beers will design, manufacture and sell premium diamond jewellery under its own brand name. The diamonds bearing De Beers brand name will be sold exclusively through De Beers stores. De Beers has opened a flagship store in London (Oxford Street) and have plans for further openings in New York and Paris.

Source: information and news on **www.diamonds.net**

Questions

1. What could be De Beers' motives for making this 'forward integration' into the retail and consumer market?

2. Is it a wise decision?

3. How should De Beers develop its Internet strategy following this 'forward integration' strategy?

4. Would it be possible for De Beers, with its branded diamonds, to standardise the international marketing strategy across borders.

CASE STUDY 17.2   Konka Group

Will an aggressive strategy help the Chinese television manufacturer to penetrate US retail distribution?

The Konka Group (**www.konka.com**) has about 9,000 employees, 18 production lines, and its annual output is approximately 6 million colour TV sets. By setting up four new production bases in east, south, south-east and north-west China, with an annual output of over 1 million colour TV sets each, Konka is becoming one of the most rational production units in the colour TV industry in China (**www.konka-television.com**).

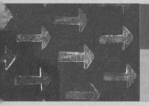

The Konka Group Company Ltd reported sales of $815.17 million for 2001, with net losses. This represents a sharp decrease of 25.1 per cent against 2000. Almost all of the company's 2001 sales (96.50 per cent) were in its home market of China.

Konka was plunged into the red for the first time in 2001 due to fierce market competition and a slack market. Then the company took a bold step and began to develop high-end new TV sets by investing in a production base for these TV sets.

In 2002 the Konka Group ended its loss-making situation and secured sales revenue of $967 million. The group sold 6 million colour TV sets and 1.6 million cellphones in 2002.

From contract manufacturing to own branding

Perseverance has helped Wei-rong Chen, now Konka's Managing Director, to grow the Chinese manufacturer, which used to make television sets for multinational corporations to sell under their own names, into China's best-known television brand.

When the Konka group started selling televisions in China under its own brand name in 1989 it was entering a tough market. Chinese consumers, who were paying as much as three years' salary for a TV, preferred foreign brands such as Sony and Panasonic, and retailers refused to carry Konka products. Undaunted, Chen ordered his salespeople to lug them into stores on their backs and beg managers to display them.

At the same time Chen began urging Konka to shift its strategy. Although the contract manufacturer had lined up seemingly lucrative deals to make televisions for General Electric and Emerson Radio, building products for other companies had failed to pay off. Chen wanted to introduce products bearing the Konka brand. 'We had worked very hard as a contract manufacturer for eight years, and we realised we made too small profits.'

That's when Chen ordered the salespeople to start lugging the televisions into retail stores. 'We knew selling them would be very difficult,' Chen says. Konka salespeople offered store managers healthy margins, and promoted the televisions' high quality and the company's commitment to service. Konka kept prices low, underselling Sony and other Japanese and local brands.

By 1993 it had captured 9 per cent of China's television market. In 2002 it controlled 25 per cent, and produced 6 million colour sets and a host of other products, including DVDs, video recorders, CD players and mobile phones.

The economic slowdown in China – and Chen's refusal to languish where he first found success – has pushed Konka abroad. In 1995 Chen began exporting Konka televisions to other Asian and southern Pacific nations, Russia, South Africa and the Middle East, before trying to woo some of the toughest customers of all: large US retailers.

Konka enters the US market

To enter the $8 billion US television market Konka first set up a research and development facility and sales office in San Jose, California, in 1998. Then it began selling traditional analogue television sets, and in 2000 Konka introduced its high-definition digital television sets, priced at $3,000 – half of what the competition currently charged – hoping that an attractive price for the masses would spark interest in Konka's products.

It put in place a nationwide service network and offered customers a free replacement Konka set in the event of any problem within a year of purchase. It planned to achieve annual sales of 1 million sets in three years and to become one of the top 10 TV brands in the United States in five years.

Konka sees itself as a '2nd-tier' supplier, below firms such as Matsushita and Sony, relying mostly on the price parameter to sell its products.

Currently the TVs sold in the United States are shipped from Chinese assembly plants, but if volumes increase Konka is considering setting up an assembly unit in Mexico. However, up until now Konka is far from achieving its goal of 1 millon television sets sold in the US market.

Source: adapted from different public sources.

Questions

1. What are Konka's motives behind its shift from being a contract manufacturer to implementing a brand strategy?

2. In what way has this shift to do with the 'vertical integration' concept covered in Chapter 17?

3. How would you characterise Konka's distribution strategy regarding market coverage?

4. In spite of all its efforts, the percentage of total sales derived from exports is still only 3.5 per cent (2.5 per cent from the US market and 1 per cent from other markets). How and to where can Konko increase its exports of television sets?

For further exercises and cases, see this book's website at **www.booksites.net/hollensen**

Questions for discussion

1. Discuss current distribution trends in world markets.

2. What are the factors that affect the length, width and number of marketing channels?

3. In attempting to optimise global marketing channel performance, which of the following should an international marketer emphasise: training, motivation or compensation? Why?

4. When would it be feasible and advisable for a global company to centralise the coordination of its foreign market distribution systems? When would decentralisation be more appropriate?

5. Do grey marketers serve useful marketing functions – for consumers and manufacturers?

6. Why is physical distribution important to the success of global marketing?

7. Discuss the reasons why many exporters make extensive use of the services of freight forwarders.

8. Discuss the implications for the international marketer of the trend towards cross-border retailing.

9. Many markets have relatively large numbers of small retailers. How does this constrain the international marketer?

10. How is retailing know-how transferred internationally?

11. What services would the manufacturer like to receive from the retailer?

References

Albaum, G., Strandskov, J., Duerr, E. and Dowd, L. (1994) *International Marketing and Export Management*, Addison-Wesley, Reading, MA.

Ariovich, G. (1985) The Economics of diamond price movements, *Managerial Decision Economics*, Vol. 6, no. 4, pp. 234–40.

Barth, K., Karch, N.J., Mclaughlin, K. and Shi, C.S. (1996) 'Global retailing: tempting trouble', *The McKinsey Quarterly*, no. 1, pp. 117–25.

Bergenstock, D.J. and Maskulka, J. M. (2001) The de beers story: are diamonds forever?, *Business Horizons*, Volume 44, Issue 3, May–June 2001, Pages 37–44.

Bucklin, C.B., Defalco, S.P., DeVincentis, J.R. and Levis III, J.P. (1996) 'Are you tough enough to manage your channels?', *The McKinsey Quarterly*, no. 1, pp. 105–14.

Cateora, P.R. (1993) *International Marketing* (8th edn), Irwin, Homewood, IL.

EIU (1995) 'The EU50: corporate case studies in single market success', Research Report, pp. 77–8.

Jain, S. (1996) *International Marketing Management* (5th edn), South-Western College Publishing, Cincinnati, OH.

Kumar, N. (1999) 'Internet distribution strategies: dilemmas for the incumbent', Mastering Information Management, Part 7, Electronic Commerce, *Financial Times*, 15 March.

Lewison, D.M. (1996) *Marketing Management: An overview*, The Dryden Press/Harcourt Brace College Publishers, Fort Worth, TX.

McGoldrick, P.J. and Davies, G. (1995) *International Retailing: Trends and strategies*, Pitman, London.

Onkvisit, S. and Shaw, J.J. (1993) *International Marketing: Analysis and strategy* (2nd edn), Macmillan, London.

Paliwoda, S. (1993) *International Marketing*, Heinemann, Oxford.

Pirog III, S.F. and Lancioni, R. (1997) 'US–Japan distribution channel cost structures: is there a significant difference?', *International Journal of Physical Distribution and Logistics Management*, vol. 27, no. 1, pp. 53–66.

Sletmo, G.K. and Picard, J. (1984) 'International distribution policies and the role of air freight', *Journal of Business Logistics*, vol. 6, pp. 35–52.

Toyne, B. and Walters, P.G.P. (1993) *Global Marketing Management: A strategic perspective* (2nd edn), Allyn and Bacon, Needham Heights, MA.

Further reading

Arnold, S.J. (2002) 'Lessons learned from the world's best retailers', *International Journal of Retail & Distribution Management*, vol. 30. no. 11, pp. 562–70.

Colla, E. and Dupuis, M. (2002) 'Research and managerial issues on global retail competition: Carrefour/Wal-Mart', *International Journal of Retail & Distribution Management*, vol. 30, no. 2, pp. 103–111.

Harvey, M. and Novicevic, M.M. (2002) 'Selecting marketing managers to effectively control global channels of distribution', *International Marketing Review*, vol. 19, no. 5, pp. 525–44.

Homburg, C., Schäfer, H. and Scholl, M. (2002) 'Wie viele Absatzkanäle kannn sich ein Unternehmen leisten', *Absatzwirtschaft*, no. 3, pp. 38–41.

Howgego, C. (2002) 'Maximising competitiveness through the supply chain', *International Journal of Retail & Distribution Management*, vol. 30, no. 12, pp. 603–5.

Jørgensen, N. (2003) 'Distribution of Danish potted plants', *International Journal of Retail & Distribution Management*, vol. 31, no. 7, pp. 365–71.

Lim, G.H., Lee, K.S., Khai, S.L. and Tan, S.J. (2001) 'Gray marketing as an alternative market penetration strategy for entrepreneurs: conceptual model and case evidence', *Journal of Business Venturing*, vol. 16, pp. 405–427.

Rugman, A. and Girod, S. (2003) 'Retail multinationals and globalization: the evidence is regional', *European Management Journal*, vol. 21, no. 1, pp. 24–37.

Wirtz, B.W. (2002) 'So binden Sie Ihre Kunden auf den richtigen kanälen', *Absatzwirtschaft*, no. 4, pp. 48–54.

Wrigley, N. (2002) 'The landscape of pan-European food retail consolidation', *International Journal of Retail & Distribution Management*, vol. 30, no. 2, pp. 81–91.

18 Communication decisions (promotion strategies)

Contents

Learning objectives

After studying this chapter you should be able to do the following:

- Define and classify the different types of communication tool.

- Describe and explain the major steps in advertising decisions.

- Describe the techniques available and appropriate for setting the advertising budget in foreign markets.

- Discuss the possibilities of marketing via the Internet.

- Discuss which points should be considered when creating a World Wide Website on the Internet.

- Explain how important personal selling and sales force management are in the international marketplace.

- Discuss how standardised international advertising has both benefits and drawbacks.

18.1 Introduction

Communication is the fourth and final decision to be made about the global marketing programme. The role of communication in global marketing is similar to that in domestic operations: to communicate with customers so as to provide information that buyers need to make purchasing decisions. Although the communication mix carries information of interest to the customer, in the end it is designed to persuade the customer to buy a product – at the present time or in the future.

To communicate with and influence customers, several tools are available. Advertising is usually the most visible component of the promotion mix, but personal selling, exhibitions, sales promotions, publicity (public relations) and direct marketing (including the Internet) are also part of a viable international promotion mix.

One important strategic consideration is whether to standardise worldwide or to adapt the promotion mix to the environment of each country. Another consideration is the availability of media, which varies around the world.

18.2 The communication process

In considering the communication process we normally think about a manufacturer (sender) transmitting a message through any form of media to an identifiable target segment audience. Here the seller is the initiator of the communication process. However, if the seller and the buyer have already established a relationship it is likely that the initiative in the communication process will come from the buyer. If the buyer has positive post-purchase experience with a given offering in one period of time this may dispose the buyer to rebuy on later occasions: that is, take initiatives in the form of making enquiries or placing orders (so-called reverse marketing).

The likely development of the split between total sales volume attributable to buyer and seller initiatives is shown in Figure 18.1. The relative share of sales volume attributable to buyer initiative will tend to increase over time. Present and future buyer initiatives are a function of all aspects of a firm's past market performance: that is, the extent, nature and timing of seller initiative, the competitiveness of offerings, post-purchase experience, the relationships developed with buyers as well as the way in which buyer initiative has been dealt with (Ottesen, 1995).

Figure 18.1 The shift from seller initiative to buyer initiative in buyer/seller relationships

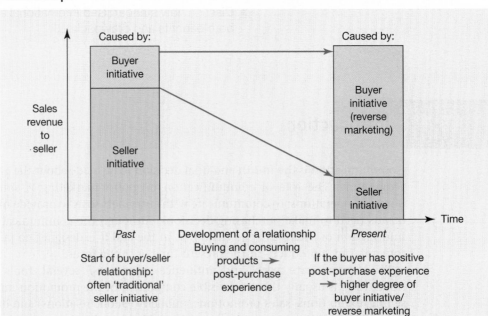

Key attributes of effective communication

The rest of the chapter will be devoted to the communication process and communicative tools based on seller initiatives. All effective marketing communication has four elements: a sender, a message, a communication channel and a receiver (audience). The communication process in Figure 18.2 highlights the key attributes of effective communication.

To communicate in an effective way the sender needs to have a clear understanding of the purpose of the message, the audience to be reached and how this audience will interpret and respond to the message. However, sometimes the audience cannot hear clearly what the sender is trying to say about its product because of the 'noise' of rival manufacturers making similar and often contradictory claims about their products.

Figure 18.2 Elements of the international communication process

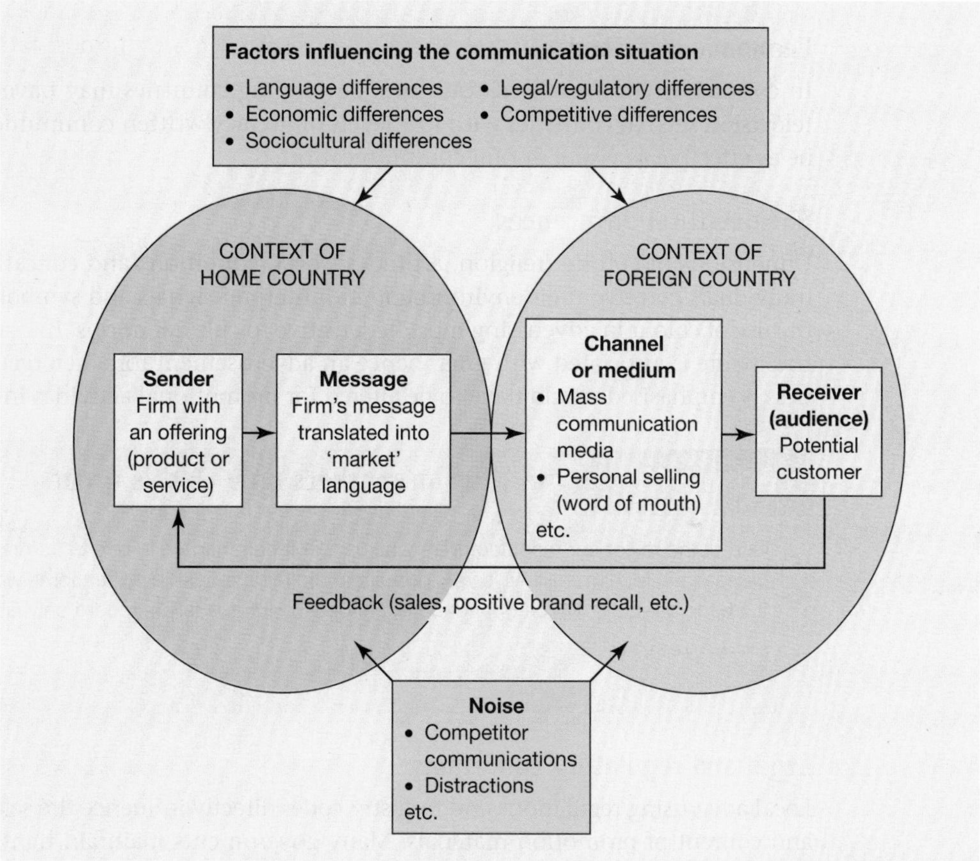

Another important point to consider in the model of Figure 18.2 is the degree of 'fit' between medium and message. For example, a complex and wordy message would be better for the press than for a visual medium such as television or cinema.

Other factors affecting the communication situation

Language differences

A slogan or advertising copy that is effective in one language may mean something different in another language. Thus the trade names, sales presentation materials and advertisements used by firms in their domestic markets may have to be adapted and translated when used in other markets.

There are many examples of unfortunate translations of brand names and slogans. General Motors has a brand name for one of its models called the Vauxhall Nova – this does not work well in Spanish-speaking markets because there it means 'no go'. In Latin America 'Avoid embarrassment – Use Parker Pens' was translated as 'Avoid pregnancy – Use Parker Pens'. Scandinavian vacuum manufacturer Electrolux used the following in a US ad campaign: 'Nothing sucks like an Electrolux'.

A Danish company made up the following slogan for its cat litter in the UK market: 'Sand for Cat Piss'. Unsurprisingly, sales of the firm's cat litter did not increase! Another Danish company translated 'Teats for baby's bottles' as 'Loose tits'. In Copenhagen Airport the following poster could be seen until recently: 'We take your baggage and send it in all directions'. A slogan thus used to express a wish of giving good service might give rise to some concern as to where the baggage might end up (Joensen, 1997).

Economic differences

In contrast to industrialised countries, developing countries may have radios but not television sets. In countries with low levels of literacy written communication may not be as effective as visual or oral communication.

Sociocultural differences

Dimensions of culture (religion, attitudes, social conditions and education) affect how individuals perceive their environment and interpret signals and symbols. For example, the use of colour in advertising must be sensitive to cultural norms. In many Asian countries white is associated with grief; hence an advertisement for a detergent where whiteness is emphasised would have to be altered for promotional activities in, say, India.

Exhibit 18.1	In Muslim markets only God is great

One of the major car manufacturers was using Muhammad Ali in one of its Arab advertising campaigns. Muhammad Ali is very popular in the Middle East, but the theme was him saying 'I am the greatest', which offended people because the Muslims regard only God as great.

Source: Harper, 1986.

Legal and regulatory conditions

Local advertising regulations and industry codes directly influence the selection of media and content of promotion materials. Many governments maintain tight regulations on content, language and sexism in advertising. The type of product that can be advertised is also regulated. Tobacco products and alcoholic beverages are the most heavily regulated in terms of promotion. However, the manufacturers of these products have not abandoned their promotional efforts. Camel engages in corporate-image advertising using its Joe Camel. Regulations are found more in industrialised economies than in developing economies, where the advertising industry is not yet as highly developed.

Competitive differences

As competitors vary from country to country in terms of number, size, type and promotional strategies used, a firm may have to adapt its promotional strategy and the timing of its efforts to the local environment.

18.3   Communication tools

Earlier in this chapter we mentioned the major forms of promotion. In this section the different communication tools, listed in Table 18.1, will be further examined.

Table 18.1 Typical communication tools (media)

One-way communication ◄──────────────────────────────► Two-way communication				
Advertising	**Public relations**	**Sales promotion**	**Direct marketing**	**Personal selling**
Newspapers	Annual reports	Rebates and price discounts	Direct mail/ database marketing	Sales presentations
Magazines	Corporate image	Catalogues and brochures	Internet marketing (WWW)	Sales force management
Journals	House magazines	Samples, coupons and gifts	Telemarketing	Trade fairs and exhibitions
Directories	Press relations	Competitions		
Radio	Public relations			
Television	Events			
Cinema	Lobbying			
Outdoor	Sponsorship			

Advertising

Advertising is one of the most visible forms of communication. Because of its wide use and its limitations as a one-way method of communication advertising in international markets is subject to a number of difficulties. Advertising is often the most important part of the communications mix for consumer goods, where there are a large number of small-volume customers who can be reached through mass media. For most business-to-business markets advertising is less important than the personal selling function.

The major decisions in advertising are shown in Figure 18.3. We will now discuss these different phases.

Objectives setting

Although advertising methods may vary from country to country the major advertising objectives remain the same. Major advertising objectives (and means) might include some of the following:

- *Increasing sales from existing customers* by encouraging them to increase the frequency of their purchases; maintaining brand loyalty via a strategy that reminds customers of the key advantages of the product; and stimulating impulse purchases.
- *Obtaining new customers* by increasing consumer awareness of the firm's products and improving the firm's corporate image among a new target customer group.

Budget decisions

Controversial aspects of advertising include determining a proper method for deciding the size of the promotional budget and its allocation across markets and over time.

Figure 18.3 The major international advertising decisions

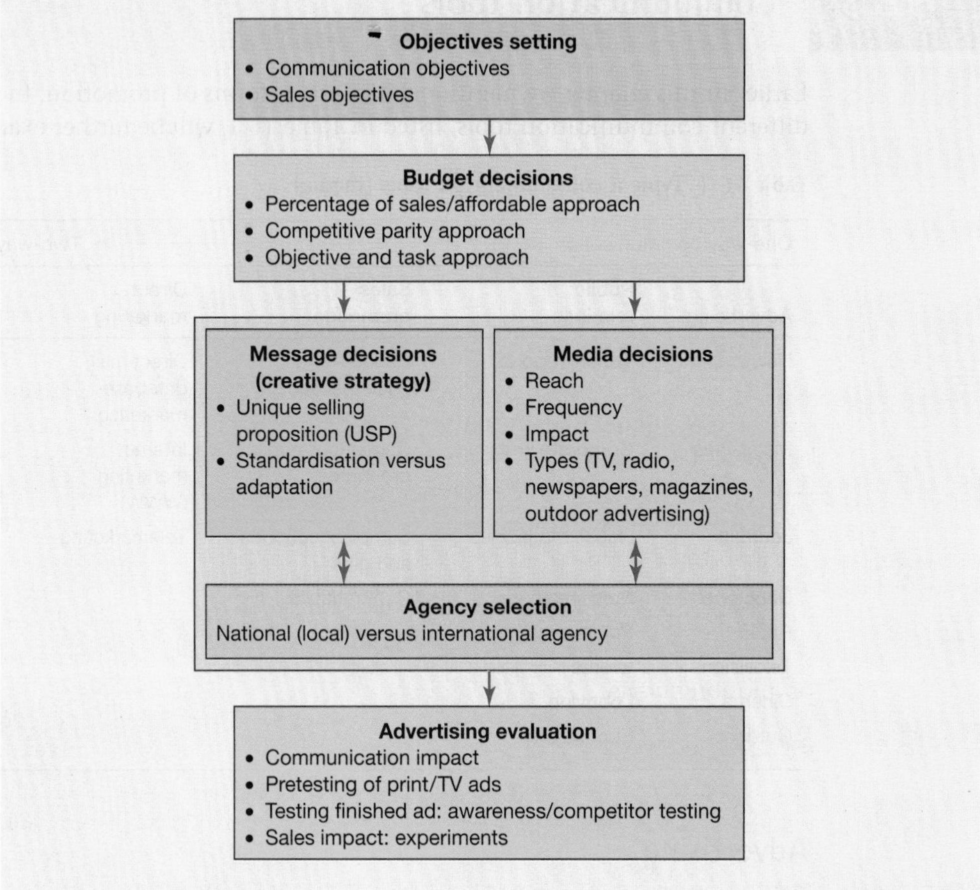

```
┌─────────────────────────────────────┐
│         Objectives setting          │
│  • Communication objectives          │
│  • Sales objectives                  │
└─────────────────────────────────────┘
                  │
                  ▼
┌─────────────────────────────────────┐
│          Budget decisions           │
│  • Percentage of sales/affordable approach │
│  • Competitive parity approach       │
│  • Objective and task approach       │
└─────────────────────────────────────┘
        │                    │
        ▼                    ▼
┌──────────────────┐  ┌──────────────────┐
│ Message decisions│  │  Media decisions │
│ (creative strategy)│ │  • Reach        │
│ • Unique selling │  │  • Frequency     │
│   proposition (USP)│ │  • Impact       │
│ • Standardisation│  │  • Types (TV, radio,│
│   versus         │  │    newspapers, magazines,│
│   adaptation     │  │    outdoor advertising)│
└──────────────────┘  └──────────────────┘
        ↕                    ↕
┌─────────────────────────────────────┐
│          Agency selection           │
│ National (local) versus international agency │
└─────────────────────────────────────┘
                  │
                  ▼
┌─────────────────────────────────────┐
│        Advertising evaluation       │
│  • Communication impact              │
│  • Pretesting of print/TV ads        │
│  • Testing finished ad: awareness/competitor testing │
│  • Sales impact: experiments         │
└─────────────────────────────────────┘
```

In theory the firm (in each of its markets) should continue to put more money into advertising, as an amount of money spent on advertising returns more than an amount of money spent on anything else. In practice it is not possible to set an optimum advertising budget. Therefore firms have developed more practical guidelines. The manager must also remember that the advertising budget cannot be regarded in isolation, but has to be seen as one element of the overall marketing mix.

Affordable approach/percentage of sales

These budgeting techniques link advertising expenditures directly to some measure of profits or, more commonly, to sales. The most popular of these methods is the 'percentage of sales method', whereby the firm automatically allocates a fixed percentage of sales to the advertising budget.

Advantages of this method are as follows:

■ For firms selling in many countries this simple method appears to guarantee equality among the markets. Each market seems to get the advertising it deserves.
■ It is easy to justify in budget meetings.
■ It guarantees that the firm only spends on advertising as much as it can afford. The method prevents 'good money being thrown after bad'.

Disadvantages of this method are as follows:

■ It uses historical performance rather than future performance.

- It ignores the possibility that extra spending on advertising may be necessary when sales are declining, in order to reverse the sales trend by establishing a 'recycle' on the product life cycle curve (see section 15.4).
- It does not take into account variations in the firm's marketing goals across countries.
- The 'percentage of sales' method encourages local management to maximise sales by using the easiest and most flexible marketing tool: price (that is, lowering the price).
- The method's convenience and simplicity encourage management not to bother investigating the relationships between advertising and sales or analysing critically the overall effectiveness of its advertising campaigns.
- The method cannot be used to launch new products or enter new markets (zero sales = zero advertising).

Competitive parity approach

This involves estimating and duplicating the amounts spent on advertising by major rivals. Unfortunately, determining the marketing expenditures of foreign-based competitors is far more difficult than monitoring home country businesses, whose financial accounts (if they are limited companies) are open to public inspection and whose promotional activities are obvious the moment they occur. Another danger in following the practice of competitors is that they are not necessarily right.

Furthermore, the method does not recognise that the firm is in different situations in different markets. If the firm is new to a market its relationships with customers are different from those of existing domestic companies. This should also be reflected in its promotion budget.

Objective and task approach

The weaknesses of the above approaches have led some firms to follow this approach, which begins by determining the advertising objectives and then ascertaining the tasks needed to attain these objectives. This approach also includes a cost/benefit analysis, relating objectives to the costs of achieving them. To use this method the firm must have good knowledge of the local market.

A research study (Hung and West, 1991) showed that only 20 per cent of companies in the United States, Canada and the United Kingdom used the objective and task approach. Although it is the 'theoretically correct' way of determining the promotion budget it is sometimes more important to be operational and to use a 'percentage of sales' approach. This is not necessarily a bad method if company experience shows it to be reasonably successful. If the percentage is flexible it allows different percentages in different markets.

Message decisions (creative strategy)

This concerns decisions about what unique selling proposition (USP) needs to be communicated, and what the communication is intended to achieve in terms of consumer behaviour in the country concerned. These decisions have important implications for the choice of advertising medium, since certain media can better accommodate specific creative requirements (use of colour, written description, high definition, demonstration of the product, etc.) than others.

An important decision area for international marketers is whether an advertising campaign developed in the domestic market can be transferred to foreign markets with only minor modifications, such as translation into the appropriate languages. Complete standardisation of all aspects of a campaign over several foreign markets is rarely attainable. Standardisation implies a common message, creative idea, media and strategy, but it also requires that the firm's product has a USP that is clearly understood by customers in a cross-cultural environment.

Standardising international advertising can lead to a number of advantages for the firm. For example, advertising costs will be reduced by centralising the advertising

---

Exhibit 18.2   **Developing the 'Me and my Magnum' campaign: the power of persuasion**

In 1989 Unilever launched the ice-cream brand Magnum in a number of European countries. A special and unique relationship arose between Magnum and the customer due to the backbone of the advertising campaign 'Me and my Magnum', which was developed in 1991–92 by Barry Day, creative consultant at Lintas, together with Langnese-Iglo's marketing director, Klaus Rabbel, and Michael Bronsten, Ice Cream Group advertising member.

The ironic thing about the advertising – and the key to its success, says Barry Day – was that 'The Magnum campaign was not dreamt up by some ad man: the consumer "wrote" it.' The advertising is based on what consumers were saying about the brand.

The advertisement contains three elements, two visual and one audio. The first visual element surrounds one particular aspect of Magnum: its size. Consumers have related that Magnum's size makes it awkward and unwieldy. Thus, they say, it cannot be eaten quickly: time is needed to consume a Magnum and this special moment should not be interrupted. They have also confessed that eating it can be

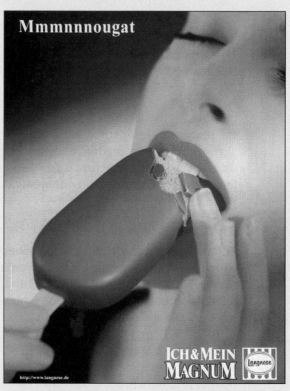

'Me and My Magnum' advertisement German Version

quite an erotic experience. These two elements come together in the second visual image: the body language of the Magnum consumer, who eats it slowly and with great care, gently toying with the crisp, cracking chocolate before teasing out the ice-cream underneath.

Binding these two visual elements together is a soundtrack that gives the consumer 'licence to indulge,' says Barry Day. It consists of genuine testimonies from consumers reflecting on what Magnum means to them. The advertisement works, Barry Day believes, because the words it uses to describe the experience of eating a Magnum really do accord with those of the consumer. This recognition is translated into a close affinity between one Magnum consumer and another. 'It gives the viewer the feeling that he or she is part of some sort of élite or club – the Magnum Club,' he explains. It is, however, a singles club. Magnum is a purely personal indulgence: people eating one are not going to share it with anyone else.

Where does the Magnum advertising go from here? Barry Day feels that future campaigns can go deeper into the psychology of the brand, but should never take away from the values that have made Magnum the success it is today.

Source: Shelly, 1995.

campaign in the head office and transferring the same campaign from market to market, as opposed to running campaigns from different local offices.

However, executing an advertising campaign in multiple markets requires a balance between conveying the message and allowing for local nuances. The adaptation of global ideas can be achieved by various tactics, such as adopting a modular approach, adapting international symbols and using international advertising agencies.

Media decisions

The selection of the media to be used for advertising campaigns needs to be done simultaneously with the development of the message theme. A key question in media selection is whether to use a mass or target approach. The mass media (television, radio and newsprint) are effective when a significant percentage of the general public are potential customers. This percentage varies considerably by country for most products, depending on, for example, the distribution of incomes in different countries.

The selection of the media to be used in a particular campaign typically starts with some idea of the target market's demographic and psychological characteristics, regional strengths of the product, seasonality of sales, and so on. The media selected should be the result of a careful fit of local advertising objectives, media attributes and target market characteristics. Furthermore, media selection can be based on the following criteria:

- *Reach*. This is the total number of people in a target market exposed to at least one advertisement in a given time period ('opportunity to see', or OTS).
- *Frequency*. This is the average number of times within a given time period that each potential customer is exposed to the same advertisement.
- *Impact*. This depends on compatibility between the medium used and the message. *Penthouse* magazine continues to attract advertisers for high-value-added consumer durables, such as cars, hi-fi equipment and clothes, which are geared primarily to a high-income male segment.

High reach is necessary when the firm enters a new market or introduces a new product so that information about, for example, the new product's availability is spread to the widest possible audience. A high level of frequency is appropriate when brand awareness already exists and the message is about informing the consumer that a campaign is under way. Sometimes a campaign should have both a high frequency and extensive reach, but limits on the advertising budget often create the need to trade off frequency against reach.

A media's gross rating points (GRPs) are the result of multiplying its reach by the frequency with which an advertisement appears within the media over a certain period. Hence it contains duplicated exposure, but indicates the 'critical mass' of a media effort. GRPs may be estimated for individual vehicles, for entire classes of media or for a total campaign.

The cost of running a media campaign also has to be taken into consideration. Traditionally media planning is based on a single measure, such as 'cost per thousand GRPs'. When dealing with two or more national markets the selection of media also has to take the following into account:

- differences in the firm's market objectives across countries;
- differences in media effectiveness across countries.

Since media availability and relative importance will not be the same in all countries plans may require adjustment in cross-border campaigns.

| Exhibit 18.3 | Co-promotion in practice: McDonald's and LEGO |

In 1994 LEGO carried out its then largest European co-promotion with McDonald's as collaborator. The family restaurant's children's menu Happy Meal contained a LEGO product for four weeks, one every week. The activity was marketed on television and in print media.

The campaign included 16 countries in Europe plus Turkey and Israel. LEGO's motives for an increasing interest in co-promotion, says brand manager Carsten Sørensen, are twofold:

- There is increasing competition in media that are becoming more and more crowded. Co-promotion offers the opportunity of getting more value for money from the marketing budget.
- In some markets LEGO needs an increased market share. The more it is in contact with consumers, the better they know the company. Co-promotion can thus be a relevant tool if a company is introducing a new product in an existing market or existing products in new markets.

Source: Nørmark, 1994.

As a way of distributing advertising messages through new communication channels, co-promotion has a strong foothold (see Exhibit 18.3).

Let us now take a closer look at the main media types.

Television

Television is an expensive but commonly used medium in attempting to reach broad national markets. In most developed countries coverage is no problem. However, television is one of the most regulated of communications media. Many countries have prohibited the advertising of cigarettes and alcohol other than beer. In other countries (e.g. in Scandinavia) there are limits on the number of minutes that TV advertising is permitted. Some countries also prohibit commercial breaks in TV programmes.

| Exhibit 18.4 | Mercedes uses Janis Joplin's hit to market its cars in the United States |

'Oh, Lord, won't you buy me a Mercedes Benz.
My friends all drive Porsches, I must make amends.
Worked hard all my lifetime. No help from my friends.
So, Lord, won't you buy me a Mercedes Benz.'

Some 30 years ago rock singer Janis Joplin begged the Lord for a Mercedes Benz. The vocal version of a poor woman's evening prayer was a hit then and is still played frequently on radio stations all over the world.

Buying power of the generation of 1968

The generation of 1968 have now reached an age with purchasing power, and the German car company has decided to let the prayer be heard as part of a huge advertising campaign. Mercedes Benz has bought the rights to use the song in its advertisements in coming years. The campaign has already been launched on US TV, where Joplin's 'whisky' voice accompanies the delicate pictures of two of Mercedes' newest luxury models. Many classic rock hits from the 1950s and 1960s have been used commercially in advertisements during recent years. But Joplin's hit is different in two ways. First, it mentions the product directly. Secondly, the song was originally a satire of the poor's dream that happiness was found in one of the day's most materialistic status symbols.

'It was never meant to be taken seriously,' songwriter Bob Neuwirth recollects, who back in 1970 helped Joplin fabricate the song in a break between two concerts. He has nothing to do with the song today and has not been asked for advice. 'But I am surprised that it took them so long to think of the idea,' he says, and maintains that Joplin had no desperate personal need for an expensive status symbol.

Drove Porsche

In those days, Joplin owned a Porsche. Mercedes Benz has chosen Joplin as part of an attempt to reach a younger audience through advertisements that, according to the director for Mercedes' North American department Andrew Goldberg, create an instant emotional and physical connection to the product.

The reactions of a test audience have documented that the song produced warm, nostalgic feelings and created a more positive attitude towards Mercedes. 'What she meant by the song 25 years ago can be freely interpreted by anyone. But when a customer sees the advertisement it is solely about emotions and not sociology,' says Goldberg.

Janis Joplin became a world name with the group Big Brother and the Holding Co. at the end of the 1960s, but died alcoholised from an overdose of heroin on 4 October 1970. Six months later her solo LP *Pearl* was released. It contained among others the Mercedes song, which a chuckling Joplin finishes with the words 'That's it,' after the famous refrain: 'So Lord won't you buy me a Mercedes Benz.' Exactly as she is doing now a quarter of a century later in the advertisement.

Source: translated from an article by Jan Lund in the Danish newspaper *Jyllandsposten*, 24 March 1995.

Radio

Radio is a lower-cost broadcasting activity than television. Commercial radio started several decades before commercial television in many countries. Radio is often transmitted on a local basis and therefore national campaigns have to be built up on an area-by-area basis.

Newspapers (print)

In virtually all urban areas of the world the population has access to daily newspapers. In fact the problem for the advertiser is not having too few newspapers, but rather having too many of them. Most countries have one or more newspapers that can be said to have a truly national circulation. However, in many countries newspapers tend to be predominantly local or regional and, as such, serve as the primary medium for local advertisers. Attempting to use a series of local papers to reach a national market is considerably more complex and costly.

Many countries have English-language newspapers in addition to local-language newspapers. For example, the aim of the *Asian Wall Street Journal* is to supply economic information in English to influential Asian business-persons, politicians, top government officials and intellectuals.

Magazines (print)

In general, magazines have a narrower readership than newspapers. In most countries magazines serve to reach specific segments of the population. For technical and industrial products magazines can be quite effective. Technical business publications tend to be international in their coverage. These range from individual businesses (e.g. beverages, construction, textiles) to worldwide industrial magazines covering many industries.

Marketers of international products have the option of using international magazines that have regional editions (e.g. *Newsweek, Time* and *Business Week*). In the case of *Reader's Digest*, local-language editions are distributed.

Cinema

In countries where it is common to subsidise the cost of showing films by running advertising commercials prior to the feature film, cinema advertising has become an important medium. India, for example, has a relatively high level of cinema attendance per capita (few have television at home). Therefore cinema advertisements play a much greater role in India than in, for example, the United States.

Cinema advertising has other advantages, one of the most important being that it has a truly captive audience (no channel hopping!). The problem, of course, is that people know that commercials will be shown before the film. So they will not turn up until the main feature begins.

Outdoor advertising

Outdoor advertising includes posters/billboards, shop signs and transit advertising. This medium shows the creative way in which space can be sold to customers. In the case of transit advertising, for example, a bus can be sold as an advertising medium. In Romania transit advertising is very effective. According to a survey by Mueller (1996), in Bucharest 91 per cent of all consumers surveyed said they remembered the content of transit advertisements, compared with 82 per cent who remembered the content of print adverts. The use of transit media is expanding rapidly in China as well. Outdoor posters/billboards can be used to develop the visual impact of advertising. France is a country associated with the effective use of poster/billboard advertising. In some countries legal restrictions limit the poster space available.

Agency selection

Confronted with the many complex problems that international advertising involves, many businesses instinctively turn to an advertising agency for advice and practical assistance. Agencies employ or have instant access to expert copywriters, translators, photographers, film makers, package designers and media planners who are skilled and experienced in the international field. Only the largest of big businesses can afford to carry such people in-house.

If the international marketer decides to outsource the international advertising functions they have a variety of options including the following:

- Use different national (local) agencies in the international markets where the firm is present.
- Use the services of a big international agency with domestic overseas offices.

In Table 18.2 the different factors favouring a national or an international agency are listed. The single European (pan-European) market is used as an example of an international agency.

The criteria relevant to the choice of a national or an international agency include the following:

- *Policy of the company*. Has the company got any realistic plans for a more standardised advertising approach?
- *Nature of the advertising to be undertaken*. Corporate image advertising might be best undertaken by a single large multinational agency that operates throughout the world via its own subsidiaries. For niche marketing in specialist country sectors a local agency might be preferred.
- *Type of product*. The campaign for an item that is to be presented in a standardised format, using the same advertising layouts and messages in all countries, might be handled more conveniently by a single multinational agency.

Table 18.2 **European agency selection: national (local) or pan-European (international)**

National (local)	Pan-European (international)
Supports national subsidiary.	Reflects new European reality and trends.
Investment in existing brand best handled nationally.	Economies of scale in new product development and branding.
Closer to marketplace.	Uniformity of treatment across Europe.
Smaller size more conducive to personalised service and greater creativity.	Resources and skills of major European or global agency.
Diversity of ideas.	Easier to manage one agency group.

Source: adapted from Lynch, 1994, Table 11-4.

Advertising evaluation

Advertising evaluation and testing is the final stage in the advertising decision process shown in Figure 18.3. Testing advertising effectiveness is normally more difficult in international markets than in domestic markets. An important reason for this is the distance and communication gap between domestic and foreign markets. Thus it can be very difficult to transfer testing methods used in domestic ones to foreign ones. For example, the conditions for interviewing people can vary from country to country. Consequently, many firms try to use sales results as a measure of advertising effectiveness, but awareness testing is also relevant in many cases, e.g. is brand awareness of crucial importance during the early stages of a new product launch.

Testing the impact of advertising on sales is very difficult because it is difficult to isolate the advertising effect. One way to solve this problem is to use a kind of *experiment*, where the markets of the firm are grouped according to similar characteristics. In each group of countries, one or two are used as test markets. Independent variables to be tested against the sales (dependent variable) might include the amount of advertising, the media mix, the unique selling proposition and the frequency of placement.

This kind of experiment is also relevant for testing other types of communication tool mentioned in Table 18.1.

Exhibit 18.5	Bailey's Irish Cream liqueur: sales expansion with market and product development

In 1993 R&A Bailey and Co. decided to increase sales of its brand in Europe by expanding usage of the drink. A cross-border television advertising campaign, 'Bailey's with ice', was developed to reinforce the contemporary all-year-round image of the drink and to distinguish it from the 'stuffy' image of traditional liqueurs with their mainly after-dinner role. The appeal was to younger consumers to drink Bailey's on a greater number of occasions. Special promotional packs were also developed, consisting of a one-litre bottle together with two free liqueur glasses.

In early 1993 Bailey's was also launched on the Japanese market after a period of test marketing. The regular brand was offered in addition to a specially developed brand for the Japanese called Bailey's Gold, which was developed with 10-year-old malt whiskey to appeal to the Japanese taste for premium-quality spirits. This Bailey's Gold was also priced at double the price of the regular brand.

Source: MacNamee and McDonnell, 1995.

Public relations

Word-of-mouth advertising is not only cheap, it is very effective. Public relations (PR) seeks to enhance corporate image building and influence favourable media treatment. PR (or publicity) is the marketing communications function that carries out programmes designed to earn public understanding and acceptance. It should be viewed as an integral part of the global marketing effort.

PR activities involve both internal and external communication. Internal communication is important to create an appropriate corporate culture. The target groups for public relations are shown in Table 18.3.

Table 18.3 **Target groups for public relations**

Publics or target groups: domestic markets	Extra international dimensions: international markets
Directly connected with the organization Employees Shareholders	Wider range of cultural issues The degree of remoteness of the corporate headquarters
Suppliers of raw materials and components Providers of financial services Providers of marketing services (e.g. marketing research, advertising, media)	Is this to be handled on a country-by-country basis, or is some overall standardisation desirable?
Customers of the organization Existing customers Past customers Those capable of becoming customers	May have less knowledge of the company The country-of-origin effect will influence communications
Environment The general public Government: local, regional, national Financial markets generally	Wide range of general publics Host governments Regional grouping (e.g. EU), world groupings

Source: Phillips *et al.*, 1994, p. 362. Reprinted by permission of Thomson Publishing Services Ltd on behalf of Routledge.

The range of target groups is far wider in public relations than it is for the other communications tools. Target groups are likely to include the main stakeholder groups of employees, customers, distribution channel members and shareholders. For companies operating in international markets this gives a very wide range of communication tasks. Internal communications in different country subsidiaries, employing people from a number of different countries, with different cultural values, will be particularly challenging.

In a more market-oriented sense, the PR activity is directed towards an influential, though relatively small, target audience of editors and journalists who work for newspapers/magazines, or towards broadcasting aimed at the firm's customers and stakeholders.

Since the target audience is small it is relatively inexpensive to reach. Several methods can be used to gain PR. Such methods include the following:

- Contribution of prizes at different events.
- Sponsorship of events (sporting, cultural, etc.). According to Meenaghan (1996), the worldwide sponsorship market grew from $2 billion in 1984 to $13.02 billion in

1994. In 1994 Europe and the United States together accounted for 32.6 per cent of worldwide sponsorship expenditure.

- Press releases of news about the firm's products, plant and personnel.
- Announcements of the firm's promotional campaigns.
- Lobbying (government).

The degree of control of the PR messages is quite different. Journalists can use PR material to craft an article of so many words, or an interview of so many seconds. How material is used will depend on the journalist and the desired story line. On occasions a thoroughly negative story can result from a press release that was designed to enhance the company image.

Hence PR activity includes anticipating criticism. Criticisms may range from general ones against all multinational corporations to more specific ones. They may also be based on a market: for example, doing business with prison factories in China.

Sales promotion

Sales promotion is defined as those selling activities that do not fall directly into the advertising or personal selling category. Sales promotion also relates to so-called below-the-line activities such as point-of-sale displays and demonstrations, leaflets, free trials, contests and premiums such as 'two for the price of one'. Unlike media advertising, which is 'above the line' and earns a commission, below-the-line sales promotion does not. To an advertising agency 'above the line' means traditional media for which they are recognised by the media owners, entitling them to commission.

Sales promotion is a short-term effort directed primarily to the consumer and/or retailer, in order to achieve specific objectives:

- consumer product trial and/or immediate purchase;
- consumer introduction to the shop;
- encouraging retailers to use point-of-purchase displays for the product;
- encouraging shops to stock the product.

In the United States, the sales promotion budgets for fast-moving consumer goods (FMCG) manufacturers are larger than the advertising budgets. In Europe, the European Commission estimates that the rate of growth of spending on sales promotions was double that for conventional advertising throughout the period 1991–94 (Bennett, 1995, p. 321). Factors contributing to the expansion of sales promotion activities include the following:

- greater competition among retailers, combined with increasingly sophisticated retailing methods;
- higher levels of brand awareness among consumers, leading to the need for manufacturers to defend brand shares;
- improved retail technology (e.g. electronic scanning devices that enable coupon redemptions, etc., to be monitored instantly);
- greater integration of sales promotion, public relations and conventional media campaigns.

In markets where the consumer is hard to reach because of media limitations the percentage of the total communication budget allocated to sales promotions is also relatively high. Here are some of the different types of sales promotion:

- *Price discounts*. These are very widely used. A variety of different price reduction techniques is available, such as cash-back deals.

- *Catalogues/brochures*. The buyer in a foreign market may be located at quite a distance from the closest sales office. In this situation a foreign catalogue can be very effective. It must be able to close the gap between buyer and seller in the way that the potential buyer is supplied with all the necessary information, from prices, sizes, colours and quantities to packing, shipping time and acceptable form of payment. In addition to catalogues, brochures of various types are useful for salespersons, distributors and agents. Translations should be done in cooperation with overseas agents and/or distributors.
- *Coupons*. Coupons are a classic tool for FMCG brands, especially in the United States. A variety of coupon distribution methods exists: door-to-door, on pack, in newspapers. Coupons are not allowed in all European countries.
- *Samples*. A sample gives the potential foreign buyer an idea of the firm and quality of product that cannot be attained by even the best graphic picture. Samples may prevent misunderstandings over style, sizes, models and so on.
- *Gifts*. Most European countries have a limit on the value of the premium or gift given. Furthermore, in some countries it is illegal to offer premiums that are conditional on the purchase of another product. The United States does not allow alcoholic beer to be offered as a free sample.
- *Competitions*. This type of sales promotion needs to be communicated to the potential customers. This can be done on the pack, in stores via leaflets or through media advertising.

The success of sales promotion depends on local adaptation. Major constraints are imposed by local laws, which may not permit premiums or free gifts to be given. Some countries' laws control the amount of discount given at retail level; others require permits for all sales promotions. Since it is impossible to know the specific laws of each and every country, international marketers should consult local lawyers and authorities before launching a promotional campaign.

Direct marketing

According to Onkvisit and Shaw (1993, p. 717), direct marketing is the total of activities by which products and services are offered to market segments in one or more media for informational purposes or to solicit a direct response from a present or prospective customer or contributor by mail, telephone or personal visit.

Direct marketing covers direct mail (marketing database), telephone selling and marketing via the Internet. A number of factors have encouraged the rapid expansion of the international direct marketing industry (Bennett, 1995, p. 318):

- developments in mailing technology, which have reduced the costs of distributing direct-mail literature;
- escalating costs of other forms of advertising and sales promotion;
- the increasing availability of good-quality lists of prospective customers;
- developments in information technology (especially database technology and desktop publishing) that enable smaller companies to produce high-quality direct marketing materials in-house;
- the increasing availability throughout the developed world of interactive television facilities, whereby consumers may order goods through a teletext system.

Direct mail

Direct mail is a viable medium in many countries. It is especially important when other media are not available. Direct mail offers a flexible, selective and potentially highly cost-effective means of reaching foreign consumers. Messages can be addressed exclusively to the target market, advertising budgets may be concentrated on the most promising market segments, and it will be some time before competitors realise that the firm has launched a campaign. In addition, the size, content, timing and geographical coverage of mailshots can be varied at will: the firm can spend as much or as little as necessary to achieve its objectives. There are no media space or airtime restrictions, and no copy or insertion deadlines to be met. All aspects of the direct-mail process are subject to the firm's immediate control, and it can experiment by varying the approach used in different countries. Direct mail can take many forms – letters, catalogues, technical literature – and it can serve as a vehicle for the distribution of samples. A major problem in the effective use of direct mail is the preparation of a suitable mailing list (marketing database).

European marketers are still far behind the United States in exploiting the medium and also with regard to the response to direct mail in the form of mail orders. Per capita mail-order sales in the United States are more than double those of any European country (Desmet and Xardel, 1996, p. 58). The use of direct mail in Japan is also below that in the United States. One reason for this discrepancy is that the Japanese feel printed material is too impersonal and insufficiently sincere.

Direct mail is not only relevant for the consumer market. However, effective use of direct mail for business-to-business purposes requires the preparation of an accurate customer profile (marketing database), including industry classification, size of target company (measured, for example, by turnover, number of employees or market share), the people to approach in each business (purchasing officer, project development engineer, product manager, etc.), industry purchasing procedures and (where known) supplier selection criteria and the buying motives of prospective customers.

Telemarketing is today used for both consumer and business-to-business campaigns throughout the industrialised world. The telephone can be used both to obtain orders and to conduct fast, low-cost market research. Telemarketing covers cold calling (unsolicited calls) by salespeople, market surveys conducted by telephone, calls designed to compile databases of possible sales prospects and follow-ups to customer requests for further information, resulting from print and broadcast advertisements. Currently, the majority of cross-border telemarketing campaigns focus on business-to-business contacts, essentially because of the combined telephone/fax/database facilities that an increasing number of companies possess and, in consequence, the greater reliability of business-to-business communications.

The administration of international telemarketing normally requires the use of a commercial telemarketing agency. Language skills are required, plus considerable skills and experience in identifying decision makers in target firms.

In some European countries cold calling of consumers is under close scrutiny in the name of consumer protection and respect for privacy. For example, Germany has prohibited calls on the grounds of privacy invasion, and this ban even applies to an insurance salesperson's announcement of a visit.

In the light of the development in Internet technologies it is very relevant to consider the World Wide Web as a direct marketing tool. This issue was discussed in Chapter 14.

Personal selling

The differences between advertising and personal selling were indicated in Table 18.1. Advertising is a one-way communication process that has relatively more 'noise', whereas personal selling is a two-way communication process with immediate feedback and relatively less 'noise'. Personal selling is an effective way to sell products, but it is expensive. It is used mainly to sell to distribution channel members and in business-to-business markets. However, personal selling is also used in some consumer markets – for example for cars and for consumer durable products. In some countries labour costs are very low and here personal selling will be used to a greater extent than in high-cost countries.

If personal selling costs on business-to-business markets are relatively high it is relevant to economise with personal selling resources, and use personal selling only at the end of the potential customer's buying process (Figure 18.4). Computerised database marketing (direct mail, etc.) is used in a customer screening process, to point out possible customers, who will then be 'taken over' by salespersons. Their job is to turn 'hot' and 'very hot' customer candidates into real customers.

Figure 18.4 Combination of direct mail (database marketing) and personal selling

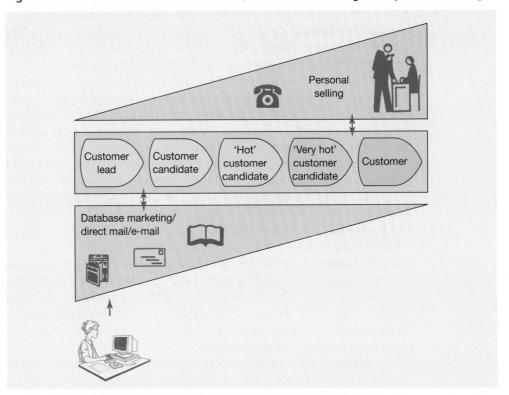

Assessing sales force effectiveness

There are five essential questions to ask in assessing sales force effectiveness:

1. *Is the selling effort structured for effective market coverage?*
   Organization.
   Size of sales force.
   Territory deployment.
2. *Is the sales force staffed with the right people?*
   Type of international sales force: expatriates/host country/third country.
   Age/tenure/education profile.
   Interpersonal skills.
   Technical capabilities.
   Selling technique.

3. *Is strong guidance provided?*
   Written guidelines.
   Key tasks/mission definition.
   Call frequency.
   Time allocation.
   People to be seen.
   Market/account focus.
   Territory planning and control tools.
   On-the-job coaching.
4. *Is adequate sales support in place?*
   Training.
   Technical back-up.
   Inside sales staff.
   Product and applications literature.
5. *Does the sales compensation plan provide the proper motivation?*
   Total compensation.
   Split of straight salary/straight commission.
   Incentive design/fit with management objectives.
   Non-cash incentives.

In the following we will go into further details with questions 1 and 2.

International sales force organization

In international markets firms often organise their sales forces similarly to their domestic structures, regardless of differences from one country to another. This means that the sales force is organised by geography, product, customer or some combination of these (Table 18.4).

Table 18.4 Sales force organizational structure

Structure	Factors favouring choice of organizational structure	Advantages	Disadvantages
Geographic	Distinct languages/cultures	Clear, simple	Breadth of customers
	Single product line	Incentive to cultivate local business and personal ties	Breadth of products
	Underdeveloped markets	Travel expenses	
Product	Established market	Product knowledge	Travel expenses
	Broad product lines		Overlapping territories/customers
			Local business and personal ties
*Customer**	Broad product lines	Market/customer knowledge	Overlapping territories/products
			Local business and personal ties
			Travel expenses
Combination	Large sales volume	Maximum flexibility	Complexity
	Large/developed markets	Travel expenses	Sales management
	Distinct language/cultures		Product/market/geography overlap

* By type of industry, size of account, channel of distribution, individual company.

A number of firms organise their international sales force along simple geographical territories within a given country or region. Firms that have broad product lines and large sales volume, and/or operate in large, developed markets may prefer more specialised organizations, such as product or customer assignment. The firm may also organise the sales force based upon other factors such as culture or languages spoken in the targeted foreign markets. For example, firms often divide Switzerland into different regions reflecting French, Italian and German language usage.

Type of international sales force

Management should consider three options when determining the most appropriate international sales force. The salespeople hired for sales positions could be expatriates, host country nationals or third country nationals. For example, a German working for a German company in the United States is an expatriate. The same German working for a US company in Germany is a host country national. They are a third country national if assigned to France.

- *Expatriate salespersons.* These are viewed favourably because they are already familiar with the firm's products, technology, history and policies. Thus the 'only' kind of preparation they would need is a knowledge of the foreign market. Yet this may be a great problem for the expatriate salesperson. Whereas some may enjoy the challenge and adjustment, other expatriate personnel find it difficult to come to terms with a new and unfamiliar business environment. The failure to understand a foreign culture and its customers will hinder the effectiveness of an expatriate sales force. The family of the expatriate may also face adaptation problems. However, very expensive items often require selling directly from the head office, which usually involves expatriates.
- *Host country nationals.* These are personnel who are based in their home country. As native personnel they have extensive market and cultural knowledge, language skills and familiarity with local business traditions. Since the government and local community undoubtedly prefer that their own nationals be hired instead of outsiders, the firm can avoid charges of exploitation while gaining goodwill at the same time. Using local sales representatives also permits the firm to become active more quickly in a new market because the adjustment period is minimised.
- *Third country nationals.* These are employees transferred from one country to another. They tend to be born in one country, employed by a firm based in another country and working in a third country.

The advantages and disadvantages of the three types of international sales force are summarised in Table 18.5.

Expatriates and third country nationals are seldom used in sales capacities for long periods of time. They are used for three main reasons: to upgrade a subsidiary's selling performance, to fill management positions and to transfer sales policies, procedures and techniques. However, most companies use local nationals as their sales personnel. They are familiar with local business practices and can be managed accordingly.

Trade fairs and exhibitions

A trade fair (TF) or exhibition is a concentrated event at which manufacturers, distributors and other vendors display their products and/or describe their services to current and prospective customers, suppliers, other business associates and the press. It appears from Figure 18.5 that trade fairs are multipurpose events involving many interactions between the TF exhibitor and numerous parties.

Table 18.5 **Advantages and disadvantages of sales force types**

Category	Advantages	Disadvantages
Expatriates	Product knowledge High service levels Train for promotion Greater home control	Highest costs High turnover High training cost
Host country	Economical High market knowledge Language skills Best cultural knowledge Implement actions sooner	Needs product training May be held in low esteem Importance of language skills declining Difficult to ensure loyalty
Third country	Cultural sensitivity Language skills Economical Allows regional sales coverage May allow sales to country in conflict with the home country	Face identity problems Blocked promotions Income gaps Needs product/company training Loyalty assurance

Source: Reprinted from *Industrial Marketing Management*, Vol. 24, Honeycutt, E.D. and Ford, J.B. (1995) 'Guidelines for managing an international sales force', p. 138, Copyright 1995, with permission from Elsevier.

Figure 18.5 **Three conceptions of trade fairs: major interactions for a local exhibitor**

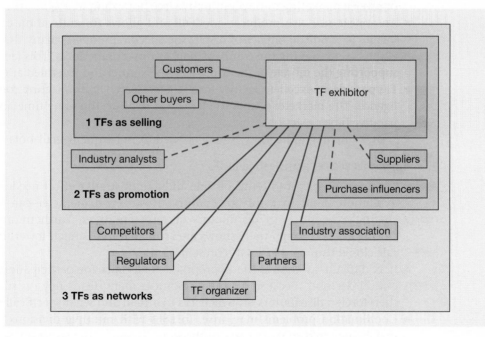

Source: adapted from Rosson and Seringhaus, 1996, p. 1181, with kind permission of P. Rossen, Dalhousie University.

TFs can enable a company to reach in a few days a concentrated group of interested prospects that might otherwise take several months to contact. Potential buyers can examine and compare the outputs of competing firms in a short period at the same place. They can see the latest developments and establish immediate contact with supplying businesses.

Traditionally TFs have been regarded as a personal selling tool, but Sharland and Balogh (1996) conclude that TFs are an excellent environment for non-selling activities such as information exchange, relationship building and channel partner assessment. TFs offer international firms the opportunity to gather vital information quickly, easily and cheaply. For example, within a short period a firm can learn a considerable amount about its competitive environment, which would take much longer and cost much more to get through other sources (e.g. secondary information).

We conclude this section by listing the arguments for and against participation in TFs.

Arguments for participation in TFs

- Marketers are able to reach a sizeable number of potential customers in a brief time period at a reasonable cost per contact. Orders may be obtained on the spot.
- Some products, by their very nature, are difficult to market without providing the potential customer with a chance to examine them or see them in action. TFs provide an excellent opportunity to introduce, promote and demonstrate new products.
- SMEs without extensive sales forces have the opportunity to present their outputs to large buying companies on the same face-to-face basis as large local rivals.
- Finding an intermediary may be one of the best reasons to attend a TF. A show is a cost-effective way to solicit and screen candidates to represent the firm, especially in a new market.
- Although many technical specialists and company executives refuse to see or take telephone calls from outsiders who try to sell them things at their places of work, these same managers often do attend trade exhibitions. The customer goes to the exhibition in order to see the seller. This is also an important aspect in the concept of reverse marketing or buyer initiative (see, for example, Figure 18.1).
- An appearance also produces goodwill and allows for cultivation of the corporate image. Beyond the impact of displaying specific products, many firms place strong emphasis on 'waving the company flag' against competition. This facet also includes supporting the morale of the firm's sales personnel and intermediaries.
- TFs provide an excellent chance for market research and collecting competitive intelligence. The marketer is able to view most rivals at the same time and to test comparative buyer reactions.
- Visitors' names and addresses may be used for subsequent mailshots.

Arguments against participation in TFs

- There is a high cost in terms of time and administrative effort needed to prepare an exhibition stand in a foreign country. However, a marketer can lower costs by sharing expenses with distributors or representatives. Furthermore, the costs of closing a sale through trade shows are estimated to be much lower than those for a sale closed through personal representation.
- It is difficult to choose the appropriate trade fairs for participation, but this is a critical decision. Because of scarce resources many firms rely on suggestions from their foreign distributors on which TFs to attend and what specifically to exhibit.
- Coordination problems may arise. In LSEs with multiple divisions more divisions may be required to participate in the same TF under the company banner. In SMEs coordination is required with distributors and agents if joint participation is desired, and this necessitates joint planning.

Furthermore, the firm faces a lot of practical problems; for example, most people visit exhibitions to browse rather than to buy. How does the exhibiting firm obtain the names and addresses of the callers who influence major buying decisions within their companies? Secondly, gimmicks may be highly effective in attracting visitors to a stand, but they can attract the wrong people. An audience may be greatly impressed by the music, dancing, demonstration or whatever is provided, yet not be remotely interested in the product. Thirdly, how can the employees who staff a stand be prevented from treating the exercise as a holiday, paying more attention to the social aspects of their involvement with the exhibition than to finding customers? What specific targets can staff be given and how can the attainment of targets be measured?

Whether a marketer should participate in a trade fair depends largely on the type of business relationship it wants to develop with a particular country. A company looking only for one-off or short-term sales might find the TF expense prohibitive, but a firm looking for long-term involvement may find the investment worthwhile.

18.4   International advertising strategies in practice

In the introduction to Part IV the question of standardization or adaptation of the whole marketing mix was discussed. Standardization allows the realization of economies of scale in the production of advertising materials, reducing advertising costs and increasing profitability. On the other hand, since advertising is based largely on language and images, it is mostly influenced by the sociocultural behaviour of consumers in different countries.

In reality it is not a question of either/or. For the internationally oriented firm it is more a question of the degree of standardization/localization. A study by Hite and Frazer (1988) showed that a majority (54 per cent) of internationally oriented firms were using a combination strategy (localizing advertising for some markets and standardizing advertising for others). Only 9 per cent of the firms were using totally standardized

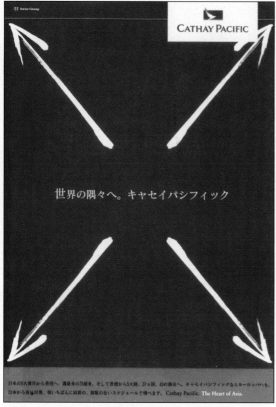
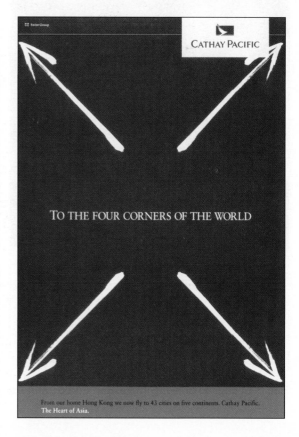

Standardized advertisements from Cathay Pacific

advertising for all foreign markets, much lower than in previous studies (Sorenson and Weichman, 1975; Boddewyn *et al.*, 1986). This could indicate a trend towards less standardization. A total of 37 per cent of the firms reported that they were using only localized advertising. Many of the global companies using standardized advertising are well known (e.g. Coca-Cola, Intel, Philip Morris/Marlboro).

The Cathay Pacific advertisements (page 579) show that the company uses a standardized strategy in the south-east Asian area. The only element of adaptation is the translation of the English text into Japanese.

Examples of adaptation (localization) strategies

Courvoisier Cognac: Hong Kong/China versus Europe

The Chinese love affair with western alcohol goes back a long way. The first imported brandy arrived in Shanghai in 1859 when Hennessy unloaded its first cargo. Then in 1949 the favourite drink of 'the Paris of the East' suddenly became a symbol of western capitalist decadence; alcohol shipments came to an abrupt halt and did not resume for the next 30 years. However, when foreign liquor once again became available in the late 1970s, cognac quickly resumed its place as a guest at the Chinese banquet table.

Today cognac and brandy still account for about 80 per cent of all imported spirits in China. Most of the imported brandy goes through Hong Kong via grey markets (see also section 17.8). Chinese awareness of brand and category of cognac is particularly high in the south, where the drinking habits of visiting Hong Kong businessmen set a strong example. This impact is reinforced by alcohol advertising on Hong Kong television, available to millions of viewers in Guangdong province.

Habits of cognac drinking in Western Europe and Asia

The key to Chinese consumption patterns lies in the importance of 'face'. Whatever the occasion, be it the father of the bride toasting his son-in-law's family in Beijing or a Shenzhen entrepreneur's night out on the town, brandy is of paramount importance. Unlike their western counterparts, who like to curl up on the couch with a snifter of brandy, the Chinese consider cognac drinking an extremely social – and conspicuous – pastime.

Two different Courvoisier advertisements are shown: the one for the western European market shows couples drinking cognac with their coffee; the Asian advertisement shows people drinking cognac from beer glasses during the meal.

Folklore as much as marketing has propelled the growth of cognac sales. Cognac has long had the inestimable commercial benefit of being widely regarded by the Chinese as enhancing a man's sexual prowess. And much to the delight of the liquor companies, the Chinese believe that the older (and pricier) the cognac, the more potent its effect.

Source: adapted from *Business Week*, 1984; Balfour, 1993.

Prince cigarettes: UK versus Germany

The Danish cigarette company House of Prince has high market share (50–90 per cent) in Scandinavian countries, but outside this area its market share is very low, typically 1–2 per cent.

The House of Prince cigarettes images show advertisements used in the UK and Germany. The UK version is based on an invitation to try the product ('I go for Prince'). The target group is also above average in education and income. The German advertisement is somewhat different. Prince is promoted as an 'original import from Denmark'. Apparently there is no 'buy German' mentality working against the use of

Advertisements for Prince cigarettes in the UK and Germany

this slogan. In the German consumer's mind Danish cigarettes are strongly positioned compared to light German cigarettes. Therefore the product's position is emphasised as 'men's business', with Viking associations and ideas of freedom. Incidentally, the two products Prince and Prince Denmark are not identical. The German Prince Denmark has a less strong taste than does Prince.

Gammel Dansk (Danish Distillers/Danisco): Denmark versus Germany

The Danish bitter Gammel Dansk has a 75 per cent share of the bitter market in Denmark. Thus the product has a high degree of recognition there (nearly all Danish adults know the label). The objective of the Danish advertisement has therefore primarily been to maintain Gammel Dansk's high degree of recognition.

Although the market share in Denmark is very high, Gammel Dansk does not have any position worth mentioning outside Denmark. In Germany the situation is totally different. Here the knowledge (and trial share) is at a minimum. The Germans have their own Jägermeister and competition is tough. The strategy behind the German campaign has therefore been to make people try Gammel Dansk by letting them fill out a coupon. By sending it in they receive a little bottle of Gammel Dansk and two original Gammel Dansk glasses.

LUX soap (Unilever): the United Kingdom versus India

The UK version of the LUX advertisement is based on the classic transborder advertising campaign, 'the beauty soap of film stars', which has been standardised to a high degree. In India the LUX campaign has been given a special local touch.

Advertisements for Gammel Dansk in Denmark and Germany

Advertisements for Lux in UK and India

The Indian version is one of three advertisements that trace LUX's association with film stars from the past era to the current stars of today and the potential film stars of tomorrow. The advertisement focuses on three past legendary beauties of Indian cinema who have endorsed the brand. The creative statement is in a cinema poster style, keeping the brand image in mind, and in a sepia colour tone to give it a nostalgic feel.

LEGO FreeStyle: Europe versus the Far East

The LEGO images show European and Far Eastern versions of an advertisement for LEGO FreeStyle. The Asian version, 'Build your child's mind', appeals to Asian parents' desire for their children to do well in school.

Advertisement for LEGO Free Style in the Far East

The Asian educational system is very competitive and only those with the highest grades are admitted to university. In many places in Asia it is a defeat for parents if their child does not do well in school. The Asian version has been run in Hong Kong, Taiwan and Korea (preferably in the local languages because the majority of consumers do not understand

English). In Hong Kong the advertisements are run in English or Chinese (depending on the language of the magazine).

The European version implies creativity when playing with the different FreeStyle bricks: 'What will your child make of it?'

Advertisement for LEGO Free Style in Europe

18.5   Implications of Internet/e-commerce for communication decisions

In the physical marketplace different communication tools are used in the buying process of customers (see Figure 18.6). Traditional mass communication tools (print advertising, TV and radio) can create awareness and this can result in consumers' identification of new needs. From then on other elements of the communication mix take over, such as direct marketing (direct marketing, personal selling) and in-store promotion. Unlike marketing in the physical marketplace the Internet/e-commerce encompasses the entire 'buying' process.

Figure 18.6 The role of Internet communication in the buying process of customers

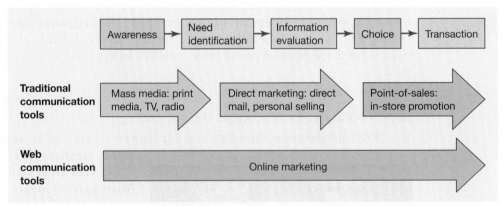

Market communication strategies change dramatically in the online world. On the Internet it is easier than ever to actually *communicate* a message to large numbers of people. However, in many cases, it is much harder for your message to be heard above the noise by your target audience. Various strategies for conducting online marketing have been developed in the past several years – from the most common (website linking) to the most expensive (banner advertising) to the most offensive (e-mail spamming), and everything in between. It is almost certain that a continual stream of new market communication strategies will emerge as the Internet medium evolves.

Although some companies do business exclusively on the Web, for most the Internet offers exciting opportunities to develop an additional sales channel. This new channel can extend a company's reach significantly, enabling it to do business with a new customer base that was previously unreachable. Customer preferences are driving e-commerce because many consumers simply prefer online shopping because of the convenience, reach and availability of products and services. Companies that do not develop an Internet presence risk losing these customers to more aggressive competitors.

Developing a successful online marketing programme boils down to the same objectives as in the physical world: how to create an audience. 'Audience development' is the preferred phrase for online marketing, because it more precisely communicates the point of the activity.

How, then, can a Web audience be created? The Web audience development process consists of the following six phases (USWeb/CKS, 1999):

1. integration;
2. design requirements that are unique;
3. techniques for audience creation;
4. methods of advertising the site;
5. effective promotions that attract attention;
6. measurement and analysis to ensure ongoing success.

1: Integration of Internet strategy into an overall business strategy

Before a company builds a site it should determine how the site will fit into the company's overall business strategy. A holistic approach does not look at the site in isolation, but in the context of overall marketing and sales efforts. Marketers must understand the role of each medium within the company's marketing mix and utilise the strengths of each. Creating the right online corporate identity is the first step for audience development, the step from which all other components of a successful Web marketing programme flow. Synergy and consistency are essential. Although individual messages may vary to apply the unique strengths of each medium, the overall flavour should be consistent across media.

All marketing and sales activities should work together, and each marketing objective should be supported across multiple media where possible. A company should cross-promote among media, for example promoting its website in brochures and print advertising.

2: Design requirements that are unique

Given the free flow of information in the *market space* and the potential for overload, the marketer with the best-designed information package will generate the competitive advantage.

While audience creation, advertising and promotions drive traffic to a site it is the design that either encourages visitors to explore or drives them away in frustration. A good design is, of course, aesthetically pleasing. More importantly, though, it engages visitors, makes it easy for them to navigate the site and compels them to explore the site further, purchase products and return another day. Attractive graphics that support the company's message are important, but large graphics that take a long time to load frustrate users. Many visitors will not wait long enough for the graphic to finish loading. Additionally, visitors are less likely to return to a site that has confusing navigational cues.

The design should use clear, consistent navigational cues that make it easy for visitors to determine where they are within the site structure. With more than a million sites competing for users' attention, first impressions are critical. A confusing, poorly organised site structure can negate even the highest quality content.

Web design differs significantly from design for other media. The most important difference is that the Web is interactive, incorporating hyperlinks and devices for immediate visitor feedback. Some sophisticated designs include dynamically generated pages that are custom-tailored to each visitor's interests, preferences and buying habits.

3: Techniques for audience creation

Developing traffic on a site requires expert knowledge of the numerous online search devices. The audience creation methods described in this section are highly cost effective for generating a large number of repeat site visitors:

- *Search engine optimization.* Search engines and directories play a critical role in Internet marketing, because the majority of Web surfers rely on these navigation guides to conduct their research. Because users typically explore only the first 10 or 20 sites on the list, an understanding of how search ranking works can make a huge difference in traffic volume. Effective optimization of search engine results requires carefully designed meta tags and other HTML code and pointer pages specialized for individual search engines.
- *Editorial placement in new media.* In addition to using the Internet as a communication tool to contact traditional journalists, companies can reach out to the new and rapidly increasing breed of 'online-only' news media. Most online stories contain hyperlinks to the sites of featured marketers. Because online stories are typically archived in news databases and indexed by search engines they provide a source of new visitors for an indefinite period.
- *Strategic linking.* A major differentiator between the Web and other media is the use of hyperlinks, in which a user clicks on a link and is instantly transported to another site. The more inbound links a company establishes on other sites, the more qualified visitors the site will attract. Unlike banner ads, links frequently stay in place for months and bear the credibility of editorial selection. Best of all, they are usually free. Some of the best investments of time marketers can make is to contact Web masters of affinity sites in an attempt to place inbound links on their sites. Web masters of many popular sites actively seek out quality sites to which they can link.
- *Interactive public relations.* Interactive public relations facilitates worldwide new delivery as well as direct interactivity with individuals. Newsgroups, mailing lists, forums, bulletin boards and other virtual communities are important sources of visitors for a site.

One method for tapping into virtual communities is to employ interactive public relations with materials such as electronic press releases or other stories that may be of interest to specific groups.

4: Methods of advertising the site

To take full advantage of the power of Internet marketing companies must understand the differences between online advertising and other, more traditional media.

- *Banner advertising.* Online banner ads use eye-catching multimedia effects such as animation, interactivity, sound, video and 3D to attract attention and draw visitors to a site. Even in-the-banner commerce transactions are becoming common.

With online advertising companies can target ads with far greater precision than with any other medium. Today's ad server technology offers highly sophisticated, automatic targeting that uses factors such as demographic data and visitor behaviour while at the site. In addition, technology is emerging that allows online ads to be tailored automatically to each individual visitor.

Marketers can take advantage of this targeting capability to place banner ads on sites that attract visitors who match the demographic profile for companies' products. As a result they can increase brand awareness among a carefully targeted audience and drive highly qualified traffic to their site.

- *Sponsorships.* Exclusive sponsorship of site content is a growing trend. Sponsoring strategic editorial content is an effective way to establish long-term brand identification among target audiences.

Sponsorship of content or pages on certain sites – for example a site maintained by an influential industry group or a leader in a particular industry – associate a company with that group or industry leader. This association lends credibility and helps increase customer interest and brand awareness.

- *Barter advertising.* In addition to paid advertising, many sites are performing banner exchanges and ad barter arrangements. Even among top content sites bartering is a common, cost-effective way to boost traffic. Companies can take advantage of this low-cost advertising method by establishing personal relationships and negotiating barter deals with other sites.

5: Effective promotions that attract attention

Promotions offer an excellent opportunity for public relations exposure and online community awareness. These promotions can take a variety of forms:

- *Contests.* Quizzes, sweepstakes and other contests are sometimes effective components of online marketing. Companies can use contests for a variety of purposes, including sales generation, brand recognition establishment, customer loyalty building and market research.
- *Loyalty programmes.* It is well known that the cost of retaining a current customer is about one-tenth that of acquiring a new one. As a result, customer loyalty programmes can have a dramatic impact on the bottom line. Loyalty programmes and similar online campaigns can help retain customers and motivate them to recruit new customers by recommending a company's site or products to friends and associates.
- *Online events.* Live events (for example live sporting events) in which users from around the world participate have proven tremendously popular with the online public. Promoters have seized on this trend to capture audiences for a variety of online events, including celebrity chats, live concert broadcasts, virtual conferences and auctions. Such events can be effective for gaining mindshare among new users and positioning a company or site at the cutting edge of its market.

6: Measurement and analysis to ensure ongoing success

The Internet is one of the most measurable of all communications media. The ability to monitor the effectiveness and continually fine-tune sites and campaigns is one of the medium's greatest benefits.

Paul (1996) argues that the Web has the ability to compile statistics about the *reach* (how many people have viewed each advertisement) and *exposure time* (how long the viewers have looked at the advertisement). This helps companies to measure the effectiveness of their advertisements.

Server logs and other performance data are valuable indicators that can be used to develop insights which are far beyond what any print circulation figures or TV ratings data can provide. It is important, however, to combine these quantitative measures with qualitative measures to achieve a meaningful evaluation of effectiveness. Tracking which external sources refer the most visitors to the home page is useful when evaluating the success of ad banners, affinity links and other promotional campaigns.

Audience qualification

Counting Web page hits alone is not sufficient to determine effectiveness of audience development strategies. It is more important to determine *who* the visitors are. Are they prospective customers or simply confused and curious surfers who will never return? How many pages past the first home page does the average visitor explore from a particular banner ad? What percentage of visitors return again, and which ones become paying customers?

Customer feedback

Perhaps the most valuable form of analysis comes not from technology but directly from site visitors. Sites that post their e-mail addresses or telephone numbers to encourage contact from visitors are sending a strong message that invites relationship building with prospects and customers. An interactive process that incorporates visitor feedback enables the company to raise the site to its full potential and keep it there.

Marketers can get information on visitors' perception of the site through online visitor surveys. Because they are convenient and even fun to respond to, response rates are typically high. For additional opinions marketers can monitor discussions about the brand and general product category on discussion boards in newsgroups as well as other independent forums. Such feedback is a natural by-product of many online marketing activities and can be effectively incorporated into the other components of audience development.

18.6　Summary

Five ingredients of international communication have been presented in this chapter:

1. advertising;
2. public relations;
3. sales promotion;
4. direct marketing;
5. personal selling.

As international marketers manage the various elements of the promotions mix in differing environmental conditions decisions must be made about what channels are to be used in the communication, the message, who is to execute or help execute the programme, and how the results of the communication plan are to be measured. The trend is towards greater harmonisation of strategy, at the same time allowing for flexibility at the local level and early incorporation of local needs into the communication plans.

Hence an important decision for international marketers is whether the different elements of the communication should be standardised worldwide or localised. The main reasons for seeking standardisation are as follows:

■ Customers do not conform to national boundaries.
■ The company is seeking to build an international brand image.
■ Economies of scale can be achieved.
■ The few high-quality creative ideas can be exploited as widely as possible.
■ Special expertise can be developed and exploited.

However, some communication tools, especially personal selling, have to be localised to fit conditions of individual markets. Another reason for the localisation of the personal selling tool is that distribution channel members are normally located firmly within a country. Consequently decisions concerning recruitment, training, motivation and evaluation of salespersons have to be made at the local level.

The process of selecting agencies has also been considered. The requisite blend of local knowledge, cultural understanding and management expertise across international markets is elusive. Too much centralisation and standardisation results in inappropriate marketing communications.

A very important communication tool for the future is the Internet. Any company eager to take advantage of the Internet on a global scale must select a business model for its Internet ventures and estimate how information and transactions delivered through this new direct marketing medium will influence its existing distribution and communication system.

CASE STUDY 18.1 Helly Hansen

Sponsoring fashion clothes in the US market

On a warm autumn day in 1997 Johnny Austad, President of the Norwegian clothing manufacturer Helly Hansen Co. (HH), arrives at the company's US subsidiary. Johnny can still not quite understand the incredible development that HH has seen in the US market. During the last couple of years Helly Hansen USA has had an increase in turnover of 10 per cent per year, but in 1996 turnover doubled, amounting to one-third of HH's worldwide sales.

How it all started
Helly Hansen Co. was founded in 1877 by the Norwegian captain Helly Juell Hansen. During the era of the sailing ship he felt the forces of nature when he had to stand at the helm in all kinds of weather. Many hours were spent oiling clothes so

they would become waterproof before rough weather set in. However, the clothes became stiff and sticky, so when Helly Juell Hansen finally went ashore he decided to develop better rain clothes for Norwegian sailors. Today HH sells its products in more than 20 countries. Production takes place in the company's own factories in Norway and Portugal, as well as in the Far East, and via contract manufacturing. Design of the new collections takes place at the company's headquarters in Norway.

From a producer of functionalistic clothes to a supplier of fashion clothes to the US 'underground'
The honourable 100-year-old Norwegian producer of functionalistic clothes for sailors has by chance

American rap group Bad Boys in Helly Hansen clothes
Source: A/S Helly Hanson

become the supplier of fashion clothes to black hip-hoppers in New York's underground. The label, which for generations has been connected with wind and waterproof leisure wear, and work clothes for the quality-conscious consumer who likes to be dressed 'sensibly', has now become a symbol of the avant-garde and the different. The young think the clothes are smart and don't care if they have taped seams and that it might be difficult to breathe through four layers of waterproof coating.

In earlier days, the first and last thing that HH thought of when making jackets was functionalism. The result was a very large collection of jackets with small specialised differences that only real enthusiasts could appreciate. HH's prices, on the other hand, became unreasonably high. By gathering several of the functions in the same jacket HH is able to make allowances for its choosy customers, as well as producing at a price that a larger part of the market is able to pay. Where HH used to direct its collections toward alpine skiers, fishermen, sea sportspeople and snow boarders, it is now beginning to look more at current fashion trends. HH is trying to link its look to street fashion and hopes that in this way its core customers will feel smarter, while new customers will be encouraged to buy because of the look of the clothes.

Before Johnny Austad gets on the plane back to Norway, the US subsidiary receives an enquiry about sponsorship from one of the most well-known rap groups in the United States. The manager of the rap group in question is seeking $200,000 from HH for Bad Boys to perform in HH clothes at all their concerts in the next six months as well as in their coming music video.

As a newly employed marketing assistant in the US HH subsidiary, you are asked to take care of this enquiry. You are specifically asked the following questions.

Questions

1. Would you recommend that HH sponsors Bad Boys? Give reasons for your answer.

2. How can an eventual sponsorship be integrated into the total marketing plan for HH clothes in the US market?

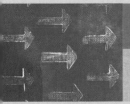

CASE STUDY 18.2   Fisherman's Friend

Is sponsoring extreme motorsport events a good promotion tool?

Lofthouse of Fleetwood Ltd, a family-owned company, first created Fisherman's Friend Original Extra Strong Lozenges in 1865 in Fleetwood, Lancashire. James Lofthouse, a Fleetwood pharmacist, devised a fluid made with liquorice, capsicum, eucalyptus and menthol to protect fishermen against the rigours of the North Atlantic fishing grounds.

Today the lozenges are available in 120 countries worldwide, and have grown to become a major international brand (**www.fishermansfriend.com**). The core proposition of Fisherman's Friend as a unique, strong-tasting medicinal sweet that comes wrapped in a paper bag remains constant globally (Fisherman's Friend Original Extra Strong Lozenges are still manufactured to exactly the same formulation as in 1865) but other elements of the marketing mix vary country by country. The lozenges are now available in eight different versions including Original Extra Strong, Aniseed, Original Tooth-friendly, Mint Sugar Free, and Lemon Sugar Free

History

The Friend was unknown outside Fleetwood until 1963. In 1969 the Lofthouse family gave up the unequal struggle of hand packing their growing orders and turned an old tram shed into a packing and distribution warehouse. The company then employed 8. Now it provides work for 250 as the town's second-largest private employer. It has a 300,000 sq ft plant with computer-controlled lines producing lozenges 21 hours a day.

By 1974 the Friend was being exported to Norway and was beginning to move into the European Community. A second flavour, aniseed, was introduced in 1976, a mere 111 years after the first. Fisherman's Friend is now one of Britain's greatest export successes, with annual sales of over 10 billion lozenges in a total of 107 countries. All in all it has been a very profitable business during recent years

Sponsorship for the the Endurance World Championship

On 23 January 2003 the Endurance World Championship announced that Fisherman's Friend had renewed its 'Associate Sponsor' agreement for the forthcoming year (**www.worldendurance.com**).

Endurance racing is probably one of the most extreme forms of motorsport. Man and machine are ridden to the limit for hours, lapping at times that are frequently little different from those seen in a World Superbike sprint length race. However, these machines cover much greater distances. Races can be based on either distance or time. The 2002 series broke new ground by having a mix of shorter 200-mile races together with the more traditional 6, 8 and 24 hour races. Although the 24 hour races are naturally the most gruelling on men and machines, the shorter races pose their own challenges with less margin for error or time to recover after problems.

If a rider is unable to continue to race, the remaining team riders may have to ride back-to-back sessions or the team may be forced to retire.

Questions

1. Which promotion tools would be the most relevant for Fisherman's Friend to use?

2. What criteria should Fisherman's Friend use for selecting the right sponsorship activity?

3. Do you think that sponsoring the Endurance World Championship is the right activity to support?

4. How should sponsoring the Endurance World Championship be supported by other promotion tools, in order to maximise the total value of the marketing expenses?

For further exercises and cases, see this book's website at
www.booksites.net/hollensen

Questions for discussion

1. Identify and discuss problems associated with assessing advertising effectiveness in foreign markets.

2. Compare domestic communication with international communication. Explain why 'noise' is more likely to occur in the case of international communication processes.

3. Why do more companies not standardise advertising messages worldwide? Identify the environmental constraints that act as barriers to the development and implementation of standardised global advertising campaigns.

4. Explain how personal selling may differ overseas from how it is used in the home market.

5. What is meant by saying that advertising regulations vary around the world?

6. Evaluate the 'percentage of sales' approach to setting advertising budgets in foreign markets.

7. Explain how the multinational firm may have an advantage over local firms in training the sales force and evaluating its performance.

8. Identify and discuss problems associated with allocating the company's promotion budget across several foreign markets.

References

Balfour, F. (1993) 'Alcohol industry: companies in high spirits', *China Trade Report*, June, pp. 4–5.

Bennett, R. (1995) *International Marketing: Strategy, planning, market entry and implementation*, Kogan Page, London.

Boddewyn, J.J., Soehl, R. and Picard, J. (1986) 'Standardization in international marketing: is Ted Levitt in fact right?', *Business Horizons*, pp. 69–75.

Business Week (1984) 'Advertising Europe's new Common Market', July, pp. 62–5.

Desmet, P. and Xardel, D. (1996) 'Challenges and pitfalls for direct mail across borders: the European example', *Journal of Direct Marketing*, vol. 10, no. 3, pp. 48–60.

Harper, T. (1986) 'Polaroid clicks instantly in Moslem markets', *Advertising Age* (special report on 'Marketing to the Arab world'), 30 January, p. 12.

Hite, R.E. and Frazer, C. (1988) 'International advertising strategies of multinational corporations', *Journal of Advertising Research*, vol. 28, August–September, pp. 9–17.

Honeycutt, E.D. and Ford, J.B. (1995) 'Guidelines for managing an international sales force', *Industrial Marketing Management*, vol. 24, pp. 135–44.

Hung, C.L. and West, D.C. (1991) 'Advertising budgeting methods in Canada, the UK and the USA', *International Journal of Advertising*, vol. 10, pp. 239–50.

Joensen, S. (1997) 'What hedder it now on engelsk?', *Politikken* (Danish newspaper), 24 April 1997.

Lynch, R. (1994) *European Marketing*, Irwin, Homewood, IL.

MacNamee, B. and McDonnell, R. (1995) *The Marketing Casebook*, Routledge, London.

Meenaghan, T. (1996) 'Ambush marketing: a threat to corporate sponsorship', *Sloan Management Review*, Fall, pp. 103–13.

Mueller, B. (1996) *International Advertising: Communicating across cultures*, Wadsworth, Belmont, CA.

Nørmark, P. (1994) 'Co-promotion in growth', *Markedsføring* (Danish marketing magazine), no. 14, p. 14.

Onkvisit, S. and Shaw, J.J. (1993) *International Marketing: Analysis and strategy* (2nd edn), Macmillan, London.

Ottesen, O. (1995) 'Buyer initiative: ignored, but imperative for marketing management – towards a new view of market communication', *Tidsvise Skrifter*, no. 15, avdeling for Økonomi, Kultur og Samfunnsfag ved Høgskolen i Stavanger.

Paul, P. (1996) 'Marketing on the Internet', *Journal of Consumer Marketing*, vol. 13, no. 4, pp. 27–39.

Phillips, C., Poole, I. and Lowe, R. (1994) *International Marketing Strategy: Analysis, development and implementation*, Routledge, London/New York.

Rosson, J.R. and Seringhaus, F.H.R. (1996) 'Trade fairs as international marketing venues: a case study', paper presented at the 12th IMP Conference, University of Karlsruhe.

Sharland, A. and Balogh, D. (1996) 'The value of non-selling activities at international trade shows', *Industrial Marketing Management*, vol. 25, pp. 59–66.

Shelly, B. (1995) 'Cool customer', *Unilever Magazine*, no. 2, pp. 13–17.

Sorenson, R.Z. and Weichman, V.E. (1975) 'How multinationals view marketing standardization', *Harvard Business Review*, May–June, pp. 38–56.

Further reading

Bayne, K.M. (2003) 'Marketing without Wires: Targeting Promotions and Advertising to Mobile Device Users' *Info - The journal of policy, regulation and strategy for telecommunications*, vol. 5, no. 3, pp. 73–5.

Blythe, J. (2002) 'Using trade fairs in key account management', *Industrial Marketing Management*, vol. 31, pp. 1–9.

Garber, L.L. and Dpotson, M.J. (2002) and Dotson, M.J. 'A method for the selection of appropriate business-to-business integrated marketing communications mixes', *Journal of Marketing Communications*, vol. 8, pp. 1–17.

Harris, G. and Attour, S. (2003) 'The international advertising practices of multinational companies: A content analysis study', *European Journal of Marketing*, vol. 37, no. 1, pp. 154–68.

Kanso, A. and Nelson, R.N. (2002) 'Advertising localization: overshadows standardization', *Journal of Advertising Research*, January–February, pp. 79–89.

Solberg, C.A. (2002) 'The perennial issue of adaptation or standardization of international marketing communication: organizational contingencies and performance', *Journal of International Marketing*, vol. 10, no. 3, pp. 1–21.

Tharp, M. and Jeong, J. (2001) 'Executive insights: the Global Network Communications Agency', *Journal of International Marketing*, vol. 9, no. 4, pp. 111–31.

CASE STUDY IV.1   Absolut Vodka

Defending and attacking for a better position in the global vodka market

On a lovely October day in 2003 Bengt Baron (the President of V&S Absolut Spirits) packs his suitcase for the third time in the month for a business trip to the subsidiary in New York, The Absolut Spirits Company Inc., which imports ABSOLUT in the US and distributes the brand through Future Brands, a joint venture with Jim Beam Brands. While packing he thinks of how hard the company must fight to keep and increase its market share for Absolut Vodka in the United States and other markets. Since March 2001 The V&S Absolut Spirits Company has controlled much more of the vodka distribution than before.

Until 1994 Absolut Vodka was distributed by Carillon Importers, with the charismatic Michael Roux in charge. In 1994 The Absolut Company entered into an agreement with the somewhat larger Seagram Co. to distribute Absolut Vodka in the United States and a number of other countries. Seagram is the world's fourth largest distributor of spirits, with worldwide sales of nearly $6 billion. Seagram distributed (in the United States) such well-known labels as Chivas Regal, Coyote Tequila and Martell Cognac. But it needed a well-known vodka label in its assortment. Seagram is an international distributor with local distributors in 150 countries.

The shift from Carillon Importers to Seagram Co. has not been without problems and drama. Michael Roux was very upset when he heard he had been fired as importer for the US market. As a countermove, he has taken the Russian competitor Stolichnaya into his assortment, thus intensifying the 'vodka war'.

In 1995 the Latin American and south-east Asian markets were transferred to Seagram. In January 1996 Canada was also transferred to Seagram. In 2000 the Seagram wine and spirits business was acquired by Pernod Richard and Diageo.

Then in March 2001 Vin & Sprit (V&S), Jim Beam Brands Worldwide and Maxxium announced a set of agreements that established new global distribution for V&S, the producer of Absolut Vodka.

V&S and Jim Beam Brands Worldwide, a unit of Fortune Brands, Inc., the US-based consumer products company, has created a joint venture for the distribution of the companies' brands in the United States.

With the creation of Future Brands LLC – the new US distribution joint venture – both V&S and Jim Beam Brands will reap the revenue and cost benefits of greater scale in a consolidating industry while retaining the ownership and marketing responsibilities for their respective brands. With a combined US sales volume of approximately 20 million 9-litre cases in 2000, the partners' brands will drive the second highest case volume in the United States. Absolut accounts for more than half of all imported vodka sales in the United States and the bourbon, Jim Beam, is the no. 1 whisky in the country.

V&S has also become the fourth equal shareholder in Maxxium – the distribution joint venture of Jim Beam Brands, Rémy Cointreau and Highland Distillers – which will handle distribution of Absolut Vodka and the other brands outside the United States.

When Bengt gets on the plane at Stockholm's airport bound for New York, there are two things that worry him:

■ Apparently the market share of Absolut Vodka in the United States has reached saturation point. Has V&S Absolut Spirits reached the top of its market share in that country or is it time for a frontal attack on the number one brand, Smirnoff?

■ Until now the market share for Absolut Vodka in Europe (especially in eastern Europe) has been a lot smaller. This can be a problem when 80 per cent of the world's vodka is consumed in Russia and the other countries of eastern Europe.

On his way over the Atlantic Bengt thinks back on the story and adventure of Absolut Vodka.

The history of Absolut Vodka

The Swedish state-owned Vin & Sprit AB can justly call the launch of its Absolut Vodka an absolute success. Absolut Vodka is probably the biggest success story in the world of spirits. It has become an icon.

The shape of the bottle

The shape of the bottle dates back to the mid-nineteenth century. Far earlier, in the sixteenth century, Swedish pharmacies sold a clear, distilled liquid as a cure for ailments such as colic or even the plague.

The custom was to ingest it by spoon, not with a shot glass.

Rediscovered at an antique store in Stockholm by Gunnar Broman, of the now defunct advertising agency Carlsson & Broman, the clear medicine bottle has since been fine-tuned by Absolut's team of shrewd marketers. The neck was lengthened, curves were adjusted and labels were replaced by printed typeface. To top it off, a medallion bearing the portrait of Lars Olsson Smith, known as 'The King of Vodka', was stamped on each bottle. In 1879 Smith successfully broke Stockholm's spirit monopoly by distilling and marketing Absolut Rent Bränvin, or Absolute Pure Vodka. His tipple was the beginning of a dynasty.

The current Absolut family consists of the following six variants/flavours:

■ *Absolut Vodka* has a rich taste, is smooth and mellow with a distinct character of grain. Introduced in 1979.

■ *Absolut Peppar* is aromatic, complex and spicy. The pepper flavour is a combination of the spicy components in the capsicum pepper family and the fresh green jalapeño pepper. Introduced in 1986.

■ *Absolut Citron* is made from citrus fruits. Lemon is dominant, but other citrus flavours are added to give a fuller flavour. Absolut Citron has a distinct

ABSOLUT PERFECTION.

ABSOLUT SQUEEZE.

character of lemon and lime with a hint of sweetness. Introduced in 1988.

- *Absolut Kurant* is made from blackcurrants, a distant cousin to the grape. It is a fragrant dark berry that grows on shrubs up to six feet in height. Absolut Kurant has a distinct character of blackcurrant, with a hint of tartness and sweetness. Introduced in 1992.
- *Absolut Mandrin* is made from citrus fruits. Mandarin and orange are dominant, but other citrus flavours are added to give a fuller flavour. Absolut Mandrin has a distinct character with a hint of sweetness. Introduced in 1999.
- *Absolut Vanilia* has a rich, robust and complex taste of vanilla with notes of butterscotch and hints of dark chocolate. Introduced in 2003.

Introduction to the US market

Independent market research in the United States concluded in 1979 that no one would buy Swedish vodka. Nevertheless the first shipment of Absolut Vodka was sent off to that country in April 1979. The destination for the first shipment of vodka was Boston. Some 90,000 litres were sold worldwide in 1979 and in 2002 worldwide sales were 67.3 million litres. About 60 per cent of this was exported to the United States. Apart from the United States the most important markets are (in decreasing order of impor-

tance): Canada, Sweden, Greece, Spain, Germany, Mexico, the United Kingdom, France and Italy.

The marketing of the bottle

For more than 25 years advertisements for Absolut Vodka have been based on the same fundamental concept, with focus placed on the product. The very first advertisement, 'Absolut Perfection', was created in 1980 and today it is one of the most often used.

Since Andy Warhol, patron saint of pop art, created his first Absolut painting in 1985 ('Absolut Warhol'), artists around the world have been asked to render their interpretation of the bottle.

In the advertisement 'Absolut Essence' magazine readers were able to fold back the cover and smell the scent of Absolut Kurant.

Distinctive advertising campaigns such as 'Absolut London', in which the door of 10 Downing Street resembles an Absolut bottle, have made the vodka brand nearly as famous as Coca-Cola or Nike. Most countries maintain strict rules concerning alcohol advertisements to consumers, but Absolut's PR machine has milked the free publicity that its advertising generates.

Bengt Baron's thoughts have become dream-like on the plane to New York, but he wakes with a start when passengers are asked to buckle their seat belts. To use his time sensibly before landing, Bengt takes

Table 1   Distribution of world vodka sales – volume and value – V&S Absolut Spirits' market share

	Volume: million litres	Value: $ million	The Absolut Company million litres	Absolut market share – volume
WORLD	3,600	16,600	67.3	1.9
	% of total	% of total	% of total	%
Eastern Europe	85.9	63.8	6.0	0.5
North America	8.7	20.7	64.0	10.2
Western Europe	3.3	11.7	14.0	6.3
Latin America	0.8	1.5	5.0	7.0
Africa & the Middle East	0.8	1.2	4.0	2.4
Asia-Pacific	0.4	0.9	4.0	10.9
Australasia	0.1	0.2	3.0	3.8
Total	100.0	100	100	

Source: adapted from Impact International and Euromonitor

a report out of his suitcase describing conditions in the US and world markets. The following is the essence of the report.

The world market for vodka

Table 1 shows that eastern European countries account for 80 per cent of the world's total vodka sales, which is matched by the area's average consumption per capita per year. In Poland the average vodka consumption per capita per year is about 10 litres, while the average in the Confederation of Independent States is 5 litres. As a comparison, average consumption in the United States is 1.3 litres and in the United Kingdom 0.6 litres. It should be noted that all these figures are based on registered sales. In addition there is home distillery, which takes place in quite a large part of eastern Europe as well as in Sweden and Finland.

The markets of eastern Europe are distinguished not only by their high vodka consumption but also by how much consumers know about alcoholic beverages and their feeling for quality. However, political uncertainty and lack of a well-functioning infrastructure in several eastern European countries make short-term developments difficult to predict.

For several years Absolut Vodka has been sold to most eastern European countries, and in 1995 the brand was introduced in Poland. Thus Absolut Vodka is now represented in all the major vodka markets of the world.

The US market for vodka

In the last 15 years the consumption of alcohol in the United States has decreased by 20 per cent. There are several reasons for this. One of the main reasons is the 'health trend' in the country, which has caused a greater consciousness of the harmful effects of alcohol. At the same time there has been a tendency towards drinking 'less but better'. Thus many people now drink cleaner and more pure alcohol. This has meant that the sale of 'super-premium' (high-quality) brands has not fallen but has been stable in the last 5 years.

Nearly all imported brands are in the super-premium segment and are the main reason that vodka imports have not fallen. Although the vodka importers' share of the total market is only 12–15 per cent, the gross margin on imported vodka represents about 40 per cent of the total gross margin of all vodka sales in the United States.

Historically vodka has not been a differentiated product, but more and more flavoured brands have gradually been introduced to the market, including Absolut Citron, Absolut Peppar and Absolut Kurant.

Today it is not without risk introducing new brands to the US market, as consumers' tastes there are so volatile. A producer can introduce a flavour one year that is unpopular the next.

Product segments

The different product segments are as follows:

- *Platinum*. The most expensive category, with prices around $20 per bottle. Labels in this category include Stolichnaya Cristall. This segment has under 1 per cent of total US vodka consumption.
- *Super-premium*. Nearly all labels here are imported. The leading labels are Swedish Absolut, Russian Stolichnaya and Finnish Finlandia. The price level is $15–16 per bottle. This category's share of the total vodka consumption in the United States is about 10 per cent.
- *Premium*. Here we find the world's most popular vodka, the US Smirnoff, sold for $9–10 a bottle. This group's share is 22 per cent of the US's total vodka consumption.

- *Standard priced*. Here the two English labels Gilbey's and Gordon's are sold for $7 a bottle. The category's share is 14 per cent.
- *Popular priced*. This is the largest group. Its share of total US vodka consumption is about 54 per cent, and the group consists of a number of local labels at about $6 a bottle.

On a worldwide level the three largest imported brands are Absolut (number two), Stolichnaya (number six) and Finlandia (number eighteen). Absolut's main competitors are Smirnoff, Finlandia and Stolichnaya. They may be characterised as follows:

- *Stolichnaya* (brand owner: Sojuzplodimport). The pioneer among imported vodka brands, this was the first vodka to be introduced in the United States, in 1972. Stolichnaya was at this time a good alternative to the USA-produced vodka brands as it tasted milder due to a more refined distilling process. But Stolichnaya's popularity has been dependent on the political climate between the United States and the former USSR. Today Stolichnaya is distributed by Absolut Vodka's former importer, Carillon Importers.
- *Finlandia* (brand owner: Alko Group). This brand was introduced to the United States in 1976. Despite many marketing campaigns, Finlandia has never been able to get a grip on the vodka market. In the trade, it is estimated that Finlandia has the most exposed position, as all new importers go for the esteemed third place, which seems to be a realistic goal for a new brand. In 2002 Findlandia celebrated its 30th anniversary in style by partnering with MGM Pictures and EON Productions' latest James Bond film, *Die Another Day*, scheduled for worldwide release in the winter of 2002. In *Die Another Day* Bond still likes his martinis shaken, not stirred, but his vodka now is courtesy of Finlandia, not Smirnoff.
- *Smirnoff* (brand owner: Diageo Plc) Diageo was created in December 1997, following the merger of Guinness Plc and Grand Metropolitan Plc. Among wine and spirits companies included in the merger were Carillon Importers Ltd, The Paddington Corporation, UDV, Glenmore, Schieffelin & Somerset, Heublein Inc., and International Distillers & Vintners North America. Guinness/UDV's primary US division is United Distillers & Vintners North America (UDVNA). In 2000 UDVNA was the second largest spirits company in the US market, with a 13.5 per cent volume share. Three of the top 10 US spirits brands in 2000 were UDVNA brands:

Smirnoff vodka, José Cuervo tequila, and Gordon's gin and vodka.

The distribution system for vodka in the United States

Generally the sale of spirits goes through the distribution system shown in Figure 1. For US producers, producer/supplier and importer/agent coincide. The retail ('off-premise') sale of wine, spirits and beer takes place through two different distribution systems. In 'open states' (licensed states) the market is free, and sale takes place in liquor stores, supermarkets or other grocery stores where the owner has a licence to sell spirits. In 'controlled states' spirits can only be sold in liquor stores owned by the state, similar to the Nordic monopoly system.

The importer/agent usually has only a minor sales force, which concentrates on selling to and servicing a distributor. An importer/agent usually cooperates with one distributor in each state (although one distributor can handle several states), and in large states a distributor can have up to 500 salespeople (geographically divided). Generally these salespeople pay for their own car and receive a low basic wage and commission.

The salesperson in the area concerned visits both the institutional market and the retail market, often once a week, taking orders and in exceptional cases delivering goods and collecting payment.

World market shares for top vodka brands – 2002 (retail channels)

If we include vodka sales through all distribution channels (retail, HORECA (HOtel, REstaurant, CAtering) and duty free) brands such as Stolichnaya

Figure 1 The general distribution system for spirits in the United States

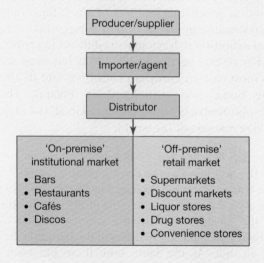

and Moskovskaya would be very highly ranked. But in reality these brands do not really exist. In Russia Stolichnaya, for instance, is produced by 800 distilleries and in various bottle and case sizes. Moreover, products differ widely between distilleries. Thus brands such as Stolichnaya are only 'brands' when exported, when control is under a single organisation, Sojuzplodimport.

Table 2 shows retail shares of the world vodka market in 2002. In the table 'virtual' brands such as Stolichnaya are not included.

The leader of the retail market for vodka is Kristal, with a 6.7 per cent share of the world market. Kristal is a local Russian brand. Diageo's Smirnoff is the leading international brand of vodka. These are the only two brands of vodka worldwide commanding more than 5 per cent of global sales.

Given the size and diversity of the Russian vodka market, the top 20 vodka brands worldwide command only around 35 per cent of global vodka sales.

Western and Eastern Europe brand shares – top 10 brands

Smirnoff, with a regional market share of 16.8 per cent, was the clear brand leader in western Europe in 2002 (Table 3). Its nearest rival brand, Gorbatschow,

Table 2 Top 20 global brands via retail channel 2002

Rank	Brand	Brand owner	% volume share
1	Kristal	Kristal	6.7
2	Smirnoff	Diageo Plc	5.8
3	Smirnov	Chernogolovka Plant	3.4
4	Topaz	Topaz	2.0
5	Dlya Druzei	PK Chernorechensky	2.0
6	**Absolut**	**V&S Vin & Sprit AB**	**1.9**
7	Goluboi Topaz	Topaz	1.7
8	Faraon	PK Chernorechensky	1.3
9	Moroz	Moroz OOO	1.3
10	Sojuzplodimport	Sojuzplodimport	1.3
11	Wyborowa	Polmos Poznan	1.0
12	Bols	Koninklijke Bols Wessanen NV	1.0
13	Luksusowa	Polmos Poznan	0.9
14	Dovgan	Dovgan Moscow	0.9
15	Ferein Gerbovaya	Ferein	0.7
16	Ost-Alko	Ost-Alko	0.7
17	Chernorechensky Russkaya	PK Chernorechensky	0.7
18	Finlandia	Alko Group Ltd	0.6
19	Popov	Diageo Plc	0.6
20	Gordon's	Diageo Plc	0.5
	Others		65.0
	Total		100.0

Source: adapted from Euromonitor and public sources.

Table 3 Top 10 vodka brands in Europe 2002

Rank	Brand	Brand owner	% volume share
Western Europe			
1	Smirnoff	Diageo Plc	16.8
2	Gorbatschow	Oetker-Gruppe	8.4
3	**Absolut**	**V&S Vin & Sprit AB**	**6.3**
4	Moskovskaya	Sojuzplodimport	4.9
5	Finlandia	Alko Group Ltd	3.3
6	Eristoff	Bacardi Ltd	2.6
7	J Grant's	Glen Catrine Bonded Warehouse Ltd	2.4
8	Renat	V&S Vin & Sprit AB	2.3
9	Explorer	V&S Vin & Sprit AB	2.1
10	Votka	Tekel	1.9
	Others		49.1
	Total		100.0
Eastern Europe			
1	Kristal	Kristal	7.9
2	Smirnov	Chernogolovka Plant	3.9
3	Smirnoff	Diageo Plc	3.0
4	Topaz	Topaz	2.4
5	Dlya Druzei	PK Chernorechensky	2.4
6	Goluboi Topaz	Topaz	2.0
7	Sojuzplodimport	Sojuzplodimport	1.6
8	Moroz	Moroz OOO	1.6
9	Faraon	PK Chernorechensky	1.6
10	Bols	Koninklijke Bols-Wessanen NV	1.2
	Others		72.6
	Total		100.0

Source: adapted from Euromonitor and public sources.

held just over 8 per cent of regional sales. Only three brands in Western Europe – Smirnoff, Gorbatschow and Absolut – held more than 5 per cent of regional vodka sales in 2002.

The vodka market in eastern Europe is large and diverse, with hundreds of brands on the market. Consequently regional leader Kristal controlled only 7.9 per cent of regional sales in 2002, with its nearest rival brand, Smirnov, holding 3.9 per cent of sales. Diageo's Smirnoff was the largest international brand on the market.

North and Latin America brand shares – top 10 brands

Diageo's Smirnoff brand was the leader of the North American vodka market in 2002, holding 18.5 per cent of regional sales. Its main rival was the premium Absolut brand, which is made by V&S Vin & Sprit AB and distributed by Seagram.

Smirnoff was also the largest vodka brand in Latin America, where it also held over 24 per cent of the regional market. Smirnoff has few serious rivals in Latin America. Its closest competitor, Oso Negro

Table 4 Top 10 vodka brands in North and Latin America 2002

Rank	Brand	Brand owner	% volume share
North America			
1	Smirnoff	Diageo Plc	18.5
2	**Absolut**	**V&S Vin & Sprit AB**	**10.2**
3	Popov	Diageo Plc	7.4
4	Gordon's	Diageo Plc	5.7
5	Barton	Barton Inc	3.9
6	McCormick	McCormick & Co	3.7
7	Stolichnaya	Sojuzplodimport	3.4
8	Tanqueray	Diageo Plc	2.9
9	Kamchatka	Diageo Plc	2.9
10	Skol	Barton Inc	2.7
Others			38.6
Total			100.0
Latin America			
1	Smirnoff	Diageo Plc	24.1
2	Oso Negro	José Cuervo SA de CV	7.4
3	**Absolut**	**V&S Vin & Sprit AB**	**7.0**
4	Orloff	Seagram Co Ltd	5.6
5	Finlandia	Alko Group Ltd	2.8
6	Baikal	Bacardi Ltd	2.3
7	Eristoff	Bacardi Ltd	2.3
8	Wyborowa	Agros Trading Co Ltd	2.2
9	Cristal	Bacardi Ltd	1.7
10	Gordon's	Diageo Plc	1.5
Others			43.1
Total			100.0

Source: adapted from Euromonitor and public sources.

from José Cuervo, held only 7.4 per cent of regional sales in 2002.

Rest of the world brand shares – top 10 brands

In the rest of the world Smirnoff is the dominant brand of vodka. It led the market in Asia-Pacific, Australasia and Africa and the Middle East in 2002.

Having read the above report, Claes G. Fick acknowledges that it is necessary to get external input on some essential strategic questions. Besides the above information you also have access to where you can find data about the competitive situation in different parts of the world. When Claes lands in New York he has written down the following questions, which he asks you to answer.

Questions

1. State the advantages and disadvantages for V&S Absolut Spirits now that is has replaced Seagram with Future Brands for the US distribution of Absolut Vodka.

Table 5 Top 10 Vodka Brands in the rest of the world 2002

Rank	Brand	Brand owner	% volume share
Asia-Pacific			
1	Smirnoff	Diageo Plc	21.1
2	**Absolut**	**V&S Vin & Sprit AB**	**10.9**
3	Suntory	Suntory Ltd	6.8
4	Stolichnaya	Sojuzplodimport	4.5
5	Taiwan Vodka	Taiwan Tobacco & Wine Monopoly	3.8
6	Romanoff	United Breweries Group	3.6
7	Danzka	Danisco AS	3.2
8	Gilbey's	Diageo Plc	2.9
9	Alcázar	Diageo Plc	2.9
10	Zubrowka	Agros Trading Co Ltd	2.0
Others			38.2
Total			100.0
Austral–Asia			
1	Smirnoff	Diageo Plc	31.3
2	Vao Sojuplodo	Sojuzplodimport	13.0
3	Karloff	Seagram Co Ltd	11.1
4	Cossack	Diageo Plc	10.6
5	Kirov	Kirov	7.4
6	**Absolut**	**V&S Vin & Sprit AB**	**3.8**
7	Tsaravich	Rémy Cointreau	3.7
8	Finlandia	Alko Group Ltd	2.8
9	Stolichnaya	Sojuzplodimport	1.9
Others			14.6
Total			100.0
Africa & the Middle East			
1	Smirnoff	Diageo Plc	51.0
2	Romanoff	Monis of Paarl Ltd	14.9
3	Count Pushkin	Distillers Corp Ltd	6.3
4	Russian Bear	Edward Snell & Co	5.5
5	Vodka Gold	Galil Wine Cellars	3.7
6	Finlandia	Alko Group Ltd	3.4
7	**Absolut**	**V&S Vin & Sprit AB**	**2.4**
8	Brilliant	Brilliant Spirit Ltd	2.0
9	Vodka Stopka	Carmel Mizrachi Wineries Ltd	1.6
Others			9.1
Total			100.0

Source: adapted from Euromonitor and public sources.

2. Which alternative marketing strategies does V&S Absolut Spirits have to increase its market share for:
   (a) Absolut Vodka in the USA;
   (b) Absolut Vodka in Europe (including eastern Europe)?
   (c) Absolut Vodka in other parts of the world (including eastern Europe)?

3. In which region of the world (country) would you recommend V&S Absolut Spirits to allocate more marketing resources?

CASE STUDY IV.2   3B Scientific

World market leader in the niche of anatomical models

As Otto H. Gies, one of the two presidents at 3B Scientific in Hamburg (**www.3bscientific.com**), drives home after work, he wonders if the company can keep up the double-digit growth rates it has had for the last 10 years and that have made 3B Scientific the biggest producer in the world in the special segment of anatomical models and biological teaching aids.

Between 2001 and 2002 the 3B Scientific group (Paul Binhold Lehrmittelfabrik GmbH) had 'only' a 5 per cent increase in sales. At the same time more and more Chinese 'no name' discount products entered the market. Even though the Chinese products are often bad copies of the 3B Scientific products, it still disturbs Otto to hear about customers who buy the copies in spite of the far better service back-up customers get from 3B Scientific.

As far as Otto H. Gies can see, the following strategic possibilities exist to lead 3B Scientific into the next millennium as number one in the world:

- to profile 3B Scientific products as global brands, so that customers are able to see and feel the difference between copies and original 3B Scientific products;
- to intensify production of certain labour-intensive products in China, perhaps in a joint venture with a competitor;
- to establish strong marketing and sales positions in the growth centres of south-east Asia and South America.

As Otto H. Gies arrives at home he has not yet made up his mind, but plans to address the problem at the next management meeting.

Company profile

The 3B Scientific Group is a family of companies specialising in the manufacture and worldwide marketing of anatomical models and biological teaching aids. The product programme includes the following:

- skeletons, torsos and human organ models;
- injection training arms, patient care mannequins and medical simulators;
- biology, chemistry and physics models;
- anatomical charts;
- anatomical software;
- anatomical gift fun products (skeletons, funny bones, t-shirts).

The 3B Scientific images show some examples from their product programme.

The 3B Scientific Group distributes products worldwide. Its customers include universities, schools, ministries of health and education, hospitals, educational and medical distributors, students and the pharmaceutical industry.

The company's website was established in 1996 so that customers can get information and regular news updates on the company and its products around the clock.

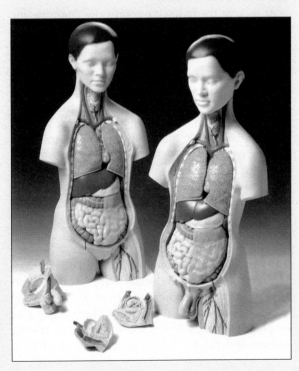

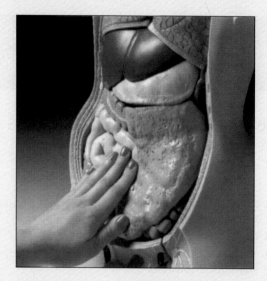

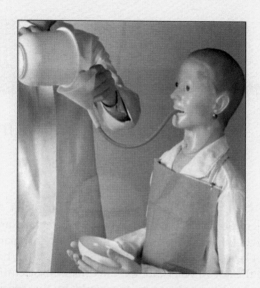

In the spring of 1995 the Binhold Group was enlarged to include a new affiliate, American 3B Scientific, founded in Atlanta, Georgia, for the purpose of expanding the Group's business in the North American market. Now Nikon 3B Scientific Japan also exists.

Throughout the 1990s the group succeeded in establishing a new company every two years. Its affiliates in Dresden and Budapest are also operating profitably, making Paul Binhold, the company's 85-year-old founder, very proud of what he has achieved: 'I set up the company and laid the foundations; it is now up to our young people to proceed and expand the business.'

At present the following companies comprise the 3B Scientific group:

- 3B Scientific GmbH, Germany (founded 1948);
- 3B Scientific Hamburg (founded in 1948 as Paul Binhold Lehrmittelfabrik GmbH);
- 3B Scientific Dresden (since 1930, DHM Lehrmittelfabrik GmbH, bought 1991);
- Biocalderoni KFT, Budapest, Hungary (since 1819, bought 1993);
- American 3B Scientific, Atlanta/GA (founded 1995);
- Nikon 3B Scientific, Niigata, Japan (founded 1997);
- France 3B Scientific (founded 1997);
- China 3B Scientific (founded in 1999);
- Brazil 3B Scientific (planned).

The affiliates are either distributing or manufacturing companies. All product improvement and new product development is carried out exclusively at 3B Scientific's HQ in Hamburg, Germany. A part of production has already been moved to eastern Europe and the Far East. The 3B Scientific Group employs around 380 people, of whom 100 are based at headquarters.

Roughly 90 per cent of 3B Scientific's sales come from export activities. Consequently the 3B Scientific product catalogues are available in 15 languages, including major Asian languages such as Japanese, Chinese, Korean and Turkish. 3B Scientific has a worldwide price guarantee: if a product of comparable quality at a lower price is available, 3B Scientific absorbs the difference. 3B Scientific considers the action a worthwhile way of gathering information on competitors' pricing practices around the globe.

The total sales of the whole group in 2002 were about €20 million, split by regions as shown in Table 1. Most of the communication from 3B Scientific's subsidiaries goes directly to the directors, especially Otto H. Gies.

Table 1 Distribution of total sales by regions 2002 (%)

Germany	10
Europe (excl. Germany)	35
North America	28
Asia-Pacific	18
South America	7
Middle East	1
Africa	1
Total	100

Now let us look at an example of how 3B Scientific attacks a new market.

Penetrating the Japanese market

At the beginning of the 1990s locally manufactured models were priced 30–40 per cent higher in Japan

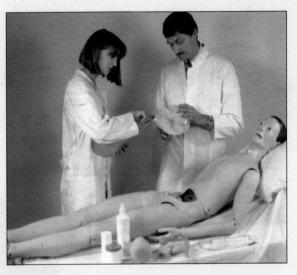

than equivalent German products, but Japanese wholesalers had shown themselves reluctant to import from Germany. Convinced that 3B Scientific had the formula for success in Japan too, Otto took up the challenge by starting to learn the language and local customs. He then had Japanese editions of the 3B Scientific catalogue printed, and embarked on personal sales calls to dealers around the country. He offered lower prices on the German-made models, resulting in bigger profits for dealers and prompting them to pressurise wholesalers to change their mind and import from Germany. The resulting success is an example of 3B Scientific's ability to adapt to the needs of individual markets. Beside printing Japanese-language versions of its sales material, the company has modified its product to accommodate torsos with Asian facial features.

As Otto H. Gies arrives at work the next morning he asks your advice on the following problems.

Questions

1. Make an evaluation of the three growth strategies considered by Otto H. Gies at the start of this case.

2. Until now 3B Scientific has primarily targeted its marketing at the educational market. In recent years it has developed a number of skeleton fun products (e.g. to be used as gifts for Halloween – see above left for the consumer retail market, but without any great success so far.

   (a) What are the key success factors for 3B Scientific in the consumer retail market? What are the arguments for and against more focus on the company marketing to the consumer retail market?

   (b) Which further products should be launched for the retail market and how should they be sourced?

3. Make an evaluation of the Internet as a distribution and communication channel for the products of 3B Scientific.

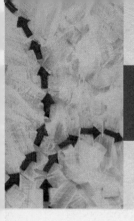
On a sunny August day in 2003 the newly appointed Executive Vice President Marketing, Tim Prescott, gets on a plane from New York bound for London where, among other things, he is going to meet megastar Dido about the marketing campaign of her new CD. Dido was BMG's best-selling artist in 2001, and Tim is looking forward to meeting the star personally. (See also case V.2.)

New in his job as Executive Vice President, Tim uses the plane trip over the Atlantic to study the global music industry more thoroughly. Tim has noticed that BMG is very proud of being one of the top five record companies in the world. Since 1995 BMG has improved from being 'only' number five to being number two in 2001 (together with AOL Warner), with a worldwide market share of 14 per cent – see Table 1. But BMG can not relax – the competitors are close behind the three leading record companies.

The holding company of BMG – The Bertelsmann Group

The Gütersloh- (Germany) based Bertelsmann Group (**www.bertelsmann.de**) originated in the nineteenth century as a Bible publisher, traditionally one of the more profitable specialisations. It is now the second-

Table 1 Global market shares of major players 2001

	Vivendi Polygram %	Sony %	AOL Time Warner %	EMI %	BMG %	Market value $ billion
Australia	13	27	18	18	6	0.7
Canada	20	13	24	10	8	1.1
US	13	14	22	10	12	11.2
Japan	13	18	7	14	8	7.0
Germany	23	12	13	22	15	3.0
UK	22	13	11	22	9	2.4
France	32	25	13	19	11	2.3
Netherlands	23	14	8	15	13	0.7
Italy	19	16	17	15	24	0.6
Korea	10	5	4	5	5	0.5
Sweden	20	19	13	26	22	0.3
Taiwan	17	5	14	6	5	0.3
Other countries	–	–	–	–	–	5.4
World	13	13	14	16	14	35.5

or third-largest global media conglomerate in terms of revenue and has over 76,000 employees. Its holdings encompass book and magazine publishing, film and music recording, online services and other interests. Sales in 2000 were approximately $20 billion (73 per cent outside Germany). Bertelsmann operates in the European Union, North and South America, Africa and Asia.

It has a controlling stake in RTL, the Luxembourg-based broadcaster (22 television stations and 18 radio stations across Europe), formed through the merger of CLT-UFA with Pearson TV. In December 2001 Bertelsmann acquired Pearson's 22 per cent in RTL.

About BMG

BMG is the global music division of Bertelsmann AG, one of the world's leading media companies. BMG's headquarters are located in New York's Times Square at 1540 Broadway, New York. The number of employees is around 5,000. BMG's total revenues are $2.8 billion.

BMG is one of the world's biggest music companies, with more than 200 record labels in 42 countries including Ariola, Arista Records, J Records, RCA Label Group – Nashville, and RCA Records. BMG is also home to one of the industry's foremost music distribution companies and one of the world's largest music publishing companies. Regarding BMG revenue by region, North America accounts for 50 per cent, Europe 34 per cent, Latin Region 5 per cent, and Asia-Pacific 11 per cent.

The top artists under contract to BMG include Christina Aquilera, Nelly, Dido, Coldplay, The Cure, Whitney Houston and Westlife.

Competition in the music industry

A handful of music companies (operating through several hundred subsidiaries and over a thousand labels) account for most records sold in the advanced economies. Music publishing – production and licensing of intellectual property rights – is even more concentrated.

Evolution in the music industry

Over the past 100 years we have seen the 'music industry' evolve through three basic stages, characterised by different technologies and different publishing organisations. Prior to the gramophone, when sheet music was the primary vehicle for disseminating popular music, the industry was dominated by music publishing houses. With the rise of recording (and subsequently broadcasting, which was driven by the availability of 'canned content'), those publishers were displaced by the record companies.

Today, increasingly the industry has involved entertainment groups that bring together a broad range of content distribution and repackaging activities – broadcast, film, video, booking and performance management agencies, records, music licensing, print publishing.

See also the value chain of the music recording industry in Figure 1.

The global market for music on CDs

Structure and competition

Global music sales fell by 5 per cent in 2001 (compared to 2000) because of the combined impact of the rapid spread of digital copying from the Internet and the economic downturn, according to industry figures. While the value of recorded music sales in 2001 fell to $33.7 billion (£23.5 billion), the total units sold also fell, by 6.5 per cent.

The IFPI organisation has estimated one in three recordings sold throughout the world is an illegal copy, costing the industry $4.2 billion ($2.9 billion). Free and unlicensed internet download services have

Figure 1 The value chain in the music industry

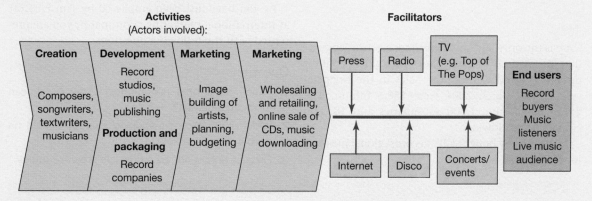

became popular among some music listeners who do not want to pay for their favourite songs. The popularity of the file-swapping service Napster, which has been shut down since last year, spawned a crop of copycat download companies (such as Kazaa and Aimster) across the Internet.

After launching a series of lawsuits against the likes of Napster for using unlicensed material, the big labels have realised they need to get themselves into the download market. Official subscription download services Musicnet and Pressplay have emerged but they are not expected to make money for at least five years. Meanwhile the battle to prevent music piracy continues, with new technology being seen as the way forward by some labels. Universal and Sony have already tested copyright protection formats for artists including Celine Dion and 'N Sync. But CD protection has received bad publicity after complaints from some fans that CDs could not be used on PCs or certain CD players.

In 2001, for every CD album sold, one copy was burned. At least half of all blank CD-Rom sales are used for copying music – only a small percentage of which is authorised by rights holders. Around a third of burned CDs contain songs downloaded from the Internet, of which 99 per cent are sourced from pirate Internet sites and unauthorised file sharing services.

Vivendi/Polygram

Paris-based conglomerate Vivendi Universal is continuing to shed major assets – and fend off speculation that it might be split up – after shareholders and analysts questioned whether they would make more money from the axe than aggregation.

French services and telecommunications giant Vivendi swallowed Seagram, the US – Canadian beverages giant that had previously swallowed the Universal entertainment conglomerate (books, theme parks, film, multimedia) and Polygram music empire, before ingesting other delicacies.

Sony

Sony is the only Japanese consumer electronics giant that has made a successful move into global content production and distribution. Sales in the financial year ended March 2001 were $58.5 billion. The group has around 1,000 subsidiaries and 181,800 employees worldwide.

In 1988 Sony bought CBS Records' global business for $2 billion.

AOL Time Warner

The 2000 merger between America Online (AOL) and Time Warner – itself the product of the merger between the Time-Life publishing group and the Warner music, film, publishing and theme parks conglomerate – has been praised by some analysts as an ideal marriage of content with carriage.

Others have been less enthusiastic, noting that the conglomerate had a market value of $300 billion in January 2000 but had slumped to $105 billion two years later.

EMI

The UK-based EMI Group comprises over 100 recording labels in all continents except Antarctica. It is the second-largest global music publisher (i.e. music scores).

During the 1960s EMI recorded the Beatles, and licensed several labels in the United States (including the MGM label).

In 1996 the ailing electronics business was demerged into a separate company, Thorn, and the music recording and retailing arms were renamed EMI Group.

BMG's basis for challenging the market leader (EMI) in the music market

BMG has traditionally been strong in markets that were geographically close to Germany, but in buying the US record company RCA in 1986 many possibilities were suddenly opened up in the United States. The new markets in eastern Europe and the Far East have also been discussed, but top management of BMG has not yet decided which marketing strategy to use in these markets.

When the plane arrives at Heathrow Airport Tim Prescott feels that BMG still needs to consider some very important strategic questions. When he enters the arrivals hall he hurries to an Internet connection to send some questions home to HQ in New York.

As you have just been employed by Tim Prescott as international marketing coordinator, you are presented with the following questions.

Questions

1. Which geographic market areas should be chosen for closer analysis?

2. Which international marketing strategy should be used in these markets?

3. Discuss acquisition as a possible growth strategy.

CASE STUDY IV.4   Dyson Vacuum Cleaner

Shifting from domestic to international marketing with the famous bagless vacuum cleaner

The Dyson history

It is impossible to separate the very British Dyson vacuum cleaner from its very British inventor. Together they are synonymous with innovation and legal battles against established rivals.

James Dyson was born in Norfolk in 1947. He studied furniture design and interior design at the Royal College of Art from 1966 to 1970 and his first product, the Sea Truck, was launched while he was still studying.

Dyson's foray into developing vacuum cleaner technology happened by chance. In 1978, while renovating his 300-year-old country house, Dyson became frustrated with the poor performance of his conventional vacuum cleaner. Whenever he went to use it, there was poor suction. One day he thought he would find out what was wrong with the design. He noted that the appliance worked by drawing air through the bag to create suction, but when even a fine layer of dust got inside, it clogged its pores, stopping the airflow and suction.

In his usual style of seeking solutions from unexpected sources, Dyson notice how a nearby sawmill used a cyclone – a 30-foot-high cone that spun dust out of the air by centrifugal force – to expel waste. He reasoned that a vacuum cleaner that could separate dust by cyclonic action and spin it out of the airstream which would eliminate the need for both bag and filter. James Dyson set out to replicate the cyclonic system.

Over the next eight years, Dyson tried to license his Dual Cyclone concept to established vacuum manufacturers, only to be turned down. At least two of these initial contacts forced him to file patent infringement lawsuits, which he won in out-of-court and in-court settlements. Finally in 1985, a small company in Japan contacted him out of the blue after seeing a picture of his vacuum cleaner in a magazine. Mortgaged to the hilt and on the brink of bankruptcy, Dyson took the cheapest flight to Tokyo to negotiate a deal. The result was the G Force vacuum cleaner, priced at $2,000, which became the ultimate domestic appliance status symbol in Japan.

In June 1993, using money from the Japanese licence, Dyson opened a research center and factory in Malmesbury, Wiltshire. Here he developed the Dyson Dual Cyclone and within two years it was the fastest-selling vacuum cleaner in the UK.

Dyson was nearly bankrupted by the legal costs of establishing and protecting his patent. It took him more than 14 years to get his first product into a shop and it is on display in the Science Museum Other products can be seen in the Victoria & Albert Museum, the San Francisco Museum of Modern Art and the Georges Pompidou Centre in Paris.

Dyson went on to develop the Root 8Cyclone, which removes more dust by using eight cyclones instead of two. In 2000, he launched the Contrarotator washing machine, which uses two drums spinning in opposite directions and is said to wash faster and with better results than traditional washing machines.

By 2001, turnover at Dyson was £235 million, up from £177 million in 1998 and £34.9 million in 1995.

In 2003, three years after the entrepreneur had abandoned earlier efforts, James Dyson revealed plans to produce a robotic vacuum cleaner; Dyson said plans for the automatic cleaner, which would move independently of any human intervention, were 'very far advanced'. His last effort with a robot cleaner, 'launched' in 1999 with three computers and 50 sensors in it, never made it to the shops after consumers blanched at the estimated £2,500 price tag. However, he insists that the new modified cleaner would be 'much cheaper than that'.

Rival Electrolux launched the first self-propelling cleaner in 2001, known as the Trilobite, and it retails for £1,000.

Marketing of the Dyson vacuum cleaner

Dyson believes the most effective marketing tool is by word of mouth, and today the company claims 70 per cent of its vacuum cleaners are sold on personal recommendation. An enthusiastic self-publicist, Dyson believes that if you make something, you should sell it yourself, so he often appears in his own advertisements.

When a Belgian court banned Dyson from denigrating old-style vacuum cleaner bags, he was pictured wearing his trademark blue shirt and holding a Dyson vacuum cleaner in a press advertisement that had the word 'bag' blacked out several times. A note at the bottom said: 'Sorry, but the Belgian courts won't let you know what everyone has a right to know'.

Dyson has sometimes shunned advertising altogether. For example, in 1996/97 the company spent its marketing budget sponsoring Sir Ranulph Fiennes' solo expedition to Antarctica, and gave £1.5 million to the charity Breakthrough Breast Cancer.

As rivals started to manufacture their own bagless cleaners, Dyson knew he would have to advertise more aggressively and in 2000 he appointed an advertising agency to promote the £2 million business. The marketing strategy, however, remains true to Dyson's original principles, with an emphasis on information and education rather than brand-building. Moreover, it seems to be working, one in every three vacuum cleaners bought in Britain today is a Dyson. See also Table 1.

The world market for vacuum cleaners

The use of vacuum cleaners is largely related to national preferences for carpets rather than floor tiles. In many warm countries instead of carpets floor tiles are more usual, and these can be swept rather than vacuumed. In countries where houses are predominantly carpeted, such as in Northern Europe, Eastern Europe and North America, the number of households owning vacuum cleaners is

Table 1 Vacuum Cleaners: Market volume and market shares (2002)

Market/%/Manufacturers (brands)	Germany	Italy	Sweden	France	Spain	UK	Netherlands	Total Western Europe	United States
Total market								+ others 2.5	
Volume (mio. units)	7.0	2.0	0.4	3.0	0.7	4.1	0.9	=20.6	25.4
% – types:									
Cylinder	67	50	94	88	73	34	80	65	9
Upright	13	30	1	5	2	62	5	25	66
Hand-held	20	20	5	7	25	4	15	10	25
Total	100	100	100	100	100	100	100	100	100
Market shares (%):									
BSH (Bosch-Siemens Hausgeräte)	18	–	9	–	–	–	30	8	
Electrolux (Eureka in US)	16	–	53	19	–	19	9	14	21
Miele	15	–	12	9	–	3	23	9	
Dyson Appliances	–	–	–	–	–	34	–	8	
SEB Group (Rowenta + Moulinex)	–	18	–	22	19	–	8	7	
Maytag (Hoover)	–	–	–	–	–	–	–	–	25
Candy SpA (Hoover)	5	12	–	–	–	11	–	6	
Philips	8	–	2	–	7	–	10	4	
De Longhi	–	15	–	–	–	–	–	2	
Matsushita (Panasonic)	–	–	8	–	27	–	–	2	
Daewoo Group	–	8	–	–	–	–	–	1	
Samsung	–	6	–	–	–	–	–	1	
Electromomésticos Solac SA	–	–	–	10	–	–	1		
Private label	8	–	15	2	–	3	3	4	10
Others	30	41	1	48	37	30	17	33	44
Total	100	100	100	100	100	100	100	100	100

Source: author's own, based on Euromonitor

Comments to Figure:
Two different companies in Europe and United States own the Hoover-brand. In United States the brand is still owned by the Maytag Corp., but in 1995 Maytag sold its European operations to Italian Candy Spa, which owns the brand in Europe.

The SEB group took over the Rowenta brand in 1988. In 2001 the SEB Group took over Moulinex SA and the SEB Group now markets the Moulinex vacuum cleaner.

Dyson Appliances are also selling in other markets than UK, but only in small numbers.

high. In 2002 over 90 per cent of households owned vacuum cleaners in Belgium, Germany, Japan, the Netherlands, Sweden, the US and the UK. Many Belgian households possess more than one vacuum cleaner, as traditional vacuum cleaners are often complemented with hand-held cleaners (cleanettes). In parts of Eastern Europe, it is also common to carpet walls, which provides additional demand for vacuum cleaners.

Few vacuum cleaners are sold in China and India. Vacuum cleaners have only been available in China for ten years, but ownership has not become widespread. In India many of the rural population do not have the means for such appliances and power supply is erratic. The Asia-Pacific market for vacuum cleaners (not shown in Table 1) is relatively small, at 10.5 million units per year.

The world market for vacuum cleaners is fairly mature and stable, and with the help of strong sales in 1999 and 2000, there was growth of 14 per cent from 1997 to 2002. As average prices fell throughout the five-year period, value growth amounted to only 3 per cent overall. In 2002 the number of vacuum cleaners sold throughout the world was 72 million units. Demand is driven mainly by replacement purchases at the end of a product's life cycle (the commercial lifetime of a vacuum cleaner is about 8 years), although new product developments such as bagless models spurred growth in some markets.

The most sold vacuum cleaner types are the upright and the cylinder types. The distinction between upright and cylinder vacuum cleaners became less clear in recent years, with the addition of hoses and tools to the upright version and cylinders mimicking uprights by adding turbo brushes to eradicate dust from carpets.

Cylinder, or canister, vacuum cleaners make up the majority of the global market, but do not take a strong lead, accounting for 65 per cent of European volume sales in 2002, compared with 25 per cent for upright models (see Table 1). As upright vacuum cleaners are more expensive, their share is higher by value, amounting to 33 per cent of the market by value.

Generally, the sales of upright vacuum cleaners grew faster than cylinders over the five-year period from 1997 to 2002. This largely reflected trends in the US, which was the world's leading market for vacuum cleaners (especially upright vacuum cleaners). Here, the addition of new features fuelled the upright subsector, including bagless operation, HEPA (High Efficiency Particulate Air) filtration and self-propulsion, which are available in various combinations on models selling for less than US$200.

In other markets, such as in Eastern Europe, cylinder vacuum cleaners are the most popular type,

as they are more practical for use on wall carpets, which are common in e.g. Russia.

The handheld vacuum cleaners do not play an important role in the market, so they are neglected in the rest of this case.

The market tends for vacuum cleaners tends to be dominated by leading white goods manufacturers. Electrolux was uncontested world leader in this sector with a volume share of 14.4 per cent in 2002, through its brands Eureka and Electrolux. However, Maytag owned the leading vacuum cleaner brand, Hoover, in the North America.

In recent years one of the most significant developments in the market was that of bagless technology. Dyson UK pioneered its dual cyclone technology back in 1993, Dyson's technology is protected by patent, but other manufacturers were quick to develop bagless versions. In the US, bagless vacuum cleaners increased their unit share from just 2.6 per cent in 1998 to 17.7 per cent in 2002.

Electrolux owes its global dominance to its leadership in both Western Europe and North American markets, though in the latter market its position is strongly contested by Maytag and Royal Appliance Manufacturing (under 'others' in Table 1). Between them, these three manufacturers accounted for 60 per cent of the North American market in 2002. Electrolux also led the emerging market in Africa and the Middle East, and ranked second in Latin America behind Swiss manufacturer Koblenz Electrica.

The Western European market is more fragmented. Dyson was some way behind Electrolux with a share of 8 per cent (see Table 1), closely followed by the premium appliance manufacturer Miele, while BSH and Candy also had strong shares.

The Asia-Pacific market for vacuum cleaners is highly concentrated, with the top five players accounting for 80 per cent of sales in 2002. These were all Japanese companies, led by Matsushita. The latter also led the Australasian market, slightly ahead of British player Dyson. Interestingly, Samsung did not rank among the top five Asian manufacturers in 2002, although it led the Eastern European market.

Competitors

In the following there is a description of the five most important players in the world vacuum cleaner industry:

BSH (Bosch–Siemens Hausgeräte)

Bosch-Siemens Hausgeräte (**www.bsh-group.com**) was established in 1967 by the merger of the domestic appliance divisions of Robert Bosch Hausgeräte and Siemens. During the 1990s, the company was largely geared towards improving its international presence. This was achieved mainly through organic growth, with a cautious approach taken towards acquisitions, e.g. Ufesa.

Ufesa is the leading manufacturer in Spain and Portugal of small appliances such as vacuum cleaners, irons and coffee makers, and has a good export network to Latin America. The acquisition allowed BSH to improve its production and distribution arrangements.

Bosch-Siemens Hausgeräte (BSH) is entirely focused on the production and servicing of domestic electrical appliances, including large kitchen appliances and small electrical appliances. Total revenue for the group amounted to €6,289 million in 2002, of which a small proportion (4 per cent) was derived from customer services. The rest came from electrical appliances. The operating profit in 2002 was €434 million.

The company is involved in all five sectors of the large kitchen appliances market, in which cooking appliances are the most important with 28 per cent of sales in 2002. This is followed by refrigeration/freezing appliances and washing/drying appliances, which each took 20 per cent of the total. Dishwashing appliances accounted for a further 16 per cent. Other business activities centred on the production of consumer products, including small kitchen appliances such as food processors and coffee makers and small appliances such as vacuum cleaners and hair dryers.

BSH remains highly focused on Western Europe, especially its domestic German market. Germany alone accounted for 28 per cent of total sales in 2002, which was down from 30 per cent the previous year. This was due to the difficult trading environment, which led to a 4 per cent decline in sales in this market.

The rest of Western Europe took a further 54 per cent of sales in 2002, up by two percentage points on 2001 as sales in the region rose by 8 per cent. This was due to particular growth in France (8per cent), the UK (10 per cent), Spain (8 per cent) and Italy (11 per cent). Turkey also continued to see very high growth of 9 per cent, despite the impact of economic and political turmoil in this market.

Sales in markets outside Western Europe were minimal, with North America, Eastern Europe and Asia-Pacific each accounting for 6 per cent of the total, and Latin America just 3 per cent. Eastern Europe recorded above-average growth rates, especially Russia with over 21 per cent.

Sales in Latin America continued to decline, due to the ongoing economic crisis in Argentina, and both Brazil and Argentina causing significant foreign-exchange-related losses. However, double-digit growth was achieved in China, where the company saw sales rise for the fourth consecutive year.

Electrolux

Electrolux (headquarters in Sweden) **www. electrolux.com** is the world's second largest manufacturer of large kitchen appliances behind American Whirlpool, in terms of revenue derived from this activity. The company produces a wide range of large kitchen appliances, as well as vacuum cleaners, and heating and cooling equipment. In addition, Electrolux manufactures products outside the scope of this report, such as garden equipment, food service equipment and chainsaws.

Electrolux dates back to 1901 when its predecessor, Lux AB was formed in Stockholm as a manufacturer of kerosene lamps. The company changed its name to Electrolux AB in 1919, following collaboration between Lux AB and Svenska Elektron AB. The company shifted into electrical appliances in 1912, when it introduced its first household vacuum cleaner, the Lux 1. In 1925, this was followed by the launch of the first Electrolux absorption refrigerator. The company was quick to expand internationally, and by the 1930s was selling refrigerators and vacuum cleaners across the globe.

Between the 1940s and the 1980s, Electrolux expanded into all areas of the large kitchen appliances, floor care and garden equipment sectors through a wide range of acquisitions. In the 1990s the company worked to expand its appliance business internationally.

From 1997, Electrolux entered into a restructuring programme to improve profitability. In line with this, several divestments were made, including industrial products, sewing machines, agricultural implements, interior decoration equipment, recycling, kitchen and bathroom cabinets, professional cleaning equipment, heavy-duty laundry equipment, leisure appliances, baking equipment and electric motors. Furthermore, the programme aimed to streamline the product portfolio down to a smaller number of well-defined brands. Concurrently, the company made some further notable acquisitions in core areas.

The company is divided into two major business areas:

■ Consumer durables, including large kitchen appliances and air conditioners, floor care products (vacuum cleaners) and garden equipment (such as lawn mowers, garden tractors and lawn trimmers).

■ Professional products, including foodservice equipment, laundry equipment for apartment/house laundry rooms, laundrettes, hotels and institutions, components such as compressors, forestry equipment such as chainsaws and clearing saws, and other products such as landscape maintenance equipment, turf-care equipment and professional-use power cutters.

In 2002 the Electrolux Group had a total sales of €14.500 million, of which €800 million was left for operating profit. Consumer durables accounted for 84 per cent of total sales, and 7 per cent came from vacuum cleaners.

Electrolux's business is largely split between Europe and North America, which together accounted for 87 per cent of sales in the consumer durables division in 2002. The company has achieved a good balance between these regions, with similar sales levels.

Miele

Miele (**www.mielevacuums.com**) is a German-based, family-run company, which produces a range of premium household appliances (e.g. vacuum cleaners), commercial appliances, components and fitted kitchens.

Carl Miele and Reinhard Zinkann established Miele in Gütersloh, Germany in 1899. The company has, since its inception, been focused on producing high-quality appliances at the premium end of the market.

The company began producing washing machines in 1900, with vacuum cleaners and dishwashers added to the product portfolio in the 1920s. During the 1950s and 1960s the company began to produce fully automatic washing machines and dishwashers, as well as tumble dryers. The 1970s saw further advances in technology, with the launch of built-in washing machines and condenser dryers and microcomputer-controlled appliances.

Since then, the company has produced a number of innovative appliances including washing machines with hand wash programmes for woollens, and during the 1990s, vacuum cleaners with the HEPA filter and Sealed System.

Over the past decade, Miele has focused on expanding its business overseas, especially in Eastern Europe and Asia-Pacific. The company opened a branch office in Hong Kong in 1998, followed by offices in Poland and Russia. In 1999, Miele opened its US headquarters in Princeton, New Jersey and in 2001 it opened sales offices in Singapore and Mexico.

Miele has made few significant acquisitions through its history. Its largest acquisition was that of Imperial in 1990, a German company specialising in built-in appliances and catering equipment.

Miele products are marketed throughout Europe and also in the US, Canada, South Africa, Australia, Japan and Hong Kong, through subsidiaries, and elsewhere in the world via authorised importers.

The company's range of domestic electrical appliances covers vacuum cleaners, large kitchen appliances such as home laundry appliances, refrigeration appliances, large cooking appliances, microwaves and dishwashers, and other small appliances such as rotary irons and coffee makers. The company specialises in producing innovative products within these sectors.

As a private company, Miele does not release detailed financial results. In 2002, company revenue reached €2,200 million, up by 3.2 per cent on the previous year. This occurred despite a difficult operating environment, particularly in its domestic market of Germany.

Miele does not publish detailed financial results by geographic region. However, for the 2002 financial year, the company reported that sales in Germany fell back by 1 per cent to reach €800 million. Outside Germany, sales increased by a strong 6 per cent to reach €1.4 billion. As a result, international sales accounted for 65 per cent of total sales in 2002.

The company lists its highest gross overseas market as the Netherlands, followed by Switzerland, France, Austria, the UK and the US. The US recorded especially swift growth at double-digit rates. Double-digit growth was also achieved in Greece, Finland and Ireland, while other markets showing above average growth, included the UK and Norway. Russia also showed extremely good growth, although to date the company has only focused on Moscow and St Petersburg.

SEB Group

SEB Group of France (**www.seb.com**) is one of the world's leading producers of small domestic equipment. The company is entirely focused on this area, manufacturing household goods (cookware), as well as small electrical appliances such as cooking appliances (steam cookers, toasters, coffeemakers, and grills), home appliances (vacuum cleaners and fans), and personal care appliances (hair dryers, scales, and electric toothbrushes). SEB's key brands include T-Fal/Tefal, Rowenta, Krups and SEB. The total sales of SEB Group in 2002 were €2,496 million.

Groupe SEB's origins date back to 1857, when the tinware company Antoine Lescure was founded. The company gradually expanded its activities to include products such as kitchen utensils and zinc tubs, beginning to mechanise its production at the beginning of the 20th century. In 1953, the company launched the first pressure cooker.

The company has since grown by acquisition. This began with Tefal in 1968, a company specialising in nonstick cookware, and continued with the acquisition of the Lyon company, Calor, a maker of irons, hair dryers, small washing machines and portable radiators in 1972. In 1973, a group structure was formed under a lead holding company, SEB SA, which was listed on the Paris Stock Exchange two years later.

Groupe SEB made a significant push into international markets when it acquired Rowenta in 1988, a German manufacturer of irons, electric coffee makers, toasters and vacuum cleaners. In 1992 and 1993, it took advantage of the opening up of Eastern Europe, setting up marketing operations to make inroads in these countries and gain a foothold in the Russian market.

In 1997–1998, Groupe SEB entered South America with the acquisition of Arno, Brazil's market leader in small electrical appliances. Arno specialises in the manufacture and sale of food preparation appliances (mixers/blenders), non-automatic washing machines and fans.

In September 2001, Groupe SEB's main domestic rival, Moulinex, filed for bankruptcy. The company submitted an offer for a partial takeover of the business assets of Moulinex, for which it finally received approval by both the European Commission and the French Finance Ministry in 2002. Moulinex had purchased one of Europe's leading brands, Krups, in the early 1990s, and was a good fit with Groupe SEB's existing businesses.

Examples of new SEB vacuum cleaners introduced in 2002 are:

- The new Neo vacuum cleaner, with a futuristic and compact design and very high performance which heralded the arrival of a new ultra-modern range.
- The relaunch of Moulinex vacuum cleaners in all market segments, including the Boogy super-compact vacuum cleaner with an automatic bag ejection system; and the Alto high-power compact vacuum cleaner.

Groupe SEB is one of the few small electrical appliance manufacturers to have achieved a truly global presence. Furthermore, the company has a good geographical balance of sales. Although its domestic market in France accounted for the highest proportion of sales, 26.4 per cent in 2002, a further 30.6 per cent of revenues was derived from other EU countries. The Americas represented 23.2 per cent of sales, with the rest of the world accounting for the remaining 19.8 per cent.

Groupe SEB has stated its intention to expand in emerging markets which offer high growth potential, such as Brazil, Korea, the CIS countries and China, although it also sees potential for development of high added-value niche products in developed markets such as the EU, North America and Japan.

Growth was achieved in all regions in 2002, which was largely due to the partial acquisition in that year of Moulinex-Krups.

Maytag Corp

Maytag (**www.hoover.com**) is a leading US manufacturer of large kitchen appliances, including home laundry appliances, dishwashers, refrigeration and cooking appliances. It operates under the premium brands Maytag, Jenn-Air, and the lower-end brands Magic Chef, Amana and Admiral.

Maytag also manufactures the leading vacuum cleaner brand, Hoover, in the US (though this brand is owned by Candy in Europe). In 2003, the company expanded its product offerings to include small appliances such as high-end blenders, mixers and irons.

The company operates mainly in the US, but has sales subsidiaries in Canada, Australia, Mexico, Puerto Rico and the UK.

Maytag Corp traces its roots back to 1893 when FL Maytag began manufacturing farm implements in Newton, Iowa. In order to offset seasonal slumps in demand he introduced a wooden-tub washing machine in 1907. The company diversified into cooking appliances and refrigerators after the Second World War in 1946. It introduced its first automatic washing machine in 1949, and its first portable dishwashers in 1966.

One of the most famous brands in the vacuum cleaner industry – Hoover – dates back to 1907, when it was developed by the Hoover family in Canton, Ohio. The Hoover Company began selling its products worldwide in 1921. Maytag took over the Hoover brand in 1989. In 1995, Maytag sold the European Hoover operations to Italian appliance manufacturer, Candy.

In the vacuum cleaner sector, Maytag operates only under the Hoover brand, which has a strong heritage and is the leading brand in the US market. Hoover manufactures a wide range of vacuum cleaners, including uprights, canisters, stick and handheld vacuums, hard surface cleaners, extractors and other home care products.

The total sales of Maytag Corp. were US$4,421 million in 2002 with an operating profit of US$396 million.

Maytag does not publish a breakdown of its sales by product, but it is believed that vacuum cleaners represent between 20 and 25 per cent of its annual revenue. The company reported that unit sales vacuum cleaners increased slightly in 2002, as strong sales in the new hard surface floor cleaner category were offset by a decline in unit sales of upright cleaners, as Maytag's market share declined with some of its lower priced products. However, sales of vacuum cleaners were reported to have suffered a decline in the first half of 2003, due to competition from cheaper products, mainly coming from Far East.

Overall, Maytag's operating and net profit margins showed a broadly declining trend over the 1998–2002 period.

Maytag operates mainly in North America, with offices throughout the US, Canada and Mexico. The company also has direct sales operations in Australia, Puerto Rico and the UK. Maytag withdrew from the Chinese market in 2001. Sales in the US accounted for 90 per cent of total revenue in 2002.

Distribution of vacuum cleaners

The situation in Dyson's domestic market, the UK, is as follows:

Department stores are the most popular source of small electrical goods in the UK, with many trusted names, Coop Home Stores, and John Lewis, who are able to stock a sufficient variety of competitively priced goods to attract consumer loyalty. Their share has increased slightly over recent years, as department stores in general have become more fashionable again.

Specialist multiples have the second largest share, although not far behind are the independents which have a larger share of the small electrical appliances market than they do of large appliances. Smaller high street stores in small and medium-sized towns attract buyers of small electrical appliances, like vacuum cleaners, since consumers are less motivated to drive to a retail park for these items, than they are say, for a fridge, for example.

Grocery multiples, such as Tesco and Asda, sell vacuum cleaners and generally offer advantageous deals on a narrow range of goods. Catalogue showrooms such as Argos also benefited from increasing their range and from low pricing and online shopping facilities.

Distribution of vacuum cleaners has become hugely extensive, with supermarkets and grocery stores stocking the cheaper to mid-end of the market. For electrical retailers still selling smaller items, their domain lies more in the pricier, higher-end of the market.

The distribution of vacuum cleaners in most other major countries is limited principally to specialist 'household appliance' store chains and department stores.

Huge retail chains like Electric City, Best Buy and Sears more and more dominate the distribution of vacuum cleaners in United States.

Latest development

During 2002 and 2003, Dyson decided to move most of its vacuum cleaner production from UK to Malaysia. The company was accused of shipping British jobs to Malaysia, inspiring some labor union people to describe it as a desperately bad example to rest of the manufacturing sector. The company's transfer to the Far East will locate its manufacturing closer to its suppliers, and Dyson also admits that the relatively high manufacturing costs in UK have partly motivated the move.

James Dyson argues that the company has created 100 new UK jobs in R&D to counteract the elimination of jobs in the manufacturing sector. However, the furore over Malaysia, and any possible damage to Dyson's 'British' brand, marks a threat to the company.

Although Dyson is still the leading vacuum cleaner brand in the UK, it is beginning to lose out to cheaper machines that have developed their own bagless technology.

The dilemma Dyson faces is dropping its own prices or reinforcing the power and quality of its brand. The loyalty of Dyson's customers has dropped off and the company's market share by volume has also decreased. However, market analysis figures show that two-thirds of Dyson owners go on to buy another Dyson. This is double the rate of its closest competitor.

Questions

1. Until now Dyson has concentrated its efforts in the UK market. In your opinion: Which new international markets should be allocated more marketing resources, in order to develop them into future Dyson growth markets?

2. Should Dyson lower its prices, in order to recapture market shares? Why/Why not?

3. How would you design the marketing mix for Dyson's entry into the US market (if necessary, make some assumptions)?

Sources: www.dyson.com; www.electrolux.com; www.mielevacuums.com; www.seb.com; www.hoover.com; http://news.bbc.co.uk

Rising from the ashes in the international motorcycle business

When Marlon Brando led a group of outlaw bikers in the 1950s film, *The Wild One*, he rode a Triumph. It was the obvious choice back then. Britain was the biggest motorbike maker in the world and led the motorcycling world in performance and engineering innovation with such bygone makers as BSA, Matchless and Vincent, to name just a few. And also Triumph was winning every race in sight. But after bad management and botched rescue attempts by successive governments Triumph went bankrupt in 1983. However, the marque is back, starring in films such as *Mission Impossible 2*. When Tom Cruise roared on to the screen on a sleek motorcycle it wasn't a Harley or a Honda but a Triumph, which is also featured in Arnold Schwarzenegger's 'Terminator 3'. It is established that the Triumph has captured approximately 75 per cent of the 'Hollywood' market, one of few US markets where Triumph is the market leader.

Product segments in the motorcycle market

Motorcycles were often classified by engine capacity in three categories follows:

- lightweight (50 cc–250 cc);
- middleweight (251 cc–650 cc);
- heavyweight (651 cc and up).

Triumph's motorcycles are in the middleweight and heavyweight category only, competing mainly with companies such as Harley-Davidson, Ducati, BMW and of course the main Japanese motorcycle manufacturers.

Motorcycles were also classified by types of use, generally separated into four groups: standard, which emphasised simplicity and cost; performance, which focused on racing and speed; touring, which emphasised comfort and amenities for long-distance travel; and custom, which featured styling and individual owner customisation. The standard models tended to have the smaller engines, while the performance motorcycles often had an engine capacity of more than 251 cc. The touring models typically had a comfortable seating position and their engines ranged from middleweight to super heavyweight types.

History

The credit for Triumph's rebirth goes to John Bloor, a builder who bought the company's remains (the Triumph brand name and the company's designs and tooling) for about $200,000. He has invested £80 million on, among other things, a new plant in Leicestershire. The product has been completely revamped. New engines were crucial. Most have a distinctive three-cylinder layout, which makes them more powerful than the two-cylinder bikes made in Europe and the United States, and more relaxing than the high-revving four-cylinder bikes made in Japan.

Bloor was betting on the nostalgic power of the Triumph brand. Back in the 1950s and 1960s, Triumph and Harley-Davidson were fierce rivals. The original Triumphs offered lighter weight and better handling than Harley's machines, and sales of the British bikes were stronger in the United States than they were in their home market. The bikes are also part of US folklore. Despite what flag-waving Harley guys in bars may mistakenly claim, Steve

McQueen in *The Great Escape* and Marlon Brando in *The Wild One* rode Triumphs. James Dean had one too. Legend and myth and the power of branding do not come any better.

Bloor's first act as a prospective motorcycle manufacturer was to hire three employees of the original Triumph company who had been involved in developing new models. Bloor realised that the engine is everything in a motorcycle, and there is no way to make a bike with a dull motor feel red-hot to the customer. So while he outsourced other parts of the bike, he put his team of engineers and metalworkers to work designing new liquid-cooled, three- and four-cylinder engines that would save costs by sharing internal parts.

Bloor's decision to keep a three-cylinder engine from the original lineup turned out to be a great marketing move, and it has helped the company stand out from the crowd. Most other bikes use two- or four-cylinder engines. Triumph's soulful three-cylinder has won a place in the hearts of many bikers, who tend to be a discriminating bunch when it comes to how an engine feels and delivers power on the road. Three-cylinder engines are also perfect for the middle-aged men who are getting back into bikes.

Today

Big-bike sales have doubled in Britain over the past five years, and the buyers are no longer youngsters needing cheap wheels but older people with the money to spend on expensive toys. Many of these born-again bikers have not touched a motorbike since their teens, and find Japanese offerings just a bit too fast and flash for their taste.

Triumph's sales have risen from 2,000 in 1991 to 33,000 in 2002 – tempting thoughts of the old Triumph's peak of 50,000 in the late 1960s. Most buyers now are aged between 35 and 55. US sales (which make up 25 per cent of the total) have soared since in 2001 Triumph introduced a retro-styled bike, called the Bonneville, and are now rising at an annual rate of 40 per cent. The Bonneville (a twin-cylinder, 800 cc machine, priced at $7–8,000) is about 85 per cent faithful to the 650 cc Bonneville of yore, which was the machine to ride in the 1960s if you were not a Harley man. Further introduction of a Harley-style cruiser bike is being considered by the Triumph management team. Taking marketing cues from Harley-Davidson, Triumph also offers a line of clothing and accessories.

Growth should be consistent. Sales are rising by 15 per cent a year, putting Triumph within sight of

European rivals such as BMW and Ducati. Bruno Tagliaferri, Triumph's Marketing Manager, reckons there is plenty of scope for growth in the United States, where 250,000 big bikes are sold each year. Triumph currently accounts for less than 5 per cent of that, compared with 12 per cent of the British market. To grab more, it needs to exploit not just its classic name but also its old race-winning reputation.

Total sales in 2002 were approximately €250 million. And the number of employees was about 650.

The downturn of the Japanese manufacturers' market shares

In 1981 Japan's motorbike industry was in a state of blissful ignorance. Its manufacturers had managed to dominate the world in not much over a decade and annual production had hit 7.4 million units. Although they did not know it, this was to be their best year.

Two decades later and Japanese manufacturers are nowhere near as dominant. While they still loom large on the global motorbike market, 1981's record domestic production has declined to just 2.4 million. This serves as a stark reminder of a painful trend for all types of Japanese manufacturers as their domestic costs have risen, their markets have matured and their rivals have sharpened their game.

In 2001 two Japanese manufacturers – Suzuki and Kawasaki – joined forces to jointly produce and develop new bikes, marking the end of the 'big four' in Japan, where they ruled alongside much bigger rivals Honda and Yamaha.

The 'hollowing out' shift to overseas production through joint ventures and wholly owned plants has also cut into domestic production in Japan.

The Suzuki–Kawasaki tie-up also serves as a symbol for what has happened to Japan's motorbike industry in the last two decades. Once-lazy and inefficient rivals such as Ducati, BMW and Harley-Davidson have found a way of replying to the competitive threat from Japan and are clawing back market share. In Europe, for example, Japan's market share has fallen from 80 per cent to 50 per cent over five years, although numbers have risen. And in the vital US market its share has fallen by 10 per cent over the past decade.

The rise and rise of the Japanese motorbike manufacturers owed as much to luck as to design. Manufacturers were servicing a huge domestic market for many years which generated the profits that financed the export drive. It also gave the

Japanese a finely honed design and production machine that churned out faster, more reliable and better-looking bikes – and did so every year. The weak yen also made Japanese exports intensely competitive.

In addition, they were up against severely weakened domestic manufacturers in the West. Triumph, BSA and Norton in the United Kingdom, for example, were spent forces, and the country was in the middle of labour disputes that generated a lazy attitude towards design and technology, producing machines that looked old-fashioned in comparison to their Japanese rivals.

But the Japanese manufacturers, perhaps complacent in their success, failed to spot a key change in the motorbike buying world. They were too obsessed with technology and assembly quality and did not recognise that motorbikes had become consumer goods which had a brand value. Harley-Davidson led the way here with branded goods ranging from desk clocks to women's thongs, feeding hugely into profits.

Japanese manufacturers based their bikes on racing models. Undoubtedly Japanese bikes are lighter and faster, but it takes a lot of skill to ride them. Western manufacturers have been designing for people who like to ride normal bikes in a normal environment. As Japan's rivals have caught up with the technology they have also managed to inject something extra.

Ducati conveys on two wheels the kind of image its Italian counterpart, Ferrari, has on four. Triumph has capitalised on its Britishness and the appeal of the marque's previous incarnation with such models as the Bonneville. Harley-Davidson has built up an appeal for weekend rebels with $70,000-plus salaries. BMW has combined engineering excellence with design flair.

But to talk of the demise of the Japanese motorbike industry would be unwise. Honda remains the largest manufacturer of motorbikes in the world. However, the Japanese are removing themselves from the big bike category. Honda, Yamaha and Suzuki are concentrating on 100–500 cc bikes for mass production in the developing countries of Asia. The bulk of Japanese-made bikes are small and service the growing economies of Asia, where having a 50 cc or 100 cc bike is the first step on a transportation ladder that eventually leads to a Toyota Corolla. India and China are huge and growing markets for the Japanese and Suzuki says it hopes its new link with its smaller rival will help its efforts in China.

The alliance between Suzuki and Kawasaki has more to do with these markets than the competition in the superbike league. It allows them to pare costs considerably by jointly procuring parts and joining forces on product design, development and production.

It also matches similar moves by Honda, which has reduced the number of its Japanese motorcycle production lines from five to two in recent years. While Japanese manufacturers may be facing competition at the top end of the market, motorbikes are a high-volume game – and in this game the Japanese are still the winners.

The global competitive situation today

The competitive market situation in the three main regions of the world is shown in Table 1.

Table 1 **The three main market areas for heavyweight motorcycles (651+ cc) number of registrations 2002**

	North America	Europe	Asia/ Pacific
Total industry (1000s)	475.0	303.5	63.9
Market share	%	%	%
Harley-Davidson/Buell	46.4	6.6	19.6
Honda	20.2	21.0	22.4
Yamaha	9.8	17.7	19.0
Kawasaki	7.1	8.5	19.0
Suzuki	9.8	14.8	9.3
BMW	2.5	15.1	4.4
Ducati	–	5.7	3.2
Triumph	2.0	4.0	1.0
Others	2.6	6.5	2.1
Total	100	100	100

Source: adapted from Harley-Davidson Financial Report 2002, p. 51, and other public sources.

For the fiscal year ended 2000 total Harley-Davidson motorcycle shipments were 204,592 units compared with 177,187 units in 1999, a 15.5 per cent increase.

Market trends

In industrialised wealthy economies such as Japan, the United States and Europe motorcycles were often purchased for recreation in addition to basic transport. In developing economies and others with low income per capita, motorcycles or smaller two-wheelers were purchased primarily for basic transport, and the market was distinctly different. Historically large touring bikes, cruisers and racers sold almost exclusively in the wealthy economies while motorcycles with small engine displacement and mopeds made up the vast majority of sales in the developing nations. Decreasing trends in the overall market in some nations were due in large part to replacement of two-wheeled vehicles by automobiles as the countries became more affluent.

The challenge

The big problem for Triumph is still the relative low unit volume of motorcycles. Triumph sells about 15 per cent of the Harley-Davidson sales volume. Being so small makes it hard to develop new bikes or to buy good components at a decent price. To maintain quality Triumph makes about a third of its components in-house, and imports many from Japan. That clobbers profits. In 2002 Triumph lost at least €8 million on sales of €250 million. Bloor's building business, which is quite profitable, can cover those losses, but that is not a long-term solution.

As a consequence the strategy is set for increasing sale and market share in the area of large motorcycles. Therefore Bloor has contacted you as an expert in this field and you should answer the following questions. As Bloor thinks that Triumph's market share in North America is not satisfactory and he considers the potential for Triumph in the United States huge. He has therefore collected the following information about US motorcycle consumers.

The motorcycle market in the United States

The Hollywood myth of the young and wild motorcycle rider became less and less a reality in the 1990s, according to Motorcycle Industry Council statistics. The 1990s' rider was more mainstream and less likely to be a part of some counterculture motorcycle gang. 'The end of the road for today's motorcyclist is just as likely to be a boardroom as a burger joint,' said Beverly St. Clair Baird, Managing Director of Discover Today's Motorcycling, a public awareness campaign of the Motorcycle Industry Council. The average motorcyclist in the 1990s was male, 32.5 years old, married, had attended college and earned $33,000 – about 12 per cent more than the average US household.

The average income of the motorcyclist of the 1990s had almost doubled since 1980 ($17,500). In 1980 less than 2 per cent of riders made over $50,000 per year. In 2000 more than 30 per cent of riders had attained that income level. Riders in the 1990s were also much older. They used their bikes more for leisure and recreation than had the riders of the early 1980s. The typical rider was interested in the outdoors. In surveys about their other interests fishing and hunting topped the list. Motorcycle use for commuting purposes was down 14 per cent since

1980 to only 56 per cent. The demographic profile showed that motorcyclists came from all walks of life and a variety of occupational, educational and economic backgrounds.

Motorcycle accidents and fatalities dropped by more than half between 1985 and 1995. In addition to state helmet laws, this was attributed in part to an increasing trend for rider education and training programmes. Enrolment in these programmes, sponsored by individual manufacturers and industry groups such as the Motorcycle Industry Council, rose dramatically in the early 1990s. Motorcyclists were likely to be more skilled and responsible than riders of the 1970s and 1980s.

Women and motorcycling

Women, though not more than 10 per cent of the US riding population, are a growing segment of the industry. The AMA (American Motorcycle Association) has had women members since 1907. In the 1990s more than half a million women in the United States rode their own motorcycles. The average female rider was almost 48 years old compared to her 32-year-old male counterpart. Of the women riders 74 per cent were married, and 44 per cent attended college. The largest segment of women riders had professional/technical careers. They belonged to a riders club and were passengers for a few years before they purchased their first bike. Most women used their motorcycles for either long-distance touring (36 per cent of riding time) or for local street use (31 per cent). Only 10 per cent of their riding time was spent commuting or running errands. More women's families positively supported their riding than the families of male riders (64 per cent vs 55 per cent); however, more men's friends than women's friends supported their riding.

Profile of the typical Harley–Davidson rider

As with the average, Harley-Davidson (H-D) has about 90 per cent male and 10 per cent female riders. However, the household average income was much higher than for the average rider, about $78,000. The manufacturer has researched the 2001 purchases of H-D motorcycles. It shows that 41 per cent previously owned a H-D; 31 per cent were competitor motorcycles and the rest (28 per cent) were new to motorcycling.

Fashion trends

Motorcycling was a major fashion trend in the 1990s. The sales of motorcycles increased 50 per cent from 1991 to 2000, and motorcycle accessories,

Table 2 Motorcycle owner profile in United States

	% of total owners		
	1990	1995	2000
Age			
<17	24.6	14.9	8.3
18 24	24.3	20.7	15.5
25–29	14.2	18.7	17.1
30–34	10.2	13.8	16.4
35–39	8.8	8.7	14.3
40–49	9.4	13.2	16.3
>50	5.7	8.1	10.1
Not stated	2.8	1.9	2.0
Median age	24.0	27.1	32.0
Mean age	26.9	28.5	33.1
Marital status			
Single	51.7	47.6	41.4
Married	44.3	50.3	56.6
Not stated	4.0	2.1	2.3
Highest level of education			
Grade school	13.5	7.5	5.9
Some high school	18.9	15.3	9.5
High school graduate	34.6	36.5	39.4
Some college	17.6	21.6	25.2
College graduate	9.2	12.2	12.4
Post graduate	3.1	5.2	5.2
Not stated	3.1	1.7	2.4
Occupation of owner			
Laborer/semi-skilled	20.7	23.2	24.1
Professional/technical	18.8	19.0	20.3
Mechanic/craftsman	23.3	15.1	13.1
Manager/proprietor	8.6	8.9	9.3
Clerical/sales	9.3	7.8	6.8
Service worker	7.1	6.4	6.6
Farmer/farm labourer	4.6	5.1	2.1
Military	1.9	1.6	1.5
Other	0.0	4.6	13.1
Not stated	5.7	8.3	3.1
Household income for prior year			
<$14,999	9.1	10.9	3.4
$15,000–$29,999	13.0	9.3	4.4
$30,000–$39,999	13.9	11.6	7.8
$40,000–$49,999	12.9	8.4	10.8
$50,000–$59,999	5.5	18.3	21.4
$60,000–$69,999	5.9	14.4	19.6
>$70,000	2.4	6.1	19.9
Don't know	30.3	21.0	12.7
Median	$32,500	$45,600	$53,100

Source: Motorcycle Industry Council.

fashions and parts followed this upward trend. Owners were making personal statements by customising their bikes with accessories, and more than 60 per cent of all owners purchased accessories in 2000 (compared to only 30 per cent in 1985). Many non-motorcycle riders or owners invested in motorcycle fashions. Men spent more on average on motorcycle fashions than women ($127 per year for men vs $117 for women). Overseas motorcyclists followed the trend as well. Motorcycle fashions and accessory sales rose in both Europe and Japan in the 1990s.

The motorcycle market in general

Motorcycle registration requires compliance with state and federal Motor Vehicle Safety Standards. Over one-third of the nation's motorcycles were concentrated in just five states: California, Texas, New York, Florida and Ohio. Over 15 per cent of the motorcycles in the United States were in California alone. Overall, there were an average of 1.5 motorcycles per 100 people in the United States in 1995. Most motorcycles in the country were registered for on-highway use, and over half of these had engine displacements over 749 cc, and more than 80 per cent over 450 cc.

Source: Stuart F. Brown (2002) 'A sweet Triumph' *Fortune Small Business*, vol. 12, no. 3/4, pp. 48–51, April; Kampert, P. (2003) 'British motorcycles "Triumphant" return – Triumph motorcycles are roaring back into the American market.' http://money.cnn.com/2003/08/04/pf/autos/triumph/index.htm

Questions

1. Design a global marketing programme for Triumph, including a suggestion for the priority of the 4Ps: product, price, place and promotion.

2. How should the marketing programme for the US market differ from your suggested marketing programme in question 1?

3. A member of Triumph's management team has proposed designing a special motorcycle for women. Do you think this is a good idea?

Implementing and coordinating the global marketing programme

PART V

Part V   Contents

Case studies

Part V   Introduction

While the first four parts of this book have considered the set-up necessary to carry out global marketing activities, Part V will discuss the implementation and coordination phase.

An essential criterion for success in selling and negotiating internationally is to be able to adapt to each business partner, company and situation. Chapter 19 therefore discusses how the international negotiator should cope with the different cultural background of their counterparts. A part of this chapter will also deal with how knowledge and learning can be transferred across borders within the company and between cooperation partners.

As companies evolve from purely domestic firms to multinationals their organizational structure, coordination and control systems must change to reflect new global marketing strategies. Chapter 20 is concerned with how organizational structures and marketing budgets (including other control systems) have to be adjusted as the firm itself and market conditions change.

19 Cross-cultural sales negotiations

Contents

Learning objectives

After studying this chapter you should be able to do the following:

- Discuss why intercultural selling through negotiation is one of the greatest challenges in global marketing.

- Discuss how learning and knowledge transfer across borders can increase international competitiveness.

- Discuss the implications of Hofstede's research for the firm's cross-cultural negotiation.

- Explain some important aspects of intercultural preparation.

- Discuss opportunities and pitfalls with global multicultural project groups.

- Explain the complexity and dangers of transnational bribery.

19.1 Introduction

To remain competitive and to flourish in the complex and fast-changing world of international business companies must look worldwide not only for potential markets but also for sources of high quality but less expensive materials and labour. Even small business managers who never leave their home countries will deal with markets and a workforce whose cultural background is increasingly diverse. Those managers with the skills to understand and adapt to different cultures are better positioned to succeed in these endeavours and to compete successfully in the world market.

Conducting business with people from other cultures will never be as easy as doing business at home.

In the early stages of internationalization SMEs may treat cross-cultural markets as purely short-term economic opportunities to be pursued in order to maximise short-term profit.

However, learning more about the nature of culture and how it affects business practices can increase the chances of success, even in the early cross-cultural business negotiations. When people from two different cultures are conducting business making assumptions about another culture is often detrimental, and can result in miscommunication. The managers in SMEs should develop realistic assumptions based on a truthful appreciation of the culture, and should refrain from any thoughts of cultural stereotyping. Exhibit 19.1 shows that cultural influences can be difficult to predict.

Exhibit 19.1	Giving gifts in China and Japan

A US businessman once presented a clock to the daughter of his Chinese counterpart on the occasion of her marriage, not knowing that clocks are inappropriate gifts in China because they are associated with death. His insult led to the termination of the business relationship. It is also bad to give one's Japanese counterpart gifts of greater value than those received.

Source: Hendon *et al.* 1999.

All successful international marketers have personal representation abroad. Face-to-face negotiations with the customer are the heart of the sales job. Negotiations are necessary to reach an agreement on the total exchange transaction, comprising such issues as the product to be delivered, the price to be paid, the payment schedule and the service agreement.

International sales negotiations have many characteristics that distinguish them from negotiations in the domestic setting. First and foremost, the cultural background of the negotiating parties is different. Successful negotiations therefore require some understanding of each party's culture and may also require the adoption of a negotiating strategy that is consistent with the other party's cultural system. It is interesting to note that Japanese negotiators, among other things, routinely request background information on US companies and key negotiators. Japanese negotiators therefore often know in advance the likely negotiating strategies and tactics of the other side.

19.2 Cross-cultural negotiations

Faced with different customs, perceptions and language the most common human tendency is to stereotype the other party in a negative way. A crucial perception is knowing what to look for and thoroughly researching the characteristics of a culture before conducting negotiations. Understanding other cultures is often based on tolerance. Trust and respect are essential conditions for several cultures, e.g. the Japanese, Chinese, Mexican, and most Latin American cultures. The Japanese may require several meetings before actual negotiation issues are discussed, while North Americans and North Europeans are inclined to do business as soon as possible. Culture affects a range of strategies, including the many ways they are implemented. The Israeli prefers direct forms of negotiation, and the Egyptian prefers an indirect form. The Egyptians interpret Israeli directness as aggressive, and are insulted, while the Israelis view Egyptian indirectness with impatience, and consider it insincere. This cultural difference endangers any negotiation between business people in the two countries.

Even the language of negotiation can be deceptive. Compromise for North Americans and western Europeans is equal to morality, good faith and fair play. To the Mexicans and other Latin Americans compromise means losing dignity and integrity; in Russia and the Middle East it is a sign of weakness. Furthermore, members of other cultures may regard the common western ideal of a persuasive communicator as aggressive, superficial and insincere.

Implications of Hofstede's work

From Hofstede's work we see that there are differences (gaps) between national cultures. Each of four dimensions is reflected in the corporate culture patterns exhibited across countries (Hofstede, 1983). In the following, implications of Hofstede's four dimensions on the firm's international negotiation strategies will be discussed (Rowden, 2001)

Masculinity/femininity

Masculine cultures value assertiveness, independence, task orientation and self-achievement. Masculine culture's strategy for negotiation is usually competitive, resulting in a win/lose situation. Conflict is usually resolved by fighting rather than compromising, reflecting an ego-boosting manner. In this situation the person with the most competitive behaviour is likely to gain the most. On the other hand, feminine cultures value cooperation, nurturing, modesty, empathy and social relations, and prefer a collaborative or a compromising style or strategy to assure the best possible mutually accepting solution to obtain a win–win situation.

Uncertainty avoidance

This dimension refers to the comfort level of a person in an unclear or risky situation. High uncertainty avoidance cultures have formal bureaucratic negotiation rules, rely on rituals and standards, and trust only family and friends. They require clearly defined structure and guidelines. Low uncertainty avoidance cultures prefer to work informally with flexibility. They disfavour hierarchy, and are likely to seek resolving solutions and compromises rather than the status quo.

Power distance

This dimension refers to the acceptance of authority differences between those who have power and those affected by power. High power distance is authoritarian, and protocol formality and hierarchy are considered important. In 'high power distance' cultures the CEO of the company is often directly involved in the negotiations and is the final decision maker.

Business negotiations between equals (low power distance) are basically a western concept and are not found in status-oriented societies such as Japan, Korea or Russia. Western Europeans and North Americans are normally informal and downplay status by using first names, dressing in casual attire, etc.

The Japanese dress conservatively – they always prefer dark business suits; to be dressed casually during negotiations with the Japanese would, therefore, be inappropriate. The Japanese do not believe in using first names unless in the very best of personal relationships. In Asia honours, titles and status are extremely important: address your counterparts by their proper titles. Frankness and directness are important in the western world, but are not desirable in Asia.

The valued European handshake is often out of place in Japan, where bowing is customary. When meeting a devout Muslim, never shake with the left hand or utilise left hand for any purpose – it is considered rude and a personal affront.

When a person from a high masculine culture negotiates with a high power distance culture conflict will most likely result if neither party takes to understand the cultural balance. Competence is valued over seniority, which yields a consultative management style. Dealings between cultures with low masculinity and low power distance usually result in more cooperative and creative behavior.

Individualism/collectivism

Individualistic cultures tend to put tasks before relationships and value independence highly. These cultures tolerate open conflict and place the needs of the individual over the needs of a group, community or society. In negotiations the individualistic society expects the other party to have the authority to make decisions unilaterally. In a highly individualist country such as the United States it is considered socially acceptable to pursue one's own ends without understanding the benefits for others. In contrast managers from a collectivistic culture, such as China, will seek a stable relationship with a long-term orientation, stressing above all the establishment of a personal relationship. A collectivistic society values solidarity, loyalty and strong interdependence among individuals, and the members define themselves in terms of their membership within groups. Collectivist managers assume that details in the negotiation process can be worked out and show more concern for the needs of the other party by focusing on group goals. Members of collectivist societies are irritated when members from individualistic societies promote their own positions and ideas during negotiations.

Different organizational models

The British model of organization seems to be that of a village market with no decisive hierarchy, flexible rules and a resolution of problems by negotiating. The German model is more like a well-oiled machine. The exercise of personal command is largely unnecessary because the rules settle everything. The French model is more of a pyramidal hierarchy held together by a united command issuing strong rules. If we look at international buyer–seller relations, the national culture is only one level in the cultural hierarchy that will influence the behaviour of the individual buyer or seller. When members of different cultures come together to communicate, whether within the sales organization or in buyer–seller encounters, they typically do not bring the same shared values, thought patterns and actions to the situation. Common ground is typically limited. This increases the degree of uncertainty about the outcome of the interaction and can limit the efficiency and effectiveness of communication. To reduce uncertainty communicators must accurately predict how others will behave and be able to explain the behaviours of others (Bush and Ingram, 2001).

The gap model in international negotiation

In negotiation situations the most fundamental gap influencing the interaction between buyer and seller is the difference between their respective cultural backgrounds (gap 1 in Figure 19.1). This cultural distance can be expressed in terms of

Figure 19.1 Gap analysis in a cross-cultural negotiation

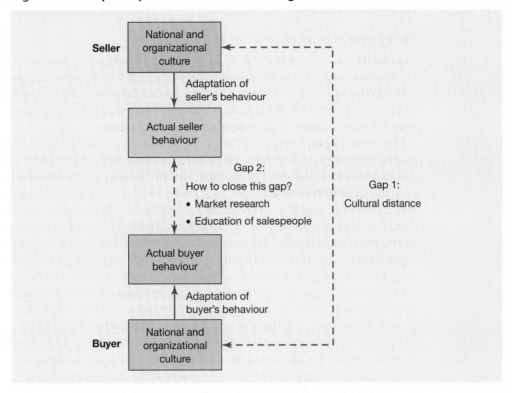

differences in communication and negotiation behaviour, the concepts of time, space or work patterns, and the nature of social rituals and norms (Madsen, 1994). The cultural distance between two partners tends to increase the transaction costs, which may be quite high in cross-cultural negotiations.

Cultural influence on persons, and thereby international negotiations, can be analysed at various levels of society. Furthermore there is a learning 'effect' in the way that a person's cultural identity formed in one specific cultural setting will affect how they view other situations in other cultural settings. Both seller and buyer are influenced by (at least) the national and organizational culture they belong to. As seen in Chapter 7 (Figure 7.2) there are probably more levels in the understanding of individual negotiation behaviour.

The influence of national culture

The national culture is the macro/societal culture that represents a distinct way of life of a group of citizens in a certain country. This national culture is composed of the norms and values that members hold, as well as their level of, for example economic development, education system, national laws and other parts of the regulatory environment (Harvey and Griffith, 2002). All these factors play an important role in socialising individuals in a specific pattern of belief (Andersen, 2003). Therefore it is typical that when individuals encounter cultural differences in their international interactions/relationships, they tend to view people from different national cultures as strangers, that is unknown people who belong to different groups. This feeling of distance can directly impact upon trust and personal bonding, which increases the probability of conflict between seller and buyer in the negotiation process. The discussion earlier of the four dimensions of Hofstede's research gives several examples of differences in national culture and how they may affect intercultural negotiations between two partners.

The influence of organizational culture

Organizational culture is the pattern of shared behaviour, values and beliefs that provides a foundation for understanding the organizational functioning processes (Schein, 1985). When two or more organizations are negotiating with each other the relative level of consistency of core elements between organizational cultures can directly influence the effectiveness of communication and negotiation.

The overall complexity of a firm's communication environment will vary tremendously when elements of national culture and organizational culture are examined. In instances where a high level of national culture distance exists between buyer and seller and the organizational cultures are inconsistent (i.e. high inter-organizational distance), then the negotiation environment will be highly complex, neccesitating careful planning and monitoring of the firm's intercultural negotiation strategies. Alternatively, when the national cultural distance is low and the cultures of buyer's and seller's organizations are consistent, both partners will find it easier to employ effective negotiation strategies without too much adaptation (Griffith, 2002).

In the case of a certain national and organizational cultural 'distance' between buyer and seller, both the buyer and especially the seller will try to adapt their own behaviour in such a way that they think it is acceptable to the other party. In this way the initial gap 1 may be reduced to gap 2, through adaptation of behaviour. To what extent the seller can adjust his behaviour to another culture's communication style is a function of their skills and experience. The necessary skills include the ability to handle stress, initiate conversation and establish a meaningful relationship.

But neither the seller nor the buyer obtains full understanding of the other party's culture, so the final result will often still be a difference between the cultural behaviour of the seller and the buyer (gap 2). This gap can create friction in the negotiation and exchange process and hence give rise to transaction costs.

Gap 2 can be reduced through market research and the education of salespeople (see next section). However, salespeople bring different 'baggage' with them in the form of attitudes and skills that result in different stages of intercultural awareness. The different stages of intercultural prepareness are highlighted in the next section. For example, if a trainer chooses to give a basic cultural awareness exercise to salespeople who are already at the acceptance stage and willing to learn about behaviour strategies, then they are likely to be bored and not see the value of some types of diversity training.

Furthermore, face-to-face communication skills remain an important topic in international sales training. This is especially true in consultative selling, where questioning and listening skills are essential in the global marketing context. However, learning about cultural diversity through training programmes should help salespeople and marketing executives be better prepared to predict the behaviours they encounter with diverse customers or co-workers. Yet many salespeople are sceptical of training and question its value. In fact employees may view diversity training as simply a current 'fad' or the 'politically correct thing to do'. However, if not prepared many salespeople may not realise the impact of cultural diversity until they encounter an unfamiliar cultural situation.

Exhibit 19.2	Euro Disney becomes Disneyland Paris – The 'American way' did not work in Europe

In preparing the opening of Euro Disney (near Paris) in 1992, Euro Disney's first chairman proudly announced that his company would 'help change Europe's chemistry'. The French ridiculed the park as a 'cultural Chernobyl'.

Several cross-cultural blunders occurred:

- Prior to opening the park, Disney insisted employees comply with a detailed written code regarding clothing, jewellery, and other aspects of personal appearance. Women were expected to wear 'appropriate undergarments' and keep their fingernails short. Disney defended its move, noting that similar codes were used in its other parks. The goal was to ensure that guests received the kind of experience associated with the Disney name. Despite such statements the French considered the code to be an insult to French culture, individualism and privacy.
- The extension of Disney's standard 'no alcohol' policy from the United States meant that wine was not available at Euro Disney. This, too, was deemed inappropriate in a country renowned for its production and consumption of wine.

It took a series of adaptions, such as renaming the park 'Disneyland Paris' and the addition of some special attractions, to make the park profitable as of 1996 and the most frequented tourist attraction of France in 1997.

In the fiscal year 1998–9, which ended 30 September, Disneyland Paris drew over 12.5 million visitors, more than any other attraction in France. Only about 41 per cent were from France, with 17 per cent from Belgium, Luxembourg and the Netherlands, 15 per cent from the United Kingdom and 10 per cent from Germany.

For the year 1998–9 Disneyland Paris reported a $24 million net profit. Though that was 46 per cent less than the year before, the drop was attributed mainly to a resumption of Euro Disney's payment of management fees to the Walt Disney Company and to stagnant attendance, which was hurt by the World Cup soccer tournament in France in the summer of 1998. Furthermore, Disneyland Paris has announced plans for a new $615 million, 62-acre park that will focus on film studios, animation and television. The official opening is planned for April 2002, 10 years after the inauguration of the first park.

However, Disneyland is not the only company which offers additional theme parks. In a few months, Warner Bros. will break ground on a $300-million theme park, Movie World, Madrid, that will supplement its existing park in Bottrop, Germany. After rejecting sites in England, Warner took advantage of Madrid's desire to 'have something that would compete with Port Aventura,' says Nick Winslow, president of the company's international recreation enterprises.

Sources: Tagliabue, J, 2000; Della Cava, M.R., 1999.

One of the main problems frequently encountered in providing salespeople with meaningful educational experience that includes cultural diversity (distance) is the inability routinely to provide on-location experiential learning opportunities. This is due to lack of time and resources. Although desirable, in many instances one cannot beforehand take the sales person to the culture to analyse and learn from their reactions. A viable alternative to this dilemma is to expose trainees to a simulated culturally diverse experience. The advantages of this approach are that it is more efficient and requires the active involvement of individuals resulting in experiential learning. Simulations based on role-plays and result-oriented learning have been very successful in teaching salespeople and managers (Bush and Ingram, 2001).

Negotiating strategies

Basic to negotiating is, of course, knowing your own strengths and weaknesses, but also knowing as much as possible about the other side, understanding the other's way of thinking and recognising their perspective. Even starting from a position of weakness there are strategies that a salesperson can pursue to turn the negotiation to their advantage.

19.3   Intercultural preparation

Many sales people may be aware that cultural diversity is an important issue in their work environment. However, as evidenced by many stories of cultural 'blunders' (see the example in Exhibit 19.2) salespeople may not realise the impact of diversity on their ability to predict behaviour in a selling situation. Thus individuals may progress through a kind of self-revelation about their own perceived skills and how these skills impact on their interactions with co-workers or buyers of culturally diverse backgrounds. Participating in such an experimental exercise can help sales and marketing personnel begin to understand the impact of cultural diversity in different ways.

General intercultural preparation

The following five-step approach is proposed to help firms with preparing their salespeople for coping with cultural diversities when entering different international markets (Bush and Ingram, 2001):

1. Build awareness about how cultural differences impact upon them in the sales organization.
2. Motivate salespeople and managers to 'rethink' their behaviour and attitude towards customers.
3. Allow salespeople to examine their own biases in a psychologically safe environment.
4. Examine how stereotypes are developed, and how they can create misunderstandings between buyers and sellers.
5. Identify diversity issues that need to be addressed in the international sales organization.

This simulation may be perceived as a valuable starting point for learning about communication styles and cultural differences. Most firms realise that cultural diversity training requires much more time than expected. One of the difficulties in educating individuals about communicating between cultures or subcultures is that individuals can not be handled in only a two-hour session. Respecting and successfully interacting with members of diverse cultures is a long-term process. By participating in a long-term exercise salespeople may begin to realise that the concept of diversity goes beyond 'the right thing to do' or satisfying affirmative action requirements. Valuing diversity can also impact the bottom line of an organization.

Specific evaluation of partner's intercultural communication and negotiation competences

To address the issues involved with the fit and reduction of 'gaps' in negotiation processes a firm must be proactive and develop specific strategies to enhance communication effectiveness. Most organizations have not formalised their management of cross-cultural communication but at least three steps are necessary in order to improve the selling firm's cross-cultural communication and negotiation competences:

1. *Assessing communication competences of salespersons:* Given the importance of a salesperson's communication competences for relationship success, it is critical that selling firms assess these persons' competences. Once the technical level (e.g. technical and standard language competences) is assessed the firm could use the above-mentioned simulation and experiential methods to gauge behavioural competences.

2. *Assessing communication competences of negotiators in the buying firm:* If possible the same procedure as in (1) above should be done for the buyers in the foreign culture. However, it might be difficult to get this information about the negotiators in the buying firm.

3. *Matching communication and negotiation competences of buying and selling firm:* Only if there is a match (and not too large a 'gap') between the communication competences of the two firms can they realistically expect success in the international negotiation and in the possible future relationship. Of course it should be noted that the selling firm is only able to control its internal competences, and not those of the buying firm.

This issue of communication assessment can also be integrated into the firm's partner selection and retention criteria. As the selling firm begins to integrate these communication competences into its partner selection and retention criteria it is also important that it shows flexibility and willingness to improve the existing competences in relation to its partner (the buying firm).

19.4   Coping with expatriates

The following discussion can be applied not only to expatriate salespeople but also to other jobs in the firm based in a foreign country (e.g. an administrative position in a foreign subsidiary). Expatriate salespeople negotiating in foreign cultures often experience a culture shock when confronted with a buyer. Culture shock is more intensely experienced by expatriates whose cultures are most different from the ones in which they are now working. What can the management of the international firm do to minimise the risk of culture shock? The following areas should be considered (Guy and Patton, 1996).

The decision to employ an expatriate salesperson

The first major decision to make is whether the use of home country expatriates is the best choice for entering and serving foreign markets. The firm should first examine its own past experience with culture shock and sales rep adjustment in other cultures. Inexperienced firms would probably be best advised to evaluate possible agents and distributors rather than using home country expatriates. Other options for firms with their own sales force are host country or third country nationals (see also section 17.3).

The firm should try to identify the elements in the expatriate sales job that suggest potential problems with culture shock. If the job is highly technical, is located in an area with other home country nationals, and involves similar tastes and lifestyles as in the home country, then the expatriate sales force may be appropriate.

If, however, the job places the expatriate salesperson in an unfamiliar job with conflicting expectations, the firm should consider other options. The chances of greater culture shock and adjustment problems increase with greater cultural distance. The greater the high context/low context contrast, the greater is the chance of difficulty. When entering a different culture many familiar symbols and cues are missing. The removal of these everyday reassurances can lead to feelings of frustration, stress and anxiety.

Selection of expatriates

Since being an expatriate salesperson is a critical task the selection process should be given considerable thought and should not be decided too quickly. The selection should not be based primarily on the technical competence of the salesperson. Substantial emphasis must also be placed on the following attributes:

- foreign-language skills;
- general relational abilities;
- emotional stability;
- educational background;
- past experience with the designated culture;
- ability to deal with stress.

Previous research (Guy and Patton, 1996) suggests that the following characteristics of the expatriate are associated with a lower level of cultural shock:

- open-mindedness;
- empathy;
- cultural sensitivity;
- resilience;
- low ego identity.

An assessment of the potential expatriate alone is not sufficient if the person has a family that will be making the move as well. Family issues that must be considered include marital stability, the overall emotional stability of family members, and family cohesiveness. In-depth interviews with at least the rep's spouse and preferably other family members as well can be very useful in determining the status of these variables.

Training

Selecting the most appropriate training programme for each expatriate requires methods for classifying people into various levels of intercultural skills. Each level needs a different training programme. The initial requirement is to train the expatriate, and any accompanying family member, to know the main sociocultural, economic, political, legal and technological factors in the assigned country.

The training activities may include the following:

- area/country description;
- cultural assimilation training;
- role playing;
- handling critical incidents;
- case studies;
- stress reduction training;
- field experience;
- extensive language training.

Obviously many firms will not be able to provide all the training needed in-house or through a single source, but they may need to coordinate a variety of methods and external programmes for their expatriates to take place before and during the foreign assignment.

Support

It is very important to provide a solid support network from the head office so that the expatriate is not simply left alone to 'sink or swim'. Support during expatriate assignment may include a number of elements:

■ Adequate monetary compensation or other benefits.
■ Constant communication from the home base regarding ongoing operations at head office and in the assigned country/area.
■ Providing opportunities for periodic travel to the home country to maintain contacts and relationships within the firm. The home base could also send copies of forthcoming job postings in which the expatriate may be interested.

The expatriate should identify and contact individuals in the host country who can become a part of the expatriate's social network. It is also important that the expatriate's spouse and family are included in a social support network.

Repatriation

Companies employing expatriates should develop an integrated career plan, identifying likely subsequent job positions and career progression. If the expatriates, during their careers, are exposed to a series of international assignments, each assignment should be selected to develop their awareness of different cultures. For example, for a UK company the first non-UK assignment would be a culturally similar or proximate country, say Germany or the United States, the next assignment might be South Africa or Australia, the next Hong Kong, then Japan and so on. In this way cultural shock is minimised, since the process encourages the ability to manage situations in more and more distant cultures.

The return of the expatriate to the home country is sometimes difficult. Lack of job guarantees is one of the most critical challenges faced by expatriates. Some months prior to return an internal position search should be started with a home visit arranged for the expatriate to meet with appropriate managers. An internal sponsor in the head office should be appointed to maintain ongoing contact and to help the expatriate secure a desirable position upon return.

Sometimes expatriated families also experience a culture shock upon returning to the home country. Therefore some support is needed during repatriation. This includes spouse job-finding assistance and time to readjust before going back to work.

| 19.5 | Knowledge management and learning across borders |

Managing global knowledge that crosses the lines between business units, subsidiaries and departments that are dispersed geographically across continents is highly complex and requires consideration of different issues and factors. The global strategy exploits the knowledge of the parent organization (headquarters) through worldwide diffusion and adaptation. The global strategy strives to achieve the slogan, 'think globally but act locally', through dynamic interdependence between the headquarters and the subsidiaries. Organizations following such a strategy coordinate efforts, ensuring local flexibility while exploiting the benefits of global integration and efficiencies, as well as ensuring worldwide diffusion of innovation (Desouza and Evaristo, 2003).

A key element in knowledge management is the continuous learning from experience (Stewart, 2001). In practical terms the aim of knowledge management, as a learning-focused activity across borders, is to keep track of valuable capabilities used in one market that could be used elsewhere (in other geographic markets), so that firms can continually update their knowledge without 'reinventing the wheel'. See also the example in Figure 19.2 for a systematic approach to global learning from transferring 'best practices' in the firm's different international markets.

Figure 19.2 'Bottom-up' learning in global marketing

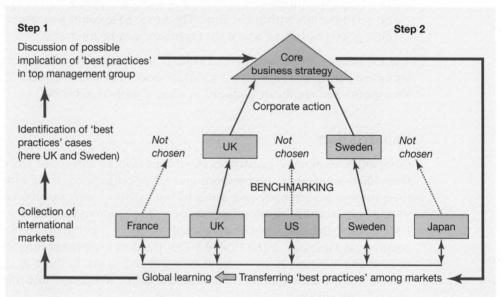

The steps in transferring the firm's 'best practices' to other international markets are as follows:

1. By benchmarking (comparing) the different procedures in the firm's international markets the firm should be able to pick up best practices – in Figure 19.2 the best practices are found in the United Kingdom and Sweden. Subsequently, the possible implications of the 'best practices' are discussed in the 'top management' group.

2. After the procedures for diffusion of the 'best practices' have been established in the top management group the next step is to see if these 'best practices' can be used elsewhere in the firm's international markets. In order to disseminate global knowledge and 'best practices', meetings (with representatives from all international markets) and global project groups should be established. If done successfully the benchmarking could result in a global learning process, where the different international marketing managers would select the most usable elements from the presented 'best practices' and adapt these in the local markets.

However, as noted earlier in this chapter, knowledge developed and used in one cultural context is not easily transferred to another. The lack of personal relationships, the absence of trust and 'cultural distance' all conspire to create resistance, frictions and misunderstandings in cross-cultural knowledge management (Bell *et al.*, 2002).

With globalization becoming a centrepiece in the business strategy of many firms – be it firms engaged in product development or providing services – the ability to manage the 'global knowledge engine' to achieve a competitive edge in today's knowledge-intensive economy is one of the keys to sustainable competitiveness. But in the context of global marketing the management of knowledge is de facto a cross-cultural activity, whose key task is to foster and continually make more sophisticated collaborative cross-cultural learning (Berrell *et al.*, 2002). Of course the kind and/or the type of knowledge that is strategic for an organization and which needs to be managed for competitiveness varies depending on the business context and the value of different types of knowledge associated with it.

Explicit and tacit knowledge

New knowledge is created through the synergistic relationship and interplay between *tacit* and *explicit* knowledge.

Explicit knowledge is defined as knowledge that can be expressed formally using a system of symbols, and can therefore be easily communicated or diffused. It is either object based or rule based. It is object based when the knowledge is codified in symbols (e.g. words, numbers, formulas) or in physical objects (e.g. equipment, documents, models). Object-based knowledge may be found in examples such as product specifications, patents, software codes, computer databases, technical drawings, etc. Explicit knowledge is rule based when the knowledge is codified into rules, routines, or standard operating procedures (Choo, 1998).

Tacit knowledge is the implicit knowledge used by organizational members to perform their work and to make sense of the world. It is knowledge that is uncodified and difficult to diffuse across borders and subsidiaries. It is hard to verbalise because it is expressed through action-based skills and cannot be reduced to rules and recipes. Instead tacit knowledge is learned through extended periods of experiencing and doing a task, during which the individual develops a feel for and a capacity to make intuitive judgements about the successful execution of the activity. Tacit knowledge is vital to an organization because organizations can only learn and innovate by somehow levering on the implicit knowledge of its members. Tacit knowledge becomes substantially valuable when it is turned into new capabilities, products, services or even new markets for the firm. Organizational knowledge creation is a process that organizationally amplifies the knowledge created by individuals in different countries and subsidiaries and crystallises it as a part of the international knowledge network of the company. There are two sets of dynamics that drive the process of international knowledge amplification (Nonaka and Takeuchi, 1995):

1. converting tacit knowledge into explicit knowledge;
2. moving knowledge from the indiviual level to the group, organizational and interorganizational levels (across subsidiaries in different countries).

A central issue in internationalized firms concerns where knowledge is created and diffused. Because of the capabilities in creating knowledge Centres of Excellence may be formed in certain subsidiaries, for example regarding specific functions such as product development or international marketing.

Global project groups

Today's business with its growing emphasis on globalization increasingly requires people to collaborate in workgroups that cross cultural and geographic boundaries. The trend to multicultural workgroups emerged as a reaction to changed economic conditions, forcing organizations to develop new structures in order to minimise costs and maximise flexibility. One consequence of these changes is that as a result of rapid knowledge growth and increasingly complex work environments more and more tasks can only be accomplished in international project groups by cooperation of functionally and culturally different experts. Based on the assumption of diversity creating value and therefore competitive advantage by bringing together different ideas and pooling knowledge, multicultural project groups have become a prevailing tendency in multinational organizations. However, the use of such groups in practice often turns out to be a lot more problematic than expected. It seems that the cognitive advantages which can be gained by a diverse workforce are counterbalanced by relational problems such as miscommunication and distrust, and therefore high turn-over rates (Wolf, 2002). Nevertheless, with today's economy facing an ever increasing need to cross all kinds of borders, the existence of culturally diverse project groups has become inevitable.

Given the communication problems and trust issues that plague ad hoc global project groups, structuring the project team is particularly critical to success. The following three questions need attention from the top management of the firm (Govindarajan and Gupta, 2001):

1. *Is the objective clearly defined?* One of the first concerns for any global project team must be explicitly to discuss the group's agenda and ensure that the objective/problem is defined clearly and correctly. Many project groups do not fully resolve and discuss the issues involved and they immediately run into problems. Different framing of the same problem can produce different outcomes. Because the project group typically has members from different subsidiaries that usually compete with one another for scare corporate resources they tend to have a high degree of internal conflict, combined with a low level of trust. As a result it is generally best to frame the problem of the project group in terms of the company's position vis-à-vis the external marketplace instead of emphasising internal issues. An external focus encourages benchmarking, fosters creativity and provides a compelling rationale for making the tough decisions inherent in any manufacturing rationalisation and workforce reduction. Given the possible communication problems in the global project group it is imperative that the members understand the agenda of the project group: the scope of the project, the expected deliverables and the timeline. Cultural and language differences may complicate the task of getting group members to agree on the agenda and the problems to be solved. Clarity is essential to promoting commitment and accountability.

2. *Choosing group members*: Another key to creating a successful global team is choosing the right group members. Two issues are of particular importance: how do you balance diversity within the team and what should be the size of the group? Normally we will see high levels of diversity. Why? First, members come from diverse cultural and national backgrounds – this refers to so-called *behavioural diversity*. Secondly, members generally represent subsidiaries whose agenda may not be congruent. Thirdly, because members often represent different functional units and departments, their priorities and perspectives may differ. The last two issues refer to so-called *cognitive diversity*.

Let us take a closer look at an example of behavioural diversity: consider, for example, a cross-border project group in a Swedish–Chinese joint venture. The norm in most Chinese teams is that the most senior member presents the team's perspective, but in a Swedish team the most junior member typically does so. Unless the members of the team are sensitised to such differences misunderstandings can easily emerge and block communication. So behavioural diversity is best regarded as a necessary evil: something that no global project group can avoid but the effects of which the group must attempt to minimise through training in cultural sensitivity.

Let us also take a closer look at an example of cognitive diversity: this diversity refers to differences in the substantive content of how members perceive the group's challenges and opportunities. Differences in functional backgrounds can account for substantive cognitive differences on issues of 'market pull' (preferred by people in marketing departments) and 'technology push' (preferred by people in engineering departments). Because no single member can ever have a monopoly on wisdom cognitive diversity is almost always a source of strength. Divergent perspectives foster creativity and a more comprehensive search for and assessment of options. But the group must be able to integrate the perspectives and come to a single solution.

3. *Selection of team leadership*: structuring the leadership of a global project team involves critical decisions around three roles: the *project leader*, the *external coach* and *the internal sponsor*. The *project leader* plays a pivotal role in cross-border project groups. They must contribute to the development of trust between the members and maybe have the biggest stake in the outcome of the project. They must possess conflict-resolution and integration skills; and expertise in process management, including diagnosing problems, assessing situations and generating and evaluating options. An *external coach* serves as an ad hoc member of the project group and is an expert in process more than content. The need for such a coach is likely to be high when the process-management skills of the best available project leader are inadequate. This might happen if the appointed leader has some major stake in the project's outcome, for example if a cross-border task force has to rationalise and decrease the number of subsidiaries around the world by 30 per cent. The *internal sponsor* of a global project group is typically a senior level executive with a strong interest in the success of the team. Among the responsibilities of the sponsor are to provide ongoing guidelines and to facilitate access to resources.

At any given time a global company will typically have many project groups working on different cross-border coordination issues. Therefore it makes sense for the company to undertake initiatives to create interpersonal familiarity and trust among key managers of different subsidiaries. For example, Unilever uses several approaches to do this – such as bringing together managers from different subsidiaries in executive development education programmes.

When a project group consists of members with distinct knowledge and skills drawn from different subsidiaries in different countries the potential for cognitive diversity is high, and this can also be a source competitive strength. But intellectual diversity will almost always bring with it some degree of interpersonal incompatibility and communication difficulty. Process mechanism that recognise and anticipate such pitfalls – and integrate the best of individuals' ideas and contributions – are needed to help the project group reconcile diverse perspectives and arrive at better, more creative and novel solutions.

19.6   Transnational bribery in cross-cultural negotiations

On first consideration bribery is both unethical and illegal. But a closer look reveals that bribery is not really a straightforward issue. The ethical and legal problems associated with bribery can be quite complex. Thus the definition of bribery can range from the relatively innocuous payment of a few pounds to a minor official or business manager in order to expedite the processing of papers or the loading of a truck, to the extreme of paying millions of pounds to a head of state to guarantee a company preferential treatment. Scott *et al.* (2002) generally define bribery as 'involving a company from an industrialized country offering an illicit payment to a developing country's public official with perceived or real influence over contract awards' (p. 2).

The difference between lubrication and bribery must be established. Lubrication payments accompany requests for a person to do a job more rapidly or more efficiently. They involve a relatively small cash sum, gift or service made to a low-ranking official in a country where such offerings are not prohibited by law, the purpose being to facilitate or expedite the normal, lawful performance of a duty by that official. This practice is common in many countries. Bribery, on the other hand, generally involves large sums of money, which are frequently not properly accounted for, and is designed to entice an official to commit an illegal act on behalf of the one paying the bribe.

Another type of payment that can appear to be a bribe, but may not be, is an agent's fee. When a businessperson is uncertain of a country's rules and regulations an agent may be hired to represent the company in that country. This person will do a more efficient and thorough job than someone unfamiliar with country-specific procedures.

There are many intermediaries (attorneys, agents, distributors and so forth) who function simply as channels for illegal payments. The process is further complicated by legal codes that vary from country to country: what is illegal in one country is winked at in another and legal in a third. In some countries illegal payments can become a major business expense. Hong Kong companies report that bribes account for about 5 per cent of the cost of doing business in China. In Russia the cost is 15–20 per cent, and in Indonesia as high as 30 per cent (Gesteland, 1996, p. 93).

Exhibit 19.3	Does bribery also cover sexual favours? The case of Lockheed Martin and a South Korean defence contract

A US court has ruled that arms maker Lockheed Martin can be sued for allegedly using sexual favours and bribes to win a South Korean defence contract. Lockheed Martin has denied the allegations.

The case was filed by the Korea Supply Company (KSC) after it lost a contract to Lockheed subsidiary Loral for the supply of an aircraft radar system to South Korea in 1996.

KSC's lawsuit claims a Loral employee, Linda Kim – a former model and singer – bribed South Korean military officers and offered sexual favours to the country's defence minister, Lee Yang Ho. He has admitted to having an 'inappropriate relationship' with Ms Kim but denies it influenced his decision making. Ms Kim's love letters to the defence minister made headline news in South Korea after they were implicated in another bribery scandal.

The US Foreign Corrupt Practices Act forbids US companies from bribing foreign officials to influence an official act or decision.

Source: adapted from BBC News, Lockheed sex suit to go ahead, 3 May 2003, **news.bbc.co.uk/go/pr/fr/-/2/hi/business/2,820,939.stm**

The answer to the question of bribery is not an unqualified one. It is easy to generalise about the ethics of political pay-offs and other types of payment; it is much more difficult to make the decision to withhold payment of money when not making the payment may affect the company's ability to do business profitably or at all. With the variety of ethical standards and levels of morality which exist in different cultures the dilemma of ethics and pragmatism that faces international business cannot be resolved until more countries decide to deal effectively with the issue.

19.7 Summary

When marketing internationally negotiation skills are needed. Negotiation skills and personal selling skills are related. Personal selling typically occurs at the field sales force level and during formal negotiation processes. Cultural factors are critical to understanding the negotiation style of foreigners.

Prior to the negotiation process between two partners there is a cultural distance between them. This cultural distance causes some transaction costs, which may be quite high. To reduce the cultural distance training of the negotiators is required.

The culture shock felt by expatriates indicates that sending negotiators and salespeople to foreign markets is often difficult and complex to implement successfully. Five important areas of implementation include: (1) making the initial decision to employ an expatriate sales force, (2) identifying and selecting qualified candidates, (3) providing adequate training, (4) maintaining ongoing support and (5) achieving satisfactory repatriation.

In global knowledge management a key element is the continuous learning from experiences in different markets. In practical terms, the aim of knowledge management as a learning-focused activity across borders is to keep track of valuable capabilities used in one market that could be used elsewhere (in other geographic markets), so that firms can continually update their knowledge without 'reinventing the wheel'.

The ethical question of what is right or appropriate poses many dilemmas for international marketers. Bribery is an issue that is defined very differently from country to country. What is acceptable in one country may be completely unacceptable in another.

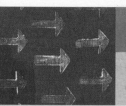

CASE STUDY 19.1 Mecca Cola

Marketing of a 'Muslim' cola to the European market

Until now the cola war has mainly been going on in North America and Europe. But a French Tunisian in January 2003 opened up a second front – by producing a carbonated drink named Mecca Cola, a new soft drink designed to cash in on anti-US sentiment, mainly in European markets. The new drink will be marketed in bottles of 1.5 litres.

Mecca Cola – a political choice

The new brand, which has a striking resemblance to Coca-Cola, is specifically intended to make a political statement. Its French label and advertising slogan translates as 'No more drinking stupid – Drink with commitment'.

The creator of Mecca Cola, prominent French political activist Tawfiq Mathlouthi, claims the drink is not competion for Coke and that his campaign is not anti-American. Instead, he says, each bottle sold is a protest against the Bush administration's foreign policy. Mathlouthi promises that 10 per cent of profits will go to Palestinian causes, humanitarian aid for Palestinian children, education and preserving the heritage. Mathlouthi hopes to make Mecca Cola the soft drink of choice for Muslims everywhere and thus push out that icon of US capitalism Coca-Cola.

Mr Masood Shadjareh, Chairman of the London-based Islamic Human Rights Commission, which is backing calls to shun US brands, predicted huge interest in the new cola. He told the *Guardian*: 'The Muslim community is targeting Coca-Cola because people feel that the only thing they can do is hit America economically. It is not only an issue for someone like me who is an activist. I bought some fizzy drinks and my children, who are 10 and 12, found out they were products of Coca-Cola and refused to drink them. I told them I'd already paid for them, but my daughter said "Look Daddy, it just won't go down".'

Meanwhile, some religious fundamentalists object to the use of the name of the Muslim holy city on a soft drink. There is no indication Mecca Cola or any other boycott product will do long-term harm to US multinationals, Coca-Cola and Pepsi-Cola. But some US manufacturers admit the boycott is having an impact on sales. And no one denies how easy it is for consumers to express their politics by simply switching brands. Coca-Cola's comment was: 'Ultimately it is the consumer who will make the decision'. Coca-Cola insists that it is 'not affiliated with any religion or ethnic group' and does not engage in politics.

Zam Zam Cola

It is not the first time Coca-Cola has been the target of a 'buy Muslim' challenge. Zam Zam Cola, an Iranian drink named after a holy spring in Mecca, has won an enthusiastic reception in Saudi Arabia and Bahrain.

US companies such as McDonald's, Starbucks, Nike and the two cola giants admit the campaign is wounding them. Sales of Coca-Cola have dropped between 20 and 40 per cent in some countries. In Morocco, a government official estimates sales of Pepsi and Coca-Cola could fall by half in the north, which is a stronghold of Islamic groups. In the United Arab Emirates, sales of the local Star Cola are up by 40 per cent over the past three months.

Zam Zam, which also produces non-alcoholic 'Islamic beer', has a long pedigree in Iran, where it was founded in 1954 and today has 47 per cent of the domestic market. For many years it was the Iranian partner of Pepsi Cola until their contract was ended after the 1979 revolution.

A Saudi firm owned by one of the kingdom's princes, Turki Abdallah al-Faisal, in January 2003 signed an agreement with the Zam Zam Group, giving the Saudi company exclusive distribution rights in Saudi Arabia, Egypt and a number of other Arab countries.

Zam Zam was taken over by the Foundation of the Dispossessed, a powerful state charity run by clerics, and today it employs more than 7,000 people in its 17 factories in Iran. It is now planning to build factories in the Persian Gulf.

Its cola is already exported to Saudi Arabia, Bahrain, Qatar, the United Arab Emirates, Oman, Kuwait, Afghanistan and Iraq, and the company says it will soon ship its drinks to Lebanon, Syria and Denmark – its first European client.

The marketing and internationalization of Mecca Cola

Other firms in the Middle East have tried creating different cola drinks, but none has turned its drink into a political weapon. The first businesses to sell Mecca Cola were what Mr Mathlouthi described as 'small ethnic shops in Muslim areas'. Now the drink can be found on the shelves of large cash and carry supermarkets in France, Belgium and Germany. The company behind Mecca Cola says the United Kingdom is also a huge market and already has orders to send about 2 million bottles a month to Britain.

Mecca Cola was originally targeted at France's Muslim community but at least one major hypermarket chain in France is now stocking the soft drink.

While Coca-Cola's revenues in the Middle East represent less than 2 per cent of its global business, it is galling for Coke to lag behind Pepsi in the region. Britain's 1.8 million Muslims have only recently begun to discover a collective voice and it remains unclear whether a boycott or a 'buy Muslim' campaign will occur.

Mecca Cola has sold 2 million bottles since its launch two months ago in France. In Muslim areas

of Paris the soft drink is sold for £1.05 ($1.7) per 1.5 litre bottle, approximately the same as its US rival Coke.

Questions

1. What are the main reasons for the success of Zam Zam cola?

2. What are the criteria for the successful implementation of Mecca Cola's international marketing strategies?

3. How should Tawfiq Mathlouthi prepare his sales force 'culturally' for selling Mecca Cola to European supermarket chains?

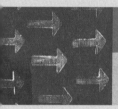

CASE STUDY 19.2   TOTO

The Japanese toilet manufacturer seeks export opportunities for its high-tech brands in United States

An average person visits the toilet 2,500 times per year, about 6–8 times per day. People spend at least three years of their lives using the toilet, and women take three times as long to use the toilet as men (**www.worldtoilet.org**).

Founded in 1917, Japanese toilet maker TOTO (**www.toto.co.jp**) is the largest toilet manufacturer in the world, producing more than 7 million toilets annually. TOTO's net sales in the financial year 2002 (ending March 31, 2003) were JPY 439,683 million (US$3,658 million). The net profits were JPY 4,000 million (US$33 million). Toto's total number of employees at the end of March 2003, were 17,000.

It seems that TOTO has made a sales success in Japan. Japanese Government statistics show that combined toilet/bidets (represented by TOTO's Washlet-brand) are now installed in 52 per cent of Japanese homes compared to just 14 per cent in 1992. TOTO, which employs around 1,500 engineers, dominates that market with a 65 per cent share. Its closest rival, Japan's Inax Corp, trails at 25 per cent. Numbers for Japan's overall toilet market share are similar. However outside Japan, TOTO's market share is only very small, with 8 per cent of TOTO's total net sales coming from overseas in 2002. The United States market is the number one

target, and China is the second, where revenues are up 14 per cent in the fiscal year 2003.

US market for toilets

The United States is the largest and most competitive market in the world, in 2002 16.3 million toilets were sold in the US market. TOTO's sales to the US, in the year 2002 rose 35 per cent to $117 million. In 1989, TOTO began to make inroads into the U.S. market with the establishment of TOKI KiKi USA, Inc., but in 2003 TOTO's overall market share of the US toilet market is still only very small – below 5 per cent.

Americans are said to move residences once every 7 or 8 years, creating a used-home market larger than that in Japan. As a consequence, remodeling is effectively the same level (or better) as that of new homes. Compared with Japan, the U.S. has stricter water conservation regulations for toilets and spurred by these regulations, industry specialists expect to see demand for replacement toilets in the future.

New housing starts are over 1.8 million annually, thanks in part to low interest rates in the US new housing market. Even when you consider the 1.1 million new housing starts in Japan, the US housing market is substantially larger in scale, and therefore has more potential. TOTO is targeting high value-added markets in the U.S. through the kitchen/bath shop and waterworks channels, and bypassing the home improvement center channel. Through the kitchen/bath shop and waterworks channels TOTO provides customers with services, including consulting, and installation for its products. In this way TOTO is hoping to capture market shares in the high-end of the US toilet market.

TOTO penetrates the US market but is facing cultural barriers

TOTO made toilet history in 1980 when, improving on a U.S. model that combined the bidet and the toilet, it produced the 'Washlet', bringing warm water to the user's nether regions. TOTO did what the American toilet makers were reluctant to try – they brought electronics into the water closet. Top-of-the-line Washlets now came with wall-mounted control panels as complex as those of stereo systems. Their manifold buttons allow adjustment of the nozzle position, water pressure and type of spray, plus blow-drying, air purification and seat warming for those cold winter mornings. Water and seat temperatures are adjustable. The controls can also be set so the lid rises as the user approaches the Washlet. Globally, more than 20 million Washlets have been sold (mainly in Japan) since their introduction in 1980. United States however, is a country without a history with the bidet. Bidets – usually stand-alone fixtures used in conjunction with toilets – originated in France and have been in use throughout the southern part of Europe since the 1700s. Ironically, more than two decades ago TOTO began importing hospital-grade bidets from United States to sell to Japan's aging population. It soon discovered there was a larger market for the fixtures and adapted the traditional bidet into a toilet seat attachment, which fits onto existing toilet bowls.

But while US consumers are just waking up to Washlets, the Japanese are going even more upmarket. TOTO's new Neorest model (introduced in 2003) gets rid of the inner rim of the bowl and brings in 'the tornado flush'. The Neorest (priced at $5,200) has all the features of TOTO's Washlet, including a heated seat for cold nights, built-in back-and-front bidet with oscillating or pulsating spray massage, and a warm-air dryer, all with temperature controls on a wall-mounted remote. Add to these features the smart toilet's built-in air purifier and motion sensors that detect your approach and automatically raise the lid. Males can lift the seat with the touch of a button and in doing so instruct the unit to flush with less water. Complete your business and the toilet automatically shuts the lid (while putting the seat down!) and flushes.

Sources:
Adapted from
Helms. T. (2003), 'The Toilet Marketplace', Supply House Times, September 2003, pp. 72–8
www.ceramicindustry.com
www.toto.co.jp
www.worldtoilet.org

Questions

1. What cultural barriers would the Japanese managers from Toto meet when negotiating with American managers from building societies about new contracts for toilets in US luxury apartments?

2. Some analysts argue that tackling cultural toilet norms and barriers is not worth the effort and that Toto would be better off pulling its Washlets and Neorests out of the United States and Europe altogether and concentrating on more receptive Asian markets like China, and of course Japan. Do you agree? Why/Why not?

For further exercises and cases, see this book's website at
www.booksites.net/hollensen

Questions for discussion

1. Explain why the negotiation process abroad may differ from country to country.

2. You are a European preparing to negotiate with a Japanese firm for the first time. How would you prepare for the assignment if it is taking place: (a) in the Japanese headquarters; (b) in one of its European subsidiaries?

3. Should expatriate personnel be used? What are some of the difficulties they may encounter overseas? What can be done to minimise these problems?

4. Compare and contrast the negotiating styles of Europeans and Asians. What are the similarities? What are the differences?

5. What are your views on lobbying efforts by foreign firms?

6. Why is it so difficult for an international marketer to deal with bribery?

References

Andersen, P.H. (2003), 'Relationship marketing in cross-cultural contexts', in Rugimbana, R. and Nwankwo S. (eds), *Cross-cultural Marketing*, Thomson, London.

Bell, D.B., Giordano, R. and Putz, P. (2002) 'Inter-firm sharing of process knowledge: exploring knowledge markets', *Knowledge and Process Management*, vol. 9, no. 1, pp. 12–22.

Berrell, M., Gloet, M. and Wright, P. (2002) 'Organizational learning in international joint ventures: implications for management development', *Journal of Management Development*, vol. 21, no. 2, pp. 83–100.

Bush, V.D. and Ingram, T. (2001) 'Building and assessing cultural diversity skills: implications for sales training', *Industrial Marketing Management*, vol. 30, pp. 65–76.

Choo, C. (1998) *The Knowing Organization*, Oxford University Press, New York.

Desouza, K. and Evaristo, R. (2003) 'Global knowledge management strategies', *European Management Journal*, vol. 21, no. 1, pp. 62–67.

Della Cava, R. R. (1999) 'Magic Kingdoms, new colonies: theme parks are staking bigger claims in Europe', *USA Today*, 17 February.

Gesteland, R.R. (1996) *Cross-cultural Business Behaviour*, Copenhagen Business School Press, Copenhagen.

Govindarajan, V. and Gupta, A.K. (2001) 'Building an effective global business team', *MIT Sloan Management Review*, Summer, pp. 63–71.

Griffith, D.A. (2002), 'The role of communication competencies in international business relationship development', *Journal of World Business*, vol. 37, issue 4, pp. 256–65.

Guy, B.S. and Patton, P.W.E. (1996) 'Managing the effects of culture shock and sojourner adjustment on the expatriate industrial sales force', *Industrial Marketing Management*, vol. 25, pp. 385–93.

Harvey, M.G. and Griffith, D.A. (2002), 'Developing effective intercultural relationships: the importance of communication strategies', *Thunderbird International Business Review*, vol. 44, no. 4, pp. 455–76.

Hendon, D.W., Hendon, R.A. and Herbig, P. (1999). *Cross-cultural Negotiations*, Praeger Publishers, Westport, CT.

Hofstede, G. (1983) 'The cultural relativity of organizational practices and theories', *Journal of International Business Studies*, Fall, pp. 75–89.

Johnson, M. (1996) 'China: the last true business frontier', *Management Review*, March, pp. 39–43.

Liu, B. (2001) 'Coca-Cola helps quench thirst during boycott of US goods', *Financial Times*, 26 October.

Madsen, T.K. (1994) 'A contingency approach to export performance research', *Advances in International Marketing*, vol. 6, pp. 25–42.

Nonaka, I. and Takeuchi, H. (1995) *The Knowledge Creating Company*, Oxford University Press, New York.

Rowden, R.W. (2001), 'Research note: how a small business enters the international market', *Thunderbird International Business Review*, vol. 43, no. 2, pp. 257–68.

Schein, E.H. (1985) *Organizational culture and leadership*. 1st edn. San Francisco, Jossey-Bass Publishers.

Scott, J., Gilliard, D. and Scott, R. (2002) 'Eliminating bribery as a transnational marketing strategy', *International Journal of Commerce & Management*, vol. 12, no. 1, pp. 1–17.

Stewart, D. (2001) 'Reinterpreting the learning organization', *The Learning Organization*, vol. 8, no. 4, pp. 141–52.

Tagliabue, J. (2000) 'Lights, action in France for Second Disney Park', *New York Times*, 13 February.

Tomkins, R. (2003) 'As hostility towards America grows, will the world lose its appetite for Coca-Cola, McDonald's and Nike?' *Financial Times*, 27 March.

Wolf, J. (2002) 'Multicultural workgroups', *Management International Review*, vol. 42, no. 1, pp. 3–4.

Further reading

Baruch, Y. (2002) 'No such thing as a global manager', *Business Horizons*, January–February, pp. 36–42.

Bonache, J. and Brewster, C. (2002) 'Knowledge transfer and the management of expatriation, *Thunderbird International Business Review*, vol. 43, no. 1, pp. 145–68.

Chang, L.-C. (2003) 'An Examination of Cross-Cultural Negotiation: Using Hofstede Framework', *Journal of American Academy of Business*, vol. 2, No. 2 (March), pp. 567–70.

Glaz, L., Williams, R. and Hoeksema, L. (2001) 'Sensemaking in expatriation: a theoretical basis', *Thunderbird International Business Review*, vol. 43, no. 1, pp. 101–119.

Heijltjes, M., Olie, R. and Glunk, U. (2003) 'internationalization of top management teams in Europe', *European Management Journal*, vol. 21, no. 1, pp. 89–97.

Katikea, E. and Morgan, R.E. (2003) 'Exploring export sales management practices in small- and medium-sized firms' (forthcoming) *Industrial Marketing Management*.

Mintu-Wimsatt, A. (2002) 'Personality and negotiation style: the moderating effects of cultural context', *Thunderbird International Business Review*, vol. 44, no. 6, pp. 729–48.

Ogbor, J.O. and Williams, J. (2003) 'The cross-Cultural Transfer of Management Practices: The Case for Creative Synthesis', *Cross Cultural Management*, vol. 10, No. 2, pp. 3–23.

Sharland, A. (2001) 'The negotiation process as a predictor of relationship outcomes in international buyer–supplier arrangements', *Industrial Marketing Management*, vol. 30, pp. 551–9.

Sparrow, J. (2001) 'Knowledge management in small firms', *Knowledge and Process Management*, vol. 8, no. 1, pp. 3–16.

Sales negotiations in China

Fan, Y. (2002) 'Questioning guanxi: definition, classification and implications', *International Business Review*, Vol. 11, No. 5, October, pp. 543–61.

Lee, D.-J. (2001) 'A model of close business relationships in China (guanxi)', *European Journal of Marketing*, Vol. 35, No. 1/2, pp. 51–69.

Reid, D.M. and Walsh, J. (2003) 'Market Entry Decisions in China', *Thunderbird International Business Review*, vol. 45, No. 3, pp. 289–312.

Standfired, S.S. and Marshall, R.S. (2000) 'The transaction cost advantage of guanxi-based business practices', *Journal of World Business*, Vol. 35, No. 1, Spring, pp. 21–42.

20 Organization and control of the global marketing programme

Contents

Learning objectives

After studying this chapter you should be able to do the following:

- Examine how firms build their organizational structure internationally and what roles headquarters can play.

- Identify the variables that affect the reorganization design.

- Describe and evaluate functional, geographic, product and matrix organizations as the key international structural alternatives.

- Explain pitfalls and opportunities with 'Global Account Management'.

- Describe the key elements of the marketing control system.

- List the most important measures for marketing performance.

- Explain how a global marketing budget is established.

20.1 Introduction

The overall objective of this chapter is to study intra-organizational relationships as part of the firm's attempt to optimise its competitive response in areas most critical to its business. As market conditions change, and companies evolve from purely domestic entities to multinationals, their organizational structure, coordination and control systems must also change.

First, this chapter will focus on the advantages and disadvantages of the main organizational structures available as well as their appropriateness at various stages of internationalisation. Then the chapter will outline the need for a control system to oversee the international operations of the company.

20.2 Organization of global marketing activities

The way in which a global marketing organization is structured is an important determinant of its ability to exploit effectively and efficiently the opportunities available to it. It also determines the capacity for responding to problems and challenges. Companies operating internationally must decide whether the organization should be structured along functions, products, geographical areas or combinations of the three (matrix). The evolutionary nature of organizational changes is shown in Figure 20.1. The following pages discuss the different organizational structures.

Figure 20.1 Structural evolution of international operations

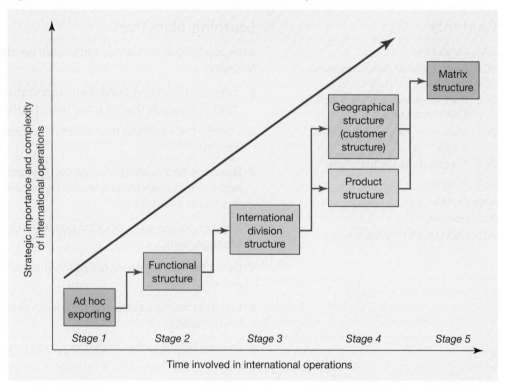

Functional structure

Of all the approaches, the functional structure (Figure 20.2) is the simplest. Here management is primarily concerned with the functional efficiency of the company.

Many companies begin their international business activities as a result of having received enquiries from abroad. The company, being new to international business, has no international specialist and typically has few products and few markets. In this early stage of international involvement the domestic marketing department may have the responsibility for global marketing activities. But as the international involvement intensifies an export or international department may become part of the organizational structure. The export department may be a subdepartment of the sales and marketing department (as in Figure 20.2) or may have equal ranking with the other functional departments. This choice will depend on the importance assigned to the export activities of the firm. Because the export department is the first real step in

Figure 20.2 **Example of the functional structure**

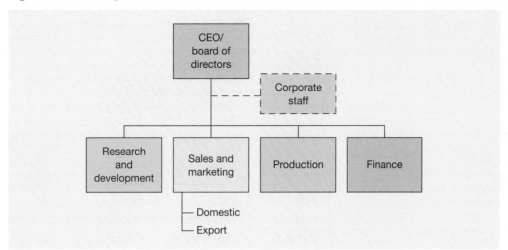

internationalizing the organizational structure it should be a fully fledged marketing organization and not merely a sales organization. The functional export department design is particularly suitable for small and medium-sized firms, as well as larger companies, that are manufacturing standardised products and are in the early stages of developing international business, having low product and area diversities.

International divisional structure

As international sales grow, at some point an international division may emerge. This division becomes directly responsible for the development and implementation of the overall international strategy. The international division incorporates international expertise, information flows about foreign market opportunities, and authority over international activities. However, manufacturing and other related functions remain with the domestic divisions in order to take advantage of economies of scale.

International divisions best serve firms with new products that do not vary significantly in terms of their environmental sensitivity, and whose international sales and profits are still quite insignificant compared with those of the domestic divisions.

Product structure

A typical product division structure is presented in Figure 20.3.

In general, the product structure is more suitable for companies with more experience in international business and marketing, and with diversified product lines and extensive R&D activities. The product division structure is most appropriate under conditions where the products have potential for worldwide standardisation. One of the major benefits of the approach is improved cost efficiency through centralisation of manufacturing facilities for each product line. This is crucial in industries in which competitive position is determined by world market share, that in turn is often determined by the degree to which manufacturing is rationalised (utilisation of economies of scale). The main disadvantages of this type of structure are as follows:

- It duplicates functional resources: you will find R&D, production, marketing, sales force management, etc., in each product division.

Figure 20.3 **Example of the product structure**

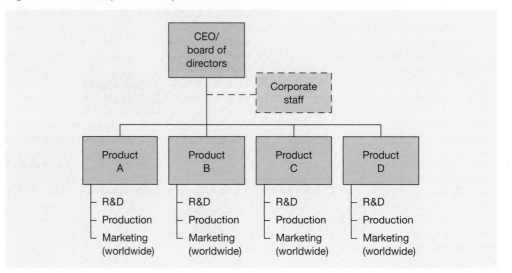

- It underutilises sales and distribution facilities (subsidiaries) abroad.
- The product divisions tend to develop a total independence of each other in world markets. For example, a global product division structure may end up with several subsidiaries in the same foreign country reporting to different product divisions, with no one at headquarters responsible for the overall corporate presence in that country.

Geographical structure

If market conditions with respect to product acceptance and operating conditions vary considerably across world markets, then the geographical structure is the one to choose. This structure is especially useful for companies that have a homogeneous range of products (similar technologies and common end-use markets), but at the same time need fast and efficient worldwide distribution. Typically, the world is divided into regions (divisions), as shown in Figure 20.4.

Many food, beverage, car and pharmaceutical companies use this type of structure. Its main advantage is its ability to respond easily and quickly to the environmental and market demands of a regional or national area through minor modifications in product design, pricing, market communication and packaging. Therefore the structure encourages adaptive global marketing programmes. Moreover, economies of scale can be achieved within regions. Another reason for the popularity of this structure is its tendency to create area autonomy. However, this may also complicate the tasks of coordinating product variations and transferring new product ideas and marketing techniques from one country to another.

Hence the geographical structure ensures the best use of the firm's regional expertise, but it means a less than optimal allocation of product and functional expertise. If each region needs its own staff of product and functional specialists, duplication and also inefficiency may be the result. As indicated in Figure 20.4, the geographical structure may include both regional management centres (Europe, North America, etc.) and country-based subsidiaries.

Figure 20.4 **Example of the geographical structure**

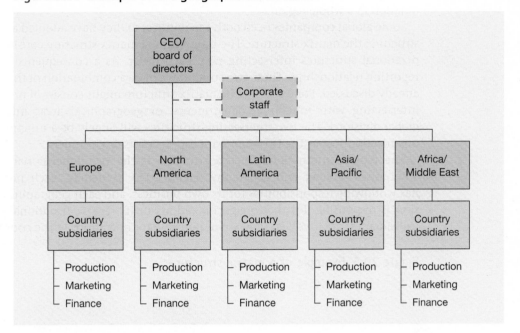

Regional management centres

There are two main reasons for the existence of regional management centres (RMCs):

1. When sales volume in a particular region becomes substantial there need to be some specialised staff to focus on that region, to realise more fully the potential of an already growing market.
2. Homogeneity within regions and heterogeneity between them necessitate treating each important region separately. Therefore a regional management centre becomes an appropriate organizational feature.

Country-based subsidiaries

Instead of or parallel to a regional centre, each country has its own organizational unit. Country-based subsidiaries are characterised by a high degree of adaptation to local conditions. Since each subsidiary develops its own unique activities and its own autonomy, it is sometimes relevant to combine local subsidiaries with an RMC: for example, to utilise opportunities across European countries.

Firms may also organise their operations using a customer structure, especially if the customer groups they serve are very different: for example, businesses and governments. Catering to these diverse groups may require the concentration of specialists in particular divisions. The product may be the same, but the buying processes of the various customer groups may differ. Governmental buying is characterised by bidding, in which price plays a larger role than when businesses are the buyers. Much of what has been said about the geographical structure also applies to the customer structure.

Matrix structure

The product structure tends to offer better opportunities to rationalise production across countries, thus gaining production cost efficiencies. On the other hand, the geographical structure is more responsive to local market trends and needs, and allows for more coordination in a whole region.

Some global companies need both capabilities, so they have adopted a more complex structure: the matrix structure. The international matrix structure consists of two organizational structures intersecting with each other. As a consequence there are dual reporting relationships. These two structures can be a combination of the general forms already discussed. For example, the matrix structure might consist of product divisions intersecting with functional departments, or geographical areas intersecting with global divisions. The two intersecting structures will largely be a function of what the organization sees as the two dominant aspects of its environment.

The typical international matrix structure is the two-dimensional structure that emphasises product and geography (Figure 20.5). Generally, each product division has worldwide responsibilities for its own business, and each geographical or area division is responsible for the foreign operations in its region. If national organizations (subsidiaries) are involved they are responsible for operations at the country level.

Figure 20.5 Example of a matrix structure

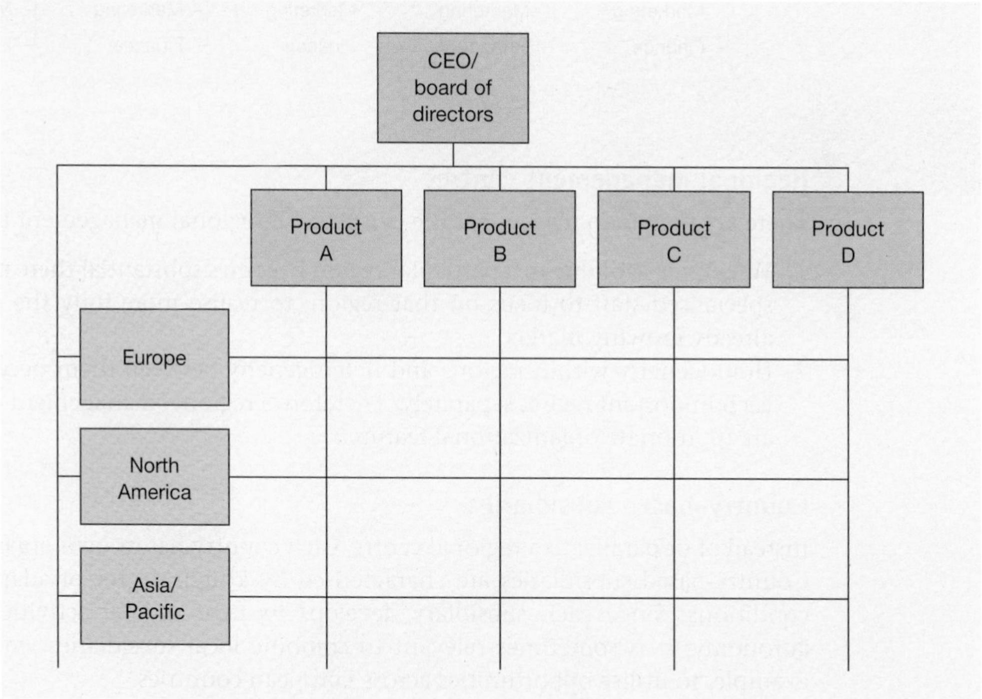

Because the two dimensions of product and geography overlap at the affiliate level, both enter into local decision-making and planning processes. It is assumed that area and product managers will defend different positions. This will lead to tensions and 'creative' conflict. Area managers will tend to favour responsiveness to local environmental factors, and product managers will defend positions favouring cost efficiencies and global competitiveness. The matrix structure deliberately creates a dual focus to ensure that conflicts between product and geographical area concerns are identified and then analysed objectively.

The structure is useful for companies that are both product diversified and geographically spread. By combining a product management approach with a market-oriented approach one can meet the needs both of markets and of products.

The future role of the international manager

At the end of the 1980s many internationally oriented companies adopted the transnational model (Bartlett and Ghoshal, 1989). It held that companies should leverage their capabilities across borders and transfer best practices to achieve global economies and respond to the local market. In this way companies avoided duplicating their functions (product development, manufacturing and marketing). However, it required that senior managers could think, operate and communicate along three dimensions: function, product and geography. Surely there are few such 'super-managers' around!

In a study by Quelch (1992) one manager says of changing managerial roles: 'I am at the fulcrum of the tension between local adaptation and global standardization. My boss tells me to think global and act local. That's easier said than done' (p. 158).

There is no universal solution to the ideal profile for an international manager, but Quelch and Bloom (1996) have predicted the 'fall of the transnational manager and the return of the country manager'. They studied behaviour of country managers in different countries and concluded that the opportunities in expanding emerging markets (e.g. eastern Europe) have to be grasped by entrepreneurial country managers. The transnational manager is better suited to stable and saturated markets, such as western Europe, with its progress towards a single market.

20.3   The Global Account Management (GAM) organization

GAM can be understood as a relationship-oriented marketing management approach focusing on dealing with the needs of an important global customer (= account) in the business-to-business market.

GAM can be defined as an organizational form (a person or a team) in a global supplier organization used to coordinate and manage worldwide activities, by servicing an important customer centrally from headquarters (Harvey *et al.*, 2002).

A global account is a customer that is of strategic importance to the achievement of the supplier's corporate objectives, pursues integrated and coordinated strategies on a worldwide basis and demands a globally integrated product/service offering (Wilson and Millman, 2003).

A global account manager is the person in the selling company who represents that company's capabilities to the buying company, the buying company's needs to the selling company, and brings the two together.

Successful GAM often requires an understanding of the logic of both product and service management. Moreover, excellent operational level capabilities are useless if strategic level management is inferior, and vice versa – the GAM approach combines strategic and operational level marketing management.

The starting point for the following is the firm that wishes to implement GAM. Afterwards the development of GAM is regarded in a dyadic perspective.

Implementation of GAM

The firm that wants to implement successful GAM with suitable global accounts may go through the following four steps (Ojasalo, 2001):

1. identifying the selling firm's global accounts;
2. analysing the global accounts;

3. selecting suitable strategies for the global accounts;
4. developing operational level capabilities to build, grow and maintain profitable and long-lasting relationships with global accounts.

1. Identifying the selling firm's global accounts

This means answering the following question: Which existing or potential accounts are of strategic importance to us now and in the future?

The following criteria can be used to determine strategically important customers:

- sales volume;
- age of the relationship;
- the selling firm's share of customers' purchase: the new Relationship Marketing (RM) paradigm measures success in terms of long-term gains in its share of its customers' business, unlike mass marketing that counts wins or losses in terms of market share increases that may well be temporary (Peppers and Rogers, 1995);
- profitability of the customer to seller;
- use of strategic resources: extent of executive/management commitment.

There is a positive relation (correlation) between the criteria and the likelihood of customers' being identified as global accounts (strategic customers).

2. Analysing global accounts

This includes activities such as analysing the following:

- *The basic characteristics of a global account*: Includes assessing the relevant economic and activity aspects of their internal and external environment. This, for example, includes the account's internal value chain inputs, markets, suppliers, products and economic situation.
- *The relationship history*: Involves assessing the relevant economic and activity aspects of the relationship history. This includes volume of sales, profitability, global account's objectives, buying behaviour (the account's decision-making process), information exchange, special needs, buying frequency and complaints. Among the above-mentioned aspects, knowing/estimating relationship value plays a particularly important role. The revenues from each global account (customer lifetime value) should exceed the costs of establishing and maintaining the relationship within a certain time span.
- *The level and development of commitment to the relationship*: The account's present and anticipated commitment to the relationship is important, since the extent of the business with the account depends on that.
- *Goal congruence of the parties*: Goal congruence, or commonality of interests between buyer and seller, greatly affects their cooperation both at the strategic and operational levels. Common interests and relationship value together determine whether two companies can be partners, friends or rivals that aims it sights lower than the sort of partnership relationship an account is looking for risks losing long-term share of that account's business.
- *Switching costs*: It is useful to estimate both the global account's and the selling company's switching costs in the event that the relationship dissolves. Switching costs are the costs of replacing an existing partner with another. These may be very different for the two parties and thus affect the power position in the relationship. Switching costs are also called transaction costs and are affected by irretrievable investments in the relationship, the adaptations made and the bonds that have developed. High switching costs may prevent a relationship from ending even

though the global account's accumulated satisfaction with the selling company may be non-existent or negative.

3. Selecting suitable strategies for the global accounts

This depends greatly on the power positions of the seller and the global account. The power structure within different accounts may vary significantly. Thus the selling company may typically not freely select the strategy – there is often only one strategic alternative to be chosen if there is a desire to retain the account.

Maybe the selling firm might prefer to avoid very powerful accounts. Sometimes the selling firm realises that accounts, which are less attractive today, may become attractive in future. Thus, in the case of certain accounts, the objective of the strategy may be merely to keep the relationship alive for future opportunities.

4. Developing operational level capabilities

This refers to customisation and development of capabilities related to the following:

Product/service development and performance

Joint R&D projects are typical between a selling company and a global account in industrial and high-tech markets. In addition, information technology (IT) applied in just-in-time production and distribution channels increases the possibilities of customising the offering in consumer markets as well.

New products developed in a partnership are not automatically more successful than those developed in-house. However, R&D projects may bring other kinds of long-term benefits, such as access to account organization and learning. Improving capabilities for providing services to global accounts is extremely important, because even when the core product is a tangible good it is often the related services that differentiate the selling company from its competitors and provide competitive advantage.

Organizational structure

The selling company's *organizational ability* to meet the global account's needs can be developed, for example, by adjusting the organizational structure to correspond to the global account's global and local needs and by increasing the number of interfaces between the selling company and the account, and thus also the number of interacting persons. Organizational capabilities can also be developed by organizing teams, consisting of people with the necessary competences and authorities, to take care of global accounts.

Individuals (human resources)

A company's capabilities related to individuals can be developed by selecting the right people as global account managers and for global account teams, and by developing their skills. The global account manager's responsibilities are often complex and varied, and therefore require a large number of skills and qualifications, which should be taken into account in the selection and development of global account managers.

It is quite common to find that the current set of global account managers may be good at maintaining their own relationships with their contacts in the account but lack the total set of skills required to lead an account team through a transition in the account relationship. Therefore an assessment of the total desired interfaces between the seller and the customer needs to be considered. It may be that a change is required by moving the relationship from a dependency on a 1 : 1 relationship (between the global account manager and the chief buyer) to a network of organizational relationships spanning many different projects, functions and countries.

Information exchange

Information exchange between the selling company and a global account is particularly important in GAM. An important relationship-specific task is to search, filter, judge and store information about the organizations, strategies, goals, potentials and problems of the partners. However, this mainly depends on the mutual trust and attitudes of the parties, and on the technical arrangements. A global account's trust is something that the selling company has to earn over time by its performance, whereas the technical side can be developed, for example with IT.

Company and individual level benefits

Successful long-term GAM in a business-to-business context always requires the ability to offer both company and individual level benefits to global accounts.

Company level benefits are rational and may be either short or long term, direct or indirect, and typically contribute to the global account's turnover, profitability, cost savings, organizational efficiency and effectiveness, and image. Individual level benefits in turn may be rational or emotional. From the relationship management point of view the global individual(s) is/are the one(s) with the power to continue or terminate the relationship. Rational individual level benefits contribute, for example, to the individual's own career, income and ease of job. Emotional individual level benefits include friendship, a sense of caring and ego enhancement.

The dyadic development of GAM

The Millman-Wilson model in Figure 20.6 describes and demonstrates the typical dyadic progression of a relationship between buyer and seller through five stages – Pre-GAM, Early-GAM, Mid-GAM, Partnership-GAM and Synergistic-GAM (Millman and Wilson, 2003).

Pre-GAM describes preparation for GAM. A buying company is identified as having key account potential, and the selling company starts to focus resources on winning some business with that prospect. Both seller and buyer are sending out signals (factual information) and exchanging messages (interactions) prior to the decision to engage in transactions. There is a need to develop networks of contacts, to gain knowledge about the customer's operations and to begin to assess the potential for relational development.

Early-GAM: at this stage the selling company is concerned with identifying the opportunities for account penetration once the account has been won. This is probably the most typical sales relationship, the classic 'bow-tie'.

Adapted solutions are needed, and the key account manager will be focused on understanding more about their customer and the market in which that customer is competing. The buying company will still be market testing other selling companies. Detailed knowledge of the global customer and their core competences, the depth of the relationship and the potential for creating relation-specific entrepreneurial value are all limited at this stage. There is an increasing need for political skills to be applied as the potential of the account is identified and the global account manager is called upon to ensure that the resources of the supplier configure to best serve the needs of the customer (Wilson and Millman, 2003). The selling company must concentrate hard on product, service and intangibles – the buying company wants recognition that the product offering is the prime reason for the relationship – and expects it to work.

Mid-GAM stage: this is a transition stage between the classic 'bow-tie' and the 'diamond' of the partnership GAM stage (see Figure 20.7).

Figure 20.6 Relational development model

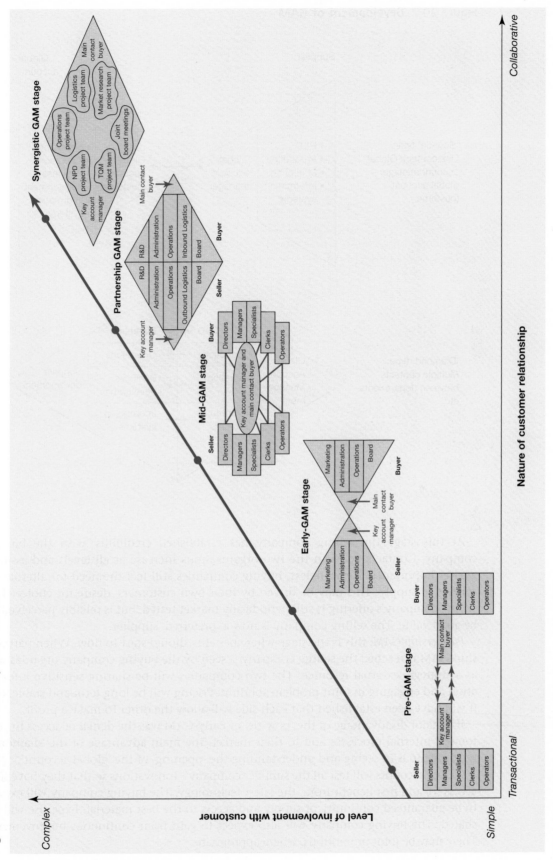

Source: adapted from Millman and Wilson (1995); Millman and Wilson (2003).

Figure 20.7 Development of GAM

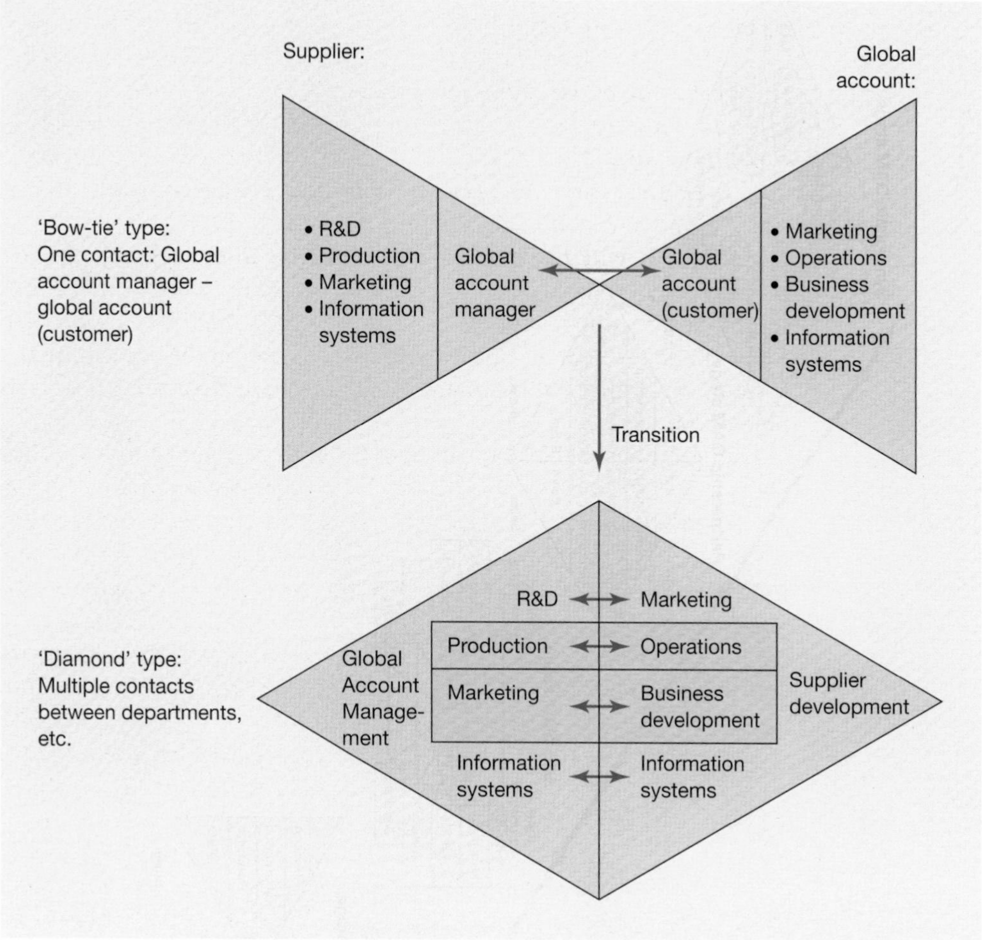

At this stage the selling company has established credibility with the buying company. Contacts between the two organizations increase at all levels and assume greater importance. Nevertheless, buying companies still feel the need for alternative sources of supply. This may be driven by their own customers' desire for choice. The selling company's offering is still periodically market tested, but is reliably perceived to be good value. The selling company is now a 'preferred' supplier.

Partnership-GAM: this is the stage where benefits should start to flow. When partnership-GAM is reached the selling company is seen by the buying company organization as a strategic external resource. The two companies will be sharing sensitive information and engaging in joint problem solution. Pricing will be long term and stable, but it will have been established that each side will allow the other to make a profit.

If a major disadvantage of the 'bow-tie' of Early-GAM was the denial of access to customers' internal processes and to their market, the main advantage of the 'diamond' relationship is in seeing and understanding the 'opening' of the 'global account'.

Global accounts will test all the supplier company's innovations so that they have first access to, and first benefit from, the latest technology. The buying company will expect to be guaranteed continuity of supply and access to the best material. Expertise will be shared. The buying company will also expect to gain from continuous improvement. There may be joint promotions, where appropriate.

Synergistic-GAM: this is the ultimate stage in the relational development model. The experience gained at the partnership stage – coordinating the team-sell, coaching the team on their interface roles – will be a good starting point for moving to synergistic GAM. The closer the relationship, the greater the knowledge about the customer and the greater the potential for creating entrepreneurial value.

The selling company understands that they still have no automatic right to the customer's business. Nevertheless, exit barriers have been built up. The buying company is confident that their relationship with the selling company is delivering improved quality and reduced cost. Costing systems become transparent. Joint research and development will take place. There will be interfaces at every level and function between the organizations. Top management commitment will be fulfilled through joint board meetings and reviews. There will be a joint business plan, joint strategies, joint market research. Information flow should be streamlined and information systems integration will be planned or in place as a consequence. Transaction costs will be reduced.

Though there are clear advantages for both partners in moving through the different GAM-stages there are also pitfalls. As the contacts proliferate through the stages, so does the speed of activity – and the risk of saying and doing the wrong things. Through the stages the key account manager changes from 'super salesperson' to 'super coach'. In the last two stages the key account manager moves on to a 'super coordinator', who conducts the orchestra.

If the key account manager does not move along then the potential of losing control is great, resulting in well-meaning but misdirected individuals following their own quite separate courses.

Key account management requires process excellence and highly skilled professionals to manage relationships with strategic customers. For most companies this represents a number of revolutions. A revolution is needed in the way activity is costed and costs are attributed, from product or geographical focus to customer focus. Currently few financial or information systems in companies are sophisticated enough to support the higher levels of key account management. A transformation is needed in the way the professional with responsibility for a customer relationship is developed, from an emphasis on selling skills to management skills, including cross-cultural management skills (McDonald *et al.*, 1997).

We end this section by assessing the advantages and disadvantages by going into GAM, seen from the supplier's (seller's) point of view:

Supplier's (seller's) advantages with GAM
- Provides a better fulfilment of the customer's global need for having only one supplier of certain products and services.
- Creating barriers for competitors – given the high switching costs global competitors (to the supplier) will have difficulty in displacing the existing supplier. If the supplier becomes the preferred supplier, the customer becomes dependent on the supplier shifting power in the relationship.
- Increased sales of existing products and services through a closer relationship with the key customer.
- Facilitating the introduction of new products/services – the Global Account (GA) is perceived to be more willing to take on new product trials and carry a more complete product line.
- Coordination of marketing/selling activities across borders may increase the total worldwide sales value to this customer – the GAM strategy enables the

supplier to coordinate global marketing programmes (i.e. standardisation) while at the same time permit local adaptation to individual country environment.

■ Perceived high potential for profit increase – due to the increased sales and global coordination – development of a strategic 'fit' between the supplier and the customer, increases the effectiveness of the supplying organization.

■ By using the learning effects the supplier has the ability to reduce the marginal cost of creating adapted programmes for every new country/region. In this way 'economies of scale' as well as 'economies of scope' can be utilised through the GAM strategy.

■ Through the global network of the customer the supplier might get access to new customers around the world.

Supplier's (seller's) disadvantages with GAM

■ The supplier will feel pressure from the global customers to improve global consistency – they may force the supplier to institute GAM to maintain their global 'preferred' supplier status.

■ Pressure to 'standardise' pricing on a global basis – the global customer may attempt to use GAM as a means to lower prices globally through telling that there should be equity/commonality of pricing throughout the global network of the customer's subsidiaries.

■ Pressure to 'standardise' all terms of trade on a global basis, and not just price. So GA increasingly demand uniformity in such issues as volume discounts, transportation charges, overheads, special charges and so forth.

■ The supplier's loss of GA due to major competitors utilising the GAM strategy – by this the supplier may feel compelled to form a GAM team to match or counteract the strategy of key customers.

■ Most often a GAM strategy is connected to the use of some kind of matrix organization. Consequently there may be multiple decision makers in the supplier organization making the same decision from different perspectives (e.g. global vs local perspective). The cost of managing may increase due to the parallel structures at global and local levels. Moreover, the parallel structures might slow down the decision-making process.

In summary, the importance of GAM strategies will grow in the future (Harvey *et al.*, 2002). The development of relational contracting with a large, global customer – the cooperation between a customer and a supplier into a long-term global relationship – has a number of positive outcomes. However, a great deal of learning is necessary upon deciding to implement a GAM strategy, because high stakes and high exit barriers accompany the implementation.

Exhibit 20.1   Sauer–Danfoss's GAM

Sauer-Danfoss is one of the world's leading companies for the development, production and sale of hydraulic power transmission systems – primarily for use in mobile work vehicles (see also Case 6.2).

One of Sauer-Danfoss's main global accounts (OEM customers), Case New Holland (CNH) is the number one manufacturer of agricultural tractors and combines in the world and the third largest maker of construction equipment. Revenues in 2002 totaled $10 billion. Based in the United States, CNH's network of dealers and distributors operates in over 160 countries. CNH agricultural products are sold under the Case IH, New Holland and Steyr brands. CNH construction equipment is sold under the Case, FiatAllis, Fiat Kobelco, Kobelco, New Holland and O&K brands.

As a result of a merger in 1999 CNH is an example of consolidation on the OEM customer side. The consequence of this consolidation is that fewer than the 10 largest OEM customers will represent more than half of Sauer-Danfoss's potential sales over the medium to long term. There is no doubt that the price-down pressure will continue worldwide. The global business culture trend is leading towards a more professional buying process on the customer side. This development requires a new way of structuring the Sauer-Danfoss organization, and the answer is GAM. As illustrated in the figure below. Sauer-Danfoss has met the requirements of CNH's worldwide production units by forming local production locations and GAM team groups in India, China, Poland, North America, Italy, Brasil, Germany and the United Kingdom. In partnership with CNH the GAM teams try to find more cost-effective solutions, rather than simply reduce prices. Sauer-Danfoss is following CNH into low cost manufacturing countries, such as India and China. At all of CNH's worldwide production units there is pressure for a higher degree of outsourcing and a request for value added packages. Sauer-Danfoss tries to fulfil this requirement by supplying pre-assembled kit packages and delivering more system solutions to CNH.

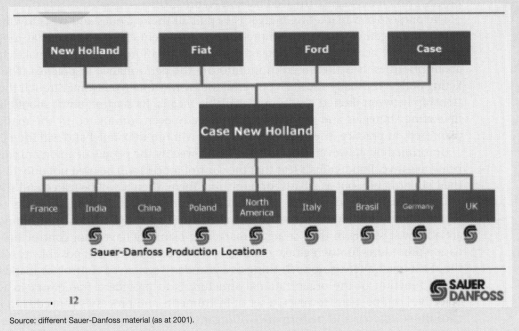

Source: different Sauer-Danfoss material (as at 2001).

20.4   Controlling the global marketing programme

The final, but often neglected stage of international market planning, is the control process. Not only is control important to evaluate how we have performed, but it completes the circle of planning by providing the feedback necessary for the start of the next planning cycle.

Figure 20.8 illustrates the connection between the marketing plan, the marketing budget and the control system.

After building the global marketing plan, its quantification appears in the form of budgets. The budget is the basis for the design of the marketing control system that may give the necessary feedback for a possible reformulation of the global marketing plan. The marketing budgets should represent a projection of actions and expected

Figure 20.8 The firm's budget and control system

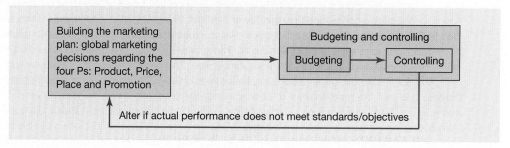

results, and they should be capable of accurate monitoring and controlling. Indeed, measuring performance against budget is the main (regular) management review process, which may cause the feed back in Figure 20.8.

The purpose of a marketing budget is to pull all the revenues and costs involved in marketing together into one comprehensive document. It is a managerial tool that balances what needs to be spent against what can be afforded and helps make choices about priorities. It is then used in monitoring the performance in practice. The marketing budget is usually the most powerful tool with which you think through the relationship between desired results and available means. Its starting point should be the marketing strategies and plans that have already been formulated in the marketing plan itself. In practice, the strategies and plans will run in parallel and will interact.

Unfortunately, however, 'control' is often viewed by the people of an organization as being negative. If individuals fear that the control process will be used not only to judge their performance, but as a basis for punishing them, then it will be feared and reviled.

The evaluation and control of global marketing probably represents one of the weakest areas of marketing practice in many companies. Even the organizations that are otherwise strong in their strategic marketing planning have poor control and evaluation procedures for their global marketing. There are a number of possible reasons for this. First of all, there is no such thing as a 'standard' system of control for marketing.

The function of the organizational structure is to provide a framework in which objectives can be met. However, a set of instruments and processes is needed to influence the behaviour and performance of organization members to meet the goals. The critical issue is the same as with organizational structures: what is the ideal amount of control? On the one hand, headquarters needs information to ensure that international activities contribute maximum benefit to the overall organization. On the other hand, controls should not be construed as a code of law.

The global question is to determine how to establish a control mechanism capable of early interception of emerging problems. Considered here are various criteria appropriate for the evaluation process, control styles, feedback and corrective action. These concepts are important for all businesses, but in the international arena they are vital.

Design of a control system

In designing a control system management must consider the costs of establishing and maintaining it and trade them off against the benefits to be gained. Any control system will require investment in a management structure and in systems designs.

The design of the control system can be divided into two groups dependent on the object of control:

1. output control (typically based on financial measures);
2. behavioural controls (typically based on non-financial measures).

Output control may consist of expenditure control, which involves regular monitoring of expenditure figures, comparison of these with budget targets, and taking decisions to cut or increase expenditure where any variance is believed to be harmful. Measures of output are accumulated at regular intervals and typically forwarded from the foreign subsidiary to headquarters, where they are evaluated and criticised based on comparison to the plan or budget.

Behavioural controls require the exercise of influence over behaviour. This influence can be achieved, for example, by providing sales manuals to subsidiary personnel or by fitting new employees into the corporate culture. Behavioural controls often require an extensive socialisation process, and informal, personal interaction is central to the process. Substantial resources must be spent to train the individual to share the corporate culture: that is, 'the way things are done at the company'.

To build common vision and values managers at the Japanese company Matsushita spend a substantial amount of their first months in what the company calls 'cultural and spiritual training'. They study the company credo, the 'Seven Spirits of Matsushita', and the philosophy of the founder, Kanosuke Matsushita.

However, there remains a strong tradition of using output (financial) criteria. A fixation with output criteria leads companies to ignore the less tangible behavioural (non-financial) measures, although these are the real drivers of corporate success. However, there is a weakness in the behavioural performance measures. To date there has been little success in developing explicit links from behaviour to output criteria. Furthermore, companies and managers are still judged on financial criteria (profit contribution). Until a clear link is established it is likely that behavioural criteria will continue to be treated with a degree of scepticism.

We will now develop a global marketing control system based primarily on output controls. Marketing control is an essential element of the marketing planning process because it provides a review of how well marketing objectives have been achieved. A framework for controlling marketing activities is given in Figure 20.9.

Figure 20.9 The marketing control system

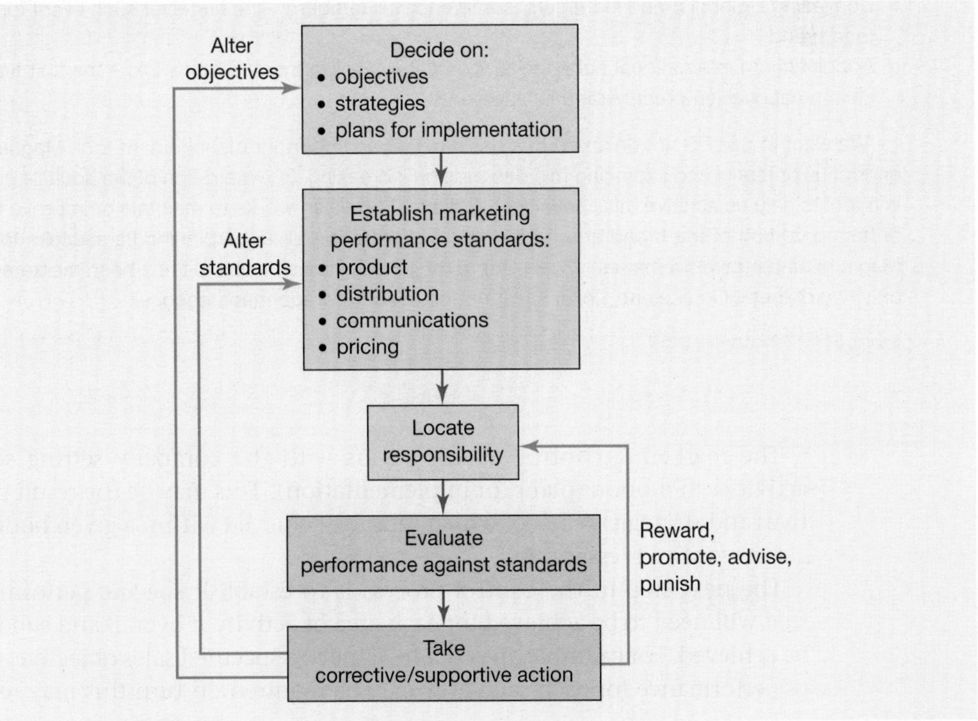

Exhibit 20.2	Unilever and its global marketing of Magnum

Unilever describes itself as a 'multi-local of multinational' company, not a 'global' company. It tries to think globally and act locally, because it does not attempt to enter all markets with the same product. Half of Unilever's business is in food, where it is essential to take a local view. Only a few products, like ice-cream, can be marketed successfuly across borders. Similarly, the formulation of detergents varies from region to region because washing habits, machines, clothes and water quality are all different. Thus, the Unilever portfolio includes a balanced mix of local, regional and international brands, which take account of the differences as well as the similarities in consumer needs.

At Unilever the major product groups are responsible for profits. As the profits are generated in cooperation with the different regions and the national subsidiaries, the international organizational structure can be described as a form of matrix structure. The following describes the organization of the global marketing strategy for one of Unilever's global products: Magnum.

The rise of a global brand: the role of the international product manager

Magnum was an immediate success when it was launched in Germany, the Netherlands, Belgium, Denmark, Sweden and Switzerland in 1989. The 'Me and my Magnum' campaign was created in 1991–2.

In 1993 the position of international brand manager for Magnum was created. 'As ice-cream is basically an emotion-led category, it is clear that the basic approach and motivation are similar across many borders,' says Chris Pomfre, senior marketing member of the Ice Cream Group. 'Taking an international approach thus offered a means of implementing best practice and enjoying economies of scale. So we agreed to appoint four international brand managers for the four core ice-cream brands, Cornetto, Carte d'Or, Viennetta and, of course, Magnum. In each case the specific role was to aid the development of what was now a global brand.'

Under the auspices of the Ice Cream Group, Jean Callanan (international product manager of Magnum) is responsible for driving the strategic development of Magnum and managing the whole of its advertising and product development. She is very much the Magnum expert. Though she is actually based at Langnese-Iglo, her clear responsibility is Magnum globally, not Magnum in Germany. Since taking up her position, her priority has been to reinforce the brand's global position. She has taken the following steps:

- Establishing a global newsletter to ensure fast spread of best practice around the world and to encourage local creativity.
- Convening a global brand managers' conference in Hamburg – the first ever such event for a Unilever food brand.
- Appointing an international public relations agency for Magnum (Shandwick) – the first time ever for an international ice-cream brand in Unilever.

'We want to use PR not on an ad hoc basis but as an important management tool. Magnum has got enormous potential and exploiting this depends on increasing its penetration of the adult population. PR is a tool to help us achieve this,' says Jean Callanan. She also works to maintain or improve the degree of harmonization of the brand around the world, a major factor underpinning its success to date. The Magnum name travels remarkably well. Out of the 38 countrries in which it has been marketed so far, in only two of them, Greece and Chile, can it not be used (for trade mark reasons).

Source: Shelly (1995); Unilever (1996).

The marketing control system begins with the company setting some marketing activities in motion (plans for implementation). This may be the result of certain objectives and strategies, each of which must be achieved within a given budget. Hence budgetary control is essential.

The next step in the control process is to establish specific performance standards that will need to be achieved for each area of activity if overall and subobjectives are to be achieved. For example, in order to achieve a specified sales objective, a specific target of performance for each sales area may be required. In turn this may require a specific standard of performance from each of the salespeople in the region with respect to, for example, number of calls, conversion rates and, of course, order value. Table 20.1 provides a representative sample of the types of data required. Marketing performance measures and standards will vary by company and product according to the goals and objectives delineated in the marketing plan.

Table 20.1 Measures of marketing performance

Product	Distribution
• Sales by market segments	• Sales, expenses and contribution margin by channel type
• New product introductions each year	
• Sales relative to potential	• Percentage of stores carrying the product
• Sales growth rates	• Sales relative to market potential by channel, intermediary type and specific intermediaries
• Market share	
• Contribution margin	• Percentage of on-time delivery
• Product defects	• Expense-to-sales ratio by channel, etc.
• Warranty expense	• Order cycle performance by channel, etc.
• Percentage of total profits	• Logistics cost by logistics activity by channel
• Return on investment	
Pricing	**Communication**
• Response time to price changes of competitors	• Advertising effectiveness by type of media (e.g. awareness levels)
• Price relative to competitor	• Actual audience/target audience ratio
• Price changes relative to sales volume	• Cost per contact
• Discount structure relative to sales volume	• Number of calls, enquiries and information requests by type of media
• Bid strategy relative to new contacts	
• Margin structure relative to marketing expenses	• Sales per sales call
• Margins relative to channel member performance	• Sales per territory relative to potential
	• Selling expenses to sales ratio
	• New accounts per time period
	• Lost accounts per time period

Source: adapted from Jobber, D. (1995) *Principles and Practice of Marketing*, pub. McGraw-Hill, reproduced with the kind permission of McGraw-Hill Publishing Company.

The next step is to locate responsibility. In some cases responsibility ultimately falls on one person (e.g. the brand manager); in others it is shared (e.g. the sales manager and sales force). It is important to consider this issue, since corrective or supportive action may need to focus on those responsible for the success of marketing activity.

In order to be successful the people involved and affected by the control process should be consulted in both the design and implementation stages of marketing control. Above all they will need to be convinced that the purpose of control is to improve their own levels of success and that of the company. Subordinates need to be involved in setting and agreeing their own standards of performance, preferably through a system of management by objectives.

Performance is then evaluated against these standards, which relies on an efficient information system. A judgement has to be made about the degree of success and failure achieved and what corrective or supportive action is to be taken. This can take various forms:

■ Failure that is attributed to the poor performance of individuals may result in the giving of advice regarding future attitudes and actions, training and/or punishment (e.g. criticism, lower pay, demotion, termination of employment). Success, on the other hand, should be rewarded with praise, promotion and/or higher pay.

■ Failure that is attributed to unrealistic marketing objectives and performance may cause management to lower objectives or lower marketing standards (Figure 19.9). Success that is thought to reflect unambitious objectives and standards may cause them to be raised in the next period.

Many firms assume that corrective action needs to be taken only when results are less than those required or when budgets and costs are being exceeded. In fact both 'negative' (underachievement) and 'positive' (overachievement) deviations may require corrective action. For example, failure to spend the amount budgeted for, say, sales force expenses may indicate that the initial sum allocated was excessive and needs to be reassessed, and/or that the sales force is not as 'active' as it might be.

It is also necessary to determine such things as the frequency of measurement (e.g. daily, weekly, monthly or annually). More frequent and more detailed measurement usually means more cost. We need to be careful to ensure that the costs of measurement and the control process itself do not exceed the value of such measurements and do not overly interfere with the activities of those being measured.

The impact of the environment must also be taken into account when designing a control system:

■ The control system should measure only dimensions over which the organization has control. Rewards or sanctions make little sense if they are based on dimensions that may be relevant for overall corporate performance, but over which no influence can be exerted (e.g. price controls). Neglecting the factor of individual performance capability would send the wrong signals and severely impair the motivation of personnel.

■ Control systems should harmonise with local regulations and customs. In some cases, however, corporate behavioural controls have to be exercised against local customs even though overall operations may be affected negatively. This type of situation occurs, for example, when a subsidiary operates in markets where unauthorised facilitating payments are a common business practice.

Feedforward control

Much of the information provided by the firm's marketing control system is feedback on what has been accomplished in both financial (profits) and non-financial (customer satisfaction, market share) terms. As such, the control process is remedial in its outlook. It can be argued that control systems should be forward looking and preventive, and that the control process should start at the same time as the planning process. Such a form of control is feedforward control (Figure 20.10).

Figure 20.10 Adjustment of global marketing strategy

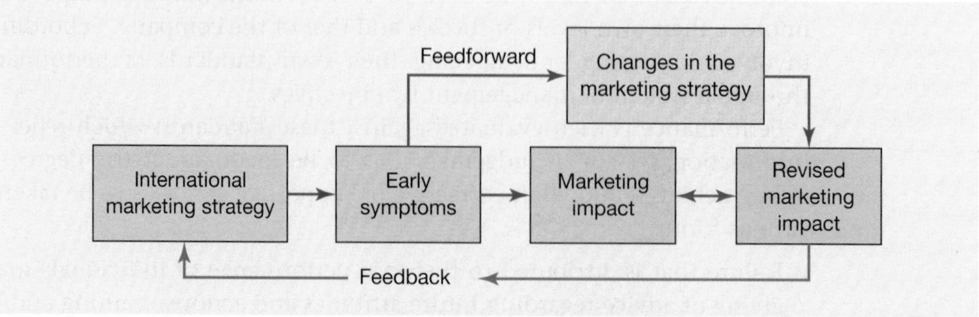

Source: Samli et al., 1993, p. 425.

Feedforward control would continuously evaluate plans, monitoring the environment to detect changes that would call for revising objectives and strategies. Feedforward control monitors variables other than performance; variables that may change before performance itself changes. The result is that deviations can be controlled before their full impact has been felt. Such a system is proactive in that it anticipates environmental change, whereas after-the-fact and steering control systems are more reactive in that they deal with changes after they occur. Examples of early symptoms (early performance indicators) are presented in Table 20.2.

Table 20.2 **Some key early performance indicators**

Early performance indicators	Market implication
Sudden drop in quantities demanded	Problem in marketing strategy or its implementation
Sharp decrease or increase in sales volume	Product gaining acceptance or being rejected quickly
Customer complaints	Product not debugged properly
A notable decrease in competitors' business	Product gaining acceptance quickly or market conditions deteriorating
Large volumes of returned merchandise	Problems in basic product design
Excessive requests for parts or reported repairs	Problems in basic product design, low standards
Sudden changes in fashions or styles	Product (or competitors' product) causing a deep impact on the consumers' lifestyles

Source: Samli *et al.*, 1993, p. 421.

Feedforward control focuses on information that is prognostic: it tries to discover problems waiting to occur. Formal processes of feedforward control can be incorporated into the business marketer's total control programme to enhance its effectiveness considerably. Utilisation of a feedforward approach would help ensure that planning and control are treated as concurrent activities.

Key areas for control in marketing

Kotler (1997) distinguishes four types of marketing control, each involving different approaches, different purposes and a different allocation of responsibilities. These are shown in Table 20.3 overleaf. Here we will focus on annual plan control and profit control, since they are the most obvious areas of concern to firms with limited resources (e.g. SMEs).

Annual plan control

The purpose of annual plan control is to determine the extent to which marketing efforts over the year have been successful. This control will centre on measuring and evaluating sales in relation to sales goals, market share analysis and expense analysis.

Sales performance is a key element in annual plan control. Sales control consists of a hierarchy of standards on different organizational control levels. These are interlinked, as shown in Figure 20.11 overleaf.

We can see from the diagram that any variances in achieving sales targets at the corporate level are the result of variances in the performance of individual salespeople at the operational level. At every level of sales control variances must be studied with a view to determining their causes. In general, variances may be due to a combination of variances in volume and/or price.

Table 20.3 Types of marketing control

Type of control	Prime responsibility	Purpose of control	Examples of techniques/approaches
Strategic control	Top management Middle management	To examine if planned results are being achieved	Marketing effectiveness ratings Marketing audit
Efficiency control	Line and staff management Marketing controller	To examine ways of improving the efficiency of marketing	Sales force efficiency Advertising efficiency Distribution efficiency
Annual plan control	Top management Middle management	To examine if planned results are being achieved	Sales analysis Market share analysis Marketing expenses to sales ratio Customer tracking
Profit control (budget control)	Marketing controller	To examine where the company is making and losing money	Profitability by e.g. product, customer group or trade channel

Source: Adapted from *Marketing Management: Analysis, Planning, Implementation and Control*. 9/E by Kotler. © Reprinted by permission of Pearson Education, Inc., Upper Saddle River, NJ.

Figure 20.11 The hierarchy of sales and control

Profit control

In addition to the previously discussed control elements, all international marketers must be concerned to control their profit. The budgetary period is normally one year because budgets are tied to the accounting systems of the company. In the following section we will further explore how global marketing budgets are developed, the starting point being the Global Account Management organization and the country-based structure of the company.

20.5   The global marketing budget

The classic quantification of a global marketing plan appears in the form of budgets. Because these are so rigorously quantified they are particularly important. They should represent a projection of actions and expected results, and they should be capable of accurate monitoring. Indeed performance against budget is the main (regular) management review process.

Budgeting is also an organization process that involves making forecasts based on the proposed marketing strategy and programmes. The forecasts are then used to construct a budgeted profit-and-loss statement (i.e. profitability). An important aspect of budgeting is deciding how to allocate the last available dollars across all of the proposed programmes within the marketing plan.

Recognising the *customer* as the primary unit of focus, a market-based business will expand its focus to customers and countries/markets, not just products or units sold. This is an important strategic distinction because there is a finite number of potential customers, but a larger range of products and services can be sold to each customer. A business's volume is its customer share in a market with a finite number of customers at any point in time, not the number of units sold.

Global marketing strategies that affect customer volume include marketing strategies that achieve the following:

- attract new customers to grow market share;
- grow the market demand by bringing more customers into a market;
- enter new markets to create new sources of customer volume.

All marketing strategies require *some* level of marketing effort to achieve a certain level of market share. Expenses associated with sales effort, market communications, customer service and market management are required to implement a marketing strategy designed to obtain a certain customer volume. The cost of this marketing effort are the *marketing expenses* and they must be deducted from the total contribution to produce a *net marketing contribution*.

Figure 20.12 is the illustration of the traditional marketing budget (per country or customer group) and its underlying determinants.

From Figure 20.12 the most important measures of marketing profitability may be defined as:

$$\text{Contribution margin in \%} = \frac{\text{Total contribution}}{\text{Total revenue}} \times 100$$

$$\text{Marketing contribution margin \%} = \frac{\text{Total marketing contribution}}{\text{Total revenue}} \times 100$$

$$\text{Profit margin \%} = \frac{\text{Net profit (before taxes)}}{\text{Total revenue}} \times 100$$

If we had information about the size of assets (accounts receivable + inventory + cash + plant + equipment) we could also define:

$$\text{Return on assests(ROA)} = \frac{\text{Net profit (before taxes)}}{\text{Assets}}$$

ROA is similar to the well-known measure: ROI = return on investment.

Table 20.4 presents an example of a global marketing budget for a manufacturer of consumer goods. Included in the budget are those marketing variables that can be controlled and changed by the sales and marketing functions (departments) in the home country and in the export market. In Table 20.4 the only variable that cannot be controlled by the international sales and marketing departments is variable costs.

The global marketing budget system (as presented in Table 20.4) is used for the following (main) purposes:

- Allocation of marketing resources among countries/markets to maximise profits. In Table 20.4 it is the responsibility of the global marketing director to maximise the total contribution 2 for the whole world.

Figure 20.12 Marketing budget 200X and its underlying determinants

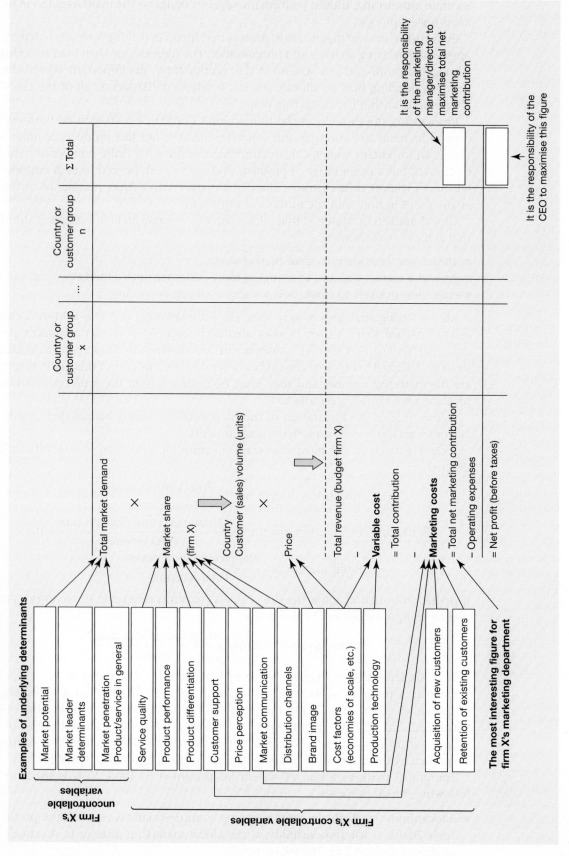

■ Evaluation of country/market performance. In Table 20.4 it is the responsibility of export managers or country managers to maximise contribution 2 for each of their countries.

Note that besides the marketing variables presented in Table 20.4 the global marketing budget normally contains inventory costs for finished goods. As the production sizes of these goods are normally based on input from the sales and marketing department, the inventory of unsold goods will also be the responsibility of the international marketing manager or director.

Furthermore, the global marketing budget may also contain customer-specific or country-specific product development costs, if certain new products are preconditions for selling in certain markets.

In contrast to budgets, long-range plans extend over periods from 2 to 10 years, and their content is more qualitative and judgemental in nature than that of budgets. For SMEs shorter periods (such as 2 years) are the norm because of the perceived uncertainty of diverse foreign environments.

Table 20.4 **An example of an international marketing budget for a manufacturer exporting consumer goods**

| International marketing budget | Europe | | | | | | America | | Asia/Pacific | | | | | |
| | UK | | Germany | | France | | USA | | Japan | | Korea | | Other Markets | |
Year = _____	B	A	B	A	B	A	B	A	B	A	B	A	B	A
Net sales (gross sales less trade discounts, allowances, etc.)														
÷ **Variable costs**														
= **Contribution 1**														
÷ **Marketing costs:**														
Sales costs (salaries, commissions for agents, incentives, travelling, training, conferences)														
Consumer marketing costs (TV commercials, radio, print, sales promotion)														
Trade marketing costs (fairs, exhibitions, in-store promotions, contributions for retailer campaigns)														
= Σ **Total contribution 2** (marketing contribution)														

B = budget figures; A = actual.

Note: On a short-term (one-year) basis, the export managers or country managers are responsible for maximising the actual figures for each country and minimising their deviation from budget figures. The international marketing manager/director is responsible for maximising the actual figure for the total world and minimising its deviation from the budget figure. Cooperation is required between the country managers and the international marketing manager/director to coordinate and allocate the total marketing resources in an optimum way. Sometimes certain inventory costs and product development costs may also be included in the total marketing budget (see main text).

20.6   Summary

Implementation of a global marketing programme requires an appropriate organizational structure. As the scope of a firm's global marketing strategy changes its organizational structure must be adequately modified in accordance with its tasks and technology and the external environment. Five ways of structuring an international organization have been presented: functional structure, international divisional structure, product structure, geographical structure (customer structure) and matrix structure. The choice of organizational structure is affected by such factors as the degree of internationalization of the firm, the strategic importance of the firm's international operations, the complexity of its international business and the availability of qualified managers.

Control is the process of ensuring that global marketing activities are carried out as intended. It involves monitoring aspects of performance and taking corrective action where necessary. The global marketing control system consists of deciding marketing objectives, setting performance standards, locating responsibility, evaluating performance against standards, and taking corrective or supportive action.

In an after-the-fact control system, managers wait until the end of the planning period to take corrective action. In a feedforward control system, corrective action is taken during the planning period by tracking early performance indicators and steering the organization back to desired objectives if it goes out of control.

The most obvious areas of control relate to the control of the annual marketing plan and the control of profitability. The purpose of the global marketing budget is mainly to allocate marketing resources across countries to maximise worldwide total marketing contribution.

CASE STUDY 20.1   Mars Inc.

Merger of the European food, petcare and confectionary divisions

Mars Inc. is a diversified multifunctional company whose primary products include foods, petcare, confectionery, electronics and drinks. Owned and controlled by the Mars family, this US giant is one of the world's biggest private companies, but also one of the most secretive.

Mars' decision in January 2000 to merge its food, petcare and confectionery divisions across Europe – and eventually with headquarters in the UK – has split the marketing industry.

The most well-known brands within the three divisions are:

- foods: Uncle Ben's rice and sauces;
- petcare: Whiskas, Pedigree;
- confectionery: M&Ms, Snickers, Milky Way, Mars Bar.

Mars UK says the decision to pool the businesses was

taken to strike at the company's international competitors in food and confectionery, such as Nestlé and Unilever. The move also coincides with plans to create a single European market and highlights the company's belief that its consumers' needs are the same across the Continent.

But the combination of food and confectionery with petcare is not clear to all industry observers. One industry analyst made the comment: 'Generally speaking, Mars is doing the right thing by merging divisions to squeeze profits out of them. Before the advent of the euro it was acceptable to run separate companies in different European countries but not any more.'

Another analyst had this opinion:

I can't imagine it marketing all three sides of the business together. They're too different.

The only visible benefit appears to be an improvement in distribution. Tastes across European markets are very different, whether you're selling products for animals or people.

It's all very well Mars saying it will tackle competitors such as Nestlé and Unilever, but they are only rivals in food and confectionery.

If Mars starts laying down too many controls by merging all its businesses – and therefore also its marketing and management strategies – it may streamline communi-cations, but could lose the creativity available in different regions.

Source: McCawley, 2000.

Questions

1. Discuss the two views of organizing Mars' European activities.

2. Did Mars Inc. do the right thing in your opinion?

CASE STUDY 20.2   AGRAMKOW Fluid Systems

Reconsidering its global organization structure

AGRAMKOW (**www.agramkow.com**) was founded in 1977 by Asger Gramkow based upon the will to become one of the world's leading developers and suppliers of filling equipment for fluid refrigerants, which are used for example in refrigerators or in car air conditioning. AGRAMKOW's mission is the following:

To improve our customers' processes and business performance – safely and reliable.

Generally AGRAMKOW has divided its business into two main SBUs: *Auto:* AGRAMKOW develops, designs and installs fluid systems for Automotive manufacturers globally; and *RAC:* AGRAMKOW develops process fluid fill systems for the refrigeration and air conditioning industries globally.

AGRAMKOW's process fluid fill system fits within the production line of a refrigerator manu-facturer. Besides the fluid fill product, AGRAMKOW

Figure 1 AGRAMKOW Organization

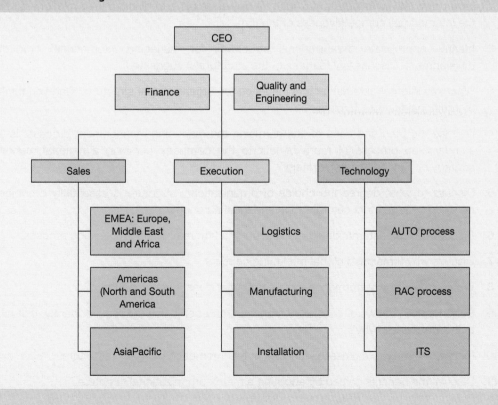

has a further department, ITS, which develops electronic control units, measure and test equipment and enterprise solutions for refrigeration and air conditioning enterprises. These solutions see to it that the end products from the production line are tested and that the whole production flow is optimised.

The current AGRAMKOW organization is as shown in Figure 1.

In the RAC business AGRAMKOW's customers are big multinational companies such as Whirlpool (US), Electrolux (Sweden), Samsung (Korea), Haier (China), Siemens (Germany) and General Electric (US). It is a fact that the company's global customers are getting fewer and bigger through mergers and aquisitions.

Local service centres

AGRAMKOW has a global network of direct and independent service centres – each staffed by trained experts. All of its service centres are stocked with a complete line of maintenance, spare and repair parts for all AGRAMKOW and related partner products.

Questions

1. What implications are there for AGRAMKOW's current organization, that its customers are getting fewer and bigger? Propose a possible new organization structure.

2. How should AGRAMKOW build up its international marketing budget (by region, country, SBU or customer)?

For further exercises and cases, see this book's website at **www.booksites.net/hollensen**

Questions for discussion

1. This chapter suggests that the development of a firm's international organization can be divided into different stages. Identify these stages and discuss their relationship to the international competitiveness of the firm.

2. Identify appropriate organizational structures for managing international product development. Discuss key features of the structure(s) suggested.

3. What key internal/external factors influence the organizational structure? Can you think of additional factors? Explain.

4. Discuss the pros and cons of standardising the marketing management process. Is a standardised process of more benefit to the company pursuing a national market strategy or a global market strategy?

5. Discuss to what degree the choice of organizational structure is essentially a choice between headquarters centralisation and local autonomy.

6. Discuss how the international organization of a firm may affect its planning process.

7. Discuss why firms need global marketing controls.

8. What is meant by performance indicators? Why does a firm need them?

9. Performance reviews of subsidiary managers and personnel are required rarely, if at all, by headquarters. Why?

10. Identify the major weaknesses inherent in the international division structure.

11. Discuss the benefits gained by adopting a matrix organizational structure.

References

Bartlett, C. and Ghoshal, S. (1989) *Managing Across Borders: The transnational solution*, Harvard University Press, Boston, MA.

Harvey, M., Myers, M.B. and Novicevic, M.M. (2002) 'The managerial issues associated with Global Account Management', *Thunderbird International Business Review*, vol. 44, no. 5, pp. 625–647.

Hollensen, S. (2003), *Marketing Management – A Relationship Approach*, Financial Times/Prentice Hall, Harlow.

Jobber, D. (1995) *Principles and Practice of Marketing*, McGraw-Hill, New York.

Kotler, P. (1997) *Marketing Management: Analysis, planning, implementation and control* (9th edn), Prentice-Hall, Englewood Cliffs, NJ.

McCawley, I. (2000) 'Can Mars bridge gaps in merger?' *Marketing Week*, News Analysis, 13 January.

McDonald, M., Millman, T. and Rogers, B. (1997), 'Key account management: theory, practice and challenges', *Journal of Marketing Management*, vol. 13, pp. 737–57.

Millman, T. and Wilson, K. (1995) 'From Key Account Selling to Key Account Management', *Journal of Marketing Practice: Applied Marketing Science*, vol. 1, pp. 9–21.

Ojasalo, J. (2001), 'Key Account Management at company and individual levels in B-t-B relationships', *The Journal of Business and Industrial Marketing*, vol. 16, no. 3, pp. 199–220.

Peppers, D. and Rogers, M. (1995), 'A new marketing paradigm: Share of customer, not market share.' *Harvard Business Review*, July–August, pp. 105–13.

Quelch, J.A. (1992) 'The new country managers', *The McKinsey Quarterly*, no. 4, pp. 155–65.

Quelch, J.A. and Bloom, H. (1996) 'The return of the country manager', *The McKinsey Quarterly*, no. 2, pp. 30–43.

Samli, A.C., Still, R. and Hill, J.S. (1993) *International Marketing: Planning and practice*, Macmillan, London.

Shelly, B. (1995) 'Cool customer', *Unilever Magazine*, no. 2, pp. 12–17.

Unilever (1996) Introducing Unilever.

Wilson, K. and Millman, T. (2003) 'The global account manager as political entrepreneur', *Industrial Marketing Management*, vol. 32, pp. 151–8.

Further reading

Arnold, D., Birkinshaw, J. and Toulan, O. (2001) 'Can selling be globalized?: The pitfalls of Global Account Management', *California Management Review*, vol. 44, no. 1, pp. 8–20.

Connell, R. (2002) 'Calculating the contribution of customers: a practical approach', *Journal of Targeting, Measurement and Analysis for Marketing*, vol. 11, no. 1, pp. 68–80.

Dibb, S. and Simkin, L. (2003) 'Marketing educators: addressing implementation in core courses', *Journal of Strategic Marketing*, vol. 11, pp. 3–13.

Dobni, B. (2003) 'Creating a strategy implementation environment', *Business Horizons*, March–April, pp. 43–6.

Dobni, B., Dobni, D. and Luffman, G. (2001) 'Behavioral approaches to marketing strategy implementation', *Marketing Intelligence & Planning*, vol. 19, no. 6, pp. 400–8.

Garau, C. (2002) 'How to calculate the value of a customer', *Journal of Targeting, Measurement and Analysis for Marketing*, vol. 10, no. 3, pp. 203–19.

Jain, D. and Singh, S.S. (2002) 'Customer lifetime value research in marketing: a review and future directions', *Journal of Interactive Marketing*, vol. 6, no. 2, pp. 34–46.

Homburg, C., Workman, J.P. and Jensen, O. (2000) 'Fundamental changes in marketing organizations: The movement toward a customer-focused organizational structure', *Journal of the Academy of Marketing Science*, vol. 28, no. 4, pp. 459–78.

Ryals, L. and Knox, S. (2001) 'Cross-functional issues in the implementation of relationship marketing through customer relationship management', *European Management Journal*, vol. 19, no. 5, pp. 534–42.

Simkin, L. (2002) 'Tackling implementation impediments to marketing planning', *Marketing Intelligence & Planning*, vol. 20, no. 2, pp. 120–26.

Simkin, L. (2002) 'Barriers impeding effective implementation of marketing plans: a training agenda', *Journal of Business & Industrial Marketing*, vol. 17, no. 1, pp. 8–24.

Sheth, J. and Sisodia, R.S. (2002) 'Marketing productivity: issues and analysis', *Journal of Business Research*, vol. 55, pp. 349–62.

Weber, J.A. (2002) 'Managing the marketing budget in a cost-constrained environment', *Industrial Marketing Management*, vol. 31, no. 8, pp. 705–17.

CASE STUDY V.1   Femilet

A SME is seeking a foothold in the European lingerie market

On a lovely Spring day in 2004, Susanne Stuhr, Managing Director of Femilet, packs her suitcase for her monthly business trip to different European countries. While packing she thinks about how the Femilet-brand (on a European level) could break through the intensive 'wall' of international lingerie brands, like Triumph, Marie Joe or Chantelle.

Femilet lingerie

Danish Femilet (www.femilet.com) is today one of the leading suppliers in Scandinavia of fashion lingerie, ladies' underwear, swimwear, and nightwear, sold under the brand name Femilet. This case study will mainly concentrate on the fashion lingerie and ladies' underwear, which together makes up the largest part of Femilet's turnover.

Femilet was founded in 1923 and was acquired by Thygesen Textile Group (http://www.s-thygesen.dk/asp/groupbody.asp) in 1995.

Over the years Femilet has developed from a production-oriented company with main emphasis on classic women's underwear in knitwear into a market-oriented company focusing on design, sales, and marketing of fashion lingerie in the upper price segment.

All products are designed and developed by Femilet in Denmark. The construction of lingerie is very complicated because the developers and manufacturers are dealing with a three dimensional product. Bras are one of the most complex pieces of apparel. There are lots of different styles, and each style has a dozen different sizes, and within that there are a lot of colors. Furthermore, there is a lot of product engineering. You've got hooks, you've got straps, there are usually two parts to every cup, and each requires a heavy amount of sewing. It is very component intensive. There is very little automation possible, compared to say a shirt where 40% of the sewing process could be automated. The average bra has up to 20 differential materials from lace, lining, foam, side panels, elastic, hooks, eyes, wire and ribbon.

Therefore the production of Femilet's lingerie is outsourced – primarily to the Far East (China). However the laces to the lingerie are typically

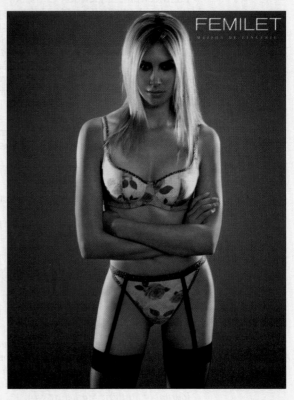

bought in France, and then sent to China for the final production process.

Femilet has own sales organizations in Denmark and Norway and importers in Spain and Holland. The company has four own sales representatives in Denmark, and two in Norway. These sales people are visiting specialized multi-brand lingerie shops, major chain stores and shops where Femilet has in-shop solutions. In total Femilet has 16 in-shop solutions in Denmark and till now one in Norway.

Femilet has about 75 employees, of which half are working in the own Femilet shops.

The franchise concept

In Denmark, Femilet has got 12 shops and two new shops are planned to open in spring 2004. One of the shops is based on a franchise concept. It is the intention that the Femilet concept shops will be extended via the implementation of a franchise model. At the moment, Femilet is actively seeking potential franchisees for expanding the number of Femilet concept shops.

Besides low investment and high profit, the franchise concept offers guaranteed territory-market protection, comprehensive training, full operational assistance for startup and on-going support to the franchisees. In the franchise concept the Femilet brand has a better opportunity of being developed to a level where it is associated with quality, consistency, service and value.

In Norway and other Scandinavian countries Femilet is also considering using the franchise model as leverage for profiling the brand and its underlying values.

Femilet's lingerie market share is relatively high in Denmark (17–20%). In Norway the market share is less than 5% and in other markets it is less than a half percent.

Further 'international marketing'-activities

Besides Norway, Femilet has recently started up with importers in Holland and Spain. In these countries (where the Femilet brand is completely unknown) importers are taking care of visiting multi-brand lingerie shops and major chain stores. The resources for marketing activities are limited but the agent's local marketing activities (e.g. advertising in local magazines or newspapers) are supported from the Femilet Headquarters with 50%.

General trends in the international lingerie market

Generally American women buy more lingerie than European women. One of the reasons is that Americans have a tendency to throw everything in the washing machine, so the wear out is quicker. Furthermore lingerie in USA is not sold through specialist shops (multibrand shops) like in Europe, but through mass distribution channels such as Wal-Mart, which is estimated to have 20% of the overall market. The US-market is also much more price driven, and lingerie (e.g. bras) cost a lot less.

In Europe there seems to be a difference between Northern and Southern countries. In Southern Europe they buy more lingerie than in Northern Europe. One of the reasons could be that women in Southern Europe place more emphasis on feeling romantic and sexy. Also the more intensive sweating in these countries may lead to more purchase of lingerie. Another explanation could be, that the northern countries are colder and women wear thicker clothes, so they are not so worried about how their underwear looks.

As in other apparel designs, the trends in lingerie have been dictated by fabric developments. This has meant that glamour, the art of seduction, and feminine charm are all ingredients in the current vogue. In addition, many bras are designed for women who partake in jogging, aerobics, tennis etc. to gain maximum benefit from their active lifestyles.

Regarding the distribution of the lingerie, more and more of the textile turnover is now going to branches other than lingerie itself. For instance, TESCO in England, is offering even fashion brands, mainly sourced from third countries, to its customers despite this practice being declared illegal by fashion brands. In Germany, for example, food retailers, drugstores and even coffee shops are also selling a significant amount of textile products. Thus in the annual list of the largest textile retailers in Germany, one finds the food discounter ALDI ranking at number nine, and TCHIBO - a chain of coffee shops, at number 13. In Germany, these non-textile retailers already have a market share of 11.8 per cent of the total textile market. They do not normally have a full assortment and only sell offers and special items, which they buy in huge quantities and sell at extremely low prices. Also, the idea of concept assortments is being used by some of them. Thus, the coffee chain Tchibo is selling every week, a completely different theme, wherein textile products are just a part of all on offer.

- Only companies with a sharp profile are successful in the market. Here are some examples of successful specialty stores:
- French group Orsay is increasing its business with their specialty concept for girlies' fashion.
- The German teeny specialist New Yorker
- H&M with their concept of top fashion products at discounted prices, has been growing in almost all countries where they are present
- Zara and Mango have also been opening stores worldwide in a remarkably short time frame for a similar target group.

Other specialty stores are also registering remarkable successes. Best examples of this can be seen in sports and sports-fashion business, where specialty stores such as Runners Point (Germany), Karstadt Sport (Germany), Foot Locker (USA), Sports Expert (Austria), Decathlon (France), Sketcher (USA) and The Sports Authority (USA) are gathering more and more market shares and expanding worldwide.

The lingerie segment, earlier a fixed part of normal textile and fashion stores, is also witnessing a fast growth. For instance, Oysho (Zara-Spain), Women's Secret (Cortefield-Spain) and even Marks & Spencer are starting their own chains of lingerie outside their traditional shops.

Generally, a polarization is taking place in the European lingerie market. The distribution of the lower priced brands are being taking over by the huge retail chains, whereas the higher priced brands are gaining market shares by using their own concept shops, where the personal service plays a much higher role. At present, the losers in the industry are the 'in-between' brands, which are 'stuck in the middle'.

Vertical integration

More and more manufacturers are opening own stores and more and more fashion retailers are selling their own retail brands.

The vertical integration is a result of increasing efficiency between production and distribution given the assumption that organization of production is best made from the POS (point of sale). Middlemen and wholesalers as well as middle activities like exhibitions, are cut out of the distribution channel to ensure that there are less costs and no losses of communication in the process. Success is more likely in cases where one company owns or controls the complete process from production to distribution. All fast expanding fashion companies are working vertically. Wal-Mart, Zara, Uniglo, Mango, H&M, C&A, Esprit – all these successful international retailers fall in this category. Frequently, they work on a completely vertical system, while at other times, they use a mixed system – selling own brands as well as manufacturer brands.

In the following three major European markets for lingerie are described: UK, Germany and France.

The UK market

Consumers, inspired by celebrity style, are buying more bras and pants and showing a tendency to trade up. The lingerie market in UK is estimated at **EURO 2.2 billion** (2002) with sales of bras accounting for around a third of that value.

The sources of competition to traditional main street chains include supermarkets, mail order and online shopping. Because of this, retail prices have become aggressively competitive. The big corporate chains are claiming growing market share with fewer, but bigger, outlets. According to the Department of Trade & Industry (DTI), the largest shops and chains control about 75% of the clothing market. The growing involvement of the grocery multiples is certainly adding low-price capacity.

Major retailers, especially Marks & Spencer, have improved their segmentation of bras and pants with more premium ranges under sub-brands, adding to the overall choice for consumers. At the same time prices are dropping. This is due to cheaper imports, especially influenced by bras and pants coming in from Eastern Europe and the Far East. This has helped the discounters to serve an even wider range of bras and pants at low prices. These two factors have both been influential in helping to stimulate demand.

Bras and pants have become a self-treat item for many women and are even a gift item at certain times of year. The branded houses have all worked hard at improving their styling, bringing in new fabrics, new construction techniques (especially for bras) and plenty of fashionable ideas.

Consumer research carried out by Mintel highlights just how an evolving interest in fashion is creating numerous opportunities for manufacturers and retailers. Women are more likely to have a 'wardrobe' of underwear, buying different styles and types for different occasions. Necessity may well drive the market but fashion influences are creating a "must have culture" and stimulating demand. When Mintel asked UK consumers what made them buy a bra and pants in the last 12 months, 62 and 60% respectively indicated replacement reasons. But 29 and 26% of respondents indicating they bought bras and then pants 'to treat' themselves. This is an important factor that both suppliers and retailers can take into their marketing.

Table 1 shows the development in the bra market from 1998 to 2000.

In 1998, the leading British main street chain Marks & Spencer accounted for 34% of UK bra sales, and similar high shares of briefs and hosiery. This has changed in downward direction since the consumers appetite for all things branded has encouraged newcomers on to the lingerie scene. In the past, most female consumers have thought of lingerie as a necessity or a commodity, and not fashion led. Even though much of the expensive and glamorous lingerie is imported from France and other European countries, US producers of upmarket and fashionable lingerie will most certainly also find a receptive audience in UK. The likes of The Gap, Benetton, and Calvin Klein have already spotted a niche in this market, and are opening standalone lingerie formats.

German market

With a total market value of **EURO 1.9 billion** (2002), Germany continues to be one of the largest European markets for lingerie. Despite economic crises German women are spending more on lingerie than ever before. In addition to new fashion lingerie styles individualism, decorative femininity and a new ethnic styling emphasize the new sleekness for the coming seasons. Fashion styles are rejuvenated by new colors and novel shapes. A surge in color is found in the mixture of deep red with pink, green

Table 1 **Brand share in the UK bra market 1988–2000**

Brand	1998 – Market share pct.	2000 – Market share pct.
Marks & Spencer	34	30
Triumph	7	7
Gossard	6	6
Playtex	5	5
Warner	3	3
Berlei	1	1
Charnos	1	1

and intense yellow. Warm colors also add more life to the fashion. Manufacturers have recognized that their lingerie collections must include innovative colors and interesting shapes.

Successful penetration of the German market depends on a continuity of efforts, regular participation in trade fairs, and the establishment of a sales office with warehousing, either in Germany or another European country. Appointment of sales agents is usually the first step.

The major country of origin for imported lingerie to Germany in 2001 were: (1) China, (2) Turkey, (3) Poland, (4) Italy, (5) Romania, (6) Hong Kong, (7) Tunisia, (8) India, (9) Czech Republic, (10) Hungary.

The absolute brand market leader in the German lingerie market is Triumph, which has also got some German roots.

The big fashion chains worldwide are grabbing more and more market share in the lingerie market from the smaller traditional fashion retailers. For example, in Germany, a quarter of the market is covered by the four largest fashion retailers (Karstadt-Quelle, Metro-Group, C&A and OTTO). The 84 large fashion retailers in Germany have with them, over 60 per cent of the total market share. According to official numbers, in Germany, every fifth small and medium-sized fashion retailer has been closing down in the past decade. This trend is also reflected in other countries. Even between the big ones, the competition is growing steadily and some of them, such as Gap, Marks & Spencer and C&A are facing problems. In the current scenario, if a retailer does not have a proper and tight concept, the market would react adversely very fast. It is only the big ones who have been able to defend themselves better with larger power and resources of their command.

French market

In 2002 French lingerie sales were estimated at **EURO 1.9 Billion**, representing approximately 20 percent of the total French women's wear sales. Although the economic recession of the past three years has been particularly difficult for the textile industry, the lingerie market segment has proven itself relatively impervious to the downward economic trends.

On average, a French woman purchases approximately five briefs and two bras per year. She renews her nightwear every year. Women, aged 15 to 34 years purchase more lingerie items than other age categories, however, they buy less expensive lingerie. The most important element for consumers is comfort.

The following lingerie trends were noted:

- *Romantic lingerie*: Importance of second skin bras for an invisible look with more microfibers lace with tulle. This romantic lingerie is made with fabrics that are smooth and is often accentuated with little touches of sophistication (pearl and embroidery).
- *Beautiful lingerie*: Sophisticated shapes with lace, floral embroidery, and cut-away effects. Necklines are back, due to the cutaway effects, strappy looks, and pretty, braided trim.
- *Sporty lingerie*: A ready-to-wear product with bright colors (red, blue, pink, yellow).

According to recent statistics, the average annual budget for lingerie per woman in France is EURO 95, and depends on the following factors:

- According to the age of consumers:
  15–24 years: EURO 140
  25–34 years: EURO 100
  35–44 years: EURO 80
  45–54 years: EURO 110
  55–64 years: EURO 90
  65 year / +: EURO 50

- According to regions:
  Paris area: EURO 95
  North of France: EURO 90
  East of France: EURO 80
  West of France: EURO 75
  South West: EURO 110
  South East: EURO 100

Advertising: A key factor in establishing a brand in France is to have an adequate advertising budget. The foreign company should be able to promote its image and reinforce its position. New products should be aggressively marketed to appeal to French women's inherent 'passion for living' which influences their fashion preferences, expressing both their sensuality and feminity. For example, Calvin Klein recently did a large advertising campaign in the Parisian underground metro system.

Together with French companies American companies dominates the lingerie market. Market leaders in France are Sara Lee (Dim, Cacharel, Playtex, Rosy), Warnaco (Warner's, Calvin Klein, Lejaby), Chantelle (Ava, Essensia Tulle, Mon Amour), Vanity Fair Corporation (Bolero, Variance, Carina, Siltex, Lou).

International competitors

In the following three of Femilet's most important competitors are described: Triumph, Marie Jo and Chantelle.

Triumph

The story of Triumph International dates back well over a century and its history parallels developments in the world of fashion.

Founded in Germany in 1886 by the Spiesshofer and Braun families, who still manage the business today, the company grew from small beginnings to Europe's biggest lingerie manufacturer and a leading garment maker throughout the world.

Production began in Heubach, Germany, with just six employees. Today the company has a turnover of 2.6 billion Swiss Francs and a workforce approaching 37,000.

Triumph's first step to international expansion came when the company was 40 years old and launched in Zurzach, Switzerland. Today Zurzach remains the financial headquarters for the corporation. By 1930 Triumph had become the largest corsetry manufacturer in Europe.

By the 1950's Triumph had become 'Triumph International' to reflect it's worldwide standing and employed 6000 staff. They expanded rapidly into countries such as Britain, Italy, Belgium and Norway. With this growth into new countries, Triumph became established as Europe's top lingerie manufacturer.

In 1960, with the step into Hong Kong, the expansion into the Asian market began. In the same year, the Triumph workforce had grown to 14,000.

Soon the company had independent subsidiaries for swimwear, daywear and nightwear.

On a global scale, Triumph International is represented in almost every country in the world and the company produces and markets foundation garments, lingerie and nightwear, swimwear and beachwear, sportswear and leisurewear.

Among the most well-known brands in the Triumph brand portfolio are: Triumph, BeeDees and Sloggi. Sold individually and in multi-packs, Sloggi's unique packaging and branding performed strongly on the shelves of leading department stores during the 90s. Sloggi's success had turned briefs into a fast-moving-consumer-goods (FMCG) market. By the late 90s, Triumph International had sold over 400 million pieces of Sloggi around the world.

Marie Jo

Textile producer Van de Velde developed from a family enterprise in Belgium to an important player in the European field of lingerie for women. Van de Velde SA designs and manufactures luxury lingerie items under three brand names: Marie Jo (feminine and fashionable lingerie), Marie Jo L'Aventure (individualistic lingerie) and Prima Donna (luxurious and comfortable lingerie for large sizes).

Van de Velde's most famous brand, Marie Jo, was introduced in 1981.

In the nineties Van de Velde introduced two new, high quality brands: Prima Donna and Marie Jo L'Aventure. Once again it was an overwhelming success. The Van de Velde image is nowadays one of creative, fashionable and stylish design combined with good quality and major emotional value. Today Van de Velde has more than a thousand employees in 5 different countries.

In 2001 Van de Velde NV acquired a controlling share in the Hong Kong lingerie producer Top Form. The strategic advantages of this move for the Belgians are easy to see - integrated management at lower costs, and an opening to the Chinese mainland market.

Van de Velde, whose turnover amounted to US$74.6 million in 2001, has production operations in Belgium, Hungary and Tunisia. However, 51% of all products designed and sold by Van de Velde were assembled by Top Form, out of Hong Kong and mainland China.

Chantelle

Chantelle lingerie is a family owned company for over 120 years. Chantelle has maintained its dedication to creating bras, panties, thongs and lingerie with the finest European laces and fabrics. Chantelle's comittment to fit, comfort, exquisite European styling, and detail has allowed Chantelle to establish themselves in over 70 countries worldwide. Its sales in 2002 was EURO 250 million.

The Chantelle brand is known throughout the world for their collections of fashionable and feminine lingerie. Delicate materials such as decorative lace and embroideries, high-end fabrics, support and comfortable cuts reflect the focus of Chantelle. Other brands of Le Groupe Chantelle include Latin-inspired Passionata and Darjeeling, for women who prefer the natural look.

Besides these three lingerie manufacturers, there is also Sara Lee Corporation, which is a market leader in the US lingerie market but they are not a very active in the Scandinavian markets. However, Sara Lee could be a serious competitor if Femilet choose to enter UK or Southern part of Europe. Sara Lee is mostly known for their Playtex lingerie or their Wonderbra.

Sources: Horne, J. (2003) 'King of Bras', FinanceAsia.com Ltd, 26 May, http://www.financeasia.com/articles/e867a971-642e-11d7-81fa0090277e174b.cfm
www.infomat.com

Questions

1. Please evaluate threats and opportunities for a company like Femilet, if they decide to enter new international markets.

2. Which of the three described European markets (UK, Germany or France) would it be most relevant for Femilet to enter in order to secure future growth?

3. Which marketing tools would be most effective in the attempt to capture market shares for the Femilet brand in the European lingerie market?

4. Would it be relevant to sell Femilet's lingerie on the internet? Please evaluate pros and cons and make a conclusion.

CASE STUDY V.2   BMG (B)

New worldwide organizational structure and the marketing, planning and budgeting of Dido's new album

After landing in London Tim hurries to the meeting with Dido, but on the way he thinks about the new global organizational structure of BMG ...

In spring 2003 BMG introduced a new organizational strategy for its music labels and corporate staff that would allow the company to focus on creating global music superstars who reach across geographical boundaries. The streamlining of the organization eliminates regional corporate groups in Europe, Asia and Latin American regions, and creates four new strategic groups within BMG: Office of the Chairman, Label Group, Territory Management and Corporate Center. All management from the groups will report directly to the Office of the Chairman, led by Schmidt-Holtz.

BMG wants to strengthen relationships with its artists. The top management of the company thinks this structure allows its creative executives to be closer to artists, while allowing managers to better support their creative executives. BMG wants an organization built on record labels with global reach. The labels and the creative executives should be able to work more closely with artists while being able to rely on effective global marketing capabilities.

Label Group will consist of US-based record labels including Arista Records, RCA Music Group, Jive/Zomba and RLG-Nashville, as well as BMG Music Publishing.

Territory Management will consist of major territories and country groups, such as Japan, Germany/Switzerland/Austria, the United Kingdom, Australia, and South Africa.

Reporting to the Office of the Chairman, Tim Prescott will serve as the company's highest-ranking marketing executive, overseeing global marketing campaigns for BMG artists. Also reporting to the Office of the Chairman are Human Resources, Strategy and New Technology and Corporate Communications. One of Tim's first tasks in the summer of 2003 is to create the worldwide marketing plan for the UK-singer Dido and her new album, 'Life for rent' released in September 2003. Hence, Tim's meeting with Dido in London. They agree that the launch of Dido's CD should start in the United Kingdom in an effort to get to the top of the charts as quickly as possible.

First some further information about the artist, Dido.

Dido – the best UK–selling artist in 2001

The singer and songwriter Dido (Armstrong) was born in London on Christmas Day in 1971. She was christened Florian Cloud De Bounevialle Armstrong. Dido lived with her poet mother and publisher father in London.

At 16 she became enthralled with the music of jazz singer Ella Fitzgerald and her brother Rollo's music collection. Rollo played in the group Faithless, and Dido appeared on the group's 5-million selling debut album 'Reverence' in 1995 on the tracks 'Flowerstand Man' and 'Salva Mea'. Dido later appeared on another Faithless album, 'Sunday 8 pm' in 1998 on the tracks 'Postcards' and 'Hem of his Garment'.

In between recording those two albums Dido met

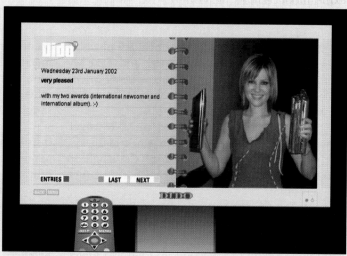

Source: http://www.didotv.com

producer Clive Davis in 1997, after he had heard demos of some of her own tracks. Dido was later signed to the record company Arista (a BMG label) and began recording her debut album 'No Angel'. Dido was also involved in the production side of her album. 'Bad boy' rapper Eminem borrowed part of her song 'Thank You' for his hit 'Stan' and she appeared as his wife in the video. The combination of Dido's angelic voice, soft acoustic guitars and great song writing, with a dash of electronica, has been a big hit with fans around the world.

The album 'No Angel' was released in the United States in 1999 and about a year later in October in the United Kingdom. Two tracks from the album have appeared in a TV show and in a film. 'Thank You' appeared in the film 'Sliding Doors' and 'Here With Me' was the theme tune to *Roswell*, a hit US science-fiction TV show, which has also been doing well in the United Kingdom. This exposure helped make 'No Angel' a huge success.

A special edition of 'No Angel' was released in January 2001 with enhanced videos of 'Here With Me' and 'Thank You'. It also included a bonus track 'Take My Hand' and a picture gallery. The album went to number one in United Kingdom and stayed there for a several weeks. It has sold more than 20 million copies worldwide.

Dido's debut single 'Here With Me' was released in February 2001 and got to number four in the UK charts. The follow up 'Thank You' was released in May 2001 and reached number three. The following month Dido appeared on another Faithless album, 'Outrospective', on the track 'One Step Too Far'. Her third single, 'Hunter' was released in September 2001, but did not do as well as the previous two, only reaching number seventeen.

A further limited edition of 'No Angel' was released in November 2001 with extra enhanced videos of 'Hunter' and live versions of 'All You Want' and 'Honestly OK'. It also included mixes of 'Here With Me', 'Thank You', 'Hunter' and 'Take My Hand' and an extra track, 'Christmas Day'. In the same month Dido won the Best New Act Award at the MTV Europe Music Awards.

A fourth and final single from the 'No Angel' album, 'All You Want' backed with 'Christmas Day', was released as a limited edition 3" CD single in December 2001. It did not enter the charts, being a limited edition.

'No Angel' was the best UK-selling album of 2001 and sold more than 2 million copies during the year. It got to number one in 13 countries and was the best-selling album in the world. In total 'No Angel'

has sold around 10 million copies around the world. In February 2002 Dido won Best British Female and Best British Album for 'No Angel' at the Brit Awards 2002.

In April 2002 'One Step Too Far', the track Dido recorded with Faithless, was released as a single and reached number six. Also in April 2002 the track that Dido co-wrote for Britney Spears, 'I'm Not A Girl, Not Yet A Woman' was released, and reached number two.

The typical value chain for a CD

The following shows how the 'value added' of a typical CD album is split among the various players in the value chain:

	£
Retail price to consumers	12
Price to retail	9
Price to distributor	6
Price to distributor (exclusive of artist royalty)	5

For a CD single the full retail price to consumers is about £2.00. But when a record is being pushed hard by the record label retailers are offered big discounts in an attempt to shift units in the all-important first week. In such circumstances singles can retail for as little as 99p.

Development

In the music industry record labels will actively seek to sign up bands and artists on long-term exclusive contracts. A key to success in development is to spot talent and to sign it up early.

Production

Production is relatively cheap in the music industry, and the cost of digital recording equipment and production of CDs is falling rapidly. Some consumers do not understand why the sale price of a CD is so much higher than the cost of producing the actual physical disc. But as described below there are many different activities and costs involved in creating songs and marketing the end result, the CD.

Distributors

Major distributors have a global network of branch offices to handle the sales, marketing and distribution process. Sometimes the distributors may outsource the physical distribution process.

Retail

Retailers put in orders to the wholesalers as and

when albums and singles are required. In the United Kingdom the retail chains are dominated by HMV, Virgin/Our Price/Smiths, Tower, etc. These chains account for about 80 per cent of the market.

The costs of a hit

Singles are released with the purpose of getting to the top of the charts. The financial risks involved in mounting an attack on the UK charts have never been greater. According to research carried out by BBC News Online, securing a top ten hit in the United Kingdom in the current climate is likely to cost a minimum of £125,000. Ever increasing amounts of financial resources are being thrown at marketing and promotion in the hope that a single will be picked up by MTV, radio and, perhaps most importantly, the major retailers, in order to secure the highest chart entry.

Biggest cost categories

Of course the most important component of a CD is the artist's effort that goes into developing the music. Artists spend a large portion of their creative energy on writing song lyrics and composing music or working with producers and A&R executives to find great songs from great writers. This task can take weeks, months, or even years. The creative ability of these artists to produce the music, combined with the time and energy they spend throughout that process, is in itself priceless. But while the creative process is priceless, it must be compensated. Artists receive royalties on each recording, which vary according to their contract, and the songwriter gets royalties too. In addition, the label incurs the costs of finding and signing new artists.

Once an artist or group has songs composed they then go into a studio and begin recording. The costs of recording, including studio fees, musicians, sound engineers, producers and others, must all be recovered by the price of the CD.

Then come marketing and promotion costs – perhaps the most expensive part of the music business today. They include increasingly expensive video clips, public relations, tour support, marketing campaigns and promotion to get the songs played. Labels make investments in artists by paying for both the production and the promotion of the album. New technology such as the Internet offers new ways for artists to reach music fans, but it still requires that some entity, whether a traditional label or another kind of company, market and promote the artist so that fans are aware of new releases.

For every album released in a given year a marketing strategy was developed to make that album stand out from the others hitting the market. Artwork must be designed for the CD box, and promotional materials (posters, store displays and music videos) developed and produced. For many artists a costly concert tour is essential to promote their recordings.

Another factor commonly overlooked in assessing CD prices is to assume that all CDs are equally profitable. In fact the vast majority are never profitable; for example, in the United States, 27,000 new releases hit the market every year. Most of these CDs never sell enough to recover costs. In the end, less than 10 per cent are profitable and, in effect, it is these recordings that finance the rest.

Marketing and promotion costs

Singles are essentially 3–4 minute adverts for CD albums. Singles' sales guarantee chart places and, in turn, radio play – and that is why music label companies persist with them. They are a kind of loss-leader for albums, where the real money is made.

The biggest expense is normally the promotional video, which for a mainstream artist starts at about £40,000 and can cost anything up to £1 million (however, this is quite exceptional, e.g. in the case of a Michael Jackson video). If the music video is to be shown on, say, MTV it has to comply with a number of requirements, which are set out by MTV (use of alcohol, sex, etc.).

It is common practice for the big retailers, HMV, Our Price and Virgin, to charge music label companies for promoting a single in their shops. This comes in form of a 'singles pack', which guarantees a prominent position for the product in the shop. There are also bonuses to be paid to the sales force to check that the single is being properly promoted in-store.

The singles chart – compiled each week by different organizations and TV stations, such as *Top of the Pops* on the BBC, has always been the cornerstone of the UK music industry. More singles are sold in United Kingdom than anywhere in the world – including the United States, where the album remains king. In 2000 it took an average of 118,700 sold singles to secure a number one spot in the UK chart. Rather than climbing the chart over a period of weeks, singles now enter high on a wave of hype and anticipation, and may drop down the following week. In order to ensure a high entry singles are given to radio stations in advance of their release date to build up anticipation. A new album (probably also the forthcoming Dido album) may be deemed a failure if the single from it does not enter the top five in the first week of release.

Here are some of the basic costs for a 'typical' UK top ten single:

	£
Recording	3,500
Promotion video	100,000–150,000
Remixes (of the original single)	5,000–10,000
Merchandising	15,000
Posters	10,000
Stickers	5,000
PR (Press)	5,000
Promotion copies to radio stations, etc.	8,000
Website	20,000
Manufacturing costs (50p per CD)	25,000

Optional costs:

Press ads	15,000
Billboard campaign	50,000
TV/radio advertising	200,000

Because of the high costs involved combined with the general decline in the sales of CDs and singles (because of the trend towards online downloading of songs), many industry insiders think the singles market can not continue in its current form. One possible escape route is the radio-only release, where a track from an album is promoted to radio stations, but is not actually available to buy. This often happens in the United States, where there is less emphasis on singles' sales, and the singles chart is largely based on radio play.

Sources: adapted from: **www.bmg.com**; BBC News Online: 'Counting the cost of a hit', 9 August 2001, **http://news.bbc.co.uk/**; Durlacher Research Ltd, 'Impacts of digital distribution on the music industry', 26 January 2001; RIAA, 'The costs of a CD', **http://www.riaa.com/MD-US-7.cfm**, 2003; BMG press release, New York, 23 January 2003.

Questions

1. What do you think of the change in BMG's organizational structure, from a geographical structure to an artist-driven organization?

2. How would you produce a sales and marketing budget for Dido's forthcoming single and album?

3. How would you control your budgets? What key figures would you monitor?

4. How would increasing digital distribution and the piracy of MP3 music files influence your budgeting and control?

5. Which marketing mix would you suggest to increase BMG's share in the UK market?

CASE STUDY V.3   Dandy/Cadbury Schweppes

This case study is solely the responsibility of the author and does not necessarily reflect the current strategy of Cadbury Schweppes

Alliance building and corporate organizational considerations in the world chewing gum market

The Danish chewing gum manufacturer Dandy is now part of the UK-based Cadbury Schweppes (www.cadburyschweppes.com). Dandy has around 2000 employees and produces about 25,000 tonnes of chewing gum per year. It sells to more than 70 countries. In 2000 Dandy's total net turnover increased to DKK 1,850 million, a 20 per cent increase on the year before. The profit in 2000 was DKK 91 million against DKK 25 million in 1999. Dandy has sales companies in 22 countries and production takes place at three factories in Vejle, Novogrod and in Africa.

Dandy's mission statement is: 'We create smiles'. And their vision is: 'To be the world's best chewing gum company'. The company will constantly offer consumers the best taste, the best products and the best experiences. It wants traders to regard it as the best chewing gum supplier. And it aims to be an attractive business partner and international workplace, through innovation, flexibility, speed and cost awareness, working together towards a common goal. It believes cooperation, networks and partnerships are the way forward.

Today Dandy is owned by Cadbury Schweppes Plc, which announced during the summer of 2002 that it had acquired 100 per cent of Dandy's branded chewing gum business from the Bagger-Sørensen family in Denmark for £201 million ($307.9 million). Dandy is the fourth largest chewing gum manufacturer in the world. Combined with Cadbury Schweppes' existing chewing gum businesses, this acquisition makes Cadbury Schweppes the second largest player in the European chewing gum market after Wrigley, with number one positions in France, Denmark, Belgium and Switzerland and number two in Russia and CIS markets.

The family behind the 'old' Dandy, Bagger-Sørensen, has kept control of that part of Dandy which develops chewing gum for big companies such as Procter & Gamble and Colgate. The new company, Gumlink, cooperates with international pharmaceutical companies in the development and production of private brands, such as Nicotinell® nicotine chewing gum, which FERTIN produces for Novartis, and the dental chewing gum Aquafresh®, produced for SmithKline Beecham.

By the end of 2002 Cadbury Schweppes Plc had completed the acquisition of Adams from Pfizer Inc. for $4.2 billion (£2.7 billion), including $450 million (£288 million) for tax benefits. The transaction brings together some of the world's best-loved brands to form the world's largest confectionery business, enjoying leadership positions in sugar and functional confectionery and the number two position in gum. Four 'power' brands represent over 70 per cent of Adams' sales – Halls medicated confectionery, Trident sugarfree gum, Dentyne Ice chewing gum and the Bubbas bubblegum range. Cadbury Schweppes also gains access to major new markets, particularly in Latin America.

Cadbury Schweppes is a major global company that manufactures, markets and distributes branded beverages and confectionery products around the world. With origins stretching back over 200 years, today Cadbury Schweppes' products – which include brands such as Cadbury, Schweppes, Halls, Trident, Dr Pepper, Snapple, Trebor, Dentyne, Bubblicious and Bassett – are enjoyed in over 200 countries around the world. With the acquisition of Adams and its brands the group now employs around 55,000 people and is the world's largest confectionery company.

Background

Dansk Tyggegummi Fabrik A/S was founded by Holger Sørensen in 1915 as an ordinary confectionery factory. His first chewing gum, Vejle Tyggegummi, was put on the market in January 1927. Holger Sørensen died in 1943 and Erik Bagger-Sørensen took charge of the company with his mother. The Second World War put a stop to any further development – restrictions and lack of raw materials slowed down production considerably. After the war Erik Bagger-Sørensen gained sole responsibility for managing the company and exports began again. Also following the war the company chose the name 'Dandy', as an expression of something new and exciting. A licence of $1,000 to import raw material was granted on condition that chewing gum was exported for 3 × $1,000.

The export office was established in 1946 and exports increased sporadically to those countries unaffected by the war.

Dandy's main brand, Stimorol, was introduced in 1956, and in 1978 it was followed up by a sugar-free version. The year 1959 was the start of a more systematic internationalization of Dandy, when it was approached by a slightly eccentric Dutch man by the name

Kamphuis. He had tasted Stimorol and believed it would be a good supplement to the tobacco products he already sold. Under Kamphuis's management, Stimorol became a success in Holland, and the product is still a market leader there.

The first sales subsidiary was established in Belgium in 1965, in a corporation with Kamphuis. In the 1970s other sales subsidiaries followed in Sweden, Switzerland, Germany and France. Today Dandy operates with distributors and agents in markets where they have no sales subsidiaries. In the 1990s (following the fall of the Berlin Wall in 1989) Dandy established several sales subsidiaries in eastern Europe. It was the first chewing gum manufacturer to establish its own production in Russia – this gave Dandy a first-mover advantage in this market, and today Dandy shares the Russian market with Wrigley.

Products

There are two main types of chewing gum: sticks (the 'oblong' chewing gum) and dragée (the tablets). The trend in the market is towards the dragée which is where Dandy has focused its resources.

One of Dandy's core competences lies in the coating process of the chewing gum. The tablets are coated with a mixture of water, sweeteners and flavourings, which form an outer shell. Coating is an advanced process requiring constant electronic monitoring of temperature and air humidity. The result of this process is the so-called dragée chewing gum.

Dandy's business is based on three brands: Stimorol®, V6® and Dirol. Stimorol is one of the biggest chewing gum brands in Europe, and in 2000 was the market leader in, for example, Switzerland, Denmark and Belgium. Stimorol is offered in many different variants.

Dirol and V6 are well-known brands in the market for dental chewing gum – protecting teeth against acid-causing tooth decay. V6 and Dirol contain the active ingredient carbamide, which neutralises acids in plaque that lead to tooth decay. The target for V6 is the 20–40-year-old age group and for Dirol® the target group is the 15–30-year-olds. V6 Junior is aimed at 5–10-year-olds and Dirol Kids 9–12-year-olds.

Stimorol, V6 and Dirol are sold through Dandy's existing distribution system (via sales subsidiaries and agents to retail chains). The brands are marketed with the aid of strong international television and cinema commercials and outdoor advertisements on posters, busses and kiosks. V6 is sold in western Europe and Dirol in eastern Europe, Central Asia, the Middle East and southern Africa.

The chewing gum market is changing a lot. From being sweet, brightly coloured and full of sugar, chewing gum today is quite a different product. The trend is changing away from chewing gum as a lifestyle product to chewing gum as a product that includes some functional benefits. Consumers will increasingly be demanding products that in addition to tasting good and adding to their sense of well-being will also, for example, provide fresh breath, help keep teeth white, reduce the acid content in the mouth after meals and protect teeth against caries, etc.

Company structure

In February 2003 Cadbury Schweppes introduced a new simpler organization structure (see Figure 1). Five geographic business units are supported by five staff functions.

Figure 1 Organizational structure of Cadbury Schweppes (2003)

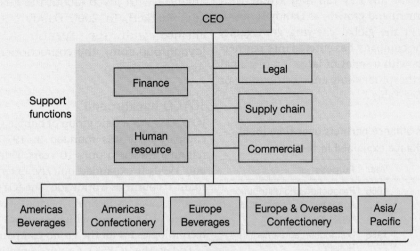

Geographic business units

Source: Adapted from information on www.cadbury-schweppes. com

Distribution of chewing gum

Chewing gum is distributed via supermarkets, shops and kiosks in nearly all countries. Chewing gum is an impulse buy. The display and position of products within shops determines which brand consumers choose. For this reason Dandy is constantly developing display stands and other advertising material specially adapted for the most strategic locations in each type of retail outlet.

Competitors

Dandy/Cadbury's main competitor is Wrigley, which also has chewing gum and other pocket confectionary

in its range (see Table 1). Wrigley is the global market leader in the chewing gum industry with a global market share of about 35 per cent. Wrigley is market leader in Europe's two biggest markets, the United Kingdom and Germany.

The chewing gum market competitive structure is very different from region to region. However, Wrigley and Cadbury Schweppes play an important role in every region, and they are true global players. Other manufacturers, such as Dandy, are regional players and are strong only in certain regions. There are also local players, such as Tong Yang, which are only local players, with presence in specific countries.

Partnerships – Dandy, a strong partner

Of all the chewing gum companies in the world Dandy has had the greatest growth over the past decade. One of the main reasons for this is the alliances that Dandy has entered into. These alliances have often been with potential competitors such as those described in this Case Study. Cooperation with Dandy means a strong partnership, from idea conception to sales to consumers. The company has a long tradition and many years' experience in the development of chewing gum, and their product development department today has considerable expert knowledge about chewing gum and flavour creation. This helps ensure the constant optimisation and development of products with the right texture, taste and flavour duration – guaranteeing high quality chewing gum with exactly the flavour the consumer desires.

Table 1 World market competitors 2003

Manufacturer	Country	Share of world market (%)
Wrigley	US	35
Cadbury Schweppes (including Dandy, Adams and Hollywood)	US	30 (the isolated share of Dandy brands is about 5% of the world market)
Lotte	Japan	10
Nabisco	US	5
Kraft Jacobs Suchard	France	4
Perfetti	Italy	3
Joyco	Spain	1
CSM Leaf	Holland	1
Others		11
		100

Source: adapted from material from Dandy.

Cooperation and networks are the way forward for Dandy. Only in this way can they ensure continued development and growth, as Dandy is only a minor 'player' in the global chewing gum game, which is why the company has entered into partnership agreements with a series of large international companies for the production and distribution of chewing gum. See Table 2.

Table 2 Dandy's alliance partners over time (bold indicates the alliance explained in this case)

Alliance	Year	Purpose
KGFF (Cadbury) France	1986	Production and distribution agreement in France and Belgium
Lotte	1986	Distribution agreement in Russia
Albert Heijn, Holland	1990	Production of private labels for own stores
Kesko	1992	Production of private label chewing gum
GlaxoSmithKline	1994	Production of Aqua Fresh (private brand) in Germany, UK, US, Denmark and Southern Europe.
Novatis Healthcare	1995	Production of nicotine chewing gum
CMS Leaf, Holland	1998	Distribution agreement for Russia/the CIS
Unilever	1998	Production of Mentadent and Signal, private brands especially for Southern Europe
Aldi in Denmark, Germany, Holland and Belguim	1998	Production of private label for own stores
Delhaize, Belguim	1999	Production of private label for own stores
Morrison, UK	2000	Production of private label for own stores
Elite, Israel	2000	Production of private label for own stores
Bergi, Italy	2000	Production of private label for own stores
Joyco, Spain	2000	Distribution agreement in Russia/the CIS. Joyco produces Dandy's bubble gum
Colgate Palmolive	2001	Production of functional chewing gum for Canada and the UK
Kroger, US	2001	Production of private label for own stores
Sweet'n Low, US	2001	Production of private label for own stores

Source: Based on talks with Dandy Management, November 2001.

In the following we will focus on Dandy's alliances with Joyco (about the Russian chewing gum market). In 2000 Dandy entered into an alliance with the Spanish JOYCO (**www.joycogroup.com**), the confectionery part of the Agrolimen Group.

JOYCO background

JOYCO is a dynamic group of bubble gum and sweet companies. It was founded in 1977 and became national leader in only 10 years. During the 1980s and 1990s it expanded quickly, extending to more than 70 countries worldwide. The JOYCO Group has its headquarters in Spain where there is a state-of-the-art R&D centre, which develops products and technologies for all the group companies.

Today the JOYCO Group comprises numerous companies, partnerships and joint ventures. The Group employs 3,600 people in 13 factories and sales offices worldwide. JOYCO has factories in the following countries: Spain, India, China, Mexico, Poland, USA, Italy, France, Philippines and Russia, and a presence in many more through commercial offices and exports.

JOYCO states that the consumers are at the heart of their vision and the company is passionate about providing the consumer with taste and fun.

History

The company started out as 'General de Confiteria', a small company with big plans concerning establishing a presence in the chewing gum and candy industry. It is known for its entrepreneurial spirit and passion for fun. In 1979 the company launched 'Bang Bang', Spain's first soft bubblegum and the company's first hit. In 1983, the company launched a new brand, 'Trex', which soon became the most popular Spanish chewing gum brand. In 1985 it followed this up with another new gum hit, 'Boomer'. At that time the company was the leading Spanish sweet maker and it was time to think more globally. In 1988 the company became the first international confectioner to enter the Chinese market. JOYCO ventured into Poland in 1992 and in 1993 the company entered into a joint venture in India and developed an extensive national distribution network. In 1995 they built a factory in India. At the same time 'Boomer' became the brand market leader in India. In 1996 the company exported to more than 70 national markets. In 2000 the company opened a new joint venture in China, with the aim of consolidating its strong market position in this country. And in 2001 JOYCO moved into a new potential market with the signing of a joint venture in the Philippines.

Products

JOYCO offers an extensive range of different products to the confectionery market. It offers some global products, e.g. 'Boomer', 'Pim Pom' and 'Solano', but a substantial part of the sales on country level originates from local brands (on **http://www. joycogroup.com/eng/index.html** you can take a look at these global and local brands).

Chewing gum brands

'Boomer' is the flagship brand of the Group. 'Boomer' offers an extensive range of variants. The brand is synonymous with its super hero Boomer. Other chewing gum brands are 'Sportsgum' (sugar free gum for sporty minded) and 'Trex', (a dental chewing gum to fight tooth decay).

Other candy brands

The most popular candy brands are 'Solano' (a traditional toffee brand), 'Pim Pom' (the company's lollipop brand), 'Dunkin' (candy with integration of a toy), 'After Dinner' (soft sugar mints), 'Duvalin' (chocolate spread) and 'Bocadin' (wafer bar with chocolate).

Some region and country details

Joyco's global presence is equally distributed in the three regions: Europe, America and Asia.

The joint venture in China is the nation's leading producer of bubblegum. The local brand 'Ta-Ta' dominates the bubblegum segment with a market share of almost 60 per cent.

In Spain, Joyco is marker leader with a 60 per cent share in the bubblegum segment ('Boomer'), but they are also a market leader in the creamy candy segment (market share of 50 per cent with 'Solano'). In addition to the global brands ('Boomer' and

'Trex'), the company has also introduced a new dental chewing gum in spain, 'Licor del Polo', based on a leading tooth hygiene brand of Henkel with 'licor del polo' which reduces dental plague.

The joint venture in Mexico is amongst the leaders in the local confectionery industry. The company has recently introduced the global brands 'Boomer' and 'Pim Pom'.

The subsidiary in Poland has established a strong distribution network. The brand 'Boomer' is market leader in the bubblegum segment.

JOYCO ITALY is the firm's oldest branch. It was set up in 1985 to serve the huge Italian confectionery Market.

The company in France features an active commercial office, complete with marketing and sales teams. JOYCO FRANCE has recently introduced a licence tracking system well equipped to track local trends.

The joint venture in the Philippines came about because of a vacancy in the market for leadership in the categories of chewing gum and lollipops in the domestic market as well as in the Asia region. In India, the gums market is highly competitive, with a presence several global players. Today the 'Boomer' brand commands a whopping 55 per cent share of the bubblegum segment, and dominates the lollipop segment with 'Pim Pom'.

Dandy's alliance with Joyco

Joyco wanted to penetrate the Russian market with their bubblegum, 'Boomer', but they had a problem

Figure 3 The Dandy–Joyco marketing and production alliance

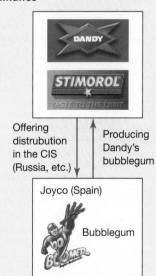

Figure 2 The Joyco–Dandy strategic distribution alliance

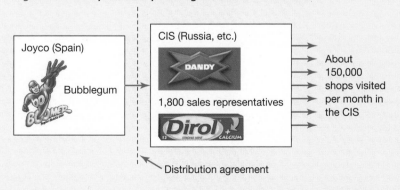

doing that in Russia. Joyco therefore became interested in using Dandy's well-established and widespread distribution network, which has about 1,800 Russian sales reps visiting all kind of shops in Russia, where shops in general are much smaller than in western Europe and North America. Thus evolved a kind of piggy-back solution whereby Joyco takes advantage of Dandy's distribution network in Russia (Figure 2). Furthermore, the alliance with Joyco was based on a 'two-way' agreement, with a 'give-and-take' situation (Figure 3).

Joyco used Dandy's distibution system not only in Russia/the CIS but also in Sweden and Denmark. In return Joyco produced Dandy's bubblegum for the northern European markets at Joyco's factories in Spain. Dandy still has some bubblegum in its product range, but now concentrates much more on the dragée type.

Questions

1. How should Cadbury Schweppes's organization be changed in order to reflect 'Global Account Management' thinking?

2. How are Dandy's competences in the value chain used in the Joyco alliance to create value for both partners?

3. How should Cadbury Schweppes implement a knowledge management system and transfer Dandy's alliance competence to the rest of the multinational organization that is Cadbury Schweppes?

CASE STUDY V.4　SKF Rolling Bearings

The automotive division is facing a big challenge in Japan*

It is Spring 2003. Outside SKF's HQ in Göteborg the grass is sprouting and growing vigorously in the fertile Swedish soil. Inside there is just as much activity. Tom Johnstone, chief executive officer of SKF, has during the last couple of years followed the explosive development taking place in the Far East. Asia has shown the fastest economic growth in the world. By the end of the 1990s the increase in China's GDP exceeded 10 per cent per year. In Korea and Taiwan growth was 5–10 per cent.

As a consequence of this Tom Johnstone and the top management group have decided to focus more on the Asian and especially the Japanese market. However, some problems have arisen from combining an organizational structure based on geography with one based on products. At the same time Tom Johnstone has doubts about whether it is possible to increase SKF's market share in bearings in the Japanese market from its present level of 1 per cent (see Table 1). The reason for the low market share is, of course, that Japan has some of the world's largest producers of bearings for the car industry. But SKF has been able to take the lead over the Japanese in all other markets, so why not challenge the Japanese manufacturers in their home market?

Background

A basic form of ball bearing existed even in early Roman times. One was discovered in the remains of a ship dating from the reign of the emperor Caligula in AD 40. But the breakthrough did not occur until the nineteenth century, with the invention of the pedal cycle. In order to ease the effort of the rider, the wheels had to rotate easily. This accelerated the development of the ball bearing. In 1907 Sven Wingquist, a bright young Swedish engineer,

Table 1 The bearings market in 2003: worldwide market shares of top manufacturers

Europe		North America		Latin America		Asia (excl. Japan)		Japan	
Manufacturer	%	Manufacturer	%	Manufacturer	%	Manufacturer	%	Manufacturer	%
SKF (Sweden)	30	Timken/ Torrington (US)	30	SKF (Sweden)	30	SKF (Sweden)	20	NSK (Japan)	34
INA/FAG (Germany)	20	SKF (Sweden)	15	INA/FAG (Germany)	20	NSK (Japan)	15	NTN (Japan)	26
				Timken/ Torrington (US)	15	NTN (Japan)	15	Koyo	27
Japanese manufacturers	20	Japanese manufacturers	20	Japanese manufacturers	10	Timken/ Torrington (US)	10	SKF (Sweden)	1
Others	30	Others	35	Others	25	Others	40	Others	12
Total	100	Total	100	Total	100	Total	100	Total	100

*This case is solely the responsibililty of the author and does not necessarily reflect SKF's current strategies in the Far East. In recent years SKF has focused a lot more on the Chinese market.

developed the world's first self-aligning ball bearing. In the same year that it became a commercial reality Svenska Kullager Fabriken (SKF) was founded.

Over the next six decades SKF grew to become the world leader in bearing technology and its applications. In 1926 production of cars was started by a subsidiary of SKF, AB Volvo. In 1935 AB Volvo became independent of SKF, and it later grew to become one of the major car producers in Europe. Through the 1960s and 1970s SKF was highly centralised and large economies of scale meant that huge quantities of bearings could be sold at competitive prices in the world market. In 1987 SKF's rolling bearing business was restructured into three business areas, each with worldwide responsibility: SKF Bearing Industries, SKF Bearing Services and SKF Speciality Bearings.

Today, operating in some 130 countries, SKF is the world leader in the rolling bearing business. Bearings, seals and special steels are SKF's main product areas. In addition the Group also manufactures and sells a host of other industrial precision components. The company has some 40,000 employees and more than 70 sales subsidiaries throughout the world. Its international sales network is backed up by about 7,000 distributors and retailers. SKF's major customer areas are the automotive industry, the industrial aftermarket, railways, electrical industry and heavy industry. Worldwide availability of SKF products is supported by a technical advisory service. One of the main contributors to SKF's strength is its R&D. The company's R&D strategy is to concentrate research in one high-powered centre in the Netherlands and then complement that centre with product development and testing facilities around the globe.

The SKF organization

During 2002 a new organizational structure was introduced. Originally more geographically focused, the Group's operations are now organised into five divisions (see Figure 1): Industrial, Automotive, Electrical, Service, and Aero and Steel. Each division serves a global market, focusing on its specific customer segments.

Germany and the United States each have their separate divisions, because of their importance for the whole SKF Group. In this way the top management of SKF hopes that the problems in these two main markets will be managed locally, and that all decisions can be made flexible and quick.

The automotive division is in focus here, and is characterised by the following.

Automotive division

The automotive division is responsible for sales to the car, light truck, heavy truck, bus and vehicle component industries and also for sales to the vehicle service market, as well as for product development and production of bearings, seals and related products and service solutions. The products include wheel hub bearing units, taper roller bearings, seals, special automotive products and complete repair kits for the vehicle service market.

The rolling bearings business

Of the total net sales of the SKF Group in 2002 (€4.6 billion), the automotive division accounted for around 32 per cent. The total profit in the Group before taxes was €388 million. Regarding sales by geographical area, Sweden accounts for 5 per cent, the rest of Europe for 50 per cent, North America for 26 per cent and the rest of the world for 19 per cent.

If the world market for bearings is divided into customer segments such as passenger cars, trucks, the aftermarket, etc., SKF holds leading positions within all segments with the exception of electronic motors. In general, its customers can be grouped into different categories as shown in Figure 2 (the percentages in Figure 2 are proportions of SKF sales).

Traditionally, OEM customers have been given the highest priority by SKF because of their high-volume production standards. However, profit margins are low in the OEM sector and SKF is under constant pressure to keep price increases below the rate of inflation.

Figure 1 SKF's organization

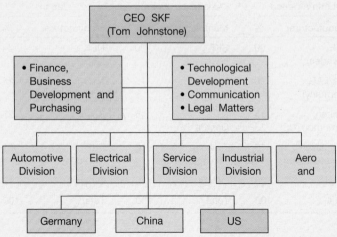

Figure 2 Segmenting customers for rolling bearings

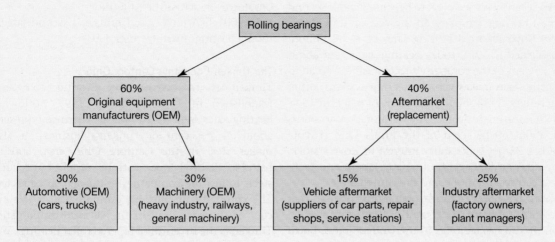

Source: SKF Annual Reports.

In the vehicle aftermarket the OEM customers (such as Mercedes, Volkswagen and Ford) may also be competitors through their own spare parts divisions. The specialist suppliers of car parts will typically buy SKF bearings and sell them under their own brand name to distributors. Overall, the largest companies in the world bearings industry are SKF, NSK Japan and NTN Japan.

Main competitors in the worldwide rolling bearing industry

In 2001 global shipments of rolling bearings were $23.4 billion. The largest five rolling bearing producers accounted for about 60 per cent of the world's bearing business. In the following, each of the main competitors will be briefly discussed:

NSK

NSK was established in 1916 and was the first Japanese ball bearing producer. The company is the largest producer of bearings in Japan and the second largest in the world, with worldwide sales of about $2.6 billion. It employs more than 23,000 people in 26 countries.

Bearings represent approximately 65 per cent of the company's total sales. NSK is inextricably linked with Japan's industrial development and prosperity and has been a global player since the 1960s. The company has gained considerable experience through the long years of operation and, as the second leading bearing manufacturer in the world, managed to achieve economies of scale. NSK in Japan serves domestic client demands as well as supporting the company's overseas bases as its global headquarters. The company carries three main categories of product and a fourth supplementary category: automotive products; bearing products; precision machine parts and mechatronics products; and other related products.

The downturn in domestic demand that still continues has had an impact on the company's performance. NSK's domestic operations posted a slight increase in sales (only in a few segments such as in the profitable precision machinery and parts), due to improvements in the production levels of manufacturing plants. Recent events have forced the company to pursue a policy of restraint shifting towards production reduction, including slashing labour costs and postponing investments. Many of the company's customers are transferring their production sites overseas, so they have to reinforce their domestic plants' functions as mother plants for their overseas production bases.

NSK was hit hard by the Japanese economic meltdown and had to retrench by closing a domestic ball bearing plant and take other bold measures to cut costs by ¥20 billion in order to return to profitability. It was especially hit by sluggish sales to automakers and general machinery producers. While closing plants, NSK intends to shift output to such countries as Indonesia, South Korea and China.

The company also operates through a network of joint ventures, which is standard practice in the industry. As an example, they have agreed with Timken, the US company, to jointly supply roller bearing products and services to Toyota Motor Corp. and its affiliates.

NSK's manufacturing presence in the United States is heavily focused on the auto industry.

E. Koyo Seiko Company, Ltd; Osaka, Japan

Koyo recently passed NTN to become Japan's second largest bearing company. In the year ending March 1999 Koyo reported bearing sales of $1.88 billion. Established in 1921, today bearings represent about 61 per cent of the company's total business. In addition the firm makes vehicle steering systems, other machinery components, and a line of machine tools for the bearing industry. The auto market accounts for about 60 per cent of the firm's sales. Toyota holds a 22 per cent equity interest in Koyo's stock. Koyo has an R&D centre in Nara, Japan, and technical centres in Europe and the United States.

Koyo has manufacturing operations in Japan that account for about 70 per cent of the firm's production. It also has factories in the United States, Brazil and the United Kingdom. In developing areas the company has production plants in China and Thailand. In 1998 Koyo acquired Romanian bearing maker S.C. Rulmenti Alexandrias SA, which was renamed Koyo Romania SA. Koyo's US plants are in Orangeburg and in nearby Blythewood, South Carolina. Both plants are high volume operations that concentrate on a relatively few parts for automotive applications.

NTN Tokyo Bearing Company, Ltd; Osaka, Japan

NTN, established in 1934, reported bearing sales of $1.86 billion for the year ending March 1999 (only $12 million less than Koyo). Bearings represent about 65 per cent of NTN's business. The firm also makes automotive components. NTN has production facilities in Japan, the United States, Canada and Europe. NTN is the third largest bearing producer in the United States, with seven factories.

INA/FAG AG; Herzogenaurach, Germany

INA, established in 1946, is a privately owned firm with estimated 1999 bearing sales of $1.94 billion. Bearings represent about two-thirds of the company's business. The company also makes auto parts, including auto carpeting. INA employs 24,000 people overall; about 16,000 make bearings. Of INA's workforce 60 per cent is concentrated in Germany and another 25 per cent in other European countries. INA accounts for about 20 per cent of the European market. The company specialises in needle bearings, although it produces other types as well. Needle bearings are used in transmissions, universal joints, cam followers, and other applications on motor vehicles. INA's major competitor in needle bearings is Torrington (see below). The two companies' major production bases are located in their home countries. Little direct competition is carried on, however, across the Atlantic.

In 2001 INA took over Germany's second largest rolling bearings manufacturer, FAG.

The Timken Company; Canton, Ohio

Timken is the largest US bearing company. Established in 1898, Timken's 1999 worldwide bearing sales were $1.76 billion. Bearings represent about 71 per cent of Timken's business. It also makes steel in the Canton, Ohio area, and in Latrobe, Pennsylvania. Latrobe supplies speciality steels to bearing companies in the aerospace sector. The company supplies an estimated 50 to 60 per cent of the steel used in the US bearing industry. Timken is the inventor of tapered roller bearings and remains the world's largest producer, representing about one-third of the world's total. Timken has 12 bearing plants in the United States and a dedicated R&D facility in Canton, Ohio. Additional plants are located in Canada, the United Kingdom, France, Poland, Romania, South Africa, India, China, Singapore and Brazil.

Timken is the largest US defence supplier. Most aircraft made in North America and Europe land on Timken bearings.

In 2003 another consolidation in the industry: Timken acquired the US number two manufacturer, Torrington.

SKF in the Japanese market – is a breakthrough possible?

SKF bearings were first introduced to Japan in 1910 in the form of samples. There was an immediate interest for the company's products, as the infant Japanese industry was absorbing all the industrial subcomponents it could find. In 1932 SKF Japan Ltd was established in Tokyo. In 1940 SKF's first overseas branch office was formed in Manchuria, China, as this was a place of significant industrial activity. The company's sales grew steadily, being supported by military demands, which not only boosted growth in sales but generated higher profit margins as well. The company's market share was more than 70 per cent, which was the highest ever achieved in Japan.

SKF at that time had 10 branch offices, not only in Japan but also in Taiwan and China, and employed about 450 people. It was, by all accounts, the most prosperous period in SKF's Japan history. The company did not have production facilities in Japan or China, but imported bearings from other SKF factories. In 1941 the Second World War severely disrupted the company's operations as it could not continue to import products via the Siberian railway and had to close all branch offices except the Tokyo headquarters. Most of the company's inventory was bought by the Japanese Navy.

When the war ended in 1946 private trade that had been banned was reinstated. The company nevertheless encountered the most difficult period of its history under the severe controls of the Japanese government, which imposed restrictions on operations and the allocation system of foreign currency, etc. The Japanese government, in its efforts to reconstruct the ruined economy, imposed strict measures on all foreign companies operating in Japan. In fact it was nearly impossible to conduct business under the circumstances, with only two salesmen. The market share dropped to almost zero. Sluggish sales continued for years.

However, as the post-war Japanese economy begun to revitalise so did the company's sales. In 1963 SKF opened branch offices in Osaka and in 1987 in Chubu. In 1990 it established the Product Service Centre in Chino, Nagano Prefecture. Furthermore, in 1998 the Asia Pacific Technical Centre was also built in Chino. At present the number of SKF employees in Japan is seven. However, the market share in rolling bearings is still 'only' 1 per cent and SKF's top managers find this figure too low for a market with such large potential.

SKF's competitors in the Japanese market

There are a multitude of bearing manufacturing companies in Japan. However, most of the market (87 per cent) is dominated by three domestic companies. The first is NSK, the market leader, which is very similar to the other two big Japanese companies, NTN and Koyo (see Table 1 and the competitor analysis above).

At the beginning of July 2003 Tom Johnstone receives an e-mail from Tryggve Sthen, the new president of the SKF automotive division. It reads:

> Hi Tom
> Good news!
> As you already know, I am in Japan at the moment negotiating a contract on our wheel bearings with Suzuki cars. I have succeeded in getting a contract involving about $5 million annually over a five-year period. We secured an order competing against very strong domestic bearing manufacturers. The order signals the start of a long-term involvement with Suzuki that I believe will benefit both our companies. Sune, I think this is a definite breakthrough in our efforts to penetrate the Japanese car industry with our products.
> Regards
> Tryggve Sthen

Tom Johnstone is, of course, very pleased on behalf of Tryggve Sthen and SKF, but is still a little sceptical about the possibilities of SKF seriously penetrating the Japanese bearings market.

As a consultant you are asked to give an independent assessment of SKF's business opportunities in Asia. You are specifically asked the following questions.

Sources: **www.skf.com**, **www.timken.com**, **www.ina.com**
http://europe.eu.int/comm/competition/mergers/cases/decisions/ m2608_en.pdf (Case no. COMP/M.2608 – INA/FAG)
http://europe.eu.int/comm/competition/mergers/cases/decisions/ m3011_en.pdf (Case no. COMP/M.3011 – Timken/Torrington)
http://www.ebearing.com/inafag.htm (the story of the INA acquisition)

Questions

1. Give an assessment of the SKF organization's ability to exploit future global business opportunites, especially the car industry in Asia and Japan. Include an assessment of the relevance of combining a product organizational structure with a geographic organizational structure.

2. How would you assess SKF's possibilities of penetrating the Japanese rolling bearing market? Consider the following:
   (a) Which kind of entry mode and penetration strategy would you advise?
   (b) What is a realistic goal for SKF's market share in bearings in Japan?
   (c) Should SKF use their resources in other parts of the world rather than in Japan?

CASE STUDY V.5   Vipp AS

A SME uses global branding to break into the international waste bin business

In 1939 the company Vipp (**www.vipp.dk**) came into existence quite accidentally when the wife of inventor Holger Nielsen needed a solid, pedal-operated waste bin for her hairdressing salon in Randers. Later on dentists and doctors became aware of the waste bin. So, for the next 50 years, the waste bin was produced for hairdressers, clinics, petrol stations, and recently also for 'designer' shops.

When Holger Nielsens died in 1992, only one other person was employed by the company. Holger Nielsen's daughter, Jette Egelund, took over the business. In 1996 her son Kasper and her daughter Sofie joined her. Today Kasper Egelund and Sofie Egelund are co-owners of Vipp and are employed as marketing manager and graphic designer respectively.

To begin with Jette tried to find time for the family business. However, in 1995 she quit her full-time job and spent the next few years trying to convince her distributors that the Vipp bin belongs in designer shops as much as it does in dentists' practices and salons.

Jette had no business experience, but little by little she got the hang of it. She tied a bin to a suitcase carrier and set out for the export markets. In Denmark the department stores Magasin and Illum turned her away, arguing that a waste bin from Randers did not belong in their product range – they would neither own nor would they have a dentist's waste bin on their stores' shelves. Every marketing expert with whom Jette Egelund spoke gave her the same advice: to stick to her present customers – dentists, doctors, hospital wholesalers, restaurants. But, believing that her father's product is a trendy, quality product, she was convinced that there would be ordinary consumers who could see the beauty of the waste bin and be willing to pay for it. If the Danes would not, the foreign countries might.

In the mid-1990s a holiday trip to London became the beginning of Vipp's internationalization process. Jette paid a visit to the international trend-setting ConranShop. It was difficult to get the English buyers' attention, but a week after her visit ConranShop placed an order for 30 bins for the shop in London and 35 for that in Paris. Not a large order, but having ConranShop among one's customers is very prestigious.

At about the same time Jette attended an international design and interior fair in Frankfurt. Here a German designer fell for the bin and advised her to contact the German mail order company Manufactum. She did, and it resulted in a full-page advertisement in their catalogue and in sales growth of 30 per cent compared to the year before.

Since then the export share has increased and is now 70 per cent of today's total sales. The only thing about the Vipp waste bin that has changed over the years is the shape of the lid. To begin with the lid

Vipp product range shown in leading design shop in Copenhagen

was produced on a lathe. In the 1950s Holger Nielsen got a hydraulic press that made it possible to produce the smooth surface.

The list of customers now includes leading design shops like Casa Shop, Illuns Bolighus and foreign design distributors such as Waterworks in New York.

Today the company has 11 employees within sales, marketing, logistics and administration. The head office and showroom are situated on Islands Brygge in Copenhagen, whereas most of the production is out-sourced to external factories. The bin is available in six sizes and as a miniature. The price to the end con-sumer varies between €170 and €340. In addition Vipp produces a toilet brush (€135) and a laundry basket (€400). The company sells approximately 150 bins a day – both to the B-t-B market and to the B-t-C market through designer shops and lifestyle stores worldwide. Approximately 10 per cent of the total sale goes to the B-t-B market, mainly in Denmark. The rest goes to the B-t-C market all over the world, mainly through designer shops.

Competitors

Vipp AS thinks that their product is special but they accept that they may have some competitors in the design and brand-oriented segment for house-hold products. Two of their main competitors are Brabantia (Holland) and Wesco (Germany).

Brabantia (**www.brabantia.com**) is one of the leading European brands in household metal arti-cles. The company was founded in Holland in 1919 when the van Elderen family, which still owns the firm, began manufacturing a range of watering cans and other household products. Today 30 per cent of the total Brabantia Group turnover (€135 million in 2002) is attributable to the UK market, where Brabantia has its own production and where the brand is also supported by TV commercials. The product range's profile has also been boosted by other valuable TV appearances. In the United Kingdom Brabantia has developed a national sales network through most of the well-known retail outlets, such as John Lewis and Tesco. The average price level for Brabantia's top waste bins are approximately 30% below Vipp (Wesco would be somewhere in-between Vipp and Brabantia.) In general Brabantia have broadened their distribution much more than Vipp.

Wesco (Westermann & Co. GmbH) (**www.wesco .de**) is a much smaller competitor than Brabantia, with only about 100 employees and a turnover of €22 million in 2002. The company was founded in 1867 as a traditional metals company. Over the

years Wesco has developed its product range into cashboxes and kitchen accessories other than the waste bin. Wesco is not an international player, as are Brabantia and Vipp, but it has strong position in the German market.

Standardised international marketing

Throughout the export markets the Vipp waste bin is sold in the same way, the only difference in the advertising from country to country is the text being translated. The Vipp images (below and overleaf) show two ads from Denmark and Holland. The text is the same though the order of the sentences is changed a little from the Danish to the Dutch ad.

Vipp believes that its international and design-aware end customers go to the same places, read the same lifestyle magazines and want the same articles for everyday use. Therefore the company is also inspired by a brand such as Coca-Cola. The corner-stone of Vipp's radical branding strategy is the product. Marketing Manager Kasper Egelund says:

> The most important thing about branding is to have a good product. Our most important asset is that we produce the original pedal-operated waste bin that is used by dentists, hairdressers and doctors. We can right-fully say that our bin is the original pedal-operated waste bin from 1939 – no copy product can beat that.

Vipp advertisement shown in Denmark

Vipp advertisement shown in Holland

We just have to make sure to tell the story to the end customers.

Source: the Danish newspaper *Erhvervsbladet*, 3 April 2003.

Today Vipp AS has a marketing budget of €270,000 a year and it will not be cut – quite the opposite. Until now the marketing budget has mainly been used for frequent 'shows' of the Vipp bin in lifestyle magazines such as the Danish *Bo Bedre*. See also

Figure 1 below, which shows the media plan (in Danish) for the so-called A markets (see below).

Change of Vipp's international sales organization

In 2001 the company changed its sales organization. For almost five years it had 10 foreign agents to manage sales outside Denmark, but now it has decided to use its own three sales representatives and a sales manager to take care of sales to retailers. Vipp will switch over to their own sales representatives as soon as the sales potential in a country can justify employing its own sales representatives. This already happens in the so-called A markets (Germany, Holland, Sweden, Belgium and Denmark), where the company itself manages sales and brand profiling through its own sales representatives. Its own sales force covers the A markets from HQ in Copenhagen. In these A markets the sales force tries to establish close relationships with larger and smaller designer shops in order to ensure that the proactive branding is implemented right through to the end customers. Vipp's own sales force helps the designer shops with in-store promotion and merchandising of Vipp products.

One of the reasons for the reorientation is that the company established only a very small growth in sales during the time the agents were employed. Vipp found that sales improved when its own representatives made the sales. On 31 March 2003, Kasper Egelund said to the Danish newspaper *Jyllandsposten*:

An agent is a kind of merchant, who opens his jacket saying: 'I sell everything; what do you want?' For us that

Figure 1 2003 VIPP ANNONCEPLAN

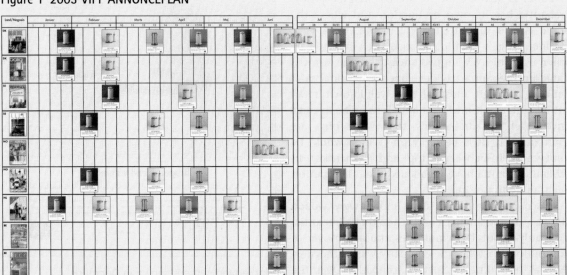

leaves a good deal to be desired. Agents are not loyal to your product; they are not enthusiastic for it.

In the so-called B markets, such as the United Kingdom or United States, the sales force visits a few key customers (retail chains), which would order larger quantities. In C-markets (overseas markets) there are no active Vipp selling efforts. However, Vipp will sell to the active information-seeking customers, who will show up at exhibitions, on the telephone, or on the internet. As an exception Vipp has an importer (with a stock of waste bins and tiolet brushes) in Australia, where the high transport costs make up a large percentage of the total product costs.

Questions

1. Vipp is considering increasing its marketing budget by €100,000 per year for its bin. What would be the break-even point of such an extra marketing cost? (Assume Vipp ex-works price of €80 and a contribution margin of 40 per cent.)

2. In your opinion, on which marketing activities should the €100,000 be used, and how should Vipp measure the effect of the marketing investment?

3. Discuss the pros and cons of using a company's own sales force as opposed to agents. Make a conclusion based on your discussion.

4. Until now Vipp's sales organization has been structured in such a way that each sales representative has been responsible for some European countries. Discuss alternative ways of structuring the sales force. Conclude on this basis with 'Which external interest groups should Vipp communicate in order to increase the long-term sales?'

5. Imagine that Vipp AS is considering online/Internet sales of its waste bin and toilet brush to end customers in B and C markets. What problems and possibilities do you see for Vipp AS in this connection?

Index